Footprint Egyp

Cherine Badawi

Fourth edition

"There is no country which possesses so many wonders."
Herodotus, 450 BC

1 **Alexandria**
Egypt's second largest city, a new library, great seafood and a mediterranean café culture

2 **Cairo**
Museums, mosques, *ahwas* and *sheeshas* in Africa's largest city

3 **Pyramids of Giza**
The world's oldest, and greatest, tourist attraction

4 **Siwa Oasis**
Take in the sound of silence deep in the desert on the shores of the Great Sand Sea

5 **Red Sea monasteries**
St Anthony's and St Paul's, two neighbouring, isolated monasteries that lie hidden in the folds of the Red Sea mountains

6 **Mount Sinai**
Where Moses received the Ten Commandments and an important pilgrimage site, best seen at dusk or dawn

7 **Dahab**
Still a place to kick back, Bedouin-hippy style, and dive

8 **Ras Mohammed National Park**
Where the land is barren, the water is an explosion of colour

9 **White Desert**
Eerie, wind-sculpted rock formations in the desert – a geologist's dream

Egypt Highlights

See colour maps at back of book

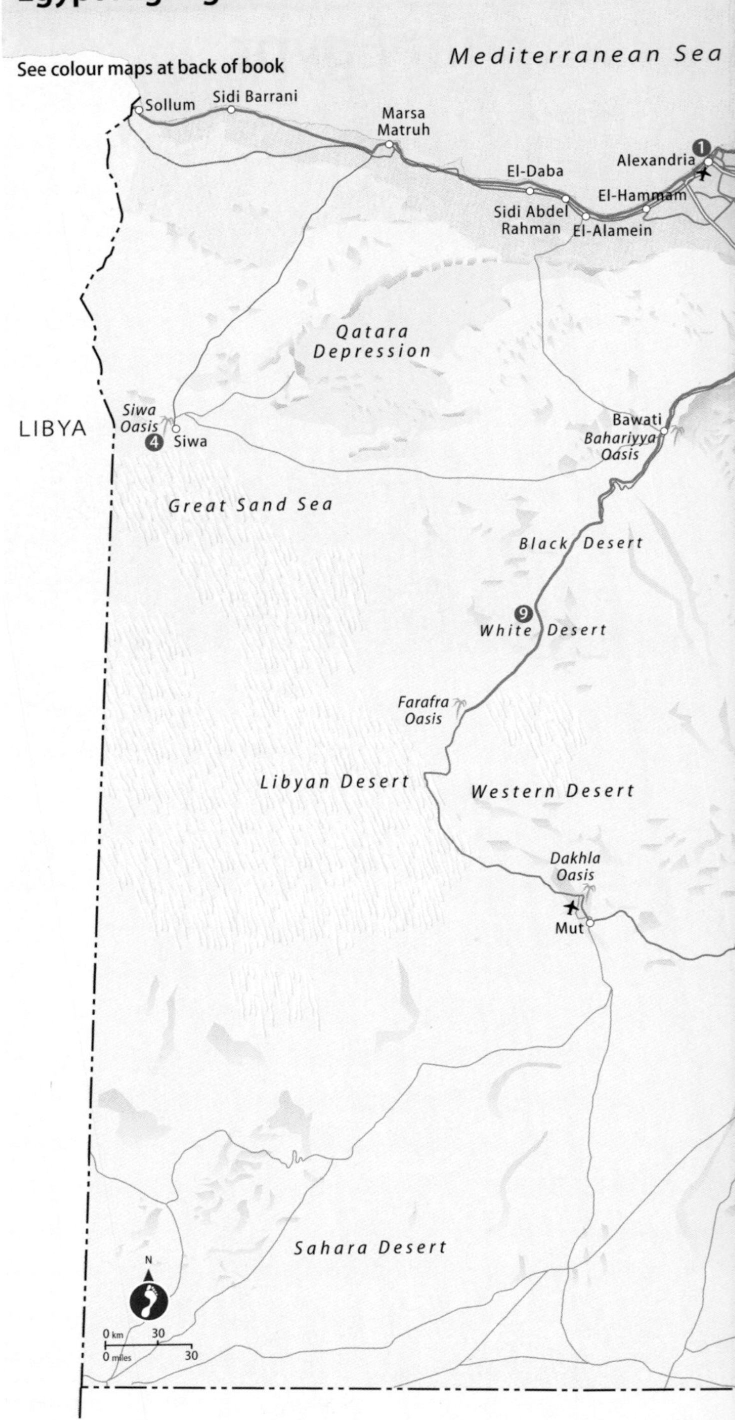

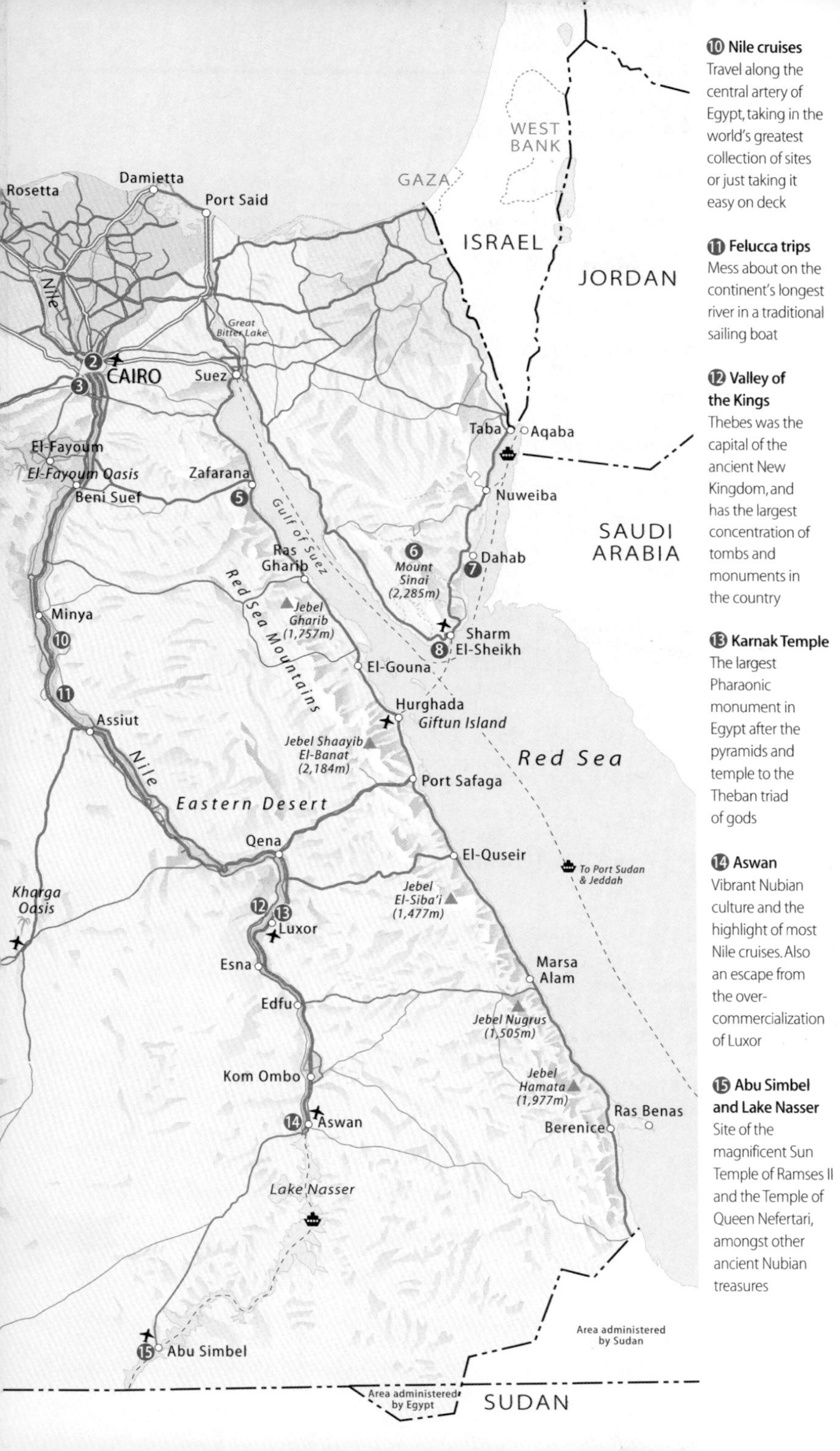

10 Nile cruises
Travel along the central artery of Egypt, taking in the world's greatest collection of sites or just taking it easy on deck

11 Felucca trips
Mess about on the continent's longest river in a traditional sailing boat

12 Valley of the Kings
Thebes was the capital of the ancient New Kingdom, and has the largest concentration of tombs and monuments in the country

13 Karnak Temple
The largest Pharaonic monument in Egypt after the pyramids and temple to the Theban triad of gods

14 Aswan
Vibrant Nubian culture and the highlight of most Nile cruises. Also an escape from the over-commercialization of Luxor

15 Abu Simbel and Lake Nasser
Site of the magnificent Sun Temple of Ramses II and the Temple of Queen Nefertari, amongst other ancient Nubian treasures

Contents

Luxor

South of Luxor

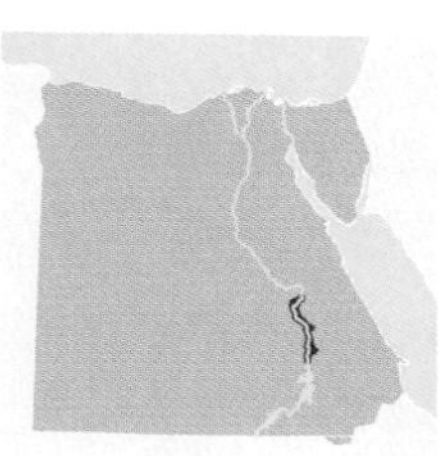

Alexandria & the Mediterranean coast

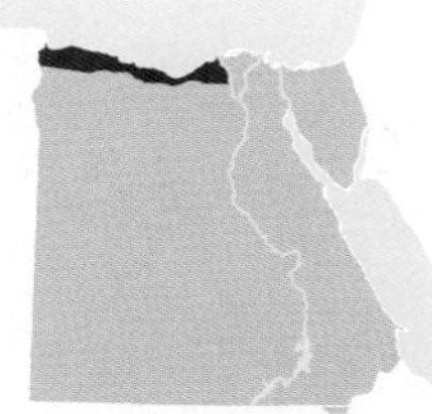

Suez Canal Zone

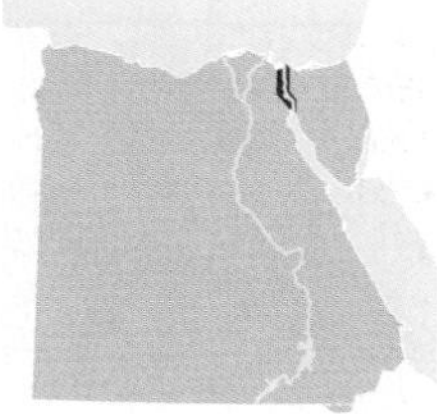

Despite appearances, share taxis are usually a very efficient way of getting around.

Sinai

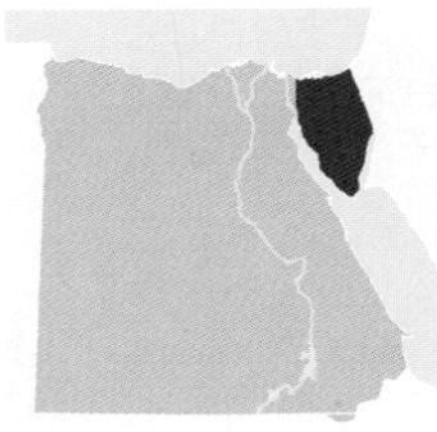

Red Sea & the Eastern Desert

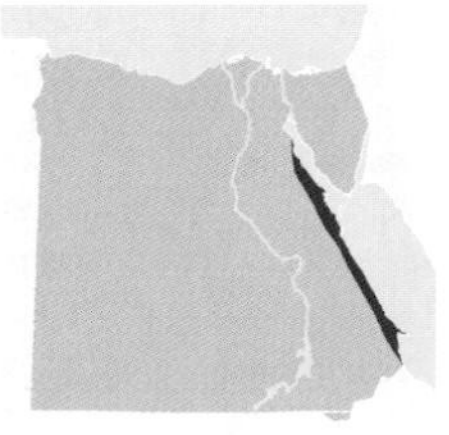

Western Desert

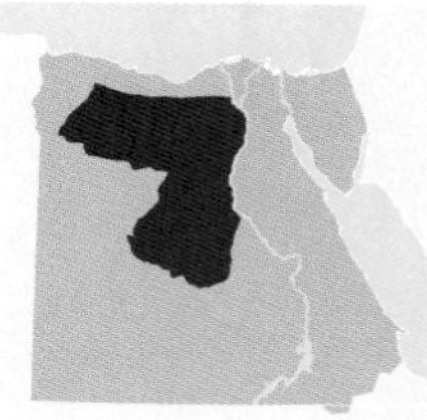

Background

Footnotes

Inside front cover

Sleeping and eating price codes

Inside back cover

Author biography

The other side of Giza

Sipping tea, puffing on a sheesha (water pipe) and watching the tourists go by from a traditional ahwa (coffee shop) in Giza.

A foot in the door

Egypt is like no other place. She mystifies and confounds. She awes and aggravates. She humbles and horrifies. What you see depends on which eyes you choose to look through; but no matter the lens, you will find paradox everywhere.

Travellers have been coming here for three thousand years to witness the magnificent temples and tombs of the old. Many still stand, humbling as ever, amid contemporary buildings not a decade old, crumbling in shambles. Locals carry on alongside the ancient monuments as they always have – just getting on.

The Nile is the central vein, still bumbling along, splitting the land mass unevenly into two vast sprawls of rugged desert. The sharp contrast between lush, green, Nile-side land and harsh, arid desert shocks in its abruptness. Much like the line between spaces populated and deserted. In crowded villages and vast urban areas, humanity seethes and oozes out of every crevice and alleyway but in the vast empty desert, life stops. The air is fresh and the silence more invasive than the strangely comforting cacophony of the cities.

When you first arrive, the sounds keep you up at night. Donkeys shriek. Horns honk. People scream a lot, whether they're haggling over the price of something, hollering their destination to a microbus driver or telling a joke. Stay long enough, and the sounds lull you to sleep. There's always laughter. And the fury of hot blood. Everyone feels strangely like family and consequently gets too involved in everyone else's business for anyone to ever have any privacy, or for anyone to ever really feel alone. God too seems ubiquitous and every other phrase reveals the spirit of Egypt. *Hamdulil'allah* (Thank God), we have what we have. *Insha'allah* (God willing), it will be better tomorrow. *Hamdulil'allah*, Egypt is blessed.

The Eternal River

'Egypt is the gift of the Nile', said Herodotus of the river. And without the mighty Nile, the many civilizations that erected the wonders of Egypt's epic past simply could not have been. As the seasonal flood inundated the valley with rich silt, the Nile became Egypt's life force. Since the erection of the Aswan and High Dams (circa 1900 and 1971, respectively), the waters, though astonishingly tamed, are still Egypt's life-giving artery.

From its dual origins of Lake Victoria and Lake Tibu, the world's longest river winds through 6,435 km of Africa, converging in Sudan before fanning out into the delta of Egypt and emptying into the Mediterranean Sea. Home to 90% of Egypt's 66 million, the countryside bounding the Nile, thrives with lush vegetation and *fellaheen* (peasants) working the land often with techniques and tools that have been used for centuries. Alongside such life, thousands of Ancient Egyptian tombs and temples dot the riverbanks, particularly in Upper Egypt (the south). Starting at Ramses II's imposing temple of Abu Simbel near the Sudanese border, passing through Aswan, a charming and beautiful city with distinctly Nubian flavour and a handful of wonderful sites, then climaxing around Luxor, the ancient capital of Thebes where the grand temple-complex of Karnak dominates the East Bank and the tomb-temple valleys of the Kings and Queens dominate the West.

Mega-malls and midans
With more than 25,000 inhabitants per sq km, Cairo has an estimated 16 million souls living in a place designed for two million.

Cruisers and *feluccas* (traditional sailing boats) stop at the major sites en route, enabling visitors to experience the contemporary life of the river amid the extraordinary remnants of Egypt's past.

Cairo

The most densely populated city on Earth, Cairo's inhabitants are a cosmopolitan mélange of Arabs, Africans, Westerners and Asians. A teeming megacity that is the result of many ancient civilizations built on top of one another, the capital is a jumble of worlds and times. In its bounds lies a journey through time, a taste of multiple ages. From the Great Pyramids of Giza, Egypt's foremost attraction, to the Egyptian Museum that hosts a pandemonium of treasures; from the narrow alleyways of Islamic Cairo, bustling with life and hundreds of Islamic monuments, to the congested remains of Babylon in Old Cairo; from the souks (traditional markets) bursting with commerce and colour to the *ahwas* (coffee shops) and cafés of the early 20th century where revolutions still brew and artists still express, there's just so much to see, smell and hear. Standing at the crossroads of Africa and Europe in the heart of the Middle East, the city has dominated the region for centuries. With so much to take in, it can be overwhelming. Wonderfully so, terrifyingly so.

Life blood

The Nile runs through Egypt like a central artery supplying water and silt to an otherwise arid, infertile land. It also supports the tourist industry as travellers sail along it in traditional feluccas or big cruise ships.

1

2

4

5

7

8

10

11

1 *Trekkers and pilgrims alike scramble up Mount Sinai to gaze at the rising sun.* ▸▸ *See page 406.*

2 *Ramses II made his mark in no uncertain terms on the Luxor Temple when he ordered these colossi.* ▸▸ *See page 215.*

3 *Ram-headed sphinxes in the avenue which links the Karnak temple to the Luxor temple.* ▸▸ *See page 220.*

4 *Sample the spice of life in the Souk Al-Attarin in Cairo. A sensory overload.* ▸▸ *See page 93.*

5 *Both glamorous and gaudy, Sharm El-Sheikh is an international tourist destination with the best diving in the world.* ▸▸ *See page 369.*

6 *Paintings over three thousand years old are still decorating tombs in the Valley of the Kings, some are simple and crude, others incredibly well preserved.* ▸▸ *See page 229.*

7 *Monument to the great feat of engineering and Egypt's pride and joy, which is the Aswan High dam, built in the 1960s.* ▸▸ *See page 287.*

8 *Feluccas (traditional Nile sailing boats) are a great way to see the many sights along the Nile.* ▸▸ *See page 40.*

9 *The richness of the Red Sea's flora and fauna knows no equal in the world.* ▸▸ *See page 418.*

10 *Hawk-headed God Horus, 'he who is far above', a deity whose image is seen in temples all over Egypt.* ▸▸ *See page 548.*

11 *Market day in Alexandria, Egypt's second city. A distinct Mediterranean feel distinguishes it from Cairo.* ▸▸ *See page 313.*

12 *A camel ride at dusk around Giza is the cooler way to catch the pyramids.* ▸▸ *See page 75.*

The Great Civilization

Egypt's chronology is of vast span, encompassing more than 5000 years of civil government. Few countries have contributed so much to the civilized world. A glut of temples and tombs, papyri and pyramids attest to Egypt's greatness. A lifetime would not suffice to see it all. Even a trip to the Egyptian Museum in Cairo would require 3 years to spend a minute in front of every piece.

Islam and Christianity: age-old heritage

Islam is a fundamental part of Egypt. It's presence is omnipotent: in the language; in the muezzin's call to prayer; in the clothes people wear and the rules they adhere to; the beliefs and the fears and the dreams that they have. Egypt contains many of the world's finest Islamic buildings that chronicle the great faith's more than 14 centuries-old history. Cairo, it has been said, is the city of 1000 minarets, splendidly speckled across the skyline adding colour to a city that is perpetually covered in dust. With a recent resurgence of restoration, the beauty of centuries past is being reawakened in scores of monuments.

Egypt also has one of the longest continuing traditions of the Christian faith, encapsulated in diverse pockets of the country. The Coptic Christians comprise almost 10% of Egypt's total population. Their history extends

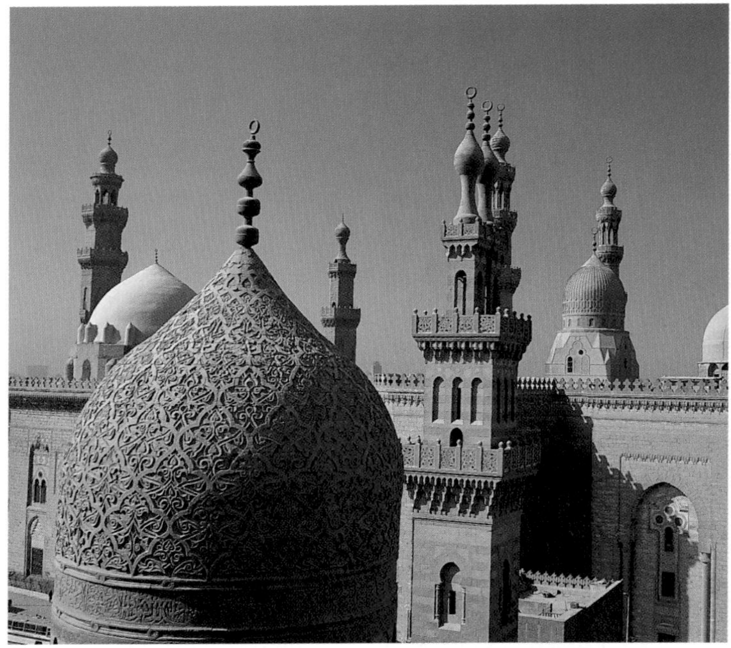

Incomparably simple and beautiful, Sultan Hassan's Mosque in Cairo.

Birqash Camel Market outside Cairo. The larger camels are generally used for transport and farming; smaller ones end up on the dinner table.

back to the time of the Pharaohs. From Old Cairo's congested townscape to the working monastic communities of the Western Desert and the unique oddity of St Catherine's old monastery in Sinai, there's a lot to see and religious tourism has taken off.

And though there is an undercurrent of tension between these age-old religions, as is often the case in a country where there is a significant minority amid a dominant majority, the world's recent tumultuous events have not tangibly impacted on the dynamic between Copts and Muslims. Egyptian Copts do not necessarily align themselves with the contemporary western perspective and in fact seem to be more politically aligned with their Muslim compatriots.

Sinai and the Red Sea

For its treasures above and below the waterline, these days the Sinai peninsula is among Egypt's foremost attractions. Along the peninsula's southern tip, the Red Sea teems with every species of life that thrives therein. Internationally recognized as one of the best diving and snorkelling spots on the planet, there are over 500 species of coral and more than 1000 types of fish. The waters are temperate year-round, visibility is consistently good, and the prolific diversity of life is nothing less than otherworldly. Sharm El-Sheikh, an upscale tourist town, and Dahab, it's laid back cousin, have particularly renowned dive sites, and a plethora of reputable dive schools. Diving and windsurfing also abound on the mainland coast of the Red Sea, where huge resort villages keen to host the influx of tourists are sprouting up rapidly. Above ground, Sinai's rugged interior, rich with historical relevance, is prime for trekking. A late night

Isolated Siwa Oasis, by the Libyan border, is surrounded by the Great Sand Sea.

hike to the peak of Mount Sinai is well worth the effort. Pilgrims come to watch the rising sun above an astoundingly beautiful and barren landscape where Moses heard the Ten Commandments.

The Oases and the Desert

Literal springs of life in the middle of the barren Sahara, there are five major oases that thrive in Egypt's western desert. The closest to Cairo and most frequented, Bahariyya and Farafra, are inundated with hot springs and offer easy access to the nearby White Desert, a bizarre landscape of bright white limestone formations set amid golden sands. Dakhla and Kharga, most easily accessed from the Nile Valley, are more densely populated and industrial. Their main appeal is their proximity to a scattering of ancient sites. Siwa, on the other hand, 60 km from the Libyan border, is doubtless the star of the oases. Isolated for centuries from the world until a road was built in the 1980s, the area has retained a culture and character like nowhere else in the world. Freshwater springs abound, alongside notable ruins and an extraordinarily kind people.

From all of the oases, it's possible to organize a safari into the surrounding desert. Spending a night under an ocean of stars, contemplating silence and big open spaces while a Bedouin guide brews sugary tea, and shares stories and jokes can be an humbling as well as fun experience. But coming prepared is essential. The desert is a wilderness, where sun beats down with glaring intensity. The air can be dusty and dry. And the flies. The sandstorms. The distinct lack of green. All of it in the dead of summer render the surrounding oases, gushing with springs and verdant life, that much more enticing a respite.

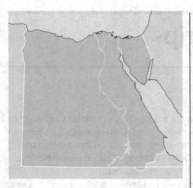

Essentials

Footprint features

Planning your trip

Where to go

One week

Egypt offers almost as wide a range of short trip possibilities as travellers exploring its wonders. If you have just a week, consider what is most important to you. You can attempt to cram as much as possible in a few days, or opt to explore a single part of Egypt's splendors and plunge in full force. Don't try to cover Cairo, the Sinai Peninsula and the Valley of the Kings in 7 days – go for just one of them.

With a little bit more time, say 10 days, plan to spend at least 2-3 days in **Cairo**, giving yourself sufficient time to explore the Egyptian museum, Islamic Cairo and the nearby pyramids of Giza. For added spice, take a sunset *felucca* (traditional sailing boat) on the Nile, or a camel ride around the pyramids. Spend an evening wandering around the markets and minarets of Islamic Cairo, sipping tea and puffing *sheesha* (water pipe) in a traditional *ahwa* (coffee shop). On day three, take a plane or train to **Luxor** and spend a couple of days around the ancient capital of Thebes. Funds permitting, book a cruise and sail down the Nile exploring tombs and temples on the way. Most trips end at or near the Nubian gem city, **Aswan**. Enjoy a day relaxing on the beautiful banks and indulging in the warmth of Nubian culture. Time permitting, spend a day visiting the nearby awe-inspiring temples of **Abu Simbel** and then fly back to Cairo from Aswan. If you're on a tight budget, from Cairo, you may wish to take the train straight to Aswan and have a 2-3 day *felucca* trip up the Nile to **Edfu**. From there, you can get the bus up to Luxor to enjoy the splendors of Thebes before returning to Cairo.

Two-three weeks

With two-three weeks, you can add a natural element to your walk through time. After 10 days exploring **Cairo** and **Upper Egypt**, travel via bus from Upper Egypt to the **Red Sea coast** and spend some time discovering its magic and the **Eastern Desert**. Alternatively, you could take a ferry across, from Hurghada to Sharm El-Sheikh, and experience the dramatic landscape of Sinai. A few days' lounging in Dahab's seaside dens, snorkeling around the virgin reefs of Ras Mohammed and climbing Mount Sinai are highlights for many travellers to Egypt.

If the Sand Sea is of greater interest, plan a safari around the oases of the **Western Desert**. There is a weekly train from Luxor to Kharga where you can commence a journey through four key oases in the Great Desert Circuit. If timing for the train is off, return to Cairo and start the desert trip in Bahariyya. Alternatively, if you want to taste the **Mediterranean coast** and the remote oasis of **Siwa**, from the Nile Valley, head north to **Alexandria** via Cairo. Spend a day or two milling about the boardwalks, eating some fish and checking out the library; then follow the coast west to the not often visited beachside community of Marsa Matruh. After a day's respite by the sea, catch a bus to Siwa to experience the desert and richness of Bedouin life in a distant and beautiful oasis before returning to Cairo.

A month or more

With a month, covering the ground fairly swiftly, you could see most of Egypt's main attractions and add a Western Desert safari to the mix.

The following is a possible route that could take a month to six weeks, depending on how fast you like to move and how extensively you intend to explore, and that includes pretty much everything. Spend your first few days getting acclimatized in **Cairo**. When you've absorbed all you can, take a bus to **Siwa** oasis for a few days

Tourist numbers waver

The number of tourists visiting Egypt fell dramatically after the massacre at Luxor in November 1997. After a very difficult time for the industry in Egypt, with the flow of visitors down to less than 1 million in 1998, the tourists began to flood back and over 4 million came in 2000.

Then 9-11 hit the country hard, along with the Al-Aqsa Intifada in Palestine – the bloodiest yet. And again, tourism plummeted. More recently, the war with Iraq has deterred wary foreigners from exploring the region. Despite the political climate globally, Islamic fundamentalists in Egypt have been in retreat since the mid-nineties. In the face of enhanced security, the situation is likely to remain quite calm. Nonetheless, since Egypt is in the centre of one of the world's hotbeds of unrest, tourism will continue to rise and fall. But history indicates that no matter how far it falls, tourists eventually come back.

respite with hotsprings, sandbaths, ruins and tranquility. On your way back, head northeast and stop in **Marsa Matruh**, a beautiful Mediterranean beach town, not often visited by foreigners. Carry on east along the coast to **Alexandria** and spend a day milling about the boardwalks, eating seafood and checking out the library. Return to Cairo and take a bus to **Sinai**. Plan to spend a week exploring this enchanting peninsula where awaits world-renowned diving, sacred sites, incredible desert trekking and abundant lounging opportunities. From Sharm El-Sheikh, take a ferry across the sea to **Hurghada** on the Red Sea coast. You may wish to head directly by bus to **Luxor**, or alternatively travel south to striking and remote **Marsa Alam**, where you can also catch a bus to the Nile Valley. Spend some time exploring the ancient vast temples of Thebes before heading south to **Aswan**. If funds allow, book a cruise, otherwise, visit the temples en route to Aswan via bus. Spend a few days enjoying the timeless pace and Nubian flavor of Aswan. (Don't miss surrounding sites like **Philae** and **Abu Simbel** and tou may also want to check out cruising and fishing opportunities on **Lake Nasser**.) From Aswan, you can cheaply and ruggedly sail a *felucca* up the Nile to **Edfu**, or if you already did a cruise, hop on a bus back to Luxor and head westward to Kharga, the closest of the **Western Desert** oases. Allow a few days to explore Bahariyya and Farafra and be sure to include an overnight desert safari to the psychedelic wonderland of the White Desert. From Bahariyya, you can easily catch a bus back to Cairo.

Another possible 'see-all-the-highlights' route: Cairo–Luxor–Aswan (and Abu Simbel)–Kharga–Bahariyya–Farafra–Cairo–Sinai–Cairo–Alexandria–Marsa Matruh–Siwa.

Public transport is available for all these areas, though the Western Desert and Central Sinai can be most extensively and easily explored with four-wheel drive vehicles. Generally, Egypt is well served by internal air transport links so that rapid transfers are possible between distant sites. Nevertheless, time permitting, there is still nothing so satisfying and memorable as bussing and training – even on the longest journeys – in company with locals.

When to go

Climate

The best time for travelling everywhere, except possibly the Alexandria region, is between October and April and especially November to February. The sun shines the whole year round and rainy days are the exception. The temperature increases as you travel south, Luxor being about 10°C warmer than Cairo. In April to May be prepared for the *khamseen* wind – the wind of 50 days – which blows sand and heat to the discomfort of those caught in the open. Relative humidity can be high (over 70%) on the coast and the Delta. Inland, humidity is not a problem with Aswan, for example, having averages of less than 50% for the whole year and a mere 30% in the summer months. At the height of the summer, humidity falls in many places to less than 20%. The best time to visit Cairo is between March and May and between September and October. In the desert, beware the high summer temperatures.

Tour operators

→ *See individual town listings for local tour operators.*

UK

* = provision for disabled
# = diving holidays

Abercrombie and Kent (*#), Sloane Square House, Holbein Rd, London, SW1W 8NS, T0845-0700610, www.abercrombiekent.co.uk. Expensive, tailor-made tours.

Amoun Travel (#), 56 Kendal St, London, W2 2BP, T020-74023100, www.amountravel.co.uk. Egyptian company doing tailor-made tours of the whole country.

Ancient World Tours, PO Box 12950, London, W6 8GY, T07071-222950, www.ancient.co.uk. In-depth cultural tours including Nile cruises.

Crusader, 57 Church St, Twickenham, Middlesex, TW1 3NR, T020-87440474, www.crusadertravel.com. The division known as **Red Sea Travel Centre** concentrates on water sports (scuba diving, wind surfing, sailing and snorkelling) – they own the Aquasport dive and water sports centres at Sharm El-Sheikh and Hurghada – and offer two-centre and tailor-made visits as well as Nile cruises.

Diving World (#), Bank Chambers, 6 Borough High St, London, SE1 9QQ, T020-74070019, www.diving-world.com.

Exodus Travel, Grange Mills, Weir Rd, London, SW12 0NE (Reg No: 1150160, VAT Reg No: 386 4160 36), admin and reservations T020-8675-5550, brochures and trip notes T020-8673-0859, www.exodus.co.uk.

Explore Worldwide Ltd, 1 Frederick St, Aldershot, Hants, GU11 1LQ, T01252-760000, www.its.net/travelscope. For hotels/camping in oases of Siwa and Western Desert, also Nile cruises, Abu Simbel, *felucca* sail-trek, Red Sea and Sinai.

Explorers Tours (#), 223 Copermill Rd, Wraysbury, TW19 5NW, T01753-681999, www.explorers.co.uk. Hotel and liveaboard diving holidays in Sharm El-Shiek and Dahab.

Goodwood Travel, St Andrews House, Station Rd East, Canterbury, CT1 2WD, T01227-763336, www.goodwoodtravel.com.

Hayes and Jarvis (*#), Sandrocks, Rocky Lane, Haywards Heath, West Sussex, RH16 4RH, T0870-8989890, www.hayes_jarvis.com.

Kuoni Travel (*#), Kuoni House, Dorking, Surrey, RH5 4AZ, T01306-747002, www.kuoni.co.uk.

Oonas Divers (*#), 30 Church St, Eastbourne, East Sussex, BN21 1HS, T01323 648924, www.oonasdivers.com. Quality liveaboard accommodation, also a fascinating Red Sea Diving Safari, involving camping and diving off the southern Red Sea coast.

Peltours Ltd (#), Sovereign House, 11-19 Ballards Lane, Finchley, N31 4UX, T020-83715200, www.peltours.com. Nile cruises, diving and other water sports.

Regal Holidays (*#), 58 Lancaster Way, Ely, Cambs, CB6 3NW, T0870-2201777, www.regal-diving.co.uk. Diving specialists for the Red Sea.

Soliman Travel (#), 113 Earl's Court Rd, London, SW5 9RL, T020-72446855, www.solimantravel.co.uk. Specialist tours to famous battlefields of Western Desert, follow route of Holy Family in Egypt.

Somak Holidays, Somak House, Harrovian Village, Bessborough Rd, Harrow-on-the-Hill, Middlesex, HA1 3EX, T020-84233000, www.Somak.co.uk. Nile cruises.

Sunbird, PO Box 76, Sandy, Bedfordshire, SG19 1DF, T01767-682969, www.sunbird.demon.co.uk. A variety of locations in Egypt with emphasis on bird life and history.

Tailor Made Holidays (*#), 5 Station Approach, Hinchley Wood, Surrey, KT10 0SP, T0208-3987424, 020-83984464, www.tailormadeholidays.co.uk. Offer Hooked on the Nile and Fishing on Lake Nasser trips. They have six boats fed by a supply boat on Lake Nasser, a civilized safari in a steel hulled boat, with ample opportunities to fish.
The Imaginative Traveller (#), 1 Betts Av, Martlesham Heath, Suffolk, IP5 7RH, T0800-3162717, www.imaginative-traveller.com. Quality camping, walking, cycling tours.
Travelbag Adventures (#), 15 Turk St, Alton, Hampshire, GU34 1AG, T01420-541007, www.travelbag-adventures.com. Cheaper end of the market, *felucca* travel, explore the Western desert by jeep and camel.
Travelscope Worldwide Limited (Gaz Tours) (#), PO Box 158, Guildford, Surrey, GU4 7GE, T01483-569453, www.its.net/travelscope. An excellent independent travel company, which has been in business since 1972, and which arranges individual and group tours to classic sites in Cairo, Luxor and Aswan and to the oases. Special tours for Christian groups can follow the Holy Family's flight from Egypt, while tours to Sinai cover all the major sites to the Israeli border.

Finding out more

Tourist information → See individual area Ins and outs sections for local tourist offices.

Depending on where you are in Egypt, the provision of tourist information is variable. If available, how helpful the services can be is also variable. The offices in bigger cities tend to be quite well-equipped and at least have an English speaker on duty. They're worth a visit if you are nearby. The particularly helpful tourist offices are noted in the relevant chapter sections in 'Ins and outs'. In Cairo, there are several, though surprisingly, they're among the least helpful in the country. Cairo's main tourist office, T02-3913454, is across the street from the tourist police, T02-3906028, downtown near Midan Opera at 5 Sharia Adly. There's also an office by the Giza Pyramids and at the airport, T02-2914255. When the tourist offices fall short, hotels, pensions and other travellers are often even better resources to access reliable travel information.

Egyptian State tourist offices abroad

Austria, Elisabeth Strasse, 4/Steige 5/1, Opernringhof, 1010 Vienna, T01-5876633, aegyptnet@netway.at.
Belgium, 179 Av Louise 1050, Brussels, T26473858, touregypt@skynet.be.
Canada, 1253 McGill College Avenue, Suite 250, Quebec, Montreal, T514-8614420.
France, 90 Champs Elysees, Paris, T1-45629442/3, Egypt.Ot@Wanadoo.Fr
Germany, 64A Kaiser Strasse, Frankfurt, T69-252319.
Italy, 19 Via Bissolati, 00187 Rome, T6-4827985.
Japan, Akasaka 2-Chome Annex, M-S Akasak 2 Chome, Minato Ku, Tokyo, T3-35890653, Tourism@ egypt.or.Jp.
Spain, Torre de Madrid, planta 5, Oficina 3, Plaza de Espana, 28008 Madrid, T1-5592121.
Sweden, Dorottningatan 99, Atan 65, 11136 Stockholm, T468-102584, egypt.Ti.Swed@alfa.telenordia.se
Switzerland, 9 rue des Alpes, Geneva, T022-7329132.
UK, Egyptian House, 170 Piccadilly, London, W1V 9DD, T020-7493 5283.
USA, 630 5th Av, Suite 1706, New York 10111, T212-3322570, egyptourst@ad.com.

Egypt on the web

www.touregypt.net A comprehensive site put together by the Ministry of Tourism. Very detailed: listings include internet cafés, dive sites off Hurghada with illustrations of wrecks, and on-line shopping from Khan El-Khalili. Also includes maps of most cities, walking routes of national parks, timetables for public transport, hotel and tour guide index and general information pertaining to life in Egypt.
www.egypt.com Extensive index of websites pertaining to Egypt – ranging from tourism to opera to the military. Excellent resource.
www.presidency.gov.eg The presidential website offers photographs of the palaces and biographies of former rulers.
www.egy.com Mine of cultural and historical information about Cairo.
www.telefax.com.eg A useful business directory aiming to cover the whole of Egypt.
www.bibalex.gov.eg Very detailed information and up-to-date news on the new Alexandria Library.
www.egyptyellowpages.com.eg Telephone directory for Cairo and Alexandria.
www.ahram.org.eg/weekly Online version of the weekly English-language sister paper to the national daily *Al-Ahram*, extensive archive with search engine.
www.cairotimes.com Online version of the weekly magazine. Succinct pieces written mostly by expats, extensive archive with search engine.
www.sinaitimes.com Information on events around southern Sinai.

Language

The official language is **Arabic**. Colloquial Arabic *(omayya)* differs significantly from the written, classical form *(fos-ha)* derived from the Arabic of religious texts. Spoken Arabic in Egypt has a dialect that varies slightly from the Arabic of other countries. For example, what is usually pronounced "j" in other Arab countries is pronounced with a hard "g" in Egypt. However, because of Egypt's once- acclaimed film industry and the significant on-screen presence of Egyptian actors, many people around the Arab world understand the Egyptian dialect and foreigners wanting to study often learn it. In addition to Arabic many Egyptians speak, or at least dabble in, foreign languages. Younger generations tend to be more proficient in **English** whereas older generations are more likely to know **French**. As tourism is such a foundation of Egypt's economy, hotel staff are generally quite fluent in English. Outside of such establishments, it is not uncommon to hear people communicating with an assortment of words taken from multiple tongues. You may find that including the occasional Arabic word in your speech will facilitate communication quite a bit. It's also helpful to learn some basic direction words, as getting around and finding the right bus often depends more on asking around rather than reading a schedule. ▸▸ *See Basic Egyptian for travellers, page 534, for a simple vocabulary.*

Specialist travel

Disabled travellers

Though many people in Egypt live with disabilities, there are few provisions for the disabled. Most budget hotels require clambering up flights of stairs. Public transport necessitates extreme finesse and is generally so crowded, wheelchairs are hard to accommodate. Though some of the newer museums have ramps and most modern buildings have lifts, access to many sites, including the Pyramids, temples and tombs, is limited. In the Sinai, there are some dive companies that accept students with disabilities. (Check out www.diveability.com for leads.) Some disabled people have been known to camel ride up the face of Mt Sinai. The best bet may be to book a tour with a company that caters to the needs of disabled travellers. *Ayman Mohammed* of **Taro Travel**, T012-3546491, leads trips into the desert that can accommodate people with some handicaps. Also check out the following websites: **Society for the Advancement of Travel for the Handicapped**, www.sath.org; and www.egyptforall.com, www.geocities.com/Paris/1502, www.access-able.com, www.wheelsup.com.

Gay and lesbian travellers

Though there are as many gay people in Egypt as anywhere else, being openly gay can be difficult. Homosexuality is forbidden in the Koran and illegal in Egypt. That said, men are strikingly open with each other. It's not uncommon to see them embracing, kissing on the cheeks or walking down the street arm in arm. Be not misled, such gestures are indicative of friendship and brotherhood, and rarely indicate anything else.

There are some rumored hotspots where gay partygoers gather. The internationally-infamous and recently-busted **Queen Boat** may still attract some foreign patrons, though the locals are probably hesitant to return. The authorities generally veer away from persecuting foreigners for homosexual behaviour, but Egyptians are not immune. Lesbian culture is so far subdued that women on the look out will have to look far. For more information about gay issues in Egypt, check out www.gayegypt.com and www.geocities.com/westhollywood/5884; for gay tours, try www.pride-holidays.com/gay-egypt.

Student travellers

Student identification cards Students are entitled to obtain an International Student Identity Card (ISIC), which is distributed by student travel offices and travel agencies in 77 countries. The ISIC card (£7) gives you more economical prices on most forms of transport (air, sea, rail, etc) and substantial discounts (up to 50%) at many Egyptian ancient sights and museums. Before you leave, contact: **ISIC**, www.isiccard.com, for details. Note that though student IDs from specific schools suffice in some places, it is worth getting the ISIC card because it is easily identified by most establishments. In Cairo, ISIC cards can be obtained from Egyptian Student Travel Services (ESTS) with proof of student status (student ID or letter from University or school). Bring a photograph and LE52. For more information, contact: ESTS, T02-5310330, 23 Sharia al-Manial in Cairo University.

Women travellers

Travelling alone as a woman can be a challenging experience in Egypt. Young Muslim women rarely travel without the protection of a male or older female, and so to Egyptians unschooled in Western culture, a single woman may automatically be regarded as strange (at best) and more often than not be considered of easy virtue. Hollywood hasn't helped – with primetime shows like Baywatch highlighting the worst of Western ways. Harassment can take many forms, from catcalls and fervent invites to inappropriate touching and threatening advances. However, with smart and sensible behaviour, it's possible to be adventurous without taking unsafe risks. Here are some gome general hints to minimize the pestering that will certainly occur. Try to walk with confidence and at least pretend that you know where you're going. Dress modestly – the less bare flesh the better (especially avoid revealing your shoulders, cleavage and legs). When in more conservative swimming areas (pretty much anywhere outside of the touristy Sinai resorts), swim in shorts and a loose opaque T-shirt rather than a bathing suit (see page 33). Ignore rude and suggestive comments and most importantly, avoid looking onlookers in the eye. In general, try to steer away from behaviours that may aggravate a situation. When riding public transport, if possible sit next to women (on the Cairo subway the first car is reserved for women only) and avoid late-night transport if alone. If seeking advice or directions outside of hotels and other touristy places try to ask a woman. If you feel exceptionally uncomfortable, deliberate embarrassment of the man in question can be a powerful weapon. You may want to don a wedding band to dissuade potential suitors. If you're travelling with a man, you can avoid a lot of interrogations and confusion by saying that you're married.

> *You can bring attention to the man harassing you by pointing and yelling "Emshee" (Go Away!).*

Note that men and women in Egypt relate to one another differently from men and women in many western countries. The western concept of 'friendship' can be misunderstood. Opt to be more conservative in the way you interact and engage, as a mere smile or question can be misinterpreted as an expression of more than platonic interest. Avoid going into the desert or other solitary places alone with a man you don't know. Most importantly, trust your instincts, be smart and keep a sense of humour. The consequences for serious violations against foreigners in Egypt are so dire that the incidence of rape and other forms of extreme harassment and violation is significantly less than in most other countries.

Working in the country

In order to work as a foreigner in Egypt, you need a special work permit. Opportunities for casual work are limited. There are a handful of English newspapers and magazines in Cairo that will employ foreigners with journalistic inclinations, but it's easiest to organize that once you arrive. If you are TEFL certified and interested in teaching English, you may find informal employment with the private sector. Those interested in diving jobs sometimes find opportunities on the Red Sea coast or in Sinai. It's best to ask around and check with dive shops to see what's available. If you plan to be around for a while, you may want to check with your respective embassy to see if there are any longer term projects available. There is no shortage of foreigners working in Egypt, but most of them are recruited from outside for specific projects.

Business travellers tend to be very well looked after. Egyptians are excellent hosts. Transport, accommodation and business facilities of the highest quality are available at the better hotels in the larger cities.

Before you travel

Visas and immigration

Passports are required by all and should be valid for at least six months beyond the period of your intended stay in Egypt.

There are few closed areas in this region but certain sensitive border zones can be mined or be restricted to military personnel. Do not stray into any clearly marked boundary or no-go areas. Details of any known sensitive areas are given in appropriate sections of this book.

Visas are required by all except nationals of the following countries: Bahrain, Jordan, Kuwait, Libya, Oman, Saudi Arabia and the UAE. Tourist visas cost around the equivalent of US$15 and, for Western tourists, can be bought easily at the airport in foreign currency. In UK this is £12 for a single entry and £18 for up to three entries. Business visas cost £53 and £91 if accompanied by a letter of authorization. Payment must be in cash or by postal order and cheques are not accepted. Visas are valid for three months from date of issue and one month from date of arrival and cannot be post dated. A renewable 30-day tourist visa can be obtained at all international airports and ports, and even on the boat (£10) but not when you are entering from Israel or Palestine.

For south Sinai visits, including St Catherine's Monastery, entrance without a visa is permitted for visits of up to 14 days. You can obtain an entry stamp free of charge when entering through Sinai entry points of Taba, Sharm el-Sheikh airport, Nuweiba and Sharm el-Sheikh seaports. Note that Sinai-only visas are not valid for Ras Mohammed or extensive trekking in Central Sinai.

Visa extensions can be obtained (with difficulty) at the Mogamma, Midan Tahrir, Cairo; Sharia Khaled Ibn El-Walid in Luxor; 28 Sharia Talaat Harb in Alexandria, and at the port in Sharm El-Sheikh. You will need your passport, two new photographs, cash to pay for renewal (£12), and receipts proving you have exchanged US$180 for each extra month you wish to extend. Overstaying by a week or so does not matter, but after 2 weeks, be prepared for a £60 fine and some hassle.

Entry into Israel, Palestine, Jordan, Libya and Sudan As part of the easing of controls on travellers in this area, most countries will issue entry visas at principal border posts. Nonetheless, for travel to another country from Egypt, it's best to consult with the corresponding embassy or consulate for details on obtaining a visa before you get to the border. Obtaining visas to travel in Libya and Sudan can be quite a process, and not always a sure bet, try to do this paperwork before entry to Egypt.

You can get a visa to Jordan on the ferry from Nuweiba to Aqaba. Crossing into Israel and Palestine may be difficult depending on the level of tension in the region.

Assuming border crossing is permitted, you can obtain a free entry visa on the border between Taba and Eilat that can last anywhere from a week to a few months depending on the border guard's inclination. Free month-long visas to Palestine and Israel are also granted from the border at Rafah. Note that visas for entry to Egypt are not granted at the Rafah border. If you plan to enter Egypt from Gaza, get a visa beforehand. If you intend to travel onward to Syria or Lebanon, do not allow your passport to be stamped in Israel or else you may not be permitted to enter (instead, ask authorities to stamp a separate piece of paper). For access to the current border situation, consult the respective embassy.

Egyptian embassies and consulates

Embassies

Australia, 1 Darwin Av, Yarralumla, ACT 2600 Canberra, T62-2734437.
Austria, 1190 Wien, Kreindll Gasse 22, Vienna 1190, T43-3681134, 3681135, 3686321, F43-368113527.
Belgium, Av de l'Uruguay, 19 1000 Bruxelles, T2-6635800, Egypt.embassy@skynet.be
Canada, 454 Laurier Ave East, Ottawa, Ontario, K1N 6R3, T613-2344958.
Denmark, Kristianiagade 19, DK - 2100, Copenhagen, Denmark, T35437070.
France, 56 Av d'lena, 75116 Paris, T1-47209770.
Germany, Kronprinzen Str, Bonn 2, T228-364000.
Greece, 3 Vassilissis Safies St, Athens, T1-3618612/3.
Ireland, 12 Clyde Rd, Dublin 4, T1-606566.
Israel, 54 Rehov Basel, Tel Aviv, T3-5465151.
Italy, 00199, Roma-Villa Savoia, Via Salaria, 267, Roma, CP 7133, T06-8440191.
Morocco, 31 El-Gazaer St, Sawmaat Hassan, Rabat, T7-731834.
Netherlands, Bad Huis Weg 92, PO Box 2587 CL, The Hague, T70-3544535, 3542000.
Norway, Drammensveien 90A, 0244 Oslo 2, T222-00010.
Portugal, Av D Vasco Da Gama No 8, 1400 Lisbon, T1-3018342.
Spain, Velazquez 69, Madrid 28006, T1-5776308.
Sweden, Strandvagen 35, Stockholm, T8-6603145.
Switzerland, 61 Elfenauweg, 3006 Berne, T31-3528012.
UK, 26 South St, London, W1Y 6DD, T020-74993304, www.egypt-embassy.org.uk.
USA Embassy and Consulate, 3521 International Court, NW Washington DC 20008, T202-8955400.

Consulates

Canada, 3754 Côtes-des-Neiges, Montréal, Quebec, H3H 7V6, T514-937781.
Libya, 5th floor, Omar El-Khayam Hotel, Ben Ghazi, T61-92488.
UK, 2 Lowndes St, London, SW1X, T020-72355684, www.MFA.gov.eg. Open 1000-1200, Mon-Fri, for visas.
USA, 1110 2nd Av, New York, NY10022, T212-7597120; 3001 Pacific Av, San Francisco, CA 94115, T415-3469700, www.egy2000.com.

Customs, duty-free and export restrictions

Declarations On arrival you may be asked to declare video cameras and computers on the D form, though this is now rarely the case. In case of theft, report to police or they will assume you have sold them and will charge you duty.

Goods may be imported into Egypt as follows: 200 cigarettes or 250 g of tobacco, 1 litre of alcohol, 1 litre of perfume or toilet water, gifts up to the value of E£500. Duty-free export of purchases can be arranged through the larger shops and tourist agencies.

Vaccinations

Vaccinations are not required unless you are travelling from a country where yellow fever or cholera frequently occurs. You are advised to be up to date with polio, tetanus and hepatitis inoculations. Evidence of an HIV test is required for visitors who intend to stay for over 30 days – although this requirement is not always enforced. » *See Health section, page 57 for further information.*

What to take

Generally, travellers tend to take more than they need. At the moment, you can find most things you might require in Egypt, though choices of products may be a bit limited. Laundry services are generally cheap and speedy. A travelpack, a hybrid backpack/suitcase, rather than a rigid suitcase, covers most eventualities and survives bus boots and roof racks with ease. Serious trekkers will need a framed backpack. The desert climate throughout the year means hot days and deceivingly cool nights. Bring loose-fitting light cotton shirts and trousers and a sweater or light jacket for evenings and cooler regions. Layers are always a good idea. Avoid tank tops and other revealing clothing that bears cleavage or legs above the knee if travelling beyond coastal areas. Sandals and comfortable shoes with socks for long walks. Women may wish to bring a headscarf or sunhat bearing in mind the modest dress norms.

Checklist Sunhat or headscarf; sun protection cream; sunglasses; bathing suit; flipflops or sandals; money belt; air cushions for hard seating; earplugs; eye mask; insect repellent and/or mosquito net; contraceptives; particular toiletry needs; International Driving Licence; photocopies of essential documents; spare passport photographs; Swiss Army knife; torch; wet wipes; zip-lock bags.

Those intending to stay in budget accommodation or take a desert safari might also include: cotton sheet sleeping sack; sleeping bag; padlock (for hotel room and pack); soap; student card; toilet paper; universal bath plug.

Health kit Antacid tablets; anti-diarrhoea tablets; anti-malaria tablets; anti-infective ointment; contraceptives; dusting powder for feet; first aid kit; flea powder; sachets of rehydration salts; tampons; travel sickness pills; water sterilizing tablets.

Insurance

Comprehensive travel insurance can offer peace of mind. Consider a plan that offers immediate repatriation for illness or accident. Claims for lost or stolen items must be backed by evidence of having reported the matter to the police. Obtaining this matter will not be easy. There is a problem of language, getting it written in English and hardest, getting someone high enough in authority to accept the responsibility.

Money

Currency

The Egyptian Pound is divided into 100 piastres. Notes are in denominations of E£1, E£5, E£10, E£20, E£50, E£100 and 5, 10, 25 and 50 Piastres. Coins (which are not worth carrying) are 5 and 10 Piastres. At the time of writing, E£1 = US$0.16 or GB£0.09.

Regulations and money exchange

Visitors can enter and leave Egypt with a maximum of E£10,000. There are no restrictions on the import of foreign currency provided it is declared on an official customs form. Export of foreign currency may not exceed the amount imported. All cash, travellers' cheques, credit cards and gold over a value of E£500 must be declared on arrival. Generally, it's cheaper to exchange foreign currency in Egypt than in your home country. It's always wise to change enough money at home for at least the first 48 hours of you trip, just in case. Nowadays though, since the destabilization of the pound and the accompanying burgeoning black market for foreign currency, US dollars in particular can get buy you most things. In fact, the Ministry of Tourism has recently imposed a new rule that requires foreigners to pay for hotels with three stars or more in US dollars (credit cards are accepted). Given the present climate in the Middle East, this could change at a moment's notice, but be prepared.

Banks

There are five national banks and more than 78 branches of foreign banks. Banking hours are 0830-1400 Sunday-Thursday; some banks have evening hours. **ATMs** are widely available but require a surcharge of between $1 and $5, and often have a daily withdrawal limit of about $500. They are also known to munch on the occasional card, so beware.

Credit cards

Access/Mastercard, American Express, Diners Club and Visa are accepted in all major hotels, larger restaurants and shops, and tend to offer excellent exchange rates. Outside of the tourist industry, Egypt is still a cash economy.

Travellers' cheques

Travellers' cheques are honoured in most banks and bureaux de change. US$ are the easiest to exchange particularly if they are well-known brands like Visa, Thomas Cook or American Express. There is always a transaction charge so a balance needs to be struck between using high value cheques and paying one charge and carrying extra cash or using lower value cheques and paying more charges. A small amount of foreign cash, again preferably US$, is useful in an emergency. Egypt supposedly has a fixed exchange rate – wherever the transaction is carried out.

Tips for saving money

If you are a student or teacher, it is definitely worth making an effort to get the ISIC card which offers extensive discounts at many attractions and on some forms of transport (see student travel on page 24). It's also a good idea, because change for larger bills is often non-existent, always to have lots of small notes on hand so you don't get short changed the odd extra pound or two when buying food on the street or taking a bus or taxi.

Cost of living

Depending on the standards of comfort and cleanliness one is prepared to accept for accommodation, food and travel, it is possible to survive on as little as US$10 per person per day. Prices and standards shift constantly according to season, political climate, inflation and location, but generally, living in Egypt is cheap. Accommodation runs from about US$3-8 for a basic double in a fairly rundown but livable hotel to well over US$100 for 5-star luxury comfort. Good eats have a comparable range. Street stall national staples like *fuul*, *felafel* and *koshari* can fill your belly for less than US$0.50. Or you can opt for a more western-style meal, a bit pricier, but still affordable at US$4-8 a plate. Coffee and tea run at about E£1, soft drinks E£0.75-E£1, beer E£6 (depending where you purchase). Transport varies according to mode. A taxi from the Cairo airport to the centre (a 30-minute ride) costs US$5-8. The Cairo metro is less than US$0.25. Local buses are even cheaper. Buses and trains between cities range in price depending on amenities and distances but are generally very cheap (for example, a bus ticket from Cairo to Sharm El-Sheikh, about a 500 km distance, runs at E£55-70 (or around US$10) on the East Delta bus company). Renting a car is a significantly more expensive option at US$40-60 per day. The price of petrol (super) has remained unchanged for years at E£1 per litre.

There are costs often not accounted for in other parts of the world that you will inevitably encounter in Egypt. Most restaurants include a 12% tax (after the service charge) on the bill and it is common practice to tip an additional 10%. Another kind of tipping, known as *baksheesh*, occurs when you are offered a small service, whether or not you ask for it. If someone washes the windows of your car, looks after your shoes in a mosque, or opens the door for you, they may expect a modest offering. Carry around several 25 and 50 piaster notes and take it in your stride, it's part of the culture.

Getting there

Air

Buying a ticket

It is possible to fly direct to Egypt from Europe, the Middle East, the USA and most adjacent African countries. There is an inordinate number of ways to buy a plane ticket and finding the cheapest among them can be a puzzling affair. A little bit of research can save a lot of money. The internet is an increasingly good resource to compare prices and shop around. Lots of websites offer access to a range of airline fares. In particular try the following: www.travelocity.com, www.cheaptickets.com, www.cheapflights.co.uk, www.flynow.com, www.travelzoo.com, www.expedia.com.

Fares vary according to season. They peak from June to September and around other holiday times. The cheapest times to travel are during November and January. As a rule, the earlier you buy a ticket, the cheaper it will be. Buying tickets at least 2-3 weeks in advance can cut down on the price significantly. It's worth checking in with a few travel agents to see if any special promotions are available. Sometimes tour companies offer cheaper fares as they buy them in big numbers. Return tickets are usually a lot cheaper than buying two one-way tickets or opting for an open-ended return. Round-the-World tickets may also be worth considering, especially if you intend to travel beyond Egypt. Prices for RTW tickets start around £900 or US$1,500.

Flights from Britain, Ireland and Europe

From London, **British Airways**, T0870-8509850, www.britishairways.com, and **EgyptAir**, see below, offer daily flights to Cairo. Flight time is about 4 hours. There are also consistent charter flights to Hurghada, Luxor and Sharm El-Sheikh. Again, prices vary depending on the season and flexibility of ticket purchased. At this time, there are no direct flights from Ireland. **Luftansa**, T0870-8377747, www.lufthansa.com, offers direct flights to Cairo via Frankfurt, **Air France**, T0845-0845111, www.airfrance.com, via Paris, and **KLM**, www.klm,com, via Amsterdam. **Austrian Airlines**, www.austrianair.com, and **Czech Airlines**, www.csa.cz, have services too, often at competitive prices. Tickets from London to Cairo range from £250 with student discount in the off-season to £400 during peak tourist season. Shop around for deals and look into discount charter flights if you don't mind starting your journey outside Cairo.

Flights from North America

From New York, **EgyptAir**, see below, offers the 11-hour direct flight to Cairo a few times per week. Ticket prices range from US$800 in the off-season up to US$1,500 during peak travel times. Most European carriers offer flights from major North American cities to Cairo via their European hubs. **British Airways** and **KLM** (see above) serve the bigger cities on the west coast. From Canada, there are no direct flights to

 Egypt, but European airlines have connecting services from Montréal and Toronto that do not necessitate overnight stays in Europe.

Flights from Australia and New Zealand

EgyptAir, see below, offers a direct service from Australia to Egypt a couple of times per week. There are no direct flights from New Zealand. Many Asian and European airlines offer service from New Zealand and Australia to Cairo via their hub cities. Tickets can be expensive, so it may be worth opting for a Round-the-World ticket, which could be comparable in price or even cheaper than a roundtrip flight. From Australia to Egypt tickets range from about A$1,750 during the off-season to A$2,500 in the peak season. **Qantas**, www.qantas.com, **Austrian Airlines**, www.austrianair.com, and **Alitlalia**, www.alitalia.com, in addition to a few Asian carriers, offer competitive prices.

EgyptAir contact details

The national airline is **EgyptAir**, www.egyptair.com.eg. **UK**, 29/31 Picadilly, London, T020-77342395. **USA**, 720 Fifth Avenue, New York 10019, T800-3346787. **Australia**, Suite 1601, 130 Pitt St, Sydney, T92326677. **Canada**, 151 Bloor Street, Suite 300, Toronto, Ontario, T9602441. **France**, 1 Bls Reu Auber, 75009, Paris, T44948530. **Netherlands**, Singel 540, 1017 AZ, Amsterdam, T6256661. **South Africa**, JHI House, 11 Cradock Ave, 7th floor, Rosebank 2196, T8804525.

Airline restrictions

General airline restrictions apply with regard to luggage weight allowances before a surcharge is added; normally 30 kg for first class and 20 kg for business and economy class. An understanding of the term 'limited' with regard to amount of hand luggage varies greatly. Some airlines can be strict and will decline to permit large or in some cases more than one item of hand luggage on board with the passenger.

Airline security

International airlines vary in their arrangements and requirements for security over electrical items such as radios, tape recorders and lap-top computers (as does the interest of the customs officials on arrival and departure). Check in advance if you can, carry the items in your hand luggage for convenience and have them wrapped for safety but available for inspection. Most airports require that travellers arrive at least 2 hours before international departure times.

Road

Bus and service taxi

For coaches to and from Israel (Tel Aviv and Jerusalem) contact: **Travco Travel Agency**, T02-7371737, 112 Sharia 26 July, Zamalek, Cairo, if the political climate is tame, they will help you book a ticket. The **East Delta Bus Company**, T02-5762293, runs three air-conditioned buses daily to Taba, at the Eilat border (times: 0630, 0800, 2200, E£55) and one bus daily to Rafah, at the Gaza border (0730, E£37).

Service taxis run between Marsa Matruh and Sollum on the Libyan border. **Arab Union Superjet**, T02-2660214/2, buses leave from Midan Almaza, T2909013, and Turgomen Station, Cairo, for Jordan, Saudi Arabia, Libya, Syria, Dubai, Kuwait, Bahrain and Qatar.

Driving

The main international road west goes to Libya and to the east under the Suez Canal via El-Arish to Palestine and Israel. As the present political climate is strained at best, and so it is essential that road travellers consult the respective consulates and embassies to ensure passage is possible. Other international routes are along the Nile Valley and along the northern Sinai and the Red Sea coasts. Entry requirements for private cars include a Carnet de Passage en Douane and an International Driving Licence. You may wish to contact the **Egyptian Automobile Club**, 1 Sharia Kasr El-Nil, Cairo, T02-5743191, 5743348. Vehicles must be petrol, not diesel. Extra vehicle insurance may be required at the border.

Sea

Ferries

The region is served by a number of ferry services, particularly across the Red Sea/Gulf of Aqaba, most catering for both vehicles and foot passengers. In general, ferries are reliable and usually moderately comfortable. Check out www.touregypt.net/ferries.htm or www.estsegypt.com/ferries.htm for the most current timetable information.

The main coastal ports are Alexandria, Port Said, Nuweiba and Suez. Ferries operating in this area can be contacted in **UK** at: **Viamare Travel**, Graphic House, 2 Sumatra Road, London, NW6 1PU, T020-74314560, www.viamare.co.uk. Ferries to Southern Europe and around the Mediterranean leave from Port Said.

In Egypt, for connections to and from **Southern Europe** contact **Mena Tours Agency**, T02-7482231, 14 Sharia Talaat Harb, Cairo; 28 Sharia Al-Ghorfa Al-Tigariya, Alexandria, T03-4806909.

For connections with **Jordan**, from Nuweiba to Aqaba there are two boats that leave daily (see the Sinai chapter for details). Reservations are generally not necessary, but it is essential to arrive early, especially for the speedier catamaran. For more information, in Cairo contact the **Cairo Navigation Agency**, T02-5745744, 7 Abdel Khalek Sarwat Street. In Sinai, the **Coral Hilton**, T069-520320, is an excellent source of information.

Given the recent political turmoil in the region, Mediterranean cruises that stop in Egypt have been significantly reduced. As things improve, they may recommence their service. In the past, the following cruise ships have called in at ports in Egypt: **Airtours Cruises**, Wavell House, Holcombe Road, Helmshore, Rossendale, Lancs, BB4 4NB, T0870-2412567, call in at Alexandria. **P&O Cruises**, 77 New Oxford Street, London, WC1A 1PP, T020-78002345, call in at Alexandria and Port Said. **Titan Travel/Costa Cruises**, HiTours House, Crossoak Lane, Selfords, Surrey, RH1 5EX, T01737-760033, www.titantravel.co.uk, call in at Alexandria and Port Said.

Ferries ply between Hurghada and Duba (3 hours) and Suez and Jeddah (2 days) in **Saudi Arabia**, contact **Mena Tours Agency**, 14 Sharia Talaat Harb, Cairo, T02-7482231.

Touching down

Airport information

Egypt's international airports are: **Cairo International (CAI)**, T02-2914255, 22 km northeast of the city (travel time 30 minutes), Terminal 1 hosts EgyptAir, the newer Terminal 2 is about 3 km away and takes all other flights, both have 24-hour currency exchange; **Alexandria Airport (ALY)**, 5 km southeast of the city; and **Luxor Airport (LXR)**, 5.5 km from the town.

Touching down

Business hours Banks: 0830-1400 Saturday-Thursday. Government offices: 0900-1400 every day except Friday and national holidays. Shops: 0900-1230 and 1600-2000 in summer and 0900-1900 in winter. Hours on Friday and Sunday vary.
Directory enquiries 140.
Emergency services Cairo Police: 122, Ambulance: 123, Fire: 125, Tourist Police: 126.
IDD 140.
Museum hours Open daily 0900-1600 but generally close for Friday noon prayers, from around 1200-1400.
Official language Arabic.
Official time GMT plus 2 hours.
Voltage 220 volts AC. Sockets take standard continental two round pin plugs. Continental adaptors are useful.
Weights and measures Metric.

Airport tax

Departure Departure tax is included in the price of airline tickets. Confirm airline flights at least 48 hours in advance. Have all currency exchange receipts easily available. Before passing into the departure lounge/area it is necessary to fill in an embarkation card. Only a limited amount of currency can be reconverted before you leave. This is a tedious process and is not possible at Luxor airport. Sometimes suitable foreign currency is not available. It is better to budget with care, have no excess cash and save all the trouble.

Local customs and laws

Though Egypt is among the more liberal and 'westernized' of the Arab countries, it is still an Islamic country where religion is deeply embedded in daily life. While Islam is similar to Judaism and Christianity in its philosophical content and the three revealed religions are accepted together as the religions of the book (*Ahl Al-Kitab*), it is wise for travellers to recognize that Islamic practices in this traditional society are a sensitive area. Public observance of religious ritual and taboo are important, just as is the protection of privacy for women and the family. Islam of an extremist kind is on the wane in Egypt but bare-faced arrogance by visitors will engender a very negative response even among normally welcoming Egyptians who generally have no tendencies towards fundamentalist views.

Islam has a very specific code of practices and taboos but most will not affect the visitor unless he or she gains entry to local families or organizations at a social level. In any case a few considerations are worthy of note by all non-Muslims when in company with Muslim friends or when visiting particularly conservative areas. (i) Dress modestly. Women in particular should see the dress code, page 33 for further explanation. (ii) If visiting during the holy month of Ramadan where Muslims fast from sunrise to sunset, dress particularly conservatively and avoid eating, drinking and smoking in public places. (iii) If offering a gift to a Muslim friend, be aware that pork and alcohol are forbidden. If you choose to offer other meat, ensure it is *hallal*, killed in accordance with Muslim ritual. (iv) If dining in a traditional Bedouin setting or context, do not use your left hand for eating since it is ritually unclean. (If knives and forks are provided, then both hands can be used.) Do not accept or ask for alcohol unless your host clearly intends to imbibe. Keep your feet tucked under your body away from the food.

Class discrepancies and the *khawagga* (foreigner)

Compared to other developing countries, there are particularly great discrepancies among Egyptians with regard to their experience, openness, education and worldliness. Some are extremely sophisticated, knowledgeable and well-travelled while others (widely known as *fellaheen* – peasants) are markedly conservative and parochial. Class is often a delineating factor, as is education and the urban/rural divide. For the traveller, maintaining awareness of social context is essential for positive and culturally sensitive interchanges with locals.

Another evident discrepancy is the cost of services for Egyptians and foreigners. If you have not yet stumbled upon the word *khawagga* (foreigner), you soon will, as it holds similar implications to the word "gringo" in many Latin American countries. Taxi fares, entries to many attractions, even the price of luxury accommodation all cost foreigners more. Bear in mind that the average Egyptian makes about US$1,500 per head per year; the average foreign tourist lives on approximately US$32,000.

The dress code

Daily dress for most Egyptians is governed by considerations of climate and weather. Other than labourers in the open, the universal reaction is to cover up against heat or cold. For males other than the lowest of manual workers, full dress is normal. Men breaching this code will either be young and regarded as being of low social status or very rich and Westernized. When visiting mosques, *madresas* or other shrines/tombs/religious libraries, Muslim men wear full and normally magnificently washed and ironed traditional formal wear. In the office, men will be traditionally dressed or in Western suits and shirt sleeves. The higher the grade of office, the more likely the Western suit. At home people relax in loose gallabah. Arab males will be less constrained on the beach where swimming trunks are the norm.

For women the dress code is more important and extreme. Quite apart from dress being a tell-tale sign of social status among the ladies of Cairo or Alexandria or of tribal/regional origin, decorum and religious sentiment dictates full covering of body, arms and legs. The veil is increasingly common for women, a reflection of growing Islamic revivalist views. There are still many women who do not don the veil, including those with modern attitudes towards female emancipation, professional women trained abroad and the religious minorities – Copts and Jews. Jewellery (see Jewellery in Background, page 508) is another major symbol in women's dress, especially heavy gold necklaces.

The role of dress within Islamic and social codes is clearly a crucial matter. While some latitude in dress is given to foreigners, good guests are expected to conform to the broad lines of the practice of the house. Thus, except on the beach or 'at home' in the hotel (assuming it is a tourist rather than local establishment), modesty in dress pays off. This means jeans or slacks for men rather than shorts together with a shirt or T-shirt. For women, modesty is slightly more demanding. In public wear comfortable clothes that at least cover the greater part of the legs and arms. If the opportunity arises to visit a mosque or *madresa*, then a *gallabah* and/or slippers are often available for hire at the door. Most women do not swim in public and if they do, they tend to dive in fully clad. If you choose to swim outside a touristy area, wear shorts and an opaque T-shirt. Elsewhere full covering of arms and legs and a headscarf is preferable. Offend against the dress code – and most Western tourists in this area do to a greater or lesser extent – and you risk antagonism and alienation from the local people who are increasingly conservative in their Islamic beliefs and observances.

Bargaining

Bargaining is expected in the souks. Most shop owners site the start price at two to three times the amount they hope to make. Start lower than you would expect to pay, be polite and good humoured, enjoy the experience and if the final price doesn't suit, walk away. There are plenty more shops. Once you have gained confidence, try it on the taxi drivers and when negotiating a room. The bargaining exchange can be a great way to meet people and practice your Arabic.

Courtesy

Politeness is always appreciated. You will notice a great deal of hand shaking, kissing, clapping on backs on arrival and departure from a group. There is no need to follow this to the extreme but handshakes, smiles and thank yous go a long way. Shows of affection and physical contact are widely accepted among members of the same sex. Be more conservative in greeting and appreciating people of the opposite sex. Do not show the bottom of your feet or rest them on tables or chairs as this gesture is regarded as extremely rude in Egypt. Be patient and friendly but firm when bargaining for items and avoid displays of anger. However, when it comes to getting onto public transport, forget it all – the description 'like a Cairo bus' needs no explanation.

Mosque etiquette

Do not enter mosques during a service and take photographs only after asking or when clearly permissible. Visitors to mosques and other religious buildings will normally be expected to remove their shoes. Women and men should remain in the areas designated solely for their respective sexes.

Photography

Photographs of police, soldiers, docks, bridges, military areas, airports, radio stations and other public utilities are prohibited. Photography is also prohibited in tombs where much damage can be done with a flash bulb. Photography is unrestricted in all open, outdoor historic areas but some sites make an extra charge for cameras. Flashes are not permitted in the Egyptian Museum in Cairo nor for delicate relics such as the icons in St Catherine's Monastery. Taking photographs of any person without permission is unwise, of women is taboo, and tourist attractions like water sellers, camels/camel drivers etc may require *baksheesh*. Even the goat herder will expect an offering for providing the goats. Always check that use of a video camera is permitted at tourist sites and be prepared to pay a heavy fee (E£100+) for permission.

Police

Report any incident which involves you or your possessions. An insurance claim of any size will require the backing of a police report. If involvement with the police is more serious, for instance as a result of a driving accident, remain calm and contact the nearest consular office without delay. Some embassies advise leaving the scene of an accident immediately and heading straight to your embassy.

Tipping

Tipping, or *baksheesh*, a word you will fast learn, is a way of life – everyone except high officials expects a reward for services actually rendered or imagined. Many people connected with tourism get no or very low wages and rely on tips to survive. The advice here is to be a frequent but small tipper. The principal of 'little and often' seems to work well. Usually 12% is added to hotel and restaurant bills but an extra tip of about 10% is normal and expected. In hotels and at monuments tips will be expected for the most minimal service. Rather than make a fuss, have some small bills handy. Tips may be the person's only income.

Beggars

Alms-giving is a personal duty in Muslim countries. It is unlikely that beggars will be too persistent. Have a few small bills ready and offer what you can. You will be unable to help everyone and your donation may be passed on to the syndicate organizer!

Prohibitions

Antiquities

Trading in antiquities is illegal everywhere. Most items for sale are fakes. Real artifacts are expensive and trading in them can lead to confiscation and/or imprisonment.

Black market

Make use of black market currency only when it is private and safe. Since the severe inflation of the pound, there is no shortage of people willing to sell Egyptian pounds for US dollars well above the official exchange rate. But be careful as Egypt, like most countries, has tight laws against currency smuggling and illegal dealing.

Documents

It's wise to photocopy all important documents just in case you lose them. Passports are lost but they are also traded for cash/drugs and officials can be very unsympathetic. Long and often expensive delays can occur while documents are replaced. Keep all forms such as landing cards and currency documents together with bank receipts for foreign exchange transactions.

! It is wise to keep a record of your passport number, travellers' cheque numbers and air ticket details somewhere separate from the actual items.

Drugs

Though there is no shortage of drugs in Egypt, drug enforcement policies are strict. The death penalty may be imposed for those convicted of smuggling or selling narcotics. Possession of even small quantities may lead to prosecution.

Firearms

Firearms including hunting guns may not be imported without prior permission. Permits can be obtained for hunting guns through the hotel/tour organizer. It is forbidden to take ivory, crocodile, snake or lizard skin into the UK.

Politics

Keep clear of all political activities. Nothing is so sensitive as opposition to the régime. By all means keep an interest in local politics but do not become embroiled as a partisan. The *mokharbarat* (secret services) are singularly unforgiving and unbridled in their action against political dissent.

Safety

The level of petty crime in Egypt is no greater than elsewhere. It is unlikely that you will be robbed but take sensible precautions. Leave your valuables in a hotel deposit box never leave them lying around around your room. Avoid carrying excess money or wearing obviously valuable jewellery when sightseeing. There will be pickpockets in crowded places. It is wise not to walk around at night away from the main thoroughfares. External pockets on bags and clothing should never be used for carrying valuables. Bag snatching and pick pocketing is more common in crowded tourist areas.

Following the war on Iraq, there is a fairly widespread anti-American and anti-Anglo sentiment, but for the most part the disillusion is not mis-targetted. Egyptians seem to separate their disdain for foreign governments from individual travellers. On the whole, Egypt is as safe a country to travel as anywhere else, especially if you maintain a sensitivity and awareness of your surroundings. Nonetheless, with such a volatile political climate around the world, it's always wise to check with your national authorities before departure for Egypt. If coming from the UK, for travel advice, check the Foreign and Commonwealth Office at www.fco.gov.uk; from the US, check the Dept of State at www.travel.state.gov.

As care for foreign visitors is vital to keep the tourist industry alive, the government has worked hard to ensure safety in more touristy locales and there have been no attacks on tourists since 1998. Still, some towns in Middle Egypt, Assiut and Qena in particular, are far more fundamentalist-inclined than others and the government has had a harder time containing the Islamic revivalist sentiment.

September 11, the war on Iraq and the 2003 attacks on foreigners in Riyadh brought about a new set of challenges for the tourist industry and reinforced the government's attempts at ensuring safety for foreign visitors. Part of the system requires most Western tourists be accompanied by a police escort (see Convoys below) on their trips to certain areas, especially if they are in a private vehicle. Tour companies and tour buses are not always immune from these regulations and some of them choose to be accompanied for security. It can be a bit of an annoyance, but not tremendously limiting. Travellers are generally expected to provide food and other essentials for the escorts. Note that, like everything in Egypt, this is always changing depending on the political climate and the whims of government officials.

Confidence tricksters

The most common 'threat' to tourists is found where people are on the move, at airports, railway and bus stations, and shipping ports, offering extremely favourable currency exchange rates, selling tours or 'antiques', and spinning hard luck stories. Confidence tricksters are, by definition, extremely convincing and persuasive. Be warned – if the offer seems too good to be true that is probably what it is.

Convoys

Egypt's security system also requires foreigners travelling in private cars, hired taxis and tourist buses to travel in police-escorted convoys when journeying between towns in certain regions. In the El-Fayoum and areas around the Eastern and Western deserts, visitors are more likely to encounter police escorts. Through the Eastern Desert and in Upper Egypt, there are regularly scheduled convoys between significant tourist destinations: at least three daily between Luxor and Aswan; three between Luxor and Hurghada, two between Aswan and Abu Simbel; two from Luxor to Dendara and back, (one of which carries on to Abydos). As schedules often change, depending on the season and number of tourists, check with the nearest tourist office for the current departure times. At present, there are no scheduled convoys in Middle Egypt. Independent travellers are best off using trains to navigate the region. If you want to drive through, inquire with the tourist authority. See box page 37.

Restricted travel

Though there are a dozen daily **trains** travelling south from Cairo to Middle and Upper Egypt, foreigners are technically only permitted to ride on three, which are guarded by policemen. For train travel once in Upper Egypt, the tickets visitors can purchase are still restricted, but it's sometimes possible to board the train and pay the conductor once in motion. It's highly unlikely you will be kicked off. **Service taxis** in Upper Egypt generally do not accept foreigners when travelling between towns so they can avoid the confines of the convoys. If a foreigner is found unescorted at a checkpoint, the drivers may be severely fined. **Buses** in Upper Egypt, if carrying more than four foreigners, are required to be in a convoy. It is essential, therefore, if travelling by bus, that you purchase your ticket in advance (where possible) to ensure a seat. Because

With friends like the tourist police

Those travelling in Egypt outside the confines of the tour bus, Nile cruise boat and the main tourist sites will often find themselves in the bear hug of the police authorities – mainly the tourist police. This is especially the case in Middle Egypt and in Upper Egypt outside of the tourist bubbles of Luxor and Aswan. You may also come upon the free escort service when travelling between the Red Sea coast and the Nile Valley, or when exploring the Western Desert and central Sinai. Individual or small groups of foreigners travelling in private cars will find their transport under rather close official guard that can be uncomfortable at times, despite the good intentions.

If you find yourself in the grip of a police escort, there is little that can be done to gain liberty. The Egyptian government is determined in the wake of the 1997 massacre at Luxor that no further tourist lives will be lost by terrorist attack. Police chiefs know that any publicized tourist deaths by Islamists in their district will mean instant transfer to an isolated Nubian village in the deep south! The best way to handle the problem is to create as profound a cordon sanitaire around your vehicle as possible; keep well out of sight line of the weapons of your watchdogs and keep as great a distance between your own car and that of your escort so as to avoid a collision. As always approach the game with a sense of humour.

of these restrictions, travel by train offers the most flexibility and reliability in the region. It's also generally faster, more consistent and comfortable.

Restricted areas Potentially risky are Egyptian border areas near Libya and Sudan, as well as off-road bits of Sinai, where landmines (usually marked by barbwire) may exist. People wishing to travel to the frontier regions will need travel permits from the Ministry of Interior's travel permit department on the corner of Sharia Sheikh Rihan/Nubar in central Cairo. Most travel agents who organize desert tours are able to obtain permits as well. Permits are also required to travel to parts of central Sinai, and far flung regions of the Western desert, including the Darb Siwa (the road connecting Bahariyya to Siwa) and the Gilf Kebir. Travel agencies that book desert tours can get permits for travel, which is a slightly more expensive but significantly easier option. Contact **Misr Travel,** T02-3930010, the huge government travel agency skyscraper in Abbaseya; **Dahab Tours,** Midan El-Nasr, T02-2632221; or **Mena Tours Agency,** 14 Sharia Talaat Harb, T02-7482231.

Safety in the desert

The Sahara is extremely varied in its topography and climate. Each day has a large range of temperature, often of more than 20°C, with the world's highest temperatures recorded here at over 55°C, and the nights sometimes below freezing. With this in mind, it is essential that you come to the desert prepared. In addition to light clothing of natural fibres, bring sufficient layers for the cooler nights. Also essential on any desert trek or expedition are: a first aid kit, hat, whistle, torch, rehydration packets, high energy foods, and extra water. Most **health** risks in the desert are avoidable. The rules, evolved over many years, are simple and easy to follow.

1 On extensive desert treks and expeditions, allow time to acclimatize to full desert conditions. Conserve your energy at first rather than acting as if you were still in a temperate climat. Most people take a week or more to adjust to heat conditions here.

2 Stay out of direct sunlight whenever possible, especially once the sun is high. Whenever you can, do what the locals do, move from shade to shade.
3 Wear natural fibre clothes to protect your skin from the sun, particularly your head and neck. Use a high Sun Protection Factor (SPF) cream, preferably as high as SPF15 (94%) to minimize the effects of UV.
4 Drink good quality water regularly. It is estimated that 15 litres per day are needed by a healthy person to avoid water deficiency in desert conditions, even if there is no actual feeling of thirst. The majority of ailments arising in the desert relate to water deficiency and so it is worth the small effort of regular drinking of water. Too much alcoholic drink has the opposite effect in most cases and is not, unfortunately, a substitute for water.
5 Be prepared for cold nights by having some warm clothes to hand.
6 Stay in your quarters or vehicle if there is a sand storm.
7 Deserts and stomach upsets have a habit of going hand in hand. Choose hot cooked meals in preference to cold meats and tired salads. Peel all fruit and uncooked fresh vegetables. Do not eat milk-based items or drink untreated water unless you are absolutely sure of its good quality.
8 Sleep off the ground if you can. There are very few natural dangers in the desert but scorpions, spiders and snakes are present (though rarely fatal) and are best avoided.

The key to safe travel in desert regions is reliable and well-equipped **transport**. Most travellers will simply use local bus and taxi services. For the motorist, motorcyclist or pedal cyclist there are ground rules which, if followed, will help to reduce risks. In normal circumstances travellers will remain on tarmacked roads and for this need only a well prepared two wheel drive vehicle. Choose a machine which is known for its reliability and for which spares can be easily obtained. In Egypt Peugeot and Mercedes are found with adequate spares and servicing facilities. If you have a different type of car/truck, make sure that you take spares with you or have the means of getting spares sent out. Bear in mind that transport of spares to and from rural Egypt might take a tediously long time. Petrol/benzene/gas is available everywhere, diesel is equally well distributed except in the smallest of southern settlements. Four-wheel drive transport is useful even for the traveller who normally remains on the tarmacked highway. Emergencies, diversions and unscheduled visits to off the road sites become less of a problem with all-terrain vehicles. Off the road, four-wheel drive is essential, normally with two vehicles travelling together. A great variety of four-wheel drive vehicles are in use in the region, Toyota and Land Rover are probably found the most widely.

Vehicles going into any desert area should have the following basic equipment:

1 Full tool kit, vehicle maintenance handbook and supplementary tools such as clamps, files, wire, spare parts kit supplied by car manufacturer, jump leads.
2 Spare tyre/s, battery driven tyre pump, tyre levers, tyre repair kit, hydraulic jack, jack handle extension, base plate for jack.
3 Spare fuel can/s, spare water container/s, cool bags.

For those going off the tarmacked roads other items to include are:
4 Foot tyre pump, heavy duty hydraulic or air jack, power winch, sand channels, safety rockets, comprehensive first aid kit, radio/telephone.
5 Emergency rations kit, matches, Benghazi burner (a double-skinned water boiler).
6 Maps, compasses, GPS, latest road information, guides to navigation by the sun and stars.

Driving in the desert is an acquired skill. Basic rules are simple but crucial:
1 If you can get a guide, who perhaps wants a lift to your precise destination, use him.

Mine peril ever present

Thirty people die from land mine explosions in Egypt each year on average. There are estimated to be as many as 21 million land mines still in place dating from the Second World War or the several Arab-Israeli wars in more recent years. Some 16.7 million lie in the Western Desert, a damaging legacy of the long campaigns in that area in the years 1940-43. Most of the remaining 5.7 million mines are in the Canal Zone and the adjacent battlefields of Sinai.

Most mines are anti-tank devices but, as they deteriorate with age, become unstable and are quite capable of detonating under the pressure of a human foot. Clearances and minefield marking are going ahead slowly but meanwhile tread with care in the following areas:

1 For 30 km either side of the Alexandria-Marsa Matruh highway and all areas around the El-Alamein battlefields.
2 The area west of the Suez Canal such as Port Said, El-Qantara and Ismailia.
3 The open country to the west of the Red Sea such as in the deserts surrounding Safaga and Hurgada.
4 Gulf of Suez.
5 The remote areas of the Gulf of Aqaba/Sinai hinterlands.
6 North Sinai around sites such as El-Arish.
7 The Sinai passes at Mitla and Giddi.

Best advice is to stay away from locations where there are no signs of previous recent entry and always heed warning markers which are posted in both Arabic and English.

2 Set out early in the morning after first light, rest during the heat of the day and use the cool of the evening for further travel.
3 Never travel at night or when there is a sandstorm brewing or in progress.
4 Always travel with at least two vehicles which should remain in close, visual contact.

Other general hints include not speeding across open flat desert in case the going changes without warning and your vehicle beds deeply into soft sand or a gully. Well maintained corrugated road surfaces can be taken at modest pace but rocky surfaces should be treated with great care to prevent undue wear on tyres. Sand seas are a challenge for drivers but need a cautious approach – ensure that your navigation lines are clear so that weaving between dunes does not disorientate the navigator. Especially in windy conditions, sight lines can vanish, leaving crews with little knowledge of where they are. Cresting dunes from dip slope to scarp needs care that the vehicle does not either bog down or overturn. Keep off salt flats after rain and floods especially in the winter and spring when water tables can rise and make the going hazardous in soft mud. Even when on marked and maintained tracks beware of approaching traffic.

In the desert border areas of Egypt, **unexploded mines** are a hidden danger. Maps of mined areas are unreliable, some were never marked. Always obey the precautionary signs. Floods can move mines considerable distances from the original site. Be warned, people do die.

Getting around

From camel to plane to *felucca*, Egypt is equipped with myriad of transport options. Congestion and chaos can be a bit anxiety-provoking on long road ventures, but with a bit of courage and flexibility, you can access most areas without too much effort. As for timetables and infrastructure, the country seems to run on magic. There are few regulations and little consistency, but somehow, people always seem to get where they want to go.

Air

Domestic airlines link the main towns. The services are reliable, but significantly pricier than other modes of transport. If time is limited or the prospect of a 12-hour train or bus ride seems too much to bear, Egypt is well-equipped with small airports around the country.

There are daily flights from Cairo to Alexandria, Luxor, Aswan, Abu Simbel, Sharm El-Sheikh and Hurghada and less frequently to Marsa Matruh, Kharga and Assuit. During high season, booking ahead is essential. **EgyptAir**, Nile Hilton, T02-5793046, 5772410, or at 9 Talaat Harb in Central Cairo, T02-3932836, 3930381, www.egyptair.com.eg.

Example flight times: Cairo to Luxor 1 hour, Cairo to Aswan 2 hours, Aswan to Abu Simbel 40 minutes, Cairo to Hurgarda 1 hour.

Boat

Ferry

Ferries connect Hurghada on the Red Sea coast to Sharm El-Sheikh in the Sinai. From Nuweiba, there are daily ferries to Aqaba, Jordan. From Alexandria and Port Said, there are boats to various destinations around the Mediterranean. The Sudanese railway operates a steamer service from Aswan to Wadi Halfa but it is often suspended due to tensions in the region.

Felucca

A long meander down the ancient and enchanting river Nile is a highlight for many exploring the mysteries of Egypt. For travellers on a budget or in search of a more rugged Nile cruise, a great way to get a taste of the river in all her splendor and take in the temples between Aswan and Luxor is on a traditional Nile sailing boat or *felucca*. Most common are the 1 day-1 night trips to nearby Kom Ombo (where the *felucca* stops immediately in front of the temple) and the 3 day-2 night trips to Edfu. From there, it's possible to carry on overland to other significant sights between Aswan and Luxor. Alternatively, you can sail on to Esna (4 days, 3 nights), or Luxor (5 days, 4 nights).

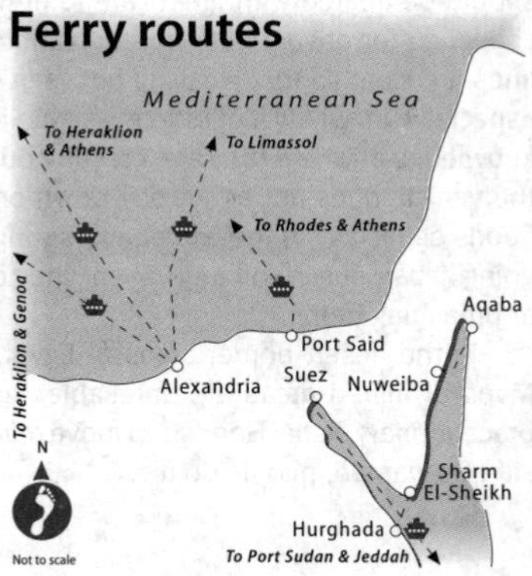

Things to consider before embarking on a *felucca* trip

1 Before agreeing to anything, make sure you check out the boat. Ensure it's well looked after and that there are life jackets for everyone and a covering to protect you from the sun. It's also wise to make sure there are sufficient blankets, mattresses, cooking necessities, etc. to accommodate everyone on board.
2 Before handing over any money, be very clear about your agreement.
3 Ensure the final destination is what you expect. Sometimes, especially in winter when the days are short and the nights too cold to sail, captains will drop their passengers 40 km south of Edfu city. Check with your captain to see what's possible given the weather and current and don't pay the entire amount up front.
4 If the price you agree upon includes all food and water, make sure you know how much bottled water you're getting. Each person will need 2-3 bottles per day. You should bring extra bottled water to be safe.
5 Ensure the captain has sufficient tap water on board for cooking; otherwise he may be dipping into the Nile to boil your pasta and brew your tea.
6 Refuse any last minute additional passengers not initially agreed upon, as supplies and comfort may grow scarce further up the Nile.
7 Ensure the captain you deal with will be on the boat and ask to meet his assistant (there are always two supporting each other). Sometimes the dealers are not the sailors.
8 Captains are required to take your passport to the police to register the trip and ensure your safety. It costs E£5. Don't hand over your passport, give them a copy.
9 Plan to pay half of what you agree upon in advance so the captain can buy your food and get permission, pay the rest after you arrive at your agreed destination.
10 In the winter, you'll need a sleeping bag, as the nights are quite cold. In the summer, it's still good to have, but not essential. If you don't have sleeping gear, ensure the boat does. It's also wise to bring sunblock, insect repellant, toilet paper (to be burned or carried with you, not buried) and a good book.
11 It's perfectly acceptable for you to change your mind about *felucca* captains. If you do, expect to forfeit your permission fee. You should get your food money back. If they say the food has already been bought, ask for the food.
12 If any problems arise, report to the tourist office who can act as an intermediary with you and the police.

Days are generally spent languidly enjoying the passing scenery, reading, and talking to fellow passengers. Nights range from lively partying around bonfires on sandy island shores to quiet sky-gazing, depending on the group and captain. Often, captains who come from villages en route will treat you to a visit to their home. There is also a scattering of interesting stops on the Nile; if the wind is pushing you on fast enough, you may want to ask your captain to dock so you can have a look around.

Passengers usually sleep on board the boat or camp on a sandy island. (The standard number of passengers is between six and eight. It's better to aim for six if you want a bit of space to move about.) Captains will stop if you need to use the 'bathroom' on shore. It's easy to hire a service taxi back to Aswan or north to Luxor from your destination and captains will often arrange it for you if you ask (bear in mind it may be a bit more expensive than what you could find on your own).

The government has established fixed prices for *felucca* trips. If there are at least six passengers, it should cost about E£25 per person to Kom Ombo, E£45 to Edfu, E£60 to Esna and E£75 to Luxor. This does not include the cost of the necessary "permission" (an additional E£5), or the cost of food and bottled water (an additional E£10-20, depending on number of days sailing and number of people on board). If you want beer or other extras, plan to bring it yourself, or ask for it and pay extra. When demand for *felucca* cruises is high, captains can ask for more; when it's low, bargaining is the norm. Beware of a captain who accepts a price significantly lower than the ones sighted because chances are the money you save is coming out of the amount allotted for your food. If your group is less than six, plan to pay a bit more to accommodate for the captain's loss.

With more than 500 *feluccas* and at least that many sailors based in Aswan, it can be a stressful experience choosing a captain, but incredibly worthwhile once you're lazily meandering down the Nile. You will be bombarded by offers as soon as you get off the train or wander for a minute along the corniche. Everyone has a favorite and most hotels organize trips (from which they'll most likely receive a commission that comes out of the money allotted to your supplies). When you're considering who you intend to share a few days with, find a captain who speaks English and has a few years' experience behind him. Be mindful that perverts and thieves thrive among good honest sailors. If you're having a hard time finding someone that feels good, check in with the tourist office for a lead. If you're looking for other passengers to share a boat with, you can leave a note at the tourist office. Also, lots of *felucca* captains and prospective passengers tend to mill about the Aswan Moon restaurant and the *felucca* docks a bit further down in the evening.

If you're only opting for a *felucca* because you're on a budget and would rather be cruising down the Nile in more luxurious style, bear in mind that it's possible to get a 4-5 star cruise ship for US$40-50/night – even less in summer. Ask at the tourist information office if they have any leads or try **Amigo Tours** directly, call Mostafa Ishazli on T010-5619700, they are the predominant budget travel company in Upper Egypt and all tours organized from Cairo generally go through them. They should be able to help you get hooked up with a good deal.

Nile cruises

Regular Nile cruises operate between Luxor and Aswan and sometimes between Cairo and Aswan for 3-5 days (standard tour), 7 days (extended tour) and 15 days (full Nile cruise). The leading Nile cruise companies are **Seti, Sheraton, Hilton, Presidential** and **Movenpick.** The quality of operator and cruise ship will, of course, be largely dependent on the price paid. If the cruise is taken as an all-inclusive package, it is recommended that, if possible, one is chosen where the overall itinerary is under the day to day control of a tour manager who is a direct employee of the cruise company. The local management of cruises can be sub-contracted to Egyptian travel agents who, should difficulties arise with the tour, may consider themselves primarily as guides and show marked reluctance to take on any wider responsibility or be fully accountable for solving problems of a more challenging nature.

Typical cruise itineraries The most popular is between Luxor and Aswan, with the journey sometimes in reverse, or a trip both ways. The itinerary will offer the following typical popular features: **Luxor**: visits to the West Bank (Valley of the Kings, Valley of the Queens, Colossi of Memnon, Temple of Queen Hapshetsut), Luxor and Karnak Temples (plus at least one alabaster factory shop!). Option of sound and light show at Karnak. **Esna**: Temple of Khnum. **Edfu**: Temple of Horus – access by calèche. **Kom Ombu**: Temple of Horus and Sobek. **Aswan**: *Felucca* boat outing to Kitchener Island, trip to Nubian village on Elephantine Island, Unfinished Obelisk, High Dam, Temple of Philae (plus at least one papyrus factory shop!). Option of sound and light show at Philae. **Dendera**: Temple of Hathor – may not be on all itineraries.

Esna lock closures Cruises from Luxor to Aswan can be disrupted by the twice-yearly closure of the lock at Esna for maintenance. Closures usually in June and December and prospective travellers are strongly advised to check these dates beforehand. When the

Nile cruisers

It is recommended for health and safety reasons that travellers use only the best grade Nile Cruise boats. The following list gives the names of Egyptian Government Five-Star grade Nile cruisers. All are based in Cairo unless otherwise noted. See also Tour operators, page 20. If you're on a budget, there are 2 and 3 star Nile cruises available, but hygiene could pose problems. Inquire with any tour operator. Further information can also be found at www.sherryboat.com.eg, www.sonesta.com, www.ie-eg.com.

Boat	Operator/Owner	No of Cabins
Alexander the Great	Jolleys Travel & Tours, 8 Sharia Talaat, Harb, Cairo, T02-5777340	60
Anni and Aton	Flash Nile Cruises, 5 Sharia Shohadaa, Mohandiseen, T02-4193451	54
Aurora	Pioneers Hotels and Cruises, 15 Sharia Hassen Sabry, T02-7380870	42
Cairo	Shalakani Tours, 36A Sharia Bahgat Ali, Zamalek, T02-7362346	65
Cheops and Cheops III	International Co for Nile Cruising, 15A Mansour Mohammed, Zamalek, T02-7364847	80
Hotp	Shalakani Tours, 36A Sharia Bahgat Aly, Zamalek, T02-7362346	65
Imperial	Seti First Travel, 16 Sharia Ismail Mohamed, Zamalek, T02-7369820	26
Isis	2A Sharia Khalifa el Maamoun, Heliopolis, T02-4503729	70
King Tut III	Oberoi Investment Ltd, Mena House Hotel, Giza, Cairo, T02-3833222	59
Lady Diana	Presidential Nile Cruises, 48 Sh Maraashley, Zamalek, T02-7350517	78
Le Scribe	Abercombie & Kent, 18 Sharia Yousef El-Guindy, T02-3936255	34
Saphire	Movenpick Hotels, Movenpick Heliopolis, T02-2919400	75
Sonesta Nile Goddess	Sonesta International, Nasr City, T02-2617100	65
Eugenie (on Lake Nasser)	Belle Epoque Travel, 17 Sharia Tunis, Maadi, T02-5169656	50

lock is closed, ships are moored at Esna and passengers are transported by coach to those points on the itinerary inaccessible by river. These makeshift arrangements can significantly reduce the pleasure and relaxation of a cruising holiday.

Meals Expect three good meals per day, often buffet style. Some meals are served on a covered deck. Meal times are likely to operate to a fairly inflexible timetable. Free tea, coffee and soft drinks are available at any time. The bar will be open most of day. Special menus can usually be organized.

Social life and entertainment Almost inevitably at some stage during the cruise there will be an evening dinner at which travellers will be encouraged to dress in local Egyptian costume – a gallabah party. Other evening entertainment may include discos, live Egyptian/Nubian music and performances by belly dancers, jugglers and acrobats.

Cabin accommodation Cabins at water level will offer limited views and, depending on position, may be more affected by engine noise and fumes. A supplement can be paid for a cabin on an upper deck. Top level cabins may have a sun deck as their roof. Obtain a plan of the vessel before you book. Bear in mind that when the ship is moored there may not be a view from the cabin whatever its level. Ships can often be berthed six or seven abreast and access to the shore is gained by walking through one ship after another. Expect to be issued with a boarding pass when going ashore.

Rail

Rail networks are limited, but travel by train can be delightful, especially to a few key destinations along the Nile. First class is significantly more comfortable with air-conditioning and sometimes sleeping accommodation. Cheaper carriages can be crowded and none too clean. Train travel also offers the advantage of views available only from the track.

The rail network extends west to Sollum on the Libyan border, south along the Nile from Alexandria and Cairo to Luxor, Aswan and Abu Simbel. There are links to Port Said and Suez. For detailed train information, contact the Cairo information office, T02-5753555. There are also several luxury, air-conditioned trains with restaurants to Luxor and Aswan with comfortable sleeping accommodation. Contact **International Sleeping Cars,** T02-5761319. Student cards offer 30% discounts on all trains (except overnight sleepers).

Approximate journey times from Cairo by train: Alexandria 2 hours; Aswan 12 hours; Luxor 9 hours; Port Said 2 hours.

Road

Bicycles and motorcycles

Bicycle hire is available in some areas, especially in highly touristed coastal towns, but the mechanical fitness of the machines is often dubious. In urban areas, traffic conditions can make cycling a very dangerous sport. Motorcycles can also be hired. The problems regarding cycles apply also to motorcycles – only more so.

Bus

Buses, the main mode and cheapest means of transport, link nearly all towns in Egypt. Air-conditioned coaches that are more expensive, but still cheap, connect the biggest cities and keep more strictly to a timetable. Book in advance wherever possible, especially on the more popular routes (like Cairo to Sinai). Smaller private vehicles (called microbuses or service taxis, pronounced *serveece*) require greater patience (see below). Inner city buses are usually dirty and crowded. Orderly queues become a jostling mass when the bus arrives. In the larger cities, buses often fail to come to complete stops so prepare to run and jump if you do not get on from a route's hub point. On Cairo buses, people enter through one door and exit through the other so getting off can be more difficult than getting on. The local buses keep to the timetable within reasonable limits. Ask a Cairene for an intra-city bus schedule and they'll laugh. The easiest thing to do is ask which bus is going to your desired destination. Using buses to travel from one city to another is a good way to get around but sorting out the routes and the fares of most innercity buses makes taking the tram, subway, or a cheap taxi, a better option.

Car hire

Vehicles drive on the right in Egypt. Where they exist, all road signs are in Arabic, with some offering the English transliteration. Cairo and Alexandria have street signs in Arabic and English on all the major thoroughfares. Road conditions vary from excellent dual carriageways to rural tracks only one-vehicle wide to far flung roads which are a rough, unsurfaced piste. Problems include encroaching sand, roads that end with no warning and lunatic drivers. An International Driving licence is required. Petrol (super) is E£1 per litre. Be aware that there are many police check points for cars in Egypt and they often request to see your papers, so have them on hand or be prepared for a hefty fine on the spot.

Car hire quality varies greatly. Car hire is not cheap, driving in the major cities can be nightmarish and the condition of vehicles can be problematic. Make sure that you are well insured as the road accident rate is exceedingly high. Some companies place restrictions on areas that can be visited. The problems of driving your own or a hired car are twofold – other drivers and pedestrians.

The main car hire firms are **Avis, Hertz** and **Budget**. See listings in each individual town transport section.

Approximate **journey times** from Cairo by road: Alexandria 3 hours; Sharm El-Sheikh 6 hours; Aswan 16 hours; Luxor 10 hours; Port Said 3 hours.

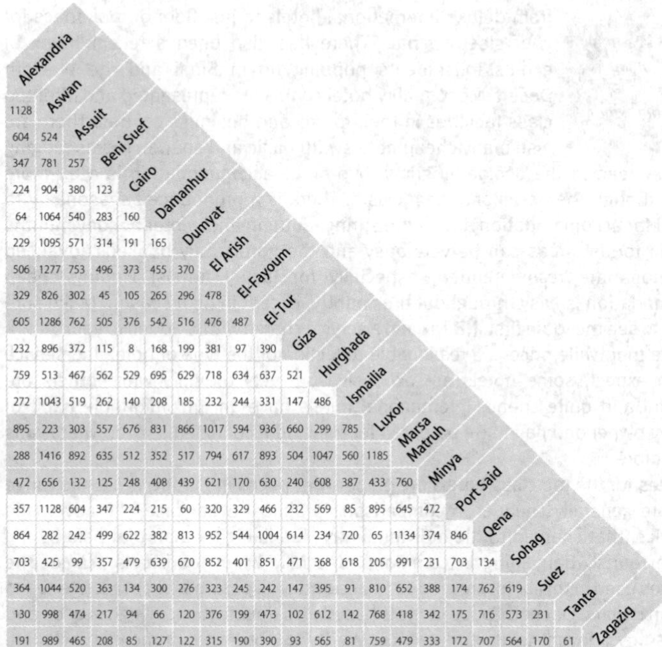

	Alexandria	Aswan	Assuit	Beni Suef	Cairo	Damanhur	Dumyat	El Arish	El-Fayoum	El-Tur	Giza	Hurghada	Ismailia	Luxor	Marsa Matruh	Minya	Port Said	Qena	Sohag	Suez	Tanta
Aswan	1128																				
Assuit	604	524																			
Beni Suef	347	781	257																		
Cairo	224	904	380	123																	
Damanhur	64	1064	540	283	160																
Dumyat	229	1095	571	314	191	165															
El Arish	506	1277	753	496	373	455	370														
El-Fayoum	329	826	302	45	105	265	296	478													
El-Tur	605	1286	762	505	376	542	516	476	487												
Giza	232	896	372	115	8	168	199	381	97	390											
Hurghada	759	513	467	562	529	695	629	718	634	637	521										
Ismailia	272	1043	519	262	140	208	185	232	244	331	147	486									
Luxor	895	223	303	557	676	831	866	1017	594	936	660	299	785								
Marsa Matruh	288	1416	892	635	512	352	517	794	617	893	504	1047	560	1185							
Minya	472	656	132	125	248	408	439	621	170	630	240	608	387	433	760						
Port Said	357	1128	604	347	224	215	60	320	329	466	232	569	85	895	645	472					
Qena	864	282	242	499	622	382	813	952	544	1004	614	234	720	65	1134	374	846				
Sohag	703	425	99	357	479	639	670	852	401	851	471	368	618	205	991	231	703	134			
Suez	364	1044	520	363	134	300	276	323	245	242	147	395	91	810	652	388	174	762	619		
Tanta	130	998	474	217	94	66	120	376	199	473	102	612	142	768	418	342	175	716	573	231	
Zagazig	191	989	465	208	85	127	122	315	190	390	93	565	81	759	479	333	172	707	564	170	61

Distances between main towns in Egypt (km)

Hitchhiking

This is really only a consideration in outlying places not served by the very cheap public transport. Rides are often available on lorries and in small open trucks but payment is always expected. Hitchhiking has a measure of risk attached to it and is not normally recommended, but in out of the way places is often the only way to travel. Women travelling alone or without male escort are strongly advised not to hitchhike, as they may be mistaken for prostitutes.

Taxis and service taxis

The larger, wagon-like long distance service taxis (Peugeots) are good value, sometimes following routes not covered by service buses and are almost always more frequent. They run on the 'leave when full' principle, which can involve some waiting around. For more space or a quicker departure the unoccupied seats can be purchased. In general these taxis are 25% more expensive than the bus but it is always possible to negotiate. Inner city taxis are smaller, rarely have a working meter, and can also be shared. In Cairo you will immediately note the hordes of black and white taxis decorated with fringe, mirrors, a Koran on the dash. In Alexandria, they are orange and black, and equally ubiquitous. In such urban centres taxis are unquestionably the easiest way to get around, and extraordinarily cheap.

Sleeping

→ *See box next page and inside front cover for price code information.*

Hotels

As tourism is one of Egypt's major industries, accommodation is widely available at the main sites and in all the major cities. With prices to suit all pockets, this varies from deluxe international hotels to just floor or roof space for your sleeping bag. There has also been a recent influx of eco-establishments popping up in Sinai and the Western Desert. Most quality hotel chains are represented and offer top class facilities in their rooms and business centres. There are also many cheap hotels with basic and spartan rooms ranging from the clean to the decidedly grimy. Mid-range accommodation is a bit more limited, though the occasional gem exists. There is a pronounced seasonality to demand for accommodation and in the spring, autumn and winter holiday months the main tourist areas can be very busy and the hotels fully booked. Advanced reservations are recommended, especially for luxury hotels. Finding cheap accommodation is easy throughout the country, except in high season. Make sure you ask to see the room first. **NB** Tax and a service charge will be added to your bill.

Abbrevations in listings:
a/c = air conditioning
T = telephone
'Bath' denotes bath and/ or shower.

Note that while price is a reasonable reflection of the type of hotel and service you can expect, some hotels are expensive but very ordinary while others are wonderful and quite cheap. International hotels have an uncomfortable habit of changing owner and name. Be prepared for this and if confused ask for what it was called before.

Prices for the top class hotels are on par with prices in Europe while mid-range hotels are generally cheaper in comparison. In almost every case, the advertised room price, that charged to the individual traveller, is higher than that paid by the package tourist. Bargaining is common, especially when tourism is scarce. The categories used in this book are graded as accurately as possible by cost converted to American dollars. Our hotel price range is based on a double room in high season and includes any relevant taxes and service. We try to note when a meal is included. Please be aware that prices for hotels are constantly shifting, sometimes significantly, depending on the season and the political climate. As we have quoted

Hotel price codes and facilities

AL **US$150+** 5 star Luxury hotels. All facilities for business and leisure travellers are of the highest international standard. Mostly chain hotels but a few privately-owned gems.
A **US$100-150+** 4-5 star Central heated, a/c rooms with WC, bath/shower, TV, phone, mini-bar, clean linen daily. Usually have a choice of restaurants, coffee shop, shops, bank, travel agent, swimming pool, parking, sport and business facilities.
B **US$75-100** 4-star As A but without the luxury, reduced number of restaurants, smaller rooms, limited range of shops and sport facilities.
C **US$50-75** 3 star Best rooms have a/c, TV, private bath/shower and WC. Usually comfortable, and with bank, shop, and pool.
D **US$25-50** 2-3 star Expect clean rooms with private bath, a/c, and satellite TV. Depending on management will have room service and a choice of cuisine in its restaurant.
E **US$10-25** 2 star Simpler provision. A/c is probable, fan is certain. May not have restaurant. Most rooms with private bath/shower and WC.
F **Under US$10** None-1 star Very basic accommodation, generally shared toilet facilities, variable in cleanliness, perhaps noisy and sometimes in dubious locations. If under US$5, we have specified it in our listings. The range of cheap accommodation is extreme. It's possible to find great deals in lovely environs, as well as some real dives. If you're on a tight budget, your best bet is to shop around, if you have the time.

high season prices, expect to find costs equal to, or less than, the prices indicated. When in doubt, always ask as prices can literally be sliced in half in the hot summer months. Also, note that as a result of the floating Egyptian pound, the Ministry of tourism recently requested that hotels classified as 3-stars and higher accept only foreign currency – generally US dollars. Bur, like everything in Egypt, this rule is variable, not followed by all, and could well change at a moment's notice. None the less, it's always wise to have foreign currency on you, as dollars are ever harder to get and they can get you out of most binds. At hotels 3-stars and higher, credit cards are almost always accepted.

Normally the facilities indicated in the box above will be available and are therefore not repeated in the descriptions.

Youth hostels

Information from **Egyptian Youth Hostels Association,** 1 El-Ibrahimy Street, Garden City, Cairo, T02-7940527, www.iyhf.org. There are 17 hostels (in Egypt's main historic and tourist towns) which are open year round. Overnight fees range from E£5-50 and often include breakfast. Visitors may stay more than three consecutive nights if there's space. Although cheap meals are available, all the big hostels have a members' kitchen where guests can prepare meals for themselves (use of the kitchen is free). Holders of membership cards can obtain significant reductions on train journeys. Rules generally include no alcohol or gambling, single sex dormitories, lights out between 2300-0600. Booking is recommended during peak travel times.

Camping

There are only a few official campsites with good facilities and guards. Sites of varying quality exist around Cairo, Sharm El-Sheikh, Farafra and Marsa Matruh. It's possible to stake out an unofficial campsite in the oases of the Western Desert, but always ask if you appear to be on someone else's land, and offer them a tip before you leave. Beware of veering too far off road in regions that are desolate as landmines are still widely scattered around some regions, especially Sinai and along the Red Sea coast. Camping Bedouin-style under virgin sky in the pristine Western Desert is a highlight of many travellers' journeys.

A few popular destinations, Dahab (Sinai) and Bahariyya (Western Desert) among them, have what are misleadingly called 'camps,' but which are generally very cheap and sometimes charming grounds that offer small concrete rooms or simple bamboo huts for a dollar or two per night. They often include bedding and a shared bath.

Eating

→ *For eating price categories see the inside front cover.*

Bearing in mind the suggestions in the Health section on food best avoided in uncertain conditions, a wide choice still remains. Forget the stories of sheep's eyes and enjoy the selection of filling, spicy and slightly unusual meals. Less adventurous, Western-style food (other than pork) can be found in many restaurants and most hotels.

Food

Egyptian food is basically a mixture of Mediterranean cuisines, containing elements of Lebanese, Turkish, and Greek cooking, with few authentic local dishes.

Breakfast is usually ***fuul***, fava beans simmered slowly overnight, the national dish and a cheap meal at most cafés. These are served in a thick spicy sauce, either with an egg on top or in a sandwich. Equally cheap and popular is *taamaya*, deep fried balls of ground fava beans spiced with coriander and garlic, again often served in a sandwich garnished with *tahina* (sesame seed dip) and *torshi* (brightly coloured pickled vegetables such as turnips, carrots, and limes). These constitute Egyptian fast food with the addition of *shawarma*, sliced lamb kebab sandwiches, and *fitir*, which is sold in special *fatatri* cafés, where the thin dough pancake is made to order with either sweet or savoury fillings.

Bread is the staple of the Egyptian diet, its Arabic name *ai'iish*, which means life. The local *ai'iish baladi*, a brown flat loaf similar to pita, tastes good fresh and should only be eaten on the day of purchase. The white flour *ai'iish shami* is less common.

Lunch is the main meal of the day, eaten anytime between 1400 and 1700. Carbohydrates, usually rice and bread, form the bulk of the meal accompanied by fresh seasonal vegetables and either meat or fish. *Mezzas*, a selection of small salads, are served at the beginning of the meal and include *tahina*, *babaghanoug* (*tahina* with mashed aubergines), olives, local white fetta-style cheese, *warra einab* or stuffed vine leaves, and *kobeiba*, deep fried bulgar wheat stuffed with meat and nuts. Like most Middle Eastern countries, *kebab*, lamb pieces grilled over charcoal on a skewer, and *kofta*, minced lamb, are common main dishes. Chicken and pigeon are also widely available, the latter considered a local delicacy when stuffed with rice and nuts. Fish is commonly eaten in coastal regions and often superb. Try the Sea Bass or Red Snapper but watch the bones in the latter. Lobster and shrimp are relatively cheap.

> ❢ *All meat should be eaten well-done to avoid stomach upsets.*

Egyptian **main dishes** include *molokhia*, finely chopped mallow leaves, prepared with garlic, spices and either rabbit or chicken, and a good deal more tasty than its glutinous texture suggests; *fatta*, layers of bread, rice, chunks of lamb or beef, yogurt, raisins and nuts, drenched in a vinegar garlic broth; *koshari*, a poor man's feast that will fill a belly for at least 4 hours, is composed of macaroni, rice and brown lentils

Fuul for all

Fuul has been an important dish for Egyptians since banquetting scenes were painted on the Pharaonic tombs. It is nutritious and cheap and is the staple diet for low income and strong-stomached locals. In Cairo a meal from one of the 25,000 (illegal) street vendors will start the day. At 25 p per sandwich it fills an empty hole and provides protein and carbohydrates.

Fuul is also considered 'in' by the Cairo smart set, who frequent luxury outlets such as El-Gahsh, Akher Saa, El-Tabei and El-Omda to buy it with onions, pickles, lemon and fresh bread – to eat in or take away.

The *fuul* bean is grown in most agricultural areas of Egypt, as an accompaniment to a major crop – the best is said to come from Minya. Nevertheless, imports are still necessary to supply consumption demands.

Variants on *fuul* dishes include: *Fuul bil zeit el harr* – with hot oil; *Fuul bil samna* – with ghee (clarified butter); *Bisara* – with oil, onion, garlic and coriander. *Fuul* is also the main ingredient in *ta'ameya* and *felafel*.

covered with fried onions and a spicy tomato sauce; and *mahshi*, vegetables, typically black or white aubergines, tomatoes, green peppers, and courgettes, stuffed with rice and mincemeat.

Fruits, like vegetables, are seasonal although there is a wide variety available all year round. Produce is picked when it's ripe and so generally fruit and vegetables are absolutely delicious. Winter offers dates of various colours ranging from yellow to black, citrus fruits, small sweet bananas, pears, apples, and even strawberries. Summer brings plums, peaches, figs, pomegranates, guava, mangoes, grapes, melons and a brief season, for a few weeks in May, of apricots.

Traditional Egyptian **desserts** are sweet, sticky, fattening, and delicious. The best of all is *Om Ali*, or Mother of Ali, a warm pudding of bread or pastry covered with milk, coconut, raisins, and nuts. But try the oriental pastries including *atayef*, deep fried nut-stuffed pancakes; *baklava*, honey-drenched filo pastry layered with nuts; *basbousa*, a syrupy semolina cake often filled with cream and garnished with pistachio nuts and *konafa*, shredded batter cooked with butter and stuffed with nuts.

Vegetarianism is not a concept with which Egyptians are familiar. While vegetable dishes are plentiful, and the majority of Egyptians only eat any large quantity of meat once a week, it is difficult to avoid tiny pieces of meat or meat stock in vegetable courses. Even the wonderful lentil soup, like most Egyptian soups a meal on its own, often has the addition of a chicken stock cube.

Drink

Tea is the essential Egyptian drink, taken strong without milk but with spoonfuls of sugar. Tea is also prepared with mint, *chai bil na'ana*, and said to be good for the digestion. Instant **coffee**, just called 'Nescafé', is available but avoid the local *Misr Café* which tastes like sawdust. The thick Turkish coffee, which can be laced with cardamom or cinnamon, should be ordered either *saada*, with no sugar; *arriha*, with a little sugar; *mazbut*, medium; or *ziyada*, with extra sugar. Leave the thick mud of coffee grains in the bottom half of the cup. The *mazbut* is the most popular. Other hot drinks include a cinnamon tea, *irfa*, reportedly good for colds; and the less common *sahleb*, a milk drink with powdered arrowroot, coconut, and chopped nuts.

Coffee grounds, like tea leaves elsewhere, are believed to indicate the future.

Chicken for Ramadan

2 medium chickens (about 1 kg each).
Salt and pepper to season.
Mmelted butter for basting.

Filling
Butter for frying.
Heart and liver from both chickens cleaned and chopped.
1 large onion chopped finely.
200 ml of chicken stock.
150 gm of cooked rice.
Chopped mint and chopped parsley to taste.
Salt and pepper to season.

Clean the chickens and season inside and out.
Heat butter in pan, fry onion until soft, add chopped hearts and livers and cook until the meats go lighter in colour. Over a low heat add the stock, rice, herbs and seasoning and cook for 5 mins.
Divide filling and place half in each chicken. Truss to secure.
Bake in a moderate oven (180 C) for 75-90 mins, basting with melted butter. Turn the birds every 10-15 mins to ensure even cooking.

Cold drinks include the usual soft drink options of Coca-Cola, Pepsi, 7-Up, and Fanta. Of more interest are the traditional *ersoos*, licorice juice; *karkade*, made from the dried petals of the red hibiscus; and *tamarhindi*, from the tamarind. Freshly squeezed juice stands are located throughout all cities, but these may not be very hygenic. Bottled **water**, Baraka, Siwa, Nestle and others, is sold widely. Check that the seal is intact and that the bottle has not been refilled. Be prepared for shortage or restriction of water in more rural areas. Tap water in the urban centres is generally safe to drink, but so chlorinated it's intolerable for a lot of travellers. It's better to opt for bottled water which is cheap and easily available.

Although Egypt is a Muslim country, **alcohol** is available in bars and good restaurants. While five-star hotels are beginning to import beer in barrels, the local 'Stella' beer is the most popular sold, with the better-quality 'Stella Export', in half litre bottles. Nonetheless, quality for both brands remains variable depending on the batch. There are a few local wines that aren't bad. Most commonly found are Omar Khayyam, a dry red, Cru des Ptolemees, a dry white and the new Obelisque, which offers a very drinkable red and a white and rose that are mediocre. The local spirits are bottled to resemble international brands, and include an ouzo called *zibib*, a rum 'Zattos', and a 'Big Ben' gin. Beware of local liquours that don labels and names resembling western brands such as 'Jhony wakker' and the like, they have been known to contain alcohol so strong that they can cause blindness if drunk to excess.

Eating out

The better hotel restaurants serve international cuisine of a high standard and also often have Egyptian restaurants. From there the price, but not necessarily the standard, falls down to the street stalls which can offer extremely delicious meals. Each stall generally sells one or two specialities like *koshari*, *fuul* and *taameyya* sandwiches, etc. (Avoid the grungier stalls for hygiene reasons.) In between fancy hotels and street stalls are a multitude of cafés that serve a variety of local favorites, often brought out *mezze*-style with a basket of bread so you can enjoy tasting a bit of everything. In bigger cities and coastal areas, there is also a tragic abundance of Western fast food restaurants. Alexandria, offers the freshest seafood around. In Cairo, you can find cuisine from around the world.

Festivals and events

Holidays and festivals → *Local festivals are listed under individual towns.*

The Islamic year (*Hejra/Hijra/Hegira*) is based on 12 lunar months which are 29 or 30 days long depending on the sighting of the new moon. The lengths of the months vary therefore from year to year and from country to country depending on its position and the time at sunset. Each year is also 10 or 11 days shorter than the Gregorian calendar. The Islamic holidays are based on this Hejarian calendar and determining their position is possible only to within a few days.

Ramadan is a month of fasting (see below). The important festivals which are public holidays (with many variations in spelling) are *Ras El-Am*, the Islamic New Year; *Eïd Al-Fitr* (also called *Aïd Es Seghir*), the celebration at the end of Ramadan; *Eïd Al-Adha* (also called *Aïd El-Kebir*), the celebration of Abraham's willingness to sacrifice his son and coinciding with the culmination of the *Haj* in Mecca; *Mouloud*, the birthday of the Prophet Mohammed.

The day of rest for Muslims is Friday. Observance of Friday as a religious day is general in the public sector though privately-owned shops may open for limited hours. The main exception is tourism where all systems remain operative. Holy days and feast days are taken seriously throughout the country.

Ramadan, the 9th month of the Muslim calendar, is a month of fasting for Muslims. The faithful abstain from eating between dawn and sunset for the period until an official end is declared to the fast and the start of *Eïd Al-Fitr*, a 3-day celebration marking the end of Ramadan. During the fast, especially if the weather is bad or there are political problems affecting the Arab world, people can be depressed or irritable. The pace of activity in official offices slows down markedly. Travellers have to manage in these conditions by leaving even more time to achieve their aims and being more patient than usual. You may want to stay out of the area during Ramadan and particularly the *Eid Al-Fitr*, but for the patient and curious traveller, it can be a fascinating time. As the sun sets during the holy month and everyone ventures inward to break fast, it offers a rare and delightful occasion to wander through barren Cairo streets. For the rushed or impatient traveller, note that travel facilities immediately before and after Ramadan are often very congested since families like to be together especially for the *Eïd Al-Fitr*.

National holidays

1 January New Year's Day
15 March El Fayoum National Day
Sham al-Nessim (Sniffing of the Breeze, or the first day of Spring) is celebrated second Monday after the Coptic Easter Day with family picnics.
25 April Liberation of Sinai
1 May Labour Day
18 June Evacuation Day – the day the British left Egypt
23 July Anniversary of 1952 Revolution
26 July Alexandria National Day
6 October Armed Forces' Day – parades and military displays
13 October Suez Day
23 December Victory Day

Approximate dates of Islamic festivals (2004) Beginning of Ramadan 16 October; End of Ramadan (Bairam Feast) 14 November; Feast of Sacrifice 1 February; Islamic New Year 1422 21 February; Prophet's Birthday 2 May.

 Approximate dates of Coptic celebrations (2004) Christmas 7 January; Epiphany 19 January; Annunciation 7 April; Easter 11 April; Coptic New Year 11 September.

Cultural events

January Cairo International Book Fair – Nasr City, Cairo.
February 22 Ramses II Coronation – Abu Simbel.
March Cairo International Fair; Spring Flower Show – Andalucìa Gardens, Cairo.
July International Festival of Documentary Films – Ismailia.
August International Song Festival – Cairo; International Folklore Dance festival – Ismailia; (Wafa El-Nil) Nile Festival Day – Giza.
September World Alexandria Festival (every two years); International Festival for Vanguard Theatre – Cairo; International Movie festival – Alexandria; World Tourism Day; (Wafa El-Nil) Nile Festival Day – Cairo.
October International Folk festival – Ismailia; October 22 Ramses II Coronation – Abu Simbel; October 24 Commemoration of Battle of El-Alamein – El-Alamein.
November Luxor National Day; International Children's Book Fair – Nasr City, Cairo.
December International Film Festival – Cairo; Festival for Arab Theatre – Cairo; Festival for Impressionist Art (every 2 years) – Cairo.

Shopping

What to buy

Clothing, textiles and rugs

Egypt is well known for its cotton and textiles. Higher end stores in luxury hotels and shopping malls around Cairo and Alexandria (as in World Trade Centre, Nile Hilton and Marriott) have stores that sell linens and new clothes. For colourful tapestries, scarves and bags, Khan El-Khalili is a good place to start. Also of interest may be the Tent Makers' Bazaar, south of Bab Zuweila in Islamic Cairo, where it's possible to commission the making of a bedcover or a Bedouin tent. If you want a gallabiyya, formal or otherwise, wander around the shops surrounding Al-Azhar mosque in Cairo. For handmade rugs, check out the many stores lining Sharia Saqqara, near the Giza Pyramids. » *See also Cairo shopping section, page 138.*

Jewellery

In particular, gold, silver and some precious stones are cheap in Egypt. In the centre of Khan El-Khalili, as well as places scattered about Islamic Cairo, you will find exquisite gold jewellery. Sold by weight, with a bit of money tacked on for craftsmanship, you can have pieces made to order. Particularly popular are cartouches bearing your name or the name of a friend. Siwa Oasis is known for the beautiful Berber silver jewellery, though the world-renowned antique pieces are exceedingly rare.

Papyrus

Papyrus can be found, albeit of varying quality, everywhere. Ensure when you are shopping around for papyrus that it is real, not the increasingly present imitation banana leaf. Also, if you are considering investing in a substantial piece of art, make sure it really is hand painted. Dr Ragab's papyrus institute in Cairo is a bit pricey, but offers good quality trustworthy papyrus art.

Real papyrus, if you crinkle it up, doesn't crack or stay crinkled.

Caveat Emptor – the art of bargaining

Haggling is a normal business practice in Egypt. Modern economists might feel that bargaining is a way of covering up high-price salesmanship within a commercial system that is designed to exploit the lack of legal protection for the consumer. But even so, haggling over prices is the norm and is run as an art form, with great skills involved. Bargaining can be great fun to watch between a clever buyer and an experienced seller but it is less entertaining when a less than artful buyer such as a foreign traveller considers what he/she has paid later! There is great potential for the tourist to be heavily ripped off. Most dealers recognize the wealth and gullibility of travellers and start their offers at an exorbitant price. The dealer then appears to drop his price by a fair margin but remains at a final level well above the real local price of the goods.

To protect yourself in this situation be relaxed in your approach. Talk at length to the dealer and take as much time as you can afford to inspect the goods and feeling out the last price the seller will accept. Do not belittle or mock the dealer – take the matter very seriously but do not show commitment to any particular item you are bargaining for by being prepared to walk away empty handed. Never feel that you are getting the better of the dealer or feel sorry for him. He will not sell without making a profit. Also it is better to try several shops if you are buying an expensive item such as a carpet or jewellery. This will give a sense of the price range. Walking away – regretfully of course – from the dealer normally brings the price down rapidly but not always. Do not change money in the same shop where you make your purchases, since this will be expensive.

Perfumes and spices

You'll probably smell the perfume stalls before you see them. They're all over Khan El-Khalili and most carry an extraordinary variety of smells – ranging from rose to Egyptian musk to attempts at replicating famous scents. Prices range from E£8-30. Ask around at different stalls for the going price before purchasing. Also fragrant and incredibly colourful are the abundance of stalls that sell spices displayed in large burlap sacks. You will find everything from dried hibiscus to thyme, cumin to saphron, which priced higher per kilo than gold, but still comparatively cheap. For an alternative spice experience, check out Harraz Medicinal Plants Co, a store in Cairo specializing in ancient remedies and medicinal plants. Upstairs you can consult with the resident herbalist if anything ails you. Sharia Ahmed Marhir St, east of Midan Bab Al-Khalq. ▸▸ *See also box page 93.*

Photography

Most types of film are available, though they may be pricier than at home. Check the sell by date and purchase from shops that appear to have a rapid turnover of films. Bring specialist films with you and take back home all exposed film for processing. High speed film is recommended for night time photography such as the Sound and Light shows, and interiors of buildings where a flash is not permitted. Lower speed film is more suitable for the brighter, outdoor conditions. The best time to take photographs is early morning or late afternoon as the amount of reflective light in the middle of the day requires a filter. Protect your camera from the fine invasive desert sand with a sturdy polythene bag.

Other things of interest you will find in larger souks and bazaars: kitsch souvenirs galore, *sheesha* pipes, musical instruments (drums in particular) copper and brass ware, wooden boxes inlaid with intricate designs and backgammon and chess sets.

Tips and trends

Normal opening hours are summer 0900-1230 and 1600-2000, winter 0900-1900, often closed on Fridays or Sundays but shops in tourist areas seem to stay open much longer. There are department stores and malls in Cairo and Alexandria but the most interesting shopping is in the bazaars and souks. The process can take time and patience, but bargains abound. The main bazaar in Cairo, Khan El-Khalili, has a wide selection of ethnic items. It attracts tourists by the hoards, though wandering far off the main alleys will lead way to shops and corridors rarely visited. For a truly off-track shopping experience, visit one of the many fruit and vegetable souks scattered throughout the country. You'll find chickens milling about, people singing songs about their wares and dead cows hanging from storefront windows. Prices are clearly marked in Arabic numerals, usually indicating the cost of a kilogram. Bargaining is not appropriate in this context but learn the numerals so you don't get taken advantage of. In Cairo, *souk tawfiqqia*, off the corner of Talaat Harb and 26 July is a colourful place to wander.

Sports and activities

Adventure and sport run the gamut of experience in Egypt. In addition to more standard forms of entertainment like swimming and golf, you can ride a horse or camel in the desert, snorkel or dive among some of the most pristine coral reefs on the planet, or leisurely sail on an age-old *felucca*, a vessel that has been floating on the Nile for centuries. Also, in the Sinai and Western Desert, there are extensive hiking and trekking opportunities. ▸▸ *Local tour operators are listed in each town's individual Activities and tours section.*

Balloon flights

This is a splendid, albeit expensive, way to see Egypt – away from the push of people and noise and crush of traffic. Contact **Balloons over Egypt**, in Cairo, T02-7383763; or **Hod Hod Soliman,** in Luxor, T095-370116. There are also representatives at the **Hilton International**, **Sheraton** and **Movenpick Jolie Ville** in Luxor. Cost is US$150.

Normally collection is from your hotel, the flight lasts between 45 and 90 minutes and takes place on the West Bank over the Valley of the Kings and Valley of the Queens. A post-trip breakfast is often served.

NB These trips are subject to weather conditions over which there is no control. Agility is required to climb into the basket and children under 4'6" are not accepted.

Bird watching

As Egypt is at the crossroad of three continents and central to the migration routes of many birds, opportunities for bird watching abound. In Sinai, Ras Mohammed National Park is home to a wide range of bird species. Nearer to Cairo, Wadi Rayan, a picturesque manmade lake is a good spot. Also popular is the huge natural salt Lake Qarun, by El Fayoum Oasis. There are several books available on ornithology in Egypt, all available at the AUC bookshop in Cairo. You also may wish to check out www.birdingegypt.com, a good resource for enthusiasts seeking the best birding sites and seasons. ▸▸ *See also page 527 in the Background chapter for information on specific sites.*

Desert safaris and trekking

Increasingly popular in Egypt are expeditions into the desert. They range from an afternoon or late night meander up Mount Sinai to a multi-weeklong trek. The two regions most commonly explored are Sinai with its vibrant coloured canyons and ancient sacred peaks, and the Western Desert, where oases sprout amid endless dunes, bubbling hot springs and weird limestone rock formations. Many tour companies and local desert guides provide absolutely everything for as little as US$20 per person per day (and, depending on what you want, up to US$150 per person per day). Trips generally include food, sleeping bags and transport (whether it's camel or jeep) and give you the freedom to create your own adventure.

Diving and snorkelling

Climatic and geographic features make the Red Sea *the* place to scuba dive and snorkel. Diving here was pioneered in the 1950s by Dr Hans Hass and Jacques Cousteau. And so extraordinary is it that many tourists come to Egypt with no intention whatsoever of seeing the monuments on land. Scores of dive shops in Sharm El-Sheikh, Hurghada and Dahab offer relatively affordable dive courses that can have you certified in 5 days. If you lack the funds or inclination, snorkelling can be just as fulfilling. In most places along the Red Sea coast, you can rent everything you'll need to breathe underwater for about E£10 a day. Highlights include the national park Ras Mohammed, and the shoreline wonders of Dahab, Sharm El-Sheikh and Basata. From Sharm El-Sheikh and Hurghada, you can also hop on a boat for more remote diving and snorkelling opportunities. An experience not to be missed.

Today the popularity of this sport means more and more people can experience the wonders of this special environment and that greater and greater numbers threaten this fragile habitat. *See box page 388.*

A mixture of deep water fish and surface coral giving a total of over 1,000 species of fish to observe, some 500 species of coral and thousands of invertebrate reef dwellers. The clear waters ensure that the fish can be 'caught' on film. Sites to visit include sheer drop-offs, sea grass meadows, coral encrusted wrecks, gullies and pinnacles, a new world. Water temperatures vary. A 3 mm or 5 mm wetsuit is recommended for all year but something thicker for winter wear (18°C) or a prolonged series of dives may be needed.

Liveaboards This method of accessing the dive sights permits divers to reach more remote locations in smaller groups so, in theory, less disturbance is caused at these locations. It provides the diver with accommodation and the opportunity for unlimited dives a day with limited travel.

Most liveaboard agents extend all year over the northern waters from Sharm El-Sheikh and Hurghada to Ras Mohammed, Gulf of Suez, Tiran Straits and Port Sudan. In summer they chart south from Marsa Alam to the more isolated reefs and islands. Summer is the best time to dive in the south when the winds and currents are not so strong and the water temperature (here at the Tropic of Cancer) reaches about 30°C. Boats from Hurghada tend to head northwards to Abu Nawas and Thistegorm, eastwards to Ras Mohammed or southwards to Safaga. Below is a list of lliveaboard boats and their facilities. From **Sharm El-Sheikh**: Cyclone, Ghazala I, Ghazala II and Freedom II. From **Hurghada**: Emperor Fleet, Golden Diver, Alexandria, Sabrina, Miss Nouran, Amira and Loveman. From **Marsa Alam**: Shadia. Sailing out of Marsa Alam gives speedier access to the southern area.

Emperor Divers – 20-25 m long, limited facilities, civilized and comfortable with tolerance. **Emperor Pegasus** – 24 m by 7 m, max 16 persons in twin cabins. **Golden Diver** – 22 m by 6.5 m, 14 persons in twin cabins. **Crusade Travel – VIP One** – seven cabins, with private facilities, professional crew and PADI Advanced courses available. Departs from Sharm El-Maya to Straits of Tira, Straits of Gubal, Abu Nuwas and Thistlegorm and to Ras Mohammed. **Mermaid** – wooden hull, built 1998, 16 divers in twin berthed, a/c, en suite rooms, 9 crew. **Miss Nouran** – 28 m by 7 m, wooden hull, built 1997, high standard, 16 divers in ensuite cabins (6x2 and 1x4), 8 crew. Full Nitrox and rebreather facilities. Sails in the Straits of Gubal. **Royal Emperor** – 29 m by 7 m , steel hull, 14 divers in twin berthed en suite cabins. Concentration on underwater photography with lab and processing facilities on board. Built specifically for journeys to Marine Park Islands. **Cyclone** – 30 m by 7 m, wooden hull, built 1998, 20 divers in 10 twin a/c, ensuite cabins. Cruises to the Straits of Tiran.

Diving Prices 6-12 days' diving US$200-400; 5-10 days' diving US$175-350.

Diving courses The prices quoted for PADI diving courses (for which the minimum age is 12 years) should include all diving equipment and materials for the course which should take just five days, three days of theory and work in confined water/deep swimming pool to put the theory into practice and two days in the sea completing four open-water dives. After which a new underwater world waits you. Courses requiring certification are an extra US$30 per certificate for which you will require two passport photographs. You will also need a log book (on sale in diving resorts) to record your dives (US$8).

Open Water Certification US$180-320. Advanced Open Water Certification (2 days) US$190-210. Medic First Aid (1 day) US$100. Rescue Diver Certification (3-4 days) US$300-320. Dive Master Certification US$550-600. Also Under Water Naturalist US$50. Night Diver US$60. Multi-level Diver US$65. Reef Diver US$65. Wreck Diver US$100.

Fishing

This is becoming a very popular sport, especially on Lake Nasser where there are over 32 species of fish (see box page 303). Specialist operators organize camping/fishing safaris (see page 21). A permit is required both to fish and to visit the lake – costs US$65. All tackle can be hired in Aswan. There are also deep sea fishing trips on the Red Sea starting from Hurghada.

Water sports

In addition to underwater pursuits, Egypt offers excellent spots to windsurf and water ski. Moon Beach in the Sinai and Safaga on the Red Sea coast are both known for windsurfing.

Annual sporting events

January Egypt International Marathon – Luxor; National Tennis Championships.
February International Fishing Festival – Hurghada; Tennis Championships; International Bridge Tournament.
March International Marathon – Cairo-Alexandria.
May National Fishing Competition – Sharm El-Sheikh; Sharkia Arab Horse Breeding Festival – Sharkia.
July National Fishing Festival – Hurghada.
September Red Sea International Wind Surfing Competition – Hurghada.
October International Competition for Long Distance Swimming – Giza; Port Said National Fishing Competition – Port Said; Pharaoh Rally – Nationwide.
November Duck Shooting; International Yacht Regatta – Alexandria; Zahra'a Arab Horse Breeding Festival – Ain Shams, Cairo; International Fishing Championship – Sharm El-Sheikh.
December Nile International Rowing Regatta – Cairo and Luxor.

Health

The local population in Egypt is exposed to a range of health risks not usually encountered in the western world. Many of the diseases are major problems for the local poor and destitute and though the risk to travellers is more remote, they cannot be ignored. Obviously five-star travel is going to carry less risk than back-packing on a minimal budget.

The health care in the region is varied. There are many excellent private and government clinics/hospitals. But as with all medical care, first impressions count. If a facility looks grubby then be wary of the general standard of medicine and hygiene. It's worth contacting your embassy or consulate on arrival and asking where the recommended (ie those used by diplomats) clinics are. (Providing embassies with information of your whereabouts can be also useful if a friend/relative gets ill at home and there is a desperate search for you around the globe.) You can also ask them about locally recommended medical dos and don'ts. If you do get ill, and you have the opportunity, you should also ask your medical insurer whether they are satisfied that the medical centre or hospital that you have been referred to is of a suitable standard.

Before you go

Ideally, you should see your GP or travel clinic at least six weeks before your departure for general advice on travel risks, malaria and vaccinations. Make sure you have travel insurance, get a dental check (especially if you are going to be away for more than a month), know your own blood group and if you suffer a long-term condition such as diabetes or epilepsy make sure someone knows or that you have a Medic Alert bracelet/necklace with this information on it.

Recommended vaccinations

Polio if none in last 10 years; **Tetanus** again if you haven't had one last 10 years (after five doses you have had enough for life); **Diphtheria** if none in last 10 years; **Typhoid** if none in last three years; **Hepatitis A** as the disease can be caught easily from food/water.

Rabies is not generally a risk in Egypt but it has been reported in a few rural areas off the tourist trail.

Malaria

Minimal risk exists only in the El-Fayoum area. Risk is highest from June to October in both P. falciparum and P. vivax forms. Check with your doctor before you go about which prophylactic (if any) you should take if travelling in this region. Remember that it is risky to buy medicinal tablets abroad because the doses may differ and there may be a trade in false drugs.

Items to take with you

Mosquito repellents Remember that DEET (Di-ethyltoluamide) is the gold standard. Apply the repellent every four to six hours but more often if you are sweating heavily. If a non-DEET product is used check who tested it. Validated products (tested at the London School of Hygiene and Tropical Medicine) include Mosiguard, Non-DEET Jungle formula and non-DEET Autan. If you want to use citronella remember that it must be applied very frequently (ie hourly) to be effective. If you are popular target for insect bites or develop lumps quite soon after being bitten, carry an Aspivenin kit. This syringe suction device is available from many chemists and draws out some of the allergic materials and provides quick relief.

Sun screen The Australians have a great campaign, which has reduced skin cancer. It is called Slip, Slap, Slop. Slip on a shirt, Slap on a hat, Slop on sun screen.

Pain killers Paracetomol or a suitable painkiller can have multiple uses for symptoms but remember: more than eight paracetomol a day can lead to liver failure.

Ciproxin (Ciprofloxacin) A useful antibiotic for some forms of travellers' diarrhoea.

Immodium A great standby for those diarrhoeas that occur at awkward times (ie before a long coach/train journey or on a desert safari). It helps stop the flow of diarrhoea and in my view is of more benefit than harm. (It was believed that letting the bacteria or viruses flow out had to be more beneficial. However, with Immodium they still come out, just in a more solid form.)

Pepto-Bismol Used a lot by Americans for diarrhoea. It certainly relieves symptoms but like Immodium it is not a cure for underlying disease. Be aware that it turns the stool black as well as making it more solid.

MedicAlert These simple bracelets, or an equivalent, should be carried or worn by anyone with a significant medical condition.

An A-Z of health risks

Bites and stings

It is a very rare event indeed for travellers, but if you are unlucky (or careless) enough to be bitten by a venomous snake, spider, scorpion or sea creature, try to identify the creature, without putting yourself in further danger. Snake bites in particular are very frightening, but in fact rarely poisonous – even venomous snakes bite without injecting venom. Victims should be taken to a hospital or a doctor without delay. Commercial snake bite and scorpion kits are available, but are usually only useful for the specific types of snake or scorpion. Most serum has to be given intravenously so it is not much good equipping yourself with it unless you are used to making injections into veins. It is best to rely on local practice in these cases, because the particular creatures will be known about locally and appropriate treatment can be given. » *See boxes on cobras and scorpions found in Egypt, pages 310 and 463.*

Certain sea fish when trodden upon inject venom into bathers' feet. This can be exceptionally painful. Wear plastic shoes if such creatures are reported. The pain can be relieved by immersing the foot in hot water (as hot as you can bear) for as long as the pain persists or citric acid juices in fruits such as lemon is reported as useful.

Symptoms Fright, swelling, pain and bruising around the bite and soreness of the regional lymph glands, perhaps nausea, vomiting and a fever. Symptoms of serious poisoning would be: numbness and tingling of the face, muscular spasms, convulsions, shortness of breath or a failure of the blood to clot, causing generalized bleeding.

Treatment of snake bite Reassure and comfort the victim frequently. Immobilize the limb with a bandage or a splint and get the person to lie still. Do not slash the bite area and try to suck out the poison because this sort of heroism does more harm than good. If you know how to use a tourniquet in these circumstances, you will not need this advice. If you are not experienced, do not apply a tourniquet.

Precautions Do not walk in snake territory in bare feet or sandals – wear proper shoes or boots. If you encounter a snake stay put until it slithers away and do not investigate a wounded snake. Spiders and scorpions may be found in the more basic hotels. If stung, rest and take plenty of fluids and call a doctor. The best precaution is to keep beds away from the walls and always look inside your shoes and under the toilet seat.

Dengue fever

Dengue is endemic in patches around the border area with Sudan. Unfortunately there is no vaccine against this and the mosquitoes that carry it bite during the day. You will feel like a mule has kicked you for two to three days, you will then get better for a few days and then feel that the mule has kicked you again. It should all be over in seven to 10 unpleasant days. Apply all the anti-mosquito measures that you can.

Diarrhoea and intestinal upset

Symptoms Diarrhoea can refer either to loose stools or an increased frequency; both of these can be a nuisance. It should be short lasting but persistence beyond two weeks, with blood or pain, require specialist medical attention.

Cures Ciproxin (Ciprofloaxacin) is a useful antibiotic for bacterial travellers' diarrhoea. It can be obtained by private prescription in the UK. You need to take one 500 mg tablet when the diarrhoea starts and if you do not feel better in 24 hours, the diarrhoea is likely to have a non-bacterial cause and may be viral (in which case there is little you can do apart from keep yourself rehydrated and wait for it to settle on its own). The key treatment with all diarrhoeas is rehydration. Try to keep hydrated by taking the right mixture of salt and water. This is available as Oral Rehydration Salts (ORS) in ready-made sachets or can be made up by adding a teaspoon of sugar and a half teaspoon of salt to a litre of clean water. Drink at least one large cup of this drink for each loose stool. You can also use flat carbonated drinks as an alternative. Immodium and Pepto-Bismol provide symptomatic relief.

One study showed that up to 70% of all travellers may suffer from diarrhoea or intestinal upset during their trip.

Prevention The standard advice is to be careful with water and ice for drinking. Ask yourself where the water came from. If you have any doubts then boil it or filter and treat it. There are many filter/treatment devices now available on the market. Food can also transmit disease. Be wary of salads (what were they washed in, who handled them), re-heated foods or food that has been left out in the sun having been cooked earlier in the day. There is a simple adage that says 'wash it, peel it, boil it or forget it'. Also be wary of unpasteurised dairy products, these can transmit a range of diseases from brucellosis (fevers and constipation), to listeria (meningitis) and tuberculosis of the gut (obstruction, constipation, fevers and weight loss).

Hepatitis

Symptoms Hepatitis means inflammation of the liver. Viral causes of the disease can be acquired anywhere in the world. The most obvious symptom is a yellowing of your skin or the whites of your eyes. However, prior to this all that you may notice is itching and tiredness.

Cures Early on, depending on the type of hepatitis, a vaccine or immunoglobulin may reduce the duration of the illness.

Prevention Pre-travel hepatitis A vaccine is the best bet. Hepatitis B (for which there is a vaccine) is spread through blood and unprotected sexual intercourse, both of these can be avoided. Unfortunately there is no vaccine for hepatitis C or the increasing alphabetical list of other Hepatitis viruses. The prevalence of hepatitis C is unusually high in Egypt.

Leptospirosis

Various forms of leptospirosis occur throughout the world, transmitted by a bacterium which is excreted in rodent urine. Fresh water and moist soil harbour the organisms, which enter the body through cuts and scratches. If you suffer from any form of prolonged fever consult a doctor.

Prickly heat

This very common intensely itchy rash can be avoided by frequent washing and wearing loose clothing. It is cured by allowing skin to dry off (through use of powder and spending two nights in an air-conditioned hotel!).

Rabies

Remember that rabies is endemic throughout certain parts of the world, so avoid any animal, domesticated or wild, that is behaving strangely.

Treatment If you are bitten by an animal, do not leave things to chance: scrub the wound with soap and water and/or disinfectant, try to at least determine the animal's ownership, where possible, and seek medical assistance at once. The course of treatment depends on whether you have already been satisfactorily vaccinated against rabies. If you have (this is worthwhile if you are spending lengths of time in developing countries) then some further doses of vaccine are all that is required. If not already vaccinated then anti rabies serum (immunoglobulin) may be required in addition. It is important to finish the course of treatment.

Schistosomiasis (bilharzia)

Symptoms The mansoni form of this flat worm occurs in Suriname and Venezuela. The form that penetrates the skin after you have swum or waded through snail infested water can cause a local itch soon after, fever after a few weeks and much later diarrhoea, abdominal pain and spleen or liver enlargement.

Cures A single drug cures this disease.

Prevention Avoid infected waters, check the CDC, WHO websites and a travel clinic specialist for up to date information.

Sexual health

The range of visible and invisible diseases is awesome. Unprotected sex can spread HIV, hepatitis B and C, gonorrhea (symptoms: green discharge), chlamydia (symptoms: nothing to see but may cause painful urination and later female infertility), painful recurrent herpes, syphilis and warts, just to name a few. You can cut down the risk by using condoms, a femidom or avoiding sex altogether.

Sun protection

Symptoms White Britons are notorious for becoming red in hot countries because they like to stay out longer than everyone else and do not use adequate sun protection. This can lead to sunburn, which is painful and followed by flaking of the skin. Long-term sun damage leads to a loss of elasticity of skin and the development of pre-cancerous lesions. Years later a mild or a very malignant form of cancer may develop.

Cures Aloe vera gel is a good pain reliever for sunburn. The milder basal cell carcinoma, if detected early, can be treated by cutting it out or freezing it. The much nastier malignant melanoma may have already spread to bone and brain by the time it is first noticed.

Prevention Sun screen. SPF stands for Sun Protection Factor. It is measured by determining how long a given person takes to 'burn' with and without the sunscreen product on. So, if it takes 10 times longer to burn with the sunscreen product applied, then that product has an SPF of 10. If it only takes twice as long then the SPF is 2. The higher the SPF the greater the protection. However, do not just use higher factors just to stay out in the sun longer. 'Flash frying' (desperate bursts of excessive exposure), as it is called, is known to increase the risks of skin cancer. Follow the Australians with their 'Slip, Slap, Slop' campaign referred to earlier.

Underwater health

If you go diving make sure that you are fit do so. The **British Sub-Aqua Club (BSAC)**, Telford's Quay, South Pier Road, Ellesmere Port, Cheshire CH65 4FL, UK, T01513-506200, www.bsac.com, can put you in touch with doctors who do medical examinations. Protect your feet from cuts, beach dog parasites (larva migrans) and sea urchins. The latter are almost impossible to remove but can be dissolved with lime or vinegar. Keep an eye out for secondary infection.

Cures Antibiotics for secondary infections. Serious diving injuries may need time in a decompression chamber.

Prevention Check that the dive company know what they are doing, have appropriate certification from BSAC or Professional Association of Diving Instructors (PADI), Unit 7, St Philips Central, Albert Rd, St Philips, Bristol, BS2 0TD, T0117-3007234, www.padi.com, and that the equipment is well maintained.

Water

There are a number of ways of purifying water. Dirty water should first be strained through a filter bag and then boiled or treated. Bringing water to a rolling boil at sea level is sufficient to make the water safe for drinking, but at higher altitudes you have to boil the water for a few minutes longer to ensure all microbes are killed. There are sterilizing methods that can be used and there are proprietary preparations containing chlorine (eg Puritabs) or iodine (eg Pota Aqua) compounds. Chlorine compounds generally do not kill protozoa (eg Giardia). There are a number of water filters now on the market available in personal and expedition size. They work either on mechanical or chemical principles, or may do both. Make sure you take the spare parts or spare chemicals with you and do not believe everything the manufacturers say.

Further information

Websites

Foreign and Commonwealth Office (FCO) (UK), www.fco.gov.uk This is a key travel advice site, with useful information on the country, people, climate and lists the UK embassies/consulates. The site also promotes the concept of 'Know Before You Go'. And encourages travel insurance and appropriate travel health advice. It has links to the Department of Health travel advice site, see below.

Department of Health Travel Advice (UK), www.doh.gov.uk/traveladvice This excellent site is also available as a free booklet, the T6, from Post Offices. It lists the vaccine advice requirements for each country.

Medic Alert (UK), www.medicalalert.co.uk This is the website of the foundation that produces bracelets and necklaces for those with existing medical problems. Once you have ordered your bracelet/necklace you write your key medical details on paper inside it, so that if you collapse, a medical person can identify you as someone with epilepsy or allergy to peanuts etc.

Blood Care Foundation (UK), www.bloodcare.org.uk The Blood Care Foundation is a Kent-based charity "dedicated to the provision of screened blood and resuscitation fluids in countries where these are not readily available". They will dispatch certified non-infected blood of the right type to your hospital/clinic. The blood is flown in from various centres around the world.

The Health Protection Agency, www.hpa.org.uk This site has up to date malaria advice guidelines for travel around the world. It gives specific advice about the right drugs for each location. It also has useful information for those who are pregnant, suffering from epilepsy or planning to travel with children.
World Health Organisation, www.who.int The WHO site has links to the WHO Blue Book on travel advice. This lists the diseases in different regions of the world. It describes vaccination schedules and makes clear which countries have Yellow Fever Vaccination certificate requirements and malarial risk.
Fit for Travel (UK), www.fitfortravel.scot.nhs.uk This site from Scotland provides a quick A-Z of vaccine and travel health advice requirements for each country.
British Travel Health Association (UK), www.btha.org This is the official website of an organization of travel health professionals.
Travel Screening Services (UK), www.travelscreening.co.uk This is the author's website. A private clinic dedicated to integrated travel health. The clinic gives vaccine, travel health advice, email and SMS text vaccine reminders and screens returned travellers for tropical diseases.

Books
The Travellers Good Health Guide by Dr Ted Lankester, ISBN 0-85969-827-0. *Expedition Medicine (The Royal Geographic Society)* Editors David Warrell and Sarah Anderson ISBN 1 86197 040-4.
International Travel and Health World Health Organisation Geneva ISBN 92 4 158026 7.
The World's Most Dangerous Places by Robert Young Pelton, Coskun Aral and Wink Dulles ISBN 1-566952-140-9.

Keeping in touch

Communications

Internet
With over a million people online, Egypt is embracing the cyberworld in a big way. Internet facilities are found in most large cities and in all large hotels. In Cairo cyber cafés can be found sprinkled around the centre, Heliopolis, Maadi, Mohnadessin, Nasr City and Zamalek. Cost is generally between E£5-10an hour. Some budget hotels offer net access to their patrons. Even Siwa, the enchanting far-flung oasis 10 km east of the Libyan border, offers access. Connections can be tediously slow. If you're interested in finding an ISP in Egypt, there is no shortage. Most reputable at present and worthy of further investigation are tedata.net.eg and link.net. » *For cyber café listings, see individual town directories.*

Post
Local services All post offices are open daily except Friday. The Central Post Office in Cairo is open 24 hours. Airmail letters cost E£1.25 and take about 5 days to get to Europe and 1-2 weeks to get to North America, New Zealand and Australia. Local letters cost E£0.10. Blue post boxes are for international airmail; red and green boxes are for domestic mail. Postage stamps can be purchased from post offices, cigarette kiosks and from hotels, where mail can be posted too.

Parcels for abroad may only be sent from a main post office. Do not seal any package until it has been examined. Shops will sometimes arrange to send items you purchase. Receiving a parcel may involve import duty.

Telephone

Country code: 20. **Internal area codes for Governorates** are: Cairo: 02, Alexandria: 03, Aswan: 097, Luxor: 095, Sharm El-Sheikh and South Sinai: 069, Hurghada and Red Sea Coast: 065, 10th of Ramadan: 010, Ismailia: 064, 6th October: 011, Suez: 062, Port Said: 066, El-Fayoum: 084, Marsa Matouh: 046.

For **directory enquiries**, dial 140. If the operators don't speak English, they'll usually find someone who can help you.

The cheapest time to telephone is between 2000-0800. Local calls can be made from some shops (tip the shop keeper), cigarette kiosks and hotels (which normally add a premium in any case). You will also find yellow and green *Menatel* phone booths scattered throughout more urban areas. You can buy a card to use these booths at many kiosks and shops (look for a Menatel sign). Cards come in various amounts starting from E£10. Calls to England and North America cost about E£3 per minute; to call New Zealand and Australia, it's a bit more expensive. Long distance and international calls can also be made from telephone centres, but the wait and service can be tedious. Business centres at better hotels also facilitate international phone calls, for a price.

Your best bet is to invest in an international phone card before you leave your home country. From Egypt, you can access international calling cards from AT&T, T5100200.

To make **international calls** from Egypt, dial 00, country code, city/area code, and local number.

Note that **mobile phones** are very widely used in Egypt. Like Europe, they run on the GPS system. If you have roaming service, you should be able to use your GPS phone in Egypt, though be aware if people call you from outside Egypt you may incur long distance charges.

Media

Newspapers and magazines

Quite a lot of English language publications have popped up in Egypt over the last few years. The *Egyptian Gazette* is a fairly poor daily paper in English. *Cairo Times* and *Middle East Times* are weeklies that come out on Thursday and do a decent job of keeping readers informed of the political, social and cultural goings on of Cairo in particular, E£4. You can access them online at www.metimes.com and www.cairotimes.com. The most influential Egyptian daily is *Al-Ahram*. It also publishes an English language paper, *Al-Ahram Weekly*, out on Thursday, 75 piastres. There are a few English monthly glossies including *Egypt Today*, which offers an extensive up-to-date listing of hotels, businesses, restaurants and attractions around Egypt, E£10.

Radio and TV

Short wave radio guide The BBC World Service (London) and Voice of America (VOA) broadcast throughout the region. Reception quality varies greatly: as a general rule lower frequencies give better results in the morning and late at night and the higher ones in the middle of the day. TV is thriving in Egypt and nowadays, more people have access to a screen than a refrigerator. One station, *Nile TV*, offers consistent French and English language programming, with news broadcasts and analysis. There's also been a recent influx of Satellite TV increasingly available in more upscale hotels that features British and American primetime, MTV and movies.

Essentials

Telephone

[illegible]

[illegible]

[illegible]

[illegible]

[illegible]

[illegible]

Media

Newspapers and magazines

[illegible]

Radio and TV

[illegible]

Cairo

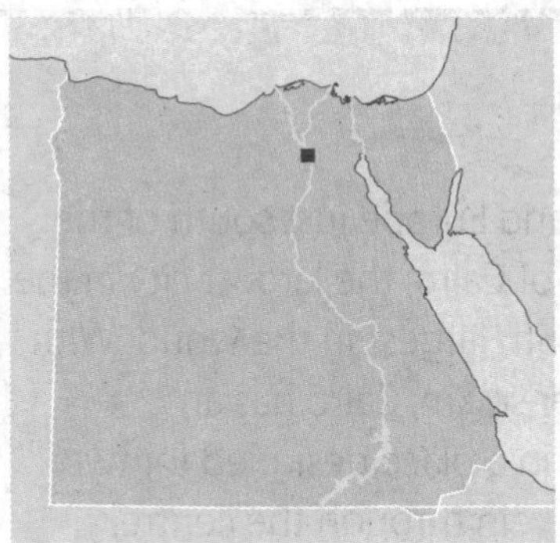

Footprint features

Introduction

At the crossroads of Asia, Africa and Europe just south of the Nile Delta stands the metropolis of Cairo, the largest city in the Middle East and Africa and the 15th largest in the world. With more than 25,000 inhabitants per sq km, Cairo has an estimated 16 million souls living in a place designed for two million. The River Nile runs like a vein through the centre, sustaining hearts and bellies as it has for millennia. On either bank extraordinary remains of civilizations past – thousands of years of Pharaonic, Coptic and Islamic history, commingle with the dwellings and lives of modern Egyptians.

Cairo has more than one face. Part of her wants to hold hands with the most cosmopolitan world cities and boast the splendours of her past; the other just wants to get by. Mega-malls and manicured *midans* (squares) sprout up with an air of contrived sophistication, but the rubble of failed building projects and the bulk of the population that concerns itself more with finding food and housing simply doesn't care about the absence of rubbish bins.

Testimony to Cairo's multiple faces is everywhere – through space and in time. A walk around the city is a walk through thousands of years: from the colossal Pyramids of Giza at the edge of the Western Desert to the Old Coptic Quarter on the east bank; through the alleys of Islamic Cairo, gushing with life and hundreds of ancient monuments to the downtown quarter where the stunning façades of 19th-century buildings remind onlookers of the profound influence of European occupiers. And in between the ancient monuments and modern buildings, souks and *ahwas* (coffee houses), bazaars and falafel stalls fill every crevice where the contagious energy of Cairo, perhaps the city's greatest attraction of all, looms on as it always has.

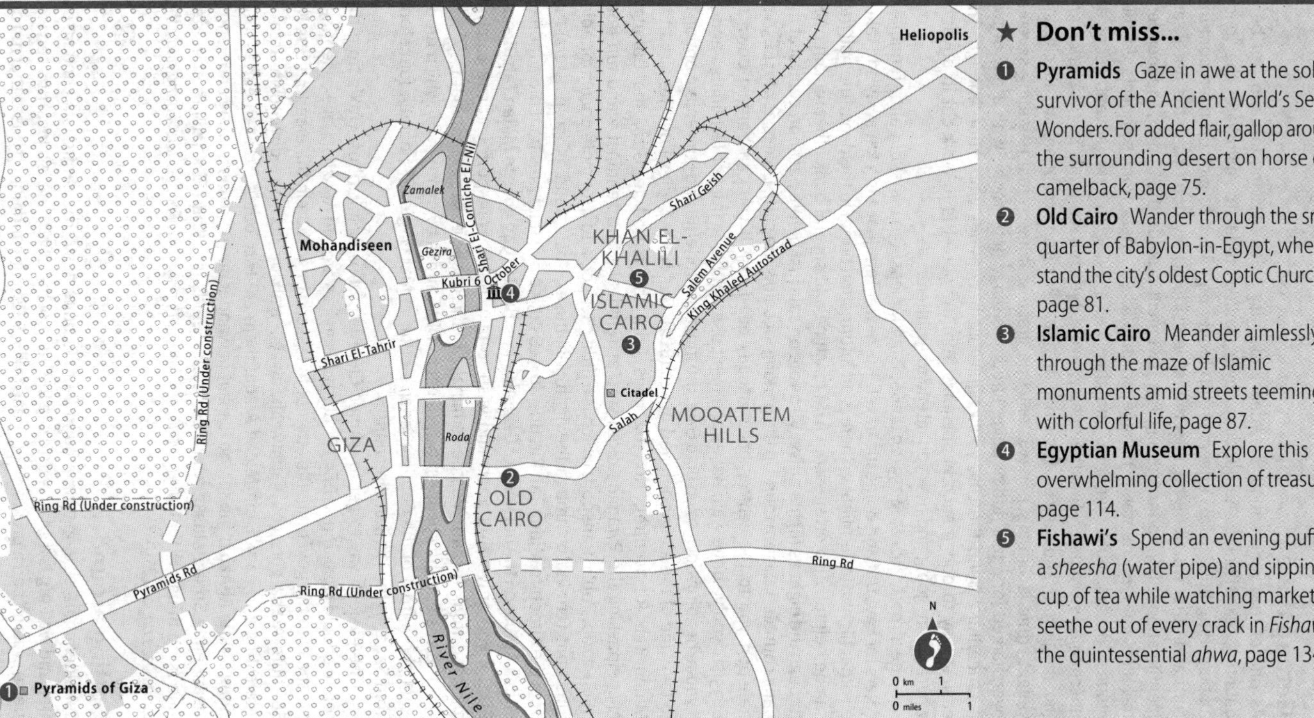

★ Don't miss...

❶ **Pyramids** Gaze in awe at the sole survivor of the Ancient World's Seven Wonders. For added flair, gallop around the surrounding desert on horse or camelback, page 75.

❷ **Old Cairo** Wander through the small quarter of Babylon-in-Egypt, where stand the city's oldest Coptic Churches, page 81.

❸ **Islamic Cairo** Meander aimlessly through the maze of Islamic monuments amid streets teeming with colorful life, page 87.

❹ **Egyptian Museum** Explore this overwhelming collection of treasures, page 114.

❺ **Fishawi's** Spend an evening puffing a *sheesha* (water pipe) and sipping a cup of tea while watching market life seethe out of every crack in *Fishawi's*, the quintessential *ahwa*, page 134.

Ins and outs → *Colour map 2, grid B2. Population: 17,000,000. Altitude: 75 m.*

Getting there

As one of the world's most crowded and noisy cities, arriving in Cairo can be a daunting experience. Authorities have worked hard to eliminate the once all-pervading hustle. Taxi drivers are no longer permitted to pick up rides from the curb and other would-be hustlers are left outside if they don't flash the necessary identification. Still, upon reaching the pavement outside the airport, independent travellers may encounter a barrage of unsolicited offers from self-declared tour guides, drivers, hotel vendors, and the like, seeking to take advantage of an unschooled newcomer. Breathe deeply, avoid eye contact, firmly say *la'a shocrun*, (no, thank you), and carry on. Bear in mind that Cairo is an exceptionally safe city and violent crime is virtually non-existent. The greatest thing to fear is getting severely overcharged for a taxi ride or being lured to a dingy hotel room. With a day or two meandering around the city, you'll figure out how things work soon enough. The easiest way to dodge such happenings from the outset is to work out in advance where you're going and how you intend to get there.

The **airport**, T02-2914255/2914266, is 22 km east (30 mins) of Cairo. Terminal 1 caters for **EgyptAir** and domestic travel. The newer Terminal 2 is 3 km away and takes all other flights. In Terminal 2, there is an information booth in the departure hall that can be helpful. Also on site is an ATM machine and several banks that remain open through the night as flights arrive. Visas are on sale just before passport control at the bank counter. Taxis are found in the parking lot below the curb. Drivers ask for E£50 to transport you to the centre, locals usually pay E£25. If you can bargain down to E£35ish, you've done well. Buses and minibuses gather in front of Terminals 1 and 2. If you're heading downtown or to Giza, the most comfortable and convenient option is to take one of the air-conditioned buses (E£2). Bus No 356 goes from the airport to **Midan Tah Rir** (centre); No 362 goes from the airport to **Giza**, the borough encompassing the Pyramids. Both stop at Terminal 1 and Terminal 2 and run from 0600-2200. Public transport, which is a little cheaper, and a lot more uncomfortable, runs from Terminal 1 through the night. Minibuses Nos 27 and 35 (50 piasters) run from the airport to **Midan Tah Rir.** Bus No 948 (25-50 piasters) runs from the airport to **Midan Ataba** (on the outskirts of Central Cairo). Bus No 949 goes to **Midan Tah Rir** and **Giza.** If you arrive after 2200 and wish to take public transport, you can catch a microbus from the curb outside Terminal 2 to the public buses in Terminal 1.

The easiest and cheapest way to get to **Old Cairo** is by metro (50p) which drops you right in front of the Coptic quarter. Get off at **Mar Girgis** (St George), four stops from **Sadat** in the Helwan direction.

The easiest way to get to **Islamic Cairo** is by taxi or microbus. (Taxis from the centre should cost around E£5.) Public bus services around Al-Azhar have essentially ceased with the government's attempt to lessen congestion in the area (but Bus No 66, from **Ataba** gets you 5-min walk away). Walking from the downtown area is interesting and easy. From **Midan Ataba**, there are two routes. You can either stroll along **Sharia Al-Azhar** (under the flyover) or wander down the fascinating and narrow meandering **Sharia Muski**, which eventually winds into **Khan El-Khalili** (both routes take 15-20 mins). » *For further details, see Transport, page 141. For Sleeping, Eating and other listings, see pages 125-148.*

Getting around

Considering its size, getting around Cairo is quite easy. The centre is a condensed area and **walking** is a good way to see the heart of the city. There is a local **bus** service, **metro** system, and a profusion of cheap **taxis**. A few air-conditioned buses that run on the major thoroughfares have been introduced to connect big tourist points and main

24 hours in the city

First stop the Citadel: visit the Mosque of Mohammed Ali Pasha, its architecture showing strong Ottoman influence. From the terrace there are excellent views over the city. On leaving, pass by the Mosque of Ibn Tulun, with its amazing spiral minaret. Near here are the Al Rifai Mosque, Cairo's most modern mosque completed in 1912, and the more ancient (1462) Sultan Hassan Mosque. Both are well worth a visit.

Spend the rest of morning in the Egyptian Antiquities Museum (go to see the treasures of Tutankhamen first before the crowds arrive).

Then head to the downtown *Felfela*'s nearby for a filling, authentic local lunch.

Next, hop on the metro and go to Old Cairo. In the heat of the afternoon the cool interiors of the museum and the churches are very welcome. Visit the Coptic Museum and either the Hanging Church or the Church of St Sergius, which is equally decorative. The beautifully restored Ben Ezra Synagogue (Egypt's oldest synagogue) is an optional extra. The Nilometer is accessible from here, but only worth seeing if you have not already seen one elsewhere.

In the early evening make your way to Khan El-Khalili (closed on Sundays) the main souk in Cairo since 1382. Stop for tea at *Fishawi*'s café just west of Midan Hussein and enjoy the atmosphere of the bustling market.

Purchases complete, cross the footbridge over Sharia Al-Azhar and walk south through the magnificent complex of Sultan Al-Ashraf Qansah II Al-Ghawri at least as far as Bab El-Zoueila for another splendid view. Take evening drinks at Mena House Oberoi before the amazing spectacle of sound and light staged at the Pyramids. Shows in English are early, allowing time to eat a dinner on a floating restaurant.

midans (squares). They are a bit more expensive than the public buses (E£2), but easier and more convenient to use. For the truly adventurous traveller, the inner-city buses and minibuses (25p-75p) cover every inch of Cairo. They are so crowded that people literally hang out of doors, and as they rarely come to complete stops, courageous riders must run and jump to hop on. There are also **microbuses** which are private van-like taxis that transport passengers through the maze of Cairo (25p-E£1). There is usually a driver and a navigator that shouts the destination out of a moving van. If it suits you, motion to the van and they'll stop. You can also shout out where you want to go and if it's en route, they will enthusiastically let you on. The metro is excellent – clean, cheap, and efficient, but with only two lines (and a third in construction), it doesn't cover the entire city. For cheaper and quicker transport, you may want to traverse the city by metro and then take a taxi or microbus for the final leg of your trip. Taxis are so inexpensive, abundant and easy, they really are the most convenient way of getting around.

Information

Main tourist office ⓘ *5 Sharia Adly, near Midan Opera, T02-3913454, 0800-2000.* The staff speak English, but except for a fairly useless map and a few colourful pamphlets they have little to offer in the way of useful information. There are tourist offices in the main airport terminals ⓘ *T02-2653640*, at **Ramses Train Station** ⓘ *T02-5790767*, and by the **Pyramids of Giza** ⓘ *T02-3838823*. The **Tourist Police** are next door. Often more helpful than the government tourist offices is the information available in hotels.

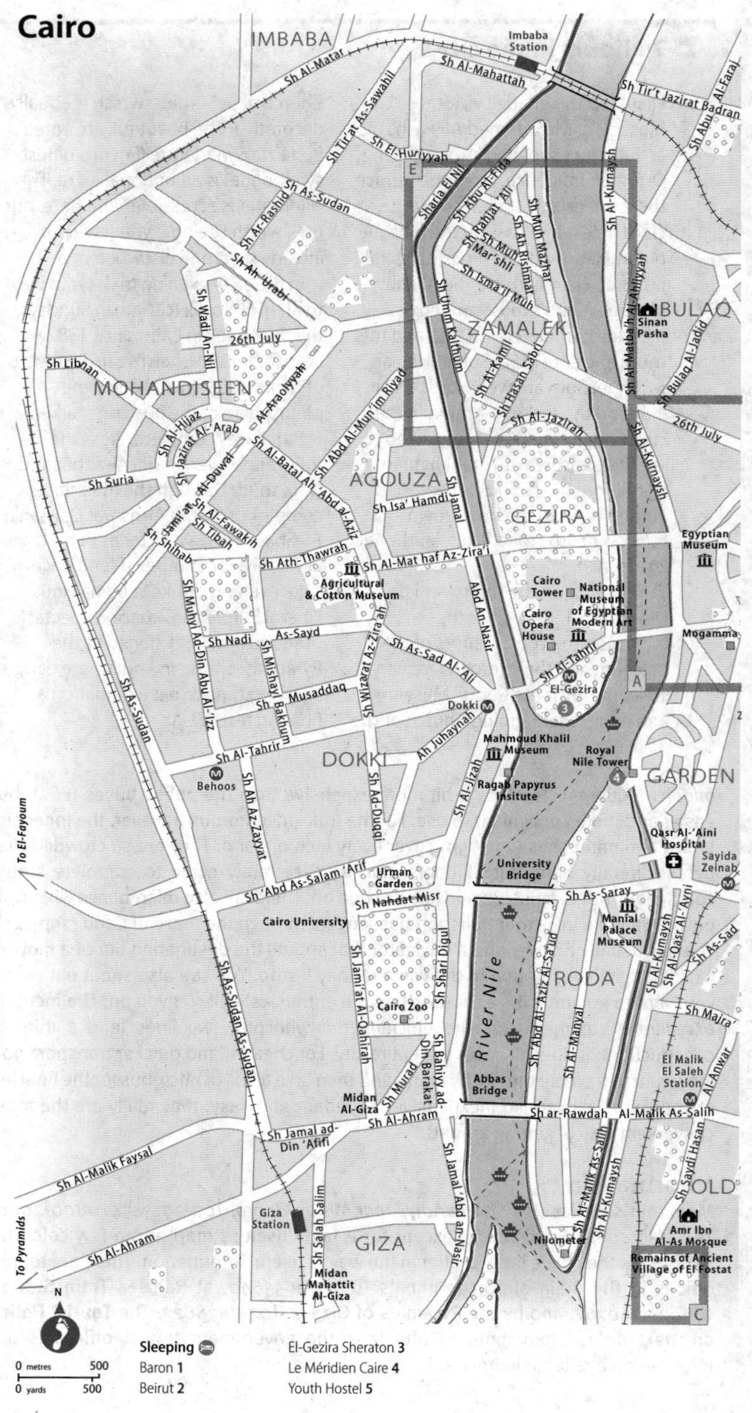
IMBABA
Imbaba Station
Sh Al-Matar
Sh Al-Mahattah
Sh Tir't Jazirat Badran
Sh Abu Al-Faraj
Sh Tir'at As-Sawahil
Sh El-Huriyyah
Sh As-Sudan
Sh Ar-Rashid
Sh Ah 'Urabi
Sharia El Nil
Sh Abu Al-Fida
Sh Rahjat 'Ali
Sh Muh Mazhar
Sh Ah Rishmat
Sh Muh Mar'shli
Sh Isma'il Muh
Sh Al-Kurnaysh
Sh Al-Matba'ah Al-Ahliyyah
BULAQ
Sinan Pasha
Sh Bulaq Al-Jadid
ZAMALEK
Sh Umm Kalthum
Sh Al-Kamil
Sh Hasan Sabri
Sh Al-Jazirah
26th July
Sh Wadi An-Nil
Sh Libnan
MOHANDISEEN
Al-Araolyyah
Sh Al-Hijaz
Sh Jazirat Al-'Arab
Sh Suria
Sh Jami'at Al-Duwal
Sh Al-Fawakih
Sh Tibah
Sh Shihab
Sh Al-Batal Ah 'Abd al-'Aziz
Sh 'Abd Al-Mun'im Riyad
AGOUZA
Sh Isa' Hamdi
Sh Jamal
GEZIRA
Egyptian Museum
Sh Ath-Thawrah
Sh Al-Mat haf Az-Zira'i
Agricultural & Cotton Museum
Abd An-Nasir
Cairo Tower
National Museum of Egyptian Modern Art
Cairo Opera House
Mogamma
Sh Muhyi Ad-Din Abu Al-'Izz
Sh Nadi
As-Sayd
Sh Mishayl Bakhum
Sh Wizarat Az-Zira'ah
Sh As-Sad Al-'Ali
Sh Al-Tahrir
El-Gezira
Sh Musaddaq
Dokki
Sh As-Sudan
Ah Juhaynah
Mahmoud Khalil Museum
Royal Nile Tower
DOKKI
GARDEN
Behoos
Sh Ah Az-Zayat
Sh Ad-Duqqi
Sh Al-Jizah
Ragab Papyrus Insitute
Qasr Al-'Aini Hospital
Sayida Zeinab
To El-Fayoum
University Bridge
Urman Garden
Sh 'Abd As-Salam 'Arif
Sh Nahdat Misr
Sh As-Saray
Manial Palace Museum
Cairo University
Sh Shari Digul
Sh 'Abd Al-'Aziz Al-Sa'ud
RODA
Sh Al-Kumaysh
Sh Al-Qasr Al-'Ayni
Sh As-Sad
Sh Jami'at Al-Qahirah
Cairo Zoo
River Nile
Sh Al-Manyal
Sh Majra
Sh As-Sudan As-Sudan
Sh Murad
Sh Bahiyy ad-Din Barakat
Abbas Bridge
El Malik El Saleh Station
Al-Anwar
Midan Al-Giza
Sh Al-Ahram
Sh ar-Rawdah
Al-Malik As-Salih
Sh Jamal ad-Din 'Afifi
Sh Al-Malik Faysal
Sh Jamal 'Abd ar-Nasir
Sh Al-Malik As-Salih
Sh Al-Kumaysh
Sh Saydi Hasan
OLD
Sh Salah Salim
Giza Station
Amr Ibn Al-As Mosque
To Pyramids
Sh Al-Ahram
GIZA
Nilometer
Remains of Ancient Village of El Fostat
Midan Mahattit Al-Giza
N
0 metres 500
0 yards 500
Sleeping
Baron 1
Beirut 2
El-Gezira Sheraton 3
Le Méridien Caire 4
Youth Hostel 5

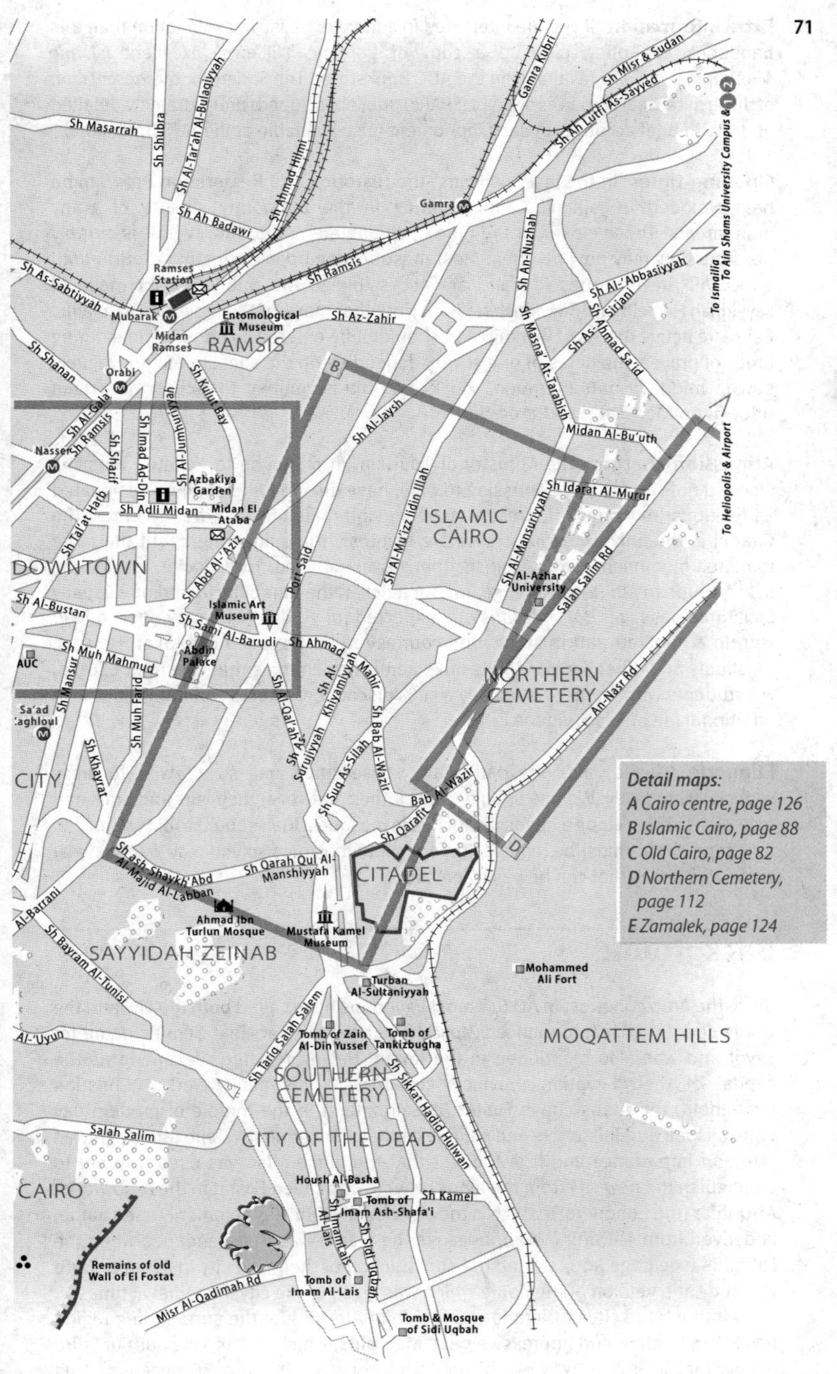
Detail maps:
A Cairo centre, page 126
B Islamic Cairo, page 88
C Old Cairo, page 82
D Northern Cemetery, page 112
E Zamalek, page 124
RAMSIS
DOWNTOWN
ISLAMIC CAIRO
NORTHERN CEMETERY
CITADEL
SAYYIDAH ZEINAB
SOUTHERN CEMETERY
CITY OF THE DEAD
MOQATTEM HILLS
Ramses Station
Mubarak
Midan Ramses
Entomological Museum
Orabi
Nasser
Azbakiya Garden
Midan El Ataba
Islamic Art Museum
Abdin Palace
AUC
Al-Azhar University
Ahmad Ibn Turlun Mosque
Mustafa Kamel Museum
Mohammed Ali Fort
Turban Al-Sultaniyyah
Tomb of Zain Al-Din Yussef
Tomb of Tankizbugha
Housh Al-Basha
Tomb of Imam Ash-Shafa'i
Tomb of Imam Al-Lais
Tomb & Mosque of Sidi Uqbah
Remains of old Wall of El Fostat
Gamra
To Ismailia
To Ain Shams University Campus
To Heliopolis & Airport
Sh Masarrah
Sh Shubra
Sh Ahmad Hilmi
Gamra Kubri
Sh Misr & Sudan
Sh Ah Lutfi As-Sayyed
Sh Ah Badawi
Sh Ramsis
Sh As-Sabtiyyah
Sh Az-Zahir
Sh An-Nuzhah
Sh Al-'Abbasiyyah
Sh Masna' At-Tarabish
Sh As-Ahmad Sa'id
Sh Shanan
Sh Kulut Bay
Sh Al-Jaysh
Midan Al-Bu'uth
Sh Idarat Al-Murur
Sh Adli
Sh Tal'at Harb
Sh Abd Al-'Aziz
Port Said
Sh Al-Mu'izz lidin Illah
Sh Al-Mansuriyyah
Salah Salim Rd
Sh Al-Bustan
Sh Sami Al-Barudi
Sh Ahmad Mahir
Sh Muh Mahmud
Sh Mansur
Sh Muh Farid
Sh Khayrat
An-Nasr Rd
Sh Bab Al-Wazir
Bab Al-Wazir
Sh Suq As-Silah
Sh Qarafit
Sh Qarah Qul Al-Manshiyyah
Al-Barrani
Sh Bayram Al-Tunisi
Al-'Uyun
Sh Tariq Salah Salem
Sh Sikkat Hadid Hulwan
Salah Salim
Sh Kamel
Misr Al-Qadimah Rd
Sh Sidi Uqbah
CITY
CAIRO

Extra information If you are interested in a more exhaustive explanation than this handbook can offer, pick up a copy of Caroline Williams' excellent *Islamic Monuments in Cairo* (available in the **AUC Bookstore**). The **Society for the Preservation of the Architectural Resources of Egypt (SPARE)** publishes superb and extremely detailed maps with brief accounts of each monument (also available at the AUC Bookstore).

Opening times In the last few years, the **Historic Cairo Restoration Programme** has exploded in Islamic Cairo resulting in the temporary closure of many monuments. Those closed at the time of writing are noted; however, it is entirely possible they may now be open. Most mosques are open from around 0800 until 2000. All the mosques in Cairo are accessible to the public except those of **Sayyidnah Hussein** and **Sayyidnah Nafisah.** Note that many of the mosques in Islamic Cairo are active places of worship and shouldn't be entered by non-Muslims during times of prayer. The times of prayer vary depending on the season, but are vaguely dawn, midday, mid-afternoon, dusk and mid-evening. Churches are open 0800-1700 Mon-Sat, 1200-1700 Sun.

Admission charges The **Ministry of Tourism**, in response to agitated Muslims who did not want to pay admission to pray, have deemed all buildings designated as religious (mosques, *madresas*, churches and mausoleums), free to enter. The Citadel is the only exception. There are some sly touts lingering about the more touristed monuments who will insist there is an entry fee. There is not. If someone asks you for an admission charge, ask for a ticket, their inability to find one usually facilitates passage. *Baksheesh* is still expected for guides (who may offer to lead you up a minaret) and it is common courtesy to tip the shoe caretaker. Houses, museums and other secular sights have admission charges that vary from E£6-20. For students with ID, there is usually a 50% discount. Cameras generally require an additional fee of E£10, videos E£100.

Etiquette Islamic Cairo is a particularly conservative area so it's wise to dress especially modestly. Women should wear clothes that cover their legs and arms and may wish to bring along a headscarf for use in mosques. Men should avoid shorts and tank tops. Shoes must be removed for entry into mosques so you may want to wear socks and shoes that can be easily removed.

Background

Since the Arab conquest in AD 641 most Egyptians have called both the city and the whole country **Misr** (pronounced *Masr*), which was the ancient Semitic name for Egypt and was also mentioned in the Koran. Having rejected Alexandria as the capital of their Egyptian province, because it was considered a Christian stronghold, the Arabs chose **Fustat** (encampment) in the middle of modern-day Cairo as their administrative and military capital. Consequently Cairo rapidly grew in size and importance and it is thought that the name Misr was used in order to distinguish the new city from the many other towns called Fustat in the Arab world. **Al-Qahira** (the Conqueror), which is the city's official but less commonly used name, is derived from Al-Qahir (Mars), because the planet was in ascendance when the Fatimids (see page 490) started the construction of their new city in AD 971. **Cairo** was the Latin version of the name which was given to the city in medieval times.

Although the city of Cairo is younger than Alexandria, the surrounding region has a very ancient and impressive past. **Memphis**, which lies 15 km south of Cairo across the River Nile, was established as the capital in 3100 BC because of its geographical and symbolic position in controlling both Upper and Lower Egypt. It

Take a deep breath – if you dare

According to UN figures lead pollution in the atmosphere in Cairo is equivalent to 1 tonne per car per year and Cairo now has over 1.5 million cars.

Egypt's Environmental Affairs Agency has reported that lead pollution and other suspended particles in the air over Cairo, which tend to manifest every autumn like a black cloud over the capital reducing visibility down to a few metres and breathing to a desperate struggle, is responsible for between 15,000 and 20,000 additional deaths annually.

USAID has funded a programme, now in its fifth year, that is addressing the problem by moving significant lead smelters out of the city, sponsoring vehicle emissions testing and tune-ups and promoting the use of natural gas (an abundant natural resource in Egypt and a much cleaner burning fuel) in public and private transport. Improvements have already been detected, but in 2000, the lead levels in the air, though lower, were still 11 times the World Health Organization's acceptable levels.

was during this period that the huge necropolis was developed across the river on the west bank first at **Saqqara** and then at the site of modern-day Giza where the largest pyramids were built.

Memphis was temporarily eclipsed by the new capital of **Thebes** (Luxor) during the New Kingdom. Then another cult centre known as On, or **Heliopolis** to the Greeks, and later Aïn Shams (Spring of the Sun) by the Arabs, was developed further north when a canal was cut between the River Nile and the Red Sea. Although the gradual westward movement of the Nile left it stranded and miles from the river, a small east bank fortress, which became known as **Babylon in Egypt**, was expanded during the Persian occupation (525-404 BC). At the time of the Roman occupation in 30 BC the fortress had been deserted and Memphis was still the country's second city after Alexandria. Recognizing the strategic importance of the site, the emperor Trajan (AD 98-117) rebuilt and reinforced Babylon and a thriving town soon sprang up around its walls. During the subsequent Christian era Memphis was completely abandoned and never rose again, while Babylon became the seat of the bishopric and the west bank village of **Giza** grew into a large town.

When the **Arabs** conquered Egypt in AD 641, they were given specific instructions by Khalifa Omar in Damascus to establish their administrative capital in Babylon rather than at the larger Alexandria. The general Amr ibn Al-As built his encampment (or Fustat) in the middle of a deserted triangular plain on the east bank which was bounded by Babylon in the south, Aïn Shams (ancient Heliopolis) to the northeast and Al-Maks (the Customs Point), which was the Arab name for Heliopolis' former port of Tendunyas and is now the site of Ramses Station, to the northwest. The Amr mosque was the first of a number of new and permanent buildings which were erected as the plain was developed and the foundations of modern Cairo were laid.

Under successive Muslim dynasties additions were made to the area, as new mini-cities, each to the northeast of the previous one, were built. By the time the Fatimid heretical Shi'a invaders arrived from North Africa in AD 969, under the military command of Gohar, only the south of the plain had been developed. Gohar therefore chose to build a new walled city (which included the Al-Azhar mosque, palaces, pavilions and gardens for the sole use of the khalifa, his family and retainers), about 1½ km north of the Fustat complex and called it Al-Qahira. Two centuries later in AD 1168 calamity struck the Fustat area when, fearing occupation by the invading Crusaders, the Egyptian vizier Shawar set fire to the city. Over 54 days the fire almost

Flinders Petrie: beginnings of systematic archaeology

Flinders Petrie applied the first systematic excavation techniques to archaeological sites in Egypt. He was born in 1853 in Scotland and arrived in Egypt in 1880 in search of measurements of the pyramids. He stayed and excavated many sites, recording in detail each item and layer of his work with consistency and accuracy – in sharp contrast to the acquisitive and unscientific digging of this and earlier periods. It was he who set the chronological framework within which most archaeologists and their colleagues later worked.

Petrie had the reputation, even as a young man, for wanting his own way and there were constant skirmishes between him and his financing committee in London. In 1886 Petrie left his employment with the Egypt Exploration Fund but remained in Egypt for a further 37 years, actively excavating and recording his finds. He eventually left Egypt in 1923 when the law on the division of archaeological finds was changed after the discovery of the tomb of Tutankhamen by Howard Carter. He died in 1942.

totally destroyed Fustat whose inhabitants fled to Al-Qahira and constructed temporary housing. Three years later the last Fatimid khalifa died and his vizier, the Kurdish-born **Salah Al-Din**, assumed control of the country and founded the Sunni Muslim orthodox Ayyubid Dynasty (AD 1171-1249). He expelled the royal family from Al-Qahira which he then opened to the public and it soon became the commercial and cultural centre of the metropolis.

Salah Al-Din actually only spent one third of his 24-year reign in Cairo. Much of his time was spent fighting abroad where he recaptured Syria and eventually Jerusalem from the Crusaders in 1187 and finally died in Damascus in 1193.

He expanded the walls surrounding the Fatimid city and in the southeast built a huge **Citadel**, which became the city's nucleus, on an outcrop of the Muqattam Hills. Under Mamluk rule (AD 1250-1517) the city grew rapidly to become the largest city in the Arab world. As the east bank of the River Nile continued to silt up, the newly elevated areas provided additional space which were developed to house the expanding population.

Under the **Ottomans** (AD 1517-1798) both Cairo and Alexandria were relegated to the position of mere provincial cities with little in the way of public building undertaken in the whole of the 17th and 18th centuries. This changed, however, with the combination of the arrival of the French in 1798 and the coming to power in 1805 of the Albanian-born Ottoman officer Mohammed Ali. As part of his ambitious plan to drag Egypt into the modern world by introducing the best that Europe had to offer, he embarked on a project which included a huge public building programme in Cairo and turned it into a large modern capital city.

The combination of very rapid population growth and extensive rural migration to the city, particularly since the Second World War, has completely overwhelmed Cairo. It has totally outgrown its infrastructure and today a city, intended to house only two million people, is home to perhaps 16 million. The result is that the transport, power, water and sewage systems are completely inadequate and hundreds of thousands live on the streets or wherever they can find shelter including the infamous 'Cities of the Dead' cemeteries. What is amazing is that, despite all its problems, this ancient city actually functions as well as it does and that in adversity the Cairenes are so good-natured and friendly.

Sights

It certainly makes sense, if time permits, to visit the major sights of this area in chronological order. Therefore, rather than rushing to the large and exhausting Egyptian Museum, start outside the city at the ***pyramids*** *and trace their development from the earliest in Saqqara (see Around Cairo chapter, page 152) to the majesty of Giza. In Cairo proper there are few remains from the pre-Christian era other than in the Egyptian Museum, so the logical sequence of visits would be –* ***Old Cairo*** *in the ancient fortress of Babylon-in-Egypt; the mosques, cemeteries and souks of* ***Islamic Cairo****; and the modern sites and museums around* ***Central Cairo****.*

Pyramids of Giza

ⓘ Daily 0900-1700. E£20 (students E£10) to enter the area, additional E£20 to enter the Pyramid of Cheops, number of tourists who can enter Cheops is limited in order to preserve the monument so arrive early (around 0800) if you want to look inside, additional E£20 to enter 2nd and 3rd pyramids, E£10 for cameras inside the pyramid, no flash photography allowed, claustrophobics should avoid the inside of the pyramids. The Sunboat is another E£20 ticket. For sound and light performances see page 138. A camel ride around the pyramids can be a fun way to take in their splendour, offer no more than E£10-15 for a short ride – to be paid after your meander. AA and MG stables at the right of the main entrance are among the more notable in Giza.

Of the Seven Wonders of the ancient world only the **Pyramids** remain. Those at **Giza** outside Cairo are by no means the only ones in Egypt but they are the largest, most imposing and best preserved. When **Herodotus**, chronicler of the Ancient Greeks, visited them in 450 BC they were already more ancient to him than the time of Christ is to us today. That the huge blocks were quarried, transported and put into place demonstrates how highly developed and ordered the Old Kingdom was at its peak. Herodotus claimed that it would have taken 100,000 slaves 30 years to have

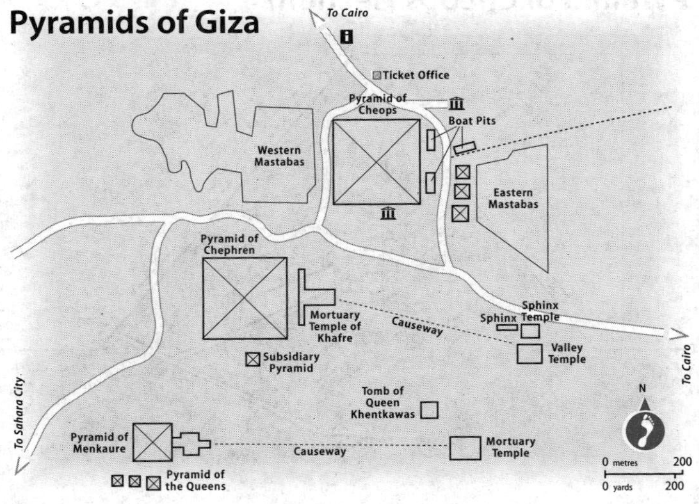

constructed the great **Pyramid of Cheops**, but it is more likely that the pyramid was built by peasants, paid in food, who were unable to work the land while the Nile flooded between July and November. Happily, the high waters also made it possible to transport the casing stone from Aswan and Tura virtually to the base of the pyramids. The enormous Pyramid of Cheops, built between 2589-66 BC out of over 2,300,000 blocks of stone with an average weight of two and a half tonnes and a total weight of 6,000,000 tonnes to a height of almost 140 m, is the oldest and largest of the pyramids at Giza. The **Pyramid of Chephren** and **Pyramid of Menkaure** date from 2570-30 BC.

A breakdown in the structure of society, and the reduction of wealth, have been proposed as reasons why other pyramids were not constructed on the same scale later in the Old Kingdom. The first thefts from tombs occurred relatively soon after the Pyramids' construction, which was undoubtedly an important factor in the preference for hidden tombs, such as in **The Valley of the Kings**, by the time of the New Kingdom.

One of the first things that visitors to the Pyramids will notice is their unexpected proximity to Cairo. The second is the onslaught of hustlers that bombard the awe-struck onlooker. Despite the increased police presence that tries in earnest to subdue the camel and horse hustlers, water and soda hawkers and papyrus and postcard vendors, they get through. Be firm with your 'no' and they'll get the point, eventually.

Pyramid of Cheops (Khufu)

Very little is known of Cheops. His tomb, which could have provided some answers, was looted long before the archaeologists arrived. He is believed to have been the absolute ruler of a highly stratified society and his reign must have been one of great wealth in order to afford so stupendous a burial site. Although he was buried alone, his wives and relations may have merited smaller *mastabas* nearby.

Originally the 230 x 230 m pyramid would have stood at 140 m high but 3 m has been lost in all dimensions since the encasing marble was eroded or removed. The entrance, which was at the centre of the north face, has been changed in modern times and access is now 15 m lower via an opening created by the plundering Khalifa Ma'mun in AD 820. From this entrance a tunnel descends steeply for about 25 m until it reaches a point where it is met by an ascending corridor which climbs at the same angle.

Pyramid of Cheops (section)

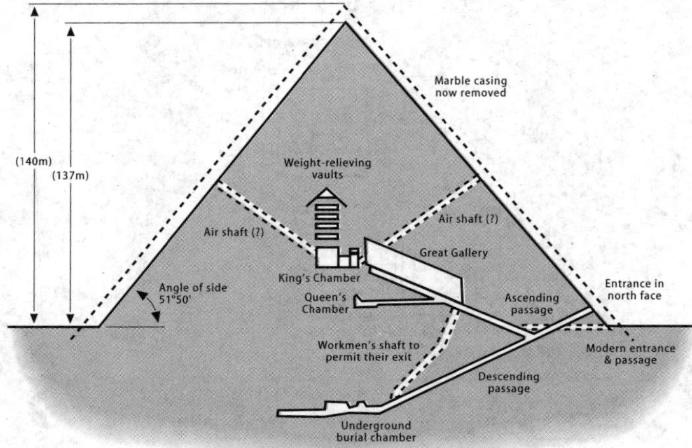

Although closed to ordinary visitors, if you continue down the very long, narrow and steep descending shaft, definitely not for those who are either unfit or claustrophobic, you eventually reach a lower unfinished chamber which lies 20 m beneath the bedrock of the pyramid's foundations. Even though the chamber is empty, except for a deep pit where the sarcophagus would have been lowered, the sensation of standing alone under six million tonnes of stone blocks is overpowering. Despite the speculation that the chamber was unfinished because of a change of plan by either Cheops or his architect, the later pyramid of Chephren follows an identical pattern.

Going up the 36 m long ascending corridor, which is 1.6 m high and has a steep 1:2 gradient, you arrive at the start of the larger 47-m long **Great Gallery** which continues upward at the same incline to the **King's Chamber** 95 m beneath the pyramid's apex. The gallery, whose magnificent stonework is so well cut that it is impossible to insert a blade into the joints, narrows at the top end to a corbelled roof which is 8.5 m high.

At the beginning of the gallery there is a second horizontal passage, 35 m long and 1.75 m high, which leads to a room misleadingly known as the **Queen's Chamber**. In fact no queen was buried there and the small room, measuring 5.2 x 5.7 m with a 6.13 m pointed roof, is more likely to be the *serdab* (cellar) which contained the icon of the Pharaoh. In 1872 two triangular holes were made by a British engineer in the chamber's north and south walls in order to discover the location of the air or ventilation shafts.

The walls of **The King's Chamber** are lined with polished red granite. The room measures 5.2 x 10.8 x 5.8 m high and contains the huge lidless Aswan red granite sarcophagus, which was all that remained of the treasures when archaeologists first explored the site. It was saved because it was too large to move along the entrance passage and, therefore, must have been placed in the chamber during the pyramid's construction. Above this upper chamber there is a series of five relieving chambers which are structurally essential to support the massed weight of the stones above and distribute the weight away from the burial chamber. A visit to the collapsed pyramid at Maidoum (see El-Fayoum, page 167) will illustrate why this was necessary. As in the Queen's Chamber, the north and south walls bear air shafts but in this case they are the original ones.

Pyramid of Chephren (section)

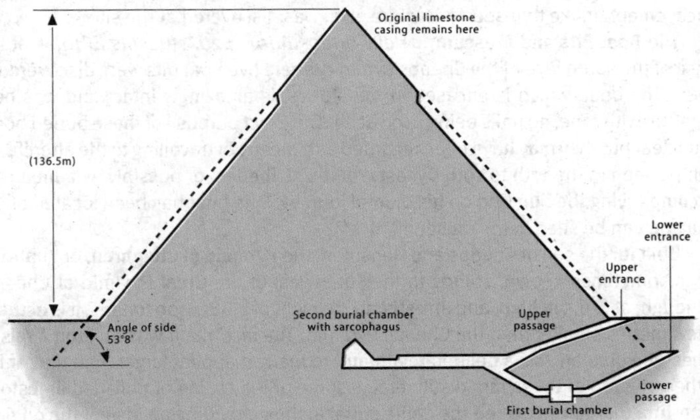

One of the great mysteries of the massive Pyramid of Cheops is the four tiny meticulously crafted 20-cm sq shafts, which travel, two from the King's Chamber and another two from the Queen's Chamber, at precisely maintained angles through the body of the pyramid to the outer walls. Obviously serving a significant function, they were originally thought to be ventilation shafts. However, Egyptologists now are more inclined to believe that they are of religious significance and relate to the Ancient Egyptians' belief that the stars are a heavenly counterpart to their land, inhabited by gods and souls of the departed.

The main feature of the ancient night sky was the Milky Way, the bright band of stars which was believed to be the celestial River Nile. The most conspicuous of bright stars which appeared in the night sky were those of Orion's Belt. Their reappearance coincided with the yearly miracle of the Nile flood and were associated with Osiris, the protector god. The brightest star in the sky, Sirius, was his consort the goddess Isis because it was bright, beautiful, and followed Osiris across the sky. Linked to the creation myth, the texts on the great pyramid's walls repeatedly tell of the dead Pharaoh, seen as the latest incarnation of Horus, the son of Isis and Osiris, travelling in a boat between various star constellations. At an angle of exactly 45°, the southern shaft of the King's Chamber points directly at where Orion's Belt would have been in the sky in ancient times. Meanwhile, the southern shaft of the Queen's Chamber points to Sirius, his consort Isis. The northern shaft of the King's Chamber is directed at the circumpolar stars, important to the Ancient Egyptians as the celestial pole because these stars never disappear or die in the sky. The 'star shafts' thus appear to be directed so that the spirit of the dead Pharaoh could use the shafts to reach the important stars with pinpoint accuracy.

Around the Cheops Pyramid

In accordance with the Pharaonic custom, Cheops married his sister **Merites** whose smaller ruined pyramid stands to the east of his, together with the pyramids of two other queens, both of which are attached to a similarly ruined smaller sanctuary. Little remains of **Cheops' Mortuary Temple** which stood to the east of the pyramid. It was connected by a causeway, which collapsed only in the last 150 years, to the Valley Temple which stands near the modern village of **Nazlat Al-Samman**. The temples and causeway were built and decorated before Cheops' Pyramid was completed.

West of the Cheops Pyramid is an extensive **Royal Cemetery** in which 15 *mastabas* have recently been opened to the public after having been closed for over 100 years. A 4,600-year-old female mummy, with a unique internal plaster encasement unlike that seen anywhere else, was discovered at the site.

The **Boat Pits and Museum** ⓘ *daily 0900-1600, E£20, students E£10*, is at the base of the south face of the Cheops Pyramid where five boat pits were discovered in 1982. The boat, which is encased in the stones, is amazingly intact and was held together with rope, no nails being used at all. The exact purpose of these buried boats is unclear but they may have been regarded as a means of travelling to the afterlife, as can be seen in the 17th to 19th Dynasty tombs at Thebes, or possibly as a means of accompanying the Sun God on his diurnal journey. One boat has been located at the site and can be seen in the museum.

Built for the son of Cheops and Hensuten, the **Pyramid of Chephren**, or Khafre as he is sometimes known, stands to the southwest of the Great Pyramid of Cheops, although, at 136.5 m high, and an estimated weight of 4,880,000 tonnes, it is actually a few metres smaller than the Cheops Pyramid. The fact that it was built on a raised limestone plateau was a deliberate attempt to make it appear larger than that of his father. The top of the pyramid still retains some of the casing of polished limestone from Tura that once covered the entire surface, thus providing an idea of the original finish. The entrance to the tomb was lost for centuries until 1818 when Belzoni located it and blasted open the sealed portal on the north side. Although he believed that it

Save our Sphinx

The carefully planned, six-year-long restoration of the Sphinx programme is in its final stage. In the 1980s over 2,000 new limestone blocks were added to the ailing body of the Sphinx and it was subjected to injections of chemicals. Unfortunately this 'treatment' flaked away taking with it parts of the original rock surface. The next attempt at restoration was certainly unkind and unscientific. Various mortars and numerous workers, untrained in restoration, carried out a six-month repair. The result was further damage and in 1988 the crumbling of the left shoulder and falling of blocks.

The present attempts to restore the Sphinx are under the control of archaeologists from the Supreme Council of Antiquities. Work has been concentrated so far on draining away the subsoil seepage which is damaging the rock and on repairing the damaged shoulder with smaller blocks more in keeping with the original size. After all, as the Minister of Culture said, "it is an objet d'art."

would still be intact, he found that it had been looted many centuries earlier. As with the Pyramid of Cheops there is an unfinished and presumed unused chamber below the bedrock. The passageway now used to enter the burial chamber heads downwards before levelling out to the granite-lined passageway that leads to the chamber. To the west of the chamber is the red granite sarcophagus, built into the floor, with the lid lying nearby. After recent restoration there is now better ventilation and new interior lighting has been provided. The number of daily visitors is also to be strictly limited.

The **Mortuary Temple of Khafre** lies to the east of the pyramid and is more elaborate and better preserved than that of his father. Although the statues and riches have been stolen, the limestone walls were cased with granite which is still present in places. There are still the remains a large pillared hall, a small sanctuary, outhouses and a courtyard.

A 500-m causeway linked the Mortuary Temple to the **Valley Temple**, ⓘ*daily 0900-1600*, which is better preserved than any other because it lay hidden in the sands until Mariette rediscovered it in 1852. It is lined with red granite at roof height which protects the limestone. Two entrances to the Temple face east and lead to a T-shaped hall supported by enormous pillars. In front of these stood 23 diorite statues of Khafre. The only one which has remained intact can be found in the Egyptian Museum. Side chambers lie off to the south of the hall. A passage which joined the causeway is now closed off.

The Sphinx

The Sphinx is next to Khafre's Valley Temple to the northeast. We are extremely lucky that it still exists because it was built of soft sandstone and would have disappeared centuries ago had the sand not covered it for so much of its history. Yet it is equally surprising that it was ever carved because its sculptor must have known that such soft stone would quickly decay. The Arabs call it *Abu'l-Hawl*, the awesome, or terrible one. Nobody can be certain who it represents but it is possibly Khafre himself and, if this is the case, would be the oldest known large-scale royal portrait. Some say that it was hewn from the remaining stone after the completion of the pyramid and that, almost as an afterthought, Khafre set it, as a sort of monumental scarecrow, to guard his tomb. Others claim that the face is that of his guardian deity rather than Khafre's own. The Sphinx was first uncovered by Tuthmosis IV (1425-17 BC) thereby fulfilling a prophecy that by uncovering the great man-lion he would gain the throne. Recent efforts to conserve the Sphinx are now complete but the rising water table threatens to accelerate its decay. Earlier attempts to restore it caused more harm than good when the sandstone was filled, totally inappropriately, with concrete. The Sphinx is incomplete. The 'beard' is exhibited in the British Museum.

The name 'sphinx', which means 'strangler', was given first by the Greeks to a fabulous creature which had the head and bust of a woman, the body of a lion and the wings of a bird. The sphinx appears to have originated in Egypt in the form of a sun god with whom the pharaoh was associated. The Egyptian sphinx is usually a lion with the head of a king wearing the characteristic wig-cover. There are, however, ram-headed sphinxes associated with the god Amun.

The Pyramid of Menkaure (Mycerinus)

This is the smallest of the three Giza Pyramids and marks the beginning of a steep decline in the standards of workmanship and attention to detail in the art of pyramid-building. At the time of the death of Menkaure, who was Chephren's successor and was later known by the Greek name of Mycerinus, it was unfinished and the granite encasement intended to cover the poor quality local limestone was never put in place by his son Shepseskaf who completed the rest of the pyramid. The base is 102 x 104 m (the original measurements much reduced by removal of stones) and rises at 51° to 66.5 m high, considerably lower than the earlier pyramids. It also differs from those of Khufu and Khafre in that the lower chamber was used as the burial tomb. The walls are lined with granite hewn into the rock below the level of the Pyramid's foundations. The fine basalt sarcophagus was discovered in the recessed floor but unfortunately lost at sea en route to Britain.

East of the Pyramid of Menkaure lies the **Mortuary Temple** which is relatively well preserved. The walls were not encased with granite or marble but with red mud bricks and then lined with a thin layer of smoother limestone. It is connected to the Valley Temple via a 660-m mud-brick causeway which now lies beneath the sand.

There is a theory that the odd plan of the three Pyramids of Giza, progressively smaller and with the third slightly offset to the left, correlates to the layout of the three stars of Orion's Belt. Highly controversial, it suggests that the Ancient Egyptians chose to reproduce, on land and over a great distance, a kind of map of the stars.

Pyramid of Menkaure (section)

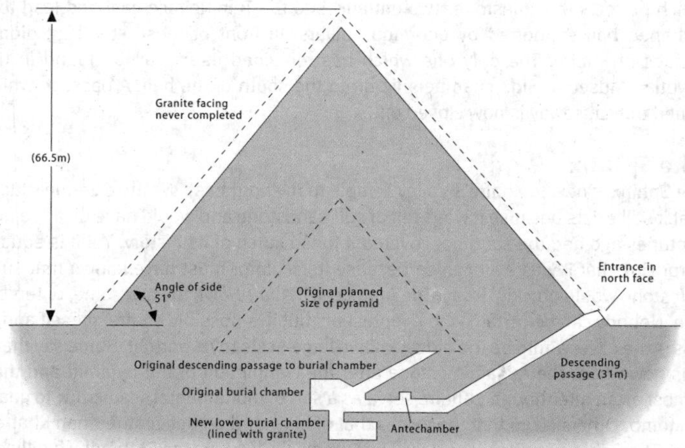

Subsidiary Pyramids

South of the Pyramid of Menkaure are three smaller incomplete ones. The largest, to the east, was most likely intended for Menkaure's principal wife. The granite sarcophagus of the central tomb was recovered and was found to contain the bones of a young woman.

The **Tomb of Queen Khentkawes**, who was an obscure but intriguing and important figure, is to the south of the main Giza pyramids. Although she appears to have been married to Shepseskaf, who was the last Fourth Dynasty pharaoh, she subsequently married a high priest of the sun god Re at a time when the male dynastic line was particularly weak. By going on to bear a number of later kings who are buried in Saqqara and Abu Sir, she acted as the link between the Fourth and Fifth Dynasties. Her tomb is an enormous sarcophagus and is linked to a Mortuary Temple cut out of the limestone.

The **Zawiyat Al-Aryan Pyramids** are roughly halfway between Giza and North Saqqara and one has to ride through the desert to see them. A visit would probably only be rewarding to the devoted Egyptologist. There are two pyramids of which the southernmost one is probably a Third Dynasty (2686-13 BC) step pyramid. The granite of the more northerly suggests that it is Fourth Dynasty (2613-2494 BC) but it would appear to have been abandoned after the foundations had been laid. The **Pyramids of Abu Sir** and the **Sun-Temples of Abu Ghurab** are about three kilometres further south (see Saqqara, page 158).

If you're interested in the Coptic Monasteries look out for the **Monastery of St Mercurius** (Abu Seifein) in Tamouh, just 12 km south of Giza, and now used as a training centre.

Old Cairo

This settlement was constructed by the Persians in about 500 BC to guard the junction of the River Nile and the canal linking it to the Red Sea. During the Christian period the fortified settlement of Babylon in Egypt grew into a large town. It was perhaps named by the fort's homesick building workers from modern-day Iraq or from the name for Gate of Heliopolis (Bab-il-On). Later the Arabs called it Qasr Al-Sham'ah (Fortress of the Beacon). Whatever its origins, it is now commonly known as Old Cairo.

Old Cairo, identified not entirely correctly by some as Coptic Cairo, is located on the east bank of the River Nile about five kilometres south of Midan Tah Rir, opposite the southern tip of Roda Island to which it was connected by a pontoon bridge. The churches do not charge admission and few request baksheesh (tips), but most have donation boxes. To get a taste of Coptic culture and heaps of Coptic Cairenes milling about from holy sight to holy sight, come on Sunday; if you are in search of a peaceful stroll through Old Cairo, it is best to avoid it on Wednesday, Friday and Sunday.

Old Cairo has been inhabited since AD 313.

*Leaving the Mar Girgis station, you are confronted by two circular **Roman towers** some 33 m in diameter which comprised the west gate of the fortress built on what was at that time the east bank of the Nile, now 400 m further west and on foundations now smothered beneath 10 m of Nile silt and rubble. Much of the original fortress was demolished as part of extensive alterations and today only its towers which supported a drawbridge and gates have survived. The new **Church of St George**, built in 1904 and the only circular church in Egypt, is actually built on top of the north tower and is part of the **Monastery of St George**, which is the seat of the Greek Orthodox Patriarchate of Alexandria. The **Convent of St George**, the **Church of the Virgin** and the remains of the original fire-damaged **Church of St George** are to the northeast.*

The Hanging Church

To the south of the Roman towers is the **Church of the Virgin** ⓘ *Coptic masses held on Fri 0800-1100 and Sun 0900-1100*, better known as the **Hanging Church** (Al Mu'allaqah or 'The Suspended One') because it stands on top of the three stone piers of the semi-flooded Roman **Water Gate** from where the Melkite bishop Cyrus, the last Byzantine viceroy, fled by boat as the Muslim army arrived. The gate below the church is reached via a stairway behind the piers, by buying a ticket at the Coptic Museum.

The original church built in the fourth century was demolished in AD 840 by Ali Ibn Yahya who was the Armenian Governor. It was rebuilt in AD 977 and modified several times, most recently in 1775. The church is approached though a wonderful narrow courtyard from which steps lead, via a 19th-century vestibule, to the church's entrance. It is divided into a wide nave and two narrow side aisles by two rows of eight columns, 15 of white marble and one of black basalt, all columns with Corinthian capitals. Look out for the odd black basalt capital. The vaulted roof is of timber. There are three supporting columns in the centre of the nave and an 11th-century marble pulpit supported by 15 delicate columns arranged as seven pairs and a leader. Examination of the marble steps up to the pulpit will reveal a shell and cross design. On examination each pair of columns is identical but no two pairs are the same. A very fine piece of work. The 13th- century *iconostasis* (wooden screen supporting icons), which separates the congregation from the three *haikals* (altar areas) behind the marble pulpit is an incredible feat of fine woodwork and appears virtually transparent. The central icon depicts Christ on the throne, with the Virgin Mary, Archangel Gabriel and St Peter to the right and John the Baptist, Archangel Michael and St Paul to the left. To the right of the altar is a room which is built over the eastern tower of the southern gateway of the old fortress. Here in the baptistry the basin is of red granite. It contains the shrine of Takla Hamanout, an Ethiopian saint, and a small room with a font. The screen dividing this room from the main church is of very

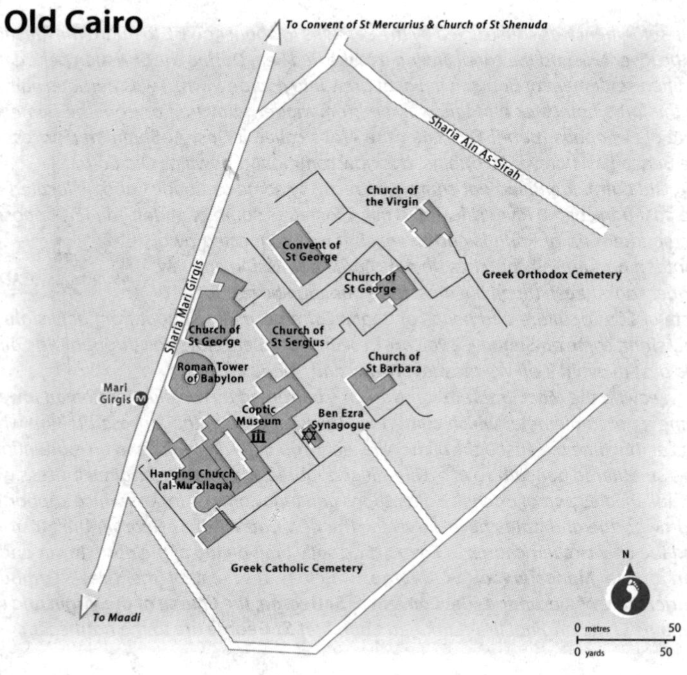

delicate woodwork – the mother of pearl inlay is enhanced by holding a candle or torch behind. To its left and right, two secret passageways lead down to the foundations. These recent discoveries are thought to be escape routes used by the Christians during times of persecution.

The Church of St Sergius

Immediately to the east of the main Roman towers, down a narrow cobbled lane, is the fifth-century **Church of St Sergius**, the oldest church in Cairo. It is dedicated to two soldiers, St Sergius and St Bacchus, who were martyred in Syria in 303. The earliest pieces of the building date from the fifth century. It lies some 3 m below street level and was rebuilt in the Fatimid period after having been virtually destroyed by fire in the eighth century. The architecture of the church, which contains many antiques recovered from ancient monuments, follows the style of a traditional basilica with the nave divided from the side aisles by two rows of six marble pillars. Eleven of these monolithic columns are marble and one is of red granite. The remains of illustrations on these pillars represented the apostles or saints. Some of the icons here are 17th century and show various scenes of the life of Christ, Virgin Mary and some of the saints.

The partially flooded crypt, to the left of the sanctuary, the only remaining vestige of the original church, is intriguing because it is claimed that the Holy Family sought refuge here during their flight to Egypt and the places where they sat are still visible. The crypt measures 6 x 5 m and is 2.5 m high. There are niches on the north, south and east walls. It has always been a popular place of pilgrimage. A special Mass is held annually on the 24th day of the Coptic month of Bechens (June 1) to commemorate the Flight into Egypt of the Holy Family. There are two smaller chapels, one on either side of the altar.

The Church of St Barbara

Just behind the church of St Sergius is the very similar 11th-century **Church of St Barbara** standing on the site of an older church dedicated to St Cyrus and St John in AD 684 which was destroyed during an Arab assault. It is said that when some Christians from Damanhur, including Cyrus and John confessed to their faith they were shot with arrows, burned in a furnace, tied to a horse's tail and dragged through the streets and survived – to be beheaded. The remains of these two martyrs are in the side chapel approached from the left of the altar. The third-century relics of St Barbara were brought to the church and are now contained in a lovely little chapel to the left of the altar. St Barbara, to which church is now dedicated, was an attractive young woman from Nicomedia in Asia Minor. In one version of her history she tried to convert her father to Christianity and he killed her. In

Church of Al-Mu'allaqah (The Hanging Church)

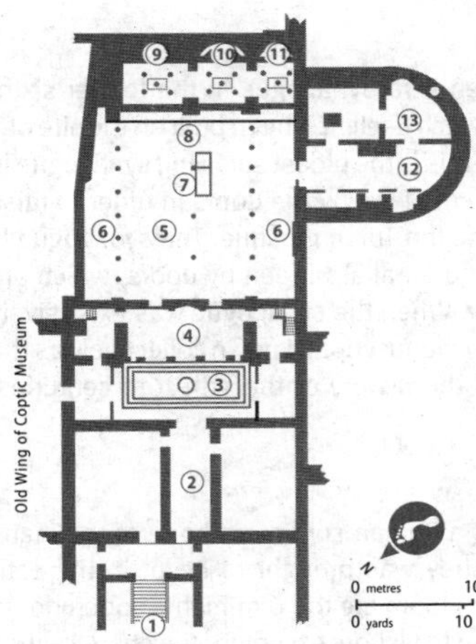

1 Entrance from Sharia Mari Girgis
2 Passage
3 Covered courtyard
4 Narthex
5 Nave (wagon-vaulted)
6 Aisle
7 Marble pulpit
8 Altar screen
9 Sanctuary of St George
10 Sanctuary of Virgin Mary
11 Sanctuary of St John the Baptist
12 Shrine of Takla Hamanout
13 Baptistry with basin

No peace for the holy either

In the grim, barren desolation of the Moqattam hills to the south of Cairo were a number of abandoned windmills. These had been used by the British army during the First World War to produce flour supplies and were no longer required.

In 1936 a monk called Mina obtained one to use as a place of retreat and prayer. With the door replaced and the roof made safe he constructed a small living area downstairs and an even smaller chapel above. His intention to devote himself to peaceful contemplation proved impossible. The monk in the windmill was good news to those needing a release from their mental and physical problems. The number of visitors increased and set times were allocated for services each day.

The area was declared unsafe during the Second World War and Mina moved, with some reluctance, to the neighbouring churches of Archangel Michael and St Mary in Old Cairo, just 3 km distance.

After the hostilities Mina purchased the land adjacent to the former windmill site and built a church dedicated to St Mina the martyr. To this was added a large monastic complex complete with accommodation where he stayed until he was elected patriach in 1971 and became Pope Shenuda III.

Whereas the monasteries in Egypt had suffered from serious decline the influence of a Pope who had spent so many years in retreat caused a revival of interest in monasticism among the Coptic community. Buildings have been restored, visitors welcomed and the number of monks has increased.

the second version she was denounced by her family when she decided to become a nun – then tortured and finally put to death by the Romans along with her faithful attendant St Juliana.

The Ben Ezra Synagogue

South of the Church of St Barbara is the Ben Ezra Synagogue in the former sixth-century Church of St Michael the Archangel, which itself had been built on the site of a synagogue destroyed by the Romans. Hence, this is the oldest surviving synagogue in Egypt. In the 12th century it was sold back to the Jews by the Copts in order to raise funds to pay taxes being raised to finance the Ibn Tulun mosque. The synagogue is built in the basilica style with three naves and an altar hidden by doors, which are wonderfully worked and encrusted with ivory. When the synagogue was extensively repaired in the 19th century, medieval Hebrew manuscripts, known collectively as the **Geniza documents** and providing details of the history of the 11th-16th centuries, were discovered.

Other sacred sights

The Convent of St George St George was a Roman soldier and one of the many Christians who fell foul of Diocletian. His body was brought to Egypt in the 12th century. One remarkable feature of the central room are the 6 m-high wooden doors which lead to the shrine. The convent is closed to visitors except for the chapel which has some interesting icons. The custodians here are very keen to display a chain which, it is claimed, was used to secure early martyrs.

Convent of St Mercurius The Convent dedicated to St Mercurius is just north of this central Coptic area. After a vision in which he was presented with a luminous sword (hence his Arabic name Abu Seifein – Mr Two Swords), with which he was to fight for the cause of Christianity, he was persecuted and killed for his faith. Relics are said to be here in the convent and also in the adjacent church. The convent has its origins in the sixth century but has gone through many stages of rebuilding especially in the 10th century. The **Church of St Mercurius,** the largest church here is actually a church and four large chapels, that on the ground floor dedicated to St Jacob (containing the font used for adult baptism) and those upstairs dedicated to St George, John the Baptist and the children killed by Herod.

Church of St Shenuda This church is adjacent to and slightly south of the church of St Mercurius. There are seven icons in the screen, the central one shows the Virgin and the others each have pictures of two apostles. This church is noted for its 18th-century icons. Shenuda is associated with the Red and White monasteries (see page 199).

Coptic Orthodox Cathedral There are more than 100 Coptic Orthodox churches in Cairo but the special pride is the new (1965) **Coptic Orthodox Cathedral** dedicated to St Mark. This is just off Sharia Ramses. It can seat 5,000 worshippers, houses the patriarchal library and accommodates the patriarch Pope Shenuda III.

The Coptic Museum

ⓘ *In front of Mar Girgis Metro, T02-363 9742. Daily 0800-1630. E£16 (students E£8), cameras E£10, video E£100.*

Beside the Hanging Church is the **Coptic Museum,** the other main tourist attraction in Old Cairo. The museum is regarded as important among Egypt's principal display of antiquities and houses a fine collection of mainly Coptic treasures. It was founded by a rich and influential Copt, Morcos Simaika, with the support of the royal court. The collection began in 1908 as a means of preserving Coptic artefacts and Egypt's Christian heritage against the acquisitive activities of local and foreign collectors. From 1931 the museum has been managed by the Egyptian Government.

Coptic Museum

New wing - ground floor

1 Architectural sculptures
2 Burial ground reliefs
3 Frescoes
4 Carved masonry
5 Stone reliefs & capitals
6 Monastery objects from Saqqara (Graeco-Coptic)
7 Graeco-Egyptian sculptures & friezes
8 Reliefs & figures of Biblical scenes
9 Christian & traditional Egyptian murals
18A Funerary stelae

New wing - upper floor

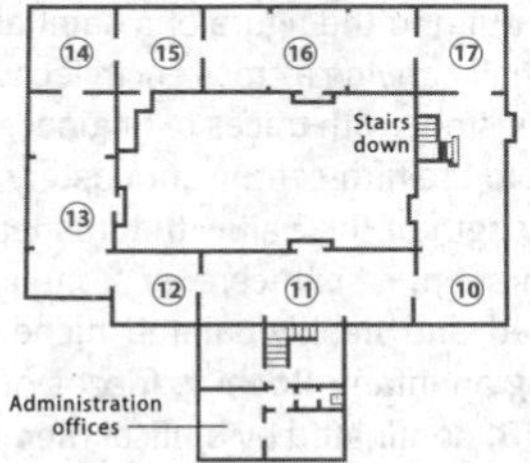

10 Mummy case & Graeco-Byzantine tapestries. Manuscripts & documents
11 Textiles
12 Religious textiles
13 Female ornaments & toiletries. Icons
14 Metalwork, silver & glass. Crucifixes
15 Eagle statue. Roman metalwork
16 Keys, door furniture & surgical instruments
17 Church wallpaintings

Old wing - upper floor

22-23 Church frescoes & furniture
24 Frescoes
25 Woodwork friezes & lintels
26 Woodwork - toys
27 Woodwork panels
28 Woodwork - doors
29-30 Ceramics & terracotta

There was an expansion programme in 1947 which enabled the collection to include a number of small but very valuable private collections of objects and items from Coptic churches throughout Egypt Much of the Coptic collection of the Cairo Museum was transferred here too. The enclosed garden is neatly laid out with benches and large pieces of old stonework. There is also a small café.

The museum gives an excellent insight into the evolution of Christian, and to some extent secular, art and architecture in Egypt in the period AD 300-1800 and shows some of the interchange of ideas with the larger Islamic community. The displays are arranged thematically, with the Old Wing of the museum holding glass, ceramics and masonry and the New Wing showing manuscripts, metalwork and textiles. Begin on the ground floor of the New Wing. Leave the museum from the ground floor of the New Wing through the garden via the steps that lead down to the Water Gate.

The most convenient way of getting the best from the displays is to circulate round each main room in a clockwise direction. Key items to look out for on the ground floor of the New Wing are in: **Room 18A**, to the right of the entrance is a pagan gravestone with intricate relief carvings; **Room 1**, pediment fragment showing Orpheus and Eurydice, another showing Pan, both from 4th century; **Room 2**, some early Christian reliefs which give strength to the suggestion that the Christian cross developed from the Pharaonic *ankh*; **Room 3**, the main semi-dome of the sixth century Bawit Monastery south of Dairut which shows a wonderful painting of Christ enthroned with four mythological creatures of the Apocalypse; **Room 4**, the classical depiction of the sacred eagle with wings spread out and the figure of a saint above and two cuddly children, naked, with lovely curly hair carrying a cross encircled with a garland; **Room 5**, complicated capital made of limestone with traces of original green colouring; **Room 6**, all the artefacts here come from the fifth-century monastery of St Jeremiah in Saqqara, huge columns march the length of the hall with lotus leaves, vines, palm fronds and acanthus leaves as decoration, a sixth-century stone pulpit (the earliest recorded), and a perfectly-preserved and freshly-painted niche with Christ floating above a sitting Virgin Mary holding an infant; **Room 7**, friezes of fruit and flowers with musicians and labourers; **Room 8**, dominated by biblical themes in which all the figures face forwards and have somewhat enlarged heads; **Room 9**, the 11th-century Fayoumi painting of Adam and Eve in the Garden of Eden is well executed and a good Coptic example of biblical stories told in pictures.

Upstairs in **Room 10** is a cabinet displaying what is claimed to be the oldest surviving book in the world – 1,600 years old. It is a small wooden-covered book containing 500 handwritten pages of the Psalms of David and here also is a fine mummy case, painted in full colour of a robed inmate, who was not necessarily a Christian. In **Room 11** there are some exquisite Coptic funeral robes carrying traditional symbols such as the sign of the fish. In **Room 12** look for the copes and other priests' garments, mainly 18th-century, with clever silk embroidery. **Room 13** displays a feast of delicate toiletry objects, including illustrations of women dressed for high days. **Room 14** has ecclesiastic paraphernalia, some, like the marvellous set of crucifixes, not to be missed. **Room 15** contains a figure of a Roman eagle from the Babylon site. **Room 16** has some heavy bolts and keys from monastery doors, musical instruments and at one side a fascinating collection of surgical instruments specifically for childbirth; also a fine collection of early Christian wall paintings from Nubia – the faces being rounder and the eyes larger than in the Egyptian illustrations.

In the Old Building, there are rewarding sights. The ceiling carvings throughout this section are from Coptic houses in Old Cairo and have been incorporated into the building along with panels and tiles. They make a magnificent background to the exhibits. Also look for the very varied and ornate woodwork, heavy work being executed in acacia and palm and finer work in imported cedar, pine and walnut. Ebony too was very popular. **Room 22** has the original Fatimid pine altar dome from the Church of St Sergius (see page 83), it is the oldest wooden altar found in Egypt. **Room 24** contains a sixth-century fresco of the head of Christ in a garland of flowers. A frieze in **Room 25** depicts a large crocodile, with flowers, suggesting a Nilotic scene, while a long wooden lintel of sycamore has a Greek inscription and numerous small figures.

The wooden toys in **Room 26** which retain some of their colouring are presumed to come from children's graves. **Room 28** has a delightful wooden litter made of ivory, bone and mother of pearl. It is almost 2 m in length and was designed to be carried by two camels. This room also displays a door from the Church of St Barbara. The wood used is sycamore and pine and the carvings are of religious scenes. The pottery in **Room 29** is arranged according to decoration and size. There are two-handled red clay jugs, small pots for make-up, a lamp with a frog decoration – all fascinating. **Room 30** has more pottery, some from the Monastery of St Jeremiah at Saqqara (see page 155). The library contains priceless manuscripts. Here is the only biblical text found in an Egyptian tomb.

Islamic Cairo

As noted in the history of Cairo (see page 72), the city was initially developed as a series of extensions and new walled mini-cities which radiated in a northeast direction from the original encampment of Fustat outside the walls of the Babylon-in- Egypt fortress. There are literally hundreds of mosques in Cairo – the city of a thousand minarets – and it is difficult to know where to begin. Broadly speaking, however, the most important places to visit in Islamic Cairo are away from the city centre and the River Nile which lies in a broad belt to the east of the main Sharia Port Said. The exceptions to this are the Amr Ibn Al-As Mosque, the oldest mosque in the country located near Babylon (visit this while seeing Old Cairo) and the Mosque of Sinan Pasha further north and nearer to the Nile. The rest of Islamic Cairo can be visited by following a series of routes, most beginning from the Al-Azhar Mosque.

Mosque of Sinan Pasha

The Albanian-born Sinan Pasha was recruited for service as a boy at the Sublime Porte in Istanbul and rose to become Sulayman the Magnificent's chief cupbearer. He was governor of Cairo between 1571-72 and is best remembered for his building activities rather than political events. He erected buildings in Alexandria and re-excavated the canal between the River Nile and Alexandria but the major buildings he initiated in Egypt were at Bulaq and included this mosque, essential as the focal point of the community, a *sabil*, a *maktab*, commercial buildings, a *hammam*, residential houses, shops, a mill and a bakery.

The small, square Ottoman mosque stands in a garden. There are entrances from three sides of the mosque into the large central domed chamber. While most of the Sinan Pasha complex has long since disappeared, the adjacent public bath (men only) is still in operation.

Mosque of Amr Ibn Al-As

The original Mosque of Amr Ibn Al-As (Gama Amr), 500 m north of Mari Girgis metro station, was built in AD 642 by the commander of the Arab army which captured Egypt in that year. Built near both Babylon-in-Egypt and the Arabs' encampment (Fustat) it is the oldest mosque in Egypt and one of the oldest in the entire Islamic world. Because of the continual enlargements, which began in AD 673 only 10 years after Amr's death aged 93, and included major restoration work in the 15th and 18th centuries and the most recent work in the 1970s, nothing of the original mud-brick 30 x 17 m thatched-roof mosque still exists. Recently repainted and cleaned, its aspect today is virtually modern. As is often the case in the older mosques the interior includes many

Islamic Cairo

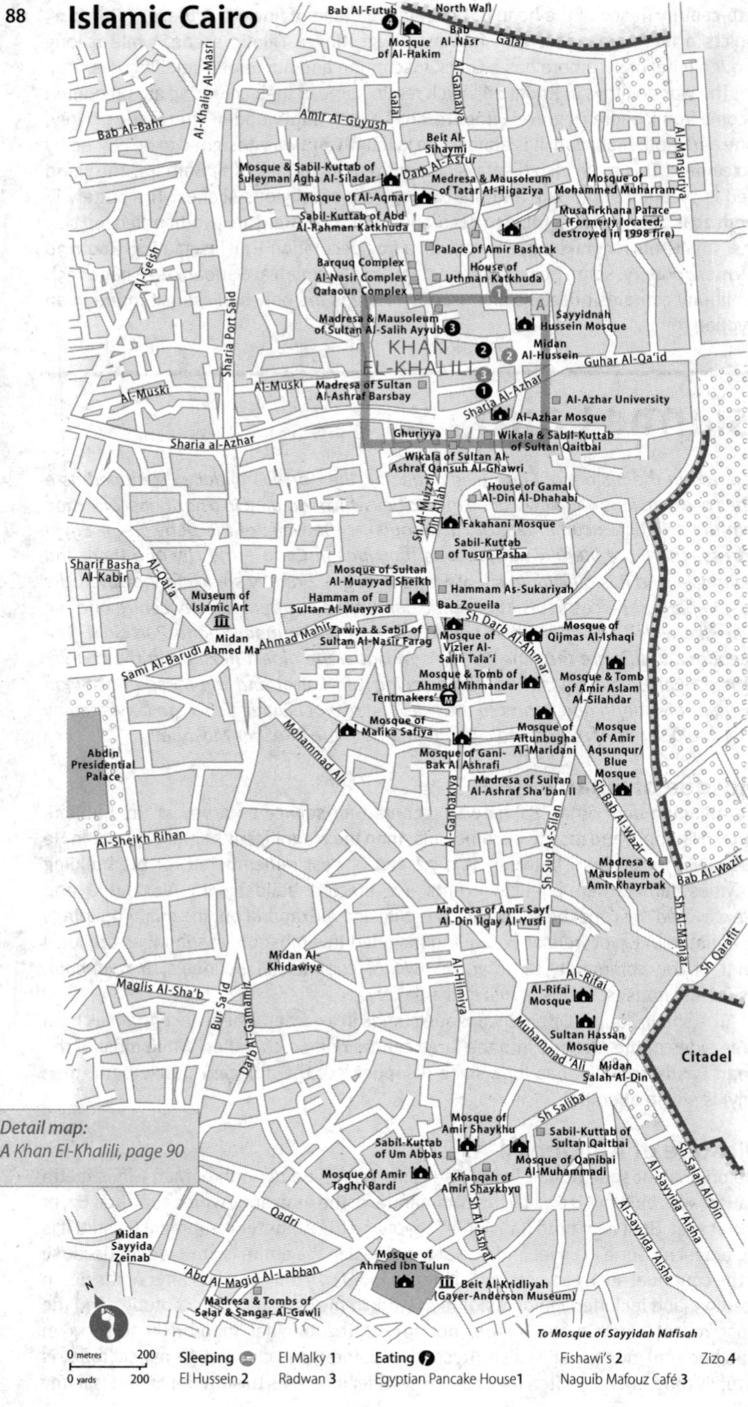
Bab Al-Futuh
North Wall
Bab Al-Nasr
Galal
Mosque of Al-Hakim
Al-Gamaliya
Galal
Amir Al-Guyush
Bab Al-Bahr
Al-Khalig Al-Masri
Beit Al-Sihaymi
Darb Al-Asfur
Mosque & Sabil-Kuttab of Suleyman Agha Al-Siladar
Medresa & Mausoleum of Tatar Al-Higaziya
Mosque of Mohammed Muharram
Al-Mansuriya
Mosque of Al-Aqmar
Sabil-Kuttab of Abd Al-Rahman Katkhuda
Musafirkhana Palace (Formerly located, destroyed in 1998 fire)
Palace of Amir Bashtak
Al-Geish
Barquq Complex
Al-Nasir Complex
Qalaoun Complex
House of Uthman Katkhuda
Sharia Port Said
Madresa & Mausoleum of Sultan Al-Salih Ayyub
Sayyidnah Hussein Mosque
KHAN EL-KHALILI
Midan Al-Hussein
Guhar Al-Qa'id
Al-Muski
Al-Muski
Madresa of Sultan Al-Ashraf Barsbay
Sharia Al-Azhar
Al-Azhar University
Al-Azhar Mosque
Sharia al-Azhar
Ghuriyya
Wikala & Sabil-Kuttab of Sultan Qaitbai
Wikala of Sultan Al-Ashraf Qansuh Al-Ghawri
House of Gamal Al-Din Al-Dhahabi
Sh Al-Muizz li Din Allah
Fakahani Mosque
Sabil-Kuttab of Tusun Pasha
Sharif Basha Al-Kabir
Al-Qal'a
Mosque of Sultan Al-Muayyad Sheikh
Hammam As-Sukariyah
Museum of Islamic Art
Hammam of Sultan Al-Muayyad
Bab Zoueila
Sh Darb Al-Ahmar
Mosque of Qijmas Al-Ishaqi
Zawiya & Sabil of Sultan Al-Nasir Farag
Mosque of Vizier Al-Salih Tala'i
Midan Ahmed Mahir
Ahmad Mahir
Sami Al-Barudi
Mosque & Tomb of Ahmed Mihmandar
Mosque & Tomb of Amir Aslam Al-Silahdar
Tentmakers'
Mohammad Ali
Mosque of Malika Safiya
Mosque of Altunbugha Al-Maridani
Mosque of Amir Aqsunqur/ Blue Mosque
Mosque of Gani-Bak Al Ashrafi
Abdin Presidential Palace
Al-Ganbakiya
Madresa of Sultan Al-Ashraf Sha'ban II
Sh Bab Al-Wazir
Sh Suq As-Silah
Al-Sheikh Rihan
Madresa & Mausoleum of Amir Khayrbak
Bab Al-Wazir
Sh Al-Manjar
Madresa of Amir Sayf Al-Din Ilgay Al-Yusfi
Sh Qarafit
Midan Al-Khidawiye
Al-Hilmiya
Maglis Al-Sha'b
Al-Rifai
Al-Rifai Mosque
Bur Sa'id
Darb Al-Gamamiz
Muhammad 'Ali
Sultan Hassan Mosque
Citadel
Midan Salah Al-Din
Detail map:
A Khan El-Khalili, page 90
Sh Saliba
Mosque of Amir Shaykhu
Sabil-Kuttab of Sultan Qaitbai
Sabil-Kuttab of Um Abbas
Mosque of Qanibai Al-Muhammadi
Sh Salah Al-Din
Mosque of Amir Taghri Bardi
Khanqah of Amir Shaykhu
Al-Sayyida 'Aisha
Sh Al-Ashraf
Qadri
Al-Sayyida 'Aisha
Midan Sayyida Zeinab
Mosque of Ahmed Ibn Tulun
'Abd Al-Magid Al-Labban
Beit Al-Kridliyah (Gayer-Anderson Museum)
N
Madresa & Tombs of Salar & Sangar Al-Gawli
To Mosque of Sayyidah Nafisah
0 metres 200
0 yards 200
Sleeping
El Malky 1
El Hussein 2
Radwan 3
Eating
Egyptian Pancake House 1
Fishawi's 2
Naguib Mafouz Café 3
Zizo 4

Islamic Cairo: suggested routes

1. North from Al-Azhar via the concentration of buildings in the **Qalaoun/ Al-Nasir/Barquq complex**, to the **Al-Hakim Mosque** at the north gates of the old city.

2a South from Al-Azhar to the **Al-Muayyad Mosque** which stands at the **Bab Zoueila** gate at the south edge of the old city and the buildings on Sharia Darb Al-Ahmar to the **Sultan Hassan Mosque** and the modern **Al-Rifai Mosque**.

2b West from the Citadel, continuing to the mosques and museums in the imposing fortress and the huge ancient **Ahmed Ibn Tulun Mosque**.

3 To the mosques and tombs in the **City of the Dead** which lies in the 'Northern Cemetery' to the east of Islamic Cairo.

The ancient **Al-Azhar Mosque (1)** and the nearby *souqs* in the **Khan El-Khalili (2)** district are at the centre of modern-day Islamic Cairo.

pillars taken from the ancient Egyptian monuments. As a result the whole mosque is a hybrid with parts of the fabric dating from before the conquest of Egypt until the 19th-century alterations. In the north corner under the dome and surrounded by a bronze screen, on the site of Amr's house in Fustat, is the tomb of his son Abdullah who was born when Amr was only 13, became a Muslim before him and was a close companion of the Prophet.

Khan El-Khalili

ⓘ *Open daily except Sun.*

Although it also refers to a specific street, Khan El-Khalili, is the general name given to this district of Cairo which has a large number of individual souks. The Arab/Islamic system of urban planning has traditionally divided the souks by professions or guilds. While the system is less rigid than formerly there is still a concentration of one particular trade in a particular area. Khan El-Khalili includes streets which almost exclusively sell gold, silver, copper, perfume, spices, cloth or any one of a number of particular products. Many of the products are manufactured within the souk, often in small workshops behind or on top of the shops. If you're lucky or courageous enough to inquire, someone may welcome you in for a look around to see how things are made.

Known to locals simply as "the Khan," this been the main souk in Cairo since 1382 when it was first created around a caravanserai by Amir Jarkas Al-Khalil, the Master of Horse to the first of the Burji Mamluk Sultans, Al-Zahir Barquq (1382-89). The caravanserai attracted many foreign and local traders and expanded rapidly, to become a base for the city's subversive groups and was consequently frequently raided. Much of the area was rebuilt by Sultan Al-Ashraf Qansuh Al-Ghawri (1501-17) but it still maintained its role as Cairo's main area for traders and craftsmen. Today the main area of the souk is occupied by tourist shops but a few of the streets to the west are more authentic and much more interesting. Here you will find gold, silver, copperware, leather goods, perfume oils, alabaster, boxes, herbs and spices. Some shops are closed on Friday and most are closed on Sunday. It is essential to bargain because the traders will always start at about double the price they actually expect. It is traditional to respond by offering them about one third of what they originally quoted. This is not so for precious metals which are sold by weight, prices for gold and silver being given daily in the paper. On a bracelet for example a small percentage is added for workmanship, and this is the only thing that is negotiable. Antique jewellery is of course more expensive.

Both Khan El-Khalili's Sharia Muski which is virtually a pedestrian precinct and the more congested Sharia Al-Azhar lead east to Al-Azhar and Midan El-Hussein.

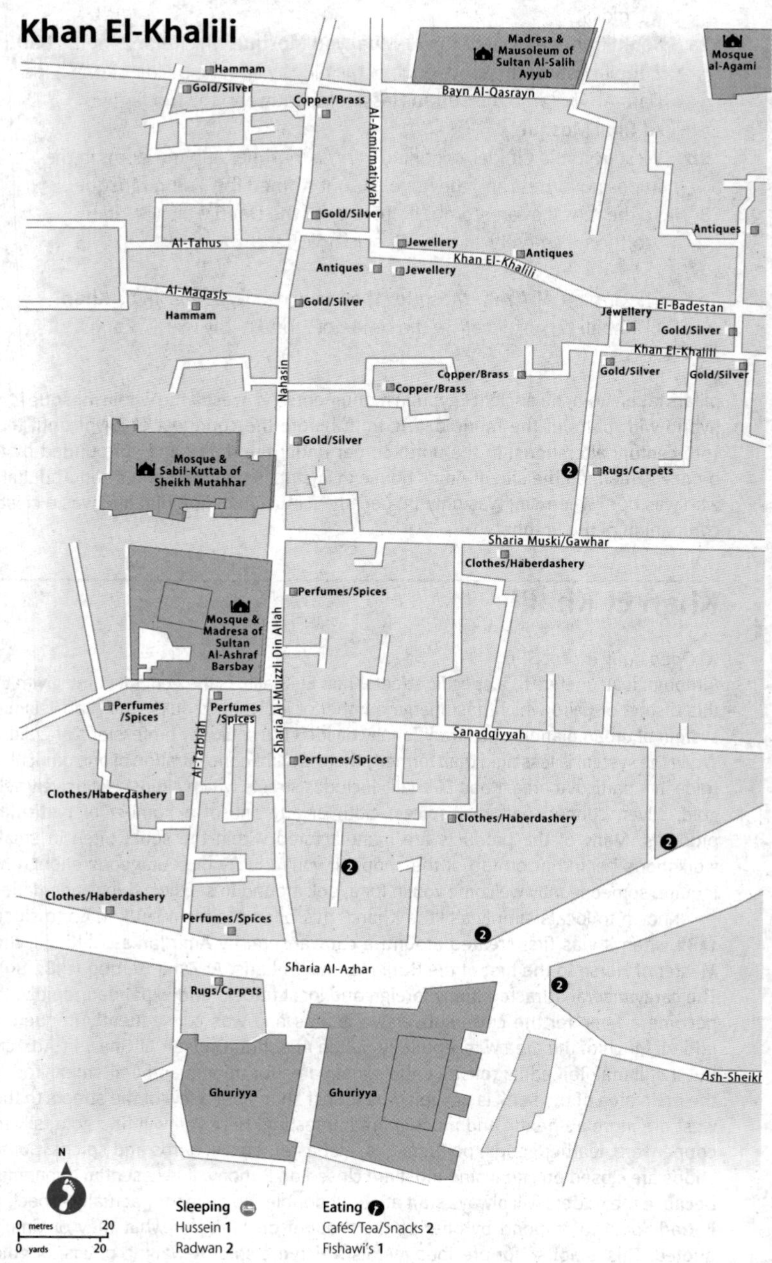

Al-Azhar Mosque → *See plan next page*

ⓘ *Sat-Thu 0900-1500, Fri 0900-1100 and 1300-1500. Tip any guides. No bare legs allowed, shawls provided for women.*

On the southwest of the Midan El-Hussein, an underpass below the busy Sharia Al-Azhar leads to the famous and very influential **Al-Azhar Mosque and University** whose leader, known as the Sheikh Al-Azhar, is appointed for life and is Egypt's supreme theological authority.

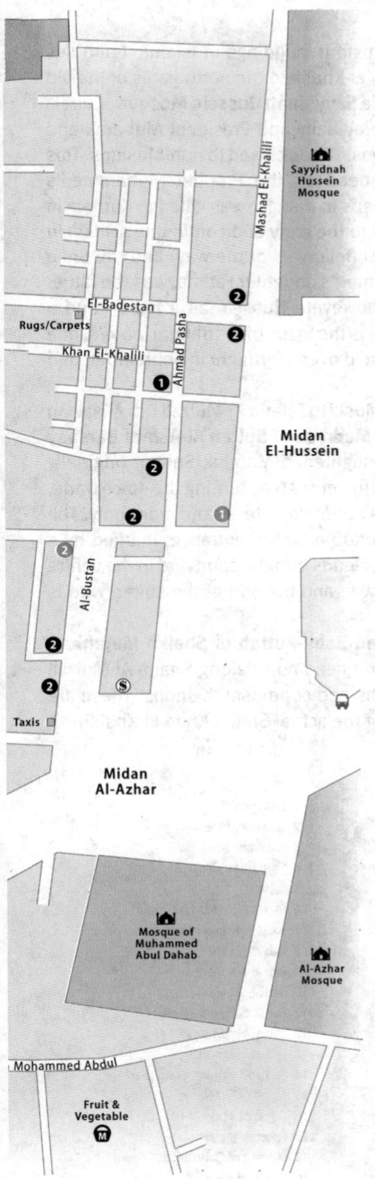

The mosque was built in AD 970 and established as a university in AD 988 which, despite a counter-claim by Fes's Qarawiyin Mosque in Morocco, may make it the world's oldest university. With the exception of the main east *liwan*, however, little remains of the original building because additions and modifications were made by successive rulers, including modern buildings to the north, designed to house the university's administration block.

During the Shi'a Fatimid era (969-1171), the university was used as a means to propagate the Shi'a faith in a predominantly Sunni city, but it fell into disrepair under Salah Al-Din and his successor Ayyubids (1171-1250) (Sunni Muslim rulers), before being reopened by the Bahri Mamluks (1250-1382) and eventually becoming a bastion of Sunni orthodoxy. Later, during the rise in Arab nationalism in the late 19th and early 20th centuries, Al-Azhar became a stronghold for independent thinkers. It is no coincidence that in 1956 President Nasser made his speech against the Suez invasion in the university.

The entrance to the mosque is through the **Barber's Gate** (where students traditionally had their hair shaved), which was built in the second half of the 15th century by Qaitbai (1468-96). This opens out on to the 10th-century Fatimid *sahn* (courtyard) overlooked by three minarets. With the exception of the Mamluk *madresa* (theological schools) surrounding the *sahn*, most of the buildings date back to the Fatimid period. Take the opportunity to climb one of the five minarets for an excellent view over the surrounding area.

Immediately to the south of Al-Azhar is an area known as **Butneya**, once notorious as the base for Cairo's underworld where drugs were openly traded by powerful and locally popular gangsters. After a major crackdown in 1988 most of them left, but the area is still home to minor local gangs who tend to prey on shops, restaurants and middle-class Egyptians rather than on tourists.

Route 1: North from Al-Azhar

The area with the greatest concentration of historic buildings in Islamic Cairo lies north from the Al-Azhar complex and the Khan El-Khalili to the north gates of the old city. On the north side of Midan El-Hussein is the **Sayyidnah Hussein Mosque**, Cairo's official mosque where some 10,000 people pray daily and President Mubarak and other dignitaries worship on important occasions. This is closed to non-Muslims. This mosque is named after, and contains the head of, the Prophet Mohammed's grandson Hussein. The rest of his body is perhaps in Iraq. He was killed at Karbala in AD 680 at the climax of the struggle which led to the early and continuing schism in the Muslim world between the orthodox Sunni (followers of the way) and the Shi'a (party) followers of Ali. Hussein, son of Mohammed's daughter Fatima, was the father of the Prophet's only direct descendants, who revere Hussein as a martyr and a popular saint like his sister Zeinab. His mosque is the focus of his annual *moulid*, one of the city's most important festivals which is held over a fortnight in September, and attracts thousands who camp in the streets.

Walk back 200 m northwest along Sharia Muski to Sharia Al-Muizzli Din Allah. On the southwest corner of the crossroads is the **Madresa of Sultan Al-Ashraf Barsbay** (1422-37) (being restored). This liberal and enlightened Mamluk Sultan, originally from the Caucasus, financed his capture of Cyprus in 1426 by turning the spice trade, which in Cairo is based just to the south of the *madresa*, into a state monopoly. The *madresa* is cruciform in plan with the *sabil-kuttab* near the entrance, marked by a splendid onion-shaped dome. An offset corridor leads into the courtyard in the centre of which are two marble tombs, those of the wife and the son of the sultan who is himself buried in the Northern Cemetery.

At the northwest corner is the **Mosque and Sabil-Kuttab of Sheikh Mutahhar**, erected in 1744. Turn right at the crossroads and head north along Sharia Al-Muizzli Din Allah passing some of the many goldsmiths and coppersmith shops. These are concentrated in the alleys to the right including the actual Sharia Khan El-Khalili.

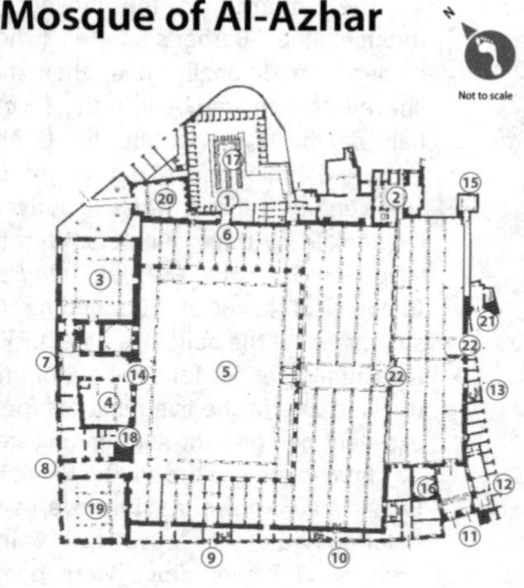

1 Entrance
2 Gawhar Medersa
3 Aqbugha Medersa
4 Taybars Medersa
5 Sahn
6 Bab Qaitbai (Barber's Gate)
7 Bab al-Muzayyinin
8 Bab al-Abbas
9 Bab al-Maghariba
10 Bab al-Shawam
11 Bab al-Saayidal
12 Bab al-Haramayn
13 Bab al-Shurbah
14 Bab and minaret of Qaitbai
15 Tomb of Sitt Nafisa
16 Tomb of Abdel al-Rahman Karkhuda
17 Toilets
18 Minaret of Qahnsuh al-Ghawri
19 Riwaq of Abbas II
20 Riwaq Al-Hanafiyyah
21 Qibla
22 Mihrab

Sugar and spice and all things nice

A visit to the spice market (Souk Al-Attarin) is highly recommended both for the visual impact and the tremendous aromas. Anything that could possibly be wanted in the way of herbs, spices, henna, dried and crushed flowers and incense are on display, piled high on the ancient pavements in massive burlap bags or secreted away in tin boxes in various drawers inside. Ask if what you want does not appear to be in stock but do not be fobbed off with old merchandise, fresh spices are always available. Prices are extremely low by western standards and shopkeepers are prepared to sell small amounts, weighing out the purchase into a little paper cornet. Saffron is the best buy, far cheaper than at home, but sometimes only the local rather than higher quality Iranian saffron is available. The main street of the spice market runs parallel to Sharia Al-Muizzli Din Allah beginning at the Ghuriyya. Here, many of the shops have been in the same family for over 200 years. Some of the owners are also herbalists (*etara*), practising traditional medicine and offering cures for everything from bad breath to rheumatism. Cairo's most famous herbalist, however, is Abdul Latif Mahmoud Harraz, 39 Sharia Ahmed Maher, near Bab El-Khalq. Founded in 1885, the shop attracts a devoted following throughout the Middle East.

The Arabic names for the more common herbs and spices are:

Allspice	*kebab es-seeny*
Arabic gum	*mystica*
Bay leaf	*warra randa*
Basil	*rihan*
Cardamon	*habbahan*
Cayenne	*shatta*
Celery salt	*boudra caraffs*
Chervil leaves	*kozbarra*
Chilli	*filfil ahmar*
Cinnamon	*erfa*
Cloves	*orumfil*
Coriander	*kosbara*
Cumin	*kamoon*
Dill	*shabat*
Fennel	*shamar*
Ginger	*ginzabeel*
Horseradish	*figl baladi*
Mace	*bisbassa*
Marjoram	*bardakosh*
Mint	*naanaa*
Oregano	*zaatar*
Paprika	*filfil ahmar roumi*
Peppercorns	*filfil eswed*
Rosemary	*hassa liban*
Saffron	*zaa'faran*
Sage	*maryameya*
Savory	*stoorya*
Sesame	*semsem*
Tarragon	*tarkhoun*
Turmeric	*korkom*

Although its façade is largely hidden by shops, at the right hand side of the street, on the site of the former slave market, is the **Madresa and Mausoleum of Sultan Al-Salih Ayyub** (1240-49) who was the last of the Ayyubid Sultans and who was the first to introduce the foreign Mamluk slave-soldiers. The *madresa* was special because it was the first built to include all four of Egypt's schools of law while the tomb is the first example where it is placed next to the *madresa* of its founder. Most significant now is the minaret standing tall above Sharia Al-Muizzli.

Opposite, with a wonderful unbroken 185-m long façade, stands an amazing complex of three *madresas* founded by three of the most influential medieval sultans, Qalaoun, Al-Nasir and Barquq. This section of the street is known as **Bayn Al-Qasrayn** (between two palaces) because of the Fatimid period's magnificent Great Western Palace and Eastern Palace which stood on either side. At the time of this writing, they are all being restored.

Qalaoun Complex

The earliest and most impressive *madresa* is the Qalaoun complex built by Sultan Al-Mansur Qalaoun Al-Alfi (1280-90). Like so many other Mamluk ('possessed') slave-soldiers he was a Kipchak Turk who used the name Al-Alfi because he was originally bought for the high price of 1,000 (or alf) dinars. He subsequently diluted the influence of his own Kipchaks amongst the Mamluks by importing Circassians whom he billeted in the Citadel. These Burgis Mamluks (*burg* = tower) were rivals to the Bahri Mamluks (1250-1382) stationed on Roda Island and eventually created their own dynasty (1382-1517). Qalaoun was constantly fighting the Crusaders and eventually died of a fever in 1290 aged 79, on an expedition to recapture Acre.

The complex was built in just over a year in 1284/85 on the site of the Fatimid's Western Palace and includes a *madresa* and mausoleum to the left and right, respectively, of the entrance with a *maristan* down a now-closed 10-m high corridor to the rear of the two linked buildings.

On the north side of the corridor is the beautiful **mausoleum** ⓘ *0900-1700*, with a 30-m high dome built in 1903 to replace the original wooden dome which was demolished in the 18th century. The tomb of Qalaoun and his son Al-Nasir Mohammed is in the middle of the room surrounded by a beautifully-carved wooden rail.

The *maristan* is now reached via an alley along the southwest wall of the *madresa*, but little remains of the original hospital except for one of the *liwans* and the remnants of a marble fountain. Since 1910 it has been the site of a modern eye clinic.

Al-Nasir Complex

To the north is the Sultan Al-Nasir Mohammed complex which was started by Sultan Kitbugha in 1295 and finished by Al-Nasir during his second reign in 1304, an era commemorated by over 30 mosques and other public buildings throughout the city. Qalaoun's eldest son Khalil (1290-94) was assassinated in 1294 and his nine-year-old brother Mohammed (1294-95) was elected Sultan. He was deposed the following year by the Mongol regent Kitbugha (1295-97) who in turn was soon forced into exile. Kitbugha was replaced by Lajin (1297-99) but he was assassinated after a short reign while playing chess. Following this chapter of 'accidents', Mohammed was restored to the throne, but was kept in terrible conditions by his regent until he escaped to Jordan 10 years later. He eventually returned with a large army the following year, executed his enemies, and ruled unchallenged for another 30 years until his death in 1341.

The complex consists of a mosque, *madresa* and tomb. Although restoration work is still in progress it is worth trying to get in to see the *qibla* wall which still has its original decoration and Kufic inscriptions. The *mihrab*, although incomplete, is also interesting because it is one of the last stucco *mihrabs*. Little remains of the mausoleum and parts of the walls have been removed to the Museum of Islamic Art. It was originally built for Al-Nasir, but he was buried next door in his father's mausoleum, and the two tombs here belong to his mother Bint Suqbay and Anuq, his favourite eldest son who died the year before his own death. The three-storey minaret is very beautiful with a richly ornamented Andalusian style first storey and the other two storeys surmounted with delicate stalactite cornices. The main door is Gothic and was brought back from the Church of St George in Acre during a campaign against the Crusaders.

Barquq Complex

This is followed to the north by the *madresa* and tomb which make up the Sultan Barquq complex which was built in 1384-86. The marble entrance and the silver-encrusted bronze-plated door are very impressive and lead through an offset corridor to the *sahn* which has four *liwans* arranged in a cruciform shape. The *qibla liwan*, to the east, is divided into three aisles by four ancient Pharaonic columns which support beautifully carved and painted ceilings. Upstairs there are cells for the Sufi monks who once inhabited the building. To the north of the *madresa* a door leads to the mausoleum where Sultan Barquq was originally buried before being transferred to the mausoleum specially built by his son Al-Nasir Farag (1399-1405 and 1405-12) in the city's Northern Cemetery (see below).

Sultan Al-Zahir Barquq (1382-89 and 1390-99), whose name means plum, reigned twice and was the founder of the dynasty of Circassian slave-soldiers who became the Burgis Mamluk rulers of Egypt. He was reportedly an enlightened ruler, who admired piety and intelligence and surrounded himself with learned scholars, before dying of pneumonia aged 60 in 1399.

Palaces and madresas

Besides the Qalaoun/Al-Nasir/Barquq complex, which is on the west side of Sharia Al-Muizzli Din Allah, there are a number of other interesting, if less important, buildings on and near the east side of the street on the route north to the Al-Hakim mosque. This area, which is the heart of Islamic Cairo, is definitely worth exploring if you have a full day.

Directly opposite the Qalaoun complex is Sharia Beit Al-Qadi. About 40 m down on the left hand side stands the modern-looking house, No 19, marked with a green plaque. Visitors should knock to be shown around in return for a little *baksheesh*. This is the remains of a palace built in 1350 but better known as the **House of Uthman Kathuda** who restored it during the 18th century.

Further north opposite Barquq's complex are the beautiful remains of the **Palace of Amir Bashtak** (Al-Nasir's son-in-law) built in 1334-39 and a fine example of the domestic architecture of the time. The original five-storey structure has been reduced to two and the windows in the rather plain façade are covered with *mashrabiyya*. It is now being restored but when open, access is via an offset courtyard; if locked, the warden is usually found at the nearby **Sabil-Kuttab of Abd Al-Rahman Kutkhuda** and should have keys to both properties.

There used to be many of the these Ottoman-influenced *sabil-kuttab*, which combine a water supply for the public at street level and a Koranic school in the building above, throughout Cairo. This elegant example, built in 1744 by a powerful *amir* seeking absolution for his former sins, stands on a triangular piece of land where two roads meet. The building is tall and slim. A beautifully carved timber screen on the upper storey protects the *kuttab* on its three open sides and the balcony permits a good view. Below, the double arches are supported by delicate columns. The *sabil* is faced with Syrian tiles.

Mosque of Al-Aqmar

About 75 m further north on the right up the main road is the Mosque of Al-Aqmar which was built in 1121-25 by the Fatimid Vizier of Khalifa Al-Amir (1101-31). It was originally at the northeast corner of the great eastern Fatimid palace. It is particularly important for three reasons: it was the first Cairo mosque with a façade following the alignment of the street, rather than the *qibla* wall, so that its ground plan was adjusted to fit into an existing urban environment; it was the first to have a decorated stone façade, the colour giving it its name which means moonlight; it introduced the shell motif and the stalactite, which subsequently became favourites in Cairo, into architectural styles.

The mosque has been restored over the centuries. Amir Yalbugha Al-Salami restored the *minbar*, *mihrab* and ablution area in 1393 and added the minaret in 1397. The minaret was apparently removed in 1412 because it had started leaning, but the current structure includes the original first storey which is made of brick covered with very uncommon carved stucco decorated with chevron patterns. Because the street level has risen since the mosque was built there are steps down to the entrance

Al-Hakim – the vanishing despot

In AD 996 at the age of 11 Al-Hakim succeeded his father as the second Egyptian Fatimid Khalifa and began a despotic reign. At the age of 15 he had his tutor assassinated and started his extremely cruel and relentless persecution of Christians, Jews, Sunni Muslims, women and dogs. He prohibited any Christian celebrations and had the Church of the Holy Sepulchre in Jerusalem demolished. He also prohibited Sunni ceremonies and tried to established Shi'a Islam as the only form of Islam. Women were forbidden to leave their homes and, in order to enforce this, cobblers were not permitted to make or sell women's shoes. At one time all of Cairo's dogs were exterminated because their barking annoyed him. Merchants who were found to have cheated their customers were summarily sodomized by his favourite Nubian slave while Al-Hakim stood on their head. Wine, singing, dancing and chess were also prohibited and the punishments for disobeying these laws were very severe and usually resulted in a gruesome death.

His erratic rule, with laws often changing overnight, led to tensions within Fustat/Cairo, particularly between the various religious communities. In 1020, the news that Al-Hakim was about to proclaim that he was a manifestation of Allah provoked serious riots to which he responded by sending in his Sudanese troops to burn down the city where they clashed not only with the civilians, but also the Turkish and Berber soldiers. An alternative story is that one particular quarter of Fustat was torched because he thought that was where his favourite sister Sitt Al-Mulk (Lady of Power) took her lovers, but when she was proved to be a virgin by the midwives he examined the ruins and asked "who ordered this?" Whatever the truth, he then sent his chief theologian Al-Darazi to Syria for safety where he is believed to have originated the theology of the Druze who consider Al-Hakim to be divine.

Despite his ruthless public acts Al-Hakim's personal life was very abstemious and he was a very generous alms-giver. He took to riding around the city and surrounding countryside on a donkey with only a couple of servants but disappeared in February 1021. Following the discovery of his knife-slashed robe, it is believed he was murdered, possibly on the instructions of Sitt Al-Mulk with whom he apparently argued because of her refusal to begin an incestuous marriage with him. The fact that his body was never discovered led the Druze to believe that he had retreated from the world to return at a later date, while the Copts believe that he had a vision of Jesus, repented and became a monk.

which is offset from the main part of the mosque. Despite its importance and unique features the original interior of the mosque is unspectacular. Around the base of the almost square *sahn* the arches bear Koranic verses in the early angular and unpointed Kufic script on an arabesque background.

The **Madresa-Mausoleum of Tatar Al-Higaziya** is in a small street which connects Sharia Al-Gamalia with Midan Beit Al-Qadi. It was built in two phases with the mausoleum, which was connected to the princess Tatar's palace, being built in 1347 for her recently murdered husband and the palace itself being converted into a *madresa* in 1360 which explains its irregular shape.

Tatar was the daughter of Sultan Al-Nasser Mohammed, the sister of Sultan Hassan and the wife of the Amir Baktimur Al-Higazi. The mosque was built on the site of the residence of Amir Qawsun who had married one of Tatar's sisters in 1347. Little else is known about Tatar except that she died of the plague in 1360. Her tomb is still visited by women seeking her blessing.

Entrance to the building is via a corridor which leads via a porch with a lovely ceiling into the *sahn*. The octagonal minaret to the southwest of the *sahn* has been missing its top for over a century. Access to the minaret, the ablution area and storage areas are all via doors off the *liwans*. The ribbed stone dome, one of the earliest in Cairo, over the mausoleum, is in the north end of the complex on the corner of two streets and passers-by can solicit a blessing or invoke a prayer via the open windows.

The restoration work carried out in the 1980s was done with care and consideration. Further east is the void where once stood the Ottoman **Musafirkhana Palace** (House of Guests). What used to be a rather fine rambling building constructed between 1779 and 1788 by the merchant Mohammed Muharram burnt to a crisp in 1998. There is talk of rebuilding it, but it probably won't happen for at least another decade. Mohammed Muharram also built the adjacent mosque, named after him, before he had the misfortune of dying from sunstroke after returning from a pilgrimage to Mecca. Mohammed Ali bought the building, which is noted as the birth place of Khedive Ismail in 1830. It is possible to enter and examine the products of the resident artists and sculptors and see the intricate *mashrabiyya* in the harem on the second storey. Note the two wind catchers which provide cool air. Return to the main thoroughfare.

Take the next right hand turn for a brief detour to No 19 Darb Al-Asfur which is 50 m along the left hand side of the street. This is the **Beit Al-Sihaymi** ⓘ *open 0900-1600, E£20,* actually two houses, built in 1648 and 1796 and inhabited until 1961, and probably one of the finest examples of a luxurious Mamluk mansion in the whole of the city. Beautifully restored, it has a lovely courtyard and a *haramlik* (harem) for the women, including a domed bathroom. An especially striking abode amid such ramshackle contemporary homes and definitely worth a visit.

Returning to the main street and continuing north, one reaches the **Mosque and Sabil-Kuttab of Suleyman Agha Al-Silahdar**, built in 1837-39 by one of Mohammed Ali's ministers who also built many other *sabils* throughout the city. The style of the building is very much influenced by the contemporary style in Istanbul including the minaret with an Ottoman-style cylindrical shaft and conical top. It is now being restored.

Mosque of Al-Hakim and the North Wall

Continuing to the north end of the street is the giant Mosque of Al-Hakim, ⓘ *entrance fee E£6 gives access to both gates, but walls being restored may limit access*, named after the third Fatimid caliph, which abuts the **North Wall** of the old city of Fustat/Cairo between the **Bab Al-Nasr** and **Bab Al-Futuh** gates and commemorates its most notorious ruler (see box, page 96). It was begun in 990 by the Shi'a Muslim Fatimid Khalifa Al-Aziz (975-996) and was eventually finished some 23 years later by his son who took the name **Al-Hakim bi-Amr Allah** (Ruler by God's Command) and ruled between 996-1021.

Possibly having a Christian wife was the reason why his reportedly tolerant and humane father Al-Aziz had been more forbearing towards Christians and Jews than towards the indigenous Sunni Muslim population. In contrast his son was very intolerant to everyone. With such a colourful history, the large 122 x 115 m mosque itself is actually rather plain. It is organized around a large central *sahn* and built of bricks with a large porch in the traditional Fatimid style. It has been restored many times throughout the centuries, notably after the major earthquake in 1302 and by Sultan Al-Hassan in 1359. Originally the two minarets stood separate from the walls; the huge salients, added in 1010 to strengthen them, are in fact hollow shells. After

The Hammam

A visit to the *hammam* or Turkish bath is still part of the way of life for many Egyptians. Some Egyptian families have no bathing facilities at home and rely on the public hammam. A ritual purification of the body is essential before Muslims can perform prayers, and even for the well-off classes in the days before bathrooms, the 'major ablutions' were generally done at the hammam. Segregation of the sexes is of course the rule at the hammam: some establishments are open only for women, others only for men, while others have a shift system (mornings and evenings for the men, all afternoon for women). In the old days, the hammam, along with the local *zaouia* or saint's shrine, was an important place for women to gather and socialize, and even pick out a potential wife for a son.

In the older parts of the cities, the hammam is easily recognizable by the characteristic colours of its door. A passage leads into a large changing room-cum-post-bath rest area, equipped with masonry benches for lounging on and (sometimes) small wooden lockers. Here one undresses under a towel.

This is the procedure. First into the hot room: 5-10 minutes with your feet in a bucket of hot water will see you sweating nicely, and you can then move back to the raised area where the masseurs are at work. After the expert removal of large quantities of dead skin, you go into one of the small cabins or *mathara* to finish washing. (Before doing this, catch the person bringing in dry towels, so that they can bring yours to you when you're in the *mathara*.) For women, in addition to a scrub and a wash, there may be the pleasures of an epilation with *sokar*, an interesting mix of caramelized sugar and lemon. Men can undergo a *taksira*, which although it involves much pulling and stretching of the limbs, ultimately leaves you feeling pretty good. And remember, allow plenty of time to cool down, reclining in the changing area before you dress and leave the hammam.

In Cairo, you can visit the 18th-century **Hammam El-Malatili**, 40 Sharia Amir El-Gyushi (0700-1900) or the back alley **Hammam El-Tabbali**, 1 km east of Ramses on Bayn El-Haret. There are also a few hammams around the Bab Zoueila. Women can visit the **Hammam Beshtak**, a cleaner newer public bath, at Sharia El-Silah (1000-1700; men 1800-0800).

the 14th century it was converted to house Crusader prisoners-of-war, then as a stable by Salah Al-Din, during the French occupation as a fortified warehouse, as a school, and in the mid-19th century to store items destined for the Museum of Islamic Art which opened in 1896. Since 1980 the mosque has been restored, practically rebuilt, in white marble by the Indian-based Bohra sect of Ismaili Muslims who claim direct spiritual descent from the Fatimid imams whom they worship. Its twin minarets have been reinforced by stone carvings.

Route 2a: South from Al-Azhar

The route south from Al-Azhar mosque has a number of very interesting buildings including the **Mosque of Sultan Al-Muayyad Sheikh** at the medieval **Bab Zoueila.** Further to the south of Fustat is the **Sultan Hassan Mosque** and the much more modern **Al-Rifai Mosque** which stand side by side below the mighty **Citadel** (see page

Adhan – the call the prayer

Listening to the first call to prayer just before the sun begins to rise is an unforgettable memory of Egypt. This is known as the *adhan* and is performed by the *muezzin*, originally by the strength of his own voice from near the top of the minaret but, today, taking advantage of technological advances, it is probably a recording timed to operate at a particular hour.

There is no fixed tune, perhaps tune is too definite a description, but in Egypt there is one particular rhythm used all over the country for the *adhan*. The traditional Sunni *adhan* consists of seven phrases, with two additional ones for the morning prayer. There are some variations which the well-tuned ear will pick up.

1. **Allahu Akbar** (Allah is most great) is intoned four times. This phrase is called *al takbir*.
2. **Ashhadu anna la ilah ill'-Allah** (I testify that there is no god besides Allah) is intoned twice.
3. **Ashhadu anna Muhammadan rasul Allah** (I testify that Mohammed is the apostle of Allah) is intoned twice. This and the preceeding phrase are called the *shihada*, a confession of faith.
4. **Hayya 'ala 'l-salah** (come to prayer) is intoned twice.
5. **Hayya 'ala'l-falah** (come to salvation) is intoned twice. This and the preceeding phrase are called *tathwib*.
6. **Allahu Akbar** is intoned twice.
7. **La ilah ill'Allah** (there is no god besides Allah) is intoned once.

The two additions to the morning prayer are: **Al-salatu khayr min Al-nawm** (Prayer is better than sleep) which intoned twice between the fifth and sixth phrases, and **Al-salatu wa'l-salam 'alayka ya rasul Allah** (Benediction and peace upon you, Oh Apostle of Allah) intoned after the seventh phrase.

105) and its various mosques. One can then head west to the huge and very old **Mosque of Ahmed Ibn Tulun** and the nearby *Gayer-Anderson Museum* before returning to the river. Allow a minimum of half a day to take in all the sites on this tour of the southern part of Islamic Cairo.

Wikalas

Immediately to the south of the Al-Azhar complex are a few of the 20 remaining *wikalas* (hostels for merchants which were usually above a bonded warehouse for their goods), which numbered over 200 in the 1830s. Directly opposite the mosque is the **Wikala and Sabil-Kuttab of Sultan Qaitbai** the first of two hostels founded by this sultan. The wonderfully preserved **Wikala of Sultan Al-Ashraf Qansuh Al-Ghawri,** ⓘ *daily (except Fri) 0900-1700 or 0900-1100 and 1400-1600 during Ramadan, E£6; being restored so access may be limited*, which was originally built in 1504, is just off the southwest corner of Al-Azhar: it now houses a permanent exhibition of desert life and is also used as workshops for artisans. Traditional handicrafts for sale.

Ghuriyya

About 50 m to the northwest, back on Sharia Al-Azhar just near the footbridge, is the Ghuriyya (24), the magnificent complex of **Sultan Al-Ashraf Qansuh Al-Ghawri** (1501-17), which is bisected by a continuation of Sharia Al-Muizzli Din Allah. The complex, made up of his domed mausoleum to the east of the street and his mosque and *madresa* to the west, was built in 1504-05 and was the last great Mamluk public building before the Ottoman conquest. He died of a stroke in 1516, aged about 76, during a battle near Aleppo against the Turks, who then immediately invaded and captured Egypt, and began their long rule lasting from 1517 to 1805. Because Al-Ghawri's body was never found, he was not buried in this magnificent and hugely expensive tomb.

Between Ghuriyya and Bab El-Zoueila

Sharia Al-Muizzli Din Allah, ⓘ *daily 0900-1400, except Fri*, between the two buildings, originally roofed, was the site of the exotic silk market. Today mainly household goods are sold in the shops. Each section of this main thoroughfare, Islamic Cairo's main street, was named after the merchandise sold in that particular stretch. For example the fruit-sellers had their own mosque, the **Fakahani Mosque** (built in 1735), about 200 m down the street on the left hand side. Make a detour by walking left from its northwest corner and then left again where, 70 m to the east at No 6, is the **House of Gamal Al-Din Al-Dhahabi**, Cairo's richest gold merchant in 1637 when this beautiful house was built. It is now being restored, but when open, it is used as a documentation centre and is open to visitors. Back to the south of the mosque, is the ornate **Sabil-Kuttab of Tusun Pasha**, built in his name by his father Mohammed Ali Pasha in 1820, also being restored. From here the south gates of the ancient city are just ahead. Before going through the gates turn left or east at the *sabil-kuttab*. About 75 m along the side street is an old 18th-century men's bath-house known as **Hammam As-Sukariyah** which was originally owned by a rich woman who also owned the nearby *wikala* and *sabil* of Nafisah Bayda. Although like the other remaining bath-houses in the city it is no longer a den of vice, it is still an interesting place to visit and relax. Today it helps the local community by allowing its fire for heating the water to be used to cook *fuul mudammas* (beans) for the locals' breakfast.

Bab Zoueila

Bab Zoueila, built by Badr Al-Gamali in 1092 when Fatimid fortifications were being reinforced, was one of the three main gates in the city walls. It is named after mercenaries from the Al-Zoueila tribe of Berbers who were stationed in the nearby barracks. The gate was soon inside the city following the successive expansions and Salah Al-Din's construction of larger walls further out from the centre. Cairo was in effect divided into two with the inner walls still in existence and both sets of gates locked at night.

Bab Zoueila also has a more popular history linked to the caravans departing both to Mecca and the south. It was not only the location of street performers including snake-charmers, story tellers and dancers, but after the 15th century it also became the site of public executions. Common criminals were beheaded, garrotted or impaled, while cheating merchants were hanged from hooks or rope. Defeated Mamluk Sultans, including the last one in 1517, were hanged and sometimes nailed to the doors. Even today the 20-m high Bab Zoueila, which comprises a 4.8-m wide multi-storey arch between two solid stone towers, is still an impressive sight particularly from the south.

Mosque of Sultan Al-Muayyad Sheikh

Immediately to the west of the gate is the Mosque of Sultan Al-Muayyad Sheikh (1412-21) built on the site of the old Kazanat Al-Shamaii prison. Al-Muayyad had been incarcerated here on a number of occasions because of his love of alcohol when he was a Mamluk slave-soldier. On being released after one particularly long and unpleasant stretch, he vowed to replace the prison with a mosque which he began in 1415 after becoming Sultan.

The mosque, now being restored, is sometimes known as the Red Mosque because of the colour of its external walls. It was one of the last to be built in the ancient large enclosure style before the Turkish style was adopted as the norm. The superb bronze-plated wooden entrance doors leading to the mosque were originally intended for the Sultan Hassan Mosque but were purchased by Al-Muayyad for his own mosque. The entrance leads into a vestibule with an ornate stalactite ceiling. From the vestibule, the door on the left leads to Al-Muayyad's mausoleum and marble tomb with Kufic inscription, while nearby is the tomb of his son, Ibrahim, who died in 1420. From the top of one of the two minarets (expect to pay for this climb), ⓘ *E£10*, there is an excellent view over the surrounding area and the adjacent Bab Zoueila.

From here a 20-minute walk or a five-minute taxi or bus ride on bus No 75 or minibus No 68 to the west of Bab Zoueila along Sharia Ahmed Maher brings you to the **Museum of Islamic Art** (see page 120).

En route immediately next to the mosque is a large and elegant building which looks like a small palace but is in fact the **Hammam Al-Muayyad** bath-house, built in 1420. This has fallen into disrepair and is now often flooded. The area between the two is known as the Bab El-Khalq after a medieval gate which has long since vanished.

From the south of Bab Zoueila there are two routes you can take to reach the **Sultan Hassan** and **Al-Rifai mosques** which stand north of the Citadel. One is to continue southwest along what is officially known as Sharia Al-Muizzli Din Allah but which, like so many other long roads, changes its name in different sections and at this point is also known as Sharia Al-Khiyamiyya, or the **Tentmakers' Bazaar** because of its colourful fabrics market. After about 1 km you reach a major crossroads where you should turn left or southeast along Sharia Al-Qala'a which leads to the rear of the two mosques. A much more interesting route includes a few nearby sites on Sharia Al-Khiyamiyya before heading east along Sharia Darb Al-Ahmar, after which the whole area is named, towards the Citadel.

Bab Zoueila to the Tentmakers

Immediately south of the gates are two buildings which are bisected by Sharia Al-Khiyamiyya. To the west is the *zawiya* (Sufi monastery) and *sabil* (public fountain) of **Sultan Al-Nasir Farag** (1405-12) who was Barquq's son and successor. To the east is the much more magnificent **Mosque of Vizier Al-Salih Tala'i** which was both the last Fatimid mosque and, when it was built in 1160, was the country's first suspended mosque resting on top of a series of small vaulted shops which, with the rise in the street level, are now in the basement. Tala'i reportedly died regretting the construction of the mosque because, being directly outside the walls of the city, it could be used as a fortress by an enemy.

In 1160 the enfeebled Fatimid Dynasty was about to fall as one child khalifa succeeded another, ruling in name only, while a powerful vizier really wielded royal authority. When the Armenian-born Tala'i ibn Ruzzik came to power he called himself Al-Salih hence the mosque's name.

The mosque, about 60 x 20 m, was originally intended as a mausoleum for the remains of the martyr Hussein which were brought to Cairo from Ashkalon when the latter was under threat from the Franks. The great earthquake of 1303 severely damaged the mosque and destroyed the minaret, which was restored together with the rest of the mosque by Amir Baktimur Al-Gukandar (Polo-Master) and subsequently in 1440, 1477 and lastly and very badly in the 1920s after the minaret had collapsed yet again.

It was only in about 1920 that it was discovered that the street level had risen so much that the mosque was suspended on the shops below. The shops – seven at the front, 12 on either side but none below the *qibla* wall – were part of the *waqf* and their rents supported the upkeep of the mosque. The northwest entrance porch, with its large portico and an arcade of keel-arches raised on ancient columns with Corinthian capitals, is unique in Cairo. The decoration around the entrance is, however, similar in style to the earlier Al-Aqmar mosque. The porch's *mashrabiyya* dates from the first restoration and the bronze facings on the exterior door are also from 1303 while the carvings on the inside of the door are a copy of the original which is now in the Islamic Museum.

From the entrance a tunnel-vaulted passage leads into the *sahn* surrounded on four sides by *liwan* but the northwest *liwan* is not original. In the northeast *qibla liwan* the tie-beams, which are inscribed with Koranic inscriptions in what is known as floriated Kufic script, are original but the ceiling is modern.

The highlight of the interior is the exquisite *minbar*, the fourth oldest in Egypt and a very fine example of Mamluk wood carving, which was donated to the mosque in 1300 by Amir Baktimur Al-Gukandar. Above is the first appearance in a Cairo mosque of a *malqaf* (wind vent) which was an ingenious early Islamic form of air conditioning.

Tentmakers' bazaar to Safiya Mosque

Further south down the street is what is probably the city's best preserved example of a **roofed market** which, because of the multitude of coloured printed fabrics sold here, is known as the **tentmakers' bazaar**. Slightly further along the street is the **Madresa-Mosque of Amir Gani-Bak Al-Ashrafi** which was built in 1426 and is named after a favourite of Sultan Al-Ashraf Barsbay (1422-37). Although the mosque has similarities to a number of other Mamluk mosques of the same period and despite the loss of both a coloured marble lintel over the portal door and the windows, its decoration even now is more ornate than other examples.

You enter the mosque from the south and pass through a serpentine corridor arriving in the central domed cruciform area with the usual *qibla* wall, *mihrab* and *minbar*. There is a two-storey minaret, to the right of the entrance, which is very plain and utilitarian.

Amir Gani-Bak Al-Ashrafi had been brought up by Sultan Al-Ashraf Barsbay and his meteoric rise to amir in 1422 naturally created many enemies. He was poisoned and died aged 25. He was such a favourite that the Sultan had his body transferred to a tomb in the Sultan's own Eastern Cemetery complex. Nearby is what little remains of the **Souk Al-Surugiyyah** (saddle-makers' market).

The **Mosque of Malika Safiya**, built in 1610, lies to the west in a small street off Sharia Mohammed Ali. It is one of the few mosques in Cairo which bears a woman's name although Queen Safiya acquired it deviously rather than constructed it herself. Safiya, who was from the noble Venetian family of Baffo, was captured by pirates along with a large party of other women in 1575 whilst on their way to Corfu where her father was governor. Because of her beauty she was presented to the Sublime Porte where she became chief consort of Sultan Murad III. He made her his *Sultana Khasski* (favourite) which gave her considerable power and influence which was increased further when she produced Murad's first-born son who succeeded his father in 1595. At her son's death Safiya was exiled to a harem where she lived in obscurity until she died in 1618.

This Turkish-style mosque, which was originally set in gardens, is entered on the southwest side via some very high steps which lead to a square courtyard.

Darb Al-Ahmar

Returning to Bab Zoueila and turning right (east) into Sharia Darb Al-Ahmar (Red Road) there is an interesting 1¼-km walk to the Citadel. The street gets its name from the incident in May 1805 when the Mamluks were tricked into going to discuss their grievances with Mohammed Ali Pasha (1805-48). He had them slaughtered as they travelled 'Between the Two Palaces' and their heads sent to Istanbul as a demonstration of his power and independence. In March 1811 he did a similar thing again on the same street when 470 Mamluks and their retainers were persuaded into going to a banquet at the Citadel to celebrate his son's imminent departure to fight the Wahabis in modern day Saudi Arabia. They were slaughtered on their return near Bab Zoueila.

About 150 m after the Mosque of Vizier Al-Salih Tala'i the road bends towards the south and on the corner of the fork in the road is the beautiful late-Mamluk era

Mosque of Qijmas Al-Ishaqi who was Sultan Qaitbai's Viceroy of Damascus, where he died and was buried in 1487. Although the mosque was built in 1480-81, it is now known locally as the **Mosque of Abu Hurayba** after the 19th-century sheikh who occupies the tomb.

At this point you can make a detour off the main road east up Sharia Abu Hurayba where the left hand fork leads 250 m to the **Mosque and Tomb of Amir Aslam Al-Silahdar** built in 1344-45 and then follow the road around southwest and back to the main Sharia Darb Al-Ahmar.

Alternatively you can forget about the detour and just continue south from the Mosque of Qijmas Al-Ishaqi along Sharia Darb Al-Ahmar. About 50 m on the right is the **Mosque and Tomb of Ahmed Al-Mihmandar**, built in 1324 but restored in 1732, but much more interesting is the beautiful, relaxing and very peaceful **Mosque of Altunbugha Al-Maridani** (1339-40) which is 100 m further along the street. This is among the most impressive 14th-century buildings in Cairo. Altunbugha (Golden Bull), who was originally from the Turkish town of Mardin, rose through the ranks to become amir and then married one of Sultan Al-Nasir Mohammed's daughters and became his cupbearer (*saqi*). After the sultan died in 1340 his successors imprisoned Altunbugha until 1342 when he was made governor of Aleppo in modern-day Syria. He died there the following year at the age of 25.

Altunbugha's courtyard mosque, which was extensively restored in 1895-1903, is one of the oldest remaining buildings in this area. The minaret, to the right of the entrance, was the first in Cairo with an entirely octagonal shaft. It was built by Mu'allim Al-Suyufi, the royal chief architect, who also built the minaret of Aqbugha at Al-Azhar. The shafts of both are decorated by two-coloured inlaid stone work. Fortunately the restoration work followed the original plans so that the bulb-crowned canopy supported on stone pillars, the earliest existing example, was retained.

Another 200 m further south past a small Turkish mosque, by which time the road is now called Sharia Bab Al-Wazir in memory of the Gate of the Wazir which once stood there, is the large **Madresa of Sultan Al-Ashraf Sha'ban II** (1363-78). It was built in 1368 when he was only 10, for his mother, who was one of Al-Nasir Mohammed's (1310-40) concubines, which is why it is known locally as *Umm Sultan Sha'ban* ('mother of Sultan Sha'ban') but he died before her and is buried there.

On the road south is the **Mosque of Amir Aqsunqur** who was the son-in-law of Al-Nasir Mohammed and later became Viceroy of Egypt. It is sometimes known as the **Mosque of Ibrahim Agha** by locals and the **Blue Mosque** by Europeans because of both the exterior's blue-grey marble and the beautiful indigo and turquoise tiling of the *qibla* wall. In the 1650s Ibrahim Agha usurped the mosque, started in 1346, and decorated it with imported tiles.

The **Madresa-Mausoleum of Amir Khayrbak** was built in stages with the earliest, the mausoleum, which was attached to his palace, being erected in 1502. Because it was squeezed between existing buildings the shape of the complex is very irregular. The complex, now being restored but still open to the public, is best viewed from the Citadel end to the south from where one can see that the minaret, undated, which has the upper storey missing (being reconstructed) and the intricately carved dome of the tomb raised above arched windows.

Unlike most Mamluk *madresas* it was initially not a Friday mosque although this was subsequently introduced in 1531 when the *minbar* was added. Documents show that the *madresa* staff included one imam, six *muezzins*, two *qari* (Koran readers) at the *madresa*, nine *qari* to recite the Koran at the windows, a sufi sheikh, 10 *qari* to perform daily in two shifts, and two *qari* at the mausoleum.

The entrance is through a corridor to the left of which is the *sabil-kuttab* and to the right of which is the portal entrance to the mosque which one enters by stepping over a piece of Pharaonic stone. From the windows of the tomb one has a good view of the ruined Alin Aq palace and Salah Al-Din's city walls.

For the record, as you admire this building, Khayrbak, who was the Mamluk governor of Aleppo, betrayed his master Sultan Al-Ghuri at the Battle of Marj Dabiq in 1516 when the Turks routed the Mamluks which led to the Ottoman occupation of Egypt. He was rewarded for his treachery by being appointed as the first Ottoman governor of Egypt where he was reportedly known for his cruelty and greed.

From here the road slopes up to the left to meet the approach road to the **Citadel** (see page 105) but we continue right to the two imposing mosques.

Sultan Hassan Mosque

ⓘ *E£12*. Directly below the Citadel are two adjacent mosques. The Sultan Hassan Mosque was started in 1356 and finished six years later during the second reign of Sultan Hassan (1354-61). The building is a masterpiece of Islamic art and is of incomparable simplicity and beauty. The main entrance is through a large, impressive doorway decorated with stalactites and finely sculpted ornaments. This leads into an antechamber connected to the main courtyard. The magnificent cruciform courtyard has an ablutions fountain at the centre covered by a large dome which was originally painted blue. Each of the vaulted *liwans* served as a place for the teachings of one of the four doctrines of Sunni Islam. The *liwan* containing the *mihrab* has richly decorated marble-lined walls and a Koranic frieze in Kufic writing carved in the plaster work. The marble *minbar* here is one of the finest in Cairo. Its height is accentuated by hanging lamp-chains. The original glass lamps from these chains can be found in the *Museum of Islamic Art* in Cairo and in the Victoria and Albert Museum in London.

From here a bronze door with gold and silver motifs leads to the mausoleum of Sultan Hassan, again a room of grand proportions. The room is dominated by a 21-m diameter dome which was actually built later during the Turkish period.

The three-section 86-m minaret by the mausoleum is the highest in Cairo, with each new section decorated at its base with stalactites. Another smaller 55-m minaret on the east side of the mosque was built in 1659 to replace the existing one which was decaying. The building also contains four *madresas* with one for each of the four – Malaki, Hanafi, Hanbali and Shafi'i – Islamic schools of law. Each *madresa* forms a virtually autonomous part of the building. The ground floor is used as a place for teaching, meditation and praying and the first floor as lodgings for the students. Sultan Hassan was murdered and his body never recovered but two of his sons are buried here.

This huge building, one of the largest mosques in the world, was at times used as a fortress, being conveniently placed for hurling roof-top missiles at enemies in the Citadel.

Mosque of Sultan Hassan

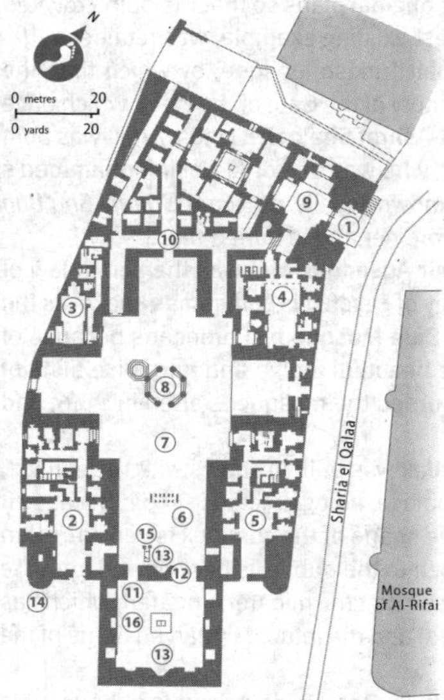

1 Entrance
2 Hanifi medersa
3 Hanabali medersa
4 Malaki medersa
5 Shafi'i medersa
6 Sanctuary/liwan
7 Sahn
8 Water for ablutions
9 Antechamber (domed)
10 Corridor
11 Bronze-faced door with gold and silver inlay
12 Qibla
13 Mihrab
14 Base of minaret
15 Minbar
16 Tomb chamber/ mausoleum

Al-Rifai Mosque

Despite its appearance, the Al-Rifai Mosque, directly to the east of Sultan Hassan Mosque, was only started in the late 19th century and was actually finished in 1912. However, the mosque, which is named after Sheikh Ali Al-Rifai who was the founder of the Sufi Muslim *tariqa* bearing his name and who was originally buried there, blends remarkably well into the surroundings. It was built over and expanded by the Dowager Princess Khushyar, the mother of Khedive Ismail who died in 1885 before it was finished, and was intended to contain the tombs of her descendants. Besides Al-Rifai and herself it contains the tombs of Khedive Ismail (1863-79), his sons Sultan Hussein Kamil (1914-17) and King Ahmed Fouad I (1917-36), King Farouk who died in exile and was initially buried in the Southern cemetery. It is also the last resting place of the last Shah of Iran (Mohammed Reza Pahlavi), who died in exile in 1980 and, on President Sadat's instructions, was buried with great ceremony in a tomb made of green marble imported from Pakistan.

The **Madresa of Amir Sayf Al-Din Ilgay Al-Yusfi** built in 1373, is on Sharia Souq Al-Salih to the north of Bab Mangak Al-Silahdar (1346-47). Sayf Al-Din Ilgay rose through the ranks to become an Amir of the Sword and eventually commander-in-chief of the army. He married Khwand Baraka, who was the mother of Sultan Shaban (1363-77), and he found himself one of the powers behind the throne. After his wife died, however, he quarrelled with the Sultan over her property and lost his influence. He had to flee the court and was drowned in uncertain circumstances while trying to cross the River Nile on horseback. His body was recovered and he was buried in the *madresa* that he had built a few years earlier in 1373. His tomb lies beneath the dome at the western corner of the mosque.

Route 2b: The Citadel

ⓘ *Daily 0800-1700 in winter, 0800-1800 in summer (except 1130-1300 on Fri). E£20, 50% student discount, camera tickets E£10 and E£100 for video cameras, tips should be reserved for guides in the museums and shoe attendants in the mosques, entrance into the museums ends at 1530, enter via Bab Al-Gabal. The Citadel can be reached direct from Midan Tah Rir by taking bus No 72 or minibus No 154; a taxi from the centre should cost E£5-7. (Tell taxi driver to take you to "Al-Qala'a", pronounced Al-ala'a.)*

The **Citadel** (also known as Al-Qala'a Al-Gabal – Citadel of the Mountain – or Al-Burg) was built by **Salah Al-Din** (1171-1193) as part of a very ambitious general fortification plan which included enclosing the whole city with a new wall which could be controlled from the main fort. The original fortress and remaining fortifications were strongly influenced by the architecture of castles built in Palestine and Syria by the Crusaders. It was built on a steep hill which stands 75 m high on the eastern side of the city. The work on the Citadel began in 1176 when pieces of demolished Fatimid mosques and tombs and blocks from the pyramids of Giza were incorporated in the defence system. It was built in two walled enclosures, linked by their shortest walls, with the military area to the northeast and the residential quarters in the southwest. Every 100 m or so along the walls there is a tower connected to its neighbours by upper ramparts and by internal corridors that run the full circuit of the walls. The whole complex is still under military control and there are large areas which are closed to the public.

Later the Citadel was abandoned until the Mamluks' arrival, when it became the Sultan's residence and the *Burji Mamluks* (1382-1517) who took their name from their base in the Citadel. In the 14th century Sultan Al-Nasir Mohammed (1310-40) added a number of buildings including a mosque and later, because of the development of warfare and the use of canons, the Turks undertook major reinforcements. The most recent modification to the Citadel was by Mohammed Ali Pasha (1805-40) who built an impressive mosque on the site of the original palaces. Today the most interesting features of the Citadel are the **Mosque of Mohammed Ali Pasha**, which provides an amazing view west over Cairo and the restored **Sultan Al-Nasir Mohammed Mosque.**

Walls, towers and gates

The Ayyubid walls and towers (1176-83) around part of the northern enclosure are from the time of Salah Al-Din. The dressed stone walls are 10 m high, 3 m thick and 2,100 m in circumference interspersed with half-round towers. Some of the larger and later towers (1207) such as **Burg At-Turfa**, which enclose parts of the wall were built by Al-Kamil (nephew of Salah Al-Din and the first Ayyubid sultan to live in the Citadel). **Bab Al-Azab** enclosed by a pair of round headed towers stands on the west side of the Citadel. It was the original entrance to the Southern enclosure and is no longer open to the public. The brass-bound wooden doors date from 1754. **Bab Al-Qullah** (16th century) connects the two separate parts of the Citadel. The original Mamluk gate was replaced after the Ottoman conquest and was widened in 1826 to allow Mohammed Ali's carriage to pass through. **Bab Al-Gadid** (New Gate) was built in 1828 and is in reality a large tunnel with a vaulted ceiling. There are guard rooms on either side.

Burg As-Siba (Lions' Tower) was built in 1207 by the Mamluk Sultan Baybars. The frieze of stone lions, the sultans' heraldic symbol, gives it its name. **Burg Al- Muqattam** (16th-century) is the largest tower in the citadel, over 25 m high and 24 m in diameter. The 7-m thick walls were built to withstand artillery attack.

Mosque of Mohammed Ali Pasha

The Mosque of Mohammed Ali Pasha, was started in 1824 but only finished eight years after his death in 1857. The architecture was strongly influenced by the Ottoman mosques of Istanbul with the characteristic high, slender, octagonal minarets and an imposing dome which had to be rebuilt in the 1930s. The marble-floored courtyard is very finely proportioned, with a beautiful central ablutions fountain. To the northwest is a small square tower for a clock which was a gift from King Louis-Philippe of France in 1846 in exchange for the obelisk now in the Place de la Concorde in Paris, but the clock has never worked. The mosque is covered by a large dome with four half-domes on each side. Once inside, it takes some time to become accustomed to the dim lighting. The white marbled tomb of Mohammed Ali is to the right after the

Mosque of Mohammed Ali Pasha

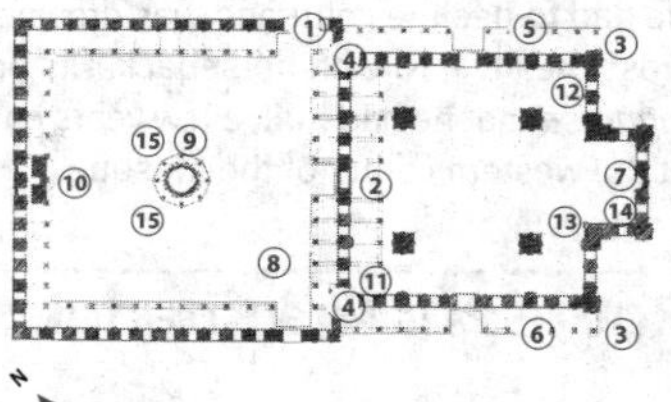

Not to scale

1 Main entrance
2 Entrance from courtyard
3 Domed turret
4 Octagonal minaret
5 Northeast arcade
6 Southwest arcade
7 Mihrab
8 Sahn
9 Ablutions fountain
10 Clock tower
11 Tomb of Mohammed Ali
12 Subsidiary mihrab
13 Minbar (1848)
14 Minbar (1939)
15 Cistern

Mosque of Suleyman Pasha, Citadel

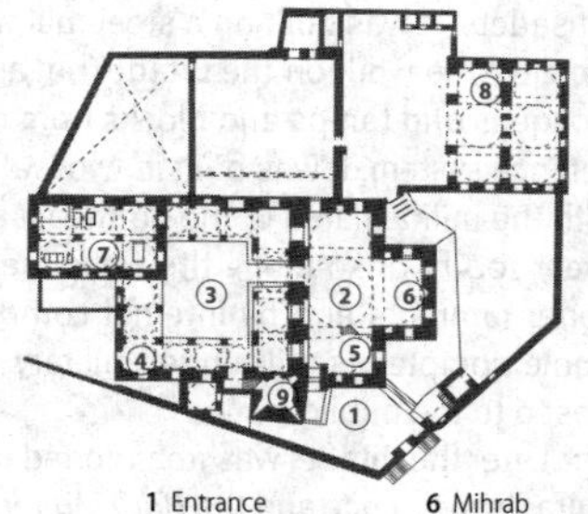

Not to scale

1 Entrance
2 Domed central area
3 Sahn
4 Roofed arcade
5 Marble minbar
6 Mihrab
7 Mausoleum of Suleyman
8 Maq'Ad
9 Minaret

entrance, behind a bronze grille. This mosque is unusual, having two *minbars*. The large wooden construction, carved, painted and gilded was installed by Mohammed Ali. It was too large to erect in the conventional space by the *mihrab* and was placed under the central dome making the weekly sermon inaudible to most of the congregation. In 1939 King Farouk installed a smaller alabaster minbar carved with a geometric pattern – to the right of the *mihrab*.

Sultan Al-Nasir Mohammed Mosque

The Sultan Al-Nasir Mohammed Mosque was built between 1318 and 1335. It is certainly the best preserved Mamluk building in the Citadel and is claimed to be one of the finest arcade-style mosques in Cairo, the arches being supported by Pharaonic and classical columns plundered from elsewhere. The two distinctive minarets, one above each entrance, are covered in the upper part with green, blue and white ceramic tiles attributed to craftsmen from Persia as are the onion-shaped bulbs on the tops of the minarets. The magnificent marble which covered the floors and lined the walls to a height of five metres was unfortunately removed on instructions of the Ottoman ruler Selim I. The *mihrab* is still in good condition.

The **Mosque of Suleyman Pasha** (1528), in the northern enclosure of the Citadel, was the first domed mosque to be built in Cairo during the Ottoman period and is believed to be dedicated to the janissary corps of soldiers of which Suleyman Pasha was earlier commander. It may have been designed by one of the architects sent to Cairo to repair the damage caused to the Citadel and the city walls by the Ahmed Pasha revolt.

The main entrance to the mosque is to the right of the minaret. Its stalactite portal leads not directly into the paved courtyard like most Ottoman mosques but into the prayer hall on its southwest side. This is due to its cramped position by the Citadel's walls. The minaret is typical of the style common in Istanbul, a tall slender cylinder with a conical top, but like the Mamluk minarets it has two galleries. Like the domes of the surrounding mosque and prayer hall the minaret's pointed cap is covered with green tiles which are similar to a number found in Cairo's mosques of the period.

The mosque interior comprises a richly painted domed central area flanked on three sides by three supported semi-domes. The *sahn* is surrounded by a shallow-dome roofed arcade and in the northwest corner is the slightly larger dome of the mausoleum containing tombs of a number of janissaries.

The frescoes on the walls were restored in the 19th century and it is uncertain how faithful they are to the original Ottoman decoration. The *mihrab* is situated under one of the half-domes. There was insufficient space here adjacent to the *mihrab* for the *minbar* which had to be placed under the central dome. The conical top of the marble *minbar*, is decorated with a Mamluk-inspired geometric pattern based on the stars and polygon forms, similar to the Ottoman minarets.

The **Mosque of Ahmed Katkhuda Al-Azab** was built in 1697, in Ottoman style on the site of an earlier mosque. The slender minaret stands tall above the ruins of the main building.

Citadel Museums

The **Carriage Museum** is in the dining hall used by British officers who were stationed in the Citadel and on display are eight carriages once used by the Egyptian royal family and some painted wooden horses.

The **Military Museum** is in the **Harim Palace** built in 1827 as the private residence of Mohammed Ali. There are three extensive wings with many halls and side rooms all decorated in lavish style. King Farouk ordered its conversion into a museum which traces the history of the Egyptian army from Pharaonic times to the present day. There are military uniforms, rifles and cannons on display. Tanks captured in the October 1973 conflict are in the courtyard.

The **National Police Museum** has some strange and interesting exhibits of policing problems ranging from assassination attempts to the protection of Egyptian antiquities. It is constructed on top of Burg as-Siba and the view from the terrace takes in the Pyramids on the left through to the minaret of the Mosque Al-Fath in Midan Ramses to the right. Absolutely breathtaking – on a clear day.

Seized Museum, provides a very interesting hour. In two small rooms the exhibits, confiscated from dealers in the antiquities black market, span the history of Egypt. The first room is set aside for Pharaonic items including a painted wooden sarcophagus and funerary beads in excellent condition. The second room is cramped with an assortment of treasures, including a collection of Byzantine, Islamic and European gold coins, a small group of beautiful books in the Arabic script, seven stunning Coptic icons and a set of official seals from the reign of the Mohammed Ali.

Qasr Al-Gawhara (Palace of Jewels) stands on the site of the palace of the Circassian Mamluk sultans. It was built in 1814 as the first of two palaces with French-style salons that Mohammed Ali built in the Citadel. It contains an impressive audience hall and guest rooms. Having been the residence of Egypt's rulers since the 12th century he predicted that his descendants would rule Egypt as long as they lived in the Citadel: sure enough, Ismail's move to the Abdin Palace foreshadowed the decline in their fortunes. Today it is a museum with displays of portraits, costumes, furniture and ornaments which belonged to King Farouk, much of which has neither beauty nor historical interest.

The **Archaeological Garden Museum** in the Northern Enclosure contains an interesting collection of bits and pieces – monuments and statues – as well as welcome benches.

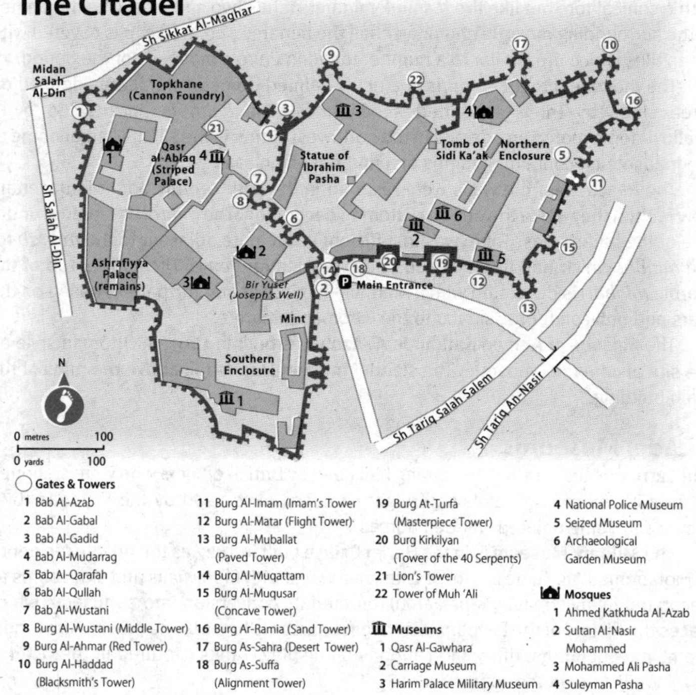

Joseph's Well built in 1183 is also known as the well of the snail as there is an enclosed spiral staircase which leads down some 87 m through solid rock to the water level of the River Nile. There are two platforms where pumps operated by oxen raised the water which was then carried to the surface by donkeys. It is possible to go down, but take great care. It was built by Crusader prisoners and provided a secure supply of drinking water for all of the Citadel. It is covered by a tower and stands just south of the Mosque of Sultan Al-Nasir Mohammed.

Qasr Al-Ablaq (Striped Palace) was built in 1315 by Al-Nasr Mohammed for official receptions. Mohammed Ali Pasha had the building torn down but a remaining portion of outer wall shows it was constructed in alternating bands of black and yellow marble, hence the name.

West from the Citadel

From Midan Salah Al-Din to the west of the Citadel and in front of the Sultan Hassan Mosque make your way west along Sharia Saliba. On the left is the second decorated **Sabil-Kuttab of Sultan Qaitbai** (1477). This is another *sabil* and *madresa* but has, unusually, no connection to a larger religious foundation. Continue west past the small **Mosque of Qanibai Al-Muhammadi** to the imposing architectural buildings with matching minarets which face each other across the Sharia Saliba. On the right, north, is the **Mosque of Amir Shaykhu** (1349) and on the left, south, the **Khanqah of Amir Shaykhu** (1355). Amir Shaykhu was the Commander-in-Chief of the Mamluk army during the reign of Sultan Hassan. The *khanqah* had small cells for up to 70 sufis around the inner courtyard and in the northeast corner of the arcaded prayer hall is Amir Shaykhu's tomb. There is an option to turn left here and travel south down Sharia Al-Ashraf. After 500 m you reach Midan Sayyidah Nafisah, on the corner of which is the Gate of Ali Pasha Hakim. Turn left through here to the modern **Mosque of Sayyidah Nafisah**, one of the very few mosques closed to non-Muslims. Sayyidah Nafisah was a direct descendant of the Prophet Mohammed. She was born in Mecca and came to Egypt with Imam Shafi where she settled in Cairo and lived on the site where this mosque now stands. She was known for her piety, her complete knowledge of the Koran and the more dubious fact that she dug her own grave. Large crowds gathered to receive her blessing and perhaps healing. She died in 824 and the first shrine over the tomb was constructed soon afterwards. The shrine has been rebuilt and enlarged many times; the present construction, the last of a series of tombs, which dates from 1893-97, was erected following a destructive fire.

Continue beyond the mosque entrance, turn right at the end of the covered passage and right again into the courtyard into the cemetery. Among the many tombs the one of note is the domed mausoleum in the centre, the mid-13th-century square tomb of the Abbasid Caliphs.

The next turning left going south down Sharia Al-Ashraf is Sharia Al-Sayyidah Nafisah which leads to the Southern Cemetery (see page 111). Return to the main route turning west (right) at the cross roads, with the **Sabil-Kuttab of Um Abbas** on the corner, passing the small but impressive **Mosque of Amir Taghri Bardi** (1440) with a carved stone dome. While the external structure of this building follows the east-west line of Sharia Saliba the interior is aligned southeast to Mecca.

Ahmed Ibn Tulun Mosque

ⓘ *Now being restored, but open daily 0700-1700. The mosque is about 15 mins west of the Citadel along Sharia Saliba on the way towards the river, alternatively it can be reached from Midan Tah Rir by bus No 72 or minibus No 154 which go to the Citadel via the Saiyyida Zeinab area and then past the mosque, although the Saiyyida Zeinab metro station is only 2 stops from Midan Tah Rir it is probably a 30-min walk from there to the mosque.*

The largest mosque in Cairo and the oldest one which retains its original features is the **Mosque of Ahmed Ibn Tulun**, it was built between 876-879 by Ahmed Ibn Tulun, the son of a Turkish slave who became governor of Egypt but who then declared independence from the Baghdad-based Abbasid Khalifas. He thereby became the first of the Tulunids (AD 868-905), at the new town of Al-Qata'i (the Concessions or the Wards) northeast of Al-Askar which, in turn was northeast of Fustat, and near the foothills of the Muqattam Hills. When the Abbasids regained power in Egypt in AD 905 they destroyed much of the town except for the mosque which fell into decay until it was restored in 1296 by Sultan Lagin who had hidden there after he was implicated in an assassination attempt against his predecessor.

The mosque was originally designed in 876 by a Syrian Jacobite Christian architect which probably explains the presence of many designs and motifs inspired by Coptic art. Legend says that the sycamore beams were brought from Mount Ararat and were part of Noah's ark. Despite the extensive restoration work by Sultan Lagin, apart from the addition of a minaret with an unusual outside spiral staircase which appears to be a copy of the one at Samarra in Iraq, no major changes were made. External measurements are 140 x 122 m making it the largest place of worship in Cairo. The central courtyard is 92 m square yet despite its huge size, the overall impression is of harmony, simplicity and sobriety. The walls have been plastered but the ornamentation is sculpted and not moulded. The long Kufic script inscriptions, almost 2 km long, of about 20% of the Koran, circle the mosque several times below the roof. The marble-plated *mihrab* is surrounded by an elegant glass mosaic frieze. Directly above is a small wooden dome. The *minbar*, presented by Sultan Lagin in 1296, is a fine work of art. The view from the top over the surrounding area is excellent and worth the climb.

Around the Ibn Tulun Mosque

The **Gayer-Anderson Museum**, which is also called **Beit Al-Kridliyah** (House of the Cretan Woman), ⓘ *T02-3647822, daily 0900-1600, except Fri 0900-1200 and 1330-1530, E£16, E£8 for students, E£10 for cameras, E£100 video*, abuts the southeast corner of Ahmed Ibn Tulun's mosque and has its own entrance into the mosque precinct. It is contained in two houses, the one on the west dating back to 1540 and the one to the east to 1631, on either side of a small alley called Atfat Al-Gami which originally belonged to the Al-Kiridli family. Originally one house was for men's accommodation (*salamlik*) and the other for women (*haramlik*). The roof area was solely for the women who crossed from one building to the other by a small bridge on the second floor. A screened balcony (*mashrabiyyah*) which overlooks the large two-storey sitting room (*qa'ah*) with its marble floor and ornately tiled fountain permitted the women to see the male visitors and the entertainments without being seen themselves.

The houses were sold to the government which in 1934 gave them to Major Robert Gayer-Anderson (1881-1945), a retired doctor and member of the Egyptian Civil Service, when he

Mosque of Ahmed Ibn Tulun

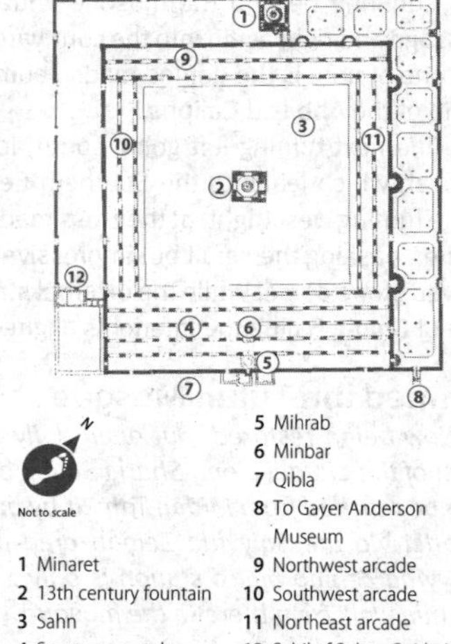

expressed a desire to restore and refurnish them with Ottoman furniture and fittings. A tour of the houses gives a good insight into the decoration and organization of a house during the Ottoman rule. Each of the main rooms has a different theme: Damascus room, Persian room, Turkish room and Byzantine room. Other rooms include a library, a writing room and a display room for the Major's collection of Pharaonic antiquities.

The **Madresa and Tombs of Amirs Salar and Sangar Al-Gawli** was once a much larger set of buildings than what you see today, but even so the remaining tombs and the *madresa* indicate some of the original grandeur. The domes over the tombs are of different sizes, that to the east being the largest. The slender minaret immediately to the right of the entrance stands about 45 m high. The first storey is square, the second is octagonal and the third is cylindrical, culminating in a cornice of stalactites capped with a ribbed dome. The entrance is up the steps through a stalactite arch into a porch. Further steps lead to the vaulted corridor and to the tombs. The Tomb of Amir Salar, 7 m squared, is encircled by a wooden frieze and has a fine marble mihrab. Note the design of the windows in the dome. The adjacent Tomb of Amir Sangar is smaller at 6.5 m squared and is less ornate than its neighbour. Still further west is a third tomb called the Tomb of the Unknown Amir. Even smaller, at only 4.5 m squared, the unnamed occupant died in 1348. Turning east from the stairs leads to the mosque. The larger courtyard had small rooms for students (the grills over the doors need some explanation) and a smaller courtyard off which is the *mihrab*.

The area to the west of the giant mosque is known as **Sayyidah Zeinab** after the Prophet Mohammed's granddaughter Zeinab (AD 628-680) who settled in Fustat/Cairo in 679 with her five children and the son of her brother Hussein who was murdered at Karbala in the Sunni-Shi'a conflict. Because of her position as closest kinswoman to the martyred Ali and Hussein the area has become a site of pilgrimage for foreign Shi'a Muslims. This is focused on the mosque built and continuously rebuilt over her tomb which is located off Sharia Bur Said but is closed to non-Muslims. Her *moulid* (saint's day) between 13-27 Ragab attracts up to half a million revellers who come to watch the wild Sufi parades and evening festivities.

Route 3: The Cities of the Dead

ⓘ *The easiest way to the Southern Cemetery from the Sultan Hassan and Ibn Tulun mosques, is to head south along Sharia El-Khalifa for about 1 km. The easiest way to the Northern cemetery is either by taking a taxi direct to Qarafat Al-Sharqiyyah or by walking east along Sharia Al-Azhar from the Al-Azhar mosque for about 15 mins until you reach the roundabout junction with the north-south dual carriageway of Sharia Salah Salem and then north for 250 m. Then cut into the cemetery and head for the dome and minaret which are clearly visible.*

The Cities of the Dead is the name given by Europeans to Cairo's two main cemeteries which spread from the Citadel. The **Southern Cemetery** is older and spreads to the southeast but there are few monuments to see. The **Northern Cemetery**, which is known locally as Al-Qarafa Al-Sharqiyyah (the Eastern Cemetery) because it was east of the old city, is much more interesting and has been the burial place of the sultans since the 14th century. It contains a number of interesting mausoleums including those of Barquq and Qaitbai.

Muslim graveyards have no flowers unless they grow wild and by chance. Instead of buying flowers to decorate family graves on their routine weekly visit, relatives will often give a simple dish to the poor to provide a meal for their children.

Warning This area is densely populated by Cairenes who live in or near the tombs. In Egypt there has long been a tradition of living close to the dead but the very large numbers are a relatively recent trend caused by an acute scarcity of housing. Consequently the people who live in the cemeteries tend to be comparatively poor and, although certainly not dangerous, it is obviously advisable not to flaunt your wealth, to dress modestly and remember that this is where people live.

Mausoleums in the Northern Cemetery

In the Northern Cemetery the **Mausoleum of Sultan Al-Zahir Barquq** (1382-89 and 1390-99) was built over a 12-year period in 1398-1411 by his son Al-Nasir Farag (1399-1405 and 1405-12). It was the first royal tomb to be built in this modern necropolis after Barquq had expressed a wish to be buried alongside a number of pious Sufi sheikhs who were already buried there. Therefore his body was moved from the *madresa* on Sharia Al-Muizzli Din Allah once the 75 sq m complex had been completed. It is square with two minarets symmetrically placed on the façade. The entrance in the southwest corner leads along a corridor to the *sahn* which has an octagonal fountain in the centre and is surrounded by four *liwans*. The north and south *liwans* have one aisle whereas the west has two, and the east, three. The east *liwan* has three very simple *mihrabs* and an extraordinarily finely sculpted stone *minbar*. Doors lead from either side of the *liwan* into mausoleums. The north mausoleum contains Barquq's own marble cenotaph which is richly decorated with Koranic inscriptions, together with the tombs of an unknown person and another intended for Farag whose body was left in Damascus after he had been assassinated on a military campaign in Syria. The mausoleum to the south holds the tombs of Barquq's wife and two granddaughters.

A little to the south is the **Madresa and Mausoleum of Sultan Al-Qaitbai** (1468-96), built in 1472-74, which is a magnificent example of 15th-century Arab art and possibly one of Egypt's most remarkable monuments from the Arab era. From the outside the building has very harmonious proportions and the dome is finely decorated with polygonal motifs. The minaret is also remarkable because it has a square base, octagonal middle section and a cylindrical top tier. The mosque is reached by climbing 17 steps to the entrance which leads into the southeast *liwan*. The cruciform *madresa*

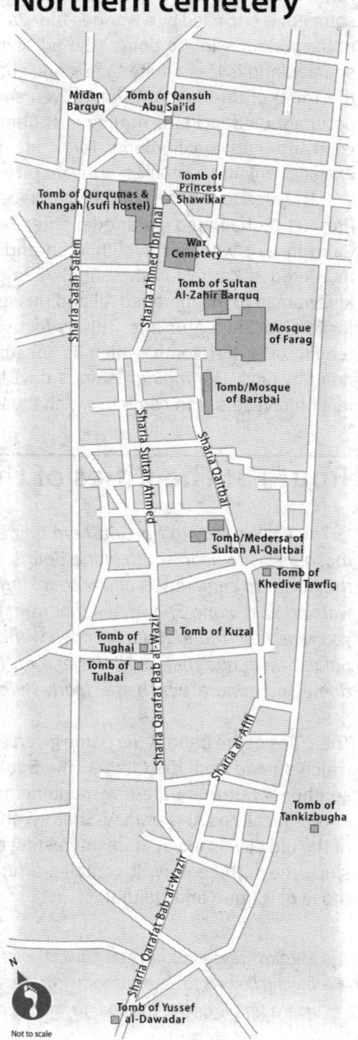

Muslim cemeteries

One of the lasting monuments in Islam is the *qarafah* or graveyard. All are different, ranging from undefined rocky areas near villages, where unnamed head and foot stones are barely distinguishable from the deserts surrounding them, to the elaborate necropoli of Cairo, where cities for the dead are established. In all cemeteries bodies are interred with head towards the *qibla* – Mecca.

In Egypt, graveyards often contain a series of simple whitewashed mud brick tombs of holy men (*marabouts*), around which his disciples and their descendants are laid. More grandly, in Cairo at the City of the Dead is the Eastern Cemetery, known as the Tombs of the Mamluks (see page 111), a set of Muslim graveyards, developed particularly from the 15th century. It contains large numbers of notable tombs, most importantly that of Tomb of Sultan Al-Zahir Barquq. A second and even more elaborate cemetery is Cairo's Southern Cemetery. This ancient graveyard includes a number of the earliest examples of Muslim funerary architecture in Egypt and is home to the Tomb of the Imam Shafa'i, the most significant mausoleum in Cairo. The Imam Shafa'i was born in Palestine in 767 and was the originator of the Shafi'ite School of Islamic jurisprudence, one of the four great Sunni Schools of Law. He spent his last years (until his death in 820) in Fustat in Cairo. Salah Al-Din set up the Shafa'i Mosque in 1180, which included the Imam's new tomb. Although subject to numerous subsequent reconstructions, the last under the Khedive Tawfiq in 1891, the tomb is in an adequate state of repair to justify a visit. The large Shafa'i complex takes in a mosque, a ceremonial gateway and the mausoleum itself. The tomb is simple but decorated at various times with silver and paintings. The mausoleum has some fine beams and a wooden cupola together with much of the inscriptions and ornamentation undertaken by Salah Al-Din's builders. Shafa'i's tomb lies to the north of the building. Its religious focus is a delicate 20th-century sandalwood screen or *maqsurah* and a marble stela. These are kissed by visiting Muslims as a sign of faith. Also entombed at the site are Mohammed abd Al-Hakim and Princess Adiliyyah, mother of Sultan Al-Kamel, while the Sultan himself (interred elsewhere) is commemorated by an uninscribed tomb in the south of the chamber. A walk along Sharia Sidi Uqbah and Sharia Imam Shafa'i takes you past a wide variety of funerary constructions, many in a sad state of decay. Also worht a visit is the Al-Basha *Housh* (house) which backs onto the Shafa'i tomb on a parallel road (Shariyah Imam Al-Lais) to the west. This is the 19th-century mausoleum of the family of Mohammed Ali Pasha.

Death and funerals are times for noisy outbreaks of wailing and crying. In traditional families, the approach of a person's death is signified by wailing, increased on actual death by the addition of the mourning neighbours and relatives. Occasionally in villages the body is laid in a large room where funeral dances are performed by mourning women, singing the praises of the deceased. Corpses are washed and wrapped in a simple shroud for interment. Mourners follow the cortege to the cemetery often in large crowds since every person who walks 40 paces in the procession has one sin remitted. At the grave side a *shedda* or declaration of Islamic faith is recited.

 has side *liwans*, and a relatively small covered *sahn* with an octagonal roof lantern. The *liwans* are very narrow but the east *liwan*, which has a modern ceiling, still has a very well preserved and finely encrusted *minbar*. A door in the south corner of the *qibla liwan* leads to the mausoleum which is decorated with the same sort of marbles as the *madresa*. Its high dome is simply decorated, in contrast with the highly ornate walls. Sultan Qaitbai's tomb is enclosed behind an elaborate wooden *mashrabiyya* while the other tomb is that of one of his sisters.

Central Cairo

Central Cairo has developed further west on both sides of the river into a modern and increasingly cosmopolitan capital. Although residential suburbs spread outwards in all directions, any visit to Cairo should include the ***Egyptian Museum*** *and the* ***Museum of Islamic Art****. The* ***Manial Palace*** *on Roda Island is also a worth a visit. Get a feel for Cairo by cruising down the River Nile on a meandering* ***felucca*** *and spending an afternoon or evening in a local* ahwa. *To see Cairo from up high, there are stellar lookout points over the city's labyrinthine sprawl from the* ***Cairo Tower****, the* ***Royal Nile Tower*** *(behind the Méridian Caire hotel) and from the* ***cliffs of Moqattem****.*

The Egyptian museum

ⓘ *The museum is in the centre of Cairo taking up the north side of Midan Tah Rir (entry is from the sculpture garden fronting the building), T02-5754319. Daily 0900-1645, Fri 0900-1115, 1330-1600, the museum remains open until 1800, but stops permitting entry at 1645 (closes at 1500 during Ramadan). The museum is best visited either early in the day or during the late afternoon since at other times it is taken over by coach parties. The Tutankhamen exhibit is particularly in demand and it might be necessary to queue for entry. From time to time rooms are closed for repair, decoration and the setting up of new exhibitions. Similarly there are changes in the lay-out of exhibits. Tickets cost E£20, E£10 for students, cameras E£10, E£100 amateur videos, no flash photography, there is an additional fee of E£40 (students E£20), for the Royal Mummy Room. It may be worth buying a detailed guide to the rooms (E£5), where the layout of displays can change from time to time (but also see plan of Egyptian Museum in this Handbook). Official tour guides wait around outside the ticket booth, some are more entertaining than others, but most seem to be quite well-informed about the contents of the museum. The going rate is E£40 per hour, but it's possible to bargain. There is a souvenir shop outside the museum on the right of the entrance and an official sales area on the left inside the main building. Café and restaurant facilities are available on the first floor.*

The Egyptian Museum (called in Arabic *El-Mathaf El-Misri* and sometimes, mistakenly, referred to as the Cairo Museum), is one of the wonders of the country. Its most famous exhibits are the world-renowned and spectacular Tutankhamen displays. It has an enormous wealth of materials covering early history, ancient Egypt and the Islamic period which is unrivalled even in the grand museums of Berlin, London, New York and Paris. For tourists and scholars alike, the museum is a must if only for a few hours.

The new museum was set up and opened in 1902, the brainchild of Auguste Ferdinand François Mariette (1821-81), a Frenchman who was a distant relation of Champollion, the decipherer of Egyptian hieroglyphic writing. He was a great scholar of Egyptology who excavated widely in Egypt throughout the second half of the 19th

Egyptian antiquities in Paris

Every serious student of Egyptology undertakes a course of study, before travel, from libraries or at museums. Most visitors from Europe have the benefit of proximity to a wide range of high calibre artefacts in their homeland. The most recent collection to come to the eyes of the public is in the Louvre which until now has had insufficient room to display its very numerous high quality possessions. Egyptian antiquities are the centrepiece of the newly opened extension there, where an amazing 30 rooms and galleries on three floors display over 6,000 objects ranging from minute scarabs to monumental sphinxes. This is just over 10% of the full collection. When, if ever, will the rest be displayed? The curators have done a fine job of balancing the needs of the casual viewer with that of the serious specialist with both thematic galleries and dynastic chronological displays, as best suit the materials and hopefully the visitor.

century. He won the confidence of the crown prince Sa'id Pasha, proposing greater preservation of monuments and artefacts and more controls on the export of antiquities. Mariette was appointed to oversee all excavations in Egypt through the Egyptian Antiquities Service and also took responsibility for the setting up of the museum of antiquities. His reign was not without its upsets since he quarrelled violently both with Egyptian officialdom and with rival archaeologists but he was successful in creating the present museum which was specially designed to house the Egyptian national collection. It remains well planned for its age and a great treasure house of objects. There are hopes of a new purpose-built museum to be established, possibly at Giza to overcome the complaint that the present rooms are inadequate to handle exhibits in a satisfactory way and that too many major objects are never seen by the public.

A visit to the museum begins in the **sculpture garden**, where there is a statue and the tomb of Auguste Mariette, a number of sphinx-headed statues and a sarcophagus. The main museum building has two floors, both with 51 principal exhibition rooms. Circulate from the entrance in a clockwise direction. The exhibits are distributed in a generally chronological order beginning in the hallway (Room 48-GF). **NB** GF = Ground Floor; UF = Upper Floor. Rooms and galleries are both described as 'Rooms'.

The museum is fairly large and you need to allow four hours for a full initial viewing of both floors and all rooms. A shortened tour of about two hours will give you enough time to take in the ground floor followed by a visit to the Tutankhamen Gallery in rooms on the upper floor. On a one-hour visit the entrance hall (Room 43-GF) and the Tutankhamen galleries would be feasible, but bear in mind that there can be queues/congestion in this area, especially in Room 3-UF where the principal treasures are stored.

Touring the museum The museum also has many other individual objects of great distinction on display. In the entrance room (**48-GF**, display unnumbered) is a cast of the **Rosetta Stone**, from which Frenchman Jean-Francois Champollion decoded the hieroglyphic writing of ancient Egypt. The original is in the British Museum. In the same room are recent additions to the museum's collection out of chronological sequence. Room **43-GF** holds a number of Early Dynastic period statues. Old Kingdom (2613-2181 BC) objects take up **GF Rooms 47, 46, 41, 42, 36, 31** and **32**. In Room **42-GF** there is a notable standing wooden statue of the priest Ka-aper and a statue of King Chephren, one of the builders of the Giza pyramids. There is also a painted stone statue of a Fifth Dynasty scribe, cross-legged on a plinth. In Room **32-GF**, display 39 is a painted effigy of Seneb the dwarf and his family. He was a keeper of the royal wardrobe in the fifth Dynasty. A well-sculpted, painted statue of Ti, a noble of the same period and other figures such as Prince Ra-hotep and his wife Nofert are also to be found in Rooms **32** and **31-GF** (display 27).

The Middle Kingdom period (BC 2050-1786) is represented in **GF Rooms 26, 21, 22** and **16**. The painted statue of King Menutuhotep is in Room **26-GF** (display 67). It was found at Bahr El-Bahari and is 11th Dynasty. Room **26-GF** also houses a series of sarcophagi of painted limestone from this period. In particular see the Sarcophagus of Dagi (display 71), a tomb beautifully illustrating objects in everyday use such as sandals and linen items together with hieroglyphs of magic spells and offerings. King Senusert I (Sesostris) is depicted in 10 limestone statues in Room **22-GF** though these are outshone for visual impact by the 56-cm wooden statuette of Senusert I (display 88) carrying sceptres in both hands to denote his royal authority. A granite statue of Amenemhat III is occasionally on show in the same room (display 105) and there is a double statue of that king as the Nile god (display 104), and several sphinxes of the same provenance in Room **16-GF** (display 102). The four sphinxes are in grey granite and come from the find by Auguste Mariette at Tanis.

The New Kingdom ran from BC 2567-1085. The exhibits in the set of galleries **11, 12, 6 and 7** are mainly from the 18th Dynasty, with more complex garments and headgear than in previous eras. Room **12-GF** is well endowed with notable objects, mainly statues in granite. Most important are the statues of Senenmut, steward of Queen Hatshepsut and tutor to her daughter. He was responsible for designing the temple of Hatshepsut at Deir El-Bahari. The examples here in Room 12-GF include his block statue (display 132) with his pupil, Princess Neferure, peering below his chin.

Egyptian Museum - ground floor

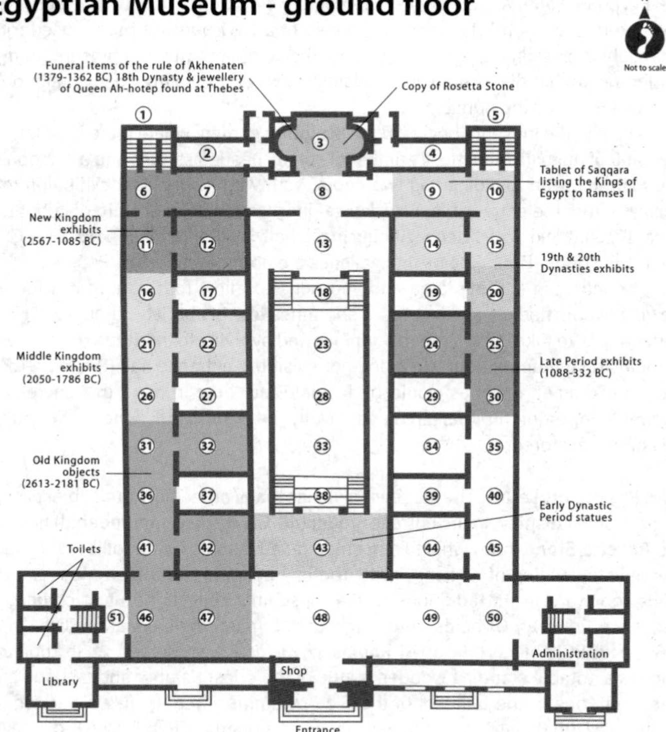

The plaque carries inscriptions of his titles and merits. Queen Hatshepsut is seen in a variety of statues (Room 12-GF, display 952) and in the remnants of her red sandstone sarcophagus (Room **28-GF**, display 131), while there is a variety of statues of Tuthmosis III and Isis, his mother. Hatshepsut is represented in a large restored statue in Room **7-GF**.

Room **3-GF** is given over to objects from the reign of Akhenaten (Amenhotep IV), who set up his capital at Tell El-Amarna (North of Assiut) and altered the mode of public art and architecture in Egypt to one of realism. There are sandstone statues of Amenhotep IV, of which the presentation of an offering tablet (display 160) is perhaps the most interesting, and a gilded coffin lid of Amenhotep's brother, Smenkhkara. Several heads of women are on display in Room 3-GF, with the unfinished head of Nefertiti (display 161) being the most famous, and the head of a princess (display 163) most exquisitely portrayed. Representations of the 'royal family' in the form of what seems to be a shrine (display 167) are also on show.

The central hall of the museum (Rooms **13, 18, 23, 28, 33** and **38-GF**) is used to exhibit giant statues of a mixture of periods. As an example, it is worthwhile to look at the 7 m statue of Amenhotep III and his wife Tyi (display 610).

Objects of the 19th and 20th Dynasties are displayed in Rooms **9, 10, 15, 14** and **20-GF**. Room 9-GF contains the Tablet of Saqqara (display 660), which lists the kings of Egypt to Ramses II. The crystalline limestone head of General Nakhtmin (display 195) is in Room 15-GF and shows fine workmanship. The painted bust of Meritamoun, daughter of Ramses II and queen in succession to Nefertari, is also in Room 15-GF, when available.

Egyptian Museum - upper floor

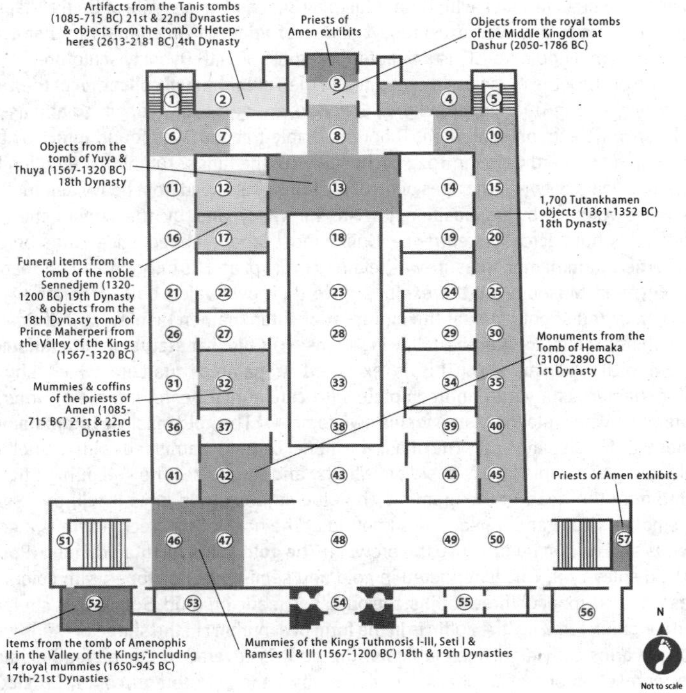

Mummy Come Home

An elegant new tomb (**46, 47**) has been constructed in the museum, its pillars supporting a deep blue ceiling studded with gold stars. This is an attempt to recreate the ambience of Thebes in around 1300 BC and provide a final resting place for some of its most famous pharoahs.

The mummies have suffered many indignities. Take Meneptah, grandson of Seti I. Having survived a spectacular first burial with all the pomp and splendour due to Egyptian royalty, tomb robbers flung his mummy aside and 21st Dynasty priests rewrapped him and placed him with eight other displaced persons in a side chamber in the Tomb of Amenhotep II. Rediscovery in 1898 was followed by transport to Cairo where he was put on view. Queen Nedjemet, another resident was slashed by the knives of those who unwrapped her. The great Ramses II unwrapped in public in 1886 in an unseemly 15 minute strip, has also found a decent home here. In 1946 public display of mummies was banned as improper. But in March 1994 the special tomb tastefully displayed these bodies neatly wrapped once again, complete with dimmed lighting and dehumidifiers to protect the desiccated remains. Among the 11 who have found, hopefully, a final resting place here beside Queen Nedjemet, Meneptah and Ramses II are Merytamum his queen and his father Seti I.

Best of the Late Period (BC 1085-332) is concentrated in Rooms **25, 24** and **30-GF**. Key items include the Psametik group of statues in greenstone of which those of the Psametik, a head jeweller, with Hathor (display 857) and of Isis, wife of Osiris (display 856), are particularly well executed. A statue of Princess Amenartais in alabaster (display 930 in Room 30-GF) is a beautiful example of 25th Dynasty sculpture.

The pride of the museum is contained in the **Tutankhamen collection** of the 18th Dynasty (years 1361-52) in rooms **3, 4, 6, 7, 8, 9, 10, 15, 20, 25, 30, 35, 40** and **45-UF** with 1,700 objects on exhibition. This remarkable treasure was found intact by the Englishman Howard Carter in 1922 in the Valley of the Kings. Tutankhamen ruled for only nine years between the ages of 9-18. His tomb was saved from heavy destruction by grave robbers by its position low in the valley and by the construction of workmen's huts across its entrance. Unlike most other archaeological finds before 1922, the Tutankhamen treasure was retained in Egypt and its full glory can be seen in the Egyptian Museum. All the exhibits have their own value both decorative and academic. You should look at the entire set of Tutankhamen displays, but if time is very short at least look at the following items. (1) **Colossal statue of Tutankhamen** (Room 9-UF, display 173). This is executed in painted quartzite which shows Tutankhamen as a youth and complete with ceremonial beard and hieroglyphs of Horemheb who stole the statue for his own tomb. (2) **The gold mask of Tutankhamen** (Room 4-UF, display 174). The mask is made of gold garnished with cornelian, coloured glass, lapis lazuli, obsidian, quartz, and turquoise. The 54-cm high figure came from the head of the mummy. The blue stripes are in lapis lazuli, there is a ceremonial beard and a headdress knotted at the back of the neck. There is a gold ureaus and vulture head above the brow. (3) **The gold coffin of Tutankhamen** (Room 4-UF, display 175). This is rendered in gold and semi-precious stones with coloured glass. It is the inner of three coffins, the outer two made in wood. Some 187.5 cm-long and weighing 110.4 kg, the coffin is in the form of a mummy in the shape of Osiris with crossed arms carrying divine emblems. The body is covered by carved feathers and the representations of Upper and Lower Egypt – the vulture and cobra. (4) **Lid of**

Never smile at a crocodile

In the Ancient Egyptian Agricultural Museum the 5 m long crocodile complete with wicked grin is fortunately very dead, as are the many other animals on display. A dog lies on its side, prostrate, seemingly sleeping in the sun and a baboon sits back resting on its haunches, huge hands hanging over its knees.

These are the animals worshipped, pampered, hunted and husbanded by the Ancient Egyptians: fat cats; even fatter Apis bulls; domesticated sheep and horses; birds ranging in size from the falcon and duck to the ostrich and the venerated ibis. The animals depicted in hunting scenes on countless reliefs and tomb paintings have not, fortunately, come to life, but their skeletal and mummified remains are on display here.

canopic jar (Room 8/9-UF, display 92), **The goddess Selket** with **The golden shrine** (Room 8/9-UF, display 177). This group of objects includes a wooden shrine gilded with gold and with silver which was in the antechamber of the king's tomb. It is ornately decorated with family and hunting scenes. The lid of the jar, containing the remains of the king's entrails, is of alabaster, carries the king's image and is lightly painted. There were four Canopic jars as miniature sarcophagi in the tomb. The golden shrine was protected by four goddesses, of which Seket, the water goddess, is displayed in gilded and painted wood about 90 cm high. (5) **Wooden funerary bed** (Room 9/10-UF, display 183). Made of stuccoed wood, these three funerary beds are gilded and painted. The most remarkable is the couch in the image of the primordial cow with cow's heads and lyre-like horns set about sun disks. (6) **The Throne of Tutankhamen** (Room 25-UF, display 179). The throne is 102 x 54 cm, made of gilded wood and ornamented with semi-precious stones. In addition to the winged serpent arms of the throne, the seat back carries a gilded and painted scene in which Tutankhamen's wife anoints him with oil. (7) **Ceremonial chair** (Room 25-UF, display 181). The finely inlaid ebony and ivory chair of Tutankhamen is regarded as among the best examples of Egyptian cabinet-making ever found. It is decorated with uraeus snakes and divinities. (8) **Funerary statues 'shawabti'** (Room 35-UF, display 182). The tomb of Tutankhamen contained 413 small, approximately 50 centimetres high, figures of the king as workers, foremen and overseers, giving one workman per day of the year. They are made of wood, which is painted and gilded. (9) **Tutankhamen with a harpoon** (Room 35-UF, display 182). Among the seven royal statuettes found in the tomb, the two gilded wooden statues of Tutankhamen hunting, in gallery 35, are most pleasing. One shows the king on a papyrus board hunting in the marshes, harpoon in hand. A second is of the king wearing the crown of Upper Egypt riding the back of a panther. (10) **Painted chest** (Room 40-UF, display 186). This is a 44 x 61 cm wooden chest, stuccoed with paintwork above. It is in a good state of preservation and carries pictures of battle against Asians and Africans and a set of hunting scenes. (11) **Anubis chest** (Room 45-UF, display 185). A carrying chest made in stuccoed wood and ornamented with black resin, gold, silver and varnish. The chest itself contained jewellery, cups and amulets. Anubis as a jackal sits on the chest ready to act as a guide for Tutankhamen in the afterworld. (12) **Ka statue of Tutankhamen** (Room 45-UF, display 180). This large (192 cm tall) statue is one of two guardians of the tomb. It is made in wood and painted in bitumen. The king holds a mace in his right hand and a staff in his left. He is wearing a **khat** head-dress and has a gilded kilt.

Long renowned for its exotic cigarettes, Egypt does not actually grow its own tobacco. In fact growing tobacco is illegal.

On leaving the Tutankhamen galleries there is much still to see in the museum, including jewellery and monuments. Important objects include the wonderful 25-piece collection of **Meketra's models**, found in the tomb of Meketra, a noble of the Middle Kingdom (2000 BC), at a site south of Deir El-Bahari.

The miniatures show the form, dress, crops, vessels and crafts of the period. The best known is the offerings bearer (display 74), 123 cm high and made of painted wood. It shows a servant, carrying a basket of vases on her head and a duck in her right hand. There are also models of fishermen, cattle, weavers and carpenters in displays 75, 76, 77 and 78 respectively. In Room **32-UF** (display 117) is a **Ka statue of King Auib-re Hor** in wood, now bereft of its stucco coating. The headdress of upraised arms symbolizes **ka**, the vital force of the king.

Worth looking out for if you have time are the **Fayoum portraits** in Room **141-UF** for the most part encaustic (wax) painted on wooden bases by Greek artists in the second century AD to leave a likeness of the deceased for his family. (See page 161.)

The Museum of Islamic Art

ⓘ *Junction of Sharia Port Said and Sharia Qala'a about equidistant between Midan Ataba and the Bab Zoueila, T02-3901520. Daily Sat-Thu 0900-1600, Fri 0900-1100 and 1330-1600. E£16, students E£8, ticket is also valid for Gayer-Anderson House,* *see page 110.* *Guides available.*

This museum contains the rarest and most extensive collection of Islamic works of art in the world. It was originally established in the courtyard of the Al-Hakim Mosque (see page 97) in 1880 but it was moved to the present building, containing over 75,000 exhibits from various Islamic periods, in 1903. The dates indicated in the museum's

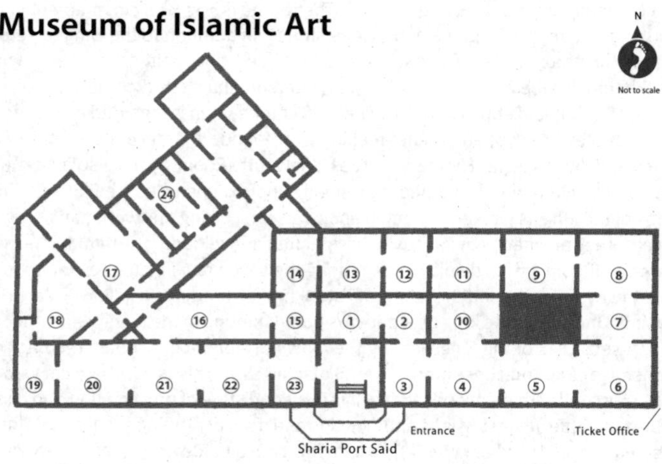

1 Mainly recent acquisitions
2 Ommayyad (7-8th century) - mainly from Fustat
3 Abbasid (8-10th century) - stucco pannels
4 Fatimid (10-12th century) - panels depicting living things
5 Mamluk (13-16th century) - woodwork & ceramics
6-10 Woodworking in chronological order
11 Chandeliers & other metalwork
12 Armour & weapons
13 A mixture - a room not to miss
14-16 Pottery
17 Upstairs from garden - textiles & carpets
18 Outdoors - Turkish headstones/tombs/sundial
19 Books & manuscripts - a changing exhibition
20 Turkish art - wall hangings, china & jewellery
21 Glass - lamps from mosques arranged in chronological order
22 Persian exhibition - mainly pottery
23 Temporary exhibitions
24 Library

exhibits are AH (After the Hegira), which is the starting point of the Islamic Calendar in AD 622 when Mohammed is thought to have fled from Mecca. The rooms follow a chronological order through from the Umayyads to the Abbasids, Fatimids, Ayyubids, Mamluks and Ottomans. Of particular interest are **Room 1** which contains recent discoveries like the very long papyrus over in the right hand corner; **Room 2** is the beginning of the Umayyad collection, considered the first true Islamic period with the first pieces of Islamic coinage in bronze and gold; **The Fatimid panels** in **Room 4** which depict animals and birds because, unlike the Sunni Muslims, the Fatimid Shi'a had no objection to portraying living things; the doors to **Room 6** which were originally from the Al-Azhar Mosque; the reconstruction of an 18th-century Ottoman patio in **Room 10**; the Mamluk astrolabe used by Muslim navigators in **Room 11**; just before leaving **Room 13** on the right the 10th century 'Fayoumi' plate in Chinese style; **Room 20** Persian carpets; the glassware in **Room 21** and the Persian art in **Room 22**. The oil lamps from the mosque of Sultan Hathor, considered one of the most beautiful exhibits in the museum, are in a central case in **Room 21**. Take refreshment in the shaded garden by a fountain moved from Roda Island and marble panels with Fatimid reliefs. Sometimes the exhibits are not illuminated; ask the custodian to turn on the light for you but do feel that you need to tip him.

Other museums

Abdin Presidential Palace Museum ⓘ *Just east of Midan El-Gumhurriya with the entrance in Sharia Mustafa Abd El-Raziq, T02-3910042, 3916909. Daily 0900-1500. E£10, students E£5, cameras E£10*. This imposing building, completed in 1872, became the official royal residence until 1952. For the previous 700 years the Citadel had housed the rulers. The rooms of the actual palace are not for viewing but 21 halls contain exhibits. The first section, President Mubarak's Hall, contains a selection of the gifts he received – a varied collection of medals, portraits, clocks and plaques. The second section is of silverware, porcelain and crystal owned by the descendants of Mohammed Ali Pasha, indicating a very luxurious lifestyle. Who lifted the 125-kg silver tray when it was laden? The Military Museum takes up 13 of the halls in the same building displaying weapons and suits of armour, as well as unusual items such as Rommel's dagger and two guns belonging to Napoleon Bonaparte. In the courtyard is a shrine to Sidi Badran.

The **Agricultural Museum** ⓘ *adjacent to the Ministry of Agriculture in Dokki (pronounced Do'ii) (metro: Dokki) at end of 6th October Bridge, T02-7608682, daily 0900-1330, closed Mon, 10 piastres*, has the distinction of being the oldest agricultural museum in world, stuffed animals, Egyptian farming practices and all. Here the artefacts are placed in context, the flax plant beside the linen, the papyrus plant beside the rope and paper. The many animals that were worshipped, hunted or eaten – cats, ostrich, Apis bulls and falcons – are there as mummies or skeletons. Unfortunately the labels, in a variety of languages, give little information if they exist at all. Next to the Agricultural Museum is the **Cotton Museum** ⓘ *free*, which gives a survey of cotton growing in Egypt.

The **Entomological Museum** ⓘ *14 Sharia Ramses, near the railway station, daily 0900-1300 except Fri and 1800-2100 Mon, Wed and Sat*, houses an old (it was founded by King Fouad) but interesting collection of Egyptian birds and insects and is very useful if you could not name what you saw, what ate your crops or what bit you.

Mahmoud Khalil Museum ⓘ *1 Sharia Kafour, off Sharia Giza, T02-3362379, daily 1000-1730, closed Mon, E£25*, has a collection of impressionist paintings and some fine sculptures.

The **Manial Palace** ⓘ *daily 0900-1600, E£10 for foreigners, E£5 for students, fee for normal cameras E£10, video cameras, E£100*, on Roda Island in the middle of the

Umm Kalthoum, Egypt's Mother Diva

The taxi driver has put his favourite cassette on. Who does that forceful voice, rising above the slithering quarter tones of the violins, belong to? It could well be that of Umm Kalthoum, the best known Egyptian of this century after Gamal Abd Al-Nasser and still the most popular Arab singer. There was nothing in her background to suggest that Umm Kalthoum was to become the greatest diva produced by the Arab world.

Born in 1904 in a small village in the Nile Delta region, Umm Kalthoum became interested in music through listening to her father teach her brother Khalid to sing religious chants for village weddings. One day, when Khalid was ill, Umm Kalthoum accompanied her father and performed instead of her brother. The guests were astonished at her voice. After this, she accompanied her father to sing at all the weddings. In 1920, the family headed for Cairo. Once in the capital, Umm Kalthoum's star rose fast. She met the poet Ahmad Ramzi and made her first commercial recordings. In 1935, she sang in her first film. She subsequently starred in numerous Hollywood-on-the-Nile productions.

In 1946, personal and health problems made Umm Kalthoum abandon her career, temporarily as it turned out. Due to her illness, she met her future husband, the doctor Hassan El-Hafnawi, whom she married in 1954. She then resumed her career. Songs such as *Al awal fil gharam wal hubb* ('The first thing in desire and love'), *Al hubbi kullu* ('Love is all') and *Alf layla wa layla* ('A Thousand and One Nights') made her name across the Arab lands. In the 1960s, her Thursday evening concert on the Cairo-based Radio Sawt Al-Arab ('Voice of the Arabs') became an Arab-wide institution. During the Yemeni civil war, the Monarchist troops knew that Thursday evening was the best time to attack the Egyptian troops supporting the Republicans as they would all be clustered round their radio sets listening to their national diva. So massive was her fame that she was dubbed 'the Fourth Pyramid'.

Umm Kalthoum's deep, vibrant voice was exceptional, of that there is no doubt. Nevertheless, the music may be difficult for western ears. Though the lyrics are often insufferably syrupy, the diva's songs continue to enjoy wide popularity and her films, subtitled in English or French are often shown on Egyptian satellite channel Nile TV. In Ramadhan 1999, a TV series on her life drew huge audiences. If there is one piece of modern Arab music you should try to discover, it has to be the Umm Kalthoum classic love song, *Al Atlal*, ('The remains of the camp fire'). The theme, a lament sung over the ashes of the camp fire for the departed lover, goes way back to the origins of Arab poetry.

Umm Kalthoum died in 1975, and her funeral cortège filled the streets of Cairo with hundreds of thousands of mourners. Her voice lives on, played in cafés and cars, workshops and homes all over the Arab world.

Nile is an oasis of tranquillity in noisy Cairo and is well worth visiting. The palace, which was built in 1903 and is now a museum, was the home of King Farouk's uncle Prince Mohammed Ali and comprises a number of buildings in various styles including Moorish, Ottoman, Persian, Rococo and Syrian. The first is the Reception Palace at the gate, beautifully decorated with polychrome tiles and stained glass. Upstairs are a number of luxurious rooms, of which the Syrian Room is the finest, and a mother-of-pearl scale model of Sultan Qaitbai's mausoleum. To the right is a mosque with a tall mock Moroccan minaret and then a revolting Trophies Museum with tatty and poorly stuffed animals including a hermaphrodite goat and a table made of elephant's ears. Much more interesting is the royal residence in the middle of the garden which is a mixture of Turkish, Moroccan, Egyptian and Syrian architectures and contains a number of rooms, nearly all of which are decorated with blue earthenware tiles. The Throne Hall behind the residence is of little interest but the Private Museum, which includes a very varied collection of Korans, manuscripts, carpets, plates and glassware, is fascinating.

The Child Museum ⓘ *34 Sharia Abou Bakr Al-Siddik, Heliopolis, T02-6399915, 0900-1400*, one of the newest museums to Egypt, this brainchild of Suzanne Mubarak brings interactive multimedia technologies to Egypt. Lots of film clips about animals that will keep young folks entertained, and an arts hall where children can paint.

National Museum of Egyptian Modern Art ⓘ *Gezirah Opera House grounds, Zamalek, daily 1000-1300 and 1700-2100, closed Mon*, includes works dating back to early 20th century and exhibitions are changed regularly.

New Egyptian Museum The foundation stone was laid in Jan 2000 on a site of 600,000 sq m on the outskirts of the city. Costing an estimated US$400 million it will be the world's largest historical gallery and will be used to display the hundreds of priceless monuments that now lie gathering dust in the store rooms of the existing museum in Cairo due to lack of space.

Post Office Museum ⓘ *Midan El-Ataba, (metro: Ataba) in annex of main post office building, daily 0900-1300 except Fri, free*, here there are displays of memorial stamps and illustrations of the ways in which the post was transported.

Railway Museum ⓘ *next to Ramses station, daily 0830-1300, closed Mon, E£1.50, Fri E£3*, automated display, coaches for Khediv Ismail's private train.

See also **Coptic Museum** page 85, **Gayer-Anderson Museum** page 110 and **Carriage Museum** page 107.

Other places to visit and things to do

The **Cairo Tower** ⓘ *T02-7357187, daily 0900-2400, E£32*, a prominent icon in the Cairo skyline, offers a bird's eye view of the city. The 187-m tower with lotus-shaped top is on Gezira Island and it is one of the city's most visible landmarks. It was built with Soviet help in 1957-62. Although the restaurant and cafeteria are OK it is the viewing platform that is most impressive. Providing the pollution is not too bad, you can look east across the modern city centre to the minarets and mosques of Islamic Cairo and the Muqattam Hills beyond; to the west the Pyramids and desert sprawl out on the horizon. It's a great view of the city at night. For a less expensive view, you may wish to try the **Royal Nile Tower** in Garden City by the Meridian hotel, complete with fully functioning revolving restaurant. For a more local view, visit the hills of **Moqqatem**, dotted with local *ahwas* along the cliff that looks down upon Cairo's labyrinth sprawl. City gazing is particularly enjoyable around sunset, as Cairo lights up.

Dr Ragab's Papyrus Institute ⓘ *in a boat moored alongside Corniche El-Nil opposite Cairo Sheraton. (metro: Dokki), T02-7488177, daily 0900-2100*, displays the processes involved in the making of papyrus. It is possible to purchase copies of illustrations and writing on papyrus found in tombs.

Dr Ragab's Pharaonic Village ⓘ *on Jacob Island 3 km south of the city centre, T02-5718675, daily 0900-2100, E£59, E£10 discount if you visit the Dr. Ragab's Papyrus Institute first*, is a great place for those with children. Numerous actors perform the daily activities of the ancient Egyptians. The show gives background to the main sites. As the pace is set by the boat tour through the village on the bullrush-fringed Nile allow at least two hours.

Nilometer on southern tip of Roda island, originally built in ninth century BC, stands in a small kiosk. There has probably been a nilometer here since ancient times but this was constructed in AD 861. The original measuring gauge remains today.

October War Display ⓘ *junction of Sharia Oruba and Ismail El-Fangari, Heliopolis, daily except Tue, shows at 0930, 1000, 1230, 1800 and 1930, E£10*, this illustrates the October 1973 War with the crossing of the Suez Canal and the attack on the Bar-Lev line, the air battle led by the Egyptian Air Force and an almost life-size painted scene of the battle to take Qantara. The commentary is in Arabic.

A trip to Egypt would be remiss without at least an hour's meander down the River Nile on an age-old **felucca**. Most *feluccas* can accommodate up to eight people – the more passengers, the cheaper the fare. Bargaining is the norm, but a standard price is around E£25 per hour. Tips are expected. *Feluccas* for hire dock in front of the *Nile Hilton* downtown, and near *Le Meridian* in Garden City. If you want to sail on a quieter and greener part of the Nile, take a taxi to the nearby suburb of Ma'adi (E£10), and ask for a *felucca* dock.

Giza Zoo ⓘ *daily 0800-1800 in summer, 0900-1700 in winter, 50 piasters*, has many claims to fame. In particular it is the biggest exhibitor in Africa, having on

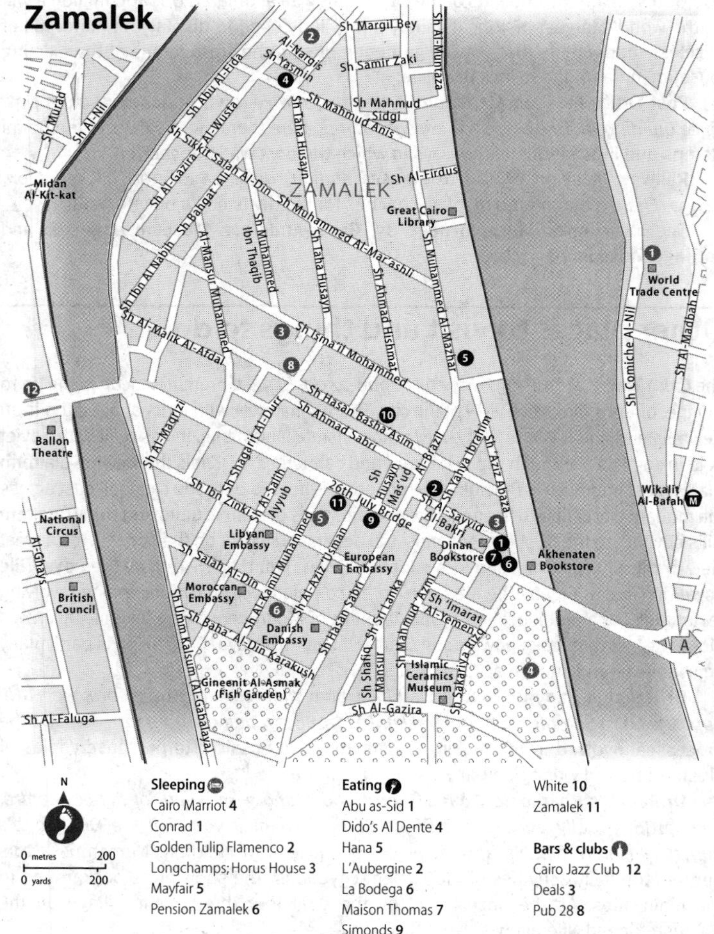

display the largest number of endangered species. Its situation near the west bank of the River Nile at Giza makes it easily accessible over El-Gamea Bridge. The zoo is organized into five huge grottos, one holding statues of rare Egyptian mammals. There are over 6,000 animals and birds on display from around 40 species. Features include the Reptile House and the Lion House. The zoo is proud of its record in breeding and returning to the wild Barbary Sheep, Nubian Ibex, Dorcas Gazelle and Sacred Ibis. Visitors used to western zoos may find a visit here very distressing.

Whirling Dervishes ⓘ *Mon, Wed, Sat, 2000, El-Gawra Theatre in the Citadel until renovation at the old venue in El-Ghoriyya is complete, it's wise to arrive an hour early to ensure you get a seat, there is a lobby with tea by the theatre. Free.* Sponsored by the Ministry of Culture, the El-Tannoura Dance Troupe puts on a spectacular, if not entirely authentic, show at the outdoor El-Gawra Theatre in the Citadel. Just watching the vibrant music and colourful spinning can put you into a trance. The performance lasts almost two hours.

Birqash Camel Market ⓘ *35 km northwest of Cairo: getting there via public transport is quite a confusing affair, as there are no direct routes, but if you want to try, take a taxi or minibus to the old camel market in Imbaba (near Imbaba Airport), from there, minibuses run to the the 'souk al-gamal'. Alternatively, hire a taxi for the morning or go with one of the many organized tours from a budget hotel. Ismailia and Sun Hotel, in Midan Tah Rir, both have weekly trips for around E£25 per person, they usually leave around 0700 and return at 1100, the earlier you arrive at the market, the more action you'll see.* Cairo's Friday camel market makes an interesting and bewildering morning trip. Shortly after the sun rises, camel traders mill about the smelly grounds in search of the biggest humps and healthiest gums they can find. Larger camels are generally used for transport and farming; smaller ones land on the dinner table.

Gardens

There are several spacious gardens where you can find some tranquillity away from the city bustle. Among them are the **Zoological Gardens** in Giza, the **Fish Gardens**, ⓘ *daily 0900-1530*, in Zamalek, with several large aquaria, popular with courting couples. The **Japanese Gardens** in Helwan, the **Merryland Gardens** in Heliopolis, a splendid place for children, with a dolphin on site, a pedalo lake, a merry-go-round and lots of good restaurants; the **International Garden** in Nasr City and the **Kanater Al-Khaireya Gardens** (the Good Barrage) about 25 km from the capital. The **River Nile Promenade**, along the Corniche downtown and on the island of Zamalek, is a lovely, if crowded, stretch for a stroll. **Manial Palace Garden** is 5,500 sq m and contains a rare collection of trees brought back to Egypt by Mohammed Ali.

Sleeping

As the largest city in Africa and the Middle East, and one of the world's great tourist destinations, Cairo has hundreds of hotels ranging from the premier deluxe accommodation of major international chains to some really rugged local dives. The listings below, which have sought to avoid the worst and include the extraordinary, provide options to suit varied budgets, though higher end mid-range accommodation is somewhat lacking in Central Cairo. As most visitors will most likely stay in the heart of the city, the listing for Central Cairo is significantly more extensive. There are abridged listings for the areas surrounding the pyramids, Islamic Cairo, and Heliopolis (the Northern borough encompassing the airport). Nearly all the notable budget and mid-range accommodation centres around Downtown (the City Centre) and Zamalek. The most exceptional expensive hotels are also in the City Centre or near the Pyramids. At the time of writing the ministry of tourism has recently decreed that all hotels deemed 3-star and above must receive payment in foreign currency. Credit cards are accepted in higher-end establishments, but if you intend to pay in cash, be prepared to have some foreign currency on hand. Take into account that the prices of accommodation in Cairo and all over Egypt fluctuate significantly depending on the season and number of tourists in the country, so the price codes indicated here could shift significantly.

For travellers on a budget, Cairo has loads of interesting and decent cheap hotels, which means fierce competition, and brutal hotel touts. Lies are part of the game. You will be told hotels are full, or closed, or have doubled in price. Take control of the situation by choosing a place in advance, or assertively spend some time wandering around the centre exploring your options. Also remember that bargaining is the norm in Egypt, especially if it's summertime or you have plans to stay for a while. Where possible, we have included specific costs for the most budget of choices.

Central Cairo *p114, maps pp71, 124, 126*

AL Cairo Ramses Hilton, 1114 Corniche El-Nil, Maspero, T02-5777444, 5744400, F5757152. 836 rooms, in heart of Cairo, overlooking the River Nile near Midan Tah Rir, within walking distance to the Egyptian museum. Tower block of 28 floors where you can do your birdwatching from the balcony. Also a pool, healthclub, plus a variety of restaurants, bars, lounges and boutiques, and a first class business centre.

AL Conrad, 1191, Corniche El-Nil, Bulaq, T02-5808000, F5808080. A bit of a hike from the town centre in a fairly uneventful area, but as one of the newest 5-star hotels in town, it offers some of the most comfortable and luxurious rooms around. There's a pool and healthclub, and a notable seafood restaurant.

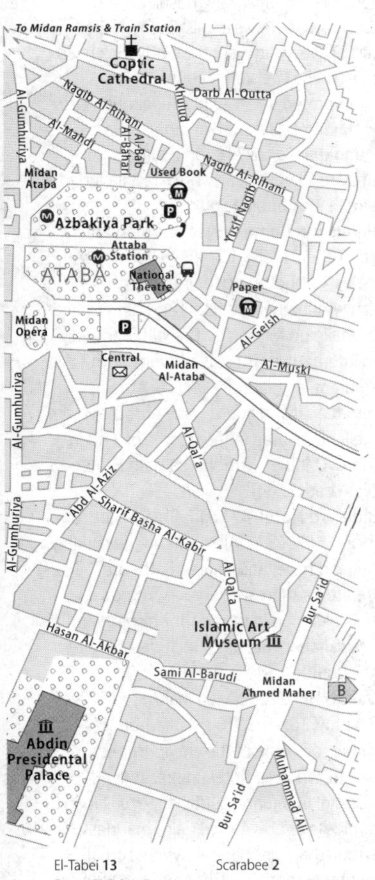

El-Tabei **13**
Fatatri El-Tahrir **7**
Felfela **9**
Fu Shing **11**
Gad **17**
Groppi's **6**
Kowloon **3**
Paprika **1**
Peking **16**
Scarabee **2**

Bars & clubs
After-Eight **4**
Cafeteria Honololo **19**
Cafeteria Stella **8**
Carrol **20**
Le Grillon **18**

AL Helnan Shepheard, Corniche El-Nil, Garden City, T02-7921000, F7921010. 270 rooms, all with good views, good Indian restaurant, pool, business centre. A modern structure named after the famous 19th-century original hotel that burnt down in 1952. *Casino d'Egypte*'s glory is fading.

AL Le Méridien Caire, Corniche El-Nil, Garden City, T02-3621717, F3621927. Very well-managed French hotel with 275 rooms and located by the River Nile on north tip of Roda Island. Lots of extras, including health club, night club and large pool. Excellent service for businessmen and tourists, and popular French restaurant. The Royal Nile Tower, attached, has a wide range of notable restaurants, including the *Hard Rock Café*, and one of the best views of Cairo. *Feluccas* congregate on the banks beneath.

AL Nile Hilton Hotel, Corniche El-Nil, Midan Tah Rir, T02-5780444, F5780475. 434 large rooms, located on the River Nile, adjacent to Egyptian Museum, recently modernized but showing its age, as it was opened in 1959 by President Nasser. Like many international *Hiltons*, it is the place for the jet set of the capital. Lots of shops and airline offices. *Jacky's* is one of the best nightclubs in the city – swinging until the early hours. *Jazz-Up/High Heels*, a new poolside evening bar with live music on most nights, is an up-and-coming hot spot in town, especially in summer where huge cooling fans yield a permanent breeze.

AL Semiramis Intercontinental, Corniche El-Nil, Garden City, T02-7957171, F7963020. 743 rooms in an ugly building and very expensive, but excellent service all around and good views of the Nile overlooking the southeast end of Gezira Island. Outdoor pool.

C Cosmopolitan, 1 Sharia Ibn Taalab, Qasr El-Nil, T02-3923845, F3933531. 84 a/c rooms including 6 suites, recently refurbished, in centre of downtown Cairo in a relatively quiet side street in an elegant building, restaurant which serves reasonable food, bars, café, nightclub, laundry service. Breakfast included.

C **Windsor**, 19 Sharia Alfi Bey, T02-5915277, www.windsorcairo.com. A historic, well-run, family-owned hotel with clean a/c rooms filled with functional antiques. Bathrooms could use a facelift. Breakfast included. One of the classiest and cosiest bars in the city, with barrel chairs, lots of wood panelling and an interesting history. Ask the bartender to share the story. Michael Palin stayed here while going around the world in 80 days. Show your *Footprint Handbook* to receive a 15% discount.

D **Carlton**, 21 Sharia 26 July, Azbakia, T02-5755181, F5755323. 60 airy a/c rooms with high ceilings and wooden floors. Near the bright bustling souk El-Tawfiqa. Hotel has laundry service, restaurant and a nice rooftop *ahwa*. Breakfast included.

D **Grand Hotel**, 17 Sharia 26 July, Azbakia, T02-5757700, F5757593. In a crowded but central location, it has retained most of its original art deco fixtures, furniture and flair. Rooms are clean with wooden floors and spotless bathrooms. A characterful place to stay and a good deal.

D **Odeon Palace Hotel**, 6 Sharia Abdel Hamid Said, Qasr El-Nil, T02-5776637, F5767971. Centrally located modern hotel with a rooftop garden bar that offers a good view of the city. 30 rooms with a/c, private bath and TV. Breakfast not included.

D **Victoria**, 66 Sharia El-Gumhoriyya, Midan Ramses, T02-5892290, info@victoria.com.eg. A large pink hotel that's been around since the 1930s. Long red carpets and loads of chandeliers make it feel Victorian. Spacious a/c rooms have all amenities, bathrooms were recently remodelled. There's a bank, internet café, bar, coffee shop and coiffeur. The place is glamorous, offers a breakfast buffet, probably the best deal for a 3-star in Cairo, though location is a bit far away from the centre of downtown.

E **Berlin Hotel**, 2 El-Shawarby St, 4th Fl, Qasr El-Nil; T02-3957502, berlinhotelcairo@hotmail.com. Centrally located small hotel on a pedestrian alley off a downtown main thoroughfare. Unspectacular rooms are clean with a/c and private shower but shared toilet. Hotel offers cheap hassle-free (but very slow) airport pickup for people who book in advance. Breakfast served in rooms. Laundry service, internet access, and tours available. Owner speaks flawless English and is well informed about budget travel options. The place feels a bit overpriced for a hotel that takes up half a floor in a rather dreary building.

E **Lotus Hotel**, 2 Sharia Talaat Harb, T02-5750966, www.lotushotel.com. 50 rooms, some with bath and a/c, in a drab but clean and comfortable centrally located hotel run by the same family as *Windsor*. Breakfast included. Restaurant and an uneventful rooftop bar and solarium. Reception is on the 7th floor. Show your *Footprint Handbook* for a 15% discount.

E-F **Lialy Hostel**, 8 Midan Talaat Harb, 3rd floor, T02-5752802, lialy_hostile@yahoo.com. A new establishment in the heart of everything, spotless, private, cheap, and homely. The staff is young, well-informed and friendly. A beautiful view over Midan Talaat Harb at night. No a/c, though there's talk of soon adding it. All baths are shared. Hearty breakfast included. Dorm E£25, double E£60.

E-F **Pension Roma**, 169 Sharia Mohamed Farid, T02-3911088, F5796243. Among the classiest of budget options, impeccably clean with hardwood floors and high ceilings that make up for no a/c. The staff is friendly and informative. There is a lounge with TV, restaurant, and laundry service. Attracts an international and age-diverse group of travellers. Located in the middle of 3 main midans. Doubles with shared bath E£58, private bath E£64.

F **Bluebird Hotel**, 42 Sharia Talaat Harb, 6th floor, T02-5756377. All rooms are reasonably clean and have fans. Shared baths are separate for men and women. There's a satellite kitchen in the common space and a shared kitchen. Breakfast included. Single E£25, double, E£40.

F **Dahab Hotel**, 26 Sharia Mahmoud Bassiouny, T02-5799104, dahabhotel@hotmail.com. One of the cheapest beds in town, this rooftop hotel is amazingly successful in offering a little taste of Dahab in the middle of downtown Cairo madness. On the roof, there are bungalows, and small, very simple rooms. Bathrooms aren't the cleanest. It's the garden that's special, a little oasis overflowing with flowers and plants, you can even hear birds chirping. Funky young atmosphere. Internet, pool table, small cafeteria. Dorms E£10, doubles E£25, add E£10 for private bath.

F Ismailia House, 1 Midan Tah Rir, T02-7963122, ismahouse@hotmail.com. Another classic budget dive in the middle of Midan Tah Rir. Even when tourism is hurting, Ismailia is buzzing. It's a friendly place with good management, clean rooms and shared baths, reliable cheap tours (also available to non-guests), and an absolutely flabbergasting view of Midan Tah Rir. News crews film from the balconies when there's action in the main square. Laundry, internet, shared kitchen, lounge with CNN always on. No a/c but all rooms have fans. Request one with a balcony. Breakfast included. Dorms E£15, double E£40, with bath E£50.

F Sara Inn Hostel, 21 Sharia Yousef El-Guindi, Bab El-Louq, T02-3922940, sarainn@hotmail.com. A quiet, intimate new hotel, centrally located with friendly staff. Warmly-decorated, communal lounge with TV and internet access. No a/c, but all rooms are very clean and have fans. Dorms E£15, doubles E£30, with private bath E£50.

F Sultan Hotel, Venice Hotel and Safari Hotel, 4 Sharia Souk El-Tawfikia, T02-5772258, 5741171, 5778692. These 3 hotels take up the first 5 floors of the same building. All are extremely cheap with dorm beds going from E£5-8, depending on how many flights of stairs you are willing to climb. Shared bathrooms can be grimy. All have laundry facilities and a kitchen. The funk and flavour of the colourful souk opposite makes up for the filth of the building. This is where it's at for backpackers on the tightest of budgets. Venice (dorms E£7, singles E£15, doubles E£20) is the quietest and cleanest of the three and offers the cheapest internet access at E£4/hr. Safari seems to have the most bustle and seems particularly popular with Japanese backpackers.

F Sun Hotel, 2 Midan Tah Rir, T02-7730087, sunhotel@hotmail.com. An old-timer on the budget scene, Sun is growing weary around the edges. Located in a convenient, if hectic spot right next to the metro, rooms are drab, carpets haggard, and bathrooms could use a makeover. Laundry, kitchen, lounge with TV, internet access, breakfast included. Dorms (E£15) are separate sex. Doubles E£40, with bath, E£50. Still a good place to come for cheap trips to nearby sights like Saqqara or the Camel Market (both E£25/person), even if you're not staying here.

E Youth hostel, 2 km south of city centre on Roda Island, 135 Sharia Abdul Aziz Al-Saud, El-Manial, near University Bridge, T02-3640729, F3684107. Location is inconvenient, though connected to the city via public transport. There's a shared kitchen with prepared meals available, family rooms and laundry. E£15-20, depending on if you share a room with 3 beds or 6. Doors closed 2400-0800. Book in advance. Places for disabled.

Zamalek *map pp 71, 124*

AL Cairo Marriott Hotel and Casino, 16 Sharia Saray El-Gezira, Zamalek, T02-7358888, F7356667. 1,124 rooms, around a lavish 19th-century Gezira Palace built to commemorate the opening of the Suez Canal and still retaining some of its splendour. 12 restaurants, bars, nightclub and Egypt's largest casino *Omar El-Khayyam* (ext 8503). Also has own sporting facilities – tennis court, health club, etc, and beautiful gardens. Simply palatial, a good place to unwind from the bustle of Cairo, non-floating restaurant and Nile cruiser.

AL El-Gezira Sheraton, Gezira Island, T02-7373737, F7355056. Opposite the *Cairo Sheraton*, circular tower, 27 floors, on the south tip of Gezira Island is one of Cairo's most distinctive landmarks, business provision is excellent. The riverfront restaurant/nightclub is a great place to take in a belly-dancing show.

A Golden Tulip Flamenco Hotel, 2 Sharia El-Gezira El-Wasta, Abu El-Feda, Zamalek, T02-7350815, F7350819. 132 rooms in a new hotel, on quieter but less scenic northwest corner of Gezira Island, though most rooms have good Nile view. High standard and spotlessly clean, Spanish restaurant, 24-hr café, cocktail bar, healthclub with cheap massage, takeaway shop, tea room, shops, bank, business centre. Cost decreases significantly in summer.

C Horus House Hotel, 21 Sharia Ismail Mohammed, Zamalek, T02-7360694, F7353182. One floor under Longchamps, this is a pricier and less appealing choice. Rooms have all the extras, the staff is friendly and there's a bar and restaurant but, compared to its bright upstairs neighbour, the hotel feels old and dreary.

C **Longchamps**, 21 Sharia Ismail Mohammed, Zamalek, T02-7352311, www.hotellongchamps.com. 30 rooms. Funky family-run long-standing hotel that feels like a home. Two lovely shaded terraces offer peace and greenery. Rooms are very comfortable with new furniture, a/c, TV, fridge and a bit of European flavour. The owner is an eclectic vivacious woman who speaks German, French and English.
E **Pension Zamalek**, 6 Sharia Salah Al-Din, T02-7359318, F7353773. Spacious warm rooms, some with a/c, most with balconies, in very tranquil nook off Zamalek's main drag. A family-run family-friendly hotel. No private baths but every 2 rooms share a spotless bath. Laundry service, TV in salon. Breakfast included. Discounts for long stays. Doubles E£85, with a/c E£100.
E-F **Mayfair Hotel**, 9 Sharia Aziz Osman, off 26 July. T02-7357315, www.mayfair cairo.com. Unspectacular rooms in quiet location. Breakfast included. There's a lobby with TV and a small terrace. Be mindful of booking tours here, as some travellers have been overcharged. Show *Footprints Handbook* for a 10% discount. Doubles E£40, with a/c and bath E£70.

Islamic Cairo *p87, map p88*

E **El Malky Hotel**, 4 Sharia El-Hussein, T02-5891093, F5896700. Unquestionably the nicest option of the three hotels around Midan Hussein, behind the El-Hussein mosque. Except for the El-Hussein mosque which sounds periodically, noise isn't a problem. Rooms and baths are reasonably clean and include TV, telephone and fan, some with a/c. Breakfast included. Make sure you request a room with a balcony, as some have no windows, and check out the view from the roof.
E-F **Hotel El Hussein**, Midan El-Hussein, T02-5918089, F5918479. In the heart of Khan El-Khalili, entry via an alley behind *Fishawi's*. A gloomy hotel and a bit run down, but if you can handle the noise, the location makes it worthwhile. Breakfast included. Request a room overlooking Midan Hussein. It's worth shelling out the extra E£10 to avoid the dank shared bathrooms.
F **Radwan**, 83 Sharia Gawhar El-Kaaid, Midan Azhar, T02-5901311, F5925287. Noisy, not advisable for single women. The dull decor and grubby bathrooms make this the least appealing hotel in the area.

Pyramids and Giza *p75*

AL **Cairo Jolie Ville Movenpick**, Alexandria Desert Rd, T02-3852555, F3835006. 240 rooms, lovely gardens and excellent food.
AL **Cairo Sheraton**, Midan Gala'a, Dokki/Giza, T02-3369700, F3364602. 660 rooms, just south of the Gala'a bridge, views of River Nile, typically high quality service, visible as twin towers on west bank of River Nile, views of the pyramids from the restaurant, circular pool.
AL **Four Seasons**, 35 Sharia Giza, T02-5731212, F5681616. 271 of the classiest rooms in town. In true *Four Seasons* fashion, the hotel offers everything you expect and then some.
AL **Le Meridien Pyramids**, Alexandria Desert Rd, T02-3830383, F3831730. 523 rooms, a/c, some with balcony, recently renovated, rooms with view of pyramids cost more, many facilities. Small charge made for shuttle bus to town centre which takes minimum of 35 mins. A really grand hotel, able to cope with businessmen and honeymooners.
AL **Mena House Oberoi**, 6 Sharia Pyramids, El-Ahram, T02-3833222, F3837777. 487 rooms in an exquisite old-style hotel built in 1869, with excellent views of Pyramids and set in 16 ha of gardens. Superb nightclubs and restaurants, disco, casino, largest outdoor pool in Cairo, tennis, a nearby 18-hole golf course, horse and camel riding with experienced instructors. Take a room in the renovated older part for preference. If out of your budget, still a delightful place to enjoy breakfast or a cup of tea opposite the pyramids.
AL **Pyramids Intercontinental Resort**, Alexandria Desert Rd, 2.5 km outside Cairo near the Pyramids, T02-3838666, F3839000. 481 rooms, good service, 4 restaurants, nightclub with oriental floorshow, pool, health club, gym, sauna, tennis, and nearby golf course and horse riding clubs.
A **Siag Pyramids Penta Hotel**, 59 Mariuteya, Saqqara Rd, PO Box 107, Ahram, T02-3856022, F3831444. 320 rooms, large hotel near, and with a good view of, the Saqqara pyramids, good room service reportedly better than eating in the restaurant.

C Pyramids Hotel, 198 Sharia El-Ahram, on the main road to the Pyramids, T02-3835100, F3831555. 144 rooms, caters for budget tours.
C Saqqara Country Club & Hotel, Saqqara Rd, Abu El-Nomros, T02-3811415, F3810571. 20 rooms outside the city near the Saqqara pyramids, well run with good food and excellent horse riding facilities. Temporary club membership available.
D Vendome, 287 Sharia El-Ahram, El-Ahram, T02-7798904, F5854138. 44 rooms, clean and comfortable family-run hotel on the way to the Pyramids.

Camping
Because Cairo has very little undeveloped earth on which to pitch a tent and since there are so many budget hotels, there is little demand for camping. The only decent real campground is called **Salma Camping**, T02-3849152. It can be reached by turning off from Harraniya village on the road between the Pyramids and Saqqara. It offers cabins, a camping ground, hot showers, a buffet and a bar. E£15 to pitch a tent; E£35-50 for a simple double cabin.

Airport and Heliopolis *p68*

In addition to the standard medley of international 5-star chain hotels surrounding the airport, there are 2 longstanding hotels worthy of note:
A Baron Hotel Heliopolis, 8 Sharia Ma'ahad El-Sahara, off Sharia El-Oraba (also known as Airport Rd), Horraya, T02-2915757, F2907007. 126 rooms in Heliopolis overlooking the palace, a good businessman's hotel. Clean and comfortable, if unspectacular, decent food and good service, 2 restaurants, 24-hr coffee shop, bar, ballrooms and discotheque.
C Beirut Hotel, 56 Sharia Beirut, T02-2911092, F4159422. 91 rooms. A decent three-star hotel with a nice dark loungey bar that's popular among guests and locals. A favourite hotel among business travellers who stay awhile.

Eating

Cairo is a cosmopolitan city with an increasingly diverse and eclectic population. The cuisine reflects such variety. You can find Japanese, vegetarian, Chinese, Italian, Indian and French, in addition to superb Middle Eastern cuisine. At the chicest of restaurants (often found in the chicest of hotels), expect to pay what you would at home for a classy meal. It's also possible to dine deliciously on the cheap. You can fill up on tasty local fare (*fuul*, *taameyya* and *koshari*) for less than a dollar. Do pay attention, though, especially when buying food on the street. If things don't seem too clean, it may be better to pay the extra few pounds and dine at a local indoor establishment where the flies and the heat are less menacing. (See Food and drink in Essentials, page 48.) Opening times and menus may change during Ramadan.

Central Cairo *p114, maps pp 71, 126*

TTT Asia House, Helnan Shepheard Hotel, Corniche El-Nil, T02-7921000. Open 1230-15300 and 1900-2300. Serves Chinese and Indian cuisine in a magnificent dining room with high ceilings and *mashrabiyya* style walls. Central fountain adds to the ambience. Food is delicious and quite authentic.
TTT Bird Cage, Semiramis Intercontinental, Corniche El-Nil, T02-7957171. Open 1230- 1630 and 1900-2400. Tasty Thai cuisine complete with live (caged) birds. Recently renovated with a neo-feng shui design and sheer curtains separating tables for privacy. Very expensive.
TTT Citadel Grill, Ramses Hilton Hotel, 1115 Corniche El-Nil, T02-5777444, 5744400. Open 1900-2300. Continental grill to the strains of house music.
TTT La Tour D'Or, Royal Nile Tower (41st floor), Corniche El-Nil, Garden City, T02-3621717 (ask for extension 2119). Opens at 2000. French cuisine overlooking a spectacular view of Cairo, reservations necessary, formal attire required.
TTT Pane Vino, Semiramis Intercontinental Hotel, Corniche El-Nil, T02-7957171. Open 1300-0100. Serves pizza and pasta, surprising modern metal and glass decor for an Italian restaurant.
TTT Paprika, 1129 Corniche El-Nil, T02-5789447. Open 1200-0100. Like the name

suggests, this place serves paprika- based dishes of mixed Egyptian and Hungarian food. Near the TV and Radio Building, it's not uncommon to spot local Egyptian celebrities like Omar Sharif on the premises.

TTT **Sea Market**, Conrad International, 1191 Corniche El-Nil, T02-5808430. Open 1900-0100. Reliably fresh tasty seafood in elegant environs, accompanied by live music on some nights.

TT **Abu Shakra**, 69 Sharia Qasr El-Eini, Downtown, T02-5316111, T02-5316222. Open 1200-0200. Among the most reputable and oldest of all local grills in Egypt. The late-lamented Muslim missionary Mohammed Mitwalli El-Shaarawi was said to order here frequently.

TT **Alfi Bey**, 3 Sharia El-Alfi, Downtown, in pedestrian precinct, T02-5771888. Open 0830-0200. Authentic Egyptian food, especially kebabs, koftas, lamb chops and shank, grilled and stuffed pigeon with pastas and rice. Smart waiters provide an efficient and friendly service, no alcohol served.

TT **Felfela**, 15 Sharia Hoda Sharawi, Downtown, T02-3922833, 3922751. Open 0800-0100. One of downtown's most popular tourist restaurants, serves good, clean, local food and beer in a dimly lit, funky environment. There is a branch in Giza near the pyramids, as well as a take away stand near the downtown restaurant.

TT **Fu Shing**, 28 Sharia Talaat Harb, Downtown, T02-5766184. A truly Egyptian-Chinese experience where the flavours of the Middle and Far East converge, if you can imagine it.

TT **Hard Rock Café** Royal Nile Tower, Corniche El-Nil, T02-5321277, 5321281. Open 1200-0400. The relatively recent grand opening of Hard Rock Café in Cairo was such an anticipated event that the Corniche was blocked for hours. You'll find all you expect from the place, standard specials, celebrity guitars, and funky costumes, live shows, karaoke, and theme nights. The dance floor gets kicking after midnight.

TT **Kowloon**, Cleopatra Hotel, 1st floor, Midan Tah Rir, T02-5759831. Open 1100-2300. Authentic Korean cuisine that delights even Korean patrons. A bit pricier than other mid-range options.

TT **Peking**, behind Diana Cinema, 14 Sharia Saraya El-Azbakia, T02-5912381. Open 1200-2400. Warm atmosphere under paper lanterns, extensive Chinese menu though not the most authentic. Some say ketchup is the secret ingredient of the sweet and sour sauce. Several chains around Cairo. The one in Zamalek features live music nightly.

T **Abu Tarek**, 40 Sharia Champollion, corner of Sharia Maarouf. Open 0800-2400. Serves up what is arguably the best *kushari* in town. A good place to land with an empty belly after 6 hrs of aimless wandering. If you've been worried about trying it on the street for fear of stomach upsets, rest assured that Abu Tarek is among the cleanest of kushari establishments.

T **Akher Sa'ai**, 8 Sharia El-Alfi. Open 24 hrs. An all-Egyptian vegetarian heaven. You can have a taste of every item they serve and pay less than E£15.

T **El-Tabei**, 31 Sharia Orabi, T02-5754211. Another cheap and good local favourite serving up mezze galore and, of course, *fuul* and *tameyya*.

T **Fatatri El-Tahrir**, 166 Sharia Tahrir, 1 block east of Midan Tah Rir. Open 0700-0100. Serves *fatir* both sweet and savoury; favoured with locals and travellers alike for being cheap, filling and open all night long.

T **Gad**, 2 locations: 13 Sharia 26 July, T02-5763583; and Midan Lazoghly, T02-7958677. Open 0900-0200. Always crowded and open late. Tasty, cheap local grub including, among other things, *fatir*, *fuul*, *tameyya*, and acclaimed liver sandwiches. Will deliver, almost anywhere.

Floating restaurants

Scarabee, Corniche El-Nil, alongside Helnan Shepheard, T02-3554481. Meals are from 1430-1630, 2000-2200, 2230-0030. The evening cruises include a belly dancer and band. E£90 per person.

Ahwas and cafés

Café Riche, 17 Sharia Talaat Harb. Classic café that has seen the face of virtually every Arab intellectual and artist of the last century. Renovations have altered the feel of the place and now it's more of a tourist haunt than a revolutionary den, but it's still worth a visit, especially if you can get the story from an old timer.

El-Horraya, Sharia El-Felaki, Downtown. You can smell the scent of coffee seeping out of this old institution from 3 blocks away. One of the few very local *ahwas* that serves beer. Everyone comes here, old and young, foreign and local to spew thoughts on the state of the country, play chess, and puff on the cheapest *shisha* in town (if sanitation is a concern, bring your own mouthpiece as they are not provided here). Women are welcome, but will be more comfortable if dressed conservatively and accompanied by a man.

Groppi's, Midan Talaat Harb, Downtown. This landmark used to be the place to meet, but the recent renovations have dimmed the classic café's former charm. The coffee isn't great but the pastries are ok, and with several chains sprouting up around the city, the location is often agreeable when you're ready for a break.

Zamalek *maps pp71, 124*

TTT Ciao Italia, *Gezira Sheraton*, T02-3411333. Open 1200-1500 and 1900-2400. Excellent cuisine, well-presented food, slick service. Desserts are superb. Very expensive.

TTT The Four Corners, 4 Sharia Hassan Sabri, Zamalek. Something for every palate with several restaurants, all offering 5-star service and superb beautifully presented cuisine in restaurants with true ambience.

TTT Justine, T02-7362961. Open 1230-1500 and 2000-2300. Noted for high quality French food.

TTT La Bodega, 157 Sharia 26 July (1st floor), T02-7362183, 7361115. Open 1200-0200. Excellent and arty international cuisine amongst an amiable, mustardy ambience featuring rotating works from local artists. The bar is cosy and well-stocked, with a vibrant evening happy hour. There's also a separate lounge with plush leather chairs and private rooms. Popular with local expats. The desserts are delicious.

TTT La Piazza, T02-7362961. Open 1230-0030. Brings Italy to Egypt. The deserts in particular are stellar.

TTT Seafood Market, Saraya El-Gezira, T02-7378300, 7376800. Open 1100-0200. Seafood with a Thai twist, family-orientated dining environs.

TT Abu as-Sid, 157 Sharia 26 July, Zamalek, T02-7359640. Open 1300-0200. Authentic Egyptian cuisine served in a substantially classier – and more expensive – space than your average koshari joint. Egyptian men admit that Abu as-Sid is as close as it gets to their mum's cooking. Try the *molokhayia*, a uniquely Egyptian slimy green soup. Their choice of house music is also splendid. Minimum charge E£30.

TT Ali Hassan El-Hati, 8 Sharia 26 July. Open 1100-2200. Another among the ranks of the best local grills. The fish and kebab are particularly worthy of mention.

TT L'Aubergine, 5 Sharia Sayed El-Bakry, T02-7380080. Open 1100-0200. The only officially vegetarian restaurant in Cairo. *L'Aubergine* changes its menu almost every 2 weeks. Maybe you can catch the peanut butter burger before they replace it with something more eccentric. The mushroom quartet is an old-time classic that never seems to move. There's also a modest separate menu for carnivores. Downstairs, the vibe is laidback, dimly lit and mellow. The bar above starts kicking around 2200. Popular with local expats.

TT Hana, Sharia Mohamed Mazhar, T02-7382972. Open 1200-1100. A fairly authentic Korean restaurant that also serves some Chinese dishes. The *kimchi* and hot and sour soup are good. One of the few restaurants in town that cooks up edible tofu. Serves beer.

TT Maison Thomas, 157 Sharia 26 July, T02-7357057. Open 24 hours. Bistro and pizzeria. The most authentic Italian pizza in Egypt. The caramel chocolate cake and cheesecake are scrumptious if you have room for dessert. The place can use a better ventilation system, but the cheap delicious food compensates, and they deliver. Branches also open in Heliopolis and Mohandiseen.

TT Roy's, Marriott Hotel. Open 1200-2400. Serves American-style burgers and some Mexican food. A good place to go if your kids want a taste of home.

TT White, 25 Sharia Hassan Assem, T012-2304404. Open 1200-0300. Going for a 70s-esque theme, this all-white new loungey dive is popular among rich young Cairenes. Besides the bar, there's an eclectic menu offering such delights as salmon spinach crêpes alongside fresh sushi. A goat's cheese and caper kind of place.

T Dido's Al Dente, 26 Sharia Bahgat Ali, Zamalek, T02-7359117. Open 1000-0130. This cute little pasta place can use more space, but if you're in the mood for tasty cheap Italian fare, it's worth the cram. Popular with AUC students who live in the hostel nearby.

Zamalek Restaurant, 118 Sharia 26 July, near intersection with Sharia Al Aziz Osman. Open 0600-0200. A sit down *fuul* and *ta'ameyya* joint on Zamalek's main drag.

Floating restaurants

Fish Market, Marriot Marina, Sharia Saraya El-Gezira, Zamalek, T02-7358888. Open 1300- 0100. Serves fresh tasty expensive seafood upon the river Nile. Also a branch in Mohandiseen.

Le Pacha, on Le Pacha 1901, 1901 Sharia Saraya El-Gezira, T02-7356730. Open 0700-0300. Superb east Asian cuisine on the floating, not cruising, Pacha, a delightful, albeit pricey dining experience.

Le Steak, on Le Pacha 1901, Sharia Saraya El-Gezira, T02-3406730. Open 1200-0200. An elegant Nile River boat, steaks plain or with all the trimmings. Book to get a river view seat.

The Nile Maxim, T02-3408888. Two nightly cruises at 2000 and 2300; weekend lunch at 1430. Wide choice of menu, fish specialities, live entertainment and show at weekends, moored opposite entrance to Cairo Marriott Hotel.

Ahwas and cafés

Garden Promenade Café, Marriott Hotel, Zamalek. A large and lovely outdoor café shaded by trees overflowing with singing birds. A nice place to come for some peace and beauty in the middle of the city. Popular with Gulf Arab tourists. Alcohol, mezze and coffee on offer. Expensive.

Simonds, Sharia 26 July, Zamalek. Open 0730-2130. One of the oldest stand-up coffee shops in Cairo. The deteriorating surroundings reflect the age. Famous for its cappuccino.

Islamic Cairo *p87, map p88*

Naguib Mafouz Restaurant and Khan El-Khalili café, 5 Sikkit El-Badestan, 40 m west from El-Hussein Mosque, Khan El-Khalili, T02-5903788. Open 1000-2000. The classiest place to breath after a day's wander through Islamic Cairo. Oberoi- managed (with a/c), serves western and Egyptian mezze and meals. Prices for tea and coffee are inflated, but the surroundings justify going. Live oriental music is featured on occasion. Minimum charge E£15.

Egyptian Pancake House, 7 Midan El-Azhar, T02-5908623. *Fiteer* galore, savoury and sweet. Tuna, cheese, eggs, meat, chicken, cream, and even turkey cock are available fillings. Price range from E£10-15 depending on size and filling.

Zizo, Midan Bab El-Futouh, T02-5926530. Open 1200-0700. Facing the north wall of Islamic Cairo. Said to have the best liver sausage and fried brain in town. There's a shabby indoor sitting area, and outside seating opposite Bab El-Futouh. Very cheap and open through the night.

Ahwas and cafés

Fishawi's, smack bang in the middle of Khan El-Khalili. Open all the time. Fishawi's is Cairo's longest-standing *ahwa*, claiming never to have closed since it first opened in 1773. If you only go to one coffee shop in Egypt, let it be this one. The place is filled with atmosphere, dangling chandeliers, cracked mirrors and characters that have been here for decades. *Shisha*, fresh juice, tea and Turkish coffee.

Mohandiseen

Flux, 2 Sharia Gam'et El-Nasr, off Sharia El-Khartoum, T02-3386601. Open 1900-0200. One of Cairo's chicest restaurants. Serves international fusion dishes in an arty, intimate, dimly lit setting. Minimum charge E£50.

Papillon, Sharia 26 July, T02-3471672, 3035045. Open 1200-0100. An authentic Lebanese experience. Come hungry and order as many mezze as you can stomach.

Raousha & Kandahar, 3 Sharia Gam'et El-Dewal, T02-3030615. 1200-2400. Another Oberoi-owned restaurant split in two. Lebanese and Indian cuisine. Overlooks one of the busiest streets in Cairo. Attentive service.

Ataturk, 20 Sharia Riyadh, T02-3475135. Open 1000-0200. Turkish food, served with steaming fresh bread. No alcohol. There's a branch in Heliopolis.

Cortigiano, 44 Sharia Michel Bakhum. Open 1300-0100. Pizzas and Italian specialities continue to delight customers. Hefty portions. Good choice of desserts. No alcohol. Has a branch in Dokki.

Maroush, 64 Midan Lebanon, T02-3450972. Open 0900-0200. Restaurant and *ahwa*. Large comfortable outdoor seating area overlooking the midan. Authentic Lebanese cuisine. Most people come here for *shisha* and tea, and order some mezze to accompany. A very local place. No alcohol served.

ΨΨ Mr Maxim, Sharia El-Shaheed Abdel Moneim Riyadh, T02-3606121. Open 1200-0200. Wide range of decent food including French, Lebanese, Moroccan and Greek food, and sea food specialities.

ΨΨ Tia Maria, 32 Sharia Jeddah. Open 1200-0100. A quiet Italian restaurant. All meals are made with fresh meats and vegetables. Seafood dishes are unconventional and creative. Live entertainment some nights.

Ψ El Omda, 6 Sharia El-Gezira, behind Atlas Hotel, T02-3452387. Open 1200-0200. Famous for traditional food, especially *fuul* and *koshari*, served very speedily. For carnivores, try the kebab, kofta and shish tawook.

Ahwas and cafés

Coffee Roastery, Sharia Nady El-Seed, Mohandiseen, T02-7498882, 7600735. 0730-2430. Western-style coffee shop with extensive breakfast and drinks menu. Good lattes and a/c. Offers respite that local *ahwas* can't.

Tornado, 3 Midan Aswan, Mohandiseen, T02-3454394, 3461500. Open 1000-0200. Juice bar, crêpes, good coffee and tea, and *shisha*. A local *ahwa* with western flair, appeals to young Cairene hipsters. E£15 minimum charge.

Giza and Pyramids *p75*

ΨΨΨ Amici, 20 Sharia El-Haram, T02-3830088. Open 1000-0100. Spanish/ Italian food spiced with a view of the Pyramids. Best choice is the seafood, choose your own fish. Limited takeaway menu. Price reflects the location so stay and eat.

ΨΨΨ Moghul Room, Mena House Oberoi, T02-3833222. Open 1200-1445 and 1930-2345. Authentic Indian food, sophisticated atmosphere, live Indian entertainment every evening.

ΨΨ Christo, 10 Sharia El-Haram. Open 1100-0300. Another choose-your-own-seafood restaurant with a view of the Pyramids. Often busy at lunchtimes with tour groups.

Ψ Andreya, 59 Mariuteya Canal, T02-3831133. Known for its pigeon dishes. Outdoor eating. A family-friendly place with lots of open space for children to play.

Floating restaurants

Golden Pharaoh, 138 Sharia El-Nil, Giza, T02-5701000. Cruising times are 1430-1630, 2015-2215, 2245-0045. With distinctive gold painted hulls, the Golden Pharaoh is operated by the Oberoi Hotel. Plan to arrive early and call to confirm times, as they shift with the season. Lunch cruises feature live Middle Eastern music. Dinner cruises feature a belly dancer.

Airport and Heliopolis *p68*

ΨΨΨ Al-Sarraya, Movenpick Hotel, T02-2470077. Open 1800-2400. Gourmet French cuisine specializing in seafood, live piano.

ΨΨΨ Baalabak, Sonesta Hotel, 4 Sharia El- Tayarn, T02-2625111. 1900-0300. This is a place where you can find good Lebanese food and live entertainment. Live show starts at 2230.

ΨΨΨ Chinois, Sheraton Heliopolis, T02-2677730. Open 1300-0100. East Asian cuisine, stir fried at the table. Leave room for fried toffee bananas. Good service.

ΨΨΨ Starlight, Baron Hotel, 8 Sharia Maahad El-Sahari. Open 1930-0030. International food, panoramic views.

ΨΨ Chantilly, 11 Sharia Baghdad, T02-2907303. Open 0700-2400. In the centre of Heliopolis, a long-standing establishment popular with wealthier locals. Continental menu with a good salad bar. Serves alcohol.

ΨΨ Chili's, 18 Sharia El-Thawra, T02-4188048. Open 1100-0100. Spicy, and perhaps overpriced, Mexican food served up in huge portions. Large outdoor patio with cooling fans. Popular hangout spot in Heliopolis after the sun sets. Extensive dessert menu, including banana splits and brownies. No alcohol.

ΨΨ Mashawina, 3 Sharia Abdel Moneim Hafez, T02-4158442. Open 1300-0100. Lebanese grilled food and extensive *mezze* menu, though limited choices for vegetarians. Good value.

Ψ El-Shabrawi, Sharia El-Ibrahimy. Features a huge salad bar, all the traditional *mezza*, and possibly the best *fuul* and *ta'amiya* in Cairo. You can't get any more local. A safe bet for sensitive stomachs.

Bars and clubs

Central Cairo *p114, map p126*

After Eight, 6 Sharia Qasr El-Nil (past a kiosk down a little alley), T02-5740855, 5765199. Open 1200-0300. A new hotspot on the downtown scene, this smoky little dive is one of few places in Cairo to hear good live music. Right now, a funky eclectic band called *Wust El-Balad* (Downtown) plays Arabic-Latin jazz you can dance to every Sun and Thu in a packed house. The owners plan to add new bands in the months to come. There is a cover charge of E£60 on Thu and E£40 on Sun (spend it as you wish, just spend it). Fully stocked bar, a bit pricey, standard mid-range menu serving variety of meats and pastas through the night.
Barrel Lounge, Sharia Alfi Bey, on the first floor of the *Windsor Hotel*. A truly delightful place for a drink. The bar staff are friendly and the ambience charming despite, or perhaps because of, the fading anglo decor.
Crazy House, Cairo Land Entertainment Centre, T02-3661082. Popular among drug-crazed young local folk.
Hard Rock Café, see page 132. Also offers space to boogie.
High Heels; Jazz Up, Nile Hilton, Downtown. Another new bar in town, classier than most. Set outdoors amid dim lights and huge fans that maintain a perpetual breeze. Popular with sophisticated expatriot Cairenes.
Jacky's, a much-frequented disco among locals and expats, is in the same hotel if you're interested in a late night.
Le Grillon, 8 Sharia Qasr El-Nil, Downtown; T02-5764959, open 1200-0300. Delightful covered garden, restaurant, bar and ahwa, very popular spot for local intellectuals and artists. Conversations about revolutions and poetry continue into the wee hours of the morn over shisha and beer. The food is mid-priced and quite good, lots of meats, soups and salads, fairly standard Egyptian fare. It's a local place that is comfortable for single women.
Odeon Rooftop Bar, Odeon Palace Hotel, 6 Sharia Abdel Hamid Said. Open 24 hrs and offers a great view of the city. A nice place to come to wind down after a rowdy evening.

See also 'Hotel discos' below.

Local drinking holes

Locals' bars are generally haunted by men only, and not recommended for women on their own. Try:
El-Horraya, (see page 132);
Cafeteria Stella, downtown on the corner of Sharia Talaat Harb and Hoda Sha'arawi. This tiny hole-in-the-wall of a bar is as local as it gets. On offer: basic mezze, E£7.50 stella, and rum and brandy which is probably better avoided. As the government forbids the word 'bar' in the names of establishments, most go under the guise of 'cafeteria'.
Cafeteria Honololo, Sharia Mohammed Farid across the street from Pension Roma. A taste of Cairo's seediest: Stella, sheesha, Heinekein, and bar girls.
Carrol Restaurant, 12 Sharia Qasr El-Nil. The food is expensive and the ambience extraordinarily gaudy. After midnight, there's a live show, performed by the only women who frequent the place.

Hotel discos

Most 4- and 5-star hotels have discos that appeal to a range of affluent and Westernized Egyptians.
Castle, Helnan Shepheard, T02-7921000, open 2200-0400;
Churchill, Baron Hotel, Heliopolis, T02-2915757, open 2200-0300, closed Mon;
Jacky's, Nile Hilton, T02-5780444, has a dance floor that is usually hopping after midnight;
Saddle, Mena House Oberoi, Giza, T02-3833444, requires E£40 to enter.

Zamalek *map p124*

Cairo Jazz Club, 197 Sharia 26 July, Mohandiseen, T02-3459939. The place in town for live local music. Each night has a theme or regular act. Find the schedule in *Cairo Times*. Loungey and hip, with plush decor and a small dance floor that doubles as a stage. On occasion there's real jazz, and it's often quite good.
Deals, 2 Sharia El-Maahad El-Swissri, Zamalek. A noisy buzzing basement-like bar with cheap beer and lots of fried fare.
Harry's Pub in Cairo Marriott Hotel. A

longtime hotspot for Cairo's expat gay community, this classy wood-panelled pub has karaoke on some nights and serves good continental food at reasonable prices.
Pub 28, 28 Sharia Shagar Al-Durr, Zamalek. One of the oldest pubs in Zamalek. Attracts an older crowd of expats and gay men, wood panelling, loud music, cheap beer and bar food. Always crowded, dark and smoky. Restaurants that double as late-night bars include: **La Bodega**, with a great early evening happy hour; the **Hard Rock Café** (which also has dance floor), **Aubergine**, a black box bar popular with local university students and **White**, a slick and pricey uptown bar.

Entertainment

Bellydancing shows

Besides floating restaurants, ritzier hotels house the main venues for bellydancing shows. There's usually a cover charge (E£100-300, depending on the venue) that includes the show and a multi-course meal. At present, the **Semiramis Intercontinental**, T02-7957171, hosts the most acclaimed dancer in town, every Thu night.
Other 5-star hotel venues that feature belly dancing include:
Aladin and **Casablanca**, Cairo Sheraton Hotel, T02-3369700, shows on Sun and Fri, 2000-2400;
Barracuda, Le Méridien Heliopolis, T02-2905055, shows on Thu only;
Empress, Cairo Marriott, T02-7358888, shows on Sat, Mon, Thu;
La Belle Epoque, Le Méridien Cairo Hotel, T02-3621717;
Shishow, Sheraton Heliopolis Hotel, T02-2677730, open 1000-0400, closed Mon.

Casinos

Found in the following hotels (make sure you bring your passport):
Cairo Heliopolis Movenpick, **Cairo Marriott**, **Cairo Sheraton**, **El-Giza Sheraton**, **Mena House Oberoi**, **Nile Hilton**, **Ramses Hotel**, **Semiramis Intercontinental**, **Helnan Shepheard Hotel** and **Sheraton Heliopolis**.

Cinemas

Current information on cinema performances is given in the *Egyptian Gazette*, *Cairo Times* and the monthly glossy *Egypt Today* magazine. Commercial cinemas change their programmes every Mon so check the schedule. Arabic films rarely have subtitles. The World Trade Centre offers two venues, **Upstairs** and **Katcho's**.

Cinema in English

Al Tahrir, 122 Sharia Al-Tahrir, Dokki, T02-3354726. Daily at 1000, 1300, 1500, 1800, 2100.
Cairo Sheraton, Sharia Giza, T02-7606081.
Cosmos 1 and Cosmos 2, 12 Sharia Emad El-Din, Downtown, T02-5742177. Shows at 1030, 1300, 1530, 1830 and 2130.
Drive In, entrance to Shourouk City, Cairo-Ismailia Desert Rd, T02-4971400.
El Haram, 147 Sharia El-Haram, near the Pyramids, T02-3858358. Shows at 1230, 1530, 1830, and 2130; midnight shows Thu, Fri and Sat.
French Cultural Centre, 1 Sharia Maddraset El-Huquq El-Faransiya, Mounira, T02-7953725. Start at 1900, English subtitles.
Goethe Institute, 5 Sharia El-Bustan, Downtown, T02-5759877. Start at 1830 with English subtitles.
Italian Cultural Centre, 3 Sharia Sheikh El-Marsafi, Zamalek, T02-7358791.
Karim I/Karim II, 15 Sharia Emad El-Din, Downtown, T02-5924830. Shows at 1000, 1300, 1500, 1800 and 2100.
Metro, 35 Sharia Talaat Harb, Downtown, T02-3937566.
MGM, 4th Floor Maadi Grand Mall, T02-5195388. Shows at 1230, 1530, 1830 and 2130, with midnight shows Thu and Fri.
Odeon, Downtown, T02-5765642.
Ramses Hilton Cinema, 7th floor of the hotel's shopping annexe, T02-5747436.
Tiba 1 & Tiba 2, 75 Sharia El-Nasr, Nasr City, T02-2621089.

Galleries

Cairo Opera House Art Gallery, Gezira, T02-7398131. Daily from 0900-1600 and 1630-2030, except Fri.
Faculty of Fine Arts, Helwan University, 4 Sharia Mohammed Thakib, Zamalek, T02-7357570.
French Cultural Centre, 27 Sharia Sabri Abu Alam, Midan Ismailia, T02-7953725.
Hannager Arts Centre, Opera House Grounds, Zamalek, T02-735686. Daily 1000-2200.
Khan El-Maghraby Gallery, 18 Sharia El-Mansour Mohammed, Zamalek, T02-7353349. Saily except Sun, 1030-2100.
Mashrabiya Gallery, 8 Sharia Champollion, T02-5784494. Daily, except Fri 1100-2000.
Townhouse Gallery for Contemporary Art, 10 Nabrawi St off Champollion, Zamalek, T02-5768600.

Sound and light shows

Three performances daily at the Sphinx and Pyramids, Giza: at 1830, 1930 and 2030 in winter; 2030, 2130, 2230 in summer. Entrance E£33. Information T02-3841062.
Mon: English/French/Spanish
Tue: English/Italian/French
Wed: English/French/German
Thu: Japanese/English/Arabic
Fri: English/French
Sat: English/Spanish/Italian
Sun: Russian/French/German

Theatres

Current information for theatre performances is given in the *Egyptian Gazette*, *Cairo Times* and the monthly *Egypt Today*. Apart from the Opera House, all performances are likely to be in Arabic.
Balloon Theatre, Sharia Corniche El-Nil, El-Agouza, near Al-Zamalek Bridge, T02-3471718.
El-Fann Theatre, 22 Sharia Ramses, Downtown, T02-5782444.
El-Felaki Theatre, The American University in Cairo, T02-7976373.
El-Gomhouriya Theatre, T02-3907707.
El-Haram Theatre, Sharia El-Haram, Giza, T02-3863952.
El-Talee'a Theatre, T02-5937948.
Hannager Theatre, on Opera House grounds, T02-7356861.
The National Theatre, Midan Ataba, T02-5917783.
Opera House, in the Gezira Exhibition Grounds at the end of Qasr El-Nil bridge, T02-7398132. Has a hall with 1,200 seats for opera, ballet and classical music performances, a second hall with 500 seats for films and conferences and an open air theatre. Advance booking recommended. Men must wear jacket and tie.
Puppet Theatre, Azbakiah, El-Ataba, T02-5910954.
Zamalek Theatre, 13 Shagaret El-Dorr and Sharia 26 July, Zamalek, T02-7360660.

Festivals and events

Jan International Book Fair. (7) Christmas, Coptic Church. (19) **Epiphany**, Coptic Church.
Mar International Fair: Annual Spring Flower Show.
Apr (7) Easter, Coptic Church. (15) Annunciation, Coptic and Roman Catholic.
Jun Pentecost, Coptic Church.
Jul International Festival of Documentary Films.
Aug International Song Festival. Nile Festival Day at Giza.
Sep International Festival of Vanguard Theatre. Nile Festival Day in Cairo.
Nov International Children's Book Fair at Nasr City.
Dec Festival for Arab Theatre. Festival of Impressionist Art (alternate years). International Film Festival.

Shopping

Clothes

Egypt's low labour costs mean that a number of western clothing chains manufacture high quality cotton goods in the country including: **Benetton**, **Naf Naf**, and **Mexx**. Prices are considerably lower than in the West. Visit Cairo's trendiest shopping mall, **The World**

Trade Centre, 1191 Corniche El-Nil, Maspero, for the full selection.
Atlas, near Nagib Mahfouz Café in Khan El-Khalili, T02-5906139. Moiré silk handmade shoes. Or try in the **Semiramis Intercontinental Hotel**.

Crafts and souvenirs

Among the most attractive areas to shop is the **Khan El-Khalili Bazaar** and **Sagh** comprising an array of shops dating from the 14th century. Renowned for craftsmanship in silver and gold, embroidered cloth, copper ware, leather and ivory inlaid goods. (Remember that the import of ivory is forbidden into most Western countries.) The Kerdassa village, east of Giza, is noted for its embroidered cotton and silk dresses, *galabeyas*, and other handmade goods while Haraneya, west of Giza, is the main centre for quality carpets. See Shopping in Essentials for more info on shopping.

Bookshops

As the largest publisher of Arabic books in the world, Cairo is a haven for Arabic literature enthusiasts. There are dozens of bookshops scattered around downtown. For secondhand books, (some of which are in English) try the huge book market in the northeast conre of Azbekiya Gardens, by Midan Ataba. The following are shops selling books and periodicals in European languages:
Academic Bookshop, 121 Sharia El-Tahrir, Dokki, T02-7485282, open daily 1000-1900, Thu 1000-1500, Fri off;
Al-Ahram, 165 Sharia Mohammed Farid, Downtown, in Nile Hilton, open daily 0900-1700, closed Fri;
American University in Cairo Bookstore, Mohamed Mahmoud St, Downtown, on main campus, T02-7975377, open 0830-1700, Sat 1030-1700, closed Fri, Sat evening and all Aug (also has a store in Sharia Mohammed in Thakeb, Zamalek, T02-7397045, open 1000-1700, in addition to an extra hour on Tue, Wed, and Thu, closed Fri);
Anglo-Egyptian Bookshop, 165 Sharia Mohammed Farid, Downtown, T02-3914337, open 0900-1330 and 1630-2000, closed Sun;
Baron Books, Méridien Heliopolis Hotel, T02-2915757, open 0830-2330;
Dar El-Bustan, 29 Sharia Faggala, Downtown, T02-5908025, open 0900-1700, closed Sun;
Diwan, 159 Sharia 26 July, T02-7362578, open daily, 0900-2300, coffee shop inside, children's literature section, French, English and Arabic books on offer, occasional cultural events in the evenings;
El-Shoroque, Midan Talaat Harb, Downtown, T02-3938071, 3912480, open 0900-2200 daily;
Lehnert & Landrock, 44 Sharia Sherif, T02-3927606, open 0930-1330 and 1530-1930, closed Sat afternoon and Sun. Books in German and English;
Livres de France, 36 Sharia Qasr El-Nil, T02-3935512, open 1000-1900, Sat 1000-0130, closed Sun, Ma'adi branch at 2 Road 23, near Ma'adi Grandmall, opens daily 1100-1900, except Sun;
Madbouli, Midan Tala'at Harb, Downtown, T02-5756421, open daily, 0900-2300;
Readers' Corner, 33 Sharia Abd El-Khalek Tharwat, T02-3928801, open 1000-1500, closed Sun;
Zamalek Bookstore, 19 Sharia Shagaret El-Dorr, open 0830-2000, closed Sun.

Activities and tours

Bowling

Cairo Land, 1 Sharia Salem. 1000-0100.
El Omana'a, 125 Sharia El-Nil, Giza, T02-3361637.
International Bowling Centre, Behind 6 October Panorama, Salah Salem.
Maadi Family Land, Corniche El-Nil. 1000-0200.
MISR Bowling Centre, 9th floor, Al Bustan Centre, Bab El-Louk.

Diving instruction

Maadi Divers, 18 Rd 218, Maadi, T02-5198644.
Nautilus Diving, 4 Sharia Omar Shabban, off Sharia El-Nozha, Ard El-Golf, Heliopolis, T02-4176515.
Seascapes Diving and Safari, 1/2 Sharia Lasilky, New Maadi, T02-5194930, www.seascapesegypt.com.

Golf

Katameya Heights Golf Course, 23 km southeast of Cairo. Here the annual membership is E£5,000 with a restriction of 600 players. Currently it has 18 holes with another 9 being constructed.
Mina House Oberoi, Pyramid Park Sofitel.

Gym and health clubs

Cairo Sheraton Health Club, Cairo Sheraton Hotel, Galaa Square, Giza, T02-3369700/800 ext 599/177. Fully Equipped gymnasium and other facilities.
Creative Dance and Fitness Centre (for adults and children), Samia Alouba, 6 Sharia Amr, off Sharia Syria, Mohandiseen, T02-3020572. Gym, steam room, gymnastics, martial arts, and fitness classes.
Golden Tulip Flamenco Hotel Health Club, 2 Sharia El-Gezira El-Wosta, Zamalek, T02-7350815. Open from 0800-2200, closed Sun. Gymnasium, sauna, jacuzzi, and massage.
Gold's Gym, 8th and 9th floor, Maadi Palace Mall, T02-3803601, 3588634. 3,000 sq m including a mixed gender gym and a ladies only gym and 2 pools.
Health Club, Siag Pyramids Hotel, Saqqara Rd, Giza, T02-3856022, 3853005. Gymnasium, sauna, massage, swimming pool and tennis courts.
Nile Hilton Health Club, Nile Hilton Hotel, Midan Tah Rir, T02-5780444/666 ext 207. Gymnasium, sauna, Turkish bath and massage. Separate sections for men and women, tennis, squash, swimming.
Sacha, 29 Sharia Ahmed Hishmat, Zamalek, T02-7356167. Aromatherapy, reflexology, acupressure, nutrition, personal training, aerobics and gymnasium.
Spa and Wellness Centre, Four Seasons Hotel Cairo at the First Residence, T02-5672040. Full-service spa, eight treatment rooms and extensive exercise facilities. Specializes in Cleopatra milk baths, Nefertiti facials, papyrus wraps and private spa for couples.

Horse riding

It's most pleasant to ride in the desert by the pyramids, particularly for sunrise or sunset. Avoid the haggard-looking horses lined up for tourists by the pyramid's gate and head for the stables in Kafr El-Gabal (straight on past the entrance to the Sound and Light). **AA Stables** and **MG Stables** are the most highly recommended, have regular western clients, and offer a variety of excursions from the standard hour-long ride around the pyramids (E£15), riding lessons (E£20 per hour) to a trip to Saqqara (E£60). More elaborate excursions and night rides need to be booked in advance.

Swimming

Use the pools at the hotels. Those in the 5-star establishments cost more. **Heliopolis**, **Giza** and **Gezira** sporting clubs have pools. In the Heliopolis club, daily (E£20) and monthly (E£250) membership available. Public pools are cheap, but not always clean. Hotels with good pools include: **Marriott Hotel** in Zamalek (E£65 per day); **Pyramids Park Inter-Continental** Cairo-Alexandria Desert Rd;
Semi-Ramis Intercontinental, Downtown (E£84 per day).

Tennis

Katameya Tennis Resort, 23 km southeast of Cairo. Has 10 clay and 2 grass courts.

Tour operators

Abercrombie and Kent, 5 Sharia Bustan, Tahrir, T02-3936255.
American Express, 21 Sharia Giza, Nile Tower Building, T02-3703411.
Astra Travel, 15 Sharia Demashk, Mohandiseen, T02-3446445.
Etam Tours, 3 Sharia Qasr El-Nil, T02-5754721. Egyptian Tourism and Medical Services. Ask for Dr Bishara. A long-established firm offering specialized handling of disabled visitors.
Gaz Tours, 7 Sharia Bustan, Downtown, T02-5752782.
Hermes Travel, 310a Sharia Sudan, Sahafeyeen, T02-3451474.
Isis Travel, 48 Sharia Giza, Orman Bldg, T02-7494326.
Mena Tours, El-Nasr Bldg, Sharia El-Nil, Giza, T02-5740864, and 14 Sharia Talaat Harb, T02-3962497.

Misr Travel, 1 Sharia Talaat Harb, T02-3930010, and 7 Sharia Talaat Harb, T02-3930168.
Seti First Travel Co, 16 Sharia Ismail Mohammed, Zamalek.
Spring Tours, 11 Sharia Talaat Harb, T02-3922627.
Thomas Cook Overseas. Head Office: Sharia Nabil El-Waqqad, Ard El-Golf, Heliopolis, T02-4171363; 7 Sharia Baghdad, El-Korba, Heliopolis, T02-4173511-4, 4140625/6; 17 Sharia Mahmoud Bassiouny, T02-5743955/3967, 5743776; Forte Grand Pyramids Hotel, Cairo-Alexandria Rd, T02-3822688; 10 Sharia 26 July, Mohandiseen, T02-3467187.

Transport

Air

Cairo International Airport, is 15 km northeast of Midan Tah Rir in downtown Cairo. Cairo is a popular stop en route from the East to the West and Terminal 2 serves most international airlines. **Egypt Air**, which operates mainly from Terminal 1, offers regular flights to the following domestic destinations: **Abu Simbel** (US$242), **Alexandria** (US$58), **Assuit** (US$87), **Aswan** (US$184), **El-Arish** (US$87), **Hurghada** (US$138), **Luxor** (US$135), **Marsa Alam** (US$184), **Kharga** (US$150), **Sharm El-Sheikh** (US$138) and **Taba** (US$161). Approximate round-trip prices are quoted.

Airline offices

Air Canada, 26 Sharia Mahmoud Bassiouny, T02-5758939, daily 0900-1700. **Air France**, 2 Midan Talaat Harb, T02-5758899. **Air Sinai**, Nile Hilton Hotel, T02-5760739, 5772949, daily 0830-1930. **Alitalia**, Nile Hilton Hotel, T02-5765127, 5767109. **Austrian Airlines**, 5th Floor, 4 Sharia El-Gezira, Zamalek, T02-7352777, Mon-Thu and Sun 0830-1630. **British Airways**, 1 Sharia Abdel Salam Aref, Midan Tah Rir, T02-5780742, daily 0800-1600. **CSA Czech Airlines**, 9 Sharia Talaat Harb, T02-3920463, 3930395. **Cyprus Airways**, 10 Sharia Talaat Harb, T02-5797300, 7400, 7500, daily 0900-1630. **Delta**, 17 Sharia Ismail Mahmoud, Zamalek, T02-7362039, 7359770, daily except Fri 0830-1700. **EgyptAir**, 9 Sharia Talaat Harb, T02-3932836, T02-3927664, or Nile Hilton, T02-5793049. El-Al, 5 Sharia El-Makrizi, Zamalek, T02-7361795, daily except Fri 0830-1700. **Emirates**, 18 Sharia El-Batal Ahmed Abdel Aziz, Mohandeseen, T02-3361555, daily 0830-1700. **Ethiopian Airlines**, Nile Hilton Arcade, T02-5740603, daily 0900-1330. **Iberia**, 15 Midan Tah Rir, T02-5795700, (Airport T02-4177297). **KLM/ Kenya Airways**, 11 Sharia Qasr El-Nil, Cairo, T02-5805700- 5747-5757. **Lufthansa**, 6 Sharia El-Sheikh El-Marsafi, Zamalek, Cairo, T02-7398339, Mon-Thu and Sun 0830-1630. **Malaysia Airlines**, Nile Hilton Arcade, T02-5799714-5, daily except Fri 0900-1630. **Malev**, 5 Sharia Talaat Harb, T02-3915083, Mon-Thu, Sat and Sun 0900-1600, Fri 1130-1300. **Olympic Airways**, 23 Sharia Qasr El-Niel, T02-3931318, daily 0830-1600. **Orascom Aviation** (charter to El-Gouna), 66 Sharia Abuel Mahassen El-Shazli, Agouza, T02-3052401. **Royal Air Maroc**, 9 Sharia Talaat Harab, Downtown, T02-3934574. **Singapore Airlines**, Nile Hilton Arcade, T02-5750276, daily 0900-1600. **Swiss Airlines**, 4 Mamar Behler, off Sharia Qasr El-Nil, T02-3961733-734. **Tunis Air**, 14 Sharia Talaat Harb, Cairo, T02-5753420, (Airport 2680188). **Turkish Airways**, Nile Hilton Arcade, T02-3804451, daily except Fri 0900-1700.

Bus

Local

Only recommended for the truly adventurous or extremely broke traveller, public buses in Cairo guarantee an experience to write home about. The old buses are ancient gas-spewing sardine tanks, stuffed with dirt and humanity. That said, the public bus network succeeds surprisingly well in connecting the labyrinth of streets that make up Cairo's many boroughs. Before setting off, beware: except for the main hubs in **Tah Rir**, **Ramsis** and **Ataba** where the lines start and stop, the buses often fail to come to complete stops and require extraordinary agility to mount and descend. When mounting a bus, get on from the back, pay your ticket to the attendant and plan to descend from the front. Since they're so cheap and the way most Cairenes get around, buses are always crowded – especially during commuting hours from 0700-1000 and 1500-1900. Be mindful of yourself and your belongings as pickpockets and groping may occur. Note that bus numbers are generally posted above the dashboard or on a plate in the window. Do not confuse the vehicle identification number (sometimes in English) with the route number. As bus numbers are not in English, it's a good idea to learn the numerals (read as in English from left to right). Some bus routes have slashes through the digits, which indicate a wholly different route. The slightly smaller and newer public buses are a bit more manageable since there is no standing room and only one door (not to be confused with the even smaller private microbuses which look more like vans). Buses operate daily from 0530 to 2430 with extended hours during Ramadan and cost 25-50p, minibuses cost 50p-E£1.

Minibuses

The **CTA** air-conditioned buses are significantly more comfortable and a good way to get to the airport and pyramids (pick-up from in front of the Egyptian Museum). They cost a flat E£2, no matter how far you ride. When in doubt, ask a station chief located in a box in the middle of all main bus hubs. They may not speak English, but state your destination and they'll point you in the right direction.

Long distance

Intercity Buses Cities in Egypt are well connected by buses that are quite comfortable and inexpensive. When tourist season is high, it's wise to buy tickets in advance, especially to key destinations like the Sinai and the North Coast. You must buy tickets at the bus station; phone reservations are still not possible. There are several bus stations in Cairo that cover different regions of Egypt. **Turgoman** is the main bus terminal. It's huge and offers service to virtually everywhere in Egypt (except El-Fayoum), and to international destinations. Ironically, though, it's not readily connected to public transport, but it's a frequent microbus stop and within walking distance of Ramsis (500 m). By taxi, it's a E£3 ride from Midan Tah Rir. **Aboud Station**, Sharia Ahmed Helmi 3 km north of Ramsis - a E£3 taxi ride from Ramsis, E£5 from Downtown, or a quick microbus hop, operates daily buses at least once an hour from 0600 to 2000 to **El-Fayoum**, the **Delta**, **Middle and Upper Egypt**, and **Alexandria** (Specific cities: **Alexandria**, **Damanhur**, **Tanta**, **Benha**, **Mansura**, **Damietta**, **Zagazig**, **Fayoum**, **Mina**, **Assuit**, **Sohag**, **Luxor** and **Aswan**). Note that those going to Middle and Upper Egypt may want to opt for the comparably cheap and significantly more comfortable and convenient train.

Major bus companies

Superjet, T02-2660214/2 (in Turgoman behind East Delta area) a step above in quality and price, operates buses to prime tourist destinations and to international destinations in **Jordan**, **Israel**, **Saudi Arabia**. **West Delta**, T02-6331846, 6351057 (Turgoman, Aboud). East Delta, T02-2611882/3 (Turgoman, Aboud), runs buses to the **Sinai**, the **Canal cities** and the **Delta**. Upper Egypt Travel, T02-5760261, (Turgoman), runs buses to the **oases**, **Luxor** and **Aswan**.

The following schedules are for your reference. Do not rely too heavily on them as times and prices change constantly in Egypt depending on the number of tourists and a million other variables. You can always call the respective bus station to inquire about departure times – try to have an Arabic speaker nearby as few operators are proficient in English. Note that prices are quoted in ranges because later buses tend to be a few pounds more expensive than early morning buses.

From Turgoman East Delta - Sinai Service To: **Taba**, then **Nuweiba** 0630, 0930, 1015 (E£55-E£58); **St Catherine** 1030 (E£37); **Sharm** 0630, 0715, 1000, 1300, 1500, 1700, 1900, 2300, 2330, 2400, 2415 (E£55-65); **Dahab**, continuing from Sharm 0715, 1300, 1700, 2415 (E£62-E£75); **El-Arish** 2 daily; **Delta** and **Canal Zone** at least every hour from early morning until 2000 to **Port Said**, **Suez**, **Ismailya**, **Mansura**, **Damietta**, **Tanta**, **Mahalla**.

West Delta operates buses every hour to **Alexandria**. Five buses go to **Marsa Matruh**: 0700, 0830, 1430, 2030, 2230 (E£30-36).

Cairo bus routes

Note that there are hundreds of buses, many of which go to these destinations and are not listed here. Ask, people will be thrilled to help you.

From Abdel Mounim Abd Riyad Bus Station (Near Metro: Sadat)
(2 'terminals' 1 – in front of Ramses Hilton; 2 – behind Egyptian Museum; M denotes Minibus)

To	Bus No	A/C (CTA) Bus No
Citadel	M154; 160 (1); 72 (1); 951 (2)	-
Heliopolis	M27; M35 (1); 940; 510 (2)	356
Pyramids/Harem	M82; M83 (1)	357; 355 (stops in front of E Museum)
Zamalek	M49 (1)	-
Mohandiseen	99 - Midan Lebnan (1); 363	-
Airport	M27 (2); 400 (2)	356 (2)
Al-Azhar/Khan	951 to Attaba, then 66; from here, 5 mins walk to Hussein	-
Moqattem	951; 983 (2)	-
Midan Giza	109; 124; 900 (1)	-
Attaba	951	-
Imbaba Airport	173; 174 (1)	-
Ramsis	Many including: M30;M35; M32;M27 (2)	-
Turgoman	M2 (2)	-
Badrasheen	987	

From Ramses (near Metro: Mubarak)
(M denotes Minibus)

To	Bus No	A/C Bus (CTA)
Attaba	M50; 401; 407; 160	-
Tah Rir/ Abdel M.	Many, M58; 95; 409	-
Citadel	M50;160; 174; 406	-
Heliopolis	940; 500; 400; 105 (from beside mosque in sq)	356
Airport	M27, 400; 949	356
Zamalek	M47; M72; M73	-
Mohandiseen	M72, 888	-
Badrasheen- (to Saqqara)	982; 987	-
Old Cairo	87; 95	-
Moqattem	407	-
Giza Midan	888, 30	-
Sayyidah Zeinab	174	-

Cairo Transport

Metro stops of particular interest

Sadat: Tah Rir; downtown.
Mubarak: Midan Ramses; Ramses Train Station.
Attaba: closest stop to Islamic Cairo, can walk to Al Azhar and Khan El-Khalili from here.
Mar Girgis: in the heart of Old Cairo, definitely the best way to get here.
Maadi: lots of expats live in this accessible suburb, some good restaurants and access to services not as available in other parts of Cairo; good library and prettiest part of the Corniche with lots of Nile-side restaurants and coffee shops; also a good spot to commence a *felucca* ride (will have to take a taxi from the metro stop – about E£4 to the Nile).

Upper Egypt Travel operates buses to the **Western Desert**: **Bahariyya**: 2000 (E£20). **Farafra** and **Dakhla**: 0700, 1600 (E£40, E£45). **Kharga**: 0900, 2100 (E£40-50). The **Red Sea Coast**: 12 buses daily to **Hurghada**; 5 on to **Safaga**; 4 to **El-Khousir** and **Marsa Alam**; 2 to **Selateen**; and 1 to **Halaeb** and **Luxor** 2100 (E£60) (**Aswan** from Aboud Station).

Superjet, T02-2660214/2, operates buses to: **Alexandria** at least once an hour (E£20); **Hurghada** 4 a day (E£55); **Sharm El-Sheikh** 4 a day; **Marsa Matrouh** 4 a day (E£37). Also runs buses at least once a week to **Libya**, **Jordan**, **Syria**, **Kuwait**, **Saudi Arabia** and **Dubai**.

Car

Car hire

Avis, 16 Sharia Ma'amal El-Soukkar, Garden City, T02-3689400. Also at Hotel Méridien, Nile Hilton Hotel, Hotel Jolie Ville and Sheraton Hotel. **Budget**, 5 Sharia El-Maqrizik, Zamalek, T02-2652395. Another branch at 1 Sharia Mohammed Ebeid, Heliopolis, T02-2918224. **Hertz**, 195 Sharia 26 July, Mohandiseen, T02- 3472238. Also at Ramses Hotel, Sonesta Hotel, Maadi Hotel and Semiramis Intercontinental.

Metro

Marked with big red "M" around the city. Signs are clearly marked in both English and Arabic. There are 2 functioning lines: **El-Marg-Helwan** and **Shobra-Giza**, with a third still in construction. Easy, efficient, clean and cheap (50p for 9 stops or less; 75p for up to 22 stations; E£1, everything above). When you buy your ticket, tell the attendant where you want to go and they'll charge you the appropriate amount. There is a separate ticket line just for women. Make sure you hold on to your ticket, you'll need it to exit. During rush hours (0700-1000, 1500-1900) it can be uncomfortably crowded, hot and pushy. Still, the metro is more manageable and reliable than the buses and often quicker than a taxi. The first car is reserved for women and children only.

Taxi

There is a profusion of the black and white chequered cars in Cairo. They're ramshackle, but easy to use and by western standards, extraordinarily cheap. To hail a taxi, simply wait on the side of the street, extend your arm, and say '*taxi*!'. Before entering, tell the driver your desired destination. Though most cabs are required to have a meter, they rarely function, and if they do, the prices are so antiquated, it's laughable. Most locals know the fair charge from one place to another. It's best to enquire at your hotel or with the tourist authority to get an idea of the standard rates. In general, travelling from one point of the centre to another shouldn't cost more than E£3-5. From one borough to another, E£10-12. To the **pyramids**, from downtown expect to pay E£15-20 and to the airport, E£25-35, depending on your bargaining skills. In general, taxis waiting outside hotels expect more money so it's best to walk a hundred metres and hail a taxi from the street. If you want to avoid a haggling fuss, agree on a fare before entering the taxi. Otherwise, be prepared for a struggle.

NB In Egypt, there is basic etiquette when riding in a taxi. Single women always sit in the back seat, at a diagonal to the driver. If a man is present, he generally sits in the front, next to the driver. Note that it is not uncommon for people going to different destinations to share taxis. If you do not want to share, simply notify your driver, bearing in mind he may expect more money.
As well as private and shared private taxis, there are service taxis (pronounced *'servees'*), which follow specific routes and carry up to 7 passengers. They function in the same way as microbuses (see transport section in Essentials) and can be flagged down from anywhere en-route. Fares range from 25p-E£1.

Trains

The main railway station in Cairo, **Ramsis Station**, T02-5753555, in Midan Ramsis, is a E£3 taxi ride from Tah Rir and most easily accessible via metro station **Mubarak**. It's a bit confusing, with several different ticket counters selling tickets for different destinations. There is a telephone point where you can make international phone calls, and a helpful English-speaking tourist office attendant in the back of the station (T02-5790767, open 0800-2000) who can assist you in sorting out train schedules and ticket counters. In short, if you are facing the main platform, tickets to **Alexandria** are purchased in the back left corner; to **Middle and Upper Egypt**, platform 11 outside to the left; to **Port Said/Ismailiya**, across the street behind you. In addition to the tourist office, there's an information booth in the middle of the station that can guide you in the right direction.

The trains are comfortable and reliable. There are several different classes. Authorities often won't sell third class tickets to foreigners. First and second class are significantly more comfortable and still cheap, anyway. First class almost always has a/c and larger seats. Second class sometimes has a/c and slightly smaller seats, about the size of coach-class in an aeroplane. Third class never has a/c and can be quite cramped and dirty. There is a 30% discount for students with ID on all trains except

Cairo Metro

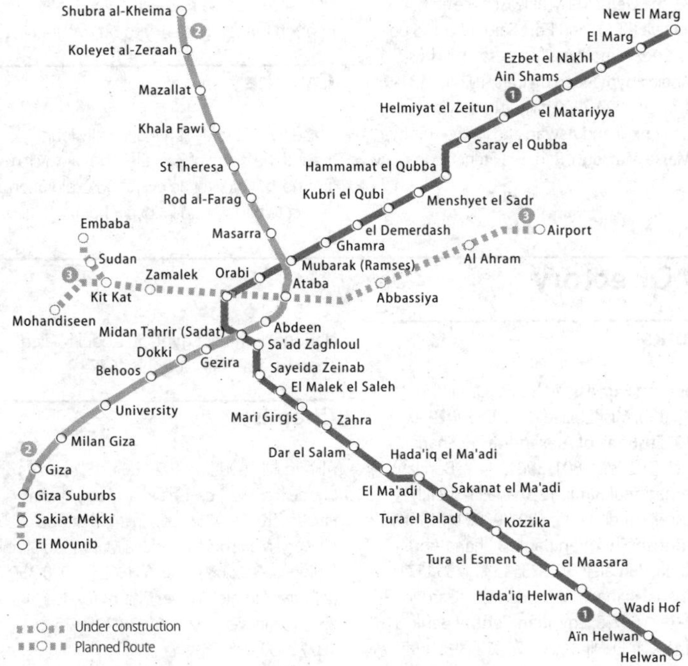

Train routes

	Dep	Arr	Dep	Arr
Train No 84	Cairo	Luxor	Luxor	Aswan
Daily	2000	0505	0515	0815
Train No 85	Aswan	Luxor	Luxor	Cairo
Daily	1830	2130	2140	0645

	Dep	Arr	Dep	Arr
Train No 82	Alexandria	Cairo	Luxor	Aswan
Daily	1720	2030	0525	0850
Train No 83	Aswan	Luxor	Cairo	Alexandria
Daily	1700	2015	0535	0910

the sleeper cars to Aswan and Luxor. Some cars are non-smoking – specify what you want when you buy your ticket. Long distance trains generally have food and beverages available. More trains run to the North Coast during summertime. Note that prices are scheduled to increase for foreigners at the end of this year.

Trains of all classes go at least once an hour, daily, to **Alexandria** (1st class E£32, 2nd E£25). If you are Alexandria-bound, try to get on an express train which has fewer stops. Trains also cover the **Delta** (daily, at least once an hour), **Ismailiya** (E£11) and **Port Said** (E£26), (5 per day). **Suez** is more easily accessed via bus.

Abela Egypt Sleeping Cars, T02-5761319/954, open 0900-2000 daily, run daily sleeping cars to **Luxor** and **Aswan** and, in the summer, to **Marsa Matrouh**. Run by a French company and claiming 4-star status, the sleepers are a clean, comfortable way to travel. You can get off the train for 48 hrs in **Luxor** and get back on to **Aswan** with the same ticket. During peak season, it's wise to buy your ticket in advance. Each train has a 'club' area and restaurant. Price US$50/person in double; US$70 for single; US$37.65 for children – prices include dinner and breakfast. Add around US$4 for trips to and from Alexandria. Credit cards and Egyptian pounds are NOT accepted, so make sure you have enough foreign currency to buy your ticket.

Calèche

Horsedrawn carriages are generally found around the island of **Zamalek**. Not a way to get around, but nice for an evening's exploration. Expect to pay around E£25 per hour.

Directory

Banks

American Express, 72 Sharia Omar Ibn El-Khatab, Misr El-Gedida, T02-2902990, 2919120; **Bank of Alexandria**, 49 Sharia Qasr El-Neil, T02-3926801, 3961124-3; **Barclays International Bank**, 12 Sharia El-Sheikh Youssef, Garden City, T02-7900014/15/17/18; **British-Egyptian Bank**, 3 Sharia Abu El-Feda, Zamalek, T02-7351341, 7354571; **Citibank**, 4 Sharia Ahmed Pasha, Garden City, T02-7921607-8; **Egyptian Central Bank**, 31 Sharia Ksar El-Nil, T02-3921662, 3921637; **National Bank of Egypt**, 50 Abdel Khaleq Tharwat, T02-3904360, 3904677.

Chemists

Ali and Ali, 9 Outlets, T02-7604277, open 24 hrs, delivery service; **Isa'f Pharmacy**, Sharia Ramses, T02-5743369, open 24 hours, no delivery; **Maa'soud**, 29 Sharia Mahmoud Shahk, Heliopolis, T02-6332630, 6333635, 0900-1500, delivery; **Zamalek Tower Pharmacy**, 134 Sharia 26 July, Zamalek, T02-7361338, 1030-1530, 1800-2300, delivery.

Couriers

DHL, 16 Sharia Lebnan, El-Mohandseen, T02-3029801/2/3/4; **Federal Express**, 16 Sharia Khaled Ibn El-Walid, Masaken Sheraton, Nasr City, T02-2687888, and 1079 Corniche El-Neil, Garden City, T02-7940520; **TNT** (International Express), 33 Sharia El-Doki, T02-7499850-1; **UPS**, 7 Sharia Hussien Zohdy, Masr El-Gededa, T02-4141456/7; **Western Union** (Money Transfers), 8 Sharia El-Slamlek, Garden City, T02-7920741, 7921691.

Embassies and consulates

Most consulates take a 2-day weekend, between Thu and Sun. **Australia**, World Trade Centre, Sharia Corniche El-Nil, T02-5750444; **Austria**, 5 Sharia Wisa Wasef, El-Riad Tower, Giza, T02-5702975; **Belgium**, 20 Sharia Kamel El-Shenawi, Garden City, T02-7947494; **Canada**, 26 Sharia Kamel El-Shenawi, Garden City, T02-7943110/9; **Denmark**, 12 Sharia Hassan Sabri, Zamalek, T02-7356490, 7356973; **France**, 29 Sharia Morad, Giza, T02-5703919; **Germany**, 8B Sharia Hassan Sabri, Zamalek, T02-7350283, 7353687; **Israel**, 6 Sharia Ibn Malek, near El-Gamaa Bridge, Giza, T02-7610388, 7610528; **Jordan**, 6 Sharia El-Basem El-Kateb Off Sharia El-Tahrir, Dokki, T02-7499912; **Kenya**, 29 Sharia El-Qods El-Sharif, off Sharia Shehab, Mohandiseen, T02-3453628; **Kuwait**, 12 Sharia Nabil El-Waqqad, Dokki, T02-7602661; **Lebanon**, 22 Sharia El-Mansour Mohamed, Zamalek, T02-7382823; **Libya**, 7 Sharia El-Saleh Ayoub, Zamalek, T02-7351269; **Morocco**, 10 Sharia Salah El-Dein, Zamalek, T02-7359849; **Netherlands**, 18 Sharia Hassan Sabri, Zamalek, T02-7395500; **Saudia Arabia**, 5 Sharia El-Gehadya, Garden City, T02- 7958111; **South Africa**, 21 Sharia El-Morad, Nile Tower, Giza, T02-5717234; **Spain**, 41 Sharia Ismail Mohammed, Zamalek, T02-7353652, 7355813; **Sudan**, 3 Sharia El-Ibrahimi, Garden City, T02-7949661; **Switzerland**, 10 Sharia Abdel Khalek Sarwat, Downtown, T02-5758284; **Syria**, 18 Sharia Abdel Rehim Sabri, Dokki, T02-3358320; **Tunisia**, 26 Sharia El-Gezira, Zamalek, T02-7368962; **UK**, 7 Sharia Ahmed Raghab, Garden City, T02-7940852; **USA**, 5 Sharia America Al-Latiniya, Garden City, T02-7972301, 7957373.

Hospitals

Cairo Medical Centre, Midan Roxi, Heliopolis, T02-4504903/4; **Al Salam International Hospital**, Corniche El-Maadi, T02-5240077; **Anglo-American Hospital**, by Cairo Tower, Gezira, T02-7356162/6164. For public ambulances call 123.

Internet

4U Internet Café, 6 Midan Talaat Harb, Downtown, T02-5796819, open 0830-1300, E£5/hour; **Café Internet**, 8 El-Mamar El-Togary, Sour Nady El-Zamalek, Mohandiseen, T02-3050493, open 1000-2400, E£6/hour; **Future Access**, 13 Osman Towers Corniche El-Nil, Maadi, T02-5261081, open 1100-2400, E£4/hour; **Hany Internet Café**, 16 Sharia Abdel Khaleq Tharwat Midan, Downtown, T0122748334, E£5/hour; **Internet Egypt**, *Nile Hilton*, Downtown, T02-5796819, open 0900-2400, E£12/hour; **Starnet Cyber Café**, 18 Sharia Youssef El-Guindy, El-Bostan Centre, Downtown, T02-3910151 ext 117, open 1000-2400, E£6/hour.

Language schools

Arabic classes available at: **The Arabic Language Institute**, 113 Sharia El-Qasr El-Einy, Tah Rir, T02-7975055; **Berlitz Worldwide**, 21 Sharia Tesaa, El-Maadi, T02-3584328; **British Council**, 192 Sharia El-Nil, Agouza, T02-3031514; **International Language Institute**, 4 Sharia Mahmoud Azmy, off Ahmed Orabi, Mohandiseen, T02-3463087.

Places of worship

Anglican/Episcopalian All Saints **Cathedral**, 5 Sharia Michel Lutfalla, behind *Marriott Hotel*, Zamalek, T02-7368391, international English-speaking congregation, Sun services, Holy Communion 0800 and 1030 on 1st/3rd/5th, Matins at 1030 on 2nd and 4th, Evensong 1915 on 2nd and 4th Sun, for weekday services enquire by phone; **Armenian Church**, 28 Sharia Sabri Abu Alam. Sun 0815-0915, 1930; **Heliopolis Community Church**, interdemoninational and international, T02-4142409; 10 Sharia Seti, off Sharia Baghdad, Heliopolis, Eucharist Sat at 1830, Sun at 1030 and 1930 in Arabic and 1800 in English. **Christian Science Society** 3 Midan Mustafa Kamel, Sun at 1900 and Wed at 1930, reading room available. **Coptic/Orthodox** Church of St Anthony and Girgis, Heliopolis, Mass in English 3rd Sun in month at 0800; First Baptist Church, 28 Sharia Khalafawi, Shubra; Sun at 1000 and 1930. **German Evangelical/Lutheran Church** 6 Sharia Gaber Ben Hayyan, Dokki, 1st and 3rd Sun at 1730. Quaker, alternate Sun at 1900. **Roman Catholic** St Joseph's Church, 2 Sharia Bank Misr, Downtown, Mass in French daily at 0730 and 1830, also Sun in French 1100, and 1900, in Arabic at 1000, and English at 1900; St Joseph's Church, 4 Sharia Ahmed Sabri, Zamalek, Mass (English) Sun 1800; St Theresa Catholic Church, Coptic Rite Mass and Latin Rite Mass at 0630/1730, confessions in Arabic, French, Italian, Spanish, English and Maltese.

Post office

Cairo's main post office is in Midan Ataba, open daily from 0800-2100, except Fri (Ramadan 0900-1600). The post office at Midan Ataba also has a *poste restante* office, that will hold mail for a month, free. Enter via Sharia El-Badek and look for the "private boxes" counter. There are other branches, but they tend to be more crowded. Major hotels often provide the same services. If you have an American Express card, you can send mail via AmEx on Shari Qasr El-Nil. Stamps available at post offices and from hotel shops and cigarette kiosks. Postcards and letters cost E£1.25 to send anywhere in the world. Packages are best sent off from the Midan Ramses post office. Bring your parcel unsealed so it can be searched. Packaging is possible in the post office for a few extra E£.

Telephone

Besides the international telephone and fax services at all major hotels, there are several public telecom centres where it's possible to make international phone calls for cheaper, but the wait can be long. Main offices are at Sharia Adly, near the tourist office, Sharia Ramses, near Sharia Tawfiqia, and 13 Midan Tah Rir. To avoid the hassle of the telecommunication centres, you can buy a public or private phone card. Public cards can be bought from the telecom centres (E£10-20) and can be used from any telephone with or without a direct line to call long distance. Make sure you specify if you want a card for street booths or a home phone. There are also private prepaid cards available from every kiosk and supermarket. Most pervasive around Egypt are the yellow and green *Menatel* booths. Cards range in price from E£5-20. A E£10 card will cover about 20 mins of local calls. International calls can cost up to E£10 per minute.

Useful addresses

Fire: T125. International reverse charge call: T146. Medical emergencies: T123. Police: T122. Major police offices: at Railway Station, Cairo Airport, Midan Tah Rir, Sharia 26 July/ Mansour Mohammed. Pyramids office: T02-3850259. Tourist Police: T126 or T02- 5715167, 5715169. Tourist Police Head Office: T02-3906027.

Cultural centres American, US Embassy, 5 Sharia America Al-Latiniya, T02-7949601, closed Fri and Sat; Amideast, 23 Sharia Mossadak, Dokki, T02-3378277, 3383867; Austrian, Austrian Embassy, Riyadh Tower, corner of El-Neil and Wisa and Wissa Wsef sts T02-5702975, British, British Council, 192 Sharia El-Nil, Agouza, T02-3031514, closed Sun; Canadian, Canadian Embassy, 5 Sharia Sarayal Kubra, Garden City, T02-7943110, only Tue and Wed; Dutch, 1 Sharia Dr Mahmoud Azmi, Zamalek, T02-7382527; Egyptian Centre for International Cultural Co-operation, 11 Sharia Shagaret El-Dor, Zamalek, T02-7365410; French, 1 Sharia Madraset El-Hoquq El-Faransia, Mounira, T02-7953725, 7941012, 7679105; German, Goethe Institute, 5 Sharia Abd El-Salam Arif, T02-5759877, 5779479; Israeli, Israeli Embassy, 92 Sharia El-Nil, Dokki, T02-3488995, 3496232; Italian, 3 Sharia Sheikh El-Marsafi, behind Marriott Hotel, Zamalek, T02-7358791, closed Fri and Sat; Japan, Japanese Cultural Centre, 106 Sharia Qasr El-Hoq El-Faransia, Mounira, T02-7953962-4; Swiss, Swiss Embassy, 10 Sharia Abdel- Khalek Tharwat, T02-5758284/8133, closed Fri and Sat.

Around Cairo & the Nile Delta

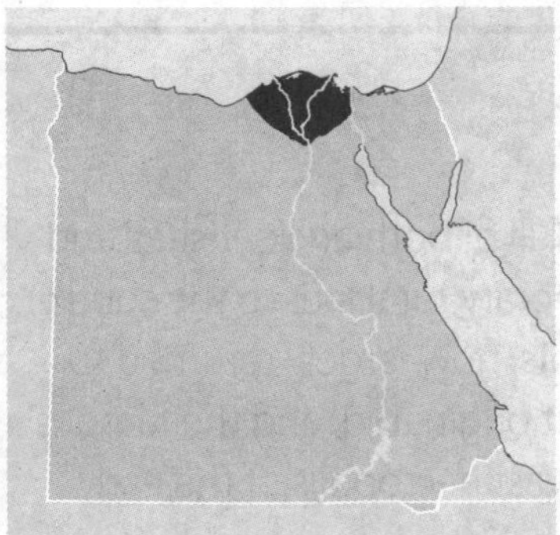

Footprint features

Introduction

The region surrounding Cairo is full of both ancient sites and communities typical of contemporary rural life. To the south lie the ancient capital of **Memphis**, now largely returned to the silt of the Nile from whence it originated, and the famous step pyramid of **Saqqara** in the vast necropolis of the early pharaohs. It is undoubtedly worth visiting Saqqara before going on to Giza (although tourists rarely do) in order to see the development from the simple underground tomb to the audacious concept of the Pyramid of Cheops. But whether sooner or later, when you come to Egypt, this is the site to visit. Further south, the harsh desert gives way to the beautiful pseudo-oasis of **El-Fayoum**, a lush expanse of fields and palms offering sanctuary to some of the richest birdlife in Egypt as well as respite from the pollution and heat of Cairo.

Beyond Cairo, the two main tributaries of the Nile continue northwards to meet the Mediterranean near **Damietta** and **Rosetta**. On either side, and between the two branches, the flat, green and fertile land fans out to create, with the help of some of the world's oldest and most efficient irrigation systems, the Nile Delta, Egypt's agricultural heartland and its most heavily populated region. The fertility of this area has enabled this scorched desert country, of which less than 4% of its land is cultivatable, to support a huge population and to export large quantities of fruits and vegetables. Because of the lack of hard stone and the very high population density, successive generations plundered old buildings for stone and built new ones on top of ancient sites. As a result there are no outstanding monuments here – life in the Delta revolves around the land. Beyond agriculture, the Delta is known for its many **moulids** or popular religious festivals that serve as the main appeal for the relatively few foreign tourists that visit the region.

★ Don't miss...

❶ **Saqqara** Explore Egypt's largest archeological site, rugged ruins amid the tranquil surrounding sands, a sight to behold – especially on horse or camel back, page 152.

❷ **El-Fayoum and Lake Qaroun** Take a break from Cairo's heat at the man-made oasis, irrigated by water channeled from the Nile, and watch out for the birds at Egypt's largest salt water lake, page 160.

❸ **Rosetta** Meander through the quaint Delta fishing village, once known as 'the city of a million palms and dates,' and enjoy the exquisite Ottoman architecture, page 177.

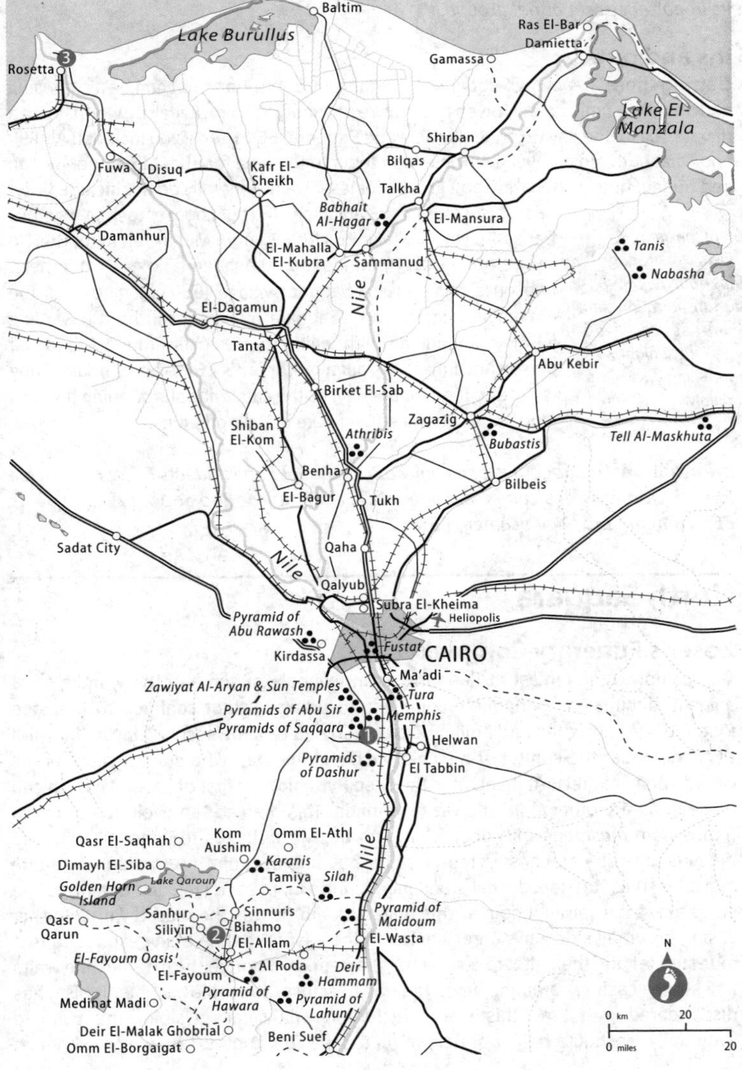

Memphis and Saqqara

→ Colour map 2, grid B2

Saqqara, which faces Memphis (the oldest known imperial city on earth) across the River Nile, was the enormous necropolis for the first pharaohs. With many tombs believed to be still undiscovered it is currently Egypt's largest archaeological site, spanning more than 7 sq km. From its inception it expanded west into the desert until the Fourth Dynasty (2613-2494 BC) when the Giza plateau superseded it. At the end of the Fifth Dynasty (2494-2345 BC) a more systematic construction of pyramids and mastabas *began, which resulted in many splendid monuments around Saqqara. In 1883 a Middle Kingdom (2050-1786 BC) necropolis was found to the east but it was not until the New Kingdom (1567-1085 BC) that Saqqara is thought to have regained its importance as a burial ground.*

Ins and outs

Getting there Reaching Saqqara or Memphis by public transport can be a confusing and time-consuming affair. Given the relative proximity to Cairo, it may be worth hiring a private taxi for the day (E£70-80 for Giza and Saqqara; E£80-100 if you included Abu Sir and Dhashur). Most travel agencies book tours to the area for about E£50 per person and budget hotels often transport groups for less. Tours generally do not include ticket prices, so inquire in advance. If you choose to brave public transport, you can take Bus No 987 from Midan Tah Rir or Bus No 121 from the Giza Pyramids to Badrasheen (E£0.35). From there, hop on a microbus to Saqqara village (E£0.50), and walk the remaining 3 km. Giza to Saqqara by camel can be a rewarding journey. Round trip with waiting time costs around E£150 per person and takes 4-5 hours; by horse it's E£100 and 2 hours. Bring water and food for the day, as the cafeterias surrounding the area tend to be overpriced and bare in their offerings.

Most of the areas described here are easy daytrips from the capital. Public transportation can sometimes be difficult to come by late at night, so plan your agenda accordingly.

Information ⓘ *Saqqara is open daily 0800-1600. E£20, students E£10, camera fee E£10, E£100 for video cameras. Memphis is open daily 0800-1600. E£14, students E£7, camera E£10, video camera E£100.*

North Saqqara

Zoser's Funerary Complex

This complex, the largest in Saqqara, is an example of some of the world's most ancient architecture. The whole complex, including but not confined to the **Step Pyramid**, was designed and built by **Zoser** (2667-48 BC), the second king in the Third Dynasty, under the control of his chief architect Imhotep who some regard as the world's first architect. At its heart is the **Step Pyramid**, the first of its kind, which can be seen as a prototype for the Giza Pyramids. This marked the evolution of burial tombs from *mastabas* with deep shafts for the sarcophagus to imposing elevated mausoleums. It was constructed in steps building up from the traditional square *mastaba* (1) of Tura-faced local stone measuring 71.5 m each side and 8 m high. The sides faced the cardinal points. This original tomb (1) was then faced with a further casing (2) on all sides and an extension to the east (3) before being expanded to a four-step (4) and then later to a six-step (5) pyramid. Although the external fine white limestone casing, brought from quarries across the Nile at Memphis, has disappeared over time this step structure is still clearly visible. The pyramid eventually reached a height of 62.5 m on a base 109 m by 121 m, which, although small by comparison with those at Giza, is still an amazing feat because of the primitive building techniques. The advances represented by Zoser's Pyramid were not in the building techniques or materials, which were already established, but the concept, design and calculations involved which made such a monument possible.

The entrance is in the north face. In accordance with the traditional *mastaba* technique, the Royal Tomb lies 28 m underground at the bottom of a vertical shaft. The shaft was then sealed with a 3-tonne granite block but this still did not prevent the tomb from being looted. Another 11 shafts were found, 32 m deep, under the east side of the Pyramid, which lead to the tombs of the queens and royal children. Unfortunately these are no longer open to the public.

The whole funerary complex was completely surrounded by buttressed walls which were over 544 m long, 277 m wide and 10.4 m (20 cubits) high. Although 14 fake doors were built, only the one in the southeast corner, which leads into the colonnade **Hypostyle Hall** actually gives access to the site. It is thought that the area was walled in order to deter intruders and thieves, and to provide space for the Pharaoh's *ka* (spirit) to live in the afterlife. Before entering the colonnade, observe the fake door complete with hinges and sockets in the vestibule on the right. The Colonnade leads through to the **Great Court** or **Southern Court**, on the south side of which there is a frieze of cobras. This represents the fire-spitting goddess of destruction Edjo who was adopted as the Uraeus, the emblem of royalty and of protection, which was worn on the pharaonic head-dress (see box Cobras, page 310).

Further along this south wall is a deep shaft at the bottom of which lies **Zoser's Southern Tomb** which some believe held the King's entrails. More importantly there is a relief, depicting the King running the Heb-Sed race, which illustrates the purpose of the surrounding buildings and monuments. The buildings in the funerary complex, some of which are mere façades like a Hollywood film-set, simply represented a pastiche for the afterlife of this crucial ceremony. Their intended purpose was to eternalize the symbol of the unification of a greater Egypt and the power of the pharaoh even in death.

This symbolism is echoed in the lotus and papyrus capitals on top of the columns fronting the **House of the South** and the **House of the North** which represent the heraldic emblems of Upper and Lower Egypt, respectively. The **House of the South** is interesting because its columns, which are precursors of the Greek Doric style, and its New Kingdom graffiti offer a fascinating reminder of the continuity of human civilization.

The Step Pyramid at Saqqara

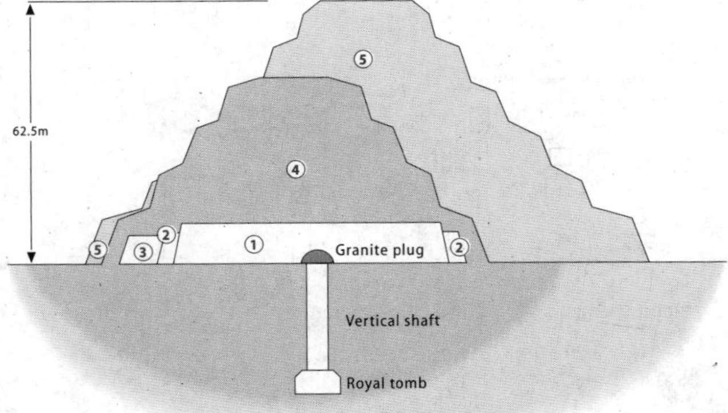

On the north side of the Step Pyramid there is a stone casket, known as the **Serdab** (cellar), containing a copy of a life-size statue of Zoser. The original is in the Egyptian Museum in Cairo. The Serdab has two cylindrical holes to enable the statue to communicate with the outside world and to preserve the Pharaoh's *ka*. To the west of the Serdab the **Funerary Temple** is in ruins but some of the walls and the entrance can still be seen. A tunnel originally linked it with the royal tomb.

South of Zoser's Funerary Complex

The Pyramid of Unas, which was built for the last pharaoh of the Fifth Dynasty (2494-2345 BC), appears from the outside to be a heap of limestone rubble but the inside is still very well preserved and contains some beautiful hieroglyphs. Originally when clad in its granite casing it stood 44 m high but is now reduced to 19 m. As always, the entrance is from the north side down a passageway leading to the Burial Chamber. This was originally closed off with three granite portcullises. This is largely undecorated except for the star-covered ceiling and the sarcophagus which is made from a single block of black basalt and bears no inscriptions. The most interesting inscriptions are in the passageway, painted in green and organized in vertical lines. The hieroglyphs are magic formulae and prayers, known as the Pyramid Texts, for the pharaoh to ease his passage into the afterlife. They were the first to be found inside a tomb and formed the basis for the *Book of the Dead* (see Valley of the Kings, page 228). To the east, a few remnants of the **Funerary Temple** can be seen, some granite columns with palm capitals and pieces of granite floor. Beyond this the remains of a causeway linking the Funerary Temple to the Valley Temple 700 m away has been discovered. The pyramid was excavated and opened as a tourist attraction in 1881 by the director of antiquities Gaston Maspero with financial sponsorship from Thomas Cook & Son.

To the north of the Pyramid the **Mastaba of Queen Nebet**, who was Unas' wife, is also fascinating and well preserved. It is divided into three rooms, the second being

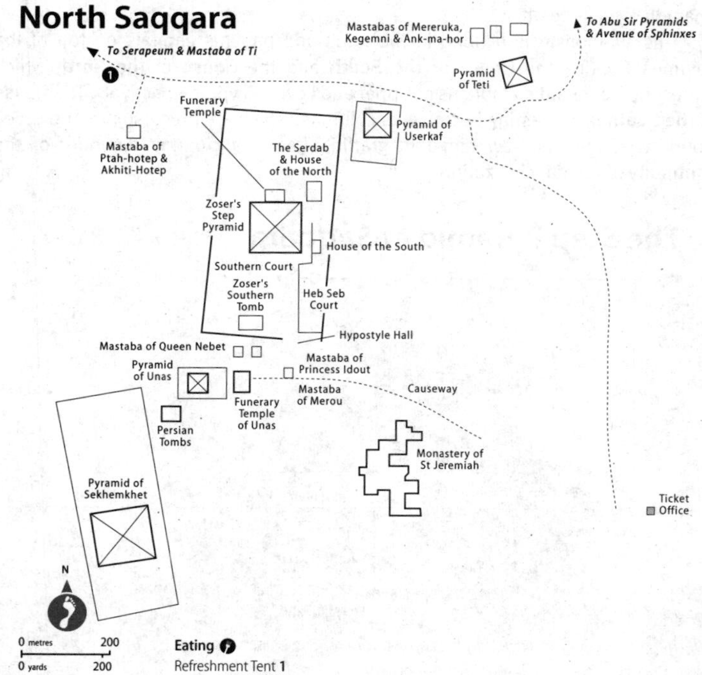

the most interesting because it contains some rare scenes of Nebet in the women's quarters, or harem, in the palace. From here, a door leads to a gallery with beautifully decorated walls.

Opposite, to the northeast, is the **Mastaba of Princess Idout**. The tomb is divided into 10 rooms but only five are decorated. The wall paintings give a glimpse of life in Idout's day with many tableaux of rural and domestic scenes. Two rooms are dedicated to the offerings to the Princess and are designed to provide for her in the afterlife.

Slightly to the east is the **Mastaba of Merou** containing some exceptionally well-preserved paintings. In the **Grand Offerings Room** the paint scarcely seems to have faded, thereby giving a good idea of the original splendour of these tombs.

South of the Pyramid of Unas a stone hut covers the access to three small **Persian Tombs** 25 m underground and composed of two shafts. In order to lower the heavy sarcophagus, an ingenious system was devised involving the use of an additional smaller shaft. The main shaft was dug out, then filled with sand. The sarcophagus was then placed on top of the sand which was gradually removed from below via the smaller shaft. The tombs dating from the 27th Dynasty (525-404 BC) are interesting because they have very similar inscriptions to those found in Unas' Pyramid constructed over 2,000 years earlier.

To the southwest are the remains of the **Pyramid of Sekhemkhet** which was at the centre of an unfinished and unused funerary complex, very similar to that of his predecessor Zoser, which was only discovered in 1950 and to which there is no public access.

To the east of the Pyramid of Sekhemkhet can be seen the remains of the **Monastery of St Jeremiah** which was founded in the fifth century but destroyed by the Arabs five centuries later. Following its discovery in 1907 many of the paintings and other items of interest were removed and are now on display in the Coptic Museum in Cairo.

Northeast of the Funerary Complex

The **Pyramid of Teti**, the founder of the 6th Dynasty (2345-2181 BC), was discovered by Mariette in 1853 but is now little more than a pile of rubble in constant danger of being submerged by sand. It is entered via a steep pathway leading to the funerary chamber in which the ceiling is decorated with stars.

To the north are a number of well-preserved ***mastabas***. The most outstanding is that of **Mereruka**, who was Teti's vizier, chief judge and inspector – an important person in Sixth Dynasty society. This is one of the largest Old Kingdom *mastabas* to have been found. Its 32 rooms are divided into three parts for Mereruka (21 rooms), his wife (six rooms) and his son (five rooms). In the main entrance passage Mereruka is depicted painting the three seasons which leads to the next room containing some interesting hunting scenes. Particularly worth noting is the indication of the types of animal that they hunted and the techniques being used. Scenes of everyday life are beautifully depicted throughout the tomb, giving a valuable insight into contemporary life. The largest room, with six pillars, has a statue of Mereruka to the north and some unusual mourning scenes on the east wall. On the left are scenes of Mereruka carried by his son and surrounded by dwarfs and dogs. To enter Mereruka's wife's rooms go back to the main entrance and take the door on the left.

To the east, the **Mastaba of Kagemni** who was also a vizier and judge of the Sixth Dynasty has some excellent reliefs and paintings of a much a higher standard, but

The Heb-Sed race took place during the festival held to mark the 30th anniversary of Zoser's reign. He would sprint between two altars (representing Lower and Upper Egypt) thereby not only re-enacting his coronation in both parts of the coutry and symbolizing unification but also demonstrating his continuing vigour.

 unfortunately less well preserved, than those in Mereruka's tomb. Further east is the **Mastaba of Ankh-ma-hor**, the vizier and overseer of the Great House in the Sixth Dynasty. It is also known as the Doctor's Tomb because of the paintings depicting circumcision and an operation on a broken toe! The other rooms are interesting and show the usual scenes of the preparation and transportation of the offerings and various representations of hunting and daily life. Look on the south wall for the mourners fainting at the burial ceremony.

Northwest of the funerary complex

About 200 m south of the road to a refreshment tent is one of the finest of all the *mastabas*. The **Double Mastaba of Ptah-Hotep and Akhiti-Hotep** contains some of the finest Old Kingdom art and some fascinating unfinished work which demonstrates the techniques used in painting reliefs. Ptah-Hotep was a priest of Maat in the reign of Djedkare, who was Unas' predecessor. His son Akhiti-Hotep was vizier, judge, and the overseer of the treasury and the granaries.

The entrance leads into a long corridor decorated with unfinished agricultural scenes. The red paint indicates the preliminary drawing before the wall was carved and painted. The outstanding masterpiece, however, is in the **Sanctuary** dedicated to Ptah-Hotep. On the walls behind the entrance Ptah-Hotep is seated watching a concert while his servants wash and manicure him. Other walls bear scenes of Ptah-Hotep receiving offerings. On the left wall, which is the most interesting and impressive, the figure in the first boat is being given water by a boy. The inscription describes him as the Chief Artist, who is thought to have been Ankhen-Ptah, and this scene may well represent the first known example of an artist's signature.

The Serapeum The Serapeum is 300 m to the northwest of the refreshment tent and is one of the most impressive sites in Saqqara. This was a burial place for the sacred Apis Bulls which were believed to be manifestations of Ptah's blessed soul and were identified with Osiris after his death. They were given full honours in a ceremony worthy of any pharaoh or important noble and were then embalmed and the mummified body placed in a sarcophagus and buried in the Serapeum. The sarcophagus was then sealed off from the main gallery by means of a richly decorated wall. The high priests would then start searching for the new Apis Bull within the sacred herd. It had to be the only calf of its mother, be black in colour except for a white diamond-shaped marking on the forehead and have a scarab symbol on its tongue. The cult was a significant one and the Serapeum represents an important funerary complex which, besides the tombs themselves, included the priests' quarters, schools and inns catering for passing pilgrims. The cult of the Apis Bulls lasted well into the Ptolemaic period.

The Serapeum is reached via a long, sloping path, at the bottom of which a door leads to the three galleries. Only two are accessible, and the 24 surviving sarcophagi are set in small galleries on either side of the main one. Each sarcophagus was made from a single piece of rock and weighed around 60 tonnes. Only three of the enormous basalt or granite sarcophagi bear inscriptions, and these are marked with the cartouches of different pharaohs, Amasis, Cambyses and Khababash. The Serapeum was discovered in 1851 but, with the exception of one tomb, most had already been looted. The artifacts discovered are now displayed in the Musée du Louvre, Paris.

The Mastaba of Ti One of the wonders of the Old Kingdom, this *mastaba*, with its beautiful reliefs provides some interesting insights into life during that period. Ti was a Fifth Dynasty royal hairdresser who married well and became steward of the sun temples of Neferikare and Nouserre and whose children later bore the title of 'royal descendant'. The *mastaba* stands 400 m north of the refreshment tent, very close to

The Sacred Scarab

Scarabaeus sacer, a dung beetle, is the celebrated beetle held sacred by the ancient Egyptians. They were fascinated by the beetles' strange habit of fashioning perfectly round balls from animal-droppings. (These balls, larger than the insect itself, are moved backwards using the rear legs, the head being thrust against the ground to give purchase. The balls are then buried with newly laid eggs and provide food for the developing larvae.) The scarab was used too as a symbol of the sun god as Egyptians thought the sun was pushed round the heavens just as the beetle pushed the ball of dung.

The dung beetle is called Kheper in the Egyptian language and is associated with the verb *kheper* which means to come into being. Models of the beetle made in clay were supposed to have healing powers while live beetles, secured by a small chain through the wing-case, were actually worn as decoration.

The scarab seal was used to stamp letters into the clay seal on letters, bottles, wine jars etc with the owner's mark.

the Serapeum, and is centred around a square pillared courtyard. The entrance is through a vestibule with portraits of Ti on the two entrance pillars. The reliefs in the courtyard have been damaged but their representations of daily life – breeding birds (north wall left), Ti on his litter with dogs and dwarfs (east wall, centre), and Ti with his wife (west wall centre) – are still worth seeing. In the centre of the courtyard an undecorated shaft leads to the tomb. A corridor leads from the southwest corner through to the main shrine. On the left of the corridor, just after the door, servants are depicted bringing offerings while on the right are musicians and dancers. Further on, to the right, is a false door bearing a representation of Ti's wife.

Further down the corridor on the right is a storage room and then the main hall of offerings and shrine which has a number of scenes depicting the offerings ceremony, the brewing of beer and the baking of bread. The main shrine is remarkable for its abundance of scenes depicting daily life including one illustrating boat construction. Note the extreme simplicity of the tools used.

The south wall holds the **Serdab**, where a copy of Ti's statue, the original being in the Cairo Museum, can be seen through the slit. Around the two slits there are scenes of daily market life, carpenters, tanners, and various other artisans. Around the second slit, Ti is entertained by musicians while servants burn incense. These paintings should be taken on one level as literal depictions of Egyptian life but it is also important to realize the importance of symbolism and allegory. The north walls show Ti in a boat observing a hippopotamus hunt in the Delta region. The hippopotamus was symbolic of evil so there is probably more to the picture than meets the eye.

Pyramids of Abu Sir

The **Pyramids of Abu Sir** are 2.5 km northeast of the Mastaba of Ti. The site originally contained 14 Fifth Dynasty pyramids but only four are still standing. The temples are solidly constructed with black basalt floors and red Aswan granite pillars and are well worth visiting. When arriving from the main Saqqara complex the **Pyramid of Neferefre** is the first to be encountered. It was never finished and is now in very poor condition. The next (also unfinished) pyramid to the north was built for **Neferikare** and towering over the others is, at 68 m, the tallest of the group. To the northeast, the **Pyramid of Nouserre** is worth noting for its **Funerary Temple** which, although originally built for the Neferikare, was used by Nouserre because of Neferikare's premature death. About 100 m to the northeast lies the tomb of **Ptah-Cepses**. The *mastaba* is not in good condition and has been closed for safety but from outside the columns with lotus capitals (which are the oldest so far discovered) can still be seen.

The remaining one, **Sahure's Pyramid**, is directly north and its **Funerary Temple** is not too severely damaged. Excavation work around it has led to the discovery of the remains of a 240-m ramp which connected it to the **Valley Temple**. Sahure was brother to Userkaf whose pyramid is at Saqqara. The ceilings of this Funerary Temple were yellow stars on a blue background and the reliefs carved on the limestone walls showed the king's defeat of his neighbours in the desert and those from Asia. Some have been removed and placed in museums, but a few remain and are quite well preserved.

Sun-Temples of Abu Ghurab

The Sun-Temples of Abu Ghurab, built in the Fifth Dynasty when the solar cult had been declared the state religion, are about 1 km northeast of Sahure's Pyramid. Unlike earlier temples their purpose was solely devotional and the pharaohs who built them were not buried in them. There were twin temples but only the **Sun-Temple of Nouserre** remains with the **Sun-Temple of Userkaf** being little more than rubble. Fortunately because they were identical little is lost.

At the western end of an enclosed courtyard a massive 70-m obelisk once stood. The obelisk was the symbol of the primordial mound, the sun's resting place at the end of the day. An alabaster altar stands in the centre of the courtyard which would have been at the eastern side of the obelisk's base. Animals were sacrificed at the northeast corner of the courtyard from which channels cut in the paving carried the blood to 10 alabaster basins, nine of which survive.

South Saqqara

This completely separate necropolis, founded by the pharaohs of the Sixth Dynasty (2345-2181 BC), is about 1 km south of the Pyramid of Sekhemkhet, which is the most southerly of all the pyramids in North Saqqara. It has a few interesting tombs, based on the Pyramid of Unas as an architectural model, but sadly has been plundered by unscrupulous stone masons or their suppliers. The pyramids of **Pepi I** and **Merenre** are in ruins.

To the east of the latter lies the **Pyramid of Djedkare,** known in Arabic as the Pyramid of the Sentinel, which is 25 m tall and is open to visitors. The entrance is on the north side through a tunnel leading into the funerary chamber but there is comparatively little to see.

The most important and interesting tombs are further south. The **Pyramid of Pepi II** is surrounded by an entire funerary complex. The inside chamber is decorated with stars and funerary inscriptions. Within the complex are a number of other smaller pyramids belonging to his queens. They are all based on the same design as Pepi's pyramid and contain a miniature funerary complex. The **Pyramid of Queen Neith** is interesting and has some wonderful inscriptions and decorations.

To the east is the **Mastaba Faraoun**, the tomb of **Shepseskaf,** the last pharaoh of the Fourth Dynasty (2613-2494 BC). The inside is interesting but undecorated and the walls are made from large blocks of granite. From the outside the tomb looks like a gigantic sarcophagus and the exterior was originally covered in a thin layer of limestone. About 1 km further south are two more pyramids. The first is the brick **Pyramid of Khendjer** which has a funerary chamber made out of quartzite. The second is larger, but unfinished, and bears no inscriptions or signs of use. It has impressive underground white stone chambers and a quartzite funerary chamber.

The Pyramids at Dhashur

ⓘ *There is unrestricted access for E£20, E£10 for students, camera E£5.*

The Red Pyramid and The Bent Pyramid lie about 2 km south of the Mastaba Faraoun. They were constructed by Snefru (BC 2575-51) first ruler of the Fourth Dynasty, at the time of the great pyramid construction. He built the two pyramids in Dhashur and was perhaps responsible for the pyramid at Maidoum. His constructive tendencies were continued in his son Cheops.

The **Red Pyramid** to the north, named after the reddish local limestone used in the core, is considered to be older. It is thought to be the first true pyramid to be constructed with sloping sides rather than steps. Each side measures 220 m, the slopes measures 43°40' and the total height is 101 m. Some of the original Tura limestone facing-stones still remain on the eastern side. Limestone fragments of the monolithic pyramidion exist. The entrance 28 m above the ground on the north side leads down to two corbelled antechambers from the second of which the burial chamber can be reached. The **Bent Pyramid** (also known as the Southern Shining Pyramid) which lies further south was constructed of local limestone with a casing of polished Tura limestone, the casing blocks slope inwards making them more stable

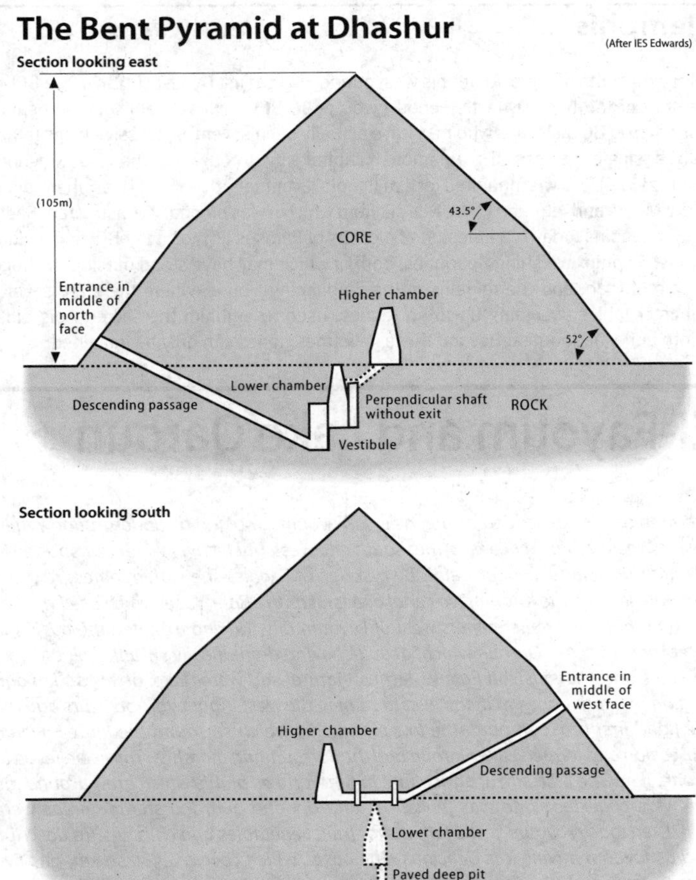

and also difficult to remove. The side at the base measures 188.6 m and the height is 97 m (originally 105 m). If construction had continued at the original angle it would have been 128.5 m high.

The pyramid is unique on two counts. First the angles change. The lower angle is 52° enclosing some 70% of the bulk of the pyramid. It then reduces to 43.5° up to the peak. There is a number of theories for the unusual shape. Some think that the builders got tired and changed the angle to reduce the volume and so complete it sooner. Others suggest that the change in slope indicated a double pyramid – two pyramids superimposed. It is also suggested that the architect lost his nerve for this pyramid was being built when the pyramid at Maidoum collapsed. That too had an angle of 52° so a quick rethink was necessary. A pyramid with two entrances is also unique. The first entrance in the middle of the north face is about 12 m above the ground and leads to the upper chamber. The second in the west face is only just above ground and leads to the lower chamber. Both chambers are corbelled and the floors of both were built to a depth of 4 m with small stone blocks.

There are three other pyramids here (from north to south) belonging to the 12th Dynasty Kings, Amenemhat II, Senusert III and Amenemhat III.

Memphis

Just 15 km south of Cairo, Memphis was founded in the First Dynasty (3100-2890 BC) at the start of the Early Dynastic Period (3100-2686 BC). It was established sometime around 3100 BC by Menes who may have actually been several successive kings rather than a single person. The pharaohs' capital city throughout the Old Kingdom (2686-2181 BC), it was inhabited for 4 millennia. Eventually the old city was abandoned by the Moors and returned to the Nile silt from which it was originally constructed. Sadly all that remains today is a limestone Colossus of Ramses II (1304-1237 BC) and a giant alabaster sphinx weighing 80 tonnes, both of which may have stood outside the huge Temple of Ptah, and the remains of the Embalming House, where there are several alabaster tables, weighing up to 50 tonnes, used to embalm the sacred Apis bulls before burial at Saqqara. Beyond these its former glories can only be imagined.

El-Fayoum and Lake Qaroun

→ *Colour map 2, grid C2.*

Although usually described as an oasis, El-Fayoum is not fed by underground water, like the Western Desert oases further south and west, but by river water transported to this natural triangular depression by a series of canals. The water comes from the River Nile leaving the Ibrahimeya canal at Assiut as the Bahr Yusef which itself divides into a number of smaller canals west of Fayoum City. Having irrigated the oasis the water runs into Lake Qaroun which, despite having dramatically shrunk over the past few thousand years, is still Egypt's largest natural salt-water lake, at 215 sq km and ranging in depth from 5 m in the east to 12 m in the west. About 70,000 years ago the Nile flood first broke through the low mountains which surround the large Fayoum depression and formed Lake Qaroun and the surrounding marshes. This is believed to be one, if not the first, site of agriculture in the world as plants which grew around the lake were collected, land was fenced in, and dry and guarded storage areas were built. Even today Fayoum is still famous for fruit, vegetables and chickens. To describe food as fayoum means it is delicious. The oasis, which covers 4,585 sq km, has five main centres and 157 villages. It is 8% water, 39% cultivated area and 63% housing and desert. » *For Sleeping, Eating and other listings, see pages 167-169.*

Fayoum portraits

While excavating in a cemetery in the vicinity of the Hawara pyramid Sir Flinders Petrie found 146 quite remarkable hand-painted portraits varying in quality of style and preservation. These funeral masks or portraits were executed in tempera or encaustic – a mixture of paint and wax – on slices of cedar or other wood. They were of children, men and women of all ages. They date from Graeco-Roman times, 30 BC to 395 AD, and are among the earliest portraits known. It is assumed that they were commissioned during the person's lifetime and used as decoration in the home until required. When the deceased was embalmed the portrait would be attached to the coffin or mummy case. Examples can be seen in the museum in Cairo.

Ins and outs

Getting there Fayoum City is the main town in the oasis and the province's capital, 103 km southwest of central Cairo and 85 km from Giza and the Pyramids, an estimated 1-hour journey along the 4-lane carriageway. The Cairo-Fayoum City **bus** leaves Cairo every 30 min 0600-1800 from Midan Ahmed Helmi behind Ramses Railway Station with a stop at Midan Giza en route. Tickets cost E£4 and can be purchased in advance from the building behind the grey church in the middle of the square. **Service taxis** bound for Fayoum (E£5) tend to congregate around Midan Ramses and Midan Giza. There are 4 daily **trains** from Ramses to Fayoum, but only 3rd class (E£2) and it can take up to 4 hours. Another option is to hire a private **taxi** from Cairo to chauffeur you around, which isn't a bad idea if you can afford it, as the oasis is quite spread out. Private taxis to Fayoum should cost around E£100 per day.

Getting around The Bahr Yusef canal bisects Fayoum. Buses and taxis from Cairo terminate close to the canal under a bridge, about 2 km from the centre of town. If you don't want to walk, you can hire a taxi or *hantour* (horse-drawn carriages, E£2-5, depending on where you're going) to your destination. Local buses and service taxis serving the oasis are found at the Al-Hawatim terminal to the south of the Bahr Yusef canal. Private taxis cost about E£10 per hour and can be hired through the tourist information kiosk, Hotel Auberge du Lac and the Kom Aushim museum.

Tourist offices The main office, 2 km north of town, T084-342313, is accessible by minibus No 5. The staff's English is somewhat lacking, and at present all they offer is a fairly useless map and the usual glossy pamphlets. There's also a small office by the water-wheels, T084-343044, 325211, along with the tourist police. Note that **tourist police** often insist on accompanying foreign visitors through the oasis to ensure their safety. If you plan to stay overnight in Fayoum, you will probably be paid a visit by the police who will attempt to clarify travel protocol in Fayoum. Do not be alarmed, as their intentions are to protect you. If you want to be independent, tell them your plans and return by nightfall. It may be best to rent a bicycle in order to dodge the many checkpoints in the area.

Background

The 12th Dynasty pharaoh Amenemhat I (1991-62 BC) first drained part of the marshes to develop the area for agriculture and also dug a large canal from the River Nile controlled by a regulator at El-Lahun to the northwest of Beni Suef. The result of this and further developments by Amenemhat III (1842-1797 BC), who showed great interest in the area and built a pyramid at Hawara (see page 166), was Lake Moeris

(Great Lake), twice the present size and teeming with fish, and an agricultural area to the south renowned for its rich and varied crops.

The Romans, who called the area **Crocodilopolis** (because of the ever-present crocodiles) changed Fayoum's previous system of crop rotation and forced the area to supply grain exclusively to the Roman market. Muslims believe that the prophet Joseph developed the area during his captivity in Egypt through the canalization of the Bahr Yusef River and by building the world's first dam. Although Fayoum's national strategic importance diminished with the canalization of the Nile Delta it remains one of the most productive agricultural areas in the country.

The water level in Lake Qaroun had been falling for about 2,000 years as it received less and less water until the construction of the Aswan High Dam led to far greater stability in the level of the River Nile. By medieval times the lake had become far too salty to sustain freshwater fish and new species were introduced. The shrunken lake now lies 45 m below sea level and 40 m lower than its original level of 70,000 years ago and is one sixth of its original size. It appears that the water table is rising again as houses and fields at the lakeside have been flooded in recent years. Evidence of this is clear in notices excusing the rising damp in the walls of the Auberge du Lac and the raised sills over which one must step to gain access to hotels along the lake shore.

Despite its stagnant and polluted water the beach resorts around Lake Qaroun still attract the more affluent visitors to the region. The oasis is declared free from bilharzia, a recommendation in itself. The number of visitors is increasing and while half are Egyptian about a third are European. The season runs all year round, but from January-April it is considered too cold to swim. As part of its efforts to persuade tourists to visit areas outside the Nile valley the Egyptian Tourist Association is trying to encourage tours from Cairo, via Fayoum and the Middle Egypt sites, to both the Red Sea coast and Upper Egypt.

The majority of the oasis' population of 1.8 million people are not Nile Valley Egyptians but settled and semi-nomadic Berber people who are related to the Libyan Arabs. Although few reminders of its ancient past have survived it is still a relatively attractive town though visitors are not advised to stay in the city for long but rather to enjoy the peace and tranquility of the oasis' gardens and the lake. In addition, the

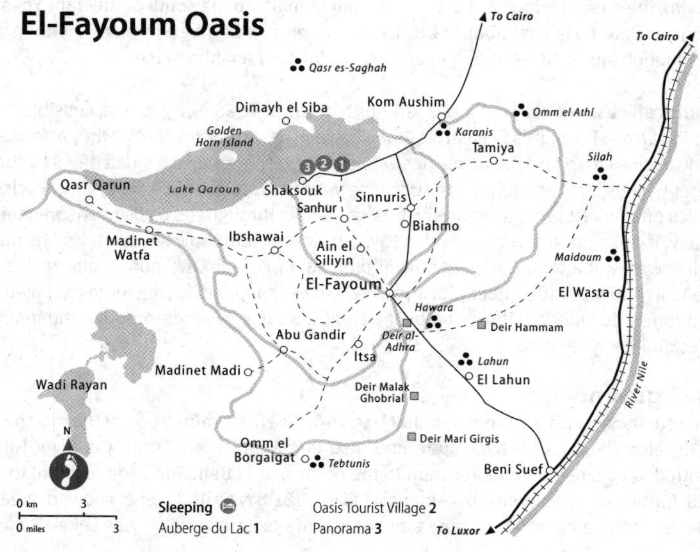

climate is splendid. The summers are not as hot as Luxor/Aswan and the winters are not as cool as Cairo or the Delta.

In the quieter areas there is a rewarding amount of wildlife to observe. While the fox is common in the town, the wolf is found only on the desert periphery. Sightings of wild cat are very rare. Thousands of egrets roost in the oasis, herons are common and many migrating birds take a rest here in spring and autumn.

Fayoum City

There is comparatively little to see in Fayoum City itself although the covered *souk* and the adjacent street of goldsmiths, **es-Sagha**, found across the fourth bridge to the west of the central tourist office, are worth a visit. A little further west along the south side of the Bahr Yusef is the attractive **Mosque of Khawand Asal-Bay** believed to have been built in 1490, or earlier, making it the oldest in the oasis. It was built by the Mamluk Sultan **Qaitbai** (1468-98) who was noted as a warrior, a builder and a torturer, for Asal-Bay who was not only his favourite concubine but also the mother of his assassinated successor Mohammed IV (1496-98), sister of Qansuh I (1498-1500) and wife of Janbalat (1500-01) who were both deposed and murdered. When, however, Tumanbay I (1501-01) married Qaitbai's official wife Fatima he insulted and disgraced Asal-Bay but he was soon deposed and exiled. Remains of its former impressive structure, most of which fell into the Bahr Yusef in 1892, include the dome supported by ancient pillars, some with Corinthian capitals, the rather plain *mihrab* and the gilded teak *minbar* elaborately carved and inlaid with ivory from Somalia. A small plaque on the wall by the *mihrab* gives information about the construction of the building.

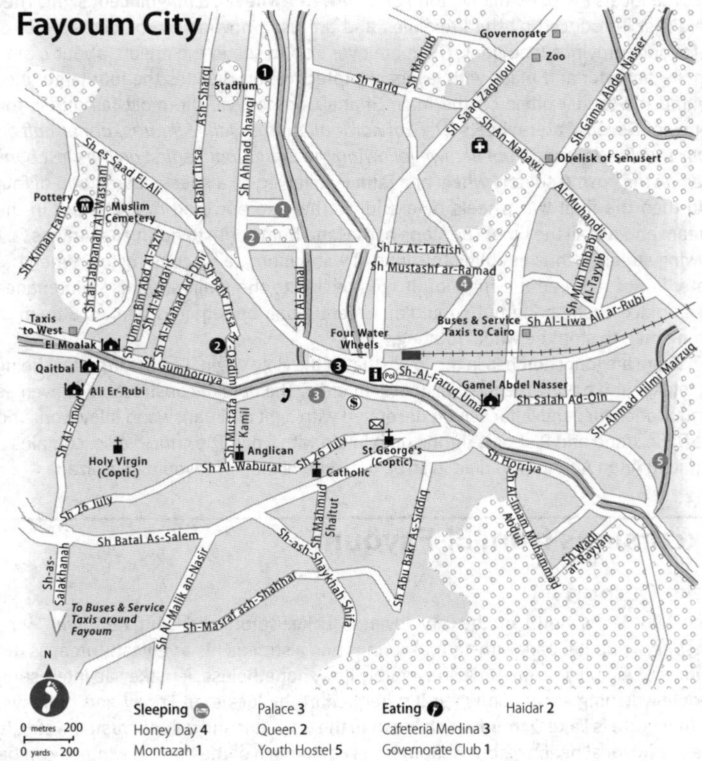

> **“” El-Fayoum is believed to be one of, if not the first, sites of agriculture in the world as plants which grew around the lake were collected, land was fenced in, and dry and guarded storage areas were built...**

Other mosques are worth visiting in town, particularly during the *moulids* (see page 170). The **Mosque and Mausoleum** in honour of **Ali El-Rubi** has a large plain white dome and a minaret. The entrance leads into a covered courtyard at the far right hand corner of which is the door to the mausoleum. The birthday feast of Ali El-Rubi is a very important *moulid* in this area. The so called **Hanging Mosque** or **El-Moalak Mosque** was constructed in limestone in 1375 by Prince Soliman Ibn Mouhamed. It is built above five arches, each of which housed a workshop, and with a double flight of steps leading to the main door. It is north of the Bahr Yusef up a small street.

The 13-m red granite **Obelisk of Senusert I** (12th Dynasty) to the northeast of town, estimated weight over 100 tonnes, serves as a useful point of reference. Originally it was in the settlement of Abgig to south but now it stands in the middle of a traffic roundabout.

The locals are particularly proud of their **water-wheels**, a magnificent sight. They were first introduced by the Ptolemies and are used now as the official symbol of El-Fayoum province (see box). There are over 200 to see in the region, about 4 m to 5 m in diameter and black with layers of protective tar. Besides the four large ones behind the tourist office on the main Sharia Gumhoriyya, the most famous is the series of **Seven Water-wheels** ⓘ *3 km north along the Bahr Sinnuris, about half an hour's walk. Walk north out of town following the Bahr Sinnuris first on the west bank then on the east.* A solitary wheel at a farm is followed by a spectacular group of four and then the final two wheels by a bridge. They are powered by the water in the stream and run all the time. The slope of the land from south to north encourages fast flowing streams, thus enabling this type of water lifting to be constructed. When the water is not required for irrigation it runs back into the main stream. Maintenance takes place each spring but should an urgent repair be required it takes a team of strong men to stop the wheel rotating.

There are four **churches** in the town, that of the Holy Virgin (Coptic Orthodox) being the oldest and having the most historical interest. The date of construction is given as 1836. Notice the large altar screen decorated with light and dark wood inlay work and the Bible stand and Bishop's throne both inlaid with ivory. The church also contains a shrine to Anba Abram who died in 1914, one time Bishop of Fayoum and Giza.

Excursions from El-Fayoum

Lake Qaroun

Nine kilometres north of the city towards Lake Qaroun lies **Aïn Al-Siliyin** ⓘ *25 piastres*, a popular park with natural springs and a stream. It's a very tatty area, as the springs of Aïn Siliyin and Aïn Alshayr rarely flow; nonetheless, it makes an interesting people-watching excursion when it's frequented by locals on Friday and holidays. Further north is **Lake Qaroun** which, despite the stagnant and salt-encrusted water, is a favourite local beach resort. Although it is calm much of the time, in winter it can be

The Groaning Water-wheels of El-Fayoum

Because the land in the El-Fayoum oasis varies from +26 m to -42 m in three main steps, self-powered water-wheels were essential and the construction of one particular type, which is exclusive to El-Fayoum, began in Pharaonic times. There are often whole series of these *sawaqih al-Hadir* (or 'roaring water-wheels'), which produce a perpetual groaning noise. There are over 200 in the oasis which has adopted the water-wheel as its official symbol.

In January each year every canal undergoes cleaning and repair. The sluices are shut, silt is dredged, walls are strengthened and the water-wheels, now white with dead algae, are lifted and overhauled. Although the wheels are considered to be ancient in fact no part is more than about 10 years old. It is said the state of the canals is a mirror of the condition of the whole country.

quite rough and teeming with ducks and geese which bring the hunters to the lakeside hotels. Qaroun means 'Lake of the Horn'. It is possible to negotiate a rowing boat from the *Auberge du Lac* to the barren **Golden Horn Island** or to the north shore.

Qsar Qarun, to the west end of the lake, has the remains of the Graeco-Roman city of Dionysias, and a well preserved limestone Ptolemaic temple dedicated to a crocodile god and decorated with a symbol of a winged sun. The date is not certain as there are no inscriptions. It is a small structure but inside there are many small rooms, corridors, cellars and tunnels. It is fun to explore – with a torch. Watch out for scorpions. There are two spiral staircases up to the roof, which provides a superb view.

Dimayh El-Siba would have been on the north coast of the lake which is now almost 3 km away. This old Ptolemaic city with ruins of a small temple dedicated to Soknopaios (crocodile) was once the starting point of a camel trade route to the oases of the Western desert. The goods first crossed the lake by boat, still a good way to reach this site.

Karanis

ⓘ *Daily 0900-1600 in winter and 0900-1700 in summer. E£16.* ⓘ *Museum Tue-Sun 0900-1600 in winter and 0900-1700 in summer, E£6.*

To the east of the lake and 25 km from the city on the main road towards Cairo, **Kom Aushim** is adjacent to the site of the ancient city of **Karanis**. Karanis, founded in the third century BC and inhabited by mercenaries of Ptolemy II, was once the centre of a large agricultural area exporting cereals to Rome via Alexandria. Of the two Roman temples, the **Temple of Pnepheros and Petesouchos** (yet more crocodile gods) is bigger and more interesting. Look for the oil/wine presses, tank for crocodiles, Roman baths with evidence of heating pipes, a row of headless sphinxes and the former residence of British High Commissioner Sir Miles Lampson. The site is very large, has a café, play area and offers **camping sites** with 50 tents available. The results of excavations carried out in the 1920s by the University of Michigan are displayed, together with exhibits from other sites around the Fayoum, in a small circular **museum** The most interesting exhibits are the carefully restored pottery and glassware, the central mummy, the necklaces and the minute statues. Trips to **Qasr es-Saghah** and the ruins of the Ptolemaic settlement of Soknopaious Nesos, which used to be on the lakeside but is now 11 km away, 65 m above the current lake, can be arranged at the museum.

Omm El-Athl, east of Karanis is the ruins of Bachias city, 700 mud brick houses and a small mud brick temple dedicated to a crocodile god. Pedestals of **Biahmo** – two 6-m high stone pedestals that once supported a seated colossus of Amenemhat

 III, can be seen in Biahmo village, 7 km north of Fayoum. Records suggest that each statue of red quartzite was 13 m above the top of its pedestal and each colossus and pedestal was surrounded by a huge solid wall.

Madinet Madi

Madinet Madi, about 30 km southwest of Fayoum City, contains the ruins of a 12th Dynasty temple, built by Amenemhat III and Amenemhat IV dedicated to Sobek the crocodile god and Renenutet the serpent goddess. This site retains an attractive avenue of lions and winged sphinxes. The walls are constructed of limestone, a soft medium for the many reliefs including one of Sobek on the outside wall at the back. The cartouches of both Amenemhats are in the sanctuary with the elegant feet and ankles (all that remains) of several statues. Access by normal vehicle. The El-Qasmiya bus departing from Al-Hawatim southwest of Fayoum city centre can drop you off.

Omm El-Borgaigat, with the ruins of **Tebtunis**, is 30 km south of Fayoum. This temple was dedicated to Sobek and was constructed of locally quarried coarse limestone. Little remains of the walls though some paving remains. A cache of mummified crocodiles was found here at the beginning of the last century.

The pyramids of El-Fayoum

There are four separate pyramid sites in the vicinity. **Hawara** pyramid, about 10 km southeast from Fayoum is a mud brick **pyramid of Amenemhat III** of 12th Dynasty, 58 m high and one side of the base measures 100 m. All the decorative casing has long since been removed. Contrary to normal practice the entrance was positioned on the south side in an unsuccessful attempt to confuse looters. Adjacent to this pyramid is the legendary **Labyrinth**, a mortuary temple built by Amenemhat III, covering an area of 105,000 sq m. It was half carved into the interior of the rock and was composed of over 3,000 rooms but today few traces remain of this spectacular construction. Nearby is the tomb of his daughter Princess Sobek-Nefru Ptah which was discovered intact in 1956.

The ruined **Pyramid of Senusert II** (1897-78 BC) near **Lahun** was built by Amenemhat III's grandfather. It was built on a rocky outcrop on which limestone pillars were constructed and then covered over with mud-brick and finally encased in stone. A 'sponge' made of sand and flint was placed around the base in order to prevent any

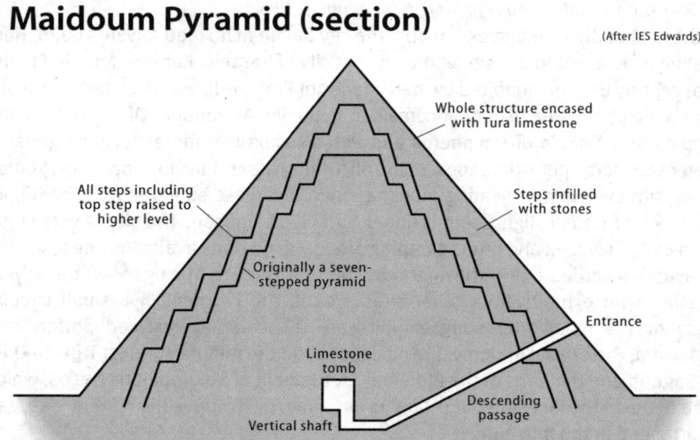

flooding. Once again the unusual south-facing entrance did not deter the tomb robbers who looted Senusert's sarcophagus but left some wonderful jewellery which is now in the Egyptian Museum and New York's Metropolitan Museum. The walled pyramid complex also includes the ruins of a subsidiary pyramid for the queen, the mortuary temple and the *mastaba* tombs of other members of the royal family.

The collapsed **Maidoum Pyramid**, ⓘ *to the northwest of El-Wasta on the River Nile, and most easily reached from there by a 1-hr early morning train journey followed by a 15-min taxi ride to the village of Maidoum and a short walk.* Originally it was 144 m sq and 42 m high but over the centuries the imposing pyramid, which is built on the edge of an escarpment above the cultivated area, has collapsed leaving only a central three-stepped core of stone standing 65 m high which looks rather like a medieval fort. The difficult entry is up a 30-m stairway on the north side from which visitors descend into a long 57-m sloping passage which levels out to reach a short vertical shaft leading to the limestone-lined and corbel roofed burial chamber which is on the same level as the pyramid's foundations.

While it is generally agreed that the Maidoum Pyramid housed the first Fourth Dynasty (2613-2494 BC) pharaoh Snefru, because he also had two other pyramids at Dashur, it is now believed that it was started by his father Huni and completed by Snefru. The theory as to why it collapsed is that, unlike the pyramids at Giza which distributed the stresses inwards, this has incorrectly calculated outward stresses – part of the trial and error evolution from the early step-pyramid to the later standard pyramid.

Slightly further north are the rubble remains of the **Seila/Silah** step pyramid of limestone from Second Dynasty and adjacent rock tombs, thought to be Christian. This excursion requires four-wheel drive, a guide and a short walk.

The monasteries of El-Fayoum

Saint Anthony (AD 251-356) acted as an inspiration for hermits and there were soon numerous monasteries throughout the country including the Fayoum depression. A number still stand today. The 12th-century **Deir Al-Adhra** (**Monastery of the Virgin**), just off the road to Beni Suef about 6 km outside Fayoum City, is the most accessible. It was inhabited until the 18th century then fell into disuse. Bishop Anba Abram was buried here in 1914. The *moulid* of the Virgin is celebrated here each August and the number of pilgrims, already large, is increasing each year. Further south is the beautiful seventh-century Coptic **Deir Malak Ghobrial** (**Monastery of the Angel Gabriel**) on the desert escarpment at Naqlun above the cultivated lowlands. There is a large number of cells in the area – cut into the hillside – which were accommodation for the monks. The last rebuilding/refurbishment took place this century, so today pilgrims to the annual celebration find more comfortable places to stay in the monastery buildings which surround the church. The church is of a simple classic design. Elements of older buildings have been incorporated giving an impression of greater antiquity. There are icons from the 19th century. **Deir Hammam**, which was originally built in the sixth or eighth century, is 6 km northeast of Lahun and Coptic **Deir Mari Girgis** (**Monastery of St George**) can be reached by boat from Sidmant Al-Gabal which is 15 km southwest of Lahan. Even more isolated is **Deir Anba Samwail** (**Monastery of St Samuel**) which is about 30 km south of the rim of the Fayoum depression and can only be reached by pack animal or four-wheel drive vehicle.

Fayoum City *p163, map p163*

E **Honey Day Hotel**, Sharia Gamal Abdel Nasser, Fayoum Entrance, T084-340105. A bit of a walk from the town centre en route to the Obelisk of Senusert. A cheap clean 2-star hotel with its own restaurant and coffee shop. Friendly staff. Rooms have a/c, TV and fridge. There's a 25% discount for groups.

E **Palace Hotel**, on Sharia El-Horiyya, T084-351222, very central, overlooking the Bahr Yusef. 35 reasonably clean rooms with optional bath and a/c. Breakfast included. Owner speaks English and is a good source of information. Cars, motorbikes and bicycles for hire.

E-F **Queen**, Sharia Manshat Luftallah, Fayoum City, T084-337828. A newish hotel with gleaming rooms that surround a quaint courtyard. All rooms have private bath but there's an extra charge for a/c and TV. Breakfast included. A quiet and comfortable place to stay, particularly if you're in town for a while.

F **El-Montazah**, Manshat Lutfallah, Fayoum City, T084-324633. Next to the Bahr Sinnuris canal in a quiet area north of the town centre, run by Copts. A decent budget hotel, though rooms have seen better days. Some have a/c. Bicycles and motorbikes for hire.

F **Fayoum Youth Hostel**, Flat No 7, Housing Block No 7, Hadaka, ask for *Beit El-shebab* to find it. 46 beds, self-catering facilities. Breakfast included. Inconveniently located and often empty. Still, at E£8 per person, the price is the cheapest in town and anyone can stay here.

Lake Qaroun *p164*

A-B **Auberge du Lac**, Lake Qaroun, T084-572001, F572003. Has 77 a/c rooms with telephone, TV and bath, laundry, 24-hr room service, 4 restaurants (open 0600-2300 in season), disco (open 2200-0300 in season). Also tennis, squash, 2 pools, water sports, boats for hire, duck shooting, poorly equipped gym and health club, parking, facilities for handicapped, major cards accepted. Comfortable, but not luxurious. The view from the more expensive rooms is blocked by the cheaper chalets built in the gardens beside the lake. King Ibn Saud and Winston Churchill met here in 1945; ask to have a look at the suite used by King Farouk, faded and well past its former glory, much like the hotel at large.

B **New Panorama Shakshuk Village**, Lake Qaroun, T084-701314, F701757. Has 66 a/c rooms with balcony and lake view, TV room, pool, water sports, fishing, wind surfing, waterskiing, duck shooting, garden, restaurants inside and out, seafood speciality. Rooms were recently remodelled.

D **Oasis Tourist Village**, Lake Qaroun, T084- 830666. Lakeside location, 28 rooms, 2 restaurants (1 over the lake), pool over lake, cheerful staff, caravan and camping facilities.

Eating

Fayoum City *p163, map p163*

† **Governorate Club**, on the grounds of Nadi Al-Muhafzah, reached by *hantour* or minibus No 9. There's a E£3 entrance fee to the club. Food is cheap and tasty, with kebab, chicken, and steak, spaghetti, and standard local mezzes. The tahina is particularly good.

† **Haidar Restaurant**, near Bahr Yusef, with an English sign. Serves stewed lamb and grilled chicken. Not a lot of options for vegetarians.

Lake Qaroun *p164*

††† **Café Gabal El-Zinah**, Lake Qaroun. Play areas for children, boat landing, fish is main item on menu.

††† **Auberge du Lac**, Lake Qaroun. Provides average quality food in attractive surroundings.

†† **Café Al-Louloua**, Lake Qaroun. At major junction, serves reasonable Westernish food.

†† **Lake Plage Café**, Lake Qaroun. Has 1.5 km of beach, play areas for children, adequate but unimaginative.

Shopping

Fayoum chickens, fresh fruit and straw baskets are available in the **city** and the village of **Tunis**, a farming community transformed into a sort of artist's haven, is renowned for exquisite local pottery.

Transport

Fayoum City *p163, map p163*

Bus

To **Cairo's** Ahmed **Helmi** and **Giza** stations, buses leave every 30 mins between 0630-1830 from the main bus station east of the town centre by the bridge. There are also regular buses south to **Beni Suef** with connections south up the **Nile Valley**.

Taxi

Service taxis are quicker but more hair-raising than buses and leave the depot next to the bus station for central **Cairo** via **Midan Giza**, and for **Beni Suef**.

Train

There are several daily trains to **Cairo** and **Beni Suef**, but the service is slow and limited to 3rd-class travel.

Directory

Fayoum City *p163, map p163*
Banks Bank of Alexandria, Banque du Caire, Banque Misr, (with ATM machine) and National Bank of Egypt, in town centre. **Places of worship** There are 4 churches in El-Fayoum where services are held in Arabic or Coptic/Arabic. **Post office** Central post office is on the south side of the Bahr Yusef canal opposite the central tourist office. **Useful numbers** Ambulance: T123; Fire: T180; Hospital: T084-342249. Police: T122.

Eastern Delta

→ *Colour 2, grid A/B 2/3*

The branching of the River Nile divides the Delta into three interlocking areas. The best Pharaonic ruins including Tanis and Bubastis are in the Eastern Delta. The main road (H1) from Cairo to Damietta runs north through the Central Delta via Tanta before striking northeast through El-Mansura but there are other more interesting routes. Turning east in Benha, a road goes through Zagazig to the ancient sites of Nabasha and Tanis from which a minor road continues to the coast or north through the intensive cultivation to El-Mansura. Damietta gives access along the coast either east to Port Said (see page 359) at the northern end of the Suez Canal or west to the coastal resorts of Ras El-Bar, Gamassa and even the isolated Baltim.

The main road is normally very busy with a mixture of agricultural traffic and vehicles bound for the ports. On Fridays and holidays it can be even busier with private cars. Shamut Oranges between Tukh and Benha is a very popular spot for picnics. Pigeon towers of varying designs are common in the delta region. The pigeons provide free fertilizer and are the main ingredient in 'pigeon sweet and sour', a speciality dish. ▸▸ *For Sleeping, Eating and other listings, see pages 173-174.*

Land and sea merge at the fringes of the delta creating a mixture of lagoons and fragile mudflats – so there can be no possibility of a coastal road. The first inland paved route winds its way for over 300 km from Alexandria to Port Said.

Benha

About 48 km north of Cairo, Benha is the first major town on the H1 highway. It's a stop on the Cairo-Alexandria train line, and accessible by bus every 20 minutes (0600-2100) from Cairo's Aboud terminal, where it's also possible to catch a service taxi. Close by lie the remains of the ancient town of **Athribis** which was once the capital of the 10th Nome and associated with the worship of the black bull. Although it pre-dates the Greeks, its greatest importance was during the Roman period. Its orderly layout, like that of many Delta towns, was built around two intersecting roads. Little remains of the town today except traces of 18th-26th Dynasty temples and an extensive Graeco-Roman cemetery. A cache of 26th-30th Dynasty silver ingots and jewellery from the site is now in the Egyptian Museum in Cairo.

Zagazig

The provincial capital, 36 km northeast of Benha, 80 km from Cairo, was founded in 1830 and was the birthplace of the nationalist Colonel Ahmed Orabi who led the 1882 revolt against the British. It can be reached by bus or service taxi from Cairo. Trains bound for Port Said stop at the local station. The small **Orabi Museum** ⓘ *daily*

Moulids – Festivals in the Delta

Officially, *moulids* are festivals in commemoration of a specific saint when pilgrims obtain their *baraka* or blessing by visiting their shrine. There is usually a parade of devotees, carrying banners and dressed in turbans and sashes in the colours of their saint, which is followed by chanting and dancing that goes on for hours. In addition, however, the most important *moulids* are like a giant medieval fair where pilgrims meet their friends and eat, drink and celebrate. They stroll amongst the stalls and rides watching the magicians, jugglers, acrobats, snake charmers, animal trainers and other traditional entertainers.

0900-1300 except Tue, contains some interesting archaeological exhibits. However, most visitors stop in Zagazig to see the large ruins of Bubastis which lie 1 km southeast of the town.

Bubastis

ⓘ *To reach the site, walk the km south along Sharia Farouq, or hail a taxi (1E£) or microbus (25p).*

This was the capital of the 18th Nome of Lower Egypt and was known to the Ancient Egyptians as Pr Baset (House of Baset). The name is derived from the worship of the Egyptian cat goddess Baset who was believed to be the daughter of the sun-god Re. During the Old Kingdom she was originally associated with the destructive forces of his eye and was symbolized as a lion. Later, during the Middle Kingdom, this image was tamed and she was represented with a brood of kittens and carrying the sacred rattle. The ancient Egyptians worshipped cats and mummified them at a number of sites including Bubastis because they believed that they would be protected by Baset.

The town was begun during the Sixth Dynasty (2345-2181BC) with the granite **Temple of Baset** ⓘ *daily 0800-1600, E£10*, which was enlarged over the centuries until the 18th Dynasty (1567-1320 BC) and was excavated in the 19th century. Herodotus described it as the most pleasing in the whole of Egypt but also criticized the antics of up to 700,000 pilgrims who attended the licentious festivals. Near the site is an underground **cat cemetery** where many statues of Baset have survived. You may (if you're lucky) find a guide to get you in.

El-Mansura

About 55 km north of Zagazig, El-Mansura is an attractive River Nile city which was founded comparatively recently (AD 1220) by the great Salah Al-Din's nephew Sultan Al-Kamil (AD 1218-38) during the Siege of Damietta by the Crusader forces during the Sixth Crusade. Despite its name, which means 'the victorious', the Crusaders reoccupied Damietta in 1249 and then, following the death in El-Mansura of Kamil's son Sultan Ayyub (1240-49), which was concealed by his widow in order not to demoralize his troops, the Crusaders captured the town. However, when the Crusaders were weakened by a vicious bout of food poisoning, the Muslims counter-attacked and captured not only El-Mansura but also France's King Louis IX before he was eventually ransomed for the return of Damietta.

Today Mansura is better known as the centre of the cotton industry. During harvest time it is interesting to see the activity in the fields, but the incredibly overladen carts bring road traffic to a standstill.

Herodotus: the historian

Herodotus lived in Greece in the fifth century BC. His great achievement was his history of the Greek wars against the Persian Empire. His origins are obscure but it is believed that he was a Greek born in Asia Minor in approximately 485 BC. He developed the great tradition of Greek historical research in which questions were asked and answers to them sought in the available written evidence. He became an avid collector of information – stories and travel data – which he eventually assembled into his *History*, writings on the wars against the Persians. He travelled widely in Asia Minor, the Black Sea region and the Mediterranean islands.

Perhaps his most famous journey was to Egypt. He began in the Nile delta and voyaged to Memphis, Thebes and the first cataract. He was deeply interested in the topography of the Nile Valley and in the nature of the Nile flood. He is attributed with the saying that, "Egypt is the gift of the Nile". Like all geographer-historians of the early period, he mixed scientific evidence and serious observation with myths, fables and tall tales. His readers were given all the excitement of the grotesque and supernatural wonders of the world, though he rarely entirely gave up rational explanations for historical events he wrote about including those in Egypt. His works were widely accepted in Athenian society and today are regarded as an important development in the establishment of history as an academic study (he was a contemporary and companion of Sophocles). In his later life he moved to a new Greek city colony in Thurii, Italy, where he is buried.

Tanis

While most travellers from Zagazig head north to El-Mansura, those going east towards the Suez Canal might make a detour to the ruins of an Old Kingdom city better known by its Greek name of **Tanis (Djane)**. It is located near the modern village of San El-Hagar, 167 km from Zagazig. It once lay alongside the now dry Tanite branch of the River Nile, which is how it got its name. In the **Second Intermediate Period** (1786-1567 BC) Asiatic settlers to the region, known as the Hyksos kings or 'princes of foreign lands', established the 15th Dynasty (1674-1567 BC) until they were expelled from Egypt and chased back to Asia by indigenous Theban kings from Luxor.

Until earlier this century it was believed that Tanis was Avaris, the capital of the Hyksos Kingdom, but Avaris has now been discovered further to the southwest at the modern day site of Tell El-Dab'a. Instead Tanis was the birth place of Ramses I (1320-18 BC) an ambitious local prince who become pharaoh and founded the 19th Dynasty (see page 233). The area is dotted with ruins, scattered and broken statues and stones which are the only remnants of the **Temple of Amun**. To the south of the temple is the **Royal Necropolis** which is closed to the public. Six tombs of the 11th and 22nd Dynasties were found here. They were almost intact.

Tell Al-Maskhuta

Another ruined site on the eastern edge of the Delta is **Tell Al-Maskhuta** which lies just south of the main Zagazig (70 km) to Ismailia (11 km) road. It has been identified as the site of the ancient town of **Tjehu** which was the capital of the 8th Nome of Lower Egypt and was often known by its Biblical name of **Pithom**. Archaeological excavations have revealed the foundations of the ancient city, a temple structure and brick chambers for single and multiple burials together with children's bodies buried

Sacred cats

Cats were first domesticated by the Egyptians and it seems probable that the breed they domesticated was the *Kaffir* cat, a thin, poorly striped, grey cat common all over Africa. Numerous tomb drawings and mummified bodies have been discovered which date from the very early Egyptian dynasties.

The cat was held in great awe and worshipped in the form of the cat-headed goddess Bast (or Pasht) from which it has been suggested the word 'puss' is derived. Egyptians believed that all cats went to heaven: there was a choice of two heavens, the more aristocratic creatures having a better class destination. If a family cat died the household members would all go into mourning and shave off their eyebrows.

in amphorae. A well preserved sphinx and a statue of Ramses II were also uncovered and are now in a museum in Ismailia.

Damietta

Back near the River Nile the easiest way north from El-Mansura is to cross the river to the Central Delta town of Talkha and head up the main H8 highway to the coastal town of **Damietta** (or **Dumyat**). It is on the east bank almost at the mouth of the Damietta branch of the River Nile and is 191 km from Cairo, 122 km from Zagazig and 66 km from El-Mansura. Furniture-making is an important craft, while production of confectionery and fresh fruit and vegetables adds to the economy.

The town is in many ways similar to Rosetta, 50 km east of Alexandria (see page 177). Damietta flourished as a trading port throughout the Middle Ages but suffered greatly during the Crusades. The Christian forces occupied the town in 1167-68 and again in 1218-21 when St Francis of Assisi accompanied the invaders. Sultan Al-Kamil's attempts to recapture it followed. (See El-Mansura, page 170.) Worse was yet to come, for the Mamluks destroyed the city in 1250 and made the river impassable as a punishment for suspected disloyalty and to prevent further invasions. The Ottomans revived the town and, as in the case of Rosetta, many of their attractive buildings are still in good condition. The last Ottoman Pasha here surrendered to the Beys in 1801 before the time of Mohammed Ali. Although the construction of the Suez Canal shifted trade to Port Said, 70 km to the east, Damietta is still a small and successful port although it has little to attract visitors.

As well as looking at the Ottoman buildings, visit the new Coptic church of St Mary opened by Pope Shenuda in 1992. Out of town is the huge **Lake El-Manzala** which in winter teems with migrating birds including flamingoes, spoonbills and herons (see birdwatching information, page 527). On the other side of the branch of the River Nile there are three beach resorts, **Ras El-Bar**, **Gamassa** and **Baltim** which, although technically in the Central Delta, are most easily reached from Damietta.

Ras El-Bar

Ras El-Bar is a reasonably attractive resort popular with middle-class Egyptians who want to get away from Cairo's summer heat. It's easily accessible from Damietta. During the summer, service taxis and special a/c buses run direct from Cairo's Aboud bus station. **Al-Jirbi**, just 2 km from Ras El-Bar has a therapy centre for the treatment of gout, sciatica, polio and rheumatism, but it's only open in the summer months.

Gamassa

Further west along the coast about 20 km from Damietta, Gamassa is another resort with a long beach, some 25 km, of fine sand. A new development of apartments and holiday homes has encroached on the beach which could be cleaner. Locals sunbathe here. The sea is dark – with iodine. The town is accessible by bus from Damietta or directly from Cairo. Alternatively catch a train to El-Mansura or Shirban from where a bus can be caught.

Baltim

This was once the most inaccessible and quietest of the three resorts, actually about half way between Damietta and Rosetta and, although it can be reached from Damietta it may be easier by direct coach from Cairo. Once the playground of the rich and leisured it is now a resort which caters for those who do not expect such high standards of service or cleanliness. Litter is a problem here. Take a Delta East bus or the train to El-Mansura and complete the journey by bus.

Sleeping

Zagazig *p169*
There aren't many choices and you may be better off venturing here from Cairo or Alexandria on a day trip. If you do get stuck in town, you can try the:
F **Opera**, near the train station, T055-2303718. Said to be none better in town.

El-Mansura *p170*
There are a few cheap and simple hotels in El-Mansura including:
D **Marshal El-Gezirah**, Sharia Gezirah El-Ward, T/F050-2213000. West of town centre on the corniche is the best in town.
E **Cleopatra**, 13 Souk Toggar, El-Gharby, T050-2246789; F2241234. 39 rooms.
F **Abu Shama Hotel**, Sharia Bank Misr, T050-2245227, F2245227. 31 rooms.
F **Marshal**, Midan Om Kalsoum, T050-2233920; F2233920. 57 rooms.
F **Mecca Touristic**, Sharia El-Abbas, Corniche, T050-2249910. 54 rooms.
F **Royal**, 40 Sharia El-Thawra, T050-2257575. 24 rooms.

Damietta *p172*
The only government registered hotel is:
F **El-Manshi Hotel**, 5 Sharia El-Nokrashy, T057-323308. 20 rooms, which are barely comfortable.
There are a few other even cheaper hotels along the Corniche.

Ras El-Bar *p172*
There are lots of cheap beach hotels catering for Egyptian tourists. The best of a mediocre bunch are:
D **Green House Hotel**, 41, Sharia Port Said, T057-528751, F528752.
E **Abu Tabl**, 4 Sharia 17, T057-528166. 34 rooms.
E **El Medina El-Monawara**, 1 Sharia 29, T057-527261. 34 rooms.
E **El-Mina Hotel**, end of Sharia 61, El-Shatee, T057-529290. 50 rooms.
The standard of the hotels shifts as often as the management. Inspect a few rooms before you settle anywhere.

Gamassa *p173*
There are a number of hotels which range from those detailed below to unofficially registered ones with cabin-like chalets.
E **Amoun**, El-Souk area, Gamassa, T050-760660, located on the beach. Best in town.
E **Beau Rivage**, Gamassa, T050-760268. 86 rooms.
F **Hannoville**, Shagaret El-Dor Area, Gamassa, T050-760750. 50 rooms.

Baltim *p173*
There are two very basic simple hotels that cater mainly for Egyptian summer tourists. Both charge E£10 per night.
F **Baltim Beach**, El-Narguess Area, Baltim, T047-501541. 30 rooms.
F **Cleopatra Touristic**, Baltim Beach. 28 rooms.

The Pied Kingfisher

The Pied Kingfisher (*Ceryle rudis*) is very common in Egypt – wherever there is water. Like all kingfishers it is recognized by its larger than expected head with a rather insignificant crest, a long, sturdy, sharp beak and by its short tail and short legs. The bird, 25 cm long, is found in both salt and fresh water. It is a superb diver, fishing from a hovering position over the water or from a perch on a convenient branch. The sexes are similar in sizes in colouring, being black and white – a white band over the eye reaching to the back of the head, a mottled crest, a white throat and neck. The back is mottled, the feathers being black with white edges. The wings are mainly black with a white central band. It has a white breast and under surface except for two black bands (only one black band on the female). It nests in holes in the river bank.

Transport

Zagazig *p169*

Bus Buses leave for **Tanta**, **El-Mansura**, **Benha**, **Alexandria**, **Ismailia** and **Port Said**. **Taxi** Service taxis congregate by the railway station. They go all over the **Delta** as well as to **Cairo** and the **Canal region**. **Train** Trains from Zagazig run daily to **Cairo**, (13 daily, 1-hr), **Benha** (13 daily, 45 mins) **Ismailia** (13 daily, 1-hr), and **Port Said** (7 daily, 2 hrs).

El-Mansura *p170*

Bus Buses run twice hourly (0600-2100) to and from **Cairo**, **Alexandria**, **Zagazig**. From the International bus station, it's possible to take a bus directly to the **Sinai** and the **Canal Zone** cities. **Taxi** Service taxis cover the same destinations as buses, and depart from the bus stations.
Train From El-Mansura, there are slow trains that run regularly to **Cairo** (3 hrs, 4 daily), **Zagazig**, **Damietta** and **Tanta**.

Damietta *p172*

Bus and service taxis There are hourly buses and service taxis to **Cairo** either down the main H8 highway via **Tanta** and **Benha** or the east route via **El-Mansura** and **Zagazig**. **Port Said**, 70 km east along the causeway which divides the lake from the Mediterranean, is most easily reached by service taxi. **Train** Although they are slower, there are trains to **Cairo**, **Alexandria**, **Tanta** and **Zagazig**.

Central Delta

→ *Colour 2, grid A/B 2*

There are fewer sites in the Central Delta but it does include two of Egypt's largest cities and features some of the biggest annual moulids. If you want to explore the area for a few days, it's probably best to base yourself in the large but charming town of Tanta, which has a wide range of services, and is also holds Egypt's largest moulid*; from there, it's easy to make day trips to the various sites. If you're aiming for the Central Delta's small coastal resorts of Gamassa and Ras El-Bar, they are more easily reached from the Eastern Delta coastal town of Damietta.* ▸▸ *For Sleeping, Eating and other listings, see page 176.*

Tanta

This town maintains its rural atmosphere despite being the fifth largest city in Egypt and having a major university. It is 94 km north of Cairo and 130 km southeast of Alexandria on the main agricultural route between the two cities. The H1 highway from Cairo to Benha crosses the Damietta branch of the River Nile and continues northwest via Birket El-Sab to Tanta.

High Noon at Damyanah – Martyrs' Calendar

Damyanah, who was the daughter of Rome's regional governor in the time of Diocletian (AD 284-305), chose celibacy rather than marriage and took refuge with 40 other virgins in a palace built for her by her father. When her father renounced the worship of the Roman gods and converted to Christianity both he and all of the women were executed on the orders of Diocletian. His persecution of the Christians was so great that the Copts date their era, known as the Martyrs' Calendar, from the massacres of AD 284. The first shrine to Damyanah is believed to have been built by St Helena who was the mother of emperor Constantine (AD 306-337).

Although it is an interesting city, worth visiting for a taste of contemporary Egyptian life without the glories of past eras and masses of tourists, there is little or nothing to see in Tanta itself for most of the year. It really comes alive, however, in late October at the end of the cotton harvest, during the eight-day festival or **Moulid of Sayid Ahmed El-Badawi** when the population swells to over two million as pilgrims pour in from throughout Egypt and the Muslim world.

Sayid Ahmed El-Badawi (AD 1199-1276) was the founder of one of Egypt's largest Sufi *tariqas* (brotherhoods/orders) which is known as the Badawiya. Born in Fes, Morocco, he emigrated to Arabia and then travelled to Iraq where he joined the Rifaiyah brotherhood. After being sent to Tanta in 1234 as its representative, he received permission to establish his own *tariqa* which soon flourished. Although the mosque built by his successor and containing his tomb was demolished in the mid-19th century, a large, new, rather undistinguished one was built by pasha Abbas I (AD 1848-54) and is the focus of Badawi's annual *moulid*.

El-Mahalla El-Kubra

The fourth largest city in Egypt, is 25 km northeast of Tanta and 120 km north of Cairo. The only decent hotel is **E Omar El-Khayyam**, Midan 23 July, T040-2234299, 36 rooms. To the west of the nearby riverside town of **Sammanud** lie the remains of the red and black granite **Temple of Onuris-Shu**, rebuilt by Nectanebo II (360-343 BC) for Tjeboutjes, the capital of the 12th Nome of Lower Egypt. Further northeast some 10 km from Sammanud along the main H8 highway towards **Talkha** there is the modern town of **Bahbait Al-Hagar** and what little remains of the great **Temple of Isis** in the ancient town of **Iseum** or **Pr-Hebeit** as it was known to the ancient Egyptians.

Monastery of St Damyanah

Continuing further along the H8 highway 25 km past Talkha, is the town of **Shirban** which has a bridge to the east bank of the Rosetta branch of the River Nile. Leaving H8 and travelling 12 km west along H7 is **Bilqas** where, 3 km to the north, is the Monastery of St Damyanah (Deir Sitt Damyanah). St Damyanah was put to death, along with another 40 maidens, under Diocletian's purges against the Christians. Normally it is isolated and difficult to reach except during the annual **Moulid of Damyanah** between 15-20 May, which is one of the country's largest Christian *moulids*. Thousands of pilgrims flock to the four 19th- and 20th-century churches on the site in the hope of being healed. Women praying for increased fertility and those who have lost young children are common visitors here.

El-Bagur

The only claim to fame of **El-Bagur**, which lies at the extremity of the Central Delta to the south of **Shiban El-Kom**, is that it is President Mubarak's small home town. The only place to stay is **E Nice Tourist Village**, El-Bagur Minufiya, T040-384072, 25 rooms. Mubarak's predecessor President Anwar Sadat, who was assassinated by Islamic fundamentalists in 1981, came from the nearby village of **Mit Abu El-Kom** which is close to Quweisna on the main Benha-Tanta highway.

Sleeping

Tanta *p174*

Unless you are visiting specifically for the *moulid* when it is essential to book well in advance, there should be no problem in finding a room.

D **New Arafa Hotel**, Midan Station, T040-3336952, F3331800. 58 recently renovated spacious rooms, with a/c, TV, and a restaurant, directly outside the train station.

D **Green House**, Sharia El-Borsa, Midan Gumhoriyya to the east of the train station, T040-3330761, F3330320. 30 good a/c rooms with TV and fridge, restaurant, splendid central location. Worth trying if New Arafa is full.

F **Youth Hostel**, Sharia Mahala El-Kobra, T040-3337978. 24 beds, parking.

Eating

Tanta *p174*

Besides the very acceptable restaurants in the aforementioned hotels, there are numerous cheap food stalls around town, especially during the *moulids*.

Transport

Tanta *p174*

Air EgyptAir, T040-3321750. **Bus** The bus station, 2 km north of the city centre, has hourly service (0600-2100) to all the towns mentioned in this section, plus a few morning buses to **Port Said**. **Taxi** Service taxis run regularly from the bus station to **Cairo** and **Alexandria**. **Train** There are 8 trains daily to **Cairo**, **Alexandria**, **Benha** and **Damanhur**, and frequent services to **Mansura**, **Damietta**, and **Zagazig**.

Directory

Tanta *p174*

Banks Delta Bank may cash your TCs and **Banque Misr** has an ATM. Both banks are in Midan Gumhoriyya.

Western Delta

→ *Colour map 2, grid A1*

Across the wider Rosetta branch of the Nile is the Western Delta. The main attractions are the port of Rosetta and a couple of moulids *held in and around the town of Damanhur. This route, like most in the delta, goes through an interesting mixture of scenery: fields of cotton, sugar cane and patches of vegetables, tiny clusters of houses, old fashioned water-lifting devices (see Delu well in Background, page 522). The area bustles with carts, donkeys, and people working in the fields. It is an ever-changing scene of rural Egypt, yet most travellers rush straight on to Alexandria. The taming of the Nile in the late 19th century, enabling perennial irrigation, enables the cultivation of three or four crops a year in this extremely fertile region.*

Ins and outs

Getting there and around There is one train per day to and from **Alexandria** (2 hrs, E£4). Minibuses to Rosetta also depart from Alexandria. There's no direct transport from Cairo. The easiest way to arrive by public transport is to travel via Damanhur, where you can catch a **service taxi** to Rosetta (1-hr, E£2).

The Hoopoe

The Hoopoe *Upupa epopsis* is like no other bird – it is the only one in its species. It is a resident breeder, fairly common especially in the Delta area. The sexes are similar, both 28 cm in length. You will see it on lawns and in parks and oases where it disturbs the ground searching for grubs. It also eats locusts, moths, spiders and ants. It nests in holes in old trees or ruins (plenty of scope in Egypt) laying up to six eggs.

In general the colouring is buff/ pink with very distinctive black and white bars in a striped pattern (like a zebra) on the wings and tail. It has a long and slender down-curving bill with a black tip, a square tail and broad rounded wings, striped with black tips. A distinctive, large erect crest runs from front to back of the head, the feathers having quite marked black tips. This crest is raised when it alights and is evident in mating displays. The call is a distinct 'Hoo-poo-oo'.

Damanhur

Mid-way between Tanta and Alexandria, Damanhur lies in the middle of the Western Delta, 160 km northwest of Cairo. This sleepy provincial capital and textile town, which was once the site of the ancient city of Tmn-Hor dedicated to Horus, has little to offer the visitor. In November, however, there is the **Moulid of Sheikh Abu Rish** which follows the more important one in Tanta. Extending over two days in January is Egypt's only **Jewish moulid** at the shrine of a 19th-century mystic called **Abu Khatzeira**. For security, non-Jewish Egyptians are denied entrance to the festival; most attendees are Europeans and Israelis who bring sick relatives or bottled water to be blessed at the shrine.

Rosetta

ⓘ *Ticket for the museum in Kili House E£20, students E£10, cameras E£10, daily 0900-1600. Tickets to other sites (including Ramadan House and Hammam Azouz) are purchased in the tourist office near Beit Kili and cost E£12, students E£6.*

Rosetta (Rashid), formerly known as 'the city of a million palms and dates', used to be the principal port in Egypt. Since ancient times its fortunes have been linked with the ebb and flow of those of its neighbour Alexandria, 64 km to the west. When one waxed, the other would wane. Mohammed Ali's Mahmudiya Canal project linking the River Nile to Alexandria marked the end of Rosetta's significance as a port. And whilst Alexandria is now Egypt's second city, Rosetta is little more than a fishing village. Nonetheless, it is famous for the 1799 discovery of the **Rosetta Stone**, the key to our understanding of hieroglyphics and, consequently, much of what we know of Egypt's ancient civilization. (See box Breaking the Code.) The stone is inscribed, in Greek, hieroglyphics and demotic Egyptian with a proclamation by Ptolemy V Epiphanes. Today it rests in the British Museum of London.

There is also some striking architecture in the town from the Ottoman period, recently renovated, that offers a taste of Rosetta's splendid past. Many of Rosetta's houses are made of distinctive red and black brick and incorporate recycled stones and columns from earlier eras. Many too have delicately carved *mashrabiyyas*. The **Ramadan House**, is open for visitors and exemplifies the most stunning of Rosetta's fine architecture. A ticket inside will also grant access to the beautifully restored 19th-century bathhouse, **Hammam Azouz**, which offers a sense of the splendor of old traditional bathhouses. Also worth noting is the house of **El-Fatatri** just off the main street to the north of the town and **Beit Kili** (18th-century), at the west end of Midan El-Gumhoriyya. The latter is now a museum noted for its delicately handcrafted

Breaking the code

Jean-Francois Champollion was born in the village of Figeac in France in December 1790. He was a precocious learner of difficult foreign languages and from an early age became involved with studies of Greek, Latin and the Coptic languages.

Like other scholars before him, in the 1820s he began deciphering Egyptian hieroglyphs and by 1822 evolved a virtually complete set of hieroglyphic signs and their Greek equivalent, using the information on the Rosetta Stone.

The Rosetta Stone was found near Rashid in 1799 by soldiers of Napoleon's expedition to Egypt. The huge, irregularly shaped piece of granite weighing 762 kg was embedded in the wall of El-Rashid fort, a piece of recycled fortification. It is thought to have been written by one of the high priests of Memphis in the ninth year of Ptolemy V's reign (196 BC) and is originally a decree of Ptolemy V declaring the benefits he, as a monarch, conferred on Egypt. Its importance was not in its content – though it did establish, amongst other things, that Ptolemy reunited the country – but in its presentation of three scripts: Greek script below and hieroglyphs; demotic and cursive Egyptian languages above.

The Swede Akerblad and the Englishman Thomas Young had made some progress in deciphering the Rosetta Stone but it was Champollion, using his knowledge of Egyptology, Greek and Coptic languages, who finally broke the code. He was unique in understanding that individual Egyptian hieroglyphs stood for individual letters, groups of letters and even for entire objects.

Champollion undertook archaeological work in Egypt in 1828 with the Italian Ippolito Rosellini, recording a whole series of sites in the Nile Valley. He died suddenly in 1832 age 42 years having been curator of the Egyptian collection of the Louvre and professor of Egyptian antiquities at the highly esteemed Collège de France. His brother Jacques-Joseph prepared and published his works after Jean-Francois's death.

woodwork. Other buildings to look out for are **Thabet House**, **Amasyali House** and the **Abu Shahin Mill**. The mosques are worth a visit for their coloured tilework. The huge **Zaghloul Mosque**, (around 1600), a block north of the main road to Alexandria, is a double mosque. The brighter and smarter half to the west is noted for its arched courtyard while the other half, with over 300 columns, sadly suffers from partial submersion. The **Mohammed Al-Abassi Mosque** (1809) standing to the south of the town by the Nile, has a distinctive minaret. A lively **market** is held in the main street to the north of the town towards the station.

Near Rosetta, there is the **Qaitbai Fort** (Fort St Julien) ⓘ *0900-1600 (closes at 1500 in Ramadan), 7 km out of town, most easily accessed by taxi (E£15-20 roundtrip) or taxi boat slightly more (E£25-30).*

The 18th-century mosque of **Abu Mandur**, 5 km upstream, is accessed by boat taxi or felucca (E£15-20).

Wadi Natrun

→ *Colour map2, grid B1*

Wadi Natrun is a natural depression of salt lakes and salt flats lying in the desert west of the Nile Delta. It is a birdwatchers' paradise brimming with age-old Coptic monasteries. The wadi is aligned on a northwest-southeast axis immediately west of the Giza-Alexandria desert road at approximately Km 100. Wadi Natrun became the centre of a series of monastic groups principally in the fourth century AD. Insecurity, the plague and attacks by Bedouin led to the decline of some scattered communities but also led to some centralization of Christians into monasteries, four of which remain populated to the present day.

Ins and outs

Getting there Without a private vehicle (a taxi from Cairo for the day should cost around E£150-200, depending on your itinerary), the only way to get there is to hop on a West Delta bus to the village of Bir Hooker from Cairo's Turgoman Station (hourly 0600-2100, E£3). From the village, you can either hire a taxi to take you around the monasteries (around E£20), or you can hitch a pick-up bound to the monastery Deir Anba Bishoi (E£1). You may also be able to hitch a ride with Coptic pilgrims venturing though.

Sights

The **Monastery of St Makarios (Deir Abu Maqar)** ⓘ *this monastery is not open to visitors*, lies 3 km off the desert highway. It comprises the meagre remains of a once-great site in which a reconstruction programme is under way. Its significance is linked to the importance of St Makarios (St Makarios the Egyptian, AD 300-390) the son of a village priest who arrived at Wadi Natrun in AD 330 and became the spiritual leader of the Christian hermits and monks in the area. He was ordained and made his name as a prophet and preacher of the ascetic way of life. He was buried at the monastery in the Wadi Natrun. Another nine patriarchs of the Church are also interred at the site.

The site itself is made up of several **churches**, frequently destroyed and rebuilt. The main church, that of St Makarios, is basically a much-restored building on ancient foundations with some small survivals like the 11th-century dome and vestiges of the side chapels from the seventh-ninth centuries. Those of St Benjamin and St John are among the most ancient of the original fabric. The main site contains the Cell of the Chrism, the fluid used to embalm Jesus Christ, and there is a belief that some of this original material was stored here at Deir Abu Maqar. A small bakery for making the host is located in a small room still standing in its original form on the north wall. Behind the churches, there's an 11th-century three-storey defensive tower. Note the religious paintings in the tower's smaller chapels.

Wadi Natrun

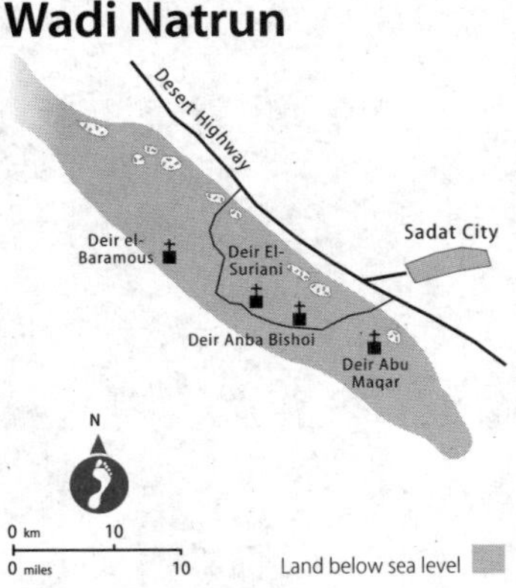

To the northwest lie two other living monasteries – **Deir Anba Bishoi (Pschoi)** and **Deir El-Suriani.** Deir Anba Bishoi was named after the patron saint who went to the wadi following a divine revelation and lived there in solitude. These two sites are easily reached and offer no problems for visitors who wish to walk around. The mainly 20th-century buildings at Deir Anba Bishoi are run by a thoroughly modern community of monks. The layout of the ancient church is cruciform, with a central nave leading to a choir, through doors to the altar sanctuary. Small side chapels (Chapel of the Virgin to the left and Chapel of St Istkhirun or Ischyrion to the right) lie on either side of the sanctuary.

Deir El-Suriani (Monastery of the Syrians) is thought to be an 11th-century foundation by orthodox monks who resisted a schismatic movement at Deir Anba Bishoi. The site was acquired by a devout Syrian Christian in the eighth-ninth centuries and thus took its now popular name since the schism had ended and the monks had returned to their centre at Bishoi. Built over the cave used by St Bishoi, the Church of the Virgin Mary, Deir El-Suriani's main structure, is open to visitors. The church has two main sections – the nave and the choir-sanctuary separated by buttresses and a doorway. The nave has a basin for the washing of feet, a stone screen and houses some religious relics, reputedly including hair from the head of Mary Magdalene, in a niche where St Bishoi lived in ascetic contemplation. In a semi-dome above the west door there is a picture of the Ascension. The altar is a very dark marble.

It is the choir which is most famous, however, for its wonderful 10th-century black, wooden doors with their ivory inlays. Unfortunately the two three-panel doors between the choir and the sanctuary are in poor condition. Note the paintings in the semi-domes, the death of the Virgin to the left and the Annunciation and the Nativity to the right. There is a library of over 3,000 books and many valuable manuscripts. There is also a small museum on site which contains a large selection of 16th-17th century icons. Check before visiting, as the monastery is closed to the public at times of important religious ceremonies.

Deir El-Baramous also known as the Monastery of the Romans is the fourth monastery of the group and the oldest of the sites. It is somewhat isolated to the north end of the Wadi Natrun, and gaining entry, though worthwhile, is not always possible. Legend has it that Maximus and Domitius, two sons of the Roman Emperor Valentinian died young of self-imposed fasting at this place and that St Makarios set up the new monastery to commemorate them. The five churches are dedicated to the Virgin Mary, St Theodore, St George, St John the Baptist and St Michael. The church of St Michael is on the second floor of the keep. There is a drawbridge to the keep held in position by an unusual key/pin known as an Egyptian lock. The now unused refectory has a special 6-m long stone table, carved all in one piece.

Middle Egypt

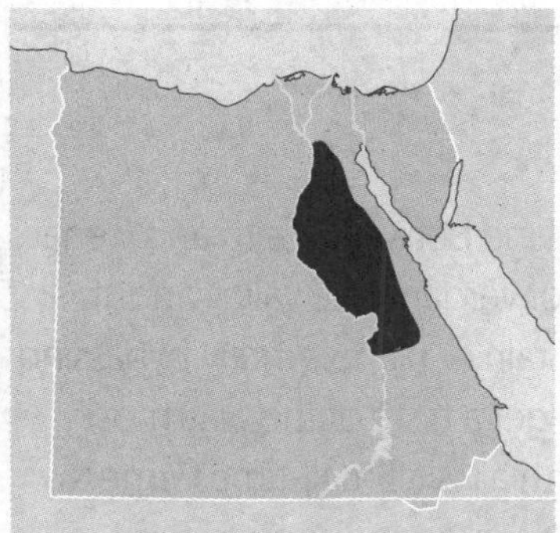

Footprint features

Introduction

Most travellers cross the stretch of land between Cairo and Qena gazing out at the striking contrast of verdant Nile valley and stark gold desert from the window of a train or plane, wholly bypassing the heartland. But if you're keen to get a taste of the way most Egyptians live, Middle Egypt is worth a visit. Small-time farmers work the land using traditional techniques and age-old tools. Women wash their clothes in the river. Children play in every available green space. The provincial pace is slow and the frenzy of Cairo far away. So unfrequented a destination are the depths of this region, that you may well be the only foreign face you see.

The area known as Middle Egypt, so dubbed by 19th-century archeologists, is tangibly distinct from Upper Egypt to the south. It has a large Coptic Christian population (at 20%, it's twice the national average), and an economy that is based much more on agriculture (mostly sugar cane) than tourism. Though the security policies of the government (see page 184) may suggest otherwise, the threat of Islamist militants has largely abated.

The prettiest city in the area is **Minya**, the provincial capital hailed the "the Bride of Upper Egypt". Though she's matured a bit, Minya is still a sleepy, romantic place, with a stunning Corniche, lots of Nile-side cafés and Middle Egypt's most notable ancient sights all within range (save Abydos and Dendera). **Qena**'s recent facelift encompassing a hearty street-cleaning effort and lots of new trees, has improved the demeanour of the city tremendously. Its proximity to the magnificent temples of **Abydos** and **Dendera**, the unquestionable highlights of the region, make it another convenient base, though the perpetual police presence may make Luxor a more inviting option, as both temples can easily be viewed on a daytrip.

★ Don't miss...

❶ **Minya** Smoke a *sheesha* and watch the sunset from a Nile-side café on one of the most beautiful stretches of corniche in the country, page 185.

❷ **Tell El-Armana** Meander around the vast and mysterious remains of the ancient city of heretical Pharaoh Akhenaten, page 190.

❸ **Abydos** Journey to the cult centre of the god Osiris, and join the ranks of ancient Egyptians who made the pilgrimage in life, or death, to be buried by the desert hills the ancient Egyptians thought were the entrance to the Underworld, page 199.

❹ **Temple of Hathor** Explore Dendara's stunning temple, a fantastic and almost fully intact complex with mysterious chambers, rooftop views and underground passages, page 204.

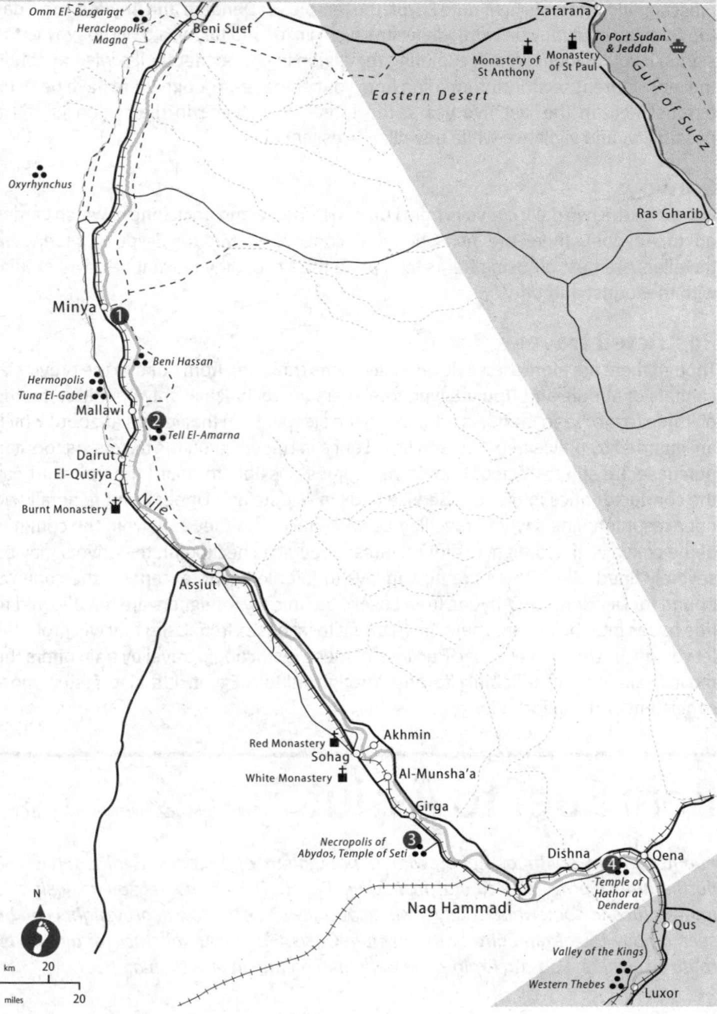

Ins and outs

Warning

Since the terrorist attacks that began in Middle Egypt in 1992 and climaxed with the 1997 massacre at the Hatshepsut Temple in Luxor, Middle Egypt and, for a brief time, Egypt at large, has been on the travel advisory lists of the US State Department and Britain's Foreign Office. In order to remedy the tourism slump, the government trampled on the Islamist uprising and developed a security system to ensure tourists' safety. As a result, visitors to the region will find themselves under the constant protection of Tourist Police. Though the extent of this protection is highly variable, you may find yourself escorted around town by a young guard and confined to your hotel after nightfall. It can be quite an annoyance and a bit of patience and humour go a long way. Luxor and Aswan (see pages 215 and 279) are security 'bubbles' in the Nile Valley, and as such do not require the perpetual presence of tourist police. Since the most significant sights in Middle Egypt, the temples of Dendara and Abydos, are a day trip from Luxor, it may be worthwhile staying in Luxor and taking a daily convoy to the sights. If you're interested in exploring the region in greater depth, it's wise to obtain the most current security information from your embassy. Though there have been no terrorist acts in the last five years, the threat of violence in the region is still a possibility, and vigilance while travelling is essential.

Convoys

Except for the two daily convoys from Luxor to Dendara and back (one of which carries on to Abydos), there are no scheduled convoys in Middle Egypt. Independent travellers are best off using trains to explore the region. If you want to drive, inquire with the tourist authority.

Restricted travel

Though there are more than a dozen daily **trains** travelling from Cairo to the provincial capitals of Middle and Upper Egypt, foreigners are technically only permitted to ride on three (0730, 1230, 2200, in addition to the sleeper train that leaves at 2000) which are guarded by policemen. For train travel once in Upper Egypt, the tickets visitors can purchase are still restricted, but it's sometimes possible to board the train and pay the conductor once in motion. **Service taxis** in Middle and Upper Egypt generally do not accept foreigners when travelling between towns so they can avoid the confines of the convoys. If a foreigner is found unescorted at a checkpoint, the drivers may be severely fined. Since there are no convoys to Middle Egypt (except for the convoys bound for Dendera and Abydos from Luxor), technically foreigners are not allowed to ride **buses** into the region. There are frequent local buses from Cairo that will probably let you on, but you never know. Because of these restrictions, travel by train offers the most flexibility and reliability to and through Middle Egypt. It's also faster, more consistent and comfortable.

Beni Suef to Assiut

→ *Phone code: 082. Colour map 2, grid C2.*

About 130 km south of Cairo, with a population of 86,000, Beni Suef is the northernmost provincial capital in Middle Egypt. There's no reason to visit this uneventful and somewhat rickety town, especially since the few nearby sights can be seen on day trips from Cairo or the Fayoum Oasis. But if you get stuck for a night en route elsewhere, you can explore the Beni Suef on foot in less than an hour.

Female circumcision

Though the practice is illegal, Egypt has one of the highest FGM rates in the world. In 2000, USAID funded another health survey in Egypt that found 97% of women of reproductive age have undergone the practice. Some progress was shown in terms of percentage of the women's daughters (78% of whom had undergone circumcision in 2000; 83% in 1995). There is no doctrinal basis for the practice in either Islam or Christianity. And though high officials and the minister of health have publicly spoken against the procedure (there was even a public health TV campaign for a while), some local religious authorities still support it. Furthermore, many Egyptians believe circumcision helps to maintain female chastity and cleanliness.

Minya, 110 km south of Beni Suef and 245 km from Cairo on the West Bank of the Nile, is by contrast among the most picturesque and charming cities of Egypt. The people are warm and relaxed. There's a wide green patch that runs alongside the river, and at night and on weekends locals flood the corniche with their families to picnic, play and sleep.

Not the most prepossessing of places, Mallawi is nevertheless the starting-off point for some important archaeological sites in the form of Antinopolis and Tell El-Amarna.
▸▸ *For Sleeping, Eating and other listings, see pages 196-199.*

Beni Suef

Except for the **Maidoum Pyramid** (see page 167) ⓘ *getting there from Beni Suef via private taxi costs around E£80,* easily seen on a trip from the Fayoum Oasis or even Cairo, there is little to see save a small museum and the ancient, poorly preserved cities of **Heracleopolis** and **Oxyrhynchus** ⓘ *15 km west of Beni Suef and 9 km west of Beni Mazar on the route to Minya. Expect to pay a taxi around E£50 for the round trip, depending on how long you intend to visit. Agree on the price before setting off to avoid a struggle.* Excursions can also be made from here to the **monasteries** of **St Anthony** and **St Paul** (see pages 421 and 422).

Minya

The centre of Minya is bounded on the east by the Nile, running southeast-northwest; the railway line and the Ibrahimiya Canal run parallel to the west. Further on lie fields of farmland giving way to a small mountain chain announcing the desert beyond. Though Minya and nearby Mallawi were at the centre of militant Islamist attacks in the mid-90s, the last five years have seen relative peace. Nonetheless, the security efforts are among the most intrusive here. Some hotels are off-limits to foreign visitors and security guards often insist on following independent travellers everywhere they go.

Ins and outs

Getting there and around All **trains** running between Cairo and Luxor stop in Minya. Perhaps because there are so few tourists, authorities don't seem to care what train you hop on, which makes train travel the easiest and least restrictive way of getting around. The train station is in the town centre, on Sharia Gumhoriyya, the main street, which runs northeast to the riverfront about 1 km away. **Buses** stopping at Minya depart from Cairo's Turgoman station daily (5 hrs). There's a direct bus service from Minya to Assiut (hourly) and Cairo (every 2 hrs), but foreign visitors are dissuaded from using it. **Service**

 taxis to Minya leave Cairo from Midan Giza (4 hrs). The main service taxi depot and the bus terminal are both 5 mins' walk to the right (south) of the railway station exit along the parallel Sharia Sa'ad Zaghloul. The service taxi depot for Abu Qirkus, the jumping-off point for Beni Hassan, is 250 m further south, just across the railway and the canal bridge. ▸▸ *For further details, see Transport, page 198.*

Information The Minya provincial government is now very keen to promote tourism and the **tourist information office** ⓘ *open daily 0800-1400 and 1700-2200, T086-320150*, on the corniche is worth a visit.

Temple of Hatshepsut

ⓘ *To get there, you can hire a hantour or walk the picturesque 3 km south along the track by the riverbank.*

About 3 km south of town, in an area popularly called Istabl'Antar lies the Temple of Hatshepsut. The temple/shrine is dedicated to a lioness goddess called Pakhet. The outer court has/had eight columns, the four at the front being wider in girth. It is thought that the capitals represent Hathor's head. The back wall has remains of scenes of Hatshepsut with gods. The inner hall (access in the centre of this back wall) contains a high level niche with a rough stone statue of Pakhet.

Beni Hassan (Beni Hassan Al-Shurruq)

ⓘ *Daily 0700-1700. E£12, E£6 for students, E£10 to take photographs. To reach Beni Hassan, you can try to hail a service taxi (although possibly unlikely to transport foreigners) to the small town of Abu Qirkus on the main Minya-Mallawi road, cross over the canal and walk about 1 km straight down its main street until the road forks from where you can take a E£0.25 pick-up to the banks of the Nile where you can find the ferry to the site. Now, the only sure way of getting to Beni Hassan is by hiring a private taxi to take you to the ferry landing and await your return. Depending on how long you intend to stay and how good your bargaining skills, it should cost E£40-60. Buy tickets for the ferry and the site before crossing the river. The ferry costs E£8 per person, less if you are in a group. You will encounter many guards who will unlock the tombs for you, all of whom expect a tip of E£3-5. Have lots of baksheesh on hand to facilitate this. Entry is permitted to four tombs.*

Named after an ancient Arab tribe, Beni Hassan is the site of a neat row of almost 40 11th- and 12th-Dynasty (2050-1786 BC) tombs which were dug into the rock face of hills overlooking the River Nile. The tombs are important because they were the first to show illustrations of sports, games and the daily life of the people of the Middle Kingdom (rather than those of offerings and magic formulae for reaching the afterlife which are more commonly associated with the royal tombs) and because they mark a stage in the evolution of tomb design from the lateral Old Kingdom (2686-2181 BC) style *mastabas* to the deep New Kingdom (1567-1085 BC) royal tombs of the Valley of the Kings (see page 229). These were not royal tombs but were built for regional rulers and military leaders. Some of the earlier tombs have no vestibules and consist only of a simple chamber carved in the rock while the later ones contain a vestibule and a more intricate arrangement of the chamber. Of the 39 tombs only 12 were decorated and only four can currently be visited.

Tomb of Amenemhat (No 2) Regional governor and commander-in-chief at the time of Senusert I (1971-28 BC), Amenemhat's tomb has a columned portico facade and a lintel bearing a list of his titles. The texts inside the door relate to his numerous military campaigns south to Kush and praise his administrative skills. Particular reference is made to a year when there was heavy flooding of the River Nile but taxes were not increased. The main chamber has a vaulted roof which is supported by four columns and decorated in a chequered pattern. To the back of the chamber the niche

Ibis – the sacred bird

This bird has been held in great esteem by man for over 5,000 years and was considered sacred by ancient Egyptians as a representation of Thoth (see page 553). It is depicted in coronation scenes listing the years of the king's rule. The birds' 'ability' to write is traced to the movements of the beak in the water and the resemblance of that beak to a held writing implement.

The main cult centre of the ibis-god Thoth was Hermopolis Magna (see page 188) but mummies of the sacred ibis have been found all over the country (though now the bird is rare in Africa north of the Sahara). They were found in tombs of kings and queens and in cemeteries set aside just for ibis mummies. A simple explanation equates the annual flooding of the Nile with the arrival of this bird and its disappearance as the water receded. Ceremonies to greet the rising water incorporated large flocks of these migrating birds.

once contained a statue of Amenemhat. The chamber walls are finely decorated with a cooking scene on the right of the south wall. In the middle Amenemhat is seated during an offering ceremony, while the north wall has scenes of hunting and military preparations. On the east wall there are pictures of wrestling, an attack on a fortress and boats sailing towards Abydos.

Tomb of Khnumhotep (No 3) This tomb is very similar and is that of Amenemhat's successor Khnumhotep who was also governor of the Eastern Desert. The façade has a proto-Doric columned portico leading into a central chamber with a niche for his statue at the far end. Inscriptions of great historical importance about feudal life in the 12th Dynasty were discovered in the tomb. Clockwise around the tomb there are scenes of ploughing, the harvest, and his voyage to Abydos. Below the next scene of desert hunting on the north wall is the lower register showing the arrival of an Asian caravan which offers gifts to the governor. All is shown in minute detail. This is followed by Khnumhotep and his wife, who are shown fishing and fowling in the marshes on the left, and harpooning fish from a punt on the right of the niche for the statue. On the south wall he inspects boat-building and then sails to Abydos while other registers show dyers, weavers, carpenters and other artisans.

Tomb of Baqet III (No 15) The tomb of the governor of the Oryx Nome, is much simpler than the others and dates back to the 11th Dynasty (2050-1991 BC). In the chamber are two columns with lotus capitals. On the north wall are scenes of a desert hunt with four mythological animals in the midst of the normal animals (including some copulating gazelles). On the east wall there are illustrations of 200 wrestling positions while the south wall illustrates scenes from Baqet's turbulent life including an attack on a fortress.

Tomb of Kheti (No 17) Baqet's son and heir's tomb is quite similar to that of his father. The same wrestling scenes are to be found on the east wall and there are very similar representations of craftsmen and desert hunts. On the south wall Kheti is shown watching agricultural scenes and receiving offerings from under a sunshade attended by his servants and a dwarf.

> Egyptians traditionally went to visit their dead relatives and took a meal or spent the night in the mausoleum...

Mallawi

Since Mallawi was replaced by Minya as the regional capital in 1824, it has sharply deteriorated. Today its littered streets make it a town to avoid, particularly because Minya is just up the road. Nonetheless, the important archaeological sites in its proximity has persuaded the regional tourist authority to plan two new three or four star hotels located beside the Nile, mercifully outside the town. They will have berthing facilities for nine tourist boats and chalets to accommodate more than 400 tourists. The effort is still in the planning phase.

Antinopolis

ⓘ *It is necessary to travel north from Mallawi to take the ferry east across the Nile to visit the village of Sheikh Abada, neighbouring the ruined Roman town of Antinopolis.*
Construction started here in AD 130 in memory of Antonius, a favourite who was accompanying Emperor Hadrian on an official visit to the area. It is said that he drowned himself in the River Nile to prevent a danger prophesied for the Emperor. (It had been foretold that someone of importance would drown in the Nile on this visit.) Early travellers described the splendid columns and archways, now dismantled and dispersed, but the plan of the town can still be traced.

Hermopolis Magna and Tuna El-Gabel

ⓘ *Daily 0900-1700. E£12. The Tuna El-Gabel Necropolis is 6 km west across a very hot and empty desert road from the small town of that name and 10 km southwest of Hermopolis.*
Today little remains of the ruined seventh-Dynasty (2181-73 BC) city of Hermopolis Magna and its necropolis at nearby Tuna El-Gabel northwest of Mallawi, about 50 km south of Minya. Hermopolis Magna was the ancient city of Khmunu, the capital of the Hare Nome. Ruled by the High Priest, it had a dual function as both a secular and religious centre. It was once quite large, extending to both sides of the Nile's banks, with a temple surrounded by a 15-m thick wall at its centre. The town regained importance under the Ptolemies, who associated the ibis-god Thoth with their god Hermes and gave the town its name.

At the same time a vast necropolis, now known as **Tuna El-Gabel**, was established west of the town. Today, however, little remains of the city except a large mound of rubble, some mud bricks and 24 rose granite columns. There is comparatively little to see above ground because most of the tombs lie below the sand dunes which would soon cover the whole site if it were not for the workers' constant efforts to keep them at bay.

Tuna El-Gabel is best known for the **Sacred Animal Necropolis**, to the right of the entrance. It is set in catacombs which are thought to stretch as far as Hermopolis, but only a small area is now open to the public. Many mummified remains of baboons and ibises, which were formerly bred here, were discovered, but the best preserved among them have been relocated to museums around the country. These were deemed sacred animals because they represented the two living images of Thoth.

Hermopolis – The City of Thoth

Hermopolis was the city of Thoth, the gods' scribe and vizier, the reckoner of time, the inventor of writing and, following his association with Khonsu, a moon-god with mastery of science and knowledge. Thoth is depicted either with a man's body and the head of a sacred ibis or as a white and very well-endowed baboon. Although his cult originated further north in the Nile Delta, its greatest following was in Middle Egypt.

In the city's complex creation myth, known as the Hermopolitan cosmogony, the chaos before the world's creation was thought to have had four characteristics: water, infinity, darkness and invisibility, each represented by a male and a female god who collectively are known as the Hermopolitan Ogdoad (company of eight). A primordial mound and the cosmic egg arose from the chaos and hatched the sun god who then began to organize the world from the chaos. While most people believed the Ogdoad itself produced the cosmic egg, Thoth's devotees credited him alone with having laid it and therefore having been connected with the creation of the world. A modern interpretation of the link between his representation as a baboon and his role in the Creation is associated with baboons' habit of shrieking at sunrise and thus being the first to welcome the sun. The baboon was also connected with the moon and there are often statues of baboons with moons on their heads. This is probably because of the ancient Egyptians' love of puns and word-play because the word for 'to orbit' was apparently similar to that for 'baboon'. Although by the New Kingdom this Hermopolitan version of the Creation myth had been supplanted by the Heliopolitan cosmogony, Thoth's cult continued until the later Ptolemaic era.

A few hundred metres south is the main part of the **City of the Dead,** modelled on a real city with streets and some tombs that resemble houses. Egyptians traditionally went to visit their dead relatives and took a meal or spent the night in the mausoleum. Some of the tombs therefore have more than one chamber and a few have an additional floor or even a kitchen. The City of the Dead's most interesting building is the splendid tomb-chapel of **Petosiris** who was the High Priest of Thoth at Hermopolis. His exquisite inlaid wooden coffin is on display in the Museum in Cairo. Built in 300 BC, the chapel's wall decorations are a blend of Pharaonic and Greek artwork, illustrated by the Greek clothes. The mausoleum was a family tomb. The vestibule has illustrations of traditional activities; farming, wine- and brick-making, wood-working and jewellery-making. The inner shrine is dedicated to the father and brother of the tomb owner. On either side of the door to the shrine are offering and sacrifice scenes. In the shrine are colourful illustrations from traditional Egyptian funerary texts with the east wall depicting a funerary procession. The actual burial chambers, where three generations of high priests were buried, is 8 m below the shrine.

Much of the important material found at these two sites is in the museum in Cairo but the Mallawi museum (open mornings only) also features a number of items from here.

Another interesting two storey tomb-chapel is that of **Isadora** which dates from 120 BC and still contains the well-preserved mummy of a young girl. Her death by drowning in the sacred River Nile led to the brief establishment of a cult for her. Also worth a visit is the tomb known as the **House of Graffiti** which has been restored and contains a kitchen, various rooms and a chamber where the deceased was exposed before being buried in the funerary shaft.

Tell El-Amarna

Midway between Minya and Assiut, 12 km south of Mallawi, Tell El-Amarna is the East Bank city founded by Pharaoh Amenhotep IV (1379-62 BC). Better known as **Akhenaten**, he left Thebes (Luxor) to establish a totally new and heretical monotheistic religion. Although little remains today because most of the temples and palaces were destroyed by subsequent pharaohs who reverted back to the previous polytheistic religion, the site still has plenty of atmosphere. There is another school of archaeologists who believe that, far from introducing a radical new monotheism, Akhenaten chose to ignore the religion that through a multiplicity of myths and images presented a surprisingly complex view of the world.

Ins and outs

Getting there Though some adventure tour groups are returning to the area, independent travellers are rare, in part because of the extensive restrictions around public transport. Unless you have your own car, you will probably have to hire a private taxi and be escorted by a policeman from Minya or Assiut (E£40-60). Independent drivers, who will also almost certainly require a police escort, should head south from Mallawi to the village of Deir El-Mawas and then east to the ferry crossing. When travel restrictions ease up, the river can easily be accessed by catching any southbound bus or pick-up from the depot just south of the Mallawi train station at the bridge between the canal and the railway tracks. Pick -ups cost 50p. You can cross the river by motorboat, car ferry (50p), *felucca* or tourist boat (E£4 round trip).

Information Once arriving at the East Bank village of El-Till, adults and children hawking basketwork and other handicrafts greet you in hordes. The ticket kiosk is just to the left of the landing stage and there is a little café to the east of the village.

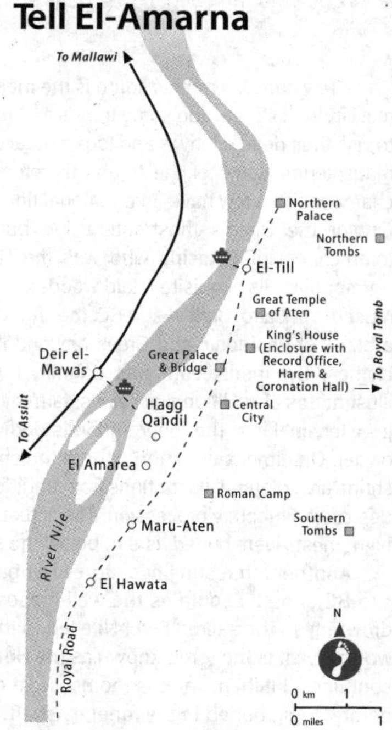

History

Amenhotep IV was the son of Amenhotep III (1417-1379 BC). His dark-skinned and possibly Nubian 'chief wife', Queen Tiy, may have ruled jointly for 12 years with her son after he ascended the throne in 1379 BC. Early in his reign, Amenhotep espoused the worship of the cult of Aten, an aspect of the sun god depicted as human and mentioned in early texts. Some scholars suggest the belief was adopted from his father who may have privately subscribed to such ideas. Amenhotep IV, however, espoused it so strongly, at the expense of Amun and the other gods, that it upset the high priests of Amun in Thebes (Luxor). As a result, in the fifth year of his reign in 1374 BC, he and his wife Nefertiti moved the capital to Akhetaten ('horizon of Aten') halfway between Thebes and Memphis at Tell El-Amarna in order to make a clean break with previous traditions. (For those of a romantic disposition the large gully or

Revolutionary Art: Akhenaten and Nefertiti's New Designs

The new settlement of Akhetaten was not only revolutionary in its religion but also in the arts. A number of excellent craftsmen and artists were recruited to work on the decoration of the new city. Rather than focusing almost exclusively on the theme of resurrection and the afterlife they also depicted daily life and nature in greater detail than before. There were two main art styles with the first depicting Akhenaten with an elongated face, protruding stomach, and feminine thighs, as demonstrated by the famous colossi from his temple at Karnak which are now in the museum in Cairo, while the later style is much less distorted. It has been suggested, although not proven, that the earlier distortions were partly due to the difficulties that the artists had in radically altering their style. Alternatively it may have been that the decoration was undertaken too hastily using inferior limestone and varying quality carvings.

It has been suggested that Akhenaten intended that the depictions of himself and his family, which appear in the shrines of private houses in Tell El-Amarna, should be worshipped and that only he could directly mediate with the god. The Aten disc is only shown when he or the Royal family are present. While the pharaoh was always, at least nominally, accepted as a god or the gods it appears that Akhenaten may have been particularly literal about this convention.

Very unusually, in scenes of royal dinners both the pharaoh and his wife were depicted and the presence of both their cartouches almost as co-rulers demonstrated the difference in Amenhotep IV's approach. Wives had never previously been portrayed as equal to the pharaoh and their names had never appeared side by side.

river *wadi* cutting through the eastern cliffs have been likened to the Egyptian symbol for the horizon. It has been suggested that it was because the sun rose from behind these cliffs that Akhenaten chose this as the site for his new city of Akhetaten.)

On arriving in Akhetaten he changed his name to Akhenaten or 'servant of Aten' while Nefertiti became Nefernefruaten or 'beautiful are the beauties of the Aten'. In the 12th year of his reign he adopted a more confrontational approach to the old cults and his decision to close down all the old temples probably led to unrest because of the detrimental economic effect caused by the temple being closed. There is some evidence that Akhenaten was criticized for not defending Egypt's borders and for jeopardizing the territories previously won by his expansionist father.

How Akhenaten's reign ended is still a mystery. One theory is that Akhenaten rejected his wife Nefertiti and made his son-in-law Smenkhkare the co-regent. Some have interpreted the fact that the two men lived together, and some of their poses in the murals, suggest proof of a homosexual relationship. Smenkhkare, who was both the husband of Akhenaten's eldest daughter and his half-brother, is thought to have continued ruling for a year after Akhenaten's death in 1362 BC but soon died himself. The other, more contentious, interpretation of events is that, far from splitting up with Nefertiti, the pharaoh actually made her co-regent and his equal. She may then have adopted Smenkhkare as her official name and been illustrated in a different way. However, only the cartouches can be used to identify the figures, which makes the theory a suitably interesting alternative. The reality is that no-one knows the truth which may be very dull compared with these stories.

Worship of Aten did not long outlive its creator. In 1361 BC Smenkhkare was succeeded by Tutankhamen (1361-52 BC), another of Amenhotep III's sons and Akhenaten's half-brother, who returned to the Thebes-based cult of Amun. He and his successors attempted to eradicate all traces of Akhenaten and the city of Akhetaten was subsequently destroyed and completely pillaged by Seti I (1318-04 BC) so that nothing was known of the city or its cult until the second half of this century.

Apart from the romantic story of Akhenaten, the importance of the city lies in its short history. Although about 5 km long, the city was built and occupied for no more than 25 years. When abandoned, a record of late 18th-Dynasty life remained, depicting everything from peasants in small houses to the official buildings and palaces. Most urban sites in Egypt have either been lost under modern towns and villages or have been badly damaged and so Tell El-Amarna offers a unique record.

The site

ⓘ *Daily 0700-1700. E£12, students E£6. The ticket office also sells bus rides to the sites. There's a tour of the Northern Tombs (E£8, plus entrance fees); the Southern Tombs (E£23, plus entrance fees), shared among up to eight people; and the Royal Tomb, (E£35) for up to eight people.* The huge site is made up of a number of different areas – the **city ruins** to the south of El-Till; the **Northern Tombs**, 5 km to the east; the **Royal Tomb**, 5 km further away up a hidden valley; the more rarely-visited **Southern Tombs**, southeast of El-Till; and the **Northern Palace** near the riverbank north of the village. Plan at least half a day for a sufficient taste of the site.

The Northern Tombs

The most interesting site at Tell El-Amarna was the necropolis for the nobles, many of whom were not originally from Thebes but were elevated to their position by Akhenaten after he arrived at Akhetaten. Most of the tombs also devote more space and decoration to Akhenaten himself than to the occupant. Even though there is electric lighting in the Northern Tombs, it's advisable to bring a torch.

Tomb of Huya (No 1) Huya was the superintendent of the Royal Harem and Steward of Akhenaten's mother Queen Tiy and may have died during her visit to Akhetaten in 1367 BC. At the entrance he

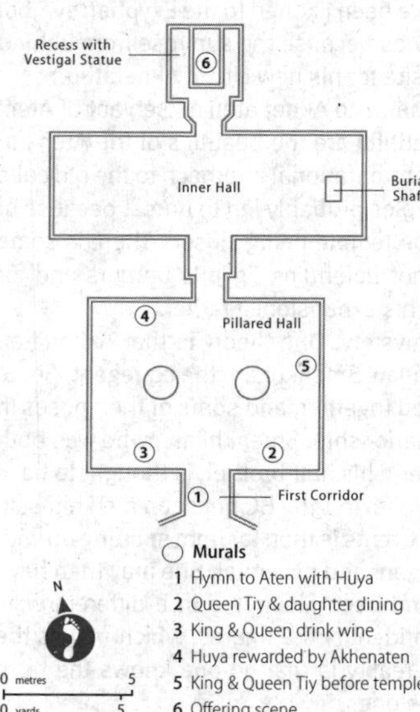

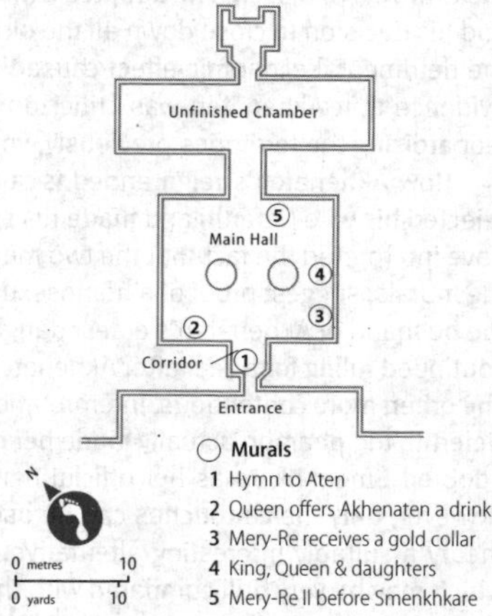

is pictured praying next to a hymn to Aten and on either side of the door are highly unusual scenes of Queen Tiy drinking wine with Akhenaten, Nefertiti and princesses. On the left wall is a scene showing Akhenaten in a procession being carried on his litter towards the Hall of Tribute where ambassadors from Kush and Syria await his arrival. To the left and right of the entrance to the shrine are somewhat damaged scenes of Huya being decorated by Akhenaten from the Window of Appearances with the sculptor's studio below. On the right hand wall Akhenaten leads Queen Tiy to see the temple he has built for his parents while the staff who worked on the temple are displayed below. The shrine is undecorated but the niche has some scenes of funerary offerings, mourning, and a curious representation of the funerary furniture.

Tomb of Mery-Re II (No 2) This tomb of the Royal Scribe, Overseer of the Two Treasuries and Overseer of the Harem of the Great Royal Wife Nefertiti, was started during Akhenaten's reign but finished by Smenkhkare and follows a similar plan to Huya's tomb. After the now destroyed Hymn to the Aten at the entrance, Mery-Re is shown worshipping the Aten and then to the left Nefertiti offers Akhenaten a drink next to three young princesses. Further along, the upper register depicts Mery-Re receiving a golden collar from Akhenaten, while foreigners look on, and then being acclaimed by his household. On the right wall Akhenaten, Nefertiti and their daughters are at the centre of a scene divided into three subjects. The first shows black slaves, with their faces painted red, carrying gold bars and coins. The tables are heaped with piles of gold and a number of slaves are shown carrying their children. In the second scene, Asian people pay homage to Akhenaten and bring him treasures and a number of female slaves. The last scene shows a double procession with the empty royal litter and the royal guard while treasures are offered to the Pharaoh. The rest of the tomb was never finished except for a defaced scene on the back wall of Mery-Re being rewarded by Smenkhkare and his wife.

Tomb of Ahmose (No 3) The tomb of Akhenaten's fan bearer, who therefore had the right to a noble's tomb, is with another group of four tombs just beyond the next valley. The tomb was unfinished and some of the scenes are damaged. Most of them depict aspects of the palace including the throne room, the royal apartments and some of Akhenaten's army preparing for battle.

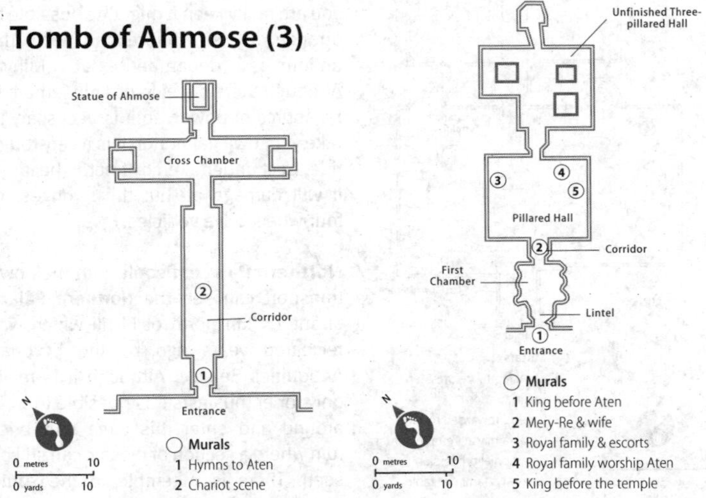

 Tomb of Mery-Re I (No 4) The High Priest of Aten and the father of Mery-Re II, has three chambers and is probably the best of all. On the entrance wall he is shown in adoration before Aten while in the columned and flower-decorated vestibule Mery-Re and his wife Tenro are shown in prayer. On the left hand wall of the main chamber, which now only has two of the original four columns, Mery-Re is invested with the High Priest's gold collar by Akhenaten. The royal family and escorts are then portrayed in an important scene (because it shows the height of the buildings), leaving the palace for the Great Temple in chariots. There are hymns to Aten and offering scenes above the entrance to the unfinished inner chambers. On the right of the main chamber Akhenaten, accompanied by Nefertiti and two of their daughters, is in the Great Temple making sacrifices to Aten. Other scenes show Akhenaten after the sacrifice with his daughters playing musical instruments while beggars await alms in the corner. Below is a scene which has given archaeologists a rare insight into the original appearance of the city. Mery-Re is seen showing the Pharaoh the stocks in the temple with views towards the port, a stable and the royal boats on the River Nile.

Tomb of Pentu (No 5) and Tomb of Panehsi (No 6) The nearby tomb of the royal scribe and chief physician (No 5), is badly disfigured and it is better to see the Tomb of Panehsi (No 6): which is 500 m to the south. This High Priest's tomb, which has four columns in each of the two chambers, was later transformed by the Copts into a chapel but many of the original decorations are still in place. In the first chamber are scenes of Akhenaten decorating Panehsi. On the left hand wall, the royal family worship Aten in front of their household. There are further scenes of Akhenaten including one on the far wall on the left behind a Coptic baptistry and one by the stairs leading down to the funerary chamber, showing him with Nefertiti and their daughters in their chariots surrounded by troops. The rest of the tomb is either unfinished or has been damaged.

Tomb of Panehsi (6)

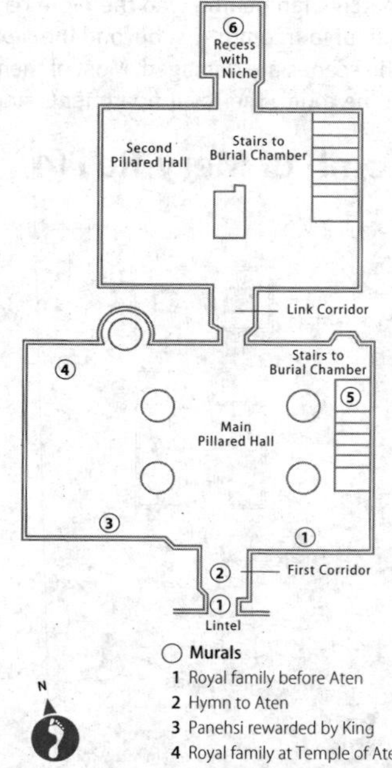

The Royal Tomb This tomb, which is in a secret valley 5.5 km east of the main plain, has been closed since 1934 and cannot normally be visited. Although if you are really keen it might be possible to arrange a visit beforehand with the antiquities department at Minya. Although there are electric lights, there is no source of power, so it is necessary to take your own generator. It is a very rough ride, best undertaken by tractor, because it will damage all but the strongest of four-wheel drive vehicles.

Northern Palace People with their own transport can see the **Northern Palace** about 1.5 km north of El-Till which was recleared years ago by the Egyptian Antiquities Service. Although it is really only for enthusiasts it is possible to walk around and enter this large mud-brick ruin where a section of mosaic can still be seen. There is a temple to the south called Kom El-Nana which is being excavated by a British mission but it is not accessible or currently open to the public.

The Southern Tombs

Visitors to the Southern Tombs usually travel on the north-south road along the edge of the cultivated area which almost exactly follows the ancient 'royal road' linking all Akhetaten's official buildings. The tombs are spread over seven low hills in two groups but only about five of the 18 tombs are of any real interest. Among them is the **Tomb of Ay** (No 25) (1352-48 BC), Akhenaten's maternal uncle and vizier to Amenhotep III, Akhenaten and Tutankhamen whom he succeeded as pharaoh when he died. There are unproven theories either that his wife Tey was Nefertiti's wet-nurse or that the couple conceived Tutankhamen. Despite this, the southern tombs are rarely visited by tourists.

Leaving El-Till you pass the remains of the massive **Great Temple of Aten** on the right which is now partly covered by the modern cemetery. There are then the vague ruins in the sand of a mixture of administrative and residential buildings until one reaches the **Small Temple of Aten**, currently being re-excavated by the Egyptian Exploration Society. Although it is not yet open to tourists a good view of the temple can be had from a local tractor.

Just before the temple there is a large mud-brick structure on either side of the road. This is the remains of the **bridge** which crossed the road and connected the **King's House** to the east with the so-called **Great Palace** to the west which runs along and partly under the cultivated area. This area, including the palace, temple and ancillary buildings is the **Central City** which was the administrative and religious centre of the ancient city.

Assiut

Assiut, 109 km south of Minya, is the largest city south of Cairo. A noisy, aggressive and rather unpleasant place, it was one of the Islamic fundamentalist strongholds and the scene of some of Egypt's worst and longest standing communal violence. The fighting has for the most part subsided and a new attraction since appeared. In autumn of 2000, the local church of St Mark became the chosen site of the regular apparition of the Virgin Mary. Witnesses claimed the miracle manifested itself as an ethereal light above the church tower. Beyond that, Assiut has little to offer the tourist save a few interesting monasteries, some decent hotels, and Nile valley access to the Western Desert oases. For those who have the misfortune to be stuck in the city here are a few of the essential details.

Ins and outs

Getting there and around There is a small **tourist office** ⓘ *T088-310010, Sat-Thu, 0830-1400*, in the Governorate building on the Corniche that may be of help, but be warned: if you have managed to dodge police protection thus far, a visit here will ensure you a permanent companion.

In Assuit, police protection will be provided – whether you want it, or not.

The train, bus and service taxi stations are all on Sharia El-Geish and most of the best hotels are on or near the same street. Roads in front of the stations run to the Nile; roads behind the railway station lead to the souks. The airport, 10 km northwest of the city, has no bus connection. » *For further details, see Transport, page 198.*

Sights

There is little to see in Assuit itself. The **Nasser Museum** in the village of Beni Marr just to the south of the city is worth a visit, as is the large **Monastery of the Virgin** *(Deir*

 El-Adhra), 12 km west of Assuit. The monastery, incorporating cave and mountain, was originally built by Empress Helena in AD 328. Copts believe the Holy Family sought refuge from Herod in the caves at Dirunka. Every year in August, up to 50,000 pilgrims come to witness the icons paraded around the cave-church during the **Moulid of the Virgin.** It is claimed that the **Church of the Blessed Virgin Mary** was the first church built in Egypt, although the current church was constructed in 1964 and badly damaged by Islamic extremists in 1988. Further afield, 42 km north of Assiut, 5 km out of El-Qusiya lies the **Burnt Monastery** *(Deir El-Muharraq)*. Dating back to the fourth century AD, the monastery gets its name from its location on the edge of the burning, roasting desert; given the attacks on Coptic churches by the area's Islamic fundamentalists, it's a particularly apt name. The Burnt Monastery is the largest and wealthiest in Middle Egypt. It is considered a place of healing and the location of the **Feast of Consecration**, the annual *moulid* involving up to 50,000 pilgrims, that takes place before Easter.

Sleeping

Beni Suef *p185*

D Semiramis, Sharia Safir Zaghloul, Midan El-Mahat, T082-322092, F316017. 30 rooms, a poor quality hotel just north of the train station, but with two official stars it's the best in town. For safety and comfort, but not gastronomic delight, eat here.

E Bakri Palace, Al-Riyadhi St, next to Banque Misr, T082-332329. Equipped with glass lift, the hotel offers decent a/c rooms with private bath. The restaurant has an extensive menu of reasonable fare, including seafood.

F Deshisha, Sharia Shehatta, east of the train station, T082-325528. A cheap and last-resort establishment that may be useful if held up in Beni Suef.

F Rest House, west of canal on Sharia Port Said.

Minya *p185*

C Nefertiti, Corniche El-Nil, T086-341515, F326467. Commonly still known by locals as the Etap. River-side location about 2 km north of the town centre on the beautiful tree-lined corniche. Recently expanded with the hope of attracting more foreign guests, it has 96 rooms (30 decent rooms in main building, 24 garden chalets without a river view, and 42 chalets adjacent to the Nile), 3 restaurants (La Palma, Banana Island and Darna), though they're not always open, bar, coffee shop, nice swimming pool, tennis, sauna, small gym. Efficient and very friendly staff. Reduction in tourism has resulted in some facilities being closed.

E Akhenaten, Corniche El-Nil, a 10-min walk from the train station, T086-365917, F365918. Clean, comfortable rooms with a/c, TV and fridge, most with balcony and good Nile views. Excellent breakfast buffet. A good second choice if the old Etap is out of your price range.

E Hotel El-Shata, 31 Sharia El-Gumhoriyya, T086-362307. 32 rooms and 2 suites, a/c with bath, good location by the river.

F Ibn Khassib, 5 Sharia Rageb, near the station, T086-364535. Has 20 rooms with decrepit antiques and old high ceilings, of varying quality, some have a/c and cramped private bath, there's also a restaurant and bar with billiards.

F Lotus, 1 Sharia Port Said, T086-364541, F364576. Pleasant hotel, 1 km from both the station and the river, with restaurant that sells alcohol, 42 clean rooms with rather noisy a/c and bath.

F Omar Al-Khayam, behind Akhenaten on Sharia Dawaran, T086-365666. Mediocre rooms have private bath and satellite TV. Breakfast included. A cheap deal, but management is not always inclined to accept foreign visitors.

F Savoy Hotel, just across the train station in Midan Mahatta, T086-363270. Some rooms equipped with private bath, TV and fridge. Management says they will only take groups of tourists.

Assiut *p195*

If you have to stay in Assiut most decent hotels are around the train station. The long-promised luxury hotel is not yet completed.

C Badr Touristic, Sharia El-Thallaga, near the train station, T088-329811/2, F322820. Has

44 tacky but well-equipped rooms, with a/c, TV and fridge. A comfortable hotel with decent restaurant and bar.

D **Assiutel Hotel**, 146 Sharia Nile, T088-312121, F312122. 31 fairly comfortable rooms with a/c, TV and fridge, Nile views, restaurant and bar.

D **Casa Blanca**, Sharia Mohammed Tawfik Khashaba, T088-337662, F336662. 48 rooms, cheaper but lacking the views of the Assiutel.

E **Akhenaten Touristic**, Sharia Mohammed Tawfik Khashaba, T088-327723, F321600. A clean but unspectacular budget hotel, 35 rooms come with private bath, a/c and TV.

E **Reem Touristic**, Sharia El-Nahda, near the train station, T088-311421, F311424. Weathered, but cheap, hotel with 40 rooms.

F **Al-Nahr Hotel**, 41 Shari Mohammed Ali Makarem, T088-344175. Cosy rooms with a/c and private bath. Restaurant, bar and cafeteria.

F **El-Salam**, Sharia Thabet, T088-332256. 40 rooms.

F **YMCA**, Sharia El-Gumhoriyya, about 10 mins' walk from the train station, T088-323218. Clean and quiet, cheap a/c rooms, pool.

F **Youth hostel**, Building 503, Sharia El-Walidia, 2 km from station, T088-324846. 40 cheap but tattered beds, E£6 per person.

Camping

It is possible, but unadvisable to camp near the Assiut barrage (built by the British in 1898-1903), at the **Officers Club** (T088-323134) and the **Sporting Club** (T088-233139) or on **Banana Island** where there are no facilities.

Eating

Beni Suef *p185*

Outside of the hotel restaurants, have a stroll along Sharia Riyadhi. The centre of the Beni Suef's bustle, it's aligned with lots of shops, pharmacies, juice joints, and *fuul*, *taamiyya* and *kushari* stalls. For a *sheesha* or pastry, try **Coffee Shop Si Omar**, near the Bakri Palace.

Minya *p185*

Besides restaurants in the Nefertiti and Lotus hotels, which offer standard but reasonably priced good quality food and good views, try:

ΨΨ **El-Fayrouz**, on the Corniche about 150 m north of Sharia El-Gumhoriyya, which provides excellent meat dishes and juices.

ΨΨ **Ibn Khassib**, is cheap but has a limited menu.

ΨΨ **Ali Baba**, offers decent kebab meals for E£15.

ΨΨ **Nefertiti Port**, across from the end of Sharia El-Gumhoriyya (on the Corniche) is a stationary boat with a restaurant on the upper deck that has decent kebab and *kofta* (grilled minced meat) meals for about E£20.

Good cheap food can be bought at many of the other local cafés, for example:

Ψ **Cafeteria Ali** on the corniche north of Sharia Port Said.

At Midan Mahatta and along Sharia Mahatta, there's a scattering of more cheap restaurants, traditional *ahwas* and juice stalls.

Ψ **Qasr Al Shoq** on Sharia El-Gumhoriyya, is a coffeeshop/internet café that resembles a miniature palace.

Assiut *p195*

All the better hotels have restaurants which offer decent food as do the various clubs which usually admit better-dressed tourists.

ΨΨ **Badr** is the best, but there is little competition.

There are a number of good cheap and cheerful restaurants between the back of the station and the souk in the main commercial district. Cheap restaurants that offer a fairly similar local menu of the usual grilled chicken and stewed vegetables include:

Ψ **Express Restaurant**, Ψ **Cairo Restaurant** and Ψ **Mattam Al-Azhar**, as well as others along Sharia Talaat Harb and Sharia 26 July.

Ahmed Wagdy is a good coffee shop.

Shopping

Minya *p185*

While the more up-market shops are on Sharia El-Gumhoriyya the best and main shopping streets bisect it about half way between the station and the river. There has been a Monday market since Ottoman times.

Transport

Beni Suef *p185*

Bus

Buses run to **Cairo** and **Fayoum** every 30 mins throughout the day. There is less frequent direct service to **Alexandria** and a few major destinations in the Delta. The bus station is south of the railway station, across the canal.

Taxi
Service taxis congregate at the depot by the bus station. They run regularly north to **Cairo**, west to **Fayoum**, south to **Minya** and east to **Zafarana** on the Red Sea. Whether or not they will transport you is unpredictable, but it may be worth a shot.

Train
It is easy to make a quick getaway from Beni Suef because virtually every express and standard train travelling north and south through the Nile Valley stops at the station in the city centre.

Minya *p185*
Hantour
Minya is small enough to easily explore on foot. It's also possible to take short trips around town with a *hantour*, (horse-drawn carriage). No in-town trip should cost more than E£5. Expect to pay around E£20 for an hour's meander.

Bus
Almost hourly buses from the terminal on Sharia Sa'ad Zaghloul to **Cairo** (5 hrs) or south to **Assiut**.

Taxi
Service taxis, which are quicker but still cheap, can be caught to the same destinations from the nearby depot under the railway arch. Those for **Abu Qirkus** (30-45 mins), the jumping-off point for **Beni Hassan**, can only be caught 250 m further south just across the railway and the canal bridge. Be forewarned that bus travel for foreign visitors may be restricted and travel by service taxi is highly unlikely.

Train
Most intercity trains stop at Minya so it is easily possible to travel north to **Cairo** (4 hrs) via **Beni Suef** or south to **Luxor** via **Assiut** and **Qena**.

Assiut *p195*
Air
Internal flights to **Cairo** (2 per week) and **Kharga** (2 per week) from the airport, 10 km northwest of the town.

Bus
7 daily buses **Cairo** (7 hrs), 5 to **Kharga Oasis** (5 hrs) which go on to **Dakhla** (8-9 hrs), 4 to **Qena** (4 hrs), as well as buses every 2 hrs (0600-1800) north to **Minya** (2 hrs) and south to **Sohag**.

Taxi
Service taxis run to every town between **Minya** and **Sohag**, as well as to **Kharga** (5 hrs), and if accepting foreign travellers, are easy to catch from the depot in the mornings but are less frequent later in the day. Be forewarned that bus travel for foreign visitors may be restricted and travel by service taxi is highly unlikely.

Train
Run almost hourly to **Cairo** (7 hrs) via **Mallawi** (2 hrs), **Minya** (3 hrs), and **Beni Suef** (5 hrs). 12 per day to **Luxor** (6-7 hrs) and **Aswan** (10-12 hrs) via **Sohag** (2 hrs) and **Qena** (4-5 hrs).

Directory

Beni Suef *p185*
Banks Bank of Alexandria in Midan El-Gumhoriyya. **Banque Misr** and **Banque du Caire** are next to each other on Sharia Riyadhi, each equipped with ATM, opening hours Sun-Thu, 0830-1400. **Post office** Opposite the **Semiramis Hotel** in Midan El-Mahat. **Telephone** At railway station.

Minya *p185*
Banks There is **Banque du Caire** on Sharia El-Gumhoriyya, open Sun-Thu 0830-1400, and **National Bank of Egypt** on the corniche at the end of Sharia El-Gumhoriyya, where you can find an ATM, open Sun-Thu 0800-1400. **Post office** In the main square called Midan Sa'a, directly outside the railway station, open Sun-Thu 0830-1400 and 1700-2200.

Assiut *p195*
Banks There are a number of banks, including the **Alexandria Bank** (open Sat-Thu 0830-1400 and 1800-2100, Fri 0900-1230

and 1800-2100) in the commercial district around Talaat Harb. **Banque du Caire** on Sharia Nemis has an ATM. **Internet** Cafés are scattered all over the city. Maro on Sharia Yusri Ragheb is recommended. E£2 per hr. **Post office** Near the railway station and open Sun-Thu 0830- 1400 and 1700-2200. **Telephone** There is a telephone beside the railway station. **Useful numbers** Emergency police: T088-322225, Hospital: T088-323329.

Sohag to Dendera

→ *Phone code: 093. Colour map 3, grid C2.*

A small agricultural and university West Bank town, 97 km south of Assiut along the Nile, Sohag has a large Coptic community among its 90,000 population. Although it has a few minor sites it is not really geared toward tourists (who receive no encouragement to stay) but it does have the advantage of being relatively close to the beautiful temple at Abydos and within a half day's journey from Dendera. Bear in mind though, that it's possible to visit both these sites on a daytrip from Luxor. ▸▸ *For Sleeping, Eating and other listings, see pages 206-207.*

Sohag

The small White Monastery (Deir Al-Abyad) and Red Monastery (Deir Al-Ahmar), at 10 km and 14 km south of Sohag are interesting. The **White Monastery**, with light-coloured limestone walls was founded in the fifth century by St Pjol and dedicated to St Shenuda, one of the most prominent figures in the history of the Coptic church. It once had a population of over 2,000 monks. There is a *moulid* each July. The church, which dominates the monastery, is divided with decorated columns into a central nave and two aisles. The three altars are dedicated to St Shenuda (in the centre), St George and The Holy Virgin. St Shenuda worked in the White and Red Monasteries for over 80 years. (He is believed to have lived for well over 100 years.) He introduced both spiritual and social support for the local community as well as medical help.

Three km north is the smaller **Red Monastery** founded by St Bishoi, a disciple of Shenuda. It is built of burnt brick, hence the name. It is said to have been the centre of a monastery of 3,000 monks. The church of St Bishai has some interesting wall paintings and a sanctuary screen with icons of St Bishai, St Shenuda and St Pjol.

Akhmin, across the Nile from Sohag is an interesting, ancient town worth a wander round. **Deir Al-Shuhuda** (Monastery of the Martyrs) is an important place for pilgrims. It is here that papyrus scrolls containing the Book of Proverbs was found. In the town too is **Deir Al-Adra** (Convent of the Holy Virgin) with a *moulid* on 22 August.

Abydos

Abydos, on the west bank of the Nile, 12 km southwest of El-Balyana halfway between Sohag and Qena, is home to the stunning Temple of Seti I. As the holiest town of all for the ancient Egyptians, pilgrims have been making the journey to Abydos from the Seventh Dynasty (2181-73 BC) until well into the Ptolemaic era (323-30 BC).

It was the cult centre for **Osiris**, the god of the dead who was known as 'Lord of Abydos' because, according to legend, either his head or his whole body was buried at the site (see Temple of Isis, Aswan, page 290). Abydos which looked out over the Western Desert, was considered the door to the afterlife. Initially, in order to achieve resurrection it was necessary to be buried at Abydos but the requirement was later changed to a simple pilgrimage and the gift of a commemorative stela.

There are cemeteries and tombs scattered over a very wide area in Abydos but there are only a few buildings left standing. Among them are the Temple of Seti I, the Osirieon (Cenotaph) and the Temple of Ramses II.

The **Temple of Seti I** ⓘ *daily 0900-1600, E£12*, was constructed in fine white marble by Seti I (1318-04 BC) as an offering in the same way that lesser individuals would come on a pilgrimage and make a gift of a stela. Most of the work on the temple and its convex bas-reliefs, among the most beautiful of all New Kingdom buildings, was carried out by Seti I, but when he died his son Ramses II (1304-1237 BC) completed the courtyard and façade. This can be seen from the quality of workmanship which changes from Seti I's beautiful bas-reliefs to Ramses II's much cruder, quicker and therefore cheaper sunken reliefs. It is a very unusual temple because it is L-shaped rather than the usual rectangle and because it has seven separate chapels rather than a single one behind the hypostyle halls. This may have been because of the water table or the presence of the older Osirieon behind the temple.

The temple was originally approached via a pylon and two forecourts, built by Ramses II below the main temple so that the concept of the temple sloping upwards from the entrance to the inner sanctuary was maintained, but they have now been largely destroyed. The temple's front is now the square-columned façade behind 12 rectangular pillars decorated with Ramses welcoming Osiris, Isis and Horus. Originally there were seven doors through the façade which led on to the seven chapels but Ramses altered the construction and only the central one is now unblocked.

Temple of Seti I, Abydos

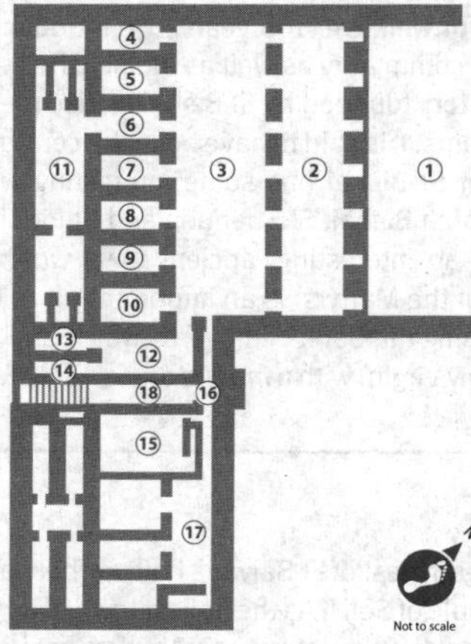

1 First & second court (destroyed)
2 First hypostyle hall
3 Second hypostyle hall
4 Chapel/Sanctuary of Horus
5 Chapel/Sanctuary of Isis
6 Chapel/Sanctuary of Osiris
7 Chapel/Sanctuary of Amun-Re
8 Chapel/Sanctuary of Re-Harakhiti
9 Chapel/Sanctuary of Ptah
10 Chapel/Sanctuary of Seti I
11 Suite of Osiris
12 Suite of Sokar & Nefertum
13 Chapel of Sokar
14 Chapel of Nefertum
15 Hall of the Books
16 Gallery of the Lists
17 Hall of Sacrifice
18 Corridor of the Bulls

Temple of Ramses II, Abydos

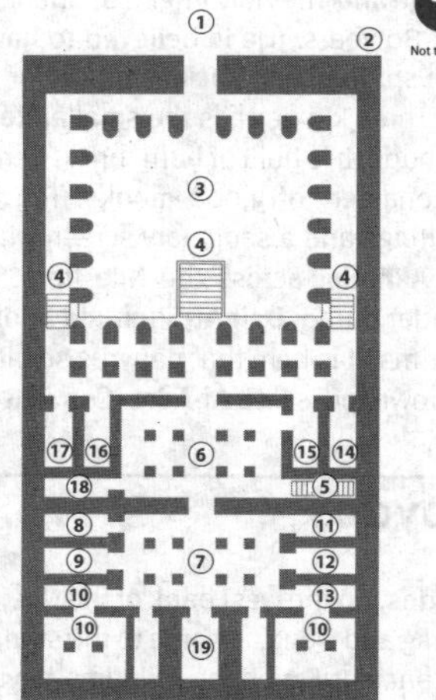

1 First pylon & first courtyard (in ruins)
2 Second pylon
3 Second courtyard with square pillars
4 Steps to raised courtyard
5 Stairs to roof (no roof now)
6 First octosyle hall
7 Second octosyle hall
8 Chapel to Osiris
9 Chapel to Min
10 Chapel to Onuris
11 Room for linen
12 Room for ornaments
13 Room for offerings
14 Temple to Seti
15 Temple to Royal Ancestor
16 Temple to Ennead
17 Temple to Ramses II
18 Temple to Onuris
19 Main sanctuary

Americans in the Nile Valley

Although the history of enquiry into Egyptology in the 18th and 19th centuries was largely determined by the Europeans, the Americans put in a late but important appearance. There was a consensus that the work of recording the reliefs and paintings of the Nile Valley sites was among the most pressing of tasks before theft, looting and other damage could take too great a toll. This task, the accurate recording of inscriptions or epigraphy, was begun with British encouragement by the Archaeological Survey in the 1890s. Among its most scholarly members was Norman de Garis Davies and his wife Nina, working first for the (British) Exploration Fund and later for the Metropolitan Museum of Art, New York. His work inspired US interest and led to the foundation of Chicago House at Luxor in 1924.

The arrival of US academic concern was the achievement of James Henry Breasted. He was born in Rockford, USA, in 1865 and rose to become the USA's first professional Egyptologist at the University of Chicago in 1894. He began the process of recording all known Egyptian hieroglyphs and continued his work in a series of scientific expeditions to Egypt and Nubia in the period 1905-07. He was particularly concerned to record all inscriptions that were at risk of damage or decay. His enthusiasm was rewarded by JD Rockefeller Jnr, who funded the establishment of an Oriental Institute at Chicago. The Institute's field centre in Egypt was sited in Luxor and a comprehensive study of a number of sites was accomplished, most famous being those of Medinet Habu and the Temple of Seti I at Abydos. Breasted died in 1935 after major archaeological successes for the Institute both in Egypt and Iran.

An American businessman, Theodore Davis, became a major backer of archaeological work in Egypt, eager to find new tombs and artifacts. He was a generous sponsor of excavations but impatient with the academic requirements of good archaeology. He fell out with all the inspectors of antiquities appointed by the Antiquities Service – Carter, Quibell and Ayrton – and was responsible for more haste than discipline in the excavation of some sites, notably that of the tomb of Smenkhare, brother, it is thought, of Tutankhamen. Davis did, however, use his money to finance the publication of many books on the archaeology of the sites he paid to have excavated. Davis died in 1915 sure that the Valley of the Kings was exhausted of new archaeological finds.

The theme of the seven separate chapels is evident in the **First Hypostyle Hall,** built and decorated by Ramses II's second-rate craftsmen, where the columns with papyrus capitals depict Ramses with the god represented in the corresponding sanctuary. In the much more impressive **Second Hypostyle Hall,** built by Seti, the first two rows of columns also have papyrus capitals but the last row have no capitals at all. On the right-hand wall Seti is pictured before Osiris and Horus who are pouring holy water from vases and making offerings in front of Osiris' shrine as five goddesses look on. The quality of the work in this hall contrasts sharply with the rougher decoration in the outer hall which was probably because Ramses had ordered all the most skilled craftsmen to concentrate on his own temple!

Behind the inner hypostyle hall there are seven separate **Sanctuaries** or chapels which are dedicated to the deified Seti I, the Osiris triad of Osiris, Isis and Horus, and the Amun triad of Amun, Mut and Khonsu. Many of the wonderful bas-reliefs are still coloured, which gives a good idea of the temple's original decoration, but some of the finest are unpainted and show the precision and great artistry used in the moulding. The sanctuary to the left is dedicated to Seti and contains a beautiful scene of the Pharaoh being crowned by the goddess of Upper and Lower Egypt.

Each of these sanctuaries would have contained the god's barque as well as his stela placed in front of a false door. The sanctuary was locked and only High Priests had access because the Ancient Egyptians believed that the gods lived in their sanctuaries. The daily rituals which were carried out included a sacrifice as well as the dressing and purification of the stelae. Unlike the others, the **Sanctuary of Osiris** does not have a false door at the back of the chapel but connects with the pillared **Suite of Osiris.** It is decorated with scenes from the Osiris myth and has three shrines on the west wall dedicated, with magnificent and incredibly vivid paintings, to Seti, Isis and Horus. The Mysteries of Osiris miracle play would have been performed in the hall and in the unfinished and partially destroyed **Sanctuary of Osiris** which is reached through a narrow entrance on the opposite wall.

Back in the Second Hypostyle Hall the temple changes direction on the left-hand or southeast side with two entrances leading to a number of other halls. The nearest is the three-columned **Hall of Sokar and Nefertum**, northern deities subsequently integrated into the Osirian cult, with the separate **Chapel of Sokar** and **Chapel of Nefertum** at the back. Through the other entrance is the narrow star-decorated **Hall/Gallery of Ancestors/Lists** which, very usefully for archaeologists, lists in rows the names of the gods and 76 of Seti's predecessors although, for political reasons, some, such as Hatshepsut, Akhenaten and his heirs, are omitted. The gallery leads on to the **Hall of Barques** where the sacred boats were stored, the **Hall of Sacrifices** used as the slaughterhouse for the sacrifices, and other storerooms: they are currently closed to visitors. Instead it is best to follow the side **Corridor of the Bulls**, where Ramses II is shown lassoing a bull before the jackal-headed 'opener of the ways' Wepwawet on one side and driving four dappled calves towards Khonsu and Seti I on the other, before climbing the steps to the temple's rear door and the Osirieon.

The **Osirieon**, built earlier than the main temple and at water level, which has led to severe flooding, is sometimes called the Cenotaph of Seti I because it contains a sarcophagus. Although it was never used by Seti I, who is actually buried in the Valley of the Kings in Luxor (see page 237), it was built as a symbol of his closeness to Osiris. Many other pharaohs built similar 'fake' tombs, which were modelled on the tombs at Luxor, in Abydos but were eventually buried elsewhere. The Osirieon is the only remaining visible tomb but is unfortunately inaccessible because of the inundation of sand and the flooding caused by the rise in the water table.

The small **Temple of Ramses II** (see plan page 200), near the village, 300 m northwest from the Temple of Seti I across soft sand, is naturally an anticlimax after the scale and sheer beauty of the Temple of Seti I. However, it was originally a very finely built shrine, erected in 1298 BC for Ramses' *Ka* or spirit in order to give him a close association with Osiris. The workmanship is better than in most of Ramses II's monuments because it was probably decorated by craftsmen trained in his father's era. Although the temple was reportedly almost intact when first seen by Napoleon's archaeologists, it has since fallen into ruin except for the lower parts of the limestone walls which are still brightly coloured.

South of Nag Hammadi in the curve of a meander of the River Nile stands a complex known as the **Monastery of St Palomen**. This is a rich agricultural area and the bell tower can be seen from quite a distance. There are three churches, St Palomen, St Mercurius and St Damyanah. St Palomen died of excessive fasting. To the north of here the famous Gnostic codices were discovered in 1947 (see page 85, Coptic Museum).

The Nile ran red

As the story goes – Re, the sun-god, creator of all men and all things, began to grow old and the men he had so carefully created began to mock him. They criticized his appearance and even complained about his neglect of them. Re was very angry at their lack of reverence due to his position, after all, he was their creator. He called a secret council of gods and goddesses (Geb, Shu, Tefnut, Nut and Hathor), where it was agreed that they would destroy all mankind and halt the unnecessary aggravation.

The task of destruction was handed to Hathor, the daughter of Re. She seems to have been happy in her work, 'wading in blood' as the story goes. The gods realized, almost too late, that without the men the tasks on earth in the temples would not be performed. It was essential, therefore, to protect those who remained from slaughter. The drug mandrake was mixed with freshly brewed beer and the blood of the already slain making 7,000 vessels in all. This liquid was poured out across the land (symbolic of the Nile floods) and Hathor, waking, mistook this liquid for blood, drank it all and was too stupefied to complete her gruesome task.

Qena

→ *Colour map 4, grid A2.*

The town of Qena, just 58 km north of Luxor, despite being the provincial capital, is not very welcoming to foreign visitors. Services are lacking, and often unavailable to foreigners. Though the town has undergone a bit of a makeover recently (complete with rubbish bins), it's not particularly friendly and police escorts can't be dodged. The main reason for stopping in Qena is to see the magnificent temple at Dendera about 8 km from the centre of town but also worth a look if you make it here is the lovely Abdur Rahim mosque on the main road in town.

Ins and outs

Getting there and around From the train station, the adjacent bus station and the southbound service taxi depot, on either side of the main canal, Sharia El-Gumhoriyya leads southeast to a major roundabout and the town's main street, to the west end of which is the northbound service taxi depot, near the River Nile. To get to Dendera from the centre of Qena, tourist police generally insist that independent travellers hire a private taxi to take them to the temple and back. If you can dodge security, service taxi pick-ups (50p) bound for Dendera converge at a depot by the large intersection near the Nile. Alternatively, if inter-city service taxis will accept foreign travellers, you can hop on a northbound ride to Sohag and get dropped at Dendera village, and walk the remaining 1 km to the temple. From Luxor, two convoys leave daily, the first at 0800, carries on to Abydos before returning in the afternoon; the second leaves at 1400 to Dendera (and back) only. Confirm convoy departure times with the tourist office in Luxor, see page 212. You can take a coach tour from one of the many tour companies along the corniche, or you can hire a private taxi for about E£100 (can seat five) for the day. Novotel also offers a daylong cruise for E£180 per person, which includes lunch and a tour of the temple. Expect delays from the additional security procedures associated with visiting this area – the intervention of the tourist police can result in a lengthy wait (30 mins or more) at both ends of the journey. » *For further details, see Transport, page 207.*

Brick making in Egypt

Sun dried bricks were made from the dried Nile mud. This mud shrinks a great deal when it dries and has to be protected from the sun and the wind to prevent the brick collapsing even before it is used. To reduce the breakage rate the mud was mixed with chopped straw or reeds.

The Bible tells of the Israelites being forced to make bricks while in captivity in Egypt. Each brick-maker had a daily target with only whole bricks being counted. Making bricks without straw meant more journeys to collect mud as it was then the only ingredient and the bricks were fragile and more frequently broken.

Dendera

ⓘ *Daily 0700-1800. E£12, students E£6. Use of cameras and video recorders free.*
Dendera had been the cult centre of Hathor since pre-dynastic times and there are signs of earlier buildings on the site dating back to Cheops in the Fourth Dynasty (2613-2494 BC). Hathor, represented as a cow or cow-headed woman, was the goddess associated with love, joy, music, protection of the dead and, above all, of nurturing. Her great popularity was demonstrated by the huge festival held at Edfu (see page 271) when her barque symbolically sailed upstream on her annual visit to Horus to whom she was both wet-nurse and lover. As they reconsummated their union the population indulged in the Festival of Drunkenness which led the Greeks to identify Hathor with Aphrodite who was their own goddess of love and joy.

The **Temple of Hathor**, which was built between 125 BC and AD 60 by the Ptolemies and the Romans, is the latest temple on the site with the first being built by Pepi I in the Sixth Dynasty (2345-2181 BC). The enclosing wall of the temple is of unbaked bricks laid alternately convex and concave, like waves of a primeval ocean – perhaps this had some religious significance. The huge, well-preserved temple dominates the walled Dendera complex which also includes a number of smaller buildings. Even although it was built by non-Egyptian foreign conquerors it copies the earlier Pharaonic temples with large hypostyle halls leading up, via a series of successively smaller vestibules and storerooms, to the darkened sanctuary at the back of the temple. There are also two sets of steps leading up to and down from the roof sanctuaries.

At the front, the pylon-shaped façade is supported by six huge Hathor-headed columns and reliefs showing the Roman emperors Tiberius and Claudius performing rituals with the gods. Through in the **Hypostyle Hall** there are 18 Hathor-headed columns, capitals of which are sistra-rattles associated with music and dance. These are organized into groups of three, and are identical to those on the façade. The magnificent ceiling, which is illustrated with an astronomical theme showing the mystical significance of the sky, has retained much of its original colour. It is divided between day and night and illustrates the 14 days' moon cycle, the gods of the four cardinal points, the constellations, the zodiac, and the elongated goddess Nut who swallows the sun at sunset and gives birth to it at dawn.

Holes at the base of the pillars here were reputedly used as tethering points for animals kept by the Copts whilst in hiding in the temple.

The next room, which is known as the **Hall of Appearances** and is supported by six columns, is where the goddess 'appeared' from the depths of the temple as she was transported on her ritual barque for the annual voyage to Edfu. On either side of the doorway there are scenes of offerings and the presentation of the temple to the gods.

Around this Hall are six small rooms (all lit by sunlight from holes in the roof). The first on the left was the **laboratory**, used for the preparation of balms and the nine oils used to anoint the statues, which has several inscriptions with the recipes and instructions for their preparation. The next two rooms were used as **store-rooms** for offerings such as flowers, beer, wine and poultry. On the right of the hall's doorway is the **Treasury** which has scenes on the base of the walls representing the 13 mountainous countries where the precious minerals were found. The second room called the **Nile Room**, has river scenes and an exit to the back corridor and the well outside. Next is the first vestibule which was known as the **Hall of Offerings** because it was there that the priests displayed the offerings for the goddess on large tables. The food and drink was then divided among the priests once the gods had savoured them. On the left a stairway leads to the roof sanctuary. The second vestibule called the **Hall of the Ennead** contained the statues of the kings and gods which were involved in the ceremonies for Hathor while her wardrobe was stored in the room on the left.

This leads on to the **Sanctuary of the Golden One** which contained Hathor's statue and her ceremonial barque which would be carried to the river each New Year to be transported on a boat upstream to the Temple of Horus at Edfu. The south and north walls of the independently roofed sanctuary depict the Pharaoh in various phases of the ceremony. The so-called **Corridor of Mysteries** around the outside of the sanctuary has nine doors which lead to 11 small shrines with 32 closed crypts below the back shrines including the crypt where the temple's valuables would have been stored.

The walls of the stairway from the left of the Hall of Offerings to the **Roof Sanctuaries** (which, unlike anywhere else, have been completely preserved at Dendera), depict the New Year ceremony when the statue of Hathor was carried up to the roof to the small open **Chapel of the Union with the Disk** pavilion to await the sunrise. The scenes on the left of the stairs represent Hathor going up and those on the right going down. In the northwest corner of the roof terrace is **Osiris' Tomb**, where ceremonies commemorating Osiris' death and resurrection were carried out. In the east corner there are two rooms with the outer one containing a plaster-cast copy of the original **Dendera Zodiac** ceiling which was stolen and taken to the Louvre in Paris in 1820. The Zodiac was introduced to Egypt by the Romans and, although Scorpio's scorpion is replaced by a scarab beetle and the hippo-goddess Tweri was added, this circular zodiac held up by four goddesses is virtually identical to the one used today.

The views from the uppermost level of the roof terrace are superb and

Temple at Dendera

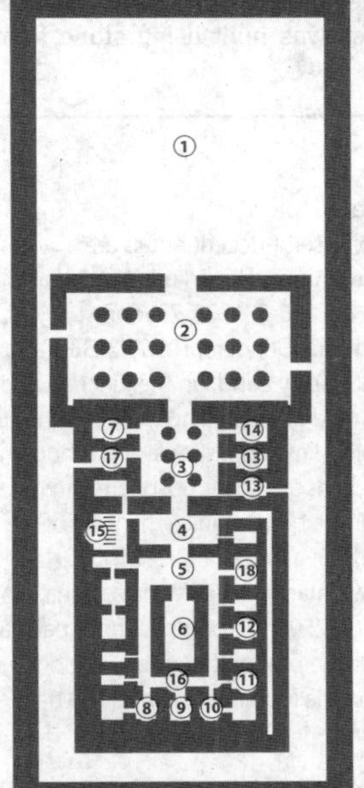

Not to scale

1 Court
2 Pronaos/First Hypostyle Hall
3 Second Hypostyle Hall/ Hall of Appearances
4 First Vestibule/ Hall of Offerings
5 Second Vestibule/ Hall of Ennead
6 Sanctuary
7 Treasury
8 Per-Neser Chapel/ House of Flame
9 Per-Ur Chapel/ Shrine of Egypt
10 Per-Nu Chapel
11 Sacred Serpent
12 Seat of Repose
13 Harvest Rooms
14 Laboratory
15 Stairs to roof
16 Stairs to crypts
17 Nile Room
18 Hathor's Wardrobe

provide an excellent opportunity to appreciate the overall scale and layout of the temple buildings, the extensive outer walls and the intensively cultivated countryside surrounding Dendera. From the northern edge of the upper terrace there are good views looking down on to the sanitorium, the two birth houses and the Coptic basilica (see below).

Back downstairs in the temple enclosure on the exterior south wall of the temple there are two damaged reliefs depicting Cleopatra and her son Caesarion, and beyond a number of small ruined buildings surround the main temple. At the back is the small **Temple of Isis** which was almost totally destroyed by the early Christians because of the fear that the worship of Isis as the universal Egyptian goddess might spread. At the front of the main temple to the right is the **Roman Birth House**, or Mammisi, which has some interesting carvings on its façade and south walls. It was built to replace the older 30th Dynasty **Birth House of Nectanebo** (380-362 BC) which was partially destroyed when the Romans built a wall around the temple. The **Sanatorium** between it and the main temple was where pilgrims, who came to Dendera to be healed by Hathor, were treated and washed in water from the stone-lined **Sacred Lake** to the southwest of the main temple, which is now drained of water. Between the two birth-houses is a ruined fifth-century **Coptic Basilica**, one of the earliest Coptic buildings in Egypt, which was built using stone from the adjacent buildings.

This is the only surviving relief depicting Cleopatra in the whole of Egypt.

Sleeping

Sohag *p199*

A stay in Sohag is not to be recommended, but if necessary the best is:

D Merit Amoun Hotel, T093-601985, F603222. 30 rooms, across the Nile by the Governorate building.

D Cazalovy Hotel, beyond the Merit Amoun, T093-601185. A 3-star hotel and the Merit Amoun's primary rival, is also decent and a bit cheaper. Both are on the East Bank.

There are also 4 rundown and fairly filthy cheap hotels directly outside the railway station. The best two are:

F Al-Salam, by the train station, T093-333317, marginally more sanitary than the nearby Andolous (below);

F Andolous, across from the train station, T093-324328. Both are noisy budget hotels which mainly cater to Egyptian train travellers. There are fans, and only grubby shared shower and toilet facilities.

F Youth hostel, 5 Sharia Port Said 1.5 km from station, T093-324395. Has 28 beds and parking.

F Youth hostel, on road from Assiut to Sohag in front of El-Manzalawy factory, T/F093-311430. Has 72 beds, family rooms, disabled facilities, parking, kitchen, laundry.

Qena *p203*

The only semi-decent hotels are:

D Aluminium, Aluminium, Naga Hammadi, Qena, T/F096-581320, 72 rooms;

F Dendera, Dendera, T096-322330, also called **Happy Land**, on the junction of the main road to Sohag and the turnoff for the temple 1 km away, simple and rundown, but retains a bit of atmosphere and is certainly a better choice than any of the grubby dives in Qena;

F New Palace, Midan Mahata, Qena, T096- 322509, 75 rooms, far from palatial, it's still the best of the grubby options, behind the Mobil garage near the train station.

Camping

Located next to the Hotel Dendera, the campsite has hot showers, electricity and a kitchen.

Eating

Sohag *p199*

Cazalovy and **Merit Amoun** hotels have restaurants.

There are a number of small cheap restaurants and cafés in the streets around the railway station including:

El-Eman to the north of Andolous hotel. There's also a decent kebab place in Midan Aref, not far from the station as well as the usual scattering of *fuul*, *taameyya* and *kushari* stands around the train station.

Qena *p195*
Besides *kushari* and *fuul* stalls, there are a few small cheap restaurants, including: **El-Prince**, **Hamdi** and **Maradona** all located around the main street in town. None of them is particularly good.

Transport

Sohag *p195*

Bus
There are 7 daily buses north to **Minya** carrying on to **Cairo** and 1 daily south to **Luxor** carrying on to **Aswan**. There is also frequent bus service to **Assiut** (2 hrs), **El-Balyana** (for **Abydos**) and **Qena** (3 hrs). The bus depot is a 5-min walk south from the train station.

Taxi
Service taxis run north as far as **Assiut** and south to **Qena** via **El-Balyana** and **Nag Hammadi**. Be forewarned that bus travel for foreign visitors may be restricted and travel by service taxi is highly unlikely.

Train
Travel by train is preferable, and offers the least restrictions. All trains travelling between **Cairo** and **Luxor** stop in **Sohag**.

Qena *p203*

Bus
There are 2 a/c **Superjet** buses to **Cairo**, via **Hughada** and **Suez**, as well as service to other Red Sea destinations like **Safaga** and **Quseir**. Though buses also go to Nile Valley hub towns like **Assiut**, **Sohag** and **Minya**, they are more easily accessed by train.

Taxi
Service taxis, if open to foreign travellers, make a quick and easy way to travel, though now it's highly unlikely as all foreigners are required to travel through the region in convoys. If you can manage it, though, southbound service taxis to **Luxor** and all points in between depart from the square just across the canal behind the railway station. 500 m away there are service taxis to **Safaga** and **Hurghada**. Northbound service taxis along the West Bank to **Sohag** via **Nag Hammadi** and **El-Balyana**, can be caught from the depot near the river in the southwestern part of town.

Train
At least 6 daily trains northbound to **Cairo** via **Sohag**, **Assiut**, **Minya** and **Beni Suef**, and south to **Luxor** (40 mins) and **Aswan**.

Directory

Sohag *p195*
Useful numbers Emergency/Police: T093-324239. **Passport office**: T093-323746.

Qena *p195*
Post office At the canal end of the main street, open Sat-Thu 0800-1400 and 1800-2000. **Telephone** Open 24 hours. **Useful addresses** Police in the train station.

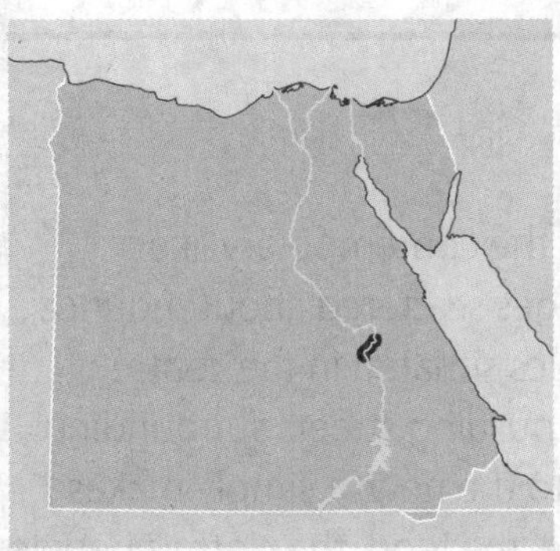

Footprint features

Introduction

In Luxor, the ancient exists amid the contemporary like nowhere else. Life thrives in villages scattered about mounds of Theban tombs. Colossal temples situated in the centre of everything cast shadows on the bustling streets surrounding them. The old doesn't give way to the new; it simply makes space. Evident in the architecture, the food, the clothes people wear, the things they sell and the games they play, Luxorians are remarkably capable of integrating layers of history with the present and future.

Second only to the Pyramids as Egypt's most visited attraction, Luxor, the New Kingdom's ancient capital of Thebes (1567-1085 BC), is among the world's oldest tourist destinations. A city built upon cities of millennia past, the area has been inhabited for at least 6000 years. With an overwhelming number of well-preserved sandstone temples and elaborate tombs, many deem Luxor the world's greatest open air museum. Among the too-many-to-count sights surrounding the city, highlights include the remains of **Karnak Temple**, a vast and beautifully-preserved temple complex built over the span of more than 1000 years, just 2 km north of the city centre. In the centre, the **Luxor Temple**, once a refuge for every great religion that thrived in ancient Egypt, rises gracefully alongside the Nile and the chaos of the nearby souk. At night it is splendidly lit and open to visitors. Across the river on the west bank, the **Valley of the Kings and Queens**, spotted with tombs and magnificent mortuary temples, yields a taste of the profound and vital journey to the next life. It also serves as a convenient base for day trips to the temples of Dendera and Abydos to the north, and the temples of Esna and Edfu, to the south.

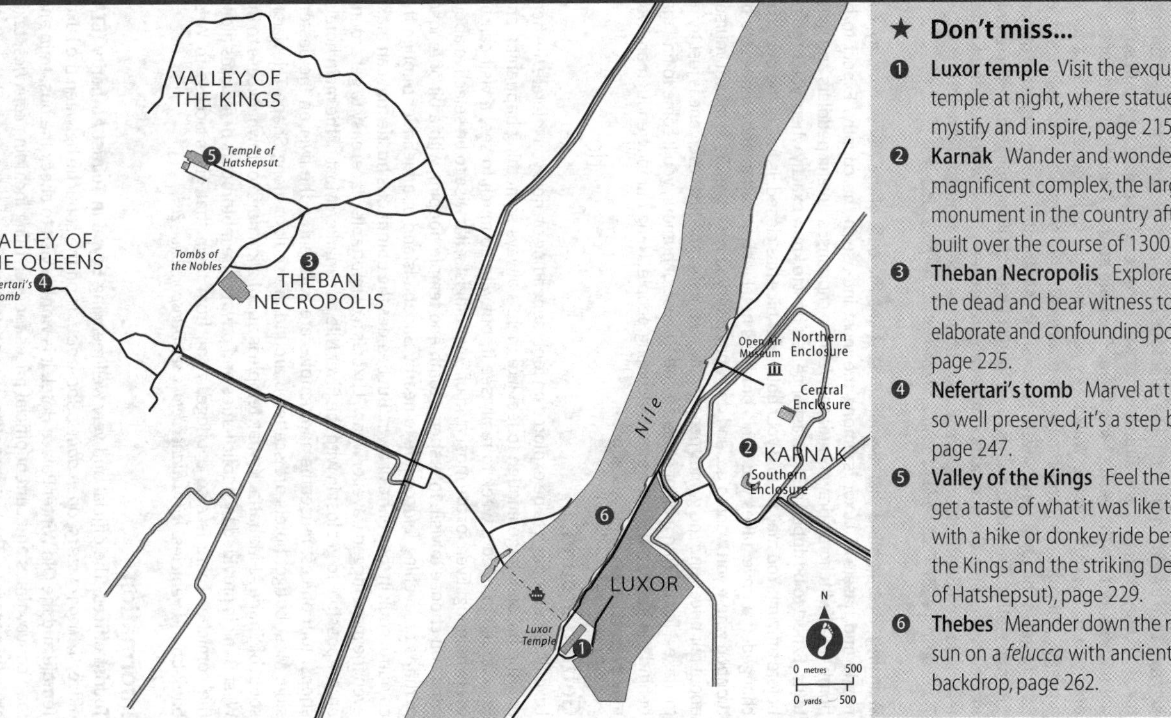

★ Don't miss...

1. **Luxor temple** Visit the exquisitely beautiful temple at night, where statues and shadows mystify and inspire, page 215.
2. **Karnak** Wander and wonder through the magnificent complex, the largest Pharaonic monument in the country after the pyramids, built over the course of 1300 years, page 219.
3. **Theban Necropolis** Explore the eerie city of the dead and bear witness to the Pharaohs' elaborate and confounding portals to the afterlife, page 225.
4. **Nefertari's tomb** Marvel at the glorious colours, so well preserved, it's a step back in time, page 247.
5. **Valley of the Kings** Feel the land's majesty and get a taste of what it was like to be a grave robber with a hike or donkey ride between the Valley of the Kings and the striking Deir El-Bahri (Temple of Hatshepsut), page 229.
6. **Thebes** Meander down the river into the setting sun on a *felucca* with ancient Thebes as your backdrop, page 262.

Ins and outs → *Colour map 4, grid A2. Population: 45,000.*

Getting there

Luxor is 676 km south of Cairo, 65 km south of Qena and 223 km north of Aswan. The **airport** is 7 km east of the town centre. Visas are on sale just before passport control. From the airport, a taxi to the town centre should cost E£15-20. Or you can haul your luggage 1 km toward town and hail a microbus or covered pickup from the main road for 25p. Other than that, the airport is not well connected to public transport so taxis are unquestionably the easiest way to go. The **train** station is in the middle of town, only 500 m from the centre. Walking is easy enough, or if you're hauling a lot of luggage, you can take a *calèche* (horse-drawn carriage) or taxi anywhere in town for E£5. To get to the town centre, walk down Sharia Al-Mahatta, the street just in front of the train station. The **bus** terminal is on Sharia El-Karnak, just behind the Luxor temple in the town centre. **Service taxis** congregate in between the town centre and Karnak temple just off Sharia Karnak, about 1 km from the town centre. » *For further details, see Transport, page 261. For Sleeping, Eating and other listings see pages 253-263.*

Warning Bear in mind that as tourism sustains the bulk of the city's economy, the hustle and hassle in Luxor is among the most intense in the country. Expect to be bombarded with horse-drawn carriages, *felucca* captains, souvenir peddlers and hotel touts. Expect to be ripped off, at least once. It is best to know exactly where you're going before arriving. You may be told your hotel of choice has closed, is full, or the price has changed. If a driver takes you to his brother's hotel instead, adamantly request to be dropped where you want to go, and don't pay until you get there. Try to inform yourself about fair prices and the games people play, and remember that everyone is just trying to make a living. With a bit of patience and a sense of humour, you'll come to find that behind the frenzy thrives a warm, welcoming people. Hang out long enough and you may even get a wedding invitation.

Getting around

Luxor is small enough to be explored on foot (depending on how you tolerate the heat and the hassle), large enough to feel like there's always something happening and full enough to need a week to really see it; but with so much to see, a visit can be overwhelming. Even for the most avid of Egyptologists, it's wise to be selective about what you choose to visit. Intersperse tomb and temple hopping with a bit of repose, perhaps an evening *felucca* ride to nearby Banana Island or a meander through the colourful souk in the centre of town. But besides the ubiquitous hustle that can make even the most rugged traveller weary, Luxor is a comfortable place, easy to get around and impossible to get lost in with the River Nile as a marker. Most of the main hotels, shops, tour offices, museums and temples are adjacent to the river on the eastern side. Most budget hotels are scattered around the souk or along Sharia Televizion, south of Sharia Al-Mahatta. Karnak temple is about 2 km north of town. Access to the West Bank is provided by public ferries and private hire motorboats or *feluccas* along the corniche. There is also a bridge, 7 km from town that gives access to West bank-bound vehicles. » *For further details, see Transport, page 261.*

Information

Tourist offices The official and very well-meaning **Egyptian Tourist Authority (ETA)** office, ⓘ *T095-372215, open daily 0800-2000*, is on the corniche between the Luxor Temple and the Old Winter Palace Hotel. It is worth a visit to check the bus, train and road convoy times and current official prices for everything including *calèches*, taxis and other services. The **tourist police** ⓘ *T095-373294*, are in the same building. Both also have branches at the airport and the railway station. **Visa extensions** are

24 hours in Luxor

If you only have one day, a sample of major monuments can be seen.

At first light, stroll along the **corniche** from the Old Winter Palace to Hotel Pharaon. If you haven't booked a tour or found a guide in advance, catch the ferry across the river and hire a taxi for the day. Plan to take in at least the highlights of the **Valley of the Kings and Queens** (which change depending on which monuments are closed for 'resting'). If possible, shell out the extra charge for the magnificent **tomb of Nefertari**. Also visit **Deir El-Bahri** before heading back to the East Bank for lunch. Spend the late afternoon wandering through the superb **Luxor Museum**. Before sundown, take a *felucca* to catch the emerging shades of evening and watch the birds fly along the river in squadrons to roost. Complete your day with the sound and light show at **Karnak** – a striking way to view the complex of temples, with modest temperatures under an ocean of floodlight.

relatively easy to get in Luxor. The **passport office** is south of town, on a side street off of the Corniche (which turns into Sharia Ibn Khalid El-Walid), opposite the Meridian. ⓘ *Hours are supposedly 0800-2000 everyday except Fri. Arrive early.*

Best time to visit

Tourist season extends from October to March, peaking around Christmas and the New Year, when the weather is sunny and sublime. In the summer, the midday heat can be unbearable, but if you can handle it, the crowds taper off giving the independent traveller a chance to gaze upon ancient wonders without swarms of tour groups milling about. Most monuments and museums in and around Luxor open at 0600 and close at 1600 in the winter, 1700 in the summer. Students with an ISIC card receive a 50% discount to everything except the Karnak sound and light show.

History

For an account of who's who in Ancient Egypt among the kings, queens and gods, see page 540 in the Footnotes chapter.

On the site of the small present-day town of Luxor stood the ancient city which the Greeks called **Thebes** and which was described in Homer's *Iliad* as the 'city of a hundred gates'. Later the Arabs described it as *'el-Uqsur'* or 'city of palaces' from which it gets its current name.

The town and the surrounding limestone hills had been settled for many centuries but during the Old Kingdom (2616-2181 BC) it was little more than a small provincial town called Waset. It first assumed importance under Menutuhotep II who reunited Egypt and made it his capital but it soon lost its position. It was during the 18th-20th Dynasty of the New Kingdom (1567-1085 BC) that Thebes reached its zenith when, except for the brief reign of Akhenaten (1379-62 BC), it was the capital of the Egyptian Empire which stretched from Palestine to Nubia. At its peak the population reached almost one million. Besides being the site of the largest and greatest concentration of monuments in the world it was, for the ancient Egyptians, the prototype for all future cities.

When the capital later shifted elsewhere it remained a vibrant city and the focus for the worship of Amun ('the Supreme Creator'). Although there is no obvious connection with the Greek city of Thebes the name was subsequently given to the city by the Greeks. It was a shadow of its former self during the Ptolemaic (323-30 BC) and

The hassle, haggle and hustle

Since 11 September 2001 and the War on Iraq, the number of tourists in Luxor has dropped by 40%. In a town where most people's bread is connected to tourism, the impact has been dire. As a result, everyone is doing everything they can to get as much as they can. Sometimes it means budget hotels cut their rates in half just to earn a few pounds. Calèche and taxi drivers accept fares that they might have totally dismissed in the past. Tour guides offer the same tour to one hard haggler for 100 pounds less than to another. When bargaining for a cheaper deal, bear in mind that less is not always best and the quality of your experience may suffer if you take advantage of this situation. Be fair and realistic and try to maintain a sensitivity to the people on your back. Especially when the season is slumping, every tourist counts. Most tour guides and *felucca* captains will make a chunk of money in a day and not see another chunk for a long spell. Bargain hard, be aware of the scams that circulate and try to maintain a sense of humour and relaxed attitude toward the scene. This is how people get by.

Roman (30 BC-AD 640) periods but, unlike ancient Memphis to the south of Cairo, it was never abandoned and it became an important regional Christian settlement. In the Luxor region a number of temples became Coptic monasteries. For example at both Deir El-Medina and Deir El-Bahri Egyptian monuments have been taken over and converted for Christian use.

After the Muslim conquest in AD 640, the town continued to decline and it was not until the beginning of the 19th century, during Napoleon's expedition to Egypt, that its historical importance began to be recognized. The display of some of its treasures in Paris's Louvre museum (see box, page 115) sparked off considerable interest from the world's archaeologists who still continue to explore the area almost 200 years later. Since 1869, when Thomas Cook took his first party of travellers to Egypt for the opening of the Suez Canal, Luxor has become the most important tourist destination in Upper Egypt. Today, although it has become an important administrative town, the economic livelihood of Luxor is, as the sudden collapse in business during the 1990/91 Gulf war and as the mass exodus of thousands of tourists in November 1997 demonstrated, almost totally dependent on the tourist industry.

Sights

There is a reason Luxor is deemed the world's biggest open air museum: it brims over with extraordinary sights. In the thick of summer, it's best to visit tombs and temples in the early morning hours, although the heat of the mid-afternoon, if you can bear it, does wonders to drive away the hordes of tourists and touts. Visit Luxor Temple at night, it's beautifully lit and easily accessible as it's right in the middle of town. On the West Bank, depending on your interest, it could take a morning to cover the major highlights or up to two full days to visit in its entirety. In brief, on the ***East Bank****, the Luxor Temple (page 215), Luxor Museum (page 218) and Karnak Temple complex (page 219) are essential stops. Although the* ***West Bank*** *is dominated by the Theban Necropolis (page 225) and the Valley of the Kings (page 229), there are also some fascinating temples and monuments above ground worth exploring.*

Luxor and the East Bank

Luxor Temple

ⓘ *The temple, in the centre of town on the corniche, is open daily 0600-2100 in winter, 0600-2200 in summer. E£20, students E£10, cameras free. Allow a few hours to see this in detail. Luxor Temple is particularly striking at night and one of the few ancient sights in Egypt that permits a post-sunset wander.*

Like the much larger Karnak Temple, Luxor Temple is dedicated to the three Theban gods Amun, Mut and Khonsu. **Amun** is usually depicted as a man wearing ram's horns or a tall feathered Atef crown. His wife **Mut** was considered to be the mistress of heaven and **Khonsu** was their son who was believed to travel through the sky at night assisting the scribe god.

Because it is smaller, more compact and fewer pharaohs were involved in its construction, Luxor Temple is simpler and more coherent than Karnak Temple a few kilometres away. Although the 18th-Dynasty (1537-1320 BC) pharaoh **Amenhotep III** (1417-1379 BC) began the temple, his son **Amenhotep IV**, who changed his name to **Akhenaten** (1379-62 BC) by which he is better known, concentrated instead on building a shrine to Aten adjacent to the site. However, **Tutankhamen** (1361-52 BC) and **Horemheb** (1348-20 BC) later resumed the work and decorated the peristyle court and colonnade. **Ramses II** (1304-1237 BC) completed most of the building by adding a second colonnade and pylon as well as a multitude of colossi. The Temple subsequently became covered with sand and silt which helped preserve it, although salt encrustation has caused some damage. Because the ground level has risen 6 m since its construction the temple now stands at the bottom of a gentle depression. An avenue of sphinxes, a 30th-Dynasty (380-343 BC) addition,

Temple of Luxor

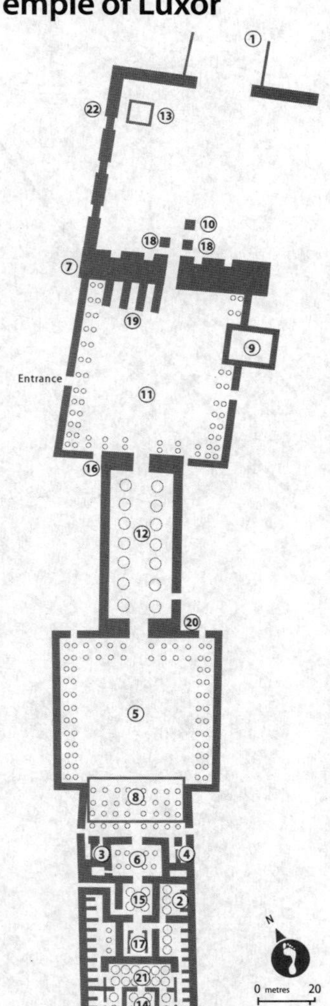

1 Avenue of human-headed sphinxes
2 Birth room
3 Chapel of Khonsu
4 Chapel of Mut
5 Court of Amenhotep III
6 First antechamber or Roman sanctuary
7 First Pylon of Ramses II
8 Hypostyle hall
9 Mosque of Abu el-Haggag
10 Obelisk
11 Peristyle Court of Ramses II
12 Processional Colonnade of Amenophis III
13 Roman shrine to Sarapis
14 Sanctuary to Amun-Re
15 Second antechamber/ offering room
16 Second pylon
17 Shrine of Sacred Barque
18 Statues of Ramses II
19 Temple to Thebian Triad/ triple shrine
20 Third pylon
21 Transverse hall
22 Walls of Roman brick

Luxor

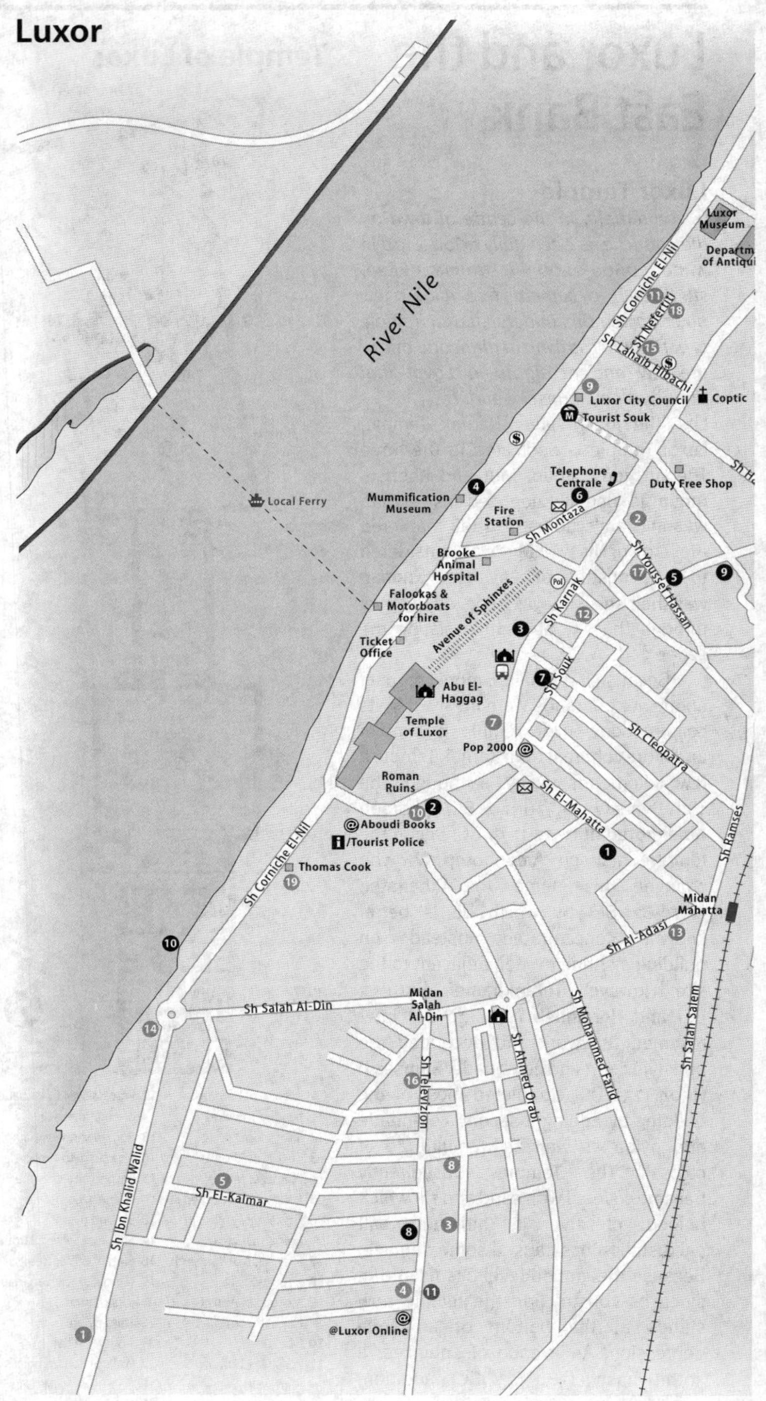
River Nile
Local Ferry
Luxor Museum
Department of Antiqui
Sh Corniche El-Nil
Sh Nefertiti
Sh Lahaib Hibachi
Luxor City Council
Coptic
Tourist Souk
Telephone Centrale
Duty Free Shop
Mummification Museum
Fire Station
Sh Montaza
Brooke Animal Hospital
Sh Youssef Hassan
Falookas & Motorboats for hire
Avenue of Sphinxes
Sh Karnak
Ticket Office
Abu El-Haggag
Sh Souk
Temple of Luxor
Sh Cleopatra
Pop 2000
Roman Ruins
Sh El-Mahatta
Aboudi Books
/Tourist Police
Thomas Cook
Sh Corniche El-Nil
Sh Ramses
Midan Mahatta
Sh Al-Adasi
Sh Salah Al-Din
Midan Salah Al-Din
Sh Salah Salem
Sh Mohammed Farid
Sh Ahmed Orabi
Sh Televizion
Sh Ibn Khalid Walid
Sh El-Kalmar
@Luxor Online

lines the approach. This avenue once stretched all the way to the Karnak Temple complex. The entrance to the temple is through the First Pylon. In front of the pylon are the three remaining colossi of Ramses II, two seated and one standing and, to the left, a single obelisk 25 m high.

The **First Pylon** gives an impression of how awe-inspiring the temple must have looked in its prime. The 22.8 m-high second Obelisk, which was given to France by Mohammed Ali Pasha in 1819 and was re-erected in the Place de la Concorde in Paris, and another three of Ramses II's six original colossi have been removed. The reliefs on the First Pylon depict Ramses's victory at the Battle of Kadesh with later embellishments by Nubian and Ethiopian kings.

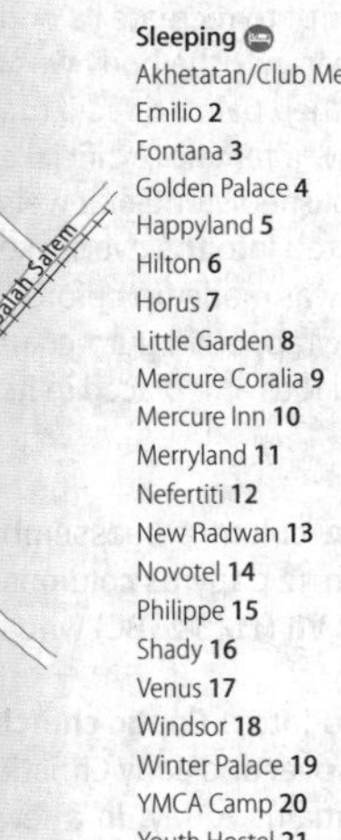

Passing through the pylon, the **Peristyle Court** is set at a slight angle to the rest of the temple and encompasses the earlier shrine of **Tuthmosis III** (1504-1450 BC) which is also dedicated to the Theban triad. The east end of the court has not been fully excavated because it is the site of the **Mosque of Abu El-Haggag**, the patron saint of Luxor and, although another mosque with the same name has been built nearby, this one is still preferred by locals. While most of the mosque is 19th-century the northern minaret is very much older. At the south end of the court, the portal flanking the entrance to the colonnade supports two black granite statues bearing the name of Ramses II, but the feathers of Tutankhamen.

The **colonnade** of 14 columns with papyrus capitals was built by Amenhotep but decorated by Tutankhamen and Horemheb. Beyond it is a **Court of Amenhotep III**, which is the second peristyle court with double rows of columns flanking three of the sides. It was built by Amenhotep III for the deity Amun who he claimed was his father. None of the original roof remains, but the columns are well preserved. Because the rising water table has undermined the foundations of this court, an extensive restoration programme has recently been

Mummification

The ritual of mummification reached its zenith during the New Kingdom at the same time as the Luxor and Karnak temple complexes were being built. It was developed because the ancient Egyptians believed that in order for a person to reach their heavenly aspect or *Ka* in the afterlife, it was essential that both their name and body survived thereby sustaining their cosmic double or *Ka* which was transported from one life to the next. In order to achieve this, the mummification ritual developed into an extremely complex means of preserving bodies. The dead were placed in tombs together with any food and utensils thought necessary to accompany the person's Ka for the journey to the underworld. Although we know quite a bit about the most commonly used New Kingdom mummification methods, others are still being revealed. For example, a recently opened princess's tomb in Giza revealed that the body had been hollowed out and lined with very fine plaster. The mummification method found in and around the Valley of the Kings, however, usually involved removing the brain through the nose (it was discarded because the heart was thought to be the centre of intelligence). The entrails and organs were then extracted and stored in jars, known as Canopic jars, while the corpse was soaked in natrun salts for 40 days until it was dehydrated, at which point the embalming process began. In an attempt to recreate its original appearance the body was packed and then painted red if male and yellow if female. Artificial eyes, made of polished stone or jewels were inserted into the eye sockets and the face was made up before the body was wrapped in gum-coated linen bandages and placed in its coffin.

completed, the floor has been relaid and the 22 columns reassembled in their original positions. It leads to the **Hypostyle Hall** with 32 papyrus columns which were taken over by **Ramses IV** (1166-60 BC) and **Ramses VII** (1148-41BC) who took no part in their erection but still added their cartouches!

Look out for the chamber which was converted into a **Coptic church** during the fourth century. The Pharaonic reliefs were plastered over and early Christian paintings covered the whitewash although little of these remains today. In a few places the stucco has crumbled away and some of the original reliefs are revealed.

Beyond is a smaller second vestibule, the **Offerings Chamber**, with its four columns still in place. Further on, in the **Sanctuary of the Sacred Barque**, the doors were made of acacia and inlaid with gold. Alexander the Great (332-323 BC) rebuilt the shrine in accordance with Amenhotep III's original plans. The east passage leads to the **Birth Room** built because of Amenhotep's claim that he was the son of the god Amun, who is depicted as entering the queen's chamber disguised as Tuthmosis IV (1425-17 BC) and breathing the child into her nostrils. The furthest hall has 12 poorly maintained papyrus bud columns and leads on to the small **Sanctuary** where the combined god Amun-Min is represented.

Luxor Museum

ⓘ *The Luxor Museum is on the corniche half way between Luxor and Karnak temples. Daily winter 0900-1300 and 1600-2100 (last tickets 1230 and 2030), summer 0900-1300 and 1700-2200 (last tickets 1230 and 2130). During Ramadan: 1300-1600 only. E£30, students E£15. E£10 for use of a camera.*

The few exhibits in this modern museum are tastefully displayed, centred around a small garden, with a large ground floor and a smaller upper gallery. The most important and of particular interest are the New Kingdom statues which were found in a cache at Karnak in 1989 but the exhibits range from pharaonic treasures to the Mamluk period (AD 1250-1517).

Of the statues on the ground floor the most striking are the large pink granite head of Amenhotep III (1417-1379 BC), an alabaster crocodile-headed Sobek, and two memorable busts of Akhenaten. A few choice exhibits from Tutankhamen's tomb are also displayed including a gold-inlaid cow's head of the goddess Hathor (see box page 203), a funerary bed and two model barques. The prints showing how the sites looked in the 19th century are also interesting.

On the second floor is the wall of Akhenaten, 283 sandstone blocks found at the Ninth Pylon at Karnak. Here Akhenaten and Nefertiti are shown worshipping Aten.

Museum of Mummification

ⓘ *Daily, summer 0900-1300 and 1700- 2200, winter 0900-1300 and 1600- 2100. Ramadan: 1300-1600 only. E£20, students E£10. Cameras not permitted.*

Right on the banks of the River Nile this museum tells the story of mummification, as practised by the ancient Egyptians, as an integral part of their religious belief in the afterlife. This museum, considered to be the first of its kind in the world, contains a comprehensive display. Exhibits include several human, reptile and bird mummies as well as stone and metal tools used in the mummification process. It is well set out and is certainly worth a visit. Note the examples of canopic jars for storing the liver, lungs, stomach and intestines.

Karnak Temple complex

ⓘ *Daily winter 0600-1730, summer 0600- 1830 (last tickets sold half an hour before closing). E£20, students E£10. Cameras free. To get to Karnak, you can walk or bike the 2.5 km north along Sharia Karnak. Microbuses (25p – for everyone, pay after you arrive) with Karnak en route are found around the train station or behind Luxor Temple (look for the yellow signs on the dashboard, yell out 'Karnak', if they're going, they'll stop for you). Calèches and private taxis from town officially cost E£5. If they wait and bring you back, it's E£10 and some baksheesh. Expect to bargain hard. The walk or ride along the corniche is quite pleasant. In order to see as much of the site as possible, aim to arrive very early or just before sunset when it is relatively cool and less crowded. Allow half a day to see this in detail and if possible return in the evening for the Sound and Light show. E£33 and E£50 for video cameras.*

The Karnak Temple complex, the largest pharaonic monument in the country after the Giza Pyramids and covering almost 25 ha, is an entertaining, albeit a bit overdramatic experience. Some find it kitschy and others enjoyable. (See 'Sound and light', page 260.) Known in earlier times as **Iput-Isut** 'the most esteemed of places', the extent, scale and quality of the remains is astonishing. The complex's temples vary greatly in style because they were constructed over 1,300 years. Their only common theme is worship of Amun, Mut and Khonsu who make up the Theban Triad of gods.

At the heart of the complex is the enormous **Temple of Amun** which was altered and extended by successive pharaohs. For example, although the heretical **Akhenaten**, who converted to the world's first monotheistic religion and moved the capital from Thebes to Tell El-Amarna (see page 190), replaced the images of **Amun** with representations of **Aten**, these were later erased by his successors and Amun's images were restored. Included in and surrounding the main temple are numerous smaller but magnificent ones including the **Temple of Tuthmosis III**, the **Temple of Ramses III** and the smaller **Shrine of Seti II**.

Temple of Amun

The Temple of Amun is approached via the **Avenue of Ram-Headed Sphinxes (1)** which used to link it to the Temple at Luxor. The imposing **First Pylon (13)** is 130 m wide and each of the two unfinished towers are 43 m high and, although incomplete, nothing else matches its enormous scale. Dynasty after dynasty added to it and there is speculation about which ruler oversaw each of the various sections. Moving towards the inner core of the temple, which is the oldest section, one is moving back in time through successive dynasties. The entry towers are thought to have been constructed by the Nubian and Ethiopian Kings of the 25th Dynasty (747-656 BC) while recent work has revealed that several levels were built during the later Greek and Roman eras.

For a little baksheesh it may be possible to climb the stairs up the north tower and marvel at the fantastic view it offers of the complex.

Arriving through the First Pylon, you come to the **Great Forecourt (15)** which was begun in the 20th Dynasty (1200-1085 BC) but completed some time later. Immediately on the left is the very thick-walled rose-coloured granite and sandstone **Shrine of Seti II (27)** (1216-10 BC) which was a way-station for the sacred barques of Amun, Mut and Khonsu as they were taken on ritual processions. The west wall had to be subsequently rebuilt because it collapsed when the First Pylon was under construction. The outer façade portrays Seti II making offerings to various deities. In the middle of the Great Forecourt are the 10 columns of **Taharga** which once supported a 26½ m high kiosk or small open temple.

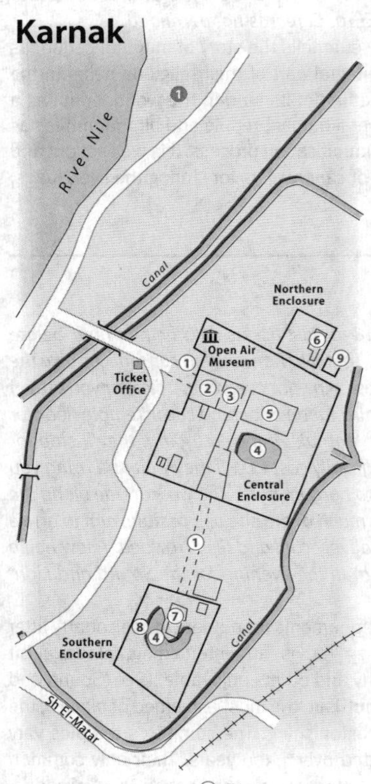

To the right of the forecourt is the small **Temple of Ramses III (33)** (1198-66 BC) which would have stood in solitary splendour in front of the **Second Pylon (25)** when it was first built in honour of Amun. Like the Shrine of Seti II, it was used as another way-station for the sacred barques. Part of an inscription in the interior reads: "I made it for you in your city of Waset, in front of your forecourt, to the Lord of the Gods, being the Temple of Ramses in the estate of Amun, to remain as long as the heavens bear the sun. I filled its treasuries with offerings that my hands had brought."

To the left of the Second Pylon is the 15 m high **Colossus of Ramses II (7)** (1304-1237 BC) with his daughter Benta-anta standing in front of his legs. On the right of the pylon is the **Bubastite Portal (3)** named after the 22nd-Dynasty (945-715 BC) kings from the Delta town of Bubastis. Through the Second Pylon is the immense 5,000 sq m (102 x 53 m) and spectacular **Hypostyle Hall (16)** which is probably the best part of the whole Karnak complex. Its has 134 giant columns, which were once topped by sandstone roof slabs, the 12 largest of which make up the central processional way to the other chambers are 23 m high and 15 m round. The other 122 smaller columns, which have papyrus bud capitals and retain some of their original colour at the higher levels, cover the rest of the hall. They are decorated by dedications to various gods, but particularly to the many different guises of Amun and the Theban Triad, and are also inscribed with the cartouches of the pharaohs who contributed to the hall. The south side was decorated by Ramses II with vivid but cheap and simple concave sunk-reliefs, while the north is attributed to Seti II whose artists painstakingly carved delicate convex bas-reliefs on the walls. Ramses is shown, on the south side of the internal wall of the Second Pylon, making offerings before the gods and seeking their guidance, while on the left is a beautiful representation of Thoth inscribing Seti's name on a holy tree.

Karnak central enclosure - Temple of Amun

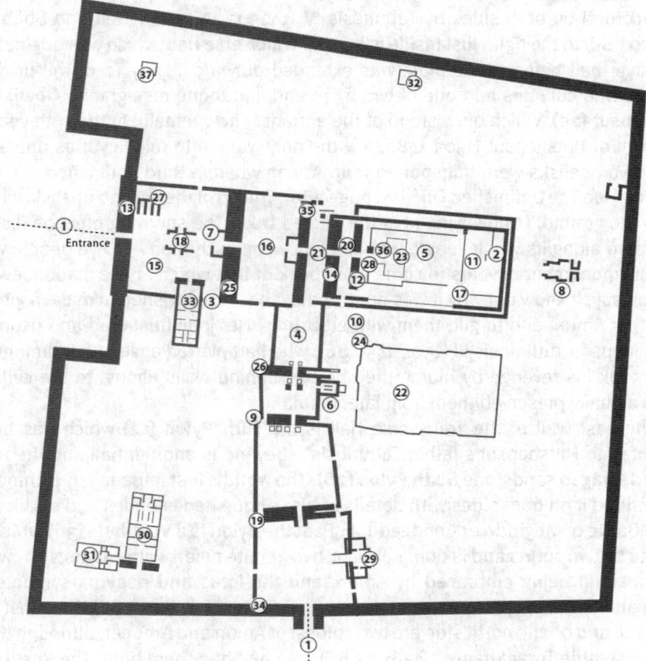

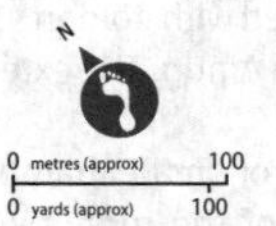

1 Avenue of ram-headed Sphinxes
2 Botanical vestibule
3 Bubastite portal
4 Cachette court
5 Central court
6 Chapel of Tuthmosis III
7 Colossus of Ramses II
8 Eastern Temple of Ramses II
9 Eighth pylon
10 Fallen Obelisk of Hatshepsut
11 Festival Hall of Tuthmosis III
12 Fifth pylon
13 First pylon
14 Fourth pylon
15 Great forecourt
16 Hypostyle hall
17 Karnak Table of Kings
18 Kiosk of Taharqa
19 Ninth pylon
20 Obelisk of Hatshepsut
21 Obelisk of Tuthmosis
22 Sacred lake
23 Sanctuary of sacred boats
24 Scarab statue
25 Second pylon
26 Seventh pylon
27 Shrine of Seti II
28 Sixth pylon
29 Temple of Amenhoptep II
30 Temple of Khonsu
31 Temple of Opet
32 Temple of Ptah
33 Temple of Ramses III
34 Tenth pylon
35 Third pylon
36 Vestibule
37 White Chapel of Sesostris

Seti II is depicted on both sides of the Third Pylon but the south wall running along the right of the hall was mainly decorated by Ramses II. He is shown being crowned by Horus and Thoth and then being presented to Amun while the Theban Triad is also pictured.

The **Third Pylon (35)** was constructed by Amenhotep III (1417-1379 BC) on the site of several earlier shrines which were moved to the Luxor Museum and the Open Air Museum within the walls of Karnak. On the inner east face is a text of tribute and a scene showing the gods' sacred boats. Amenhotep III built a small court to enclose four **Tuthmosid Obelisks (21)** in the narrow gap between the Third and Fourth Pylon which at that time represented the entrance to the Temple. Of the four, only one pink granite obelisk (23 m high, weighing 143 tonnes and originally tipped with electrum) built by Tuthmosis II (1512-04 BC) now remains and the stone bases and some blocks from two other obelisks built by Tuthmosis III (1504-1450 BC) are scattered nearby.

Moving towards the earlier centre of the temple is the limestone faced sandstone **Fourth Pylon (14)**, built by Tuthmosis I (1525-12 BC). Texts describing later restorations are recorded on both sides by Tuthmosis IV (1425-17 BC) to the left and Shabaka (716-702 BC) to the right. Just inside is a small **Transverse Hall** which was originally a hypostyle hall before the temple was extended outwards. Only 12 of the original papyrus bud columns and one of two 27 m and 340 tonne rose-granite **Obelisk of Hatshepsut (20)**, which once stood at the entrance, now remain. In the 16th year of the reign of Hatshepsut (1503-1482 BC), the only woman to rule Egypt as pharaoh, these two obelisks were transported from Aswan where a third unfinished one still remains (see The Unfinished Obelisk, page 280). The tip of the second obelisk, which fell to the ground, is now lying near the Sacred Lake. The surviving erect obelisk is decorated along its whole length with the following inscription – "O ye people who see this monument in years to come and speak of that which I have made, beware lest you say, 'I know not why it was done'. I did it because I wished to make a gift for my father Amun, and to gild them with electrum." Her long-frustrated and usurped infant stepson Tuthmosis III (1504-1450 BC), who had plotted against her during her reign, took his revenge by hiding the obelisks behind walls almost to the ceiling, which actually preserved them from later graffiti.

The east wall of the Transverse Hall is the **Fifth Pylon (12)** which has been attributed to Hatshepsut's father Tuthmosis I. Beyond is another hall and then the badly damaged sandstone **Sixth Pylon (28)**. The world's first imperialist, Tuthmosis III inscribed it on both sides with details of his vanquished enemies and his victory at the Battle of Megiddo or Armageddon. Past the pylon is a **Vestibule (36)** which is flanked by two courts and is dominated by two granite pillars with carvings showing Tuthmosis III being embraced by Amun, and the lotus and papyrus symbols of Upper and Lower Egypt. A seated statue of Amenhotep II (1450-25 BC) is against the west wall and on the north side are two colossi of Amun and Amunet, although their faces resemble Tutankhamen (1361-52 BC) who had had them built. The Vestibule leads to the Granite Sanctuary built by Alexander the Great's moronic half-brother and successor Philip Arrhidaeus (323-317 BC). The ceiling is covered with golden stars on a dark base while the walls depict scenes of Philip with the god Amun. The exterior walls are decorated in a similar fashion.

North of the Sanctuary beyond the granite door is a series of small chambers built by Hatshepsut but later altered by Tuthmosis III. Some of the rooms were walled up by her son to conceal Hatshepsut's influence and consequently the bright colours have been very well preserved although Hatshepsut's face has been cut away whenever it appeared.

Further to the east is Tuthmosis III's **Festival Hall (11)** which, with its central tentpole-style columns symbolizing the tents used during his campaigns, is unlike any Egyptian building. It was built for his jubilee festivals which were intended to renew the pharaohs' temporal and spiritual authority. Access is via a small vestibule which leads to the central columned hall. The columns in the central aisle are taller than the side ones and would have supported a raised section of the roof thereby permitting sunlight to enter. The hall was later used as a Christian church and early paintings of the saints can still be seen on some of the columns.

Off to the southwest is a small chamber where the original stela, or standing block, known as the **Karnak Table of Kings (17)**, minus Hatshepsut, was found. The original is in the Louvre in Paris, the one on display here a replica. The series of interconnecting chambers beyond is dedicated to the Theban Triad and further north is an attractive chamber known as the **Botanical Vestibule (2)**. Its four columns have papyrus capitals and are carved with the unfamiliar plants and shrubs discovered by Tuthmosis III during his Syrian campaign. Surrounding the small chamber on the far east wall is the small and badly decayed **Sanctuary of Amun**, built by Hatshepsut and originally decorated with two raised obelisks on either side of the entrance – only the bases now remain. The nearby **Chapel of Sokar**, which is dedicated to the Memphite god of darkness, is better preserved.

To the south of the main temple is the **Sacred Lake (22)** (200 m x 117 m), which has been restored to its original dimensions but has become stagnant since the inundation which used to feed the lake by underground channels from the River Nile ceased after the construction of the Aswan Dam. Today the lake is totally uninteresting but it has the Sound and Light Show grandstand at the far end and a café on the north side. A Nilometer is attached to the lake and there is a statue of a giant scarab beetle which childless women walk around five times in order to ensure that they soon bear children.

While the main temple runs from west to east there is a secondary axis running south from the area between the third and fourth pylons. It begins with the **Cachette Court (4)** which received its name after the discovery between 1903 and 1906 of 17,000 bronze statues and 780 stone ones which had been stored in the court during the Ptolemaic period and the best of which are now in the Egyptian Museum in Cairo. The reliefs on the outside wall of the Hypostyle Hall, northwest of the court, depict Ramses II in battle. On the east walls, close to the **Seventh Pylon (26)**, is a replica of a stela now in the Egyptian Museum which shows the only reference to Israel during Pharaonic times. The Seventh Pylon was built by Tuthmosis III and shows him massacring his prisoners before Amun. In front of the façade are parts of two colossi of Tuthmosis and in the courtyard to the left is the small chapel of Tuthmosis III.

Although restoration work continues on the nearby **Eighth Pylon (9)** and others further along, it may be possible to have a quick look in return for a small tip to the guard, either early or late in the day when there are fewer people. The Eighth Pylon was built by Tuthmosis II and Hatshepsut and contains extensively restored reliefs and cartouches. As in so many other places, Hatshepsut's name has been erased and replaced that of Tuthmosis II, while Akhenaten's name was systematically erased by Seti I. The south side of the pylon has four of the original six **Seated Colossi**, two of which are Tuthmosis II and one is Amenhotep I.

The **Ninth Pylon (19)** and the **Tenth Pylon (34)** were built by Horemheb (1348-20 BC) using materials from the demolished Aten Temple. The Tenth Pylon has two colossi of Ramses II and his wife Nefertari usurping the original colossi of Amenhotep III. On the south side of the pylon there are two quartzite colossi of Amenhotep III. The pylon is part of the outer enclosure and marks the start of the ram-headed sphinx-lined road to the southern enclosure.

In the far southwest corner of the central enclosure are two fairly well preserved temples, but they of limited interest. The **Temple of Khonsu (30)** was built by Ramses III and Ramses IV and dedicated to the son of Amun and Mut. Many of the reliefs show Herihor, high-priest of Amun, who ruled Upper Egypt after Ramses XI (1114-1085 BC) moved his capital to the Delta and delegated power to the high-priest. In the courtyard Herihor's name is inscribed on every pillar and all the scenes depict him venerating the gods and making offerings to them. The **Temple of Opet (31)**, the hippopotamus-goddess, is normally closed to the public.

Southern Enclosure

To the south, enclosed by a mud-brick wall are the much over-grown remains of the Temple of Mut and associated buildings. They are worth a quick visit. The entrance is in the centre of the north wall. Outside the enclosure and to the east are the ruins of a temple and to the west remains suggested as a barque sanctuary. Inside the enclosure, in a central position between the entrance and the Sacred Lake, and orientated north-south, stands the **Temple of Mut (5)**, consort of Amun. Little remains of this construction accepted as the work of Ptolemies II and VII except a number of diorite statues of the lioness-headed god, Sekhmet. To the northeast is the **Temple of Amenhotep III (4)**, later restored by Ramses II. Little remains except the bases of the walls and pillars and the feet on wall decorations which certainly leaves much to the imagination. To the west of the Sacred Lake stands the **Temple of Ramses III (6)** with some military scenes on the outer walls and a headless colossus on the west side.

Northern Enclosure

On the north side of the central enclosure, the **Temple of Ptah (32)** leads on to Karnak's northern enclosure which includes two temples, a sacred lake (now dry) and some chapels. The **Temple of Montu**, the god of war, was built by Amenhotep III, some of whose cartouches survive, and restored by Ramses IV. He left his mark too. Also in this small enclosure (150 sq m) to the west is a **temple to Amun (7)**. At the southern wall, six small gateways give access to six small chapels of which the **chapels of Amenortais and Nitocris (2 and 3)** are the best preserved.

This precinct does not have the splendours of the more famous temples and is best appreciated by real enthusiasts.

To the east outside the enclosure is the **Treasury of Tuthmosis I (10)**, while to the west stand the remains of a **Temple of Osiris (9)**.

Karnak southern enclosure - Precinct of Mut

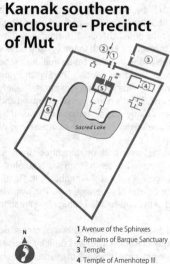

N

0 metres 100
0 yards 100

1 Avenue of the Sphinxes
2 Remains of Barque Sanctuary
3 Temple
4 Temple of Amenhotep III
5 Temple of Mut
6 Temple of Ramses III

Karnak northern enclosure - Precinct of Montu

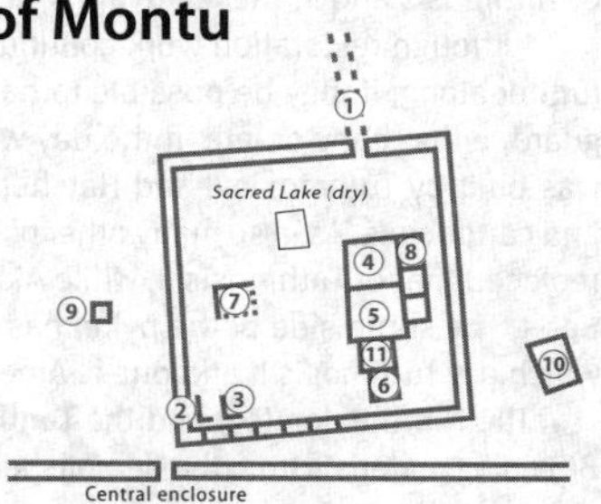

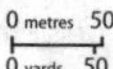

1 Avenue of Human-headed Sphinxes
2 Chapel of Nitocris
3 Chapel of Queen Amenortais
4 Forecourt of Temple of Montu
5 Hypostyle Hall
6 Sanctuary
7 Temple of Amun
8 Temple of Harpre
9 Temple of Osiris
10 Treasury of Tuthmosis I
11 Vestibule

Open Air Museum

ⓘ *Daily 0700-1800 summer, 0700-1700 winter. E£10, students E£5. Tickets sold at the temple ticket booth.*

To the northwest of the complex, this museum contains 1,300 blocks from the foundations of the Third Pylon and 319 stone blocks reassembled into Hatshepsut's **Sanctuary of the Barque**. Another barque sanctuary built by Amenhotep I is also on display, but the most beautiful monument is the lovely 12th Dynasty (1991-1786 BC) **White Chapel** built by Senusert I (1971-28 BC) which is divided into four rows of five pillars and includes some wonderful convex bas-reliefs and an interesting geographic list of the Middle East. The rest of the chapel is dedicated to offerings to a phallic Amun-Min who is embraced by Senusert.

West Bank and Theban Necropolis

Ins and outs

Getting there and around Direct road access from Luxor to the West Bank is possible via the relatively new and controversial Nile Bridge, about 7 km south of town. With such a roundabout journey, if travelling over the bridge by coach or minibus, it takes about 40 minutes to get from the centre of Luxor to the Valley of the Kings. (The new bridge was built so far to the south in an attempt to dissuade and restrict the construction of large buildings on the West Bank. Authorities are trying to avert the development of water, drainage and sewage systems that may have detrimental effects on the condition of the tombs as a result of capillary action and alterations to the water table.) Since September 11 2001 and the bombing at the Temple of Hatshepsut, authorities have also taken new measures to curb the threat of terrorism. If you take this road, notice on the ride that while the land is cultivated up to the road edge (mostly sugarcane), no tall crops grow adjacent to the main roads; they are set back to reduce cover for terrorists. The quicker and easier way to get to the West Bank is by public ferry, (E£1 for foreigners) which leaves from in front of the Luxor temple. Alternatively, you can hire a private motorboat or *felucca* (E£5-10) to take you across.

Bike Though bikes are for rent on the West Bank, it's better to rent one from East Bank for the day, they're generally a bit cheaper and less raggedly. You can take it on the ferry with you. Be aware that are some steep hills on the West Bank that are quite challenging, especially in the thick of summer. Guards at the various sights will keep an eye on your bike for you. You may want to offer a bit of *baksheesh*.

Donkey Travelling by donkey can be memorable, if a bit hard on the bum. It does afford some amazing views as you climb up to the Valley of the Kings. You can organize a donkey tour through most hotels, or hire your own at the ferry landing. For a morning meander, expect to pay about E£30.

Organized tours Many tourists and travellers alike opt to explore the West Bank with an organized tour. The advantage of this is that they generally provide transport from your hotel on the East Bank to the West Bank and between the sights (about an 8 km loop if you want to take in everything). Most tours also include a certified tour guide that can elucidate some of the mysteries and secrets of the ancients and their civilization. In the summer, the pricier tours offer the respite of an air-conditioned coach. The disadvantage is that you're being trucked along with a herd of other folk and your time in each place is dependent on your guide and group rather than your own inclination. Tours can be booked from any of the countless travel agents along the corniche (there is a dense handful near the Winter Palace, see tour operators page 261 for listings). For a tour of the West Bank's highlights (that usually includes Valley of the Kings, Valley of the Queens and the Temple of Hatshepsut), expect to pay about E£120-150 per person. West Bank tours are also aggressively pushed by virtually every budget and mid-range hotel in town. Some offer transport in minibuses (generally not air-conditioned) and some organize donkey tours. Cost fluctuates significantly with the season and is always negotiable. Aim for E£45-60 for a guided tour of the highlights, E£35 for a few hours' donkey tour (which usually involves taking the public ferry across the Nile and meeting your donkey there). If you want to hire a private guide, everyone has a brother who's a tour guide. Ask for leads at the tourist office or try your hotel, and make sure whoever you end up with is licensed.

Around Luxor

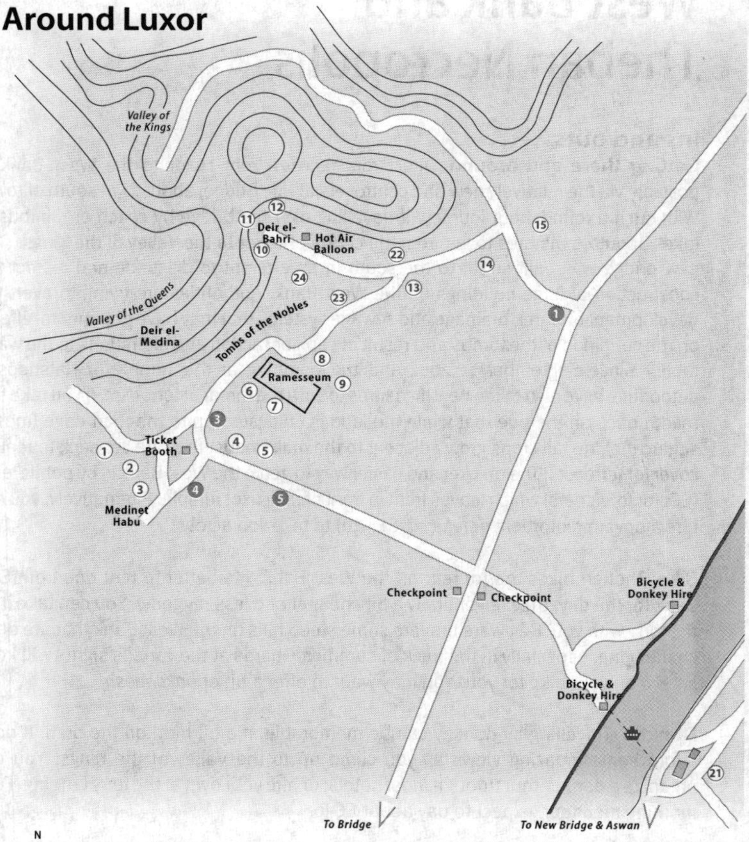

Valley of the Kings
Deir el-Bahri
Hot Air Balloon
Valley of the Queens
Deir el-Medina
Tombs of the Nobles
Ramesseum
Ticket Booth
Medinet Habu
Checkpoint
Checkpoint
Bicycle & Donkey Hire
Bicycle & Donkey Hire
To Bridge
To New Bridge & Aswan

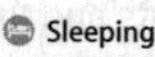

N
0 metres 500
0 yards 500

Sleeping
1 Abul Kassem
2 Hilton
3 Marsam
4 Resthouse, Queen & Medinet Habul
5 Memnon

Sites
1 Temple of Ramses III
2 Temple of Tuthmosis III
3 Pavillion of Ramses III
4 Temple of Amenophis III
5 Colossi of Memnon
6 Temple of Tuthmosis IV
7 Temple of Merneptah
8 Temple of Tuthmosis III
9 Temple of Amenophis II
10 Temple of Mentuhotep
11 Temple of Tuthmosis III
12 Temple of Hatshepsut
13 Site of Ramesside Temple
14 Temple of Amenophis I & Ahmes Nefertari
15 Temple of Seti I & Ramses II
16 Great Temple of Amun
17 Temple of Montu
18 Temple of Ramses III

Taxi If you want to see the sights at your own pace and have a ride, you can hire a taxi for a few hours. Rather than hailing one from the East Bank, it's a lot cheaper and faster to take the public ferry across the Nile and pick one up from the landing. You will be bombarded with offers. Expect to pay about E£50 to be shuttled around the major sights for three to four hours. Bargain hard.

Walking If it's cool enough, walking around the West Bank is certainly feasible for those with stamina. Except for the Valley of the Kings, which is 8 km from the Colossi by road, all main sights are within 3 km of the Colossi, which is about 3 km from the ferry landing. The public ferry leaves every 10 minutes or so from in front of the Luxor Temple and costs foreigners E£1. Whether or not you cover the entire West Bank on foot, it's worth taking the off-road path that connects the Valley of the Kings to the Temple of Hatshepsut. Ask a guard to point out the trailhead. It's a 45-minute walk that offers stellar views of the valley and tombs.

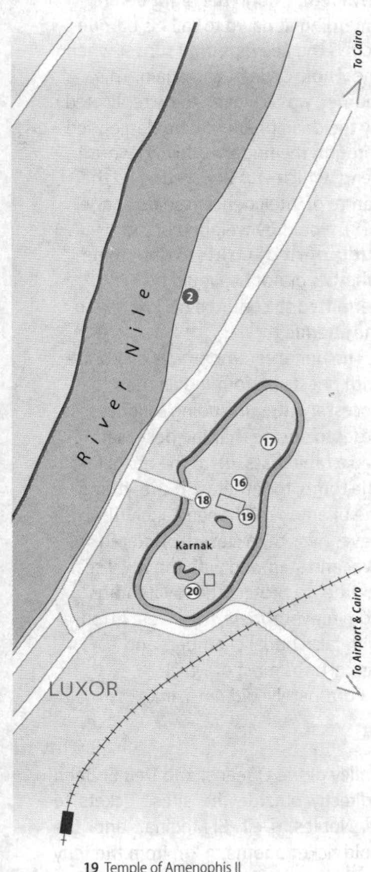

Tickets and visiting information

Although 62 tombs have been opened so far, many are closed to the public, some for restoration and others for rest. A system has been devised to reduce wear and tear on the more popular tombs – by closing them at intervals. The changes happen so often that the guards who work in the Valleys have a hard time keeping up. Always check if you have a particular destination in mind. A list of open tombs is displayed by the ticket booths. There are always at least 12 tombs open in the Valley of the Kings and three open in the Valley of the Queens. The Ministry of Tourism tries to ensure at least a few of the more remarkable tombs are always open. Expecting to see every single tomb and temple on the West Bank is impractical unless you intend to visit every day for a week. If you don't have a guide and want to know which open tombs are most worth seeing, ask at the ticket booths around the sights. In order to avoid the heat and the rush it is best to go as early as possible, particularly during the summer. In the winter, there tend to be less people in the afternoon. Make sure you bring a supply of water and snacks; though they're available on the West Bank, they're twice as expensive. It's also wise to bring a torch to see shadowed places and lots of small notes to offer as *baksheesh* (either to take advantage of a guard's knowledge or to be left alone).

Theban Death Rites and the Book of the Dead

In order to fully appreciate the Theban Necropolis in the soft limestone hills opposite Luxor it is important to understand a little about the celebration and rituals of death in Ancient Egypt.

The **Book of the Dead** (see box page 231) is the collective name given to the papyrus sheets which were included by the ancient Egyptians in their coffins. The sheets contained magic spells and small illustrations to assist the deceased in the journey through the underworld to afterlife. In total there are over 200 spells though no single papyrus contained them all. Some of the papyrus strips were specially commissioned but it was possible to buy ready-made collections with a space left for the relevant name.

Some of these spells came from the **Pyramid texts**. They were the oldest written references to this passage from one life to the next. They were found on the walls of pyramids constructed during the fifth to seventh Dynasties (2494-2170 BC). Later the text and descriptions of the rituals which were involved were written on the actual coffins of commoners, not kings. The spells were written in vertical columns of hieratic script. Eventually lack of space on the sarcophagi led to only the ritual prayers and offerings being listed. When papyrus began to be used during the New Kingdom (1567-1085 BC) written texts were enclosed in the coffin and they became known as the Book of the Dead. Many copies of the writings, including the Book of the Caverns and the Litany of Re, were subsequently discovered.

The ancient Egyptians believed that at sunset the sun-god Re descended into the underworld and voyaged through the night before emerging at dawn to sail his barque across the heavens until sunset when the whole cycle began again. This journey was believed to be replicated by the dead pharaoh who descended through the underworld and whose heart, which was believed to be the centre of intelligence (see box page 218), would be weighed in the **Judgment of Osiris** to determine whether or not he would be permitted to continue his journey to the afterlife.

The burial ceremony was elaborate with priests performing all the necessary rites, including sacrifices, in order to ensure that the deceased had a rapid passage to the next life. The tomb, together with everything the pharaoh might need, including slaves, was then closed, plastered over and stamped with the royal seal. In order to protect the royal tombs from graverobbers, they were fitted with false burial chambers and death-traps most of which, unfortunately, did not work.

Tickets Tickets to the Valley of the Kings, the Valley of the Queens, and Deir El-Bahri (Hatshepsut Temple) can now all be bought directly outside the sites. Tickets to everything else, including the Tombs of the Nobles, Deir El-Medina, and the Ramesseum must be bought in advance at the old ticket booths, 3 km from the ferry landing, 200 m after the Colossi of Memnon. Booths are open from 0600-1600. Sites are open 0600-1800 summer, 0600-1700 winter. Students with ISIC should receive a 50% to all sights. At present, photography of all sorts is prohibited inside all tombs. This is a new rule and it very well may change again, so inquire. Note that flash photography can seriously damage the pigment in the tombs. Resist all temptation.

Entry to the Valley of the Kings is E£20 and gives you access to three tombs of your choosing, except for Tutankhamen's tomb, which costs E£40 extra. If you want to see more than 3 tombs, you'll have to buy another E£20 ticket. In the Valley of the Kings, video cameras are held at security.

In the **Valley of the Queens**, Nefertari's tomb has been closed, but is scheduled to reopen some time 2004. There is a rumour that the price may double. Currently, the tickets for Nefertari's tomb cost E£100 and are limited to the first 150 visitors of the day. A visit to the other three tombs open to the public costs E£12.

The **Tombs of the Nobles** are divided into seven groups of pairs and triads. A ticket to each group costs E£12. The most important group of tombs is 100, 96, 55 and 52: the next important is 69, 56, and 57.

Tickets for the **Deir El-Bahr** and the **Ramesseum** both cost E£12. Tickets for the **Deir El-Medina** cost E£12 for both Sennedjem and Inherkhau and an additional E£10 for Peshedu. There is no charge to see the **Colossi of Memnon**.

The Valley of the Kings

Also known as Wadi Biban El-Muluk, the Valley of the Kings is one of many necropoli in the limestone hills on the West Bank of the River Nile. The area first became a burial site during the New Kingdom rule of Tuthmosis I (1525-1512 BC) in the hope that the tombs would be safe from looters. The kings' tombs are not actually confined to the single valley and it is believed that there may be others still waiting to be discovered. Those already discovered are numbered in the chronological order of their discovery

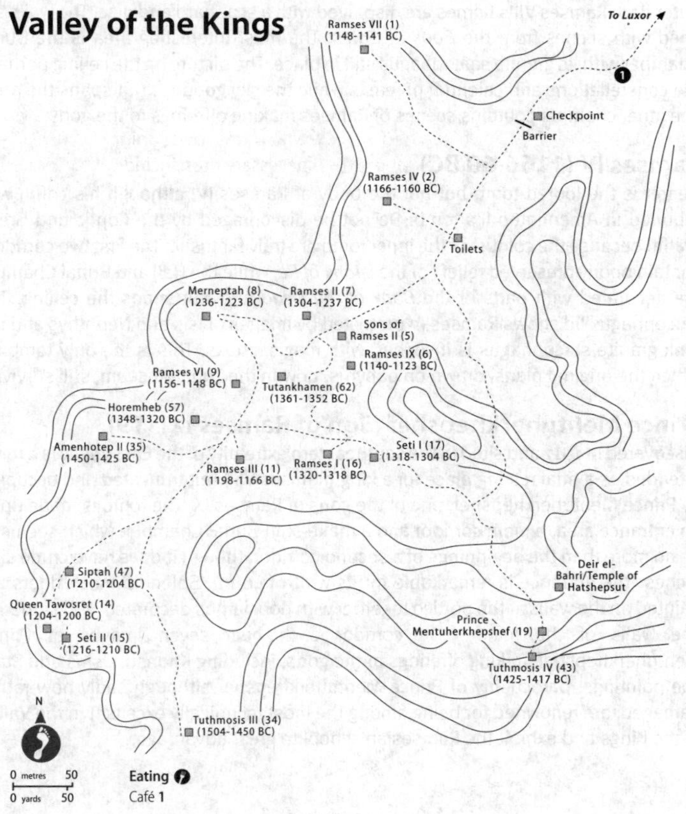

 rather than by location. Although some are simple and comparatively crude the best are incredibly well preserved, stunningly decorated and illustrate their intricate craftsmanship. Most of the discovered tombs are in the East Valley but the Tomb of Ay in the West Valley (Valley of the Monkeys) is worth a visit.

The tombs generally follow two designs. The early 18th-Dynasty (1567-1320 BC) tombs are a series of descending galleries followed by a well or rock pit which was intended both to collect any rain water and deter thieves. On the other side of the pit there were sealed offering chambers and then the rectangular burial chamber built at right angles to the descending galleries. The later tombs, from the late 18th to the 20th Dynasties (1360-1085 BC), were built in the same way but the galleries and burial chambers were on the same axis, being cut horizontally but deeper straight into the rock face.

There was obviously no need, originally, for light in the tombs and today the authorities maintain the lowest possible light levels. Take a torch, it will enable you to read this book, to admire the outstanding wall decorations and illustrations, and to avoid tripping on the uneven ground!

Allow a day to explore in some comfort and a little depth. There is a small **kiosk** at the entrance to the Valley of the Kings, it's only just adequate but it does have drinks, literature and toilets if you are desperate. The tuf-tuf bus from here (cost E£1 per ride) saves some of the tiresome walking in the heat.

Ramses VII (1148-41 BC) (1)

This later style, single horizontal plane, and poorly preserved tomb lies in a small valley to the right after the entrance gate and is seldom visited by tourists. Above the outer door Ramses VII's names are displayed with a scabbard and disc. The walls are lined with scenes from the *Book of Gates*. The most interesting area is the Burial Chamber with its granite sarcophagus still in place. The picture on the ceiling portrays the constellations and calendar of feasts while the sky goddess Nut spans the area. The inner chamber contains scenes of Ramses making offerings to the gods.

Ramses IV (1166-60 BC)

Nearer is the looted tomb but not the body of Ramses IV, although his coffin was reburied in Amenhotep II's tomb. Do not be discouraged by the Coptic and Greek graffiti because the colours of the inner tomb are truly fantastic. The first two corridors contain poorly preserved reliefs of the *Litany of Re*, while the Hall and Burial Chamber are decorated with parts of the *Book of the Dead* and Nut spans the ceiling. The sarcophagus lid shows Ramses IV protected by images of Isis and Nephthys and the pink granite sarcophagus is inscribed with magical texts. This is the only tomb for which the original plans, drawn on papyrus, now in the Turin Museum, still survive.

Prince Mentuherkhepshef (Son of Ramses IX) (19)

Discovered in 1817 and sited in the southeastern extremity of the East Valley is a tomb intended as a final resting place for a king (Ramses VIII) but truncated and occupied by Prince Mentuherkhepshef, one of the sons of Ramses IX. The tomb is made up of an entrance area, a main corridor and a make-shift Burial Chamber, which seems to be no more than the beginnings of a second corridor, though it does have crude side niches. The entrance is remarkable for its width (3.6 m). Splendid mock doors are painted on the walls at the portico together with door jambs decorated with serpents. The walls of the main 3 m corridor each bear seven images of Prince Mentuherkhepshef making offerings to the gods, including Khonsu, Osiris and Ptah. The paintings, particularly of Prince Mentuherkhepshef although sadly now rather damaged, are renowned for being among the most technically excellent in the Valley of the Kings and exhibit the Ramsesian school to great advantage.

Books of the Afterlife

The Egyptians believed that the journey to the afterlife was through *Duat*, the underworld, and to combat the monsters and other evils there, a series of prayers and some magic spells were necessary. These were written in the *Book of the Dead* which also contained a map of Duat.

Book of the Dead Called *The Book of Coming Forth by Day* by the Egyptians. This is a collection of mortuary texts, spells or magic formulas which were placed in tombs and intended to be of help in the next world. They are thought to have been compiled and perhaps edited during the 16th century BC. They included texts dating back to around 2000 BC (Coffin Texts) and 2400 BC (Pyramid Texts). Selected sections were copied on papyrus by scribes (illustrated versions cost more) and sold for inclusion in one's coffin. Many selections have been found and it is estimated that there were approximately 200 chapters. Extracts appear on many of the antechamber walls of the Ramessid tombs. Nearly 12 chapters are given over to special spells – to turn the deceased into any animal shape.

Book of Am-Duat Called *The Book of the Secret Chamber* by the Egyptians. It deals with the sun's journey through the underworld during the 12 hours of the night. Selections are found in many tombs. Full versions are inscribed on the walls of the burial chambers of Tuthmosis III and Amenhotep II.

Book of Gates Refers to the 12 gates which separate the hours of the night and first appears on tombs of the 18th Dynasty. The inscriptions in the tomb of Ramses VI give the most complete version. This has the same journeying theme as the book of Am-Duat but the Duat is not comparable other than for the fact that is has 12 segments.

Book of Caverns A full version of this is found in the tomb of Ramses VI.

Litany of Re This deals with Re (see page 552) in all his 75 different forms.

Books of the Heavens Describes the passage of the sun through the 24 hours of the day and includes the *Book of the Day*, the *Book of Night* and the *Book of the Divine Cow*. These texts were first used during the New Kingdom and there are several pieces inscribed in the tomb of Ramses VI.

For further details refer to *The Ancient Egyptian Book of the Dead* by RO Faulkner.

Tuthmosis IV (1425-17) (43)

This large tomb was discovered in 1903 by Carter, but others had been there before and everything moveable had been taken. Many of the walls and pillars are undecorated and the impression is rather austere. The well room has scenes of Tuthmosis paying homage to various gods and receiving the key of life from various deities including Hathor. The antechamber has illustrations of a similar theme and both have a ceiling of yellow stars on a dark blue sky.

Ramses IX (1140-23 BC) (6)

Immediately to the left of the barrier, this tomb is of the typical later long, deep style which became the established style by the end of the New Kingdom. The reliefs on the corridor walls depict Ramses before the gods and this is followed by three chambers. The four pillared Offerings Chamber leads to the richly decorated Burial Room but the sarcophagus is missing. The ceiling in yellow on a dark blue background depicts a scene from the *Book of the Night* with jackals, watched by Nut, drawing the barque through the skies to the afterlife.

Meneptah (1236-23 BC) (8)

Set back against the cliff face on the other side of the road is a long steep 80 m tomb with a wonderfully preserved false Burial Chamber. The ceilings of the five corridors are decorated with flying vultures and other forbidding reliefs. Looters abandoned the sarcophagus lid, which portrays scenes taken from the *Book of Gates* and the *Book of Am-Duat* similar to those in the hallway, in the antechamber. Steep steps lead down to the Burial Chamber where the pink granite inner sarcophagus lies, decorated with intricate designs from the *Book of Gates*. It is claimed that Meneptah was pharaoh during the time of the Exodus.

Ramses VI (1156-48 BC) (9)

The discovery of this tomb, which was usurped from his predecessor Ramses V (1160-56 BC) and enlarged, became one of the longest in the valley, shed light on some aspects of pharaonic beliefs which were not previously understood. The corridor displays reliefs from unknown and long since lost *Books*. Egyptologists were fascinated at their revelation of pharaonic concepts, more usually associated with India, and of reincarnated birth into a new life. One does not, however, have to be an expert to appreciate the graphic designs and the colours beyond the graffiti drawings in the first two corridors.

The themes on the corridor ceilings are predominantly astronomical while the walls are largely devoted to the *Book of Gates* and the entire version of the *Book of Caverns*. In the Offerings Hall there is a relief of Ramses making libations before Osiris. The pillars are devoted to the Pharaoh making offerings to other gods including Amun. Descending deeper within the tomb, the passage leading to the Burial Chamber is guarded by serpents of Nekhbet, Neith, Meretseger and Selket. Further on illustrations from the *Book of the Dead* predominate. Just before the entrance to the Burial Chamber, cryptographic texts adorn the ceiling. The Burial Chamber is supported by four pillars but two are damaged. Astronomical scenes from the *Book of Day* and the *Book of Night* cover the ceiling and the sky goddess Nut observes from above. The sarcophagus, shattered by grave robbers centuries ago, lies broken in the centre of the room.

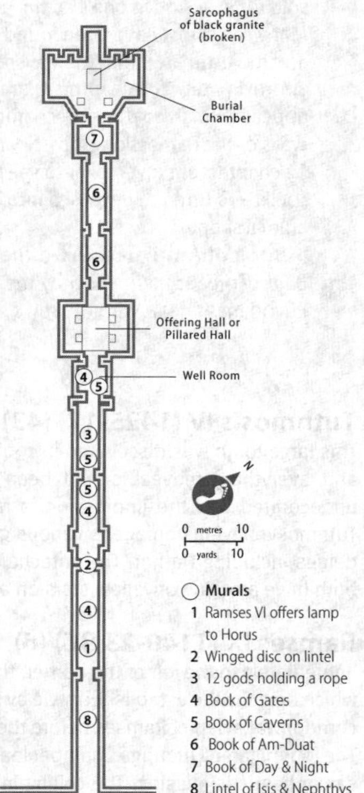

Ramses III (1198-66 BC) (11)

Also known as 'Tomb of the Harpists', this particularly beautiful and exceptionally large tomb is unusual because, unlike those of most Pharaohs, it illustrates scenes from everyday life as well as a wonderful scene of two harpists from which the tomb's other name is derived. It was originally intended for Sethnakht (1200-1185 BC), but the angle of digging was such that it coincided with another tomb and was abandoned. Later Ramses III restarted the work by digging into the rock face from a different angle. The lintel with a disc and Re shown with a ram's head accompanied by Isis and Nephthys can be seen at the entrance. Ten side chambers – five to the left and five to the right – which were for storing objects that the Pharaoh would require after his death, lead off from the entrance corridor. Only part of this tomb has lighting. One section of the tomb is closed because of a collapsed ceiling.

Ramses I (1320-18 BC) (16)

Despite being the founder of the 19th Dynasty, his short reign meant that this Ramses did not merit a larger tomb but it still has beautifully ornate and sophisticated designs which are preserved on the blue-grey foundation. The granite sarcophagus in the burial chamber is decorated with yellow while the wall relief depicts scenes of the Pharaoh with local deities and divisions from the *Book of Gates*. The eastern wall of the entrance corridor is decorated with 12 goddesses depicting the hours of the night. This is one tomb not to be missed

Tomb of Tuthmosis III (1504-1450 BC) (34)

Hidden away high up a side valley furthest from the main gate this is one of the oldest tombs. Its simple design is balanced by the interesting layout. After the second steep corridor, it veers sharply to the left into the antechamber. The walls here are lined with lists of 741 deities who are portrayed as tiny stick figures. The burial chamber, shaped, unusually, like a cartouche, is entered down a set of oval shaped steps. The walls here are dominated by sections of the *Book of Am-Duat* with an abridged version also inscribed on two pillars. The Pharaoh is depicted on one of the pillars with his mother standing behind him in his boat. A beautiful carving of Nut, effectively embracing the mummified Tuthmosis with her outstretched arms, lines the inside of the red granite sarcophagus. His mummy is in the museum in Cairo.

Siptah (1210-04 BC) (47)

This interesting tomb is in the east valley of the Valley of the Kings (Wadi Biban El-Muluk). Siptah was a monarch of the late 19th Dynasty, probably the son of Amenmesse. He reigned for six years until 1204 BC. The tomb was discovered by Edward Ayrton in 1905. The tomb was constructed from a stair entry leading to a long corridor decorated with formal scenes of the Litany of Re on the right and left, with images of Mut and other scenes such as a fine representation of Siptah before Re-Horakhte. The first corridor, consisting of three linked passages, is plastered and painted to a good standard but both the intermediate pillared hall/stairway and the second corridor with its antechamber are undecorated. The same applies to the third short corridor leading from the antechamber to the burial chamber off which there is a dead-end tunnel on the left hand. The burial chamber is rough-hewn with four pillars and contains a red granite sarcophagus. The sarcophagus bears jackal and demon figures. The cartouches appear to be reworked. The tomb was disturbed at one time – possibly during the 21st Dynasty – and the mummified body of Siptah was found in a cache of royal mummies in the tomb of Amenophis II (35) in 1898, the withered left foot of King Siptah clearly visible.

Tawosret (1204-00) and Sethnakht (1200-1198 BC) (14)

Sited in Wadi Biban El-Muluk, close by the tomb of Tuthmosis I, this is one of the longest (112 m) axial tunnels in the Valley of the Kings – belonging to Tawosret, wife of Seti II from the 19th Dynasty. The monument was later taken over by Sethnakht, the first ruler of the 20th Dynasty, who lengthened the tomb and removed the remains of Tawosret, it is suggested, to the cache in Tomb KV35. The ownership of the first

Howard Carter

Howard Carter was born at Swaffham in Great Britain in 1873. When he was only 17 years old he was taken on by the Archaeological Survey of Egypt under Flinders Petrie and later became Inspector General of Antiquities in Upper Egypt in 1899 for the Antiquities Service. Carter was responsible for excavation of the Valley of the Kings and discovered the tombs of Hatshepsut and Tuthmosis IV in 1902 for the American Theodore Davis. After a dispute with Davis he moved to Saqqara in 1903 but then left the Archaeological Service to open a studio in Luxor where, in 1907, he met and began his archaeological association with the wealthy Earl of Carnarvon, whose own efforts at excavation had failed. When Theodore Davis gave up his concession to excavate in the Valley of the Kings in 1914, Carter, backed by the Earl of Carnarvon, took it up and continued digging, locating six more royal tombs. In 1922, Carter's last year of sponsorship by Lord Carnarvon, he came across a set of remains of workmen's houses built across a stairway to a tomb. Carter waited for Lord Carnarvon to arrive at the site and then dug away the remaining rubble to reveal the entrance to the Tomb of Tutankhamen. Eventually Carter's men cleared the way to the anteroom which was full of interesting cloths, furniture and other materials. The burial chamber that Carter found was once again packed with valuable objects but none more so than the gold-laden coffins and mummy of Tutankhamen. Carter remained at the site for a further 10 years supervising the cataloguing activity of so great a find. He died in London in 1939.

Howard Carter will be known principally as the discoverer of the Tomb of Tutankhamen. But his imprint on Egyptology went far deeper. He was among the first archaeologists, following Flinders Petrie, to apply scientific principles to the recording of his excavations. Remarkably, the treasure trove of objects found in 1922 has still to be studied in full and, to Carter's great disappointment, there were in any case no parchments or manuscripts to explain historical events surrounding the boy king and the court politics of the day.

corridor of the monument is still apparent, with male deities bearing female designations but many scenes of the owner before the gods were usurped by Sethnakht. There are scenes in the second and third corridors and in the First Hall of passages from the *Book of the Dead*. The Well Room and anteroom to the Burial Chamber by contrast carry images of the deities. In the Burial Chamber of Tawosret itself, comprising an eight section pillared hall, there are scenes from the *Book of the Dead*, the ceremony of the opening of the mouth and the *Book of the Gates* together with a finely-drawn scene of facets of the Sun God Re as a disc and ram-headed eagle from the *Book of the Caverns*. Beyond the Burial Chamber of Tawosret is the extended royal tomb of Sethnakht along broad corridors decorated with scenes from the *Book of the Secret Chamber*. The Burial Chamber of Sethnakht has a barrel-domed ceiling with a painted astronomical finish while the walls are decorated with scenes from the *Book of the Caverns* and *Book of the Gates*. The eight pillars of this Burial Chamber carry representations of the king and the deities. The granite sarcophagus is shattered but still in place and has probably been taken over from a previous incumbent.

The Curse of Tutankhamen

Tutankhamen's tomb's fame and mystery was enhanced by the fate of several of those who were directly connected with its discovery. The expedition's sponsor Lord Carnarvon, who had first opened the tomb with his chief archaeologist Howard Carter, died shortly afterwards in April 1923 from an infected mosquito bite. Howard Carter supposedly protected himself by not entering the tomb until he had performed an ancient ritual. A subsequent succession of bizarre deaths added weight to British novelist Marie Corelli's unproven claim that "dire punishment follows any intruder into the tomb". However, such alleged curses have done nothing to deter the tens of thousands of visitors who still visit the site despite the fact that most of the treasures are now in the Egyptian Museum.

Seti II (1216-10 BC) (15)

The tomb of Seti II has been open since antiquity. It was also a hastily completed monument but is important in that it has a number of innovations which became standard practice in subsequent works in the Valley of the Kings. The wall niches in the antechamber to the first pillared hall (the well room) are much more pronounced than in earlier tombs while the entrance is cut into the hill face lacking the previously used wall and stairway. The burial chamber is crudely adapted from what was to have been a passage to a larger room that was never excavated. There are conventional decorations on the entrance doorway of Ma'at, the goddess of truth and beauty (see page 549), and scenes from the *Litany of Re* are shown in a variety of reliefs on both the left hand wall of the first and second corridors. Beyond the first corridor the walls are unplastered and generally painted in an attractive but peremptory fashion. The antechamber to the first pillared hall has an unusual format of figures of deities in which a representation of the king is shown riding on a panther and a picture occurs of the king hunting in a papyrus boat. In the pillared hall itself there are formal scenes from the *Book of the Gates*. Over the site of the sarcophagus there is a fine picture of Nut, goddess of the sky, with outreaching wings. There is little of the sarcophagus that remains. The mummy of Seti II was among the kings found in the cache of royal mummies at the tomb of Amenophis II (35).

Amenhotep II (1450-25 BC) (35)

Over 90 steps lead down to the Burial Chamber of one of the deepest tombs in the valley. Here for once the tactics of building false chambers and sunken pits actually worked and the mummified body was found in the sarcophagus, together with another nine royal mummies which had been removed from their original tombs for safety's sake, when the tomb was opened in 1898. Amenhotep's mummy was originally kept in the tomb but after a nearby theft it was removed to the Egyptian Museum in Cairo. Steep steps and a descending corridor lead into a pillared chamber where the tomb's axis shifts 90° to the left, after which the walls and ceiling are decorated. Further steps and a short passage lead to the enormous two-level Burial Chamber.

The entrance passages are rough-hewn and each led down to by flights of stairs, entirely without formal decoration. In the well room – its painting unfinished – there is a shaft to a sunken but plain chamber. The first decoration of note is found in the two-pillared hall with paintings on only two adjacent walls. The Burial Chamber at the end of a short corridor is made up of a six-pillared hall with a sunken area of which are the sarcophagus and storage rooms, the western (right side) areas being where the cache of mummies was found in 1898. The ceiling is coloured blue with an

The 'Lost' Tomb

Explored and looted decades ago, dismissed as uninteresting by Egyptologists, and used as a dump for debris from the excavation of Tutankhamen's tomb, **Tomb 5** in the Valley of the Kings was about to become a car park. However, the final exploration in May 1995 unearthed a major discovery, certainly the largest and most complex tomb ever found in Egypt and possibly the resting place of up to 50 sons of Ramses II. Excavations are expected to take at least another five years, but the tomb's unusual design is already apparent. Instead of plunging down into the steep hillside, Tomb 5 is more like an octopus with at least 62 chambers branching off from the central structure. There may be more chambers on a lower level and it is hoped that some of the mummies may still be entombed. No treasure is expected: robbery of the tomb was documented as early as 1150 BC, but the elaborate carvings and inscriptions along with the thousands of artifacts littering the floor, including beads and fragments of jars used to store the organs of the deceased, nevertheless offer a wealth of information about the reign of one of ancient Egypt's most important kings.

Egyptologists have never before found a multiple burial of a pharaoh's children and in most cases have no idea what happened to them. This find thus raises the question of whether Ramses buried his children in a unique way or that archaeologists have overlooked a major type of royal tomb. And where are Ramses' dozens of daughters? Are they buried in a similar mausoleum, perhaps in the Valley of the Queens?

astronomical star design in yellow and the walls delicately decorated with passages from the *Book of the Secret Chamber*. Columns show pictures of the king with deities – Anubis, Hathor and Osiris.

Amenhotep's sarcophagus remains in place, indeed his mummy was found undisturbed by Victor Loret who first found his way into the tomb in the 19th century. Look out in particular for the beautiful image of Isis in sunk relief at the end of the highly decorated quartzite sarcophagus, still with its lid in situ. The sarcophagus is still in place in the centre of the pillared chamber.

Horemheb (1348-20 BC) (57)

After the long, steep and undecorated descent is the Well Room where the reliefs begin. Colourful scenes portray General Horemheb who, despite lacking royal blood, was the effective regent during Tutankhamen's short rule and leader of the Theban counter-revolution against Akhenaten's monotheistic religion, being introduced to Isis, Osiris, Horus, Hathor and Anubis. The scenes are repeated in the antechamber which is dominated by the huge red granite sarcophagus. Point a torch inside the sarcophagus for a glance at some bones. Some guides suggest that the base black lines in the sanctuary indicate the first draft of the decorating, while the red marks are corrections. Horemheb died too young for the artists to finish.

Tutankhamen (1361-52 BC) (62)

The tomb owes its worldwide fame not to its size or decoration, which is small and ordinary, but to the multitude of fabulous treasures that were revealed when it was opened in November 1922. The scale of the discovery was so vast that it took 10 years to fully remove, catalogue and photograph all of the 1,700 pieces.

The funeral objects in this tomb were lavish in the sense that the boy king reigned for a mere 9-10 years and was a comparatively minor pharaoh. The burial chambers too were relatively limited in size, so when Carter broke through into the tomb it felt as though the rooms were crowded and that there was an abundance of artifacts. The hoard was additionally rich because it had not been significantly robbed – unlike most other pharaonic tombs.

If Tutankhamen's tomb was important above average, it was because he had rejected the heresy (monotheism) of his predecessor, though it is probably right to assume that tombs of more dominant pharaohs were, before being looted, even more lavishly furnished.

The short entrance corridor leads to four chambers but only the Burial Chamber, which is the second on the right, is decorated. Around the room from left to right murals display Tutankhamen's coffin being moved to the shrine by mourners and officials after which his successor Ay (1352-48 BC) performs the ceremony of the Opening of the Mouth and makes sacrifices to sky-goddess Nut. Tutankhamen is then embraced by Osiris and is followed by his black-wigged *Ka* or spirit. A scene from the *Book of Am-Duat* on the left hand wall depicts the Pharaoh's solar boat and sun-worshipping baboons. The quartzite sarcophagus is still in place, with its granite lid to one side, and inside is the outermost of three coffins.

Seti I (17)

Seti I is regarded as the most developed form of the tomb chambers in the Valley of the Kings. At some 100 m it is among the longest, though it is closed at present, perhaps permanently for conservation purposes since its decorations suffer from condensation produced by visitors. Throughout the tomb there are paintings/reliefs of fine workmanship on nearly every surface, though not all were completed. In particular look out for the picture of Osiris in the pillared hall and the depictions of tomb furniture in the side chamber. The mummy can be viewed in the museum in Cairo. The sarcophagus is in London.

Ay (1352-48) (23)

This monument dates from the 18th Dynasty and was opened up by Bellzoni in 1816, cleared by Schaden in 1972 and opened to the public in recent years. The entry shaft at first has a shallow incline but then after a second flight, steps become steep. Flat shoes are a necessity here on the ramp-like corridors. There is good lighting provided the generator is turned on.

Ay was the counsellor of Tutenkhamen and his successor to the throne. The tomb had probably been built for King Tutenkhamen but was incomplete at the time of his sudden death. Ay had no claims to royal descent and was not even high-ranking in the priesthood. His tomb is important for its unusual pharaonic hunting scene in the burial chamber.

The tomb is constructed with a strong linear alignment as a single corridor with a flight of very steep steps down to the small chamber which leads into a burial chamber. The burial chamber itself is approximately 7 m by 10 m and about 4 m high but off to the right of the axis of the tunnel. A small canoptic room terminates the tomb.

Only the Burial chamber is decorated but even here there has been extensive damage to the paintings and the roof is just rough-hewn rock without decoration. Throughout almost all of the tomb the cartouches have been defaced. On the entry wall to the left of the door is the famous hunting scene with the deceased shown clubbing birds and plucking reeds as if he was an ordinary being rather than a deity. On the north wall is a painting representing 12 baboons (hence the name Tomb of the Monkeys) or hours of the night from the *Book of the Secret Chamber*. On the west wall look for the image with Ay before the gods, including Osiris, Nut and Hathor. A well worked but slightly damaged boating scene is shown on the south wall above passages from the *Book of the Secret Chamber*. On the lintel area above the door to the canopic chamber is a fine representation of the four sons of Horus, which you will not see anywhere else in the Valley of the Kings. The sarcophagus is in place, made out of quartzite, and nicely tooled in reliefs of deities, Neith, Nephthys and Selkis. The sarcophagus was formerly in the museum in Cairo and was transported back to the tomb for display to the public in 1994. Its lid is intact and there are wings of four goddesses – one at each corner with wings wrapped round the sarcophagus for protection.

Deir El-Bahri

ⓘ *E£12, cameras and videos free of charge.*
Meaning 'northern monastery' in Arabic, Deir El-Bahri derives its name from the fact that during the seventh century the Copts used the site as a monastery. It is now used as the name for both the magnificent **Mortuary Temple of Hatshepsut** and the surrounding area.

Queen Hatshepsut was not only the only female Pharaoh to reign over ancient Egypt (1503-1482 BC) but also one of its most fascinating personalities. She was Tuthmosis I's (1525-12 BC) daughter and was married to his successor Tuthmosis II (1512-04 BC) but was widowed before she could bear a son. Rather than give up power to the son of one of her husband's minor wives she assumed the throne first as regent for the infant Tuthmosis III but then as queen. Tuthmosis III, who later hugely expanded the Egyptian Kingdom and was the first imperialist, was only able to assume office when Hatshepsut died 21 years later in 1482 BC. He naturally resented her usurping his position and removed all traces of her reign including her cartouches. Consequently the truth about her reign and the temples she built both here and at Karnak was only fully appreciated by archaeologists relatively recently. As a woman she legitimized her rule by being depicted with the short kilt and the false beard worn by the male pharaohs.

Hatshepsut's imposing temple which was only dug out of the sand in 1905 was designed and built in the Theban hills over an eight-year period between the eighth and the 16th year of her reign, by **Senenmut** who was her architect, steward, favourite courtier and possibly the father of her daughter Neferure. The temple's three rising terraces, the lower two terraces lined with fountains and myrrh trees, were originally linked to the River Nile by an avenue of sphinxes which was aligned exactly to Karnak. A pair of lions stood at the top and another at the bottom of the ramp which leads from the ground level first terrace over the first colonnade to the large second terrace.

The scenes on the restored left-hand south side of the first colonnade columns depict the transportation of the two obelisks from Aswan to Karnak temple. Behind its columns on the right-hand north side is a relief defaced by Tuthmosis III in which Amun can be seen receiving an offering of four calves from Hatshepsut whose face has been erased. The original stairs from the second terrace to the second colonnade have now been replaced by a ramp. Hatshepsut's famous voyage to **Punt**, which was known as 'God's Land' by the ancient Egyptians, and various texts to Amun are depicted on the left-hand (or south) side of the second colonnade. Voyages to Punt, now believed to be modern-day Somalia, had been undertaken since the Old Kingdom (2686-2181BC) in order to find the incense and myrrh which was required for temple rituals.

Further to the left is the large **Chapel of Hathor** where the goddess is depicted both as a cow and as a human with cow's ears suckling Hatshepsut. This area was badly damaged because Tuthmosis removed most, but not all, traces of Hatshepsut and Akhenaten later erased Amun. The reliefs on the colonnade to the right-hand (or north) side of the ramp portray Hatshepsut's apparent divine conception and birth. She claimed that her father was the supreme god Amun who visited her mother Ahmose disguised as Tuthmosis I just as Amenhotep III (1417-1379 BC) made similar claims later on (see Luxor Temple, page 215). Further to the right is the fluted colonnade and the colourfully-decorated **Chapel of Anubis**, who is portrayed in the customary way as a man with a jackal mask, but the images of Hatshepsut are once again defaced.

The ramp leading to the smaller and recently-restored upper terrace (unfortunately closed) is decorated with emblems of Upper and Lower Egypt with vultures' heads guarding the entrance. There are suggestions that this was originally a Hypostyle Hall and not a terrace. The columns were originally round but were squared off by Tuthmosis III in an attempt to replace her name with his own and that of his father Tuthmosis II. Beyond the Osiride portico to the left is the **Sanctuary of Hatshepsut** with its enormous altar and to the right is the **Sanctuary of the Sun**. In the middle at the back of the whole temple is the **Sanctuary of Amun** which is dug into the

Temple of Hatshepsut

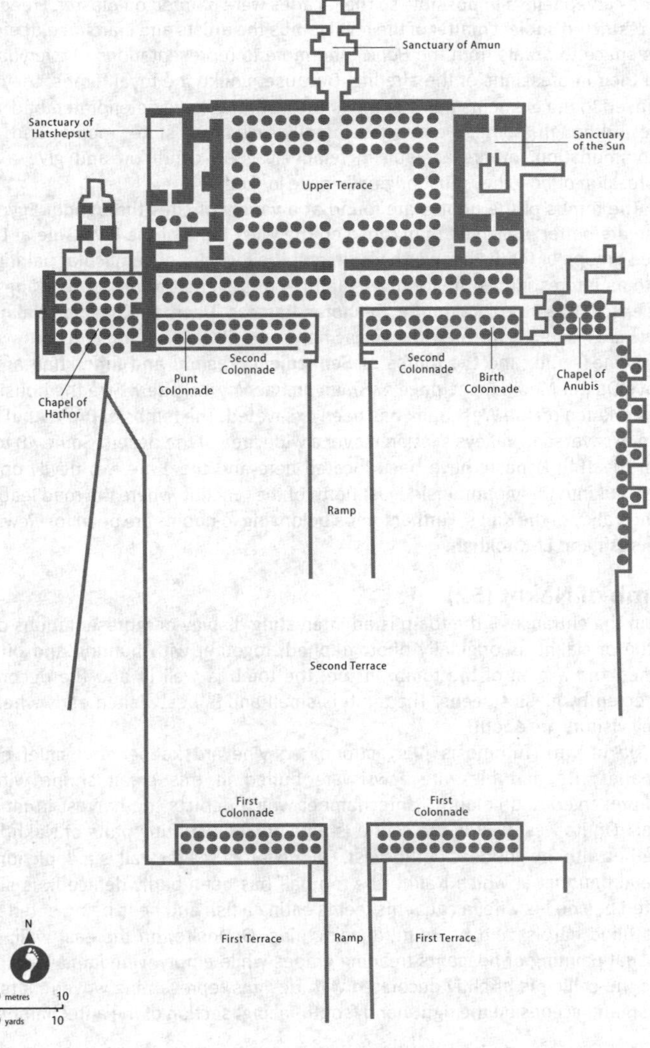

cliff-face and is therefore connected to the Valley of the Kings which lies on the other side of the hill. Hatshepsut's burial chamber lies underneath but it is unclear whether she was actually ever buried there.

Tombs of the Nobles

ⓘ *The entry fee for each pair or triad of tombs is E£12. There are cafés and shops throughout the area, which also still has local modern village housing – inhabitants sell bric-a-brac and genuine artefacts to passing tourists.*

While the pharaoh's tombs were hidden away in the Valley of the Kings and were dug deep into the valley rock, those of the most important nobles were ostentatiously built at surface level overlooking the temples of Luxor and Karnak across the river. Their shrines were highly decorated but the poor quality limestone made carved reliefs impossible so the façades were painted on plaster. Freed from the restricted subject matter of the royal tombs the artists and craftsmen dedicated less space to rituals from the *Books* and more to representations of everyday life and their impressions of the afterlife. Because, unlike the royal tombs, they were exposed to the elements many of the nobles' shrines have deteriorated badly over time. Although some were subsequently used as store rooms and even accommodation, others are still in relatively good condition and give a clear impression of how they must originally have looked.

The tombs of the nobles are found at a variety of sites throughout Egypt but none are better preserved than those on the West Bank of the River Nile at Luxor. Three groups of tombs are worth visiting for their wealth of vernacular paintings – quite as interesting as the formal sculptures of the great tombs of the Kings and Queens. The tombs of **Rekhmire, Sennofer, Ramoza, Userhat, Khaemet, Nakht** and **Mena** are located in the area known as Sheikh abd El-Qurna, north and northwest of the Ramesseum, and the tombs of **Sennedjem**, **Peshdu** and **Inherkhau** are just above Deir El-Medina (see page 248), an archaeological site where the housing of the workmen on the West Bank has been excavated. The tombs of **Dra'a Abul Naga** were excavated in valleys scattered over a wide area of the desert. Some 48 tombs from the 18th Dynasty have been located here and there are two newly opened ones, cut into the mountainside just north of the junction where the road leads left to the Valley of the Kings. Further tombs belonging to nobles are open for viewing at **El- Asasif** and **El-Khokhah**.

Tomb of Nakht (52)

Set in the entrance of the tomb is an interesting display of representations of the statue of Nakht as originally photographed, together with hunting and offering scenes and a plan of the tomb. Inside, the tomb is well lit and the decoration protected by glass screens. The tomb is small and is best visited early when not many visitors are about.

Nakht was Tuthmosis IV's astronomer, vineyard keeper and chief of his granaries. He and his wife Tawi were buried in this small shrine with its well-preserved and colourful antechamber which depicts the harvest in intricate detail. On its west wall in the centre is a painting illustrating parts of Nakht's life together with the goddess of the west. On the left of the far wall is a depiction of a funeral banquet at which Nakht (the top half has been badly defaced), is shown seated beside his wife, a cat at his feet is eating a fish and he is being entertained by a blind harpist and beautiful dancing girls. Opposite, on the east wall, is an unusual painting of peasants treading grapes while empty wine jars await filling. Here the ceiling is brightly decorated with designs representing woven mats. The marshland scenes on the right-hand (south-facing) section of the antechamber are exceptionally fine – the fish are wonderfully depicted. In the inner chamber there is a small niche with a replica of a statue of Nakht bearing a stela with a hymn to Re. Unfortunately the original was lost in 1917 when the SS Arabia, which was transporting it to the USA, was torpedoed by the Germans in the Atlantic. There is a deep shaft leading to the inaccessible burial chamber.

Tomb of Ramoza (55)

Ramoza was Vizier and Governor of Thebes at the beginning of the Akhenaten's heretical rule in 1379 BC and the tomb illustrates the transition in style between the worship of Amun and Aten (see Tell El-Amarna, page 190). The impressive and excellent workmanship of the shrine is probably because it was built by Ramoza's brother Amenhotep who was the chief of works at the family's home town of Memphis. Only the main columned hall can be entered, since the inner hall and false sarcophagus area are separated. This is one of the few tombs where the forecourt is still preserved and the central entrance leads into a broad columned hall. The tomb was carved out of solid limestone and all the decoration carved on polished rock. On the wall to the right are depictions of Ramoza with his wife and opposite on the back wall Akhenaten and Nefertiti stand at their palace windows giving a golden chain to Ramoza. On the left-hand wall are scenes of Ramoza and his wife worshipping Osiris. Beyond is an undecorated inner hall with eight columns and the shrine at the far end. There is a second gap on the left of the end wall leading to the actual sarcophagus chamber. Within each hall are the gated entrances to dark and dangerous tunnels which end with a 15 m drop to the burial chamber.

Tomb of Userhat

Userhat who, in the reign of Amenhotep II (1450-25 BC), was a royal tutor and scribe was buried in a small but pinkishly-decorated tomb which was partially damaged by early Christian hermits. At the extremity of the outer hall on the left is a small stela showing the purification by opening of the mouth. At the opposite end of this hall look out for the representation of the double python, a symbol of protection. **NB** The interesting representation of rural life on the left on the way into the hall, the façade of the snake-headed harvest goddess Renehat on the right of the back wall, and a realistic hunting scene in the desert on the left of the inner hall.

Khaemhet (57)

Khaemhet, another royal scribe and overseer of the granaries in the period Amenhotep III in the 18th Dynasty, adopted a raised relief system for the carved and painted decoration of his tomb-chapel which is well worth seeing for its variety. The tomb is entered through a courtyard off which there are other tomb entrances largely blocked off. The Khaemhet tomb is made up of two transverse chambers joined by a wide passage. In the outer chamber there are rich reliefs depicting rural scenes, some of the originals now only to be seen in Berlin. The passage has funeral scenes (south wall) and the voyage to Abydos (north wall), while both the transverse chambers, though mainly the far one, have statue niches of Khaemhet and his family. There is a small room annexed to the inner transverse chamber, possibly added later.

Antefoker (60)

Antefoker was the Governor of Thebes and his tomb-chapel deserves a visit. The tomb is structured as a main corridor which carries a series of scenes of farming, the life of the marshes and hunting at the time of the 12th Dynasty at the time of Senosert 1. Domestic scenes of servants and gifts for the New Year are all contained within the main corridor. The inner chamber has figures carrying offerings and in front of the niche at the head of the tomb is a statue of Antefoker's wife.

Tomb of Mena (69)

This tomb has been undergoing restoration and, although Mena's eyes have been gouged out by rivals to prevent him seeing in the afterlife, the paintings are in good condition. He was an 18th-Dynasty scribe or inspector of the estates in both Upper and Lower Egypt. In particular, visit this tomb to see the following items: on the end wall on the right-hand side of the outer hall is a depiction of a series of gods, notably Hathor and Isis. On the adjacent wall is a fine painting of Mena and his wife giving flowers. Opposite is a vignette of the younger members of the family making gifts to their father. In the left-hand limb of the outer hall note the depiction of Mena's wife in an elegant dress and jewellery as she stands with her husband before Osiris. In the inner hall there is a niche for a statue of Mena and his wife. Elsewhere in the inner hall are well-preserved paintings of the gods, presentation of gifts, funeral and judgement scenes. Look out for the finely-executed paintings of hunting and fishing scenes on the right-hand wall close to the statue niche, which are extremely well done with crocodiles, wild cats and fish. The ceilings are brightly coloured and represent woven cloth.

Horemheb

Horemheb was a scribe in the reign of Tuthmosis III-Amenhotep III. His tomb-chapel is made up of a rectangular entrance hall and a main corridor leading to a four-pillared hall. The main corridor of his tomb is decorated with scenes of his official life in the military and decorations in the entrance hall show a concern with funeral affairs.

Ineni

Ineni was the architect of Tuthmosis I and in charge of the granary of Amun. His main work is thought to have been building the tomb of Tuthmosis I and the monarch's obelisk at Karnak. The temple-tomb spans the period Amenhotep I-Hatshepsut of the 18th Dynasty. The tomb is constructed with a transverse corridor defined on the southwest by six large square pillars. The corridor is decorated with rural scenes of farming and hunting. The inner chamber has the normal offering, banqueting and funeral procession. Additionally, at the northern end, it has statue niches for Ineni, his wife and family.

Tomb of Sennofer

At the time of Amenhotep II (1450-25 BC), Sennofer was, among other things, Mayor of Thebes, overseer of the granaries and gardens, and chief vintner. In the antechamber of this tomb there is an excellently clear set of diagrams etched on the glass showing the layout of the tomb and its decorations, accompanied by explanations. Look at these first. The entire tomb has discreet electric lighting. The ceiling is covered in illustrations of vines and the tomb is known locally as the 'Tomb of Vines'. The antechamber is rough and irregular in shape. Pass into the pillared main chamber under a low beam. Within the four-pillared hall Sennofer is shown making offerings to the deities and on his journey into the afterlife he is accompanied by his wife Meryt. A double figure of the jackal-headed Anubis looks down on the whole chamber from above the entrance. There is a false door painted on the east (right-hand) wall with the god Anubis and the goddess Isis. Facing the entrance arch look to the right for a depiction of Sennofer's wife, son and daughters. On the north (end) wall Sennofer and his wife cross to the west bank of the river by boat, accompanied by a funeral offering of wine, flowers and food. On the west wall are the goddess Hathor and Osiris in dark colours of the dead. On the same wall to the left is the funeral furniture for use in the afterlife. There is a small niche for a statue now absent. Above, note the vultures with wings spread for protection of the tomb. On the pillars are formal representations of mummification, cleansing rites and offerings.

Tomb of Rekhmire (100)

This crucifix-shaped tomb should not be missed because its highly decorative paintings and inscriptions reveal some of the secrets of Egypt's judicial, taxation and foreign policy at that time. Rekhmire, who came from a long line of viziers and governors, was the vizier at the time of Tuthmosis III's death in 1450 BC when he then served his successor Amenhotep II. The tomb is in good order, though lit only by hand-held mirrors (held by the man at the door who will require a tip), which means that the visibility is not great. Walking left or clockwise around the whole tomb from the entrance wall of the transverse corridor you can see: Egyptian taxes, Rekhmire being installed as vizier, foreign tributes being received from Punt, Crete, Nubia, Syria and Kush, then along the main corridor the inspection of the various workshops, the voyage to Abydos, the various gods of the dead, and the end niche which would have contained a statue of Rekhmire. The ceiling has deteriorated but some of the original plaster work remains, with a continuous line down the centre of the main north-pointing chamber. Look out too for the splendid marsh/woodland scene which, with a small lake and trees, has a warmth and realism to it that contrasts nicely with the formal and predictable decoration in praise of the gods (notably Osiris) and Tuthmosis III. On the way out along the other corridor wall are pictures of the afterworld and then, back in the transverse hall, illustrations of hunting and fowling, wine-making, Rakhmire's wives and ancestors, and finally more taxes being collected.

Tombs at Dra'a Abul Naga

Roy (255) Opened to the public in 1999, this finely decorated tomb was prepared for Roy, the royal scribe, steward of the estates of Horemheb (1348-20 BC) and of Amun in the 18th Dynasty. This is a small tomb consisting of an open entry court and a hall from which there is a shaft. It is one of the most beautiful tombs here because its scenes and colours are remarkable. The southern wall is decorated with ploughing, pulling flax and the deceased and his wife worshipping at the tomb with Ennaed (the nine gods of the cosmonogy of Heliopolis). Also Horus leading them to Osiris with the weighing scene, a funeral procession, friends and mourners led by Anubis at the pyramid tomb. The northern wall is decorated by offering scenes and a libation scene before the deceased and his wife. There is a niche containing stelae with the barque of Re adorned with baboons and the deceased and his wife and a Hymn to Re. On the left side the deceased is adoring western Hathor in the form of a tree goddess with Ba (the soul) drinking. On the right Roy's wife is worshipping.

Shuroy (Suroy, Shoray) (Ramessid 13) Also north of the road at Dra'a Abul Naga is the tomb of Shuroy, the head of the brazier bearers. The tomb is newly opened and worth a visit since the entry chamber is brightly coloured with many scenes in a good state of preservation – as bright as the day they were drawn. It is well lit and the decoration easy to see.

The monument consists of a court and two halls forming a 'T' shape. The first hall on the left is decorated with sketches of the deceased and his wife adoring divinities, adjacent is the *Book of Gates*. A representation of Zed appears on a pillar. On the right the deceased and his wife adore Macet and Re-Horakhte and there are gates decorated with demons. In the second hall the door jambs carry sketches of the deceased on the right and of his wife on the left. The left side of the chamber is decorated with offerings-bearers and a funeral procession including a child mourner before a mummy and the deceased kneeling with braziers before Hathor the cow on a mountain. On the right side there are scenes representing offerings-bearers before the deceased and his wife and a banquet with clappers and bouquets.

There is a niche offset to the right with a squatting woman on the left, and on the right the deceased bearing a brazier, followed by his wife.

Tombs at El-Asasif and El-Khokah

Kheruef (192) This tomb made for Kheruef, the Steward of Amenhoptep III's wife Queen Tiye, is of great interest because it is one of the few tombs at El-Asasif which survived the rapacious activities of the tomb robbers, largely because it was filled with compacted debris. There is added importance arising from its decoration, which is not only good quality but also unusually illustrates the festivals of the Jubilee, an affirmation of a king's power in the land towards the close of the 18th Dynasty.

The architecture of the tomb is sophisticated, with a short entry tunnel leading into a large, square, open courtyard at the west side of which is a four-pillared portico over three steps down to a decorated wall. In the centre of the west wall there is a narrow entrance (with locked gate) to the 30-pillared hall, where only one fluted column approximately, 3-4 m high, is left standing at the extreme left side. This remnant does, however, give some idea of the original grandeur of this chamber before its ceiling collapsed. A doorway leads to an extension to an unfinished second hall, where two pillars are in place.

The decoration of the tomb is worth some attention. To the right, after the entrance under a picture of Amenhotep, are nine vignettes of nations conquered by the pharoah, each being a representative of a different race and city. On the portico wall is a set of scenes of stick fighting, sports, dancing, men driving cattle as part of the festival of the pharaoh's jubilee in which Kheruef is keen to show his important role. Also there is a picture of the king and priests worshipping Jed, husband of Nut, on a adjacent pillar. At the left-hand end of the portico is another set of images showing the king and queen sailing at the end of the jubilee festival and decorated, large-scale figures of Amenhotep and his queen. There are wonderful impressions of ladies clapping, musical instruments such as flutes being played, and ladies dancing during the jubilee celebrations – all very beautifully and graphically done. Look out for Nubian dancing ladies even though some of the colouring is now faded. These figures are mainly on the bottom two registers, the high levels being scraped and broken and in very bad condition.

At the very end of the blue-ceilinged access tunnel to the pillared hall, on the right-hand side, is a large panel of the king and queen in boat crossing to Abydos but it is badly damaged. On the right of the corridor, about 2½-3 m from the end and about 1 m from ground, is a small cartoon in black of Sinmootè, one of the great craftsmen of the period, and it leads specialists to suspect that this area was used as a trial ground for the workers who built the main Hatshepsut temple.

Anch-hor (414) This 26th-Dynasty tomb in El-Asasif was prepared for the chief steward of the divine votaress of Amun, and Overseer of Upper Egypt. It is much restored with the main pieces saved represented by the relief at the entrance and the very deep burial chambers – repaired by the Austrian Archaeological Institute in 1971-81. The tomb is cut heavily into the strata. Down a long flight of stairs is a set of 10 rooms and an open courtyard. The main chamber or western hall has eight square columns and leads to a deep antechamber and thence to a small burial chamber with a niche in the west end.

Two items of interest in the decoration are the change in style of wigs at this late stage as Mediterranean influences penetrated to Thebes. Secondly, there is a unique scene of the art of bee-keeping. (**NB** This tomb can become unpleasantly warm.)

Nefersekhru (292) This is among some 60 tomb chapels from the Ramessid period at El-Khokha. There is a descent down a long ramp of stairs cut in the rock to the entrance of the tomb, discovered in 1915 by Mond. Nefersekhru was the scribe of the divine offerings of all of the gods. He married three wives who are represented in the tomb. The monument has a short corridor leading to a single chamber some 2 m x 10 m aligned on a north-south axis. In the west wall of chamber at the north end is a barred entrance with steps to a set of undecorated burial chambers. The main tomb is well lit and the images screened behind glass.

On the entrance corridor walls of this tomb are scenes on the right of Nefersekhru and his wife coming into, and on the left the wife and the deceased coming out of, the main chamber. Inside there is a ceiling of highly coloured panels in geometric designs, probably representing a carpet. To the south of the door on the entrance wall is a formal picture taken from the *Book of the Gates* and scenes of Nefersekhru before deities. On the back wall opposite the entrance are more decorated panels – beautifully coloured and designed. The owner of this tomb is shown in his leopard skin on a panel on the top left. The middle panel on the back wall exactly opposite the doorway has three registers, of which the left one, more or less intact, shows a wife. Of special note are the dominating image of Osiris, the king of the dead – sadly scarred – and the statues of Nefersekhru set in niches in the middle section. On the right inset and slightly damaged is another highly-detailed female figure.

On the right wall at the end is well-executed sculpture of two wives and the deceased sitting on a bench. On the back wall under a lintel is a scene of feasting with the deceased and one of his wives handing out gifts, including flowers, to visitors. There are agricultural scenes on the left-hand side of door on entry to the chamber.

The western side chamber leads to another Ramessid tomb chapel (295) of unknown ownership with a shaft in its north eastern extremity. The ceiling of this side room has a spectacular carpet design.

Nefermenu (365) In the same cutting are other tombs such as that of the 18th Dynasty Nefermenu (365), Overseer of the wig-makers of Amun at Karnak, now firmly closed. Peer in through grill on door to a large but undecorated chamber.

Neferrompet (178) This small but famous tomb temple to the Scribe of the Treasury is open for public viewing in El-Khokha. It lies to the right at the bottom of the stairs leading to the tomb of Nefersekhru. Discovered in 1915 by Mond it dates from the time of Ramses the Great (II) (1304-1237 BC). The monument is made up of two chambers joined by a narrow doorway. The first small chamber is 3 m by 2.5 m. Lights in the tomb are good. The walls are protected by glass.

Decoration is typical of the Ramessid tomb type. On the centre outer lintel of entrance the door are cartouches of Ramses II, while in the thickness of the entrance door the deceased and his wife are shown, respectively entering and leaving, worshipping with hymns to Re. In both rooms the frieze represents Hathor's face and Anubis. The first hall has a ceiling with beautiful carpet-like paintings bearing geometrical designs with flowers. The most interesting decoration is a representation of 14 scenes from the *Book of the Gates* with Neferrompet and his wife drinking from the pool, a weighing scene with deceased and wife led by Anubis, a harpist singing before Neferompet and Mutemwia and his wife playing draughts. His wife has beautiful hair styles and is wearing attractive dresses. In places the garment appears so fine that the outline of her arm shows through the cloth. Look for the cat with a bone in the far left hand corner!

In the second chamber are five panels showing adoration of the gods.There is a much-noted panel showing Neferrompet keeping a tally of/storing offerings given to the temple, which is in excellent condition and illustrates the life in the treasury at that time. On the end wall is a series of four statues cut from the rock and decorated, showing perhaps Mutemwia and daughters or possibly priestesses.

Valley of the Queens

ⓘ *One ticket costing E£12 gives entry to three tombs of your choosing. A separate ticket costing E£100 is required for tomb 66 (Nefertari), if it is open.*

Like the Valley of the Kings, the Valley of the Queens, about 3 km south from the tombs of the nobles, can be reached via another road which cuts northwest through the main northeast-southwest escarpment. It was once known as the 'Place of Beauty' and was used as a burial site for officials long before the queens and their offspring, who had previously been buried with their husbands, began to be buried there in the 19th Dynasty (1320-1200 BC). It contains more than 80 tombs but many are still unidentified. The tombs are generally quite simple with a long corridor, several antechambers branching off and the burial chamber at the end. The most famous tomb is that of Ramses II's wife Nefertari.

Queen Sit-re (38)

Queen Sit-re's tomb-chapel is in the south quadrant of the Valley of the Queens. The tomb is normally closed and official permission must be sought to gain entry. The Queen was the wife of Ramses I and this is among the earliest tomb-chapels built in the valley. The elemental structure comprises an outer hall chamber and an unfinished burial chamber. The decorations include (in clockwise order in the hall chamber): scenes of the sons of Horus, the queen at a shrine, a water scene with a Lion-headed god.

Prince Seth-Hir-Khopshef (43)

Prince Seth-Hir-Khopshef was a son of Ramses III who died of smallpox when very young. He was ceremonial charioteer of the great stables. His tomb-chapel is decorated with a series of scenes of the gods, clockwise from the entrance to the corridor including Ramses III and Seth-Hir-Khopshef in front of Osiris and other deities, the sons of Horus, Osiris enthroned, Ramses III and Prince Seth-Hir-Khopshef offering gifts, Ramses and the prince before a set of deities.

Valley of the Queens

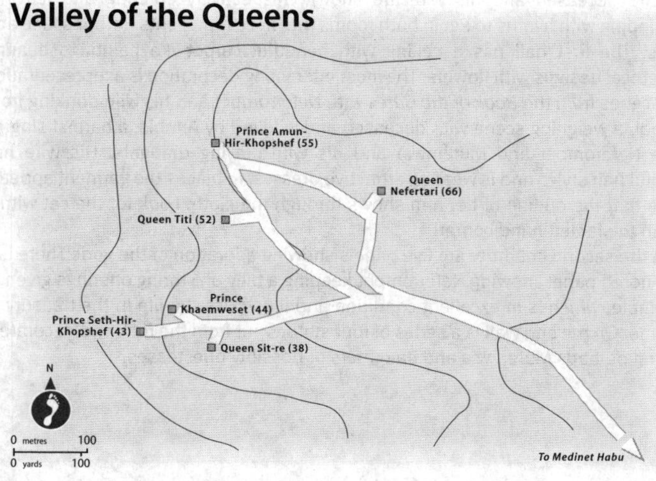

Prince Khaemweset(44)

Although the tomb is dedicated to one of Ramses III's (1198-66 BC) young sons who died of smallpox, it is dominated by the pharaoh himself. The reliefs depict the young boy being led to the underworld by his father who is offering sacrifices and helping his son through the underworld and the judgement of Osiris to the Fields of Yaru.

Queen Titi (52)

Queen Titi was the daughter, wife and mother of a succession of the 20th-Dynasty (1200-1085 BC) pharaohs called Ramses but it is uncertain to which one she was married. Although the tomb is open to the public the reliefs are faded and damaged. A corridor leads to a square shrine which branches into three antechambers with the badly preserved burial chamber on the left being dedicated to the four sons of Horus and Osiris. The central chamber features the Queen before the gods and the shrine is dominated by animal deities with pictures of jackals, baboons and guardian lions. The right-hand chamber is the best preserved and depicts the tree goddess and Hathor as a cow goddess rejuvenating the Queen with Nile water.

Prince Amun-Hir-Khopshef (55)

Prince Amun-Hir-Khopshef was the eldest son of Ramses III who like his younger brother Seth-Hir-Khopshef (43) died young. Descent to the tomb is via a stairway into the main hall from which there is a corridor to the burial chamber. The tomb is elaborately decorated with fine illustrations which remain in good condition. The scenes show excerpts from the *Book of the Gates* and Ramses III leading his son in a course around the stations of the gods. An oddity is the sarcophagus which contained the remains of a foetus, thought to be one of the prince's stillborn infants. This foetus is displayed in a glass cabinet in one corner of the burial chamber.

Nefertari's Tomb (66)

ⓘ *In order to control humidity levels, only 150 visitors are allowed inside per day. The temple is closed periodically to ensure preservation. Separate tickets are required (E£100 or E£50 for students). There is a rumour circulating that the cost of entry may double next year.*

The most famous and outstanding tomb, Nefertari was the favourite wife of Ramses II. It was opened to the public for the first time, since its discovery in 1904, in November 1995. Even the most tomb-resistant visitor to Egypt should try to see this for the bright clear paintings are a sheer delight. One of the most sophisticated pieces of artwork created during the New Kingdom, it stands, like the Taj Mahal, as a final testamant to a king's love for his wife. Small, compared to the tombs in the Valley of the Kings, its 430 sq m of fine reliefs were nearly completely destroyed by flood damage

Tomb of Nefertari (66)

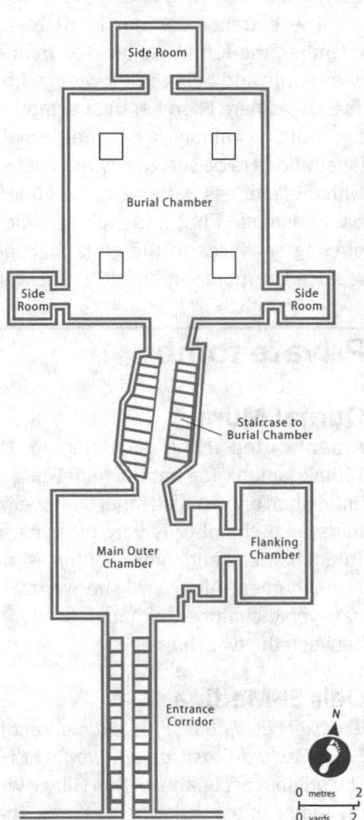

Calling on Nefertari

Although this tomb was discovered in 1904 the delicate condition of the tomb walls and fragile nature of the ornate reliefs have prevented Nefertari from receiving visitors. After six years of intense labour and the outlay of over US$2 million, Nefertari became fit to entertain, but on her own terms. Though open to visitors without a break for a few years, nowadays, the tomb is also frequently closed for rest, as the influx of hot, wet breath has already had a detrimental effect on the exquisite colour. When open, access is restricted to 150 visitors per day, 10 at a time, for 10 minutes each.

Nefertari was the favourite wife of Ramses II and her tomb was decorated with 430 sq m of the finest wall paintings ever produced. Sodium chloride seeped into the plaster which covered the limestone walls and salt crystals developed. As they grew in the damp atmosphere they forced the painted plaster off the walls and the murals fell to the floor in fragments. With the help of photographs from the museum in Turin and those taken by Ernesto Schiaparelli, who discovered the tomb, the carefully cleaned pieces of mural were replaced on the wall, a huge Egyptian jigsaw.

and leaching of the salt crystals in the tomb's limestone bedrock which caused the plaster to buckle and crack. After a US$6 million, 6-year restoration project by the Getty Conservation Institute, the tomb is ready for public display.

The entrance corridor leads to a main outer chamber and a small flanking chamber, the former dominated by the image of a smiling Nefertari holding hands with Horus and being acknowledged by Isis, the vivid colours splendidly preserved. The stress here is on her beauty rather than good works. The staircase descends to the burial chamber and three small side rooms. Among the immensely rich illustrations to be seen are Queen Nefertari bearing gifts and the Queen hand in hand with the goddess Hathor and the god Horus. Unfortunately the downstairs reliefs are badly damaged but it is still possible to see that in the burial chamber Nefertari, offering sacrifices to the gods, becomes solemn and her fashionable clothes are replaced by more sombre attire. The wall texts are chapters from the *Book of the Dead*.

Private tombs

Qurnat Murai

Amenhoptep (Huy) Amenhoptep (Huy) was the Viceroy of Kush in the reign of Tutankhamen. The tomb-chapel is cruciform with a transverse chamber and an unfinished or damaged inner chamber with four irregular pillars. The decoration of the transverse chamber is very pleasing, showing scenes of Nubians offering gifts to Tutankhamen, and Amenhoptep is depicted among the Nubians and also with Tutankhamen. Almost all the worthwhile decorations are in the west wing of the transverse chamber, although sections of Hymn to Ptah occur in the small corridor between the two chambers.

Deir El-Medina

ⓘ *Tickets available at the main ticket office. Entry to Sennedjem and Inherkhau costs E£12, Peshedu costs an additional E£10.*

The original occupants of this village were the workers who excavated and decorated the tombs in the Valley of the Kings. The neat remains are certainly worth exploration (no entrance fee) and beginning at the north end is recommended. A narrow street, in places little more than a metre wide, runs south with the houses tightly packed on either side. The foundations show how small these dwellings were, and often they were subdivided, but remains of stairs indicate an upper storey and sometimes a cellar. Some houses were a little larger and contained a kitchen. Further south the street turns to the left and right, marking the limit of the 18th-Dynasty town.

Above the site of Deir Al-Medina, now partially excavated, there are three tombs open at present, those of Sennedjem, in the 19th Dynasty, Peshedu and Inherkhau, Foreman of a construction team of the 20th Dynasty. All, but especially the tomb of Sennedjem, are beautifully-preserved and have outstanding paintings. Normally guides are not allowed to conduct their groups into the comparatively small chambers.

Sennedjem Sennedjem's tomb was found undamaged in 1886 by Gaston Maspero, then head of the Antiquities Service. It is a small, simple, rectangular burial chamber, 6 m by 3 m, with narrow stairs leading into it and a slightly domed ceiling. On discovery it held intact the mummies of Sennedjem, his wife, son and two daughters-in-law. There was a handsome range of funeral materials. Unfortunately, the mummies and funerary objects were dispersed across the museums of the world so that a compehensive view is no longer possible. The wall decorations shown in the burial chamber and now protected by glass are first rate in colour, style and present condition and are worth travelling to see. The domed ceiling is wonderfully decorated with snakes, pictures of the gods and a golden orb. Clockwise round the chamber are hunting/forest scenes in the lower register and, above, a mummy on a bier with the goddesses Isis and Nephthys protecting it. On the side wall Sennedjem and his wife stand before the gods and, on the back wall opposite the entrance, the masterpiece of the tomb, the body of Sennedjem lying on an ornamental bier is embalmed by Anubis. On the east wall is a double painting of the barque of Re above and a view of life in eternity below. The south wall (right of the door) shows Sennedjem and his wife, Iyneferty, facing the Deities of the Gates. The usual offering scenes are shown. Of great appeal is the depiction of the tree of life from which a goddess is appearing bearing an offering table.

Inherkhau This is another brilliantly-painted tomb in excellent order and accessible down a steep flight of steps to a small anteroom with a low ceiling into a chamber with decorated plastered walls bearing coloured paintings, now considerably damaged by efflorescence and exfoliation of the limestone rock. From this chamber are two exits, one into a rough rock-cut burial chamber. The second exit leads down steps under a low lintel to the main decorated chamber itself. This room is vaulted and is approximately 5 m by 2 m. On the left-hand side is a painting of a stork, the god Anubis, and a fine depiction of the family with hair left down in funeral form. At the north end, slightly damaged, is a full-scale representation of Inherkhau and his family with offerings. The right-hand side wall also carries more pictures of Inherkhau's family, children naked and with hair curled round their ears to denote immaturity. The ceiling is vaulted and painted in bright colours – ochre, yellow, gold, bearing cartouches and a detailed list of events in the life of Inherkhau.

Peshedu (Ramessid 3) Peshedu's tomb is highly decorated and in very good condition. It celebrates the life of the "servant in the place of truth" and was opened for visits in 1998. The tomb is very light and airy, with the coloured scenes protected by transparent screens and a cooling fan. It is entered down a very steep flight of stairs, with a low roof – take care! Eventually a narrow entrance is reached which leads to the first large chamber which is not decorated. After about 6 m it narrows down into a low gateway just 1½ m high. This is where the wonderful decorations begin – all in good condition on panels on both sides with hieroglyphics above. On the sides of the entry corridor are images in very good colour of Anubis as a jackal lying on an altar. Within the burial chamber there is a wealth of decoration. Above the doorway the god Ptah-Sokaris is shown as a winged falcon under the eye of Horus. The two human figures are Peshedu on the right and his son on the left. Inside the burial chamber to the left the upper register shows a beautiful image of a female (probably the goddess of the sycamore) carrying water up the tree and below right are rows of Peshedu's attendants in fine detail.The long left-hand wall carries an image of Peshedu and his wife with two children standing before Horus with passages of *Book of the Dead* around them.

The right-hand wall of the burial chamber shows Peshedu and his child before Re-Horakhte and three other gods. Surrounding these images are passages from the *Book of the Dead*. Inside the burial chamber to the left is the now famous scene of Peshedu beneath a date palm in fruit by the side of the water.

Other temples and sites

The Ramesseum

ⓘ *Tickets available at the main ticket office, E£12.*

While most tourists confine themselves to the two valleys and Hatshepsut's temple there are a number of other interesting West Bank ruins closer to the river. Of these, among the most impressive was the Ramesseum, a 19th-century name for what was effectively a state cult-temple, on the opposite side of the road near the tombs of the nobles. Today only scattered remains and faded reliefs are left of the great temple which once stood there and reportedly rivalled the splendours of the temples at Abu Simbel.

Ramses II (1304-1237 BC) built this mortuary temple, on the consecrated site of Seti I's (1318-04 BC) much smaller but collapsing temple, in order to impress his subjects but he failed to take account of the annual flooding of the River Nile. The result was that this enormous tribute to Amun and himself was less eternal than he expected!

The first two pylons collapsed and only a single colonnade remains of what would have been the First Courtyard. On its south side is a palace where Ramses stayed when he attended religious festivals on the West Bank. In front of the ruins of the Second Pylon is the base of the enormous colossus of Ramses which was originally over 17 m high but it is now much eroded and various parts of his anatomy are scattered throughout the world's museums. The forefinger alone measures more than 1 m in length. The upper part of the body crashed into the second court where the head and torso remain. Three smaller colossi stood next to the three stairways leading to the Hypostyle Hall but only one fragmented one now remains.

Although it is now roofless, 29 of the original 48 columns still stand in the Hypostyle Hall. The centre of the roof would have been higher than the sides in order to allow shafts of sunlight to enter the hall. To the left of the entrance is the famous relief of the Egyptian victory over the Hittite city of Dapur in the battle of Kadesh. Around the base of the west walls some of Ramses' many sons are depicted. At the far end of the hall a central door leads into the Astronomical Room renowned for its ceiling which is illustrated with the oldest-known 12 months' calendar. Because the temple was dedicated to Amun it is thought to represent a solar year. Two other vestibules, a library and a linen room, lead to the ruined sanctuary which is the temple's highest point.

The Mortuary Temple of Ramses III

The Mortuary Temple of Ramses III (1198-1166 BC), which lies west of the Colossi of Memnon and south of the Valley of the Queens at a place known in Arabic as **Medinet Habu,** was modelled on that built by his forefather Ramses II (1304-27 BC) near by. It is second only to Karnak in terms of its size and complexity and within the enormous enclosing walls are a palace, a Nilometer and several smaller shrines with some pre-dating the temple itself.

When Thebes was threatened, as it was during the 20th Dynasty's Libyan invasions, the enclosing walls sheltered the entire population. Although Ramses III named his temple the 'House of a Million Years', the smaller shrine that already occupied the site next to the south enclosure walls was in use long after the main temple shrine had fallen into disuse.

The small temple, which was constructed by Hatshepsut but later altered by Tuthmosis III who, as ever, erased her cartouche, was built on a platform from which there are good views in all directions. Until the 18th century a grove of acacia trees led to the Colossi of Memnon. The site, known as Jeser Ast or 'Sacred Place', was venerated because it was thought that the waters of chaos had divided and the primeval mound erupted here. During Akhenaten's rule, Amun's images were destroyed but they were later replaced by those of Horemheb and Seti I.

Ramesseum site

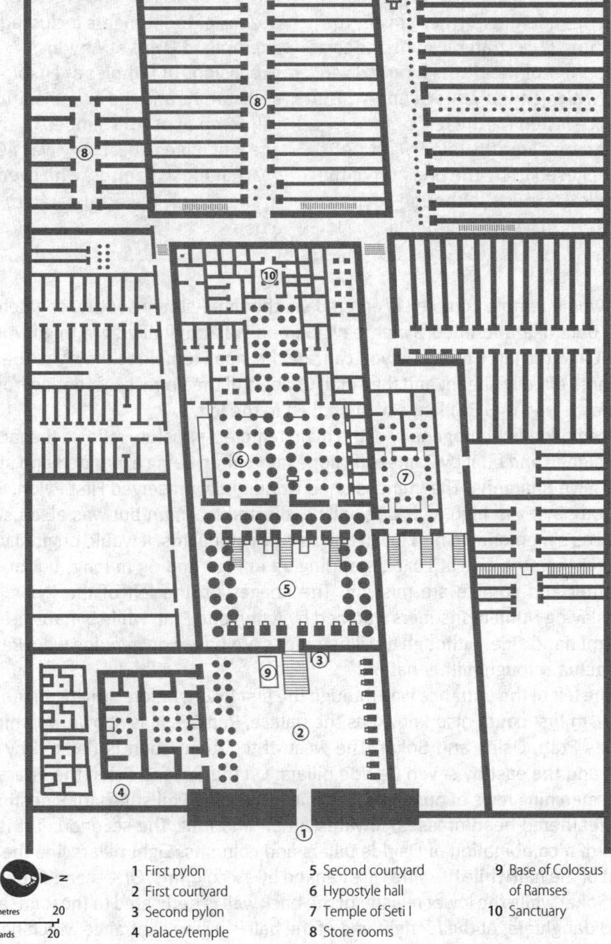

Ramses The Great (1304-1237 BC)

Known by the Egyptians as Ramses Al-Akbar (the great), a name that would no doubt have pleased him, the achievements of Ramses II, arguably Ancient Egypt's most famous king, were majestic. During his 67-year reign, the pharaoh presided over an empire stretching west from present-day Libya to Iraq in the east, as far north as Turkey, and south into Sudan. While his military feats were suitably exaggerated for posterity in the monuments of his day, Ramses also engineered a peace treaty with Egypt's age-old northern rivals, the Hittites, by a strategic marriage to a daughter of the Hittite king in 1246 BC which ended years of unrest. The peace lasted for the rest of the pharaoh's lengthy reign. Ramses II is believed to be the pharaoh of the biblical 'exodus', although Egyptian records make no mention of dealings with Israelite slaves. His massive fallen statue at the Ramesseum inspired Shelley's romantic sonnet *Ozymandias*, a title taken from the Greek version of Ramses' coronation name *User-maat-re*. Egypt's most prolific pharaoh (siring at least 80 children), he was also a prodigious builder. He began building soon after ascending the throne at the age of 25, having discovered that the great temple his father Seti I had begun at Abydos was a shambles. During the rest of his reign he erected dozens of monuments including a temple to Osiris at Abydos, expansions of temples at Luxor and Karnak, and the awe-inspiring cliff temples at Abu Simbel. In an age when life expectancy was 40 years at most, Ramses, who lived to 92, must truly have appeared to be a god.

The whole temple complex is entered via the three-storey southeast gatehouse which is built like a fortified Syrian pavilion and was originally 22 m high. Arriving through it into the large forecourt you can see the small temple to the right, the huge main temple directly ahead, and the small Chapels of the Votressess, dating from the 25th Dynasty (747-656 BC) kings of Kush, just to the left.

The remarkable homogeneity of the main temple's structure reflects the fact that it was designed and built by Ramses III alone rather than being expanded and altered by successive pharaohs. The immense and wonderfully preserved First Pylon, which is 65 m long by 27 m high, was originally dedicated to Amun but was also used by Ramses II as a memorial to his Libyan and Asiatic campaigns. It would originally have been larger than the one at Luxor, standing 27 m high and 65 m long, but now the north corner and cornice are missing. The images on the left of the Pylon show Ramses slaying Nubian prisoners watched by Amun and Ptah while Syrians are slain on the right hand side. Although the illustrations are based on genuine wars Ramses III never actually fought either nation!

On the left of the entrance way through the first Pylon, before arriving in the large 48 m x 34 m first court, also known as the palace, Ramses III is shown worshipping the deities Ptah, Osiris and Sokar. The west of the great court is flanked by eight columns and the east by seven Osiride pillars. On the Second Pylon the Pharaoh is depicted marching rows of prisoners, the third row being Philistines (or Palestinians) wearing feathered head-dresses, towards Amun and Mut. The second court is also made up of a combination of Osiride pillars and columns. Eight pillars line the back and front of the hall while the sides are flanked by six columns. One scene depicts the Feast of Sokar while the lower register of the back wall is dedicated to the Ramses III's sons and daughters. At the far right end of the hall is a small entrance which has two

The Singing Colossus of Memnon

The northern gigantic sandstone colossus was broken off at the waist by the earthquake in 27 BC after which it was reputed to sing at dawn. This phenomenon, which was most likely caused by the wind or the expansion of the broken stone in the morning sunlight, attracted many visitors including the Roman emperors Hadrian in AD 130 and Septimus Severus (AD 193-211). The latter decided it should be repaired, after which it never sang again.

interesting illustrations. One shows the Pharaoh before Seth, but this was later defaced to change him into Horus, while above the door Ramses is shown kneeling on the symbol of the united Upper and Lower Egypt.

The west door connects to the ruins of the severely damaged Hypostyle Hall. Above the door the Pharaoh can again be seen kneeling over the symbol of Upper and Lower Egypt and at the base of the entry wall are 13 princesses and 10 princes. The central aisle of the hall would have been raised, in the same way as at Karnak, to allow Re's sunlight to enter.

A multitude of side rooms would originally have led off from the hypostyle hall but little now remains because of the severe damage caused by the major earthquake in 27 BC. The best-preserved room is the Treasury to the north where the walls are adorned with scenes of the Pharaoh making offerings of gold to Amun. Another small room shows the Pharaoh wearing the Osiride symbols of the Atef feathered crown, a crook and flail.

The outer walls are better preserved and some of the reliefs are clearly visible. At the far end of the south wall is a calendar of religious feasts which is believed to be the longest such inscription. Further along is a portrayal of all the benefits with which Ramses III was blessed by Amun. The rear west wall is dedicated to the Pharaoh's victories in battle. In the northeast corner of the enclosure near the small temple is a small sacred lake where childless women came to bathe at night and pray to Isis that they might conceive. Close by stand the remains of the Nilometer that was originally fed by a canal which branched off from the Nile.

On a more modern theme – the **Monastery of St Theodore** lies to the southwest of the Temple of Medinet Habu and is within easy reach. The religious pictures are quite modern. Theodore was one of the many Christian soldiers who fell foul of Diocletian's oppression.

Colossi of Memnon

These two gigantic sandstone colossi, which are located on the main road 1.65 km from the river and next to the student ticket kiosk, represent Amenhotep III (1417-1379 BC). They once stood in front of his mortuary temple which collapsed and was plundered for stone long ago. Although the faces and crowns have been eroded the two colossi make a strange spectacle seated in splendour in the midst of the desert and are well worth a visit (see box above).

Sleeping

As the second biggest tourist destination in Egypt, Luxor has thousands of beds – from the most luxurious to the dingiest of crash-dives. As a result, when tourism wanes due to the intense heat of summer or tension in the region, competition is fierce. Prices get sliced, sometimes in half, and bargaining is the norm. If you're travelling in peak season (Nov-Feb), it's wise to book ahead; otherwise, shop around. The 5-star hotels are mostly located along the Nile, some quite far from the town centre. Mid-range hotels tend to be scattered both north and south of Sharia Mahatta, the central vein that runs perpendicular to the Nile from the train station. Most offer swimming pools and rooftop terraces with bars. Budget hotels are concentrated around the souk, at the town centre and along Shari Televizion to the south. Virtually all budget hotels in Luxor include breakfast and virtually all breakfasts consist of exactly the same thing: bread, jam, cheese, tea or coffee, and a boiled egg. In the listing that follows, it is only noted if breakfast is extraordinary or not included.

East Bank *p215, map p217*

AL Le Meridian Corniche El-Nil, T095-369999. The newest 5-star hotel in town, next to the Sonesta, with rooms overlooking the Nile. Absolute elegance.

AL Luxor Hilton, New Karnak, north of town with free courtesy bus, T095-374955, F376571. Has 261 rooms with twin beds, rather small, but magnificent views from private balcony. Unprepossessing exterior hides an excellent interior with reportedly the best hotel management in the town. Three restaurants provide wide choice of excellent food and there's a coffee shop, a heated pool (necessary for comfort in winter) with a sundeck which overlooks the river, a casino, *feluccas* to rent (E£40 per hr), and a new mini-gym and billiards. **NB** Sleep may be disturbed by cruise liners which moor alongside and run engines all night.

AL Luxor Sheraton Hotel and Resort, Sharia El-Awameya, T095-374544, F374941. A well managed hotel with 298 rooms in main building with views of River Nile (more expensive) or bungalows in garden (very comfortable). Shopping arcade, hairdresser, disco, tennis courts, heated pool, *feluccas* to rent (E£35 per hr). Caters for tour groups which receive reduced rates, the service is consistently excellent.

AL Movenpick Jolie Ville Luxor, Crocodile Island, T095-374855, F374936. The only tourist village in Luxor with 320 rooms in 20 bungalow pavilions. Lush flowering gardens sprout up on this beautiful island 4 km south of Luxor. Connected to mainland by bridge and to town centre by a free ferry and more frequent free shuttle bus. Under 16s can sleep free in their parents' room. Good restaurants – Movenpick, Jolie Ville, Garden Terrace, Sharazade Nile Terrace, Crocodile Bar, and the Sobek Hall for banquets, functions and conferences. There's also a good pool, horse riding, fitness centre and private *felucca* on the island.

AL Sofitel Winter Palace Hotel, Corniche El-Nil, T095-380422, F374087. The oldest and most famous luxury hotel in Luxor whose guests have included heads of state, Noel Coward and Agatha Christie. There are 110 unusual but rather basic rooms in the old building and 260 in the new, overlooking the Nile. Also 2 restaurants, terrace bar in splendid position overlooking corniche and river, and a shared pool.

AL Sonesta St George Hotel, Corniche El-Nil, T095-382575, www.sonesta.com. A modern 7-storey building where the lower level terrace overlooks the Nile. Serapis restaurant, Beban coffee shop, elegant dining room with excellent food and attentive service, Mikado Japanese restaurant, Nobles pub, poolside bar with light refreshments, nightclub and disco, sport and fitness centre.

A Akhetaten Village, Sharia Ibn Khalid El-Walid, T095-380850, F380879. Run by Club Med with its unique and stylish atmosphere. Pool overlooks the Nile. Popular with French tourists and groups.

A Pyramisa Isis Hotel, Sharia Ibn Khalid El-Walid, in extensive grounds to the south of town (courtesy bus), T095-373344, F372923. The largest hotel in Upper Egypt with 520 large, clean, well-decorated rooms set in 3 wings round the garden and 2 large pools (one is heated) where non-residents can swim for E£15. Italian and seafood restaurants, plus 3 other specialist restaurants, 2 bars. Excellent facilities but slow service. Sports facilities include clay tennis courts and squash.

B Mercure Luxor Hotel, Corniche El-Nil, T095-380944, F373316. Hotel on the river front with 306 quality rooms with bath. An attractive atmosphere and very well run. Has 2 restaurants with live entertainment. 24-hr coffee shop. Most guests are tour groups who are mainly British in summer and German in the winter high season when the hotel is always full. Popular disco with an acclaimed belly dance floorshow.

C **Novotel Luxor**, Sharia Ibn Khalid El-Walid, T095-380925, F380972. 185 rooms, emphasis on friendly service, 2 restaurants (1 floating, takes trips to Dendera (E£150), conference and fax facilities, most guests are tour groups.

D **Emilio Hotel** and **New Emilo Hotel**, Sharia Yusef Hassan, T095-386666, F374884. Roof garden with popular pool, in town centre, 111 a/c rooms with bath and TV, 2 restaurants, 3 bars, disco, pool, small shop, exchange, international phone lines, friendly service. In winter, it's wise to make reservations as the place swarms with European tour groups.

Sharia Ibn Khalid El-Walid

River Nile
Sh Ibn Khalid El-Walid
Social & Sport Club/ Olympic Pool
Passport Office
To 5
To 6 & Banana Island

0 metres 200
0 yards 200

Sleeping
Le Meridian **3**
Movenpick Jolie Ville **6**
Pyramisa Isis **4**
Sheraton Resort **5**
Sonesta St George **2**
St Joseph **1**

Eating
A Taste of India **7**
Classic **1**
Dragon Class **4**
Jem's **6**
Kings Head Pub **2**
Murphy's Irish Pub **3**
Seven Days Seven Ways **8**
Sinouhe **5**

D **Philippe Hotel**, Sharia Dr Labib Habashi, T095-373604, F380050. 40 rooms some with slight Nile view, most look onto Windsor's pool next door (see below). Rooms are carpeted and include TV, a/c, and fridge. Some rooms have remodelled bath, some have balcony. They vary significantly in size so look at your room before booking. Atmosphere of the place feels a bit congested. Pool is murky, but the terrace and bar surrounding it are nice.

D **Windsor Hotel**, Sharia Nefertiti, just behind the Corniche, T095-375547, F373447. 40 rooms, used to be the best 3-star hotel in town, but it's growing grimy around the edges and in need of a serious spring-clean. Roof garden has a fountain and bar with river view. Sauna and Jacuzzi only function in winter. Rooms are comfortable with tiled floors and clean baths, TV and a/c, but nothing spectacular. Staff are friendly and the atmosphere bright. A child-friendly establishment. On site there's a bank and 2 international telephone lines, several restaurants and bars. The 'disco' feels more like a dungeon. Price of rooms drops by half in summer.

E **Golden Palace**, Sharia Televizion, T095-382972, F38274. A good 3-star hotel with popular roof terrace (that features live music on occasion), mid-sized pool and clean, comfortable rooms including a/c, fridge, TV. Probably the nicest mid-range hotel on this street.

E **Horus**, Sharia El-Karnak, T095-372165. Centrally located but rather noisy budget hotel with 25 clean, a/c rooms, a friendly staff and a decent breakfast. Often has vacancies. Rooms significantly reduced in the summer.

E **Little Garden**, Sharia Radwan, off Sharia Televizion, T095-389038. A quaint, very new hotel that feels like a big villa. Rooms are simple and spotless, bathrooms fresh. The garden is indeed little, but lovely, with lots of fruit trees and flowers. Restaurant serves cheap pastas and Oriental food, wine and beer. Internet E£5 per hour for guests. Rooftop is cosy, Bedouin-style seating and *ahwa* with shisha.

E **Merryland**, Sharia Nefertiti, across from the Windsor, T/F095-381746, 376903. This place has lost its grandeur. It used to offer stellar Nile views, but the construction of a huge concrete bank immediately in front means the 4 rooms with Nile view are looking through a cage to see it. The rooftop bar is high enough to still provide one of the best views around. Rooms are dark, but reasonably comfortable and clean.

E New Radwan, Sharia Al-Adasi, next to the train station, T095-373604. Spotlessly clean family-run hotel that offers 3-star quality rooms for 2-star prices. All rooms overlook the small but clear pool and have gleaming private baths and a/c. There is a mosque next door. Poolside restaurant is ok, no alcohol. If you don't mind being half a km from the Nile and incessant background muzak, Radwan offers an excellent deal.

E Shady, Sharia Televizion, T095-381262, F374859. A seedy, but reasonably comfortable centrally located 3-star hotel equipped with murky rooftop pool, bar, billiards and disco. All rooms come with a/c, TV, and fridge.

F Fontana, Sharia Radwan, off Sharia Televizion, T095-380663. Doubles with a/c and private bath E£25, singles E£15, subtract E£5 for shared bath or fan. Rooms are simple and clean. Spacious bathrooms include toilet paper and towels. Washing machine and kitchen available for guests. Lots of tours on offer and helpful information board displayed. Mr Magdy, the manager, tries to add something new every year – now he's working on a rooftop terrace.

F Happyland, Sharia El-Kamar, near Sharia Televizion, T095-371828. Doubles with a/c and private bath E£30, singles E£23, dorms E£7. An all-round excellent budget hotel. Rooms are simple, but clean. Bathrooms include towels, shampoo and toilet paper. Bikes for rent (E£7.50 per day), internet (E£5 per hr), laundry service, message board, nice rooftop terrace but no view. Luggage storage and use of facilities for guests after check-out. Buffet breakfast with fresh fruit, cornflakes, and an omelette. Guided tours to the West Bank (E£45).

F Nefertiti, look for a huge painted sign off Sharia Karnak around the tourist bazaar, T095-372386, www.nefertitihotel.com. Doubles with a/c and private bath E£40. The centrally located hotel offers the best budget roof in town with a stellar view of the avenue of the sphinxes and the Nile. At night, the surrounding streets are filled with lively local *ahwas*. All rooms have a/c and clean, though cramped bathrooms, with towels and linens replaced daily. Breakfast is a step above most with the option of Egyptian (*fuul* and *felafel*) or continental (includes Cornflakes) fare. Game room has billiards, tawla (backgammon), TV, internet (E£9 per hr) and basic weight room equipment. Family-like warm atmosphere offers nice respite for weary travellers.

F Venus, Sharia Yusef Hassan, T095-372625. In the middle of the souk makes the location convenient, if frantic. Basic double rooms have fans (E£20) or a/c (E£40). All rooms have their own bath, but some are outside the room (E£20 cheaper). Not the cleanest of budget options. Camping on the roof is allowed (E£5). Used to be the most popular backpacker hotel in town until the former management rented it out. They reclaimed it a year or so ago and the friendly owner, Mr Hassan, insists he is doing what he can to bring back its past glory. The bright and funky Mars Bar on the 2nd floor has a TV, football table, tiny dance floor and sells cheap food and beer (Stella E£6).

F IYHF Youth Hostel halfway between Luxor and Karnak Temples at 16 Sharia Karnak Temple, T/F095-372139. Clean, spartan 275 beds. Meals available, family rooms, laundry, There are many cheap hotels which offer more comfortable and convenient accommodation without the 1000-1400 lockout and 2300-0600 curfew.

Camping

Rezeiky Camp Sharia Karnak, T095-381334, www.rezeikycamp.com. Offers tent sites (E£10), and fairly cheap a/c rooms (doubles E£50). It's a bit of a hike to town. On site, there's a swimming pool, internet café, washing machine and garden with bar and restaurant.

YMCA Sharia Karnak, T095-372425. Tent sites and space for caravans (E£4). Clean bathrooms with a lot of showers and cheap compared to the **Rezeiky**, but offers far fewer amenities and is quite inconveniently located.

West Bank *p225, map p227*

In recent years, a few charming hotels have sprung up on the West Bank. Though the area has a lot less action than the East Bank, and fewer services, people in search of a more tranquil Luxor experience may find this appealing. The cheap public ferry makes transport across the Nile easy, but if you're planning to have an exceptionally late night, you'll have to hire a private motorboat (E£5).

AL El-Moudira, Dabaiyya, on the edge of the desert, 5 km from the bridge connecting the East and West bank, T012-3928332. This relatively new palatial hotel is exquisite and far away from everything except serenity. Built with natural materials, each room is unique. Bathrooms are lavish. Requires a taxi from the ferry landing.

E Nile Valley Hotel, from the ferry, turn left on the main street and walk 150 m, the hotel will be on your right, T/F095-311477, karinkhalifa@hotmail.com. A cheery intimate clean hotel in front of the Nile with a view of the Luxor temple. Rooms are new, bright, comfortable, and overlooking a lovely garden. All have a/c, tiled floors and spotless bathrooms.

Eating

East Bank *p215, map p217*

Luxor has dozens of fairly cheap Middle Eastern restaurants that all have virtually identical menus (kebab, chicken, moussaka, etc) concentrated around the souk and Luxor Temple. They tend to be quite inexpensive, safe and quite good. Prices increase with a Nile view or a license to sell alcohol. There's also a growing European expatriate community that has introduced some delicious new mid-range eateries to Luxor in recent years.

TTT Expensive restaurants and fine dining experiences seem to be generally confined to 5-star hotels. Try the **Sonesta St George** for Japanese, the **Sheraton** for Italian, and the **Movenpick** for a good buffet breakfast.

TTT **Anubis Restaurant**, adjacent to Museum of Mummification on the corniche, T095-387320. Open 1000-2400. Serves European and Middle Eastern food that is decent but extremely overpriced. Better to come here for the Nile and a good drink. The cappuccino is excellent. Extensive juice bar and beer on offer. There's also a pool table on the boardwalk.

TTT **The Classic Restaurant**, Sharia Ibn Khalid El-Walid, look for the yellow sign. Good food – European or Middle Eastern – and service, but often overloaded with large tour groups. Features a belly dancer on Fridays if there are enough people in town to warrant it.

TT **A Taste of India**, Sharia Ibn Khalid El-Walid, across the street from Seven Days, T010-5341221. Open 1600-2300. An English-run restaurant that specializes in Indian food but also features an English and Middle Eastern menu. The atmosphere is intimate, dimly lit with soft yellow walls. The curry is outstanding and the chapatti fresh and delicious. Lots of vegetarian options. As of yet, they have no licence to serve alcohol, but will gladly buy you a beer from the shop next door.

TT **Dragon Class**, 19 Sharia Ibn Khalid El-Walid, near the Meridian, T095-368902. A fairly upscale new Chinese restaurant with everything you'd expect on the menu. Good quality food. Alcohol served. They'll create a buffet for groups of 10 or more.

TT **Jamboree**, 29 Sharia El-Montazah, T012-2415510. A classy restaurant, also with British proprietors, that offers a daytime snack menu (1030-1430) featuring omelettes, soups, sandwiches and jacket potatoes. Dinner is served from 1800-2200. Entrées include an excellent salad bar (by itself, E£12.50). The food is tasty, but not always hot. Also on offer are milkshakes (E£8.50) and Movenpick ice cream.

TT **Jems**, Sharia Ibn Khalid El-Walid, T012-2261697, on the 2nd floor. The atmosphere isn't quite as quaint as its neighbouring restaurants but guests love the food and keep coming back. The policy is, if you return more than once in the course of the week, you are offered a modest discount that gets bigger every time you return. There are set vegetarian meals, a hodgepodge of Middle Eastern and British fare and an extensive bar. The *shish tawook* comes highly recommended. Tables by the window offer good views of the action on the street.

TT **Lotus**, in the heart of the souk on the 2nd floor, T095-380419. Serves a selection of Middle Eastern and European dishes including spinach canneloni, fish and chips and a variety of vegetarian options. Large windows look down on thriving alleyways. 15% discount for students. The service is good, but if the restaurant is full, it can take a while. The chocolate mousse is delicious.

Seven Days and Seven Ways, Sharia Ibn Khalid El-Walid, T095-366265. Open 0900-2300. Quite far down in the area that is turning into a bit of a restaurant midan. It's rather quaint to find such an English restaurant here. A warm welcome, good for travellers seeking a bit of home after all the temples and tombs – braised beefsteak with onions, shepherd's pie, wide selection of alcohol with the Royal Oak Pub upstairs. Desserts of the home-made variety. Special Sunday roast dinners for E£28 (3 seatings that fill up fast so book ahead). Run by two Englishmen, both named John.

Abu Ashraf, Sharia Mahatta, half way between the station and the souk. Sells tasty Koshari (E£2), shish kebab, roasted chicken, and lots of salads. Nothing exceeds E£10 and the place is clean.

Ali Baba Café, Sharia Karnak, enter on side street. Rooftop dining that offers a lovely view of Luxor temple, particularly at sunset and in the early evening when the temple is lit up. The food is standard Egyptian fare, but the servings are quite small. Stella E£8, local wine E£15/glass.

Amoun, the best of the touristy restaurants in a courtyard by the temple. Indoor and outdoor seating areas. Offers a variety of cheap good food including pizza, seafood, and all the usuals. Excellent juice bar and ice cream. Friendly service that will keep the hustlers away as you watch all the people go by.

Chez Omar, Sharia Yousef Hassan, smack bang in the middle of the souk, T095-367678. This place offers cheap decent food and fast friendly service in an oasis-like setting. Surrounded by trees lit up with green lights at night, it's a good place to breathe after a long day. E£15 gets you a 5-course dinner including soup, salad, rice, vegetable, dessert and a meat of your choice. Stella E£8, shisha, E£5.

Chicken Hut, takeaway at the junction of Sharia Mohatta and El-Souk. Sit-down meals half way down Sharia Mahatta, chicken, kofta and other Egyptian fast food sandwiches (E£3-5), popular with locals and travellers.

Felfela, by Luxor temple. Shares the name of the Cairo restaurant, but no relation. Tasty cheap *felafel* and *fuul* sandwiches.

Mish mish, Sharia Televizion. Serves up tasty cheap pizza with fluffy crust, although the local cheese doesn't melt like mozzarella (E£6-10), a medium should fill you up unless you're famished. Also serves pastas, sandwiches and other standard Middle Eastern dishes. Student discount. A longtime popular eatery among backpackers.

Oum Hashem, a block away from Chez Omar in the souk. A good Egyptian restaurant popular with locals and travellers alike. Menu is traditional, features a variety of casseroles, pigeon, veal and other meat, as well all the standard mezze. Known by locals for the *shish kebab*. Frequented by tour groups.

West Bank *p225, map p227*

A number of good cheap restaurants have sprung up on the West Bank.

Africa Restaurant, immediately opposite the ferry landing, T095-310311. Open 0800-2400. Serves up the standard Luxor Middle Eastern menu in a delightful outside courtyard. Surrounded by fruit trees and mint the friendly staff will pick to accompany your tea. As the menu differs somewhat for English speakers, if there's a local dish you want that you don't see, ask for it. Serves a good traditional Egyptian breakfast. Beer available. Spotless bathrooms.

Nile Valley Restaurant, part of a quaint hotel. Open till 2400. Offers a nice covered roof sitting area with a wide range of food including soups, sandwiches, salads, fish, and lots of meat. *Shisha*, beer and wine by the glass on offer.

The Tutankhamun, from the ferry landing, turn left on the main road and walk 200 m to the motorboat landing, then follow the signs. One of the oldest on the scene, selling all the standards. No alcohol.

Cruising restaurants

Le Lotus, at Novotel, well-organized dinner cruises offering international cuisine, book to get a good seat, also day cruises with high quality lunch while travelling to Dendera and Esna (E£150/person). There's only one functional floating restaurant on the Nile at present.

Tiba, near the Novotel. Just got a bright yellow paintjob with the hopes of attracting more visitors. The menu offers standard Middle Eastern fare. Dinner costs E£50-60.

Bars and clubs

In the winter, all 5-star and most 4-star hotels have some kind of 'live' music or belly dance floor show. In the summer, they're less frequent, it depends how many people are in town. The **Sheraton** and **Winter Palace** are particularly acclaimed, but drinks are expensive. The **Mercure** (locally still known as the "ETAP") offers belly dance shows and sells E£10 beers. The **Abu Hameed Club and Restaurant** features a belly dance show accompanied by Middle Eastern food. Discos also exist in the major hotels, but with the exception of **Sinouhe**, they seem to remain quite empty. The disco in **Novotel** is popular with younger people. There are quite a few surprisingly authentic pubs and bars that have sprung up over the last few years, much to the delight of travellers and expats alike. Most are centred around the southern end of the corniche and are close enough to one another to warrant an evening tour of Luxor pub life (which doesn't stop until people leave). Besides the bars, Luxor is a lovely town to stroll around at night. There are dozens of *ahwas* scattered about the souq where local men smoke *shisha*, sip tea, watch loud Arabic movies and play dominoes and *tawla* (backgammon) into the wee hours of the morn. In addition to pubs, there are several hotels that have rooftop bars offering exquisite views of the town and Nile, particularly at sunset.

For luxury, try the **Old Winter Palace**; and the bars at **St Joseph** and at the **Golden Palace** are also good.

The King's Head Pub, Sharia Ibn Khalid El-Walid, T095-380489. Open 1000-until late. The most longstanding and happening pub in town, and for good reason. It's a true taste of England except that the place stays open until people are ready to go home (at least till 0200) and serves dozens of cocktails with specials like "Sex on a felucca". Though the king in question is Akhenaten, you'd think it Bob Marley with the number of his pictures plastered on the wall. There's a free pool table in the back. The menu is extensive and includes a wide variety of hot and cold mezze (E£6-8), curries, sandwiches and English standards (fish and chips E£27). Stella E£10, cocktails E£14.

Murphy's Irish Pub, Sharia El-Gawazat, near the passport office off Sharia Khalid Ibn El-Walid, T095-388101, www.murphyirishpub.com. Huge 2-floor pub with billiards and TV upstairs. 80s music wafts in the background quiet enough to hear yourself speak. It's a nice place with comfy chairs and lots of wood, but a bit pricey, with Stellas going for a whopping E£17. Guinness is on the menu, but as yet, not in the bar. Several whiskys are available and there's an extensive pub menu that includes a veggie burger (E£12), a variety of jacket potatoes (E£9) and a loads of soups, salads and pastas.

The Royal Oak Pub, Sharia Ibn Khalid El-Walid, upstairs from Seven Days and Seven Ways Restaurant. Intimate friendly pub with red walls and sofa seating. The menu is the same as the restaurant. Currently, there's a buy one cocktail, get one free deal.

Sinouhe/ Red Lion Pub, Sharia Ibn Khalid El-Walid, opposite the Meridian Hotel, T095-370246, 379244. Located on the 2nd floor. Pub and disco with black lights, red walls a disco ball and pumping 90s music, probably the hippest dance floor in town. The action doesn't get started until after midnight. Stella E£12.50, cocktails E£19, small selection of food available through the hotel restaurant.

Entertainment

Casino

Luxor Hilton, open 2000-0200, has the only casino in Luxor offering roulette, blackjack and lots of slot machines. Open only to non-Egyptians over 18 years, have your passport available.

Egypt's 12 highest earning belly dancers pay a total in annual taxes equivalent to US$250 million. This makes them the country's fifth largest source of income. Only receipts from traffic on the Suez Canal, tourism and oil and cotton exports are more important.

Sound and light

The sound and light show at Karnak is a bit melodramatic but many visitors still find it entertaining. There are 3 shows daily with a late night slot for a fourth to accommodate any large tour groups that may be in town. In winter, shows happen daily at 1830, 1945, 2100. In summer, 1945, 2100, 2215. At present, the schedule is as follows:
Mon English/French/German;
Tue English/French/Italian;
Wed German/English/ French;
Thu English/French/Arabic;
Fri English/French/Spanish;
Sat French/English/ Italian;
Sun German/English/Italian/French.

Festivals

The **National Day** is in **Nov** and the **Nile Racing Regatta** is in **Dec**. Both are moveable dates.

Shopping

Shopping in Luxor can be stressful. A leisurely meander through the souk is almost impossible when countless kitschy souvenirs are being thrown in your face and everyone is hollering at you to have a look. But there is a lot to look at. The souk in the town centre is the most interesting place to stroll. Spices, dried herbs and nuts and lots of colourful scarves are all over the place. Laser printed T-shirts are at **Venti** on the corner of Sharia Mohammed Farid.
Local alabaster carved into vases (E£25 small), clay pots and tagins are cheap (E£2 medium size). An unusual collection of unpolished precious and semi-precious stones, many believed to have healing properties, can be found at the **Zaghloul Bazaar** by Luxor Temple.
There's a duty free shop on Sharia Yusef Hassan, near the Emilio Hotel. On the southern end of the corniche around the strip of 5-star hotels, there are some upscale stores that promise no hassle and sell beautiful gold jewelry and high quality Egyptian cotton clothing. For the independent traveller, there's an abundance of fresh fruit and vegetables around the souk in the town centre and in the **Sharia Televizion Market** on Tue. Generally the further away from the river, the lower the prices and the less the hassle.

Bookshops

Bookshops are found at all major hotels but the top in town is unquestionably **Aboudi Books** near New Winter Palace on Corniche El-Nil, T095-373390, which may be the best bookshop for non-Arabic readers outside of Cairo. It offers an extensive collection of fiction and historical books in English, German and French. It also has lots of maps and guidebooks to specific areas in Egypt. and a decent selection of cards and secondhand paperback novels, many in English. Open 0800-2000 except Fri. Internet café upstairs, E£10/hour.
Al-Ahram, by the Museum of Mummification on Corniche El-Nil. Open 0800-2200. Has a good selection of books, also maps and cards and newspapers.
Gaddis Bookshop, by New Winter Palace on Corniche El-Nil, T095-372142. Open 0800-2130. Books in English, French and German. Foreign newspapers are sold in a kiosk in the middle of the street outside the Old Winter Palace Hotel. There is a good chance that these will also be offered for sale by street vendors along the corniche where the cruise ships are moored.

Activities and tours

Balloon flights

Becoming a popular activity for those who can afford it, there are now 3 hot air balloon companies in Luxor.
Balloons over Egypt, Sharia Ibn Khalid El-Walid, opposite Isis Hotel, T/F095-376515. The oldest company in town offers trips in British-built hot air balloons that hold 8 people (US$250 per hr). Leave your hotel at 0500, total excursion time is 4 hrs, flight 45-90 mins, breakfast served in desert or leave your hotel at 1430 and return after a desert 'sundowner buffet'. Insured by Lloyds of London and full refund if weather conditions prevent flight.
A little cheaper are:
Hod hod Soliman, T095-370116, for US$200/person; and
Magic Horizon, T095-365060, for US$150. All 3 will pick you up from your hotel on the morning of your flight, just call to book.

Calèche

All over the place (you can't avoid them if you try), often in queues. Go to the one in front, when he's done, he will return to the end of the queue. E£5 should be enough to get you across town; E£20 for an hour's ride.

Cycle hire

Reliable and expensive bikes are for hire from Hilton Hotel or Mercure Inn Luxor Hotel for E£5 per hr. Cheaper and fairly roadworthy cycles can be found along Sharia Mahatta, or on the corner of Sharia Yousef Hassan and Sharia El-Karnak near the Emilio Hotel.

Horse riding

Horse riding on West Bank has become popular, usually passing through villages and some monuments towards the mountains (E£20 per hr, E£100 per day). Camel and donkey excursions are also possible.

Motorcycles

Motorcycles (E£50-60 per day) are available for hire from some bike shops and hotels, ask around or try the Sherif.

Swimming

An exceptionally important activity after a hot day's temple exploring, especially in the summer. An impressive and brand new Olympic Pool, the highlight of a government sponsored sports club, will soon be open to foreigners for E£9 per day. Find it along the corniche between the Meridian and Sonesta St George. It also has a large children's pool. For an extra fee, you can use the health club. Additionally, most hotels with pools offer day use for a fee. On the cheaper (murkier and smaller) end, try the New Radwan, Shady or the Windsor hotels, all for E£10 per day. The Sheraton, and Pyramisa Isis hotels charge E£20 per day. Club Med requires a minimum charge of E£40 to enjoy its beautiful Nile-side pool.

Tour operators

Most travel agencies and tour operators are concentrated on the corniche around the Old Winter Palace and the tourist information office. The lesser-known agencies often offer the best deals.

Abercrombie and Kent, Sharia Sayed Youssef, T095-370444.

Eastmar Travel, Corniche El-Nil, **Old Winter Palace**, T095-373513.

Misr Travel, Corniche El-Nil, also near **Winter Palace Hotel**, T095-373460.

Nawas Tours, by the tourist office, T095-370701/2. A cheaper local agency selling Hurghada-Sharm ferry tickets.

Thomas Cook, Corniche El-Nil, near Winter Palace Hotel, T095-372407.

Transport

NB Check all transport times with great care – timetables are often a printed figment of someone's imagination.

Air

Egyptair, in Winter Palace Hotel, T095-380580, 380588, offers frequent daily flights, particularly in the winter high season, to **Cairo** (US$116 one-way), **Aswan** (US$50 one-way), and **Abu Simbel** via **Aswan** (US$140 Aswan-Abu Simbel return). 3 flights a week go to **Sharm El-Sheikh** (US$100 one-way). Fares change depending on the season. Book your tickets well in advance. There are also several weekly charter flights to/from European cities including **London**, **Paris**, **Frankfurt** and **Brussels** with Egyptair and several European carriers. **Airport information:** T095-374655.

Airline offices EgyptAir, T095-380580. **Luxor international airport**, T095-374655.

Bus

Local Microbus: a cheap (25p) and easy way to get across town and to the Karnak Temple. Call out your destination to microbuses passing by. A popular route, Sharia Karnak-Sharia Mahatta-Sharia Televizion, includes the train station to Karnak temple. Microbuses with a yellow sign on the dashboard should be bound for Karnak Temple.

Long distance The buses leave from the station behind Luxor Temple, T095-372118. Reserve tickets in advance at the station. Convoys are sometimes necessary for foreigners travelling around Upper Egypt by bus. Currently, there is 1 bus daily to **Cairo** at 1900 (10 hrs, E£60). 1 bus daily to **Dahab** at 1700 (14-17 hrs, E£100) via **El-Tur** (E£85) and **Sharm El-Sheikh** (13-16hrs, E£90). 1 bus daily to **Port Said** at 2000, via the **Red Sea Coast** (E£63). 8 buses per day (from 0630 to

2000) go to **Suez** (8 hrs, E£45-50) via **Qena** (1 hr, E£3), **Safaga** (3 hrs, E£12-18) and **Hurghada** (4 hrs, E£15-21). Buses in the early morning are the cheapest and they go up in price throughout the day. 5 daily buses to **Aswan** 0715, 0930, 1130, 1400, 1430, 2000 (4 hrs, E£9.50) via **Esna**, **Edfu** and **Kom Ombo**. There are 2 buses per day to **El-Balyana** (**Abydos**) leaving at 1030, 1315 (3 hrs, E£7).

Convoys From Luxor to **Aswan**, 3 convoys daily leaving to **Hughada** (via **Dandera** and **Abydos**) at 0700, 1100, 1500. 3 convoys daily leaving at 0800, 1400, 1800 to **Aswan** (via **Esna**, **Edfu** and **Kom Ombo**). More convoys may be added as tourism increases. Hours and times change often. Check with tourist information or the train station for the most current schedules.

Ferry

Feluccas Are numerous on this most beautiful stretch of the Nile. Travel is limited to the southward direction, but this also has the most attractive scenery. Sunset is the best time to ride but bring a sweater and protection against mosquitoes (E£20 per hour if you're a hard bargainer). The most popular local sail takes you around the nearby **Banana Island**, lets you off for an hour to explore and brings you back. The trip takes about 3 hrs. *Feluccas* are available as you walk down Corniche El-Nil. For longer *felucca* trips, it's better to start from Aswan and head north with the current; otherwise, you could be waiting days for the wind to blow.

Taxi

Local Taxis congregate around the train station and can easily be hailed from all major thoroughfares; E£5 to get anywhere in town; E£15-20 to the airport.

Long distance **Private taxi**: sample charges: E£150 to **Aswan** with stops in **Esna**, **Edfu** and **Kom Ombo**; E£250 round trip to **Dendera** and **Abydos** (requires convoy). **Service taxi**: from the terminal just off Sharia El-Karnak, half way between the Luxor town centre and Karnak temple, these are quicker and more convenient than trains or buses but they may be required to travel with convoys if carrying foreigners long distances.

Train

Foreigners are technically restricted in their choice of trains. (Train information: T095-370259, office hours 0900-1400, 1700-2000.) To **Cairo**, there are 3 'secure' trains per day, all with a/c and restaurants on board. The 1st class service on the Cairo trains offers plenty of leg room and is a pleasant way to see the Egyptian countryside. 2nd class is comparable to coach class in an aeroplane. It is essential, particularly in the high winter season, to reserve your seat at the station a few days before you travel. 1st/2nd class trains to **Cairo** (10 hrs, E£62/35; 30% discount for students with ISIC) leave daily at 0915, 2115, 2310. If you are travelling as a family or group, you can buy 4 seats (E£60/each) in a Nefertiti Cabin (which seats 6 privately) and the other 2 won't be sold. The 0915 Cairo-bound 1st/2nd class train stops at **El-Balyana** (**Abydos**, 3 hrs, E£28/E£13), **Sohag** (3 hrs, E£26/16), **Assiut** (4 hrs, E£36/22) and **Minya**. There is 1 daily 2nd class direct train to **Alexandria** at 1530 (16 hrs, E£28) but it stops absolutely everywhere en route. Better to take a train to Cairo and switch as trains run almost every hour between Alexandria and Cairo. 1st/2nd class trains to **Aswan** (3 hrs, E£30/21) leave daily at 0715, 0930, 1720 and stop in **Esna** (1 hr), **Edfu** (1 hr) and **Kom Ombo** (2 hrs). There is a 3rd class train to **Kharga** that leaves every Thu around 0700 (E£10). Privately-run **sleeper** trains (T095-372015) depart daily to **Cairo** 2130 (9 hrs, US$50, payable in hard currency only) and sometimes to **Alexandria** via **Cairo** at 2015 (13 hrs, US$53, payable in hard currency only). There are no student discounts for sleeper trains and they do not accept credit cards.

Directory

Banks Bank of Alexandria, north of Sharia Nefertiti and Sharia El-Karnak intersection on Corniche El-Nil. **Banque Misr**, on Sharia Dr Habib Habashy, Sun-Thu 0830-2100, ATM. **Egyptian American Bank**, in Novotel on Corniche El-Nil. **National Bank of Egypt**, Corniche El-Nil, just south of the Old Winter Palace Hotel, open Sat-Thu 0830-1400 and 1700-2000, Fri 0830-1100 and 1700-2000, ATM.

Internet Cafés are popping up all over the place, even on the West Bank. The going rate at present is around E£8-12 per hr. **Rainbow Net**, in the souk, look for the bright sign on Sharia Yousef Hassan, T095-387938. The oldest, cheapest, and fastest in town; E£6 per hr; E£4 per half-hour, open till 0200. **Aboudi Books** near New Winter Palace on Corniche El-Nil, T095-373390, 0800-2230, has internet café upstairs, E£12/hr, serves cheap drinks.

Hospitals Luxor International Hospital, T095-387192. **Maged Pharmacy**, 24 hr, Sharia Aly Ibn Abi Taleb, T095-370524, will deliver.

Post office Main post office (Sun-Thu 0800-1400) is on Sharia El-Mahata on the way to the railway station, T095-372037. Hotels sell stamps.

Places of worship The Holy Family **Church**, 16 Sharia Karnak Temple, holds Mass in Italian with multilingual readings each Sun at 0900 and 1800.

Useful addresses Passport Office: on Sharia Ibn Khalid El-Walid, just south of and opposite Hotel Isis, T095-380885, visas extended. **Useful telephone numbers** Fire: T180. **Police**: T095-372350. **Tourist Police**: T095-376620.

South of Luxor

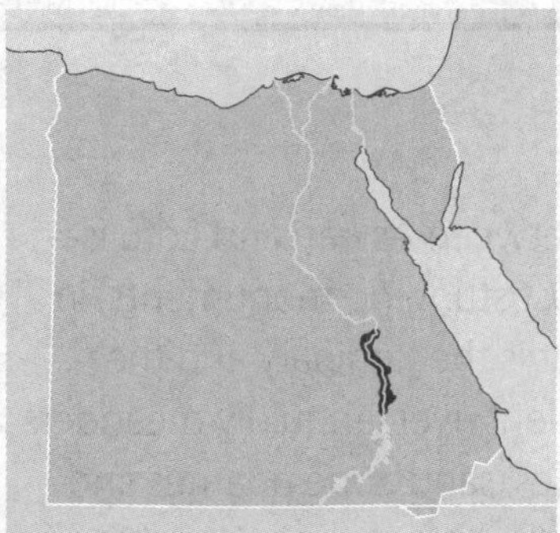

Footprint features

Introduction

Though the Nile Valley stretch between Aswan and Edfu is home to some of the world's most stunning monuments, in this region, it is the River Nile that is the luminary and the central vein. For 228 km, the ancient river languidly meanders along past Graeco-Roman temples, sandstone quarries and lush vegetation with vibrant small villages and a rich array of birdlife dotting the way. The area is best explored by boat – from the deck of a cruiser or felucca, the Nile is so close you can feel her as she mumbles and sighs, still as glass in the morning and raging like a rough sea by midday. At times the silence is so profound, one's breath feels invasive, until the next bend yields another bit of humanity seeping through the cracks of an ancient riverside temple.

Among the highlights of Uppermost Egypt are the striking Graeco-Roman temples of **Esna**, **Edfu**, **Kom Ombo** and **Philae**, all placed at strategic and commercial centres near the river. After the Pyramids and the Sphinx, **Abu Simbel**, adorned with four enormous colossi of Ramsis II (the builder), is the most famous sight in Egypt. Just 40 km north of the Sudanese border, the temple was erected as testimony to the pharaohs' might for anyone who dared approach from the south. Three millennia later, the monument's sheer size still inspires awe.

The further south one ventures, the more apparent the melding of Africa and Arabia. **Aswan**, the provincial capital, is a highlight all its own. Populated largely by Nubians, a taller and darker skinned people with a unique language and tradition, the city is among the most peaceful and laid back in Egypt. You can spend a week just quietly wandering through the streets, visiting the nearby islands, walking amid the Nubian villages and along the west bank.

★ Don't miss...

❶ **Daraw** Watch thousands of camels be flaunted and scrutinized as they have for centuries at the Daraw camel market, a key stopping point on one of the world's oldest caravan routes, page 276.

❷ **The River** Sail a *felucca*, for hours or days, on the ancient River Nile, and feel the pulse of a flow that has sustained life for millennia, page 276.

❸ **Nubia** Experience a bit of the depth and beauty of Nubia with a look at Aswan's excellent Nubian museum, a stroll through a Nubian village on Elephantine Island, and a superb meal at the Nubian House, a cliff top restaurant overlooking Aswan, page 280.

❹ **Philae temples** Visit the romantic island sanctuary of Philae in Aswan, where stands a stunning tribute to the goddess Isis, almost lost to the rising waters of Lake Nasser, but salvaged by a UNESCO-led international effort, page 288.

❺ **Old Cataract Hotel, Aswan** Enjoy a cup of tea during sunset upon the Nile-side terrace of Egypt's most famous hotel, as featured in Agatha Christie's *Death on the Nile*, page 293.

❻ **Temple of Abu Simbel** Be awe-struck by the might and ego of Ramses II at this humbling temple set amid the stark and beautiful backdrop of sapphire Lake Nasser waters and golden Sahara sands, page 299.

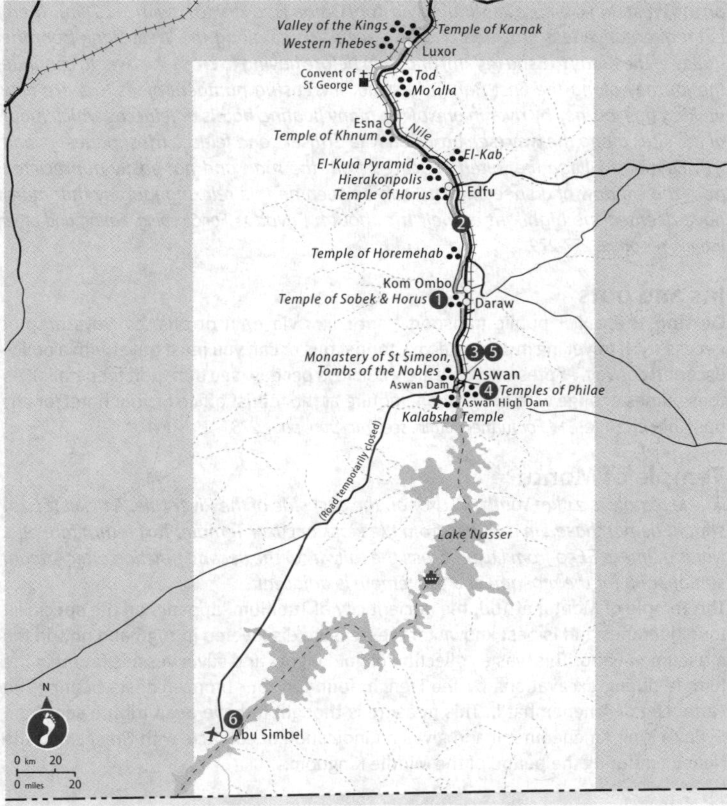

Ins and outs

Getting around Travel in Upper Egypt, at present, is fairly straightforward. With no terrorist attacks since 1997, there is little to worry about. Nonetheless, outside of the 'bubble' of Aswan, local authorities require foreigners travelling overland to move in convoys when venturing between the major sights. As such, accompanying a tour (which is sometimes just a ride) is often the easiest and most hassle-free way to go. There are many options, catering to both piaster-pinching backpackers as well as tourists with more resources see pages 296 and 311. For information on *felucca* trips on the Nile, see Essentials page 40.

Best time to visit Most people visit the area between October and March, and around Christmas in particular. There is a running joke in Aswan, 'we have the best weather in the world...in the winter.' And it's true. In December, temperatures average a lovely 30 degrees. Come July, though, they rise to a scorching 40. Be forewarned and prepared.

South of Luxor to Aswan

→ *Colour map 4*

The main road follows the River Nile along its East Bank from Luxor, past Edfu (115 km) on the West Bank, before continuing via Kom Ombo (176 km) to Aswan (216 km). There is an alternative less crowded and less scenic route along the West Bank from the Valley of the Kings to Esna (55 km) and Edfu before having to cross the river to continue the journey along the East Bank to Aswan. Increasing numbers of visitors are now making this journey by river in one of the many floating hotels or feluccas which moor at the sites along the way (see boxes on Nile Cruisers and felucca trips, pages 43 and 41). Egyptian village life, often obscured from the road and not easily appreciated from the window of a speeding car, can be seen on this relaxing journey that many have deemed the highlight of their trip though Egypt. » *For Sleeping, Eating and other listings, see pages 277-279.*

Ins and outs

Getting there For public transport from Luxor via train or bus, convoys are not necessary. If travelling in a private taxi, tourist bus or car, you must travel with a police escorted convoy. At present, there are 3 convoys per day (see transport for details). As these times change with the season, inquire at the tourist office or your hotel for any possible changes. » *For further details, see Transport, page 278.*

Temple of Montu

ⓘ *The temple is 21 km south of Luxor on the east side of the River Nile. A ticket (E£20) should be purchased in advance from the kiosk at Luxor Temple. Taxi return fare plus waiting time is E£50 from Luxor. Cross the railway at the second junction after Armant station, aim for the mosque and the temple is adjacent.*

The Temple of Montu, at Tod, the ancient city of Tuphium, appears on the specialist tour itineraries and is best known for the treasure discovered in 1936 and now in the museum in Cairo. This was a collection of gold ingots and silver vessels found in the temple during excavations by the French, found in four bronze chests bearing the cartouche of Amenemhat II. This treasure is thought to have been tribute sent from Syria to King Amenemhet II and gives an indication of contacts with Greece and the Near East during the period of the Middle Kingdom.

The original building, a mud brick chapel, was constructed here in the Fifth Dynasty. A granite pillar bearing the cartouche of King Userkaf of that time was found here but the main temple to Montu (god of war) was constructed consecutively by Mentuhotep II, Mentuhotep III and Senusert I (2050-1928 BC). Only fragments of this structure remain. Tuthmosis III (1504-1450 BC) erected a barque shrine for Montu that has undergone much rebuilding. Many of the blocks from here were recycled – to build the nearby church to the east of the site. Ptolemy VIII built the new temple (170-145 BC) and a Kiosk was added later in the Roman period.

Mo'alla Cemetery

ⓘ *Before visiting this site buy your tickets at the kiosks on the West bank, at the Luxor Museum kiosk or be prepared to pay an informal fee of some E£20 to the guardian. Travelling from Luxor, after the Nagga Abu Said station take the first turning left, cross the bridge over the canal then take the unsurfaced track which swings left towards the cliffs and the cemetery.*

There are rock-cut tombs in the cemetery of Mo'alla on the east bank 40 km south of Luxor dating from the First Intermediate period. Four tombs are located here, cut into the cliffs. All entrances face the west and the River Nile.

The tomb of Ankhtifi (1) Ankhtifi was one time governor of the area between Edfu and Armant. He was a very important man in his time and noted for feeding the people in neighbouring areas during a time of famine. The tomb is of slightly irregular shape and cut directly into the rock. On entry there is a rectangular chamber which originally had 30 pillars in three rows of 10. The chamber is 6 m wide and 20 m long and shaped to fit in with the harder veins in the rock strata. Some of the pillars have disappeared though it is clear that a number of pillars were round and others hexagonal in form. Most pillars are decorated with fine plaster work and those pillars near the doors carry the best examples of coloured hieroglyphs.

An amusing fishing scene on the wall immediately to the right of the entrance door shows a huge fish being caught by spear. There is also a small picture of the deceased and his beautiful wife in very good condition about 50 cm square. There are other interesting scenes of daily life, one on the wall facing the entrance with lines of animals carrying food to relieve a local famine and another with a line of spotted cattle to indicate Ankhtifi's wealth. A burial chamber lies at a lower level in the centre rear of the main hall. Much of the roof has been hidden by recent protective material.

Tombs 2 and 3 These comprise small chapels cut into the rock. No 3 is about 5 m square with a burial chamber to the left and a little off centre. Very little decoration remains – mind your head as you go down into the chambers!

The tomb/chapel of Sobekhotep (4) This monument to another regional governor lies a short way to the north in the cemetery. It is entered (or seen into) via a metal door. There are vestiges of decoration on the door jamb but the best known decoration is on the back wall where there are representations of trees and a man taking animals as offerings. The three pits inside the grill have over them on the left a picture of the owner in full size carrying a staff and on the right a scene with eight ladies. The three pits inside are cut some 600 mm x 300 mm x 300 mm deep with burial chambers under the rock face.

Convent of St George

Half-way between Tod and Mo'alla on the other side of the River Nile to the edge of the desert is the Convent of St George. It is not easy to miss as the surrounding walls are about 2 m high. The annual feast day is celebrated in November when thousands of pilgrims, including the Bishop of Luxor, attend. The main church which has 21 domes also has six altars dedicated (from north-south) to St Pachom, St Mercurius, The Virgin Mary, Saint George, Saint Paul of Thebes and Saint Michael.

Esna

This small market town lies about 55 km south of Luxor on the West Bank of the Nile. Besides its Temple of Khnum, it's mainly known for the sandstone dam across the river, built in 1906 at about the same time as the first Aswan dam. Today cruise ships and barges usually have to queue for a number of hours for their turn to pass through its locks. The town and the temple are certainly worth a couple of hours' visit.

The **Temple of Khnum** ⓘ *daily 0700-1800, E£10, students E£5, service taxis and buses stop about 10 mins' walk from the temple which is in the centre of town, walk to the river and then south along the corniche to the ticket kiosk, the railway station is in the centre of town and it's a short walk or calèche ride from here to the temple*, lies partially exposed in a deep depression in the centre of town. The excavation began in the 1860s but did not continue because the area above was covered in houses. Over the centuries since its construction the annual Nile flood has deposited 10 m of silt over the temple site so that all that is visible today is the **Hypostyle Hall**. The part of the temple that can be seen today is Ptolemaic/Roman and was built on the foundations of a much older shrine which was also dedicated to the ram-headed deity Khnum. He was believed to have created man by moulding him from River Nile clay on a potter's wheel. Later, when Amun became the principal deity, Khnum's image changed and, in conjunction with Hapy, he came to be regarded as the guardian of the source of the River Nile.

The hypostyle hall's **Outer Façade** is decorated from left to right with the cartouches of three Roman emperors Claudius (AD 41-54), Titus (AD 79-81) and Vespasion (AD 69-79) (1, 2 and 3). Above the entrance, at the very top, on the lintel, is the winged sun disc. Inside the tall hall 18 columns with capitals of varying floral designs support the **Astronomical Ceiling** which, although once a beautiful and complex spectacle, is barely visible today because it was blackened by the wood fires of a Coptic village once housed within the temple. In places various deities and animals, including winged dogs, two-headed snakes and the pregnant hippo-goddess Taweret (see background page 553) can be seen intermingled with signs of the zodiac. Enter and turn left passing a tiny enclosed space built into the walls (4), perhaps the doorkeeper's chamber. In the first corner the pillar is decorated with rams (5) and the side wall on the second register Roman emperors Septimus Severus (he is second from the left), Caracella and Greta making offerings to Khnum (6). At the back, opposite the entrance, the walls of the original Ptolemaic temple (7) are incorporated in this hypostyle hall. The hall's columns are inscribed with texts detailing the temple's various festivals. On the lighter side look out for the cross-legged pharoah (8), frogs on top of the capital (9) representing the goddess Heqet (see page 548) and a god being offered a laurel wreath (10) which shows Greek influence. On the right-hand wall pharoah with Horus and Khnum netting fowl and demons is illustrated (11) and in the last corner the column has countless crocodiles (12). Around the northern outer walls at the back of the temple are texts of Marcus Aurelius (AD 161-180) (13) while Titus, Domitian and Trajan slay their Egyptian enemies on the eastern and western outer walls (14 and 15).

The **Convent of the Holy Martyrs** lies 6 km to the southwest of Esna. It commemorates 3,600 Christians who refused to sacrifice to the Roman gods and died for their faith c249-251. The

Temple of Khnum

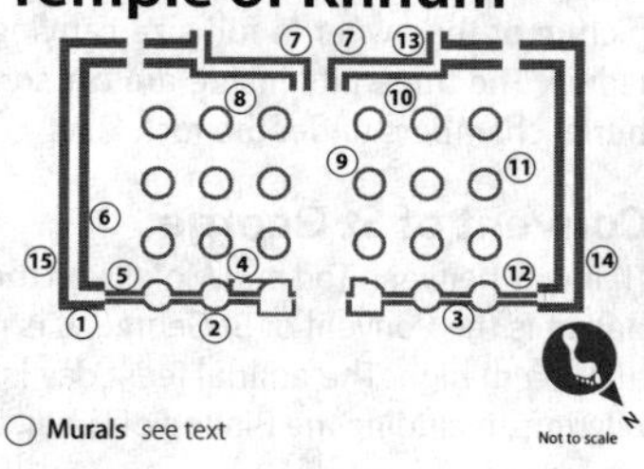

7 7 13 8 10 9 11 6 15 5 4 12 14 1 2 3

○ **Murals** see text

Not to scale

N

Horus – The First Living God-King

Horus who was originally the Egyptian sky-god and falcon-god was later identified as the son of Osiris and his sister Isis. He subsequently avenged his father's murder by his uncle Seth in an epic fight at Edfu in which Horus lost an eye and Seth his testicles. It was not until Isis intervened that Horus prevailed as good triumphed over evil. Osiris pronounced his judgment by banishing Seth to the underworld and enthroning Horus as the first living god-king. Each Pharaoh claimed to be an incarnation of Horus and the annual Festival of the Coronation, at Edfu's now destroyed Temple of the Falcon in front of the main temple's grand pylon, followed by a crowning ceremony in the temple's main forecourt, symbolized the renewal of royal power.

older church in the complex dedicated to the martyrs was first built in 786 but has been destroyed and rebuilt on a number of occasions. It has some interesting wall paintings. The **Church of the Holy Virgin Mary** is of more recent construction (1931).

El Kab

The mud-brick walls of El-Kab, 32 km south of Esna, stand on the western bank of the River Nile. The ramparts are very solid and in places measure 12 m thick. The important ruins here are the **Temple of Thoth** built by Ramses II and the later **Temple of Nekhbet** the vulture goddess who was worshipped on this site. The inclusion of stone blocks from earlier periods in the building of these temples is an example of pharaonic recycling. Cut into the hills to the west of the old town are a number of **tombs**. ⓘ *The keys are held in Edfu (below), so make arrangements to visit in advance.*

Edfu and the Temple of Horus

ⓘ *Summer 0700-1800, winter 0700-1700. General entry E£20, student entry E£10. The temple is west or inland from the river along Sharia Al-Maglis and can be reached by calèche, many of which are drawn by emaciated and badly treated horses, or taxis which await the arrival of the tourist cruise ships. Taxis and pick-ups to the temple linger around the train station, just across the Nile bridge;the service taxi terminal at the town-side west end of the bridge is a 20 minutes walk or short ride to the temple. Inter-city buses drop their passengers on Sharia Tahrir or the parallel Sharia El-Gumhoriyya about half way between the bridge and the temple.*

Edfu, 60 km south along the West Bank almost equidistant from Luxor (115 km) and Aswan (106 km), is the site of the huge, well-preserved Ptolemaic cult Temple of Horus the most complete in the whole of Egypt. Edfu Temple (as it is also known) was the focus of the ancient city of Djeba. It was begun in August 237 BC by Ptolemy III and took 25 years to complete, with the decoration taking another five years. Because of a revolt in Upper Egypt it was not until February 176 BC that the opening ceremony took place under Ptolemy VII, and further additions were still being made into Ptolemy XIII's reign. Like Esna's Temple of Khnum, it was completely buried (except for its huge pylons) under silt and sand and its top was covered with houses until the 1860s but, unlike Esna, the whole site has been excavated. It had been severely damaged by the town's inhabitants and it was not until 1903 that the excavation work was finally completed.

The whole complex is entered from the ticket office in the northwest corner at the rear of the main north-south axis temple, which one walks along to reach the **entrance** at its south end. Just to the southwest is the small east-west axis birth house called the **Mammisi of Horus**, which was built by Ptolomy VII and VIII. The inner sanctuary is surrounded by a peristyle of foliage capped columns, topped by pilaster capitals showing the grotesque figures of Bes, god of joy and birth. His frightening appearance was thought to dispel evil and to protect women in labour (see page 546). Each year there is a performance of the miracle play which represents Horus' birth at the same time as the birth of the divine heir to the throne of Egypt. At the southwest corner of the birth house there are reliefs of Isis suckling Horus (in infancy) and an erect Amun. On the pillars of the colonnades in the forecourt Hathor beats a tambourine, plays the harp and suckles Horus (in adolescence).

The main temple is entered through a gateway in the huge **Grand Pylon** on either side of which are grey granite statues of the hawk-god Horus. A tiny Ptolemy stands in front of him. On the left outer wall of the pylon Ptolemy XIII (88-51 BC), who was also known as Neos Dionysus and had usurped the pylon from its original builder Ptolemy IX (170-116 BC), is shown killing his enemies before Horus and Hathor (1). The right wall has the same illustration in mirror image. Above are carved decorations and niches which were cut into the walls, as supports for the flagpoles. On its inner wall in the upper register the barge of Horus tows the barque of Hathor (2) and on the other side (3) the waterborne procession continues in the lower register. (No sails are required as the journey is downstream.) Celebrations for the gods' arrival are seen at (4). The pylon also contains the usual guardians' quarters and stairs up to the roof.

The giant **Court of Offerings,** at a slightly lower level, is lined with 32 columns with paired capitals behind which, on the west side, Ptolemy IX makes offerings to Horus, Hathor and Ihy, their son (5), and on the right (east) Ptolemy X appears before the same three (6). At the north end of the court is the **First Hypostyle Hall**, built by Ptolemy VII (180-145 BC), with its 18 once brightly-painted columns supporting the roof. There are three different types of capital, repeated on either side of the hall. Before the entrance of the Hall stands another large statue of Horus, in grey granite. At the entrance to the Hypostyle Hall is the small Chamber of Ungents to

Temple of Horus at Edfu

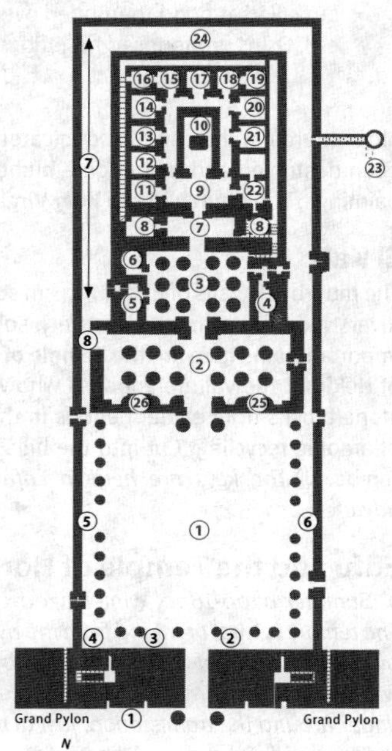

N

0 metres 20
0 yards 20

1 Court of offerings
2 First hypostyle hall
3 Second hypostyle hall/ festival hall
4 Offering hall: liquid offerings
5 Offering hall: solid offerings
6 Laboratory
7 First vestibule/hall of offerings
8 Stairs to roof
9 Second vestibule/ Sanctuary of Horus
10 Main sanctuary dedicated to Horus with altar
11 Chapel of Min
12 Chamber of Linen
13 Chamber of the Throne of the Gods
14 Chamber of Osiris
15 Tomb of Osiris
16 Chamber of the West
17 Chamber of the Victor (Horus)
18 Chapel of Khonsu
19 Chapel of Hathor
20 Chapel of the Throne of Re
21 Chapel of the Spread Wings
22 Sun Court
23 Nilometer & well
24 Passage of victory/ ambulatory
25 Library
26 Chamber of Ungents

◯ **Murals** see text

the left with reliefs of flowers and recipes for consecrations and a small library, where the names of the guests for the day's festival would be kept, to the right. Here many rolls of papyrus were found. The foundation ceremonies are illustrated on the walls of the hall.

Leading north from the hall is a smaller 12 slender columned hypostyle hall, known as the **Festival Hall**, the oldest part of the building dating back to Ptolemy III (246-222 BC) and completed by his son, where offerings entered the temple and were prepared. Recipes for offerings are found on the walls of the laboratory. These were then carried through into the **Hall of Offerings**, or first vestibule, where the daily offerings would have been made at the many altars and tables bearing incense, juices, fruit and meat. From here there are steps to the east which were used for the procession up to the roof where a **Chapel of the Disc** once stood. The stairs are illustrated with pictures of the priests carrying the statues of the gods to the roof to be revitalized before returning down a separate staircase (not safe to climb) to arrive back on the west side of the Hall of Offerings. Today all the roof offers is an excellent view of the surrounding area.

The Offerings Hall leads to the inner vestibule called the **Sanctuary of Horus**, where engravings show Ptolemy IV (222-205 BC) making offerings to the deities while others show Horus and Hathor in their sacred vessels.The sanctuary holds a low altar of dark syenite on which stood the barque and behind is the large upright shrine of Aswan granite where the statue of the god was placed. The sanctuary is virtually a separate temple within the main temple and is surrounded by a series of 10 minor chambers with doors, then immediately behind the sanctuary containing a lifesize model of the sacred barque. (The original is in the British Museum.) The chapel of the Throne of Re shows Horus with a serpent, Horus in the sacred tree and Horus with monkeys. These chambers, many of which originally served as vestries and store rooms, are better examined with a torch. Horus' defeat of Seth, who is portrayed as a hippopotamus, is illustrated in the middle of the west wall of the ambulatory (7). Note how the hippo gets smaller and smaller as the tale is repeated to the north. On the same side where the ambulatory narrows to the south the pharoah helped by gods pulls close a clap net containing evil spirits portrayed as fish, birds and men (8). There are some interesting water spouts jutting into this area, some in better repair than others, carved as lions' heads.

On the dimly-lit northeast wall of the outer corridor are the remains of a Nilometer (see Aswan, page 283) and a well.

The **Monastery of St Pachom** is in the desert about 6 km to the west of Edfu. It may be worth a visit if you are in the area – but not worth a special journey.

Kom Ombo

Kom Ombo was the ancient crossroads where the '40 Days Road' caravan route from western Sudan met the route from the eastern desert gold mines. It was also the site of the training ground for the war elephants used in the Ptolemaic army. It is 66 km south of Edfu and only about 40 km north of Aswan, and is a small East Bank town known today for its sugar refinery which processes the cane grown in the surrounding area. It is home for many of the Nubians who were displaced by the flooding which followed the construction of the Aswan High Dam. Most tourists stop here to visit the Temple of Sobek and Horus which stands on the banks of the River Nile 4 km from the town.

Kom Ombo Temple, is the more usual name given to the small but beautiful **Temple of Sobek and Horus**. ⓘ *Daily 0600-1800. E£10, students E£5. To reach the temple, leave the service taxi to Aswan at the turnoff 2 km south of Kom Ombo town from where the signposted 'tembel' is only 1.5 km away. In the town itself, buses and service taxis stop on the north-south Sharia 26th July, 300 m apart. Cheap pick-ups to the temple can be caught from behind the white mosque, one block away from the*

Luxor-Aswan road on Sharia El-Gomhoriyya. These days most visitors arrive by felucca or cruiser, both of which dock on the river bank directly below the temple.

The temple faces the Nile at a bend in the river and is unusual because it is dedicated to two gods rather than a single deity. **Sobek** was the crocodile god which, given the fact that the nearby sandbanks were a favourite basking ground for crocodiles until the construction of the Aswan Dam, was particularly appropriate. On its right hand side Sobek-Re, who is identified with the sun, his wife in another form of Hathor, and their moon-god son Khonsu are honoured. The left hand side is devoted to a form of **Horus** the Elder or Haroeris known as the 'Good doctor', his consort Ta-Sent-Nefer ('good sister') and his son Horus the Younger, who was known as Pa-Heb-Tawy ('Lord of the Two Lands'). A healing cult developed and pilgrims who came to be cured would fast for a night in the temple precinct before participating in a complex ceremony with the priest of Horus in the heart of the temple.

The present temple, like many others along this stretch of the River Nile, is a Greco-Roman construction, built of sandstone. Ptolemy VI started the temple, Neo Dionysus oversaw most of the construction while Emperor Augustus added some of the finishing touches. Its proximity to the Nile was a mixed blessing because, while its silt assisted in preserving the building, the flood waters eroded the First Pylon and Forecourt which were falling into the Nile before they were strengthened by the Department of Antiquities in 1893.

Like so many others, the temple lies on a north-south axis with the main entrance at the south end. In front of it to the west on the riverbank itself is the **Mamissi of Ptolemy VII** (180-145 BC) which has been virtually destroyed by flooding. To the east of the main temple is the **Gate of Neos Dionysus**, who is believed to have been Ptolemy XIII (88-51BC) and the father of Cleopatra, and the tiny two-room **Chapel of Hathor** which is now used to display mummified crocodiles found near the site.

With the Pylon and much of the **Forecourt** now destroyed by water erosion, one enters the main temple at the forecourt which was built by Tiberius (AD 14-37). Unfortunately only the stumps of the colourful columns, with a high-water mark

Temple of Sobek & Horus at Kom Ombo

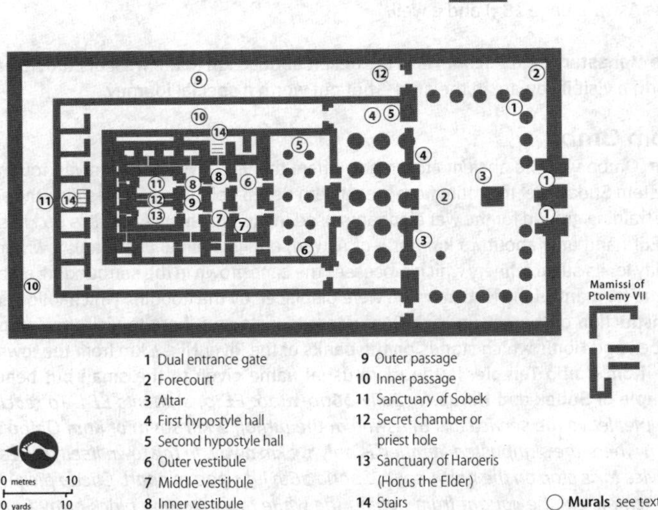

clearly visible at about 2.5 m, and a few pieces of its walls now remain. Continuing the theme from the rest of the temple the twin deities are divided so that the left-hand columns are dedicated to Horus the Elder and the right-hand ones to Sobek-Re. In the centre of the forecourt is the base of a huge square altar which is flanked by two granite basins set into the paving. On the column in the far corner (1) note the eye socket in the relief of Horus. Once this was inlayed for greater decoration. Behind this column, right in the corner (2), a staircase rose up to the roof level. At the north end is the double entrance of the **First Hypostyle Hall** with one door for each deity. On the left wall of which (3) Neos Dionysus undergoes the purification ritual overseen by Horus and on the right (4) the same ritual is overseen by Sobek. The capitals are brightly decorated with floral arrays while the bases are decorated with lilies. The reliefs on the lintel and door jambs show the Nile gods binding Upper and Lower Egypt together.

The five entrance columns and the 10 columns inside the Hypostyle Hall and its wall reliefs are attractively decorated and the curious mixture of the two deities continues. Part of the roof has survived on the east side of the Hall and flying vultures are clearly depicted on the ceiling (5). The rear walls leading to the older **Second** or **Inner Hypostyle Hall**, which has two entrances and 15 columns, five incorporated in the front wall, show Ptolemy VII holding hymnal texts before the Nile gods. Inside he is shown offering sacrifices to the god. The most striking relief is adjacent on the left of the north wall where Horus the Elder presents the *Hps*, the curved sword of victory to Ptolemy VII, while Cleopatra II and Cleopatra III, his wife and sister respectively, stand behind him (6).

This is then followed by three double **Entrance Vestibules**, each progressively smaller and higher than the last, also built by Ptolemy VII. The outer vestibule shows the goddess of writing Sheshat measuring the layout of the temple's foundations (7), while the middle chamber served as an **Offering Hall** to which only priests were allowed entrance. Look for the long list or calendar detailing the temple gods' various festivals, one for each day (9). Two small side rooms originally served as the library for the sacred texts and the other as a vestry for the altar clothes and the priests' robes. As in Edfu, a staircase originally led to the now-destroyed Chapel of the Disk on the roof.

The inner vestibule has two doors leading to the two separate **Sanctuaries of Horus and Sobek** and between the doors the gods give a Macedonian cloaked Ptolemy a notched palm branch from which the Heb Sed, or jubilee sign displaying the number of years of his reign, is suspended (9). Khonsu, who is wearing a blue crescent around a red disk, is followed by Horus in blue symbolizing the air, and Sobek in green representing the water. The sanctuaries, built by Ptolemy XIII (88-51BC), are in a bad state and are much smaller than those at Edfu. Within each was an altar upon which a portable shrine would have stood. Beneath the sanctuary are the crypts which are empty but, unusually, are open to the public.

A small **secret chamber** or priest hole lies between the two sanctuaries, in what would have appeared as a very thick wall. This chamber was connected to the small room behind and to a space above the altars.

On the inner wall of the **outer corridor** (10) is the first known illustration of instruments, including bone-saws, scalpels, suction caps and dental tools, which date from the second century AD. A seated figure of a god accepts these as offerings. While your guide may tell you that complicated operations were carried out 1,800 years ago it is most probable that these were instruments used in the mummification process. Adjacent to the left is a repeated relief of Isis on a birthing stool. Nearby the temple corridor floor is marked with graffiti which were drawn by patients and pilgrims as they spent the night there before the next day's healing ceremonies.

Also in the outer corridor, at the back of the temple (11), Horus and Sebek stand either side of a small niche/shrine now empty. Above and around are mystic symbols of eyes, ears and animals and birds each sporting four pairs of wings. Continue round

What colour is a camel?

With a deal of imagination it is possible to distinguish five different colours of camel. The white camel is the most beautiful and the most expensive as it is claimed to be the fastest runner. The yellow version is second best – and slightly cheaper. Looking for a solid, dependable beast to carry the baggage? Choose red. A blue camel, which is really black but is called blue to avoid the problems of the evil eye, is not high in the popularity stakes. And a creature that is a mixture of white, red, yellow and black is just another unfortunate beast of burden.

the corridor to (12) where the traditional killing of the enemies scene, much eroded, this time includes a lion.

In the northwest corner of the temple complex is a large circular well which has a stairway, cistern and rectangular basin which are believed to be connected in some ways with the worship of the crocodile god Sobek. The temple is particularly attractive to visit at dusk when it is floodlit and many of the beautiful reliefs are shown at their best, especially in the first and second hypostyle halls. Taking a torch with you at this time of day is wise.

Daraw Camel Market (Souk El-Jamaal)

ⓘ *8 km south of Kom Ombo. The camel market is on Sun and Mon from 0700-1400. It's most lively in the early morning. The livestock market is on Tue (there's another one in Kom Ombo on Thu, same hours). To get there, take a train (45 mins, buy ticket on board, 0600, 0730, 0845) or bus (hourly) from Aswan to Daraw, they will drop you on the main road, from there, walk north across the tracks (take a right as you exit the train station, walk 200 m, and take another right to cross the tracks), follow the road for about 3 km, after you pass the open fields and see houses, turn right and follow the sounds and scents, if you want to take a private taxi from Aswan, you will need to join a convoy, the trip should cost around E£100 return. If you're on a felucca, ask the captain to drop you in Daraw and hire a pick-up to take you to the market and back (about E£10 for your group).*

An easy stop if you're sailing a *felucca* up the Nile is the village of Daraw. Except for one of the most interesting and unforgettable camel markets in the world, there's not much to see in the dusty little town. Sudanese merchants and Bishari tribesmen wrangle and haggle with Nubian farmers and Egyptian *fellaheen* (peasants) over camels that have walked for weeks by caravan along the 40 days' road to be showcased. When they reach Abu Simbel, trucks usually bring the camels to the veterinarian in Daraw where they receive the necessary inoculations to ensure good health before heading to the market. Once in the market, camels go for E£2,000-5,000 depending on their age, sex, and general well being. Strong healthy females tend to be worth the most, for their reproductive capabilities. Only the males are killed for their meat. After being sold in Daraw, many camels end up at the camel market in Birqash, about an hour north of Cairo. In addition to milk and meat, camels are used for working the fields and carrying tourists around. There's also a twice-weekly livestock market in Daraw that attracts villagers from all over. Hundreds of cows, chickens, sheep, and goats mill about as their proud owners try to strike up a good deal.

Silsila

In between Kom Ombo and Daraw as limestone gives way to sandstone and the river narrows, the ancient sandstone quarries of Silsila come into sight. In use from the 16th to the first century BC, the quarries were the source of literally tons of stones used in temple building. Temple builders cut the huge blocks from the cliffs and transported them on the Nile to sacred sights around Egypt. You can still see holes carved into the rock where the ancient boats were moored. The cliffs are decorated with graffiti and stellae. Small temples and statues were also carved in the surrounding rock. On the west bank you can visit the colorful **Temple of Horemheb** ⓘ *entry into the temple is E£15, students E£7.50; open 0600-1700 in winter, 1800 in summer, arriving by land is a bit more of a challenge, it's really only worth the trek if you have a lot of time and a lot of interest, the closest town is Faris, from there, you will need to take a ferry to west bank where you can hire a private taxi for E£10 to bring you to the temple.* If you're on a boat and have the chance to stop, it's defiantly worth exploring, even after hours. For a bit of backsheesh, the guard will show you around. The cliffs of Silsila are particularly beautiful around sunset.

Sleeping

Esna *p270*

Esna is so close to Luxor, it's best to hop on a bus or train and find a decent place to sleep nearby but if you're really hard up for a place to stay, you could try:

F Haramin, about 1 km south of the ticket kiosk along the corniche, T095-400340. Doubles E£14. It's very basic but probably the best of three not very nice options.

(There is also **F Al Medina** in the central square and **F Dar as Salaam** closer to the temple.)

Edfu *p271*

There are no good hotels in town and most tourists are either only passing through or are staying on cruise ships which moor on the river bank from where calèches take them to the temple.

There are a few cheap hotels including:

F El-Medina, just off the main roundabout on Sharia El-Gumhoriyya, T097-711326, doubles E£40, friendly but shabby; and

F El-Magdi, further down Sharia Al-Maglis.

Kom Ombo *p273*

Kom Ombo is so close to Aswan, it is worth making the trek not to stay here. If you're really desperate, there is the:

F Cleopatra Hotel, is near the service taxi depot on Sharia 26th July.

Eating

Esna *p270*

There are a few cafés and stalls sprinkled around the central square, but no real restaurants.

Edfu *p271*

In addition to the standard food stalls, there is a pricey cafeteria by the temple.

Zahrat El-Medina Restaurant, on the Corniche across from El-Medina, is a cheaper place to sit down for a bite.

Kom Ombo *p273*

Besides the small stalls which serve *fuul*, *taameyya* and *kebab*, there are a couple of cafeterias by the Nile serving meat standards.

Shopping

Esna *p270*

When the cruise ships reach the locks here the traders appear in a flotilla of small rowing boats and attempt to sell a wide variety of clothing and table clothes, etc. Goods are hurled from the small boats in a polythene bag with great accuracy onto the top deck of the ship for the purchaser to examine and then barter over the price by shouting to and fro. Rejected goods are expected to be thrown back (although these are not always dispatched with the same accuracy as they were received!). If a price is agreed and a purchase made, a small garment to act as ballast, again in a bag, is then thrown up on deck with the expectation that payment will be placed inside the package and returned to the sender below.

Edfu *p271*

The main tourist bazaar is next to the Edfu temple complex and offers a colourful selection of cheaply-priced goods, particularly *gallabahs*, scarves, tablecloths and other local souvenirs. Not surprisingly, the calèche drivers taking tourists from the cruise ships will drop you and collect you from this area.

Kom Ombo *p273*

There is a small but colourful tourist bazaar in the street below the entrance to the temple. Scarves seem to be the specialty here and bargaining with the stallholders tends to be a more relaxed and good- natured experience as you travel further south towards Aswan.

Activities and tours

Felucca trips See Essentials, page 40.

Transport

Esna *p270*

Bus

From **Luxor** to Esna and further south buses are cheap and frequent but crowded in the morning, and they stop a lot, which makes service taxis a quicker option.

Ferry

Esna is also on the itinerary of most Nile Cruisers (see box p43), but most *feluccas* embarking from **Aswan** don't make it this far north.

Taxi

Service taxis to/from **Luxor** (1-hr, E£3), **Edfu** (1-hr) and **Aswan** (2-3 hrs). From the service taxi drop off point in Esna, you can either walk the kilometre to the temple, or hire a carriage for E£5. Depending on the political climate, be aware that police may require you to travel in a private taxi with a convoy.

Train

Virtually all trains heading south from **Alexandria** and **Cairo** to **Aswan** stop at Esna, as do northbound trains from Aswan. The station is an awkward 5 km out of town on the opposite bank of the Nile.

Edfu *p271*

Bus

Buses arriving in Edfu sometimes stop on the east bank opposite town, which requires further transport into town, again with the covered pickups (25p to the bridge, and another 25p for a pickup across the bridge). You can catch a bus out of town north to **Luxor** through Esna (2 hrs, E£5) or south to **Aswan** via **Kom Ombo** (1-hr, E£3) from Sharia Tahrir halfway between the bridge and the temple. There is also a daily morning bus to **Marsa Alam** that is supposed to leave at 0800 (3 hrs, E£8). Check with the cafés on the east bank to be sure.

Convoys

Convoys en route from **Aswan** to **Luxor** top at the Edfu temple for about an hour and carry on at 1130 and 1630.

Taxi

If foreigners are permitted to ride in them, service taxis are the quickest and simplest option. Find them at the west end of the bridge. Prices are comparable to the public buses. North to **Esna** (1-hr) and **Luxor** (2 hrs), or south to **Kom Ombo** (45 mins) and **Aswan** (1-hr).

Train

As with **Esna**, trains to and from **Luxor** and **Aswan** stop at Edfu, but the station is 4 km from town on the other side of the Nile. From the station, you can take a covered pick-up to the bridge and then another to town (25p each), or hire a private pick-up for E£5.

Kom Ombo *p273*

Bus

Buses running between **Aswan** and **Luxor** usually stop in town on Sharia 26th July about 350 m south of Sharia El-Gumhoriyya. From here, hire a covered pick-up (25p) to take you to the temple; alternatively, ask the bus driver to drop you at the road to the temple and walk or hitch the remaining 2 km there.

Ferry

If you're travelling on the river, *feluccas* and Nile Cruisers dock just below the temple.

Taxi

Service taxis north to **Edfu** (1-hr) or south to **Aswan** (45 mins) are found by the terminal on Sharia 26 July just south of Sharia El-Gumhoriyya.

Train

To/from **Luxor** and **Aswan** stop at Kom Ombo station just across the highway.

ⓘ Directory

Esna *p270*

Banks One bank open Sat-Thu 0830-1400, Sun 1800-2100, and Wed 1700-2000, 1000-1330 during Ramadan.

Edfu *p271*

Banks Sharia El-Gumhoriyya in the centre of town is open Sun-Thu 0830-1400. **Post office** Near the temple on Sharia Tahrir on the south side of the main roundabout.

Kom Ombo *p273*

Banks Next to the mosque, open Sun-Thu 0830-1400 but 1000-1330 during Ramadan.

Aswan

→ *Colour map 4, grid B2. Population: 350,000. Altitude: 193 m.*

Aswan, Egypt's southern frontier town, in its delightful river setting is the highlight of any Nile cruise. It is a stunningly beautiful, charmingly romantic, and wonderfully relaxing escape from the over-commercialization of Luxor. This is the sunniest city in Egypt, hence its popularity. It is not too large to walk around in the cooler part of the day and pace of life is slow and so relaxing. From the cool and inviting corniche, where dramatic desert cliffs merge with palm lined Nile waters, you can see the tall masted feluccas handled masterfully by a tiny crew and listen to the Nubian musicians. In the late evening you can watch the flocks of egrets skimming the surface of the Nile as they go to roost before you feast on freshly-caught Nile fish. In the early morning you can watch the sun rise behind the city and hear the call of the muezzin. With the outstanding Nubian museum, a local souk that is among the country's most vibrant and colourful, as well as proximity to several notable temples and the nearby High Dam, the city deserves more than a stopover en route to Abu Simbel. People aren't so pushy and the sales aren't as hard. The place feels ancient, enchanted. ▸▸ *For Sleeping, Eating and other listings, see pages 292-298.*

Ins and outs

Getting there The railway station is at the north end of the town, about 5 mins' walk from the corniche heading west, or 5 mins' walk from the heart of the souk, heading south. Most mid-range and higher end hotels are by the Nile. Budget hotels are scattered around the railway station and in the souk. The inter-city taxi depot is nearby, just one block to the south of the railway station. The inter-city bus station is about 4 km out of town. To get to town from the bus station, hire a covered pickup (25p) or a private taxi (E£5). *Feluccas* and cruise boats moor along the corniche. Aswan's desert airport is 24 km south of town. There is no bus service connecting the airport and town. A hired taxi costs about E£25 for a hard bargainer. ▸▸ *For further details, see Transport, page 296.*

Tourist offices There are two tourist offices in Aswan, quite close to one another. The primary one ⓘ *T097-312811, daily 0900-1500 and 1900-2100*, is by the train station in a white domed building. Shukri Saad and his assistant Hakeem Hussein offer possibly the best and most informative tourist office in the country. They will happily assist you in navigating the area, giving you the most recent of the ever-changing schedules and prices of transport, tours and entertainment. They can also help in booking trustworthy and suitable accommodation, *felucca* trips and tours. Shukri has a million stories and quite a bit of wisdom floating around his head. If time permits, you may want to indulge in a cup of tea and some conversation.

Background

Aswan's indigenous inhabitants are the ethnically, linguistically and culturally distinct **Nubians** who are more African than Arab. Despite being frequently invaded and conquered by their northern Egyptian neighbours, the Nubians actually controlled Egypt during the 25th Dynasty (747-656 BC). Cleopatra was a Nubian from the modern-day Sudanese town of Wadi Halfa. Indeed, the term Nubian is equally applicable to the Sudanese who live along the Nile as far south as Khartoum. The later Nubian kingdom of Kush, whose capital was the Sudanese town of Merowe and which included Aswan, remained largely independent from Egypt. Having been the last region to adopt the Christian faith, Nubia became a sanctuary for Coptic Christians fleeing the advance of Islam and it remains a Christian stronghold today.

For many centuries a sleepy backwater, Aswan assumed national importance when it became the headquarters for the successful 1898 Anglo-Egyptian re-conquest of Sudan. With the 1902 construction of the first **Aswan Dam** the town became a fashionable winter resort for rich Europeans who relished its dry heat, luxury hotels and stunning views, particularly from the *feluccas* sailing on the River Nile at sunset. With the completion of the Aswan High Dam in 1970, the Nubian villages to the south of Aswan were submerged by the rising waters of Lake Nasser and many of those who were displaced joined in swelling the population of the ever expanding town. Despite the subsequent construction of a number of heavy industries in Aswan, to take advantage of the cheap hydro-electric power generated at the dam, the town has retained its attractive charm and relaxed atmosphere.

Sights

In town

In the town itself, besides watching the beautiful sunset either from the corniche or from the terrace of the Old Cataract Hotel, it is well worth visiting the exotic **souk** which, with the exception of Cairo, is probably the best in the country. Running parallel to the corniche there are stalls selling food and a wide range of fresh produce, best bought in the morning, as well as jewellery, textiles and a host of oriental herbs and spices which are best bought after sunset.

The **Nubian Museum** ⓘ *T097-313826, winter hours 0900-1300 and 1700-2100, summer 0900-1300 and 1800-2200, E£20, students E£10*, stands on a granite hill to the south of the town on the road to the airport. If you visit any museum in Aswan, let it be this one.

The construction is of sandstone and incorporates features of Nubian architecture. There are two storeys where 2,000 artefacts trace the area's history. The colossal statue of Ramses, the remaining part of a temple at Gerf Hussein, dominates the entrance, a reminder of his positive presence in Nubia. There are 86 explanatory panels and a huge diorama. The displays include the oldest skeleton – unearthed in the southern area of Toshka. The pre-history cave depicts the first attempts at rock carvings and the use of tools. The Pharaonic period demonstrates the importance of this region to the rulers of Egypt as a gateway to the south. There are sections devoted to the Graeco-Roman, Coptic and Islamic influences to irrigation, and the UNESCO project to save the monuments.

The colourful exhibition of the folk heritage emphasizes the individuality of Nubian culture. The most common crafts are pottery and the weaving of baskets and mats from palm fronds.

On the outskirts of Aswan about 2 km along the highway south, is the **Unfinished Obelisk** ⓘ *daily 0600-1800, E£10, students E£5, you can walk the 2 km, hire a bike, or take a taxi for E£10 return*, in the quarries which provided red granite for the ancient temples. The huge obelisk, which would have weighed 1,168 tonnes and stood over

41 m high, was abandoned before any designs were carved when a major flaw was discovered in the granite. It was originally intended to form a pair with the **Lateran Obelisk**, the world's tallest obelisk which once stood in the Temple of Tuthmosis III at Karnak but is now in Rome. When it was discovered in the quarry by Rex Engelbach in 1922 the unfinished obelisk shed light on pharaonic quarrying methods, including the soaking of wooden wedges to open fissures, but shaping and transporting them remains an astounding feat. NB It's easy to combine a visit to the Unfinished Obelisk with a trip to the High Dam or the Philae Temple, see pages 286 and 288.

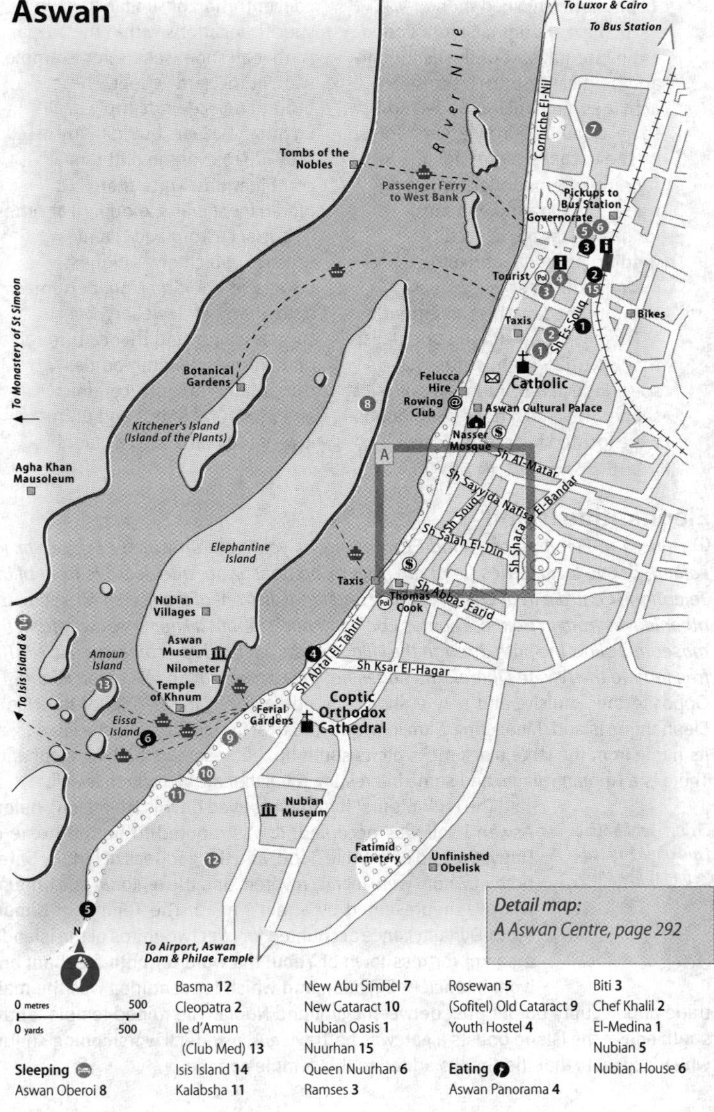

The Souk

The souk or bazaar economy of North Africa has distinctive characteristics. In Egypt a series of large souks continues successfully to exist while bazaar economies elsewhere are faltering. In Egyptian cities as a whole, such as Aswan (see Sharia Sa'ad Zaghloul), Islamic ideas and traditional trading habits have remained strong.

The bazaar originally functioned as an integral part of the economic and political system. Traditional activities in financing trade and social organizations were reinforced by the bazaar's successful role in running international commodity trade. The bazaar merchants' long-term raising of credits for funding property, agricultural and manufacturing activities was strengthened by this same trend.

There is a view among orientalists that Egyptian/Islamic cities have a specific social structure and physical shape. The crafts, trades and goods were located in accordance with their 'clean' or 'unclean' status, and whether or not these goods could be sold close to the mosque or *medresa*. Valuable objects were on sale near to the main thoroughfares, the lesser trades, needing more and cheaper land, were pushed to the edge of the bazaar. There was a concentration of similar crafts in specific locations within the bazaar so that all shoe- sellers, for example, were in the same street. These ground rules do not apply in all Egyptian bazaars but in many cases they are relevant in different combinations. Thus, there is a hierarchy of crafts, modified at times by social custom and Islamic practice, which gives highest priority to book-making, perfumes, gold and silver jewellery, over carpet-selling, and thence through a graded scale of commodities through metal-work, ceramics, sale of agricultural goods and ultimately low-grade crafts such as tanning

Elephantine Island

ⓘ *Felucca to Elephantine Island E£10 per hr as your captain waits; E£15 per hr for sailing; or two local ferries (25p) run from 0600 until 2400, one docks in front of the Telephone Centrale near Egypt Air office and lands in front of the Aswan Museum, the other leaves from in front of Thomas Cook and docks about a kilometre away from the museum. Follow the path through the village to the left until you come upon it. NB The free ferry to the Aswan Oberoi Hotel does not give access to the rest of the island.*

Opposite the corniche and only a short ferry ride away in the middle of the Nile is Elephantine Island. Measuring 2 km long and 500 m at its widest point, the island gets its name from the large black rocks off its south tip that resemble bathing elephants. There is a Nubian village, and some interesting ruins that are well worth a visit.

Locals on Elephantine Island are often thrilled to accompany you though the island, share a bit of their village and practise English.

The region's first inhabitants lived on this island long before Aswan itself was occupied. It was reputed to be the home of Hapy, the god of the Nile flood, and the goddess of fertility Satet, both of whom were locally revered, and the regional god Khnum, who was represented by a ram's head. The **Temple of Khnum** (30th-Dynasty) once accounted for over two-thirds of the island's 2 sq km fortress town of **Yebu**, the word for both elephant and ivory in ancient Egyptian and which for centuries was the main trade and security border post between Egypt and Nubia. The ruined temple, at the south end of the island boasts a gateway portraying Alexander II worshipping Khnum which suggests that the Greeks added to this temple complex.

The island has a number of less impressive ruins, and temples have been built here for four millennia. Make time when visiting to take advantage of an outstanding high viewpoint from which to enjoy the beautiful panorama of the Aswan corniche to the east, including the picturesque Old Cataract Hotel, the islands and the River Nile itself. To the west the Aga Khan Mausoleum (see page 283) is clearly visible and to the south, look for the pink fronted Hotel Amun, set on its own island amongst palm trees and exotic gardens.

You can see a **Roman Nilometer** if you take the pathway southwards to the left of the museum entrance. This fascinating device, rediscovered on the southeast tip of Elephantine Island in 1822, was designed to measure the height of the annual River Nile flood. This enabled the coming season's potential crop yield to be estimated and the level of crop taxation to be fixed. Besides Roman and very faint pharaonic numerals, there are also more recent tablets inscribed in both French and Arabic, on the 90 walled stairs which lead down to a riverside shaft.

The **Aswan Museum** ⓘ *daily winter 0800-1600, summer 0800-1700, E£10, students E£5 and E£10 for camera, price includes entrance to the museum, view of ruins and walk down steps of the nilometer*, was established in order to display relics salvaged from the flooded areas behind the Aswan dams, which is ironic because the villa and gardens originally belonged to Sir William Willcocks, designer of the first Aswan Dam. Its brief was subsequently expanded to act as a museum of the region's heritage. It offers a spread of exhibits of phaoronic material, Roman and Islamic pottery, jewellery, and funerary artefacts. The arrangement is logical and names are clear. When the Nubian material is transferrred to the newly open Nubian museum there will space to display the wealth of material found on Elephantine island itself. The ground floor is arranged in chronological order with items from the Middle and New Kingdoms, including pottery, combs and some jewellery, while the basement displays a series of human and animal mummies and an impressive gold sheathed statue of Khnum.

In addition to the museum, Nilometer and temple ruins, there are several small **Nubian villages** in the middle of Elephantine Island. A wander here gives a taste of contemporary life, albeit not much changed in centuries. The spirit and generosity of the Nubians becomes fast apparent. If you're lucky, you may be invited into someone's home. And if not, you can always visit Mohammed (T097-315509) at his beautiful **Nubian House**, (aka the crocodile house, since two little crocs live in a bucket by the door) next to the museum (ask anyone to point it out). Decorated with traditional Nubian handicrafts, you can enjoy a cup of tea or a bite to eat on his colourful roof.

Kitchener's Island

ⓘ *Daily from 0800 until sunset. E£10, accessible by felucca.*

Kitchener's Island lies north of the larger Elephantine Island and, originally known as the 'Island of Plants', it has a magnificent **Botanical Garden**. The beautiful island was presented to Lord Kitchener, who had a passion for exotic plants and flowers from around the world, in gratitude for his successful Sudan campaign and the gardens have been maintained in their original style. The atmosphere on the island, which is almost completely shielded from the bustle of Aswan by Elephantine Island, is very relaxed and its lush vegetation, animals and birds make it an ideal place to watch the sunset. There is an expensive café at the south end of the island.

Agha Khan Mausoleum

The beautiful Agha Khan Mausoleum ⓘ *not open to the public*, on a hill on the West Bank of the River Nile opposite the town, was built of solid marble for the third Agha Khan (1877-1957) who was the 48th Imam of the Ismaili sect of Shi'a Muslims. He was renowned for his wealth and was given his body-weight in jewels by his followers for his 1945 diamond jubilee. As an adult he visited Aswan every winter for its therapeutic climate, having fallen in love with its beauty and built a villa on the West Bank. Until her recent death, his widow lived in the villa every winter, and erected the mausoleum on the barren hill above the villa. Its is a brilliant white marble building, closely resembling a miniature version of the Fatimids' mausoleums in Cairo, with virtually the only hint of colour being the fresh red rose that was placed daily on the sarcophagus by his wife. Outside, the views of the desert and of Aswan across the Nile are particularly breathtaking at sunset.

Necropolis of the nobles

ⓘ *The tombs are open from 0700-1600 (-1700 in summer). E£12, students E£6. Access by felucca or ferry (25p) from the dock in front of the governate building in the northern part of town, the ticket office is above the ferry landing. Wear a strong pair of shoes and take a torch. There is a guide on duty to show the way, unlock the tombs and turn on the electric lights, his services are part of the entry fee but a small tip is also a good idea.*

The Necropolis of the Nobles at Qubbet Al-Hawwa (dome of the wind) is further north along the West Bank of the Nile (west being the world of the dead and east the world of the living). The riverside cliff is lined with tombs from various periods which have been discovered during the last century.

The necropolis is illuminated at night by hidden spotlights – magnificent when viewed from the Aswan side of the River Nile.

Just above the water-line are the Roman tombs, and higher up in the more durable rock are those of the Old and Middle Kingdoms. The majority of the dead are believed to have been priests or officials responsible for water transport between Egypt and Nubia. Most tours begin at the southern end with the tombs of Mekhu and Sabni. Most of the tombs are numbered in ascending order from south to north. Only the more interesting ones are mentioned here.

Tomb of Mekhu (No 25) Mekhu was a chief overseer in Upper Egypt at the time of the Sixth Dynasty and was killed while on official duties. His son Sabni mounted an expedition to reclaim his father's body and successfully returned to Aswan to give Mekhu a ceremonial burial. The tomb of Mekhu comprises two chambers, a narrow antechamber roughly decorated with family and farming scenes (1 and 2). The main chamber is cut out of solid rock leaving 18 slightly tapering columns, themselves decorated with reliefs of the family and fragments of other funeral scenes. The inner wall to the left carries a series of false doors inscribed to Mekhu. There is an offering table in the middle of this main chamber.

Also accessed from here (the original entry is blocked) is a memorial to **Sabni** (No 26) son of Mekhu. To the right of the main chamber is a large false door and a depiction of fishing and fowling from river craft.

Tomb of Sarenput II (No 31) Sarenput, who was governor or Guardian of the South at the height of the Middle Kingdom, has the largest, most elaborate and best preserved tomb in this necropolis. It is well lit and comprises two axial chambers, linked by a corridor with niches. The first hall is rectangular with six rock-cut pillars and a small granite offering table. The ceiling is decorated and there is a distinctive stripped, coloured door lintel. Steps lead to a narrow connecting corridor which has six niches with statues of Sarenput II. In the inner chamber there are four pillars with the deceased represented on the inward facing sides of each. A niche at the head of the tomb is surrounded by depictions of Sarenput and his family. In a small recess at the rear of the tomb there is an elaborate relief portraying him with his wife, son and mother in a beautiful garden.

Harkhuf (alongside No 32) (This tomb has no artificial lighting.) Harkhuf was Guardian of Southern Egypt and a royal registrar in the Sixth Dynasty. He achieved great fame as a noble of Elephantine and leader of diplomatic/military expeditions in the south and west of Aswan. His tomb-temple is modest, being made up of a (now) open entrance area with a doorway centrally placed. On this entrance wall to the main chamber, on the right-hand side, are the remains of a verbatim copy of a letter from Pepi II commending Harkhuf and, around the doorway, offering scenes. Inside there is a small rock-cut chamber with four columns, inner faces of which carry pictures of the deceased and biographical texts. On the inner wall there are two niches, the left- hand one with a false door bearing offering scenes and the right-hand one also with a false door/painted stela below which is a small offering table. An inclined shaft leads to the burial chamber, while to the left-hand side is a second passage, thought to have been used for a later burial.

The tomb-temple of **Pepinakht**, which lies adjacent to that of Harkhuf is currently closed while a German excavation is in progress.

Around Aswan

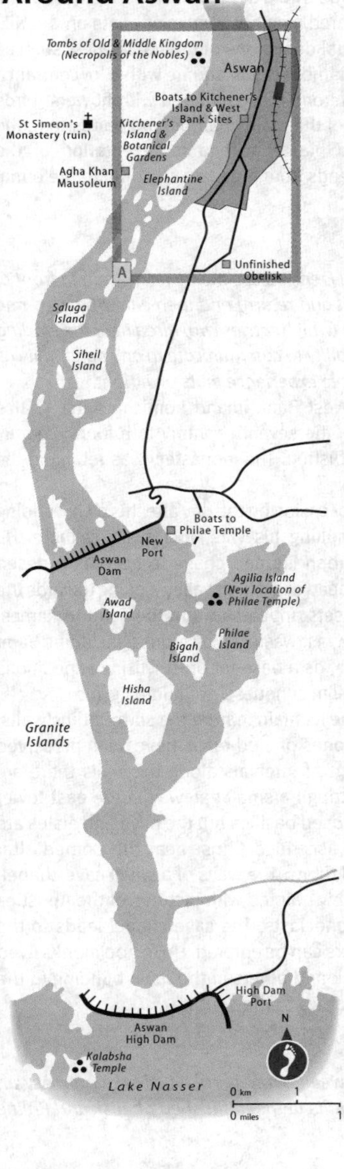

Tomb of Sarenput I (No 36) (The tomb-temple is well lit.) The grandfather of Sarenput II (in No 31), was both Guardian of the South and also the overseer of the priests of Khnum and Satet during the 12th Dynasty (1991-1786 BC). The tomb is one of the largest, and consists of three major chambers with joining corridors, but unfortunately many of the reliefs are badly decayed. You enter through a doorway decorated with excellent reliefs carved on polished limestone. On either side of the doorway are damaged depictions of a seated Sarenput I. Pass into an antechamber with six columns in a line close to the inner wall, which originally carried a finely decorated portico. On the right column there are carvings on all faces of a likeness of Sarenput. There are small niches in the side walls of this antechamber which contain representations of Sarenput and his wife. The inner wall carries important scenes in good condition. On the left is a scene of the deceased spearing fish, his wife clutching him, apparently lest he fall, and his son on the adjacent bank. Above are farming scenes with oxen. On the right of the inner wall are pictures of Sarenput, his wife, mother and family. An inner hall is entered through a narrow doorway, a modest room with four pillars. The pillar decorations have almost vanished in this room and the paintings on the plaster work of the walls have also all but disappeared. Fragments show scenes of fowling, boating and women at work. A narrow corridor has been cut into the west wall rising a little to the small burial chamber with two columns. In this room is a niche and shrine for Sarenput. Two breaks in the rock in the walls of this chamber have no access.

Tomb of Ka-Gem-Em-Ahu To the north of these tombs is a separate tomb-temple, to Ka-Gem-Em-Ahu, reached by a sandy path. Ka-Gem-Em-Ahu was the high priest of Khnum in the late New Empire. His tomb was discovered by Lady William Cecil in 1902. The outer courtyard measures 10 m wide with a depth of some 7 m. Most of the plaster work has been lost from this six-pillared area but scenes of boats on the Nile can still be made out with one or two residual depictions of funeral scenes, such as the weighing of the heart. The main tomb chamber is 7 m square with a low entrance doorway and four pillars. The ceiling is quite ornately decorated with flowers, birds and geometric designs. Although the walls of the main chamber are quite plain, the left-hand side inner pillar carries painted plaster with a representation of the deceased and his wife. A sloping passage leads from the main chamber to the burial chamber below which is difficult to access.

Monastery of St Simeon

ⓘ *Daily from 0700-1600 (-1700 in summer). Free. Accessible by ferry (from in front of the Governate building, or felucca (E£30 wait and return) and then either by a 20-min walk through soft sand or a 10-min camel ride (which carries two) hired near the landing stage. The guide here is well known for his ability to communicate to any nationality as he practically mimes his account, a memorable experience in its own right.*

This desert monastery, which lies on the West Bank inland from the Agha Khan's Mausoleum, was founded and dedicated in the seventh century to a fourth-century monk Anba Hadra, who was later ordained bishop. The monastery was rebuilt in the 10th century.

Following an encounter with a funeral procession on the day after his own wedding Simeon decided, presumably without consulting his wife, to remain celibate. He became a student of St Balmar, rejected urban life and chose to become a desert hermit. The fortress monastery stands at the head of a desert valley looking towards the River Nile and from where the dramatic sunsets appears to turn the sand to flames. Until Salah Al-Din destroyed the building in 1173 it was used by monks, including Saint Simeon about whom very little else is known, as a base for proselytizing expeditions first south into Nubia and then, after the Muslim conquest, north into Egypt.

Although the monastery is uninhabitable its main feature the surrounding walls, the lower storeys of hewn stone and upper ones of mud-brick, have been preserved and the internal decorations are interesting. At intervals along the walls there are remains of towers. Visitors are admitted through a small gateway in the east tower which leads to a church with a partially collapsed basilica but the nave and aisles are still accessible. There is a painting of the ascended Christ near the domed altar recess. Near him are four angels in splendid robes. The walls of a small cave chapel, which can be entered via the church, are richly painted with pictures of the Apostles which were partially defaced by Muslim iconoclasts. The cave chapel leads to the upper enclosure from which the living quarters can be entered. Up to 300 monks lived in simple cells with some hewn into the rock and others in the main building to the north of the enclosure, with kitchens and stables to the south.

Aswan Dams

ⓘ *E£5 per person to cross the High Dam between 0700-1700. A taxi here from Aswan costs E£20 return, if the taxi takes you and waits at the unfinished obelisk and Philae*

The Great Dams of Aswan

Although it has since become a cliché, the River Nile really is 'the lifeblood of Egypt' and the combination of a restricted area of agricultural land and an ever expanding population has necessitated the very careful management of what limited water is available. The theory behind the construction of the Aswan dams was that, rather than years of low water levels, drought and famine being followed by years when the Nile flooded and washed half the agricultural soil into the Mediterranean, the flow of the River Nile could be regulated and thereby provide a much more stable flow of water. Unfortunately, although the two dams did control the Nile waters and thereby boost both hydro-electric power and agricultural production, the mushrooming population outstripped the gains and Egypt now imports almost half of its cereal requirements. At the same time it is now recognized that the High Dam was planned and built when the level of the River Nile was particularly high. Whether it is because of climatic change or simply part of an apparent 20-30 year cycle the volume of water reaching Aswan is decreasing and if the trend continues it may be necessary to pipe natural gas from the Gulf of Suez to generate the electricity at the giant 2,100 mw power station at Aswan.

The original Aswan Dam was built by the British between 1898-1902 and was then raised twice in 20 years to make it the largest dam in the world. Although no longer used for storage or irrigation the dam, which is crossed by the road to the airport, is now mainly used to provide local power. After the 1952 Revolution, the new leaders recognized that massive population pressure meant that a more radical solution was required both to control the waters of the River Nile and generate sufficient electricity for the new industrial sector and bring power to every Egyptian village. To finance the construction of the planned High Dam, following the withdrawal of a World Bank loan under US pressure, Nasser nationalized the Suez Canal and persuaded the USSR to help build the dam. Construction started in 1960 and was completed in 1971 after Nasser's death in September 1970.

Although it took a number of years to fill, the most visible effect of the dam was the creation of Lake Nasser. This has enabled Egypt, unlike Sudan or Ethiopia, to save water during times of plenty and have an adequate strategic reserve for times of shortage. The extra water from the dam significantly increased the area of land under permanent irrigation and allowed over one million feddans (about 400,000 ha) of desert to be reclaimed. In addition, the extra electric power facilitated the expansion of the industrial sector not only around Aswan but throughout the country.

There were, however, major environmental implications of the dam's construction because the rise of Lake Nasser flooded the homeland of the Nubians who were forced to migrate north to other towns and cities (to date they have been offered negligible compensation). Another drawback is that the lake accumulates the Nile's natural silt which used to fertilize the agricultural land downstream from Aswan. Consequently farmers in Lower Egypt are now having to rely heavily on chemical fertilizers, destabilizing the whole food chain. In view of its expanding population, however, Egypt would be in an absolutely hopeless situation without the dams.

David Roberts – painter of Egypt

David Roberts was a remarkable man whose oriental paintings brought to life Egypt and its heritage for many people in the Western world. His pictures are full of atmosphere and wonderful colour. Among the most famous are the *Temple of Dendera, Island of Philae, Nubia* and *A Street in Cairo* together with his paintings of the Temple of Ramses II at Abu Simbel.

Roberts, born in 1796, had a difficult childhood as the son of an impecunious Edinburgh cobbler. He eventually became known as a painter of theatrical scenery at the Old Vic and Covent Garden before making his name as a picture painter with items such as The Israelites leaving Egypt and scenes of his travels in Spain.

David Roberts arrived in Egypt in 1838 and spent 11 months travelling through the Nile Valley and visiting the Holy Land. He was a prolific sketcher of sites and left six volumes of lithographs of this visit, including several scenes of Cairo. Many of these and other scenes were later translated into oil paintings. Roberts returned to Great Britain where, in his absence, he had been made an associate of the Royal Academy. He lived to 69 years and produced many masterpieces based on his travels in Egypt, incidentally providing a wonderful record of the state of Egyptian monuments of the time.

There are many inexpensive cards and books with copies of his illustrations. It is certainly useful to have one with you when visiting the major sites. They show very clearly parts that have disappeared, parts that are now too high to view and give an excellent idea of the coloured decorations.

temple (around a 3-hr trip), it should cost around E£40. Note that you will also have to pay for the motorboat to transport you to and from the island of Philae, an additional E£20. Getting these prices may require some bargaining, but they are fair rates.
There are in fact two Aswan Dams but it is the so-called **High Dam**, just upstream from the original 1902 British-built Aswan Dam, that is Egypt's pride and joy and which created Lake Nasser, the world's largest reservoir. In fact the High Dam is so big (111 m high, 3,830 m long, 980 m wide at its base and 40 m at its top) that it is almost impossible to realize its scale except from the observation deck of the lotus-shaped Soviet-Egyptian Friendship tower or from the air when landing at nearby Aswan airport. It is claimed that the structure of stones, sand, clay and facing concrete give it a volume 17 times that of the Pyramid of Cheops. To help appreciate the scale and consequences of the dam's construction, the visitors' pavilion, which includes a 15 m high model of the dam and photographs of the relocation of the Abu Simbel temple, is worth a visit. Occasionally, crossing the dam is prevented for security reasons. The contrast, however, between the view of the narrow river channel looking towards Aswan on the downstream side of the dam and the vast area of Lake Nasser, almost like an open sea, as you look upstream could not be more marked.

Philae Temples

ⓘ *Summer 0700-1700, winter 0700-1600. E£20, students E£10, permit for commercial photography E£10, there is no charge for video recorders. The easiest way to get to Philae is to join one of the many cheap organized tours from Aswan or take a taxi to the dock (E£30 return) and then a motorboat to the temple. The boats seat eight people and cost E£3 per person or E£20 per private boat for the return journey including a 1-hr wait at the temple.*

Temples of Philae, Agilkia Island

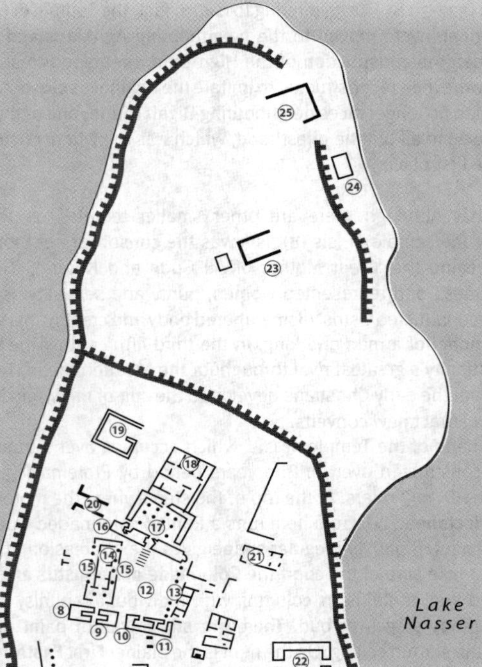

Lake Nasser

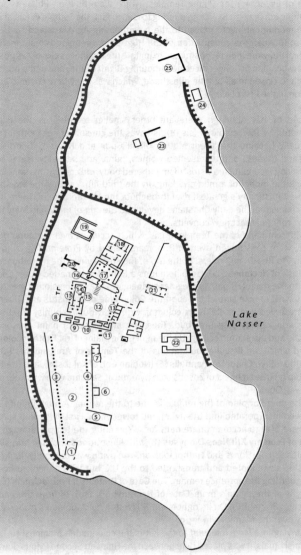

1 Kiosk of Nectanebo
2 Outer court
3 Western colonnade of Augustus Tiberius
4 First eastern colonnade
5 Temple of Arensnuphis
6 Chapel of Mandulis
7 Temple of Imhotep

Temple of Isis
8 First pylon (Ptolemy XIII, Neo Dionysus)
9 Entrance to mammisi
10 Gate of Nectanebo II
11 Gate of Ptolemy II, Philadelphus
12 Inner court
13 Second eastern colonnade
14 Mammisi (birth house)
15 Composite columns with Hathor's heads
16 Second pylon
17 Hypostyle hall
18 Inner sanctuary
19 Temple of Harendotes
20 Hadrian's Gate
21 Temple of Hathor
22 Roman Kiosk of Trajan
23 Temple of Augustus
24 Roman arch
25 Gate of Diocletian

0 metres 20
0 yards 20

 Few would dispute that among the most beautiful and romantic monuments in the whole of Egypt, are the Philae Temples, which were built on Philae Island in the Ptolemaic era (332-30 BC) as an offering to Isis. In fact, the Temple of Isis and the rest of the monuments were moved to the neighbouring **Agilkia Island** by UNESCO in 1972-1980 when the construction of the High Dam threatened to submerge Philae forever. They were then reconstructed to imitate the original as closely as possible but the new position no longer faces neighbouring Bigah island, one of the burial sites of Osiris and closed to all but the priesthood, which was the whole raison d'être for the location in the first place.

Temple of Isis Although there are other smaller temples on the island it is dominated by the Temple of Isis (8). Isis was the consort of her brother Osiris and eventually became the 'Great Mother of All Gods and Nature', 'Goddess of Ten Thousand Names', and represented women, purity and sexuality. Isis is attributed with having reconstructed Osiris' dismembered body and creating his son Horus, who became the model of a man and king. In the third-fifth century the worship of Isis became Christianity's greatest rival throughout the Mediterranean. There have even been claims that the early Christians developed the cult of the Virgin Mary to replace Isis in order to attract new converts.

Different parts of the Temple of Isis, which occupies over a quarter of the new island, were constructed over an 800 years period by Ptolemaic (332-30 BC) and Roman (30 BC-AD 395) rulers. At the top of the steps where the motorboats arrive is the **Kiosk of Nectanebo (1)**. From here runs a Roman colonnaded Outer Court which leads to the main temple. Its irregular shape gives the impression of greater length. On the west or lake side of the court the **Colonnade of Augustus and Tiberius (3)** is well preserved and contains 31 columns with individual capitals, plant shaped – papyrus in various stages of bud. There are still traces of paint on some of the columns and the starred ceiling. On the right is the plainer **First Eastern Colonnade (4)** behind which are first the foundations of the **Temple of Arensnuphis (5)** (Nubian God), the ruined **Chapel of Mandulis (6)** (Nubian God of Kalabsha), and the **Temple of Imhotep (7)** (the architect of Zoser's step pyramid at Saqqara who was later deified as a healing God).

The irregular plan of the temple is due to the terrain. A huge granite intrusion has been incorporated into the right hand tower of the First Pylon and steps to this pylon are also to accommodate hard rock. You enter the temple through the **First Pylon of Ptolemy XIII Neos Dionysus (8)** with illustrations showing him slaying his enemies as Isis, Horus and Hathor look on. The pylon was originally flanked by two obelisks, since looted and transported to the UK, but today only two lions at the base guarding the entrance remain. The **Gate of Ptolemy II Philadelphus (11)**, just to the right of the pylon's main **Gate of Nectanebo II (10)**, is from the earlier 30th Dynasty (380-343BC). On its right is graffiti written by Napoleon's troops after their victory over the Mamluks in 1799.

Arriving in a large forecourt to the left is the colonnaded **Mammisi (14)**, used for mammisi rituals. It was placed here between the First and Second Pylons due to lack of space. It was originally built by Ptolemy VII and expanded by the Romans which explains why images of Isis with Horus as a baby are intermingled with the figures of contemporary Roman emperors. In the inner sanctum of the Mammisi itself are historically-important scenes of Isis giving birth to Horus in the marshes and others of her suckling the child-pharaoh. A curiosity to note on the outer western wall of the birth house is a memorial to men of the Heavy Camel Regiment who lost their lives in the Sudanese Campaign of 1884-85. The tablet commemorates the nine officers and 92 men who were killed in action or died of disease. Look carefully at the Hathor headed columns facing into the Inner Court from the walls of the Mammisi. At far end her face is straight but at the near end she is smiling. On the opposite side of the forecourt from the Birth House is the late Ptolemaic **Second Eastern Colonnade (13)** behind which are a number of attractive reliefs and six small function rooms including a library.

The axis of the temple is changed by the **Second Pylon (16)**, set at an angle to the first, which was built by Ptolemy XIII Neos Dionysos and which shows him presenting offerings to Horus and Hathor on the right tower (some of the scenes on the left tower were defaced by the early Christians). Beyond the Pylon a court containing 10 columns opens onto the **Hypostyle Hall (17)**, much reduced in size for normal plan due to lack of space. These columns have retained few traces of their original colour although the capitals are better preserved. The ceiling in the central aisle has representations of vultures which were symbolic of the union of Lower and Upper Egypt. The rest of the ceilings have astronomical motifs and two representations of the goddess Nut. On either side of the wall, backing onto the Second Pylon, Ptolemy VII and Cleopatra II can be seen presenting offerings to Hathor and Khnum. The crosses carved on pillars and walls here provide evidence of the Coptic occupation. From the entrance at the far end of the Hypostyle Hall is a chamber which gives access to the roof. The interconnecting roof chambers are all dedicated to Osiris and lead to his shrine. Vivid reliefs portray the reconstruction of his body.

Continuing upwards and north from the chamber, linked to the Hypostyle Hall, are three rooms decorated with sacrificial reliefs representing the deities. The central room leads to a further three rooms linked to the **Sanctuary (18)** in which is a stone pedestal dedicated by Ptolemy III which formerly supported the holy barque (boat) of Isis. Reliefs portray Isis and her son surrounded by Nubian deities. The temple's exterior was decorated at the direction of the Emperor Augustus.

Hadrian's Gate (20), which is west of the Second Pylon, has some very interesting reliefs. The north wall on the right depicts Isis, Nephthys, Horus and Amun in adoration before Osiris in the form of a bird. Behind is the source of the Nile which is depicted emerging from a cavern and Hapy, a Nile god, in human form with a headdress of papyrus is shown pouring water from two jars, indicating the Egyptians' knowledge that the Nile had more than one source. Hapy is crouched in a rocky aperture (encircled by a serpent) under huge boulders representing cliffs, indicating that this is the first cataract. The south wall depicts a mummified Osiris lying on a crocodile together with another image of the reconstructed Osiris seated on his throne with his son Horus.

Smaller shrines can be seen throughout the island dedicated to both Nubian and local deities. East of the temple of Isis is the small **Temple of Hathor (21)**. Two columns depict the head of Hathor at their capital while, in a famous relief, the local deities play musical instruments. Much of the later additions to the buildings on Philae were Roman due to its position as a border post (ie extension of walls, huge gates, kiosks). The **Kiosk of Trajan (22)**, built in AD 167, further south, has 14 columns with floral motifs and stone plaques on the lintels which were intended to hold sun discs. It was never completed. Only two walls have been decorated and these depict Osiris, Horus and Isis receiving offerings from the Emperor Trajan. It is thought that the Kiosk originally had a wooden roof. From here looking southeast towards the original Philae Island it is possible to see the remains of the coffer dam which was built around it to reduce the water level and protect the temple ruins before they were moved to Agilkia. At the northeast end of the island is the ruined **Temple of Augustus (23)** and the **Gate of Diocletian (25)** which were next to a mud brick Roman village which was abandoned by the archaeologists when Philae was moved because the water had already caused such severe erosion.

Sound and light show ⓘ *Usually there are shows daily at 2000, 2115 and 2230 in summer (end Apr-end Sep) and 1800, 1915 and 2030 in winter. However, at present, due to the serious decline in tourism, there are only two shows per night, but this should increase as tourists return. Check with the tourist office or your hotel for the* *latest schedule. Mon English/French; Tue French/English; Wed French/English; Thu French/Spanish; Fri English/French; Sat English/French; Sun German/French. Cheap tours from Aswan abound, check with the tourist office or your hotel, they should also have the most recent language schedules (around E£50 per person all inclusive). If you want to go alone, tickets cost E£33, but you'll have to pay for a taxi (E£20 return) and the motorboat (E£3 if you can share with a group, E£22 on your own. Give yourself at least 45 mins to get there from your hotel in Aswan.*

Like most big temples in Egypt, Philae has its own Sound and Light Show. This one is an informative and melodramatic hour-long floodlit tour through the ruins. Some find it kitchy, and others majestic. Arriving before sunset in time for the first show can be especially memorable. Travelling out from the harbour in a small flotilla of boats, watching the stars come out and tracing the dark shapes of the islands in the river silhouetted against the orange sunset sky is a stunning prelude to the beauty of the ancient floodlit ruins.

Sleeping

Aswan *p279, maps p281 and p292*

As a primary destination for visitors to Egypt, accommodation in and around Aswan runs the gamut of quality and budget. There are 5-star resorts that controversially lay claim to their own islands and there are some very comfortable budget options around the souk. You can also find surprisingly cheap rooms on the corniche with stunning views of the Nile. Note that the prices for accommodation in Aswan especially, fluctuate significantly. In the summer, prices

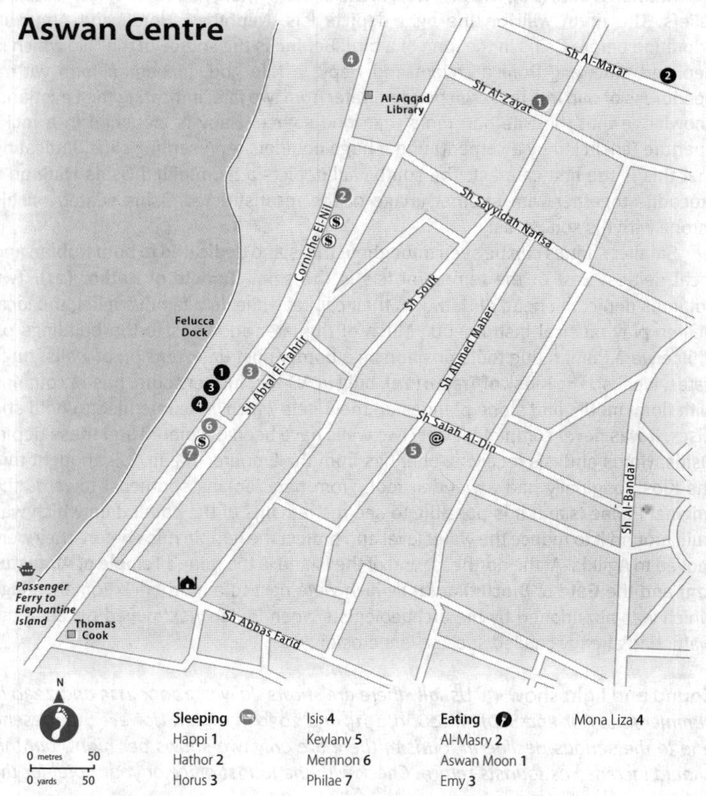

decrease up to 50%. Use the following price codes to get a general idea, but definitely inquire further. Plan to bargain. Even in mid-range and more expensive hotels, you can strike a deal.

AL Aswan Oberoi, Elephantine Island, PO Box 62, T097-314667, F323485. 160 rooms with balcony, excellent location in middle of river, reached by a free ferry which runs to/from the **Isis Hotel**. Stunning views particularly at sunset, restaurants offering Indian, Egyptian and continental food, coffee shop, bar, nightclub, health spa, gym, also tennis and pool which non-residents can use.

AL Isis Island Aswan Hotel, T097-317400, F317405. 382 rooms spread over its own island to south of town at the 1st cataract, access by private ferry. Every facility imaginable including a 9-hole mini golf course, picturesque setting, a most relaxing atmosphere, an excellent place to get away from it all.

AL New Cataract, Sharia Abtal El-Tahrir, T097-323377, F323510. 144 rooms, an unfortunate slab of a building overlooking the Nile about 5 mins' walk south from town centre, connected by a series of gardens to, and shares many facilities with, the **Kalabsha Hotel**, and the famous **Old Cataract Hotel**. Choice of restaurants, 24-hr coffee shop, pool, bar and disco.

AL Sofitel Cataract Hotel, Sharia Abtal El-Tahrir, opposite Elephantine Island, about 5 mins' walk south from town centre, T097-323434, F323510. 136 rooms, Edwardian Moorish-style hotel, universally known as the 'Old Cataract Hotel' and featured in Agatha Christie's book *Death on the Nile*. Connected to **New Cataract Hotel** and **Kalabsha Hotel**, opened in 1899. One of Egypt's oldest and most famous hotels. Large a/c rooms, some with river view, friendly service but faults due to age are reported. Full range of facilities including classic **1902 Restaurant**, nightclub, lounge bar, shops, tennis, croquet. There are minimum charges for non-residents taking drinks on the terrace (E£25) and in the Elephantine Bar (E£15). Afternoon tea, which includes sandwiches and cakes, is recommended, given these minimum charges, than morning coffee.

A Basma Hotel, Sharia El-Fanadek, T097-310901 F310907. 187 rooms, perched on Aswan's highest hill, commanding breathtaking views of Elephantine Island and Aga Khan's mausoleum. Amazing views of the sunset justify being away from the town centre. A 4-star hotel with the usual amenities, breakfast included.

A Isis Hotel, Corniche El-Nil, T097-315200, F315500. 126 rooms, a bit overpriced for quality, but excellent on the river, facing Elephantine Island. Offers a/c bungalows in a small garden with a pool and all the usual 4-star amenities, riverside terrace and restaurant.

C Ile d'Amun, Amun Island, T097-313800, F317190. 56 rooms, excellent location on its own lush island in the middle of the River Nile, opposite the Old Cataract Hotel. A free ferry operates to/from the dock in front of the EgyptAir office. A Club Mediterranée resort with top standard of food, service and facilities amid beautiful gardens.

C Kalabsha Hotel, Sharia Abtal El-Tahrir, about 5 mins' walk south from town centre, T097-302666, 302999, F305974. 120 rooms, on hill overlooking the Nile. Shares the pool and other facilities with New Cataract and Old Cataract Hotel. Built in 1963 for Russians working at the High Dam, comfortable reception and lounge but bedrooms are ugly. The starkly-furnished restaurant serves a good breakfast included in the cost of rooms.

D Cleopatra, Sharia Sa'ad Zaghloul, Aswan, T097-314001/003, F314002. 130 rooms, located centrally in the heart of the souk. Lobby is quite chic in a 3-star kind of way with a fountain, coffee shop, souvenir store, internet terminal and bar. Carpeted rooms and beds are comfortable and include balcony overlooking town and all the usual facilities (fridge, TV, a/c etc). Bathrooms are nothing special, but clean enough. Pool on top floor with juice bar and Nile view is open to non-guests for E£10/day.

E Hathor, on the Corniche El-Nil, T097-314580, F303462. Excellent location. A/c rooms are decent with clean tiled baths, if a bit cramped, but as with most budget hotels on the corniche, it's really only worth staying here if you get a Nile view. The rooftop pool is open to non-guests for E£5 per day.

E Memnon, Corniche El-Nil (entrance is from the back street). The a/c rooms are reasonably clean, if a bit tattered and the management is especially friendly. Price includes breakfast. There's a small pool on the roof.

E Philae, Corniche El-Nil next to the Memnon, T097-312090, F324089. 70 rooms with bath, a/c, TV. Dusty and a slight step below the Memnon, but could be worth staying here if you get a room with Nile view.

E-F Happi Hotel, Sharia Abtal El-Tahrir, T097-314115; F307572. 66 rooms in town centre near the Corniche behind the Misr Bank. Nile views from the rather cramped single and more spacious double rooms. Bathrooms are very clean and quite lovely. Some rooms have TV. Hotel serves beer and decent food. Guests can use the pool at Cleopatra's.

E-F Ramses Hotel, Sharia Abtal El-Tahrir, T097-304000, F315701. Hotel is a bit gaudy but has 112 small clean a/c rooms with bath, satellite TV and fridge. Unspectacular but comfortable, small balconies overlooking Nile, from some rooms you can see the Tombs of the Nobles. Breakfast included and there's a bar in the hotel. Popular with tour groups.

F Keylany, 25 Sharia Keylany, at the southern end of the souk down a side street, T/F097-317332, 323133. Probably the best budget hotel in Aswan. Super-clean, friendly hassle-free management. Rooms have a/c and comfy firm beds. Bathrooms are small but spotless with reliable hot water and toilet paper. Breakfast included. The only potential disadvantage is that it's a bit of a walk from the railway station and town centre, but that also lends to extreme quiet. Doubles E£45, singles E£30. Aswanet, the best Internet café in Aswan is located here. Get reliable access for E£6 per hr.

F New Abu Simbel Hotel, Sharia Abtal El-Tahrir, T097-306096. Set in the far northern part of town, away from the bustle and tourist centre, has a beautiful garden where you can indulge in a nice cool brew at the end of a hot day's wandering. Can be a happening place when it's crowded in town. Colourful rooms are simple and a bit dusty, with a/c, private bath, and telephone. There's a TV and pool table in the lounge. Breakfast is included. Doubles E£40, singles E£30. Across the street from a strip of quaint local *ahwas*.

F Nubian Oasis Hotel, 234 Sharia Sa'ad Zaghloul, T097-312123, F312124, Nubianoasis_ hotel@hotmail.com. Simple and comfortable budget hotel located in the middle of the souk (near the Cleopatra). Reception is on the second floor. Rooms are simple and dark with ragged carpets but have clean linens and good fans. The bathrooms have toilet paper. Some rooms on higher floors have good views of town. Lounge offers cable TV and pool table. Serve decent cheap food. Beer available on rooftop terrace with impressive views for E£6. Internet E£8 per hour. Doubles E£15, singles E£10. For private bath or a/c, add E£5. Experienced with backpackers needs, very helpful and informed staff.

F Nuurhan, Sharia Saad Zagloul (off a little side street, look for the sign or ask), T097-316069. Another cheaper option in the middle of the souk. Reasonably clean and comfortable rooms with wooden dresser, price varies depending on what you want (fan or a/c private or shared bath). Doubles with a/c and private bath E£25, E£15 without either. Includes breakfast. Discounts available for students. *Felucca* tours will be pushed on you.

F Queen Nuurhan Hotel, Sharia First of Atlas, 2 blocks from the train station to the right, T097-326069. Look for the pink building. Still feels very new. Has lift, lobby with coffee shop and pleasant atmosphere. Rooms have modern amenities – a/c, fridge, private bath. The 3rd and 4th floors have slight Nile view.

F Rosewan, near the train station on Sharia Kamal Nur Din, T097-304497, rosewan20@ hotmail.com. One of the cheapest choices in town. The rooms and lobby are quite drab and unimpressive. What makes this place worth mentioning is the artwork scattered about. The owner, an eccentric artiste, has displayed his psychedelic drawings and sculptures all around brightening up this dark dingy place. Rooms have fans and private baths that are a bit grimy. Includes breakfast. Management is delightfully friendly. Doubles E£25, singles E£12. The hotel's pizza and fatir restaurant next offers a markedly different atmosphere – clean, bright, and charming with delicious grub, and cheap.

F Youth Hostel, 96 Sharia Abtal El-Tahrir, 3 mins from railway station, T097-302313. 76 beds, overnight fee E£8, free kitchen. Usually empty, except when Universities let out and then it becomes a popular spot for Egyptian college students. There are so many more colorful inexpensive options around town, it's really not worth staying here. Open all year, midnight curfew casually imposed.

Eating

Aswan *p279, maps p281 and p292*
For expensive and exceptionally chic dining options, there's really nothing outside the resort hotels. There are, however, a number of mid-range and cheap restaurants that serve good food. In addition to the numerous *koshari* and *shishkabob* stalls, some local restaurants serve up fresh seafood with a Nubian flair. There are also a few notable *fatir* and Italian-style pizza joints, and, of course, the sit down cafeterias, some floating on the Nile, that serve up the standard chicken kebab entrées.

1902 Restaurant, in the Old Cataract Hotel. Offers international food spiced with Nubian dancers in classic decor. Even budget-conscious visitors may want to indulge in a cup of tea or a glass of wine at sunset on the terrace. It really is an institution.

Darna Restaurant, New Cataract Hotel. Serves an impressive Egyptian buffet in a restaurant resembling an Egyptian house.

Nubian Restaurant, on Eissa Island south of Elephantine, T097-302465. Offers set Nubian meals for E£55. Wine and beer are available, but pricey. The restaurant offers a free boat that leaves from the dock in front of EgyptAir. Reputably the most romantic place to dine in Aswan.

Orangerie, Oberoi Hotel (take the free ferry). Classic European-style buffet.

Aswan Panorama, on the corniche. A garden setting in which to indulge in the not very creative, but decent fare, all cooked in traditional clay pots. Beer and lots of herbal teas available.

Nubian House, on a hill behind the Basma Hotel, T097-326226. A popular intimate restaurant. Serves authentic and delicious Nubian food for E£10-20 per entrée. *Sheesha* also on offer, but no alcohol. Outdoor seating with stunning panoramic views over all of Aswan make it worth the modest trek from the centre of town, especially around sunset.

Aswan Moon, on the corniche. The most acclaimed of the floating restaurants (all next to each other). The food is OK, but it's better to come here for the Nile-side setting and colorful atmosphere. It's 10 degrees cooler by the river than on the street so it's a good place to cool off with an afternoon beer or *sheesha*. More lively at night. Sometimes there's entertainment in the summer. A good place to meet *felucca* captains and other travellers. Wine is also available.

Al Masry Restaurant, Sharia Al-Matar. Spotless a/c restaurant popular with locals and tourists alike. Offers huge portions of fish, chicken, kebab and pigeon. Meals cost E£20-25.

Chef Khalil, in the souk. Serves tasty seafood by the weight – you pick what you want. Choices include lobster, prawns and sole, and various fillet of other locally caught fish. All meals accompanied by tahina, salad and chips or rice. Entrées are E£25-40. If this tiny restaurant is full, hang out, it's worth the wait.

El-Medina, in the heart of the souk. Clean, reknowned local joint that serves up good homemade cooking. Mostly meat dishes, but they will prepare you a veggie plate. Cheap and popular among budget travellers. Meals are E£5-15.

Biti, in the main midan in front of the train station, T097-300949. A new *fatir* and pizza restaurant. A charming new restaurant with three levels, the 2nd floor has a/c, the 3rd is on the roof. Excellent pizza and *fatir*, good service; most delightful is the view over the square. Open late, good place to people watch once the sun sets.

Rosewan Pizza, next to the Rosewan hotel, near the train station. This gem of a restaurant is decorated in an Italian-style and highlighted by the work of the eccentric artist who owns it. Good cheap pizza and *fatir*. E£4 for a small simple pizza up to E£24 for family size.

Entertainment

Aswan *p279, maps p281 and p292*
There are **nightclubs** in the Kalabsha, New Cataract and Oberoi hotels among others that offer Nubian and Western floorshows when enough tourists are in town. During the winter, except on Fri, there are nightly

performances (2130-2300) by the Nubian Folk Troupe at the **Cultural Centre**, T097-323344, at the north end of the *Corniche*. Other big hotels have discos, but they always seem to be empty. An evening in Aswan is better spent wandering through the ever- thriving souk, puffing on a *sheesha* in a local *ahwa*, strolling by the Nile or taking in a beer or cup of tea in a riverside restaurant. Families tend to congregate in the midan across from the train station. There are a few local restaurants with rooftops that offer great people-watching possibilities.

A night time *felucca* sail is always a romantic way to spend an evening, especially in Aswan where the riverbanks are among the most beautiful. Keep your ears open for celebratory sounds as you may well run into a wedding party – which you will very likely be invited to join.

Shopping

Aswan *p279, maps p281 and p292*
Aswan has what is perhaps the most colourful souk in all of Egypt outside of Cairo. Musical instruments, spices and nuts from the depths of Sudan, tempting baked goods moved along by eager boys on carts, fruits and veggies fresh and dried, shimmering scarves and embroidered *gallebeyyas*, ancient stereos and local music to play in them – all of it can be found among the narrow alleys that make up the maze of the souk. Aswan is a good place to look for the often acclaimed Nubian music. Most music merchants blare tunes from their humble sound systems. If you want to listen to a particular album, just ask and they'll be happy to play it for you. There is also a duty free shop on the corniche (near the EgyptAir office), as well as a large departmental store on Sharia Abtal El-Tahrir. There are bookshops in the Oberoi and Isis arcades.

Activities and tours

Aswan *p279, maps p281 and p292*
The major hotels have good sports facilities but remember that with temperatures as high as 50°C (122°F) in the summer Aswan is not the place to be engaging in a lot of movement.

Felucca trips See Essentials page 40.
Hiking Lots of good walks to be had if the weather is suitable. A walk around Elephantine Island is a good place to start (about 2 hrs depending on your pace).
Horse riding Can be arranged on a short or long term basis. Try at the large hotels for the safest mounts.
Watersports Available at the Rowing Club on the corniche above the Isis Hotel.

Tourist transport and tour operators

In addition to the famous tour companies, all hotels organize transport to Abu Simbel and other nearby sites. Be aware that most hotels pool their guests. What that means is one person may pay E£30 for a ride to Abu Simbel in one hotel and someone else may chock up E£60 in another to wind up on the exact same bus. Your best bet is to shop around a bit and bargain hard, especially when the season is low. Cheaper places tend to book cheaper trips.

For people with more money to spend, there are numerous travel agencies and guide companies around town who are all touting for your booking. Tours and treatment don't differ much. Half-day tours usually include a trip to the unfinished Obelisk, the High Dam and the Temple of Philae. Expect to pay around US$30. Travel agencies can also organize *felucca* trips to the nearby islands if you have a group of at least three (about E£40 per person).
Try **Eastmar Travel**, Corniche El-Nil, T097-323787, or **Misr Travel**, one block behind corniche on way to railway station, adjacent to Tourist Information.

Transport

Aswan *p279, maps p281 and p292*

Air

Airport, T097-480307, the easiest way to leave Aswan is by air. (Taxi to the airport E£20.) There are regular daily flights both to **Luxor** (30 mins, US$50 one way) and **Cairo** (1-hr, US$160 one way). There are 3-4 daily flights to **Abu Simbel** – usually booked by tour groups (see transport, Abu Simbel, page 311).
Airline offices EgyptAir, southern end of Corniche, T097-315000.

Bicycles

Bicycles are becoming very popular for short distances. There are several hire shops around the souk and corniche and an especially reliable one behind the train station. Cross the railway station via the bridge, walk ahead and you'll find the bike shop on the first corner to the right, near the mosque. The going rate is E£15 per day.

Bus

Don't be misled by the lot of parked buses in town. Though once the Aswan bus station, it is now just a garage. The official bus station is 3.5 km north of the town centre. A taxi there will cost you E£5, or you can grab a covered pick-up by the train station for 25p. Before deciding to leave town by bus, note that with the authority's attempt to 'protect' foreign visitors, the unwritten rule decrees that buses leaving Aswan can only carry up to 4 foreigners, or else they have to join a convoy. Add to that the fact that bus tickets cannot be purchased in advance and it makes it a frustrating proposition for the traveller. If you arrive early enough, you may be a lucky one. Currently, there are 5 buses a day to **Abu Simbel** (see page 299) at least 4 buses go to **Hurghada** (7 hrs, 0600, 0800, 1530, 1700, E£35) 3 of which carry on to **Suez** (0600, 0800, 1700, E£50), 2 go to **Cairo** (the quicker one leaves at 1530, takes 12-14 hrs, doesn't stop in Suez; the other leaves at 1700, is a bit cheaper, and stops in Suez; both should have a/c and TV, E£60). There are hourly buses heading north to **Kom Ombo** (1 hr, E£2), **Edfu** (2 hrs, E£4) and **Esna** (3 hrs, E£6), arriving in **Luxor** (4 hrs, E£10). You can also reach **Sohag** and **Assuit** by bus. Hours, prices and even routes change constantly. For the most current bus schedule, check with the tourist office or the drivers that linger outside the garage in the middle of town. Be prepared for stops at several checkpoints when travelling by bus in

Nubian Temples cruise

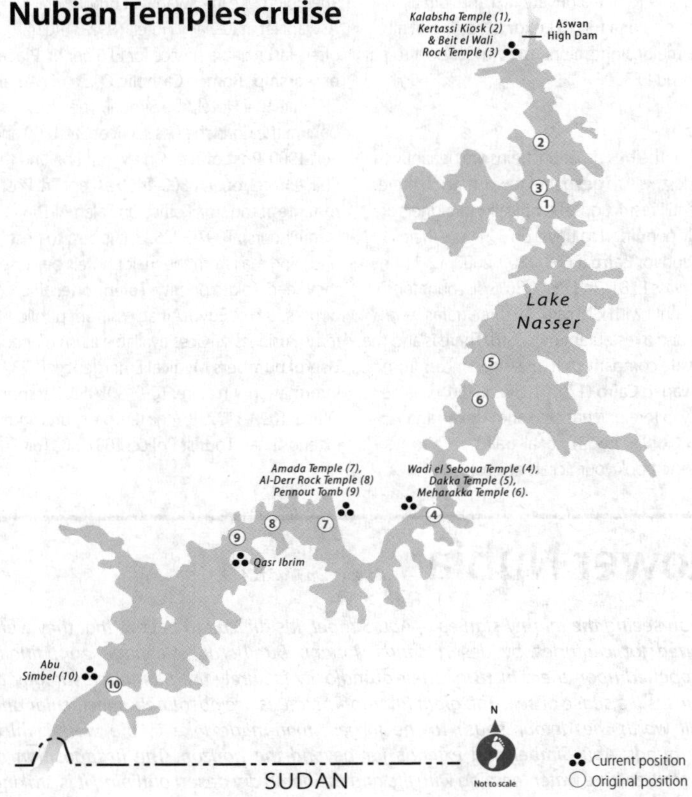

this region. Have your passport ready and don't worry, it's standard procedure.

Ferry

Feluccas Official prices, regulated by the government, charge E£15-20 per hour for a *felucca* while it's sailing and E£10-15 per hour as it waits. For example, if you sail to Kitchner Island, Agha Khan Mausoleum and Elephantine Island, and spend a couple of hours wandering around, a 3-hr trip with 1 hour of sailing time should cost around E£40-50. If there are more passengers, prices usually go up. Haggle hard. For longer *felucca* trips along the Nile, see the box on page 41. *Feluccas* can be found on Corniche El-Nil, if the men with the *feluccas* have not found you first!

Taxi

Service taxis have security restrictions and are presently not permitted to carry foreigners from Aswan. They get stopped and fined at the police checkpoint on the way out. It's possible to hire a private taxi and join a convoy. For a trip to **Luxor**, stopping at all the major sights along the way, expect to pay around E£300.

Train

Given the bus situation, trains are defiantly the easiest way to get out of town, though there are still restrictions. Technically, foreigners are only permitted to travel on 3 'secure' trains bound for **Cairo** (0600, 1800, 2000, 12-15 hrs). 1st class E£81, 2nd E£47; 30% discount for students with ISIC card. All three trains have a/c and a restaurant on board. There is also the private company that runs sleeper cars from Aswan to **Cairo** (1700, 1830; US$50, payable only in foreign currency) and **Alexandria** (1700 only; US$53). For all trains to Cairo, it's wise to book your tickets at least 1 day in advance. 2nd class trains to Cairo (13 hrs; E£47) via Luxor (3 hrs; E£15) leave at 0730, 1600, 1900, 2100; E£15. They usually stop in **Kom Ombo**, **Daraw**, **Edfu**, and **Esna**. As these trains are not supposed to carry foreigners, plan to buy your ticket on the train. Check with the tourist office or train station for the most current schedule.

Directory

Aswan *p279, maps p281 and p292*

Banks Besides the major hotels which change money, there are numerous branches of most of the Egyptian banks on the corniche or Sharia Abtal El-Tahrir. The **National Bank of Egypt**, on the Corniche, near the Memnon Hotel has an ATM. **American Express**, Old Cataract Hotel, T097-302909. **Thomas Cook**, Corniche El-Nil, T097-304011, best for Tcs. **Hospitals** **German Hospital**, on the corniche, T097-302176. **Internet** Email facilities at all major hotels and scattered all around town. The going rate in Aswan is E£6/hour. AswanNet at Keylany Hotel, T097-314074, offers fast reliable service for E£6 per hr. **Places of worship** **Roman Catholic**, 89 Sharia Abtal El-Tahir, near Hotel Abu Simbel, one block behind the Corniche has services Sat 1800 and Sun 1900. **Post office** On the road behind the Philae Hotel, open 0800-1400 except Fri. Post restante at the small office on Salah Al-Din (same hours), T097-323533. It is best to post outgoing mail from the major hotels because they seem to get priority. **Telephone**: office 2 doors south of **EgyptAir** across from public ferry. Business services available at *Isis Island*. **Useful numbers** Medical Emergency: T123. Information: T16. Fire: T097-303058. **Passport Office**: T097-312238, registers passports and extends visas. **Tourist Police**: T097-303163.

Lower Nubia

→ *Colour map 7, grid C4.*

Upon seeing the mighty statues of Abu Simbel, it's difficult to believe that they were buried for centuries by desert sands. Johann Burkhardt, see page 299, finally happened upon them in 1813. Their grandiosity is surely the ultimate testimony to Ramses II's sense of self. The giant Pharaonic statues are absolutely spectacular and well worth the detour south to the largest man-made lake in the world which surrounds Abu Simbel and extends far beyond the horizon. The juxtaposition of crystalline blue water teeming with life and the harsh dry desert outlining it is striking

Burckhardt the Explorer

The Anglo-Swiss geographer and explorer, Johann (John) Ludwig Burckhardt was born in Lausanne, Switzerland on 24 November 1784. He studied at London and Cambridge and between 1806 and 1809 lived in Syria, where he learned Arabic and became a follower of Islam, taking the Muslim name Ibrahim Ibn Abd Allah. He left Syria, en route for Cairo and the Fezzan (Libya) from where he was to attempt to cross the Sahara. Local Bedouin spoke of the ruins of a 'lost city' in the mountains. Knowing that the legendary lost city of Petra was in the vicinity of Aaron's tomb on Jebel Harun he persuaded his guides of a desire to sacrifice a goat in honour of Aaron at his tomb. His scheme succeeded and on 22 August 1812 he was guided through the Siq and into the valley where he saw the Al-Khazneh and the Urn Tomb and thus saw enough to recognize the City of Petra.

When he arrived in Cairo he could find no immediate transport to Fezzan so instead he journeyed up the Nile and discovered the Temple of Ramses II at Abu Simbel. He next travelled to Saudi Arabia, visiting Mecca. He returned to Cairo where he died on 15 October 1817, before he was able to complete his journey.

and makes Lake Nasser a treat to explore. Besides the wide variety of migrating birds, there are fox, gazelle and huge crocodiles (up to 5 m long) that live off the shallows and shores of the lake. Fishermen travel from afar to partake in extraordinary fishing (the rich silt that once nourished the riverbank of the Nile now nourishes the bellies of the lake's inhabitants). There is also an magnificent collection of Nubian temples scattered around Lake Nasser's shores and the Lake Nasser cruise, while expensive, is incredibly rewarding. *» For Sleeping, Eating and other listings, see pages 310-311.*

Temples of Abu Simbel

ⓘ Daily 0600 – 1700 in the winter, 1800 in the summer, entrance E£36, students E£21, flash photography inside the temples is strictly prohibited.

Abu Simbel, 280 km south of Aswan and only 40 km north of the Sudanese border (virtually closed to all traffic), is the site of the magnificent **Sun Temple of Ramses II** and the smaller **Temple of Queen Nefertari**. With the exception of the temples, hotels and the homes of tourist industry employees, there is almost nothing else here.

The two temples, which were rediscovered in 1813 completely buried by sand, were built by the most egotistical pharaoh of them all, Ramses II (1304-1237 BC) during the 19th Dynasty of the New Kingdom. Although he built a smaller temple for his queen Nefertari, it is the four gigantic statues of himself, which were carved out of the mountainside, which dominate Abu Simbel. It was intended that his magnificent and unblinking stare would be the first thing that travellers, visitors and enemies alike, saw as they entered Egypt from the south. Behind the statues is Ramses II's Temple of the Sun which was originally built to venerate Amun and Re-Harakhte but really is dominated by, and dedicated to, the pharaoh-god Ramses II himself.

Although it had become the highlight of the trip for the relatively few intrepid travellers who ventured so far south, it was not until the monuments were threatened by the rising waters of Lake Nasser that international attention focused on Abu Simbel. UNESCO financed and organized the ambitious, costly (US$40 mn) and ultimately successful 1964-68 operation, to reassemble the monuments 61 m above and 210 m behind their original site.

Ramses II's Temple of the Sun

The entrance steps lead up to a terrace, with alternate statuettes of the king and a falcon to mark the edge, where the imposing façade of the main temple (35 m wide by 30 m high) is dominated by the four-seated **Colossi of Ramses II**, each wearing the double crown. Each figure was originally 21 m high but the second from the left lost its top during an earthquake in 27 BC. There are smaller statues of some of the members of the royal family standing at Ramses' rather crudely sculptured feet which contrast with the ornately chiselled and beautiful faces of Ramses. There is graffiti, written by Greek mercenaries about their expeditions into Nubia, on the left leg of the damaged statue.

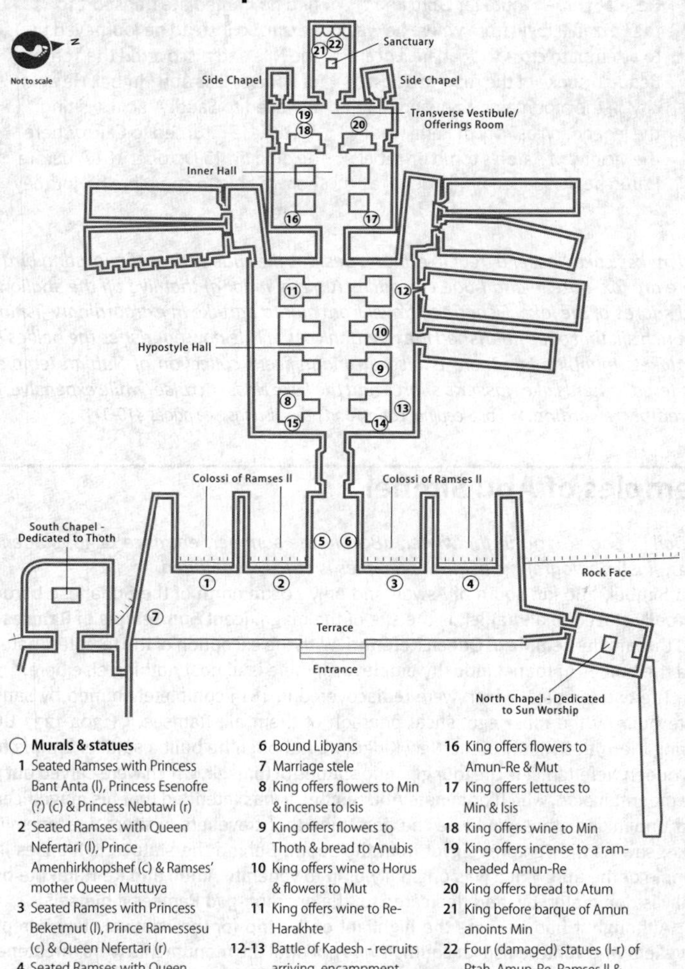

Murals & statues

1 Seated Ramses with Princess Bant Anta (l), Princess Esenofre (?) (c) & Princess Nebtawi (r)
2 Seated Ramses with Queen Nefertari (l), Prince Amenhirkhopshef (c) & Ramses' mother Queen Muttuya
3 Seated Ramses with Princess Beketmut (l), Prince Ramessesu (c) & Queen Nefertari (r)
4 Seated Ramses with Queen Mother Muttuya (l), Princess Merytamun (c) & Queen Nefertari (r)
5 Bound Nubians
6 Bound Libyans
7 Marriage stele
8 King offers flowers to Min & incense to Isis
9 King offers flowers to Thoth & bread to Anubis
10 King offers wine to Horus & flowers to Mut
11 King offers wine to Re-Harakhte
12-13 Battle of Kadesh - recruits arriving, encampment, town of Kadesh, enemy chariots
14 Libyan prisoners
15 Nubian & Hittite prisoners
16 King offers flowers to Amun-Re & Mut
17 King offers lettuces to Min & Isis
18 King offers wine to Min
19 King offers incense to a ram-headed Amun-Re
20 King offers bread to Atum
21 King before barque of Amun anoints Min
22 Four (damaged) statues (l-r) of Ptah, Amun-Re, Ramses II & Re-Harakhte

A bit of Nubian lingo

Hello *raigri*
How are you? *Er meena bu?*
Good *A denma*
Thank you *Gas si raykum*
Goodbye *Inna fee ya-der*
Hot *Joogri*
Cold *Od*
Come here *In day gerta*
Beautiful *A sheerma*

The sides of the huge thrones at the entrance to the temple are decorated with the Nile gods entwining lotus and papyrus, the plants representing Upper and Lower Egypt around the hieroglyph 'to unite'. Below are reliefs, called the **Nine Bows of bound Nubians** on the south side (5) and **bound Asiatics** to the north side (6), representing Egypt's vanquished foes. In the niche above the main doorway is a figure of Re-Harakhte. Lining the façade, above the heads of the four Ramses, is a row of 22 baboons smiling at the sunrise. There are two small chapels at either end of the façade. The smaller chapel with altar to the north was dedicated to the worship of the sun and that to the south was dedicated to Thoth. A **marriage stela** (7) commemorates the union of Ramses II with Ma'at-Her-Neferure, daughter of the Hittite king.

At the entrance into the temple's rock **Hypostyle Hall** is a door bearing Ramses II's cartouche. Having entered the temple the eye is immediately drawn to eight statues of Ramses, 10 m high and clad in a short kilt typical of the Nubian Osiride form, which are carved in the front of the eight enormous square pillars which support the roof. The four statues on the right bear the double crown and those on the left the white crown of Upper Egypt. Each pillar depicts the kings before the gods. See where he is presenting flowers to Min and incense to Isis (8), wine to Horus and flowers to Mut (9), flowers to Thoth and bread to Anubis (10), wine to Re-Harakhte (11). The hall's ceiling is crowded with vultures in the central aisle and star spangled elsewhere. The reliefs on the walls are colourful and well preserved. The north wall is the most dramatic with four different scenes depicting the Battle of Kadesh against the Hittites in 1300 BC (12, 13, l and m) which, despite the scenes on the wall, was not an unqualified Egyptian success. The depictions of chariots and camps are particularly revealing of ancient battle methods but, more interestingly, Ramses's double arm lancing a Libyan may have been an attempt at animation. The slaughter of prisoners, generally small in size, is a common theme (14 and 15).

There are also **side chambers**, probably originally used to store vases, temple linen, cult objects and Nubian gifts, branching off from the hall. Their walls are lined with reliefs of sacrifices and offerings being made by Ramses to the major gods including Amun.

The **Inner Hall** has four columns depicting the pharaoh participating in rituals before the deities. On the far left, Ramses can be seen before Amun (16). Lettuces, considered an aphrodisiac, are being offered to Amun (17). In both these scenes a deified Ramses II has been inserted at a later date. Two sandstone sphinxes, which originally stood at the entrance to the hall, are now in London's British Museum.

Further in and in front of the inner sanctuary is the **Transverse Vestibule** where offerings of wine, fruits and flowers were made. The **Sanctuary** itself, which was originally cased in gold, has an altar to Ramses at its centre, behind which are now statues of Ptah, Amun-Re, Ramses II and Re-Harakhte, unfortunately mutilated. Ramses is deified with his patron gods. Before the temple's relocation the dawn sunrays would shine on all but Ptah (who was linked with death-cults), on 22 February and 22 October. Despite what your guide will say there is no scholastic evidence to connect these two dates with Ramses' birthday and coronation day. A sacred barque (boat) would have rested on the altar and the walls beside the door portray the barque of Amun and Ramses. The adjoining side chapels were not decorated.

Despite its magnificence and beauty for many visitors to Abu Simbel there is a slight tinge of disappointment because of the combination of a sense of familiarity and artificiality. The latter is heightened when at the end of the official tour one is led through a door and into the hollow mountain on which the temple was reconstructed when it was moved. At the same time, however, the combination of Ramses' egoism and the scale of the magnificent feat of saving the temple from the rising waters of the Nile make the trip from Aswan worthwhile.

Temple of Queen Nefertari

Although dedicated to the goddess Hathor of Abshek, like that of her husband, the queen's temple, 120 m north of Ramses II's temple, virtually deifies the human queen Nefertari. Unsurprisingly it is much smaller than that of Ramses II but is nevertheless both imposing and very, very beautiful. It is cut entirely from the rock and penetrates about 24 m from the rock face. The external façade is 12 m high and lined with three colossi 11.5 m high on either side of the entrance. Nefertari stands with her husband and their children cluster in pairs at their knees. From left to right – Ramses II with Princes Meryatum and Meryre (1), Queen Nefertari shown as Hathor has the solar disc between the horns of the sacred cow with Princesses Merytamun and Henwati (2), Ramses II with Princes Amunhikhopshef and Rahrirwemenef (3). The same groupings appear in reverse order on the other side. The king wears various crowns. To show the importance of Queen Nefertari her statues are of similar size to those of her husband. Just within the entrance are the cartouches of Ramses II and Nefertari. There is one simple **Hall**, with six square pillars. On the aisle side of each is depicted a Hathor head and sistrum sounding box while the other three sides have figures of the king and queen making offerings to the gods. The ceiling bears a well-preserved dedication inscription from Ramses to Nefertari. The reliefs on the hall walls are rather gruesome – the pharaoh slaying his enemies while Nefertari and the god Amun look on (8). The walls backing the entrance depict Ramses killing a Nubian and a Libyan.

Three corridors lead from the rear of the hall into the **Vestibule**, the central one passing directly into the **Sanctuary**. The back walls of the Vestibule portray reliefs of Ramses and Nefertari offering wine and flowers to Khnum and Re-Harakhte on the right (18) and to Horus and Amun on the left (17). Vultures protect the Queen's cartouche on the door above the sanctuary (19) which is dominated by the figure of Hathor in the form of a cow watching over Ramses. On the left wall, Nefertari can be seen

Temple of Queen Nefertari

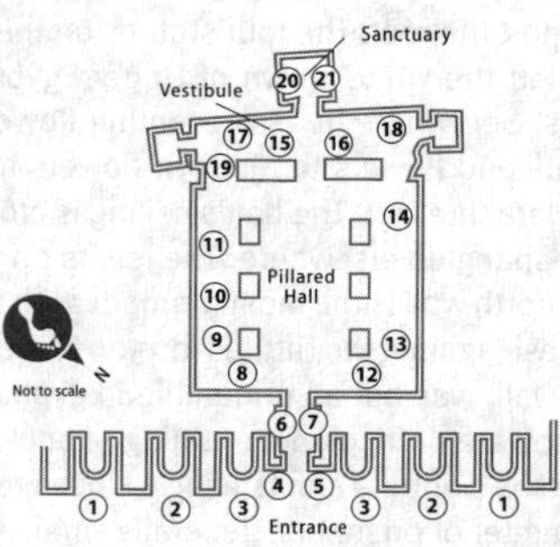

○ **Murals & Statues**

1 Ramses II with Princes Meryatum & Meryre
2 Queen Nefertari shown as Hathor with Princesses Merytamun & Henwati
3 Ramses II with Princes Amunhikhopshef & Rahrirwemenef
4 Lintel where King offers wine to Amun-Re
5 King offers incense to Horus
6 King offers flowers to Hathor
7 Nefertari offers flowers to Isis
8 Ramses II smites Nubian prisoner before Amun-Re
9 Ramses II receives necklace from Hathor
10 Ramses II crowned by Horus & Seth
11 Nefertari offers flowers & musical instrument to Anukis
12 Ramses II smites Libyan prisoner before Horus
13 Ramses II with offerings
14 Nefertari before Hathor of Dendera
15 Nefertari between Hathor & Isis
16 Ramses II & Nefertari give flowers to Tawere
17 Ramses II offers wine to Horus & Anu
18 Ramses II offers wine to Re-Harakhte & Queen offers flowers to Khnum
19 Nefertari's cartouche between vultures
20 Nefertari offers incense to Mut & Hathor
21 Ramses II worships deified image of himself & Nefertari

Fishing on Lake Nasser – an old sport in a new area

Lake Nasser is the result of flooding 496 km of the Nile valley with the construction of the Aswan Dam. The extraordinarily rich silt that once coated the valley during the seasonal flood is now at the bottom of the lake, sustaining the marine environment. As a result of the extreme nourishment, the fish have grown to huge sizes and Lake Nasser has become a popular destination for keen fishermen from around the world. There are over 6,000 sq km to fish in and 32 species to catch (the two most popular being Nile perch and Tiger fish).

Nile perch (*Lates niloticus*) are found in the River Nile and other rivers in Africa, but grow to their greatest size in large bodies of water like Lake Nasser. They are large mouthed fish, greeny-brown above and silver below. They have an elongated body, a protruding lower jaw, a round tail and two dorsal fins. They are one of the largest freshwater fish in the world and can be over 1.9 m in length and 1.5 m in girth. The record catch in Lake Nasser is a massive 176 kg.

The most common of the **Tiger fish** caught is *Hydrocynus forskaalii*. They have dagger teeth that protrude when the mouth is closed. They resemble a tiger in both appearance (they have several lengthwise stripes) and in habit (they are swift and voracious). They can grow to 5.5 kg.

Catfish are represented by 18 different species in the lake but the two of interest to anglers are *Bagrus* and *Vundu* of which the largest caught in Lake Nasser to date is 34 kg.

The main methods of fishing are: **trolling** – restricted on safari to six hours a day which covers a wide area and can result in a bigger catch of bigger fish; or **spinning** or **fly fishing** from the shore, generally in the cool of the morning, which is a delight and a challenge as it requires more skill as well as a strong line and heavy-duty gloves.

All fishing on Lake Nasser is on a catch and release policy, except those needed for the evening meal.

offering incense to Mut and Hathor (20) whilst on the opposite side Ramses worships the deified images of himself and Nefertari (21).

Other Lake Nasser Temples

ⓘ *These monuments were previously almost inaccessible. However, Belle Epoque Travel, now organizes a relaxing tour of Lower Nubian antiquities aboard its elegant cruiseboat Eugenie (see page 310), constructed in 1993 in the style of a Mississippi paddle steamer. Pampered by the luxurious surroundings, high calibre guides and excellent service, travellers can sit back and appreciate the sheer vastness of desert and lake, a sharp contrast to the lush scenery and teeming villages of the Nile valley. Few more tranquil places exist. The boat's passengers have the monuments almost to themselves. Memorable features include a private sunset tour of Abu Simbel followed by a candlelit dinner on board for which the temples are specially lit.*

Originally spread along the length of the Nile, the important Nubian antiquities saved by UNESCO from the rising waters of Lake Nasser were clustered in groups of three to make for easier visiting. Many of the Nubian monuments do not have the magnificence of those north of the High Dam though their new sites are more attractive. A number were erected in haste with little concern for artistic merit, for the sole reason of inspiring awe in the conquered people of Nubia.

Kalabsha Temple

ⓘ *Daily 0600-1800. The easiest way to reach it is by taxi from Aswan or possibly as part of a half-day tour which would include the Unfinished Obelisk, the Aswan Dams and Philae. Negotiate with the boatmen with motor launch at the west end of the High Dam near the canning factory if the waters of the lake cover the pathway from the shore. Pay at the end of the return trip after about an hour on the site.*

Kalabsha Temple, the largest free standing Nubian temple and the second largest Nubian temple was also relocated when the High Dam was built and is now semi-marooned on an island or promontory (depending on the water level) near the west end of dam. It is rarely visited by tourists.

The original site of the temple, which was built in the 18th Dynasty (1567-1320 BC) in honour of Marul (Greek *Mandulis*), was about 50 km south of Aswan at Talmis which was subsequently renamed Kalabsha. Mandulis was a Lower Nubian sun god of fertility equated with Horus/Isis/Osiris and usually shown in human form with an elaborate headress of horns, cobras and plumes all topped off with a sun disc. Over the centuries the later **Temple of Mandulis,** a Ptolemaic-Roman version of the earlier one, developed a healing cult as did those of Edfu and Dendera. It was moved from Kalabsha to its present site in 1970 by West German engineers in order to save it from the rising waters of Lake Nasser.

Leading up to the First Pylon is an impressive 30 m causeway, used by pilgrims arriving by boat, but it is not known why the causeway and first pylon are set at a slight angle to the temple. In order to align the structure, the first court is in the shape of a trapezium, with the pillars on the south side grouped closer together. At either end of the pylon a staircase leads up to the roof. Within the thickness of the walls are four storage rooms, two at each side.

Temple of Kalabsha

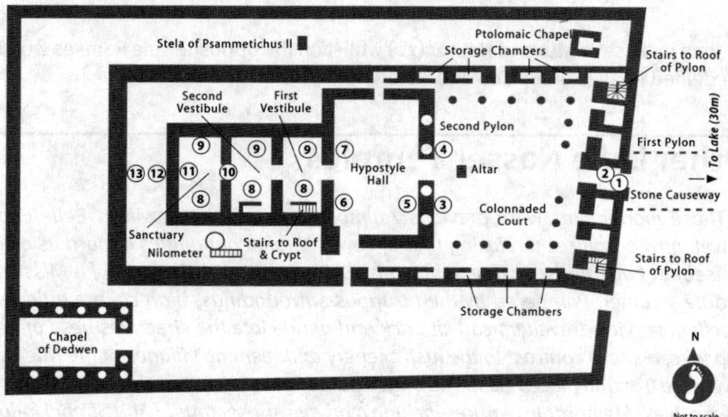

Murals ○

Lintel with sundisc **1**
Emperor Augustus with Horus **2**
King being purified with sacred water by Horus & Thoth **3**
Decree in Greek regarding expulsion of pigs from temple **4**
Coptic crosses carved on wall **5**
Second register - a pharaoh offers a field to Isis, Mandulis & Horus **6**
Second register - Amenophis II offers wine to Mandulis & another **7**
Procession of gods, the King in the lead, before Osiris, Isis & Horus **8**
Procession of gods, the King in the lead, before Mandulis, a juvenile Mandulis & Wadjet **9**
Lintel with sundisc **10**
King with various gods **11**
King with deities - double picture **12**
King before Mandulis **13**

Worship of the Nile crocodile – Crocodylus niloticus

These huge creatures, the largest reptile in Africa, were worshipped as the god Sobek (see page 553), who was depicted as a man with a crocodile's head. The Ancient Egyptians kept them in lakes by the temples which were dedicated to Crocodile gods (see page 165) and fed them the best meat, geese and fish and even wine. Special creatures were decked with jewels, earrings, gold bracelets and necklaces. Their bodies were embalmed after death (which for some came after more than 100 years). It is suggested that they were worshipped out of fear, in the hope that offerings and prayers would make them less vicious and reduce the dangers to both man and beast.

The problem was these cold blooded creatures needed to come out of the river to bask in the sunshine and feed – and they could move at a surprising speed on land. The long muscular tail was used as a rudder and on land could be used to fell large animals at a single blow. Small humans were easy prey.

In other regions they were hunted, eaten and considered a protector as they prevented anyone from swimming across the Nile.

It is fortunate that today these 900 kg creatures can no longer reach the major part of Egypt. They cannot pass the Aswan dam but they exist to the south of this barrier in large numbers.

The left portico, beside the entrance to the Hypostyle Hall, portrays the pharaoh being purified and anointed with holy water by Thoth and Horus, while on the right is inscribed a decree from Aurelius Besarion who was Governor of Ombos and Elephantine ordering the expulsion of pigs from the temple precincts. The Hypostyle Hall has lost its roof, but the eight columns are still in good condition. The capitals are ornate and flowered, some paintings having been preserved with their original colours, though not all are complete. On either side of the doorway leading to the vestibule is a relief of Trajan making offerings to Isis, Osiris and Mandulis on the left and Horus, Mandulis and Wadjet on the right.

Beyond the hall are the vestibules each with two columns and south access to the roof. Most of the decoration has survived and on the entrance wall the pharaoh can be seen offering incense to Mandulis and Wadjet, and milk to Isis and Osiris. The south wall depicts the emperor making libations to Osiris, Isis, Horus, Wadjet and Mandulis. The statue of Mandulis has long since vanished, though he is pictured on the walls amongst the other deities.

Near the lakeside just south of the Temple of Kalabsha is the Ptolemaic-Roman **Kiosk of Kertassi** rescued by UNESCO from its original site 40 km south of Aswan. It is a single chamber with two Hathor-headed columns at the entrance on the north side. Hathor was associated with miners and quarrymen as patroness. Dedicated to Isis, the temple is undecorated except for one column in the northwest whose reliefs on the upper part depict the pharaoh standing before Isis and Horus the child.

Beit El-Wali

In the hillside behind the Kalabsha Temple stands a small rock temple, **Beit El-Wali** (House of the Governor), again part of the UNESCO rescue mission. This was originally situated northwest of Kalabsha Temple and possessed a long causeway to the river. Built during Ramses II's youth by the Viceroy of Kush it is believed to have been erected in honour of Amun-Re as he is depicted most frequently. The reliefs in the temple's narrow forecourt depict Ramses II victorious against the Nubians and

 Ethiopians (south wall) and defeating the Asiatics, Libyans and Syrians (north wall). In fact a great deal of smiting and defeating is illustrated. In particular the tribute being offered on the east wall of the entrance courtyard is well worth examination, while on the wall opposite look out for the dog biting a Libyan's leg. The reliefs and residual colours are well preserved making this an interesting visit.

The two columns in the vestibule are unusual in a Nubian monument – being fluted. When this building was used as a Christian church the entrance forecourt was roofed over with brick domes.

Wadi El-Seboua

The isolated oasis of Wadi El-Seboua, 135 km from the High Dam, contains the Temple of Wadi El-Seboua, the Temple of Dakka and the Temple of Maharakka. The giant Temple of Wadi El-Seboua (valley of the lion) is named after the two rows of sphinxes which line its approach. It was constructed between 1279 BC and 1212 BC under Setau, the supervisor of the Viceroy of Kush. It is dedicated to Amun, Re-Harakhte and the deified Ramses II.

A huge statue of Ramses II and a sphinx stand on either side of the entrance. The base of each is decorated with bound prisoners, a reminder of Egyptian supremacy.

There are six human headed sphinxes in double crown in the First Courtyard and four falcon headed sphinxes in double crown with small statue of the king in front in the Second Courtyard. Again the bases have illustrations of bound prisoners. Steps lead up to the main part of the temple. The massive statue on the left of the First Pylon is of the wife of Ramses II and behind her leg their daughter Bint-Anath. The corresponding statue from the right of the entrance now lies in the sand outside, damaged when the temple was converted into a church.

The carved reliefs by local artists in poor quality sandstone, are crude but much remains of their original colour. Around the court are roughly carved statues of Ramses II unusually portrayed as a Nubian, holding the crook and flail scepters displayed against the 10 pillars – but most have been damaged. Along the lower register appear a procession of princes and princesses, estimated at a total of over 50 of each.

From the far end of the First Pillared Hall the temple is cut into the rock and this inner section has decorations better preserved and with better colours. The Christians who used this as a church covered the reliefs with plaster to permit their own decoration, thus preserving the earlier work. In the Sanctuary a relief on the wall shows Ramses II presenting a bouquet to the godly triad but early Christians defaced the figures and Ramses II now appears to be offering lotus flowers to St Peter.

Unfortuately a number of the sphinxes have been decapitated and the heads illegally sold to treasure hunters.

Temple of Dakka

Uphill is the Ptolemaic-Roman Temple of Dakka, reconstructed on the site of an earlier sanctuary. In fact several rulers contributed to its construction and decoration. It was started by the Meroitic King Arqamani, adapted by the Ptolemies Philopator and Euergetes II and changed again by Emperors Augustus and Tiberius (see key). What a history!

Like many temples it was used for a time by the Christians as a church and in some places fragments of their decorations remain. This is the only temple in Egypt facing north, an orientation preserved by UNESCO, pointing to the home of Thoth but perhaps an error by the foreign-born Ptolemaic builders. The pylon is still in good condition, standing an imposing 13 m in height. The gateway has a curved cornice with a central winged sun disc on either side and a high level niche at each side intended to hold a flag pole while on the left of the doorway is graffiti in Greek, Roman and Meriotic (ancient Nubian). Inside the doorway a king makes offerings to Thoth, Tefnut and Hathor (b). Stairs in either side of the pylon lead to guard rooms and the roof from which a fine view is obtained. Deep incisions in the inner pylon wall were probably made by locals convinced that the stone possessed healing properties. The main temple building is across an open courtyard but before you enter, turn back and admire the view to the north.

There are four interconnecting rooms, many of the decorations being of deities receiving assorted offerings. A staircase leads off the vestibule on the west side up to the roof. Off the sanctury is a small room to the east side leading, it is thought, to a now-choked crypt. Here the decorations are in quite good condition – two seated ibises, two hawks and two lions. The lioness being approached by the baboons (6) needs some interpretation. As an animal could approach a lioness without danger except if she was hungry but a human was in danger at any time the humans assumed animal form to worship in safety. The king is seen worshipping gods including Osiris and Isis (5) and Horus and Hathor (7). The large pink granite casket in the sanctuary once held the cult statue of Thoth.

Temple of Maharakka

Less impressive is the unfinished Roman Temple of Meharakka, dedicated to Isis and Serapis. This stood on the southern border of Egypt in Ptolemaic and Roman times. Rather plain inside, bar the Roman graffiti from travellers and soldiers fighting Nubian troops in 23 BC, the temple illustrates the union of Egyptian and Roman styles. Isis is depicted full frontal, instead of the more common profile, while her son Horus wears a toga. Other surviving carvings depict Osiris, Thoth and Tefnut. The temple consists of one room – six columns on the north side, three columns on the east and west side and six on the south side joined by screen walls. The capitals (floral?) of the columns were never completed. For stair access to roof, from which there are spectacular views, enter temple and turn right. This is the only known spiral staircase in an Egyptian building. Look east to the pharaohs' gold mines.

Temple of Dakka, Nubia

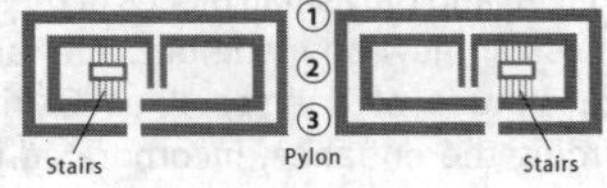

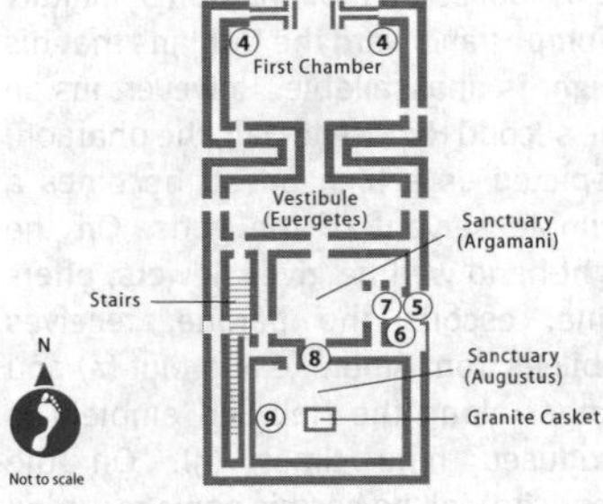

◯ **Murals**
1 Winged sun disc
2 King before Tefnut, Thoth & Hathor. King offers field to Isis
3 Winged sun disc
4 Sacred cobras
5 King offers gifts to Isis & Osiris
6 Thoth as baboon worships Tefnut as lioness
7 King offers sacred eye to Horus & Hathor
8 Winged sun disc. King receives life from Thoth & Hathor
9 Thoth as ape sitting under sycamore tree. Nile god pours water

Temple of Amada

Some 40 km further south in the Amada Oasis, is the oldest temple in Nubia, the sandstone Temple of Amada, dedicated to Amun-Re and Re-Harakhte. It was built by Tuthmosis III and Amenhotep II, with the roofed pillared court added by Tuthmosis IV which accounts for the many scenes of Tuthmosis IV with various gods and goddesses on the walls and pillars of this hall. At the left of the entrance hieroglyphics detail the victorious campaigns of Meneptah (3) against the Libyans. Opposite is the cartouche of Ramses II (4). Before entering the next doorway look up at the Berber grafiti of animals high on the wall at both sides (14). Inside turn right. Reliefs show the Pharaoh running the

Heb-Sed race (17) (see page 155), cattle being slaughtered and presented as offerings as heads and haunches (16). Opposite (15) are the foundation ceremonies, an interesting depiction of the way a site for a building was marked out, foundations dug, bricks manufactured and the construction eventually completed and handed over to the owner. In the central section are more offering, of pomegranates, very realistic ducks and cakes (18). The stela at the back of the the sanctuary tells of the temple's foundation during Amenhotep II's time. The holes in the roof allow light in so one can see, also on the back wall, Amenhotep dispensing justice to six Syrian captives (19), a prisoner turned upside down and crucified (20), a grisly reminder to his remote Nubian subjects of pharaoh's treatment of enemies.

Temple of Amada

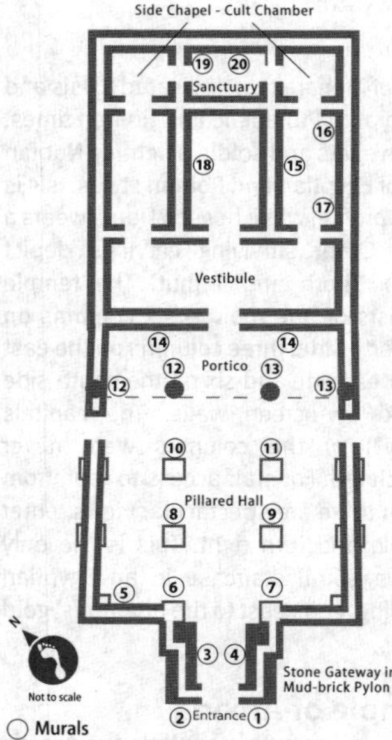

○ **Murals**

1 Tuthmosis III with Re-Harakhte
2 Amenhotep II with Re-Harakhte
3 Hieroglyphs detail Mereneptah's successful campaign against the Libyans
4 Cartouche of Ramses II
5 Inscription of Tuthmosis IV as 'beloved of Senusert'
6 Tuthmosis IV & Anukis
7 Tuthmosis IV & Khnum
8 Tuthmosis IV & Khepri
9 Tuthmosis IV & Amun
10 Tuthmosis IV & Atum
11 Tuthmosis IV & Ptah
12 Column with titles of Amenhotep II
13 Column with title of Tuthmosis III
14 Berber graffiti
15 Foundation ceremonies
16 Slaughtered cattle as offerings
17 Pharaoh running Heb-Sed race
18 Offerings of fruit & poultry
19 Inscription of Amenhotep II. Amenhotep dispensing rough justice
20 More rough justice

Rock temple of Al-Derr

Here too is the Rock Temple of Al-Derr, built in honour of Amun-Re, Re-Harakhte and the divine aspect of the pharaoh, notable for the excellent colour and preservation of its reliefs. It is the only temple on the east bank of the Nile in Nubia. In the first hypostyle hall the temple's builder Ramses II stands in the Tree of Life and presents libations to Amun. Ibis, the eternal scribe, behind, records the pharaoh's years and achievements. The decorations here are, however, very damaged and only small pieces of these scenes can now be made out. The four large statues of Ramses II as Osiris, guarding the entrance, incorporated in the last row of columns here, are reduced to legs only. The other columns in the hall are very reduced in size too. The majority of the reliefs on the outer walls boast of the pharaoh's military triumphs and warn the Nubians that his might is unassailable. However, inside the second Hypostyle Hall, the pharaoh, depicted as a high priest, becomes a humble servant of the gods. On the right-hand wall he gives flowers, offers wine, escorts the barque, receives jubilees from Amun-Re and Mut (4) and further along the Heb-Sed emblem is produced nine times (5). On the opposite wall he has his name recorded on the leaves of a tall acacia tree. Entering the sanctuary on the left Ramses is putting in a plea to live for ever (7). In the sanctuary on the back wall there were originally four statues as in the larger temple at Abu Simbel (see page 302), now nothing, but on the wall decorations the king continues to offer perfumes, cake and flowers.

The rock-cut **Tomb of Pennout**, Chief of the Quarry Service, Steward of Horus and viceroy of Wawat (northern Nubia) under Ramses VI, is a rare example of a high official buried south of Aswan. The ancient Egyptians believed that their souls were only secure if their bodies were carried back and buried in Egyptian soil. The tomb's wall paintings rather poignantly reflect this conviction, expressing Pennout's desire to be laid to rest in the hills of Thebes. The walls are decorated with traditional themes, including the deceased and his family. Before entering on the left the deceased and his wife Takha in adulation, on the main wall the judgement scene with the weighing of the heart against a feather and below the traditional mourners pouring sand on their heads. On the end wall Horus leads the deceased and wife to Osiris, Isis and Nephthys for a blessing but the lower register has all disappeared. To the left of the inner chamber representation of the solar cult. There is no entry into the inner chamber but the three badly mutilated statues of Pennout, and his wife with Hathor between can be viewed. The actual burial chamber lies 3 m below. Above on the lintel is the sun-god barge and howling baboons. What is left of the decoration on the wall to the right shows Pennout with his wife and six sons while on the end wall Pennout in golden colours is in his illustrated biography which continues on toward the exit. It is very disappointing to note that almost all the wall decorations were intact when this temple was moved here and even more disappointing to note that the damage had been caused by illegal removal from the monument.

Rock Temple of Al-Derr, Nubia

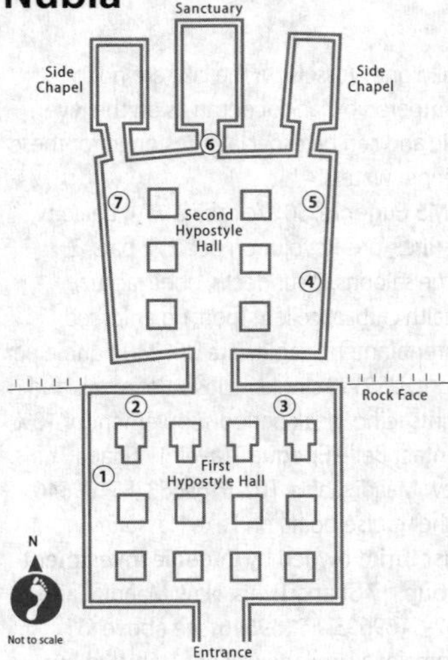

◯ **Murals**

1 Lower part of Ramses II in horse-drawn chariot
2 King with ka & pet lion smiting enemies before Amun
3 & before Re-Harakhte. Procession of royal children below
4 King as high priest acts as servant to gods
5 Heb-Sed emblem repeated nine times
6 Thoth writes King's name in sacred tree
7 King receives symbol of life from Amun-Re (l) & Re-Harakhte (r)

Qasr Ibrim

ⓘ *No access permitted.*

The fortress of Qasr Ibrim, 40 km north of Abu Simbel, is on its original site, once a plateau, now an island. It is noted for an exceptional length of continuous occupation, from 1000 BC to AD 1812. The ancient city included seven temples to Isis and a mud-brick temple built by the Nubian king Taharka, ruins of which are visible in the centre of the island. In the pre-Roman period construction of a massive stone temple, similar to the structures at Kalabsha, turned the garrison city into a major religious centre. A healing cult developed and Qasr Ibrim became 'the Philae of the south'. Footprints, carved by pilgrims to commemorate their visit, are still visible in the temple floor. A tavern, 400 BC, on the north side of the island is recognizable by the large piles of pottery shards. The temple was destroyed by early Christians who built an orthodox cathedral on the site in the 10th century AD in honour of the Virgin Mary, the Christian version of Isis. Three walls remain standing. By the steps to the burial crypt are numerous fragments of red (Roman) and glazed (Ottoman) pottery. Bosnian troops loyal to the Ottoman Sultan invaded the site in 1517 whereupon the cathedral was converted

Cobras

The Egyptian Cobra occurs on every kingly brow. The *Uraeus*, the cobra's head and the neck with the hood spread, as worn in the head dress of Egyptian divinities and sovereigns, is a sign of supreme power.

Fortunately this is the only place you are likely to see an Egyptian Cobra (although Cleopatra conveniently found one in the environs of her palace).

All cobras are potentially very dangerous although the venom is used to catch prey rather than eliminate humans. Yet these creatures, though infrequently seen are not considered in danger of extinction.

There are other cobras in Egypt. The smaller Black-necked Spitting Cobra sprays venom up to the eyes of its attacker – causing temporary blindness and a great deal of agony. The black refers to the distinctive bands round the neck. Sightings are confined to the region south of Aswan. The Innes Cobra is exceedingly rare, recorded in particular around St Catherine's Monastery.

into a mosque, and their descendants inhabited the site for the next 300 years. The fortress was brought under central control in 1812.

Sleeping

Abu Simbel *p299*

AL Mercure Seti Abu Simbel, T097-400720, F400829. The fanciest place to stay in Abu Simbel – for a price. In addition to the regular 5-star amenities, there's satellite TV and a swimming pool.

A Nefertari Abu Simbel, T097-400509, F400510. 122 a/c rooms, built in 1960s, near the temples and overlooking Lake Nasser. It offers all the regular 4-star amenities and has a swimming pool and decent restaurant.

C Nobaleh Ramses Hotel, T097-400294, F400381. 40 rooms with TV, a/c and fridge. Comfortable but spartan hotel with a cheap buffet breakfast. 2 km from the temples.

D Abu Simbel Village, T097-400092, F400179. The cheapest and newest choice in town. In summer, and if tourism is in a slump, they're known to offer significant discounts. Not far from the temple, all rooms have a/c and private bath.

Cruise boats on Lake Nasser

Since the construction of the High Dam the upper part of the Nile has been effectively cut off to navigation from the lower reaches. The only solution to getting a good vessel on the lake was to set up a shipyard and build one. Vessels on the lake are not hampered by lack of depth as on the River Nile and can be especially designed for these deeper waters.

A MS Eugenie, 50 a/c cabins with balcony, 2 suites, pre-Revolution decor, 2 bars, 2 large saloons, 2 sundecks, pool, jaccuzi, health club, excellent food, no enforced entertainment, cabins are US$240 double per night, US$190 single inclusive of meals and sightseeing, peak period supplement of 10%, contact **Belle Epoque Travel**, 17 Sharia Tunis, New Maadi, Cairo, T02-5169653, F5169646.

Other cruise boats on Lake Nasser:

Kasr Ibrim owned by **Eugenie Investment Group**, 17 Sharia Tunis, New Maadi, Cairo, T02-5169653, F5169646, see above, 65 rooms of a similar excellent standard but without the ancient charm;

MS Nubian Sea owned by High Dam Cruises, 15 Sharia El-Shahud Mohammed Tallat, Dokki, Giza, T02-3613680, F3610023 which has 66 cabins and suites;

MS Prince Abbas launched 1998, 38 standard cabins, 18 junior suites and 4 royal suites;

MS Tanya, Sharia 26 July, Zamalek, Cairo T02-3420488, F340520, good quality, 31 rooms.

Camping

Sometimes the **Abu Simbel Village** and the **Nefertari Abu Simbel** permit camping on their grounds, but call ahead to be sure, as it often depends on the tourist traffic.

Eating

Abu Simbel *p299*

Because of Abu Simbel's position in the middle of the desert, most supplies come from Aswan and consequently there are often problems with the range of foods available. Outside of the hotel restaurants, there are a few cafés with humble offerings in town. If you're coming for a day, it's better to bring your own snacks. There are bare provisions available in some stores, but the prices are severely inflated. Bring what water you'll need from Aswan.

Activities and tours

Abu Simbel *p299*

Felucca trips

See Essentials, page 40.

Organized tours

Travel agencies and hotels in Aswan all daily run trips to Abu Simbel. Most esteemed agencies generally transport their passengers in an a/c coach and may include a tour guide. They can also book day trips via plane.

For people on a budget, hotels offer 2 basic trips incorporating Abu Simbel (the short, E£40-50 and the long, E£50-60). The short trip picks you up from your hotel at 0330 in the morning, transports you to the temple and gets you back by 1300. The long trip stops at the High Dam, unfinished Obelisk, and Philae Temple on the way back and finishes around 1530. It's tempting to stick it all in one day, but the long trip feels very long. Price usually only includes transport in a minivan – some with and some without a/c. If you are visiting in the summer, it is worth shelling out the extra few pounds to ensure you are in an aircon vehicle, the heat is intense and you are generally sandwiched in with 12 other passengers. Admission fees are generally not included.

Both tours usually join the convoy that departs at 0400 in the morning and arrives at the temples around 0800. You have about an hour and a half to look around before being bussed back to Aswan or on to the next stop on your tour. Bring the food and water you'll need for the morning and use the bathroom before you get on the bus, as the ride is 3 hrs long and the convoy will not stop.

For **hunters**, **fishermen** and **bird watchers**, there are a few companies that specialize in nature and adventure safaris on Lake Nasser. Check with the tourist office in Aswan to see who's running trips or try **African Hawk**, T012-3424101, or **Safari Adventure**, T097-311011, their office is by the EgyptAir office in Aswan.

Transport

Abu Simbel *p299*

Air

EgyptAir runs numerous daily flights to Abu Simbel during the winter high season: from **Cairo** (2 hrs) via **Luxor** (1-hr) and direct from **Aswan** (30 mins, US$140 roundtrip). During the summer when the season slumps, there are still at least 2 flights per day and about 3 during the summer low season. Book a ticket as early as possible, especially in the peak season. Most tickets are sold on the assumption that you will return the same day but it is possible to include overnight stopovers. Seats on the left hand side of the aircraft usually offer the best views as it circles the temples before landing at Abu Simbel. There are free buses from Abu Simbel airport to the site of the temples.

Bus

Currently, the only way to visit Abu Simbel by road unaccompanied by a convoy is to take the public bus, which can only hold 4 foreigners, as the unwritten rule goes. Public buses depart from the main **Aswan** bus station (3.5 km north of town) 5 times per day at 0600, 0800, 0900, 1100, 1600, tickets cost E£30 roundtrip and you can't buy them in advance. Don't take the last bus unless you intend to stay the night. Since the organized transport is significantly more convenient (they pick you up directly from your hotel) and still very cheap, it's probably the best idea. Depending on the number of visitors, there are 1-3 convoys per day. At present, they depart at 0400 and 1100.

Alexandria & the Mediterranean coast

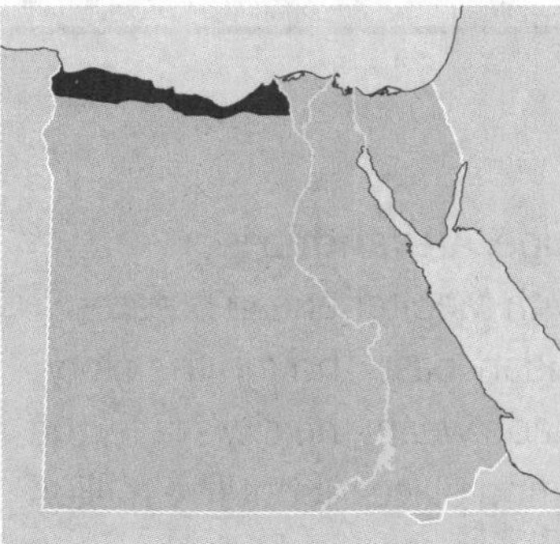

Footprint features

Introduction

Some 20 km long but only 3 km wide, **Alexandria** is an emphatic waterfront city, swept with Mediterranean breezes and tangible nostalgia for its legendary past. Though the glory days are long gone and age has made weary the city's face, the modern metropolis is still a fascinating place. About five million people speak at least five different languages and live along a seashore on the edge of east and west, creating a world that is in between. Where else can you indulge in a British ale and some Greek souvalaki followed by a sheesha and French espresso with the call to prayer and Lebanese pop music in the background? That said, Egypt's second city has a distinctly European flavour. The hassle and bustle is less than the capital and the many waterside cafes, coffee shops and stylish boutiques convey a more sophisticated – and somewhat snobbish – demeanour.

Heading west from Alexandria, the Mediterranean Coast stretches 500 km to the Libyan border, passing the neighbouring beach resorts of **El-Agami** and **Hannoville**, the site of the huge Second World War battle at **El-Alamein**, and the newer beach resorts towns of **Sidi Abdel Rahman** and **Marsa Matruh**. There, a road winds inland to the Siwa oasis (See Western Desert Chapter), before finally arriving at the Libyan border, near Sollum. Considering the rapid development trend of the Red Sea, the relative lack of development on the Mediterranean Coast is striking. A shortage of fresh water coupled with bureaucratic hurdles have thus far saved the stunning shoreline from being gobbled up by resorts. With largely domestic tourism, the beach culture on the North Coast is considerably more conservative than that of the Red Sea and women may find that outside of the larger resorts with private beaches, hassles abound.

★ Don't miss...

1. **Catacombs of Kom El-Shoquafa** Spook yourself with a visit to an eerie subterranean necropolis filled with ancient carvings and lurking spirits, page 323.
2. **Library** Visit the new Bibliotheca Alexandrina and view the world's largest reading area in an extraordinary modern edifice. Though it was Alexandria's old library that earned the city the epithet of "most learned place on earth," the new library seems keen to reclaim it, page 329.
3. **Fish** Enjoy a delicious 'so fresh it's almost moving - pick your own fish' meal at one of Alexandria's many outdoor fish restaurants, page 335.
4. **Café society** Indulge in an espresso at one of Alexandria's age-old cafés that remain literary centres and revolutionary converging points, page 336.
5. **Diving** Plunge into the depths of the Mediterranean Sea around Alexandria and dive amid the wrecks and ruins, among which are remnants of the Royal Quarter and a German fighter plane, page 338.
6. **Beaches** Marvel at the waters of the Mediterranean Sea where there are too many shades of blue to count off the white, sandy, wind-swept beaches around Marsa Matruh. Agibah is the most divine, page 346.

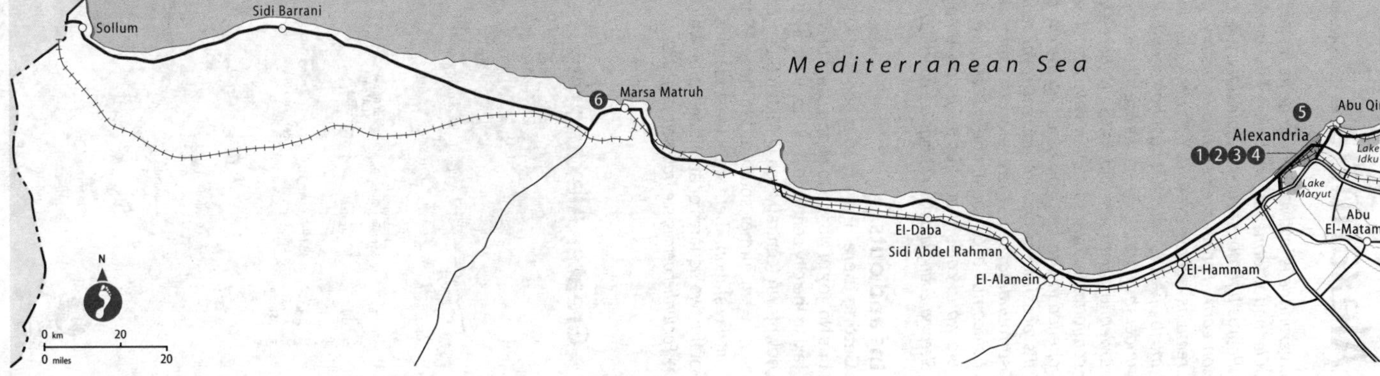

Alexandria

→ *Colour map 2, grid A1. Population: 3,700,000.*

Alexandria is mythical: old stage for historical characters like Alexander the Great and Cleopatra; former sight of one of the world's seven ancient wonders, the legendary Pharos lighthouse, and the old library, once the container of all knowledge available on earth. For an area so rich in history, perhaps what's most striking is how little remains – above ground. With book-burning patriarchs and earth-shattering quakes, much of Alex's splendid past has been burnt to crisp, toppled into the sea or buried under the earth. Excavations are all but impossible with millions of people thriving in towering apartment blocks. Still, there's a lot to see and do and Alexandria is a comfortable town to stay in with lots of services. The new Bibliotecha Alexandrina opened in October, 2002, putting the city back on the global map. If you scuba dive, it's possible to explore ancient royal remains that have been submerged in the surrounding sea. There are also some excellent intimate museums, the creepy Catacombs of Shoqafa, and scores of wonderful seafood restaurants and charming old-world cafés that offer a window onto the city's multifaceted personality. » *For Sleeping, Eating and other listings, see pages 332-341.*

Ins and outs

Getting there The airport is about 10 km from the town centre which is reached by bus No 307 or No 310 to Midan Orabi or No 203 to the nearby Midan Sa'ad Zaghloul. A taxi to the city centre costs E£12. Intercity buses to Alexandria stop in the heart of the downtown (central) area in Midan Sa'ad Zaghloul while buses from the Delta towns stop 1 km further south at the huge Midan El-Gumhoriyya outside the main Misr railway station. There are at least 12 trains daily from Cairo. Service taxis stop at either of the two squares or at Midan Orabi, which is 750 m west of Midan Sa'ad Zaghloul. » *For further details, see Transport, page 339.*

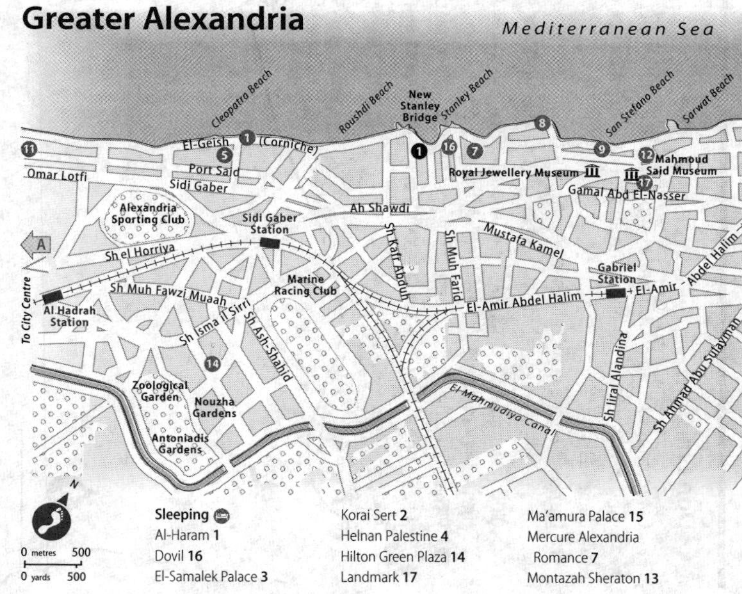

Getting around Alexandria is a thin ribbon-like city whose residential areas are still largely bound by the El-Mahmudiya canal and Lake Maryut. At the city's western end is the El-Anfushi peninsula which divides the giant functional Western Harbour and the beautiful sweeping curve of the Eastern Harbour and its corniche. To the east is a series of beaches which stretch to the Montazah Palace and on to Ma'mura beach and eventually Abu Qir, site of Nelson's 1798 victory over the French fleet. The city's main downtown area, its main transport terminals and many of the hotels are in the blocks around Midan Sa'ad Zaghloul in El-Manshiya which is in the western end of the city just inland from the Eastern Harbour. There is a tram service around the city and taxis abound. Considering its size and the population that more than doubles in the summer, Alexandria is remarkably easy to navigate. Places aren't too far distant and with the coast to the north, locating attractions and oneself is simple.

Tourist offices Main office ⓘ *southwest corner of Midan Sa'ad Zaghloul, T03-4851556. Daily 0800-1800, 0900-1600 during Ramadan.* There are also tourist offices at the **Misr Railway Station**, T03-3925985, the **Borg Al-Arab airport**, T03-4485119, and the **port**, T03-4803494. For practical advice visit **Misr Tours** on Saad Zaghloul St, T03-4809617, 4808776. **Tourist Friends' Association**, T03-5962108, 5866115, offers all services needed by tourists, introduces them to local customs and provides multi-lingual guides.

Best time to visit The Mediterranean climate diverges radically from the rest of Egypt. The northern winds deliver quite a chill in the winter, just as they offer utmost respite in the summer. Alexandria is the only place in Egypt you may need a jacket in July.

History

Having conquered Egypt by 332 BC, **Alexander the Great**, who was then only 25 years old, commissioned his architect Deinocrates to construct a new capital city on the coast. He chose a site near the small fishing village of Rhakotis. Its natural harbour and proximity to his native Macedonia offered significant strategic and commercial

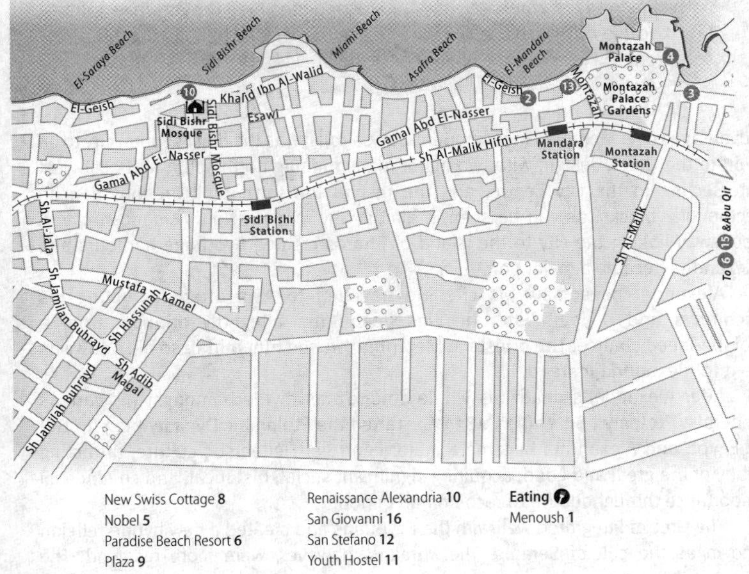

New Swiss Cottage **8**
Nobel **5**
Paradise Beach Resort **6**
Plaza **9**
Renaissance Alexandria **10**
San Giovanni **16**
San Stefano **12**
Youth Hostel **11**

Eating
Menoush **1**

Seeing the light – Ancient Alexandria

The **Mouseion**, from which the word *museum* is derived, meaning Temple of the Muses, was a vast centre of learning standing at the main crossroads of the city. It was commissioned by Ptolemy I, Soter and the important library was collected under the sponsorship of Ptolemy II, Philadelphus. As well as an observatory, laboratories, lodgings and a refectory for hundreds of scholars, it housed the famous library, **Biblioteca Alexandrina**, which by Caesar's day contained nearly a million papyrus volumes. Obviously the material on a scroll of papyrus was shorter than a modern book but nevertheless the amount of information was outstanding. There is no evidence that it was destroyed by the Christians mobs – or by any other group – it is more likely that it gradually declined over a period of time due to lack of support. (A few years back the international community pledged US$65 million to rebuild the library and make Alex once again the centre of the civilized world. See page 329.)

The fire from the immense **Lighthouse of Pharos** could be seen from 55 km across the open sea. It was 135 m high and stood at the mouth of the Eastern Harbour where Sultan Qaitbai's fort now stands. The first storey was square, the second octagonal and the third circular, topped by the lantern. At the very top stood a statue of Poseidon, god of the sea, trident in hand.

It was still in use at the time of the Muslim invasion over 900 years after its construction and was mentioned by Ibn Battuta in 1326 (more than 1600 years after its construction) as being used as a fortress.

The idea for the lighthouse may have come from Alexander the Great but it was actually built in 279 BC by Sostratus, an Asiatic Greek, during the reign of Ptolemy II (284-246 BC). According to popular myth an immense mirror lens made it possible to view ships far out at sea while the fuel to feed the fire is said to have been hydraulically lifted to the top of the lighthouse. Upkeep was a serious problem. Ibn Tulun attempted some repairs but the great earthquakes of 1100 and 1307 destroyed the ancient foundations and the stones lay abandoned until the Ottoman Sultan Qaitbai decided to build the fort on the site in 1479 AD.

advantages over Memphis (near modern-day Cairo). It was the first Egyptian city to be built to the Greek design, with two major roads running north-south and east-west intersecting in the city centre, and the rest of the town built around them in rectangular blocks, as can be seen in almost any modern North American city. A causeway linking the city to the island of **Pharos** created two huge harbours and Alexandria became a major port.

Alexander never saw his city. He travelled to Asia after instructing his architects and 8 years later he was dead after allegedly drinking from a poison-laced chalice. The priests at Memphis refused him burial, so his body was sent to Alexandria instead.

After Alexander's death his whole empire was divided amongst his various generals. **Ptolemy I Soter** (323-282 BC) started the Ptolemaic Dynasty (323-30 BC) in Egypt, and Alexandria became a major centre of Hellenistic culture, attracting many of the great and good, acquiring significant social, historical, and commercial importance throughout the Graeco-Roman period.

The Greeks integrated well with the Egyptians and created a new hybrid religion known as the cult of Serapis. The Romans, however, were more reserved. The

Ptolemy history in brief

Following the death of Alexander the Great, Ptolemy, *satrap* (governor) of Egypt soon gained control of the country. He took the title of king and founded a dynasty that lasted from 323 BC to 30 BC. There were 14 monarchs in all, ending with Cleopatra's son but the first three members of the dynasty were the most important.

Ptolemy I 367-283 BC known as Ptolemy Soter (saviour) was a great soldier with administrative ability who built roads and canals, founded the famous Library of Alexandria, wrote a scholarly account of Alexander's campaigns and abdicated at 82 in favour of **Ptolemy II** 309-246 BC, surnamed Philadelphus, a cultivated man whose court has been compared to that of Louis XIV at Versailles. He was not a soldier but supported Rome against her foes. **Ptolemy III** 281-221 BC, like his grandfather, was a vigorous warrior, supreme controller of the eastern Mediterranean who reopened the war against the Seleucids. He was a known as a just ruler especially noted for his leniency towards Egyptian religion and customs.

The later members of the dynasty were described as decadent and dissolute, due largely to the increasingly incestuous convention of the king marrying his own sister.

influence of later Ptolemies declined steadily and they relied on the Romans for support. **Cleopatra VII** (51-30 BC), the last of the Ptolemies, seduced first Julius Caesar and then his successor Mark Antony in order to retain her crown. Mark Antony and Cleopatra held sway in Egypt for 14 years until they were deposed by Octavian who became the Emperor Augustus.

Tradition has it that the Gospel was first preached in Alexandria by Saint Mark in AD 62. Whatever the accuracy of this date, **Christianity** was certainly established around this time and Alexandria remained the centre of its theology for three centuries. However, its presence was still sufficiently threatening to the Muslim conquerors three centuries later to make them move their administration and theological capital inland to Cairo. Although Alexandria was still important as a centre of trade its decline as a city was inevitable when the power base, along with the customary baggage of wealth, learning and culture went south.

With the 16th century discovery of America and the sea route around Africa to India and the Orient, which made the land route via Egypt virtually redundant, Alexandria lost its former magnificence. The decline during the Ottoman period was so great that while Cairo continued to flourish, the population of Alexandria fell to a mere 5,000 people by 1800.

Just in time, a saviour was found in the shape of **Mohammed (Mehmet) Ali** (1805-48). He organized the construction of the **El-Mahmudiya Canal** starting in 1819 and linked the Nile and Alexandria's Western Harbour, reconnecting the city with the rest of Egypt, whilst simultaneously irrigating the surrounding land, which had been badly neglected. With a trade route open, the city prospered once more and now it is only surpassed by Cairo itself. Foreign trade grew apace with the Egyptian merchant fleet and was later maintained by the British. Being further north and nearer to the sea, the city is cooler than Cairo in summer and each year the administration moved to the coast during this hot season. The British invested in many building projects including, true to the Victorian obsession, a sea-front promenade.

Population growth and industrialization have altered Alexandria since **Nasser's** revolution (see History of Egypt, page 494) in 1952. Today it is a modern city with much to recommend it. Although the outer areas have suffered from too rapid rural-urban migration, the busy central area is small enough to walk around and become familiar with the main squares and landmarks. Although Alexandria's opulent heritage is no longer so obvious, the atmosphere of the town which inspired

Alexandria

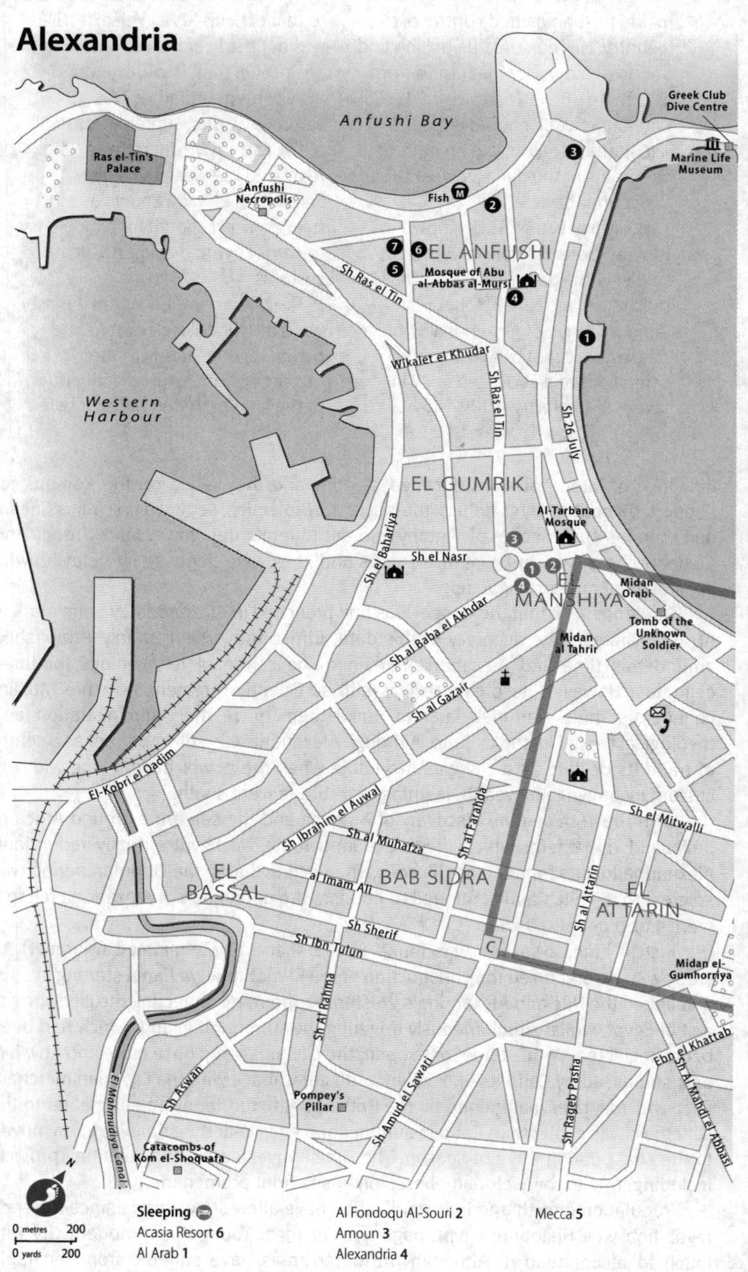

such literary classics as Lawrence Durrell's *Alexandria Quartet* still remains. So don't rush immediately to all the places of interest. It is as important to absorb the atmosphere as it is to view the sights.

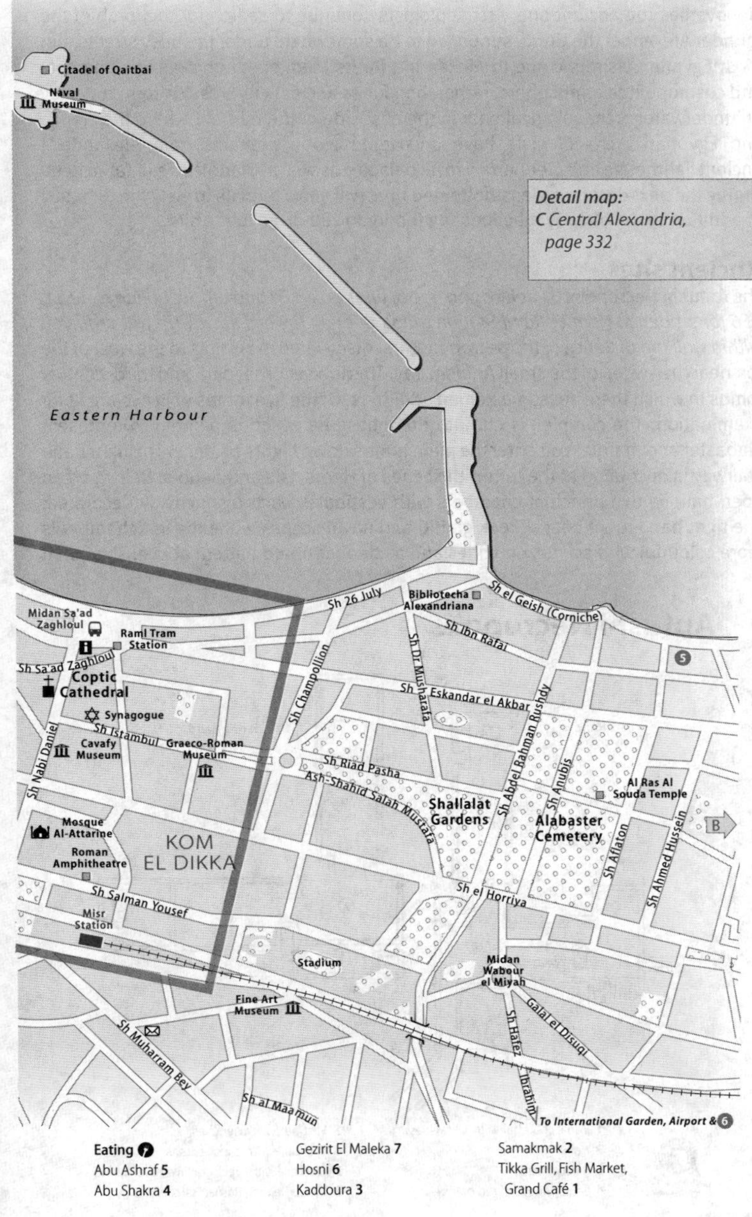

Sights

Historical remains in Alexandria today are pale shadows of their former glories, chief amongst which were the **Mouseion** (see page 318) and the **Lighthouse of Pharos**, one of the Seven Wonders of the Ancient World. For a city with such a magnificent past history there is, unlike Cairo, comparatively little to see today because the modern city overlies the ancient one. Archaeologists continue to search for the tomb of the founder Alexander the Great, supposed to be somewhere under the busy streets, but most Egyptian visitors come to Alexandria for its Mediterranean beaches and cool and cosmopolitan atmosphere, rather than for its ancient cultures. Visitors can enjoy an underwater archaeological park in the east side of the harbour where the French and Egyptian archaeologists have uncovered 7,000 artefacts from Alexander's ancient lighthouse and Cleopatra's royal palace – as well as Napoleon's ill-fated fleet. During the next decade a glass-bottomed boat will allow tourists to view the remains, in addition to the already functionaling for organized dives to the site.

Ancient sites

The **Anfushi Necropolis** ⓘ *daily 0900-1700, till 1500 on Fri and official holidays, E£12, E£6 for students, from El-Raml Station trams 15 or 25 toward Ras El-Tib will drop you within walking distance of the necropolis,* first discovered in 1901, is to the west of the fort near the sweep of the small Anfushi Bay. This is a set of second- and third- century tombs in which there are some Roman additions. Of the five tombs only two are fit for examination. The complex is cut into the limestone which is painted to represent alabaster and marble. You enter the main tombs down flights of steps. The right hand stairway is decorated at the turn with scenes of Horus, Isis and Anubis. Below, off an open hall, lie two principal chambers with vestibules each distinctively decorated. The right hand room bears Greek graffiti and naval scenes while the left chamber is more colourful with scenes of deities and a chequer-board pattern above. The burial

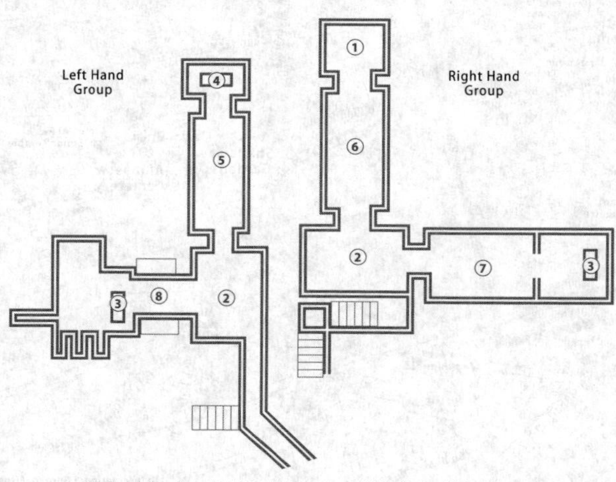

chamber, with matching wall decoration, is guarded by sphinxes. Inside the left hand group there is an entrance hall off which are two vestibules and tomb chambers. The right hand vestibule has benches and leads to a chamber with a red Aswan granite sarcophagus. In the left hand room the layout was modified in the Roman period to house a series of sarcophagi.

The **Catacombs of Kom El-Shoquafa** (Mounds of Shards) ⓘ *T03-4865800, daily 0900-1800 in summer, and 0900-1700 in winter, E£12, E£6 for students, plus E£10 for camera,* in Karmouz, where many of the houses are 120-200 years old, were originally second-century private tombs which were later extended in order to serve the whole community. Three styles of burial are represented here – in sarcophagi, on shelves and as ashes in urns. They have been extensively excavated since their rediscovery in 1900. Another case of the stumbling donkey. Sadly, water has flooded the lowest of the three levels and caused some deterioration. A large spiral staircase serves as the entrance to the tombs, below which passages lead to interconnecting tomb shafts. Immediately to the left of the entrance is a corridor leading to the more recent tombs. The main passage from the stairwell runs into a large rotunda with a domed roof. Branching from this is a banqueting room or triclinium for those visiting the deceased! Here in the triclinium the short granite pillars pushed away in the corner once supported the central banqueting table. A burial chamber leads off the rotunda opposite the dining area. As it was considered unlucky to remove dishes taken into the tombs for banquets these were smashed and left – hence the mound of shards. Within the chamber are many niches in which one or more bodies were sealed. A fourth passage leads to another stairway from which further ornate chambers branch off. The mixture of Graeco-Roman decoration with Egyptian – in columns and on wall illustrations indicates – the mingling of the two cultures. In places red paint can be found below the niches bearing the name of those encased within. The eerie atmosphere is intensified by the ornate serpents and Medusa heads that lurk above doorways and passage entrances. Also on the site is a **Hypogeum** containing over 30 murals.

At the very end of the peninsula, in a most imposing position stands the **Citadel of the Mamluk Sultan Qaitbai**. ⓘ *T03-4809144. Daily 0900-1700. E£12, students E£6, camera E£10, video camera E£50. Can be reached directly by taking minibuses 706 or 707 from Midan El-Khartoum.* It was built in 1479 by Sultan Qaitbai (AD 1468-96) on the ancient site of, and probably with the stones of, the Lighthouse of Pharos and stands at the far end of the Eastern Harbour as one of a series of coastal forts. It is one of the city's major landmarks and is now the property of the Egyptian Navy. The Citadel is approached up a wide causeway which ends at the original gateway between two half-round towers, both with interior rooms. Unfortunately today's entrance, further to the east, is less impressive. From the causeway notice the antique granite and marble columns incorporated in the fabric of the west facing wall. Three sides of the enclosed courtyard were given over to storage and accommodation for animals and troops. The north-facing wall has emplacements for a score of cannon and the higher look-out tower gives a commanding view over the Mediterranean. The keep houses a small mosque which, unusually for the Delta region, is built in the shape of a cross. The entrance to this mosque is through a huge gateway flanked by pillars of red Aswan granite. Nearby a complex cistern stored water in case of siege. The fort's greatest attraction is the view from the battlements back over the open sea toward Alexandria.

See plan of the Citadel on the next page.

The Yacht Club beside Qaitbai's Fort hires boats.

Further southwest on the way to the El-Mahmudiya Canal and Lake Maryut in an area of cheap markets is **Pompey's Pillar**, ⓘ *just east of Sharia Al-Rahman, T03-4865800; daily 0900-1700, E£6, students E£3. Can be reached direct by bus No 709 fromEl-Raml Station.* It is a 27-m high and 9-m thick column of red Aswan granite topped by an impressive Corinthian capital. This pillar, Alexandria's tallest ancient monument, is a rather bizarre spectacle and its origins are the subject of speculation. It certainly does not originate from Pompey and is thought to have come from the **Serapis Temple** (40 km to the west) and to have been erected in AD 300 in honour of **Diocletian** (AD 284-305). It may have supported his statue. Extensive archaeological excavations surround the site. See the three granite sphinxes among a jumble of columns and Coptic crosses and some underground cisterns to the west of the ridge.

To the east of the Nabi Daniel mosque and to the north of the Misr railway station is the **Kom Al-Dikkah (Hill of Rubble)** ⓘ *T03-3902904, daily 0900-1700, E£6, students E£3,* thought to be the ancient site of the Paneion ('Park of Pan', a hilly pleasure garden), which has been under excavation since 1959. Instead a small semi-circular 700-800 seat **Roman Amphitheatre** or **Odeon** behind Cinema Amir was discovered with 12 rows of seats faced with Italian marble focussing on a columned stage which still has the remains of its mosaic flooring. Some of the seats still show their numbers. A residential quarter with Roman baths from the third century is currently being excavated to the north. The site is one of the few in Alexandria to indicate the wealth of the city's heritage and it is well worth a visit. An annexe of the Graeco-Roman Museum displays local discoveries such as desalinated blocks from the harbour bed.

Citadel of Qaitbai

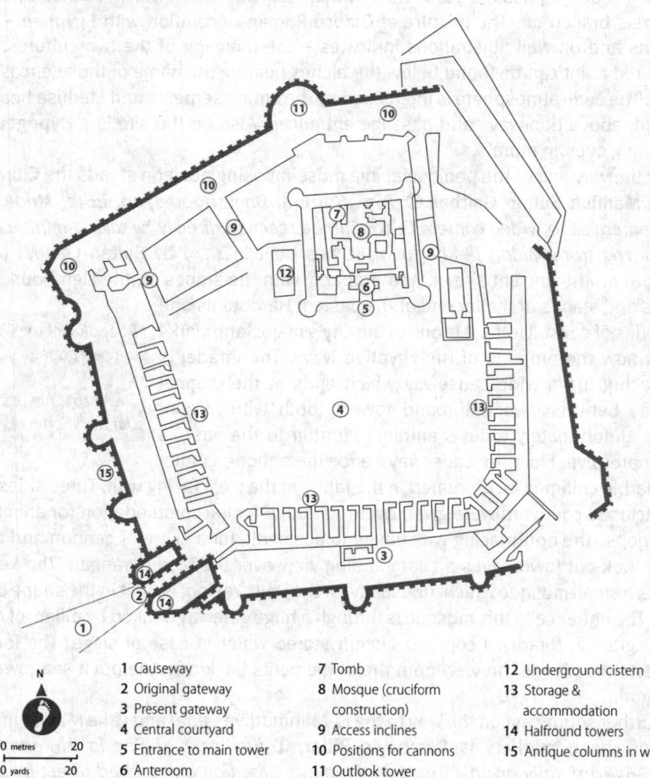

Mosques

Inland from the peninsula towards the city centre is the old Ottoman area of Anfushi and some of the most important mosques including the **Mosque of Abu Al-Abbas Al-Mursi** ⓘ *north off Sharia Ras El-Tin. All mosques are open from the dawn until the last prayer of the day which is held approximately an hour and a half after sunset. Trams 15 or 25 from El-Raml Station will take you there directly. Note that women are only permitted entry into a room at the back of the mosque. Both men and women should dress conservatively; women are advised to wear a head cover.* Ahmed Abu Al-Abbas Al-Mursi (1219-87) was an Andalusian who came to Alexandria to join and eventually lead the Shadhali brotherhood. He is the 'patron saint' of Alexandria's fishermen and sailors. His mosque and tomb, which is still here, were renovated in 1775 by a rich Maghrebi merchant but was then demolished and rebuilt in 1943 and is now the largest mosque in Alexandria. The current layout is octagonal with Italian granite supporting the roof arches, four decorated domes and the slender 73-m minaret rising in tiers which gives the modern mosque a pleasing weightless aspect. This is one of Alexandria's foremost religious buildings and is well worth a visit.

Further south down the street is the French Cultural Centre where the Mouseion once stood and then the **Mosque Al-Nabi Daniel** ⓘ *to get there via public transport, the mosque is just a five-minute walk down Sharia El-Nabi Daniel from the main Misr railway station.* Although popular myth claims that it houses the remains of the prophet Daniel it actually contains the tomb of a venerated Sufi sheikh called Mohammed Danyal Al-Maridi who died in 1497. Excavation works around the tomb have revealed another tomb from a 10th- or 12th-century Muslim cemetery and also revealed that the site is likely to have been that of the Great Soma Temple which was erected over the tomb of **Alexander the Great**.

Further south in this Ottoman part of the city is the **Al-Tarbana Mosque** on Sharia Farnasa to the east of Sharia Al-Shahid. It has undergone major alterations since it was built in 1685 by Hajji Ibrahim Tarbana. The minaret is supported by two antique columns which stand above the entrance whilst a further eight columns support the ornamental ceiling. The original Delta style façade is almost completely obscured by plastering.

The **Attarine Mosque**, on Mesijd Al-Attarine, dates from the 14th century and stands on the site of the once famous Mosque of a Thousand Columns. It was from here that Napoleon removed the 7-tonne sarcophagus which now is displayed in the British Museum in London.

The **Ibrahim Al-Shurbaji Mosque**, east of Midan Sa'ad Zaghloul, was built in 1757. The internal layout is similar to that of the Al-Tarbana Mosque. A courtyard to the rear creates a pleasant impression of space. There have been many modifications, but the *mihrab* is still decorated with the original Kufi inscriptions. To complete the examination of mosques don't omit the small mosque in the Citadel.

Turn south from the sea to Midan Sa'ad Zaghloul and walk down Sharia Nabi Daniel to the **Coptic Orthodox Cathedral**. ⓘ *T03-4835533. Entry welcome – leave a small donation. To get there, with your back to El-Raml Station, go down Safiya Zaghloul Street and turn right on the Coptic Orthodox Cathedral street where the cathedral will immediately face you.* This is a very recent establishment (1950-87), and presented as a large arched vault is a fine example of ecclesiastical architecture. It is dedicated to five saints, in particular St Mark whose head is reputed to be buried at this site together with the remains of early patriarchs of the Egyptian church including St Menas (see page 342). A sunken chapel, beyond an interesting recent mosaic of incidents in the life of St Mark, gives access to their tombs.

Nearby, and over 145 years old, is the main **Synagogue**, ⓘ *69 Sharia Nabi Daniel, daily from 1000-1300.* The previous building was destroyed by Napoleon. The synagogue which serves the remaining 90-100 Jews who live in Alexandria is not

Alexander the Great – Greek King of Egypt

Alexander the Great and his army entered Egypt in November 332 BC. He made a sacrifice to Apis in Memphis, taking at that time the twin crowns of Lower and Upper Egypt. He remained in Egypt for some months setting up control of the Egyptian army and founding the city of Alexandria on the coast of the northwest of the Nile delta. In the spring of 331 he marched along the Mediterranean coast to Paraetonium (present-day Marsa Matruh) and thence through the Western Desert to Siwa.

His visit to Siwa was to consult the oracle of Zeus-Amun. The Temple of the oracle at Siwa (see page 471) is situated to the west of Shali, the new town, at the old site of Aghurmi. There are elaborate stories of Alexander's visit to the oracle temple of Amun but what is clear is that he was received by the priests at Siwa as a pharoah and had a private audience at the oracle. His concern was his expedition against his enemies, the Persians, but he gave no word to his followers on the outcome though in a letter to his mother he promised to tell all when he saw her again (which he never did!). Much later it was reported that Alexander was saluted by the oracle as the son of Zeus which effectively led to his deification and assured him of success in Asia, certainly, Alexander retained a deep belief in the powers of the god Amun and a flow of gifts continued to come during Alexander's lifetime to the temple priests at Siwa.

He went on in 331 to attack Babylon and by 330 had control of the Persian empire and thereafter moved his armies into Central Asia and in 327 to India. Within 10 years he was master of the known world. He died unchallenged in this role aged 33 on 13 June 323. He was buried in the Egyptian city of Alexandria. (See also page 475.)

normally open to the public and the security guards are quite off-putting: but with gentle, polite persistence one can get through to the lady curator and into the ornate building. Ask to see some of the 50 ancient 500-1,000-year-old Torah scrolls held in worked silver cases in the arc. They are fascinating.

Palaces

To the east of downtown Alexandria lie 17 km of beaches stretching to the beautiful 160-ha gardens of **Montazah Palace** ⓘ *(see gardens, page 331), 1-day passes can be purchased at the gate for E£4, minibus 770 from Misr railway station, and minibus 736 from Orabi Square, go there directly,* now a state guesthouse. It was constructed in the 19th century by the visionary Mohammed Ali as a palace for the engineers who built the barrages which are so important for the irrigation of the Delta. It was later inhabited by King Farouk. The original construction had been halted, and was completed later in the century, on a grander scale, by Sir Colin Scott-Moncrieff.

Further west along the peninsula are formal gardens and then **Ras El-Tin's Palace** (Cape of Figs Palace) which overlooks the Western harbour but which is now the Admiralty Headquarters and is unfortunately closed to the public. It was built so that Mohammed Ali (1805-48) could review his fleet and was reconstructed in the European Turkish style by Fouad I (1917-36) to serve as the government's summer seat. It was therefore ironic that his son King Farouk signed his abdication at the palace on 26 July 1952 before boarding a yacht bound for exile in Italy.

Greco-Roman Antiquities Museum

ⓘ *5 Sharia El-Mathaf; To3-4865820. Daily 0800-1700. E£16, students E£18.*

In downtown Alexandria the Greco-Roman Antiquities Museum contains an interesting collection of around 40,000 relics from the Graeco-Roman period, mainly taken from local tombs dating from about 300 BC to AD 300. The most significant cult was that of Serapis which was a hybrid of the Greek god Dionysus and the Nile god Osiris. Serapis was depicted as a bull and is directly associated with the ancient Egyptian cult of the Apis bull. Take the rooms in chronological order, beginning in **Room 6** with the centrally placed magnificent sculpture of the black granite Apis bull (see Deities, page 546). The inscription dates it at AD 117-138. The white marble sculpture of Serapis was, like the bull, found near Pompey's Column. This room has some attractive mosaics.

Canopus, now reduced to rubble, was on the coast to the east of Alexandria and the artefacts from there in **Room 7** seem to be a collection of headless statues, sandstone sphinxes and basalt goddesses. Ramses II put his name on the huge red granite statue. **Room 8** has mummies differently decorated and an example of a Fayoum portrait (see box, page 161 Fayoum portraits) while **Room 9** has a mummified crocodile and other pieces from the Temple of Pnepheros, all connected with the crocodile worship practised there. **Room 11** illustrates how the mixture of Greek and Egyptian influences produced some interesting sculptures excavated from Athribus near Benha in the Central Delta. On the fragments of tomb paintings in **Room 15** is a *saqiya* or water-wheel with jars to collect and lift the water (see section on the Nile and man, page 520). The sculptures in **Rooms 16-16A** are some of the most worthwhile exhibits in the museum. Look particularly at the Persian god, the lion-headed Mithras; the giant eagle from the Aegean; the graceful figure of Aphrodite and the carefully executed male and female torsos. There are six marble sarcophagi in **Room 17**, most

Graeco-Roman Museum

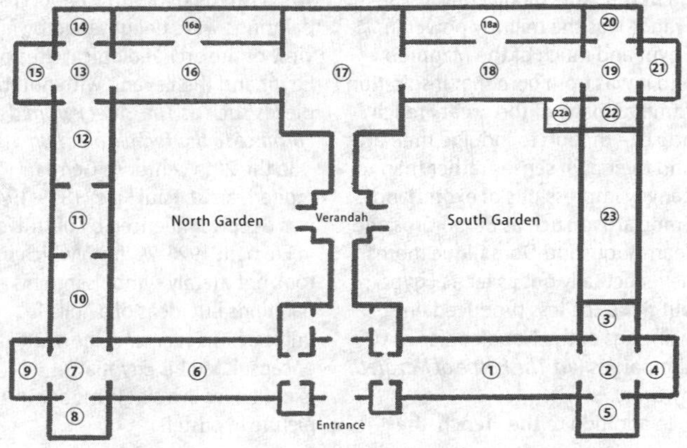

- **1-2** Coptic earthenware & architectural elements
- **3** Jewellery
- **4** Textiles
- **5** Coptic stucco
- **6** Cult of Serapis
- **7** Artifacts from ancient Canopus
- **8** Mummies & sarcophagi
- **9** Crocodile worship in El-Fayoum
- **10** Late Pharaonic - Sir John Antoniadis collection
- **11** Statues & fragments from Athribus near Benha
- **12-14** Miscellaneous sculptures of Graeco-Roman period
- **15** Tomb paintings
- **16-16a** Hellenistic sculpture
- **17** Monolith & sarcophagi
- **18** Pottery & glass
- **18a** Miniature Tanagra terracotta figures
- **19** Statues, funerary urns & pottery
- **20** Chatby collection
- **21** Ibrahimeya collection
- **22** Coloured glassware
- **22a** Bronze & other metals
- **23** Coins

Not to scale

Western artists in Egypt

Egypt has rarely been an independent country. The Ottoman Empire lasted until 1805, though the first direct intervention in Egypt began in 1798 with the Napoleonic invasion. A great entourage of scientists, writers and artists accompanied the French occupation of Egypt, which went on until 1801 opening this hitherto largely protected Islamic country to a new and interested audience.

The orientalist artists and writers of the 19th century were confronted in Egypt, and elsewhere in North Africa, with sights and scenes of what appeared to be a startlingly different culture. They recorded what they saw for an audience at home that was eager to catch glimpses of these unknown lands. By the end of the century, a new breed of artists found their way to the new territorial possessions that their countries had acquired in the great grab for colonial purposes. France was the military power in Egypt and much of the Maghreb and it was from here that inspiration came to many of the great French artists – though to indulge their art and their own senses rather than to convey impressions of exotic lands. Some artists such as Baron Gros and Jean-Augustine-Dominique Ingres never actually got as far as Egypt but none the less produced fine paintings of the Napoleonic campaigns (viz *The Battle of Nazareth* by Gros).

In addition to the French, the British imperial mission was important in 19th-century Egypt and brought its own harvest of 'orientalist' works of art. John Frederick Lewis (1805-75) spent 10 years in Egypt and was a prolific British painter of watercolours of ancient monuments such as Edfu, Upper Egypt and scenes of contemporary Cairo life such as *A Turkish School in the vicinity of Cairo*.

David Roberts (1796-1864) was another British master of the sketch and oil painting who voyaged along the Nile in 1839, see page 288. His sketches, reproduced as lithographs, are still popular and provide a wonderful catalogue of the major Nilotic sites in the mid-19th century. *Temple at Dendereh* and *The Island of Philae* are fine examples of his work.

Later comers to Egypt were William Holman Hunt (1827-1910), who was a founder member of the Pre-Raphaelite Brotherhood and who visited Egypt in 1854-56. His paintings were enlightened by his view of the archaeological sites of Egypt and the Levant, with notable pieces such as *The Great Pyramid* and *Entrance to the Temple of Amun*.

In the 20th century a German modern artist, Paul Klee (1879-1940), was deeply influenced by his travels in Egypt in 1928-29, from which he took not merely symbols into his paintings but ideas of a holistic universe. His *Legend of the Nile* encapsulated his Egyptian experiences in a single modern picture in pastel.

with intricate carvings and one with scenes from the Greek myths, keeping company with what is claimed to be the largest statue ever carved in porphyry (even though it has no head). The tiny terracotta figures from Greece displayed in **Room 18a** were associated with burials of young people and provide interesting detail about the dress and fashions of the time. Local Alexandrian excavations provide the displays in **Rooms 19-21**. Look particularly at the figures of the happy god Bes and Min (see Deities, page 545). **Room 22** is a reminder that Alexandria was a centre for glass-making. **Room 23** has an interesting display of coins.

> **It took a couple of millennia, but a new Bibliotheca was finally inaugurated on 16 October, 2002, about 100 m from the location of the old one. It boasts the largest open reading area in the world...**

Rooms 1-5 are devoted to Coptic artefacts. There are objects relating to St Menas' Monastery (see Abu Mina, page 342), including numerous pilgrims' flasks. The textiles have delightful designs, the Copts being recognized as fine weavers. Take time to examine the larger items displayed in the garden. Some of the statues are very fine. There are rock-cut tombs in the South Garden and the parts of the Temple of Pnepheros (Room 9) in the North Garden.

Bibliotheca Alexandrina

ⓘ *T03-4830346, 4830342. Sun-Thu 1100-1900, Fri and Sat 1500-1900, closed Tue. E£10, E£5 for students, US$60 for annual membership and US$30 annual membership for students.*

Bibliotheca Alexandrina, a 10-minute walk on the corniche east of El-Raml station, gives way to the striking concrete sun disc design, that rises by the Mediterranean symbolizing the dawn and rise of knowledge that has no end. The first library in the world was situated but a stone's throw away. Construction of the ancient knowledge centre was initiated in 288 BC by Ptolemy I, and finished during the reign of Ptolemy II. The old library housed 700,000 scrolls (equivalent to about 100,000 books). It caught fire twice – first from the infringing sparks of the Alexandria war and later from the residue of a fire commanded by a bishop intended to burn all pagan books in a daughter library nearby. It took a couple of millennia, but a new Bibliotheca was finally inaugurated on 16 October, 2002, about 100m from the location of the old one. The idea was conceived in the head of Dr. Mostafa Abeydi, a History Professor of the University of Alexandria in 1972. It took a while, but eventually UNESCO and the Egyptian government organized a competition to determine the proposed ediface's design. In 1989, a Norwegian's proposal was accepted and construction finally began in 1995. The effort, funded by Egypt, and a handful of other mostly Arab countries, cost US$220. The new library boasts the largest open reading area in the world. The complex is comprised of the main library building, a conference hall, and a planetarium. At present, it holds only 230,000 books, with the bottom floor hosting the roots of knowledge sprouting up through time to the top floor where new technology books are situated. There isn't yet a checkout system, but the premises have already become a hub for cultural activities. There are two permanent exhibitions, one featuring the impressive collection of Mohammed Awad, the contemporary architect, encompassing old photos, drawings and maps of ancient Alexandria; the other featuring a collection of the famed filmmaker/renaissance man Shadi Abdel Salam, with his drawings, books and antiques. You can pick up a free monthly bulletin with the schedule of music concerts, visiting exhibitions, public seminars, and lectures taking place at the library from the entrance of the conference building. Also on site are the **Archaeological Museum**, the **Manuscripts Museum**, and the **Science Museum** and **Planetarium**. Ask for a free guided tour at the information desk, available in English, French, Italian, Spanish and soon German.

How plump is the planet?

Eratosthenes lived in Alexandria. He was an eminent astrologer cataloging 675 stars and a mathematician but his fame came from measuring the circumference of the Earth.

At Aswan on the Tropic of Cancer at noon on midsummer's day the sun is directly overhead and casts no shadow. Eratosthenes, who was in Alexandria, measured the shadow cast there and was able to work out the angle of the sun's rays on the same day at the same time. Using information gathered from travellers he had previously concluded that the distance from Aswan to Alexandria was about 800 km. These two facts he used to calculate the circumference of the earth as 40,000 km, an error of only 75 km. He went on to work out the distance from the Earth to the Sun and the Earth to the Moon. His calculation of the angle of tilt of the axis of the Earth at 23° 51'14" was truly amazing.

Other museums and sights

Cleopatra's Empire and Second World War ruins were recently discovered **underwater** east of the Citadel of Mamluk Sultan Qaitbai. Excavations revealed Cleopatra's castle, her sun boat, a Second World War plane, and some 2000 monumental pieces. **Alexandra Dive** ⓘ *24 Sharia 26th of July, near Tikka Grill in El-Anfushi, T03-4832045, 010-6666514, www.alexandra-dive.com; US$45 for a single dive,* is a local dive centre which recently inaugurated the commercialization of the sites. It's possible to dive amid the underwater ruins, swim through columns and plane wrecks. Make sure you check the currents and visibility before committing, as the currents and undertow of the Mediterranean can be significantly stronger and more turbulent than the Red Sea.

The **Cavafy Museum** ⓘ *4 Sharia Sharm El-Sheikh, daily 1000-1500, 1800-2000 Sun and Thu, closed Tue, free,* has recently moved from the Greek Consulate building. It is now housed in the building where the great Alexandrian poet Constantine Cavafy lived for the last 25 years of his life. He died in 1933. Lying to the east of Sharia Nabi Daniel in the street parallel to and just north of Sharia El-Horiyya, it is marked with a plaque. Two of the rooms have been arranged with his household furniture, books and manuscripts to give an idea of the place when he was in occupation.

On the ground floor of the **Fine Art Museum** ⓘ *18 Sharia Menasce, T03-3936616, 4865800, daily 0900-1300, 1700-2000 on special exhibit days, free, take minibus 700 from Midan Khartoum to Sharia Moharram Bey, then take Sharia Ahmed Ismail off of Moharrram Bey to the museum,* there is a permanent exhibition of 20th-century Egyptian painting, while the upper floor is dedicated to temporary exhibitions which are generally of modern Egyptian art. It is a venue for concerts and the film club meets here every Wednesday.

The **Marine Life Museum** and **Hydro-Biological Institute** near Sultan Qaitbai's Fort on Anfushi Bay houses a rare collection of fish and marine life. ⓘ *T03-4807140, 4807138. Daily 0800-1500, 0800-2300 in summer, E£1.* The **Naval Museum** ⓘ *Daily 0900-1500 except Fri,* nearby contains artefacts from Roman and Napoleonic sea battles which are likely to appeal more to specialists than to the casual tourist.

The **Royal Jewellery Museum** ⓘ *21 Sharia Ahmed Yehia Pasha, Gleem, T03-5828348 (behind the Governor's residence), daily 0900-1700, Fri 0900-1130 and 1330-1600 (although closed for renovations at the time of writing), E£20, video E£150,* originally belonging to Fatma El-Zahra, granddaughter of Ibrahim Pasha, was formerly one of King Farouk's palaces which, with its garden, covers an area of over 4,000 sq m. It now houses a glittering collection of treasures from the time of Mohammed Ali

Lift your eyes from the jewels to admire the ceilings.

through to King Farouk. There are jewels, clearly labelled in Arabic and English, on everything in cases. Statues and paintings are also on display. The mansion in which these are housed is almost of equal interest. It contains 10 stained glass doors and many stained glass windows depicting stories of European history. The bathrooms, cordoned off but on view to the public, are an inspiration. The items in the collection considered the most important include: from Mohammed Ali, a gold plated, enamelled and inscribed snuff box; from King Fuad, a gold knob inlaid with diamonds, gold medals and decorations, a platinum crown inlaid with diamonds and sapphires with other pieces of jewellery to match; from King Farouk, a gold chess set enamelled and inlaid with diamonds, a gold tray inscribed with the signatures of 110 pashas; from Queen Safinaz, her crown of platinum inlaid with diamonds, gold and platinum brooches inlaid with diamonds. This is just the beginning of the catalogue.

Mahmoud Said Museum ⓘ *6 Mahmoud Said St, Ganaclis, T03-5826688, 5851245*, a beautiful intimate collection opened in 2000 to celebrate Said, a pioneer of Egyptian modern art. Set in the artist's former home, a stunning villa in a suburb just east of the city, the museum features a wide array of Said's work, highlighting scenes of traditional and rural life.

Beaches

Anywhere along the Corniche the beach is very pleasant and there are all the facilities nearby. **Stanley Beach** is among the best in town. To the east is the beach of the **Montazah Gardens** (see below) and another at Ma'amoura. **Abu Qir**, a small fishing village further east again offers a pleasant beach and the opportunity to sample the extremely fresh fish and shell fish.

Gardens

The **Antoniadis Gardens** ⓘ *near the El-Mahmudiya Canal and the zoo, T03-4243325, 4291757. Daily 0900-2000 in summer, and 0800-1830 in winter. E£2.* The house, originally owned by a wealthy Greek family is now used for meetings of state. The gardens contain beautiful arrangements of trees and flowerbeds as well as several Greek marble statues. The **Montazah Palace Gardens** ⓘ *open 24 hrs, entrance E£4*, cover almost 160 ha. These formal gardens are a welcome respite from the bustle of the city. Originally built in 1892, this palace only dates from 1926, when it became the summer residence of the Egyptian royal family. The adjacent beautiful beach makes this the most popular garden here. **Nouzha Gardens and Zoo** ⓘ *Sharia Smouha, T03-4280079, 4282255, both open daily 0830-1730 in summer, and 0830-1630 in winter, 25pt, you can get there directly by taking tram 10 from St. Catherine's Square*, has many interesting birds and animals in the zoo. Adjacent gardens have picnic areas. **Shallalat Gardens** ⓘ *to east of city centre, open 24 hours, free*, are lovely and have varying levels, rockeries and waterways. **Alexandria International Garden** ⓘ *open daily 0800-sunset. Tickets are between 50-75pt depending on day of the week. Minibus 781 from El-Khartoum Sq drops you off directly at the garden.* At the entrance of the Desert Road lies 130 acres of gardens that provide recreational and cultural activities such as water sports. The garden also contains models of famous Alexandria tourist attractions and sites.

Canopus

To the east and 5 km along Ma'mura Bay is Canopus which bears few traces of the Delta's chief market which flourished before the development of Alexandria and was best known for its **Temple of Serapis**. Canopic jars were produced here, see box on Mummification on page 218. The motivation for building a city in the area was the Canopic branch of the River Nile which has long since dried up. The city is claimed to have been built by Menelaeus's pilot Canopus on his return from the Trojan wars who was venerated by the local population after his death from snakebite. Today little remains of the site. The destruction is a recent phenomenon, apparently mainly caused by British occupation during the First and Second World Wars. The ancient remains which have survived, including several statues of Ramses II, are now in the Graeco-Roman Museum in Alexandria. Two **abandoned forts** to the east of Canopus can be explored.

Further east from Canopus, submerged under the waters of the Mediterranean Sea and 2 m of silt are the remains of the ancient cities of **Herakleion**, the main port of entry into Egypt before Alexandria was founded, and **Menouthius**, the centre for the cult of Isis. Recent elaborate excavations have verified the position and extent of these lost cities and produced some fascinating artefacts.

Sleeping

Alexandria is Egypt's 2nd largest city and as the major domestic resort for Egyptian tourists, it boasts hotels to suit every budget and taste. Besides the main downtown hotels there are others east along the coast toward the exclusive El-Montazah area and beyond. Hotels on the Corniche tend to suffer from traffic noise – day and night.

AL El-Salamlek Palace Hotel & Casino, PO Box 258 Montazah Palace, T03-5477999, F5473585. Built like an Alpine chalet for the Khedive's Austrian mistress. Once a royal guesthouse/study for King Farouk, now a very exclusive and newly renovated hotel, 6 rooms and 14 suites, 2 restaurants – French, Italian, and a health club. Also on offer: water sports, tennis, golf, bowling, fishing, and sailing. The hotel supports business

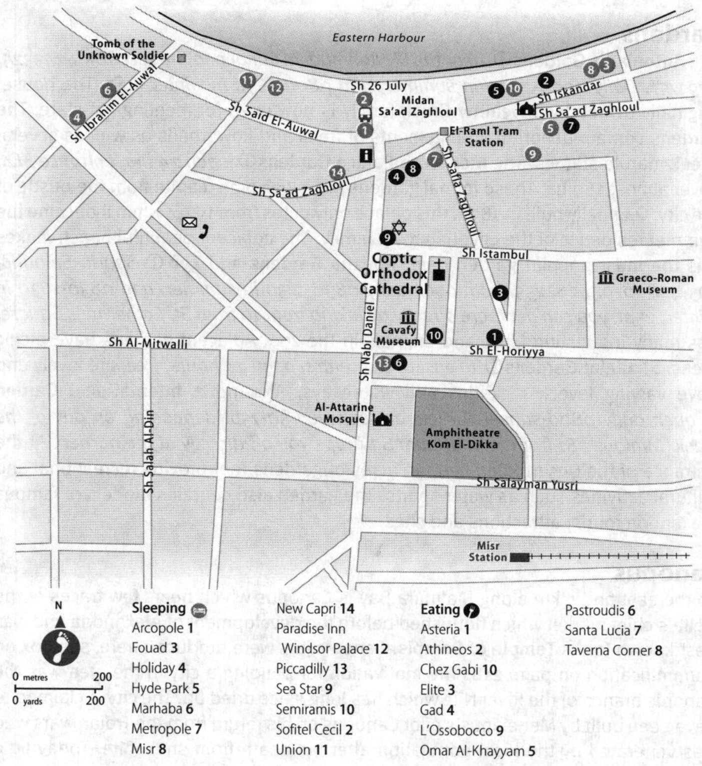

activities. There is a conference hall and secretarial service.

AL Helnan Palestine, Montazah Palace, El-Montazah, T03-5473500, F5473378. Recently renovated, 232 rooms, also in the grounds of the Montazah Palace with a lagoon, beautiful gardens and an excellent beach nearby. Very comfortable, charming staff and a most pleasant place to stay. Water sports from private jetty into Mediterranean.

AL Mercure Alexandria Romance, 303 Sharia El-Geish, Saba Pasha, T03-5840911, F5870526. Very comfortable, modern 5-star hotel with 55 recently renovated suites. Also 2 notable restaurants featuring French and Chinese cuisine.

AL Metropole, 52 Sharia Sa'ad Zaghloul, El-Raml Station, T03-4821466, F4822040. 70 centrally located rooms just renovated in dramatic fashion. Wonderful Greco-Roman decor. Established in 1902.

AL Montazah Sheraton, Corniche, El-Montazah, T03-5480550, 5481220, F5401331. More than half of the 311 rooms have been renovated and as a result are more expensive. Located outside the grounds of the walled Montazah Palace, with excellent sea views, private beach. For luxury and convenience this place cannot be faulted. Features 2 Italian restaurants, 2 coffee shops and a beauty salon, 1 adult and 1 children's pool.

AL Paradise Inn Windsor Palace, 19 Midan Saad Zaghloul, El-Raml Station, T03-4866510, 4866550, F4860049. 76 rooms with a breath-taking sea view, and close to main most main city attractions. Similar to Cecil in its feeling of recent antiquity, but more regal. Egyptian Minister of Culture stays here.

AL Renaissance Alexandria Hotel, 544 Sharia El-Geish (on coast road 12-15 km from town centre), Sidi Bishr, T03-5490935, F5485590. 171 very comfortable rooms and suites, excellent restaurant with panoramic view of the Mediterranean. Features a lovely new library with current periodicals and history books about Alexandria. Tours arranged upon request. Offers all the comforts of a good international hotel and the charm of well-trained staff, but the rooms seem a little worn for 5-star status. Check your room for traffic noise.

AL Sofitel Cecil, 16 Midan Sa'ad Zaghloul, T03-4807055, 4877173, F4855655. 86 rooms, guests have included Winston Churchill, Noel Coward, Lawrence Durrell, Agatha Christie, and Mohammed Ali Clay. Has 3 restaurants and a casino. The architecture and ambience transports you back a century. While the Cecil offers the convenience of being in the centre of town in the former European quarter, it lacks the peace of the other high quality hotels in El-Montazah.

A Hilton Green Plaza, Sharia 14th of May, Somouha, T03-4209120, T03-4209140. Despite the name, the 224 rooms overlook nothing green. The rooms are by far the most luxurious in all of Alexandria, but the distant location reflects the slight reduction in price. The best view is on the food court, which holds some 18 restaurant outlets and 11 coffee shops. The complex, fairly new to the scene, fast became young Alexandrians' favourite evening hang-out with its proliferation of stores, food, movie theatres, and arcade. No need to worry about the noise, all rooms are perfectly soundproofed.

A Paradise Beach Resort, Ma'amoura Beach, T03-5479602, 5650152, F5650153. 55 rooms surrounding a tropical pool with bar. Private beach with beach games five steps away from the pool. Health club available with animation team holding daily aerobics classes. Ideal for groups or couples with children, Day care nanny available. A real treat.

A Plaza, 394 Sharia El-Geish, Zizinia, T03-5838714, F5835399. 134 modern rooms in good condition, clean and with a sea view. A place for groups.

A San Giovanni, 205 Sharia El-Geish, Stanley, T03-5467775, F5464408. A beach hotel about halfway between downtown Alexandria and the Montazah Palace with 30 rooms. Overpriced for a 3-star hotel, despite the midway location between downtown and Montazah.

B Landmark, 163 Sharia Abdel Salam Aref, Midan, San Stefano, T03-5827850, 5840500, F5840515. 150 rooms, conveniently located about halfway between central Alexandria and the Montazah Palace. Better value than the San Giovanni.

C The quality of hotel varies considerably in this price range. A change of management or staff can make a big difference. Always ask to see the room first.

C Acasia Resort, Sharia Acasia, Behind Alexandria International Garden,

T010-1353131, F3934620. A recently-established country club-style resort with a motel. Day use and hotel residents are entitled to all facilities including tennis and squash courts, 6 swimming pools, health club, water games, restaurants and cafés. Recommended for families and travellers planning to stay for extended periods.

C **Alexandria**, 23 Midan El-Nasr, El-Manshiya, T03-4801447, 4837694, F4823113. Family-run central hotel with 108 rooms and attentive, personal service. Overlooking a busy square so ensure you request a quiet room.

C **Desert Home**, Sharia Omar El-Mokhtar, King Mariout, T03-981315, F4914939. One of a few places, and probably the only decent one, to stay in King Mariout, a 30-min drive out of Alexandria. Has 14 cosy rooms.

C **Ma'amura Palace**, El-Ma'amura, T03-4573108, 5473450, F5473383. 75 rooms and suites, good standard, modern, decent street views, in the exclusive El-Ma'amura area east of the Montazah Palace. Access to a clean beach, free for guests. A classical place to stay in Ma'amoura. Several Egyptian movies shot honeymoon scenes in the hotel. Recommended.

C **Marhaba**, 10 Midan Orabi, El-Manshiya, T03-4800957, 4809510. 33 rooms with a great partial sea view overlooking El-Manshiya Square. The central location might compensate for the slightly dirty bathrooms. For backpackers with a bit of money to spend.

D **Amoun**, 32 Midan El-Nasr, El-Manshiya, T03-4818228, 4807128, F4807131. 96 rooms overlooking a busy district. Rooms on top floors are somewhat secluded and quiet. There's a playstation room and pool table for entertainment. Chinese restaurant with separate management available in the lobby. Good value.

D **Al-Haram Hotel**, 16 Sharia El-Geish. 221 somewhat eerie rooms. If you don't mind the strange use of space or the green walls and plastic flowers, you'll appreciate the relatively cheap price and extremely friendly staff.

D **Hyde Park House**, 21 Sharia Amin Fikri, El-Raml Station, T03-4875667. 60 rather tired-looking rooms. If you can get a room overlooking the historic Qua'id Ibrahim Mosque and square, it may be worth the stay.

D **Mecca**, 44 Sharia El-Geish, Camp Caesar, T03-5923935, 5923925, F5919935. 105 very clean and recently renovated small rooms with direct sea views. Bathrooms are tacky but sparkling.

D **New Swiss Cottage**, 346 Sharia El-Geish, Gleem, on coast road about half way between downtown Alexandria and the Montazah Palace, T03-5835863, F5830455. Sixties-style beach furniture, plastic chairs and tiled floors. There is a sense of community among the friendly staff and the guests who often keep their room doors open to the corridor.

D **Semiramis**, 180 Sharia 26th July, T03-4846837, T03-4870824. 60 somewhat claustrophobic rooms, many of which have a sea view. Extremely overpriced compared to other options in the same price category.

E **Arcopole**, 27 Sharia El-Ghorfa Al Togariyya, El-Raml Station, T012-3737692. 37 stuffy rooms with dirty shared bathrooms. Still, seems quite popular among city-thriving travellers. Management organizes tours upon request.

E **Dovil Hotel**, 274 Sharia El-Geish, Stanley, T03-5454805, F5454806. 41 recently renovated clean rooms, overlooking a spectacular view of the new Stanley Bridge across the Stanley Bay. From the hotel roof terrace, you can spot the contents of a military museum not open to the public that includes gigantic ruins pulled out of the sea. Simple, comfortable and highly recommended.

E **Holiday**, 6 Midan Orabi, El-Manshiya, T03-4803517, F4801557. 41 double rooms suitable for backpackers. Bathrooms are a bit grubby, but the central location might justify the stay.

E **Korai Sert Hotel**, 802 Sharia El-Geish, El-Mandara, T03-5480996. 28 rooms with a noisy direct sea view. Overpriced for the standard of rooms and location, but just across the street from a public beach.

E **Nobel Hotel**, 152 Sharia El-Geish, T03-5464845, F5473374. 38 small cosy rooms with clean bedding. Nice sea view from small balconies. Some rooms have air conditioning. Friendly staff.

E **Sea Star Hotel**, 24 Sharia Amin Fikri, El-Raml Station, T03-4871787, 4805343. 59 rooms with a side sea view. Rooms are tidy, relatively clean and comfortable. Staff are helpful.

F **Al Arab Hotel**, 36 Sharia El-Nasr, El-Manshiya, T03-4804868. A bit rough, but cheap. For E£6-10, you can get one of 16 beds with clean sheets. All rooms open out to a terrace with a panoramic view of the main port and busy streets. The place has a charm to it, but not much else.

F Al Fondoqu Al Souri, 46 Sharia El-Nasr, T03-4811625. 51 rooms close in standard to Al Arab Hotel but not as clean. Bedrooms are also connected with a panoramic balcony overlooking busy streets and a bit of the sea. E£10 a bed.

F Fouad Hotel, 1 Sharia Degla, El-Raml Station, T03-4870684, 4879117. 11 very charming well-lit rooms with a breathtaking sea view of the Eastern Harbour. Located in a historical building. Great value if you don't mind the sharing a bathroom.

F Hotel Misr, 1 Sharia Degla, El-Raml Station, T03-4868386. In the same building as Fouad Hotel and shares the same spectacular view, but rooms are not as clean or tidy. 14 rooms. E£30 per double; E£20 per single; bargaining is possible.

F New Capri, 23 El-Mina, Sharia El-Sharkia, El-Raml Station, T03-809310. The 32 rooms are spacious and bathrooms are gleaming. Some rooms overlook the busy, yet central, Saad Zaghloul Square, downtown. Located in the tourist police building.

F Piccadilly, 11 Sharia El-Horiyya, El-Nabi Daniel, T03-4934802. 33 rooms, a 6th-floor exceedingly cheap hotel, near the railway station. A bargain.

F Union Hotel, 164 Sharia 26th July, El-Raml Station, T03-34807312, 4807771, F4807350. By far the best value for its price category. Rooms are spacious and clean. Management seems a bit conservative and might politely and indirectly reject mixed gender groups or unmarried couples sharing rooms.

F Youth hostel, 32 Sharia Port Said, 2 km northeast of city centre, Shatbi, El-Raml, T03-5925459, F5914759. 200 beds, meals available, train 3 km, ferry 5 km, family rooms, laundry, facilities for disabled, self catering available.

Camping

At Sharia Bahr Al-Mait in Abu Qir which is about 20 km from downtown Alexandria about 5½ km east of the Montazah Palace.

Eating

For the greatest concentration of restaurants and cafés, try the area bounded by Sharia Sa'ad Zaghloul, El-Raml station and Eastern Harbour by Midan Sa'ad Zaghloul. The restaurants in the higher grade hotels are reliable and serve Western and Egyptian cuisine.

TTT Abu Ashraf, 28 Sharia Safar Pacha, Bahari, T03-4816597, 4842850. Down the street from Gezeirit El-Maleka (see below), the menu and quality of food is comparable, but Abu Ashraf is more famous. The Crown Prince of Denmark is an annual regular.

TTT Alexander's, Renaissance Alexandria, 544 Sharia El-Geish, Sidi Bishr, T03-866111. Good service, excellent fish, and a panoramic view of the Mediterranean to boot.

TTT Al Farouk, El-Salamlek Hotel, Montaza Gardens, T03-5477999. Egyptian dishes and seafood served in elegant surroundings. Older, experienced waiters provide attentive and classy service.

TTT Chinese Restaurant, Cecil Hotel, T03-4877173. It's a pleasure to eat here. Authentic, albeit pricey, Chinese food with a the great view.

TTT Gezeirit El-Maleka, 46-48 Sharia Safar Pacha, Bahari, T03-4858886, 4831243. One of the best, and most laid back, seafood restaurants in all of Alexandria. For less than E£50 you can have a sample of every item on the menu. Drop the etiquette and comfortably use fingers to pick at the crab and clams. Freshness guaranteed. Bustles with people from all walks of life; families, groups, couples, tourists. Highly recommended.

TT Athineos, 21 Midan Sa'ad Zaghoul, T03-4860421. An all-time Alexandria classic, established more than a century ago by a Greek. Today the restaurant and café has added a few Egyptian dishes to its mainly Greek menu. There's a lovely pavement area with sea view. Alcohol served with meals and at bar.

TT Chez Gabi, 22 Sharia El-Horiyya, behind Cinema Royal, T03-4874404, 4874306. Italian cuisine. Pizzeria with diffused lighting and a lot of style. The first place to introduce pizzas to Egypt in 1979.

TT Denise, 1 Sharia Ibn Bassam, off El-Raml Station, T03-4861709. Open 0900-0100. Select your own fish from the freezer. Alcohol served.

TT Dynasty, Renaissance Alexandria, 544 Sharia El-Geish, Sidi Bishr, T03-5483977. A

Chinese restaurant a little out of town but worth the journey for the food and the sea view.

ƳƳ **Elite**, 43 Sharia Safia Zaghloul, T03-4863592. Open 0900-2400. Opposite Santa Lucia. A taste of the 60s and 70s. The unrenovated decor is sure to make you nostalgic. A great place for loners longing for a quaint reading spot, or for people in search of a quiet place to converse over a beer.

ƳƳ **Hosni**, Sharia Gamal Abdul Nasser, El-Mandara, T03-5507799, 5506655, and another branch on Safar Pach Street, Bahari, T03-4812350, 4843488. By far the best grill in the city. An authentic Egyptian haven for carnivores. Great value for the price.

ƳƳ **Kaddoura**, 33 Sharia Beirum El-Tonsi, Bahar, T03-4800405. This used to be *the* seafood place, with chains in Alexandria and Cairo, but the charm seems to have faded with commercial expansion.

ƳƳ **Pastroudis**, 39 Sharia El-Horiyya, El-Raml Station, T03-3929609. Resembles a 1950s movie set. A typical Mediterranean joint; dimly lit, wooden decor, and high ceilings. In spite of its charm, the place often seems to be empty.

ƳƳ **Samakmak**, 42 Sharia Ras El-Tin, T03-4811560, 4809523. Italian decor but mainly Egyptian seafood dishes. Cosy, inviting atmosphere.

ƳƳ **Santa Lucia**, 40 Sharia Safeya Zaghloul, T03-4860332, 4864240. Open 1200-1600 and 1900-0100. Excellent seafood and French cuisine. Serves wine and beer. This is where the classic song *Mustafa Ya Moustafa* made its debut.

ƳƳ **Seagull**, Sharia El-Agami, T03-4455575. Beachside Egyptian seafood restaurant. Excellent food and highly recommended, but way out of town in western industrial area.

ƳƳ **L'Ossobuco**, 14 Sharia El-Horiyya, T03-4872506. Recently renovated and very stylish French restaurant and pub which, perhaps surprisingly, also has a quite a few vegetarian options on the menu.

ƳƳ **Tikka Grill**, El-Kashafa Building, near Abul Abbas Al-Mursi Mosque, T03-4805119, 4805114. Open 1300-1700 and 2000-0200. View overlooking Eastern Harbour. Beautifully presented, spicy Indian grill with salad bar.

Ƴ **Cafeteria Asteria**, 40 Sharia Safeya Zaghloul next door to Santa Lucia, T03-4822293. Open until 2400. Serves a range of tasty cheap Italian and Greek dishes in charming, classic environs.

Ƴ **Fuul Mohammed Ahmed**, 17 Sharia Abdel Fattah El-Hadary, near El-Raml station, T03-4873576, a block east of Midan Sa'ad Zaghloul, beyond Bank of Alexandria and a block south of Sharia Safia Zaghloul. Open 0600-2400. A totally authentic, cheap and delicious Egyptian dining experience and a haven for vegetarians.

Ƴ **Gad**, 1 El-Raml Station, T03-4860135. The original Egyptian stand-up fast food chain, with several branches in Cairo. Serves great *fuul* and *ta'amiya* as well as *fiteer* and all the other standard meaty local specialties. Reliably good, clean and cheap.

Ƴ **Taverna Corner**, at El-Raml station, T03-4874591. Open 0730-0200. Greek-owned tasty fish dishes and pizzas with salad bar.

Cafés

There's 24-hr service in better hotels including Sheraton, Ramada Renaissance, Plaza, Landmark and San Giovanni. Good atmosphere at Cecil Hotel by bus station. Minimum charge E£8 per person, mouth-watering pastries.

Athineos, by the station. Classical décor, gets noisy in the evenings.

Baudrot, 23 Sharia Sa'ad Zaghloul, El-Raml, T03-4869751, 4865687. Classic Western style coffee shop. The indoors area isn't that inviting, but there's a heavenly terrace with a ceiling made of grape vines. The place is calm, secluded, ideal for a quiet morning. Serves drinks and some desserts.

Brazilian Coffee Shop, 44 Sharia Sa'ad Zaghloul, by the tourist office, T03-4865059. Very old coffee roaster and stand-up coffee joint. Great cappuccino. A real taste of Alexandria.

Coffee Roastery, Sharia Fouad, T03-4805119, 4805114. If you're longing for a piece of home, this is the best Western-style coffee shop near the city centre and the best branch of the chain. Chose from an extensive menu of coffee and all sorts of funky fruit drinks.

Délices, 46 Sa'ad Zaghloul, T03-4861432, 4865460. Licensed French-style coffee shop and patisserie. Serves snacks in a high-ceilinged, spacious area. An Alexandria classic.

El-Sultan Hussein, intersection of Sharia El-Sultan Hussein and Sharia Safiya Zaghloul. A typical Egyptian *ahwa* with *sheesha*, backgammon, hot and cold drinks. Spacious and open to the pavement.

Faroul, Sharias Ismail Sabri and Mohamed Korayyim, T03-4803103. Same management as El-Sultan Hussein *ahwa* and similar offerings. The ambience is more regal. High ceilings and marble walks.

Grand Café, El-Kashafa Building, Bahari, T03- 34805119, 4805114. Another western-style café. Although open-air and close to the sea, there's no seaside. More of an evening hang-out.

Jungle, Sharia Acasia, behind the Alexandria International Garden, T03-5388024, 010-1250917. An open-air night café with lots of greenery and jungle-like decor. There is a beautiful swan lake in the middle of the place. Offers *sheesha*, Egyptian food and drinks.

Sofianopolo, 18 Sharia Sa'ad Zaghloul, El-Raml Station, T03-4871417. Stand-up coffee shop and roaster. Similar to Brazilian coffee shop but more spacious and sells packaged products like cocoa powder and instant juice.

Trianon Le Salon, east end of Midan Sa'ad Zaghloul under Hotel Metropole, T03-4860986, 4860973. Another of Alexandria's classics. Very elegant. Don't confuse it with the new Trianon chain that sprawled across Egypt less than 5 years ago.

Welad El-Zawat Café, Sharia Victor Emanuel, Semouha, T03-5245455. Western-style coffee shop, most lively after sunset. Features board games and Karaoke nights every Saturday.

Other seaside western style cafés and *ahwas* are scattered along the Corniche often less than 50 m apart. Some are noisier than others.

Bars and clubs

Most of the large hotels have some evening entertainment, though not with the style of the capital.

Aquarius, Sheraton Montazah, T03-5480550. Has a belly dance competition every Monday and occasionally a Russian dancing show.

Café Royal, 22 Sharia El-Horiyya, next door to Chez Gabi Restaurant, T03-4874404, 4874306. Pub, nightclub and restaurant. There's a dance floor and DJ on most nights. Occasionally features live bands. Excellent French cuisine.

Calithea, 82 Sharia 27th of July, El-Raml Station. Greek style 2-storey seaside pub. Famous for *mezze* and Greek seafood.

Cesar, Montazah Sheraton Hotel. Piano bar, sometimes live bands, and a dance floor.

Dolphin Nightclub, Palestine Hotel. Open 2200-0330. Features live singing. Dance floor and music.

Mermaid, 38 Sharia El-Geish, a 5-min walk from El-Raml Station, T03-4844822, 4847764. A quaint little beach side pub and restaurant with a dance floor and DJ upstairs.

Palace Suite, Plaza Hotel. Open 2200-0430. Cocktail bar. Features belly dancing and live music.

Sheikh Ali Bar (officially Cap D'Orbar), 4 Adib St, T03-4875177, 012-4489704. One of Alexandria's oldest. Very cheap, laid back all-Egyptian bar. Waiters are extraordinarily cheerful. Try the *besaria mezza*; deep-fried salted sardines. The actual bar is a 1919 antique.

Entertainment

Cinemas

Amir, 42 Sharia El-Horiyya, T03-3927693.

Metro, 26 Sharia Safia Zaghloul, T03-4830432.

Radio, 22 Midan Sa'ad Zaghloul, T03-4870282.

Rialto, 31 Sharia El-Horiyya, T03-4864694.

Rio, 37 Sharia El-Horiyya, T03-3929036.

There are four **Renaissance** cinemas inside Zahran Mall, T03-4240844, 424086. At the Green Plaza Mall, Sharia 14th May, Somouha, there are 6 massive screens, but it's a bit of a haul from the city centre.

Concerts

Alexandria Conference Centre, in Great Hall – contact Les Amis de la Musique et Des Arts, T03-5862325 for programme.

Theatre

Alexandria's old opera house opposite Cinema Royal presents plays, concerts and ballets, T03-4865110.

El-Anfushi Cultural Centre Theatre, T03-4804805.

El-Salam Theatre, Sharia El-Geish, Mustafa Kamel, T03-5436543.

Mohamed Abdel Wahhab Theatre, Sharia 26th July, El-Raml Station, T03-4863637.

Puppet's Theatre, Sharia El-Geish, Mustafa Kamel, T03-5436543.
Sayed Darwish Theatre, Sharia 22 El-Horiyya, T03-4800092.

Festivals and events

Feb International Book Fare, at the Fine Arts Museum. **Mar** International Marathon, Cairo-Alexandria. **Jul 26** Alexandria National Day. **Sep** International Movie Festival. **Sep** (every other year) World Alexandria Festival. **Nov** International Yacht Regatta.

Shopping

Alexandria has a wide range of shops but lacks the famous souks of Cairo. The main area is south and west of Midan Sa'ad Zaghloul. **Leather goods** including shoes are of good quality and good value. Look also for silk and cotton material and clothes. **Zan'it El-Sittat** in El-Manshiya is a historical shopping spot with a hodge podge of sewing accessories and cheap beauty items. The public sector chain stores are well represented; among them, **Omar Effendi**, **Haute Couture Co**. and **Couture Moderne Co**. Among the many malls are: **El-Samalek**, El-Samalek Palace Hotel, Montazah Gardens; **El-Wataneya**, Sharia Shaarawi, Loran; **Mena**, Sharia Bilouz, Ibrahimia; **Zaharan**, Sharia Victor Emmanuel, Semouha; **Green Plaza Mall**, at the Hilton Green Plaza Hotel.

The **Fish Market** further west on Anfushi Bay is easy to find, just follow your nose. Go early to see this small area teeming with fish and people. You can also watch ships being made; workers are friendly and welcome tourists.

Bookshops: **Al-Ahram**, 10 Sharia El-Horiyya, T03-4874000; **Book Bazaar** in Renaissance Hotel, open 0900-1200; **Book Centre**, 49 Sharia Sa'ad Zaghloul, T03-4872925, has best choice of books in English, French and German; **Dar El-Mostakbal**, 32 Sharia Safeya Zaghloul, T03-4872452, books and magazines in English, French and German; **Nile Christian Bookshop**, 4 Sharia Anglican Church, Attarine.

For **fresh fruits and vegetables** have a meander around El-Manshiya Square. Supermarkets and grocery stores are scattered all around the city and are easy to spot. For Western-style shopping there's a **Metro Market** in the Zahran Mall, and another branch in Cleopatra just after the Cleopatra Tunnel.

Activities and tours

Beach and water sports facilities are available at all major hotels. Non residents can, with permission and a not-always requested modest fee, use pools at major hotels like the Sheraton Montazah and the Renaissance.
Alexandria Sporting Club, T03-5433627/8/9. Golf, tennis, bowling and horse riding but you may need to befriend a member to be able to get in.

Horse racing

Racing Club, Sharia 14th May, Semouha Club, T03-4274656.

Tour operators

Atlantic Tours, 40 Sharia Safeya Zaghloul, T03-4830119.
Egyptian International Travel, 16 Sharia Talaat Harb, T03-4845882, 4848881.
Fayed Travel, 7 Sharia El-Fath, Wezarah Station, Fleming, T03-5870579.
Misr Tours, 28 Sharia Sa'ad Zaghloul, T03-4809617, F4847995.
North African Shipping Co, 63 Sharia Nabi Daniel, T03-4870059.
Passant Travel, 164 Sharia El-Horiyya, Camp Caesar, T03-5916091, 5917378.
Sporting Tours, 178 Sharia Omar Lutfi, Sporting, T03-5918964.
Thomas Cook, 15 Midan Sa'ad Zaghloul, T03-4867830.

Water sports

Alexandria Yacht Club, adjacent to Sultan Qaitbai's Fort, T03-4802563. Gives sailing lessons and holds an annual regatta in Nov, boats available for hire.
Alexandra Dive, 24 Sharia 26th July, near Tikka Grill in El-Anfushi, T03-4832045; 010-6666514, www.alexandra-dive.com. Organize diving around the ruins of Cleopatra's Empire and a war plane wreck. One dive costs around US$45. Check the currents and visibility before committing, as the currents and undertow of the Mediterranean can be quite strong.

Transport

Air

The airport, southeast of the city off the main Delta road to Cairo on land reclaimed from Lake Maryut, has 5 flights per week to **Cairo** and **Jeddah** (Mon, Wed, Thu, Fri); 2 per week to **Hurghada** and **Sharm El-Sheikh** (Mon and Fri); 2 per week to **Athens** and **Kuwait**; and 1 per week to **Abu Dhabi**, **Beirut**, **Benghazi**, **Dammam**, **Doha**, **Dubai** and **Riyadh**.

Considering the time wasted at airports and the travel time to and from it is certainly as quick, and much, much cheaper to travel by road to Cairo.

Airline offices El-Nozha Airport, T03-4271036, 4272021. **Air France**, 22 Sharia Salah Salam, T03-4878901. **Alitalia**, 6 Sharia Mahmoud Azmy, T03-4870847. **British Airways**, 15 Midan Sa'ad Zaghloul, T03-4876668. **EgyptAir**, 19 Midan Sa'ad Zaghloul, T03-4868701. **Lufthansa**, 9 Sharia Talaat Harb, T03-4875983. **Olympic Airlines**, 19 Midan Sa'ad Zaghloul, T03-4847295. **Royal Dutch Airlines (KLM)**, 6 Sharia El-Horiyya, T03-4868547.

Bus

Long distance All Western Delta Buses, T03-4270916, and **Superjet**, T03-4289092, arrive and depart from the 15th May Station behind the Sidi Gaber train station. Accessible by minibus from town centre or tram No 2. West Delta and Superjet buses leave every 30 mins to **Cairo**. Tickets cost E£16-E£20, depending on departure time and final destination. For an additional E£5, you can be dropped off at Cairo International Airport. **Siwa**: West Delta, 0830, 1100, 1400. E£27. **Marsa Matrouh**: West Delta, hourly service, E£15 with stops, E£20-23 for direct trips. **Port** Said: West Delta, 0600, 0800, 1100, 1600, 1800, E£18-22. **Safaga**: daily 0630, E£65, via **Ras Ghareb** (E£50), **Zafarana** (E£50) and **Hurghada** (E£60) then **Safaga** (E£65).

International **Cyprus**: service has ceased as of late due to low demand. This very well may change. For the latest information contact, **North African Shipping Company** (NASC), 63 Sharia Nabi Daniel, T03-4870059. **Aquaba-Jordan**: daily, 0600; ferry ticket is an additional US$75, via **Cairo** and **Nuweiba**.

Local Public buses are the most used form of transport by Alexandrians. Tickets cost 25p to E£1, depending on how far you ride. They are almost always crowded and you are very unlikely to find a seat. Not recommended for long trips. Some popular routes from **El-Raml** Station are: No 1 to **San Stefano**, **Sidi Gaber Train Station** and **Sidi Bishr**; No 2 to **Zahra' El-Agami**; No 3 (special a/c bus) to **Hanovillle beach** in El-Agami; No 12 (special a/c bus) to **Bitach beach** in El- Agami; No 555 (special a/c bus) to **Borg El-Arab Airport**.

Minibuses offer a slightly less rugged way to travel inside the city, and you are much more likely to find a seat. Some popular routes from **Midan El-Khartoum** are: No 700 to the new bus station/ service taxi terminal in **Moharram Bey**; No 750 to **Bitach beach** in El-Agami; No 760 to **Hanoville beach** in El-Agami; No 781 to **Alexandria International Garden**; No 706 and 707 to the **Citadel of the Mamluk Quait Bay**; No 215 to the **Marine Public Bus Station** (El-Mahatta El-Bahariyya).

From **Midan Orabi**: No 703 to **El-Nozha Airport**; No 736 to **El-Montazah** and **El-Ma'amoura**; No 729 to **Abu Qir**; No 724 to the **15th** of May Bus station in Somouha (where are West Delta and Superjet buses are based).

From **Misr Railway Station**: No 768 to **Abu** Qir via the Corniche; No 770 to **El- Montazah** and **El-Ma'amoura**; No 778 to **El-Madara**; No 728 to **Abu Qir**, Sharia El- Horiyya.

Calèche

A ride in a horse-drawn *calèche* along the Corniche or from outside the Misr railway station is a slower and more expensive alternative; E£15-20 for 30-min meander.

Car hire

Avis, Sofitel Cecil, T03-807532. **Budget**, 59 Tariq El-Geish, T03-5971273. A/c Fiat costs E£125 per day including tax and insurance, deposit of E£300 required. **Limousine**, 25 Sharia Talaat Harb T03-4825253.

Taxis

Long distance Service taxis depart from **Moharram Bey terminal**, on the outskirts of town, (in Arabic known as *El-Mogaf gedida* or the new terminal). Accessible by minibus from

Midan El-Gumhoriyya, (25p) or taxi (E£5) the terminal serves all North Coast tourist destinations. Drivers call out their destinations. There is regular service to: **Marsa Matruh** (hourly, 0630-2100, E£10-15); **King Mariout** (0800-1800); **Mar Mina Village** (hourly, 0800-1800); **El-Alamein** (hourly, 0800-1500); **Borg El-Arab** (every half-hour, 0630-2000); **Abu Sir** (0700, 1430); **Rosetta/Rasheed** (hourly, 0700-1900); **Wadi Natrun** (hourly, 0700-1600).

Local Metered black and orange city taxis can be caught throughout the city. Taxi rides in Alexandria are cheaper than in Cairo. Like Cairo, the meters are rarely on. In Alexandria, expect to pay around E£4 for a 10-min ride, E£8 for 20 mins, etc.

Train

Long distance Alexandria has 2 train stations. The main **Misr Station**, T03-3921233, is in Midan El-Gumhoriyya in the city centre. **Sidi Gaber Station** is to the east, about a 15-min taxi ride from El-Raml station. Trains to and from Cairo stop at both stations. To **Cairo**, there are more than 12 trains a day (2-3 hrs), via **Sidi Gaber**, **Tanta**, **Banha**, and **Damanhour**. Although slower and less frequent, there are also a few west bound trains to **El-Alamein** and **Marsa Matruh**, but you're better off taking the bus. When demand is sufficient, the French-owned **Abela** train company, T03-3932430, runs an overnight sleeper from Sidi Gaber Station to **Luxor** and **Aswan** via **Cairo** (departs daily at 1720, US$74.70 for a single and US$53.25 per bed in a double, payable in foreign currency only, no credit cards, duration is about 12 hrs).

Local **Trams**: from El-Raml station just to the east of Midan Sa'ad Zaghloul. A cheap way to cut long distances across the city but can be painfully slow and crowded, although they are a nice way to tour the city if you can afford the time. They run from dawn until 2400. Popular tram routes are: No 15 from El-Raml Station to **Ras El-Tin**; No 25 from Sidi Gaber to **El-Raml Station** and Ras El-Tin; No 3 from St Catherine's Square to **Maharram Bey**; No 10 from St Catherine's Sq to **El-Nozha**; No 16 from St Catherine's Sq to **Karmouz**.

Directory

Banks

There are branches of most domestic banks. Central branches of **Bank of Alexandria** at 59 Sharia Sa'ad Zaghloul, T03-4878588, and 6 Sharia Salah Salam, 4864056. Open Sun-Thu 0830-1400. **Bank Misr**, 9 & 18 Sharia Talaat Harb, T03-4870629, 4868612. **Banque du Caire**, 16 Sharia Sisostris and 5 Sharia Salah Salam, T03-4866273, 4861243. Foreign banks include: **American Express**, 10 Sharia Beatrice Lumumba, T03-3950918; **Citibank**, 95 Borg El-Silsila, El-Azarieta, T03-4875236, T03- 806376; **NSGB**, 240 Sharia El-Geish, Roshdi, T03-5452352; **Thomas Cook**, El-Raml Station, recommended for changing travellers' checks.

Cultural centres

American, 3e Sharia Pharana St, T03-4861009. **El-Anfushi Culture Centre**, T03-4804805. **British Council**, 9 Sharia El-Batalsa, Bab Sharaqi, T03-4860199. **French**, 30 Sharia El-Nabi Daniel, T03-3918952. **German**, 10 Sharia Batalsa, Bab Sharaqi, T03-4839870. **Italian**, Italian Consulate, Midan Sa'ad Zaghloul, T03-4874924. **Jesuit Culture Centre**, 298 Port Said St, Cleopatra, T03-5423553. **Russian**, 5 Sharia Batalsa, Bab Sharaqi, T03-4865645. **Spanish**, 101 Sharia El-Horiyya, T03-3920214.

Embassies and consulates

Denmark, 20 Sharia Beatrice Lumumba, T03-3921818. **France**, 2 Midan Orabi, T03-4809038. **Germany**, 5 Sharia Kafr Abdu, Roushdi, T03-4867503. **Netherlands**, Sharia Mohamed Mas'oud, T03-4264877. **Spain**, 101 Sharia El-Horiyya, T03-3939185. **Sudan**, 48 Sharia El-Horiyya, T03-4879920. **Switzerland**, 8 Sharia Mokhtar Adbel-Hamid Khallaf, T03-5832978. **UK**, 3 Mena Roshdi, T03-5467001. **United States Consulate**, 3 Sharia El-Farana T03-4861911.

Hospitals

Armed Forces Hospital, Sharia El-Geish and Sharia Port Said, T03-5430747. **Egyptian-British Hospital**, Sharia Mohamed Baha' El-Deen El-Ghatwari, Semouha, T03-4227722. **German Hospital**, 56 Sharia Abd El-Salam Arif, T03-5841806, 4204845.

Somouha Medical Centre, Sharia 14 May, Semouha, T03-4272652. **University Hospital**, Kolleyet El-Tib St, T03-4861861. **El-Salama Specialized Hospital**, T03-4863471.

Internet
Cyber cafés are constantly going in and out of business, but there are so many in Alexandria that you should not have any problem spotting one. Try: **Bonzzi**, 7 Sharia Abdel Hamid El-Deeb, T03-5844188, open 1000-2300; **ICC Internet**, Sharia Safiya Zaghloul, downtown, T03-4874459, open 1000-2200; **NetServ**, Sharia Abu Quir, Loran, T03-5832269, open 1200-0500.

Pharmacies
El-Ahram, 56 Aziz Fahmy St, T03-5455099. **Gleem**, 15 Moustafa Fahmy Street, Gleem, T03-5825820. **Hisham**, 40 Sharia Moharram Bay, T03-3936263. **Oxford**, 10 Sharia Kolleyet El-Teb, T03-4876720. **Rushdi**, 423 Sharia El-Horiyya, T03-5428018. **El-Razzi**, 67 Sharia Sidi Gaber El-Sheikh, T03-5423794.

Places of worship
Anglican/Episcopal All Saints' Church, Stanley Bay, services Sun 1800 (in Arabic) and Fri 1030 (in English); **St Mark's**, Midan El-Tahrir, El-Mansheya, at 1030 each Sun. **Catholic** St Catherine's Cathedral, 3 Midan Saint Catherine's, El-Manshiya El-Soghra, T03-4864546, Sun 0830 in Arabic, 1200 in French and 1800 in Italian. **Synagogue**, 69 Sharia El-Nabi Daniel, Fri afternoon and Sat morning, temporarily closed.

Post office
Open Sat-Thu 0800-2000 at Midan El-Raml. Sidi Gaber Train Station has a post office, T03-5465169. **DHL**, 14 Sharia Omar Lutfi, Sporting, T03-4271148. **FedEx**, Sharia 281 El-Horiyya, Sporting, T03-4272312.

Telephone
There are **Menatel** and **Nile Card** telephones on every street (sometimes every hundred metres). Cards can be purchased from supermarkets, pharmacies, and kiosks for denominations of E£5, E£10, E£20. International calls from the exchange at El-Raml Station, open 24 hrs. International calls from hotels are trouble free but slightly more expensive. Calls are always cheaper after 2000.

Useful numbers and addresses
Ambulance, T123; Fire, T180; Police, T122; Port, T03-4800100, 4800201. **Passport Office**, 25 Sharia Talaat Harb, T03-4847873, for registering arrival and renewing visas, open Sat-Thu 0800-1430. **Tourist Police**, Midan Sa'ad Zaghloul, T03-4873378, and in grounds of Montazah Palace, T03-5473395, and at the Citadel of Qaitbai, T03-4809144.

West to Libya

→ *Colour map 1, grid A2/3.*

From Alexandria, the Mediterranean Coast stretches 500 km west to the Libyan border passing through El-Alamein, Alexandria's local beach resorts of El-Agami and Hannoville, and the new beach resorts of Maraqia, Marabilla, Sidi Abdel Rahman and Marsa Matruh (from where a road leads inland to the Siwa oasis, see page 471), before finally arriving at the Libyan border near Sollum. The first few kilometres are the worst, as the road west out of Alexandria is complicated and very badly signposted. There are two roads going west: it is best to take the more scenic coastal route. For the first 30 km a series of developments, more attractive to stay in than to look at, lie between the road and the sea. ▸▸ *For Sleeping, Eating and other listings, see pages 346-348.*

Beach resorts west of Alexandria

El-Agami and Hannoville

About 20-25 km west of Alexandria, are these two beach resorts, popular with wealthy Egyptians, which tend to be packed during weekends, especially in the summer. They can be reached easily and cheaply from Alexandria by bus, service taxi; or microbus which leave El-Gumhoriyya and Moharram Bey station every 10-30 minutes.

Abu Sir

Abu Sir, 43 km from Alexandria, is halfway between Alexandria and El-Alamein. Here the important but neglected archaeological site of **Taposiris Magna** dating back to the 27th Dynasty stands to the south of the road. Remains include a necropolis, two temples, a 10th-century church and the **lighthouse**. In the Ptolemaic period a string of beacons lit up the coast from Pharos in Alexandria to Cyrenaica in Libya. The **Borg Al-Arab** (Arab Tower) just to the east of Abu Sir, is the sole survivor. The 17-m high lighthouse has the same three-tier construction as Pharos but is just a tenth of the size. The cylindrical top collapsed but it still gives an accurate impression of the appearance, if not the scale, of the Wonder at Pharos. The ancient temple dedicated to Osiris was of Ptolemaic design except for the gate at the east which had a more traditional Pharaonic structure. The series of colonnades were thought to resemble Karnak temple.

A second temple was discovered here at the beginning of the century by Italian archaeologists. This was dedicated to the ibis, the sacred bird of Egypt. This was hewn out of the rock and is well enough preserved for the illustrations of birds and animals on the walls to be quite clear today. There is much concern, however, about the continuing deterioration of the buildings due to erosion; the dampness and salt in the atmosphere being harsh enough to make some places of critical concern. There is worry too about the stability of the remains of the church. Many damaged stones have been replaced and a safe walkway for visitors has been cleared.

The mound has been excavated – following the discovery during the Second World War of an engraving – and it is here the necropolis is buried, parts dated as Graeco-Roman and others going back to the 27th Dynasty. All the sarcophagi found here were anthropoidal in shape. Abu Sir was once an important coastal town, surrounded by great walls which have long since crumbled, so now only the gates remain. From the top there is a beautiful view over the Maryut marshes to the sea.

Abu Mina

Abu Mina, 48 km southwest from Alexandria and about 15 km inland from Abu Sir, beyond the new town of Mobarak, was once the most important destination in the east for Christian pilgrims, thanks to **Deir Mari Mina**, one of the largest Coptic monasteries. **St Menas**, an Egyptian-born Roman legionary, was martyred in Asia Minor in AD 296 for refusing to renounce Christ. He had rather a bad time. Legend says that first they tore off the soles of his feet, then poked out his eyes before pulling out his tongue. None of these assaults prevented him from standing up to address the crowd. In the end the Emperor himself struck the fatal blow and the body was placed in a lead coffin and sunk out at sea. The coffin was washed ashore, discovered by passing Bedouins and loaded on to a camel. He was buried here when the camel carrying his coffin would go no further. When miracles occurred at the site of his tomb the news travelled across Christendom, via the camel trains, that the tomb of Abu Mina and the Holy Waters nearby could cure sickness and suffering, and his sanctity was assured. Successive emperors built temples and basilicas around the shrine but when the waters dried up in the 12th century the town fell into decay. Excavations have revealed the remains of the basilicas and shrines and much of the surrounding pilgrim town. Most pilgrims left carrying a small amount of healing water in a small clay bottle – marked with the image of a St Menas and two kneeling camels. These are common enough to appear in your local museum. Saint Menas' day is now celebrated on 11 November and the town is the site of an austere concrete Coptic monastery which was built in 1959, easily recognized by its two white towers.

El-Alamein

El-Alamein, 106 km west of Alexandria, owes its fame to what was, until the 1967 Arab-Israeli war, the largest tank battle in history. In July 1942 the Allies under Britain's Field Marshal Montgomery halted the German-Italian advance towards the River Nile and, in British eyes, if not in those of the Soviet troops at Stalingrad, turned the course of the Second World War. Winston Churchill later wrote, not entirely accurately, "Before Alamein we never had a victory. After Alamein we never had a defeat". (See The North Africa campaign, page 344.) Unless you are a military historian or have a personal interest in the battle, there is little to see and it is probably best to combine a visit here with other sights on the journey from Alexandria to El-Alamein. ▸▸ *For Sleeping and other listings, see page 346.*

Ins and outs

El-Alamein is a fairly short car or bus ride away from Alexandria. The trains are slow and upon arrival there's a 2 km walk north from the station to town. Buses and service taxis are faster and more frequent. From Alexandria, you can hop on any bus or service taxi bound for Marsa Matrouh and disembark near the War Museum at El-Alamein. To get back to Alexandria or carry on to Marsa Matrouh, you'll have to flag down a vehicle, as there's no bona fide station or depot in town. Alternatively, you can rent a car in Alex or hire a car with driver from a tour company. With Thomas Cook it's around US$60 per car.

Sights

El-Alamein was the site of the battle between Germany's Afrika Korps and the Allied Eighth Army which turned the Second World War in the Allies' favour and marks the closest that the Axis forces got to the Nile valley. The results of the encounter can be seen adjacent to the town in the huge **war cemeteries** (about 11,000 were killed and 60,000 wounded). The Greek war memorial is passed first. The **Commonwealth cemetery** ⓘ *daily 0700-1630 but books of remembrance not available Friday, free,* lies to the east of the town to the south of the road. Through the arch and beyond the gardens silent lines of over 7,000 white headstones commemorate those who fought and died supporting the Allied cause. Despite the sombre surroundings the gardens here encourage migrant birds – and bird watchers. The **German cemetery** lies about 4 km to the west of the town between the road and the sea. Here in a sand coloured building resembling a castle there are 4,200 graves. The man with the key will see you coming. He lives nearby. The **Italian cemetery**, the only one in North Africa, lies a further 6 km west of the town on the sea side. The white memorial tower is dedicated to 4,800 Italian soldiers, sailors and airmen. Just walk in.

El-Alamein has a fairly good beach but heed the danger signs for unexploded mines! Large parts of the coast and the desert are fenced off because they are still littered with them. Use common sense and keep to the main roads and beaches.

A **museum** ⓘ *daily 0800-1800, 0900-1500 in Ramadan, E£5, E£5 for camera,* to the west of the settlement contains maps of the campaign and some of the uniforms and weaponry used in Egypt by both sides. A clever map/model display with lights and commentary (choose your language) explains the North Africa campaign. There is also information here about the war between Egypt and Israel in 1973.

Marsa Matruh → *Population: 25,000*

Marsa Matruh (178 km west of El-Alamein, 288 km west of Alexandria and 512 km northwest of Cairo), has been transformed from a sleepy village (noted for sponge

The Desert War 1940-43

Italy, the colonial power in Libya at the outbreak of the Second World War, invaded Egypt in the closing weeks of 1940 thus beginning a long period of fighting between the Axis powers and Great Britain in North Africa. Italian, and later German, strategic plans were the displacement of Great Britain from Egypt, the destruction of Britain's imperial communications links through Suez, and the opening up of the Middle East oilfields to Axis penetration. The local Arab and Berber peoples of North Africa played a remarkably small role in events. The damage and disruption of the war were considerable and their negative effects (see Box 'Mine perils ever present', page 39) persisted for many years after the end of hostilities.

The Italians were soon expelled from Egypt and much of eastern Libya but were powerfully reinforced in Tripolitania in February 1941 by the arrival of German troops and armour which rapidly drove the British back to the Egyptian frontier by April. The German formations were led by General Rommel with skill and audacity. Air power favoured the joint German-Italian armies in the earlier part of the campaign. Rommel's eastward advance was slowed by the protracted resistance of the garrisons, first Australian then British and Polish, at Tobruk. Meanwhile, the main armies fought pitched battles around the Libyan-Egyptian border until Rommel withdrew temporarily in December 1941. He used his improved lines of communication in the west to prepare a counter attack and pushed east again as far as Gazala, near to Derna, in January and February 1942 and, after a pause, into Tobruk and deep into Egypt in June though his advance was finally held at El-Alamein after a fierce battle. Rommel made a final attempt at Alam Halfa east of El-Alamein to push aside British and Commonwealth forces and break through to the Nile Valley in August 1942 but failed in the face of strong defensive effort and his own growing losses of men and equipment.

The balance in the desert war changed in mid-1942 as the allies gradually won superiority in the air and had more freedom of movement at sea. The Germans and Italians began increasingly to suffer from shortages of equipment, while the health of Field Marshal Rommel gave rise to concern. On the allied side, General Montgomery took over leadership of allied forces and began a build-up of the Eighth Army sufficient to overwhelm the well trained and experienced Afrika Korps. Montgomery opened his attack at El-Alamein on 23 October 1942 and after 11 days of hard fighting the Axis army was beaten back and retreated by rapid stages to the west to make a last, unsuccessful, stand in Tunisian territory.

fishing) and minor port into a popular, low-grade, summer resort for domestic tourists with a plethora of tatty beach-side tented areas belonging to trade and government groups. Despite the government's attempts, it has not – and is unlikely to be, turned into the new mass tourist Mediterranean beach destination for European tourists. Although there are some good beaches in the area and the lagoon has potential, if correctly developed, the little town with a population of around 25,000 has none of the holiday facilities and nightlife that tourists expect. ▸▸ *For Sleeping, Eating and other listings, see pages 347-348.*

Ins and outs

Getting around Marsa Matruh's streets are on a grid pattern with most of the hotels being on the streets behind and parallel to the Corniche. Buses and service taxis stop at the main station, 2 km south of the Corniche. Taxis to the town centre cost E£2. Shared covered pick-ups cost 25p. From the train station, you can walk or catch a taxi or pick-up. The airport is close to the south of town. Getting around town is easy. It's small enough to walk. For places a bit out of the way, hire a taxi for E£3-5, or take a donkey cart. A trip to the Rommel Museum from the town centre should cost around E£5. ▸▸ *For further details, see Transport, page 348.*

Sights

There are really only two reasons for visiting Marsa Matruh: either to travel to the magnificent desert oasis at Siwa (see page 471) or a rest en route to Libya. Most of the area's much-advertised beaches are a severe disappointment. Except for the *Beau Site* hotel's private beach, almost all beaches are public. Western women can still experience problems from both voyeurs and exhibitionists who are more used to seeing fully-clothed Egyptian women swimming and sunbathing, although the situation is improving as the locals become more accustomed to foreign visitors. No serious attempt has been made to solve the major litter problem on those beaches closest to town.

The beaches in the town's bay are protected by two sand spits which will eventually meet and form a lagoon. **Lido Beach** and **Beach of Lovers** curve around the bay to the west of the town while in the other direction **Rommel's Beach** and its small military museum in a cave hewn in the rock, are beyond the small port and are almost facing the town on the landward side of the east spit. **The Rommel Museum** ⓘ *daily in summer 0930-1600,* gives details of this famous field marshal in the Second World War campaign. Offshore from the beach is a red buoy, 25 m beyond which is a sunken German U-boat, which can be seen if you have suitable underwater swimming gear.

The better and cleaner beaches are those to the west of the town: among them is **Cleopatra's Bath** (7 km), where Cleo supposedly soaked in a rock engulfed by Mediterranean turquoise, a sort of natural tub. Surrounded by cliffs, the sea gets deep very suddenly. *Cleopatra St Giovanni* (see page 347), the nicest and newest hotel in town, recently opened its doors here. There's also **El-Obeid Beach** (20 km) with beautiful white sand that resembles sugar and **Agibah Beach** (28 km), the most striking of all, which is surrounded by dramatic rock formations and totally undeveloped. It's aptly named – *Agibah*, 'a wonder'.

Marsa Matruh to Sollum

This last 215 km of road to Libya has little to recommend it. There are some new developments and sundry Bedouin settlements. Sidi Barrani was the site of fierce battles during the Desert Campaign of the Second World War. **Sollum**, the ancient port of Banaris, is the border town with Libya. The British and Commonwealth cemetery at the eastern side of the town has 2,060 war graves.

Border crossing

At present, there is only one bus a week from Marsa Matruh, which leaves on Tuesdays at 1430. As traffic to and fro increases, this will most likely change. Inquire with the tourist office or at the bus station. The trip costs E£10 and takes around 4 hours. *Hotel Al-Ahram* is for those who get stuck. **Visas for Libya** are not readily available at the border and are best obtained in Cairo. They are £20 sterling for UK nationals and are valid for one month, but must be used within 45 days. The border is 12 km west of the town and service taxis, E£2-4 are available. Service taxis go to Al Bardia. The bus from here goes to Benghazi. If you plan to drive in a private car, come armed with passport and car papers, as you will be stopped at numerous checkpoints en route.

Sleeping

Road to El-Alamein *p343*

A-B Aida Beach Hotel, Km 77 on Alexandria to Marsa Matruh road, T/F046-4102820. 200 rooms in the hotel, 40 apartments and 22 villas. Sports equipment and courts to hire, jet skis and windsurfing. Not as close to the beach as the name suggests but nevertheless recommended for its high quality service and entertainment facilities.

Marina, just 10 km beyond Aida Beach. This is a 3-km stretch of up-market 2-storey villas. Some of these villas are for rent at about E£4,500 a month. The beach is beautiful but the reason why it is so clean is the strong sea currents – be warned.

C Atic Hotel, Km 90, Alexandria to Marsa Matruh road, T046-4106183, F4106182. 64 double rooms, 16 km east of El-Alamein. Good standard of service, pool, private beach, mainly Egyptian guests. This hotel is recommended as it has plenty of space – the rooms are large, the beds are large and so are the dining room and the pool and the beach. The sports facilities are not up to the standard of *Aida Beach*. Compensate by enjoying the lively nightlife, the good food (try the fish food, the pizzeria or the coffee shop in addition to the main Omda restaurant). Used by day guests who are not quite so restrained.

D Agami Palace, Al-Bittash Beach, El-Agami, 20 km west of Alexandria, T046-4330230, F4333503. 56 rooms, tasteful decor, pool.

E New Admiral, Hannoville, El-Agami, T046-4303038. 44 rooms, on beach.

F Costa Blanca, Sharia Hannoville, El-Agami, about 25 km west of Alexandria, T046-4303112. 36 rooms, located on rather polluted and crowded beach. Day-trippers from Alexandria flock here every weekend.

El-Alamein *p343*

As there are no decent hotels in El-Alamein, we recommend making the day trip from Alexandria or stopping en route to Marsa Matruh or other resort areas along the coast. If you are desperate, try:

Al-Amana Hotel, near the museum, T03-4938324/5.

West of El-Alamein

A El-Alamein, Sidi Abdel Rahman, El-Dabaa Centre, T046-4680140, F4680341. 209 rooms and villas with own seaside barbecue, very good standard, located on the beautiful white sands of the isolated up-market resort of Sidi Abdel Rahman about 25 km west of El-Alamein, early reservations essential, open Apr-Nov. Prices have been reduced slightly but rooms and general facilities are not really up to price standard. Day use of beautiful beach E£350.

Camping

There are no specific camp sites but the *El-Alamein Hotel* has a tourist camp equipped with all necessary services.

Marsa Matruh *p343, map p345*

Considering Matruh is the prime beach destination on the Mediterranean Coast, there are relatively few nice places to stay. Most hotels are overpriced for what's on offer, and except for the newest of the bunch, are growing rough at the edges. Still, during the tourist season that peaks July and August, it's wise to make reservations, especially if you are particular about where you want to stay.

A-B Cleopatra St Giovanni, Cleopatra Beach, 7km west of town, T046-4947600. Beautiful private beach, rooms are lovely and very new. Rate includes half board with open buffet, bar, disco, live band on beach in the evenings, coffee shop, fully equipped health club, jet skis for rent.

B Beach House Hotel, Sharia El-Shatee, T046-4935169/70, F4933319. 20 suites here sleeping 3/4, overpriced, but nice for families or small groups.

B-C Beau Site, Sharia El-Shatee, 2 km west of Sharia Iskandariya on the Corniche, T046-4932066. Rooms have a/c, satellite TV and a view of a splendid blue lagoon with private beach. Highly recommended. The food is reportedly excellent, also rents out chalets for 3-8 persons. Rates include buffet breakfast. Unquestionably the nicest place to stay in town.

C Negresco, Corniche, T046-4934492. 68 clean rooms with a/c, TV and fridge. A decent hotel with good views, but like most hotels in the area, considerably overpriced. Breakfast included. Open year round.

C Riviera Palace, Sharia Gala'a, Market Area, T/F046-4933045. 32 recently renovated rooms with all the extras. A downtown 3-star hotel, good restaurant, no alcohol. Popularity with tour groups sometimes makes rooms unavailable during the summer months.

E Adriatika, Sharia Gala'a, just north of the tourist office, T046-4935195/6. Closed in winter. 55 rooms with bath and balcony, good. Inexpensive, yet facilities include 24-hr room service, laundry, bar, cafeteria and TV.

E Arouss El-Bahr, Corniche, T046-4942419. Closed in the winter. Small hotel with 54 clean simple rooms, some with balconies and sea views, helpful staff, restaurant. Some bungalows for 4 people.

E Reem, Corniche, T046-4933605, 4933608. 58 unspectacular but clean rooms, some with sea view and balcony. Good value. Breakfast included.

E Rommel House, Sharia Gala'a, T046-4945466, F4932485. 60 large rooms with fans, TV and fridge. Good café. Breakfast included. Prices may be reduced in the winter.

F Ghazala, Sharia Alum Rum, T046-4933519. Basic doubles, triples and quads available. There's a sink in the room, but no toilet. Shared baths are clean, though in summer may not have hot water. E£10 per person, E£15 for a private room. The most popular stop for backpackers.

F Youth hostel, behind 4 Sharia Gala'a, Sollum Rd, T046-4932331. 52 beds, kitchen, meals, parking, facilities for disabled, overnight fee E£10, train 2 km. The grotty shared rooms have bunk beds.

Camping

It's possible to camp for free on the beaches in the town of Marsa Matrouh but it's essential to obtain permission from the tourist police first since the beaches are patrolled by armed officers at night. Camping without permission is risky.

Eating

Marsa Matruh *p343, map p345*

Besides the hotel restaurants, most notably the Beau Site and Riviera Palace, there are a few cheap downtown restaurants around the intersection of Sharia Iskandariya and Sharia Gala'a.

Abdu Kofta, by Hammo Al-Tamsah. Serves the best kofta and kebab in town. A good place to experience authentic Egyptian molokhiyya, the slimy green soup.

Hammo Al-Temsah, Sharia Zaher Galal, an excellent fish restaurant that serves up deliciously spiced grilled and fried fish and prawns. Open late.

Restaurant Panayotis, Sharia Iskandariya. An old-time restaurant on the scene, opened by a Greek family a few generations back. They serve good seafood and salads, and cheap beer.

Alexandria Tourist Restaurant, Sharia Iskandariya. Offers a cheap solid meal. Lots of options, the fish is good.

Entertainment

Marsa Matruh *p343, map p345*
There are nightclubs and bars in the larger hotels and discotheques at the *Beau Site, Cleopatra, St Giovanni and Radi* hotels, in summer. Marsa Matrouh also has a couple of cinemas, (showing only Arabic movies), and a local circus.

Transport

Marsa Matruh *p343, map p345*
Air In the summer, **EgyptAir**, Sharia Galaa, T046-4934398, offers 3 flights a week between Marsa Matruh and **Cairo**. At present, they fly on Sun, Thu and Fri, but check with the tourist office or EgyptAir office to be sure. A 1-way ticket costs around E£160.

Bicycle The **nearby beaches** can be reached from town by hiring a bicycle. Bike shops are scattered around **Sharia Iskandariya**. E£5-7 per hr.

Bus Local transport to the beaches of **Cleopatra**, **El-Obeid** and **Agibah** leave every 15 mins during daylight from Midan Al-Gala'a. To **Alexandria**, there are a/c buses every hr from 0700-2400 (3-4 hrs, E£20-23). Buses to Alexandria can drop you off at **Sidi Abdel Rahman** or **El-Alamein**. To **Cairo**, there are a/c buses with toilet every hr on the half hr (0730-2330) (8 hrs, E£33-36). It's wise to book your seat in advance. To **Siwa**, there are 4 buses daily leaving at 0730, 1400, 1600 and 1930 (4 hrs, E£12). There is one bus per week to Libya that leaves on Tue at 1430. **West Delta Buses**, T046-4932079.

Service taxis and pick ups The more distant beaches to the west can be reached in summer by service taxi, microbus or pick-ups which shuttle back and forth (0800-sunset) from Midan El-Gala'a. E£1-3, depending on how far you go. To get back to town, just flag one down from the street. Service taxis are quicker and cheaper but less comfortable than the express buses to **Alexandria**. Taxis to **Siwa** (4 hrs), E£15, leave early morning or in the afternoon to avoid the midday heat. It is difficult but not impossible to take one of the service taxis, which carry Egyptian expatriate workers, to the **Libyan border** (230 km east of Marsa Matruh) via **Sidi Barrani** (150 km) and **Sollum** (220 km) but it is essential to have a Libyan visa.

Train There are 2 daily trains that run between Marsa Matrouh and **Cairo**, via **Alexandria**. They leave Matrouh for Cairo at 1330 and 2300. The late night train has sleeper cars. There are also tediously slow daily 2nd and 3rd class trains to Alexandria at 0700 and 1545. **Railway Station**, T046-4933036.

Directory

Marsa Matruh *p343, map p345*
Banks Most of the town's banks are west of the EgyptAir office and are open daily 0900-1400 and 1800-2000. **Banque du Caire**, east of the main north-south Sharia Iskandariya. 0830-1430 and 1800-2100. **National Bank of Egypt**, across the street from EgyptAir in the west of town. **Post office** Sharia Ash-Shatta, east of Sharia Iskandariya. Daily 0900-1500. **Telephone** 24-hr telephones opposite the post office on Sharia Ash-Shatta. **Tourist office** Corner of Sharia Iskanderiya and the Corniche, T046-4931841. Sat-Thu, 0830-1500. Staff speak English and are reasonably well-informed about accommodation and surrounding sites. **Useful telephone numbers** Emergencies, T125. Ambulance, T046-4934370. Police, T046-4933015.

Suez Canal Zone

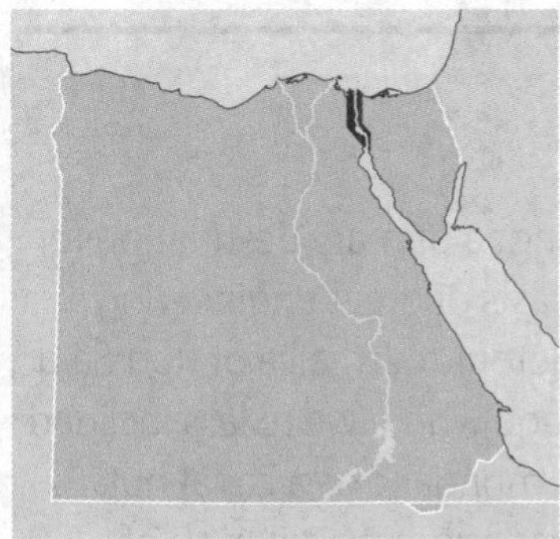

Footprint features

Introduction

Although the Suez Canal Zone is not a primary destination for most visitors to Egypt, for enthusiasts of great engineering feats or travellers with time, the detour to Ismailia or Port Said is worthwhile. We may live in an age where we're less inclined to be impressed by something as mundane as a canal but, seen in context, the Suez Canal was as great a triumph of engineering in the 19th century as the Pyramids were in their day. As one of the world's most heavily trafficked shipping lanes, the canal is among Egypt's greatest riches (toll revenues are a consistent source of income that fluctuate less than the more volatile tourist industry). Convoys of vessels glide along it as if floating on the desert. Viewed from the comfort of a hotel window or waterside restaurant in Port Said, they become a fascination that's almost addictive. Come nightfall, the riding lights of container vessels mark the line of their movement. Only one thing can improve on this – a journey through the canal itself.

Port Said, **Ismailia** and **Suez** collectively make up "The Canal Zone". The three cities essentially grew up with the construction of the canal alongside the British colonial presence that hung about until the 1956 war. Soon after, the region's proximity to Israel resulted in a temporary mass departure. With such a dramatic and distinct history, the area has a feel that sets it apart from much of Egypt, but each city has managed to retain its own separate character. Of the triad, Ismailia, a sleepy romantic little town more popular among local honeymooners than foreign tourists, is unquestionably the prettiest. The former base of the Suez Canal Company's headquarters, streets brim with gardens and façades of worn Victorian villas. The canal cities are particularly inviting in the summer, where the cool waterside breezes offer respite from the inland heat.

★ Don't miss...

❶ **The Canal** Get mesmerized by gazing at massive ships plying over the Suez Canal, one of the greatest engineering triumphs of history, page 354.

❷ **Ismailia** Wander through the Victorian-flavoured city of Ismailia, where many honeymooners and few foreigners mingle along the streets and shores amid verdant gardens and buildings of a colonial past, page 356.

❸ **Port Said** Enjoy the Mediterranean breeze, waterfront fish restaurants, abundant shopping opportunities and maritime feel of Port Said, page 359.

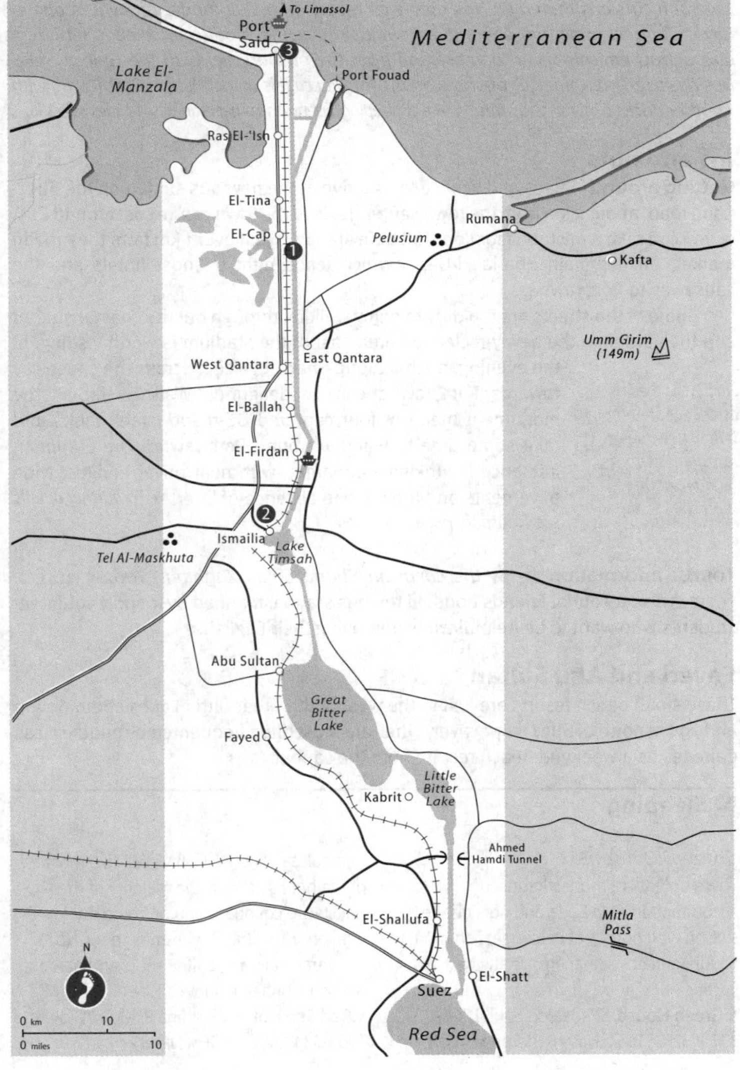

Suez and around

→ *Colour map 2, grid B4. Population: 458,000.*

Suez's friendly demeanour compensates in part for what it lacks in looks. The city was badly hit by an Israeli siege in 1973 and though the mess has largely been cleaned up and mines have been cleared, Suez is still a dirty town, more of a transit spot than a destination. The city lies at the southern end of the Suez Canal, just 134 km from Cairo. During the Ptolemaic period, the city was known as Klysma and in the Middle Ages the walled city, then known as Qulzum, became prosperous thanks to the burgeoning spice trade and the many pilgrims bound for Mecca. In the 15th century it became a naval base. The opening of the Suez Canal in 1869 ensured the city's survival and development. Almost totally destroyed through conflict with Israel in 1948, and in several incursions thereafter, the area was rebuilt with Gulf funds. Today it is one of Egypt's largest ports and an important industrial centre producing cement, fertilizers and petrochemicals using domestic oil from the offshore fields in the Gulf of Suez. Besides a ferry terminal for pilgrims bound for Mecca it is also linked to Port Tawfiq with its other docks and ferry terminals. ▸▸ *For Sleeping, Eating and other listings, see pages 352-356.*

Ins and outs

Getting around Buses and service taxis arrive at the new bus station on the Suez-Cairo road, about 2 km from the town centre. Taxis to the town centre cost around E£5, or you can take a microbus for 50p. The train station is just over 1 km from the Arba'in market, off the main Sharia El-Geish which leads right to most hotels and the causeway to Port Tawfiq.

Some of the streets are too dirty to enjoy walking through but the coastal quarter and the garden in the newly-reclaimed area east of the stadium is worth visiting. In the evening, a stroll along Sharia El-Geish across the causeway towards Port Tawfiq can be delightful. Walk as far as the monument made of four captured US-made Israeli tanks and take some time to wander around Port Tawfiq. The European influence is strikingly apparent, with neat privet hedges, wide pavements and the relative absence of litter. ▸▸ *For further details, see Transport, page 355.*

Excursions to the Monasteries of St Anthony and St Paul (see page 421) can be organized from Suez. Enquire at the tourist office.

Tourist information ⓘ *By the canal on Sharia Sa'ad Zaghloul, T062-331141/2.* There is also a **Tourist Friends** booth at the bus station, manned by friendly volunteer students who want to be helpful while improving their English.

Fayed and Abu Sultan

These small beach resorts are just to the west of the Great Bitter Lakes about 60 km and 70 km north of Suez respectively. They are most often frequented by middle class Cairenes as a weekend beach respite from the capital.

Sleeping

Suez *p352, map p353*
There's plenty of modestly-priced accommodation in Suez, and outside the Hajj season with hordes of passengers en route to Saudi Arabia by sea, there are always vacancies.

C Green House, Sharia Port Said, T062-331553, F331554. Has 48 rooms with a/c, minibar, satellite TV, Gulf views. Like most of the hotels in Suez, the majority of the guests are Egyptians and oil company workers. Hotel has a swimming pool. No bar, but restaurant, coffee shop, and garden. Breakfast buffet included.

C Red Sea Hotel, 13 Sharia Riad, Port Tawfiq, T062-334302, F334301. Has 81 clean comfortable rooms, with TV and a/c. Good restaurant, open 24 hours and has an excellent view of the canal. Breakfast included.

C **Summer Palace**, Port Tawfiq, T062-224475, F321944. 90 rooms, good Gulf views, pool, restaurant with views. A bit overpriced, despite the views.

E **White House**, 322 Sharia El-Geish, T062-331550, F223330. Rooms are growing old, but they're clean and have bath, a/c, and TV. The telephone is often out of service, but the hotel's still alive. Beer served. The top of budget options.

F **Sina**, 21 Sharia Banque Masr, T062-334181. Centrally located, decent budget hotel. Rooms have fans. No private baths but shared baths are clean enough.

F **Star**, 17 Sharia Banque Masr. Another decent budget hotel that's a bit cheaper than the Sina nearby. Rooms are varied in quality and cleanliness. All have fans and some come with private bath.

F **Sharia Tariq El-Horiyya youth hostel**, near sports stadium in front of Hawgag village, T062-339069. Women are only permitted to stay in the family rooms (3 beds per room, E£13 per person). E£1 extra for non-members. Dorm beds for men are E£7. Lockout from 2400-0800. Kitchen available.

Fayed and Abu Sultan *p352*

B **Bonita Village** in Kabrit, T064-600674, 442266. A new resort with 60 comfortable a/c rooms, good restaurant.

B **Helnan Morgan Village**, Km 54, Ismailia/ Suez Rd, Fayed, T064-661718, F661719. 92 good double rooms, excellent views, good

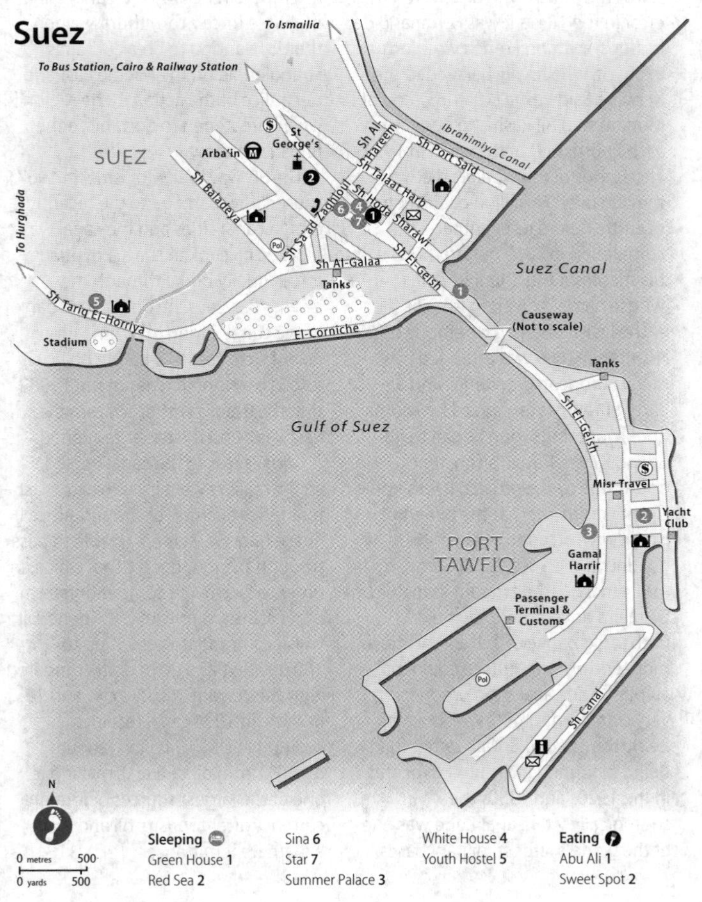

The Suez Canal

Since its completion in 1869 the Suez Canal, which at 167 km is the third longest in the world, has enabled ships to pass from the Mediterranean to the Indian Ocean via the Red Sea without sailing around the African continent. There had been many previous attempts to build a canal including those during the 26th Dynasty by Necho II (610-595 BC) and the Persian Emperor Darius I (521-486 BC). Napoleon's engineers vetoed their own plan to build the canal after calculating (incorrectly) that the sea level in the Red Sea was 10 m lower than in the Mediterranean. Although it was the British who discovered their error in the 1840s it was Ferdinand de Lesseps, a young French vice-consul in Egypt, who finally persuaded the Khedive Said Pasha (1854-63), son of Mohammed Ali Pasha, to begin work at the north end of the canal in 1859. Thousands of the workers died moving over 97 million cubic metres of earth, before its eventual completion in 1869 during the rule of his successor the Khedive Ismail whose name is given to Ismailia.

The lavish opening ceremony on 17 November 1869 was attended by many European dignitaries and a party of tourists organized by Thomas Cook, but things soon began to go wrong. Given Britain's constant opposition to the project, it was ironic that it was to her that the bankrupt Ismail was forced to sell his 44% holding in the Suez Canal Company for £4 million (the amount loaned to Disraeli's government by the Rothschild bankers), before the much more enthusiastic France could make an offer. The canal soon produced very significant profits which were being remitted to Britain rather than being ploughed back into Egypt and in the 1920s and 1930s the strategically vital Canal Zone was one of the world's largest military bases.

Since 1945 the canal has been the subject of both important political disputes and serious armed conflicts. Britain reluctantly agreed to remove its troops in 1954 but refused to give a larger share of the revenues to Egypt. The West vetoed World Bank loans to help finance the construction of the Aswan Dam because of the Soviet Union's offer to rearm Egypt after its 1948 defeat by Israel. In reply Colonel Gamal Abdel Nasser nationalized the Suez Canal on 26 July 1956. Britain and France used the pretext of an agreed and pre-planned Israeli invasion of Sinai in October 1956 in an attempt to reoccupy the Canal Zone but were forced to withdraw when the US, wanting to break Britain's stranglehold on the Middle East and get a slice of the action in the region itself, threatened to destabilize the British economy.

The Six Day War with Israel in 1967 caused new damage to the recently rebuilt canal cities and the canal was blocked by sunken ships. Egyptian forces briefly broke through the Israeli's Bar-Lev Line on the east bank of the canal during the Yom Kippur war of October 1973 before being forced back and it was not until 1982 that the Israelis withdrew from the East Bank and the canal reopened.

With access to the canal denied, super-tankers were built to carry vast quantities of crude oil around Africa. These huge vessels are unable to pass through the reopened Canal which, in order to face fierce competition from other routes, is now to be widened. It will accommodate vessels up to 180,000 dwt and 20 m draft compared with the current 150,000 cwt and 19 m draft. In 1994 canal receipts brought in US$1.9 billion (about 35-40% from oil tankers), making it one of the largest sources of foreign currency after tourism, oil and expatriate remittances.

Suez Canal in numbers

- About 7% of all sea-transported trade goes through the canal. 39% is shipped to and from the Far East; 35% is shipped between the Red Sea and Arabian Gulf ports; 20% shipped to or from India and Southeast Asia
- Total length of canal: 193 km
- Canal depth: 21 m
- From Port Said to Ismailia: 78.5 km
- Width at water level: 300-365 m
- Navigable width: 180-205 m
- Maximum permissible draught for ships: 17.68 m

pool and beach, a real 'find' in this area. Recommended.

C **Shamoussa**, Km 59, Suez Canal Rd, Great Bitter Lakes, T064-661525, F661009. 54 rooms of good standard.

E **El Safa Hotel**, Farana, T064-661659. 30 rooms, cheapest place in town.

Eating

Suez *p352, map p353*

Except for seafood, which is available at virtually every place that serves grub, options are limited in Suez.

Abu Ali is a particularly good fish restaurant in the town centre where you can pick your own from the day's catch.

The Sweet Spot, down the road serves up good *shawerma*. (For a beer, try the **St George**, nearby.)

Standard stall food abounds around Sharia Talaat Harb and the Arba'in Market. Cost depends on weight.

Tour operators

El Salaam Transport Company, T062-326252. **Mena Tours**, in Port Tawfiq, T062-228821.

Transport

Suez *p352, map p353*

Bus

Buses leave the terminal (2 km west of the city) every 30 mins between 0600-2030 to/from **Cairo's Turgoman Station** (2 hrs, E£8). There are also frequent buses every 30 mins to **Ismailia**, (just under 1 hr, E£5) and almost every 2 hrs 0700-1500 to **Port Said**, (2 hrs, E£10). It's also possible to head straight to the Sinai from Suez. There are 6 buses daily to **Sharm El-Sheikh** (0830, 1100, 1330, 1500, 1700, 1800, 4 hrs, E£27), the 1100 bus carries on to **Dahab** (9 hrs, E£32); the 1500 carries on to **Nuweiba**, (5-6 hrs, E£32) then **Taba** (6-7 hrs). There is also one bus daily that goes direct to **St Catherine's Monastery** (1400, 6 hrs, E£27). There are 4 buses daily to **Alexandria**, (0700, 0900, 1430, 1700, 6 hrs, E£25). 9 buses daily from 0600-2200 to **Hurghada**, (7 hrs, E£25) most via **Ain Sukhna**. There are also 6 buses daily to **Luxor**, (0500, 0800, 1030, 1400, 1700, 2000, 6 hrs, E£37) and 3 to **Aswan** (0500, 1200, 1700, E£42). Prices vary depending on the time you depart.

Ferry

The vehicle ferry service, taking 2-3 days, from **Port Tawfiq** to **Port Sudan** is supposed to be weekly but because of operational and political problems it is often less frequent, if it runs at all. Contact **Telstar** in Cairo, T02-7944600, for the latest on times and prices. Ferries shuttle more reliably to and from **Jeddah** in Saudi Arabia. For details, in Suez, contact **El-Salaam Transport Company**, T062-326252; in Cairo contact **Telstar**. There are 2-3 boats per week. The journey lasts 3 days (1st class E£410, 2nd class E£350).

NB Be wary of attempting this journey during the Hajj when thousands of pilgrims make the trek across the sea. You must have the necessary visas in order to purchase a ticket.

Taxi

Service taxis travel to all of the same destinations as the buses, although foreigners may be requested not to travel in these taxis – for their own protection. Costs are comparable to the buses. Though service taxis are speedier, they are often not as comfortable as the a/c buses and will not depart until full.

Train

There are 6 trains run to/from **Cairo** en route to/from **Ismailia** daily, but they're hot and slow. You're better off opting for the bus.

Fayed and Abu Sultan *p352*

Taxi

Taxis running between **Suez** and **Ismailia** stop at Fayed.

Directory

Suez *p352, map p353*

Banks Bank of Alexandria, Sharia El-Geish changes money. **Post office** Sharia Hoda Sharawi, 1 block away from the main Sharia El-Geish, near the causeway to Port Tawfiq. Open Sat-Thu 0830-1400. **Telephone** The telephone office is further south on Sharia Sa'ad Zaghloul. **Useful addresses** Passport office for registration or extending a visa is on Sharia Tariq El-Horiyya.

Ismailia

→ *Colour map 2, grid B4. Population: 600,000.*

Ismailia, 120 km east of Cairo, 90 km north of Suez and 85 km south of Port Said, is the largest and most attractive of the three main Canal Zone cities. Named after Ismail Pasha, Khedive of Egypt, it was built as a depot by the Suez Canal Company in 1861 on the west shore of Lake Timsah (Crocodile Lake), one of Egypt's largest lakes (covering 14 sq km). The town is divided by the railway track: the attractive and tranquil Garden City built for the company's European employees to the south; the poorly-constructed apartment blocks, financed with Gulf money, to the north. The Sweetwater Canal was dug from its source in Lake Timsah to provide fresh water during the construction of the Suez Canal and the calm, clear water and many sand beaches of the lake make Ismailia a popular weekend destination for Egyptian tourists. The rare desert-weary traveller who ventures here will find the orchard gardens and trees a delight. There is very little nightlife but blissful days can be spent sitting on the beach watching ships go by. ▸▸ *For Sleeping, Eating and other listings, see pages 358-359.*

Ins and outs

Getting there Ismailia's bus station is a few kilometers from town on the ring road across the street from the Suez Canal University. A taxi to the city centre costs around E£3-4. The train station is in the centre of town. Sharia Ahmed Orabi, outside the station, runs straight down to the lake. Most hotels and restaurants are found in close proximity to the train station, north of the Garden City area. ▸▸ *For further details, see Transport, page 359.*

Getting around With its wide tree-shaded pavements and functional traffic rules, Ismailia is easy to walk around and most sights can be reached on foot. In summer it's possible to hire a horse-drawn carriage to see the sights. For destinations a bit further away, bicycles can be hired from the streets off Mohammed Ali Quay. Private taxis shouldn't cost more than E£3-5 to get anywhere in town.

Information **Tourist office** ⓘ *T064-321072, 321076, open Sat-Thu 0900-1400*, is a bit of a walk from the town centre, upstairs in the Mahefezah building, the district authority head office. Hotels in town are often a better source of information.

Sights

A number of minor sites, although comparatively unimportant, are worth visiting while in town. In the attractive Garden City (**Mallaha Park** is over 200 ha of trees, flowers and grass) is the huge **Suez Canal University** opened in 1997, the **Catholic church** built in 1930 to a unique architectural design, and the **El-Rahman mosque** to the west of town constructed post 1973. Also some 7 km south of Ismailia on the west bank is the memorial to the unknown soldier, recalling the First World War. An unusual memorial of 6 October 1973 is located on east bank of the canal near the ferry crossing – a fixed bayonet. The **Ismailia Regional Museum** ⓘ *Sat-Thu 0900-1600, Fri 0900-1100, 1400- 1600 daily during Ramadan 0900-1400, E£6, E£3 students, labels in French*, near Fountain Park (established 1932) is in the north of the Garden City. Although it has some minor ancient Egyptian pieces it is the mosaics and other pieces amongst its collection of 4,000 Graeco-Roman artifacts which are the museum's highlights. Permission is necessary from the museum to visit the Garden of Stelae nearby which holds a number of Pharaonic artefacts and obelisks, mainly from the period of Ramses II.

Left off Sharia Ahmed Orabi on Mohammed Ali Quay next to the Sweetwater Canal is the **House of Ferdinand de Lesseps** ⓘ *Wed-Mon 0900-1600*, which, although officially a museum, is sometimes used as a government guest house, at

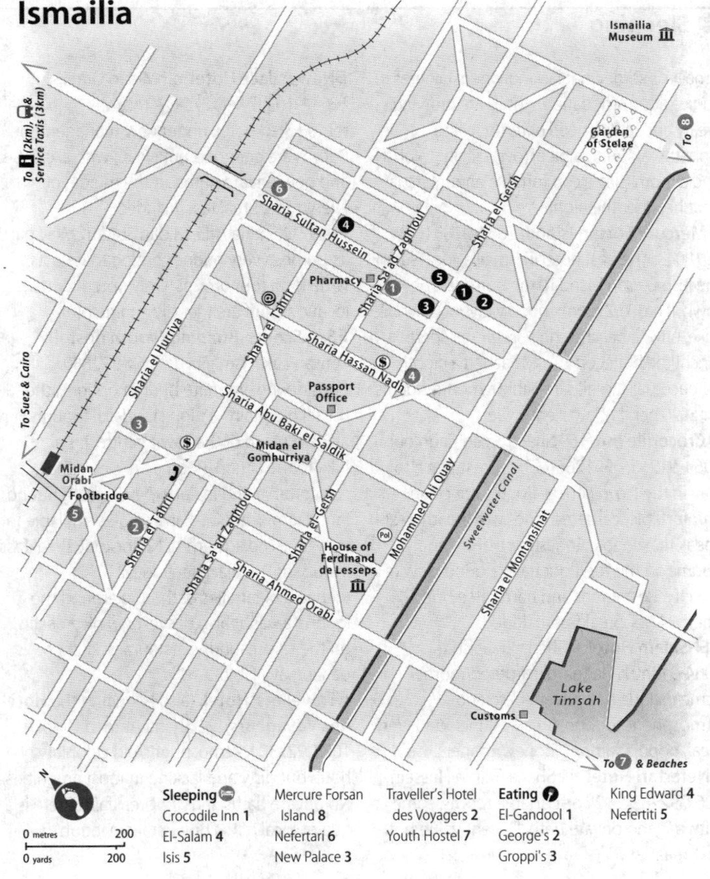

“” The rare desert-weary traveller who ventures here will find the orchard gardens and trees a delight.

which times it is closed to the public. It displays many of his personal possessions, his diaries and his private carriage.

About 7 km north of the city is the main car ferry across the Suez Canal to Sinai and the **Bar-Lev Line**, which is the impressive 25-m high embankment built by the occupying Israelis to stall any Egyptian advance across the canal and into Sinai. Although Egyptian forces managed to break through the line at the beginning of the October 1973 war, by using the element of total surprise and high pressure water hoses, the Israeli counter-attack across the Great Bitter Lakes virtually succeeded in surrounding the Egyptian army and, under pressure from the super-powers, both sides were forced to the negotiating table.

There are some pleasant public beaches around **Lake Timsah**. Use the private beach and pool on Forsan Island for E£20 per day. Picnicing is popular in the park between Lake Timsah and Sweetwater Canal.

Sleeping

Ismailia is somewhat lacking when it comes to choice accommodation. Hotels are growing weary and in dire need of remodelling. Nonetheless, with a bit of 'overlooking', you'll find a room that is comfortable enough to lay your head for the night.

B **Mercure Forsan Island**, T064-916316, F918043. The best hotel in Ismailia, located on the lush Forsan Island to the northeast of town. It has 152 rooms, good views of Crocodile Lake, private beach, tennis and water sports, a lunchtime buffet on Fri and Sat and a nightly barbecue, all facilities available to non-residents for E£20 per day, excellent value.

D **Crocodile Inn**, 169 Sharia Sa'ad Zaghloul, T064-912555, F912666. The nicest place to stay in the town centre. Rooms are clean, comfortable, carpeted, and with a bath. Staff speak reasonable English and are friendly. Rooms on the top floor have a good view of the city. Restaurant and bar/coffee house open 24 hrs. Breakfast included.

E **El-Salam Hotel**, 9 Sharia El-Geish, T064-914401. Haggard, carpeted rooms, some include a/c, private bath and TV. Atmospheric lounge. Breakfast included. Very local, popular among honeymooners.

E **Nefertari Hotel**, 41 Sharia Sultan Hussein, T064-922822. 32 comfortable rooms, some with a/c and private bath. Decent value but no breakfast.

E **New Palace Hotel**, off Midan Orabi, T064-916327, F917761. A recently remodelled hotel, under new management. Rooms are cramped but clean, with a/c, TV, and new private baths. In the middle of everything. Breakfast included.

F **Isis**, 32 Sharia Adli, Midan Station. Way past its prime, a very budget option that hosts large local tour groups. Only noted for its location. Staff are friendly and helpful.

F **Sea Scouts' Building (youth hostel)**, Timsah Lake, Ismailia, T/F064-922850. Considering alternate budget options, the hostel maintains a high standard, though at 2 km south of the town centre, it's a hike to the action. Rooms are clean and comfortable and include private bath but no fans. Dorms, doubles and singles available for everyone (no age limit). No lockout. Breakfast included. The place feels local, with lots of families gathering around the lounge areas. It also has its own nice beach on the lake. Laundry, restaurant, kitchen, parking available.

F **Travellers' Hotel**, (also known as the **Hotel des Voyageurs**), 22 Sharia Ahmed Orabi, T064-923304. Atmospheric old colonial-style hotel but dirty and lacking in most amenities. No private baths, fans, or breakfast. There is a quaint local *ahwa* downstairs, though.

Eating

The only hotel that offers a relatively expensive classy dining experience is the Mercure (see above). There are many places to eat in town and along the beaches. Among the particularly good restaurants are:

King Edward on Sharia Tahrir just off Sharia Sultan Hussein;

George's Restaurant and Bar, 11 Sharia Sultan Hussein, open daily 1100-2300, famous for its seafood;

Nefertiti Restaurant, across the road, open daily 1200-2400, cheaper, family-owned, also specializes in seafood;

El-Gandool, off Shari Sultan Hussein, offers a wide range of local grub at a wider range of prices, huge grilled meat platters and cheap spaghetti dishes on offer.

Zahran, Sharia El-Geish, has an outdoor barbecue grill and rotisserie and often cheap decent kofta, lamb chops and chicken.

Groppi's Patisserie, across the road from George's. A branch of the famous Cairo Café, where the coffee and sticky cakes are good.

Festivals

The International Folklore Dance Festival takes place each **Aug** and the International Festival of Documentary Films each **Jul**.

Tour operators

El-Ghamri Travel, 211 Sharia El-Hurriya, T064-911725.

Transport

Bus and service taxis

Regular buses and service taxis run between towns in the Canal Zone and Delta. Catch them from the depot by the bus station or northwest of the train station a block north of Sharia El-Hurriya. From the bus station on the ring road, there are hourly buses to **Suez** and **Port Said** (from 0630-1830, E£5-6, each 1 hr); **Cairo** (every 45 mins, 0630-2000, E£8, 2 hrs); **Alexandria** (0700 and1430, E£10, 4 hrs); **El-Arish** (8 per day, from 0830-1700, E£9, 3 hrs); **Sharm El-Sheikh** (8 per day, from 0630-2400).

Train

There are 7 daily trains to **Cairo** (3-4 hrs).

Directory

Hospitals The huge Suez Canal University Hospital, opened in 1993, has 350 beds and all the latest equipment. **Post office** Beside the railway station, open Sat-Thu 0900-1500.

Port Said

→ *Colour map 2, grid A4. Population: 526,000.*

Port Said, with its grand promenades, attractive seafront architecture and perpetual Mediterranean breeze, is an inviting maritime town. In 1975 when it was declared a duty-free zone, it began to rival Alexandria (after Alexandria it's Egypt's second largest port and fourth largest city) as a leading domestic tourist destination – a place where cheap shopping and beach lounging could be combined. However, in early 2002, the government removed the extended free zone status (though visitors are still required to pass through customs) and the result has been something of an economic downturn for the city. The main appeal for most visitors nowadays is a stroll along the waterfront where giant supertankers crawl through the astounding desert passage. There is little to see beyond the canal but the lack of Western tourists makes it another relaxing place to sit on the beach and get a taste of Egyptian life for a few days. As this is still a duty-free zone, have passports ready to enter and leave. ▸▸ *For Sleeping, Eating and other listings, see pages 362-364.*

Ins and outs

Getting there Port Said is 225 km from Cairo and 85 km north of Ismailia. Most visitors arrive either at the new bus terminal at the entrance of town, off the Ismailia

Road or at the railway station and service taxi depot near the Arsenal Basin. The city's main streets are Sharia Filistine (Palestine) along the waterfront, and the parallel Sharia El-Gumhoriyya. From the train station, it's a short walk to the corniche and centre; from the bus station, a taxi to the waterfront costs E£3. » *For further details, see Transport, page 364.*

Getting around It is easy to walk around town. Most services and places worthy of a visit are along the main thoroughfares near the waterfront.

Information **Tourist office** ⓘ *43 Sharia Filistine, T066-235289*, is easily accessible and quite helpful.

Sights

The city was founded in 1859 as a harbour and named after Said Pasha (1854-63) who began the construction of the canal. Like the other Canal Zone cities there is less to see compared with the major tourist destinations but there are one or two landmarks/buildings to note. See the **Abd El-Rahman mosque** on the main street, **El-Salam Mosque** by the *Helnan* and *Sonesta* hotels, the **base of de Lesseps's statue,** and the **Obelisque memorial** in front of the Government Building. The three shiny green domes of the **Suez Canal Authority Building** on the canal side on Sahria Mostafah Kamal are another landmark in the town. The many Egyptian and few Western visitors who come here stroll around the main shopping streets by day and promenade along the canal and sea-front in the evening. There is a free ferry (15 minutes) across the canal to **Port Fouad** and its yacht basin. It is one of Port Said's suburbs, on the eastern side of the Suez Canal, and thus part of Asia. It still retains some of the colonial feel, fairly quiet residential areas with green spaces, a number of sports clubs and a popular beach.

Building the Suez Canal

Ferdinand de Lesseps was a French citizen through whose vision and perseverance the Suez Canal was constructed. He was born in France in 1805 and served as a senior diplomat in the French Foreign Service. His first visit to Egypt was in 1832 when he was the French consul in Alexandria. At this time he became acquainted with proposals for a canal across the Isthmus of Suez by a French engineer, Le Père, with whom he had served during the Napoleonic invasion. De Lesseps was deeply convinced of the economic and strategic utility of a Suez Canal and was encouraged to press the scheme's merits by the then ruler of Egypt, Mohammed Ali. De Lesseps transferred to Cairo as French consul in the years 1833-37 when he became a friend of the ruler's eldest son, Said Pasha. Said Pasha in 1854 invited de Lesseps back to Cairo to pursue the Suez Canal scheme, granting him a concession for construction of the canal in the same year.

Within two years de Lesseps had engineering designs prepared, raised the necessary capital and overcome British political reservations. On 25 April 1859 the project for the Suez Canal (*Qanat es-Suways*) was begun. The canal ran for 168 km from Port Said to Suez, using the path of Lake Menzala and the Bitter Lakes. It was 8 m deep and 22 m wide with passing places every 25.5 km. The project saw the excavation of great volumes of material and the building of port and ship-handling facilities at sites along the canal. Although de Lesseps had hoped to finish the scheme in six years, in the end it took 10 years to complete, delayed by environmental difficulties, labour problems and disease.

The Suez Canal came into full use in 1869, run by the Suez Canal Company which had a 99-year concession to manage it. The new company was 52% French, 44% Egyptian and 4% internationally owned. In 1875 the Egyptian government's financial troubles led to its holding being bought out by the British. De Lesseps welcomed the British involvement and kept a close interest in the affairs of the company. De Lesseps also sponsored the construction of the Panama Canal but his company became caught up in engineering and commercial problems. But despite this shadow, de Lesseps remains a monumental figure in Egyptian history for his foresight and determination in creating the Suez Canal which still contributes generously to Egypt's foreign exchange earnings, employs thousands of workers and which brings prosperity to the entire zone along its banks.

The **Port Said National Museum** ⓘ *Sharia Filistine, Sat-Thu 0900-1700, T066-237419, E£12, students E£6*, is near Nora's Floating Restaurant in a cool, uncrowded building. Its collection is well presented, though at the time of writing, it is undergoing extensive restoration. The ground floor is dedicated to early history and Pharaonic times including sarcophagi, statues, and two well-preserved Pharaonic mummies beside utensils and pots. The second floor is Islamic and Coptic material, textiles, coins and manuscripts. The coach used by Khedive Ismail during the inauguration ceremonies of the Suez Canal in 1869 is also on display. Also worthy of note is a hand-worked shroud and a tunic decorated with images of the apostles.

The **Military Museum** ⓘ *Sharia 23 July near the corniche, daily 0900-1700, E£4*, displays exhibits from the various conflicts fought along the length of the Suez Canal. These include not only the 1956 Suez crisis with some very lurid paintings and dioramas (look for the headless figures in the scene of Nasser at Al-Azhar), but also the successive wars with Israel: the 1973 storming of the Bar-Lev line receives pride of place and is on display in a separate room.

The base of the **statue of Ferdinand de Lesseps** stands on the quay by the canal he constructed. The statue was pulled down in 1956 – no way to treat the person who brought prosperity to the region. (You can take a **Port Cruise**, T066-326804, to see the ship convoys going through De Lessep's canal, from the jetty opposite the museum.)

Port Said is the access point for **Lake El-Manzala**, an excellent spot for fishing and watching migrating birds and those that overwinter on the shores.

Beaches Public access to the Mediterranean is everywhere. The ritzier hotels in the area may clean their own beach-fronts, which make them a bit more inviting. Chairs and umbrellas are for hire every few hundred metres (75p). As Port Said is less accustomed to seeing foreign bathers than other coastal towns, scantily clad women will find they attract a lot of unwanted attention. You are advised to wear shorts and a loose fitting opaque tee-shirt over your bathing costume.

Cemeteries These lie to the west of town, Muslim, Christian and one maintained by the Commonwealth War Graves Commission with over 1,000 graves from the First World War.

Sleeping

There are quite a few expensive and cheap hotels, but the happy medium is lacking.

A **Helnan Port Said**, Sharia El-Corniche, T066-320890, F323762. 2,200 good rooms with sea views, restaurant, 2 pools, health club and sauna, 'private' Mediterranean beach, splendidly located around the convergence of canal and sea.

A **Nora's Beach Hotel**, Sharia El-Corniche, T066-329834, F329841. 384 rooms, the first tourist village in Port Said, a bit worn around the edges. Rooms have all amenities and village includes several pools and a health club. Popular with large Egyptian family groups.

A **Sonesta Port Said Hotel**, Sharia Sultan Hussein, T066-325511, F324825. More intimate than the nearby Helnan, the Sonesta is another high quality hotel. It has no beach but offers stellar views of the canal. There's a nice pool that non-guests can use for E£20 per day.

D **Holiday**, 2/3 Sharia El-Gumhoriyya, T066-220713, F220710. A decent 3-star hotel with 81 rooms and all the usual amenities. Popular with Egyptian families.

D **New Concord**, corner of Sharia Salah Salam and Sharia Mustafa Kamel, near the train station, T066-235341, F235930. Hotel with 60 shabbily-carpeted rooms with bath and TV. Worn, but reasonably comfortable.

D **Palace Hotel**, 19 Sharia Ghandy, T066-239490, F239464. 84 a/c rooms, near the governorate building just off the main coast road, good access to the beach.

D **Panorama Hotel**, Sharia El-Gumhoriyya/ Sharia Tarh El-Bahr, T066-325101-2, F325103. Rooms come with a/c, TV, and private bath. They're growing weary with age, but still offer good views.

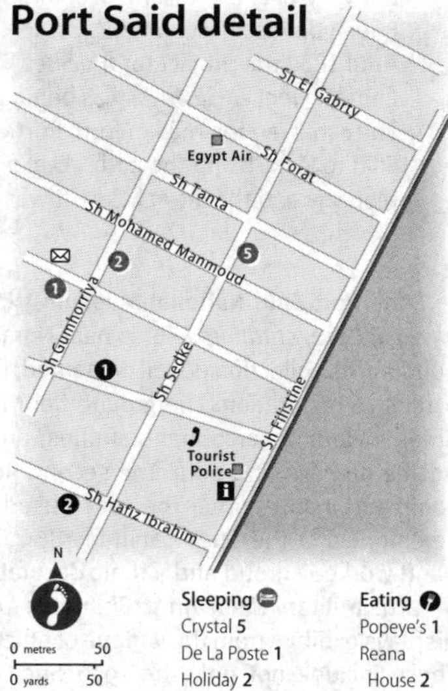

E De La Poste, 42 Sharia El-Gumhoriyya, T066-224048. The glory of this hotel is fading, despite relatively recent renovation. Prices of rooms vary depending on amenities. Still, it's the the most distinctive of the budget options. All rooms have fans and baths. TVs and fridges cost extra.

F Akry Hotel, 24 Sharia El-Gumhoriyya, T066-221013. The cheapest choice in town. 26 rather shabby rooms, with shared facilities and very little hot water. Restaurant on roof but breakfast not included.

F Crystal, 12 Sharia Mohammed Mahmoud, T066-222747. 70 a/c rooms in a huge imposing construction. Not very atmospheric, but cheap and reasonably comfortable.

F El-Nasr Hostel, Sharia El-Amin and El-Corniche (near sports stadium), T066-228702, F226433. 145 beds, family rooms, kitchen, meals available, parking, train 2 km, bus 3 km, overnight fee E£18.50 per dorm bed. Breakfast included. Clean, but dispiriting place to stay and a bit far away from town.

Eating

There are numerous restaurants serving fairly decent if unspectacular Western food. Most notable, though, is the seafood.

Maxim, upstairs, in the shopping centre adjacent to the Sonesta, T066-23433. Has the priciest fish in town. The view over the canal is outstanding, and the shrimp curry quite good.

Nora's Cruising Restaurant, T066-326804, operates from Sharia Filistine in front of the *National Museum*. Try this place if you'd rather be cruising on the canal than gazing at it. It leaves twice daily, for lunch (winter 1400; summer 1500) and dinner (winter 2000, summer 2100). Meals cost E£30-60. It's E£10 just to ride. Cruising time is 1-2 hrs.

Other seafood restaurants are scattered about Sharia El-Gumhoriyya and the Corniche, along the Mediterranean:

Abu Essam, also on the Corniche, near the Helnan, serves good fish in modern funky environs.

El Borg Restaurant, on the seafront, T066-323442, with advertisements everywhere, is a good choice.

Kastan Restaurant, Sharia El-Corniche T235242, specializing in shell fish, locals say this is the best fish place around, open 24 hrs daily, in season.

Pizza Pino, Sharia El-Gumhoriyya, T066-239949, a fairly fashionable place, good for tasty Italian fare just behind the National Museum.

Popeye's Café, further south along Sharia El-Gumhoriyya, T066-224877. Really a burger bar.

Reana House, a bit further down Sharia El-Gumhoriyya, serves large helpings of Korean and Chinese food.

Shopping

As Port Said was until recently a totally duty- free port, visitors, excluding ship's passengers, are still supposed to pass through customs when entering and leaving and it is therefore necessary to declare all valuable items on arrival to avoid being charged a hefty tax when leaving. Many shops still offer an array of imported goods at fairly competitive prices. Items of Egyptian origin that may be of interest include: oriental dresses and fine scarves; silver and gold jewellery; leather work; and paintings on papyrus.

Sharia El-Togary, organized like a typical Egyptian market, sells a wide variety of goods.

Sharia Filistine has a European-style shopping centre equipped with parking, restaurant and café, and a wide range of high quality imported goods.

Sharia El-Gumhoriyya and **Sharia El-Nahda** further west are important commercial streets with some shops.

Activities and tours

Sporting clubs

El Uonani Club, by Yacht Club, T066-240926.

Fishing Club, north end of Sharia El-Gumhoriyya, T066-236870. (Places to fish include: Al-Jameel bridge, Hagar Said, Lake el Manzala, Al-Tafri'a and Port Fouad bridge.) There's a National Fishing Competition each Oct.

Port Said Club, west end of Sharia 23 July by stadium, T066-221718.

Yacht Club, Sharia El-Tirsana/El Baharia, across canal in Port Fouad, T066-240926.

Tour operators

EgyptAir, Sharia El-Gumhoriyya, T066-224129.

Menatours, T2257442.

Misr Travel, 16 Sharia Filistine Mondial, 16 Sharia Filistine, T066-338853/226610.

Nasco Tours, Sharia Filistine, T066-229500, 02-3914682 (Cairo).

Port Said Tourist, Sharia Filistine, T066-329834.

Thomas Cook, 43 Sharia El-Gumhoriyya, T066-227559.

Transport

Bus

Both **East Delta**, T066-226883, and **Superjet**, T066-228793, bus companies serve Port Said. Buses depart hourly from the bus station to **Cairo** (2-3 hrs, E£15) from 0600-2220. There is also regular service to **Alexandria** (4 hrs, E£20). To get to **El-Arish**, head to **Ismailia**. From there, there's no shortage of Sinai-bound buses and service taxis. It's wise to book your tickets in advance.

Ferry

Free ferry crosses to **Port Fouad**, a smarter suburb of Port Said founded in 1920s. It leaves every 10-15 mins – returning immediately. **Princess Marissa** provides a twice weekly ferry service to **Limassol, Cyprus** usually leaving Port Said on Tue and Fri evenings in the winter (Sat in summer). Its sister ship sometimes goes on to **Athens** via **Rhodes**. For more information or tickets, try **Nasco Tours** on Sharia Filistine, T066-229500; 02-3914682, or **Menatours**, T066-2257442.

Taxi

Regular and quick service taxis run frequently to **Cairo** and **Alexandria** from the depot on Sharia El-Sbah, near the railway station. Depending on demand, service taxis also offer service to other destinations in the Canal Zone, Delta and across the canal to **El-Arish**.

Train

There are 5 slow and dirty trains a day to and from **Cairo** via **Ismailia** (4-5 hrs, E£5-14 depending on class). Buses and service taxis are a faster and more frequent option.

Directory

Banks Bank of Alexandria, Central Bank, Bank of Cairo or Thomas Cook all on Sharia El--Gumhoriyya, open 0900-1800. **Embassies and consulates** There are a number here as it is an important port: **Belgium**, main shopping centre, T066-223314; **France**, main shopping centre, T066-322875; **Greece**, 52 Sharia El-Gumhoriyya, T066-222614; **India**, 12 Sharia El-Gisr, T066-226865; **Italy**, Sharia Salah Salem, T066-223755; **Norway/ Sweden/Denmark**, 30 Sharia Filistine, T066-336730, 224706, 336740; **Spain**, 19 Al-Gabarty/El Geish, T066-233680; **UK**, main shopping centre, T066-231155; **USA**, 11 Sharia El-Gumhoriyya, T066-222154. **Passport office** in Government Building, T066-226720. Open 0800-1400 Sat-Thu. **Places of worship** Church of St Eugenie founded 1869, Sharia Ahmed Shawki; **Roman Catholic Cathedral** founded 1931, Sharia 23 July. **Church of St George** (Mari Girgis), founded 1946, Sharia Mohammed Ali. **Post office** Main post office, with International Telex and Fax, open daily 0700-1700, is on the corner of Ferial Gardens near the bus station, T066-225918. **Shipping agents** All on Sharia Filistine: **Assuit Shipping Agency**, T066-2203551; **Aswan Shipping Company**, T066-220662; **Canal Shipping Company**, T066-220790; **Damanhour Shipping Agency**, T066-220351; **El-Menia Shipping Agency**, T066-220351. For **Arab Express Shipping Co** contact head office in Alexandria, T03-4939142. **Useful numbers** Passport office in Port Police Building, T066-224811. **Port Said Harbour Authority**, Sharia Filistine, T066-223783.

Sinai Peninsula

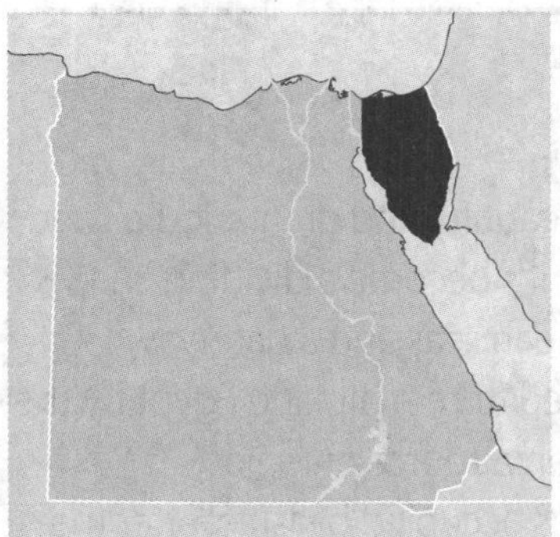

Footprint features

Introduction

Sinai is a mysterious land, stark, beautiful and dramatic. Formed by a literal collision of continents, it's become a dividing line between the Red and Mediterranean seas and a gateway between Africa and Asia. Separated from mainland Egypt by the Suez Canal, the peninsula has been a source of major contention in recent history. It was occupied by Israel after the war of 1967 and returned to Egypt in 1982 with the signing of the Camp David Accords. But continued turbulence in the region has had an impact on tourism.

It has been said that the triangular wedge of earth, home to just 340,000, is but '24,000 square miles of nothing', yet with its mystical past, dazzling seas and layers of desolate, majestic peaks, travellers fast come to find that in 'nothing,' there is so much. The southern coastal region features some of the best diving in the world. Scuba classes are affordable, the beaches are wide and inviting and the weather on the coast is always good. **Ras Mohammed**, Egypt's first officially declared protected area at the peninsula's southern tip, is a sanctuary to every species of life that thrives in the Red Sea and a fantasy for divers and snorkellers around the world. Sinai's rugged **interior**, too, is magical, where sun and wind and water have converged to paint pictures in the rock and carve jagged peaks that fade endlessly into the horizon in a million shades of pink. Trekkers and pilgrims journey from afar, some donning dirty rucksacks and others limping along with canes, to scramble up the splendid face of **Mount Sinai**, gaze at the rising sun and marvel at the sacred spot where Moses received the Ten Commandments. In the north, the less-visited Mediterranean coast with its fine palm fringed white sandy beaches, colourful Bedouin markets and relaxed pace offers pristine refuge for travellers and sea turtles alike.

★ Don't miss...

❶ **Sharm El-Sheikh** Take a break from antiquities and rugged romping in Sharm where you can party past dawn and partake in all the luxurious comforts of a fine international resort, page 369.

❷ **Diving** Discover colours and creatures you never imagined with a dive or snorkel in the underwater world of Ras Mohammed, page 371.

❸ **Dahab** Lose your watch and sense of time as you laze about Dahab, chilling out in waterside cafés, cooling off with the occasional snorkel and slumbering in cheap funky camps, page 374.

❹ **Desert Safari** Explore the hidden springs, valleys, canyons and peaks of the enchanting rugged interior on a Bedouin-led safari or extended desert trek in Central Sinai, page 390.

❺ **Mount Sinai** Humble and mystify yourself with a pre-dawn hike to watch the sunrise, page 406.

❻ **El-Arish** Escape the tourist hordes and enjoy the sandy, white, palm-lined beaches, diverse birdlife and laid back Bedouin culture of Northern Sinai, page 412.

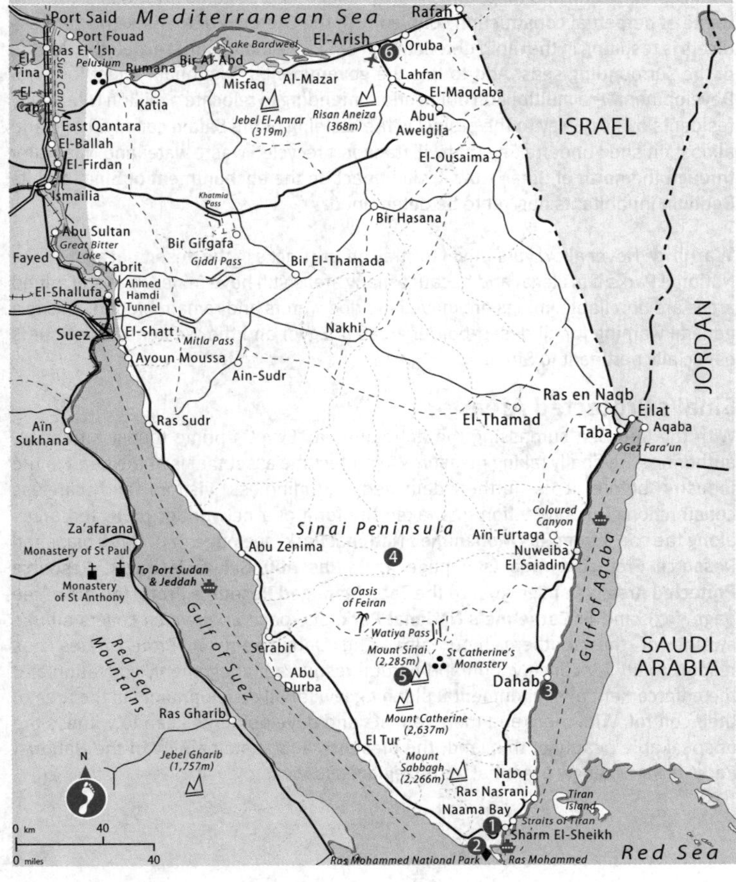

Background

Since the beginning of civilization, the Sinai has been one of the most important crossroads to human expansion. The Pharaohs created a path through the peninsula connecting Egypt to Jerusalem. Along the Mediterranean coast, the Sinai connected the Nile Valley with Mesopotamia. The Romans and Nabateans used an east-west desert route across that later became the *Darb El-Hajj*, or the pilgrim's way, to Mecca. For the Pharaohs, Sinai served as an easily protected barrier allowing ancient Egypt to blossom unthreatened. Later in third century BC, it was the stage for the Israelites' exodus out of Egypt. In recent history, Sinai's role as a crossroad grew even more pronounced with the completion of the Suez Canal. The strategic significance of this desert wedge and the many people that lay claim to it still yields clashes in the region.

While most backpackers and more rugged travellers journey overland from Cairo or Israel, or by ship from Hurghada or Jordan, many now fly to Sinai direct via Sharm El-Sheikh airport. And although this tourism is generating jobs and bringing in lots of foreign currency, the hasty pace of development in Sinai is of great concern to many. Since the peninsula was returned to Egypt in the early 80s, South Sinai alone has seen the onslaught of almost 25,000 hotel rooms. With 50,000 more under construction and thousands more planned, there seems no end in sight. The waste of perpetual construction coupled with the overload of tourists and careless divers is resulting in the rapid deterioration of Sinai's main tourist asset: the rich life of the surrounding seas. Add to this the government's "National Project for Sinai Development" – a multibillion dollar effort intending to relocate 3 million Nile Valley residents by 2017. Key to the project is the building of the Salam canal, a huge and almost finished undertaking that will transport recycled waste water and Nile water through the north of Sinai. How it will impact on the enchantment of Sinai and its Bedouin inhabitants has yet to be determined.

Warning Never allow your driver to stray off the tracks in the desert because in the National Parks it is illegal and because many areas still have mines. Maps of mined areas are unreliable, mines are moved in flood waters and remain hidden. This is a general warning for all desert-border areas of Egypt and the Western Desert but is especially pertinent to Sinai.

Sinai's Protected Areas

With the Red Sea surpassing the antiquities as Egypt's prime tourist attraction, authorities are finally taking measures to protect the asset that is at the heart of the industry before it is further damaged by mindless visitors and careless construction. This protection has taken the form of a network of protected areas along the coast from **Ras Mohammed National Park** (see page 371), **Nabq Managed Resource Protected Area** (see page 373), **Ras Abu Galum Managed Resource Protected Area** (see page 394) to the **Taba Managed Resource Protected Area** (see page 397), and **St Catherine's National Park** (see page 403) which covers a huge swathe of the southern mountains. The Department of Protectorates has responsibility for conservation and natural resource management, education and the enforcement of environmental planning law for all developments in the area of their control. With more and more tourists and developments keen to witness the unspeakable beauty of this land, the presence and sustainability of the National Parks is increasingly essential to the region's survival.

Sharm El-Sheikh to Dahab

➔ *Colour map 3, grid A/B6.*

The east coast of Sinai from Ras Mohammed to Taba boasts the most attractive shoreline coral reefs in the northern hemisphere. The climate, tempered by the sea, varies from pleasant in winter to hot but bearable in summer. To the east lie white sand beaches, rugged cliffs and views to Saudi Arabia and Jordan; the west holds the barren interior. The road journeys north from Sharm El-Sheikh to Dahab (98 km – 1-1½ hours) and passes the airport before turning inland through beautifully rugged scenery past a Bedouin school, a water-drilling camp, a manganese quarry, the tomb of an Israeli general and the remains of his bombed-out vehicle before entering Dahab. ▸▸ *For Sleeping, Eating and other listings, see pages 376-392.*

Sharm El-Sheikh

Known by locals and regulars simply as 'Sharm', this name misleadingly encompasses both the town of Sharm El-Sheikh and the resort of Na'ama Bay (7 km further north). The area has developed very rapidly in recent years becoming an international resort destination, at once glamorous and gaudy. Besides the wide sandy beaches and pristine blue sea, Sharm offers a spectacular and exceedingly popular diving area. There is over 60 km of rainbow-coloured vibrant reef teeming with hundreds of different underwater species, dramatic drop-offs and breathtaking formations unparalleled anywhere else in the diving world. The rich rugged interior is also accessible through countless tour operators eager to share the wonder of their desert with nomads of a newer and richer sort. As the region is increasingly brimming over with Western tourists, local people are growing more accustomed to their ways; and, as a result, there is significantly less hassle on the beaches. Sharm is one of the few areas in Egypt where bikinis, beer and booty-shaking are completely the norm.

Ins and outs

Getting there Most travellers landing in Sharm El-Sheikh airport have already booked a tour that will transport them to their destination. Individual travellers must rely on service taxis (around E£40-E£50) into town from the airport, about 10 km north of Na'ama and 17 km north of Sharm. Buses from Cairo (470 km) to Sharm via Suez (336 km) and the rest of Sinai can be caught from Cairo's Turgoman Station on either the **Superjet** service, T02-2660214, or a slightly cheaper and less comfortable **East Delta Bus**, T02-5762293. All buses terminate either at the bus station in the town of Sharm (at the bottom of the hill) or at the newer bus station behind the Mobil Petrol station half way between Sharm El-Sheikh and Na'ama Bay. To get to Na'ama Bay from there, you can take a taxi (a ludicrous E£10) or hail one of the many mini buses that run up and down the road from Na'ama to Old Sharm (50p-E£1, from 0630-2400). They will drop you off wherever you want to go. Ferries from Hurghada arrive at Sharm El-Sheikh port. ▸▸ *For further details, see Transport, page 392.*

Getting around Take a minibus or taxi to travel between the town of Sharm and Na'ama Bay. Minibuses also run up and down the hill to Hadaba in Sharm. In Na'ama, the minibus effectively gets you across the bay but walking around is pleasant and easy, as the area is quite compact. Getting to the East Delta Bus Station, behind the Mobil station, requires either minibus or taxi from both Sharm and Na'ama. Many of the major hotels in the town of Sharm offer shuttle buses to Na'ama Bay for free or for a nominal sum and will normally carry any visitor.

Information There is no tourist authority in Sharm El-Sheikh but all the major hotels can provide detailed tourist information. The tourist police is in Hadaba, up on the hill across the street from the mosque.

Sharm El-Sheikh town

The town of Sharm El-Sheikh, which existed pre-1967 as a closed military zone was used by the Israelis. The small community dubbed, by some 'Old Sharm', is rapidly shedding its previous dilapidated image. Now it has an airport, bus station, marina and docks, several banks, post office, telephone exchange, hospital, police station, supermarket, garages with repair facilities, souvenir shops galore, hotels, diving centres and a number of small restaurants. In the last few years, more high quality hotels have been built around Hadaba, the hilltop neighbourhood between the town and resort area. While Sharm cannot compete with its neighbour Na'ama Bay for beach access and general leisure facilities, it has the advantage of being an Egyptian

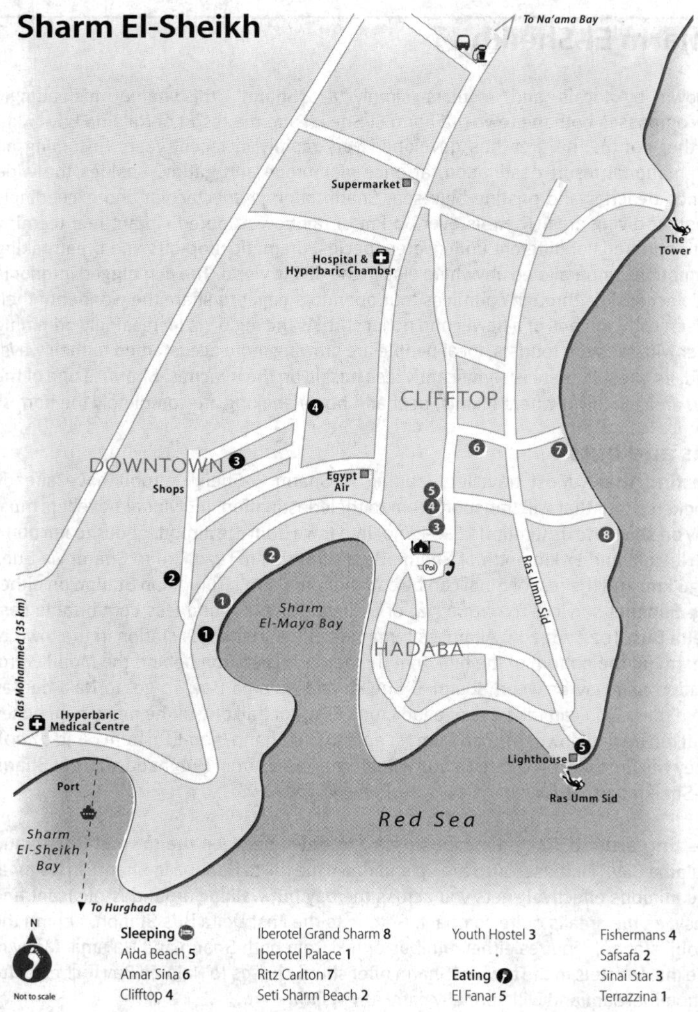

town rather than an international playground. In recent years, its cheaper property prices and proximity to Ras Um Sidd, a spectacular shore diving spot, has attracted a growing international community of diving instructors and the like.

Na'ama Bay

Purely a tourist resort, Na'ama Bay, or 'God's blessing' in Arabic, is considered by many to be more attractive than the town of Sharm. Renown for its smooth sandy beach, chic and pricey modern hotels, an attractive vehicle-free corniche and some of the best diving facilities in the world, Na'ama is rivalling the ancient wonders by the Nile as a leading tourist attraction in Egypt. Relative to other locales in the Sinai, Na'ama Bay caters to tourists with money to spend. Many visitors book packaged tours from their home countries, which often include diving opportunities, in addition to airfare and accommodation for very reasonable rates. But for a true taste of Egypt, Na'ama is lacking. There are restaurants and shops for divers and other visitors but little or no indigenous Egyptian life. Indeed the vast majority of the hotel workers come not from Sinai but from elsewhere in Egypt. If respite and beauty are what you seeks, spectacular views across the clear blue waters of the Red Sea to the mountains of Saudi Arabia make Na'ama Bay an inviting place for relaxation, partying and play in sea and sand. (You don't have to be interested in diving but it helps.) Outside of the sea and surrounding desert peaks, there is very little to see. Bedouin villages that may be of interest are more accessible from Dahab. ▸▸ *For diving and other actvities listings, see page 386.*

Day trips from Sharm El-Sheikh

From Sharm El-Sheikh, it is possible to book daylong trips and tours to see parts of Sinai's breathtaking desert interior. Most of the people who opt to explore the desert from Sharm, however, are of the package tourist sort. It's best to set off from Dahab or Nuweiba if you want a more authentic and rugged desert experience. For those who lack the time or inclination, though, you can rent a jeep or book a tour to **St Catherine's Monastery**, (10 hours, see page 404) which may include a trek to the summit of **Mount Sinai** (see page 406) and a visit to a Bedouin village. Tour prices vary from US$50-100 depending on content and number of people. For US$30, a jeep will transport you to **Wadi Ain Kid**, a lush canyon filled with fruit trees and funky rock formations just 40 km north of Na'ama. Or for about US$50, you can visit the enchanting **Coloured Canyon** and take the hour-long hike to its depths. Most large hotels book these trips and some include Bedouin-style tea or dinner under the stars. The Pigeon House (see page 379) comes highly recommended for those looking for a more affordable and rugged experience.

There are many boat trips to nearby coral reefs and a ferry that runs four times a week across the Red Sea to **Hurghada** (see page 392), **Thomas Cook** books tickets, T069-601808. Day trips to **Cairo** and **Luxor** (0600-2130) are organized by **Sun 'N' Fun**, T069-601623 (see page 390) as well as the Sonesta Beach Resort (see page 378).

Ras Mohammed National Park

ⓘ *The national park is open from sunrise to sunset while the visitors' centre, which includes a restaurant, audio-visual presentations, first aid, shops and toilets, is open from 1000 to sunset. US$5 equivalent plus US$5 per car. There are colour-coded signs that lead visitors to the various attractions. Also crude toilets between Main Beach and Observatory Beach. Bring your own water bottles from Sharm El-Sheikh. Taxis to Ras Mohammed from Sharm El-Sheikh cost E£60 one way but it is advisable to keep the taxi for the day – around E£100-150 – as there are no taxis at Ras Mohammed. A 4-wheel drive vehicle is a better bet – although you cannot go off road. Vehicles pass through UN checkposts. Passports are scrutinized at the Egyptian checkpoint where*

Israelis or any non-Egyptians who came in through Taba may experience delays. Note that Ras Mohammed is beyond the Sinai-only visa jurisdiction, so you will need a full Egypt tourist visa to enter. Beyond deserted Israeli trenches are the gates of the national park and nature reserve.

Collection of or damage to any natural resource, hunting, driving on vegetation or in a prohibited area, spear fishing or fish feeding are prohibited. Rules are strictly enforced by the park's English-speaking rangers.

Ras Mohammed National Park, Egypt's first national park, was designated in 1983, and subsequently expanded in 1989. A terrestrial and marine area covering 480 sq km, 53 km south of Na'ama Bay, and just 30 minutes from the mania of Sharm, the park offers an underwater spectacle unsurpassed anywhere on the planet. The area includes all marine and terrestrial areas at Ras Mohammed and the island of Tiran as well as the shorelines between the Sharm El-Sheikh harbour and the southern boundary of the Nabq protected area.

Ras Mohammed is a small peninsula which juts out from Sinai's most southerly tip and is the point where the waters of the shallow (95 m) Gulf of Suez meet the deep waters (1,800 m maximum) of the Gulf of Aqaba. The result is a truly extraordinary ecosystem that encompasses virtually every life form thriving in the Red Sea. Besides the huge variety of brightly coloured fish that live on the coral reef, deep water species like sharks, tuna, barracuda and turtles also come to feed. The beaches around the marine gardens are beautiful. There are some clean shallow sheltered coves perfect for snorkelling as well as more exposed stretches where wind and strong currents necessitate caution. With more than 20 acclaimed sites, the **diving** in Ras Mohammed is internationally renowned. (To ensure care of the area, authorities are limiting the number of dive boats coming in so try to book ahead. If you would rather dive from shore, plan to bring a diving guide and your own gear with you.)

Home to a stunning variety of forms and colours in the corals and reef fish, the area is also famous for manta ray and turtle. Two of the reefs in the Straits of Tiran, which fall under the Ras Mohammed National Park, are the permanent residences of **Hawksbill turtles** and there are also turtle nesting beaches within the restricted areas of the National Park. Particularly good fossil reefs dating back 15,000 years can be found all around Ras Mohammed but are especially vivid around the mangrove channel and the visitors' centre.

Ras Mohammed is remarkable too for its rare northerly **mangroves** which lie in a shallow channel at the tip of the peninsula, in an area with many rock pools and crevices in the fossil reef that shelter shrimp, among other stranger creatures. The famous Hidden Bay confuses visitors, because it appears and disappears with the changing tide. The Saline or Solar Lake is interesting for its range of salt-loving plants and bird watchers will also find this a delightful

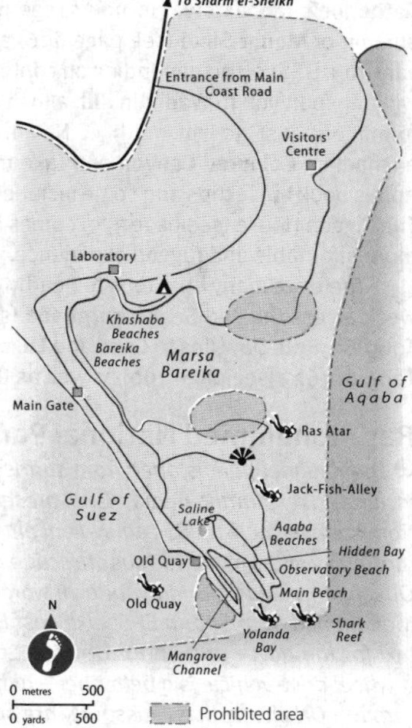

> Egypt's first national park, was designated in 1983, and subsequently expanded in 1989. The park offers an underwater spectacle unsurpassed anywhere on the planet...a truly extraordinary ecosystem that encompasses virtually every life form thriving in the Red Sea...

spot. In late summer months, thousands of White Stork stop over to rest during their annual migration to East Africa. The Park is also an important area for four heron species – Grey, Goliath, Reef and Greenback – as well as gulls, terns and ospreys.

Although much of the land appears to be barren and hostile it is in fact home to a variety of life, from insects to small mammals, Nubian ibex and Desert foxes. The foxes are often seen near the main beaches and cubs can be spotted at sunset in late spring. They are harmless if approached but should not be fed.

A word of warning: expect to wander far if you seek isolation – there are over 100,000 visitors annually here.

Camping is permitted in designated areas (US$5 per person per night) but numbers are strictly limited to preserve the environment. Enquire about camping permits at the entrance to the park. The closest store is in Sharm El-Sheikh so plan to bring all your camping supplies, including water, with you.

Nabq Protected Area

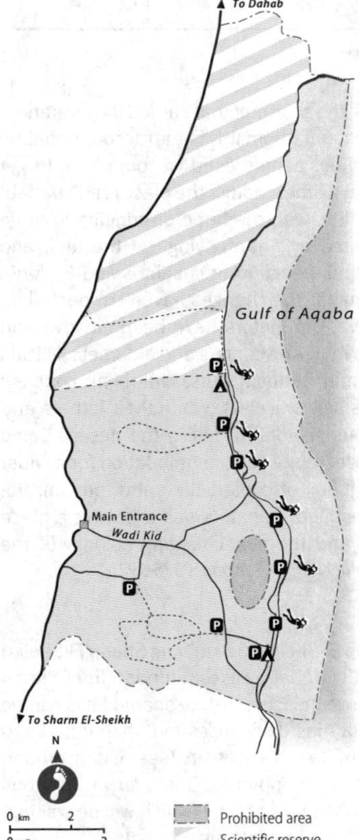

Nabq Managed Resource Protected Area

ⓘ *Free. Taxis from Sharm E£60-80 one-way but it is advisable to keep the taxi for the day at around E£150, most hotels organize day trips.*

Nabq Managed Resource Protected Area, to the north of Na'ama, 35 km north of Sharm El-Sheikh, is also an outstanding area (designated in 1992) of dense mangroves – the most northerly in the world at the mouth of Wadi Kid – and also rare sand dune habitats. The area covers over 600 sq km and contains multiple ecosystems sheltering more than 130 plant species. Much of the 600 sq km has restricted access to prevent critical damage by four-wheel drive vehicles but there is still lots to see here for the careful viewer. Among the most notable habitats of the area are the dunes at the edge of Wadi Kid and the largest mangrove forest in the Sinai. Mangroves have adapted to the saline environment. Their root systems are able to filter out much of the salt from seawater so they can receive the nourishment they need to survive. The location and density of the trees around the mouth of Wadi Kid suggest an infiltration of fresh water, which has reduced the salinity to levels tolerated by the trees. The presence of the mangroves allows for an extraordinary ecosystem and the wildlife is outstanding. Storks, herons, ospreys and raptors are quite common; mammals like foxes, ibex and gazelles are more rare. The area's warm clear waters and sandy bottom also make it a great place for swimming. The hyrax, a small rodent-like mammal which is actually the closest living relative to the elephant, can be found here in Wadi Khereiza. The diving is also superb, though little is done these days as the reefs lie at some distance.

A small Bedouin settlement, Ghargana, lies on the coast where the tribesmen continue to fish in a traditional manner. Another Bedouin village, Kherieza, is inland from the main coastal valley Wadi Kid. The parks make a sincere effort to involve the Bedouin in their work and to protect their traditional lifestyle, currently under much pressure from the rapid development in the area. Near the settlement is a more modern establishment, a shrimp farm that supplies much of the produce for the hotels and restaurants in Sharm El-Sheikh.

Though popular with safari groups, Nabq is less crowded than Ras Mohammed.

Dahab

Dahab, meaning 'gold' in Arabic, is fast losing the shimmer that earned its reputation. Known for its laxness with regard to marijuana, unfathomably cheap accommodation and food, and a super-chilled backpacker vibe, people used to come here to get stoned, go diving, and kick back – for weeks at a time. Though the place is still Dahab, things are changing. The Sinai tourist authority, with the hope of bringing in more money and the tourists who have it, initiated a "Sharm-ifying" of the area and required many establishments to trade off their beach front cushions and Bedouin style seating areas for 'proper' tables and chairs. The changes haven't impacted on the entire bay, though, and where they have, proprietors have been creative and managed to retain quite a bit of the former flavour. Newcomers and oldtimers will still find beach cafés, bazaars and mosques amid Bedouin huts, crumbling concrete camps, and palm trees. Local Bedouin girls sell bracelets, while their fathers and brothers hawk camel rides and invite curious visitors for tea in the desert. Some fancier hotels are sprouting up, offering a wider range of accommodation for a wider range of humanity. Thankfully, despite the influx of construction and tourism, the magic of the sea, sun and stars remains unsoiled. Dahab is still a gem of a place where time dissolves into tea and smoke and the ever-changing colours of the surrounding peaks. ▸▸ *For Sleeping, Eating and other listings, see pages 376-392.*

Ins and outs

Getting there Dahab is 98 km north of Sharm El-Sheikh, 82 km from Sharm El-Sheikh airport, 133 km from Taba and 570 km from Cairo. Daily buses run north from Sharm El-Sheikh (E£15) and south from Taba and Nuweiba (E£15, 10), or shared taxis can be hired from the main towns in Sinai. East Delta runs daily buses to Dahab from Cairo through Suez and Sharm (E£55-70). Because of Dahab's split site (see Getting around below), make sure you know where you want to be dropped off. Buses arrive in the bus station in Dahab in the south. To get to Assalah, a pick-up taxi (which will be waiting) will transport you for E£1-3 depending on how many people are with you.

Getting around Dahab can be divided into two distinct areas: the Bedouin village, **Assalah**, and the town of Dahab. Assalah is further divided into three parts: the actual village where locals live and the adjacent tourist areas of **Masbat** and **Mashraba** where travellers hang out. The administrative town of Dahab, or Dahab 'City', where

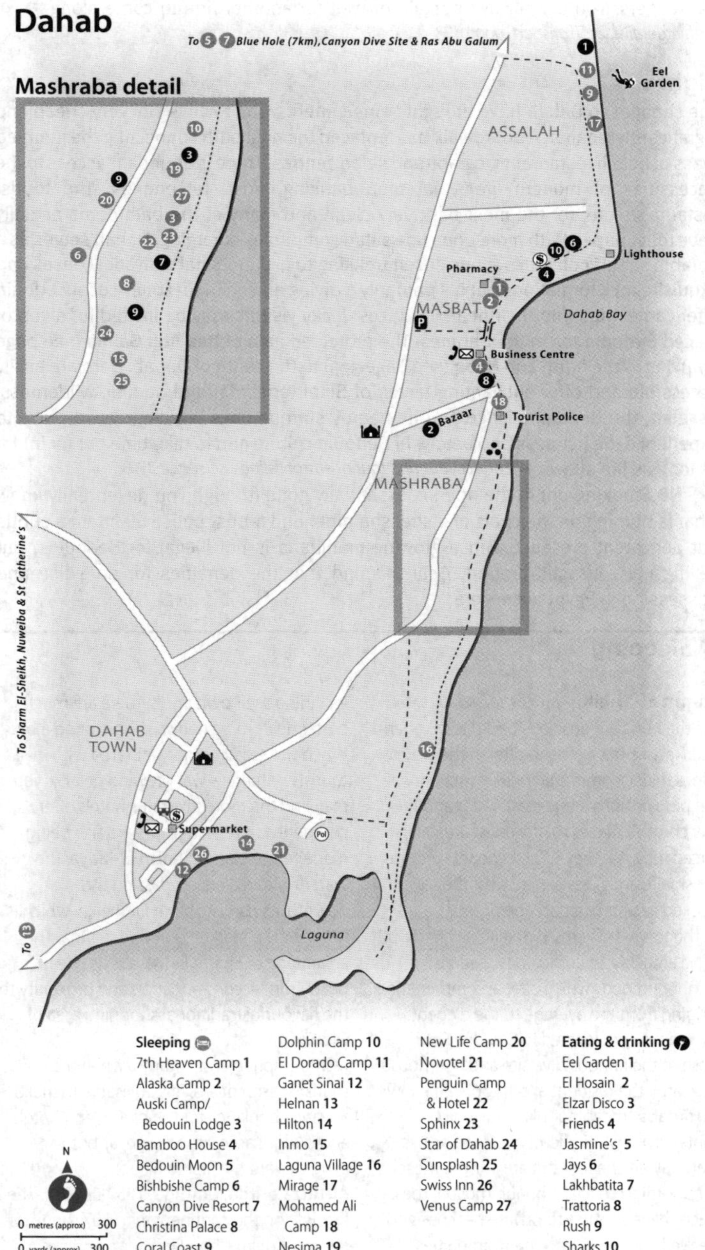

 there's a bus station, bank and post office, is about 3 km south and 1 km inland from the beach. There are also a few self-contained resorts on the water to the south of Dahab City in an area known as the **'Laguna'**. Walking is really the best way to get around, but there is no shortage of pick-ups and taxis. A taxi costs E£5 from one section of town to the other, pick-ups are a bit cheaper, depending on the number of passengers. You can always bargain or wait for another ride to come along. ▸▸ *For further details, see Transport, page 393.*

Sights

The changes to Dahab have brought some benefits. The town is still very cheap and significantly cleaner. A boardwalk has replaced the dust path connecting the jumbled mass of beach restaurants, camps and safari centres. There is abundant access to the necessities of modern life – internet, banking, post, telephones. The tourist restaurants are, for the most part, very clean and many of the bathrooms actually have toilet paper. With more bona fide safari companies emerging, Dahab serves as a notable set-off point for serious desert trekking to explore Sinai's mystical oases and exquisite rock formations but it's primarily a diving and chill-out zone. Local Bedouin offer camel trips into their nearby villages; lucky visitors may be invited for a cup of spiced Bedouin tea in their homes. The protected area of **Ras Abu Galum** (see page 394) lies to the north and **Nabq** (see page 373) to the south of Dahab. Both are easily accessible and offer enchanting tastes of Sinai terrestrial and aquatic wilderness. **Assalah**, the Bedouin village and its nearby surroundings remain a good place to experience the richness and beauty of Bedouin culture and to take time out (or in) for as long as life allows. ▸▸ *For Activties and tour operator listings, see page 390.*

NB Smoking pot in the open is essentially gone (though you never really know what is burning on the coals of a sheesha pipe) and tourist police maintain a subtle but persistent presence. Since growing marijuana is not illegal for Bedouins, but selling it is, it's still around. Bear in mind that the penalties for drug use and possession in Egypt are severe.

Sleeping

Sharm El-Sheikh *p369, map p370*

For the budget-conscious backpacker, Sharm and Na'ama have little to offer in the way of affordable accommodation. The majority of sleeping options are at least 4-star and the few cheaper places that do exist are over-priced for what they offer. In general, rooms are significantly less expensive if they are booked as part of a package or tour.

The town of Sharm El-Sheikh, 6.5 km south of Na'ama Bay, encompasses several neighbourhoods which offer accommodation ranging from the average to the elegant. Most hotels are located in **Ras Um Sidd**, close to the famous dive site and lighthouse, or nearby the residential cliff top area known as **Hadaba** (meaning "hilltop"), which contains many middle-of-the-road hotels that may be cheaper but are, for the most part, nothing special. Though most of these places have shuttles to private beaches and are well equipped with many amenities including their own pools, there are much better deals to be had so shop around a bit. When the season is not saturated with tourists or there is war brewing nearby, you may find the more luxurious hotels offer competitve rates. Attempts are also being made to popularize **Sharm El-Maya**, the waterfront area encompassing the downtown part of Sharm El-Sheikh, which is home to the market, port and marina. The advantage of Sharm El-Maya is its cheaper beachfront accommodation and proximity to the flavourful traditional shopping area of Old Sharm.

In the spring and autumn, when the tourist season peaks, it is advisable to make advance bookings for the higher end hotels and budget accommodation, as both extremes are the first to fill up.

AL Ritz Carlton, Um Sidd, T069-661919. The first Ritz on the continent with 307 rooms, is the most deluxe hotel in Sharm and has every amenity imaginable and then some. Sea and garden views, beach access, lots of restaurants – each with a different theme – athletic facilities, internet access, a spa, and diving centre.

A Iberotel Grand Sharm, 1 km from Ras Um Sidd, 3 km from downtown Sharm market, T069-663800. On a coral beach equipped with floating jetty to facilitate entry into water. Has 223 rooms fully equipped with satellite TV, a/c. Pools, restaurants, disco and athletic facilities. Good snorkelling, and dive centre in hotel. Beautiful views of the sea.

A Iberotel Palace, in Sharm El-Maya bay in front of the old Market, T069-661111. Free shuttle from airport, wonderful views from position on cliff top, extensive landscaped grounds, nearby sandy beaches, easy walk to town centre, 255 rooms. Many restaurants and sports facilities including Seafun Divers Dive Centre.

C Seti Sharm Beach, T069-660870-9, F660147. 286 rooms, offer half board, beach location with coral reefs, 2 restaurants, 2 swimming pools, tennis courts, health club, watersports and diving centre.

C Sun Rise Hotel, Hadaba on 'Motel Road' next to Aida Hotel, T/F069-661721. 106 rooms, nothing special but another hotel in a block of hotels miles from the sea. 2 pools, 2 restaurants, shuttle bus to beach, a/c, TV, fridge and Pharaoh Dive Centre.

D Aida Beach Hotel, Hadaba on 'Motel Road', T069-660719, F660722. One of the older hotels in Hadaba, overlooking Sharm El-Maya Bay. 198 large split-level rooms, restaurants, coffee shop, bars, shops, pool, sports facilities, free transport to 2 hotel beaches about 5 mins away, and Submaldives Diving Centre.

D Amar Sina, Hadaba, T069-662222. Funky architecture with domes and outdoor courtyard spaces make this the best place to stay in Hadaba. 88 rooms – each one unique, pool and jacuzzi, internet access, Colona Dive Centre – reputable and particularly popular with Scandinavians.

F Sharm El-Sheikh Youth Hostel, Hadaba, near the police station, T069-660317. 80 beds in a/c dormitories, family rooms (3 beds per room, E£55 per person), doubles available. Additional 80 beds in men-only dormitory. Open to non-members for modest extra charge, no maximum age, open 24 hrs. Kitchen, parking, food available. One of the few really cheap options in Sharm. Breakfast included in price.

Camping

F Ras Mohammed, T069-660668 (open from 0800-1700). It is possible to camp in designated sites inside the national park, but it is camping of the rugged sort, no showers. It costs about E£100 to be dropped off from Sharm and there is a fee of US$5 per person with an additional fee for cars. Bring in everything you will need including water, as it may not be available. Also note that the park is beyond the jurisdiction of the Sinai-only visa, so plan to come here only if you have obtained a tourist visa that covers all of Egypt, and bring your passport.

Na'ama Bay *p371, map p378*

The number of hotels in Na'ama Bay continues to grow rapidly. Most of them extend back from the boardwalk to the main road and some offer cheaper rooms across the highway. Almost every hotel has its own tourist office offering water sports equipment, diving information and desert safaris. Every hotel with direct beach access offers beachside bars and food. Again, the best deals to be had are through tour companies before you arrive. With the exception of the youth hostel in Old Sharm, the often-full Pigeon House and nearby Shark's Bay, accommodation for the budget-conscious in Na'ama Bay is close to nil.

AL Hyatt Regency Sharm, T069-601234, F603600. Beautiful hotel with exquisite gardens, overlooking the sea. Beach is coral-laden, and not ideal for swimming. Disabled rooms and standard 5-star amenities available. Excellent Thai restaurant, some say it's the best place to eat in the Bay.

AL Iberotel Lido, at the southern end of Na'ama Bay, T069-602603, F602099. A beautiful hotel, the Lido offers stunning views of the sea, interesting ship-like decor, and a rooftop pool.

AL Jolie Ville Movenpick Golf Hotel and Resort, further up the road from Na'ama Bay in Om Merikah Bay, T069-603200, F603225. This hotel is on its own – 5 km west of the airport and within walking distance of the 18-hole Championship Golf Course. Sea views but not on beach. Far away from the action of Na'ama, this is where President Mubarak usually stays when he visits Sharm. It has 9 restaurants and bars and a water theme park. Hotel offers regular shuttle to airport, around the golf course and also to Na'ama Bay.

AL Sonesta Beach Resort, at the northern edge of Na'ama Bay, T069-600725-30, F600733. Overlooking the bay, it's a good place to enjoy an evening drink or stay in one of the cool collection of white domes in extensive gardens. Attractive and spacious, the hotel has 7 pools (some heated and some not), dive centre, shops and boutique. The 455 split-level rooms are decorated in Bedouin style with either balcony or patio. Selection of cuisine, including La Gondola Italian restaurant, several cafés and bars, children's club (5-12 years – runs daily 1000-1600), tennis, squash, spa, 24-hr baby-sitting service.

A Ghazala Hotel, centrally located in Na'ama Bay, T069-600150, F600155. Smart, modern hotel but an old-timer in Na'ama. Houses a variety of restaurants indoors and out representing different types of cuisine and an ice cream corner, bars in lobby and by very large pool, separate children's pool, easy access to beach and all facilities, helpful tourist office located right on the boardwalk offering maps of the area and access to sports equipment, diving and desert tours.

A Hilton Fayrouz Village, centrally located near Ghazala, T069-600137-9, F770726. One of the oldest and quaintest hotels in Na'ama Bay, it offers double bungalow rooms in lovely gardens, with the largest private beach in Na'ama, a large playground for children, several bars and restaurants, excellent food, first class water sports (and dive centre), yacht, glass-bottom boat, pool, tennis, minigolf, volley ball, horse riding, massage, aerobics, disco, games room.

A Marriott Beach Resort, T069-600190, F600188. Spacious, modern hotel, large free-form pool, connected by wooden bridges and surrounded by sun terrace and gardens, spectacular waterfall in the central courtyard. In standard Marriott fashion, it offers all amenities including water sports equipment rental, dive centre and a fully equipped health club. A little further away from the action in central Na'ama so generally more quiet. Particularly popular with wealthy Egyptians.

A Movenpick Hotel Jolie Ville, smack in the middle of Na'ama bay, T069-600100-9, F600111. Very large low-level building, spreading on both sides of desert road. It's the most extensive hotel in Na'ama Bay, so

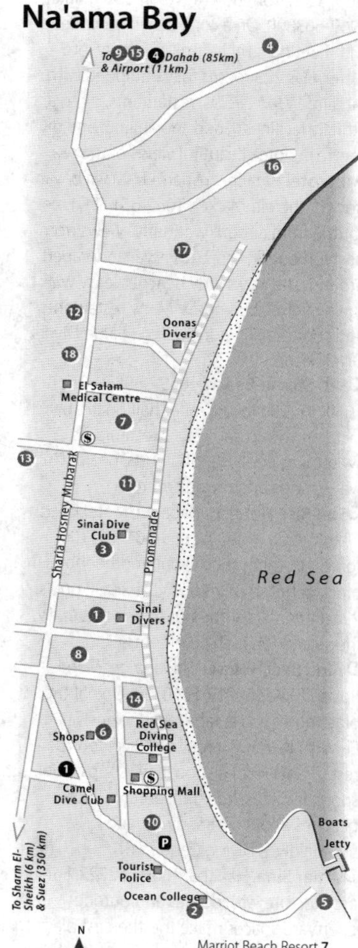

Sleeping

Ghazala **1**
Helnan Marina Sharm **2**
Hilton Fayrouz Resort **3**
Hyatt Regency Sharm **4**
Iberotel Lido **5**
Jolie Ville Movenpick **8**
Kanabesh **6**
Marriot Beach Resort **7**
Movenpick Golf Resort **9**
New Tiran Village **10**
Novotel Aquamarine **11**
Pigeon House **12**
Rosetta **13**
Sanafir **14**
Shark's Bay **15**
Sofitel Coralia **16**
Sonesta Beach Resort **17**
Tropicana Tivoli **18**

Eating

Hard Rock Cafe **1**

not suitable for those with walking difficulties. Has 337 rooms and 10 suites; the cheaper rooms, on the far side of desert road, are 5 mins walk from the beach. Large circular pool, children's pool, children's club. Excellent service, good food, modern facilities but soulless. Also home to a large casino and the disco Cactus, a popular spot for young people.

A Sofitel Coralia, T069-600081-04, F600085. A beautiful, sophisticated hotel, large pool, children's pool, diving centre for beginners and advance level skills, health club with gym, aerobics, sauna, jacuzzi, Turkish bath and massage, table tennis, archery (pay locally) and mountain bikes for hire. Shows and entertainment provided by in-house professional team, has the coral gardens called Nir Gardens just off shore. A superb Indian restaurant. Beautiful view of the entire Bay so a good place for an evening cocktail.

B Helnan Marina Hotel, T069-600170-1, F600170. Not the most glamorous hotel in Na'ama but, being the oldest, something of an institution. More than 150 rooms on the southern end of the Bay. Beach location, good sea views, helpful and efficient staff, bar service, clean rooms, buffet. In close proximity to the set-off point for dive boats and the most frequented area of the boardwalk.

B Novotel Aquamarine Hotel, T069-600173-82, F600193. More than 150 rooms, with terrace or balcony, central position, landscaped gardens, choice of restaurants, tennis, pool which often plays very loud Arabic music, very popular with Egyptian families during national holidays.

C Kanabesh Hotel, T069-600184, F600185. Another cheapish centrally located option with 64 double rooms with a/c, restaurant, café, snackbar, bar, live music, small kiosks, travel agent, dive club.

C Rosetta Hotel, across the street from the Hilton Fayrouz, T069-601888, F601999. Known for Emperor's Divers, it offers comfortable accommodation with satellite TV, a/c, several pools, beach access, good Egyptian restaurant, disco, laundry and bank.

C Sanafir, T069-600197, F600196. 90 rooms, one of the area's original hotels, a block from the beach and right in the middle of the action on the boardwalk. One of the few hotels with flavour in Na'ama Bay. Highly recommended by guests, many of whom are divers. Relaxed, friendly authentic Egyptian atmosphere, with Egyptian, fish and South Korean restaurants, snack bar, private beach, funky courtyard area with pools and bridges. Home to the hippest club in Na'ama Bay, Bus Stop, which hosts twice-weekly dance parties that rage through the night. A good place to mingle and meet people but not recommended for the tranquillity-seeker.

C New Tiran Village, next to the Helnan Marina, T069-600225, F600220. Among the cheaper options in the centre of the action, though accommodation is nothing extraordinary. Pool, restaurant and access to beach, though other hotels seem to take over the space in front (although beaches by law are open to all you may get grief from stewards for sitting on other hotels' chairs).

D-E Pigeon House, T069-600996, F600995. Cheapest room in town, 5 mins' walk to beach, rooms are small and basic but clean and comfortable. Some rooms are equipped with fans, some with a/c. There are both shared bath and private bath options. Prices of rooms vary depending on standard and number of people sharing. Lively courtyard with sheesha and beer attracts younger backpackers and divers. Use of beach at Sonesta. Anenome Dive Centre offers discounts to guests of hotel (and 4-day desert safari tours can be arranged through the dive centre).

E Tropicana Tivoli, next to Pigeon House, 5 mins walk from beach, T069-600652. Over 60 rooms built in Moorish citadel style, with white domes. Small, friendly, pool with slide (but deep and with no shallow end so not suitable for children), restaurant, billiards, all water sports available nearby. 20 mins by bus from airport, and 15 mins by hourly free shuttle bus into Na'ama Bay. Used by divers who rent the cheaper rooms, some with windows and some with skylights. All rooms a/c, studio rooms are larger with balcony.

Camping

E-F Sharks Bay Camp, 5 km north of Na'ama Bay, about 10 mins from airport by taxi, T069-600947, F600943. Offers very basic accommodation, Bedouin-style huts (bamboo cabins) with clean communal toilet and showers (hot water). Meals are taken in the excellent Sharks Bay open air restaurant where the speciality is seafood in a Bedouin-style tent by the beach. Friendly and informal, coral garden for diving or snorkelling is directly off the beach and a popular spot for novice divers. Very popular dive centre on site (run by Bedouin) offers courses and equipment. Recommended for budget travellers.

Dahab *p374, map p375*

Nowadays Dahab offers something for everyone. There are a few high-end hotels, including some fully self-contained resorts. There's also a wide range of comfortable middle-price options closer to Assalah. And Dahab is still the budget traveller's dream, with dozens of camps offering bungalows and concrete box rooms for less than US$1. For about E£50 per night, you can find a comfortable double room with fan and private bath. For US$50, expect stellar accommodation around Assalah with a/c, pool, and all the usual 4-star amenities. Hotels and resorts near Dahab are quite self-contained and intentionally separate from the Bedouin village. Their prices fluctuate depending on the season.

A Hilton Dahab Resort, near the laguna, on the beach, T069-640310. A beautiful fully self-contained resort. 163 whitewashed dome-shaped rooms with all the usual 5-star facilities, Sinai Divers' Centre, windsurfing and aquasports centre, travel agent organizes excursions into desert, 2 pools, 3 restaurants. It's the snazziest hotel around Dahab though quite isolated from the pulse of Assalah.

A Swiss Inn Golden Beach Resort, T069-640471, F640470. 147 rooms, under Swiss management, private beach with bar, 3 restaurants, pool, diving and windsurf centre, massage, billiards, bank, one of the newest fully contained resorts in Dahab.

A-C Novotel Dahab Holiday Village, PO Box 23, Dahab, T/F069-640301-5. 139 a/c rooms with private terrace, including 40 divers' cabanas, very attractive, excellent beach good for windsurfing, **A** rooms on the beach are larger and have a sea view, **B** rooms in the middle of the village, have a garden view and **C** rooms at the back are more basic. 2 restaurants, café, bar, pool (NB no shallow end), disco, bank, windsurfing, a glass boat, pedalos, canoes, tennis courts, massage, bicycle hire, volley ball, jet skis, speed boats, horse riding, safari and desert trips, shops, Sinai Divers Centre, non- residents can enjoy the facilities for E£40.

C Ganet Sinai Hotel, T069-640440, F640441. 70 chalet-style rooms with sea views, 4 suites, prices vary depending on nationality – US$10 cheaper for eastern Europeans. Dive centre, 3 restaurants, 3 pools, fitness centre and health club with sauna and jacuzzi, private beach, windsurfing school.

C Helnan Dahab Hotel, stands apart to the south, T069-640425, F640428. 200 rooms, a/c, private beach, 2 swimming pools, 2 restaurants, café, bar, tennis, squash, pool hall, watersports, dive centre, windsurfing, all rooms have sea view, good beach.

Assalah *p375, map p375*

After the luxury of the above hotels the contrast is grand. In Assalah to the north along the beachfront there are dozens of "campgrounds" varying from run-down to pleasant. They start in the south in an area dubbed Mashraba, followed by the Masbat, and then the actual Bedouin village of Assalah. Camp quality varies though all, or parts of all, have electricity, sit toilets, hot water, fans and even a/c. For the cheaper end accommodation, you will need a sleeping bag of sorts among other necessities, as most camps don't provide bedding, towels, soap or toilet paper. For the sake of security, opt for padlocked rooms. There are generally 3 categories: basic bamboo huts, concrete rooms – both with a shared bath – and rooms with private bathroom. For the hut or concrete box, expect to pay E£5-10 per person per night. If you want the private bath and maybe fan or a/c, the price varies from E£20-E£50 per night depending on extras. Some camps are on the beach, others across the road, many offer a discounted breakfast. Some only have hot water in winter. Think about what's important to you, keep in mind mosquitoes and peeping toms and look around. Don't drink the tap water – it's brackish and hard. Prices in Dahab for everything are always negotiable and better deals can be made in the low season. Each camp has its own character – some are cleaner, some are louder, some cater to divers and others to party-goers. Some campgrounds/hotels have less than desirable reputations relating to drugs, and staff who are over-friendly to women. Ask around, everyone has a favourite.

Laguna

B-C Laguna Hotel, on the beach between Dahab City and Assalah, T069-640352. 78 rooms (standard and superior), restaurant, a/c, phone, satellite TV, pool and dive centre. Near the laguna but far from the action – a little run-down for the price.

Mashraba area

Most camps and hotels in this area have views across the gulf. Mashraba tends to be quieter, more popular with families, more remote. Unlike Masbat, most establishments here have been able to retain the old-style Bedouin seating areas and flavour.

B-C Nesima Hotel, T069-640320, nesima@intouch.com. Perhaps the nicest place to stay in Assalah, and certainly in Mashraba. A true quality hotel with breathtaking views across the Gulf, 51 spacious clean rooms with a/c, private bathrooms, wheelchair access, popular restaurant and bar with happy hour, pool (open to non-residents for E£20 including beverage), beach and reef access, and dive centre. Good snorkelling. Doctor on call.

D Inmo Hotel, T069-640370, F640372, inmo@inmodivers.de. Long established quality hotel owned by German-Egyptian couple. 50 rooms, 4 categories ranging from very comfortable rooms with private bath and terrace to clean backpacker-basic. Known as a divers' hotel and a place where people keep coming back to. Organizes desert safaris with local Bedouin guides. Depending on the season there can be discounts for people staying long term and for divers using their centre. Pool, beach and reef access. Fills up fast so book ahead.

D New Sphinx, T069-640032. More upmarket than Sphinx (below), but same owner. With pool and beach access.

D The Sphinx, close to centre, T069-640032. Offers cheaper rooms without en suite bathroom.

E-F Auski/Bedouin Lodge, T069-640474. Popular well-established camp with beach access. Bedouin-run. Family-friendly. Camel, snorkelling and jeep trips can be arranged. Good views of sea. Bike rental is possible.

E-F Dolphin, T069-640018. An older camp with a reputation for cleanliness and conveniently located for the centre while maintaining the peace of a non-central position. Beach and reef access, cushioned seating area with additional wicker seating outside some rooms. Restaurant serves good, if not authentic, Indian food.

E-F Jasmine Hotel and Restaurant, beach access and some rooms have sea view. Restaurant serves up tasty Thai fare for dinner.

E-F New Life. Sudanese-run popular camp that has a good reputation with local workers, but away from the beach. Central cushioned seating area. Rooms are clean, the more expensive ones with private bath offer a beautiful view of the sea. Trips arranged. Rush, the restaurant across the street, has delicious, if pricey, food.

E-F Penguin, T069-640117, penguindivers@crosswinds.net. Offers modest hotel accommodation and camp. Has lost much of its traditional atmosphere but maintains a traditional beach seating area with reef access. If you want to know anything about anything, ask for Jimmy. He sets up desert tours, diving safaris, leg waxing, hair braiding and trips to almost anywhere. Penguin's restaurant serves excellent breakfast though it's a bit pricier than most. The dive centre is well regarded and many people who stay here dive.

E-F Star of Dahab, T069-640130. Has reef access and a beach with traditional seating where one can truly gaze at the stars of Dahab. Unfortunately the rooms are not of such good quality, but there's hot water and the shared bathrooms are reasonably clean. Candelight only in bamboo huts. Mosquito repellent needed.

E-F Sunsplash Camp, anita.sun@t-online.de, www.sunsplash-divers.com. This camp is trying to maintain the old Dahab atmosphere. Peacefully located on the edge of Mashraba you can relax on traditional seating, or within a few strides snorkel the house reef. A clean camp, including brightly-coloured wooden huts, restaurant, ladies-only sun roof, table tennis and gift shop. Anita, the owner, speaks English, German and Arabic and can organize trips into the desert away from the crowds.

F **Bishbishe**. Although located on the roadside away from the beach, the camp is clean and its courtyard is attractively arranged with young palms. A particularly safe camp for women traveling solo. There's a cushioned seating area, soft drink sales and guest kitchen. Snorkelling, St Catherine's, jeep and camel trips can be arranged. Snorkel and fin hire, US$1.

F **Venus**. Traditional-style camp with café and basic rooms. Clean around the edges only but with a lovely and quiet beachfront café and lounge area.

Masbat area

The Masbat, sandwiched between Mashraba and Assalah, begins at about the big white building that houses the tourist police and extends northward to the lighthouse. Not the place to be if you are in search of tranquility, this is where the action lies. Bars, restaurants blaring Bob Marley, tourist shops, camel rides and hawkers selling everything and nothing at all loom large. Bedouin seating in this area in particular has given way to tables and chairs in most restaurants.

D **Bamboo House**, T069-640263, F640466. The only new-ish real hotel right in the middle of everything, very comfortable rooms with TV, fridge.

F **Alaska Camp**, T069-641004, dahabescape@hotmail.com. Hip young camp that offers cheap huts for the usual price and slightly more costly a/c rooms. Centrally located, next to Seventh Heaven (below), pleasant courtyard where guests linger and share travel tales.

F **Seventh Heaven**, T069-640080. Clean, safe camp in the centre of things. Huts and double/triple rooms with shared bath, some rooms with private bath, balcony and view. All rooms include fan and screens on windows. E£5 breakfast for guests. Fills up fast so call ahead if possible. Internet access E£3/hr, laundry, dive centre, travel services.

Assalah area

The Assalah area starts at the lighthouse and extends north up the coast all the way to the acclaimed dive sites of Canyon and the Blue Hole. The shoreline is dotted with an array of accommodation ranging from a few cheap camps to more comfortable middle-of-the-road accommodation. The hippy vibe of Masbat turns a bit New Age as you wander north. Several hotels in this area offer yoga, rebirthing in the desert and massage. Inland lies the non-touristy village where Bedouin, longtime foreign implants and other Egyptians live.

C-D **Coral Coast**, T069-641195/6. Beautiful and comfortable hotel in front of the Eel Garden dive site. Bedouin-run and owned, rooftop restaurant and bar, all rooms have sea view and private balcony or terrace, most with a/c. Bedouin tent, on-site dive centre and daily excursions to the desert. Attempting to create an eco-conscious sustainable establishment.

C-D **Mirage Village**, T069-640341. A former camp with courtyard and sunken BBQ, good view, beach access, breakfast additional. Apartments available. These camps are accessed from the dirt road in front of the Lighthouse camp.

F **El Dorado**. A small intimate camp with basic cheap rooms, fans available upon request. Bathrooms are regularly cleaned. Beach access. Cushioned seating area and café that serves *sheesha*. A cheaper option for this area with great access to the Eel Garden.

F **Marine Garden**, aqualife@euronet.nl. Old style, Dutch-run establishment with very basic rooms, some with corrugated roofs. Bathrooms clean.

Between Assalah and Blue Hole dive site

D-E **Bedouin Moon**, T069-640695, bedouinmoon@menanet.net. Beautiful Bedouin-owned and run hotel situated solemnly amid mountains and sandy each. Rooms have private bath and domed ceilings, 3-person dorms available. Prices vary depending on extras which may include a/c, fan, sea view. Highly acclaimed dive centre, Reef 2000, attached. Excellent restaurant. A few kilometres north of Masbat, good place to stay if you're here for the diving and peace.

E **Canyon Dive Resort**, next to dive site of the same name, 8 km north of Dahab. Decent accommodation but it's so far out, the only reason to stay here is to dive the Canyon. Dive centre attached.

Eating

Sharm El-Sheikh *p369, map p370*

In addition to a number of traditional food stalls bearing the usual *fuul* and *ta'ameyya* sandwiches, and a range of buffet-style hotel restaurants, there are a few good restaurants in town that are often frequented by locals and dive masters.

TTT **Al-Fanar**, at Ras Um Sidd lighthouse, T069-662218. Under Italian management, serves excellent, albeit pricey, Italian food with a variety of wines. The atmosphere is majestic, open-aired, with a stunning view of the sea and mountains of Ras Mohammed. A good place to see the sunset. There is live music most evenings.

TT **Safsafa**, market area. Delicious seafood, only 8 tables, no alcohol, meals starting at around E£25. Has a counterpart in Na'ama Bay – but this is the original and most people in the know say it's better, and cheaper.

TT **Terrazzina**, next to Iberotel Palace. Enjoy fresh and excellent seafood with your toes in the sand, used to be mainly locals but opening up to more visitors.

T **Sinai Star**, in market area of Sharm, T069-660393. Offers tasty fish, prices have increased as this place gathers fame, but still cheap.

T **Fisherman's**, another seafood dive, 500 m away. Similar feel to how Sinai Star used to be before it got saturated with tourists.

Na'ama Bay *p371, map p378*

TTT **Wings and Things**, at Oonas Divers' Inn. For a special occasion meal.

TTT **Hard Rock Café**, T069-602665. Standard International Hard Rock offerings and atmosphere, good nachos, beer, children's menu, the bar gets kicking after midnight. Dishes start around E£30. Upstairs, you'll find Tabasco, a pub with decent international fare, opened by the same owner of the sister establishment with the same name in Cairo – appeals to rich Egyptian youth.

TTT **Rangly**, at the Sofitel, T069-600081. Excellent Indian in a beautiful setting with a stunning view of the Bay, but arrive early – after 9 the animation team gets loud and ruins any chance of romance.

TTT **Sala Thai**, at the Hyatt Regency, T069-601234. Offers authentic and delicious, though expensive, Thai cuisine. Entrées start around E£40.

TT **Franco Pizzeria**, at Ghazala Hotel. One of the longer-established Italian restaurants in Na'ama. Serves good standard Italian fare.

TT **Peking**, at Sanafir Hotel. An Asian restaurant that has undergone many incarnations since its original inception. Serves decent, though not necessarily authentic, Chinese food. Part of the Peking chain that also has several branches in Cairo.

TT **Viva La Vista**, at the Divers' College (Sultana). Serves reasonably priced, no-nonsense food.

TT **Viva Restaurant**. Friendly, new and spacious a/c restaurant and bar on the beach which serves good quality reasonably priced food.

T Except for beach-front stalls serving most varieties of takeaway food and the tragic array of fast food restaurants, there are few cheap eats in Na'ama Bay.

T **Tam Tam**, atop the Ghazala Hotel. Really the last cheap place in Na'ama. It serves very good Egyptian food with a large selection of salads – both local and conventional – on a lovely rooftop setting outdoors.

Dahab *p374, map p375*

The traditional places to eat and chill out in Assalah are at the beach side cafés, on bright coloured cushions or close-to-the-ground chairs. While shaded under palms, travellers can indulge in Dahab's favourite pastime – talking to people from all corners of the globe, sipping tea and puffing on whatever. Menus are quite similar from café to café though each place offers its speciality – be it food or atmosphere.

If you're looking for a buffet meal or high-end indoor eating experience, check out the array of restaurants at the Hilton or Swiss Inn. Most hotels in Dahab open their buffet dinners to non-residents.

Mashraba

TT **Lakhbatita**, off the promenade in Mashraba. Superb cuisine, open only for dinner, offering the freshest seafood, a cheap and excellent salad bar and a wide array of authentic Italian dishes. Run by an Egyptian and Italian couple, no alcohol as the owner is a devout Muslim – waiters actually stop working at the call to prayer. Beautiful romantic atmosphere interestingly decorated with doors and oddments from the Delta.

Indoor and outdoor seating area a metre from the sea.

ΤΤ **Nesima Hotel**, T069-640320. Restaurant serves alcohol, good standard of more expensive food in an intimate atmosphere, if you choose the right seat.

ΤΤ **Rush**, next to Nesima's street entrance, T012-3198267. Excellent food and very clean kitchen, extensive vegetarian offerings, fresh French bread shipped in daily from Sharm, small market that sells delicacies ranging from sundried tomatoes to asparagus, a/c, funky atmosphere blaring good tunes and the cleanest toilets on the block.

ΤΤ-Τ **Dolphin Café**, next to Dolphin camp in Mashraba. In addition to solid breakfast fare, the dinner menu includes Indian and vegetarian dishes for under US$3, Bedouin-style seating, good samosas and curries – a refreshing respite from the normal Dahab fare (the nan is a little less authentic). Get there early to avoid the techno pumping from the Elzar disco next door.

ΤΤ-Τ **Jasmine**, far into the Mashraba. Jasmine offers a quiet setting to enjoy tasty Thai food.

ΤΤ-Τ **Penguin**, very clean restaurant with Bedouin-style seating right on the sea, hip young vibe, excellent service, good place for breakfast, a bit more expensive than most but worth the extra couple of pounds.

Masbat

ΤΤ-Τ **Friends**, one of the few restaurants in Masbat that won't hassle you, a very pleasant atmosphere, fires on cold nights, beautiful clean beach-side setting, good music, excellent service, extensive salad bar. Waiters will go down the road to bring you a beer or bottle of wine, just ask. The food is consistently good and the fresh juice isn't watered down or sugared up.

ΤΤ-Τ **Jays**, in the northern end of Masbat away from the sea, T012-3353377. Great food with an extensive menu, always a veggie option, fresh menu every night, tasty desserts. Atmosphere is pleasant enough with Bedouin-style seating and palm trees about, but not on the beach. Reservations are sometimes necessary. Run by English-Egyptian couple.

ΤΤ-Τ **Trattoria Pizzeria**, near the Police Station in the Masbat. Serves thin crust pizzas and fish on terraces overlooking the sea for around US$6.

Τ **El Hosain**, near the pick-up/taxi drop-off in Masbat. Less touristy, with typical Egyptian food like a basic chicken meal.

Assalah

ΤΤ-Τ **Eel Garden Stars**, friendly restaurant in quiet pristine setting, with excellent access to snorkelling around Eel Garden. Lots of crèpes, both sweet and savoury on offer. Generous portions, excellent food, try the fried aubergines.

ΤΤ-Τ **Sharks**, run by an Australian-Egyptian couple is a friendly, popular joint known for its huge portions. Quality has gone down somewhat over the years but the shakes and pancakes are still stellar.

Bars and clubs

Sharm El-Sheikh *p369 map p370*

Nightlife in Sharm largely centres around Na'ama Bay. For details on events and parties, check out www.sharmevents.com or www.sinaitimes.com.

Oriental floorshows and bellydancers are largely confined to the major hotels but new independent bars and restaurants are opening (and closing) all the time in Na'ama Bay.

Pirates Bar, in Fayrouz Hilton. An old favourite among the expat local divers' community. Standard pub fare with guaranteed cold brew. Evening happy hour starts at 1900 ish.

Bus Stop at Sanafir Hotel. Where it's at for dancing. E£20 entry includes a drink and is open until the wee hours with lots of noise, dancing and billiards downstairs.

Echo Temple, a venue in the middle of the desert. Hosts special events (on some nights) from concerts to movies, organized through Sanafir.

Hard Rock Café. With a family-friendly atmosphere in the early evening, the bar starts raging later alongside dance music in typical Hard Rock fashion.

Tabasco, upstairs from the Hard Rock Café. The counterpart of its Cairo equivalent. Good food and drinks, quite popular among young Cairenes, especially during Egyptian holidays.

The Camel Bar, by the Camel Dive Centre. Buzzing most evenings. A funky and happening spot with typical bar fare, good music and reasonably priced drinks. Very popular with divers and beer enthusiasts young and old.

For a more traditional evening, there are a handful of cafés and *ahwas* offering *sheesha*, **Arabic music**, **tea** and **coffee** alongside the boardwalk near Sanafir.

Dahab *p374, map p375*

Nightlife mainly revolves around the restaurants and cafés in Assalah which are open until people leave.

Adam's Bar, north of the lighthouse. Serves the cheapest beer in town. You can sit inside or out and enjoy a fairly substantial selection of libations.

Blue Moon, also north of the lighthouse. Offers the closest thing to a real pub, equipped with TV airing football. It's not as cheap as Adam's, but no more than Tota.

Nesima Hotel bar, Mashraba. Popular, particularly with divers, and has a happy hour from 1900-2100. There is a DJ there on some evenings.

Crazy House, next door. Retains a slightly more refined air. Both establishments are having a price war and sell Stella at US$1.

Elzar, next to Dolphin Restaurant, Mashraba. Disco blaring music late into the night. Generally appeals to a young crowd.

Swiss Inn Golden Beach Resort in Dahab City. Has occasional belly dancing shows.

Tota, Masbat. Popular, despite the tacky boat decor and waiters donning sailors suits. After midnight, the restaurant/bar turns into a disco.

Entertainment

Sharm El-Sheikh *p369, map p370*

Casinos

Na'ama Bay has several late-night casinos based in the chicer hotels. Oldest among them is the **Movenpick's Casino Royale**. Bring your passport if you intend to gamble.

Cinemas

Renaissance Cinema, on the road to the airport. Shows films sometimes in Arabic, sometimes in English. Two showings most nights – 2200 in the evening and 0100 in the morning. Check out www.sinaitimes.com to see what's playing.

Shopping

Sharm El-Sheikh *p369, map p370*

Most shops in Na'ama Bay are linked to the hotels and are well stocked with provisions for beach lounging or diving and snorkelling accessories. Tourist shops are scattered along the boardwalk selling tee-shirts, perfume bottles, sheesha pipes and Bedouin jewellery. Souvenirs are significantly cheaper in old Sharm, where you can also find the best stocked food market in town. **Sheikh Abdullah supermarkets** offer imported western foods and a good range of produce, (one in Hadaba on the hill in Sharm and another in Hay El-Nour – halfway between Sharm town and Na'ama Bay – you'll need a taxi or minibus).

There's also a spattering of shopping strips that offer a variety of more conventional stores. Na'ama Centre, on the northern side of Na'ama Bay near the crowded Sanafir strip is overflowing with fashion and upscale jewellery shops and rooftop restaurants.

Bookshops

Bookshops in Sharm Mall, Movenpick, Sanafir, Ghazala and Fayrouz Hilton hotels.

Photography

You can hire an underwater camera at most diving centres. There are several **Kodak** stores that sell and develop film scattered throughout Na'ama Bay. **Sanafir Hotel** has a shop where film can be developed within 1 hr.

Dahab *p374, map p375*

There are a few small supermarkets in Assalah, which are open 0730-2400. They stock most of the basics including bottled water and toilet paper. Fresh **fruit and vegetables** are harder to come by – there's a shop on the road next to Lighthouse camp and sometimes a stall near Bishbishe. **Ghazala market**, near the police station is well equipped with most essentials. **Rush**, the restaurant next to Nesima by the street entrance, sells harder-to-find imported goodies.

There are a few easy-to-spot **pharmacies** scattered about the Masbat.

Necklaces, tie-dyes, skirts and bags etc, the hallmark **souvenirs** of Dahab, are available in the small bazaars on the main bay and by the taxi drop-off. Don't shop when the Sharm El-Sheikh tourists are in town – everything doubles in price. Bedouin girls sell cotton bracelets in the beach cafés, but barter hard. **Henna tattoos** and **hair braiding** are available along Masbat. You'll also find **spice stalls, carpet sellers** and **music shops** blaring the latest Arabic hits and offering a wide range of Western and traditional music.

Activities and tours

Sharm El-Sheikh *p369*

Dive centres

Water sports in general, and diving in particular, are the main attractions in south Sinai. The reefs off the Gulf of Aqaba coast are some of the best in the world with incomparable coral reefs and colourful marine life. The waters are warm year round, currents are relatively benign and visibility is consistently good. Most divers from Europe book a package before they leave, including diving courses and safaris in combination with accommodation and airfare. This is usually the most economical way to go. If you are an independent traveller, there is no shortage of dive centres available to accommodate you. Most of Sinai's main dive centres are based in Na'ama Bay but organize daylong offshore dive trips to all of the region's major reefs. Many also book week-long liveaboard safaris that traverse the wonders of the Red Sea. Dive centres generally organize all transport to and from Sharm. All offer courses ranging from the beginner's open-water to instructor level. A standard open-water course costs US$300- 350 and takes 4 days. Sometimes the certificate requires an extra fee of US$30. PADI is the most common certificate granted and a world-known diving accreditation. Do your research before you commit to a dive school, as some are safer and more reputable than others. Be aware that some dive schools try to cram the open-water course into as few as 2 or 3 days. Though it may be cheaper, we do not recommend it. Most large hotels have their own dive centres, the following is a list of some good choices.

Camel Dive Club, centrally located in Na'ama Bay, T069-600700, F600601. One of the longest established dive centres in Na'ama, slick and friendly service with a 3.5-m training pool. Popular bar inside the dive club area and internet café. Appeals to young cosmopolitan crowd. There is a hotel with 38 rooms in the dive club – comfortable and convenient if you're here to dive, but not cheap. Lots of daily dive trips.

Ocean College, Na'ama Bay and Hadaba, T069-663378, T600802 (in Na'ama, the college is under the big wooden boat-shaped building in front of the Helnan Marina). Presently expanding; offers cheap packages from the UK.

Oonas Divers, near the Sonesta at the far northern end of Na'ama Bay, T069-600581-2, www.oonasdivers.com. Mainly European instructors and divers. Offers reasonably cheap courses. Overseas bookings which include flights can be made through **Oonas Divers UK**, 23 Enys Rd, Eastbourne, Sussex, T01323-648924, F738356.

Red Sea Diving College, in the centre of the beach, Na'ama Bay, T069-600145, F600144, www.redseacollege.com. PADI 5-star fully equipped IDC centre. Joint project between Sinai Hotels & Diving Clubs and Scubapro Europe. Opened 1991, at least 10 multi-lingual PADI instructors from a good purpose-built facility. Like Oonas, it's one of the cheaper and more reputable places to take a dive course. Good beachfront restaurant, Viva.

Shark Bay, Shark Bay Resort, T069-600947. Local-style architecture, right on beach, very basic and laid back, bamboo bungalows sleep 2, shared shower and facilities, excellent fish restaurant on the beach. The only PADI dive centre with its own private jetty, ideal for the more adventurous who can live a bit more ruggedly. Bedouin-run. Offers access to many other water sports.

Sinai Dive Club, in Hilton Fayyrouz, Na'ama Bay, T069-600140. Smaller dive club offering liveaboards and all PADI courses. Excellent service, kind and knowledgeable dive instructors.

Sinai Divers, in Ghazala Hotel, Na'ama Bay, T069-600150-4, F600158. Claims to be the largest diving centre in Na'ama Bay, certainly one of the most established. Germans make up half the divers in summer (May-Oct) while about 60% of the winter divers are British. Book in advance in the winter high season. Sinai Divers consistently runs week-long liveaboard boats in addition to lots of daily dive trips. Offers the full range of PADI certified courses.

Dive sites

Against all the odds of decades past, **Ras Mohammed** and the surrounding reefs are still among the world's top dive sites. The diving opportunities around Sharm are so varied and rich, you'd need a book to highlight them all. The guide that most local dive masters use is Alberto Siliotti's *Sharm El-Sheikh Diving Guide*, which is available in dive shops. The following is a list of some key sites.

Ras Mohammed In efforts to preserve this pristine marine garden that offers some of the best snorkelling and diving in the world, access to some areas is restricted and there are limits on the number of boats that can approach. Of the 20 dive sites in the park, **Shark reef** is worthy of note. Hanging on the southernmost tip of the Sinai peninsula, currents split along the site resulting in a hugely varied spectacle of life. Depending on the season, you'll see whatever you could see in the Red Sea: sharks, turtles, thousands of schools of fish, a wonderland. **Yolanda**, another popular dive site in Ras Mohammed, is a seabottomed wreck from the early 1980s that resulted in countless toilets sprawled around the ocean floor. It is nothing short of surreal to wander amid the wonders of the sea and a bunch of porcelain toilets.

As there are no dive centres on the grounds, the best way to dive in Ras Mohammed is to join a dive centre daytrip from nearby Sharm or Na'ama Bay. It is possible to camp for a modest fee in some designated areas, see page 377.

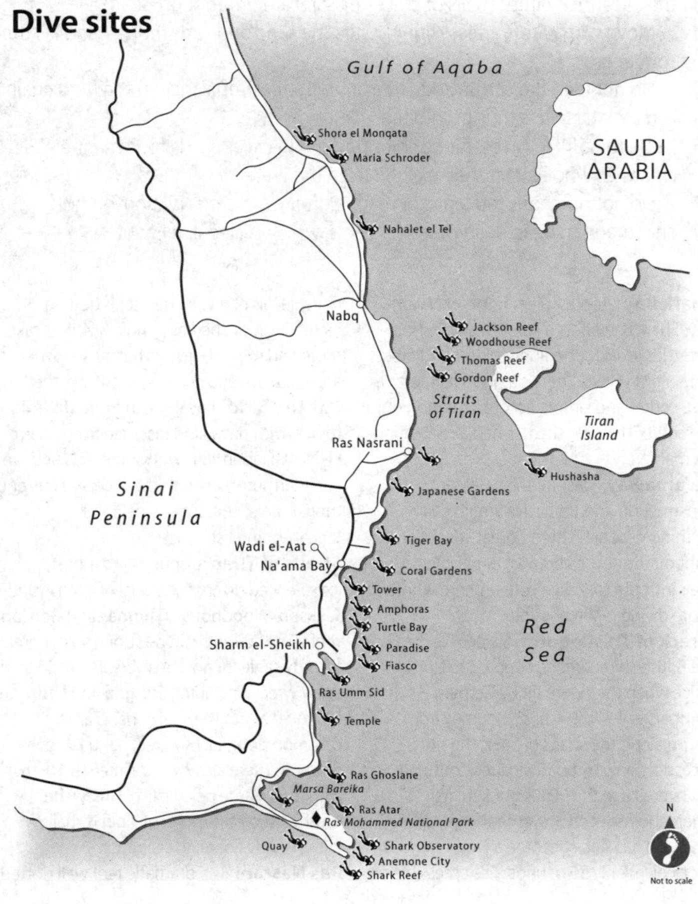

Responsible diving

There has been a great deal of unnecessary damage caused to the coral reefs around the coast. Divers taking trophies, anchors being dropped onto the living corals, rubbish being thrown into the water. The regulatory bodies set up to prevent this damage to the environment have had little effect – it is up to those who delight in this area to preserve it for the future.

Code of responsibility for reef divers:

1. Check you have the correct weights. As the Red Sea is a semi-enclosed basin it has a greater salt content than the open ocean. The extra salinity requires heavy weights, thus buoyancy checks are essential.
2. Avoid all contact with coral. These living creatures can be damaged by the slightest touch. Many reef fish are inedible or poisonous – but the reef needs them to survive.
3. Remove nothing from the reef. Shells and pieces of coral are an integral part of the reef. In Egypt this is taken so seriously that boat captains can lose their license if either shells or pieces or coral are brought on board.
4. Move with care. Careless finning stirs the sand and can smother and kill the softer corals.
5. Do not feed the fish. Introducing an unnatural imbalance to the food chain can be fatal and is thus prohibited.
6. Be mindful in caves. Air bubbles trapped in caves can kill the marine creatures who extract their oxygen from the water.
7. Do not purchase souvenirs of marine origin. Aid conservation, do not encourage trade in dead marine objects, which is illegal in Egypt.

Shark Bay About 10 km north of Na'ama Bay, Shark Bay offers a smooth slope shore entry. It's ideal for beginner divers and first time night divers. There's a good restaurant, dive centre and simple accommodation on the shore. The dive site has had a reputation for manta rays.

Na'ama Bay Despite the incessant construction and traffic, Na'ama is still teeming with life. There's great snorkelling right off the shore and a lot of people do their introductory dive courses here where shore diving is still possible.

Wreck of Thistlegorm Six people died on the British ship bringing supplies to North Africa when they were hit by German bombers in 1941. A 4-hr sea journey from Sharm along the straits of Suez, the site is accessible only by boat. Jacques Cousteau discovered it in the 1950s but kept its whereabouts secret. It was rediscovered in 1993 and has since become a world-famous wreck dive. Only 30 m under, it's accessible to many levels of divers. The site is getting increasingly trashed as mindless visitors take more and more souvenirs but it's still an amazing dive and certainly worthy of the trip.

Ras Um Sidd Local site in front of the light tower, within walking distance from Sharm El-Sheikh, abundant with soft corals and fan corals. In summer, with the colliding currents, there is an abundance of pelagics (ocean-going fish) passing.

Straits of Tiran Popular with more experienced divers, the straits of Tiran include **Jackson**, **Woodhouse**, **Thomas** and **Gordon reefs**. The currents can be strong so this area is not advisable for novice divers. The residue of a few wrecks including **Sangria** and **Laura** are scattered about the strait. Sharks are a common sight. Jackson reef has a 70-m drop-off. There are also coral reefs at 10-15 m, with many large pelagic fish. **Hushasha**, southwest off the island of Tiran is shallow with a sandy floor and sea grass.

Ras Nasrani Is a dramatic reef wall dotted

with caves. There are 2 spots worthy of note: **The Light**, a 40-m drop off, with large pelagic fish; and **The Point**, with hard coral boulders. Be mindful of the currents.

The Tower Steep wall, 60 m, large caves with colourful array of fish. The Tower has been so over-dived in recent years that the spot has lost some of its old splendour, but the wall and colours are still impressive.

Amphoras/Mercury Unnamed Turkish wreck with a cargo of mercury still evident, on the sandy floor at 25 m. A relatively easy dive.

Liveaboards

Liveaboards are boats that offer accommodation and diving on week-long expeditions. There is a huge variety of boats to choose from, ranging from the tolerable to the luxurious. They sleep anything from 8 to 20 people and all include a dive instructor, dive master and cook. The main advantage of liveaboards is that they cover all the same dive sites as the daily boats but tend to hit them at different times, which means a lot less people in the water and a more intimate diving experience. Another advantage is that divers need not swim very far to dive because the boat is already above the site. A few days offshore also gives divers an opportunity to travel to more remote sites like the waters around Gubal Island. Most visitors to Sharm book a liveaboard in advance with a tour company from their home country but it's also possible to book with a local diving centre. Booking ahead is advisable as these boats tend to fill up fast and have very specific departure/arrival times. Individual travellers should enquire with specific diving centres to find a suitable safari.

Royal Diving, T069-660627, www.royaldiving.com. A reputable British- managed liveaboard fleet, offers trips that can accommodate divers with disabilities. Check out www.divability.com for more information.

Snorkelling

A cheaper, easier, and less bulky way to enjoy the magic of the sea is by hiring or investing in a snorkel. Equipment can be rented at diving centres and purchased in many beachfront stores. Despite development, there is still excellent snorkelling literally off the sands of Na'ama Bay. For more remote snorkelling spots, you can follow Na'ama Bay on foot, North beyond Oonas toward the area known as "**The Coral Gardens**". Look for easy entry into the water so you won't have to splice your feet and kill the coral on your way in. Access is significantly easier during high tide. In the shallows, you will find a vast array of wondrous creatures, corals that open and close, fish that kiss your goggles, exquisite rainbow colours and patterns. Nearby **Ras Um Sidd** is another exquisite place to mill out in the blue with its extreme and diverse drop-offs where currents collide and bring in a wide array of fish. **Ras Mohammed**, too, is a splendid place to snorkel with warm waters and sheltered coves offering homes to over a thousand different kinds of sea life.

Other water sports

In addition to snorkelling and diving, there are countless other ways to enjoy the sea. **Glass bottom boats** are offered from most hotels along Na'ama Bay's boardwalk, where you can also rent **windsurf boards**, **hobicats** and masks and fins. The **Marina Sharm**, **Fayrouz Hilton**, and **Ghazala** hotels all offer a wide range of equipment and activities, to name a few. The **Movenpick** offers **parasailing**. Aside from the hotels, there is only **Sun 'N' Fun** (T069-601623, F600602) which seems to have a monopoly of sorts on sea and sand excursions. You won't miss their bright yellow logo, every few hundred metres along the beach and boardwalk. **Jetskis** were banned in Sharm a few years back when two Italian tourists died as a result of another tourist's carelessness.

Bowling

Mas, just outside Na'ama Bay up the hill from the Hard Rock Café. Also offers billiards and ice skating on a plastic ring.

Bungee jumping and trampolining

In front of Helnan Marina in a parking lot at the southern end of Na'ama Bay. Reverse bungee in a seat built for 2, get strapped in and catapulted into the air. Or bounce up and down on a trampoline strapped in for 5 minutes. Look for the towering poles.

Horse riding

Sofitel, T069-600081. Has good stables and relatively healthy horses that can be hired per hour or per day. They also offer overnight desert trips on horseback.

Quad bikes

Safari Tours, behind the Pigeon House Hotel. Bikes can be rented by the hour (about US$35) or by the trip for short desert rides.

Go-karts

Ghibili Raceway, near the Hyatt Regency on the road to the airport, T069-603737. It's really fun and really expensive. US$20 buys you 10 mins on the track.

Desert safaris

Most hotels in Na'ama Bay offer a sort of desert safari, but for the most part they're intended for tourists who want to look at the desert through the window of an air-conditioned bus. Expect to pay about US$50 for a daylong trip to nearby desert attractions like **St Catherine** or the **Coloured Canyon**. For half of that, you can get a ride to **Ras Mohammed** if you'd rather a hotel organized it, though it's cheaper just to hail a taxi. Outside of the big hotels, **Sun 'N' Fun**, T069-601623, F600602, has the monopoly in Sharm on desert trips. Their prices are comparable to the hotels. They host a Sunset trip into the desert to drink tea with Bedouin. Hotels and Sun 'N' Fun also offer very dense daytrips to Cairo and Luxor for about $US275. If you're trying to cram Egypt into your beach experience, you may want to explore this option, but a day really doesn't suffice to even get a taste of these places.

If you're interested in a more extensive desert experience, talk to the folks at **Anenome Dive Centre** in the Pigeon House. Eid Soliman, a local Bedouin guide, leads multi-day trips into the desert for about US$60 per person per day. Look for him at Anemone or call him on T010-1436127. The best bet for the desert adventure seeker is to set off with a real Bedouin guide from Dahab or Nuweiba.

Tour operators

There are travel agents attached to almost all the major hotels, as well as a few independent ones that can book transport, hotels, sightseeing, desert trips and other excursions. Some better known and reputable agents:

Nass Tours, Plaza Mall, T069-601258/9.
Spring Tours, Mall 8, T069-600131.
Thomas Cook, Gafy Mall, T069-601808. Helpful with travel arrangements to other cities, reserves tickets on the ferry to Hurghada.
Travco, Iberotel Palace Hotel, T069-661111.

Dahab *p374*

Diving

Some of the best diving in Dahab is accessible by land. There are more than 40 diving centres in and around Assalah that rent equipment and run PADI diving courses. Of those not all are considered to be safe. Accidents occur on a daily basis and every year there are a number of deaths. Ask around before choosing a dive centre and ensure whoever you choose to study or dive with is PADI certified, reputable and experienced. See also the point about responsible diving on page 388.

There are many stunningly beautiful and interesting dive sites close to Dahab that are generally less crowded than Sharm El-Sheikh and Hurghada, and since most are shore dives, they don't require the added expense of a boat, which keeps the prices down a bit. Following is a list of recommended centres, but remember managers and instructors do change and with them so may the quality of the centre. Prices range from US$40-60 for one day's diving with full equipment. PADI Open Water courses are in the region of US$260-320. Some dive centres don't include the US$30 certificate fee in the cost of the course so enquire. Most of the centres have instructors catering for a number of languages, including English, French and German.

Inmo, Inmo Hotel and Dive Centre, T069-640370, inmo@inmodivers.com. Mashraba diver community, people keep coming back here.
Fantasea, at the northern end of Masbat bay, near the lighthouse, T069-640043, ide@intouch.com. Also rent windsurf boards.
Nesima, Nesima Hotel, Mashraba, T069-6400320/1, nesima@intouch.com. Reputable dive centre.
Club Red, in front of the Mohammed Ali camp next to the Tourist Police in the Masbat, T069-640380. An old-timer dive school.

Reef 2000, Bedouin Moon Hotel, between Dahab and Blue Hole, T069-6400087, www.reef2000.com. Catering mainly for the British market. Offers camel safari to Ras Abu Ghalum, includes food and 2 dives, US$100.

Dive and snorkel sites near Dahab

North from the lighthouse:

Eel Garden A 15-min walk north of lighthouse, off Assalah, good snorkelling area and a safe shallow spot for beginner divers. Sandy bottom with a garden of eels.

The Canyon Opposite Canyon Dive Centre a few kilometres north of Dahab. Accessible from the shore, you snorkel along the reef through a narrow break before diving into the canyon. A popular spot for more experienced divers, it bottoms out at 50 m.

The Blue Hole 7 km north of Dahab, the most famous – and infamous – dive in the area. The hole is over 80 m deep and just a few metres from the shore. About 60 m down, there's an arched passageway to the other side of the hole. Attempting to go through it is strongly discouraged. Every year there are stories of advanced divers who die from nitrogen narcosis or carelessness while attempting this dive. At 60 m, you can't see anything anyway, the majesty and life of the place is closer to the surface. Be advised that the Blue Hole is difficult, dangerous and only for very experienced divers.

Overnight trips to see the **nocturnal lobsters** at the Blue Hole, and possibly eat one the next day are popular. Hamid, the "Lobster Man", is famous for organizing such adventures and can be found at the Crazy Camel Camp in the Masbat.

The Bells Just north of the Blue Hole, along a coral cliff that leads to the hole. A good place to snorkel. Rich with colourful coral and large fish.

South from the lighthouse:

The Islands An enchanting and pristine site just south of Dahab near the Laguna. Close to town and easily accessible from shore. Offers multiple routes in a maze of pathways through delicate rainbow coloured corals and fish.

A bit further out than the aforementioned sites lies **Ras Abu Galum** (see page 394), a majestic and remote protectorate area that shelters some of the richest marine life in Sinai. Beginning about 15 km north of Dahab, this stretch of 30 km is only accessible by camel or 4-wheel drive. There are 3 main dive sites with virgin reefs and a wide array of marine life. Most of the listed dive centres lead day-long trips to Ras Abu Galum that include camel transport and 2 dives. Costs range from US$60-100 per day depending on the season, number of dives and if you need gear.

Some dive centres in Dahab lead trips to the **Thistlegorm**. Enquire at **Inmo**, **Fantasea** or **Club Red** (see above).

Snorkelling

Amazing opportunities for snorkelling abound right off the coast of Assalah. Though a coral reef follows the rim of the entire bay, the best spots are right in front of the lighthouse and further south along the reefs of Mashraba. Be aware that despite the reef's proximity to the shore, the currents can be very strong. All the dive sites listed above are excellent snorkelling areas, particularly popular are Ras Abu Galum, the Eel Garden and the Blue Hole. All dive centres in Dahab rent snorkel, mask and fins for around E£20 per day. You can also rent them directly at the Blue Hole.

Windsurfing

A consistently strong and steady breeze makes Dahab among the top places to windsurf in Sinai. Several of the high end hotels, including the **Hilton** and the **Novotel** with its perfect private windsurfing beach, offer surfing schools with introductory classes up to 3-day courses. In Assalah, **Fantasea Dive Centre** rents boards.

Desert safaris

Dahab is a good place to set off for the interior by camel or jeep. You can venture inland on a camel with a Bedouin for a few hours, enjoy a cup of tea, and come back to civilization, or you can go for days or weeks at a time to trek around the Sinai, explore the surrounding oases, and dine under diamond studded sky on coal-cooked grub and fresh Bedouin bread. Camels and Bedouin tend to herd around the sandy median area in the middle of the Masbat where a bridge is being constructed. Like most things, the going rate varies depending on the season, but expect to pay about E£30 per hr for a camel ride and about E£40 per hr for a horse led by a beach-wandering guide. For day- long safaris with food included, it's E£100 per day. Popular destinations on camel include **Wadi Gnay**, a nearby oasis with a few palms and a brackish spring; **Nabq**, in between Dahab and Sharm, a protectorate area that offers the largest mangrove forest in Sinai (see page 373). By jeep, for E£300 per day, you can see the **Coloured Canyon**, a beautiful rift with spectacular rock formations covered with swirls and pictures painted over millennia with countless shades of pink. The trip generally includes the hour-long trek down the canyon. Due to its increasing popularity, be forewarned that it can be quite crowded. Note that from Nuweiba, there is cheaper and easier access. The **White Canyon**, often included on day-long jeep trips with the Coloured Canyon, has cloud-white smooth rocks you can hike up. Virtually all the camps and large hotels can either organize the short safaris to nearby attractions or point you in the right direction. Overnight trips and more extensive safaris cost E£120 per day. The following are a few notable safari companies based in Dahab which may be bit more expensive, but are safe, experienced and well equipped to organize long distance journeys into remote areas.

Embah Safari, in the middle of the Masbat near Tota, T069-640447, www.embah.com. Highly recommended. Co-run by an Irish-Egyptian couple with the intention of bridging Bedouin and western cultures to build understanding and mutual appreciation, they provide tailor-made excursions for days or weeks at a time and offer both educational and adventure safaris. Guides specialize in a variety of particular interests including rock climbing, trekking, geology and history. An extremely professional, safe and respectable choice. Booking ahead is advisable.

Best Friends Safari, T069-641211, www.bestfriendsafary.com. Another decent option. The owner, Ahmed, is a vibrant, friendly man who knows the desert deeply and has worked with local Bedouin for years. He will help you create the trip you want.

Transport

Sharm El-Sheikh *p369, map p370*

Air

Ras Nasrani Airport, T069-601140/1, F600416, is further along the coast 10 km north of Na'ama Bay with direct flights to and from an increasing number of European cities as well as internal flights to **Cairo** (daily at 0645), **Hurghada** and **St Catherine**.

Airline offices Egyptair, Hotel Movenpick, T069-600314, 600100. Sharm market area, along the road leading to Na'ama Bay, T069-661058, airport, T069-600408, 660664.

Bus

The bus station in Sharm El-Sheikh, T069-660600, is at the bottom of the hill. At least 8 trips daily to **Cairo**, running from 0730 in the morning till midnight. As the schedules are constantly changing, it's best to call and confirm departure times. Costing E£55-E£65, trip is 7-9 hrs. Other destinations include: **Suez** (E£25-35) very frequent about one an hour, takes 5-7 hrs; **Dahab** at least 6 buses a day running from 0630-2330 (E£10, takes 1 hr), of which the early morning bus goes on to **St Catherine** (E£25, takes 4 hrs), and of which 2 go on to **Nuweiba** (E£15-25, takes 2½ hrs) and 1 of these to **Taba** (E£35, takes 3½ hrs). **Shared taxis** cover all these routes on a leave-when-full basis – they may cost more but take much less time, avoiding the tedious stops in each town.

Car hire

Avis, Sonesta Hotel, T069-600979. **Europecar**, Fayrouz Hilton, T069-600140/50. **Flying Car**, Ghazala Gardens, T069-601197. **Hertz**, Royal Mall, T069-600457. **Shark Limousine**, Sharm Movenpick Jolie Ville, T069-603023. **NB** Drivers beware: there is only one petrol station on the 81 km route between Dahab and Sharm El-Sheikh.

Sea

Ferry Ferry to **Hurghada**, T065-447571/2, on Sat, Mon, Tue and Thu at 1800 (from Hurghada to Sharm, same days but leaves Hurghada at 0800), takes 1 hr, costs US$40 or E£180, depending on the state of the pound. To secure a spot, make reservations a day in advance at a hotel or private travel agent like

Thomas Cook, T069-601808. Ferry leaves from the Sharm marina.

Private vessels Entry procedures for Sharm El-Sheikh port. Visas may be obtained for boats and crews from Egyptian consulates in country of origin. It is possible but more hassle to get one in Sharm El-Sheikh. It is as well to give clear advance (at least 1 week) notification of your intention to berth. The Port Commander must be notified upon arrival. The course of the vessel, in national waters, must be filed and approved by the Port Authority.

Dahab *p374, map p375*

Bus

The **East Delta bus station**, T069-640250, is outside the Bank of Egypt in Dahab; there are 5 daily buses south to **Cairo** (E£55-70, takes 8 hrs) via **Na'ama Bay** and **Sharm El-Sheikh** (E£12, takes 1½ hrs); 2 buses go north to **Nuweiba** (E£8, 1 hr) and 1 carrying on to **Taba** (E£20, 3 hrs), and 1 goes east to **St Catherine** (E£15, 1-hr). Bus schedules are posted around most camps. Overnight buses tend to be a bit more expensive.

Taxi

Service taxis Faster than the bus, another way to get around from city to city is to hire a service (pronounced *servees*) taxi. If you are travelling en masse or can team up with some other wanderers, you can bargain with a driver to take you almost anywhere.

Taxis A necessary expense for getting between Dahab town and the beaches. Tourists are usually charged more than Egyptians. To and from the bus station costs E£5. If you join others or take a pick-ups, it's cheaper. To the Blue Hole, E£30 – the driver will wait and bring you back.

Directory

Sharm El-Sheikh *p369, map p370*

Banks In the town of Sharm El-Sheikh there are several banks including the **National Bank of Egypt**, **Banque du Caire**, which both have ATMs and the **Bank of Alexandria**, T069-660355, which will permit you to charge money on your Visa or Mastercard for currency. Mon-Sat 0800-1400 and 1800-2100, Sun 1000-1200. In Na'ama Bay, there are also several banks including the **National Bank of Egypt** in the Ghazla, Movenpick and Marina Sharm, and **Misr International Bank**, T069-601667, in Na'ama centre. You can use your ATM card there, in the Movenpick lobby and in front of the Ghazala hotel. There is also a **Western Union**, T069-602222, at the Rosetta Hotel. **Thomas Cook**, T069-601808, in the Gafy Mall, offers travellers' cheques and other banking services. Most big hotels exchange money at the standard rate. **Hospitals** Sharm **El-Sheikh International Hospital**, 24-hr emergency room, hyperbaric chamber, T069-660894/5, 661625/4, F660891, midway between Sharm and Na'ama Bay, looks like a pyramid. **Hyperbaric Centre**, Dr Adel Taher is the local expert on diving-related health matters, T069-661011/660922/3. For emergencies T012-2124292. For non-emergency cases there are doctors on call at the larger hotels. The Movenpick Hotel runs a daily clinic (1900-2000) and their doctors are on 24-hr call, reached through hotel reception. Fayrouz Hilton has a doctor living on the premises. **Internet** Internet Service **Provider**, T069-662245. **Future Net**, in the Gafy Mall, T0123507041. Internet cafés are scattered all over Na'ama Bay. The **Camel Bar** is a particularly popular spot as you can enjoy a brew while you check your email. Cost all around Na'ama is about E£20 per hr. **Pharmacies** Pharmacy Sharm El-Sheikh, Hadaba, T069-660388. **Na'ama Bay Pharmacy**, T069-600779. **Post office** At the top of the hill in Sharm El-Sheikh, T069-660518. Sat-Thu 0800-1500. All the major hotels have mail services. **Telephone** The main telephone exchange is in Hadaba, on the hill opposite the Grand Mosque. In Na'ama Bay, Menatel card phones are available. **Useful numbers** Ambulance: Sharm, T069-660554, Na'ama T123. Fire: T069-660633. **Police**: T069- 660415. **General information/directory enquiries**: T16.

Dahab *p374, map p375*

Banks **Bank of Egypt** near the bus station, in Dahab town accepts travellers' cheques and ATM cards. Daily 0830-1400 and 1800-2100. In Assalah in the northern part of the Masbat, there is a **National Bank of Egypt** that accepts travellers checks and exchanges money. There's a **Western Union** that offers all sorts of business services, next to the

Bamboo Hotel in the Masbat. The Golden Beach Resort also has a bank.
Internet Service is widely available in Assalah, try Seventh Heaven Camp in the Masbat or Sharks Bay Internet across the street from Nesima. The going rate is E£3 per hour. **Post office** In Dahab town centre. Sat-Thu 0830-1500. In the Masbat, you will also find a phone and post shop near the Bamboo House/Western Union by the Neptune Restaurant that sells stamps and will deliver your mail. **Telephone** Office near bus station. In Assalah, there is an office that will facilitate international faxes and phone calls across the street from the supermarket. **Useful numbers** Tourist Police: T069-640188 near Novotel.

East coast north of Dahab

Ras Abu Galum

In addition to pristine marine gardens Ras Abu Galum, another protectorate area, designated in 1992, along the coast between Dahab and Nuweiba, holds some of the most striking above-ground scenery in Sinai. High mountains and long winding valleys run right down to the sea. From the Blue Hole you can hire a camel for E£40, or better still, walk the magical 7 km to a nearby village only accessible on foot (you are strongly recommended not to visit without a guide and certainly never to leave the marked trails). Although the Protectorate is valued mainly for its rare plant life, the diving here is also superb. It should be noted, however, that access to the underwater cave network at Ras Mamlah is strictly forbidden. Many divers have died here and their bodies remain unrecovered.

There are a handful of huts on the beach and a couple of restaurants, see page 398. There is also a solar-powered information centre, sometimes open, that offers maps and information about the local wildlife and people. Bright-eyed Bedouin children will ask you to buy their jewellery along with a million other questions. If you want to come with gifts, bring them pens or gum (of the sugar-free sort, as their teeth are fast deteriorating). Ras Abu Galum is a majestic tranquil spot with a welcoming Bedouin community and silky white sand beaches unspoiled by the stomping of tourism. Walk softly and assist in maintaining its magic.

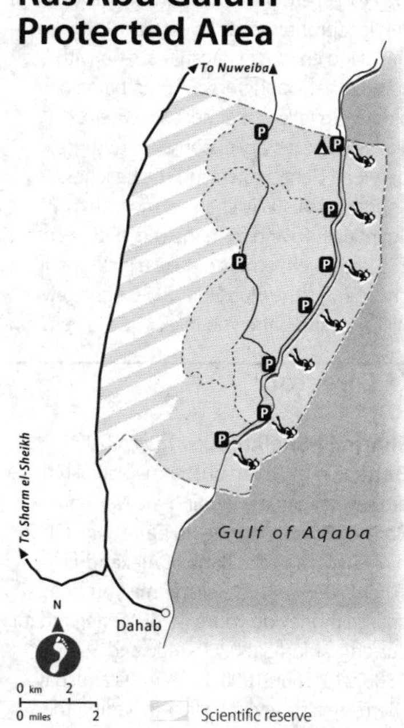

Nuweiba

Nuweiba lies 69 km north of Dahab and 64 km south of the Israeli border at Taba on a beautiful stretch of coast. From the shore you can see Saudi Arabia painted pink on the horizon as the Gulf of Aqaba narrows towards the north. Nuweiba's Moshav or co-operative village used to be a major destination for Israeli tourists during the occupation but has long since been surpassed by Na'ama Bay as the

Sinai's primary resort destination. As a result, the town has little to offer and is becoming increasingly dull. Still, Nuweiba has some splendid sandy beaches with comfortable hotels that tend to be cheaper than Sharm El-Sheikh's and are in close proximity to the Israeli border, Jordan, and amazing desert wonders and colourful reefs. ▸▸ *For Sleeping, Eating and other listings, see pages 398-403.*

Ins and outs

Getting around The town is divided into three distinct areas: the centre, the port to the south, and the Bedouin village of Tarabeen to the north. Nuweiba port is the set-off point for the ferry across the gulf to Aqaba. All the buses arrive at Nuweiba port and some continue on to the town centre or vice versa. From the port you can hop on a minibus (E£1) heading toward Taba, get off at Tarabeen and walk the kilometre or so toward shore, or take a taxi which will deliver you directly to town or the village. Taxis in these parts have an unspoken camaraderie and tend to charge foreigners exhorbitant prices for transport. Standard fare from the port to town centre is E£5-10, from the port to Tarabeen, E£15-20, and from Tarabeen to the town centre E£10. Bargain hard and keep a sense of humour. ▸▸ *For further details, see Transport, page 402.*

Sights

Apart from the lounging on the beach there is little to see or do in Nuweiba. Tarabeen (see below) offers billiards galore and there are sometimes travelling musicians that jam and lead singalongs by the water. There is also a handful of enterprising local Bedouin who organize camel treks and jeep safaris into the magnificent interior for daytrips and more extensive overnight safaris. Many take short trips to Petra in Jordan via the ferry to Aqaba. Nuweiba is also home to Oleen, a wild **dolphin** that has become something of an attraction over the last decade. Ten years ago she befriended Abdullah, a local deaf Bedouin. The stories of their union are varied. Some say she was mourning the loss of her beloved companion who was accidentally shot by hunters. Abdullah jumped in the water to comfort her and play and so began their friendship. Others say her wounded mother washed up on the shore years back and local Bedouin tried to nurse her to health. The mother died, but Oleen stayed and connected deeply with Abdullah. She's been around ever since. No one really knows why she stays. Scientists speculate that she was probably rejected from her pod and is in need of interaction. Since her time in the bay, she has since given birth to two calves. Sadly, one of them died and the other disappeared. For better or worse, tourists are bused in daily from as far away as Sharm to have their five minutes' swim with the dolphin. Abdullah has made quite a good living off his friendship and local folks say his hearing has improved dramatically, because of the

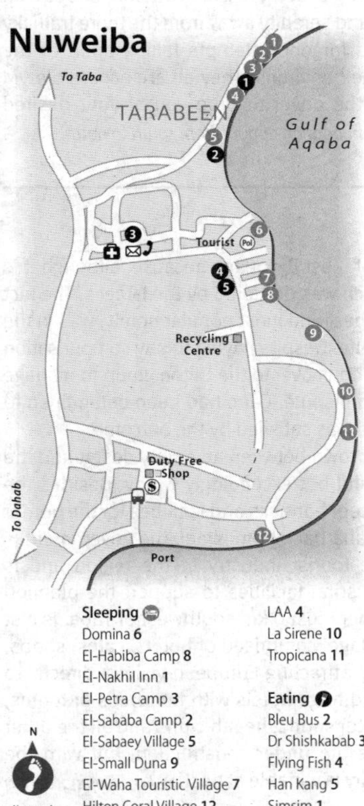

 dolphin. As of late, Oleen's presence has been increasingly sporadic. In winter, she often ventures south to warmer waters. Ask around to see if she's in the bay. If you do choose to swim with her, be sure not to wear any suntan lotion or cream. Oleen lives in an area that has come to be known as Dolphin beach. It's a 20-minute walk south from Nuweiba port, or you can hire a taxi from town for E£10. It costs E£10 to hire snorkel and fins, and another E£10 to swim with her. If Abdullah is in the water with you, she's more likely to come close.

Tarabeen

A 20-minute walk along the beach, north of Nuweiba city lies the Bedouin settlement sprawled along a stunningly beautiful sandy bay. Reminiscent of Dahab a decade back, there are dozens of 'camps', Bedouin-style restaurants and a few hotels scattered about a dirt road alongside countless mini bazaars and camel-ride hawking Bedouin. Notable differences are the white sandy beaches and a distinctly lacking presence of tourist police. In the last few years, Tarabeen suffered quite a loss. Since the outbreak of the Intifada in late September, 2000, Israelis, which make up over 80% of the tourism around Nuweiba, have stopped coming. As a result, many camps and restaurants have closed. Trash is washing up on the shores, huts are collapsing and there is a tangible air of sadness and despair around. ▸▸ *For Sleeping and Eating listings, see pages 399-402.*

Between Nuweiba and Taba

Along the striking stretch of shore between Nuweiba and Taba where rugged red mountains twist and turn and pour down to the sea, there is a scattering of Bedouin camps and tourist villages that offer respite and serenity away from the more trafficky resorts of the south. Some are dilapidated forgone attempts falling apart at the seams, others are gems and sensitive to their environs. They all are accessible via bus, service taxi or microbus; simply ask the driver to drop you at your desired destination. ▸▸ *See page 399 for interesting accommodation options from south to north.*

Taba

This town has a special place in the hearts of most Egyptians because, although it is only tiny, it was the last piece of territory which was occupied by the Israelis. The fact that the luxury Sonesta hotel, one of Israel's best and most popular hotels, was in the Taba enclave no doubt complicated the dispute. Despite having to pay compensation to the Sonesta's owners, before handing the hotel over to the Hilton group to manage and despite the very small size of the area in dispute, Cairo had been determined to retrieve every centimetre of Egyptian land and was satisfied by the outcome.

Taba is unusual, an international border town between an empty desert and the bright lights of Eilat. The coastline is beautiful but exceedingly windy. Besides the hotel there is little else in the tiny enclave except barracks and facilities for the border guards and customs officials. Having won Taba back from Israel, the government is now concentrating on development of the tourist industry in the region and is building power stations and other infrastructural facilities to support the planned influx. **Taba Heights**, a new tourist development just 9 km southwest of Taba, is just such an attempt. The vision is to build a 'village' comprised of hotels, cafés, shops, casinos, and a dive centre, with the hope of attracting European visitors directly to Eilat airport in Israel. To date, a few high-end huge hotels with hundreds of rooms, private beach, pools, restaurants, shops, water sports, health clubs and all the other usual 5-star amenities are open, and more are under construction, but with the political situation across the border, popularity is variable at best. ▸▸ *For Sleeping, Eating and other listings, see pages 400-403.*

Ins and outs

Getting there and around The easiest way to reach Taba, 390 km from Cairo and 260 km from Sharm El-Sheikh, is via Israel's Eilat airport which is only 15 km across the border. Guests of the Taba Hilton and Nelson Village do not have to pay Israeli Departure Tax. These hotels will provide a pass to allow free movement through the border during time of stay. Taxis and buses run to the border and the hotel is just a few steps on. Buses approach Taba from Nuweiba. ▸▸ *For further details, see Transport, page 402.*

Sights

Sightseeing in Taba is limited to trips to the beautiful interior, **Pharaoh's Island**, ⓘ *ferry to the island costs E£15, admission to the fort is E£20,* with the ruins of Salah Al-Din's (Saladin's) fortress (the most important Islamic remains in Sinai), and across the Israeli border to Eilat. The fortress was originally built in 1115 by the Crusaders to guard the head of the Gulf of Aqaba and protect pilgrims travelling between Jerusalem and St Catherine's monastery. It was also used to levy taxes on Arab merchants travelling to and from Aqaba. Salah Al-Din took it over in 1171 but abandoned it in the face of European attacks 12 years later. There is a cafeteria on the island but it is absurdly expensive and not always open. The Salah El-Din Hotel also organizes snorkelling trips around the island's surrounding reefs, but beware – the currents can be strong.

A visit to the island, a short boat ride (400 m) from the Salah el-Din hotel, is especially worthwhile around sunset.

Taba Managed Resource Protected Area is the newest and largest in the network of coastal and inland protected areas (designated in January 1998). It lies south and west of Taba and includes the Coloured Canyon (see page 392). There is a wealth of ancient writings and carvings on rock walls in the area that span the history of Sinai, the crossroads between Asia and Africa. The scripts include Arabic, Semitic, Greek, Nabatean and other, unknown, languages.

Road to Suez and Cairo

The Ahmed Hamdi Tunnel ⓘ *The tunnel under the Suez Canal costs E£1.50 for cars and E£3 for buses.* The road journey across the centre of the Sinai peninsula from Taba to the Ahmed Hamdi tunnel under the Suez Canal takes about 4 hours. The turn-off just to the south of Taba is the main road to the tunnel 270 km away. Ras El-Naqb airport, 20 km further south, serves Taba and Nuweiba which is 80 km away but only has a few flights a week from Cairo. From the airport the road proceeds onto a flat plain and to both UN and Egyptian checkpoints. About 190 km from the tunnel there is a small, dirty site which includes a petrol station, mosque, restaurant, radio mast and semi-finished houses. Further along the route there are pillboxes, burnt-out trucks from the fleeing Egyptian army in 1967, and lots of road building. At **Nakhl** there is a petrol station, police post, garage, mosque, as well as cafés and stalls which have fresh fruit. At a crossroads 126 km from the tunnel there are turn offs to El-Arish (151 km) and El-Hasana (63 km). The maximum speed limit is 90 kph for cars and 80 kph for buses. About 70 km from the tunnel there is turn off for Ras Sudr one way and El-Hasana the other way. Further on is the **Mitla Pass** and its trenches, pillboxes and other war debris, which was the site of one of the largest tank battles in history. Closer to the tunnel there are turn offs for Ras Sudr, Wadi El-Giddi, El-Tur and El-Qantara.

Immediately after the Ahmed Hamdi Tunnel there is a crossroads to Ismailia, Suez and Cairo where there are some rather dirty cafés and a petrol station. The road to Cairo across an empty featureless desert plain passes lots of quarries, a coal stockpile and army camps, including one with candy-striped huts, and follows the railway line from Suez to Cairo. After a major traffic police checkpoint the dual carriageway is a very good road. About 100 km from Cairo there is a Red Crescent station. Towards the east of Cairo there are some large industrial works and the air becomes noticeably more polluted.

Taba tug of war

Taba is an enclave of land of no more than 1 sq km on the Gulf of Aqaba seized by the Israelis in the war of 1956 but, unlike the rest of Sinai, not returned to Egypt. Assuming that the Taba strip would be forever Israeli, an international hotel complex was built there (now the Taba Hilton). In 1986 agitation by Egypt for a final settlement of the international border at Taba led the dispute being put to arbitration.

This revealed that the border post at Ras Taba, 1 of 14 put in place after the 1906 Anglo-Turkish agreement, had been moved by the Israeli side.

In one of the oddest of cases concerning the delimitation of an international border this century, it was found that the Israeli army had cut away part of the hill at Ras Taba to enable Israeli artillery to have a good sweep of the Sinai coast road as it approached the port of Eilat. At the same time the Israeli military engineers removed the border post which rested on the top of Ras Taba. This gave the Israeli government the excuse to claim that, despite Israeli maps to the contrary, the old border had always run south of the Taba strip. In 1989 the arbitrators returned Taba to Egypt, though it remains virtually an enclave with border posts on all sides.

Border crossing to Israel

Although the checkpoints are always open it is better to cross between 0700-2100 and to avoid crossing on Friday just before the Israeli Sabbath when almost all businesses close and transport ceases. Free one-month Israeli entry visas are available for most Western tourists. **NB** Make sure that your **entry card** and **not** your passport are stamped because an Israeli stamp, and even an Egyptian entry stamp from Taba, may disqualify you from entering some Arab countries. Once on the Israeli side of the border you can catch a service taxi or No 15 bus into Eilat.

Sleeping

Ras Abu Galum *p394, map p394*
In recent years, a group of Bedouin built about 15 modest huts on the beach that can be rented for E£10-15 per night. There are a few clean squat toilets but no cars, running water or electricity. Water and other basic necessities are available at inflated prices and there are a couple of restaurants.

Nuweiba *p394, map p395*
Nuweiba has a few nice hotels on the shoreline between the town centre and port. There is also a range of comfortable camps and simple hotels in Tarabeen a few kilometres south. See also the listings below for a scattering of magical tourist settlements along the coast between Nuweiba and Tarabeen that offer more remote, tranquil accommodation.

A **Nuweiba Hilton Coral Village**, on the beach just north of the port, T069-520321-6, F520327. Choice of restaurants, spread over 115,000 sq m of beachfront, water sports, camel and horse riding, safaris, bicycles, squash, tennis, children's facilities, 2 heated pools, bank, internet access, travel agency, disco. A stylish resort, very relaxing, ideal for recuperating, rather isolated from rest of Sinai resorts. Excellent snorkelling just 30 m off shore where there is a coral garden. Aquasport Dive and Watersport Centre on the beach, one of the best diving centres in Nuweiba.

B **Domina**, formerly the **Helnan Hotel**, T069-500401-3, F500407. Under new Italian management, 127 comfortable rooms with all the extras, disco, private beach, mainly package tours, restaurant, sports facilities, campground and dive centre under construction.

B **Tropicana**, T069-520056-9, F520022. Perhaps the best deal in Nuweiba, a very comfortable spotless hotel with lush gardens surrounding large pool, all rooms have a/c, TV, phone and sea or pool view, outside disco, bar and good restaurant.

D **La Sirene**, T069-500701/2. Simple and a bit rundown, but rooms are cosy enough – some have their own rooftop terrace, Bedouin-style restaurant directly on beach, no pool, excellent snorkelling on the coral reef, dive centre (T069-500705).

D-E **El-Habiba**, T069-500770. Well-cared for high-end camp with fully equipped a/c bungalows and cabins, some with private bath, known for tranquil beach, well-stocked bar and superb beachfront restaurant.

D-E **El-Waha Touristic Village**, T/F069-500420. 38 rooms and wooden bungalows with a/c and TV right on beach, just south of Domina, owner sometimes permits camping on the beach, buffet restaurant, old, rundown and overpriced, but among the cheapest options in Nuweiba town.

F **El-Small Duna, Sun Beach Camp**, T069-500198. There are a few cheap camps run by Bedouin from the Mzeina tribe which offer E£10 huts on the shoreline between the town centre and port (in between El-Waha and La Sirene). They used to be clean and enchanting places, offering proximity to town and a quieter respite from nearby Tarabeen, but since the decline in Israeli traffic they have become quite run-down.

Tarabeen *p396*

Tarabeen offers a range of possibilities. For E£10, you can get a hut in a one of the dozens of camps. They are quite comparable in quality, though some have cleaner bathrooms and offer extras like hot water, fans and mosquito nets. Look around before you choose. For E£50, a bit more if it's during the peak season, you can expect to find a room with a/c and private bath. There are a few pricier places that offer nicer quality rooms with all the expected amenities.

C **El-Nakhil Inn**,T069-500879, F500878. A relatively new hotel in the northern part of the bay, beautiful outdoor sitting area, quiet spot with private beach, good snorkelling, very comfortable spacious rooms with all amenities, bar (open to residents only), indoor and out-door restaurant, desert and diving excursions, dive centre (closed in off-season, but offers trips to Ras Abu Galum when open). Unquestionably the nicest place to stay in Tarabeen.

D **El-LAA**, T069-500679. Very central, not the prettiest, but offers clean, comfortable rooms with a/c, satellite TV, private bath, billiards, restaurant under shelter and on beach, closest thing to a hotel besides El-Nakhil Inn in Tarabeen.

D-F **El-Sabaey Village**, T069-500373. A clean and well-kept place offering a range of accommodation from cheap bungalows to rooms with a/c and private bath. Very central. Home to Samira, a pink pelican who has been kept in the place for good luck. Nice gardens, with nearby supermarket, bar and restaurant.

F **El-Petra Camp**, T069-500086. Run by a young Bedouin lawyer, this place is well-managed and hip, attracts lots of young Israelis, offers clean, comfortable huts, well-kept shared bathrooms with hot water, good food.

F **El-Sababa Camp**, T069-500855. An old timer in Tarabeen, the very helpful owner Salama knows everything about the area, all huts have doors painted with yin yangs and oms from hip New Agers of yesteryear, as well as fans, mosi nets, electric outlets and sheets on the mattresses, some have sea view, bathrooms are clean and the water is hot. Good restaurant, though pricier than most. Clean beach. Desert excursions.

Camping

F **El-Simsim**, T069-500616. Run by incredibly knowledgable Sudanese man named Abdullah, allows camping on beach and roof. Simsim also offers billiards and some of the best seafood on the bay, can't get any fresher as Abdullah casts his fishing nets daily. Plans to remodel the place include an African bazaar and beach bar.

Between Nuweiba and Taba *p396*

Ras Shitan, which means 'Devil's Head,' is an area named for a peculiar rock formation that rises 12 km north of Nuweiba. Nearby are a string of Bedouin camps with exquisite beaches under an amazing virgin Sinai sky.

C **Bawaki Beach Hotel**, 18 km north of Nuweiba, 1 km from Nuweiba-Taba road and 47 km from Taba, T069-500470. 36 rooms, beach location, attractive, well built chalet hotel, friendly and helpful staff, cheap restaurant, bar, beach café, seawater pool, mainly European guests in winter and locals in summer, some problems with fresh water, power and telephone facilities, hire of fishing boat, cruise boat (E£100 per hour), speed boat for water skiing (E£40 per hour), windsurfing, and good snorkelling with submerged coral reef just offshore.

D **Aquasun**, a few kilometres north of Basata, T069-530391. A 90-room resort with a sandy beach and reef excellent for snorkelling; resident dive centre offers beginners' diving courses. Also on offer are camel and jeep desert safaris.

D-E **Basata Ecolodge**, 23 km north of Nuweiba, T069-500481, www.basata.com. Basata (meaning 'simplicity' in Arabic) has become one of the most frequented tourist resorts in Sinai. Since its establishment in 1986, German-educated owner, Sherif El-Ghamrawy has worked to create an environmentally-conscious retreat. Water for the lodge is desalinated and the byproduct is used to flush the toilets. Solid waste is recycled – organic waste feeds the lodge's garden and menagerie. There is no electricity in the 16 simple clean beachfront huts. Camping is permitted. A communal kitchen runs on an honour system where guests are invited to take what they want and write it down. There are some steadfast rules – no drugs or alcohol, late night noise, nudity, or sleeping in the common area. The result is a respectable, family-friendly environment. Optional dinners are served to lodge guests every evening. The beach is sandy and there's a good reef for snorkelling offshore. Sherif organizes desert treks and tours for groups and individuals. It's wise to book ahead, as the huts are often reserved months in advance – especially during national holidays.

E **Sally Land Tourist Village**, T069-530380, F530381. A bit further north from Aquasun, in a Bedouin settlement called Bir Zuir, tastefully planned, 68 attractive chalets, beautiful white sandy beach, courteous and efficient staff, mainly European guests, restaurant, café, bar, shop and beach snack bar, snorkelling and windsurfing equipment for hire.

E-F **Castle Beach**, next to Ayaash (below), T012-7398495, www.castlebeach_sinai.com. A bit more comfortable with bungalows that each have electricity and their own terrace. Sheets and towels can also be provided. The bathrooms are cleaned every few hours, restaurant is excellent but more expensive than most. Desert trips with experienced guides available.

F **Ayaash's Camp** (also known as '**Ras Shitan**'), T010-5259109. Is the first camp from Nuweiba and lies directly in front of the 'head'. Accommodation is extremely simple, wall-less huts are scattered about the hills and shore, some are only a few metres from the waterline. There is no hot water or electricity. Desert safaris are available and it's possible to rent snorkel and fins to explore the reef offshore. There's also a busy restaurant that often is the gathering spot for late night jam sessions.

Taba *p396*

In addition to the huge resorts at Taba Heights, there is the longstanding deluxe Hilton that has dominated the area for years.

A **Taba Hilton**, Taba Beach, Taba, T069-530140-7, F5787044. High rise hotel, private beach, pool, water sports, 5 floodlit tennis courts, billiards room, use of facilities at the sister hotel Club Inn just across the border in Eilat, there are 5 restaurants and 3 bars a nightclub, and casino attracting cross-border business from Israel, a variety of shops, bank, travel agency and car rental service. There is an excellent coral reef just off the shore with Aquasport Dive and Watersport Centre (T069-520329).

B **Nelson Village**, T069-530140, F530301. Designed using natural materials to blend in with the surroundings. An extension of the Taba hotel, with a private beach, garden and sea view. Lounge and coffee bar, restaurant offers Tex/Mex cuisine, also more standard fare. Guests have use of facilities of Taba Hilton.

C **Salah El-Din Hotel**, 5 km south of Taba, T069-530340-2, F530343. 50 double well-equipped chalets, view of Pharaoh's Island, large portions of simple food, friendly staff.

Eating

Nuweiba *p394, map p395*

Outside the resorts in Nuweiba good restaurants are scarce.

Habiba, T069-500770. Open until midnight. Excellent beachside restaurant that cooks up fresh Bedouin bread, can get busy from midday as it caters to tourists on daytrips from Sharm.

Han Kang, in the town centre, across the street from Domino. A notable Asian restaurant that has been around for years.

Flying Fish, near Han Kang in the town centre. Serves up fresh fish and traditional Egyptian chicken and meat dishes in a nice outdoor courtyard.

Dr Shishkabab, in town centre. Open late. Has lost some of its acclaim in recent years but still serves up a cheap shishkabab and other traditional grub. Popular eatery and meeting spot for budget travellers.

There are a few small stores, fruit stands and surprisingly good bakeries in and around Nuweiba town centre. A few street food stalls selling the usual *fuul* and *taameyya* sandwiches are by the port.

Tarabeen *p396*

Bleu Bus. A popular restaurant with a pleasant beach area to enjoy mid-priced pizzas, pastas and fish.

Sababa Camp, extensive menu including pizzas, pastas and good fresh fish.

Simsim. Abdullah takes great pride in his restaurant, which is always spotless. Fish straight from the sea served up.

In Tarabeen, there are a few small super-markets scattered around the village that sell fruit and other necessities; one of the most substantial is outside El-Sabaey Village.

Taba *p396*

Taba Hilton restaurants: **Palm Court, Marhaba Oriental, Casa Taba Italian, Surfer's Deck**. All are expensive but of a high standard.

Salah Al-Din Hotel. See above.

Bars and nightclubs

Nuweiba *p394, map p395*

Nightlife in Nuweiba is very limited and revolves around the hotel beach bars.

Pool Cave Bar. Has occasional live music.

Nuweiba Hilton Coral Village. Popular darts bar.

Tropicana and **Domino** have discos.

Tarabeen *p396*

In Tarabeen several restaurants have billiard tables and there always seems to be someone banging on a drum or strumming a guitar in the beachfront restaurants.

Taba *p396*

Outside of the large hotels, there isn't much in the way of evening entertainment.

The Hilton (see above) has a disco, bar and an extremely popular casino.

Nelson Village (see above) also has a disco.

Activities and tours

Nuweiba *p394*

Besides diving and desert safaris, sports equipment and facilities are only available at the large hotels.

The Hilton (see above) rents **jetskis** and **kayaks**.

Diving

Nuweiba is known more for sandy beaches than diving, but, because its waters are quiet and clear, it makes a suitable spot for beginners. There are some good snorkelling areas offshore, the most famous is the **Stone House**, just south of town. There are a few dive centres around, all of which offer trips to nearby sites that are more impressive than the few reefs off Nuweiba shores.

Dive Point, based in the Hilton Coral Resort, T069-520327. Offers beginners' courses and excursions.

SCUBA Divers, based in La Sirene, T069-500705. Has an international staff of certified instructors that offer beginners' courses and rent diving and snorkelling gear.

Desert safaris

Desert safaris and excursions are widely available from Nuweiba and the nearby camps and tourist villages. Virtually every hotel and camp has connections with experienced Bedouin that know the desert like their hands. The cost is fairly consistent around town – by camel it's E£120 per person per night including food. A jeep costs about £E250 per day but price varies depending on the number of people and destination. Costs generally do not include water, so plan to bring all you need, as it's scarce in the interior.

Abanoub Travel, T069-520201. If you can't find a Bedouin guide that feels good, this, though a bit more expensive, is a reputable local tour company that has organized safe camel and jeep safaris for years.

Soliman Travel, at the Hilton Coral Village,

T069-350350. Books cheap travel to St Catherine and other Sinai cities, Aqaba and Cairo.

There are countless majestic spots in the Sinai interior, some much more frequented than others. Most visited is the **Coloured Canyon**, a stunning site even in the midst of tour buses. From Nuweiba, you should be able to find a ride in a jeep for E£50. Other striking spots often included on camel and jeep safaris are **Ain Um Ahmed**, a large fertile palm-laden oasis fed by the snowmelts from far-off peaks; **Ain Khudra**, or 'green spring', is a magical and tranquil destination easily accessible in a day by jeep; and **Wadi Ghazala**, a valley where gazelle are known to graze.

Tarabeen *p396*
Nakhil Inn, T069-500879. Has a dive centre open during tourist season that leads regular trips to Ras Abu Galum.

Taba *p396*
Aquasport Dive and Watersport Centre, T069-520329.
Taba Hilton (see above). Has more sports facilities and can arrange onward travel and provide car hire.

Transport

Nuweiba *p394, map p395*

Bus

T069-520370-1. There are various daily buses from **Cairo**, **Suez**, **Sharm El-Sheikh** and **Taba**, which call at the port and sometimes the town centre. Departure times from Nuweiba are always changing so ask at any hotel or camp or call to confirm departure times. Buses leave for **Cairo** (E£50, 0900, 1100, 1500, 6 hrs); **Sharm El-Sheikh** (E£15, 0630, 1530, 2 hrs), via **Dahab** (E£10, 1 hr); **Taba** (E£10, 0600, 1200, 1 hr). For **St Catherine**, catch the morning bus to **Cairo**. **Microbuses** offer cheaper and sometimes quicker transport. They operate on a leave-when-full policy and travel north and south along the main highway as well as to **Cairo**. Negotiate prices before setting off. Women travelling solo should sit in the front seat.

Ferry

T069-520216, US$30. There is a slow ferry to **Aqaba** in Jordan that leaves every day some time between 1300 and 1400 and takes 3-4 hrs to get across (barring potential obstacles). Foreigners must buy the US$30 first class ticket and pay in US dollars. There is also a speedboat which is a more reliable, comfortable and less crowded choice. It costs US$45, leaves daily at 1300 and only takes 1 hr. Arrive 2 hrs early to secure tickets for the departure. To confirm departure time, which may switch with the season, call the Coral Hilton, T069-520320. Two-week or 1-month Jordanian visas are issued on board or immediately on arrival in Aqaba, with charges varying according to nationality.

Taxis

Service taxis With passengers sharing the cost of the journey, these are available from Nuweiba port to **Taba** and other towns in the region.

Taba *p396*

Air

Eilat airport (15 km from Taba) has direct daily flights to major European cities. (No problem at Egyptian border but customs officials at airport are very thorough.) The local **Ras El-Naqb airport** 39 km away has only a few flights a week from **Cairo**. Orascom, T02-3052401 (in Cairo), has plans for more frequent flights as the new hotel complex develops and increases in popularity.

Bus

East Delta Bus Co runs daily buses to and from **Cairo**, **Sharm El-Sheikh** via **Nuweiba** and **Dahab**, and **Eilat** across the border in Israel.

Taxis

There are also hordes of **service taxis** driven by local Bedouin that regularly transport visitors to **Nuweiba**, **Dahab** and **Sharm**. They are more frequent, more comfortable, and quicker than buses – but marginally more expensive. Assuming the car is full, expect to pay around E£30 per person to **Tarabeen** and **Nuweiba**, E£50 to **Dahab** and E£80 to **Sharm El-Sheikh**.

Directory

Nuweiba *p394, map p395*
Banks Both Domino Hotel and the Hilton have banks open in the morning and evening. There is also a Bank Misr with an ATM in front of the bus station near the port. **Internet** Is available in the Hilton for E£20 per hr, and at Habiba Camp. **Post office** In the town centre. **Useful numbers** Tourist Police, T069-500231 next to Domino Hotel in Nuweiba City.

Taba *p396*
Banks Bank Misr, on the Egyptian side of the border. The Taba Hilton also has a bank that is always open and changes Israeli money. **Post office** Taba Hilton sends mail via adjacent Eilat rather than distant Cairo.

The interior

→ *Colour map 2, gridB/C 6.*

The largest single protected area in Sinai is St Catherine's National Park (designated in 1987), which covers a roughly triangular area of the mountains south from St Catherine's Monastery. This Greek orthodox monastery at the base of Mount Sinai, where God is believed to have revealed the Ten Commandments to Moses, has attracted pilgrims and visitors for centuries and despite its location in the heart of the Sinai wilderness, it's one of the most important tourist sites in the country. As well as containing the monastery of St Catherine and Mount Sinai, a site holy to Christians, Muslims and Jews, the park also contains ibex, gazelle and hyena, hyrax, leopards and possibly cheetahs. Bedouin have been recruited as community guards to help the rangers patrol this immense expanse of mountains, wadis and desert and although the park has not been long established, it has already had noticeable success, particularly in clearing the area of the previously abundant rubbish and providing information and nature trails. Another peak nearby (Egypt's highest) with some great hiking potential and another monastery is Mount Catherine and further west is the welcome flash of green of Wadi Feiran. Further west still from the top of Jebel Serabit, you'll find more striking views out over this jagged parched wilderness. ▸▸ *For Sleeping, Eating and other listings, see pages 408-410.*

Ins and outs

Getting there The road journey from Dahab to St Catherine, which is generally very good with little traffic, takes about 1½ hours. On the way, at the top of a very steep hill there is a breathtaking view over the desert. The coaches and taxis stop here and Bedouins attempt to sell fossils, sand-roses and other souvenirs. You then pass through one UN and two Egyptian checkpoints. There is a small run-down cafeteria 55 km from St Catherine, trenches (25 km), the El-Salam Hotel (15 km), and Masr petrol station (10 km), Morgan Land camping (8 km), and a Bedouin village and encampment just before arriving in St Catherine. While all of the organized tours to St Catherine stop at the monastery itself, the normal buses services stop in the small village of St Catherine about 2 km below the monastery.

Information St Catherine's National Park administration office/visitors' centre, near the monastery, T069-470032. Has information on shorter walks, and a few books and maps of the area. Alternatively access walking tours and maps online at **www.touregypt.net/walkingtours.**

Best time to visit St Catherine is very cold in winter with a metre of snow a few times a year, and snow sometimes until March, but it is very hot in summer. Despite the environment there are no problems with water or electricity.

St Catherine's Monastery

ⓘ Cairo office T02-4828513. Mon-Thu and Sat 0930-1200, but closed Fri, Sun and public holidays, free. Visitors to the inside of the monastery must dress modestly. Shorts are not allowed – for either men or women. There is no dress code for visiting the outside.

The **Burning Bush**, through which God is said to have spoken to Moses, holds religious significance for Jews, Christians and Muslims and in AD 337 Empress Helena, mother of Constantine, decreed that a sanctuary was to be built around what was thought to be the site of the bush. It became a refuge for an increasing number of hermits and pilgrims who sought the wilderness of the Sinai Valley over the following centuries. Between 537 and 562, Emperor Justinian expanded the site considerably by building fortifications and providing soldiers to protect the residents and adding the Church of the Virgin and the Basilica of the Transfiguration. The monastery and its community which then, as today, was controlled by the Byzantine Church was tolerated by the subsequent Muslim conquerors.

The number of pilgrims dwindled until a body, claimed to be that of the Egyptian-born St Catherine, was 'discovered' in the 10th century and was brought to the monastery, which attracted many pilgrims during the period of Crusader occupation (1099-1270). The numbers of both pilgrims and monks, who are now restricted to Greeks mainly from the Mount Athos area, subsequently waxed and waned until today there are only 25 monks, but the thousands of international pilgrims and tourists actually make the monastery too crowded in the high season.

Although an official tour guide, who will explain the history and symbolism of each part of the monastery, is a bonus he is not essential if you buy the monastery's guide book in the small bookshop near the entrance.

The site The ancient gate on the western face has been walled up (but the funnel above, for pouring oil on unwary attackers, remains) and a newer entrance constructed alongside. Visitors now enter through the north wall. The outer wall, constructed of local granite by Justinian's builders, is 2-3 m thick and the height, which varies due to the uneven topography, is never less than 10 m and in places reaches 20 m. The southern face has some interesting raised Christian symbols.

The highlight of the walled monastery, which includes the monks' quarters and gardens which are not open to the public, is the highly decorative and incense-perfumed **St Catherine's Church** including **St Helena's Chapel of the Burning Bush**. The church was built between AD 542-551 in memory of Emperor Justinian's wife. The building is of granite in the shape of a basilica. It has a wide central nave and two side aisles reduced by the construction of side chapels and a vestry. Its 12 enormous pillars, six on each side, each a single piece of granite, are free-standing and decorated with beautiful icons representing the saints which are venerated in each of the 12 months of the year. A candle is lit below the relevant icon on each saint's day. Examine the capitals for their Christian symbols. The walls, pillars and cedar wood doors of the church are all original (by comparison, the 11th-century doors made by the Crusaders seem almost new). The ancient roof is hidden above a more recent (18th-century) ceiling with reliefs of animals and plants. Above them the inscription (in Greek) reads – "This is the gate to the Lord; the righteous shall enter into it." The gable window in the western end of the church is made in the form of a cross. This, with the palm tree reliefs on either side, is better observed from outside. The iconostasis is dated at 1612. In the apse is one of the delights of this building, a magnificent mosaic illustrating the Transfiguration. It is the earliest and one of the finest mosaics of the Eastern Church. The theme is taken from St Matthew's Gospel. Christ is in the centre with Moses and Elijah at each side and Peter, James and John at his feet. Around these are further figures identified as the 12 apostles, the 12 prophets, the abbot in church at the time of the mosaic's construction and John of Climax, the deacon. The three-tiered bell tower at the western end of the church was built in 1871. There are nine bells, each of a different size. They came as a gift from Russia. These bells are used for special services. The original wooden bell, older than the metal bells, is used daily.

At the far side of the north aisle is **St Helena's Chapel of the Burning Bush** which, although it was the site of the original sanctuary, was not included in Justinian's original building but was only enclosed later on. A silver plate below the altar marks the site where the bush is supposed to have stood.

West of the church is a small 11th-century **mosque** which, originally a guesthouse, was converted apparently in order to placate the Muslim invaders and to encourage them to tolerate the monastery. The detached minaret which faces the church is 10 m high. Significantly, however, the church steeple is considerably taller.

The **Old Refectory**, east of the church, is an interesting room. The ceiling is arched and the stones supporting the arches are decorated with symbols attributed to the Crusaders. A 16th-century mural decorates the eastern wall and the long refectory table has intricate carvings worth examining.

The **Library** is one of the monastery's most unusual features. It has an almost unrivalled collection of precious Greek, Arabic, Syriac, Georgian, Armenian Coptic, Ethiopian and Slavonic manuscripts, reputedly second only to that of the Vatican. There are over 5,000 books and over 3,000 manuscripts, mostly in Greek, including the famous Codex Syriacus, a fifth-century translation of the gospels. The icon gallery contains 2,000 priceless icons in the collection, of which 150 are unique and date from fifth-seventh centuries. Some are on display in the narthex of the church. Look out for the icons which show Moses receiving the commandments and Moses taking off his shoes before the **Burning Bush**.

Monastery of St Catherine

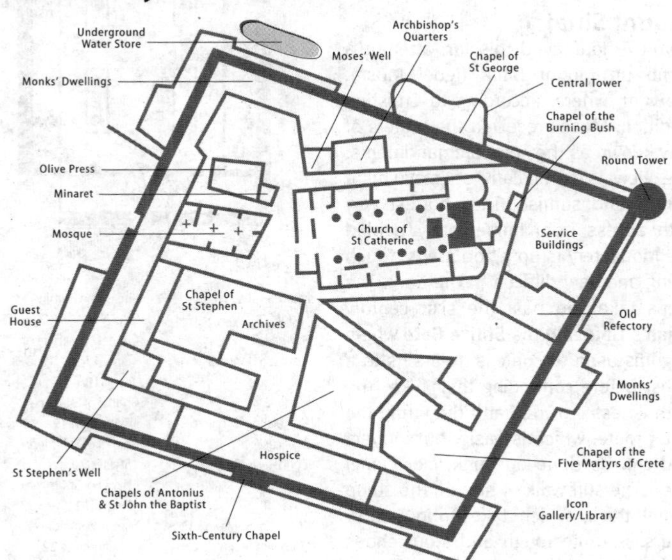

The monastery's small **museum** contains a collection of the gifts presented to the monastery over the centuries. The treasures were randomly scattered throughout the monastery until their accumulated worth was calculated by Friar Pachomius who then carefully gathered and preserved them in one place, but many of the more interesting items have been lost over the ages.

Because the monastery's **cemetery** in the gardens was so small, a custom was developed of storing the overflow of monks' skeletons in the crypt of the Chapel of St Tryphon. This serves as the ossuary of the **Charnel House** which was in the monastery gardens. When a monk died his body was buried in the cemetery in the place of the oldest body which was then removed to the Charnel House. The remains of the archbishops are kept separate in special niches. You can visit this rather macabre room full of skeletons and skulls.

The monastery gardens are small. All the soil was carried here by the monks who also constructed the water tanks for irrigation. It contains olive and apricot trees, plums and cherries with vegetables growing between. Immediately to the right of the monastery's main entrance at **Kleber's Tower**, which is about 15 m high and 3 m thick, is **Moses' Well** which it is claimed has never dried up. It is supposed to be the site where the 40-year-old Moses, who was fleeing from Egypt, met one of Jethro's seven daughters, Zipporah, whom he subsequently married. Just around the corner to the left of Kleber's Tower is a rather unimpressive overgrown thorny evergreen bush which is claimed to be a transplanted descendant of the **Burning Bush** from which God allegedly spoke to Moses.

Mount Sinai

If you've journeyed this far, attempt a climb up Mount Sinai (Jebel Musa), 2,285 m, where, according to Christian tradition, Moses received the tablets of Law known as the Ten Commandments. The view is particularly spectacular at sunset and sunrise. The shortest way with access from immediately behind the Monastery is up 3,700 steps, tough going and very difficult in the dark. The steps take you past the sixth-century **Elijah's Gate** and the **Shrive Gate** where pilgrims used to confess their sins to a priest before continuing their hike. The path is less crowded and dirty than the other route, which is easier but indirect and can be done on donkey or camel back. The stiff walk or ride up the steep camel track, which takes about 2 ½ hours, is quite rough and stout shoes and warm clothing are essential. Camels can be hired from behind the monastery for E£35. One way takes you three parts of the way up in 1 ½ hours. The last 700

Church of St Catherine

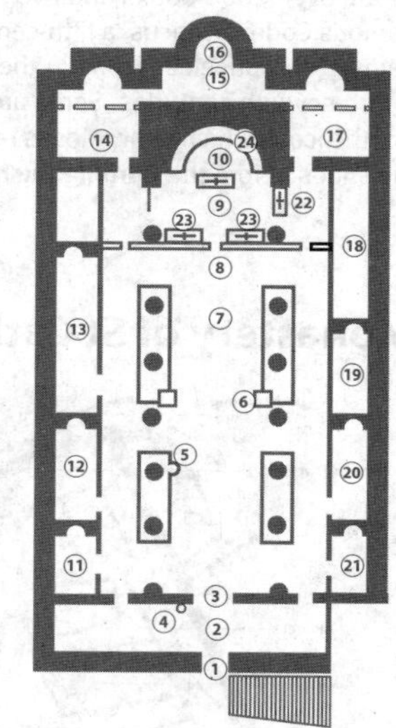

Fatimid Crusader doors **1**
Narthex **2**
Justinian doors **3**
Holy water **4**
Pulpit **5**
Archbishop's chair **6**
Basilica **7**
Iconostasis **8**
Holy altar **9**
Apse **10**
Chapel of St Marina **11**
Chapel of Sts Constantine & Helena **12**
Chapel of St Antipas **13**
Chapel of St James **14**
Chapel of the Burning Bush **15**
Site of the Burning Bush **16**
Chapel of Martyrs of Sinai **17**
Vestry **18**
Chapel of Sts Anna & Joachim **19**
Chapel of St Simeon Stylites **20**
Chapel of St Cosmas Damian **21**
Marble coffin of St Catherine **22**
Sarcophagi of St Catherine **23**
Mosaic of the transfiguration **24**

Blazing bushes and Catherine Wheels

Mount Sinai marked the half way point of the flight of the Jews from Egypt to the 'promised land'. Moses was clearly an inspirational leader for the incident of the burning bush led him to return to Egypt to lead his people to the land of milk and honey. But despite calling down from God the 10 plagues (frogs, lice, locusts, hail and fire among them), he failed to persuade the Pharaoh to release them from their slave labour. Finally the 80-year-old Moses asked God to strike the Egyptians with the passover when the Jews marked their houses with lamb's blood and were spared the massacre of all first born children. As a result, the Pharoah banished the 600,000 Israelite men, women and children from Egypt. Their epic journey is related in the Book of Exodus in the Bible. They were pursued by the Egyptians (drowned after the Red Sea divided to allow the Israelites across), faced starvation (rescued with manna from heaven) and thirst (saved when a spring flowed from a rock Moses had struck with his staff) and defeated an attack by the Amaleks.

On Mount Sinai, Moses received the wisdom of the Ten Commandments which have formed the code of practice for human behaviour for centuries.

The supposed site of the burning bush was developed into a monastery and in the 10th century named after Saint Catherine. According to legend Saint Catherine, who was born in AD 294 and was from a noble family in Alexandria, was a Christian convert who was martyred in the early fourth century for refusing to renounce her faith. She herself converted hundreds of people to Christianity and accused Emperor Maxentius of idolatry. When he tried to have her broken it was claimed that she shattered the spiked (Catherine) wheel by touching it, so Maxentius resorted to having her beheaded in Alexandria. After her execution her body vanished and according to legend was transported by angels to the top of Egypt's highest mountain, (2,642 m) now named after her. Three centuries later this body was 'discovered', brought down from the mountain and placed in a golden casket in the church where it remains to this day.

steps, which you must walk up take 30 minutes. Although there are refreshment stalls on the way up, which get more expensive nearer the summit, it is advisable to take at least 2 litres of water per person if making the ascent during the day but it is best to start the ascent at about 1700, or earlier in winter, in order to arrive at the summit at sunset. On Mount Sinai is a chapel where services are performed on some Sundays by the monks and a mosque where a sheep is sacrificed once a year. Camping is possible (see Sleeping below) and blankets and mattresses are available for hire (E£5, E£10) around the summit.

Mount Catherine

At 2,642 m Mount Catherine or Jebel Katrinahth is Egypt's highest peak. It is about 6 km south of Mount Sinai and is a 5-6 hours' exhausting but rewarding climb. En route you pass the deserted **Monastery of the Forty Martyrs.** On the summit there is a small chapel dedicated to St Catherine with water, a two-room hostel for overnight pilgrims and a meteorological station. The path up to the summit was constructed by the monks who laid the granite staircase up Mount Sinai.

Surrounding sights

About 50 km west of St Catherine lies **Wadi Feiran** ⓘ *accessible by taxi from St Catherine for E£70*, a lush winding valley filled with palms and wells. Some say this is where Moses left his people when he went to collect the Ten Commandments. A convent lies at the valley's centre and there are several good and challenging hikes nearby.

Further to the west is **Serabit El-Khadim** which, in the Pharaonic period, was an area well known for the mining of the semi-precious stone turquoise. Here on the summit of Jebel Serabit (850 m) are the ruins of the Temple of Hathor erected for the 'Lady of Turquoise', with a small chapel to Sopdu, who was guardian of the desert ways. The views over the desert region from here are outstanding. It's possible to arrange a tour to Sarabit from Sharm El-Sheikh or Dahab. Alternatively, you could hire a guide and four-wheel drive, which are essential, in Wadi Feiran. Bring lots of water.

Sleeping

St Catherine *p404*

Most tourist facilities lie 3 km away from Mt Sinai and the monastery in the village of St Catherine. Shared taxis between the two cost E£5. The bus station is in the village's main square, along with the tourist police, bank, post office and hospital.

B **Catherine Plaza**, T069-470288. A strange site in town, 4-star hotel with over 120 very comfortable a/c rooms, pool, and several bars and restaurants.

B-C **St Catherine Tourist Village**, Wadi El-Raha ('Valley of Repose'), St Catherine, T/F069-470333. Unrestricted views of the monastery 2 km up the road. 100 clean twin-bed chalets of local stone, the shape of a Bedouin tent. Mainly European, US and Japanese guests who stay 1 night (it's normally full in high season). Restaurant, coffee shop, gift shop, library, video hall, tennis, billiards, and table-tennis. Price includes half-board.

C **Daniella**, St Catherine, T069-470379, F3607750. 54 rooms in a simple, comfortable hotel (but not enough blankets in winter). Set in in nice grounds and provides good packed lunch for climbing mountains.

C **El-Karm Eco-lodge**, to make reservations or for more information, call the St Catherine Protectorate administration office, T069- 470032. Recently opened deep in the St Catherine's Protectorate, a 2-hr walk from the monastery or by jeep with 4-wheel drive. E£40 per person per night, fully managed and operated by local Bedouin; objective of lodge is to preserve the habits and traditions of Bedouin culture and teach the necessity of environmental protection to visitors and other Bedouin.

C **El-Salam**, 15 km from St Catherine on the road from Dahab, T069-470409, 470409, F2476535. 35 rooms, expensive 2-star hotel.

C **Monastery Hostel**, T069-470353/F470343. The hostel at the monastery has transformed into more of a guesthouse in recent years and increased substantially in price. Cost for 2 people sharing a double room is US$50, includes half-board. Also on offer are triples and dorm beds. Rooms are comfortable, warm and have private baths. Restaurant serves beer and wine. Reserve ahead in peak season, especially during common pilgrimage months of Apr and Aug.

D **El Wadi El-Mouquduss**, T069-470225, F2632021. 58 rooms, next to Daniella.

E-F **Morgan Land**, 6 km from monastery, T069-470404, F470331. 92 rooms each sleeping 3/4 dorm-style, shared bath, restaurant.

E-F **Zeitouna Camp**, 5 km from monastery, T069-470409. A range of accommodation offerings including stone huts, shared showers, restaurant.

F **Fox of the Desert Camp**, 1 km from town centre, T069-470344. Cheapest choice in town, clean concrete huts with blankets – E£10 per person, tea around campfire at night, run by 2 local Bedouin brothers who also organize trips to surrounding desert sites.

Camping

There is no specific camp site at St Catherine but it is possible to spend the night on Mt Sinai to see the sunrise. The altitude makes for sub-zero night-time temperatures for much of the year – a torch, sleeping bag and warm clothing are absolutely essential. It is possible to rent blankets and mattresses around the summit for E£10.

Eating

St Catherine *p404*
Besides the meals provided by most places to stay and the restaurants in more expensive hotels like at St Catherine's Tourist Village, there are a few virtually identical cafés in town serving decent standard fare of chicken and rice with vegetables for around E£10.
The Resthouse, near the bus stop, T069-470374. A popular spot, serving up big plates of filling, wholsome grub for less than E£10.

Shopping

St Catherine *p404*
Supermarket Katreen, a grocery store, bakery, bazaar and petrol station.

Activities and tours

St Catherine *p404*
Trekking
Besides the well-trampled peaks of Mt Sinai and to a lesser extent, Mt St Catherine, trekking opportunities in Central Sinai abound. Information is available at the St Catherine's National Park administration office/visitors' centre, see page 403.
Some highlights of the area include: **Galt El-Azraq**, a striking and beautiful 7-m deep spring-fed crystal clear pool nestled in the rock, a 2-day trek from St Catherine's; **Wadi Nugra**, a rocky valley with rain-fed 20-m high waterfall that trickles off mossy boulders into pools perfect for cooling off, in between Nuweiba and St Catherine's, a 3-day trek from St Catherine's; **Sheikh Awad's Tomb**, a picturesque oasis with Sheikh Awad's tomb, a well and a small Bedouin community, a 3-day trek from St Catherine; **Blue Valley**, a bizarre sprawl of desert 12 km from St Catherine interspersed with boulders painted blue by a Belgian artist in the late 70s. Claims as to why he did it vary, there's a common saying in Arabic, "There will be peace with Israel when the sky meets the desert", an impossibility, of course. So the artist, in attempt to make real the impossible, met with both Prime Minister Rabin and President Sadat to offer his idea in the name of peace, and painted the rock blue to bring the sky to the desert. A noble true tale, or was he trying to replicate landscape artists before him? Who knows... Ask your guide for his version of the story.

To explore in depth any of the surrounding peaks, you must have a Bedouin guide. **Mountain Tours**, T069-470457, headed up by Sheikh Musa, organizes most trips in the area. You can call ahead to reserve or find his office in El-Milga, uphill past the square and petrol station. Sheikh Musa will take your passport, (which must have a full Egypt visa, the Sinai-only visa will not suffice) and secure the necessary permit, guide, camels, food and equipment. Tell him how much time you have and what you want to see and he'll help create an itinerary. Cost is around US$35 per person per day, including everything, for a group of at least 3. You may wish to bring water purification tablets if drinking spring water is a concern.

Transport

St Catherine *p404*
Bus
There are direct buses for the 8-hr journey between St Catherine town and **Cairo's Sinai terminal** (0600, E£37) via **Suez**, and others to **Dahab** (1300, E£25), **Nuweiba** and **Sharm El-Sheikh**. Check at the nearby Resthouse Restaurant (see above) for the latest bus schedules.

Taxis
Service taxis Travellers can share the cost of hiring a 7-seat service taxi to **Dahab** (E£150 per car), **Sharm El-Sheikh** (E£200), **Nuweiba** (E£200), or other towns in the peninsula, but the prices almost double once the last bus has left St Catherine.

Directory

St Catherine *p404*
Banks Bank Misr branch on the main street in St Catherine town is open daily from 0830-1400 and 1830-2030. **Hospital** Next to the tourist police opposite the bus station.

Post office Is opposite the bank in town, open Sat-Thu 0800-1400. **Telephone** There is an international telephone exchange in town open from 0800-2400 near the post office. **Useful addresses** St Catherine's Protectorate Administration Office, T069-470032, very helpful info source about the area. Tourist Police, T069-470046, in main square opposite the bus station.

The west coast → *Colour map 2, B/C5.*

The west coast of Sinai on the Gulf of Suez is far less attractive than the Gulf of Aqaba coast. It has been spoilt by the oil industry which, while being one of Egypt's sources of foreign exchange, has transformed this region into a mass of oil rigs and gas flares and made it unsuitable for another foreign exchange earner – tourism. The largely featureless coast has become polluted with oil industry debris and is far more interesting to the industrialist than to the tourist. ▸▸ *For Sleeping, Eating and other listings, see pages 411-411.*

El-Tur

During the third and fouth centuries El-Tur was an important Christian centre with a monastery (now in ruins) built by Justinian. But now, although it is the administrative capital of south Sinai, the seedy and dilapidated coastal town, 108 km from Sharm El-Sheikh and 170 km from Suez, has little to recommend it: the best hospitals are located here as it was the quarantine stop for pilgrims from Mecca; El-Tur airport handles small planes; the port, which has always been of some significance, can accommodate medium-size ships.

If you do end up here, though, have a look at the **Fortress of El-Tur**, built by Sultan Selim I in 1520 AD and the **Temple of Sarabit Al-Kahadim** which stands on a small hill to the north of the town. To the east of the town are several caves such **Cave of Hathor**, built during the reign of King Snefru, and **Cave of Souidu**, the God of War.

Ras Sudr

Near the northern end of the Gulf of Suez, Ras Sudr, 190 km from Cairo and 250 km from St Catherine, is both an oil company town and the site of a noxious oil refinery and also a year-round destination for middle class Egyptian tourists. **Moon Beach** offers internationally acclaimed windsurfing opportunities, and the resort has a notable school.

Nearby sites include **El-Shatt point** (41 km), **Ayoun Moussa** – the springs of Moses mentioned in the Bible – and the place where the Hebrews rested after their exodus from Egypt and God provided honey dew and quails. Seven of the springs still exist and plans are afoot to make this into a new tourist resort. Situated 5 km from El- Tur, the pool is at the foot of a small mountain where hot water springs spew out water 26 degrees Centigrade. There's also **Hammamat Pharaoun** (50 km), south of Ras Sudr on a 494-m mountain that rises like a natural pyramid. Some Bedouins call it *Jebel Hammam Firaun Malun*, the Mountain of the Baths of the Cursed Pharaoh, believing it was here the King of Egypt drowned in the Red Sea with his army when he was pursuing Moses and his people. A very hot sulphur spring spews out of the mountain at 72 degrees centigrade and flows to the sea. Bedouins have visited these baths for centuries to cure rhematism. You can bathe in the steamy waters, or in the sea where they fall. Plans to build a spa are in the works. **Sarabit El-Khadem** and the rock temple here (130 km) is also accessible from this area. (South of Ras Sudr, you will find a small port community called Abu Zenima. A few kilometres south, a small road opens on the left and leads to the turquoise mines of Maghara. A few kilometres further south, from the main road, a small road turns off to the right, offering access to Sarabit El-Khadem.)

Sleeping

El Tur *p410*

E **Delmoun**, T069-771060. 75 rooms with a/c, private bath, breakfast included, not on beach.

E **Tur Sinai**, T069-770059. A/c, private bath, 24 rooms, 5 suites, next to bus station.

Ras Sudr *p410*

B **Moon Beach Resort**, about 40 km south of Ras Sudr, T069-401501/2, www.gybemasters. co.uk. All 72 bungalows have a/c and a fridge. Price includes half board; on site there is a restaurant, bar, disco, water sports and acclaimed windsurfing school with British instructors. School offers equipment and lessons for beginners and advanced surfers – by the hour and by the week.

C **Concord Royal Beach**, formerly the Helnan Beach Resort, just to south of town, T069-400101-3, F400108. 72 beds in the best hotel in town. US$22 per person per night, half-board, on beach, restaurant, bar, horse track, water sports, trips to nearby sights, Bedouin night in desert.

D **La Hacienda Beach Hotel**, 20 km south of Ras Sudr, T010-1177200. 25 rooms, plus suites and villas that can sleep 7, half-board, on beach, games room, bar and restaurant, disco, cinema and coffee shop in hotel.

Eating

El Tur *p410*

Only the restaurants in the hotels can be recommended.

Ras Sudr *p410*

There are a few *fuul*, *taameyya* and *koshari* restaurants in town but only the restaurants in the hotels are recommended.

Activities and tours

Ras Sudr *p410*

Incessant gusts of wind throughout the day all year round make this area an excellent spot for **windsurfing**.

Moon Beach Resort, T069-401501. Operates a very repuatable British-run windsurfing school that provides lessons for beginners and equipment for the more advanced.

Transport

El Tur *p410*

Bus

T069-770029. The most important information about El-Tur is how to get out of town. There are buses to **Cairo** almost every hour until evening and several a day to **Sharm El-Sheikh** (1130, 1300) and **Suez** (1130, 1500).

Ras Sudr *p410*

Bus

The daily buses between **Suez** and **Sharm El-Sheikh** stop at Rus Sudr. If you want to go to a hotel or resort further on down the road, tell the driver and he will drop you in front.

Directory

El Tur *p410*

Useful numbers Ambulance: T069-770350. Hospital: T069-770320 (0900-1400).

Northern Sinai

→ *Colour map 2, grid A5.*

Although the majority of tourists only visit the Gulf of Aqaba coastline and St Catherine's Monastery, the northern part of the peninsula has a number of attractions both in El-Arish and along the 210 km Mediterranean coastline which stretches from Port Said to the border at Rafah. Distinctly different in feel from the red rugged south, Northern Sinai is softer, with palm-fringed beaches and creamy sand dunes that melt into Mediterranean lagoons. (The main beaches on the north coast of Sinai are at El-Arish, Oruba, further east beside Rafah and Lake Bardweel, which is really a lagoon on the central north coast, famous for its fishing.) Fortunately for those trying to escape the hordes, while the region is appreciated by Egyptian tourists, most foreigners only see the area from the bus window as they speed to or from the Israeli border. » *For Sleeping, Eating and other listings, see pages 413-414.*

Ins and outs

Getting there Access from the west is across the Suez Canal or from further south, through the Ahmed Hamdi Tunnel.

Pelusium and Lake Bardweel

ⓘ *0900-1600 daily. Measure carefully 15 km from the junction of the road from El-Qantara with the road from the Ahmed Hamdi Tunnel. There is no road sign but the walls are very ornate. Turn north. The road is surfaced until it crosses a small canal. Turn left on to the next (unsurfaced) road. This road is not passable after rain so be prepared to walk from the tarmac.*

If you have your own transport you can visit the Roman ruins of Pelusium, also known as Tel El-Farame. The site covers a wide area, littered with ancient rubble, stone, bricks and columns. This city was situated on a now dry distributary of the River Nile and guarded the access from the east and acted as a customs post. It is mentioned in the Bible as "the stronghold of Egypt". The Persians came through here and both Pompey and Baldwin I ended their days here in tragic circumstances.

Lake Bardweel (66,500 ha) is important for fish such as mullet and seabass as well as migratory birds but access to the shore is often difficult. At the eastern end is the **El-Zaraneek Reserve** where over 200 species of migrating birds have been recorded. Take the track north at the hamlet of Al-Sabeka. (**NB** The sign says keep to the road but forgets to mention the landmines.) This area is of such significance that it has been preserved as a wetland under the auspices of UNESCO.

El-Arish

This town, 180 km east of the Suez Canal is the governorate capital of North Sinai and was noted for its 30 km of palm-lined fine white sand beach. It's a quiet, bumbling sort of place, good for family getaways or groups of friends who may wish to rent a somewhere on the beach and enjoy one another's company and not much else. The Bedouins of Northern Sinai weave beautiful fabrics and rugs, which are brightly displayed at the weekly souk. Al-Nakheel to the east is the best beach at El-Arish with famous but depleted palm trees extending the length of the shoreline.

Ins and outs

Getting around The town consists of two main streets, Sharia Fouad Abu Zakry, which runs along the beach, and the Sharia 23rd July, which veers off, and then runs perpendicular to, Sharia Fouad Abu Zakry. From the bus and taxi station, at the southern end of Sharia 23rd July in Midan Baladiya it is a 2-3 km walk or minibus ride (50 piasters) to Fouad Abu Zakry and the beach, which is the site of most hotels. This area is very popular at weekends. » *For Sleeping, Eating and other listings, see pages 413-414.*

Information There is an **Egyptian General Authority for the Promotion of Tourism** office in El-Arish, T068-363743, in the same office as the **Tourist Police** station, T068-353400, 359490, just before the beach on Sharia Fouad Abu Zakry. There is also a small, helpful **tourist information office** on the dual carriageway to the west, about 12 km out of town.

Sights

You can visit the Thursday Bedouin market (**Souk El-Khamees**) in the oldest part of town selling north Sinai embroidered cloth, plants and Bedouin handicrafts. This is best reached from the coast road turning south just by the Semiramis Hotel. **El-Arish Fortress**, is on a plateau to the southwest of the town on the remains of an ancient Pharaonic castle. Follow signs to Souk El-Khamees and beside the pieces of aqueduct, and hidden behind wooden walls (absolutely no entry) where excavations are taking place, are the ruins of the fort rebuilt by the Turk Sultan Sulayman Al Qanouni in 1560 and demolished in the First World War by British bombardment. Otherwise life in town revolves around the beach.

Out on the Rafah road there is the **Sinai Heritage Museum**, ⓘ *T068-324105, opening hours fluctuate with the season, but generally 0900-1400, closed on Fri, tickets E£4*, filled with Bedouin handicrafts and stuffed Sinai wildlife. There is a small zoo, also east of town, but it's not worth the visit. Between Abi-Sakl to the west and the zoo to the east is the **harbour** of El-Arish, used mainly by fishing vessels. (Fishing permits may be granted.) The **Zaranik Protectorate**, ⓘ *cost is US$3 per person and US$3 per car; several campsites are available for US$5 per person per night, for more information, contact the Egyptian General Authority for the Promotion of Tourism office, T068-363743*, around 30 km east of town, encompassing the eastern shore of Lake Bardaweel and extending north to the sea, is a wildlife haven protected since the mid-1980s. In September, thousands of birds stop here en route from Europe to Africa. At the entrance of the protectorate, there is a cafeteria and an informative visitors' centre.

Border crossing to Palestine and Israel

From El-Arish, you can ride the 41 km to **Rafah** by microbus or service taxi (E£5) or hire a private taxi, (E£20). From Rafah, there are frequent buses and service taxis to the international border (known as the Gate of Salah Al-Din) 4 km east of town. It is best to avoid crossing on Friday. Whenever you cross, try to leave El-Arish in the morning to avoid getting caught in the Gaza Strip at night in case a curfew is in place. There is a free one-month Israeli visa for most Western tourists. **NB** Make sure that your **entry card** and **not** your passport are stamped because an Israeli stamp, and even an Egyptian entry stamp from Rafah, disqualifies you from entering some Arab countries. Once on the Palestinian side of the border you can catch a service taxi into the Israeli side of the divided town of Rafah and then on to Khan Yunis and Gaza City's Palestine Square from where there are service taxis to Jerusalem and Tel Aviv. If **entering Egypt** at Rafah be sure to have a visa in your passport because they are not granted on arrival here.

Sleeping

El-Arish *p412*

Hotels along the beach range from the luxurious to the basic. During the Jul-Sep high season it may be difficult to find a room without pre-booking, but during the winter most hotels are very quiet.

A **Coral Beach Resort**, 20 km west of El-Arish, T068-331000. Very romahtic resort with 54 chalets built on islands in an artificial lake and some seafront buildings. Attracts wealthy Egyptians and foreigners. Has 2 restaurants, a health club and spa, 2 pools, a large private beach, no bar but alcohol available, *ahwa*. Entertainment in the summer.

B **Hotel Egoth Oberoi**, Sharia Fouad Abu Zakry, T068-351321/7, F352352. 219 rooms, most with sea view, breakfast included, sports and recreation facilities including health spa, tennis and squash courts, windsurfing, pedal boats, a private beach, 2 pools, one of the few bars in town, certainly the best stocked.

D **Semiramis Hotel**, Sharia Fouad Abu Zakry, T068-364167/8. 170 rooms, on both sides of the coast road, breakfast included, a/c, TV, private bath, most rooms have sea view.

E **Sinai Beach Hotel**, Sharia Fouad Abu Zakry, T/F068-361713. 30 rooms some with sea view.

F **Sinai Sun Hotel**, Sharia 23 July, T068-361855. All 54 rooms with a/c and shower. Used predominantly by Egyptians.

F **Youth hostel**, adjacent to Governorate Building.

Camping

Camping is permitted in the Zaranik Protectorate, US$5 a night. It may be possible to camp on the beach if you can get permission from the police.

Eating

El-Arish p412

Besides the hotels and a series of stalls by the beach that sell *fuul* and other standards, there is an outdoor restaurant near the Egoth Oberoi and a number of cheap restaurants and *ahwas* (with sheesha) in and around Midan Baladiya.

Basata, in the western part of town. Offers a pleasant atmosphere with good seafood for around E£20, geared more for tourists.

Sammar and **Aziz** at the coast end of Sharia 23 July, serve up good cheap grilled food with a variety of salads.

Entertainment

El Arish p412

Nightlife in El-Arish thrives around the cafés of Midan Baladiya, where no matter the night, you will find people puffing on *sheesha* pipes, sipping tea and playing backgammon. El-Arish is a rather conservative community and there aren't many places that serve alcohol.

Egoth Oberoi has a well-stocked bar and a nightclub.

Shopping

El Arish p412

There are some rather sleazy tourist shops on Sharia 23 July but for quality items it is better to bargain at the Bedouin market.

Transport

El Arish p412

Air

During the summer, **EgyptAir**, T068-356092 offers flights to and from **Cairo** on Sun and Thu. The airport is along the Bir Lahfan road to the south of the town.

Bus

East Delta Bus Co, T068-325931 (Cairo T02-5762293), runs frequent daily buses between El-Arish and **Cairo** (6 per day from 0800 to 1800, 5 hrs, E£16-25), and others to the Suez Canal cities of **El-Qantara** and **Ismailia** (E£10). There are also daily buses to **Alexandria**. Bus station off Midan Baladiya near the mosque.

Minibuses Constantly run back and forth from the souk to the beach (50 piastres)

Taxis

Service taxis to/from Midan Koulali Terminal in **Cairo** (5 hrs, E£30): Midan El-Gomhoriyya in **Ismailia** (3 hrs, E£15) or by the Suez Canal in **Qantara** (2½ hrs, E£12). **Rafah** (30 mins, E£4). Taxis to **Cairo** leave early morning. Taxis around El-Arish shouldn't cost more than E£5, if you stay in town.

Directory

El Arish p412

Banks Bank of Alexandria, T068-353041; Misr Bank, T068-351881; National Bank of Egypt, T068-351556, are available in town; the main hotels will also change money. **Hospitals** El-Arish General Hospital, Sharia El-Geish, T068-361077/ 360010. **Pharmacies** Ibn Sinai Pharmacy, T068-360706, open 0800-2400 except Fri. **Post office** The post office and the international telephone exchange are off Sharia 23 July between the Sinai Sun Hotel and Midan Baladiya. **Useful addresses** The main police station is on Sharia El-Geish on the way to Rafah. Tourist Police, T068-353400, 359490, off the beach to the left of the main intersection (Fouad Abu Zakry and 23 July) if facing the sea. Tourist office: T068- 363743, in the same building as the tourist police, speak English fluently and are very helpful. **Useful numbers** Ambulance: T068-360123.

Red Sea Coast & the Eastern Desert

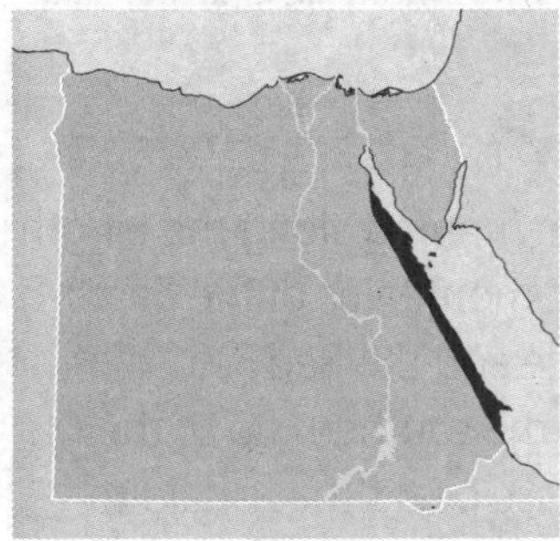

Footprint features

Introduction

The slowly widening major fault line running along the length of the Red Sea created the dramatic mountains of the **Eastern Desert**, a belt between the River Nile and the Red Sea stretching for about 1,250 km from the southern tip of the Suez Canal. It is the red colour of these peaks that is said to have inspired the name for the adjacent sea and deep in their folds thrive ibex, gazelle, and a scattering of ruins dating back to the Ptolemaic and Roman eras. But most visitors traverse or overlook the scorching, virtually uninhabited region to get to the coast, one of the fastest growing tourist regions in the country, even amid the current economic recession.

The eastern rim of the **Red Sea** shelters a thriving expanse of brilliantly-coloured fish, corals and other marine life. With no rivers flowing into the sea to disturb the translucent waters, the corals blossom unimpeded. The shoreline is also famous for its wind, so steady in force that a windfarm with 50 towering turbines opened in 2001 by the town of **Zafarana**. For tourists, the ever-blowing wind is the main appeal for windsurfers. **Safaga**, in particular, is internationally acclaimed for its first class facilities. Sadly, the optimal conditions for such water delights is yielding hasty development. With the Marsa Alam/El-Quseir airport opening in 2001, the southern region is also even more accessible – and it's taking a toll. Incessant construction coupled with careless, excessive diving and fishing is resulting a serious imbalance in the ecosystem, especially around Hurghada, the area's most visited coastal resort town. Thankfully, in regions further south, the government is striving to protect the marine area, insisting on eco-friendly practices for all new tourist developments. Though regulating and maintaining such worthy edicts is often a fait-ill-accompli in Egypt, the efforts are certainly a start, and hopefully sufficient to preserve the extraordinary, fragile underwater environs.

★ Don't miss...

1. **Diving** Plunge into the Red Sea's translucent turquoise depths and transport yourself to another realm, page 418.
2. **Monasteries** Explore the oldest monasteries in Egypt, St Anthony's and St Paul's, near Zafarana, where monks still live in sanctity, page 421.
3. **Hurghada or Safaga** Indulge in a few days of 5-star comfort at knock down prices in one of the coastal resorts, page 426 and 439.
4. **El-Quseir** Visit the quaint old port town where the old Ottoman fortress towers over the town centre, page 440.
5. **Southern coast** Marvel at the unrivalled beauty of the pristine mangroves before they are swept away by the encroaching tourist industry, page 441.
6. **Eastern Desert** Get isolated and awe-struck by a trek into the remote and mysterious Eastern Desert, where await spectacular sunsets, secluded wildlife and ancient ruins still unearthed, page 445.

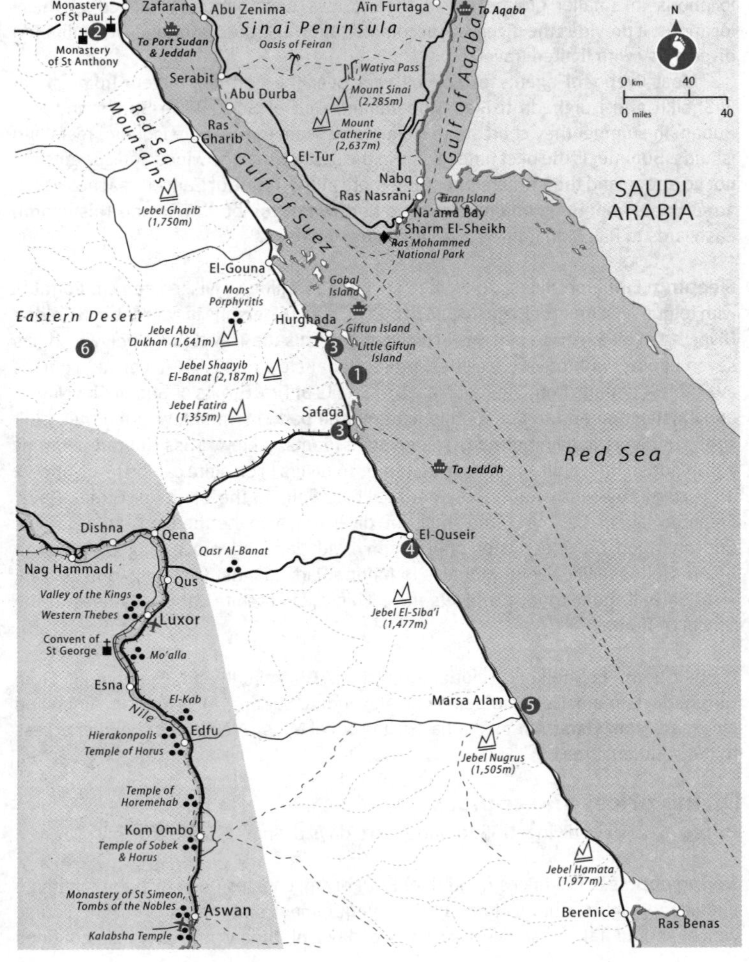

Diving in the Red Sea

Diving here was pioneered in the 1950s by Dr Hans Hass and Jacques Cousteau. Today the popularity of this sport means more and more people can experience the wonders of this special environment and that greater and greater numbers threaten this fragile habitat.

A mixture of deep water fish and surface coral give a total of over 1,000 species of fish to observe, some 500 species of coral and thousands of invertebrate reef dwellers and the clear waters ensure that the fish can be caught on film. Sites to visit include sheer drop-offs, sea grass meadows, coral encrusted wrecks, gullies and pinnacles. Water temperatures vary. A 3 mm or 5 mm wetsuit is recommended for all year but something thicker for winter wear (18°C) or a prolonged series of dives may be needed.

Liveboard

This method of accessing the dive sights permits divers to reach more remote locations in smaller groups so, in theory, less disturbance is caused at these locations. It provides the diver with accommodation and the opportunity for unlimited dives a day with limited travel.

Most liveboard agents extend all year over the northern waters from Sharm El-Sheikh and Hurghada to Ras Mohammed, Gulf of Suez, Tiran Straits and Port Sudan. In summer they chart south from Marsa Alam to the more isolated reefs and islands. Summer is the best time to dive in the south when the winds and currents are not so strong and the water temperature (here at the Tropic of Cancer) reaches about 30°C. Boats from Hurghada tend to head northwards to Abu Nawas and Thistegorm, eastwards to Ras Mohammed or southwards to Safaga.

Sleeping **Emperor Divers**, 20-25 m long, limited facilities, civilized and comfortable with tolerance. **Emperor Pegasus**, 24 m by 7 m, max 16 persons in twin cabins. **Golden Diver**, 22 m by 6.5 m, 14 persons in twin cabins. **Crusade Travel** (*VIP One*), which has seven cabins, with private facilities, professional crew and PADI Advanced courses available – departs from Sharm El-Maya to Straits of Tira, Straits of Gubal, Abu Nuwas and Thistlegorm and to Ras Mohammed marine park. **Mermaid**, wooden hull, built 1998, 16 divers in twin berthed, a/c, en suite rooms, 9 crew. **Miss Nouran**, 28 m by 7 m, wooden hull, built 1997, high standard, 16 divers in en suite cabins (6 x 2 and 1 x 4), 8 crew, Full Nitrox and rebreather facilities. Sails in the Straits of Gubal. **Royal Emperor**, 29 m by 7 m, steel hull, 14 divers in twin berthed en suite cabins. Concentration on underwater photography with lab and processing facilities on board. Built specifically for journeys to Marine Park Islands. **Cyclone**, 30 m by 7 m, wooden hull, built 1998, 20 divers in 10 twin a/c, en suite cabins. Cruises to the Straits of Tiran.

(From **Sharm El-Sheikh**: Cyclone, Ghazala I, Ghazala II and Freedom II. From **Hurghada**: Emperor Fleet, Golden Diver, Alexandria, Sabrina, Miss Nouran, Amira and Loveman. From **Marsa Alam**: Shadia. Sailing out of Marsa Alam gives speedier access to the southern area.

Diving prices and courses

Prices 6/12 days diving: US$200-400. 5/10 days diving: US$175-350.

Diving courses The prices quoted for PADI diving courses (for which the minimum age is 12 years) should include all diving equipment and materials for the course which should take just five days, three days of theory and work in confined water/deep swimming pool to put the theory into practice and two days in the ocean completing four open-water dives. After which a new underwater world waits you.

There are three main sections: **theory** – written test after reading the manual and watching a training video; **pool work** – confined water training; **open water qualifying dives** – in the sea.

Courses requiring certification are an extra US$30 per certificate for which you will require two passport photographs. You will also need a log book (on sale in diving resorts) to record your dives (US$8).

Open Water Certification: US$180-320. Advanced Open Water Certification (2 days): US$190-210. Medic First Aid (1 day): US$100. Rescue Diver Certification (3-4 days): US$300-320. Dive Master Certification: US$550-600. Under Water Naturalist: US$50. Night Diver: US$60. Multi-level Diver: US$65. Reef Diver: US$65. Wreck Diver: US$100.

Wrecked ships

Satellite images indicate over 180 wrecks on the bed of the Red Sea. By far the most wrecks are to be found around the dangerous **Straits of Gubal** at the mouth of the Gulf of Suez. Access is easiest from Hurghada or Sharm El-Sheikh.

Thistlegorm, was a 126 m long, 5,000-tonne English cargo ship which was damaged on 6 October 1941 by a long range German bomber and sank without firing a defensive shot or delivering her goods to the awaiting British troops fighting in the North Africa campaign. Nine of the crew lost their lives. She lies on the massive Sha'ab Ali reef, on the northern edge of the Straits of Gubal, under 30 m of water just as she went down, complete with an incredible cargo of armaments. There are jeeps, trucks, motorbikes, tanks, train cars, a locomotive and an 'explosive' collection of ammunition ranging from rifle bullets to mortar shells, along with uniforms and regulation boots. She was 'discovered' by Jacques Cousteau in 1956 but visits by casual divers to this war grave only began in the last eight years.

Dunraven, a 82 m sail-equipped steam ship has been lying on the reef of Sha'ab Mahmood just south of Beacon rock since 1876 and is now covered with soft corals and sponges and each year looks more attractive. She lies bottom up with the bow 15 m and the stern (propeller still in place) 28 m below the surface. Her journey from Bombay to Newcastle on Tyne remains incomplete. This English merchant ship carrying a cargo of spices and exotic timber is now home to lion fish and other colourful inhabitants.

Carnatic, once a 90 m luxurious Greek steamship is a sad tale. With a passenger list numbering 230 and a cargo of gold reported to be then worth £40,000, she hit the reef at Shab Abu Nuas on 13 September 1869. The conditions were calm, the ship remained upright and life for the passengers remained as normal until the vessel snapped in two without warning. Survivors were taken to Shadwan island but 27 people were drowned. £32,000 worth of gold was rescued, but where is the rest? Perhaps it is still there waiting for the lucky diver. The abundance of sponges and corals and the favourable light conditions make this a popular for underwater photography.

Giannis D was another Greek vessel, 99 m long and full of cargo. She ran aground on the reef at Shab Abu Nuas on 19 April 1983 and later broke in two and sank. The shallowest remains are just 8m under the surface allowing easy access to the bridge and the engine room in the stern. Giannis D, now covered with soft corals, is considered one of the best wreck dives.

Aida II was sunk in 1957 to the northwest of Big Brother Island. The stern section of this supply ship, all that now remains, is encrusted with hard and soft corals and is gradually becoming part of the reef that caused it to sink. At between 30 m and 70 m it makes an interesting dive, but only for the experienced diver, and the schools of barracuda add to the interest.

Chrisoula K was a 106 m Greek cargo ship carrying Italian tiles which struck the northwest corner of Shab Abu Nuas reef at full speed. The wreck remains upright but at an angle with the bow nearer the surface. The hull and much of the superstructure can be visited with safety but the badly damaged bow section should be avoided in rough weather. (Adjacent to the Chrisoula K is an unnamed wreck sloping down from the lighthouse.)

Other wrecks Off El-Quseir, at **Brothers Islands**, are two wrecks. One is an unnamed freighter at the depth of about 80 m with its stern firmly wedged into the sea bed. There are strong currents and viewing the corals on this wreck is only for experienced divers. Further offshore, between **Golbal Island and Tawila** lies a British 4000 ton steamer which was sunk on 8 October 1941 (see date for Thistlegorm above). The cargo of coals being carried from Cardiff remains with the wreck which lies at a depth of 50 m, the deck at 30 m and the funnel at 18 m. Hurghada port has its own wreck, an Egyptian minesweeper sunk in 1973 during the Arab-Israeli war, by friendly fire. It is at a depth of 28 m.

South of Suez

→ *Colour map 2, grid B4*

Aïn Sukhna

Only 2 hours from Cairo, on the Red Sea about 60 km south of Suez, the shoreline of Aïn Sukhna is a popular getaway for middle class and wealthy Cairenes seeking respite from the chaos of the capital. Although it lacks the breadth of sea life that thrives further south, and the horizon is perpetually dotted with huge oil tankers, it still retains the beauty of a Red Sea shoreline and makes a convenient beach stop for anyone based in Cairo if time is limited. It's supposed to be a region of hot springs, hence its name (which literally means hot springs), but the appeal centres much more around the sandy beaches and resort culture. The location of Sukhna also makes it a popular spot for bird watchers, as it's on the raptor migration route. There are several resorts, most offering water sports, snorkeling, fishing and lots of restaurants. If you want solitude, avoid Sukhna on the weekends. ▸▸ *For Sleeping, Eating and other listings, see pages 422-426.*

Zafarana

The small community of Zafarana is 62 km south of Aïn Sukhana on H44 at the junction to Beni Suef. For travellers, it's really just an access point to the two neighbouring isolated monasteries of St Anthony's and St Paul's, the oldest in Egypt, that lie hidden in the folds of the Red Sea Mountains. Pilgrim tours to these monasteries are organized by St Paul's Cairo residence, Kineesa El-Morqosiyya, a church just south of Midan Ramsis. Tourists are welcome to spend the night at St Paul's, but advanced booking with the Cairo office is required. T02-5900218. The monks at St Anthony's are less open to welcoming visitors who are not Coptic pilgrims, though neither is likely to leave you bed-less in the desert if you make the trek without a reservation. ▸▸ *For Sleeping, Eating and other listings, see pages 422-426.*

Ins and outs

Getting there Day tours to the monasteries are offered by a number of Hurghada travel agents including Misr Travel, see page 438. Otherwise a group can negotiate a single price with a local taxi in Hurghada. Provided it is not too hot and you take enough water it is also possible to get there from Beni Suef by service taxi or the Hurghada to Cairo or Suez bus at the turn offs for the respective monasteries, and then hitch or walk the remaining distance. For St Paul's turn off the north-south desert road approximately 24 km south of Zafarana at the small blue and white signs indicating the monastery and follow the rough track for about 13 km. For St Anthony's drive inland from Zafarana and after 32 km turn left at the blue and white sign which indicates the monastery. There are still 15 km more to go.

St Anthony's Monastery

ⓘ *Daily 0900-1700, except during Lent and between 25 Nov-7 Jan.*

Known locally as Deir Amba Antonyus this is the more important of the two monasteries. It has recently reopened to the public having been closed for a year for cleaning and restoration of the ceiling and entrances to the church. In particular the fabulous wall paintings and icons have been carefully preserved.

St Anthony (AD 251-356) was born in the small village of **Koma Al-Arus.** He became a hermit after he was orphaned at 18 just before the height of the persecution against the Christians by emperor Diocletian (AD 284-305). By AD 313 not only was Christianity tolerated but it had also been corrupted by becoming the state religion. This led to increasing numbers of hermits following Anthony's example and seeking isolation in desert retreats (see St Catherine's monastery, page 404 and El-Fayoum, page 160). After his death, at the reported age of 105, the location of his grave was kept secret but a small chapel was erected which became the foundation of the monastery. St John the Short sought refuge at the monastery 200 years later and died there.

In the course of its history it has been subject to attacks from the Bedouin tribes in the eighth and ninth centuries and the Nasir Al-Dawla who destroyed it in the 11th century. It was restored in the 12th century by monks from throughout the Coptic world, only to be attacked again in the 15th century when the monks were massacred and the buildings badly damaged by rebellious servants. Syrian monks were sent to rebuild it in the mid-16th century and it was then inhabited by a mixture of Coptic, Ethiopian and Syrian monks. Its importance rose and many 17th-19th century Coptic patriarchs were chosen from amongst its monks: by the 18th century it was receiving increasing numbers of European visitors. The result has been that the five-church monastery has developed into a large and virtually self-sufficient modern village which draws water from an ancient spring and grows most of its own food, mills its own grain and bakes its own bread. The whole complex is enormous with the outer walls spanning 2 km. Rituals observed here have hardly changed in the last 16 centuries.

St Anthony's Church, parts of which date back to the 13th century, is the oldest church in the complex. It consists of a central nave, two side chapels and an antechamber. While inside try to identify the apostles in the picture on the south wall! There are four other churches in the complex. **St Mark's Church** dates from 1766 and is reputed to contain the relics of St Mark the Evangelist in a chest on the north wall.

Cave of St Anthony, 276 m above and 2 km northeast of the monastery, is a steep 1-2 hours' walk but the view alone from the cave, 690 m above the Red Sea, justifies the climb. The cave, where St Anthony is supposed to have spent the last 25 years of his life, consists of a terrace, chamber, tunnel and balcony. The decorations on the walls are medieval graffiti often complemented by more recent additions in the shape of supplications stuck into the cracks of the walls by visiting pilgrims.

St Paul's Monastery

ⓘ *Daily 0900-1700 except during Lent and 25 Nov-7 Jan.*

The smaller Monastery of St Paul, which lies to the southeast of St Anthony's monastery, and is reached via the main coastal road, was built around the cave where St Paul the Theban (AD 228-348) spent his life. Although the dates do not actually match, he is supposed to have fled the persecution of **Decius** (AD 249-251) and arrived in the eastern Desert from Alexandria at the age of 16. He is the earliest hermit on record and was visited by St Anthony to whom he gave a tunic of palm leaves. St Paul apparently acknowledged him as his spiritual superior and St Anthony's Monastery has always overshadowed that of St Paul both theologically and architecturally.

The larger of the two churches is dedicated to St Michael and there are two sanctuaries. The south one is dedicated to St John the Baptist where a strange 18th century gilded icon depicts the saint's head on a dish. The **Church of St Paul** contains the actual cave where he lived and what are claimed to be his relics which were preserved during the many raids on the monastery. On the third floor of the keep is the **Church of the Virgin** which is unfortunately closed to the public because its wooden floor is dangerous.

El-Gouna

This is a new up-market resort, with a very attractive coastline, just 25 km (40 minutes in a taxi) north of Hurghada. Compared with the bustle of Hurghada Gouna is a peaceful place to visit. The coastline is a series of lagoons giving privacy for the hotel developments and private villas all of which have been constructed in a Nubian/Arabesque style. There are many uninhabited islands and coral reefs which are exposed only at low tide. The development boasts its own private airport for small planes, a post office, museum, observatory, eco-farm, aquarium and an amphitheatre. There's also a casino, a hospital with hyperbaric chamber, and two marinas. Abydos Marina, built in 1992, hosts up to 40 boats. The newer Abu Tig Marina, designed by Italian architect Alfredo Freda, is the first private, sailing marina on the Red Sea. With its own collection of chic restaurants and cozy inns overlooking a harbor brimming with colorful sails, a stroll down the boardwalk is a delight. Shuttle buses marked Downtown 1 and 2 run from hotels to heart of El-Gouna to shops and restaurants. » *For diving information for the Red Sea, see page 418.*

Sleeping

Aïn Sukhna *p420*

AL **Hilton Aïn Sukhna Resort**, Km 142, Cairo/Hurghada Rd, T062-290500. Rooms surround a huge pool; there are also privately-owned villas, each with their own pool, that may be available for long-term rent. Family orientated 5-star resort with a playground and trampoline on the beach for kids. There's a nice outdoor coffee shop/restaurant and a well-stocked store for picnic items and beach accessories.

A **Stella Di Mare**, on the Suez road (part of *Swiss Inn* chain), T062-250100, F250001. A quality resort, with open air restaurant, water sports, bowling centre, commercial centre, 700 m of beach, lagoons. The disco is the meeting spot for young people.

B **Aïn Sukhna Portrait Hotel**, Km 59, Suez/Zafarana Rd, T062-325561/2, F322003. It's white walls have browned with time, the strange architecture feels too rigid for the surroundings. This time-share place has lost popularity with the openings of newer resorts. Still, rooms are comfortable enough, with sea view. In addition to the beach, tennis, swimming pool and water sports are available.

El-Gouna *p422, maps p423 and p424*

AL/A **Movenpick**, shuttle bus 30 km from airport, T065-544501-2, F545160. Private airfield, hotel built in terracotta, in tropical gardens with tropical plants and palms framed by the desert behind and the lagoon in front. There are 2 large pools, health club, Turkish bath, disco, a selection of bars and restaurants including El-Sayadin on the beach, children's club, children's pool, baby sitting. Associated within the hotel complex is Nautic Dive Centre with the latest facilities. Non-divers may join the day boats at US$22 per day. Parasailing, pedalos, snorkelling and water skiing.

AL/A **Sheraton Miramar**, T065-545606, T580100-3, F545608. 338 deluxe rooms, 6 Junior Suites and 4 executive suites. Designed by Micheal Graves (the man who designed Disneyland). Bold colours and unique structures. Beach front on 9 separate islands in the lagoon, diving centre in the hotel, health club, beauty salon, choice of restaurants, golf course.

AL/A **Steigenberger Golf Hotel**, T065-580141-5, F580149. Set in a golf course, between the lagoon and the mountains retaining a cosy, warm atmosphere. Built round the central pool area. The interiors have been decorated with detail, old golfing prints, and beautiful carpets. Health club fully equipped. 18-hole USPGA Championship German-run golf course. Club house has outdoor terrace and a la carte restaurant with breathtaking views.

B **Sonesta Paradisio**, T065-547934/9, F547933. The first hotel built in Gouna, it's a sprawling beachfront resort 20 mins from the Hurghada airport with its own private strip for small planes. 3 restaurants, 2 lounges, private beach, 3 pools, water sports, tennis, horse riding.

El-Gouna

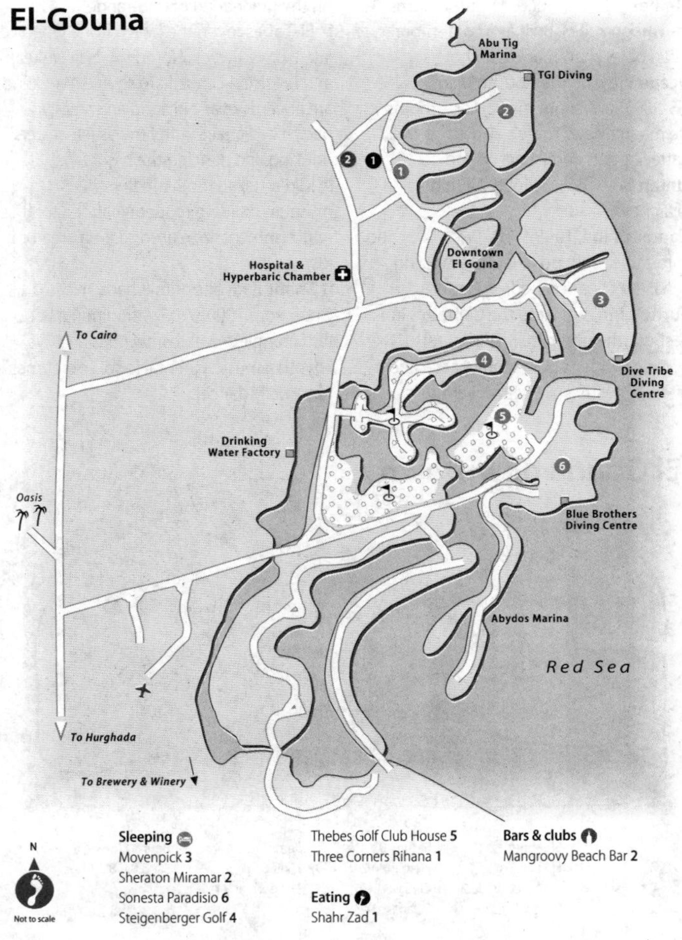

Sleeping
Movenpick **3**
Sheraton Miramar **2**
Sonesta Paradisio **6**
Steigenberger Golf **4**
Thebes Golf Club House **5**
Three Corners Rihana **1**

Eating
Shahr Zad **1**

Bars & clubs
Mangroovy Beach Bar **2**

B **Three Corners Rihana Resort**, in central Gouna. T065-580025-9, F580030. Striking Nubian-style architecture, 1 main restaurant, shuttle bus to beach. 183 rooms, 14 for handicapped, 15 suites with kitchenettes. Low building – just 2 floors, constructed 1999. Freshwater pool, children's pool. All water sports here, other sports in village including horseriding and go-karting. No pets allowed.

B **Dawar El-Omda**, central Gouna, T065-545060. A smaller hotel, with comfortable rooms furnished in traditional Egyptian style. Suites also available. The hotel's name literally means 'Omda's home,' (chief's home) and as such, the design resembles an Egyptian community leader's house. Rooms are furnished in traditional Egyptian style.

C **El-Khan**, T065-545060. 21 guest rooms, 4 honeymoon suites. Built as a contemporary version of "el khan" Canvasary hotels.

C **Ocean View**, in the Abu Tig Marina, T065-580350. A slight misnomer – rooms have marina view. There's also an open-air theatre, 2 pools and 2 bars on site.

C **Sultan Bey**, T065-545600. All domes and arches.

D **Captain's Inn**, T065-580170/71. Cozy and comfortable rooms, overlooking Abu Tig Marina; the cheapest beds in Gouna.

D **Turtle's Inn**, similar to the **Captain's Inn** in feel, another intimate 3-star motel on the Marina with its own sandy beach and rooftop bar with a nice view over the marina.

Eating

El-Gouna *p422, maps p423 and p424*

Among the most upmarket resorts in Egypt, dining well in El-Gouna takes little effort. Restaurants tend to congregate around each other which makes menu perusing easy. Outside the hotels that feature the more expensive fare, most restaurants are in the central area and the Abu Tig Marina. Unless stated otherwise, the following hotels are situated around the centre.

TT **Biergarten**, varied menu from wurst and sauerkraut to spaghetti. Dancing on Wed.

TT **Bleu Bleu**, Abu Tig Marina, T065-549702-4. Unquestionably Gouna's most elegant restaurant, the French cuisine is superb and set in lovely environs. Prices are on the higher end of mid-range.

TT **El-Tabasco**, on the beach front. Open very late 7 days a week. Noted for its fillet steak and irresistible chocolate souffle. Weekends are advertised as big, loud and smoky party-filled affairs with Egypt's jet- setters drinking and dancing the night away.

TT **Kiki's**, Italian food, top floor of museum building reopened after a total refurbishment, increased seating area but just as cosy.

TT **Shahr Zad**, opposite Rihana Hotel. Open from 1800-0300. A traditional Bedouin tent complete with camel rides and live Egyptian music. Oriental food. Sometimes has a belly dancer.

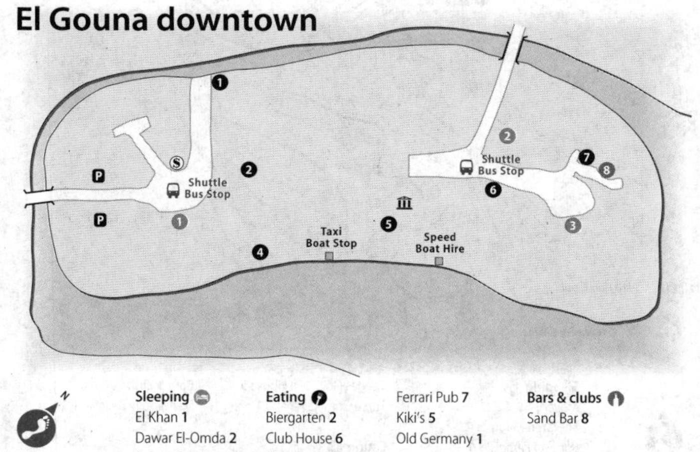

¥¥-¥ Club House, opposite Dawar El-Omda. Try the lunch selection of Italian food, freshly prepared. Beach parties in the evening.

¥¥-¥ Paradisio Bakery and Café. Open at 0600. For the early bird or very late night snack – sugar-coated Danish pastries, muffins and croissants.

¥ Ferrari Club. Stays open later than anyone else. Serves the usual Italian cuisine, pizza, tortellini, gnocci while the TV provides entertainment. Take away provision.

¥ Maison Thomas, Abu Tig Marina. The stellar pizza joint has opened a branch in El-Gouna. The water view is fantastic.

¥ Old Germany. Open 1700 for an early start to the evening. German-run restaurant provides a hearty meal and traditional desserts of mousse and Weckel pudding. Take-away available.

¥ Tamr Henna Food Court. Outdoors only. Mixture of Turkish, Egyptian and Italian dishes. Something for everyone.

Bars and nightclubs

El-Gouna *p422, maps p423 and p*

Besides the standard hotel bars, there are a few funky places to go for a drink.

Sand Bar Pub, next to Sultan Bey Hotel. Small in size but lively atmosphere, cheap draught beer, good selection of wine and tasty bar snacks, cold beer and loud music, very popular with divers.

Barten, at the end of the marina. Intimate bar with modern funky decor highlighted by redlights and minimal furniture. Popular with young trendy Cairenes.

Mangroovy Beach Bar, special seafood dinners with dancing round the bonfire at weekends in season. Access by shuttle bus. Enquire in town.

El-Arena, is open-air, built in Greco-Roman style, with dancing Thu and Fri nights.

Activities and tours

El-Gouna *p422, maps p423 and p424*

Above the water's surface there is **horse riding**, **tennis** and an international grade 18-hole **golf course**. The El-Gouna Tourist Information Office, near Tamr Henna, can organize afternoon trips into the nearby desert to sip tea with the local Bedouin and watch the sunset. Open daily from 0011-1400 and 1600-2300. **Go-Karts**, El-Gouna, T065-549702.

Diving

This location provides for the visitor some flora and fauna not normally found any further north and gives opportunity for day boats to reach dives normally accessed only by liveaboards. Dives may include the 2 wreck sites as well as the coral gardens and pinnacles. Diving Clubs in El-Gouna include:

Blue Brothers Diving Centre, Divers' Lodge, T065-545161.

Subex Paradisio, T065-547934.

Other watersports featured on the beaches include: windsurfing, sailing, parasailing and power boats (T065-580580).

TGI Diving, T065-549702.

The Dive Tribe at Movenpick.

See also diving section, page 418.

Transport

Aïn Sukhna *p420*

Bus Buses bound for Hurghada will stop if you request them to (though you may have to pay the full Hurghada-bound fare). The bus from **Suez** is E£6. There are also plenty of microbuses running along the coast between **Suez** and **Hurghada**, just hitch a ride, if there's a seat, they'll stop. Since there's no real bus stop in Sukhna, the police checkpoint south of the Portrait Hotel is a good place to wait if you're trying to get back to Suez or Cairo.

El-Gouna *p422, maps p423 and p*

Air

Orascom fly turbo prop to **Cairo** but tickets are available only during holidays and special events US$125 return. At just 20 km away, Hurghada airport is so close, and flights so frequent, it's easier to just hop on a bus and transfer between towns. Taxis from Hurghada airport cost E£50-70, depending on your bargaining skills.

Bus

Local Shuttle buses around El-Gouna cost E£5 for daily ticket and E£10 weekly ticket.

Long distance There are several buses commuting between Gouna and **Cairo** daily, run by the **El-Gouna Bus Company**,

T065-541561. Buses bound for Gouna leave from the Hilton Ramsis in central Cairo. In the summer there are buses that leave every few hours during the day and a nightly bus that departs around midnight. It's essential to buy your ticket in advance. The ticket booth is next to the **Superjet** sale's counter at Mastiro Mall on the museum side of the Ramsis Hilton, downtown. Buses bound for **Cairo** leave from Gouna at 0930, 1200, 1500, 1630, 0030, 0130. Tickets are E£50, except for the 1500, which is only E£35. Buses to **Hurghada** leave every 15 mins from 0700-0045, E£5 per day.

Taxi

Taxis running between El-Gouna and **Hurghada** cost E£50-70.

Directory

El-Gouna *p422, maps p423 and p*

Bank There are 3 banks, each open daily from 0900-1400. Money may also be changed in the hotels. **Hospital** El-Gouna Hospital, T065-580012-18. **Internet** Café near Tamr Henna; internet club at Abu Tig Marina. **Pharmacy** Open daily from 0900-1400 and 1800-2100. **Post office** Central; open daily from 0900-1400, closed Fri. **Useful telephone numbers** Emergency: T065-580011; **Hyperbaric chamber**: T012-2187550.

Hurghada

→ *Phone code 065. Colour map 3, grid B5.*

People generally end up in Hurghada, 506 km southeast of Cairo, 395 km south of Suez and 269 km northeast of Luxor, for one of two reasons: either they landed an absurdly cheap package tour, or they're a diver. Extending along the coast for 25 km, the area is especially popular with Eastern European tourists, particularly Russians, who often manage to score an airfare, a week's accommodation in 5-star resort and a diving package for around US$500 per person per week. In some ways it is an ideal location for a new tourist development: it is in a virtually uninhabited region, a long way from the Islamic fundamentalist strongholds; the hotels and holiday villages that have been built are largely self-contained, with the exception of fresh water which is supplied from the Nile valley; and they employ workers from the major cities. Unfortunately, however, although there are many very good hotels, in its dash for growth the government has allowed the 'get-rich-quick' private sector to erect some less attractive accommodation. In truth the area has been developed too quickly since the first constructions in 1992 and frequently without adequate planning controls. While Hurghada's facilities undoubtedly offer good, cheap, beach holidays it has been partially achieved by removing any trace of local Egyptian culture and the Egyptian government has pledged considerable further investment to create more leisure facilities here. ▸▸ *For Sleeping, Eating and other listings, see pages 430-439.*

Ins and outs

Getting there and around Most visitors arrive at Hurghada from the airport, 6 km southwest of the town centre. A taxi to/from town costs E£25-30. Arriving at either bus station (with **Superjet** or **Upper Egypt Bus Co**) you will need to take a short minibus ride unless you plan to stay at the hotels near the Upper Egypt Station. Expect to pay 25pt-E£1, possibly 50pt-E£1 for baggage, especially if it takes up seating. Public transport will drop you in Dahar, west and north of the area's main physical feature, a barren rock outcrop known as Ugly Mountain.

Dahar is the old fishing town that lingered long before the beach resorts started gobbling up the coast. As the base for most locals and backpacking travellers, cheap eats and budget accommodation abound here. The public beach and the Red Sea lie to the east. Two kilometres south, the area known as **Sigala** begins, satiated with

Diving in Hurghada – tales and tips

- A majority of diving centres in the area cater for the German market, so if you want to take any qualifications make sure your instructor can speak your mother tongue. You can't be safe if you cannot understand the instructor. "We all speak the same language underwater", is a sign you should be looking elsewhere.
- Be careful in choosing your dive centre – safety, environmental impact and price should be on your agenda. Bargain basement prices could mean that short cuts are being made.
- Make sure you are insured to dive.
- Fly-by-night operators do exist. Always be on your guard. Go to an approved operator and watch out for scams, eg non-PADI centres flying PADI flags.
- The best options are those centres which have regular guests on dive holidays flying in from abroad.
- Common tricks include: cheap deals, making you feel guilty or rude if you refuse, sudden loss of understanding of your language, free desert/restaurant trips, offers of marriage! Also talk of donations to the decompression chamber, Sinai National Parks and Giftun Islands – these are virtually all compulsory and it is the diver that pays. (The government has introduced a US$1 a day charge for the decompression chamber and a US$2 tax for the Giftun Island Reef).
- HEPCA (Hurghada Environmental Protection and Conservation Association), T065-446674, hepca@hepca.org, is concerned about environmental destruction. It organizes clean ups at various Red Sea sites. Some dive centres are members, but this is not necessarily a guarantee of safety.
- Membership of the Red Sea Diving and Watersport Association and the Egyptian Underwater Sports Association is not proof of safety either. Membership is a requirement of law.
- Contact PADI, BSAC, CMAS and SSI while at home for advice and check out the international diving press.
- Check whether dive centres will pick you up or if you will have to arrange your own transport.

mid-range hotels inland and more expensive ones by the seaside. The 'heart' of package-tour Hurghada, the area is filled with fancy restaurants, dive clubs, cafés and nightlife haunts.

Although it is easy to walk around the relatively compact town it may be necessary, when trying to get to the port or the holiday villages to the south of town, to take cheap local buses and minibuses or the town's taxis which are among the most expensive in the country. Alternatively cars and bicycles can be hired from some of the hotels.

Ferries to Sharm El-Sheikh and Duba depart from the port at Sigala's northern tip. Further south, high-end 5-star resorts wind down the coast back to back with no end in sight. The road continues south all the way to the Sudanese border. ▸▸ *For further details, see Transport, page 438.*

Information The **tourist office** ⓘ *T065-444420-1, open daily 0830-1500*, is the once- smart new building opposite the Marine Sports Club on the west side of the main road. But it now falls short of its glossy beginnings. Given the intense competition between travel agencies and dive centres, there is little additional information that the office provides.

Who sells sea shells?

The answer is nobody should sell shells because nobody wants to buy.

The sale of shells and coral is illegal, and large fines and long prison sentences can be the result if you are successfully prosecuted. Removing anything living or dead from the water in Protected Areas is forbidden. Fishermen are banned from these areas. Continuing to plunder the marine environment will cause permanent damage.

The Environmental Protection Association, along with operators of dive centres and hotels are desperately trying to educate visitors. Unfortunately, they know they have a better chance of educating the tourists not to buy than the locals not to sell.

Sights

Hurghada is more than another place to toast on the beach. It's an international resort that boasts stellar water sports facilities and excellent diving. There are two harbours, one for the local fishing boats and in the other, the marina, boats associated with these sporting activities, excursions and the ferries to Sharm El-Sheikh and Duba. A few hotels have coral gardens actually on their site and there are plenty of coral islands offshore from which to study the hidden life below the warm blue waters. Nightlife is booming as European tourists shake their bellies and their booties into the wee hours of the morning.

The **Marine Museum** ⓘ *T065-500103, daily 0800-1700, E£5 for the museum and its adjacent Red Sea Aquarium*, is about 7 km to the north of the town centre (take a taxi) and is associated with the National Institute of Oceanography and Fisheries. A good place to begin learning about the marine life of the area with stuffed examples of coral reef fish, shark, manta rays and associated bird life as well as samples of coral and shells. **The Aquarium** ⓘ *daily 0900-2300, E£5, camera E£2, video E£10*, on Sharia El-Corniche adjacent to Three Corners Village, is quite small but has live specimens in well-marked tanks and may be worth the E£5, especially if you are not a diver.

Time can be spent wandering around the **bazaars** of Dahar even if you don't intend to buy. In the short term it's an interesting experience for all your senses. The noise and jostle of people, bikes, donkeys, cars, bright tacky souvenirs, tired white donkeys, gallabahs and flip flops and veils aside scantily clad Russian tourists, the smell of shisha pipes, herbs, carpets, dead chickens and bad drains.

If you want to observe a bit of the real life of Hurghada residents take a stroll around the "Egyptian areas" behind the Three Corners Empire Hotel, near the "mountain" behind Sharia Abdel Aziz, and various other side streets in Dahar or by the ferry port in Sigala. The housing is pretty crumbly and the streets strewn with litter. Here you will find women staying at home. They are traditionally dressed (well covered), scruffy children play in the dirt of the streets, boys are bold and loud and girls in *hejabs* wander from school in demure, giggly groups. It's always noisy: cockerels, car horns and cart vendors continuously calling to sell their wares. There's been a bit of a move to clean up these areas because of the tourists but you can still get a glance of life as it really is in the rest of Egypt.

The **old harbour** area is an interesting stroll as well, dotted with bright coloured fishing vessels, boat construction yards and small shops catering to locals. In the autumn there are some spectacular sunsets so try and head for a view of the mountains.

Dive sites

Among the best dive sites are **Um Gamar**, 1½ hours north, a plateau of beautiful soft and hard corals with a good drop off and cave. Also has a kingdom of poisonous snakes. Dives are made onto a slope that drops gradually from 50 feet to 250 feet. **Sha'ab Al-Erg**, is 1½ hours north. There's a coral plateau including table coral and, if you are lucky, manta rays and dolphins. At the **Careless Reef** you may see shark. There is a spectacular drop off and ergs. This site is for advanced divers only, due to the currents. The island stands over three columns of rare corals resting originally on a 10 to 15 m surface. **Giftun Islands** are close to Hurghada and thus very popular, and fast deteriorating. Fortunately they possess a number of reefs still teeming with plenty of fish including moray eels. **El-Fanadir**, is a popular site close to Hurghada with a pretty reef wall and drop off with nice soft corals. **Sha'ab Abu Ramada**, 40 minutes south, with a good drop off, has lots of fish and coral. Usually a drift dive. The corals shapes are unique: round and brain-like.

Further afield are a series of islands including **Shadwan**, **Tawlah** and **Gubal**, around which there are less spoiled dive sites with chances of seeing pelagic fish and dolphins.

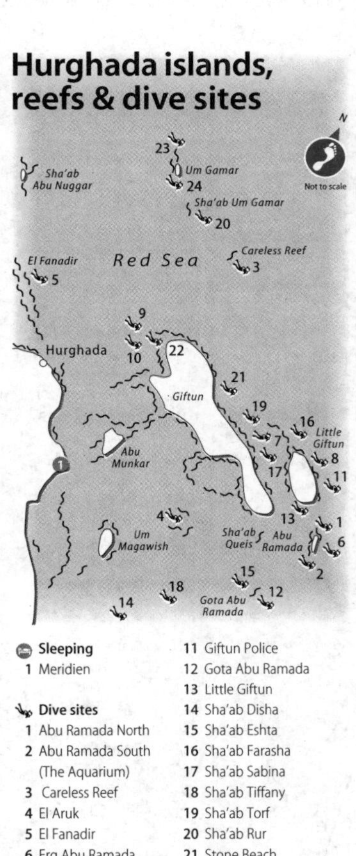

Hurghada islands, reefs & dive sites

Sleeping
1 Meridien

Dive sites
1 Abu Ramada North
2 Abu Ramada South (The Aquarium)
3 Careless Reef
4 El Aruk
5 El Fanadir
6 Erg Abu Ramada
7 Erg Sabina
8 Erg Somaya
9 Fanous East
10 Fanous West
11 Giftun Police
12 Gota Abu Ramada
13 Little Giftun
14 Sha'ab Disha
15 Sha'ab Eshta
16 Sha'ab Farasha
17 Sha'ab Sabina
18 Sha'ab Tiffany
19 Sha'ab Torf
20 Sha'ab Rur
21 Stone Beach
22 Turtle Bay
23 Um Gamar North
24 Um Gamar South

Beachs and etiquette

There are public beaches ⓘ *E£2*, which are rather dirty at Dahar near the Three Corners Empire, around the Port at Sigala and after the V junction on Sharia Sheraton Sigala. At all three, and in particular the first two it is socially unacceptable, and inadvisable to wear a bathing costume or less. In any case you will invite attention. Women sit in a proper manner on upright chairs and if they do venture into the sea, they are fully clothed. Men can wear shorts.

If you are not staying at a hotel with beach access, the only option is to pay to use one of the resorts' beaches. This costs between E£20-50 daily. Resist temptation to bathe at building sites and bits of derelict beach as you will almost certainly invite harassment.

Excursions from Hurghada

By boat It's possible to take a trip to **Tobia Island** with its sandy lagoons and untouched (for how long?) corals surrounded by turquoise water. THere's also a sea cruise via **Shadwan Island**, the **Gulf of Suez**, and even Ras Mohammed (see apge 371). The trip takes at least 6 hours and costs about E£200 – check with local travel guides, see page 438.

By land A day trip to the Roman ruins of **Mons Claudianus** near Jebel Fatira (1,355 m) is possible from Hurghada. There's evidence here of Roman military presence, a Roman road and columns as well as a Roman settlement with houses, stable and temple to Serap and the Roman Fortress of Om Dikhal. It's also a mixture of quarry and fortress – you can see the remains of the cells used to house the workers/prisoners who quarried the stone.

Before venturing into the desert, hire suitable transport, take sensible provisions and a local guide. Travel agents and hotels can help.

It's also possible to get to **Mons Porphyritis**, 55 km northwest of Hurghada at foot of Jebel Abu Dukhan (1,641 m), where there's a ruin of a Roman temple and ancient quarries for porphyry, a popular stone used for sarcophagi and facing walls.

Sleeping

Hurghada *p425, maps p430 and p432*
There are as many officially registered hotels in Hurghada as there are non-registered ones – and new ones springing up all the time. Although most visitors pre-book their accommodation as part of a package with their flight there should be no problem, except perhaps during the winter high season, for independent travellers to find a room. All of the hotels have roof tanks to store fresh water piped in from the Nile Valley but, depending on their capacity and electricity supplies, there are on occasion problems with the water provisions. If the

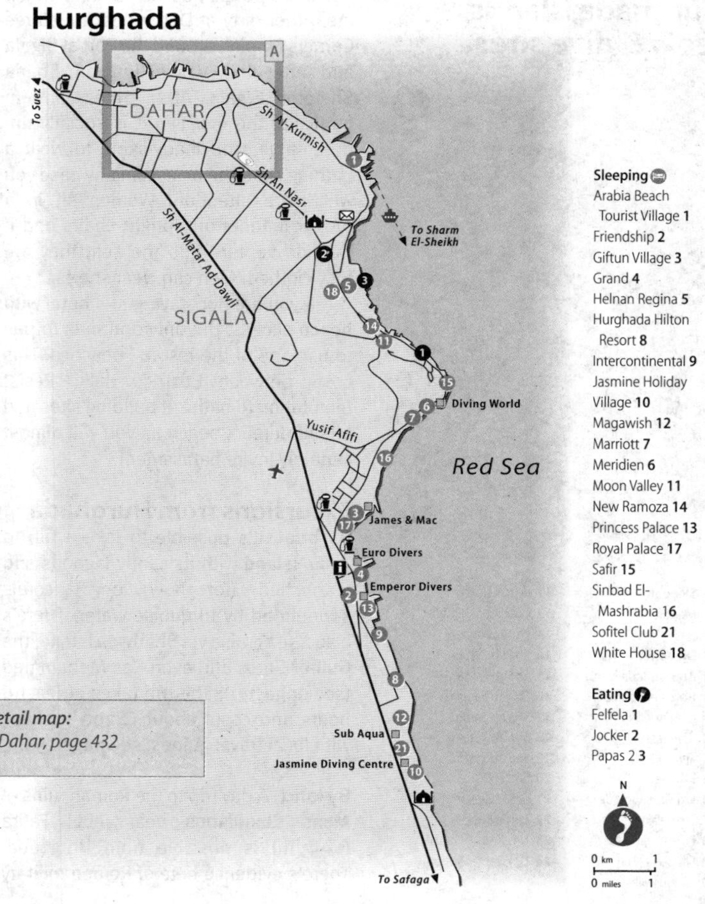

Hurghada
A
DAHAR
To Suez
Sh Al-Kurnish
Sh An Nasr
Sh Al-Matar Ad-Dawli
To Sharm El-Sheikh
SIGALA
Diving World
Yusif Afifi
Red Sea
James & Mac
Euro Divers
Emperor Divers
Sub Aqua
Jasmine Diving Centre
To Safaga
Sleeping
Arabia Beach Tourist Village 1
Friendship 2
Giftun Village 3
Grand 4
Helnan Regina 5
Hurghada Hilton Resort 8
Intercontinental 9
Jasmine Holiday Village 10
Magawish 12
Marriott 7
Meridien 6
Moon Valley 11
New Ramoza 14
Princess Palace 13
Royal Palace 17
Safir 15
Sinbad El-Mashrabia 16
Sofitel Club 21
White House 18
Eating
Felfela 1
Jocker 2
Papas 2 3
N
0 km 1
0 miles 1

Detail map:
A Dahar, page 432

planned tourist developments along the coast towards Safaga go ahead it will be necessary to build at least one desalination plant. The water supply is the main obstacle to more major expansion along the coast, and the main source of relief to environmentalists and reefs in need of a break from reckless building and mindless tourists. That said, there are still more than 100 good quality hotels to choose from. Bear in mind the best deals often come from outside Hurghada in the form of package tours. Like everywhere else in Egypt, prices change, sometimes drastically, depending on the number of tourists in the region, so treat these prices quoted as variable. Also bear in mind that hotels in Hurghada change management and ownership frequently. Sharia Sheraton, the main drag, was so named for the hotel that towered above it, one of Hurghada's first luxury resorts. It no longer exists, though the street name hasn't changed, but the *Meridien* has seized its old edifice. It may be confusing, but fear not, the beds remain, in numbers too big to count. Single female travellers should be on guard when staying at budget hotels.

AL **Conrad International Resort**, 10 mins from airport and 15 mins from centre, shuttle bus to centre, T065-443250-7, F443258-9, foconrad@menanet.net. Many restaurants: La Palma for breakfast and buffet dinner; Chinese menu in Ginger House; El-Khan for local flavour and colour; Sunrise pool-side bar; Café Trottoir, a French-style coffee house overlooking gardens and sea; Poseidon, recommended for fish and seafood. There's also a disco bar and Trocadero piano bar for relaxation. Sports facilities include volleyball, a huge pool, billiards, 2 all-weather tennis courts, basketball, health club and a diving centre. Other assets are money exchange, shops, same-day laundry and medical clinic. Very friendly staff.

AL **Hurghada Hilton Resort**, 10-15 mins from airport and from town centre, T065-442116-8, F442113, hurghada_resort@hilton.com. Good range of high standard facilities, 161 rooms round the main pool and near the beach, 40 garden rooms in the hotel block on the desert side of the road all with a/c, bath/shower. All the usual Hilton facilities, free day time shuttle to town centre, 2 pools, private marina, tennis, squash, health club, dive centre. Selection of restaurants, bars, tennis, pool. The good service one would expect from this chain of hotels.

AL **Intercontinental**, T065-446911, F446910. Highly recommended as the best in town – and one of the best in Egypt. Relatively new, opened 1996, secluded bay, large pool, 3 restaurants, bars, health club, 3 floodlit tennis courts, 2 squash courts, billiards, medical centre, horse riding, shops, diving centre. Sheer luxury.

AL **Marriott**, T065-443950, F443970. Tranquil and relaxed, large pool, 3 bars, shops, water sport and dive centre, health club, 2 flood-lit, tennis courts, 2 a/c squash courts.

AL **Royal Palace Hotel**, T065-443660-6, F443661, royalpalace@hurghadaie.eg.com. 120 rooms, private beach, 3 restaurants, good food, guests are 80% German and 20% British tour groups. With its Sonesta Diving Centre (with 8 instructors) and easy access to the beach for disabled people, this is among the best hotels in Hurghada.

A **Grand Hotel**, T065-447490, F447649. Rooms all have balcony/terrace. Hotel has a private sandy beach, several restaurants, coffee shop, bars, disco, tennis, health club, water sports. A very comfortable and lively beach resort.

A **Hilton Plaza**, off Corniche, T065-549745-7, F547597, hrghitwrm@hilton.com. 217 quality rooms, private beach and marina, reputable diving centre, 4 restaurants: La Gondola serving Italian food; Sea Grill on the beach; Coral Café in Lobby and Terrace Grill by the pool.

A **Meridien**, T065-442000-2, F442333. Distinctive art deco circular main building, formerly the Sheraton, recently renovated. In addition to stand rooms, there are 9 pool-side cabanas and 10 2-storey 4-room chalets on 2 very good beaches. All the usual luxury facilities: 3 restaurants, bars, large pool, tennis, water sports, boat cruises, glass bottomed boat, fishing trips and barbecue.

A **Sofitel Club**, El-Corniche, T065-447261-69, F447260, sofitel@hurghadaie.eg.com. Directly on beach, just 20 mins' drive from airport. 312 rooms with balcony, many interconnecting, most have sea view, all facilities, various restaurants, bars, disco, fitness club, spa with jacuzzi and steam bath, tennis, squash, shops, outdoor amphitheatre for entertainments, kids club, pool, horse riding. Free activities include archery, gymnastics, kayaking, water gym. Pay ones: water skiing, wind surfing, catamaran sailing. Ideal for families and very cosmopolitan. Restaurants including The Terrace with German food, German music and German beer, also O'Reilly's Irish Pub with Irish beer (Guinness) and Irish food.

B **Arabia Beach Tourist Village**, 9 km from centre, T065-548790, F544777. Large, well-equipped, new, hotel with mainly German guests. Saltwater pools, tennis and squash courts, jetski, water-skiing, fitness centre, and Nautico Diving Centre with 6 instructors.

B **Hilton Villas**, on desert side of the road opposite main Hilton. 22 2-storey villas with 4 bedrooms, 3 bathrooms (shower), 2 lounges and a kitchen sleeping up to 12 people, built round a pool. Bar plus full use of all facilities at Hilton Hotel. Excellent value for groups. See Hurghada Hilton Resort above for more details.

B **Magawish Tourist Village**, south of the airport, T065-442620-2, F442759, magawish@link.com.eg. 314 rooms, excellent standard, private bay and beach to south of port, offers all the normal facilities plus a wide range of water sports and children's activities.

B **Safir**, El-Corniche, on its own beach-front lagoon, 10 mins drive from airport, T065-442901-3, F442904. 123 rooms with usual facilities, variety of restaurants, bars, shops, billiards, pool with sun deck and a marina with aqua sports centre, a lively hotel, comfortable.

B **Shedwan Golden Beach**, town centre, T065-547044, F548045. Reasonable standard hotel with 152 rooms, restaurant, bar, disco, banking, private beach, pool, tennis, squash, dive centre, guests mainly French, Belgian and German.

B **Sinbad El-Mashrabia Village**, Sharia Sheraton, to south of the port, T065-443330-1, F443344. Very good Moorish-

Dahar

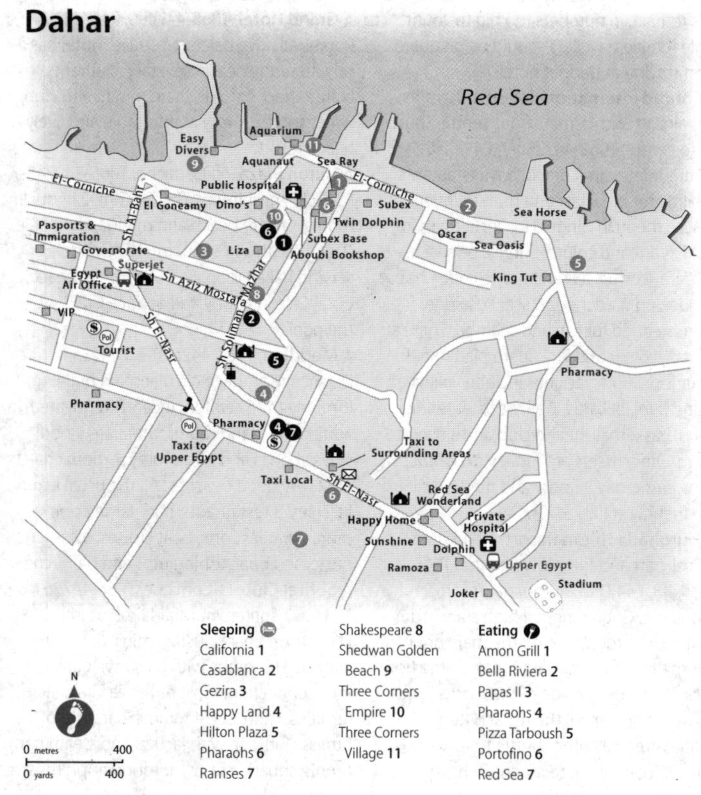

style, 4-star hotel with140 rooms, 3 pools, parasailing and excellent watersports, guests are 75% German.

B Three Corners Empire, town centre adjacent to the Khan El-Khalili shopping centre, T065-549200-9, F549212. Deluxe hotel with 366 rooms and several bars, hence lively atmosphere. It's a bit of a blemish in the area, but the location compensates for this a bit. 3 restaurants: international, seafood and oriental. Diving at Khan El-Khalili shopping centre; windsurfing and snorkelling at Three Corners Village, 2 outdoor freshwater pools, beach at 200 m is pebble here, bank, laundry.

C Giftun Village, T065-442665, F442666. 391 comfortable bungalows set in a vast private sandy beach a little out of town. Pool, squash, tennis and all water sports are free except diving, windsurfing and tennis lessons. Main restaurant provides buffet meals and there are bars and discos for evening entertainment. Barakuda Dive Centre within the hotel.

C Jasmine Holiday Village, T065-446442, F442441. Big, good standard hotel with 362 rooms. But it's so large that it is a long walk from the main building to the beach. Has its own diving centre.

C-D Three Corners Empire, central near hospital on Shari Sayed Karim, T065-549200, F3369049. Hotel with 82 rooms, 2 pools, bar and 2 restaurants, 200 m to the beach. Use of facilities at Three Corners Village.

C-D Three Corners Village, El-Corniche, T065-547816-7, F547514. Belgian management, part of the empire, centrally located and situated on a beautiful sandy beach. Has 136 rooms with magnificent views and good facilities, 2 restaurants, 2 bars, freshwater pool, dive centre, windsurfing centre, volley ball, minigolf.

D Gezira, off Sharia El-Bahr, in northeast of town near the poor public beach, T065-547785, F543708. Hotel with 30 good rooms built around a courtyard. There's also a restaurant, bar and disco.

D Moon Valley, Sharia Sheraton, to south of port, T065-442811, F443830. Former backpackers' retreat with 30 rooms, which has moved up-market. Has a private beach, and diving courses around a small coral reef. Recommended.

D Princess Club/Palace, about 3 km south of town, T065-443100, 447701-3, F447708. 160 spacious rooms, 2 separate parts directly opposite one another. Palace offers better accommodation than the cheaper Club, but both offer good service in a cool, relaxing atmosphere. The main building has European and Egyptian buffet restaurants, or you can also eat at the hotel's private beach or by main swimming pool. The Fox and Hounds serves drinks and the Vienna serves snacks. There are also shops, bank, squash, tennis, (flood-lit), gym, pool, private beach, windsurfing with instruction, hire of jetskis, waterskiing, pedalos, British-managed Red Sea Scuba School located in Princess Village, Emperor Divers within the complex.

E Friendship Village, T065-443100-2/ 447701, F447800. Budget hotel with 129 clean and spacious rooms and the use of facilities at Princess Club (see above). Large open-air restaurant, pizzeria, shop, laundry service, buffet breakfast, 2 tennis courts, pool table, use of beach and, doctor on call.

E Mena House, T065-442303. Budget hotel with 20 rooms which caters mainly for students. Facilities include: restaurant, bar, oriental cabaret and belly dancing, private beach, windsurfing, diving with multi-lingual instructors and day trips to Giftun Island.

E-F Ramses Hotel, on dirt road from Sharia Arab El-Dahar. Among the better budget deals in the area, rooms are quite clean, though toilets not so. A/c available in some rooms.

F California, Dahar, T065-549101. Good location for reaching the centre or the sea on foot. Some rooms have balconies, some with sea view. Reasonably clean. Breakfast available.

F Casablanca, on the Corniche in Dahar opposite the public beach, T065-548292. Generally the rooms are quite large. Some overlook the sea. The bathrooms are a little grimy.

F Happy Land Hotel, El-Sheikh Sebak St off 23rd July St, T065-547373. A dismal place, but rooms with bathroom are clean. Shared facilities reasonable.

F New Ramoza, Sigala. 43 rooms with a/c or fans and balconies, good value, popular with students, small private beach, TV lobby and disco.

F Old Ramoza, next door to New Ramoza. Has 24 rooms with fans, communal showers, guests are students or Egyptians.

F **Pharaohs**, around the corner from California (see above). Rooms vary in quality, best are on top floor where a sea view is available.

F **Shakespeare Hotel**, on the edge of the Three Corners area by the roundabout on Sharia Sayyed, T065-546256. Large, but dingy rooms. Some rooms have a/c and are better than others, communal lounge areas with fridge.

F **St George Hotel**, off Sharia El-Nasr, 2 blocks behind Bank Misr, from where it's signposted, T065-548246. Rooms dingy, but hotel is pleasant with roof view.

F **White House**, Sharia Sheraton, near old harbour, T065- 443688, F442085. Very clean, up-market budget hotel, German-owned, 45 comfortable a/c rooms with bath and balconies, decent restaurant, TV lounge, guests can use facilities of Giftun Village which is a short taxi ride away – for divers this transfer is free.

Camping

There are so many cheap hotels that camping is unnecessary. However, **National Youth Camp**, 5 km north of town, E£5 per night, is the site most recommended.

BEWARE If camping on the coast, large areas of shoreline are still mined, enter fenced-off areas at your peril.

Ras Abu Soma

A new tourist complex has sprouted up just 48 km, 45-min drive, south of Hurghada on the peninsula of Abu Soma. A few are already open and there are plans for 13 new luxury hotels still in the works. The 18-hole golf course covering 400,000 sq m and designed by Gary Player, is on the highest point of the peninsula, almost 22 m above sea level and offers stunning views. The intention has been to attract 'well-to-do' visitors, such as Japanese who love golf,

into their 60-room club house. Other activities are provided by a fresh water swimming pool, lots of watersports, the Sheraton's dive centre and the seven coral reefs in the vicinity. There's also a marina on sight. A 4 km long promenade is in the works.

AL **Sheraton Soma Bay**, T065-545915. Constructed in Pharoanic style, looks like the first pylon of a huge temple, white sandy beaches, 277 rooms, 35 suites, all with quality facilities and sea view, rooms for disabled, 18-hole golf course, 4 pools, 3 restaurants, 6 bars, tennis, squash, even desert safaris.

Eating

Hurghada *p425, maps p430 and p432*

Expensive dining experiences in Hurghada are pretty much confined to the resorts and upscale hotels. But beyond their gates, good restaurants in Hurghada are as plentiful as good hotels. Many are in the central area (in Dahar) but there's also a substantial scattering in Sigala and along the southern most resort stretch.

Jocker Fish Restaurant, Midan Sheraton, Sigala. Has a long-standing reputation. Pick your own fish, pay by weight. Frequented by tourists and locals alike. A no-frills kind of fish joint.

Lagoona, at Hilton Resort, T065-443567. Open daily 1930-2330. A fish restaurant and international dishes. Open aspect gives breathtaking views.

Portofino, by General Hospital, Dahar, on Sharia Dr Said Koraiem, T065-546250. Friendly atmosphere with sublime pasta dishes. Besides Italian, the menu also features seafood and some Egyptian specialties.

There are several restaurants, cafés and food stalls in the centre of **Dahar**, of which the best are:

Amon Grill, by trees on Sharia Sayyed, has the cheapest burgers and shishtawook, take away available;

Felfela, Sharia Sheraton, T065-442411, popular chain that got its start in the capital offers modestly-priced authentic Egyptian food, overlooking the sea, a little out of town around the resort strip, but worth it for the view, and the good quality food;

Golden Spur Restaurant, opposite Marriott Hotel, T065-444414, steaks and burgers and Mexican food;

Nefertiti, at the south end of Sharia Abdel Aziz Mustafa;

Pizza Tarboush, opposite Restaurant Bella Riviera, T065-548456, student discount, over 20 types of pizza generously and cheaply served, plus salads, seafood and standard grilled fare;.

Pharaohs, Sharia 23rd July, near Red Sea I, fish, meat and kebabs, beer also available;

🍴 **Pronto**, up the dirt road opposite the supermarket near 🍴 **Papas 2**, frequented by locals, fare is the standard local bread, salad and meat (kofta, chicken, pigeon or fish), fresh juices are heavenly, from US$1-4;
🍴 **Quick Cook**, Sharia Al-Horreya, where you can sit and watch the chaos of the bazaar and enjoy a cheap and quick has shawerma;
🍴 **Red Sea Restaurant**, near El-Dahar square on the market street, T065-547704, vibrant rooftop terrace, popular with package tourists wanting a change of atmosphere from their buffet dinners, excellent fresh fish dishes;
🍴 **Restaurant Bella Riviera**, on Sharia Abdel Aziz opposite Pizza Tarboush, T065-548985, authentic food and friendly atmosphere, serves a variety of meat and seafood dishes, as well as pizza.

In **Sigala**, try the following:
🍴 **Agra Roma**, opposite Papa's Beach in southern Sigala, offers reasonable Indian food for modest prices, it's also a pub;
🍴 **Tamar Hena Café**, under the Golf Hotel, a good place to watch the bikes and donkeys;
🍴 **Rossi Pizzeria**, Sharia Sheraton, Sigala, T065-446012. Traditional Italian cuisine and sandwiches with a decent salad bar;

Ahwas and cafés

Authentic local *ahwas* are in Dahar. There are a number by the small mosque in the centre. Strictly speaking they're generally patroned by local men only, but with so many foreigners around, few take offence if visitors enjoy a *shisha* or a cup of tea and gaze at the world on the streets around you. There are also numerous tourist cafés including those mentioned here as restaurants and bars. Try the sugar cane juice E£1, fresh orange E£3, or whatever fruit is in season, at the best juice shop in Hurghada on Sharia Sayyed, next to Supermarket Rashidy.

Grand Café, Sharia Sheraton Sigala, just after the V junction, is a pleasant place to stop for awhile. Dimly lit with a soothing fountain, the cafe overlooks the beach and sea. Fish is served from about E£15. Whilst you're enjoying the lack of hassle you could ask owner Kelal to tell you tales of how it used to be in Hurghada before major tourist expansion.

La Torta, Sharia Sheikh Sabak, T065-549504, has nice cakes, good ice cream and Ramadan sweets.

Bars and nightclubs

Hurghada *p425, maps p430 and p432*

Bars

At the last count there were over 100 bars in Hurghada.

Cheers, open 24 hrs at the Shedwan Hotel. The place to go for late night munchies.

Chill, near New Ramoza Hotel, Sigala. A very chilled out vibe by the sea, frequented almost exclusively by divers. Has BBQs, a dance night, full moon party and diver/ tourist volleyball matches.

Fisherman's Pub in Giftun Village.

Papas 2, on the V junction of Sharia Sheraton and El-Hadaba in Sigala. Dark, wooden decor, live music on occasion.

Peanuts Bar, next to Empire Hotel. Copious amounts of peanuts available to supplement copious amounts of beer, a happening spot with package tourists from the nearby Three Corners.

The Pub, Hilton Resort, T065-443567. With a variety of draught beers, and local drinks, live music most nights, open 1700-0200.

Papa's III, Sigala. Papa's newest effort, has proven quite successful. It's a happening waterside bar, and a delightful place to have drink after a day of diving and beach lounging.

Clubs

As a major tourist resort there is less concern about offending Islamic sensibilities. As a result, besides the main hotel restaurants which feature discos and serve alcohol, there are many clubs in town. There are plenty of belly dancing shows at all the big hotels on a nightly basis, mostly performed by Russian women.

Calypso, on the Hill (Sharia Hadaba) at the southern end of Sigala, toward the resort strip. A bonafide disco with a like it or not Russian show everynight at 0130. Still, the music is good, and the place usually packed. Minimum charge is E£30.

The Blackout, a bit of a haul from the city centre, at the southern part of the resort strip on the way out of town. It's worth the trek on Tue, though, when a popular foam party has the place pumping (minimum charge E£50).

Kalaboush, Arabella Hotel, which claims the first karaoke bar, is another popular spot to go dancing.

Shopping

Hurghada *p425, maps p430 and p432*

Hurghada has very few local shops although all of the major hotels and holiday villages have shopping arcades which cater for tourists' requirements. Souvenir stands are plentiful. T-shirts, towels, carpets, jewellery, scarabs, Shisha pipes, papyrus, pyramids, stuffed camels – the list is endless. If buying gold or silver make sure it's stamped and you get a certificate of authenticity. Remember trade in coral and some animals and fish is illegal. Herbs here are much cheaper than at home, but if your travels will take you beyond Hurghada, better deals exist elsewhere. The bazaar area is lively but the stalls around the Red Sea Restaurant (go straight at each junction) tend to have better bargains. Duty free goods can be bought at the Pyramid at the roundabout in Sigala and next to the Royal Palace and Ambassador hotels. Bear in mind that passport stamps for duty free are only valid for one day. There are supermarkets on Sharia Sayyed, Three Corners and Sharia Abdel Aziz.

Small shops, selling limited provisions, such as **Andalus** shop on Sharia Sayyed can be found throughout Dahar. Fruit and vegetables are easy to get in the Mosque square and by Quick Cook in the centre.

It is now possible to obtain most toiletry and feminine requirements although, as these are imports, they are considerably more expensive than you might expect. If you are travelling further south this is your last chance to stock up on products such as shower gel, moisturizer, tampons, contact lens solution and hair conditioner.

Bookshops

Aboudi Bookshop, near Three Corners Empire. Good selection of European books, maps and guides.

Al Ahram, T065-443401, near Sindbad Hotel. Open 0900-1300 and 1800-2200.

Jetline, in Arabia Beach. Has a good selection of books on the Red Sea.

Pyramid Bookshop, in Jasmine Village. With international newspapers.

Hotel Intercontinental, T065-446911. Has daily newspapers in Arabic and English (sometimes just 1 day old). You can also find the Hurghada Bulletin, an informative magazine that offers the latest listings.

Activities and tours

Hurghada *p425, maps p430 and p432*

Diving

Though the terribly rapid development of tourist sites and the excessive underwater traffic from thoughtless divers keen to take a piece of the Red Sea home has yielded tragic destruction in the reefs around Hurghada, the area still boasts some of the best diving in the world. The waters are warm year round, visibility is always good, and currents are mild. In addition to a wide variety of coral, vast schools of sparkling tiny fish and large pelagic swimmers along the seabed's deep walls, you may have the chance to swim with dolphins, hammerheads and manta rays. This is a selection of the better diving clubs available. All teach accredited dive courses and offer liveaboard safaris to nearby sights, daily and extended trips. Shop around a bit before you commit, make sure you can get on with your dive instructor and that s/he speaks your language. Choose with care as diving can be a dangerous sport, check the qualifications, see what safety precautions are in place. Cheap may not be best.

Bubbles Diving College, in Andrea's Hotel, Sigala, T065-442057, www.bubbles-diving.com. In addition to Scuba, specializes in free diving.

Dive Point, at Coral Beach, T065-447162, T0123165708, hurghada@dive_point.com.

Diver's Lodge, at Intercontinental, T065-446911, www.divers_lodge.com. Excellent reputation.

Diving World, Le Meridien, T065-442000.

Easy Divers, Three Corners Village, T065-548816, easydive@intouch.com. Has good reputation, caters for all levels with instructors speaking numerous languages.

Euro Divers, Grand Hotel, T065-443751.

James and Mac, Giftun Village, T065-442665, info@ james/mac.com. Good reputation.

Jasmine Diving Centre, Jasmine Village,

T065-446455, info@jasmin-diving.com. A German-run centre, among the best in the area.

Sub Aqua, Sofitel and Conrad T/F065-442473, www.subaqua-diveteam.de.

Subex, opposite Sandbeach Hotel, T065-547593, redsea@subex.org. Swiss-run, very good reputation, 3 branches: in Dahar, Gouna and Quseir.

Red Sea Scuba Schools, Hilton, T065-444854, www.red-sea-scuba-schools.com. Also known as **Empire Divers** and has branch in Sharm El-Sheik.

Voodoo Divers, Mirette Hotel on the coastal road between Sigala and El-Dahar, T065-548159, www.voodoodivers.com.

(See pages 55 and 427 for more diving information and tips.)

Boat trips

All-day boat excursions to **Giftun Island**, now often overcrowded with boats anchored offshore, are available from most hotels which usually add a 20-25% commission to include rental of snorkelling equipment. Expect your tour to include a fish barbecue and perhaps a trip in a glass bottomed boat. From the marine port, you can find a spot on a boat for E£35-40. If booked through a hotel, the average price to the island is around E£50. For around E£400, you can rent a private boat from the port or the athletic marine club.

Some tour operators and hotels, including: **Flying Dolphin Sea Trips, Nefertiti Diving Centre** and **Sunshine Sea Trips**, also organize longer boat trips including 3-day trips to **Gobal Island**, overnight excursions to **Giftun**, and expeditions to the deeper reefs such as the **House of Sharks** (20 km south) where experienced divers can see hammerheads, tiger sharks and other exotic marine life.

To view the underwater world and keep dry there is the Finnish-built a/c 44-seater **Sinbad Submarine**, T065-444688/90, offering a 3-hour roundtrip including an hour underwater. Should be booked the day before. Transfer by boat 30 mins, out to submarine, which goes down to 22 m with diver in front attracting fish with food (not a recommended procedure). Carries 44 passengers. Trips everyday leaving from 1000-1200. Price US$45-50 for adults and US$22.50 for children under 12.

Aquascope has a deep hull with glass sides. Transfer to it from the Marine Sports Club near the Grand Hotel. It travels to **Magawish Island** and back. Operates 1000-1400 and each trip takes 2 hours, costs US$30-40; $15 for children, reservations necessary, T065-444146.

Horseriding

At Hotel Intercontinental.

Quad bike

For a short, and expensive desert trip, **Friendship Village**, T010-1567571.

Volleyball

At most of the beachside hotels and the **Chill Bar**.

Watersports

Windsurfing is particularly good thanks to the perpetually gusty winds, usually 4-8 on Beaufort Scale. Equipment of varying weights can be hired from a number of outlets. Many hotels offer equipment but much of it is outdated. Ensure your choice of centre has a rescue boat that works. The best equipment is found at centres offering windsurf holiday packages. Try:

Planet Windsurf, at Three Corners Village; **Happy Surf**, at Magawish, Jasmine Village, Giftun Village and Sofitel (German-run). Expect to pay about E£50 per hr, E£150 for 1 day and E£610 for a week.

Jet skiing and **water skiing** Jet skis can be hired for E£200 per hr and waterskis from E£220.

Snorkelling Boats with motors to tow or for fishing or snorkelling are also for hire. Three Corners, Shedwan and Coral Beach hotels all have house reefs, but the best reefs are offshore. With a tour, a day's snorkelling, including lunch, costs from US$20-40. It is cheaper to take your own lunch and water if that is an option. Good snorkelling sites include **Giftun Islands**, **Fanadir**, **Um Gamar**. **Sailing boats** are available too.

Catamarans and **toppers** are best found at the windsurf schools. **Pedalos** and **banana boats** can be found at the larger hotels.

Fishing **Marine Sports Club**, next to the Grand Hotel, T065-442974. Remember spear fishing is illegal in the Red Sea.

Tour operators and travel agents

Besides the independent travel agents there is at least one in each major hotel. With the Nile Valley only a few hours away, many travel agencies organize daylong tours to Luxor that depart Hurghada with the early morning convoy at 0600 and return in the early evening.

Eastmar, 12-13 Shopping Centre, T065-444581.
Menatours, Midan Sigala, T065-444465.
Misr Travel, at Tourist Centre, T065-442130.
Thomas Cook, in Midan Sigala, T065-541870.
Travco, T065-446623/4.

Transport

Hurghada *p425, maps p430 and p432*

Air

International flights go to **Dusseldorf**, **Frankfurt**, **Geneva**, **Milan**, **Munich**, **Rome**, **Vienna** and **Zurich**. There are regular daily flights from Hurghada to **Cairo** at 0845 and a frequent service on other days during the week. Flights also go direct to **Luxor**, Tue, Wed and Sat and to **Sharm El-Sheikh** on Fri, Sat and Sun. Times and numbers of flights change daily so it is best to visit **EgyptAir** in person, as the phones are rarely answered. Flights to Cairo and Sharm El-Sheikh are approximately E£500. Airport: T065-442831/442594.

Airlines EgyptAir, in the square with the new mosque and a branch on Sharia Sheraton, T065-447503-7/442831. Open 0800-2000.

Bicycle

Bikes can be rented from the street next to Bank Misr and on Sharia Abdel Aziz.

Bus

Local Minibus and microbuses make regular circuits of Dahar. A ride from Dahar to Sigala and the resorts should cost E£1-2.

Long distance The bus station is on the main north-south road to the south of the main town. Bus companies include **Upper Egypt Bus Co**, T065-547582; **El-Gouna**, T065-541561; and **Superjet**, T065-544722.

Upper Egypt runs regular daily buses north to **Suez** (every hr, 0600-2400; 5 hrs; E£20-25) and **Cairo** (0800, 1000, 1130, 1300, 1430, 1730, 1930, 2030, 2200, 2330, 0130; 6-7 hrs, between E£30-50 depending on time of departure), and southeast to **Luxor** (5 hrs; E£15-22), via **Qena** (3 hrs; E£8) 8 per day every couple of hours; 4 of which carry on to **Aswan** (1030, 1530, 2230, 0030; 8 hrs; E£20 daytime, E£40 overnight). There are also 6 daily buses to **El-Quesir** (2 hrs; E£10- 15) via **Safaga** (0500, 1530, 1930, 2030, 0030, 0200, E£5-7) all except the 1530 and the 0200 carry on to **Marsa Alam** (4 hrs, E£20) and **Bir Shalatein** (E£35, 5 hrs).

Superjet, T065-544722, runs 3 daily buses to **Cairo** at 1200, 1430, 1700 (6 hrs, E£50) and 1 to **Alexandria** at 1430 (9 hrs, E£80).

El-Gouna, T065-541561, runs 5 daily buses to **Cairo** (via **El-Gouna**) at 0900, 1430, 1600, 240, 010 (6 hrs, E£50, except for 1430 which is E£35).

Car

Car rental Most agencies are scattered around Sharia Sheraton. **Budget** is based in the Marriott, T065-446950.

Ferry

High speed a/c ferry to **Sharm El-Sheikh** on the Sinai peninsula (1½ hrs, though weather can impact duration), booking is essential through your own hotel or **Spring Tours** on Sharia El-Nasr, **Thomas Cook**, T065-541870, in Midan Sigala, or **Travco**, T065-446623/4. One-way fare costs E£180. Presently, ferries leave Hurghada for Sharm El-Sheikh at 0800 on Sat, Tue, Thu and at 0500 on Mon. They depart from Sharm El-Sheikh back to Hurghada on the same days at 1800.

There is also regular ferry service to **Duba**, in Saudi Arabia (3 hrs, departs daily at 0900 but you should be in the port at 0700, E£260, more if you have a car). Contact **Menatours**, T065-444465, to book a ticket or for more information.

Taxi

Local Minimum charge would be E£5-10 within Dahar.

Long distance Service taxis operate to destinations south, north and west, although as a foreigner you may not be allowed in those travelling to the Nile valley. You need to go to the service taxi station across the roundabout from the Telephone Centrale. Service taxi fares are approximately E£3-5 to **Safaga** (1-hr), E£15 to **Marsa Alam** (3 hrs), E£30 to **Cairo** (5-7 hrs), E£20 to **Suez** (4 hrs).

You may have to wait some time for the car to fill up (7 people, microbus 14). If you're in a rush, you can pay for empty seats in order to leave sooner. If you want to take a service to **Luxor** (4 hrs) or **Aswan** (6 hrs), you'll need to get a group together and work it out privately, as the drivers will have to join a convoy to transport foreigners in order to avoid having their licenses taken away. For long distances, fares and travel times are less than the bus but more dangerous as drivers often speed quite fearlessly.

Police convoys For independent travel to the Nile Valley in private car or with a contracted service taxi, foreigners are required to travel in police-escorted convoys. At present, there is 1 per day that departs from Hurghada's southern-most checkpoint at 0600. When demand is high, there is another one later in the morning. Check with the tourist office for the most up to date times, as they often shift.

Directory

Hurghada *p425, maps p430 and p432*

Banks Commercial International Bank, in front of Grand Hotel, T065-448680/4. Other banks on the main road in Hurghada are: Bank of Alexandria, T065-546559/549575; Banque Misr, T065-546624; Islamic Investment Bank; and National Bank of Egypt, T065-548199/549199, Sharia Sheraton. Only Banque Misr, T065-546624, and National Bank of Egypt, offer cash advances on Visa/Mastercard and only the National Bank of Egypt has an ATM. Banks open from Sun-Thu 0900-1300, 1800-2100, Fri and Sat 0900-1330. Money transfer can be arranged through Thomas Cook, T065-541870, and Western Union, T065-442772, both in Sigala shopping centre. **Hospitals** Safa Hospital, T065-546969, El- Salam hospital, T065-548785, and the Public Hospital on Sharia Aziz Mostafa to El-Corniche, T065-546740. El-Gouna Hospital, T065-580014. **Decompression chamber**, El-Gouna, T065-580011; and at Naval Hospital, T065-449150. VHF code 16. **Internet** Try to go to internet cafés when the locals are at work. Expect connections to be slow and unreliable. Internet Egypt, in Sigala behind the Pyramid, yellow sign on balcony. Aboudi Bookshop, on Sharia Aziz Mostafa near Three Corners Empire. Internet café at Papas Bar in Sigala. E£8-10 per hr. Business services available at Hilton Resort. **Places of worship** Coptic Church, Fri and Sun 1000, at El-Anba Shenouda. **Post office** Next to the tourist police on Sharia Al-Central to the south of the new mosque, T065-546372. Open 0800-1400 daily except Fri. Special post by Federal Express, T065-442772, in Sigala shopping centre. **Telephone** Outside of the hotels, Telephone Centrales are on the main roundabout of Sharia El-Nasr, in Dahar, and on Sharia Sheraton and Midan Shedwan, in Sigala. There are also Menatel phone boxes scattered everywhere. Buy their cards in any shop or supermarket with the Menatel sticker. **Useful telephone numbers** Air Ambulance: T101541978. Ambulance: T065-546490. Fire: T065-546814. Police: T065-546723. Tourist Police: T065-447774. Visa extensions at Passports and Immigration Office north of the town on Sharia El-Nasr, open 0800-1400, closed Fri, T546727. Telephone Centre: T16. Telephone Directory: T140.

South of Hurghada

→ *Colour map 3, grid C5.*

Safaga

Safaga stands a long 567 km from Cairo, 65 km (45 minutes by taxi) south of Hurghada's airport, where the coastal road meets the main road across the Eastern Desert to Qena. Though the town isn't particularly beautiful, it has this stretch of the Red Sea's usual attractions: diving, snorkelling and perhaps the most famous wind on the coast. The stiff breezes which favoured the trading vessels along these shores now provide excellent conditions for windsurfing, generally cross-shore in the morning and side-shore in the early afternoon. (The Windsurfing World Championships were held here in 1993.) Safaga has also seen an upsurge in health tourism as of late, with many psorisis and arthritis sufferers journeying from afar to roast in the mineral enriched black sands. With such geological riches, the area does not rely totally on tourism. It has local phosphate mines that export the mineral overseas. The small port is also busy importing grain, much of it US food aid, which is currently trucked inland to the Nile Valley.

Most travellers simply pass through in a convoy on their way between Hurghada and the Nile Valley. Outside of the sea, there is very little to visit other than a small fort which overlooks the town and offers good views. **Tourist information**, T065-451785. ▸▸ *For Sleeping, Eating and other listings, see pages 441-446.*

El-Quseir

Further south is El-Quseir, 650 km from Cairo and 80 km south of Hurghada (2 hours by road), an old Roman encampment and busy port. Far enough away from the hoards of package tourists in Hurghada and Safaga, the small southern port town has managed to retain a bit of its ancient charm. People are friendly and move a little slower. The surroundings are still pristine and the diving is superb.

El-Quseir has had a long history as a major port of the Red Sea. It was from here that Queen Hatshepsut departed on her famous expedition to the Land of Punt (see page 542). This was also once the most important Muslim port on the Red Sea. In the 10th century it was superseded first by Aydhab, which is the ancient name for the Halaib in the currently disputed triangle on the Egyptian-Sudanese border, and then by Suez after the canal was opened in 1869. Now the port's main function revolves around the export of phosphates. The 16th-century fortress of Sultan Selim (rebuilt by the French in 1798) still standing dominates the town centre and creates a sort of mystique that no other Red Sea village quite has. Though the unspoiled diving and snorkelling are the main appeal, the town is well worth a visit for its dry land charm too.

Located in a small inlet sheltered by a coral reef, the road inland from El-Quseir to Qift, just south of Qena, follows the ancient pharaonic road that was built at a time when almost a hundred small but very rich gold mines operated in the region. Some of these mines have been reopened with the help of modern technologies. ▸▸ *For Sleeping, Eating and other listings, see pages 441-446.*

Sights The partly ruined **fortress** was built by Sultan Selim to protect the Nile Valley from attacks from the sea – until 1710. At that time it became the main departure point for Egyptian pilgrims on their annual journey to Mecca. There was conflict here too at the end of the 18th century – during the French campaign. Also between the British Indian Army coming in from Bombay and the Egyptian campaign to the Arabian Peninsula headed by Ibrahim Pasha in 1816. (See box on Mohammed Ali and family page 493.) During the Ottoman era it had been used as an administrative office and today the ancient structure is sufficiently repaired to be used as a police station. Some of the inscribed verses from the Koran can still be read. There are other buildings from this earlier period including the mosques of Al-Faroah, Abdel-Rehim Al-Qenay and Al-Sanussi and a number of tombs, mainly by the fortress, of holy men considered important by the inhabitants.

All of the hotels can help you organize jeep and horseback **safaris** into the surrounding mountains to visit nearby oases and a number of ghost cities created when the mines were abandoned. ▸▸ *For dive sites and listings, see Activities, page 444.*

Wadi Hammamat, about 100 km along en route to Qift, has some fascinating Pharonic graffiti – Heiroglyphic inscriptions – including the names of Pepi, Sesostris, Seti, Cambyses and Darius. The inscriptions lie along an ancient trade route where remains of old wells and watch towers are also detectable.

Marsa Shagra

This remote bay, 113 km south of El-Quseir and 13 km north of Marsa Alam, has transformed into a small village celebrated by divers. There is an extensive underwater cave system to explore, and some outstanding coral formations. It's also near a group of striking offshore reefs with great sloping walls, the mysterious **Elphinstone Reef** among them, where in its dark depths some say lie the remains of an unknown Pharoah. ▸▸ *For dive sites, see Activities, Marsa Alam, page 445.*

Marsa Alam

A tiny fishing village 130 km south of El-Quseir, Marsa Alam is a gem of the southern coast. The village is also a way station between the Nile Valley and the Red Sea since a road through the Eastern desert connects it to Edfu, 250 km to the west. The small harbour is nestled in a beautiful area where the coast is lined with rich mangrove swamps that encourage rich bird and marine life. These mangroves are protected and all newdevelopments are supposed to be eco-conscious in order to ensure the preservation of the fragile environment. Though the place has thus far escaped the onslaught of tourism so rampant further north, foundations are being laid and plans declared. Even amid the current economic slump, development in these parts is imminent. ▸▸ *For dive sites, see Activities, page 445.*

Berenice

A very ancient city – named by Ptolemy II, Berenice became a trading port around 275 BC. The ruined temple of **Semiramis** is near the modern town. Inland there are remains of the emerald mines of Wadi Sakait which were worked from Pharonic to Roman times. Berenice is noted for both quantity and quality of fish and having a climate reputed to promote good health. The coast is lined with mangrove swamps and there are some beautiful coves which are completely isolated.

Offshore is the **Zabargad**, a most unusual volcanic island. Evidence of its origin is found in the (olive-green) olivine mined as a semi-precious gem stone. Mining has been active here on and off since 1500 BC. **Peridot Hill** (named after another semi-precious stone) offers breathtaking views of the surrounding area. A wonderful place to watch the dolphins and, in season, the migrating birds. Once off limits to visitors, Zabargad Island was finally declared a Protected Marine Park by the Egyptian government. Sometimes a permit is required for this area, though a bit of baksheesh to the right people can often grant access. ▸▸ *For Sleeping, Eating and other listings, see pages 441-446.*

Excursions inland There is one interesting excursion possible from here into the interior, but a guide is essential. The restored tomb and mosque of **Sidi Abul Hassan Al-Shazli** lies some distance inland. The track/road is a distance of 110 km southwards off the main road west towards Edfu. Al-Shazli (1196-1258) was an influential sufi sheikh originating in the northwest of Africa but spending much of his life in Egypt. He had a large and important following and was noted for his piety and unselfishness. He travelled annually to Mecca for which Marsa Alam was convenient. His *moulid* is popular despite the isolation of the site. The buildings are modern, being last restored on the instructions of King Farouk after his visit in 1947.

Sleeping

Safaga *p439, map p442*
As with most Red Sea accommodation, prices fluctuate depending on the number of tourists circulating so use our price guide just to get an idea.

A Holiday Inn, T065-252821/31, F252825. Usual facilities associated with this hotel chain, spacious, well-tended gardens, perfect for sports enthusiasts, health club, tennis, volleyball, large pool, 2 restaurants, bars, shopping arcade. Most expensive hotel in town.

B **Lotus Bay Beach Resort**, T065-251040/1, F251042. Whitewashed clusters with gardens between, all rooms have sea view, usual room facilities, choice of restaurants, tennis, squash, volley ball, freshwater pool, cycle hire, horse and camel riding, water sports facilities, Barakuda International Diving Club.

B **Menaville Village**, about 5 km north of Safaga port, T065-251760/2 F251764. A better choice. 100 hotel/villa rooms, 48 chalets and 33 suites, villas in gardens, by pool or adjacent to the very good beach, all rooms a/c, telephone, minibar and terrace or balcony, villas sleep 4/5 and have lounge and small kitchen. Shops, bank, laundry, clinic. TV lounge, 24-hr cafe, private beach, cycle hire, billiards, table tennis. Has own Barakuda Dive Club (German management) with private jetty. Unlimited shore diving from hotel reef and boat dives available with all equipment for hire.

B/C **Shams Safaga Village**, T065-251781/6, F251780. Designed and built in local style, 135 bungalow rooms and 150 hotel rooms with a/c, bath, terrace/balcony, TV, private sandy beach within a protected, secluded, natural bay, and spacious, well-tended gardens, restaurant, 3 bars, tennis, squash, mini golf, health club, parasailing, all water sports, large pool, small children's pool, play area and baby sitting. Shams diving centre on site. Reputable diving centre and famous Club Mistral offers windsurfing with full range of instruction from beginners to slalom stylists. A rescue boat is on hand. Advantage for disabled is flat access to beach.

E **Cleopatra Hotel**, T065-253926. An adequate hotel in the town centre near the port. The 48 rooms all have private baths that are clean enough. There's a hotel in the bar and a pizza restaurant next door.

F **El-Eez**, in central area near port, T065-252312. Offers cheap accommodation frequented by truckers. A double with fan going for around E£45. The shared bathrooms are grimy and English is not spoken. Unless really in a crunch, you're better off spending the extra money on the Cleopatra Hotel.

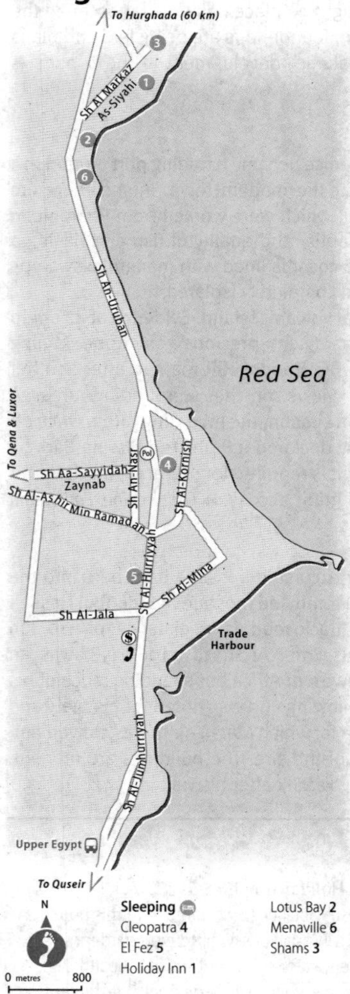

El-Quseir *p440*

A-D **Movenpick Serena Beach**, El-Quadim Bay, T065-332100-102, F4332128. Unbeatable value and perhaps the coastline's most stunning hotel with a coral reef running the entire length of the private beach. You can almost snorkel from your room. Moorish style, environmentally conscious, lovely gardens and beach, large pool, 3 restaurants of which Orangerie is recommended, 4 bars, 2 floodlit tennis courts, squash, archery ranges with coach, gym, mountain bikes to hire, horse and camel riding. Children's pool and club. All

175 rooms have usual facilities from sea view to hair dryer. Subex Diving Centre.
B Utopia Beach Club, a bus is needed to get into El-Quseir, 20 km away but taxis are available. New, right on the beach, restaurant, pool with snack bar, lobby bar, disco, billiards, volleyball, tennis, table tennis, windsurfing and pedalo hire, children's pool and small size tennis court, doctor on call. Some spectacular dives just off the beach, others reached by jeep. Dive centre on sight organizes marine safaris of the area.
B Mangrove Bay Resort, 29 km south of town, T065-334507/9. Comfortable 3-star with a beautiful white sandy beach, colourful reefs and a dive centre.
B/C Fanadar Beach Hotel, 1 km south of town, T065-331414, F331415. 50 little bungalows.
F Sea Princess Hotel, 1 km south of town, T065-331880. The only really budget option in town, the rooms are cramped and the bathrooms grubby. Staff don't speak much English.

Marsa Shagra *p441*
Though several establishments have sprouted up in these parts in recent years, the oldest among them is still at the top, both for its comfort, facilities and experience, as well for its environmental sensitivity.
Red Sea Diving Safari, reservations in Cairo T02-3371833, in Shagra, T0195-100262, www.redseadesertsafari.com. Set back from the beach to the west of the coast road (so as not to spoil the view), the construction in local red sandstone is very sympathetic. A central domed area containing all the main facilities is surrounded by separate chalets, huts and tents with lots of space. During high season (Aug – May), prices are €50, 40, 35 per person, including full board; during low season, they drop €5. All are spotlessly clean and very comfortable but only the chalets have private bath. There is no pool or bar, but the bay boasts a stunning beach with a fantastic house reef, good for shore dives and snorkelling. The owner, Hossam Helmi, is a pioneer in the area, and one of the foremost environmentalists on the coast. He's also a diving enthusiast and knows the surrounding seas better than most. Extensive diving day-long safaris are organized from the hotel, as its name suggests. Two offshore dives cost €35/person plus €35/boat all inclusive.

Marsa Alam *p441*
A Shams Alam, reservation office in Cairo, T02-4170046. A comfortable resort, south of Marsa Alam. Accommodation is in white 2-storey bungalow-like complexes with domed roofs. There's a lovely private sandy beach with a bar as well as a fresh water pool with a bar. The Wadi Gamal Dive Centre on site specializes in diving safaris to more remote reefs in the south. Price includes half-board.
B Kahramana Resort, 6 km south of town, office in Cairo, T02-7604820, mobile in Marsa T012- 7454105. A quaint 4-star, that's been around a while with mustard coloured buildings and a nice beach. The best of the tackier options in the area. There are 2 pools, a well-stocked bar and one of Marsa Alam's better restaurants. Price includes half-board.

Further south, Hossam Helmi (see Marsa Shagra above) has also opened up two other high-end camps, each with their own bay and liveaboards.
Marsa Nakari, 18 km south of Marsa Alam, offers chalets, huts and tents at the same prices as the Red Sea Diving Safari.
Wadi Lahami, 142 km south of Marsa Alam. Permits to the seldom visited area are arranged for clients. Only tents are on offer, for €40 per night, full board. Diving safaris are organized from the site, with a 3-day liveaboard program at €85 per person per day all inclusive (food and dive gear). Reservations to both camps are made through the Cairo office, T02-3371833.

Camping
Coral Cove, Sharia Marsa Alam, 8 km north of Marsa Alam, T02-3647970. Rent a camp spot on the beach for E£15 per night or use one of the camp's tents, that can accommodate 2, 3 or 10 persons. The atmosphere is peaceful, and the shared baths clean. Particularly popular with backpacker divers. Full and half board available.
Also recently sprung up is a stretch of old Dahab-style camps with cheap simple backpacker accommodation about 12 km south of Marsa Alam. The camps are on

a beautiful sandy beach and are quite eco-orientated.

Eating

Safaga *p439, map p442*
As Safaga is significantly less touristed than nearby Hurghada, most restaurants are confined to the hotels, as are the bars and discos. There are some cheap cafeterias selling standard grilled fare along the main drag Sharia Al-Gomhuriyya. The Menaville's is at present, the most popular.

El-Quseir *p440*
Food choices are limited. For standard stall food like *fuul* and *taamiyya*, look around the seafront. There is a scattering of traditional cafeterias in town. The widest options are available in the hotels, most of which welcome non-guests to their buffet dinners.

Marsa Alam *p441*
Choices in the small village are very limited. Outside of the hotels, there's really only one local cafeteria that's clean enough to warrant a recommendation. It's at the entrance to town on the right side of the main road, across from the port. There is no name, but you'll see it. Order whatever's on the stove.

Activities and tours

Safaga *p439, map p442*
Diving *(see also Sleeping, p441)*
The best dive sites around Safaga are **Panorama**, where a sloping hill leads to a dramatic drop off and sharks and mantas often linger; and **Abu Qifan**, a remote and pristine site that leaves behind the traffic of Hurghada liveaboards. The prolific marine life is an underwater photographer's dream. There are frequent sightings of dolphin, ray, barracuda, reef and leopard shark. All dive centres in Safaga organize day trips and half-day to the nearby sites. A standard PADI open water course, all inclusive, costs €300-320.

Diving clubs *(see also Sleeping, p441)*
Barakuda, at Lotus Bay, T065-251041.
Menaville, T065-251760/3.
Duck's Dive Centre, Holiday Inn, T065-252821. Instruction in English, German and Italian. PADI open water certification €320.
Shams Safaga Diving Centre, Shams Safaga Village, T065-251781. Instruction in German and English. PADI open water certification €300.

El-Quseir *p440*
Diving *(see also Sleeping, p442)*
Shallow dives Off the shore at **Movenpick's Subex Dive Centre** (very professional and eco-conscious, but extremely expensive, see p442) is **El-Qadima Bay** with a variety of topography and fauna; about 10 km further south is the more sheltered **El-Kaf**.
Deep dives The islands **Big Brother** and **Little Brother** are about 1 km apart, 67 km off the shore northeast of El-Quseir. They were off limits for a few years until authorities developed a protection plan. They reopened in the late 1990s as part of a newly-decreed Protected Marine Area. Two exposed parts of the same reef, the Brothers offer what some

Safaga islands, reefs & dive sites

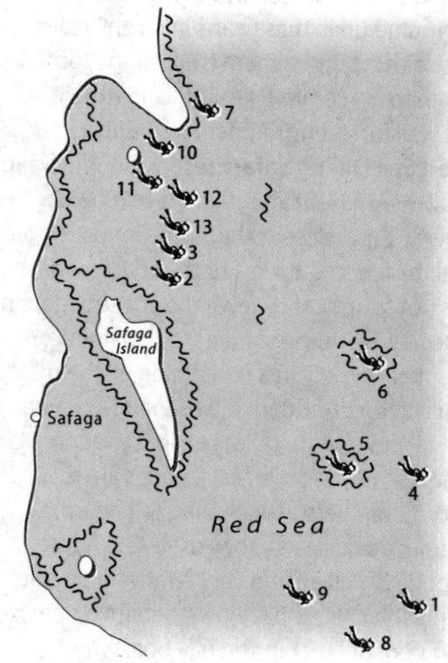

say is the best diving in the Red Sea. Divers pilgrimage to make the plunge, and special permission is required
as the area is strictly regulated. Access is by liveaboard. The walls are a vertical 900 m. On Big Brother, the larger of the two, there's a stone lighthouse constructed by the British in 1883 (and still working). To the northwest of Big Brother are two **wrecks**. The unnamed cargo vessel with its shattered bow can be reached at 5 m (and then deeper as it is at an incline). The other wreck is Aida II (see box on Wrecks, pXXX). The strong currents around the Little Brother are home to vast fan corals and caves, and sharks are of various sorts are often seen. Along with stunning corals, these two dives offer an impressive range of fish.

Marsa Shagra *p441*

Desert

Though most venture this far south for the underwater splendors, the surrounding majesty of the desert and turquoise sea makes the place ideal for reflection and respite above ground. There's also a burgeoning desert safari effort, **Red Sea Desert Adventures**, www.redseadesertadventures.com, led by an experienced Austrian man named Thomas and his marvellous Dutch partner, Karen, who has been in the area for more than 20 years living among the local Bedouin. They lead both day treks and overnight expeditions that last up to 10 days to some extraordinary sights, many of which have yet to be fully uncovered.

Diving *(see also Sleeping, p443)*

Should you need a **decompression chamber**, in emergency, VHF code 16, or call Hossam Helmi, the owner, at T012-2187550.

Marsa Alam *p441*

Diving *(see also Sleeping, p443)*

Live-board dive locations south from Marsa Alam: **Elphinstone Reef**, 12 km off shore; **Daedalus Reef**, 96 km off shore; **Sha'ab Sharm**; **Dolphine Reef**, 15 km to the northwest of Ras Banas; **Zabargad Island**, 45 km southeast of Berenice.

Decompression chamber – see above.

Transport

Safaga *p439, map p442*

Police convoys For independent travel to the Nile Valley in private car or with a contracted service taxi, foreigners are required to travel in police-escorted convoys. At present, there is 1 per day that departs from Hurghada's southernmost checkpoint at 0600 and stops at a large lot on the northern side of Safaga off the main road around 0645. When demand is high, there is another one later in the morning. Independent travellers bound for the Nile Valley on public buses are generally OK (ie won't get kicked off) if there are only 4 or less on board.

Bus

Buses via **Hurghada** (E£3-5) to **Suez** (E£20-40) every 1-2 hrs of which 5 go on to **Cairo** (7-8 hrs, E£50). Buses to **Qena** (E£10), **Luxor** (E£15-20) and **Aswan** (E£30-40) 4-5 times a day, currently at 0100, 1100, 1400, 1630, 2330. Buses to **El-Quesir** (2 hrs, E£8) and **Marsa Alam** (3 hrs, E£10-15) leave at 0600, 1600, 2100, 0130, 0200.

Ferry

Sea passenger boats leave here for **Duba** daily. During the *haj* there are passenger boats to **Jeddah** (not advised). Check at the port or with the **Telestar** office in town.

Taxi

Service taxis follow all the bus routes – change at **Suez** for **Cairo**. Prices are comparable to bus costs, but the journeys tend to be a bit faster (and more terrifying).

El-Quseir *p440*

Air

There is an **airport** 60 km south of town that also serves Marsa Alam.

Bus

The bus **station** is in the town centre on Sharia Port Said. Please check all times and destinations as schedules change often. There are 5 daily buses to **Cairo** (E£55) via **Safaga** (E£5-8) and **Hurghada** (E£10-15) at 0500, 2030, 2100, 2200, 2300; 2 pass through **Suez** (E£25). There is at least 1 daily bus to **Qena** (4 hrs, E£11) via **Qift** that presently departs at 0500. From there, you can easily find a bus to Luxor and Aswan. As with other cities on the coast, independent travellers bound for the Nile Valley on public buses are generally OK (ie won't get kicked off) if there are only 4 or less on board. There's also a morning bus to **Marsa Alam** (E£12) that leaves at 0800. Sometimes there are evening buses, check to be sure.

Taxi
Service taxis and microbuses that congregate in the southern part of town go to all these destinations throughout the day (on a leave-when-full basis), change at **Suez** for **Cairo**.

Marsa Alam *p441*
Air
There is an **airport** 60 km north of Marsa Alam that also serves **El-Quseir** with flights to **Cairo**, **Hurghada** and **Luxor**.

Bus
Buses leave **Cairo** for Marsa Alam at 2000 and 2300 (11 hrs, E£55). To get out of Marsa Alam, ask the locals about the latest schedules once you get to town, as things change with the winds. At present, from Marsa Alam to **Cairo**, there is an early morning direct bus that stops in **Safaga** and **Hurghada**; otherwise, it's easy to catch a ride to Hurghada and transfer. Crossing the road to **Edfu** from Marsa Alam is supposedly difficult for tourists, as many get kicked off the public buses or service taxis at one of the 3 check points, but if you want to try and trust the unspoken 4 tourists or less rule, the public bus heads west around 0700 from the T-junction. The safest and surest way across is to join the convoy in Safaga, where tourist buses congregate at 0630 daily, bound for the Nile valley via Qena. There are buses every few hours throughout the day to **El-Quseir**, where many more northbound and westbound buses depart from.

Taxi
Service taxis (Peugeot-style) run up and down the coast regularly, on a leave-when-full basis. They are comparable in price to the buses, but faster and more frequent.

Berenice *p441*
Berenice is 908 km from Cairo, 400 km from Hurghada and 258 km from El-Quseir. Access is by road only. The nearest airport is El-Quseir, with Hurghada a bit further north.

Directory

Safaga *p439, map p442*
Banks Banque Misr, El-Qseir-Hurghada Road.

El-Quseir *p440*
Banks There is a bank in the town centre near the main midan where the 24-hr telephone centrale is situated. **Post office** The post office is close by, towards the sea.

Marsa Alam *p441*
South of the T-junction a small settlement there's a pharmacy and telephone.

Western Desert

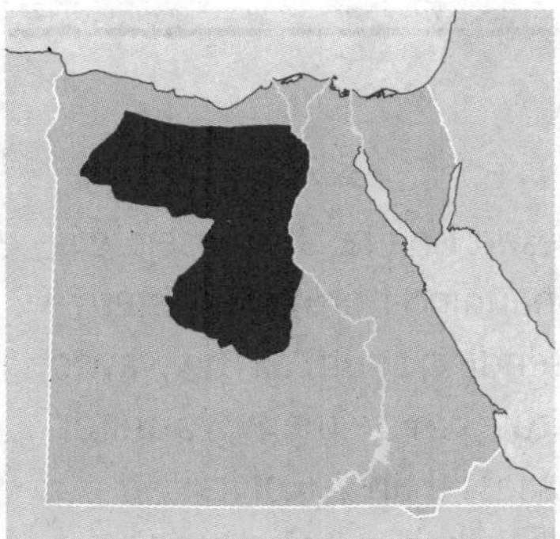

Footprint features

Introduction

Wherever you are in Egypt, the desert isn't far. Its presence is tangible, omnipotent, mystical. Spanning from the western banks of the Nile to Libya and extending south all the way to Sudan, the Western Desert constitutes more than two-thirds of Egypt's total area, and supports less than 2% of its population. Though more accessible than ever before, the region is still not a tourist destination, it is a traveller's destination; and only travellers of a particular sort are drawn to this wild and captivating land: travellers in search of a rich, rugged, adventure filled with beauty, challenge and insight.

There are five major oases that make up what has come to be known as the Great Desert Circuit: Bahariyya, Farafra, Dakhla, Kharga and, in the northwest, the more removed Siwa. **Bahariyya**, swarming with desert guides keen to capitalize off the sharing of its many hot springs and interesting sights, is an easy setoff point for safaris. **Farafra**, a bit more remote, is a quieter village, clutching onto tradition. Between Bahariyya and Farafra lies the **White Desert**, a psychedelic wonderland with limestone sculptures that resemble minarets and mushrooms. Also accessible directly from Luxor are Dahkla and Kharga, key points on ancient camel caravan routes. Significantly larger than the other oases, both have airports. Though **Dakhla** with its soft pink sands, enchanting medieval settlements and warm demeanour has managed to retain a village feel, the government's "New Valley" reconstruction project of the 1970s and 80s infiltrated **Kharga** with hordes of Delta workers and hideous concrete structures. **Siwa**, brimming with rolling dunes, crumbling temples, fields of palms, bubbling springs and a language and culture all its own, personifies the enchantment of the oasis experience. Furthest from Cairo, it's most easily reached via the North Coast road.

★ Don't miss...

❶ **White Desert** Transport yourself to another planet with a visit to the limestone sculptures carved by millennial efforts of sand and wind, page 456.

❷ **Dakhla Oasis** Get lost in the enchanting 10th-century mud brick labyrinth city of Al-Qasr. It protected inhabitants from heat, sand and intruders for centuries, page 457.

❸ **Siwa Oasis** Mingle with the inhabitants who have been isolated by an ocean of sand for centuries; take in a sunset over a crystalizing salt lake at Fatnas Island; seek your true nature at the sight of the Oracle where Alexander the Great asked if he was indeed the son of Amun; hike up Jebel Dakhrour and gaze in awe at the blanket of palms below, page 471.

❹ **Bir Wahed** Relax your weary muscles in one of the numerous hot springs scattered around the oases. Bir Wahed in Siwa, nestled amid rolling golden dunes, is among the best, page 477.

❺ **Safari** Explore desert depths with an overnight safari by jeep or camel from Siwa, Bahariyya, Farafra or Dakhla and gaze in awe at a virgin desert sky with more stars than you ever though possible.

❻ **Sand dunes** Nourish your inner child with a hike up and a roll down a great sand dune around Siwa or Dakhla.

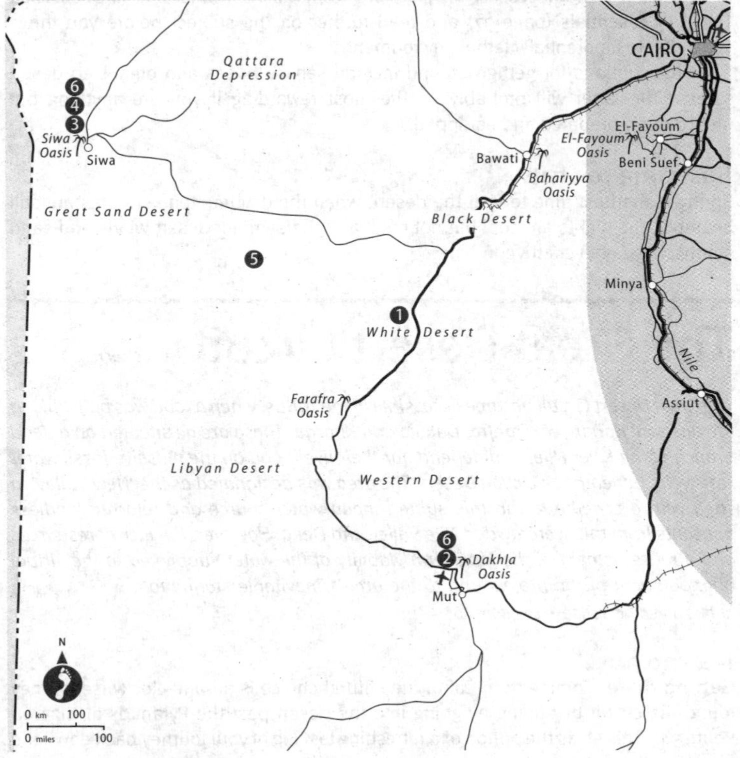

Ins and outs

Getting around and permits

Travel around the oases is straightforward and unimpeded. For overnight safaris, permits are generally not required, but signifcant detours from the main roads and extended travel on less-frequented routes (like the Darb El-Siwa, a desert road connecting Bahariyya and Siwa) may require a permit. Virtually every travel agent that organizes safaris into the desert can obtain permission to travel. **Misr Travel** (see page 141) heads up the process.

If time is short, El- Fayoum (see page 160) and Wadi Natrun (see page 179), give a taste of the desert's mystique and both can be seen in a day-trip from Cairo. The oases of the Great Desert Circuit require a more substantial commitment.

If you are interested in an extended desert expedition, it is essential to plan in advance. Obtaining a **permit** requires photocopies of the important pages of your passport and the Egyptian entry stamp, two passport photos and an outline of your trip itinerary. Depending on the political climate, Egyptian authorities require that some nationalities travel with a military escort before issuing permits. If such is the case, be prepared to provide food and all essentials for the escort.

Make sure you take enough **cash** with you. Credit cards will not do, indeed, you will be lucky to find a bank.

When **planning** a drive NEVER underestimate the potential dangers of the desert. It is said that in 524 BC Cambyses, the Persian conqueror of Egypt, managed to lose an entire army of 50,000 men without a trace! Always carry more than enough fuel, food and water. There are no service stations between towns. You need the right type of vehicle, and the necessary driving skills to handle it in this terrain. See Desert Travel in Essentials (page 37) and read further on the subject before you throw yourself into a potentially lethal environment.

Other options for gettign around include service buses and organized desert safaris. The latter will probably be the most rewarding if you are anything but meticulously prepared and equipped.

Best time to visit

Spring is the best time to visit the desert, when the daytime temperatures are still bearable, the nights are cool but not cold, and the summer desert winds and sand storms, have not yet arrived.

The Great Desert Circuit → *Colour map 1*

The Great Desert Circuit became accessible in the 1980s, when a road was built linking the oases of Bahariyya, Farafra, Dakhla and Kharga. These are all situated on a dead branch of the River Nile, and depend, for their livelihood on the massive fossil water reservoirs beneath the Libyan Desert. The area was designated as the 'New Valley' in 1958 with a scheme to tap this subterranean water source and relocate landless peasants from the overcrowded Nile Valley and Delta. However, the lack of resources and a reassessment of the long-term viability of the water supply led to the virtual abandonment of the project and to the area's inevitable stagnation. » *For Sleeping, Eating and other listings, see pages 465-471.*

Ins and outs

Getting there Coming from Cairo, the natural choice is an anti-clockwise journey round the circuit beginning by going into the desert past the Pyramids at Giza on Route 341. This gives the option of a refreshing last leg of your journey back down the

"" The call of the desert for the thinkers of the city has always been irresistible. I do not think they find God there, but that they hear more distinctly in the solitude, the living verb that they carry within themselves. (TE Lawrence)

Nile. It's also possible to start your exploration from **Kharga**, accessible from Luxor by train once weekly, or from Assuit (see page 195) via bus. Driving conditions have improved significantly over the years, but there are still relatively few places to stop for petrol, food or water so fill up on all essentials before beginning your trek. The oases are well-connected via public transport in both directions. **Upper Egypt Travel** (see page 144) runs several daily a/c buses between Cairo and the oases. There are also dozens of microbuses circulating so finding a ride is rarely a problem. If you intend to travel by coach, though, it is wise to buy your ticket at least a day in advance to ensure a seat. Also bear in mind that public transport in the remote oases can be less consistent and less reliable than other parts of the country so double check all schedules and call upon a bit more patience than usual. If you lack the time, or the inclination, for all this you can fly direct from Cairo to **New Valley Airport** at Kharga, where it's possible to get a taste of the desert, but you will be missing far more. It may be true that Kharga has more interesting monuments than some of its neighbours, but the desert itself is the star of this chapter and Kharga, with it's sprawling modern town, is undoubtedly a disappointment.

Siwa is most easily accessible from the North Coast road that passes through Alexandria and Marsa Matrouh before winding inland toward the oasis and Sollum at the Libyan border. There is a desert road connecting Siwa to **Bahariyya**, but it's not served by public transport. Road conditions can be poor due to shifting sands and independent travellers with private vehicles need a permit (see above) to make the journey. It's possible to organize a safari across from both Siwa and Bahariyya with four-wheel drive, but it's a pricey venture.

Depending on the level of security precautions taken by the Egyptian authorities you may find yourself accompanied by armed guards for part of your journey throughout the oases. Generally these concern themselves with travellers in self-drive vehicles or cars with hired drivers. They cause no problems though the effectiveness of their protection is questionable. » *For further details, see Transport, page 469.*

Bahariyya Oasis and Bawati

This is the closest oasis to Cairo in distance and the furthest in historical time, dating back to the Middle Kingdom. At 2,000 sq km and with 33,000 inhabitants, it is the smallest of the four depressions and has the great advantage of having water just 7 m below the ground, not 700 m as is common in the other oases.

Ins and outs

Getting there The journey to Bahariyya Oasis from Cairo, 310 km west of the Pyramids of Giza, along Route 341 takes 6-7 hours by bus, with one stop en route, 5-6 hours by service taxi or 4-4½ hours in a four-wheel drive. After taking the turn to

Chameleonic camels

There are two kinds of camel, *Camelus Dromedarius*, the Arabian camel with one hump and *Camelus Bactrianus*, the Bactrian which has two. Arabian camels, introduced into North Africa in the fifth century BC, though only as domestic animals, are about 3 m long and about 2 m high at the shoulder. They range in colour from white to black.

Interesting physical characteristics which allow these animals to survive in the desert include hairs inside the ear opening as well as the ability to close the nostrils between breaths, both preventing sand infiltration; thick eyebrows to shade the eyes from the sun's glare; a pad of skin between the two large toes on each foot forming a broad, tough 'slipper' which spreads the animal's weight over a larger area and prevents sinking in the loose sand; large bare leathery areas on legs and chest that act as cushions when the animal kneels down; and the ability to survive for long periods without food or without water. Each eye has three eyelids, the upper and lower lids have very long eyelashes to protect the eyes from sand whipped up by desert winds, while a third, thinner lid blinks away dust from the eyeball. The skin inside a camel's mouth is so tough that cactus thorns do not penetrate, hence a camel can eat anything, 'even its owner's tent'.

Camels can go for many days without food as the hump can store up to 35 kg of fat as emergency rations. They can go without water for even longer, depending on the weather and the kind of food available. As camels do not sweat but instead function at a higher body temperature without brain damage, their demands of fluid are less. At a water hole they drink only enough to balance their body moisture content.

Less pleasant camel characteristics include a most unpredictable nature, especially in the mating season, which includes nasty habits like using its long sharp teeth to bite people and other camels, viciously kicking with the back legs, spitting and being generally awkward. When a camel stands up it moves in a series of violent jerks as it straightens first its hind legs then its front legs. When a camel walks, it moves both the legs at one side at the same time, giving a very rolling motion.

Camels are unwilling beasts of burden, grunting and groaning as they are loaded and generally complaining when being made to lie down or stand up. Once underway though, they usually move without further protest.

These large, strong beasts are used to pull ploughs, turn water wheels and carry large loads for long distances across difficult terrain. They can carry up to 400 kg but usually the load is nearer 200 kg. Despite moving at a mere 6-7 km an hour, camels can travel 100 km in a day. They also provide their owners with hair for cloth, rich milk and cheese, dried dung fuel and eventually meat, bones for utensils and hides for shoes, bags and tenting.

October 6th City the dual carriageway becomes a new black top three-lane highway. (Running parallel to the road is a private railway that takes iron ore from the country's most important mine at Managum to the giant Helwan steelworks near Cairo. This was the catalyst for Egypt's industrial development in the 1950s.) 155 km from Giza there's a resthouse with petrol. Bus and service taxis generally stop here, 31 km after the resthouse is the new road north to El-Alamein marked by five signs – of the petrol companies involved.

As the road begins its descent towards the oasis the first huge black topped **inselburgs** appear, protruding through the yellow sands. The **Managum mines** are announced by a sign at 150 km from the resthouse but it is a further 10 km before houses for the workers appear on the right. The head office of the mines, down the road to the left is reported to have a **museum** but getting beyond the guard at the gate could prove very difficult.

Pause at the top of the scarp for a really magnificent view of the Bahariyya depression.

Information The official **Egyptian Tourist Authority (ETA)** office, ⓘ *T02-8473039, open daily 0800-1400*, is in the government building on the main street near the Popular Restaurant (which is actually often a better source of information than the office). The **tourist police**, ⓘ *T02-8473900*, are also on the main street, about 1 km away at the beginning of town if you're coming from Cairo.

ⓘ *At the time of writing, the following sights in Bahariyya are officially open to the public: the Temple of Alexander, Aïn Al-Muftillah, the tombs of Zad-Amun ef-Ankh, Bannentiu and Amunhotep Huy and the Antiquities Inspectorate's 'museum' that houses the acclaimed Golden Mummies. One ticket (E£30) purchased in the Antiquities Inspectorate make-shift museum covers admission to all sights, except for the Valley of the Mummies, which is "officially" off-limits. Cameras require an additional ticket, E£25, videos E£100.*

Background

Bawati is the oasis's main settlement. Throughout their history the people of the oasis have prevaricated between independence and co-operation with the current regime. They converted to Islam soon after the Muslim invasion but returned to a Berber Emirate during the 10th century before being incorporated once more into the Islamic state by the Fatimids a century later. In the last few centuries they have co-operated fully with the ruling regimes but have maintained a slightly independent stance although they are generally very welcoming to visitors. The farmed areas, producing dates, olives and wheat, are owned by small landowners. Problems of falling water tables in the oases were solved by tapping the subterranean aquifers held in the Cretaceous sandstones, but the interesting underground water channels (similar to those found as far afield as Morocco and Iran) formerly used in Bawati are now dry and a very depressing sight.

The other small settlements are all worth visiting to see how these sturdy people combat the elements. Once on the floor of the depression take the track to the south of the road which continues beyond **El-Harrah** (rock cut tombs) and its ponds, used by the locals for duck breeding, to the gardens round the spring of **Aïn Yousef**. Further west along the main road the ruins of **Muhrib** are out of bounds at present but a tarmacked road opposite on the right leads to **Gabala** where the encroaching sands have been spreading over the oasis gardens for the last 20 years and have covered the rest of the road. Approaching closer to Bawati, again on the right, is **Aïn Hemma** with **Mandesha** beyond, also fighting a losing battle against the encroaching sand. The last turn right before Bawati leads to **Agouz**. A guide from the village is an asset when visiting these small settlements. Ask for school teacher Badry Macpool.

Bawati

Bawati is built along the main road and the parallel oasis road to the south. There is a circular walk worth taking along the main road and the oasis road through the gardens, by **Aïn Bishmu**, the Roman springs, where the hot water is used for bathing and washing clothes. Cultivation of fruit – apricots, dates, figs and melons – takes place in these gardens. The women who work in the gardens and also contribute to the household finances by selling embroidered goods. The hill to the southwest of the town is known as the **'Ridge of the Chicken Merchant'** as here in underground passages are small recesses, which are the burial sites of a great many mummified ibis and hawks, dating from the 26th Dynasty and clearly relating to worship of Thoth and Horus. South of the village in a dominant position stands **Jebel Hafuf**, Bahariyya's highest mountain, made of dolerite and basalt. Also of interest may be the Naghi family's **camel breeding farm**. ⓘ *17 km from Bawiti on the slopes of Pyramid Mountain. Inquire at the Popular Restaurant or tourist office.* You can see how camels are bred and buy camel blankets and products. The Naghis also organize camel tours of the desert.

Museums **Oasis Heritage Museum** ⓘ *opening times are erratic, entrance is free, but a donation requested.* At the entrance to the village lies this intimate museum highlighting the artwork of Mahmoud Eed, a local self-taught Bedouin artist. Clearly inspired by the old-timer, Badr of Farafra, Eed molds clay to depict his experience of life in the oasis. The museum also houses scenes from the oasis that offer a view of daily life in Bahariyya. At the store, visitors will find beautiful embroidered dresses and locally-made silver jewellery.

The **Antiquities Inspectorate Museum**, known to some as the Bawati museum, and to others still as the Mummy Hall, shelters some of the finds from surrounding ruins. Among them are four of the acclaimed "golden mummies", so dubbed for their guilded coffins (see box).

Tombs and temples The **Tomb of Amenhotep-Huy,** mayor of Bahariyya oasis in the 18th-19th Dynasty, rests on a ridge called Qarat Hilwa, a few kilometres northwest of town. It's quite hard to spot without a guide.

In Bawati proper, nestled on the small hill of Qarat Qasr Salim inside the village are the colorful tombs of **Banentiu**, a wealthy merchant and **Zed-Amon-Iuf-Ankh,** his father, both from the 26th Dynasty.

Bawati (Bahariya Oasis)

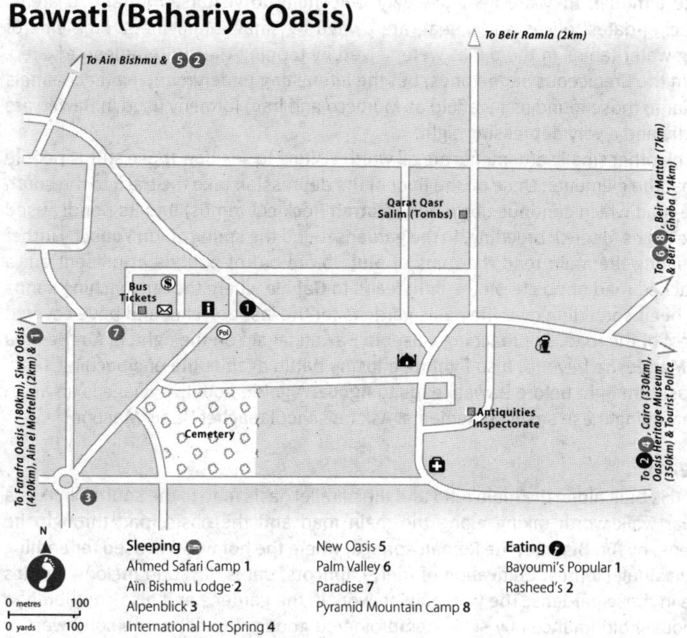

The Golden mummies of Bahariya oasis

It is widely reported that the 'recent' find of these mummies in 1996 was in fact discovered almost four years earlier and that in that time the discovery was supressed to allow some 'private' excavations. Be that as it may, these golden mummies are as exciting a find as Tutankhamen's Tomb. It seems this cemetery was in use from the construction of Alexander's Temple to the fourth century AD. The mummies are all different – individual men, women and children. The mask and upper bodies of many were coated with gold, others decorated with painted scenes. Each mummy has, unusually, a painted smile.

It will be some time before this site is open to the public and then it is unlikely that the mummies will be on view. In the meantime five mummies are on display in the makeshift museum of the Antiquities Inspectorate.

There are three kinds of mummies: The first is wrapped in linen without a sarcophagus;

The second is laid to rest in a pottery coffin;

The third is characterized by its decorations – pasteboard made of linen or papyrus, from the head to the waist on which artists have depicted scenes, or those wearing gilded masks and often surrounded by funerary artefacts.

The **Temple of Aïn El-Moftella**, 2 km west of town, built in the 26th Dynasty during the reigns of Kings Apries and Amasis (Ahmose II). The temple has four ruined chapels decorated with deteriorating scenes of the king presenting offerings to the gods.

The **Temple of Alexander the Great,** at Al-Qasr Allam built in 332 BC and occupied perhaps until the 12th century AD, stands at the northern end of the site where the mummies were discovered (see box). The temple is unique – being built to honour a living person. It consists of two chambers within an enclosing wall. Behind the temple the priests' houses were built. The administrator lived to the east of the building and to the front were 45 store rooms made of mud brick where a small statue of the priest to Re was found. The temple itself is constructed of local sandstone. The front faces south and the stone gateway in the enclosing wall is here. A granite altar over 1 m in height was erected to the south of the entrance. The altar is inscribed with Alexander's name and can be viewed in the museum in Cairo. In the inner sanctuary Alexander, with the mayor who built the temple, is shown making offerings to Amun-Re and other gods.

Hot springs One of the delights of visiting Bawati is a soak in one of its sulphury steaming springs. Closest to town is **Aïn Bishmu**, about a 10-minute walk from Bayoumi's Popular Restaurant. It offers a splendid view over the oasis, but as it's used as a local laundry, it's not an ideal place to swim. For a boiling soak, check out **Bir Ramla**, a scalding 45 degree centigrade spring, only 2 km from Bawiti. **Bir el-Mattar**, 7 km northeast of Bawiti, is cooler, but not particularly beautiful, where luke warm water pours out of a viaduct into a small cement pool. Men bathe here by day, and women by night. **Bir Al-Ghaba**, 7 km further down the road, is the best spot to bathe in Bahariyya. Locals often splash around here when the sun's out, but come night, men and women travellers can soak undisturbed under in stunning moonlit environs. ⓘ *Women swimming in Bir Ramla and Bir El-Mattar should wear an opaque loose-fitting tee-shirt over a bathing suit.*

Al-Qasr lying west on the road to Siwa, is Bawati's sister village, beneath which lies Bahariyya's ancient capital. Here you will see stones from a 26th Dynasty (664-525 BC) temple reused for house building and the remains of a Roman triumphal arch that stayed intact until the 19th century.

NB A much-improved but still fairly uncomfortable track, known as the **Darb El-Siwa**, leads west from here to **Siwa** (see page 471). Permits, which can be obtained through most travel agents working with desert tourism in Cairo, are required to travel this road. A four-wheel drive is essential, as sand dunes have blocked the road at points. A guide is recommended. It's also wise to check at the Tourist Information office (see page 453) before you leave, to inquire about the road's conditions, which are often shifting. » *For Sleeping, Eating and other listings, see pages 465-471.*

Bahariyya to Farafra

Just 12 km beyond the outskirts of Bawati is the **Runi shrine of Rene Michael**, the Swiss explorer who lived in the village for seven years, rediscovered the area and was so enchanted by the beauty of the place that he wanted to be buried here in the desert. Beyond lies the **Black Desert**, the pebbles of dolerite darkening the land. The road begins to rise out of the Bahariyya depression through a bright rainbow canyon and a checkpoint at **El-Hayz**, a collection of hamlets rather than a specific place, about 35 km to the south. Some Roman finds have been reported including a church dated to the 5th/6th century BC, a military camp and evidence of dwellings. A second checkpoint is just beyond the village of **Aïn El-Izza**, a place to stop for a drink. On the plateau are numerous erosion features known locally as 'lions'. Of special note are the small mountains of calcite. One, just 10 m to the left of the road, is called *Jebel El-Izza* or **Crystal Mountain**, more like a big hill and with a flower-like growth of crystal formations sprouting forth around the small arch in the centre. The road cuts through the escarpment and descends towards the Farafra depression. Of the flat topped outliers, two are particularly prominent to the east of the road, and are known as the **Twin Peaks**.

Beyond is the fabled **White Desert** where many travellers stop and camp for the night. By moonlight, the eerie wind-sculpted landscape has been compared to the Arctic wasteland, and sunrise here is the highlight of many trips. These strange shaped rocks have caught the imagination of countless travellers – intrigued by them and inspired by them. Geologists will delight in the huge calcite crystals, the chalk fossils and the accumulations of pyrites. To the north of Jebel Gunna a road goes west to **Aïn Della** (Spring of the Shade). An extra permit may be required for this journey.

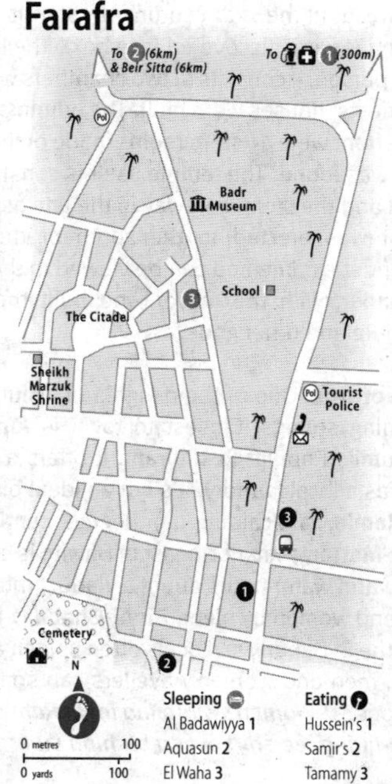

Farafra Oasis

Farafra offers a good starting point for safaris into the nearby White Desert and a thorough taste of oasis life, much unfettered by the onslaught of tourism. It is the smallest and most isolated of the oases in the Western Desert though the deep depression in which it lies suggests that it was once larger. To the northwest steep cliffs rise dramatically out of the desert while to the south there is a gentle incline. The village of **Qasr El-Farafra** was based around a large 116-room mud brick fort or castle (*qasr*) from which it got its name. This was used by all the villagers when they were under attack until it collapsed in 1958. The village is a lovely slow-moving place, with palm-lined roads and traditional, decorated houses.

The inhabitants of Farafra, who spawn mainly from two extended families, have been involved in trade and contact with the Nile Valley since earliest times. Until quite recently, residents in Farafra numbered less than 5,000, before a wave of *Saidis* (Upper Egyptians), migrated to the isolated oasis to exploit the vacant fertile land. Now there are more than 15,000 people living peacefully together, though the separation of quiet-natured Farafrans and more animated Saidis is apparent in the local *ahwas*. ▸▸ *For Sleeping, Eating and other listings, see pages 466-471.*

Sights

There are no ancient sites to visit in this oasis. Nearby desert landscapes are the real attraction of this region. However, **Badr's Museum** ⓘ *entry is free, though donations are appreciated, usually open, but if not, inquire with anyone in the village and someone will lead you to Badr*, with its eccentric displays is a highlight of all the oases. Badr is the first of several oasis artists who has been invited to share his work, spirit and culture in galleries around the world. Badr built the museum, a work of art in itself, with his own hands. Set up like a traditional Farafran home, the rooms are overflowing with sculptures, sand paintings and watercolours. Badr's art is filled with sadness, depth and longing. It's mythic, surreal and an earnest reflection of life in the desert and among the people of Farafra. If you're lucky, you'll meet Badr's brother Gamal, a superb *urghul* (traditional flute) player who accompanies a band of impressive local musicians. Ask Badr if he's playing at any weddings or celebrations during your visit.

Bir Sitta, a steaming hot spring 6 km out of town, is a blissful spot to soak. Camping is also permitted, though mosquitoes can be quite an annoyance. Taxis there and back cost around E£15-20.

Dakhla Oasis and Mut

Moving on southeast from Farafra, the much larger Dakhla oasis, with a population of around 70,000 in 14 settlements, sprouts up 310 km from Farafra. Buses make the journey in 4-5 hours; cars in 3-4 hours. The first 100 km of the journey are through unoccupied oases and open areas of sand which in places extend over the road. Beyond, the sand dunes increase in size. After a huge vegetation filled *wadi*, you'll find another check point at **Maghoub**, sheltered under Jebel Edmonstone. As you come upon the oasis, primary colors explode. A million shades of pink in the cliffs meld with bright golden sand dunes, wide blue sky and the lushest fields in all the oases.

Known as the "pink oasis", Dakhla is a magical place that has managed to dodge the extreme urbanization of nearby Kharga. The people are among the friendliest and most sincere in all of Egypt. They welcome travellers with curiosity and hospitality as they openly share their traditional way of life that has remained much unchanged for centuries. With the capital Mut, at the centre, there are some notable ancient sights to both the east and west. Dakhla is also a good place to venture into the desert for star-gazing and overnight exploration. Like Bahariyya, there's no shortage of eager guides who will organize everything from a day's hop around the sights to an 11-day camel trek to Farafra. ▸▸ *For Sleeping, Eating and other listings, see pages 466-471.*

One kilometre south of Maghoub is **Deir El-Hagar.** ⓘ *Tickets E£20. 0800-1700, expect to have to offer baksheesh to guards. Without your own transport, getting here requires a bit of effort. You can hire a taxi from nearby Al-Qasr (8 km, E£10 roundtrip) or take a pick-up (50p) and ask to be dropped at the 'trail' head to the temple, follow the road to the nearby small village and then find the dirt road that will lead you over a small ridge and to the temple.* This small sandstone temple was built during Nero's reign (AD 54-68) to honour the triad of Thebian gods: Amun Ra', Mut and Khonsu. Nero's successors, Vespian, Titus and Domitian elaborated upon the temple, but it was still never completed. The site, surrounded by a wall intended to deflect drifting sand, is well preserved – due, ironically, to being enveloped by sand for much of its more recent history. In the 1960s, Ahmed Fakhry began excavation and in 1992, the Canadians funded extensive rehabilitation and preservation efforts.

The temple consists of a two-columned court and a hypostyle court with four columns, a vestibule and a sanctuary. Each of the columns in the hypostyle hall has inscriptions to Emperor Titus, the columns in the sanctuary to Domitian, Vespasian and Nero. There are some interesting inscriptions representing religious life. Notice the smoke-covered columns near the sanctuary, thought to be residue of ancient rituals. Also, ask the guard to point out the Coptic graffiti, a clear indicator that the temple was later used as a church. The responsibility for the site now lies in the hands of the Supreme Council of Antiquities, who are actively encouraging visitors.

The Roman period **Muzawaka Tombs** (Hill of Decoration) ⓘ *free but baksheesh expected, without your own vehicle, you can get here by taxi or private pick-up from Al-Qasr (5 km, E£10) or take a public pick-up (50p) and asked to be dropped off at the dirt road leading to the tombs*, the larger one of **Petosiris** (AD 54-84) and the other of **Sadosiris**, his wife, are vividly painted tombs depicting contemporary myths relating to the afterlife and a striking zodiac ceiling. Unfortunately, these tombs have been officially closed for years, awaiting restoration that has yet to begin. The sight is still worth a visit, though, as a bit of baksheesh will yield an unbelievable viewing of mummies – the closest you'll ever get. Notice the hands of the males rest by their sides while the hands of the females cover their genitalia. There is one tomb with the skeleton of a child that is frequented by local woman wanting to conceive.

Al-Qasr

ⓘ *Al-Qasr is 32 km north of Mut, if you're coming from Farafra, you can ask to be let off here; from Mut, take a pick-up for 50p.*

This old Islamic settlement built, upon the foundation of an older Roman settlement, is Dakhla's fortified medieval capital. The narrow streets of the old quarter, covered as protection from the sand and sun, reflect the antiquity of the area. Ancient wooden lintels at doorways are decorated with carved inscriptions from the Koran and date back to AD 924. Wander around this enchanting ancient town and taste the timelessness of oasis life. There are still a few inhabited houses, but newcomers are no longer permitted to settle in the old town. Ask the guard to let you inside the houses of **Abu Nafri** and **Abu Misid** ⓘ *baksheesh expected.* The beautifully restored **Ayyubid madresa**, served as both a school of *sharia'a* (Islamic law) and a courtroom. Look for the holding cell and more permanent jail inside, and climb to the roof for a spectacular view. Next to the school is the **Nasr El-Din mosque**, marked by a three-storey wooden minaret that doubled as a lookout tower, 21 m high. The tomb of Sheikh Nasr El-Din is inside the old mosque, marked by a 12th-century mud-brick minaret that was destroyed and rebuilt in the 19th century. Also make sure you spot the *saqiya*, an ancient water-wheel, the huge old corn mill, and the olive oil press, where the rich scent of Farafran olives still lingers. At the edge of the old town, check out the small but informative **Ethnographic Museum** ⓘ *ask a guard to open it for you, E£5,* founded by Alia Hussein, a premier anthropologist of the oases. Photographs and crafts from all the oases are on display. There is also a **steel mill** still in use and a nearby **pottery factory**, well worth a visit, where you can witness a family making mud bricks and *zirs* (water-coolers) in the same manner they have for centuries.

Beyond Al-Qasr, the road turns south toward the ruined village of **Amheidah** where the tombs date from 22nd century BC. The road continues by the Mamluk hilltop village of **Qalamun**, where you can find striking views of the area, back to Mut.

Mut

Set in a striking landscape bursting with life, Mut (pronounced *moot*), Dakhla's capital, is pretty in a shabby, faded way. It is both lively and a laid-back town with a wide range of inhabitants from as far away as Nubia, Sudan, and Libya, all living peacefully together. With a fairly extensive range of food and accommodation, and lots to see and do nearby, this town makes a comfortable stopping point on a long journey through the oases.

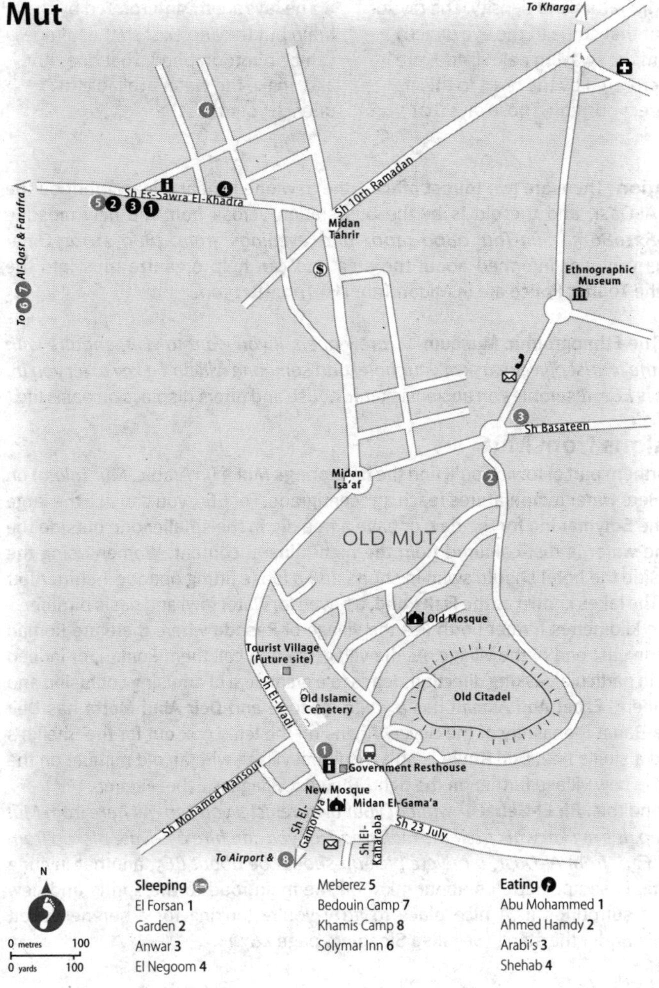

It must have been a mirage

For a fascinating optical illusion try the mirage, a feature of all romantic travellers' adventures in the desert. Most commonly they occur in hot desert regions where the distant and most welcome pool of water perhaps reflecting swaying palm trees turns out, much to the disappointment of the thirsty traveller, to be another area of parched sand.

A mirage is caused by the bending of rays of light as they pass through different layers of air which vary in temperature and density. The rays of light that come to the eye directly from the swaying palm fronds are interpreted by the brain in their correct position. Those rays that travel nearer to the hot ground surface move faster through the warmer, less dense air as they meet less resistance. They change their direction as they travel, bending closer to the ground. The brain, however, assumes the rays have travelled in a direct line and records the blue sky as a pool of water and the trees as reflections. The illusion, perhaps overused by film producers and novelists, is of wide expanses of inviting, shimmering "water".

The rays are misinterpreted by the brain but they do exist so the mirage can be photographed. That does not, alas, make the water available to quench your thirst.

Information There are two **tourist offices,** the new one is near Midan Tahrir on the road to Al-Qasr, and the old is by the bus station across from the new mosque ⓘ *T092-821686/5, Sun-Thu 0800-1400, and evenings from 1800-2100.* Omar Ahmed is very well-informed about the area and can help organize trips into the desert. The **Tourist Police** are in Midan Tahrir ⓘ *T092-821500.*

Sights The **Ethnographic Museum** ⓘ *rarely open. If you want to visit, enquire with Omar at the tourist office or ask at your hotel and someone will find a key to let you in, entrance is E£2*, resembles an ancient Islamic house and offers displays on oasis life.

Excursions from Mut

In the northern part of town, you'll find the **hot springs Mut 3** (in Arabic, *Mut Talata*) on the left. Here water temperatures reach 43° centigrade. For E£5, you can use the large pool in the **Solymar Inn** for the day, or have a free dip in the smaller one outside the hotel. The water is rust-coloured from the high mineral content. Women using the pool outside the hotel should swim in shorts and a loose fitting opaque T-shirt. After 1 km are the lakes known as the **Fish Pond,** a haven for water fowl and oasis birdlife.

Three kilometres further north lies the village of **Rashda** where there are Roman ruins at the east end of the village. As the villagers don't call them Roman, or indeed anything in particular, asking directions leads to a great deal of amusing confusion and disagreement. **Ezbet Abu Asman** has a white mosque and **Deir Abuf Matta** has Deir El-Seba'a Banat Monastery of the Seven Virgins on the left. Look out for the Sheikh's tomb and a single tree. **Bud Khulu** is an agricultural village with an old minaret on the left and the new village further on the right. The next village is Ezbet Fiteima.

Beyond this, **Bir El-Gebel** ⓘ *without your own vehicle, you can get here from Mut via pick-up, it's a 3 km walk from the main road, or you can hire a private pickup from Mut for E£20, from Al-Qasr, a private pick-up should be about E£5*, another inviting hot spring, is signposted. It's about 5 km off the main road to the spring and new camp that surrounds it. A nice place to go if you're looking for a serene desert experience under the stars. (See also Sleeping, page 467.)

Sights around Eastern Dakhla

Balat is an interesting and still inhabited old village dating back to the Turkish period, with narrow covered streets and fertile gardens dangling with vines and palms. The streets were intended to keep the city cool and safe from sand and winds as well protected from potential invaders on horse and camelback by forcing impending warriors to fight on foot. Not quite as otherworldly as Al-Qasr, Balat is still a quaint and fascinating old Islamic settlement and well worth a visit. Outside the old village, there is a good bakery and several markets selling refreshments and tea.

Nearby, **Qila Al-Dabba** ⓘ *0800-1700, entrance is E£20, students E£10, climb to the top of the French archaeologists living station for an impressive view of the area*, the ancient necropolis of Balat, offers visitors a look at several mud-brick *mastabas* which mark the tombs of sixth-Dynasty governors. One has been extensively excavated by a group of French archaeologists that continue to work on the site a few months every year. Inside the tomb, that resembles an inverted step pyramid, you can see faint coloured reliefs of daily life and images of the governor Khentika and his wife. His mummy was found here, but has been relocated to the Cairo museum.

About 1.5 km east of the Necropolis, the French have also been working for more than 17 years at **Aïn Asil.** ⓘ *Your ticket to Qila Al-Dabba should allow you access to the Aïn Asil ruins. To reach the site, turn towards Bashendi through the triumphal arch, swing left before the mosque and then right at the next through-way into the desert. The track turns off to the left to a brick hut, the excavations are behind the hut, going back towards the main road.* An Old Kingdom settlement that was abandoned around Ptolemaic times, excavations thus far have uncovered the remains of a fort and farming community.

Bashendi, on a huge arch at its entrance, describes itself as a 'model' village. It's a working community, not quite as picturesque as nearby Balat, but quaint enough with narrow streets, mud houses and lots of smiling children that excitedly ask for pens. (Riders on the Paris-Dakar route introduced this concept to the children on their frequent stops to the village where they often distribute pens and T-shirts). You need to ask around for the key to see the internal decorations of the Roman period second century AD Tomb of **Kitnes** ⓘ *entrance is E£16 and may not be worth the effort.* The original funerary reliefs depict Kitnes meeting the gods Min, Seth and Shu. The Tomb of **Bash Endi** (name derived from a medieval Sheikh from India known as Pasha Hindi) consists of a Roman base and a much more recent Islamic dome. Notice the handprints covering the walls. Local women believe that three hands on the walls of a sheikh's tomb can lift the black magic that prevents them from conceiving. The acoustics in Bashendi's tomb are remarkable. If you're not alone, have your companion whisper in the far left corner of the tomb and put your ear around the near right corner to hear.

Dakhla to Kharga

The journey from Dakhla to Kharga, 195 km in an easterly direction, takes three hours. The road, which has a good surface, passes the villages of **Sheikh Wali** and **Masara**; **Asmant** (Smint), a fortress town at 11 km; **Sheikh Mufta** at 16 km on the right; and **Qasr El-Kassaba**, at 20 km. To reach the ruins of Asmant El-Khorab (**Kellis**) turn right off the road at the sign that says 'Kharga 170 km' and drive directly into the desert for 1 km.

Immediately beyond **Teneida,** and its tombs on the left of the road, is a checkpoint. Look out now for the sandstone outcrops very near the road. On the closest, to the south, are a number of **rock inscriptions** – some purporting to be very old. Note the rock formations in the area, a particularly striking one resembles a sitting camel. This area marks the intersection of two ancient caravan routes, one between Dakhla and Kharga; the other connecting Teneida to the Darb El-Arbaeen (40 days road).

About 45 km west of Kharga a new town is being constructed by the road to the phosphate mine. (Your next point of interest is a single tree.) The road into Kharga for the last 20 km has been replaced at intervals with another to the south due to the continuing march of the dunes.

Kharga Oasis

Pre-industrial Kharga was very different from the city here today. At that time the water level was considerably higher and the route was vital for the caravan trade. The New Valley scheme has converted this attractive oasis into a modern concrete town thereby removing almost all traces of its former charm. Nevertheless, a few interesting historical sites remain in the surrounding area.

Information Tourist office ⓘ *T/F092-921205/6, Sun-Thu 0800-1400 and most evenings from 1800-2100*, opposite Kharga Oasis Hotel. The museum can also be a helpful resource in organizing tours of the area. The **Tourist Police** are next door to the information office.

Kharga

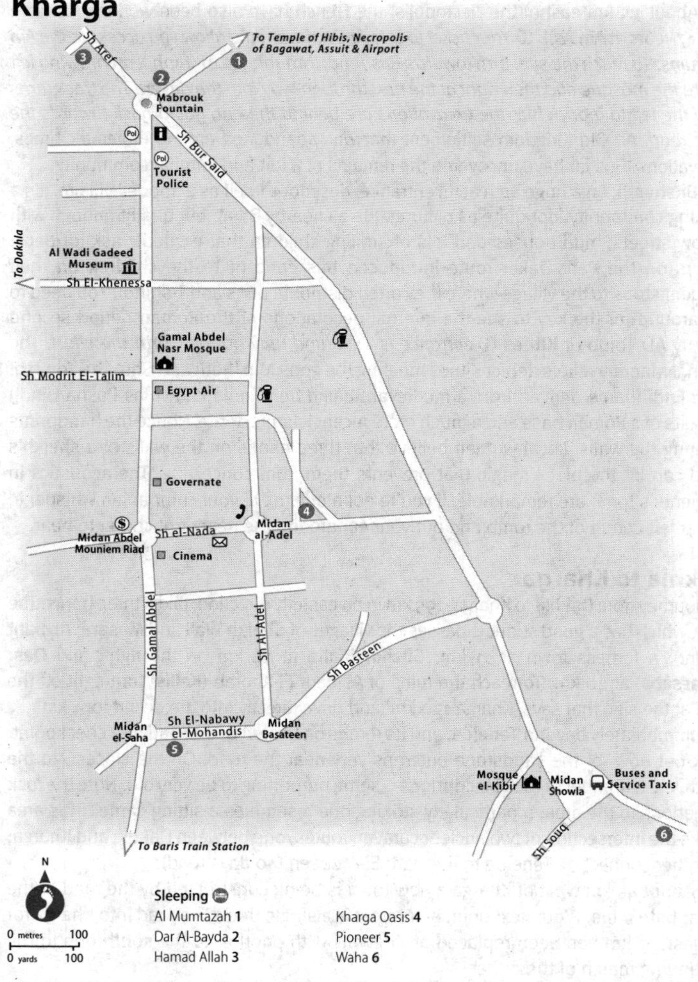

Scorpions – the original sting in the tail

Scorpions really deserve a better press. They are fascinating creatures, provided they do not lurk in your shoe or shelter in your clothes.

Scorpions are not insects. They belong to the class Arachnida as do spiders and daddy longlegs. There are about 750 different kinds of scorpions. The average size is a cosy 6 cm but the largest, *Pandinus imperator*, the black Emperor scorpion of West Africa, is a terrifying 20 cm long. The good news is that only a few are really dangerous. The bad news is that some of these are found in Egypt.

They really are remarkable creatures with the ability to endure the hottest desert climates, revive themselves after being frozen in ice, and survive for over a year without food or water and they have a remarkable resistance to nuclear radiation.

Scorpions are nocturnal. They shelter during the heat of the day and to keep cool wave their legs in the air. They feed on insects and spiders, grasping their prey with their large claw-like pincers, tearing it apart and sucking the juices. Larger scorpions can devour lizards and small mammals.

Their shiny appearance is due to an impervious wax coating over their hard outer shell which protects them from any water loss. They have very small eyes and depend on their better developed senses of touch and smell. The sensitive bristles on the legs point in all directions and pick up vibrations of movements of potential prey or enemies. This sensitivity gives them ample warning to avoid being seen by heavy-footed humans.

The oft-reported 'courtship dance' before mating is merely repeated instinctive actions. The grasping of claws and the jerky 'dance' movements from side to side are a prelude to copulation during which the male produces spermatozoa in a drop of sticky fluid to which the female is led so that they may enter her body. The male departs speedily after the 'dance' to avoid being attacked and devoured.

Scorpions bear live young. After hatching, the young crawl on to the female's back and are carried there for two or three weeks until their first moult. They gradually drop off after that time and have to fend for themselves.

Most scorpions retreat rather than attack. They sting in self-defence. The sting is a hard spine and the poison is made in the swelling at the base. The sole of the bare foot, not surprisingly, is most often the site of a sting, and the advice in the section on Health in Essentials is not to be ignored, see page 58. The African fat-tailed scorpion (we do not recommend measuring the size) is described as aggressive and quick-tempered. It is responsible for most of the reported stings to humans and most of the human fatalities. The beautifully named *Buthus occitanus*, the small Mediterranean yellow scorpion, and *Leirus quinquestriatus*, the African golden scorpion, also have neurotoxic stings that can be fatal.

Sights

Al-wadi Gadeed Museum ⓘ *Sharia Gamal Abdel Nasser. Daily 0800-1600, closed for Fri noon prayer. £E20 for foreigners, E£10 students*. Opened in 1993 and also known as the Kharga museum, it houses a collection of artifacts found from ruins throughout the oases. In particular look at the mummies, the painted sphinx and the selection of gold coins upstairs. This is a very good museum and well laid out, with most items named in English or French.

The **Temple of Hibis** ⓘ *2 km to the north of the town, to get there, you can take a covered pickup to the end of town and walk the remaining 2 km, or flag down a* *microbus/service taxi en route and ask them to drop you at the temple (ma'abad), entrance free*, dedicated to Amun, was begun in 510 BC at the beginning of the Persian occupation, under Darius and completed under Nectanebo II. It is one of the few remains from that period. It is dedicated to the triad of Thebian gods, Amun Ra', Mut and Khonsu. Unfortunately it was built on clay and suffers from subsidence. Several attempts have been made to restore the planks and reinforce the foundations. From the outer to the inner gate was an avenue of sphinxes and beyond the inner gate two obelisks of which just the bases remain. A wall, also made of local sandstone, surrounds the main temple with an entrance at the southeast into the portico of Nectanebo I and II. The first Hypostyle Hall has 16 columns in four rows and the second Hypostyle hall four transverse columns. A third Hypostyle has four columns (2x2). Around this hall are small chambers, one with stairs to the roof. The sanctuary is at the far end.

The remains demonstrate the prevailing influence of the Pharaonic era on the later empires. The ornamentation and designs within the temple are mainly animals, showing vultures, dogs and serpents intertwined with Persian and Egyptian deities. On the walls of the sanctuary is a relief of Seth overcoming a serpent.

Temple of Nadoura, ⓘ *go north from town and turn right at the triumphal arch*. This small temple of sandstone was built by Antonius Pius in AD 138 and later used as a fortress by the Ottomans. Though the temple is in ruins, a walk to its mount gives a splendid view of the Temple of Hibis and the surrounding desert. It's an excellent place to take in the setting sun.

The **Necropolis of El-Baqawat** ⓘ *daily 0800-1800 summer, 0800-1700 winter. E£20, students E£10*, was once so far from civilization that hermits came for the seclusion it offered. In 490 the Christian theologian St Athanasius was banished here. About 500 baked brick tombs, originating from an early Christian burial site, and dating from the third to the seventh centuries lie crumbling in the desert. Small chapels cover some of the tombs. The most interesting features of the burial ground are the vivid wall paintings of biblical scenes. Some are fairly crudely executed and others were defaced by the ancient Greeks. The chapels are known by the illustrations they contain which are mainly of Old Testament scenes depicting Adam and Eve, the Exodus, Daniel in the lion's den, Noah's Ark, Abraham and Isaac. (Look out for Jonah being vomited out of the whale's stomach.) From the New Testament, the Virgin Mary and St Paul feature most often. Takla Hamanout, an Ethiopian saint (see page 82), is shown here with St Paul. Some of the best preserved paintings are in locked chapels but, with a bit of negotiation and baksheesh the guard may happily let you see.

In the centre is a church dating from the fifth century AD – one of the oldest in Egypt. If you're on foot from the Temple of Hibis, you can follow can dirt track from through a palm grove into the desert. By car, just continue on the road to Assuit, you'll find the entrance less than a kilometre north of the Temple.

South of Kharga

ⓘ *Service taxis, covered pickups and public buses operate on this route.*
To the south of Kharga, on the road to Darfur is the Nasser Resthouse with campsite; **Bulaq** village with wells/springs with temperatures reaching 39°C and a primitive resthouse; **Qasr El-Ghueita** with a 25th-Dynasty Ptolemaic Temple of Amun, Mut and Khonsu; **Qasr Zaiyan** with a Ptolemaic and Roman Temple again to Amun; and **Qasr Dush** southeast of **Baris** with a Roman Temple dedicated to the Gods Serapis and Isis, also a mud-brick Turkish fortress, an ancient church and some Coptic pottery. The road to Luxor (another 225 km) turns off at Jala.

North of Kharga

To the north excursions can be made to **Aïn Umm Dabadib** with ruins of ancient settlements and a Roman castle; **Qasr El-Labeka** which is one of the largest forts in this oasis and boasts Roman tombs and a temple; and **El-Deir** where walls and towers still stand. If time is limited visit El-Deir accessible by car to within 1 km of the site, but take a guide as the route is unclear.

The cliffs here dominated the route to Assiut, and the mud brick ruins of the **Monastery of Mustapha Kachef** (Mustapha the taxman) to the west of the road just beyond the airport indicate good use was made of this position.

Arriving back in the Nile Valley at **Assiut** (see chapter Middle Egypt page 195) one can either continue the circuit back to Cairo or take the opportunity to travel south (security permitting) via the Abydos and Dendera temples to the wonders of Luxor and the Valley of the Kings.

Sleeping

Bahariyya and Bawati *p451, map p454*
New camps and second class hotels are sprouting up more quickly than ever, though higher end accommodation is still lacking. All include breakfast and most offer half and full-board options. Tours into the desert and transport to nearby springs and sights can easily be organized from all hotels and camps. Beware, if travelling by bus, there is intense competition and sometimes ugly rivalry among hotel and safari touts. You will be bombarded.

C International Hotspring Hotel, on outskirts of Bawiti, T012-3212179, F8472322, www.whitedesertours.com. German-managed spa with 29 rooms with private bath and a/c, built around a hot spring. Massage, sauna, health centre on site. Halfboard is part of the deal. Prices decrease in the summer. Alcohol available.

D Palm Valley, a few kilometres out of town in Agouz, T02-8496271. 24 spacious comfortable rooms, some with a/c. Restaurant offers half and full board. A small palm garden, view of nearby Jebel Inglees.

E Aïn Bishmo Lodge, centrally located near the Bishmo springs, T02-8473500. 20 clean rooms with fans and shared facilities, 5 rooms with a/c and private bath, breakfast included, cafeteria and shops, safaris organized, overlooking palm grove.

E Oasis Panorama, T02-8473354, www.oasispanorama.com. Tacky hotel on the main road lacking in spirit but clean in body. Rooms have private baths and fans, some with a/c. Breakfast included, with half- and full-board options. Tours organized to surrounding springs and the desert.

E-F Alpenblick Hotel, T02-8472184. The first hotel in Bahariyya, an old favorite for backpackers, although becoming increasingly run-down as age takes its toll. 22 very simple double rooms, some with grubby private showers; includes breakfast of large helpings of bread. Popular desert trips. The occasional evening tea round the fire in the courtyard makes it a special place.

F New Oasis Hotel, near the Bishmu springs, T/F02-8473030. Rooms are clean with private baths, carpeting and lots of color. Not as nice as nearby Al-Bishmu, but has a pool. Breakfast included. Popular with tour groups, especially in the winter.

F Paradise Hotel, T02-8472600. 6 basic double and triple rooms, shared bath, access to kitchen and laundry, safaris organized. Not much of a paradise, but the cheapest choice in town with some beds going for only E£5 a night.

Camping

AL Luxurious Eco-Camp, T02-4184821. A very pricey but beautiful seasonal camp set at the base of a cliff in the White Desert. Run by Waleed Ramadan, a long-time friend of the desert and the founder of the environmental NGO *Desert Pioneers*. On offer are gourmet meals, porcelain toilets and showers with running water stored in tanks. The camp boasts low impact on the environment. First class Bedouin-led safaris cater to intellectual desert-goers who appreciate comfort and a wealth of information. Camp only accommodates 14 people at a time.

E-F Ahmed Safari Camp, 3 km outside of town within walking distance to a hot spring and close to Alexander's temple, T02- 8473399.

For an explanation of the sleeping and eating price codes used in this guide, see inside the front cover. Other relevant information is found in Essentials pages 46-48.

A popular and long-standing camp in the area, offers space to pitch a tent, huts, and 21 rooms, a few with private bath; campers get access to kitchen, electricity and bath with hot water, free transport to Bawiti, bikes available, wide range of desert safaris can be organized. Beer and food available.

F Eden Camp, 10 km south of Bawiti, T02-8473727. A homey camp in a small palm garden with a hot spring and cold pool. Simple cozy huts (E£20 per person) share clean baths. 2 a/c rooms with private bath available (E£60), as well as space to sleep under the stars. A good place to stay if you're travelling with a group looking for some mellow lounging in the desert. Breakfast included.

F Pyramid Mountain Camp, at Bir Al-Ghaba, 14 km from Bawati. Hot water spring of 42°C, huts, guard, E£10 per person per night includes mattress and blankets, ask at Alpenblick Hotel for details. Take all your own supplies.

Farafra *p456, map p456*

C Aquasun, a new more chic option 6 km from town near Bir Sitta, T010-6678099, 02-3372898. A/c rooms, satellite TV and a hot spring fed pool. A quiet resort, stylish and fresh. Hitch a pickup to town for E£1-2 or hire a taxi for E£10, each way.

D-F Al-Badawiyya Hotel, T092-510060, 02-5758076, www.badawiya.com. Clean, rooms range from E£150 for large split-level double with bath and TV to E£10 per person in shared room with shared facilities.

F El-Waha Hotel, a new budget option 300 m north of town, near the Badr museum, T012-7200387, 010-3064733. Clean new rooms, singles, doubles, and triples. Every two rooms share a spotless bathroom with reliable hot water. Common lounge with TV. Friendly eager staff who lead relatively inexpensive tours of the area.

Camping

Campsite at Bir Setta, 6 km from village by the hot spring.

Dakhla and Mut *p457, map p459*

Compared to other oases, there's quite a range of accommodation in Dakhla, though most places are quite simple in their offerings. Most hotels and camps rent bicycles and will gladly arrange a tour of the area for you. Desert safaris can also be organized. 'Camps' in this area usually offer a place to pitch a tent, as well as simple bungalo accommodation.

C Solymar Inn (Mut 3), in the Northern part of town on Sharia El-Thawra, by the hot spring Mut 3, T/F092-821530. Operated by the same management as the Pioneer in Kharga, this place is absurdly overpriced for what it offers. Rooms are clean, but very basic. All have fans and private bath but only 2 come with a/c. Cost includes both breakfast and dinner. There's a 25% discount in the summer. Camping is permitted, E£20 per person and there are some tents available for hire E£60. The restaurant, across the street from the pool, offers pleasant ambiance and the exact same menu as every other restaurant in town for twice the price (lunch E£35, dinner E£54). There is a bar with the widest selection available in town. The only reason to stay here is for the pool fed by the rich spring. Since it's open to non-guests for E£5 per day, use it and find another place to sleep.

E El-Negoom, in El-Horraya near the police station, T092-820014, F8203084. Most rooms overlook a garden and are very clean. They are organized in suites of 3, each sharing a sitting area with TV and fridge. Rooms with a/c and private bath (E£57); or without (E£40). Breakfast included. Restaurant also serves lunch and dinner (E£12 and E£15). 15% discount in the summer. A step above Mebarez, Negoom feels brighter and newer, though it's a bit out of the way.

E Mebarez Hotel, Sharia El-Tharwa, T092-821524. Clean carpeted double rooms with a/c, private bath, telephone, fridge, and some with TV. Breakfast included. Management is friendly but the atmosphere a bit drab. Popular with package tours. In the winter, there's a small warm water pool available. 25% discount in summer. There's a restaurant that serves lunch and dinner (E£17, E£18).

F Anwar Hotel, in the centre of Mut between the Old and New parts of town, T/F092-820070, 821566. Friendly family-run hotel that feels quite homely. Rooms are comfortable, all with fans and some with a/c. Only 1 has a private bath. Restaurant downstairs has all the regular dishes and a *felafel* stand.

F El-Forsan Hotel, by the cemetery near the New Mosque and bus station, T092-2821343,

F821347, elforsan1@yahoo.com. Management is friendly and helpful, rooms are clean and spacious with a range of options. Rooms are E£20, add E£10 for a/c and E£10 for private bath. A coffeeshop and hilltop garden offer a good view of the area.

F Garden Hotel, in the centre of town, near Anwar's Hotel, T092-821577. Decent rooms with fans amid a verdant palm garden. A bit shabbier than other budget options, but the cheapest central hotel. Dorms can get stuffy and shared bathrooms are a bit grubby. Washing machine E£1 per load. You can rent a bike here.

F Al-Qasr Resthouse, Al Qsar. Friendly Mohammed offers rustic and reliable shared rooms with clean shared bath for E£10 per person; and camping on the roof is also possible (mattress provided, E£2). The resthouse also has a telephone and a tasty restaurant that serves ice cream and beer. It's a good place to go if you want a guide of the old city or any information on transport in the area.

Nearby is the **Al-Qasr Hotel**, on a cliff overlooking the town, T092-876802, but it's only open sporadically. There is also a classy new hotel that is scheduled to open soon.

Camping

F Khamis Camp, is 2 km south of Mut, T092-822435, run by the Garden Hotel. You can pitch a tent E£5 per night, or rent a hut for E£15. It's a quiet and remote site, surrounded by sand dunes with a nearby hot spring. The unreliable restaurant may necessitate a frequent hike to town for food.

F Bedouin Camp, near El-Douhous about 7 km north of Mut, T092-805805, F805480. 22 simple clean concrete huts on a hilltop overlooking the valley. Run by poetic and friendly Bedouin, this is a good place to come for serene desert respite. E£20 per person, most rooms include mosquito net but no fans or a/c. Baths are shared and spotless. Breakfast is included and restaurant on sight. At night, there's often a fire and Bedouin music. Extensive desert safaris can be arranged.

F Bir El-Gebel, see page 460. Accommodation in a few concrete bungalows with clean shared baths. The surroundings are majestic: lush fields and golden dunes in the distance. There is a garden and a restaurant surrounding the large pool which is fed by the hot spring.

Kharga Oasis *p462, map p462*

A Pioneer, on road out to Assiut, T092-927982, F927983. A little out of keeping with the oasis but clean, comfortable and everything works, even the satellite TV. There's a mid-sized swimming pool open to non-guests for E£30 and a 'tourist village' highlighting traditional architecture and artifacts. A Bedouin-style *ahwa* offers *sheesha* and tea at night. From the roof, you can see the Temple of Nadoura. There's also a well-stocked bar and good, albeit pricey, restaurant.

E Hamad Allah Hotel, off Sharia Abdel Mounim Riad, T092-920638, F925017. 54 clean, carpeted rooms with phone, fridge and TV. New a/c recently installed, which means if you're in Kharga in summertime, this may be a good bet. Hotel has a decent restaurant with set menu prices (lunch E£21, dinner E£25), as well as a bar and garden.

E Kharga Oasis, Sharia Gamal Abdel Nasser, T092-921500. 30 rooms, some with aged and tempermental a/c (at best). The rooms overlook a nice palm garden, which helps compensate for all the concrete that went into building the hotel. The restaurant is unspectacular, the service mediocre.

F Dar Al-Bayda, Midan Ash-Showla, T092-921717. A good and relatively clean budget place to stay in old town. Most rooms have fans and a bathroom. As it's right by the buses and the action, it can get noisy.

F Waha, Sharia El-Nabawi, T092-920393. Probably the cheapest choice in town, and a favorite overnight spot for drivers and budget travellers, Waha is cramped, but comfortable enough. Rooms have fans and clean sheets. The shared bathrooms can get grubby if there are too many guests and the hot water supply is erratic.

Guest houses

Government guest houses provide cheap (**F**) accommodation in **Al-Mumtazah** and **Mogamma**. An especially good option for groups of 4 or more. Mogamma with its 4 well-equipped chalets (each has a TV and a kitchen) is a step above Mumtazah. Book through the tourist office, T092-921205/6.

Camping

Kharga Oasis, see above. Use of hotel facilities is permitted, E£7 per night.

Nasr Wells, south of Kharga, is in a beautiful site. Although there are only a few official camping areas there is no problem camping along the route. Come prepared with mosquito repellant and sufficient water, as provisions are scarce in these parts.

Eating

Bahariyya and Bawati *p451, map p454*
Most hotels and camps serve up a decent breakfast. In town, there are a few small shops and cheap places to eat, but hygiene is a variable. The safest bet is:
Bayoumi's Popular Restaurant, truly the most popular gathering spot in town with tasty homemade food (though no menu), decent bathrooms, and an owner who is always smiling and filled with information. Also a good place to come if you're looking for a desert guide.
Rasheed Restaurant, on the main street near the Oasis Heritage Museum. Good for sweets and *sheesha*.

Farafra *p456, map p456*
Except for the snazzier restaurants in Al-Badawiya and the Aquasun hotels, all local eateries are in the town's main square.
Hussein's Restaurant serves *fuul*, omelette or tinned tuna with chips or bread with Coca Cola or tea.
Samir's, follow the smoke to find it. Serves the standard *fuul* and *taamiyya* as well as grilled chicken and kebab.
For *sheesha*, tea and coffee, there are a couple of options, a bustling *ahwa* by the 'bus stop' that is popular among *Saidi* immigrants and a quieter more local *ahwa* near the Badr museum. There is a small bakery and a few stores that sell all the basics.

Dakhla and Mut *p457, map p459*
Most restaurants offer the exact same food and few have menus. Lunch or dinner in Dakhla usually consists of salad, soup, rice, and some kind of vegetable and meat. Except for the Solymar's restaurant, the cost for a meal ranges from E£10-20. Besides the hotels, there is a stretch of restaurants on Sharia El-Sawra, toward Mut 3:
Ahmed Hamdy's, is definitely the best and most popular with tourists and locals alike. In addition to the regular dishes, they serve up delicious fresh juice. Nearby, find **Abu Mohammed**, **Arabi's** and **Shehab**, all of which offer similar fare.
Felafel is available in front of Anwar's. Fruit can be found at the market in Midan Tahrir.

Kharga Oasis *p462, map p462*
Besides the hotels and the few local cafés the choice is limited. The area around Midan Basateen has the most local eating options. For fruit or *felafel* and *fuul*, try the souk near Medan Showla.
The Pioneer, see above. Offers an extensive, good meaty menu. Entrées average around E£35.

Bars and nightclubs

Bahariyya and Bawati *p451, map p454*
Bedouin Music and Teahouse, in Agouz, T8472431. Abd El-Sadik Badromani recites poetry and plays delightful traditional music on his *simsimaya*, a classic Bedouin string instrument. He started inviting people into his home years ago but with increased traffic, he has since created a large Bedouin- style area just outside his house to host visitors. If you want to go, ask anyone for Badromani, it's a 2 km walk from Bawiti and every taxi driver knows his place. He also serves tea, coffee, and beer.

Dakhla and Mut *p457, map p459*
For beer, try **Meberez**, the **Solymar Inn** or **Abu Mohamed**. There is also a store that sells Stella near the Anwar Hotel.

Kharga Oasis *p462, map p462*
The **Pioneer** has a well-stocked bar, as does the **Hamad Allah Hotel**.

Shopping

Farafra *p456, map p456*
Shopping in Farafra is limited, but it's worth checking out the famous **Dr Socks** who has made quite a lucrative business cycling around town selling camel socks and other goods.

Activities and tours

Bahariyya and Bawati *p451, map p454*
In Bahariyya, there are over 70 people working as guides of the Western Desert.

Every hotel and camp can organize safaris, ranging from an afternoon trip to multi-week-long adventures. Most common are jeep tours, though some opt to explore by camel or on foot. The most popular safari takes 2-3days and includes Bir Ghaba, the Black desert, Crystal Mountain, and the White Desert. Depending on the quality you are seeking, prices vary significantly. For a jeep filled with 6, expect to pay about US$25 or E£150 per person per day. In addition to the hotels, there are a few particularly reputable freelance tour guides. Among them:
Lutfi Abd-el-Sayad, T02-802092. A kind character and a safe experienced desert driver and tour guide, a classic on the safari scene.
Hamuda Kilani, T02-802148. One of the foremost guides in the area, incredibly knowledgeable about the Western Desert, speaks good English and French. Great sense of humour and takes care of his clients. Specializes in walking trips.

Farafra *p456, map p456*
Tours and excursions into the surrounding desert are organized by all local hotels.
El-Waha offers the cheapest deals.
Al-Badawiyya, has been around the longest.

Transport

Bahariyya and Bawati *p451, map p454*
Bus
Buses from **Cairo** to Bawiti (4-5 hrs, E£14) leave daily at 0700, 0800, 1800. The 0700 and 1800 buses carry on to **Farafra** and **Dakhla**. Buses from Bahariyya to **Cairo** leave daily at 0700, 1500. Cairo-bound buses coming through from **Farafra** leave Bawati around 1200 and 2400 daily. You can't reserve tickets but if there's space, you can hop on. Enquire at Popular Restaurant for the most current times and routes. The ticket kiosk (hours very uncertain) is by the telephone office but only sells tickets for journeys originating in Bawati. Otherwise pay on the bus if you can get a seat.

Taxi
Service taxis and microbuses leave for **Cairo** daily as soon as they're full (E£14); service to **Farafra** as well, but not on a daily basis. Ask at the Popular Restaurant. Private taxis charge around E£600 to take the variable Darb El-Siwa, the 420 km direct route to **Siwa** via the desert. If you have a 4-wheel drive and permit, you can do it, but exercise extreme caution as the road is poorly maintained and often covered up for long stretches by mounds of sand. Note that there are no facilities on the road so come armed with sufficient essentials including lots of water and petrol.

Farafra *p456, map p456*
Bus
Buses and service taxis congregate around the Tamawy *ahwa*. 2 daily a/c buses to **Cairo** (8-10 hrs, E£27) via **Bahariyya** (2-3 hrs, E£14) are supposed to leave at 1000 and 2200. Tickets must be purchased on board. The night bus originates in **Dakhla** and is often full so arrive early. There are 2 daily buses to **Dakhla** (4-5 hrs, E£15) that leave daily around 1300 and 0100. Check the latest timetables at any hotel or *ahwa*. Microbuses to **Dakhla** and **Bahariyya** leave when full, generally quite early in the morning, fare E£15. Rarely to **Cairo**.

Taxi
Service taxis to **Cairo** are very irregular.

Dakhla and Mut *p457, map p459*
Air
Dakhla has an airport, but services have been suspended due to a lack of demand. Officials are working to reinstate it so check with **EgyptAir**, T092-822853/4, or the tourist office to find out the latest. Much more likely to be in service during the winter when tourism increases significantly.

Bicycle
Bicycles are a popular way to get around Mut and in the winter, to surrounding villages. They can be hired from most hotels and restaurants. The going rate is around E£10 per day.

Bus
Local There's also a crowded local bus, leaving from the bus station that runs to nearby villages 4 times a day.
Long distance Bus from Dakhla (Mut) to **Cairo** (E£44) via **Kharga** (2-3 hrs, E£8) and **Assiut** (6-7 hrs, E£15) daily at 1900 and 2030, takes 10-11 hrs; via to **Cairo** (E£35) via

Farafra (5 hrs, E£10) and **Bahariyya** (8 hrs, E£16), daily at 0600 and 1800, takes 12-14 hrs. All Cairo-bound buses should have a/c, but only the 2030 direct bus has a bathroom. There are additional daily buses that stop in **Kharga** and only go as far as **Assuit** at 0600, 0830, 1700, 2030, 2200. Presently, there are not direct buses to **Luxor**. You can either take a bus to Assuit and change there or aim to get on the weekly Fri 0700 train from Kharga. Buy tickets at least a day in advance to ensure a seat.

Taxi

Local Service taxis, usually in the form of shared covered pick-up trucks, connect Midan Tahrir to the nearby villages **Balaat**, **Bashendi** and **Al-Qasr** (50p- E£1) throughout the day but it's easiest to find a ride in the early morning.

Long distance There are also service taxis from the bus station to all the above destinations for about the same cost as the buses. They are a bit less comfortable, but can be a good option if the buses are full or if you want to leave at an unscheduled time. Easiest to find them in the morning and early evening.

Kharga Oasis *p462, map p462*

Air

There are 2 flights to/from **Cairo** every week. Sun mornings, direct; and Wed mornings, via **Assuit**. Flight time is 50 mins. The airport, T092-920457, is 5 km northeast of town on the road to Assiut.

Bus

Buses leave from Midan Ash-Showla. To **Cairo**, 3 each day (10 hrs) departing at 0600 (no a/c or toilet, E£24), 2100 (a/c but no toilet, E£38) and 2300 (a/c and toilet, E£38). There are 3 buses daily to **Dakhla**, 1400, 2100, 2200 (3 hrs, E£8) with a/c, coming from **Cairo** via **Assuit**. To go to **Luxor**, your best bet is to travel via **Assuit** (5 daily buses, 3-4 hrs, E£8-9) or take the weekly train. **Upper Egypt Bus Co**, T092-920838

Taxi

Service taxis and microbuses usually caught from near the bus station are about the same cost as the bus and sometimes quicker, though they generally don't leave until they're full. Easiest to find rides out of town in the morning (0600-1000) and evening (1700-2200) when it's cooler. Most popular destinations include **Assuit** (2 hrs, E£8), **Dakhla** (2 hrs, E£8), **Baris** (1-hr, E£3). You can also hitch a ride to nearby sights if a service taxi is en route. Covered pick-ups and microbuses shuffle people from one side of town to the other for 25p. A private taxi along the new road not yet used by public transport costs E£250-350, depending on your bargaining skills.

Train

To **Luxor**, there is a weekly train on Fri, 0700, 3rd class only, no a/c, E£11. There are also early morning trains to **Baris**, 0600, and back 1400, but they do not run daily, check with the tourist office for a current schedule.

Assiut *p465*

Air

There are direct flights to **Luxor** (Tue) **Cairo** (Tue, Sun) and **Kharga** (Sun) from the airport 10 km northwest of the town.

Bus

There are 7 daily buses to **Cairo** (7 hrs) as well as buses every 30 mins between 0600-1800 north to **Minya** (2 hrs) and south to **Sohag**.

Taxi

Service taxis, where permitted, run to every town between **Minya** and **Sohag** and are easy to catch from the main depot in the mornings but are less frequent later in the day. Foreigners may not be permitted to ride in a service taxi outside of a convoy which makes bus or train travel a more reliable option. Be prepared for this annoyance.

Train

Trains run 12 times a day to **Cairo** (7 hrs) via **Mallawi** (2 hrs) and **Minya** (3 hrs), and a bit less frequently to **Luxor** (6-7 hrs) via **Sohag** (2 hrs) and **Qena** (4-5 hrs). Remember that foreign visitors are restricted to designated trains, but if you hop on a local train and pay on board, it's unlikely you'll get kicked off.

Directory

Bahariyya and Bawati *p451, map p454*
Banks National bank, changes cash, closed Fri and Sat, open 0800-1400. **Hospitals** Nowadays, there are many doctors in Bahariyya, if you are in need of medical assistance, ask at the **Popular Restaurant** or any hotel and someone will help you. There's a small hospital on the road to Cairo, T02-8472390. **Telephone** Office is opposite the Paradise Hotel, though for international calls, you're better off trying the **International Hotsprings Hotel**. **Useful addresses** There are 2 **gas stations** on the main road and a **pharmacy** near by **Bayoumi's**, open daily from 0800-0100.

Farafra *p456, map p456*
Banks There's no bank in town, though you may find some local folks who will gladly buy dollars. **Hospitals** There is a relatively new hospital, T092-510047, 1.5 km out of town toward Bahariyya. **Post office** Open 0800-1400, closed Fri. **Telephone** Adjacent to the post office is the telephone office. Open 24 hrs. **Useful addresses** There is no **tourist information** office, but folks at **El-Badawiyya** and **El-Waha** speak decent English and have quite a bit of information. Museum is also a good source. There's a **petrol station** at the entrance to Qasr Farafra.

Dakhla and Mut *p457, map p459*
Banks Misr Bank, T092-820063, near Midan Tahrir, open 0830-1400 and 1800-2100 each day, takes TCs and cash. . **Hospitals General Hospital**, T092-821555, 821332.
Internet Available at the **Forsan Hotel** for E£10 per hour. **Post offices** Both open Sat-Thu 0800-1400. **Telephone** International calls are best made from the tourist office or some of the hotels. Try the **Forsan**, **Anwar** or **Negoom**.

Kharga Oasis *p462, map p462*
Banks Misr Bank, open Sun-Thu 0800-1400.
Hospitals General Hospital, T092-920777.
Useful telephone numbers Police: T122. Tourist police: T092-921367.

Siwa Oasis

→ *Colour map 1, grid A2.* *Population: 20,000.*

In the northeastern corner of the Western Desert sprouts the Siwa Oasis, a place like no other on earth. Less than 60 km from the Libyan border, isolated for centuries by hundreds of kilometres of rolling sand dunes, Siwa was inaccessible by car until a road was built in the early 1980s connecting it to Marsa Matruh. The 300 km road winds through desert oblivion and suddenly gives way to a striking shroud of green. About 82 km long east-west and 20 km north-south at its widest point, the oasis, 18 m below sea level, shelters 30,000 date palms, 70,000 olive trees and hundreds of bubbling springs to nourish them. Despite its seclusion, Siwa has drawn in visitors from afar, captivated by its singular culture and beauty since antiquity. In the early 20th century, the oasis lured an average one or two tourists a month. Now, some 7,000 tourists visit every year.

South from Siwa the Sudanese border lies across 700 km of desert. Of this 400 km is The Great Sand Sea, which, like a frozen storm with waves 100 m high, casts rolling sand dunes in every direction. Legend tells of a lost oasis and true adventurers still come in search. Perhaps the descendants of Cambyses live on... (see box, page 473).

▸▸ *For Sleeping, Eating and other listings, see pages 477-480.*

Ins and outs

Getting there It is possible to approach Siwa from Bahariyya but a reliable four-wheel drive vehicle is essential. Enquire at the tourist office on either end of the route if you want to make the 420 km journey. Safaris to Bahariyya via the White Desert can be arranged. They generally take two nights and three days, and cost about E£200 per person or E£800 per car. ▸▸ *For further details, see Transport, page 480.*

Getting around You can easily cycle, or hire a karetta. A trip to Jebel Dakhrour, Juba's Spring and the Temples of Amun can be combined as they all exist on a loop to the east of town. Take the road east from the PalmTrees Hotel. Follow it to the fork, where it veers to the right. If you want to go straight to Jebel Dakhrour, stay on the tarmac. To head first to Juba's Spring and then the Temples of Amun, go straight on the dirt road that forks off.

Information Tourist office ⓘ *at the entrance of town, across the street from the large pink hospital, west of the new mosque, T046-4602338, mahdi_hweiti@yahoo.com. Open Sun-Thu from 0900-1430*. Mahdi Hweiti, an articulate and wonderfully knowledgeable Siwi native, has been single-handedly manning the tourist office since it opened. He has a wealth of information about the oasis and some fascinating tales, ask him about his ancestors who he says were the first among the re-settlers of the oasis in the 12th century. Mahdi can arrange tours to nearby sites and help anyone who wants to make a more epic desert venture. Even if you stop by after hours, Mahdi is often hanging out around his office

NB But with its customs unchanged for centuries, untarnished by the world around, a heightened sensitivity is called for when visiting Siwa. You will quickly see how modestly Siwan women dress, covered from head to toe in a voluminous blue shawl with sheer black fabric covering their faces – and women visitors are requested to keep legs and upper arms covered. Alcohol and affection are forbidden in public.

Background

Siwans, currently numbering 20,000, have always been fiercely independent; the oasis only officially became part of Egypt in the 19th century. It has been inhabited, with reliance on the more than 200 fresh, salt, warm and cold springs, since Palaeolithic times.

The economy is based on agriculture, dates and olives. The Sa'idi date is preferred for eating. Water supply is from natural springs. No pumping is necessary but the springs are capped to provide some control. Surplus water is a serious problem and the water level is rising at about 9 mm annually. New land is taken into cultivation if demand increases, the olives bearing fruit in five years and the date palms in 10 years. Quarrying, transport, trade (and smuggling) are also important and there is an increasing revenue from tourism but labour costs are high as labourers have to be brought in and need food and accommodation.

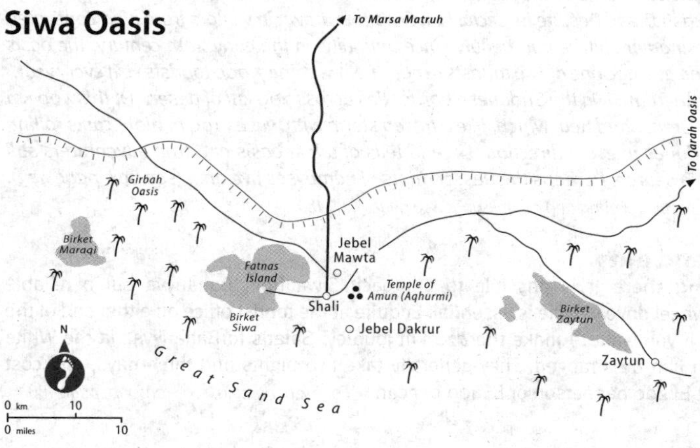

The Oracle of Amun

It was The Oracle of Amun which brought Siwa to the attention of the world, from the 26th Dynasty (664-525 BC) onward. Alexander the Great is known to have consulted the Oracle in 331 BC after wresting control of the country from its Persian rulers in order to ask it if, as he suspected, he was indeed the son of Zeus. His arrival with a large party of friends and an even larger number of soldiers must have caused quite a stir in sleepy Siwa. Unfortunately, posterity does not record the Oracle's response. Nearly 200 years earlier, Egypt's Persian ruler Cambyses (525-522 BC) is said to have carelessly lost an army of 50,000 men who were dispatched from Aïn Dalla near the Farafra Oasis to Siwa in order to destroy the Oracle. The army was simply never seen again having been either buried by a sandstorm or snatched by aliens.

The filming of the Oscar-winning *The English Patient*, has drawn attention to this area. With increased tourism, the building of an Olympic Pool and stadium that seats 20,000, and the recent upsurge of luxury hotels, there are plans to open the adjacent military airport which guards the nearby Libyan border to commercial traffic. This could increase the visitors, currently about 100 a week, to vast numbers to be accommodated in planned luxury tourist villages and almost certainly damage the very essence of this remote area. Locals dread the day. Cisit before its too late.

Sights

Siwa deserves some time. To appreciate the oasis in all its splendour, moving slowly is essential. There are hot and cold springs to swim in, ancient tombs housing mummies and beautiful paintings, the temple of Amun with the Oracle that has attracted pilgrims for centuries (Alexander the Great, among them). The people of Siwa are extraordinary, retaining customs and traditions from centuries past, as well as their own language, Siwi, a Berber dialect with Algerian roots. Their kindness and low-key nature are refreshing respite from the hustlers of other heavily trafficked destinations. And no visit would be complete without at least one night in the desert, underneath far too many stars to count and the silence of the Great Sand Sea.

The main settlement is **Shali**, until recently straddling two low hills within the depression, but now abandoned. The ruins of the old town established in 1203 are still impressive. The minaret of the 17th-century mosque remains. The mud brick walls and towers are floodlit at night, a splendid sight. New stone dwellings, mainly single storey, have been constructed. They are certainly not so attractive but probably much more comfortable. The new mosque of Faud I, a solidly built structure of stone in the pleasant style of the late 19th-early 20th century, is the natural centre of the new town. Adjacent to it is the tomb of Sidi Sliman, a local saint.

Birket Siwa salt lake and **Fatnas Island** 4 km from town, is a beautiful picnic spot and the most popular mini-excursion from Siwa. Despite the recent government irrigation effort in the middle of the lake that resulted in a significant receding of water and the death of the famed leaning palm, Fatnas (or Fantasy Island as its known in tourist lingo) has managed to retain its beauty. There is a cold spring-fed pool, perfect for swimming in (women should wear opaque T-shirt and shorts), and a small coffee

Female donkeys are not allowed in Siwa oasis. Locals find the mating behaviours between males and females to be offensive and they believe the absence of females will help the males sustain their energy. The only females on the oasis are confined to a village 30 km from Shali, around the spring of Abu Sheruf.

shop that offers *sheesha* and light snacks. The sunsets overlooking White Mountain and the surrounding *mesas* are spectacular. Camping is possible, inquire with Omran, the kind man who runs the café. If it's not too hot, the walk or bike ride is pleasant, or you can hire a *karetta* (donkey cart) for around E£10-15 to take you, wait an hour or two, and bring you back. Take precautions against the many mosquitos.

There are two **temples to Amun** here, both at the deserted village of Aghurmi 3 km east of Shali. The **Temple of the Oracle** (see box, page 473) is built on a large rock amid the remains of the village. Crudely restored by German archeologists, it dates back to the 26th Dynasty. There are stunning views to the nearby Temple of Umm 'Ubayda, Jebel Matwa and across the palm groves to the shimmering salt lakes. The site of the second temple **Umm 'Ubayda**, from the 30th Dynasty, is marked by an area of fallen blocks in which one wall, all that survived the 1877 earthquake, carefully inscribed, still stands.

Juba's Spring, also called Cleopatra's Pool although it has nothing at all to do with the lady, was mentioned by Heroditus. It is supposed to change temperature during the day but the reality is the relative difference between air temperature and the temperature of the person dipping in, and many people do. On a practical note, the spring produces enough water to irrigate 121 ha every 14 days. Women are advised to swim in a long T-shirt and shorts. You're most likely to find the pool empty early in the morning or late in the evening. Fridays are crowded.

Jebel Dakhrour, the 'mountain' that sprouts up in three mounds about 4 km east of town, is the site of Siwa's annual **Siyadha festival** in October. The summit awards stunning views of the oasis all around. The salt lake shimmers amid a blanket of

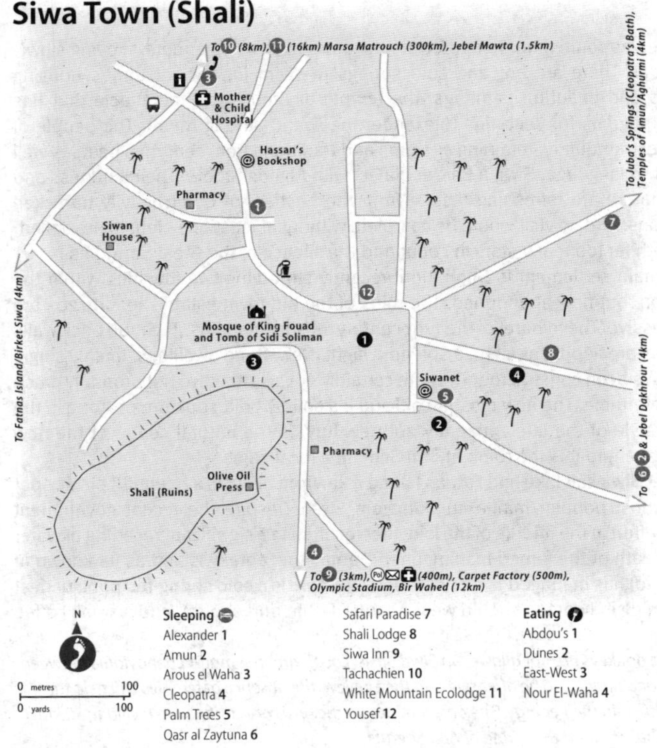

A long lost tomb?

First it was, then it wasn't, and now it probably isn't – the long lost tomb of Alexander the Great. The announcement by Greek archaeologist, Liana Souvaltzi, that she had uncovered (at Maraqi in Siwa) possibly the most important archaeological find since that of Tutankhamun's tomb created a storm of controversy. Her claim centres around a 50 m above- ground 'tomb' which Souvaltzi says bears the same markings as that of Alexander's father, King Philip of Macedonia, including his royal symbol, an eight-pointed star. Just 18 m away, lies an entrance to a tunnel guarded by two royal lion statues and three stelae. The inscriptions, she claims, describe Alexander's funeral procession to Siwa.

The find, if authentic, would rewrite history. According to ancient texts, the conqueror, who died possibly from poison in 323 BC, expressed a wish to be buried in Siwa, where he had been deified in 331 BC, but was finally laid to rest in Alexandria. A team of Greek experts, who flew out immediately to assess the find, concluded that there was "no evidence" of Alexander's tomb: the inscriptions were from the late Roman rather than earlier Hellenistic period, and the 'royal' eight-pointed star was a common theme in Macedonian monuments. Meanwhile, the burial chamber, at 76 cm wide, is too narrow for a sarcophagus to pass through. Excavations are still continuing but so far the only point of agreement is that the tomb, unusually large by Macedonian standards, is an important discovery; but of whom, it has yet to be decisively determined.

palms, with the Great Sand Sea abruptly encroaching on the edge. In July and August around midday when it's hot enough to cook a chicken outside, sufferers come from afar to be buried in the **hot sands** (sand bath: *hammam ramal*) around Jebel Dakhrour with the hopes of alleviating their arthritis, rheumatism and even impotence.

Tombs of Jebel Mawta ⓘ *there's no entrance fee but the custodian must unlock the tombs for you, baksheesh is expected, 0900-1400, closed Fri, no photographs allowed inside*, or Mountain of the Dead is a conical hill about 1½ km north from the centre of Shali. It is honeycombed with tombs from 26th Dynasty to the Roman period, varying from small chambers to large composite excavations complete with columns and wall paintings. Anything worth stealing has long since been removed. During 1940 many items were 'sold' to the visiting troops by Siwans who had moved into the tombs for security. Excavations are still in process and new tombs are regularly being discovered. Of the tombs open to visitors, that of Si-Amun, a rich local merchant is the most striking, with wall paintings of Si-Amun and his family, of Nut the goddess of the sky, and a very recognizable maple tree. Others that are open include: Tomb of Mesu-Isis; Tomb of the crocodile; and Tomb of Niperpathot in relatively poor condition, but shelter to several mummies too delicate to relocate.

Aside from the tombs, there are also splendid views from the summit of Jebel Mawta.

The **Traditional Siwan House** ⓘ *1000-1200, closed Thu and Fri, admission E£1.50*, exhibition financed by Canadians, shows in great detail the artefacts and decorations used until very recently in the houses of the oasis.

Thewre is an **olive press** ⓘ *no fee but baksheesh appreciated*, driven by donkey power, in operation only at the end of the olive season around the first week of December. Arrangements can be made at the tourist office.

The 'sacred aunt' of the Arabs – the date palm

Egypt produces about half a million tons of dates each year, though only a small portion of the total is made up of top quality dessert fruit. Even so, dates are an important part of the Egyptian rural diet and each year some 62,000 tons of dates are produced from scattered palmeries in the Delta and valley areas, though principally in the commercial plantations of the true desert or the oases such as Siwa. The date palm is among the longest established orchard trees in Egypt and was a favoured symbol on monuments from pre-dynastic times.

The prophet Mohammed called on the Islamic faithful to protect the date palm, which he called their 'sacred aunt' because of its many uses as a food, building material and provider of shade (see below). The Swedish naturalist Carl Linnaeus paid homage to the beauty and generosity of the palm tree when he classified it in the order of Principes, 'The Order of Princes'. The green and yellow foliage of the date palm is also a fine decoration in the otherwise vegetation- less squares and avenues of many Egyptian cities. In the western oases of Egypt, the palm is the tree of life, its fruit, leaves and wood the basis of the local economy. The Latin name of the date palm, *Phoenix dactylifera*, can be translated as "the Phoenician tree with fruit resembling fingers".

For the oasis dwellers, the date is so precious that they have a name for each stage of its growth. Trees may produce up to 100 kg of dates annually for a whole century. However, in order to do this, it needs manure and a lot of water, anything up to 300 litres a day.

The palm tree provides many essentials for its owner. The trunks are used to support roofs of houses, strengthen walls and in slices are used to make doors. One or two trunks make an adequate bridge over an irrigation channel, and with pieces cut out can be used as steps. The fibres on the trunk are removed and used as stuffing for saddles while the base of the palm frond, stripped of its leafy part, makes a beater for washing clothes and a trowel for the mason. Palm fronds are used to make baskets and a variety of mats such as the famous *margunah* or covered basket of Siwa. Midribs have enough strength to be used to make crates and furniture. Leaf bases are used for fuel and fibre for packing. The sap is drained and consumed as a rough but intoxicating beer *laghbi* or even as a distilled liqueur. This practice is banned for Muslims, who are forbidden alcohol and in any case drawing the sap can also kill the tree and is therefore discouraged by the authorities. The flesh of the fruit, which is rich in sugar and vitamins is eaten by man and the stone is eaten by camels (date stones can even be ground and used to supplement coffee). Best quality fresh dates are a delicacy for the rich. Dried and pressed dates stay edible for long periods and can be taken on journeys or used to sustain the nomads in their wanderings.

Siwa water bottling plant is run by an Italian company on the outskirts of Shali. It produces over one million bottles annually. **Safi water**, of equal quality, has a smaller output. **Hayat**, the newest of the bunch, welcomes visitors to its factory about 30 km from town on the road to Bahariyya. Ask Mahdi at the tourist office if you're interested. An excellent way to exploit an area with too much water.

Excursions around Siwa

Among the most beautiful spots to visit around Siwa is **Bir Wahid**, an enchanting hot spring set amid silky dunes and a lush garden, about 12 km off road from town. There is a small cafeteria that sells *sheesha* and basics, as well as a few simple tents for rent (E£5 per person). If you plan to stay more than a night, bring your own provisions and lots of water. En route most safari guides will stop at one of the natural sweet water cold pools, perfect for swimming. In the vicinity, there are plenty of opportunities to climb dunes and rocky summits, search for fossils or go sand-surfing.

Birket Zeitoun, the huge salt water lake, visible from the summit of Jebel Dakhrour, is quite a desolate place, due largely to its high salinity. Still, it's silvery water and salty edges offer a stunning setting to take in a sunset. Some 37 km southwest of town, the beautiful spring **Abu Shrouf** bubbles up invitingly. The water is a deep shade of blue and so clean, you can see the bottom and schools of little fish 10 down. It's undisputedly the nicest pool around, and often empty, save the female donkeys that are supposedly confined to the area for mating. Whenever a local loses his donkey, the first question asked is "have you been to Abu Shrouf?" Going to Abu Shrouf is also a widely known euphemism for "did you have sex?" Lone women travellers, be cautious if a man invites you to accompany him alone to the magic spring.

Across the street, the **Hayat** water bottling factory is open to visitors. The source of their water is a hot spring that empties out into a large concrete pool, suitable for a soak if you don't mind stepping on slimy algae.

Further south along the lake, there is a small Bedouin village and the ruins of **Al-Zeitoun**, an old community that once tended the lushest gardens in the oasis until an Italian bombing raid in 1940 led to its abandonment. There is the dwindling remains of a small temple and an age-old circular olive press worth a look, as well as a nearby hill dotted with old Roman tombs.

Sleeping

Siwa Oasis *p471, map p474*

p471, map p474

The range and quality of accommodation in Siwa has increased tremendously over the last few years. Now you can find royal accommodation in exquisite surroundings, as well as less-than-a-dollar beds on rooftops or under a tent surrounded by palm trees. All hotels organize tours into the surrounding desert.

AL White Mountain Ecolodge, 16 km west of town at the foot of and built into White Mountain (in Siwi, known as *Adrar Al-Milal*). Reservations must be made in Cairo, T02-7367879, F7355487. This astonishingly beautiful mud-brick complex that melds so beautifully into the surrounding landscape has been noted as one of the top 25 eco-lodges in the world. The daily rate of US$200 per person includes full board and access to the 24-hr bar, horses and stables, a stunning cold spring-fed pool, and day-long safaris to Bir Wahed and other sites. The views overlooking Birket Lake are breathtaking. There is no electricity, only candles and oil lamps. The rooms are royal, made by locals with local materials, palm and olive wood, salt, and rocks from nearby mounts. Nothing short of enchanting and worth a visit even if it's out of your budget. A restaurant and bar for non-guests is being constructed.

B Tachachien, 8 km from town on the road out to the eco-lodge, on its own island accessible by a causeway, T046-4600455. The 20 huts overlooking Lake Birket are simple and clean. A bit overpriced, but it's one of the best places around to take in both the rising and setting sun. There is a huge spring-fed pool on the island and plans for boats to transport visitors to other islands on the lake. Outdoor restaurant and cafeteria. Mosquitos can be a problem.

C Safari Paradise, 200 m from the main square, T046-4602289. Touristic village popular with large groups. Offers a range of

For an explanation of the sleeping and eating price codes used in this guide, see inside the front cover. Other relevant information is found in Essentials pages 46-48.

accommodation in a/c and bungalows with fans. Both have satellite TV, fridge and private bath. Rates include half-board and are negotiable in the summer. A bit overpriced, but comfortable. Bungalows surround the large cold spring-fed swimming pool in a garden setting.

C Shali Lodge, Midan El-Souk, 100 m from the town centre, T046-4602399, F4601799. A prototype for the ecolodge, the Shali Lodge is unquestionably the nicest place to stay in town, but with only 8 suites, it's not always possible. Built in the traditional Siwan style with mud bricks and palm wood ceilings and furniture, the gorgeous rooms are spacious and spotless, decorated with local Bedouin crafts and rugs. Unlike the eco-lodge, Shali has electricity, satellite TV, fans and natural heaters in the winter. There's a pool in the pipeline too. The restaurant features the best food in town, and the best atmosphere, set on the breezy roof under blooming palms. Excellent value.

D Qasr Al-Zaytuna, on the road to Dakrour, T046-4600037. A brand new hotel scheduled to open soon. Built and managed by a delightful Egyptian-German couple. Very tasteful, with huge soft-toned rooms, hardwood floors, high ceilings. There is a suite available with a nice kitchen. Some rooms have a/c, all have fans and lovely bathrooms. Very close to Jebel Dakrour, a good place to stay for anyone interested in sand baths or being away from the little action there is in town. There's also a pool, garden and restaurant. Trips are organized. Rates include half-board.

D Siwa Inn, 30 mins' walk from the town centre, T046-4602284, F4600405, siwainn@yahoo.com. 10 rooms surround a palm and vegetable garden with a cold spring-fed pool. All have a/c, fridge and private bath. Run by an Egyptian couple. Rates include half board. The rooms, though not built from mud brick, feel traditional and are decorated with local crafts. There's a shared lounge with TV and a large restaurant.

E Arous El-Waha, near the tourist office at the entrance of town, T046-4602100. A government-run hotel. All the rooms facing west make it impossible to bear the heat in the summer. Ragged carpet covers most of the floors. Rooms come with fans and private bath. Breakfast is included. Overpriced.

F Alexander, north of the main square, T046-4600512. Another long-standing budget hotel with a friendly staff. Rooms are a few pounds more than the Palm Trees but cleaner, all with fans, some with private bath. The restaurant is good and frequented by travellers.

F Amun, on the outskirts of Jebel Dakhrur, 4 km from town. Not a 'tourist' hotel, it's quite filthy. People who stay here are generally partaking in the sand bath therapy to soothe their rheumetism or alleviate their impotence so the atmosphere is subdued.

F Cleopatra, 200 m south of the town centre, T/F046-4602148. The best of budget offerings in town if you're looking for a clean room, though without a garden, atmosphere is lacking. The slightly pricier new branch (E£45 per double) has spotless rooms with tiled floors, private bath and fan. This old branch is cheaper (E£31 per double) and is clean enough, but a bit worn around the edges. Staff is friendly and helpful.

F Palm Trees, T046-4602304, F4600006. The rooms aren't the cleanest but the garden is the best and most happening in town. There's a range of accommodation from garden rooms with fans and private bath (E£45) at the top end, to sleeping on the roof or in the garden (E£5) at the bottom. An old-timer on the scene, Palm Trees remains a backpacker's favourite and makes a great spot to meet other travellers. Check out sunset over Shali from the rooftop.

F Yousef, in the main square, T046-4602162. Rooms are cramped but clean. All have fans and some include private bathroom and balcony. Location is central, which makes it noisy at times. The view from the roof is excellent.

Camping

This is a sensitive area close to the Libyan border, so despite the good relations, don't camp out without permission from the tourist office. Some people camp out by the hot spring behind Jebel Dakhrur. It's also possible to camp on Fatnas Island, see page 473. You can sleep on the roof or under the Bedouin tent of **Palm Trees Hotel** for E£5 per night. For more leads, or to camp in the desert, enquire with Mahdi at the tourist office.

Eating

Siwa Oasis *p471, map p474*
As far as the oases go, there's quite a range of good grub in Siwa. Most restaurants are scattered around the town centre and serve up fairly comparable food, for comparable prices (all cheap). There are the standard chicken and kebab dishes, as well as Egyptian pizzas, vegetable medleys and a surprising array of Indian curries. (The story is an Indian tourist came about 10 years ago and taught a local desert chef how to cook a curry and so the trend began, though authenticity is up for question.) Among the longest standing of all the eateries is **Abdou's**, cheerful and welcoming, though lacking on intimate atmosphere. The kebab is especially good. Safaris into the desert can be arranged. Other old-timer, good cheap eats are: **Restaurant Alexander** and the **East-West Restaurant**, which is open the earliest.
Dunes, across the street from the Palm Trees Hotel, has a lovely atmosphere with chairs and Bedouin-style seating in a Palm garden. On Fridays after midday prayer, they offer a delicious multi-course meal where local men come in droves to indulge. There's also cheap good *sheesha* (50p). A bit more expensive, but not by much, is the softy-lit **Nour El-Waha**, across the street from the Shali Lodge. Comfortable and quaint, there are candles, good food, sheesha (E£3) and lots of backgammon. For the classiest meal in town, try the restaurant on the roof of the **Shali Lodge**. It's still very modestly priced, and the atmosphere so inviting. The menu is the most diverse in town featuring various crepe and couscous dinners. With 24-hrs notice, they'll stuff a goat for you. There is no alcohol.

Festivals and events

Siwa Festival or the **Siyadha Festival**, in **Oct** just before date harvest during full moon, lasts 3 days and over 3,000 people come to celebrate with prayers and sing religious songs. A truly exceptional event that welcomes visitors. Book accommodation in advance if you intend to come.

Shopping

Siwa Oasis *p471, map p474*
Market every Fri. Siwan handicrafts of note include carpets woven from local wool, in thick bright stripes of red, yellow and blue; traditional wedding gowns in black – equally eye-catching but less popular as a purchase; traditional old Siwan silver jewellery, is in limited supply. If you walk around the village, girls and women may invite you to look at their work. There are a few shops in the main square that sell scarves, clay incense burners and ashtrays, baskets and some jewellery. There's also a **carpet factory** in town that employs 250 women who weave intricate patterns. It's open to visitors.

Bookshops
Fathy Malim Bookshop English and French books available, and internet service for E£10 per hr. Fathy recently published a very informative book on Siwa, that is available at his shop and at the PalmTrees Hotel.

Activities and tours

Safaris
Most hotels will help you organize day-long or overnight safaris around the oasis. Though rates fluctuate a bit, the margins are modest. Day-long excursions generally cost around E£40-60 per person. Overnight trips including food cost E£60-80 per person. For the 420 km journey to Bahariyya, it's E£200 per person for the 2-night/3-day trek, minimum 4 people. Bear in mind that some safari leaders are more reputable than others, those listed below are recommended.
Abdullah Baghi, an extremely articulate English speaker with fascinating tales who was personally honoured for his commitment to his community by Kofi Anan, leads trips. Ask for him around the Shali Lodge.
Ali, also based at the Shali Lodge in the mornings and his handicrafts shop in the main square in the afternoons, organizes safaris.
Omar, aka the Desert Fox, is among the most reputable of guides, especially for more extensive expeditions. If you want to find him, check in with Mahdi at the tourist office.

Mahdi also leads trips. He's especially fond of showing visitors around the nearby antiquities; his wealth of knowledge makes the visits much more meaningful.
Salah, at the Palm Trees Hotel, can arrange for you to be dropped in the desert with your provisions and picked up the following morning, with a stop at Bir Wahid if you wish.

Transport

Siwa Oasis *p471, map p474*

Bicycle

Most places are within cycling distance; virtually every hotel and restaurant rent bikes, most for E£10 per day. The **Palm Trees hotel** rents fairly rickety bikes for E£5.

Bus

The bus station and taxi halt are near the big pink mother and child hospital by the tourist office at the entrance of town, just a short walk from the centre. There are 4 a/c **West Delta buses** daily from Siwa to **Marsa Matruh** (0700, 1000, 1300, 2000, E£12), 3 of which carry on to **Alexandria** (0700, 1000, 2200, E£27). Buy your tickets at least 2 hrs in advance. If travelling on the 0700, buy them the night before to ensure you have a seat.

Donkey carts

Donkey carts, or *karrettas* as they are called here, are for hire everywhere. Expect to pay around E£10 for a quick roundtrip journey to nearby sites like the Temple of Amun or Fatnas Island. For long waits, pay an additional E£5, more at night. A ride from the bus station to a hotel in town shouldn't cost more than E£3.

Taxi

Service taxis bound for the coast leave daily, generally around mid-morning and late afternoon. For longer distances, there are service pick-up trucks that will shuffle visitors around the oasis. They are generally found in front of the tourist office. You may want to step inside and inquire about times. You'll find the most options in the early morning.

Directory

Siwa Oasis *p471, map p474*

Banks Presently, there is one under construction. It's best to arrive in Siwa with what you need but if you must change money, check in with Mahdi at the tourist office, he should be able to help. Most hotels will buy euros and dollars. **Internet** There are a few internet cafés scattered around the town centre nowadays, the most established of which is **Siwa Oasis Net**, T012-7447374, www.siwaoasis.com, next door to the Palm Trees Hotel. Mohmaed Ibrahim, runs the place and speaks excellent English. The going rate at present is E£10 per hr. Try also **Fathy Malim Bookshop**, E£10 per hr.
Post office Located with the police station just south of the Arous El-Waha Hotel.
Telephone Central phone station open 24 hrs, near the tourist office. It's also possible to use the phones at most hotels.

Background

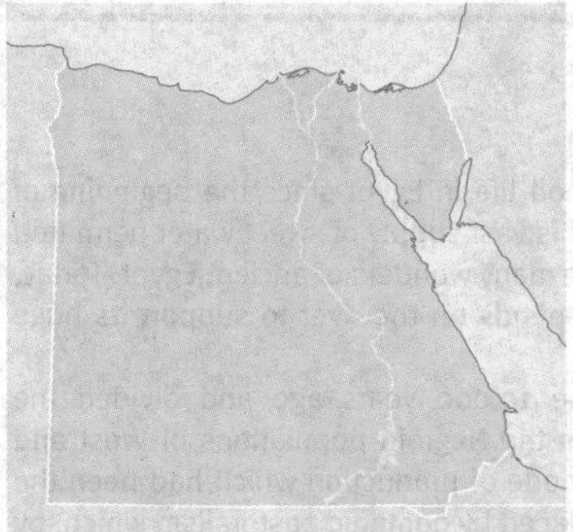

Footprint features

History

The River Nile has been the key influence on life in Egypt since the beginning of civilization many thousands of years ago. This vast supply of sweet water permitted the creation of a society which produced the many wonders of ancient Egypt. Today, no less than in the past, modern Egypt depends on the river to support its huge population. The Nile is Egypt's lifeblood.

The Sahara began to dessicate some 10,000 years ago and divided the Caucasoid populations of North Africa from the Negroid populations of West and Equatorial Africa. The original agricultural mode of production which had been the basis of settlement there was gradually replaced by nomadic pastoralism which, by around 4000 BC, had become the preserve of two groups, the Libyan-Berbers in the east part and the ancestors of the modern Touareg in the west. North African populations, all classified as part of the Hamito-Semitic group which stretched east into Arabia, soon became sub-divided into the Berbers in the west, the Egyptians in the east and the Nilo-Saharians and Kushites to the south, in what today is Sudan.

The key to the development of a complex civilization lay in the water and soils of the Nile valley. By 3000 BC, the Nile was supporting a dense sedentary agricultural society which produced a surplus and increasingly allowed socio-economic specialization. This evolved into a system of absolute divine monarchy when the original two kingdoms were amalgamated by the victory of King Menes of Upper Egypt who then became the first Pharaoh. Pharaonic Egypt was limited by an inadequate resource base, being especially deficient in timber. Although it was forced to trade, particularly with the Levant (Eastern Mediterrean), it never became a major seafaring nation. Equally, the growing desertification of Libya meant that its influence never extended west. Instead, the Egyptian Empire sought control up the Nile valley, towards Kush (or Nubia) which it conquered as far south as the Fourth Cataract (between Khartoum and Wadi Halfa in Sudan) by 1500 BC. It also expanded east into the Levant, until it was restrained by the expanding civilizations of the Fertile Crescent (the arc of territory lying between the rainfed east Mediterranean coastlands/Syria/Mesopotamia) after 2300 BC.

By 1000 BC, Pharaonic Egypt was being pressured from all sides. The Hyksos (the shepherd kings of Egypt (2000-1700 BC) who migrated to Egypt from Asia) threatened the Delta from the Mediterranean, whilst the Lebu from Libya began to settle there too. They eventually created the 21st (Sheshonnaq) dynasty of the New Kingdom in 912 BC which, for a short time, extended its power east as far as Jerusalem. In the 7th century BC, however, Egypt was conquered by its Kushitic imitators to the south in the Nubian kingdom under King Piankhy who founded the 25th Pharaonic Dynasty.

The Nubians were expelled some years later by the Assyrians, but their conquest marked the end of the greatness of Pharaonic Egypt. Thereafter, Egypt was to be a dependency of more powerful states in the Middle East or the Mediterranean. The rulers of Nubian Kush in their turn, having been expelled from Egypt, looked south from their new capital at Meroe – to which they had moved as a result of the subsequent Persian conquest of Egypt in 525 BC and later Persian attempts to conquer Kush. Kush became, instead, the vehicle of transmission of iron-working technology and of Egyptian concepts of divine political organization southwards as well.

Pharaonic Egypt

About 3100 BC, King Menes succeeded in uniting Upper and Lower Egypt into a single kingdom. His new capital at Memphis, about 15 km to the south of modern-day Cairo, was deliberately located on the border of Upper and Lower Egypt. Despite this, the rivalry between the two parts of Egypt continued until the end of the Early Dynastic Period (3100-2686 BC).

The **Old Kingdom** (2686-2181 BC) began with the Third Dynasty and ushered in a major period of achievement. A series of strong and able rulers established a highly centralized government. The 'Great House', *per-aha* from which the word pharaoh is derived, controlled all trade routes and markets. The calendar was introduced and the sun god Re was the most revered deity. Until then it was common practice for leaders to be buried in underground mausoleums (*mastabas*).

In the 27th century BC King Zoser and his chief architect Imohotep constructed the first step pyramid in Saqqara, the huge necropolis across the river from Memphis, and pyramids became the principal method of royal burial for the Pharaohs during the next millennium. The scale of organization required to mobilize the resources and manpower to build these phenomenal pyramids is testimony to the level of sophistication of this period. The three Fourth Dynasty (2613-2494 BC) giant pyramids of Cheops, Chephren and Mycerinus erected on the Giza plateau still awe the world.

By the end of the Old Kingdom, the absolute power of the Pharaohs declined. Local leaders ruled their own *nomes* (provinces) and a second capital emerged at Heracleopolis. Few great monuments were built in this very unstable **First Intermediate Period** (2181-2050 BC).

During the 11th Dynasty Menutuhotep II reunited the country and created a new capital at Thebes (Luxor). Remains from this era, the Middle Kingdom (2050-1786 BC), demonstrate its prosperity.

During the five dynasties of the **Second Intermediate Period** (1786-1567 BC), central authority again disintegrated and Egypt was controlled briefly by Asiatic kings known as the Hyksos (foreign princes), rulers who introduced horses and chariots to Egypt.

The **New Kingdom** (1567-1085 BC), spanning the 18th-20th Dynasties and based at Thebes, ushered in a period of unparalleled wealth and power. During these 400 years the kingdom prospered and expeditions led to the creation of a huge empire. Military campaigns in Western Asia by Tuthmosis III, now known as the Napoleon of Ancient Egypt, brought Palestine, Syna and Nubia into the empire and their wealth and cheap labour poured into Thebes. The temple complex of Karnak and the Valley of the Kings are but two of the astounding remains of the era. During this period (1379-62 BC), Akhenaten renounced the traditional gods in favour of a monotheistic religion based on the sun god Re but his boy-king successor Tutankhamen immediately reverted to the former religion and its principal god Amun. In 1922 archaeologists discovered Tutankhamen's undisturbed tomb and its treasures are displayed at the Egyptian Museum in Cairo. After the military dictatorship of Horemheb, a general who seized the throne, royal power was restored by Ramses I. Ramses II, a most prestigious builder, reigned for 67 years. Following the death of Ramses III, the last great pharaoh, effective power moved increasingly into the hands of the Amun priests and the empire declined. The pharoahs' power was diminished through intra-dynastic strife, decline in political grip on the levers of power and loss of control of day-to-day administration.

During the **Late Dynastic Period** (1085-332 BC), the succession of dynasties, some ruled by Nubians and Persians, became so weak that **Alexander the Great** had little difficulty in seizing the country. Although he did not spend long in Egypt his new capital city of Alexandria, where he is believed to be buried, still flourishes. His empire was divided among his generals and Ptolemy established the **Ptolemaic Dynasty** (332-30 BC) which ended with the reign of Cleopatra VII (51-30 BC), the last of the Ptolemies, before Egypt became a province of the Roman Empire.

The division of power between Rome and Constantinople resulted in the virtual abandonment of Egypt. Egypt's autonomy led to the development of the Coptic

Dynasties in Egypt up to 30 BC

Rules mentioned in text are included in the list.

Ruler	Date
Early Dynastic Period (3100-2686 BC)	
First Dynasty	3100-2890 BC (Memphis established)
Menes	
Second Dynasty	2890-2686 BC
The Old Kingdom (2686-2181 BC)	
Third Dynasty	2686-2613 BC
King Zoser	2667-2648 (Step Pyramid in Saqqara)
Huni	
Fourth Dynasty	2613-2494 BC (Pyramids of Giza)
Snefru	
Cheops (Khufu)	
Chephren (Khafre)	
Mycerinus (Menkaure)	
Shepseskaf	
Fifth Dynasty	2494-2345 BC
Unas	
Sixth Dynasty	2345-2181 BC
South Saqqara necropolis	
Teti	
Pepi I	
Pepi II	
First Intermediate Period (2181-2050 BC)	
Seventh Dynasty	2181-2173 BC
Middle Kingdom (2050-1786 BC)	
Eleventh Dynasty	2050-1991 BC
King Menutuhotep II	Creation of Thebes (Luxor)
Twelfth Dynasty	1991-1786 BC
Amenemhat I	1991-1961
Senusert I	1971-1928
Senusert II	1897-1878
Amenemhat III	1842-1797
Queen Sobek-Nefru	1789-1786
Second Intermediate Period (1786-1567 BC)	
Fifteenth Dynasty	1674-1567 BC (capital Avaris)
New Kingdom (1567-1085 BC) based at Thebes	
Eighteenth Dynasty	1567-1320 BC (Temples of Luxor & Karnak)
Amenhotep I	1546-1526
Tuthmosis I1525-1512	
Tuthmosis II	1512-1504
Hatshepsut	1503-1482
Tuthmosis III	1504-1450
Amenhotep II	1450-1425

Ruler	Date
Tuthmosis IV	1425-1417
Amenhotep III	1417-1379
Amenhotep IV (Akhenaten)	1379-1362
Tutankhamen	1361-1352
Ay	1352-1348
Horemheb	1348-1320
Nineteenth Dynasty	1320-1200 BC
Ramses I	1320-1318
Seti I	1318-1304
Ramses II	1304-1237
Seti II	1216-1210
Siptah	1210-1204
Tawosert	1204-1200
Twentieth Dynasty	1200-1085 BC
Sethnakht	1200-1198
Ramses III	1198-1166
Ramses IV	1166-1160
Ramses V	1160-1156
Ramses VI	1156-1148
Ramses VII	1148-1141
Ramses IX	1140-1123
Ramses XI	1114-1085
Late Dynastic Period (1085-332 BC)	
Twenty-second Dynasty	945-715 BC
Twenty-fifth Dynasty	747-656 BC
Shabaka	716-702
Twenty-sixth Dynasty	664-525 BC
Necho II	610-596
Twenty-seventh Dynasty	525-404 BC (Persian occupation)
Cambyses	525-522
Darius I	521-486
Thirtieth Dynasty	380-343 BC
Nectanebo I	380-362
Nectanebo II	360-343
Late Period (332-30 BC) (Macedonian Kings, capital Alexandria)	
Alexander III (The Great)	332-323
Philip Arrhidaeus	323-317
Ptolemaic Era	323-30 BC
Ptolemy I	Soter 323-282
Ptolemy II	282-246
Ptolemy III	246-222 (Edfu Temple)
Ptolemy IV	222-205
Ptolemy V	205-180 (Kom-Ombo Temple)
Ptolemy VII	180-145
Ptolemy VIII	170-145
Ptolemy IX	170-116
Ptolemy XIII	88-51
Cleopatra VII	51-30

Isis and Osiris

Myths have always played a very important part in the religion of ancient Egypt and it is not possible to separate the myths from religious rituals. The story of Isis and Osiris, one of the chief Egyptian myths, was written on papyrus some 5,000-6,000 years ago.

According to the story, Osiris was the son of Geb, the earth god and was therefore descended from the sun god Re. He was known to have been a great and good king and was particularly concerned with agricultural techniques, growing crops to provide the essentials: bread, beer and wine. He ruled wisely and when he travelled abroad Isis, his sister and wife, most competently took charge.

His brother Seth was filled with jealously and hatred for Osiris and was determined to be rid of him. This he did with the help of the Queen of Ethiopia and another 72 conspirators. Seth had constructed a most magnificent chest, which exactly fitted the measurements of Osiris. At a feast all the guests tried the chest for size and when Osiris took his turn the conspirators nailed down the lid and sealed it with boiling lead.

The sealed chest was carried to the banks of the Nile and thrown into the river where it floated out to the sea and came to land at Byblos in Syria. There a tamarisk tree grew up immediately and enclosed the chest. The size of this magnificent new tree caught the eye of the king of Byblos, Melcarthus, who had it cut down to make a pillar to support the roof of his palace.

Isis, distressed by the disappearance of her husband's body and aware that without funeral rites he could never rest in eternity, went out to search for him. It took some time to trace the route to Byblos, find the chest still encased in the trunk of the tree but now supporting a main room in the king's palace and even longer to persuade them to part with that pillar and the chest.

She made her way back to Egypt with the body of Osiris still in the chest. Here she was a little careless, for leaving the chest hidden but unguarded, she went off to be reunited with her young son. By some mischance Seth, hunting by the light of the moon, stumbled on the chest. He immediately recognized the container and in his rage cut the body into 14 separate pieces.

Seth, determined to rid himself of his brother once and for all took the pieces and scattered them through all the tribes of Egypt. Undaunted, Isis set out again, this time in a papyrus boat, to retrieve the separate pieces which she did with the help of her sister Nephthys, the gods Thoth and Anubis and some magic. At every place she found a part of her husband she set up a shrine. The severed parts where brought together and Osiris was restored to eternal life.

Horus, the son of Isis and Osiris, was brought up in secret to protect him from harm. When he reached manhood he swore to avenge the wrong done to his father and mother. Another myth describes his victory over Seth, after one or two setbacks, and how he was declared by the tribunal of gods to be Osiris's rightful heir.

church, which was independent from both the Byzantines and the Romans, and whose calendar dates from AD 284 when thousands were massacred by the Roman emperor Diocletian.

The Three Crowns of Egypt

The king was a reincarnation of a god – Re, Aten, Amun or Horus. He was addressed by the god as "my living image upon earth".

A king was recognized on illustrations by his garments and paraphernalia. The most important of these was his crown. The earliest kings wore the white bulbous crown of Upper Egypt. The red crown of Lower Egypt was even more distinctive with a high back and forward thrusting coil. A king wearing the double crown was thought to symbolize his control over all Egypt.

The ultimate sign of kingship, however, was the *uraeus* on his forehead, a rearing cobra with an inflated hood – generally in gold.

Other items of importance associated with kingship included the hand held crook and flail and the false plaited beard.

Greeks and Phoenicians

In North Africa, Egypt's failure to expand westward permitted other developments to occur. The coastal area became the arena for competition between those Mediterranean civilizations which had acquired a naval capacity – the Greeks and the Phoenicians. Indeed, this became the future pattern and resulted in the history of the region being described in the terms of its conquerers.

We do know, however, that the Greek and Phoenician settlements on the coast provoked a response from the nomadic communities of the desert such as the Garamantes around the Fezzan in Libya. These communities appear to have specialized in warfare based on charioteering and they began to raid the new coastal settlements. At the same time, they also controlled trans-Saharan commerce – one of the major reasons why the Phoenicians, at least, were so interested in North Africa. As a result, they also engaged in trade with the new coastal communities, particularly those created by the Phoenicians. Other invasions also took place, this time of northeast Africa from southern Arabia, bringing Arab tribes into Africa. The new Arab invaders spread rapidly into modern Ethiopia and Eritrea.

The Greeks had begun to colonize the Egyptian and eastern Libyan coastline as part of their attempt to control Egyptian maritime trade. Greeks and Phoenicians competed for control of the old coastal areas in Libya and eventually created an uneasy division of the region between themselves. The Greeks took over Egypt after the creation of the Ptolemaic Kingdom on the death of Alexander the Great in 323 BC and incorporated Cyrenaica (in Libya) into the new kingdom. The Phoenicians, by now being harried in their original Lebanese home base of Tyre by the Assyrians and Persians, created a new and powerful maritime commercial empire based at Carthage (in Tunisia), with outlying colonies to the west, right round to the Atlantic coast at Lixus (Larache).

The Roman Empire

Control of Egypt and North Africa passed on once again, this time to the rapidly expanding city-state of Rome. Control of the Ptolemaic Kingdom of Egypt passed to Rome because of Roman interest in its agricultural produce and Egypt became a province of Rome in 30 BC.

The difficult problem of border security for Roman administrators was solved by creating the limes, a border region along the desert edge which was settled with

The Jews in Egypt

Jewish involvement in Egyptian affairs has long historical roots. Twelve tribes of Israel were forced by famine to migrate to Egypt where they remained as an underprivileged minority until led out by Moses 13th century BC, eventually to move to Canaan in today's Palestine. During the period of dominance of Egypt by Greek and Roman cultures, the Jews became scattered around the major lands of the respective empires in the Diaspora. At that time Egypt was a major destination for the Jews in exile. It is estimated that as many as one million Jews lived in Egypt, with important centres of Jewish activity in Alexandria (see page 325), Leontopolis (north of Cairo in the eastern delta) and even in Lower Egypt as far south as Elephantine Island.

The Jewish population in Egypt declined with the passing of the Hellenistic tradition and the imposition of a less tolerant Roman government. During the Islamic era, the Jews, though subject to some social constraints and dealt with separately for tax purposes, thrived as traders and bankers in addition to their role as skilled craftsmen in the souks. Occasional violence occurred against the Jews, who tended to be associated in the Egyptian popular mind with the foreign community and thus attacked at times of anti-British or anti-French riots in the major cities, as for example in 1882, 1919, 1921 and 1924. In general, however, it was true that Jews in Egypt fared far better and were more tolerated than Jews in some countries of Europe.

This all changed dramatically with the rise of Zionism in the period from 1890 and the return of Jews to Palestine. Even before World War Two the scale of Jewish migration to Palestine provoked fears in the Egyptian body politic and there were serious riots against the Jews in eight cities, most importantly in Alexandria and Cairo in 1938-39. Foundation of the State of Israel in 1948 brought an inevitable outbreak of rioting in which the Jews were a principal target. The Arab-Israeli wars of 1948, 1957, 1968 and 1973 added to the problem. Some 29,500 Jews left Egypt for Israel alone in the years 1949-72, in the latter years in official expulsions. Under pressure from both the flight to Israel and migration elsewhere, the Jewish population in Egypt fell from approximately 75,000 in 1948 to a few families by 1998.

A return of diplomatic relations between Egypt and Israel after President Anwar Sadat's visit to Jerusalem in 1977 improved official links and economic contacts between the two sides (albeit put in jeopardy by Israel's break of faith with the peace process in 1997), but the Jews have never returned as a community to Egypt.

former legionaries as a militarized agriculturalist population. Thus, although the border region was permeable to trade, resistance to tribal incursion could be rapidly mobilized from the resident population, while regular forces were brought to the scene. The limes spread west from Egypt as far as the Moroccan Atlantic coast.

Christianity

Egyptian Christianity became the major focus of the development of Christian doctrine. The Coptic Church became the main proponent of Monophysitism (the

Coptic Monasteries in Egypt

belief that there is only one nature in the person of Jesus Christ (ie that he is not a three-in-one-being) after the Council of Chalcedon in AD 451; Donatism (direct giving, official largesse) dominated Numidia (an area approximately the size of present day Algeria). At the same time, official Christianity in Egypt – the Melkite Church (Christians adhering to the rulings of the Council of Chalcedon that there are two natures to the person of Christ and who are known as "monarchists" or "supporters of the Byzantine emperor") – combined with the Coptic Church to convert areas to the south of Egypt to Christianity. See also page 515.

The Islamic Period

In AD 642, 10 years after the death of the Prophet Mohammed, Arab armies, acting as the vanguard of Islam, conquered Egypt. To secure his conquest, the Arab commander, Amr Ibin Al-As, immediately decided to move west into Cyrenaica (part of Libya) where the local Berber population submitted to the new invaders. Despite a constant pattern of disturbance, the Arab conquerers of Egypt and their successors did not ignore the potential of the region to the south. Nubia was invaded in AD 641-42 and again 10 years later. Arab merchants and, later, Bedouin tribes from Arabia, were able to move freely throughout the south. However, until AD 665, no real attempt was actually made to complete the conquest, largely because of internal problems within the new world of Islam.

The Muslim seizure of Egypt was, despite the introduction of Islam, broadly welcomed by the Copts in preference to remaining under the Byzantine yoke. Islam slowly prevailed, as did the introduction of Arabic as the official language, although there remained a significant Coptic minority. Cairo became the seat of government and emerged as a new Islamic city. Whilst the seeds of Islam itself strengthened and blossomed there were centuries of political instability which led to the creation of countless dynasties, mainly ruled by foreign Muslim empires. The new faith was only fleetingly threatened when the Christian Crusader armies attacked Cairo and were repelled by Salah Al-Din (AD 1171-93).

The Great Dynasties and their successors

The Fatimids The first of the great dynasties that was to determine the future of North Africa did not, however, originate inside the region. Instead it used North Africa as a stepping stone towards its ambitions of taking over the Muslim world and imposing its own variant of Shi'a Islam. North Africa, because of its radical and egalitarian Islamic traditions, appears to have been the ideal starting point. The group concerned were the Isma'ilis who split off from the main body of Shi'a Muslims in AD 765.

The Fatimids took control over what had been *Aghlabid Ifriquiya*, founding a new capital at Mahdia in AD 912. Fatimid attention was concentrated on Egypt and, in AD 913-14, a Fatimid army temporarily occupied Alexandria. The Fatimids also developed a naval force and their conquest of Sicily in the mid-10th century provided them with a very useful base for attacks on Egypt.

After suppressing a Kharejite-Sunni rebellion in Ifriquiya between AD 943 and AD 947, the Fatimids were ready to plan the final conquest of Egypt. This took place in AD 969 when the Fatimid general, Jawhar, succeeded in subduing the country. The Fatimids moved their capital to Egypt, where they founded a new urban centre, Al-Qahira (from which the modern name, Cairo, is derived) next to the old Roman fortress of Babylon and the original Arab settlement of Fustat.

The Fatimids' main concern was to take control of the Middle East. This meant that Fatimid interest in North Africa would wane and leave an autonomous Emirate there which continued to recognize the authority of the Fatimids, although it abandoned support for Shi'a Islamic doctrine.

The Hillalian invasions Despite Fatimid concerns in the Middle East, the caliph in Cairo decided to return North Africa to Fatimid control. Lacking the means to do this himself, he used instead two tribes recently displaced from Syria and at that time residing in the Nile Delta – the Banu Sulaim and the Banu Hillal – as his troops. The invasions took place slowly over a period of around 50 years, starting in AD 1050 or 1051, and probably involved no more than 50,000 individuals.

The Hillalian invasions were a major and cataclysmic event in North Africa's history. They destroyed organized political power in the region and broke up the political link between Muslim North Africa and the Middle East. They also damaged the trading economy of the region. More than any other event, the Hillalian invasions also ensured that Arabic eventually became the majority language of the region.

Egypt after the Fatimids Fatimid power in Egypt did not endure for long. They were forced to rely on a slave army recruited from the Turks of Central Asia and from the

Sudanese. They found it increasingly difficult to control these forces and, eventually, became their victims. In 1073 AD, the commander of the Fatimid army in Syria, which had been recalled to restore order in Egypt, took power and the Fatimid caliph was left only with the prestige of his office.

What remained of the Fatimid Empire was now left virtually defenceless towards the east and the Seljuk Turks, who were already moving west, soon took advantage of this weakness. They were spurred on by the growth of Crusader power in the Levant and, after this threat had been contained, Egypt soon fell under their sway. Control of Egypt passed to Salah Ad-Din Ibn Ayyubi in AD 1169 and for the next 80 years the Ayyubids ruled in Cairo until they in their turn were displaced by their Mamluk slaves.

The Mamluks The Mamluks were a class of Turkic slave-soldiers. The first Mamluk Dynasty, the Bahri Mamluks, were excellent administrators and soldiers. They expanded their control of the Levant and the Hijaz and extended their influence into Nubia. They cleared the Crusaders out of the Levant and checked the Mongol advance into the Middle East in the 1250s. They also improved Egypt's economy and developed its trading links with Europe and Asia. Indeed, the fact that the Mamluks were able to control and profit from the growing European trade with the Far East via Egypt was a major factor in their economic success.

In AD 1382, the Bahri Mamluks were displaced from power by the Burgi Mamluks. Their control of Egypt was a period of instability and decline. The Ottoman Turks, in a swift campaign in 1516-17, eliminated them and turned Egypt into a province of the Ottoman Empire.

The Ottomans in North Africa

The Ottoman Occupation

The Ottomans emerged with some strength from the northwest heartlands of Anatolia in the 15th century. By 1453 they controlled the lands of the former Byzantine Empire and 65 years later took over Syria and Egypt before expanding deep into Europe, Africa and the Arab Middle East. The Syrian and Egyptian districts became economically and strategically important parts of the empire with their large populations, fertile arable lands and trade links.

Administratively, Palestine west of the Jordan Rift Valley was split into the *wilayat* (province) of Beirut along the northern coastal strip and the *sanjak* (district) of Jerusalem in the south reaching down towards the Gulf of Aqaba. The east bank of the Jordan River fell within the *wilayat* of Syria and included Aqaba. Egypt was also a valued part of the Ottoman Empire, ownership of which provided the Sublime Porte (the Ottoman Court at Constantinople) with control over the Nile Valley, the east Mediterranean and North Africa. Power was exercised through governors appointed from Constantinople, but over the centuries an Egyptian, mainly Mamluke (of Caucasian origin) elite imposed themselves as the principal political force within the country and detached the area from the direct control of the Ottomans. In most areas of the empire, the ability of the sultan to influence events diminished with distance from the main garrison towns and a great deal of independence of action was open to local rulers and tribal chiefs outside the larger towns.

The great benefit of the Ottoman Empire was its operation as an open economic community with freedom of movement for citizens and goods. Traders exploited the Ottoman monopoly of land routes from the Mediterranean to Asia to handle the spice, gold and silk from the East, manufactures from Europe and the slave and gold traffic

The arrival of the Ottomans in North Africa was the last invasion of the region before the colonial period began in the 19th century.

from Africa. Ottoman tolerance of Christian and Jewish populations led in Palestine/Syria to the growth of large settlements of non-Muslims. Arabic continued as the local language and Islamic culture was much reinforced. Elaborate mosques were added to the already diverse architectural heritage. Outside the larger towns, however, pastoralism, farming and parochial affairs remained the major occupation of the people and cultural and other changes were slow to occur.

Until the late 18th century the Ottoman Empire was wealthy, its armies and fleets dominant throughout the region, but after that date a marked decline set in. European powers began to play a role in politics and trade at the expense of the sultan. The empire began to disintegrate. During the 19th century Egypt under the Khedives, the famous Mohammed Ali and his successor Ismael, were only nominally under the sultan's control. Egypt adopted Western ideas and technology from Europe and achieved some improvements in agricultural productivity. The cost was ultimate financial and political dominance of the French and British in this part of the empire. In Palestine, too, colonial interventions by the French in Syria and Lebanon reduced Ottoman control so that by the time of the First World War the collapse of the Ottoman Empire was complete and the former provinces emerged as modern states, often under a European colonial umbrella.

The Ottoman occupation of North Africa was a by-product of Ottoman-Venetian competition for control of the Mediterranean, itself part of the boundless expansionism of the Ottomans once they had conquered Constantinople in 1453. The Ottoman attack was two-pronged, involving their newly acquired maritime power to establish a foothold and then backing it up with the janissary, land based forces that formed the empire's troops. The decrepit Mamluk Dynasty in Egypt fell to the Ottomans in 1517 and a new, centralized Ottoman administration was established there.

Egypt and Sudan

In Egypt, the Ottoman administration soon found itself struggling against the unreconstructed remnants of Mamluk society, with the province frequently splitting into two units, each controlled by a different section of the Mamluk Dynasty. By 1786, the Ottomans had destroyed the Mamluk factions and restored central control. In 1798, Napoleon's army conquered Egypt, delivering a profound cultural shock to the Muslim world by demonstrating, in the most graphic manner, the technological superiority of Europe. In 1805 Mohammed Ali was appointed governor and lost no time in breaking away from the Ottoman Empire to found a new dynasty, the **Khedivate,** which remained in power until a revolution in 1952.

Mohammed Ali sought to modernize Egypt and to expand its power. He brought in European military advisors, destroyed the remnants of the old political elite in Egypt and instituted wide-ranging economic reforms. In the Sudan, Mohammed Ali's Egypt was more successful; after the initial invasion in 1820, some 40 years were spent consolidating Egyptian rule, although, in 1881, the experiment failed (see box, page 493).

By that time, Egypt itself had succumbed to the financial pressures of its modernization programme. Borrowings from Europe began, with the inevitable consequence of unrepayable debt. In addition, Britain realized the potential importance of Egypt for access to its Indian Empire, particularly after the Suez Canal was opened in 1869. A debt administration was instituted in 1875, under joint British and French control. In 1881, a nationalist officers' rebellion against what they saw as excessive European influence in the khedivate, provoked a British take-over which lasted until 1922. Following British military commander General Gordon's death in Khartoum and the consequent British campaign against the Mahdist state in the Sudan, which culminated in the Battle of Omdurman in 1898, Britain instituted an Anglo-Egyptian condominium over Sudan.

Mohammed Ali and his successors

Mohammed Ali, the founder of the Khedival Dynasty, was born in Macedonia in 1769, came to Egypt in 1800 as an officer in the Turkish army, and was made governor under the nominal control of the Ottoman Sultan in 1805. He remained in post as a vigorous and development-orientated ruler until 1848. He died in 1849, having initiated the modernization of Egypt and the creation of a national identity, and is buried in the eponymous mosque in the Citadel in Cairo.

Ibrahim Pasha, eldest son of Mohammed Ali, was trained as a political leader as well as a soldier. He acted very successfully as his father's right-hand man but in his own right ruled for just four months in 1848. (See his imposing statue erected in Midan Opera by his son.)

Abbas Pasha (1848-54) was the son of Mohammed Ali's third son, Tusun. He organized the laying of a railway from Cairo to Alexandria with British support and encouragement. In other respects, however, he was reactionary, closing schools of advanced studies and slowing down the modernization process.

Sa'id Pasha (1854-63), second son of Mohammed Ali, served as an admiral in the Egyptian fleet and gave permission for the Suez Canal to be constructed. Sadly a large foreign debt was left as a legacy to his successor.

Khedive Ismail (1863-79), son of Ibrahim Pasha, was considered one of the great builders of modern Egypt, being responsible for the building of the Suez Canal, the Opera House, Ras El-Tin Palace and Abdin Palace. He was a man of great energy and vision. He expanded Egyptian influence in the south and east but eventually led the country deeper into debt and into subservience to the French and British.

Khedive Tawfik (1879-92) was the son of Ismail, during whose reign Egypt's financial problems led to foreign take over and, finally, the beginning of the British occupation in 1882. Manial Palace, his dwelling in Cairo, houses an important museum (see page 121).

Khedive Abbas Hilmi II (1892-1914), son of Tawfik, was noted for his interest in preservation and conservation of the country's ancient monuments. His attempts to develop a nationalist political movement came to nothing. He was deposed by the British in 1914.

Sultan Hussain Kamal (1914-17) was the second son of the Khedive Ismail. He owed his throne to the British and, despite the hardships of the war period, he ruled without challenging British power in Egypt.

King Fuad (1917-36) was another son of the Khedive Ismail, though much more an Egyptian nationalist than his brother Hussain Kamal. Egypt became more politically active and was given a form of independence in 1922 as a constitutional monarchy. However, Fuad was unable to create n political role for himself and was caught up in the political battles between the British and the nationalist politicians.

King Farouk (1936-52) was Fuad's son and the penultimate Khedival ruler of Egypt. He became, like his father, unable to manage an increasingly radical nationalist community in Egypt and the British occupiers distracted by the demands of World War Two and its legacies of change. Farouk had few political friends and he was forced to abdicate in 1952 in the face of the revolution by the Young Officers led by Gemal Abdel Nasser. Farouk's infant son, **Fuad II**, was nominally successor to the throne but lost all rights in the new constitution of 1953.

Colonialism

The British occupation of Egypt introduced a régime which, as the well known historian Ira Lapidus said 'managed the Egyptian economy efficiently but in the imperial interest'. Railways were built and widespread irrigation was introduced; the population virtually doubled in 35 years; private property was increasingly concentrated in the hands of a new elite; and the foreign debt was repaid. Industrialization was, however, neglected and Egypt became ever more dependent on cotton exports for revenue.

Social and political relations were not so smooth. The British occupation of Egypt coincided with a wave of Islamic revivalism. At the same time, a secular nationalist tradition was developing in Egypt which crystallized into a political movement at the end of the 19th century and was stimulated by Egyptian resentment at British demands on Egypt during the First World War.

After three years of agitation Britain granted limited independence in 1922. It retained control of foreign affairs, foreigners in Egypt, the Sudan and the Egyptian army, although some of these controls were abandoned in 1936.

At the beginning of the First World War, the potential vulnerability of the Suez Canal (see Box page 354) and the strategic implications of the Turkish-German alliance led Britain to increase its control over Egypt by declaring it a Protectorate. This led to the emergence, over the following 20 years, of both Arab and Egyptian nationalist movements which eventually procured nominal independence for Egypt in 1936, although Britain reserved the right to protect the Suez Canal and defend Egypt. By the end of the Second World War, this complex political system had outlived its usefulness and in 1950 Egypt unilaterally abolished the Canal Zone Treaty.

In 1952 the constraints of the British Mandates, and the frustration following the defeat in the 1948 Arab-Israeli war, led to the emergence of a new class of young army officers who staged a bloodless coup overthrowing King Farouk and ousting the remaining British troops. The new leader, Colonel Gamal Abdel Nasser, inherited a politically fragmented and economically weak state burdened with an ever-increasing demographic problem.

When the World Bank, at the behest of the USA, refused to help finance the construction of the new Aswan High Dam in 1956 Nasser nationalized the Suez Canal in order to raise the necessary revenues. This led to shock waves throughout the world and to the Suez crisis in which an Anglo-French force invaded and occupied temporarily the Canal zone. Nasser's dreams of development were hampered by Egyptian/Israeli tensions including the shattering Egyptian defeat in the 1967 war. He died in 1970 and was succeeded by Anwar Sadat. Sadat was aware that Egypt could not sustain the economic burdens of continual conflict with Israel so, despite the partially successful October 1973 war which restored Egyptian military pride, he sought peace with his neighbour. In 1977 he made a historic trip to Jerusalem and laid the foundations for the 1979 Camp David Peace Accords which enabled Egypt to concentrate on her own economic development and firmly allied Egypt with the USA. While he was applauded abroad he was considered a traitor in the eyes of the Arab world and Egypt was diplomatically isolated. His assassination by Islamic fundamentalists in October 1981 brought vice-president Hosni Mubarak to power.

Egypt factfile

Official name	Gumhuriyah Misr Al-Arabiyah (Arab Republic of Egypt)
National flag	Equal horizontal bands of red, white and black with a central emblem of Salah Al-Din's golden eagle clutching a panel bearing the country's name in its claws.
Official language	Arabic
Official religion	Islam
Statistics	Population: 66.5million. Work force: 19.5 million. Religion: Muslim (mainly Sunni) 90%, Christian 10%. Infant mortality rate: 41/1000. Fertility rate: 3.5%. Life expectancy: 67/69. Literacy: 54.6%.

Source: *Egyptian Almanac*, 2003

Modern Egypt

Government

Egypt became a republic in 1952 with a presidential system of government. The current president is Hosni Mubarak (see box page 497) who has effective control of the armed forces and the cabinet and can convene or dissolve the single tier People's Assembly virtually at will. He is also head of the ruling National Democratic Party (NDP). There have been efforts to introduce an element of democracy into government with general elections for the People's Assembly. The principal influence on the membership of the cabinet is the president. The Assembly has worked well but, until recently, was seen as a puppet organization for the regime. The speaker of the Assembly, Rifat Mahjub, was assassinated in October 1990. There was an attempt in 1991 to improve local administration with the appointment of a new minister. Regional government is carried out through four groups of administrations – the governorates for the Desert, Lower Egypt, Upper Egypt and the urban areas. Sub-districts operate from regional capitals and separately for the cities of Port Said, Alexandria, Cairo and Suez. The administration is very bureaucratic and slow. There have been generally fruitless attempts to reform the civil service but, with almost a third of the work force in public administration and defence, progress has been slow. Travellers should not have high expectations of officials and official agencies, though there are some institutions, mainly military, which function well. Personal influence is a key element in making the system work.

The government is only partially representative of the people and there are major dissident groups whose activities have in the past affected traveller. The Muslim Brotherhood – a form of fundamentalist Islamic organization – has flourished in Egypt for many years. While the Muslim Brotherhood is now the leading opposition group and is generally tolerated by the government the more extreme splinter groups, which have resorted to terrorism, are pursued by state agencies. In addition to attacking members of the government, often successfully, the extremists are opposed to corrupt foreign influences, of which the excesses of the tourist industry, including the country's 20,000 belly dancers, are seen as a key part. Opposition groups are suppressed by severe laws such as the detention regulations and by an ever-present security service, the *mokhabarat*, but see also page 516.

Heritage

Egypt's natural assets in the form of her skills and her fabric are at risk. There is now a clear need for the advanced industrialized countries to understand the basis of Islamic science and technology. Certainly this would help to bridge the growing cultural divide between themselves and their more numerous neighbours to the east. In particular, appreciation of the way in which Islamic culture has matured over the long-term is required so that the valuable skills and technologies of Egypt are not discarded for short-term gains. The pace of 21st century modernizations might all too quickly sweep away the remains and the folk memories associated with traditional culture.

There is also a risk that rapid technological change forced on a developing Egypt by the industrialized nations could lead to the indigenous technology being unnecessarily discarded instead of being used and, in the future, being deployed with advantage. The urgency of the problem of conservation or rescue of traditional Islamic technologies is acute. War and strife are depleting physical assets such as buildings and other works. Quite apart from man-made disasters, the processes of weathering on mud brick, from which many Islamic traditional constructions are made, is considerable. The comparatively recent abandonment of traditional villages, old mosques and underground water cisterns in Egypt has exposed traditional technology/material culture to destruction by natural erosion.

There is a real threat that the existing stock of examples of traditional Egyptian and Islamic technology of this kind could vanish with little trace in less than a generation.

Agriculture

Agriculture is the basis of the Egyptian economy accounting for 16% of total national output and 28% of employment. Despite very rapid urbanization, farming and the rural community remains at the cultural heart of the country. Current land patterns show the vital importance of the Nile Valley and Delta because the rest of the country is little better than waste land. Unfortunately even this very limited arable area is being reduced by the encroachment of Cairo and other urban areas.

Traditional agriculture

The great mass of Egyptian farmland is under traditional forms of agriculture and worked by the fellahin, the Egyptian peasantry. Farming is based on use of the waters of the River Nile for irrigation which are now available, theoretically, throughout the year from Lake Nasser. There has been a gradual increase in production of commercial crops but self-sufficiency is an important aim of small farmers. Wheat, rice, vegetables and fodder are the main crops, the latter to support the considerable number of draught (3.18 million buffalo), transport (two million asses and 200,000 camels) and other animals (3.23 million cattle, 3.3 million goats, 4.41 million sheep and 87 million chickens) kept mainly on farms. It is estimated that 6 million people are engaged directly in the traditional farming sector.

Land tenure

Until the 1952 land reforms, 1% of Egypt's land owners possessed 90% of the farming land. The reform stripped the former royal house of its lands and the state took the estates of the great families who had controlled rural Egypt. In their place the revolutionary authorities established centrally controlled co-operatives which substituted civil servants for the former landlords, a move which did little to alter the agricultural system or indeed benefit the peasants. At the present time the peasantry is either landless or has tiny fragments of land which are mainly uneconomic. The

President Mubarak – a four times winner

Hosni Mubarak's victory in the presidential referendum held in September 1999 won him a fourth six-year term. It might have been seen as a foregone conclusion. Voters were asked to either vote 'yes' or 'no', though there was no opposing candidate. To stand against the incumbent president an opponent needs the approval of at least two-thirds of the People's Assembly. In most circumstances Egypt's electoral system is designed to ensure that the National Democratic Party (NDP), which Hosni Mubarak leads, commands a majority in the Assembly and prevents any opposition from making a serious challenge.

There is an electoral register of 24 million, of which 19 million voted in 1999. With suspicious alacrity, it was officially announced less than 24 hours after the vote took place that 94% of voters had cast a 'yes' to a fourth term for President Mubarak. There was some skepticism about the scale of the turnout in a nation known for its political apathy. The government encouraged people to vote by offering free rail transport on the day of the election, and, for the first time, the electorate could cast their votes by email. But a four times presidential winner can afford to ignore the criticism and take credit for being a well managed political survivor.

average availability of land per cultivator is put at 0.35 ha. Attempts to reclaim land in the desert regions using underground water, newly constructed canals and high technology irrigation systems have, of yet, been of marginal use in resolving Egypt's shortage of agricultural land.

Modern agriculture

Modern farming is principally a matter of the operations of the centrally managed co-operatives on reformed land and the activities of the mixed farms on recently reclaimed land in the rimlands of the delta and the newlands in the desert interiors (see box page 499). The co-operatives are still managed with a large participation by the government, which controls cropping within the central rotation and handles credit and technical matters. These farms have been turned over to commercial crops for the most part – cotton, sugar cane, maize and rice, some destined for export. The newland farms specialize in exploiting the opportunities for early cropping for the supply of fruit and vegetables to the European market. The new farms stand out in the landscape with their contemporary buildings and rectangular field patterns.

Economic plans, potential and problems

Egypt was an early devotee of development planning, reinforced by the desire for a socialist centrally-controlled economy under Gamal Abdel Nasser, the first president after the 1952 revolution. The plans were taken seriously and great efforts were made to use national resources to beat the twin difficulties of shortages of domestic natural resources and a burgeoning population. Some successes were won but the constant involvement of the country at the forefront of the Arab-Israeli wars diverted attention, funds and materials away from the economy. Under President Sadat the dedication to centralized control was gradually watered down and the plans became little more than indicative long-term budgets. Strategies were set at the top – development of the Suez Customs Free Zone under Sadat and privatization under Mubarak. The latest

Turning back the clock – modern landlordism

Egypt set the pace in land reform in the Arab world in the 1950s, abruptly removing many of the landlords on large estates and reorganizing the basis of farmland ownership by creating a new co-operative structure in which the government played the leading management role. Rural bureaucracy did no better in raising productivity in commercial cropping than the system before land reform.

In 1997 the landlords in farming areas were free from state-imposed (and updated) rent controls and security of tenure for tenant farmers was removed. This change led to a threefold increase in rentals for tenants and liberty for landlords to remove tenants on one-year's notice. It is thought that 420,000 out of 905,000 tenant farmers lost their farms in the period 1997-2000. Many others accepted increased rental payments or remained on fragments of land they owned in their own right. Government schemes to provide new farms on which to re-settle displaced farmers have so far made only 12,000 new farms available. Rural unrest has inevitably followed this turning back of the clock in land tenancy. It is estimated that more than 85 people have died in clashes between displaced tenants and landlords with many injuries and a mass of legal complaints that are slowly being tackled by the courts.

development plans continue emphasis on growth of the private sector including the transfer to it of some state assets. The government has limited means at its disposal to promote economic expansion given the high costs of debt repayment and defence, together representing 25% of the budget in most years.

Potential

Egypt's potential is hindered by its paucity of natural resources which, besides oil and natural gas produced in large enough quantities to meet domestic demand and some exports, are limited to iron, phosphate and a few other non-hydrocarbon minerals. Another difficulty for Egypt is its meagre area of fertile land and reliance on the waters of the Nile. The growth of irrigation and hydro-electric schemes in the Upper Nile countries is putting the country's water supply at risk and there is no substitute. Industrialization has some scope for expansion but the past record here is not encouraging.

A further challenge for Egypt is that economic growth needs to exceed its 2.1% annual population increase. For some years Egypt has depended on predominantly US and European foreign aid. Though the floating pound is creating incentive for domestic growth in all sectors, foreign aid still accounts for up to 50% of food supplies needed annually from abroad that enable Egypt to feed itself.

Ultimately it seems that Egypt will have to continue to rely on its current principal sources of foreign exchange – oil, tourism, Suez Canal fees, and expatriate remittances – for its economic salvation. Unfortunately all four are to varying degrees dependent on stable political conditions in Egypt and the rest of the Middle East.

Energy

At the heart of the modern economy is the **petroleum** sector. The oilfield areas are widely distributed among the Suez/Sinai zone to the east and the more recently discovered Western Desert fields. Crude sales abroad account for about half of all exports. Egypt also benefits from employment of its nationals in the Middle Eastern oil industry, worth US$6 billion per year. **Natural gas** resources are even more significant than oil and several oil companies and governmental organizations are working to

New lands – mega-developments

Egypt hopes to increase the area of land under cultivation by 40% in the next decade, cutting into the 96.5% of the nation's territory that is unused desert. The cultivated area will, it is expected, rise from 3,000,000 ha to 5,000,000 ha – representing an explosion of farming activity such as the country has not seen since the 19th-century phase of dam building on the Nile. At the same time, there will be a vast expansion in new urban developments on lands reclaimed from the desert.

Foremost of the new projects is the South Valley Project at the Toshka, a large site close to Lake Nasser. Here 500,000 ha of farm land will be brought into use by private venture capitalists, including Saudi Arabian investors. In all it is estimated that the Toshka scheme will cost US$88 bn in the period 1999-2017.

The initiatives at Toshka and other parallel agricultural/industrial locations are a huge gamble which will need enormous foreign financial backing and great ecological care if they are to be successful. Egypt, with a population growing at 2% per year, needs every opportunity for employment and hectare of land to grow food that it can manufacture. The new projects thus carries immense implications for the country's future prosperity. Success is an imperative.

further tap into the resource, a cleaner burning fuel that is increasingly important given the state of the environment and the fact that the Aswan High Dam now supplies less than 10% of the country's total electricity use of 49 billion kwh per year.

Industry

Since the 1952 revolution, there has been a growing tendency to turn to industrialization as a means of achieving faster economic growth and providing for the needs of an expanding population. Most industries were then state-owned, carried very large work forces and were inefficient. The country did nonetheless lay the basis for iron and steel, automobile and petrochemical sectors. Industry was concentrated around Cairo and its outliers such as Helwan. In recent years Egypt has industrialized steadily through a growth of small, private and/or foreign funded plants producing consumer goods, textiles, arms and processed foodstuffs. Egypt compares well with industrial growth in emerging markets to other developing economies. Though disposable income is on the decline, the floating pound has offered more incentive with a wider domestic consumer base. Nonetheless, the country is a long way from achieving its ideal of being the manufacturing centre for the Arab world.

Tourism

Another primary source of foreign currency, tourism directly employs 1,000,000 people in Egypt, in addition to all the income tourists bring in outside their hotels and restaurants. With almost 13% of Egypt's workforce kept employed by spending visitors, the perpetual wavering of the industry has weighed heavy on the state of the economy. The 1997 Luxor massacre was the first serious blow, resulting in a drop from 4.5 million visitors in 1996 to less than 3.5 million the following year. It recovered only to slump again after 9-11 and the Al-Aqsa Intifada. The War on Iraq resulted in another serious setback. But with Israeli/Palestinian peace talks in progress and conflict, for the moment, simmering down in Iraq, people are coming back. And if the number of hotel rooms are any indicator of people's predictions, with more than 70,000 hotel rooms in mid-construction, optimism is high.

Axis to Africa

Egypt is redeveloping its links in trade and economy with the African continent. It is spurred on by the need to establish new markets for its manufactured goods and by the need to compete with the growing political intervention by neighbouring Libya into Africa south of the Sahara. The Egyptian government also sees it as an important objective to compete with South Africa for leadership of the African countries as a whole. Above all, Egypt needs to consolidate its strategic control over Nile water resources by constructing strong diplomatic links with those African states such as Sudan, Ethiopia that lie upstream astride the River Nile. Egypt will be helped considerably in future negotiations for increased supplies of Nile water if it has close and well-established relations with its southern neighbours.

Egypt has joined COMESA, a 21-member Common Market of East and Southern Africa, and is fast expanding other formal links into the sub-Sahara area to mitigate the effects of drought and encourage regional security.

The Egyptian engagement with Africa is important but will never displace the Arab world in its emotional attachment and is unlikely to out-perform growth in Egyptian commercial links with the EU under a new trade partnership accord.

Trends in the economy

Economic growth has been erratic, but mainly too low to enable the economy to reach a level of self-sustaining development. Part of the problem has been the heavy foreign debt burden. Though Egypt has reduced its trade deficit from about US$9.5 billion to US$7.7 billion, over the last few years, it's still not enough. Egypt continues to borrow overseas and the trend towards external dependence, encompassing $US2 billion per year in aid, has not been fully reversed.

In the 1990s, an IMF-backed program helped to knock down inflation and rein in the deficit. The private sector stepped up as the government increased sales of state assets. However, in recent years, economic mismanagement and rigid control of the exchange rate, compounded by a rise in regional tensions have resulted in a booming foreign-exchange black market. Another serious obstacle is widespread corruption. Fueling discontent and distrust both domestically and overseas, it infiltrates local governments as well as central ministries and the private sector. In 2002, the minister of the Giza governorate was sentenced to 16 years hard labour after a disgruntled colleague revealed he had accepted more than a million pounds in bribes.

Floating the pound

Propping up the pound at a rate of roughly E£3.5 to the dollar for so long has cost the Egyptian government about US $5 billion since 1998. In 2001, the government lifted the cap and adopted a managed peg against the US dollar, resulting in a 30% devaluation of the pound. In 2003, the pound was fully floated resulting in another big drop. The present exchange rate lingers between E£6-7 to the dollar. Most analysts agree that a truly free floating currency will ultimately boost the economy by causing a decline in interest rates and an ease on capital and trade restrictions, thereby allowing domestic companies access to imports and foreign financing. In the short term, though, folks on the street are hurting. Since so many locally-produced products are composed of imported goods, prices are up and the pound is still falling. Disposable income is on the decline. Dollars are scarce and most people are hesitant

East of Port Said: a new Egyptian port

It has been officially decided to name the giant Shark Al-Tafrea (east of Tafrea) hub port and free zone scheme the "East of Port Said Project" since the area is geographically linked to this zone. Construction of the port is moving ahead as scheduled, with the East of Port Said Development Company working on its development plans. Plots of land have also begun to be allocated to new steel, pharmaceutical and building material plants at the site.

The Egyptian Company for Port Said Region Port Development, capitalized at US$440,000,000, has to present detailed plans for the new hub port including the possibility of linking the new container port with the existing terminals of Port Said and Damietta. The port will be built by P&O Ports, a subsidiary of Australian/Dutch P&O Nedlloyd.

This is one of a number of massive infrastructure projects initiated to transform Egypt into an export-orientated, private-sector-led economy. Local and international studies on Egypt's highly inefficient and dilapidated ports have been unanimous in concluding that exports will not grow unless a major reorganization gets under way. The public sector monopoly must be opened up to cheaper and more imports and lower freight costs are needed to encourage efficient private sector operators.

It currently costs twice as much to discharge a container at Egypt's main port in Alexandria as in Cyprus and three times as much as in Lebanon. If full storage charges are also taken into account the costs are as much as six times as high. But the 30-year state monopoly in maritime services was abolished in the latter part of 1997 and privatization of state maritime companies has already begun. The effect has been immediate and now a number of major international shipping lines have begun to look afresh at Egypt's potential.

The new East of Port Said port, estimated to cost US$10 billion to build, is intended to serve as a transshipment hub for the eastern Mediterranean. Egypt hopes it will become the major port between Singapore and Rotterdam.

The army has finished clearing mines from the site of the new port. It is to be established on 2,000 feddans of land on the east bank of the eastern bypass channel of the Suez Canal. An estimated 200,000 people are eventually expected to service the area. The deep water port will be able to accommodate larger container vessels than Port Said and Damietta.

Egypt clearly has a new thrust in its ports policy with East of Port Said but whether it can compete with other ports in the Eastern Mediterranean has yet to be seen.

to exchange them, negating the benefit of floating the pound in the first place. None the less, a free floating currency will reflect well on exports, making Egyptian goods cheaper on the international market, and it will boost tourism by making Egypt a cheaper and more accessible destination. It's also an important symbol to the rest of the world that Egypt is serious about reform and becoming a bigger player in the global market. Keeping the pound afloat now will largely depend on revitalizing privatization efforts and keeping government spending down.

Egypt's ambitious 16-point economic agenda

Egypt's government set out its major economic policy goals in 2000. Prime minister Atef Obeid made ambitious and costly promises to the nation that the government would work to diminish social inequalities and to achieve high economic growth. The prime minister stressed that his government was not, as is popularly perceived, a government of big business interests, solely focused on selling off state enterprises, but has the welfare of the mass of the lower income population at heart. The main promises he made include:

1. The creation of 650,000 jobs a year. The government later said that the donor-financed Social Development Fund will create 150,000 jobs annually, by helping university graduates establish small-scale enterprises, while 500,000 jobs will be found in government ministries and enterprises.
2. The monthly £E50 pension will be doubled and extended to destitute families without a breadwinner. Some 1,000,000 families will be eligible.
3. The government will repay investors who lost money in the Islamic investment companies that went bankrupt in the late 1980s taking with them many people's life savings. An initial 10% repayment will be followed by the remainder over the next five years.
4. The government will continue to subsidize homes for the young and plans to build 100,000 housing units yearly and facilitate access to soft loans for younger families.
5. The government will continue to subsidize basic food supplies, water and electricity, public transport, low-cost housing and free education.
6. Bureaucracy is to be cut to the minimum.
7. Slum areas are to be developed, action will be taken to relieve Cairo of its rubbish accumulation problem and tenders put out for the upkeep of roads and lighting of new areas.
8. The government will improve the working conditions of its employees. All government employees and their families will be offered attractive health insurance packages. The new health insurance system will cover 10 million additional people (25 million are already covered).
9. Interest-free loans of up to £E1,000 will be extended to impoverished students. Repayment of the loans will be scheduled over 40 years.
10. Seasonal workers in both rural and urban areas will be offered soft loans to develop income-generating activities
11. Loans will be extended to non-governmental organizations to establish productive small-scale enterprises.
12. To raise the annual economic growth rate to 7% during the next decade.
13. To raise exports by 10% annually to ensure a greater supply of foreign exchange.
14. To keep the Egyptian pound at the same value relative to other currencies.
15. To strike hard against corruption, dumping, tax-evasion and the smuggling of sub-standard goods into the country.
16. To reduce the volume of foreign and domestic debt. To achieve this, the budget of the economic and public service sector authorities will be separate from the state budget in future so that expenditure can be rationalized.

Culture

Architecture

The development of the Egyptian architectural tradition is both complex in so far as many influences affected it over the country's long history and discontinuous because of alien invasions and the impact of internal economic decline. In Egypt, even more than in other states of the Middle East, the extant pre-Islamic heritage in architecture is considerable – readily visible in the pyramids, temples and tombs throughout the length of country. The Egyptian showcase reflects almost all styles from the dawn of history because Egypt lay at the crossroads of the known world for so long, across the rich and desirable nodal point of African, Mediterranean, European, Turkic, Arab and Persian influences. Even after the coming of Islam, Egypt experienced a diversity of architectural styles, as dynasty succeeded dynasty bringing new fusions of imported and local building techniques. In Egypt, Orthodox Islamic, Shi'ite, Ottoman and many other ruling elites brought in their own ideas of the function and design of public/religious buildings, often together with the craftsmen to construct them, but always interacting with local architectural traditions in a way that gave innovative results in mosques and other great building projects.

In Egypt there are not only local variations on the Islamic theme but also continuities in existing vernacular building styles and Coptic church architecture of the Romano-Greek basilica models as at St Barbara (see page 83).

The transition from felt to stone

It must be remembered that the early Islamic conquerors were soldiers and often migrant pastoralists in lifestyle. The nomadic tradition, for all its emphasis on a minimum of light, transportable materials has, over time, produced exciting artifacts in the form of tents, particularly the black tent which survive still in the desert outposts of Egypt. Immediately after the conquest of Egypt by Amr Ibn Al-As in the seventh century, the Islamic armies used the existing Egypto-Roman stock of citadels, forts and housing at Fustat (see page 72), which enabled some of the historical legacy of the area to survive.

Rapid development in Islamic technologies

But is was the remarkably rapid development of science and technology in the construction of Islamic buildings – especially the *mesjid al-jami* (Friday Mosque) – from a primitive model in Madinah built by Mohammed in AD 622 – to the building of the original city of Baghdad on the instructions of Caliph Al-Mansur in the eighth century and the contemporary expansion of Cairo. Notable in this growth of technology was the codification of knowledge by the great ninth century engineer Al-Karaji, who laid down the scientific principles on which urban water supply works should be undertaken. In the same way, the sciences developed by the Islamic surveyors of the eleventh century such as Al-Biruni were also important. It is worth recalling the architectural excitement of the technological and material innovations that stirred invention and development in Egypt in the early Islamic period.

The mosque

At the heart of Islamic architecture is the mosque. The elaboration of Islamic architecture centring on the mosque took place despite the men of the Arab conquest being essentially unlettered nomads and warriors. To redress the shortcomings of the Arab armies, their rulers imported skilled architects, masons and tile workers from established centres of excellence in the empire – Persians, Armenians and others. Together these itinerant teams of artisans and their Islamic patrons evolved a wonderful and distinct style of building form and decoration which are among the great legacies of Islam, especially in its early innovative period.

The mosque was the first and main vehicle of spectacular Islamic architecture, because it was a form based initially on the prayer building constructed by the Prophet himself and was important in enabling Muslims to conform with a need to pray together on Friday. In the Madinah mosque the worshippers faced north towards the holy city of Jerusalem but changes brought about in the first century after the death of Mohammed saw the qibla – direction of prayer – moved to face Mecca and other elaborations.

Key parts of the early mosques which were enduring elements of all mosques built since that time include: the entrance, normally large and ornate, in the north wall, the mihrab, or niche in the *qibla* wall, the *sahn*, or open courtyard, the *minbar*, or pulpit, the *maqsurah*, or wooden screen, the *liwanat*, or covered arcades, the *koubba*, or dome, which was adopted as a roof form in the Dome of the Rock at Jerusalem, from whence Mohammed ascended to heaven.

As the caliphate extended and grew wealthy, so the architecture of the main Friday mosques, made for mass worship by the faithful on the holy day, became more magnificent as exemplified in the Great Mosque of Damascus, built in the eighth century AD, which also had a square *ma'dhana*, or minaret outside the main building for the *muezzin* to call people to prayer.

The minaret of the Great Mosque of Kairouan in Tunisia, constructed in the eighth century, is the oldest minaret still standing while in Egypt the Ahmed Ibn Tulun Mosque (876-879) near the Cairo citadel has the only original standing minaret tower with an external spiral staircase in Africa.

Local mosques

In addition to the great mosques used for public prayer on holy days, there are many local mosques of plain construction, many with architectural modifications to suit regional conditions of climate, culture and the availability of building materials in Egypt. The basic layout even here is uniform, though the ornamentation and wealth in carpets in the sahn many well vary.

The non-Muslim traveller in Egypt is greatly blessed. They are allowed into nearly all mosques albeit with some restrictions on times for public access.

Understanding the mosque

For a traveller to make sense of a visit to a mosque, the following principles and guidelines might be useful. Remember that the mosque serves as a centre for congregational worship in Islam. The word *mosque* implies a place of prostration and this is borne out in the plan of every mosque. The architecture of mosques, like that of traditional Christian churches, was designed to induce quiet and contemplation, above the noise and bustle of everyday life – to induce a subjection of the individual to God, *Allah*.

Muslims pay particular attention to this solemn sanctity of the mosque. Behaviour is muted and decorous at all times, particularly during services, of which the main ones are Friday Prayers. Women are not forbidden from taking part in public services at the mosque but very rarely do so.

Most important is prayer and the *mihrab* is the niche in the mosque wall, known as the *qibla* wall, which indicates the direction of Mecca and hence the direction in which to pray. The main prayer hall is the *sahn* which can be a simple square, though more often it has (usually four) arcaded porticoes the longest and most decorated of which is the sanctuary or *liwan*. In the main Friday Mosques the porticoes can be elaborate and reminiscent of transepts in a church. A pulpit, *minbar*, is sited to the right of the *mihrab* and opposite the lectern from which readings are made from the Koran. In larger mosques there can be a screen, *maqsurah*, normally made as a wooden grill, in the sanctuary to protect the officiating *imam* from the congregation.

An outer courtyard or *ziyada* is generally found or a recess with flowing water or water jugs where people gather and perform their ritual ablutions before prayer. In the teaching mosques the *liwan* or specially created cloisters or side rooms served as classrooms or hospital sick-rooms.

Thus, while all mosques vary in detail of lay-out and decoration, the basic floor plan remains more or less uniform.

The Egyptian contribution to the mosque

Egyptian mosques in particular show great variety of decoration and some differences in ground plan. Even to the untutored eye, five principal styles of mosque can be seen in most Egyptian cities; Fatimid (967-1171), Ayyubid (1171-1250), Mamluk (1250-1516), Ottoman (1516-1905) and modern (1905-present).

The Fatimids left as their monument the great Mosque of Al-Azhar in Cairo, square in plan with a roofed and clestoried sanctuary borne on twin pillared colonnades. There were two side cloisters.

The Ayyubid buildings After the overthrow of the Fatimids by Salah Al-Din (1171 AD) a new mosque style grew up in Egypt, reflecting the mosque as a major public building by scale and ornamentation. A good example of this style is the Madresa of Sultan Al-Salih Ayyub. Unlike all previous mosques, it provided a separate teaching room for the four great schools of Orthodox Islam in a pair of mosques, each with a double liwan. Look out for the windows at ground level and for the discordance between the alignment of the adjacent street and the *liwans*, resulting from the need to set the *qibla* facing Mecca.

Legacy of the Mamluks The legacy of the Mamluks includes the Madresa of Sultan Hassan, built in 1356-60. It is an Islamic building on a giant scale with the tallest minaret in Cairo. Architecturally, it is also distinct for its simplicity and for the separate liwans, entrances to which are all offset from the magnificent *sahn*.

The Ottoman intervention The Ottomans ruled for many years (16th century- 19th century) during which Egypt experienced a flood of new architectural ideas – the use of light as a motif, and the deployment of slender pillars, arches and minarets of Turkish origin. The Mosque of Suleyman Pasha dated to 1528 was the first Ottoman mosque to be built in Cairo exhibiting these features, that of Mohammed Ali Pasha, one of the last, with its tall octagonal minaret and fine Ottoman dome.

The modern period The modern period is represented by the Al-Rifai Mosque, completed in 1911, which blends Mamluk with contemporary architecture and by the standard village mosque, small, block built, neat but uninspired.

Features of the mosque

Each architectural feature of the mosque has undergone development and change. For example, the minaret (*ma'dhana*) evolved to provide a high point from which the prayer leader (*muezzin*) could call (*adhan*) the faithful to their devotions five times each day. Construction of minarets to give a vantage point for the muezzin began in Damascus at the end of the seventh century AD. The earliest minaret that has survived is the one at the Great Mosque in Kairouan, Tunisia, built in the years eighth-ninth centuries. The minaret of the Ibn Tulun Mosque in Cairo with its external spiral staircase is dated to 876-879. There is some belief by scholars that the three-part form of the Egyptian minaret was taken from the 135 m Lighthouse of Pharos at Alexandria, of which the extant Abu Sir lighthouse 43 km west of Alexandria is a small scale copy.

The minarets of the Egyptian mosque are quite distinct despite reflecting influences from elsewhere in the Islamic world. There is great variety in the shape and architectural effects of Egyptian minarets as may be seen from the illustration of three fine minarets in Cairo, the minaret of the Ibn Tulun Mosque has an external stair-way and octagonal third section while the minaret of Sanjar Al-Gawli Madresa carries an extended square base with short and delicate second and third sections. In contrast, the splendid early 15th century minaret of the Sultan Al-Barquq mausoleum displays great variety as it evolves from square to modified cruciform to circular to octagonal. Yet there is an underlying general tendency for the Egyptian minaret to have three separate levels including a base of square section, overlain by a multifaced column usually octagonal in shape surmounted by a circular tower, itself terminating in an elaborate miniature pavilion. The finial is provided by a small gilded spire carrying a crescent.

The original brick-built minarets in Egypt used finely worked panelling and line work as on the Ottoman minaret of Sultan Hassan Madresa (1356-62BC) near the Cairo Citadel. The passage of time saw the expensive kiln brick medium dropped in favour of stone and finally rough random stone covered with a plaster rendering. These painted towers have been augmented in the recent past both in Egypt and other Muslim countries by what has become a standard modern equivalent, reproduced in new urban and country settlements, alike. It is plain and repetitive – scarcely a description of the more traditional and characterful minarets – but serves its purpose (See box page 99), and remains a principal topographic marker in the Egyptian landscape.

Madresas – Islamic colleges

Closely linked to the mosque in both religious and architectural form is the *madresa*, a college of higher education in which Islamic teachings lead the syllabus. The institution originated in Persia and developed in the West in the 13th century. The construction of places of advanced learning was a response by orthodox Sunni Islam to the growth of Shi'ite colleges but they soon became important centres in their own right as bastions of orthodox Islamic beliefs. Subjects other than theology were taught at the *madresa* but only in a limited form and in ways that made them adjuncts to Sunni teachings and acceptable to a very conservative religious hierarchy. Unfortunately, therefore, the *madresa* became associated with a rather uninspired and traditional academic routine in which enquiry and new concepts were often excluded. Muslim scholars believe that knowledge and its transmission sadly fell into the hands of the least academic members of the theological establishment. The poor standards of science, politics, arts and ethics associated with the Arab world in the period since the 13th century is put down by some Arab academics to the lack of innovation and experiment in the *madresa*, a situation which has only very recently begun to break down in Sunni Islam. It can, however, be argued that formal Islam needed firm basic teachings in the face of rapidly expanding popular Islam and its extravagant sufi beliefs.

The short-comings of the *madresa* in creative teaching terms were in part compensated for by the development of the college buildings themselves. The Egyptian style before the beginning of the tenth century was based on norms borrowed from Syria and Iraq but after that time was mainly modelled on a more Mediterranean tradition with use of a high domed roof as in the mosque of Al-Guyushi in the military area above Sharia Al-Mokatam in Cairo. The small courtyard is separated from the *sahn* by a vaulted transect. The Al-Azhar Mosque complex in old Cairo began life as a principal congregational mosque but become a great teaching university for Islam, much added to and altered and thus at the apex of the *madresa* form.

Madresas were until quite recently widely used for student accommodation and teaching. Visitor entry is restricted to specific times but fairly free access is allowed to the building. Other fine architectural works can be seen at the Sultan Barquq Madresa in Cairo with its marbled entry and wonderful four-liwan courtyard and the Madresa of Tatar Al-Higaziya with its ribbed stone dome.

The rise in awareness of Islam among the young signalled by the high tide of Islamism in Egypt has given the *madresa* an added political interest and social vitality in recent years.

Mausoleums – a very Egyptian celebration of death

One of Cairo's most eye-catching features, visible even as the traveller comes into the centre of town on the Heliopolis road, is the City of the Dead, where 15th century tombs and later additions offer an unparalleled range of Islamic funerary architecture. There are also some separate tomb-temples of the Islamic period which are now parts of larger mosque and madresa complexes such as the finely-worked Tombs of Amir Salar and Sangar a-Gawli in Sharia Saliba.

The private house

Although there was some inertia in the architectural style/practices and building techniques in Islamic Egypt, aided by the Ottoman imperial practice of adopting local building types without change, the private houses belonging to great families and powerful individuals showed much individuality but did at the same time contain strong elements of continuity. All houses had a central courtyard or *waset al-dar*, with perhaps a columned area, fountain, water basin and even trees which was reached indirectly through a corridor from the street. The house entrance was usually via a studded door to a lobby or pair of small rooms designed to ensure that no-one from the street could either view or easily enter the inner courtyard or rooms. Around the central courtyard were clustered all the principal rooms, including in large houses a collection of family rooms set around a main living space or an area to give family privacy to visitors. These groups of rooms had a small courtyard and may be seen as the successors to the peri-styles of Romano-Greek houses in North Africa or to the Perso-Ottoman *haivans*. Libraries were important in the houses of public figures, while some great houses had internal *hammam* or bath areas.

Naturally, there was a large staff and housing for it in establishments of this kind to service the kitchen, the daily needs of the resident family and the transport/guard functions necessary for a public figure. The harem was kept distant from the public rooms and often near the baths. Kitchens, stores, water well/storage, stables and accommodation for servants took up considerable space. Egyptian great houses of the 18th and 19th centuries rarely had a developed upper storey, though roof areas were accessed by stairways and used for laundry, the drying of fruits and for water gathering for the cistern below. Open space within the house was often generous in scale. A fine example of the classical Egyptian house can be seen at the House of Zaynab Khatun in Sharia Mohammed 'Abduh near the Al-Azhar Mosque. This building was first laid out in 1468 for Mithqal Al-Suduni, a minister of Sultan Jaqmaqis, and has Ottoman additions. It was restored in the 1950s and is open to the public. There are many fine historic houses in various states of repair in Cairo which are rarely seen by visitors simply because they are over shadowed by so many wonderfully attractive public buildings. As a sample of early housing, visit the Gayer-Anderson Museum entered from the southeast corner of the Ahmed Ibn Tulun. The museum is in what are two restored houses of the 16th century and 17th century, respectively, with a number of fine features such as a screened balcony (*mashrabiyyah*) and marbled sitting room. Sadly many of the older grand houses in diverse styles borrowed from France, Greece and Italy of the 18th and 19th century have been demolished and few examples remain for which there is public access. In Ismailia look out the house of de

 Lesseps on Mohammed Ali Quay as an example of "colonial period" housing.

In lower class dwellings this same formula was repeated but on a smaller scale and without the baths and libraries. Many larger houses at the present day are laid out often using an offset entry system just like the older Islamic houses, though only few modern dwellings benefit from total family privacy, thick walling, a generous central courtyard and ornamental gardens. Finding mud-brick for construction purposes is getting difficult as a result of prohibitions on brick-making so that low rise houses are roughly constructed in cement blocks. Increasingly, better off Egyptians are in any case abandoning the traditional house for apartments in tower blocks.

Art and crafts

Jewellery

The dynamic history of the region has produced imaginative traditional designs mixed with foreign elements leading to a range of decoration few regions in the world can rival. Influences from the Phoenicians, Greeks and Romans, Arabs and Andalusians have each contributed subtly to the immense range of jewellery found in this part of the world.

Although some urban dwellers have adopted Western attitudes to dress and decoration, at times of festivals and especially for marriage ceremonies, traditional dress and elaborate jewellery that has changed little since the Middle Ages is still worn. The increase of tourism, while in some cases destroying traditional values, is in fact promoting and preserving crafts, especially jewellery making, by providing an eager and lucrative market for ornaments that was rapidly declining. Unfortunately, with the changes of cultural values, changes in fashion and style also occur and unfortunately large quantities of old, exquisite silver jewellery have been destroyed to provide raw materials for new pieces.

There is a division of tastes and wealth between towns where gold is favoured and the countryside where silver predominates. Basically, traditional styles continue to be popular and jewellery tends to become more traditional the further south one goes. A general shift can be discerned away from silver towards gold, especially in Egypt, where it is now believed to be a better investment.

Despite a whole field of inspiration being forbidden to Muslim jewellers, that of the human form, they developed the art of decorating jewellery in ways that eventually merged to become a distinctive 'Islamic' style. Using floral (arabesque), animal, geometric and calligraphic motifs fashioned on gold and silver with precious and semi-precious gems, coral and pearls they worked their magic.

According to Islamic law, silver is the only pure metal recommended by the Prophet Mohammed. For the majority of Muslims this sanction is felt to apply only to men who do not, as a rule, wear any jewellery other than a silver wedding ring or seal ring.

Every town has its own jewellery souk. There is almost always a distinction between the goldsmiths and the silversmiths and there are also shops, designated in Egypt by a brass camel over the door, which produce jewellery in brass or gold plate on brass for the cheap end of the market.

The tourist industry keeps whole secions of the jewellery business in work, especially in Egypt where designs which have a historical base – the Scarab, the Ankh (the symbol of eternal life), the Eye of Horus, Nefertiti's head and heiroglyphic cartouches – predominate. The jewellery spans the entire range of taste and quality from the very cheap mass-produced pendants to finely crafted very expensive pieces. Jewellers also sell a great number of silver items at the cheaper end of the tourist market which is very popular as 'ethnic' jewellery. Gold and silver jewellery is usually sold by weight and, although there might be an additional charge for more intricate craftmanship, this means the buyer must judge quality very carefully.

The Talisman

The use of amulets and other charms was well developed in ancient Egypt when magic charms were worn like jewellery or put into the wrappings round a mummy – to ward off evil. Among the most sought-after charms was the Eye of Horus or the *ankh* (see page 464), the cross of life. Protective necklaces were particularly treasured and among the beads would be small carvings of animals representing gods – a hawk for Horus, or a baboon for Thoth. In the same way stelae (marker stones) or house charms stood at the door begging the gods to protect the family from danger.

The 'evil eye' is a powerful force in the contemporary local societies of Egypt and North Africa. It is believed that certain people have the power to damage their victims, sometimes inadvertently. Women are thought to be among the most malignant of possessors of the 'evil eye', a factor associated with the 'impurities' of the menstrual cycle. Even a camera can be considered as an alien agent carrying an 'evil eye' – so only take photographs of people where they are comfortable with the idea and be exceptionally careful about showing a camera at weddings or, more importantly, funerals. Envy too is a component of the 'evil eye' and most conversations where any praise of a person or object is concerned will include a *mashallah* or 'what god wills' as protection against the evil spirits that surround humankind.

Major victims of the 'evil eye' are the young, females and the weak. Vulnerability is seen to be worst in marriage, pregnancy and childbirth, so that women in particular must shelter themselves from it. Uttering the name of 'Allah' is a good defence, alternatively amulets are used, a practice originating from the wearing of quotations from the Koran written on strips of cloth which were bound into a leather case and then strapped to the arm. The amulet developed as a form in its own right, made of beads, pearls, horn or stone brought back from a pilgrimage. Amulets also have the power to heal as well as to protect against the occult.

In Egypt today, medicine, superstition and ornament combine to give an array of amulets worn both everyday and for specific use.

The earring is by far the most popular and convenient ornament. It appears in an infinite variety of styles with the crescent moon shape being the most common. This is closely followed by the bracelet or bangle which is also very much part of a woman's everyday wardrobe.

Most of the jewellery is worn both as an adornment and as an indication of social status or rank. It generally has some symbolic meaning or acts as a charm. Jewellery is usually steeped in tradition and is often received in rites of passage like puberty, betrothal and marriage. Women receive most of their jewellery upon marriage. This is usually regarded as their sole property and is security against personal disaster.

Many of the symbols recurrent in jewellery have meanings or qualities which are thought to be imparted to the wearer. Most of the discs appearing in the jewellery represent the moon which is considered to be the embodiment of perfect beauty and femininity. The greatest compliment is to liken a woman to the full moon. Both the moon and the fish are considered as fertility symbols. The crescent is the symbol of Islam but its use actually predates Islam. It is the most common symbol throughout the region and acquires greater Islamic significance with the additon of a star inside. Other symbols frequently seen are the palm and the moving lizard both of which signify life and the snake which signifies respect.

Amulets are thought to give the wearer protection from the unknown, calamities and threats. They are also reckoned to be curative and to have power over human concerns such as longevity, health, wealth, sex and luck. Women and childen wear amulets more frequently as their resisitance to evil is considered to be weaker than that of a man.

The most popular amulets are the Hirz, the Eye and the *Khamsa* or hand. The *Hirz* is a silver box containing verses of the Koran. Egypt in particular has a preoccupation with the Eye as an amulet to ward off the 'evil eye', usually modelled on the Eye of Horus which, as with most symbols in Ancient Egyptian jewellery, has always had mystical connotations. The *Khamsa* is by far the most widespread of the amulets. It comes in a multitude of sizes and designs of a stylized hand and is one of the most common components of jewellery in the region. This hand represents the 'Hand of Fatima', Mohammed's favourite daughter. Koranic inscriptions also form a large section of favoured pendants and are usually executed in gold and also heavily encrusted with diamonds and other precious stones.

Coins or mahboub form the basis of most of the traditional jewellery, from the veils of the bedouins of the Nile Delta to the bodices of the women from the Egyptian oases. Spectacular ensembles are worn at festivals and wedding ceremonies. Each area, village or tribe has its own unique and extraordinary dress of which jewellery, be it huge amber beads as in Sudan or hundreds of coins, forms a fundamental part.

Among the more interesting items are anklets called khul khal, worn in pairs and found in a great variety of styles. In Egypt they are mostly of solid silver fringed with tiny bells. Fine examples are expensive due to their weight. They are losing popularity among the younger generation as they are cumbersome to wear with shoes and because of their undertones of subservience and slavery. It is still possible to see them being worn by married women in the remoter villages of Egypt.

Today the main jewellery bazaar is Cairo's Khan El-Khalili (see page 89). Jewellers in all main cities sell modern versions of traditional jewellery.

Dress

Dress traditions in Egypt are a striking and colourful evidence of a rich cultural heritage. Here, as in all societies, dress is a powerful form of cultural expression, a visual symbol which reveals a wealth of information about the wearer. Dress also reflects historical evolution and the cumulative effects of religious, ethnic and geographical factors on a society.

The many influences which have shaped Middle Eastern history have produced an equally diverse dress culture in which elements from antiquity, the Islamic world and Europe are found. The heritage from earlier times is a rich blending of decorative motifs and drapery. Carthaginian material culture drew upon local tradtions of colourful geometric ornament, which is still seen in Berber clothing and textiles, and luxury goods from Egypt. Greek and Roman fashions have survived in the striking dress of the inhabitants of the deserts and mountains. The Arabs introduced a different dress tradition, influenced by the styles of Egypt and Syria. Here the main features were loose flowing robes and cloaks, wrapped turbans and headcovering which combined a graceful line, comfort and modest concealment. The establishment of Islamic cities encouraged a diverse range of professions and occupations – civil and religious authorities, merchants, craftsmen – all with their distinctive dress. Within cities such as Cairo specialist trades in textiles, leather and jewellery supported dress production. Widening political and commercial relations stimulated new elements in dress.

The Ottoman Turks introduced another feature into city dress, in the form of jackets, trousers and robes of flamboyant cut and lavishly embroidered decoration. Finally European fashion, with emphasis on tailored suits and dresses entered the scene. The intricate pattern of mixed dress styles reflects an adjustment to economic and social change.

The widest range is seen in urban environments where European styles mingle with interpretations of local dress and the clothing of regional migrants. Men have adopted European dress to varying degrees. The wardrobes of civil servants, professional and business men include well-cut sober European suits worn with shirts, ties and smart shoes. Seasonal variations include fabrics of lighter weight and colour and short-sleeved shirts and 'safari' jackets. Casual versions of this dress code, including open-necked shirts, are seen in more modest levels of urban society.

Men's city dress alternates between European and local garments according to taste and situation. Traditional dress is based on a flexible combination of loose flowing garments and wraps which gives considerable scope for individuality. One of the most versatile garments is the *gallabiyya*, an ankle-length robe with long straight sleeves and a neat pointed hood, made in fabrics ranging from fine wool and cotton in dark and light colours to rough plain and striped homespun yarn. Elegant versions in white may be beautifully cut and sewn and edged with plaited silk braid. A modern casual version has short sleeves and a V-shaped neck and is made of poly-cotton fabric in a range of plain colours. Professional men may change from a suit into a *gallabiyya* at home, while working class men may wear a plain or striped *gallabiyya* in the street over European shirt and trousers.

A handsome and dignified garment worn by high ranking state and religious officials is the *caftan*, another long robe with very wide sleeves and a round neck. The cut and detail, such as the use of very fine braid around the neck and sleeves and along the seams, are more formal than those of the *gallabiyya*. The modern *caftan* has narrower sleeves and is worn in public by men of an older and more conservative generation. Traditional dress may be completed with the addition of drapery. Examples include the *selham* or *burnous*, a wide semicircular cloak with a pointed hood and the *ksa*, a length of heavy white woollen cloth which is skilfully folded and wrapped around the head and body in a style resembling that of the classical Roman toga.

Headcoverings are a revealing indication of status and personal choice. A close fitting red wool felt pillbox cap, a *fez*, *tarboosh* or *chechia*, with a black tassle can be seen more often on older men both in traditional and European dress. The distinctive, often checked, headsquare (*kiffiyeh*) of the Bedouin is secured by a heavy double coil (*igal*) of black wool. The ends of the cloth may hang loose or be wrapped around the face and neck for protection against heat or cold. The more traditional loose turban of a length of usually white, less commonly brown, cotton is widespread in Egypt, worn by a wide selection of the working men.

Women's town dress is also a mixture of traditional and modern European forms and depends on wealth, status and personal taste. In the larger cities where women are employed in business and professions, European clothes are worn, cleverly accessorized with scarves and jewellery. Longer skirts and long-sleeved blouses are worn, a more modest form of European dress.

However, traditional dress is remarkably enduring among women of all classes. The most important garments are the *caftan* and *gallabiyya* of the same basic cut and shape as those for men. The *caftan*, as worn in the past by wealthy women, was a sumptuous garment of exaggerated proportions made of rich velvet or brocaded silk embroidered with intricate designs in gold thread. The modern *caftan* is usually made of brightly-coloured and patterned light-weight fabric and edged with plaited braid. The shape is simple and unstructured with a deep slit at each side from waist to hem. Variations can be found in texture and colour of fabric, changes in proportions of sleeves and length of side slits. The *caftan* in its many variations is always worn as indoor dress and can suit all occasions. Traditionally it is worn as an everyday garment belted over a long underskirt. A light shawl may be draped around the neck and the hair tied up with a patterned scarf. Women who normally wear European dress to work often change into a *caftan* at home. Very chic versions of the *caftan*, combined with modern hairstyles and accessories, are worn as evening wear at private and official functions.

Literature

Early Egyptian literary roots

Egypt is literature-rich. Champolleon's and his academic successors' work on the ancient languages of the Pharonic period have opened up official state and private stores of written materials on which much work remains to be done. The pre-Islamic Egyptian tradition was preserved through to the present day to an extent in Coptic liturgies and there is hope for a renaissance in a broader literature now that Coptic is again being taught in religious schools.

Arabic has been the overwhelmingly most important language in Egypt since the 17th century. Classical Arabic had been perfected long before the Prophet Mohammed but its use in the Koran, the oldest existing book in Arabic, has made it the basis of Muslim texts and liturgies, and of the Arabic exemplified in the literatures of the several Arab nations. Among the very earliest of Arabic writing is a tablet dated 512 AD found at Zabad in Syria. A considerable body of oral literature in Arabic is also known to have existed before that time – mainly poetry. In the early centuries of Islam, there was a flowering of religious, philosophical and scientific texts that in translation had an impact well beyond the boundaries of the Muslim world.

Egypt as a literary powerhouse

Cairo in the 19th century witnessed a remarkable expansion of literary activity under internal pressures of embryonic nationalism and the impact of western cultural and scientific influences in the so-called "modernist" movement. Expansion was greatly assisted by the exploitation of machine printing presses. Poetry, biography and history became the staple element in Arabic literature of the 20th century. There was also an explosion of interest in political affairs as literacy spread and anti-colonial attitudes deepened. New literary forms were adopted such as the novel, the most influential of which was Zaynab by Husayn Haykal published in 1914 dealing with human relations and the pastoral theme. By the 21st century the book stands and book shops in Egypt carry a growing weight of publications. Much is ephemeral, a great number of school and university text books are translated from western languages but there is also a goodly proportion of imaginative, religious, social science and technology writing by Arab authors. The international success of Naguib Mahfouz's novels (see illustration) is an indicator of the great strength of contemporary Egyptian literature. Meanwhile, the rising tide of literacy and education makes Arabic literature universal within the greater Arab world so that an Egyptian knows that his/her potential audience is some 100 million or more readers other than those in Egypt. Although the bulk of serious writing concerns Islam, ethics and politics, new literary effort is apparent in areas as diverse as electronics, to serve the growing revolution in communications, and an expandingly active women's press (though taking its roots from the 1890s) with books, journals, magazines and newspapers as their product. Among the most influential women writers is Nawwal El-Saadawi, who is revered among leading female writers as a feminist and political radical. Her book *Woman at Point Zero* is available in English and many other languages. She operates under constraint of the censor in Egypt. Look out for books by Ahdaf Soueif, who, although Egyptian, writes in the English language. Her best known work is *In the Eye of the Sun*, a novel based on her own up-bringing in Cairo.

Reflections of Egyptian literature in the West

Of course, the number of non-Arab Arabic readers is limited and most educated people outside the Muslim world come into contact with Egyptian literature in translation. The novels of Nobel Price winner Naguib Mahfouz are a case in point, reaching an enormous international readership. Mahfouz ran foul of the conservative religious establishment in Egypt and was very badly hurt in 1994 by an Islamist assassin responding to a judgment issued against him by a fundamentalist cleric. He has written less since that time but many more of his prolific output of novels remain to be published in translation. The Cairo-based English-language paper, Al-Ahram Weekly, publishes his column regularly.

There were also foreign residents in Egypt who were authors of international standing and who brought Egyptian society and environment to the attention of an external audience. Notable in English was Lawrence Durrell with his *Alexandria Quartet*, a series of novels that take as their subject the Alexandria of the expatriate Europeans. Lesser known is Constantine Cavafy (1863-1933), a poet whose home can be visited in Sharia Sharm El-Sheikh in central Alexandria.

Overall, Egypt is a rich mine of literary veins of many different kinds. Fortunately, the repressive activities of government and Islamists have far from extinguished a vibrant intellectual tradition in factual and imaginative writing.

Egyptian popular music

Egypt is the recording centre of the Arab world, although Lebanon is beginning to become a rival once more. Egyptian popular music dates back to pharaonic times, but it is influenced much more by the country's Arab and Islamic heritage. While Western music is popular with the cosmopolitan upper class, the vast majority of Egyptians prefer their own indigenous sounds. Arabic music is based on quarter notes rather than the Western half tone scale.

Classical Arabic music is the traditional music of the upper class with its roots in the court music of the Ottoman empire. Sung in classical Arabic, it is highly operatic, poetic, and stylized in form. It is characterized by a soloist backed by mass ranks of violinists and cellists and a large male choir. Its most famous singer by far, and the Arab world's first singing superstar, was Umm Kalthoum (see box page 122) who died in 1975. During her five-hour concerts, her endless melodic variations could ensure that one song lasted up to 2½ hours.

This tradition was lightened and popularized in the 1960s by Abdul Halim Hafez, the other 'great' of Egyptian music, whose romantic croonings in colloquial Arabic also dominated the Arab musical scene.

By contrast, **Shaabi**, or 'popular' music, is that of the working classes, particularly the urban poor. Like Algerian Rai, it has retained a traditional form but through stars such as Ahmed Adawia or more recently Shaaban Abd Al-Reim, who was catapulted into fame with his song "I Hate Israel," it broke convention by speaking in plain and often raunchy language about politics and the problems of society.

Al-Musika Al-Shababeya or 'youth music' is highly popular with the middle and upper classes and is sometimes imitated in the Shaabi. First appearing in the late 1970s, it is a mixture of Arabic and Western influences, taking typical Arabic singing and Arabic instruments such as the *dof* drum and *oud* lute and underpinning this with a Western beat of melodies. The seminal album is Mohamed Mounir's Shababik (Windows) which, in partnership with Yehia Khalil, revolutionized Egyptian pop music in 1981 by introducing thoughtful lyrics, harmonies and a jazz-rock influence into still authentically Arabic music.

In the late 1980s Hamid Al-Shaeri pioneered the offshoot **al-Jil** or '(new) generation' wave of sound whose fast handclap dance style glories in its self-proclaimed Egyptian-ness. It has spawned a new clutch of stars such as Amr Diab and Hisham Abbas but its disco style and safe lyrics have brought criticism that Egyptian pop music has become stagnant and repetitive.

Much less popular is Egyptian ethnic music, although it has its adherents particularly in the countryside. Of particular note are **Simsimmeya** music, named after its dominant guitar-like stringed instrument, which comes from Ismailia and around the Suez Canal zone; **Saiyidi** or Upper Egyptian music, the rhythms of which are based on the wooden horn, *mismar saiyidi*, and two-sided drum nahrasan; the **Delta Fellahi** or peasant music which is calmer and less sharp; and **Nubian** music, which possesses a more African feel, and, unlike Arabic music, uses the pentatonic scale. The pre-eminent Nubian folkloric singer is Hanza Alaa Eddin, who counts among his admirers Peter Gabriel and The Grateful Dead.

Recordings of Egyptian music are available in all cities from small roadside kiosks (often bootleg), market stalls, or record shops. For Saidi and Nubian albums, you'll find the largest selection in Upper Egypt around Aswan and Luxor.

People

Egypt had a population of 66.5 million in 2002. More than 90% of which is concentrated in the Nile Valley and Delta. Average densities are put at 65 people per sq km but in Cairo and the irrigated lands densities of many thousands per sq km are recorded. The growth rate of Egypt's population remains a sensitive matter given the difficulties of the government in providing jobs and feeding the people. It had seemed in the 1970s that the annual rate of increase was tailing off at 2.1% per year but there was a spurt again in the mid-1980s to 2.9% per year before falling again in the 1990s to 1.9%. The population at this latter rate will double every 37 years. In the recent past there were high levels of emigration to the oil-exporting states of the Persian Gulf. Meanwhile, the crude death rate has fallen over the last 25 years and life expectancy has gone up to male 67 and female 69, thus adding to the growth of the population size.

Racial origins

Egyptians living in the Nile Valley between Aswan and the sea have ancient origins. It is speculated that the people of the Nile Valley were of Berber origin with some Arab and Negroid admixtures. The people of the Delta had a slightly different early history and thus had distinct racial origins in which Armedoid and Arab elements were fused with the other peoples of the Nile Valley. Other racial additions were made from invasions from Libya, then from the desert lands of Arabia and Persia in the east, and finally the Mediterranean connections which are most graphically illustrated by the Alexandrine conquest and the Roman establishment in northern Egypt. Present day Egyptians see themselves as having common racial and cultural origins which increasingly are not identified absolutely with the Arabs and Arab nationalism as a whole.

Age groups

The population is youthful with 36% under the age of 15, 58% in the working age group 15-59, and 6% over 60. Literacy is high at 54%, with males at 64% being better placed than women at 39% literate.

Income per head

Egyptian income is put at US$1,200 per head of population. UN sources suggests that there was a modest level of growth of 2.5% per year in real personal incomes in the 1990s, during which labour productivity has grown slowly and labour market conditions have tended to harden.

Religion

The practice of Islam: living by the Prophet

Islam is an Arabic word meaning 'submission to God'. As Muslims often point out, it is not just a religion but a total way of life. The main Islamic scripture is the Koran or Quran, the name being taken from the Arabic *al-qur'an* or 'the recitation'. The Koran is divided into 114 sura, or 'units'. It is for Muslims the infallible word of God revealed to the Prophet Mohammed. In addition to the Koran there are the hadiths, from the Arabic word *hadith* meaning 'story', which tell of the Prophet's life and works. These represent the second most important body of scriptures.

The practice of Islam is based upon five central tenets, known as the Pillars of Islam: *Shahada* (profession of faith), *Salat* (worship), *Zakat* (charity), *saum* (fasting) and *Haj* (pilgrimage). The mosque is the centre of religious activity. The two most important mosque officials are the *imam* (leader) and the *khatib* (preacher) who delivers the Friday sermon.

The *Shahada* is the confession, and lies at the core of any Muslim's faith. It involves reciting, sincerely, two statements: 'There is no god, but God', and 'Mohammed is the Messenger [Prophet] of God'. A Muslim will do this at every *Salat*. This is the prayer ritual which is performed five times a day, including sunrise, midday and sunset. There is also the important Friday noon worship. The Salat is performed by a Muslim bowing and then prostrating himself in the direction of Mecca (*Qibla*). In hotel rooms throughout the Muslim world there is nearly always a little arrow, painted in the ceiling – or sometimes inside a wardrobe – indicating the direction of Mecca and labelled qibla. The faithful are called to worship by a mosque official. Beforehand, a worshipper must wash to ensure ritual purity. The Friday midday service is performed in the mosque and includes a sermon given by the khatib.

A third essential element of Islam is *Zakat* – charity or alms-giving. A Muslim is supposed to give up his 'surplus' (according to the Koran); through time this took on the form of a tax levied according to the wealth of the family. Good Muslims are expected to contributea tithe to the Muslim community.

The fourth pillar of Islam is *saum* or fasting. The daytime month-long fast of Ramadan is a time of contemplation, worship and piety – the Islamic equivalent of Lent. Muslims are expected to read 1/30th of the Koran each night. Muslims who are ill or on a journey have dispensation from fasting, but otherwise they are only permitted to eat during the night until 'so much of the dawn appears that a white thread can be distinguished from a black one'.

The *Haj* or pilgrimmage to the holy city of Mecca in Saudi Arabia is required of all Muslims once in their lifetime if they can afford to make the journey and are physically able to do so. It is restircted to a certain time of the year, beginning on the 8th day of the Muslim month of *Dhu-l-Hijja*. Men who have been on the Haj are given the title *Haji*, and women *Hajjah*.

The Koran also advises on a number of other practices and customs, in particular the prohibitions on usury, the eating of pork, the taking of alcohol, and gambling.

The application of the Islamic dress code varies. It is least used in the larger towns and more closely followed in the rural areas.

Christians in Egypt

The Copts take their name from a corruption of the Greek word *aigupioi* for Egyptian. They were concentrated in the region from Girga to Assiut and had a community in old Cairo until recently. Now many have moved to the metropolitan area of Cairo and its suburbs. The number of Christians of all kinds in contemporary Egypt is put officially at 3.5 million but is thought to be much larger (6 million) of which the majority (4.4

Fundamentalism

Islam has been marked over the course of history by the emergence of rigorous revivalist movements. Most have sought a return of the faithful to the fundamentals of Islam – the basic doctrines of the Prophet Mohammed – uncluttered by the interpretations of later Islamic jurists and commentators. Behind the movements was generally the idea that Muslims should go back to the simple basics of their religion. Some, like the Wahhabi movement in Saudi Arabia were puritan in concept, demanding plain lives and an adherence to the tenets of Islam in all daily aspects of life. Others imposed a rigorous schedule of ritual in prayer and avoidance of the 'unclean' in public life.

Until recent times the fundamentalist movements inside Islam arose from a desire to cleanse the religion of unnecessary ideology and to make all Muslims observe the basic pillars of the Islamic religion – prayer, belief and actions on a consistent and demonstrable basis. In the last 100 years there has been a growing tendency in the Islamic world for revivalist movements to be reactions to political, military and cultural setbacks experienced at the hands of the Western industrialized world. The aim of the reformers has been to make good the disadvantage and backwardness of the Muslim states when contrasted with the powerful countries of Europe, America and the Far East. The matter is varied and complex, depending on the particular cases involved but the clear linkage between an increasingly dominant Western culture and economy and the growth of reactive Islamic movements is inescapable.

In Egypt, the Muslim Brotherhood was an early form of revivalist movement of this kind. Founded by an Egyptian schoolteacher, Has Al-Banna in 1928, it initially tried to take Islam back to its roots and therefore to its perceived strengths but was later taken over by extremists who used its organization for political ends. It developed as a clandestine political group and harnessed religious fervour to political objectives, including the assassination of political enemies and remained the Egypt's main organization though other smaller sects were also founded.

Politically, the Egyptian government has struggled to find ways either to repress or co-opt these extreme Islamist movements which have been responsible for the murder of, and injury to, foreign tourists and Egyptians (including the 83-year-old novelist Naguib Mahfouz) over recent years.

This lack of any understanding between the government and the Islamist opposition gives Egypt's political system an unneeded air of fragility. President Mubarak has responded as a soldier to armed political attacks on his régime. Attacks on the state by the Islamists has diminished but remains a serious issue and one that is unlikely to go away at present. But for the foreign tourist, there is much less to fear. They now seem (in Egypt) to be out of the direct firing line. For the first time since they took up arms against the government in 1992, the militants have ceased to dominate the political scene. The unilateral ceasefire, announced by the Gamaa Islamiya has largely held. Brutal police repression, public hostility, and the large-scale release of Islamist prisoners by the interior ministry make the return unlikely. Gamaa leaders abroad might well find that they are now incapable of reactivating the organization should they so wish.

Islamic dietary laws

Islam has important rules governing what things may be eaten by the faithful. The Koran specifically forbids the eating of the flesh of swine and the drinking of wine. Other rules dictate how an animal may be slaughtered in proper Islamic manner and ban the consumption of meat from any carcass of an animal that perished other than in the approved way. Any food made of animal's blood such as black pudding or boudin is strictly excluded from the diet of a good Muslim. Non-muslim visitors are not included in these controls and international food is provided in all quality hotels.

The ban on wine has been interpreted as a total outlawing of all alcohol. In practice, local traditions have led to relaxations of the ban from place to place. Some areas, such as much of Turkey forbade Muslims from trading in alcohol but not necessarily from drinking it. Indeed sufi poets used wine as a metaphor for liberty and the ecstasy of truth – and perhaps often as a real stimulant to freedom of the soul! As the poet Hafez wrote:

"From monkish cell and lying garb released,
Oh heart of mine,
Where is the Tavern fane, the Tavern priest,
Where is the wine?"

In Egypt Sufism, it was a road to spiritual understanding, but the tradition of wine imbibing was never well developed here. Wine is produced in Egypt though the quality varies round the 'only fair' standard.

Fasting is a pillar of Islam, as originally of Judaism and Christianity. It demands that Muslims desist from eating, drinking and smoking for the month of Ramadan during the hours of daylight. The Ramadan fast, always followed by the faithful in Libya and Egypt, is now rigorously enforced by social influence.

Travellers are unlikely to be disconcerted by Islamic taboos on food and during Ramadan meals will be provided at normal times. However, the Ramadan fast can be very inconvenient for the uninitiated western traveller. Quite apart from a rising tide of irascibility in some of the Egyptian population, the break of fast in the evening may result in more seldom and erratic service in transport, hotels and restaurants.. The holidays that follow the fast have a similar impact as most local people meet with their extended families and leave their places of work for several days.

million) are of the Coptic Church. There are also some 90,000 members of the Alexandrian rite, affiliated to Rome and quite separate from the Coptic Church proper.

The Coptic language is no longer spoken. It originated from the language spoken in Egypt in the early Christian era, at that time written in Greek characters. Although there were regional variations in the Coptic language, by the fifth century AD they had merged into a universal form throughout Egypt. The language has been in disuse since the sixth century as a working language though it survived in use in religious rituals. Arabic is the language of the Coptic church services.

The Coptic Church is very old – for it is believed that St Mark, author of the gospel, preached in Egypt during the time of Emperor Nero and founded a church in Alexandria. He is considered the first patriarch. The Coptic Church is close in belief and form to the Armenian, Ethiopian and Syrian Orthodox rites and differs from Rome which believes in the dual nature of Christ and God while the Copts believe in the unity of the two. The Arab invasion of Egypt in the seventh century put the Coptic

The Kosheh affair – a damaging confrontation

Events in the village of Kosheh in Upper Egypt have, since August 1998, revealed an extraordinary conflict between extremist Muslims and local Copts that has led to loss of life and bad publicity abroad.

There seems to have been widespread police abuse, including torture and the victimization of over 1,000 people – nearly all Christians – to force a confession to the murder of two Coptic Christians from Kosheh. Egyptian publications, both English and Arabic, had reported the story as an act of unprecedented police brutality. The consensus was that police had concentrated on the Coptic Christian inhabitants of the village because, ironically, of fears of sectarian strife if the murderer turned out to be a Muslim.

In Western Europe the position was described as "ritual persecution" of Copts which was a sad misrepresentation of the case, as prominent Christians in Egypt were first to point out. The response of the government did not help. In a clumsy attempt at damage limitation Egyptian newspaper editors were obliged to follow the official line, reporting that no more than two dozen people in Kosheh, if anyone, received "inappropriate" treatment at the hands of the police. The interior ministry, meanwhile, denied that anyone was mistreated at all.

The real issue was lost in the publicity fracas: over 1,000 Egyptians suffered gross violations of their human rights, and Egypt is plagued by a deep-rooted problem of police brutality that touches Muslims and Christians alike.

Church under siege and made it a minority religion in the country. It survived, however, despite some persecution.

The Coptic Church is led by the patriarch of Alexandria and all Egypt from Cairo with 12 bishops. The Church runs a series of Coptic churches and monasteries throughout the country and has a foundation in Jerusalem. The Copts are heirs to a rich Christian literature going back to the third century AD. Egyptian governments have normally recognized the historical and religious importance of the Coptic community by giving cabinet posts to at least one of its members. The appointment of Boutros Boutros Ghali as Secretary General of the United Nations in January 1992 did much to highlight the strength of the Coptic role in Egypt.

Religious practices in the Coptic church Baptism of infants takes place when the child is about six weeks old, with three immersions in consecrated water in the plunge bath. Confirmation takes place at the same time. Men and women are segregated during church services (to left and right) and while men must remove their shoes before moving through the screen from the nave to the altar women are forbidden to enter that part of the church.

The most important celebration in the church's calendar is Holy Week, culminating on Easter Day. This is preceded by a fasting time of 55 days during which no animal products may be eaten, nor wine nor coffee drunk. Like the Muslims no food or drink is permitted between sunrise and sunset. Holy Week is a time of special prayers beginning with a mass on Palm Sunday, after which family graves are visited. On Good Friday altars are draped with black and many candlelight processions take place at dawn – commemorating the entry of Jesus into Jerusalem. Easter Sunday is a day of celebration. Christmas is preceded by 43 days of fasting, ending on 6 January (Christmas Eve) with a midnight service and a celebratory meal. Christmas Day, after church, is a time for visiting relations and friends.

Land and environment

Geography

Egypt lies at the crossroads of Africa and the Middle East as well as having extensive borders on the Mediterranean and Red Sea. The narrow green ribbon of the Nile cuts its way from south to north through the seemingly endless desert. There is an additional 2,000 km of Red Sea where off shore the area is fringed with teeming coral reefs. And to complete these rich offerings is the Mediterranean Sea coast. The overall area of the country is 1,002,000 sq km, which is over twice the size of Morocco.

Egypt's location in northeast Africa gives it great strategic importance arising from its position at the junction of the land routes joining Africa to the Near and Middle East and the sea routes from the Atlantic/Mediterranean and the Indian Ocean/Red Sea. Its borders abut in the north onto the Mediterranean coast and for much of the east onto the Red Sea. These two coastal reaches are separated by the isthmus of Suez, a 150 km land bridge linking the eastern outliers of the Nile Delta with Sinai. The international frontier with Israel runs northwest across the Sinai peninsula from the Taba strip at the head of the Gulf of Aqaba, to the coastal plain of the Negev with a deviation to take account of the Gaza strip. The border area is clearly marked and the area is monitored by UN forces. Off-shore in the Gulf of Aqaba care is needed not to stray across undemarcated frontiers because the Israelis are particularly sensitive about the possibility of terrorists crossing by sea from the three neighbouring Arab countries just across the water.

Egypt's 1,000 km southern border is with Sudan. There is a dispute over ownership of land and economic rights in the Halaib area immediately adjacent to the Red Sea which travellers should avoid. Egypt's 1,300 km long border with Libya on the west is one where there have always been periodic tensions. Nomads often smuggle goods across the border in the area between Siwa/Al-Jaghbub and the coastline in the territory of Ulad Ali tribe. The only easy and official crossing point is in the north on the coast road near Sollum. There is some dispute in the Egyptian-Libyan offshore zone about the alignment of the boundary but this does not currently affect either land or sea transport.

Main regions

Egypt's two largest life-sustaining regions, the Delta and the Nile Valley are both clustered close to its water supplies. The Delta lies north of Cairo and is a vast, low, flat triangle of land through which the tributaries of the Nile pass to the sea. South of Cairo the Nile is contained within a rich and fertile but narrow 2-3 km incised valley which eventually reaches Lake Nasser which is a 425 km ribbon of water extending up to and beyond the border with Sudan. The Delta and the Nile Valley contain almost 99% of the country's cultivated land and approximately the same proportion of the population. East of the Nile Valley is the Eastern Desert and the narrow Red Sea coastline. To the east of the Delta lies the formerly isolated Sinai peninsula which now has international airports and harbours and is traversed by major roads. West of the River Nile is the Libyan Desert which is often referred to as the Egypt's Western Desert. It is broken up by the occurrence of the Al-Uwenat Heights in the southwest which extend in an elongated plateau towards the lowlands of Dakhla Oasis, which has larger parallel formations in the north as the Qattara and Siwa depressions which, together with Dakhla, form the eastern edge of the Sirtican embayment. The long coastal plain between Alexandria and Marsa Matruh gets narrower towards the west as it approaches the Libyan frontier in the Gulf of Sollum.

Egypt is a country of lowlands and low-lying plateaux of which 60% is less than 400 m above sea-level. The few areas of high relief are the Al-Uwenat Heights in the southwest and in the Eastern Desert adjacent to the Red Sea coast where mountains rise to over 1,000 m. The highest mountain in the country is Jebel Katrinah next to St Catherines Monastery (see page 404) which reaches 2,228 m at its summit.

Egypt has the River Nile as its only but vital river. The total annual flow down the Nile, from the Blue Nile and River Atbara which both start in the Ethiopian highlands and the White Nile which begins in East Africa's Lake Victoria, is normally 55 cubic km. Under the 1959 Nile Waters Agreement, Egypt is entitled to take 37 cubic km but, because Sudan so far does not use its full allocation, has been able to take more. There is now growing pressure in all the upstream states for more water and another water crisis is looming.

Egypt has undertaken extensive engineering projects on the River Nile over the centuries which reached a peak with work by the British authorities in the 19th and early 20th centuries. In the modern period the Aswan High Dam, (see page 288) which was designed to give Egypt both water storage facilities and hydro-electric power for its new industries, was built with Russian assistance in the 1960s. In fact the low level of the River Nile in the late 1980s led to a major crisis and precipitated a crash programme to build power stations dependent on locally produced natural gas.

The construction of the Aswan High Dam also reduced the deposition of silt on Egyptian farmlands in the Nile Valley and the Delta. This has necessitated the use of large quantities of fertilizer and led to a decline in the offshore fishing production. Despite some initial success in the search for sub-surface water reservoirs under the deserts, the River Nile remains the very lifeblood of Egypt. There are no other perennial streams, although wadis run elsewhere after heavy rain as brief but dangerous spates.

The Nile and man

The River Nile runs for 6,435 km and drains one fifth of the entire African continent. It rises as the White Nile in Lake Victoria close to Jinja in Uganda and flows as the Victoria Nile through the tropics to Lake Albert. The Nile then begins its course through The Sudan as the Bahr El-Jebel eventually reaching the central plains of Sudan and becoming sluggish and ponding up during the annual flood in the marshy papyrus swamps of the *Sudd* (Arabic for 'dam'). Tributaries such as the Bahr El-Ghazal and the Sobat enter the Nile and north from that point the river for its next 800 km is called the White Nile. The Sobat, which takes its source in the Ethiopian Highlands, is an important water supply for the White Nile system. It joins the Blue Nile at Khartoum. The Blue Nile drains an area deep in the Ethiopian Highlands and, like the Atbara which also joins from the east bank, provides run-off from the

Slope of the River Nile from Lake Victoria to the Mediterranean

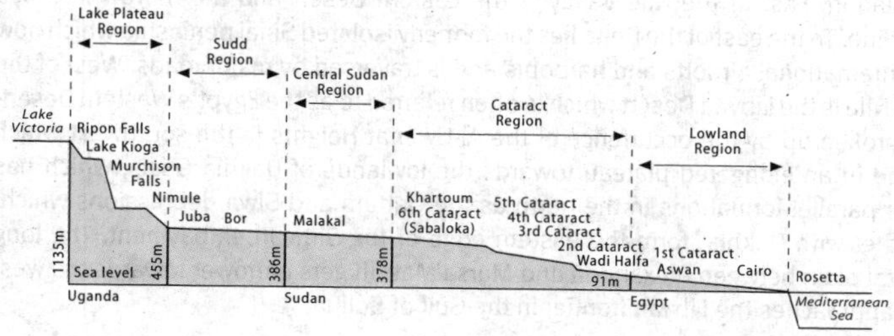

Northeast African monsoon. Between Khartoum and Åswan the river passes over six cataracts. The cataracts are wide rapids which make navigation impossible, the steepest of the cataracts, the sixth, is at Sababka 80 km north of Khartoum.

The River Nile in Egypt is entrenched in a narrow valley below the surrounding land and has only one cataract at Aswan. In its last 325 km before entering its Delta the River Nile tends to keep to the east bank with the main cultivated zone of the valley on the west bank. Most irrigation requires water to be lifted from the river by traditional means such as the saqiya, *shadoof* or by mechanical pumps.

The Nile Delta is the heartland of Egypt. It covers a great silt plain built up by the river over centuries. The Delta stretches 160 km from the vicinity of Cairo north to the Mediterranean coast and 250 km across the Mediterranean end of the wedge. The main distributaries in the delta are the Western Rosetta and Eastern Damietta 'mouths', which are the axes of intensive irrigation networks.

The flow of the River Nile has been influenced by fluctuations in rainfall in the countries where the river has its sources. It is possible that long term climatic change is involved, indicating that the flow in the river might never recover to the average of 84 cu km in the period 1900-59 from the 1984-87 level of less than 52 cu km. The water flow during floods has always varied, as we know from inscriptions in pharaonic times, but recent trends are worrying for the states that rely on the river.

Division of Nile waters is governed by the international agreements of 1929 and 1959, which ultimately gave 48 cu km to Egypt and 4 cu km to Sudan but the arrangement involved only Egypt and Sudan and excluded Ethiopia and the East African states. Argument over allocation of Nile waters continues, with Egypt's rights as the downstream state most at risk. Egyptian governments have felt so strongly on the issue of maintaining their share of Nile waters that they have threatened to go to war if the traditional division was changed against Egyptian interests. A master plan for the future use of Nile waters seems to be a distant prospect.

Finding the source of the River Nile

The ancient Egyptians believed that the waters of the River Nile came from a mystical paradise of plenty. Early exploration by the Greeks and Romans established that the River Nile ran at least from the site of modern day Khartoum. In the 17th century there began a steady stream of European explorers and adventurers seeking the source of the River Nile. Most notable was James Bruce, a Scotsman who in 1769 began a trip which led him to the head waters of the Blue Nile. He was followed by the Englishmen Richard Burton, John Speke and James Grant, who traced the River Nile back to the Lake Victoria connection and, finally, Sir S W Baker, who went further south to Lake Albert. Full mapping of the Nile Basin as a whole went on until the 1960s. The 1980s film Mountains of the Moon captures the discovery of the source of the Nile.

Traditional irrigation in Egypt

In Egypt a basic problem for farmers was lifting water from the River Nile up the river banks which enclosed it. Simple systems of lifting water included windlasses and pulleys were used initially to enable humans or animals pull up leather bags full of river water (see box page 522). Some mechanization followed in which flow-turned wheels were used. These were driven by the current of the river and had pots or wooden containers to carry the water to be deposited at a higher level as at El-Fayoum (see page 165). In much of the country where irrigation canals have little or no flow an animal powered wheel is exploited. Perhaps the classic and oldest water lifting device in Egypt is the *shadoof*, a weighted beam which is swung into the water by its operator and swung up and on to land with the help of a counter balance on the other end of the beam. In recent times water has been led to the fields by diesel and electric pumps.

The water supply system of Egypt has been much improved. Even before the construction of the Aswan Dam and the later High Dam (see box page 288) much had

The delu well – traditional well of North Africa

In the traditional oases of Egypt's Western Desert – and still in evidence today – water was lifted from shallow water tables along the coast or from depressions in the desert by means of a device called a delu. The name is taken from the word for a hide, which is made into a bag comprising an entire goatskin. Strung on a line, this is dipped into a well and drawn up full of water for both household and irrigation purposes.

The mechanism is simple and effective. A shallow 1 or 2 m diameter well is hand dug to about 2 or 3 m below the water table and lined with stone work or cement. Above ground an often ornate gantry is made of two upright stone or wooden pillars rising from the side of the wellhead. A cross beam between the top of the two pillars acts as an axle to a small pulley wheel which carries a rope tied to the mouth of the goatskin bag. The rope is drawn up or let down by the ingenious use of a ramp to ease the task of lifting water to the surface. An animal travels down the ramp when pulling up the goatskin from the bottom of the well and moves up the ramp to return the bag into the bottom of the well. Most delu wells have a secondary rope attached to the bottom of the goatskin bag which can be used when the full bag is at the top of the gantry to upend it and tip out the water.

The rate of water lifting by the delu method is obviously limited. The capacity of the bag is about 20 litres. Working from dawn to dusk, however, enough water could be raised to irrigate up to 3 or 4 ha of land – enough to feed a family and leave a small surplus for sale in the market. Most wells were equipped with a storage basin adjacent to the wellhead so that water could be raised and stored for household use and to give a reserve of water for irrigation.

The creak of the wooden pulley wheel of the delu was one of the characteristic sounds of the Western Desert oases until the 1960s. After that time diesel and electric power pumps became available and the delu system has mainly fallen into disuse. A few delu gantries remain, some as museum pieces, and only the observant traveller in the deepest south of the Saharan oases will come across this splendid and environmentally friendly technology in day-to-day operation.

been done to improve the water storage and flow control of the River Nile. Below the river works at Aswan is the Esna barrage, a masonry dam which acts as an enormous weir to raise the height of the River Nile so that water can be led off in side channels to serve the lands lying under the canal. Downstream at Assiut a diversion dam was constructed to send water throughout the year into the existing Ismail Pasha Canal. A second diversion dam was built at Nag Hammadi between Assiut and Esna. In the delta, the replacement Mohammed Ali barrage was erected on the Rosetta branch. Other dams exist at Edfina and at Sennar in Egypt and Jebel Awlia in Sudan.

The use of the River Nile for navigation has been limited by the narrow, gorge-like nature of some stretches of the upper valley, by the Sudd of Sudan and the existence of the six cataracts in the river bed downstream of Khartoum. In Egypt the River Nile unites the country and local and long-distance craft ply the waterway on a scheduled basis. A large fleet of passenger vessels transport tourists on the River Nile particularly from Luxor to Aswan to serve the great monuments of ancient Egypt (see Nile Cruisers, page 43).

Feluccas

One of the most splendid sights on the river is the local *feluccas* under sail. The *felucca* is a lanteen rigged sailing vessel for inshore or river work. It has very shallow draught so that it can safely cross shoals and can be easily rowed if the wind is absent or unfavourable. Most *feluccas*, once for transporting produce up and down the Nile, are now available for hire by tourists by the hour or the day for a suitably bargained price which will depend on the season and other factors.

The *felucca* is much smaller and less magnificent than the Nile boats of the ancient Egyptians. These ancient craft developed from bundles of papyrus reeds, woven or bound together to make a buoyant crescent-shaped hull for carrying light loads. Later in the Old Kingdom wood was the principal raw material for constructing larger vessels whose shape followed that of the papyrus craft. Most wood was imported to make a keelless craft with a sail and steering gear made up paddles at the stern. By the Middle Kingdom boats took on a more crescent-shaped silhouette, while a cabin was added to the deck immediately before the stern deck. In the New Kingdom boats on the River Nile were longer and more sophisticated, with deckhouses sited round the mast and ceremonial daises both stern and aft. The sail on the New Kingdom vessels was rigged between top and bottom spars and was much wider than earlier types of sail. An example of an Old Kingdom (fourth Dynasty) boat was found at the Great Pyramid at Giza. It was 43.6 m long and 5.9 m beam and when found was still unbuilt kit. The ship was made to be constructed with boards bound to ribs and to carry a small deckhouse and a single steering paddle. It is lodged in a store near the Cheops pyramid.

Climate

Egypt is a desert country. Even its frontage to the Mediterranean offers only a modest tempering of Saharan conditions in the vicinity of the coast in the Alexandria region. Here rainfall is at a maximum with an average of 188 mm per year with summer maximum temperatures averaging 30°C and diurnal ranges rarely more than 10°C. Moving inland brings a rapid decline in rainfall. Cairo, some 150 km from the sea, has an annual average rainfall of 25 mm, a maximum temperature of 35°C and average diurnal ranges of temperature of up to 15°C. Progression southwards brings even greater extremes. At Aswan rainfall drops away to 1 mm per year and average maximum temperatures rise to 37°C with a diurnal range of as much as 18°C. The profound aridity of Egypt outside the Nile Valley makes it absolute desert for the most part, relieved only where water occurs such as the oases of the Western Desert.

Flora and fauna

In the desert environment, annual plants have a very short life span, growing, blooming and seeding in a few short days, covering the ground, when moisture content permits, with a patchy carpet of low-lying blooms. Desert perennials are sparse, tough and spiny with deep root systems. Desert animals are rarely seen, being generally nocturnal and/or underground dwellers to avoid the heat. With water from the River Nile, an oasis or precipitation in the south, the plants are tropical and subtropical and the wildlife becomes more obvious in the form of small and medium size mammals like rats and the Egyptian mongoose. Bird life proliferates by the water, with roosting egrets, herons, kingfishers and hoopoes all very common. The birds of prey range in size from kestrels to black kites and Egyptian vultures. The number of Nile fish is decreasing but the coasts continue to teem with fish.

Papyrus

This word was the name given to the plant *Cyperus papyrus* which grew alongside the River Nile. Later it was also given to the writing material made from the plant. Papyrus is a straight, tall, reed-like plant. Its leafless, triangular stems rise to 5 m above the water being as 'thick as a man's arm' at their lower part. It is topped by drooping spikelets of insipid flowers and long, thin leaves like soft ribs of an umbrella.

To produce writing paper the pith from the stem was cut into narrow strips and arranged in alternate layers at right angles to each other. The sheets were pressed together and dried in the sun, the natural juice of the plant making the pieces stick together. The sheets were pasted together to form rolls which varied in length. An example in the British Museum is 30 m long. On the inner side of the roll the fibres went across and the writing usually went the same way as the fibres. Paper made this way was cheap. The Egyptians are recorded as using it soon after 3000 BC and the Greeks around 500 BC.

The more slender stalks were woven into baskets (Miriam made a basket for Moses out of papyrus before she hid him in the same plants by the water's edge) and the thicker ones were tied into bundles and used to construct cheap, light boats, the earliest craft on the Nile. Isis went to search for the several parts of Osiris, see page 486) in a papyrus boat. The fibre used to make ropes, matting, awnings, sails and the pith, in addition to its important use for paper, was actually used as food by the less fortunate. The dried root of the papyrus plant was used as fuel and being a harder substance, the manufacture of utensils. The papyrus plant no longer grows in Egypt but can be found in the Sudan.

See the displays at the papyrus museums by the Nile at Cairo, Luxor and Aswan.

Although predominantly desert there are many sub-regions. The northern coast of Egypt is influenced by the Mediterranean but the scrub vegetation soon gives way to semi desert; the Nile Delta area includes coastal wetlands and salt marsh; inland lakes and reservoirs provide saltwater and freshwater sites for migrating and resident birds. The limited areas of arable agriculture along the narrow Nile valley and in the extensive delta contrast with the vast expanses of scrub. The mountain ranges of Sinai provide their own climate, delaying flowering and shortening the growing season. Even the desert areas which cover so much of this region provide contrasts, the sands (*erg*), gravels (*reg*) and rock (*hammada*) being interspersed with the occasional flourishing oasis. The Red Sea provides a colourful and unusual selection of sea creatures.

Many of the habitats mentioned above are under threat, either from pollution, urbanization, desertification or advanced farming techniques. Fortunately the conservation movement is gaining pace and many National Parks and Nature Reserves have been created and programmes of environmental education set up. However, regrettably, wildlife is still regarded as a resource to be exploited, either for food or sport.

In desert regions, wildlife faces the problem of adapting to drought and the accompanying heat. The periods without rain may vary from four months on the shores of the Mediterranean to several years in some parts of the Sahara. Plants and animals have, therefore, evolved numerous methods of coping with drought and water loss. Some plants have extensive root systems; others have hard, shiny leaves or an oily surface to reduce water loss through transpiration. Plants such as the broom have small, sparse leaves, relying on stems and thorns to attract sunlight and produce food. Animals such as the addax and gazelle obtain all their moisture requirements from vegetation and never need to drink, while the ostrich can survive on saline water. Where rain is a rare occurence, plants and animals have developed a short life cycle combined with years of dormancy. When rain does arrive, the desert can burst into life, with plants seeding, flowering and dispersing within a few weeks or even days. Rain will also stimulate the hatching of eggs which have lain dormant for years. Many animals in the desert areas are nocturnal, taking advantage of the cooler night temperatures, their tracks and footprints being revealed in the morning. Another adaption is provided by the sandfish, which is a type of skink (lizard) which 'swims' through the sand in the cooler depths during the day. Perhaps the most remarkable example of adaption is shown by the camel (see box, page 452). Apart from its spreading feet which enable it to walk on sand, the camel is able to adjust its body temperature to prevent sweating, reduce urination fluid loss and store body fat to provide food for up to six months.

Mammals

Mammals have a difficult existence throughout the area, due to human disturbance and the fact that the species is not well adapted to drought. Many have, therefore, become nocturnal and their presence may only be indicated by droppings and tracks. Mammals represented here include the Red fox which is common in the Delta, the Sand fox, a lighter coloured hare, the shrew and two species of hedgehog, the Long-eared and the Desert. The appealing large-eyed and large-eared Desert fox or Fennec is less common and is often illegally trapped for sale. Despite widespread hunting, wild boar survive. Hyenas and jackals still thrive particularly in Sinai while wild cats are found in Sinai and the Delta. The leopard, formerly common in North Africa, is now extremely rare, but is occasionally seen in some isolated regions in Sinai, to the panic of the local people.

There are three species of gazelle, all well adapted to desert conditions; the Dorcas gazelle preferring the Western Desert, the Mountain gazelle inhabiting locations above 2,000 m in Sinai and the Desert gazelle locating in the reg of the northern Sahara. The latter is often hunted by horse or vehicle, its only defence being its speed. There are over 30 species of bat in the area, all but one – the Egyptian Fruit bat – being insectivorous. Recent ringing has shown that bats will migrate according to the season and to exploit changing food sources. Many species of bat have declined disastrously in recent years due to the increased use of insecticides and disturbance of roosting sites.

Rodents are well represented. They include the common House rat and the Large-eyed Sand rat, the gerbil and the Long-tailed jerboa which leaps like a tiny kangaroo. Many gerbils and jerboas, sadly, are found for sale in pet shops in Europe.

Weasels are common in the Delta region, even in urban areas such as Cairo, where they keep down the numbers of rats and mice. The snake eating Egyptian mongoose with a distinctive tuft on the end of its tail is frequently sighted but sightings of porcupines are rare and then only in the far south. The ibex too is only found in the south.

Reptiles and amphibians

The crocodile, treated as a sacred animal by the Egyptians (see El-Fayoum) who kept them in tanks by their temples, is no longer found north of the Aswan Dam. A few remain in Lake Nasser and in Sudan. Tortoises are widespread. Terrapins are less common. Both tortoises and terrapins are taken in large numbers for the pet trade. There are over 30 species of lizard in the area, the most common being the Wall lizard, which often lives close to houses. Sand racers are frequently seen on dunes, while Sand fish and Sand swimmers take advantage of deep sand to avoid predators and find cooler temperatures in the desert reg. Spiny lizards have distinctive enlarged

Prickly pears or barbary figs

Opuntia Vulgaris is the Latin name for the prickly pear cactus, with its large, flat, spined leaves, which is used for boundary hedges or less commonly shelter belts to deflect wind from delicate plants.

The attractive flowers of yellow or cyclamen occur on the rim of the leaves from May onwards and provide a bright splash of colour. If your visit occurs in July or August do not hesitate to try the fruit of the Barbary fig. Obtain them ready peeled from roadside sellers and certainly do not pick them yourself as they are protected by a multitude of fine spines, almost invisible to the naked eye, which can only be removed, painfully, by an expert.

Consume these fruits in moderation – more than two or three can cause constipation!

spiked scales round their tails. The *waran* (or Egyptian Monitor) can grow to over a metre in length. Geckoes are plump, soft-skinned, nocturnal lizards with adhesive pads on their toes and are frequently noted running up the walls in houses. The chameleon is a reptile with a prehensile tail and a long sticky tongue for catching insects. Although basically green, it can change colour to match its surroundings.

Snakes are essentially legless lizards. There are some 30 species in Egypt but only vipers are dangerous. These can be identified by their triangular heads, short plump bodies and zig-zag markings. The Horned sand-viper lies just below the surface of sand, with its horns projecting, waiting for prey. The Saw-scaled Carpet viper, which is of variegated dark camouflage colours, is twice the size but don't stay to measure, it is considered the most dangerous snake in Egypt. The Sinai or Desert Cobra, up to 2 m long, was the symbol of Lower Egypt. It too is deadly. Sand boas stay underground most of the time. Most snakes will instinctively avoid contact with human beings and will only strike if disturbed or threatened. For what to do if you are bitten by a snake, see Health in Essentials.

River, lake and marine life

There are over 190 varieties of fish in the River Nile, the most common being the Nile bolti with coarse scales and spiny fins and the Nile perch, frequently well over 150 cm in length. Bolti are also found in Lake Nasser. Other fish include the inedible puffer fish, lungfish which can survive in the mud when the waters recede, grey mullet and catfish which are a popular catch for domestic consumption but some species can give off strong electric shocks. Decline in fish numbers is blamed on pollution, over-fishing and change of environment due to the construction of the Aswan Dam. Marine fish such as sole and mullet have been introduced into Lake Qaroun which is becoming increasingly saline.

The Mediterranean Sea has insufficient nutrients to support large numbers of fish. The numerous small fishing boats with their small mesh nets seriously over-exploit the existing stock. The catch is similar to the North Atlantic – hake, sole, red mullet, turbot, whiting. Sardines occur off the Nile Delta but in much reduced quantities due to pollution. Tuna, more common to the west, are caught off Libya too. Grey mullet is fished in and off the Nile Delta while sponges, lobsters and shellfish harvested.

The fish of the Mediterranean pale into insignificance against 800 species of tropical fish in the Red Sea not to mention Tiger and Hammerhead sharks, Moray eels, Slender barracudas and Manta rays. Here, while sport and commercial fishermen chase after tuna, bonita and dolphin, scuba divers pay to explore the fringing coral reefs and view the paint box selection of Angel, Butterfly and Parrot fish and carefully avoid the ugly Scorpion fish and the even more repulsive Stone fish.

Insects

There are a number of insects that travellers might not wish to encounter – bedbugs, lice, fleas, cockroaches, sand flies, house flies, mosquitoes, wasps and ants. By contrast there are large beautiful dragonflies which hover over the river, the destructive locusts fortunately rarely in swarms, and the fascinating Black dung beetles, the sacred Scarab of the Egyptians, which roll and bury balls of animal dung as food for their larvae (see box, page 157). Scorpions, not insects, are all too common in Egypt. See box, page 463.

Birds

The bird life in the region is increased in number and interest by birds of passage. There are four categories of birds. Firstly, there are 150 species of **resident birds**, such as the Crested lark and the Sardinian warbler. Resident birds are found mainly in the fertile strip of the Nile Valley and in the Nile Delta. There are surprisingly few in the oases. Secondly, there are the **summer visitors**, such as the swift and swallow, which spend the winter months south of the equator. **Winter visitors**, on the other hand, breed in Northern Europe but come south to escape the worst of the winter and include many varieties of owl, wader and wildfowl. **Passage migrants** fly through the area northwards in spring and then return southwards in increased numbers after breeding in the autumn. Small birds tend to migrate on a broad front, often crossing the desert and the Mediterranean Sea without stopping. Such migrants include the Whitethroat, plus less common species such as the Nightjar and Wryneck. Larger birds, including eagles, storks and vultures, must adopt a different strategy, as they depend on soaring, rather than sustained flight. As they rely on thermals created over land, they must opt for short sea crossings following the Nile Valley, Turkey and the Bosphorus.

There are a number of typical **habitats** with their own assemblage of birds. The Mediterranean itself has a poor selection of sea birds, although the rare Audouins gull always excites twitchers. Oceanic birds such as gannets and shearwaters, however, over-winter here. The Red Sea coast hosts the indigenous White-eyed Gull and White-cheeked Tern, migrant pelicans, gregarious flamingos and, near Hurghada, Brown boobies. Ospreys breed on the nearby Isle of Tiran.

Wetland areas attract numerous varieties of the heron family such as the Night heron and Squacco heron, while spoonbill, ibis and both Little and Cattle egrets are common. Waders such as the avocet and Black-winged stilt are also typical wetland birds. The species are augmented in winter by a vast collection of wildfowl. Resident ducks, however, are confined to specialities such as the White-headed duck, Marbled teal and Ferruginous duck. On roadsides, the Crested lark is frequently seen, while overhead wires often contain Corn buntings, with their jangling song, and the Blue-cheeked and Green Bee-eaters. Mountain areas are ideal for searching out raptors. There are numerous varieties of eagle, including Bonelli's, Booted, Short toed and Golden. Of the vultures, the griffon is the most widely encountered. The Black kite is more catholic in its choice of habitat, but the Montagu's harrier prefers open farmland.

The desert and steppe areas have their own specialist resident birds which have developed survival strategies. Raptors include the Long-legged buzzard and the lanner, which prefer mountain areas. The Arabian rock pigeon of Sinai is a protected species. Among the ground-habitat birds are the Houbura bustard and the Cream coloured courser. Duponts lark is also reluctant to fly, except during its spectacular courtship display. The Trumpeter finch is frequently seen at oases, while the insectivorous Desert wheatear is a typical bird of the erg and *reg* regions.

Special mention must be made of the Nile Valley. Essentially a linear oasis stretching for hundreds of kilometres, it provides outstanding bird watching, particularly from the slow-moving cruise boats, which are literally 'floating hides'.

 Apart from the wide range of herons and egrets, specialities include the African skimmer, Egyptian geese, Pied kingfisher and White pelican. Even the tombs and monuments are rewarding for the ornithologist, yielding Sakar falcons, Levant sparrowhawks and the Black shouldered kite.

Bird watching locations → *Numbers refer to map below.*

1. Lake Burullus, a good location for delta birds – thousands of Wigeon, Coot and Whiskered Tern and other water birds. Access can be difficult.
2. Lake El-Manzala is in the Eastern Delta with access from Port Said. It is an important over wintering area for water/shore birds.
3. Lake Bardweel on the north Sinai coast is well known for migratory birds in their thousands, especially in the autumn, and in particular water birds, ducks and herons. Shore birds too like Avocet and Flamingo can been seen here.
4. Wadi El-Natrun. Here in the shallow lagoons may be found Kittlitz's Plover and Blue-cheeked Bee-eaters but don't expect an instant sighting.
5. Near Cairo airport at Gabel Asfar the recycling plant provides a mixed habitat with opportunities to see Painted Snipe, Senegal Coucal and the White-breasted Kingfisher. The Egyptian Nightjar may be heard but is unlikely to be seen. Cairo Zoo, Giza is recommended – for the song birds in the gardens. In cities, or any settlement for that matter, the Black Kite acts as a scavenger. Near Cairo, at the Pyramids look out for the Pharaoh Eagle Owl.
6. Suez in the perfect position for observing migratory birds – for Raptors in particular which pass over in their thousands, also Gulls, Waders and Terns. Look for the Greater Sand Plover and Broad-billed Sandpiper also White-eyed Gull and Lesser Crested Tern more often associated with the Red Sea. All these resident and migratory birds are attracted by the mud flats and conditions in Suez Basin.
7. Taba region residents include Namaqua Dove, Little Green Bee-eater, Mourning,

Birdwatching sites

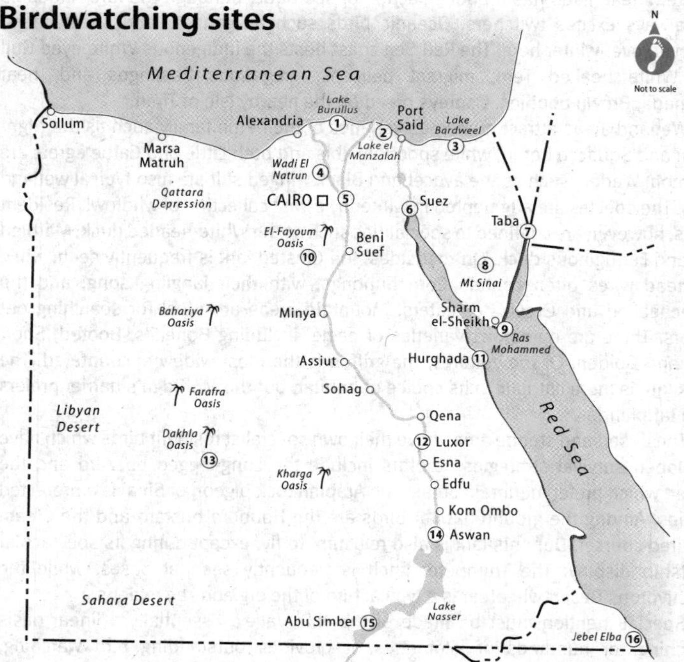

Hooded and White-crowned Black Wheatears. Migrants include Olivaceous and Orphean Warblers. White-cheeked and Bridle Tern can be seen off the coast between Taba and Sharm El-Sheikh.

8. At Mount Sinai look for Verreaux's Eagle which nest in this area. Residents include Lammergeier, Sinai Rosefinch frequently sighted near St Catherine's Monastery, Barbary Falcon, Sand Partridge, Little Green Bee-eater, Rock Martin, Desert and Hoopoe Larks, Scrub Warbler, White-crowned Black and Hooded Wheatears, Blackstart, Tristram's Grackle, Brown-necked Raven and House Bunting. There are special migrants to be observed such as Masked and Red-backed Shrikes, Olive-tree and Orphean Warblers. Look also for Hulme's Tawny Owl.

9. Try the tip of Sinai round Ras Mohammed where the Nabq protected area is recommended. Mark up Sooty Falcon seen on the cliffs nest here, Lichtenstein's Sandgrouse further inland near the recycling plant, White-eyed Gull, Bridled Tern, White-cheeked and Lesser Crested Tern (less common are Brown Booby and Crested Tern). Osprey nest in this region too. Migratory birds include White Storks which are very abundant. There is a White Stork sanctuary near Sharm El-Sheikh.

10. El-Fayoum oasis is noted for water birds and waders. It has been associated with duck hunting from ancient times. Over wintering duck, Coot and Grebe gather here in great numbers. Lake Qaroun in El-Fayoum oasis is a salt water lake and the area is now protected. In winter it is covered with water fowl. On the north shores of the lake falcons and hawks quarter the ground and in the trees see the Green Bee-eater, Bulbul and Grey Shrike. Note too Lapwing, Swallow and Senegal Thick-knee. Shore birds include Sandpipers, Curlew, Coot (never seen so many) and Grebe.

11. The Red Sea off Hurghada is a rich habitat supporting 15 species of breeding birds, both water birds and sea birds. Brown Booby, Western Reef Egret, White-eyed and Sooty Gulls, Crested, Lesser Crested and White-cheeked Terns, Red-billed Tropicbird, Bridled Tern are on the list. The islands in the Red Sea provide a safer habitat for the birds. Such is Isle of Tiran, approach only by boat, not to land. Osprey nest here, in places quite common. Sooty (a few) and White-eyed Gulls (more common) are found on the uninhabited islands further south.

12. Around Luxor look for Black-shouldered Kite, Black Kite, Egyptian Vulture, Senegal Thick-knee, Purple Gallinule with perhaps a Painted Snipe or a Nile Valley Sunbird on Crocodile Island where Hotel Movenpick has made an effort to protect the environment for these birds. On the other side of the River Nile in the Valleys of the Kings and Queens are Rock Martin, Trumpeter Finch, Little Green Bee-eater. Desert birds found anywhere in desert are represented here by Hoopoe and Bar-tailed Larks.

13. Dakhla Oasis has a large lake called the Fishpond the surface almost obscured by birds, Avocet, Stilt, coot.

14. Aswan is one of the best places for herons and kingfishers, best viewed from the river itself. Pied Kingfishers and Egyptian Geese are common. At Aswan try Saluga Island which is a protected area.

15. Abu Simbel is important due to its southerly location. After viewing the monuments take time to look for rarities including Long-tailed Cormorant, Pink-backed Pelican, Yellow-billed stork, African Skimmer, Pink-headed Dove and African Pied Wagtail.

16. Jebel Elba in the very south-east corner of Egypt has samples of sub-Saharan birds - Verreaux's eagles, Pink headed Doves and perhaps even Ostrich. This region cannot be visited without a permit, which is not likely to be forthcoming.

Books

Area-specific guidebooks

Fakhry, Ahmed *Siwa Oasis*. An extensive look at the life, history and monuments of Siwa from the premier archeologist of the Western Desert. Also look for volume two of Fakhry's *The Oases of Egypt* where he highlights his explorations into the oases of Bahariyya and Farafra.
Ghisotti and Carletti *The Red Sea Diving Guide*. Written by Italians but translated into several languages, the colourful guide includes 3-D diagrams of reefs and illustrations of more than 100 species of fish.
Vivian, Cassandra *The Western Desert of Egypt* – An Explorer's Handbook (2000, AUC Press). To date, the most comprehensive guide to the W. desert, includes maps, GPS coordinates, and loads of historical, ecological and cultural information. This book is essential to any extensive exploration in the Western Desert. Be aware, though, that parts are not entirely accurate, so do not depend solely on this guide.
Williams, Caroline *Monuments in Cairo* – The Practical Guide (2002, AUC Press). The most up to date and comprehensive guide to Islamic Cairo. Includes detailed walking tours, maps and historical accounts and explanations of all the important buildings in Cairo.

Ancient Egypt

Murnane, William J *The Penguin Guide to Ancient Egypt* (1983, Penguin Books). A comprehensive book detailing the monuments and culture of Ancient Egypt. There are loads of illustrations and descriptions of almost every major monument in the country.
Tyldestey, Joyce *Daughters of Isis: Women of Ancient Egypt* (1994, Penguin Books). "Egypt was undoubtedly the best place to have been born a woman in the whole of the Ancient World." Drawing upon archelogical, historical and ethnographical evidence, this book tells why and offers an engaging account of women's daily life in Egypt.
Quirke, S and Spencer J (eds) *The British Museum Book of Ancient Egypt*. An accessible and solid general overview of Ancient Egypt, with glossy pictures highlighting the museum's impressive collection.
The Shire Egyptology series (Shire Publications Ltd, Princes Risborough, Bucks, UK). A fascinating series (£4.99 each) including *Egyptian Coffins, Mummies, Pyramids and Household Animals, Temples, Tools & Weapons*.

Travel accounts

Edwards, Amelia B *A Thousand Miles up the Nile* (1877, Century Publishing, London). Engaging detailed travel account highlighting a journey up the River Nile, extensive writing on ruins as well as people, in the voice of a 19th century woman novelist who, after this trip, became an authority in Egyptology.
Flaubert, Gustav *Flaubert in Egypt* (Penguin). A collection of personal writings that highlight more of Flaubert's jaunts through brothels and bathhouses rather than an exploration of the monuments.
Pick, Christopher *Egypt: A Traveller's Anthology*. An interesting collection of writings from a diverse group of 19th and early 20th century writers – Gustav Flaubert, Mark Twain, and EM Forster among them.
Sonnini, CS *Travels in Upper and Lower Egypt*. Famed naturalist and frequent traveller, the Frenchman visited Egyptian 1777. The English translation of his accounts were published in 1799.

Culture and society

Abu Lughod, Lila *Veiled Sentiments: Honour and Poetry in a Bedouin Society*. A sensitive anthropological study of the Awlad Ali tribe in the Western Desert that puts forth an insightful account of Bedouin culture.
Atiya, Nayra *Khul-Khaal – Five Egyptian Women Tell Their Stories*. Compelling accounts from five women of varying socio-economic and cultural backgrounds. Offers tremendous insight into the lives of contemporary Egyptian women.

El-Sadawi, Nawal *The Hidden Face of Eve.* Written by the renown Egyptian feminist, the book details the situation of Arab women and speaks directly of female genital mutilation, divorce and prostitution. It is banned in Egypt.
Murphy, Caryle *Passion for Islam* – Shaping *the Modern Middle East: The Egyptian Experience* (2002, Scribner). An accessible and fascinating account of Islam and its ever changing role in Egypt. Offers a thorough introduction to those interested in understanding the motivation and fuel behind Islamist movements, especially amid the current political climate.
Rodenbeck, Max *Cairo: the City Victorious.* Written by the Economist's Egypt correspondent, this accessible and impressively researched book details 5,000 years of Cairo's great history and offers keen insight into the nature of Egyptians past and present.

Wildlife

Boulos, Loutfy *Flora of Egypt* (1999, AUC Press). Premier guide to plant life in Egypt, encyclopedic in scope and including over 500 drawings and pictures.
Hoath, Richard *Natural Selection – A Year of Egypt's* Wildlife (1992, AUC Press). Engaging text recounting Egypt's wide array of life throughout the varied regions and seasons, includes animal sketches by the author. Richard Hoath also writes a monthly column on wildlife for the monthly Egypt Today.
Khalil, Rafik and Aly, Dina *Egypt's Natural Heritage* (2000). A beautiful hardcover picture book offering documentation of Egypt's wildlife and scenery through images and descriptive text.
Miles, John *Pharaohs' Birds* (1998, AUC Press). Detailed guide of ancient and present day birds in Egypt, including possible safaris for avid bird watchers.

Maps and town plans

Michelin map No 154 covers Egypt. The **Oxford** Map of Egypt (OUP) is very good. Sinai printed in Switzerland by **Kümmerly and Frey** gives most of the sites. Look out for four maps produced by **SPARE** – Society for the Preservation of Architectural Resources of Egypt – with detailed information of The Citadel, Islamic Cairo and Khan El-Khalili. Several maps of the whole of Egypt and of the major towns are available from the Egyptian Survey Authority.

Footnotes

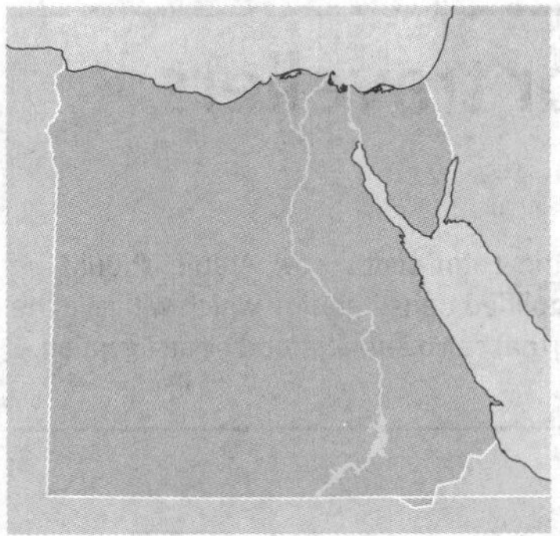

Basic Egyptian for travellers

It is impossible to indicate precisely in the Latin script how Arabic should be pronounced so we have opted for a very simplified transliteration which will give the user a sporting chance of uttering something that can be understood by an Egyptian.

Basics

Bad	*Mish kweyyis, wahish*
Can you help me?	*Mumkin tisa'idny?* (m) *Mumkin tisa'ideeny* (f)
Do you have a problem?	*Fee mushkilla?*
Do you speak English?	*Bitikalim ingleezy?* (m) *Bitikalimy ingleezy?* (f)
Excuse me	*law samaht*
God willing	*insha*'allah
Good	*Kweyyis*
He/she	*howwa/heyya*
How	*Izay*
How much	*Bikam?*
I/you	*ana/inta* (m) *inty* (f)
I don't speak Arabic	*Ma bakalimsh 'araby*
No	*la'a*
No problem	*mafeesh mushkilla*
Please	*min fadlak* (m) *min fadlik* (f)
Thank You	*shukran*
What	*Eih*
Where	*Fein*
Where's the bathroom	*Fein el hamam?*
Who	*Meen*
Why	*Leih*
Yes	*aiwa/na'am*
You're welcome	*'afwan*

Greetings and farewells

Fine	*kwayis* (m) *kwayissa* (f)
Goodbye	*ma'a el salama*
Hello	*ahlan wasahlan/assalamu aleikum*
How are you	*Izayak?* (m) *Izayik?* (f)
See you tomorrow	*ashoofak bokra* (m) *ashoofik bokra* (f)
Thank God	*il hamdullil'allah*

Numbers

0	*sífr*
1	*wahad*
2	*etneen*
3	*talaata*
4	*arba*
5	*khamsa*
6	*sitta*
7	*saba'a*
8	*tamenia*
9	*tissa*
10	*ashra*
11	*hidashar*
12	*itnashar*
13	*talatashar*
14	*arbatashar*
15	*khamstashar*
16	*sittashar*
17	*sabatashar*
18	*tamantashar*
19	*tissatashar*
20	*'ayshreen*
30	*talaateen*
40	*arba'een*
50	*khamseen*
60	*sitteen*
70	*saba'een*
80	*tmaneen*
90	*tissa'een*
100	*mia*
200	*miteen*
300	*tolto mia*
1,000	*alf*

Dates and time

Afternoon	*Ba'd el dohr*
Day	*Yom*
Early	*Badry*
Evening	*Masa'*
Everyday	*Kol yom*
Hour	*Sa'a*
Late	*Mit'akhar*
Month	*Shahr*
Morning	*El sobh*
Night	*Bil leil*
Today	*Inaharda*
Tomorrow	*Bokra*
What time is it?	*E'sa'a kam?*
When?	*Imta?*

Year	*Sana*
Yesterday	*Imbarah*

Days of week

Monday	*el itnein*
Tuesday	*el talaat*
Wednesday	*el arba'*
Thursday	*el khamees*
Friday	*el goma'*
Saturday	*el sapt*
Sunday	*el had*

Travel and transport

Airport	*el matar*
Boat	*markib*
Bus	*otobees*
Bus station	*mahatit otobees*
Bus stop	*maw'if otobees*
Camel	*gamal*
Car	'arabiya
Carriage	*karetta; calesh*
City	*madeena*
Does this go to...	*da beerooh*
Donkey	*homar*
Ferry	*'abara*
Horse	*hosan*
I want to go...	*a'yiz arooh* (m) *a'yiza arooh* (f)
Map	*khareeta*
Parking	*parking*
Passport	*gawaz safar*
Petrol	*benzeen*
Plane	*tayara*
Police	*bolice*
Street	*shari'*
Ticket office	*maktab e'tazakir*
Tourist office	*makta e'siyaha*
Train	*atr*
Train station	*mahatit atr*
Tyre	'agala
Village	*kareeya*
Visa	*visa*

Directions

After	*ba'ad*
Before	*'abl*

Far	*bi'eed*
Here is fine	*hina kwayis*
How many kilometres is...	*kem kilometers el...*
Left	*shimal*
Near	*gamb*
Right	*yimeen*
Slow down	*bishweish*
Speed up	*bisora'*
Straight	*doghry; ala tool*
There	*hinak*
Where is the...	*fein el ...*

Money and shopping

25 piasters/a quarter pound	*robe' gineih*
Bank	*benk*
Bookstore	*maktaba*
Camera	*camera*
Carpet	*sigada*
Cheap	*rikhees*
Do you accept visa?	*Mumkin visa?*
Do you have...	*'andak...* (m) *andik...* (f)
Exchange	*sirafa*
Expensive	*ghaly*
Film	*film*
Gold	*dahab*
Half a pound	*nos gineih*
How many?	*kem?*
How much?	*bikem?*
Jewellery	*seegha*
Market	*souk*
Newspaper in English	*gareeda ingleeziya*
One pound	*gineih*
Price	*se'r*
Silver	*fada*
That's too much	*kiteer awy*
Where can I buy...	*fin ashtiry...*

Food and drink

Beer	*beera*
Boil	*ighly*
Bread	*'aysh*
Chicken	*firakh*
Coffee	*'ahwa*
Coffee shop	*'Ahwa*
Dessert	*helw*
Drink	*ishrab*
Eggs	*beid*

Fava beans	*Fu'ul*
Felafel	*Ta'*ameyya
Fish	*samak*
Food	*akul*
Fruit	*fak ha*
I would like…	*a'yiz* (m) *a'yza* (f)
Juice	*'aseer*
Meat	*lahma*
Milk	*laban*
Pepper	*filfil*
Restaurant	*mata'am*
Rice	*roz*
Salad	*salata*
Salt	*malh*
Soup	*shorba*
Sugar	*sucar*
The check please	*el hisab law samaht* (m) *samahty* (f)
Tea	*shay*
Tip	*baksheesh*
Vegetables	*khodar*
Vegetarian	*nabaty*
Water	*maya*
Water pipe	*shisha*
Wine	*nibeet*

Accommodation

Air conditioning	*takeef*
Can I see a room?	*Mumkin ashoof owda?*
Fan	*marwaha*
Hotel	*fondoq*
How much is a room?	*Bikam el owda?*
Is breakfast included?	*Fi fitar?*
Is there a bathroom?	*Fi hamam?*
Room	*oda*
Shower	*Doush*

Health

Aspirin	*aspireen*
Diaharreah	is *hal*
Doctor	*dok-tor*
Fever	*sokhoniya*
Hospital	*mostashfa*
I feel sick	*ana 'ayan* (m) *ana 'ayanna* (f)
I have a headache	*'andy sod'a*
I have a stomache ache	*'andy maghas*

I'm allergic to	*'andy hasasiya*
Medicine	*dawa*
Pharmacy	*saydaliya*

Useful words

Black	*iswid*
Blue	*azra'*
Church	*kineesa*
Clean	*nadeef*
Cold	*bard*
Desert	*sahara*
Dirty	*wisikh*
Finished/done	*khalas*
Green	*akhdar*
Hot	*har*
Less	*a'al*
More	*aktar*
Mosque	*gami'*
Mountain	*gabal*
Red	*ahmar*
River	*nahr*
Sandstorm	*khamaseen*
Sea	*bahr*
Summer	*seif*
Valley	*wadi*
White	*abyad*
Winter	*shita*
Yellow	*asfar*

Common Egyptian words

Balad	country
Baladi	traditional/from the countryside
Corniche	Nile-side road
Felucca	Traditional sailboat often found on the Nile
Felaheen	Peasants

Dodging touts

You'll get hassled less and respected more if you learn a bit of Arabic.

La'a shocrun	no thank you!
U'ltilak la'a	I told you no!
Mish ay-yez (m) *mish ay-zza* (f)	I don't want; I'm not interested
Bess	enough
Khalas	finished, that's it
F'il mish mish	lit. 'when the apricots bloom' (ie 'in your dreams')!

Who's who in Ancient Egypt

Kings and Queens → *Illustrations represent monarchs' cartouches*

Akhenaten

Amenhotep IV, who later took the name of Akhenaten, ruled for 15 years around 1379-52 BC. He is remembered for the religious revolution he effected.

The authority of the priests of Amun-Re, the Sun God, the chief god of the Egyptians, had grown so great it almost rivalled that of the pharaohs. The pharaoh was regarded as the son of Amun-Re and was bound by strict religious ritual, part of a theological system understood clearly only by the priests, wherein lay their power.

Meanwhile a small religious cult was developing with the god Aten (a manifestation of the old sun-god Re of Memphis) at the centre, the sole god. This new cult appealed to the young prince and after he succeeded his father he changed his name to Akhenaten meaning 'it is well with the Aten' and moved his capital from Thebes to an entirely new city identified with the modern Tell El-Amarna, though no trace remains (see page 190).

This idea of the sole god was new in Egypt, new in the world, and Akhenaten is known as the first real monotheist. There is no evidence that the new religion appealed to the mass of the people for while the King was deeply involved in his worship his empire fell into decay.

The new religious ideas were expressed in carvings. While the pharaoh as the son of god could not be portrayed and the queen rarely appeared at all in reliefs and statues, Akhenaten changed all the conventions and his artists represented him, and his wife and family, as they were, riding in chariots, bestowing gifts to his followers, even kissing.

When Akhenaten died at the age of 41, his half brother, Tutankhaton, a young boy, succeeded him. The Court returned to Thebes, the priests of Amen returned to power, the King changed his name to Tutankhamen (see page 483) and everything possible was done to wipe out Akhenaten's 'heretical' religion.

Cheops

Cheops or Khufu was an Old Kingdom pharaoh, the second king of the fourth Dynasty succeeding his father Snefru. His mother was Queen Hetepheres. He reigned between 2549 BC and 2526 BC. He is well known as the builder of the Great Pyramid of Giza (see page 76). He is recorded as having had four wives. Three names are given – Merityetes, Hen-utsen and Nefert-kau one of whom was his sister/half-sister, and one queen is unnamed. For Merityetes and Hen-utsen there are smaller pyramids built beside his own.

Herodotus records his reign and that of his son Chephren (Khafre) as a century of misery and oppression under wicked and tyrannical kings but in Egyptian history he is considered to have been a wise ruler. Nevertheless, there certainly was misery. He shut all the temples and forbade the people to make sacrifices. At the same time he forced them to give up their livelihoods and assist in the construction of the pyramid being part of the team of a hundred thousand men who worked a three month shift. The preliminaries and actual construction took over 20 years. Part of the preparation was the construction of the oldest known paved road. Its purpose was to allow the huge granite facing blocks for his pyramid to be dragged and rolled to the site. Small fragments of the road exist today.

Cleopatra 69-30 BC

In 51 BC at the death of her father Ptolemy XIII she became joint ruler of Egypt with her younger brother. Three years later she was ousted from the throne but reinstated by Julius Caesar. It is related that while Julius Caesar was seated in a room in the citadel in Alexandria two slaves entered bearing a magnificent carpet. 'Cleopatra, Queen of Egypt, begs you to accept this gift' said one and as the carpet unrolls out sprang the 19-year-old Cleopatra. Dazzled at the sight of such loveliness, so the tale goes, the stern warrior fell in with all her plans, helping her subdue her enemies and permanently dispose of her brother.

When the daggers of the conspirators at Rome removed Caesar's protection she turned her charms on Mark Antony. Called to his presence to answer charges of assisting his enemies she came, not as a penitent but in a barge of beaten gold, lying under a gold embroidered canopy and fanned by 'pretty dimpled boys'. This certainly caught his attention and conveniently forgetting his wife and duties in Rome he became her willing slave. While Cleopatra had visions of ruling in Rome as Antony's consort his enemies at Rome prevailed on the Senate to declare war on such a dangerous woman. The battle was fought at Actium in 31 BC but Cleopatra slipped away with her ships at the first opportunity leaving Antony to follow her as a hunted fugitive.

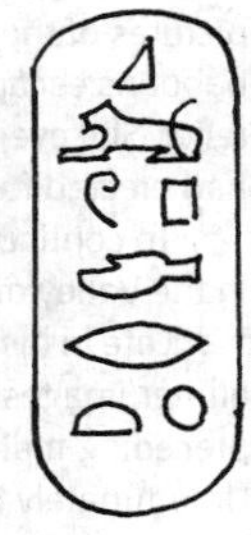

Cleopatra attempted to charm Octavian, Antony's conqueror, but he was made of sterner stuff and proof against her wiles. Antony killed himself and Cleopatra, proud and queenly to the last chose to die by the bite of a poisonous asp (an unsubstantiated fact), rather than be taken to Rome in chains. Certainly an eventful life for a woman who never reached her 40th birthday.

Hatshepsut

She was the first great woman in history living about 1503-1482 BC in the 18th Dynasty. She had immense power, adopted the full title of a pharaoh and was dressed in the full regalia down to the kilt and the false beard. She ruled for about 21 years.

She was the daughter of Tuthmosis I and Queen Ahmose and was married to her half brother Tuthmosis II who came to rule Egypt in 1512 at the death of his father. He was not very strong and at his death Hatshepsut, who had had no sons of her own, became the regent of his young son Tuthmosis III, son of a minor wife/woman in the harem. She took effective control of the government while pretending to be only the prince's regent and Tuthmosis III was made a priest of the god Amun.

Around 1503 she gave up all pretence of being subservient to her stepson and had herself crowned as pharaoh. To have reached this position and to retain it indicates the support of a number of faithful and influential officials in her government. Her steward Senenmut was well-known and may have been the father of her daughter Neferure.

Determined to expand commercially she despatched (with Amun's blessing, she said) an impressive expedition to Punt on the African coast (now part of Somalia) from

which were brought gold, ebony, animal skins, live baboons, processed myrrh and live myrrh trees to decorate her temple and that of Amun in Karnak. Tributes also flooded in from Libya, Nubia and the nearer parts of Asia.

In the name of/to honour the god Amun-Re (the main god of the region and her adopted 'father') she set about a huge reconstruction programme repairing damage caused to earlier temples and building new ones. The chapels to the Thebian Triad behind the Great Pylon of Ramses II at Luxor were built by Hatshepsut and Tuthmosis III. She renovated The Great Temple of Amun, at Karnak where she introduced four huge (30 m+) obelisks made of Aswan granite. At Beni Hasan she built a rock cut temple known as Speos Artemidos but her finest achievement was her own beautiful temple cut into the rock at three different levels.

The wall reliefs in the temple fortified her position of importance, her divine birth which is a very complicated set of scenes involving the god Amun, her mother and herself as a baby; her selection as pharaoh by Hathor; her coronation by Hathor and Seth watched over by her real father, Tuthmosis I.

Her expedition to the exotic land of Punt is depicted in very great detail with pictures of the scenery (stilt houses) and selected incidents from the voyages (some baboons escaping up the rigging). Items brought back are offered to Amun in another relief. She even had depicted the huge barges used to transport the four obelisks she had erected for her adopted father (Amun) in Karnak.

To continue her position as a pharaoh even after her death she had her tomb cut in the Valley of the Kings. It was the longest and deepest in the valley.

Late in his reign Tuthmosis III turned against the memory of Hatshepsut and had all her images in the reliefs erased and replaced with figures of himself or the two preceding male pharaohs. In many places her cartouches have been rewritten too. Unfortunately he had all her statues destroyed.

Ramses III

He reigned from 1198-66 BC, in the 20th Dynasty which was noted for the beginning of the great decline of Egypt. He was not part of the decline, however, and was considered a worthy monarch. He excelled himself in the earlier part of his reign with victories on land and victories at sea vanquishing the Cretans and the Carians. On land he used the military colonies established by previous rulers such as Ramses II and Seti I to conduct his missions further into Asia. He had little trouble subduing the tribes far into Asia but had problems nearer at home – having to fight to hold his position as pharaoh. A group of invaders made up of

Libyans, Sardinians and Italians managed to advance as far as Memphis in the 8th year of his reign but their defeat put him in a much stronger position internally.

Having had his fill of expeditions to foreign parts and no doubt having returned with sufficient booty to have made the trips worthwhile and make him a very wealthy monarch he paid off his troops and set about adding to and constructing temples and other monumental works. Of particular note are the buildings at Medinet Habu. Here there is a magnificent temple with the walls covered in reliefs depicting the engagements on land and sea in which he had been so successful. Even the gate is inscribed with reliefs showing the despatch of prisoners and where a neat design on the pylons shows a cartouche of each vanquished country surmounted by a human head and with bound arms (see page 250). This is a valuable historical record of Egypt and the surrounding lands at this time.

In brief he restored law and order within Egypt and provided some security from outside aggression. He revived commercial prosperity. His attentions to the temples of Thebes, Memphis and Heliopolis certainly enriched Egyptian architecture. He was, however, unable to turn the slow ebb of his country's grandeur which was said to be suffering from 'fundamental decadence'.

He was assassinated. Four sons, all bearing the his name, succeeded him but their reigns were not distinguished and the decline of Egypt was hastened.

Tutankhamen

He was a pharaoh of the New Kingdom, 18th Dynasty, and reigned from 1361-52 BC. He was the son of Amenhotep III and probably his chief queen Tiy and was married to Akhenaten's daughter. He was too young to rule without a visir and regent. He died in the ninth year of his reign at about 18 years of age, leaving no surviving children, his regent Ay succeeded him by marrying his widow.

He was originally called Tutankhaton but changed name to Tutankhamen to distance himself from Atun and the cult of Atun worship of his half brother Amenhotep IV (Akhenaten). He moved his capital back to Memphis and to eradicate the effects of the rule of his predecessor he restored the temples and the status of the old gods and their priests. His greatest claim to fame was his intact tomb discovered by Howard Carter in 1922, details of which are given on page 236, see also box page 235.

Tuthmosis I – the trend setter

He was an 18th-Dynasty pharaoh who ruled from around 1525-12 BC. He is noted for his expansion of the Egyptian Empire south into Nubia and east into present day Syria. He led a river-bourne expedition into Nubia to beyond the fourth Cataract (he was after the gold there) and set up a number of defensive forts along the route. His foray across the Euphrates was part of his campaign against the Hyksos who caused many problems for the Egyptians. Tuthmosis I used the Euphrates as the border over which he did not intend these enemies to cross.

He is also noted for the building and renovation works he contracted at Karnak. Much of the inner temple of Amun at Karnak is attributed to him. In particular the sandstone fourth Pylon in front of which one of his obelisks still stands, and the limestone fifth Pylon which marked the centre of the temple at the time, and behind which was the original position of the sanctuary of Tuthmosis I.

He was born in the era when burial in a pyramid was 'out of vogue' and being buried in a secret tomb in the rocks of the surrounding hillside was just coming 'in'. (See box below Pyramids out of fashion.) It is suggested that his tomb was the first in the Valley of the Kings and he certainly set a trend. Even so his red quartzite sarcophagus was found in the tomb of his daughter Queen Hatshepsut and is now in the museum in Cairo.

Zoser

This was a king of the Old Kingdom, the second king of the 3rd Dynasty. It is hard to piece together his history. He succeeded his brother and perhaps reigned for 19 years between 2667-48 BC. Two of his daughters were called Intkaes and Hetephernebti, their names taken from steales in the complex.

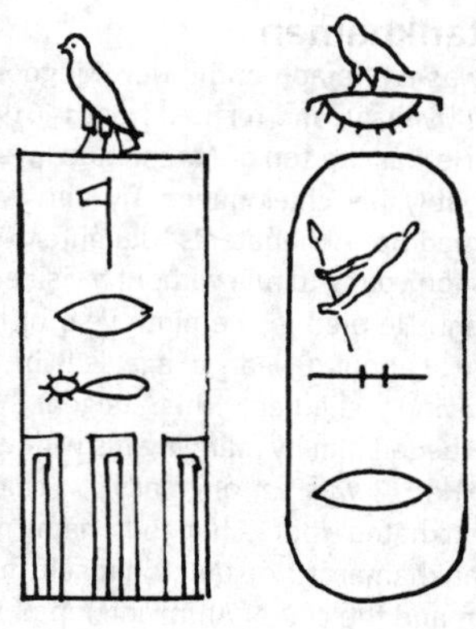

His funerary complex at Saqqara (see page 152) is an example of some of the world's most ancient architecture and it was all, not only the Step Pyramid, but also the huge enclosure wall and the subsidiary temples and structures, designed by Zoser, under the charge of his talented architect/chancellor/ physician Imhotep. This building was important being the first large scale building to be made completely of stone. In addition it was of an unusual stepped design. Many of the buildings in the surrounding complex were never intended for use but were replicas of the buildings used by the pharaoh on earth so that he could use them in eternity. Eventually he was buried under his Step Pyramid. So what was the other tomb for in the complex? Perhaps it was for his entrails as it was too small for a royal person?

He made Memphis his capital which gave impetus to the growth in importance of this town which eventually became the political and cultural centre.

Travellers interested in seeing his likeness must visit room 46 in Cairo Museum which has the huge seated figure of King Zoser taken from the complex.

Deities

There were hundreds of gods and goddesses worshipped by the ancient Egyptians. Over time some grew in favour and others became less important. In addition each district of the country had its own deities. It is useful to have an idea of their role in ancient Egypt and to recognize them on the wall paintings and carvings. Unfortunately they could be represented in more than one way, being different aspects of the same god.

Aker

He was an earth god often shown with the head of a lion. He guarded the east and west gates of the afterworld.

Amun

He was first worshipped as a local deity in Khmun in Middle Egypt in Hermopolis and later when his cult reached Thebes his importance spread to all of Egypt. He was believed to be the creator of all things, to order time and the seasons. When he sailed over the heavens he controlled the wind and the direction of the clouds. His name means 'the hidden' or 'unseen one'. At times he was identified with the sun-god Re, hence Amun-Re, and as Amun-Min was the god of fertility. He was often drawn as a human form with twisted rams horns and two tall feathers as a headdress, a sceptre/crook in one hand and a ceremonial flail in the other, an erect phallus and a black pointed beard.

The sacred animals with which he was identified were the ram and the goose (the Great Cackler). As the ram-headed god he renewed the life in the souls of the departed. He was part of the Thebian Triad with Mut his wife and Khonsu his adopted son.

Anubis

This god was responsible for the ritual of embalming and looking after the place where the mummification was done. Indeed he was reputed to have invented embalming, his first attempt of this art being on the corpse of Osiris. When Anubis was drawn on the wall on either side of a tomb's entrance the mummy would be protected. He helped Isis to restore life to Osiris. He was also included in scenes weighing the dead person's heart/soul against the 'feather of truth', which was the only way to enter the next world. In the earlier dynasties of the Old Kingdom he held an important position as lord of the dead but was later overshadowed by Osiris. Later he was better known simply as a conductor of souls. He was closely associated with Middle Egypt and bits of Upper Egypt. He was depicted as a recumbent black dog/fox/jackal or a jackal-headed god. On any illustration the ears of the creature were alertly pricked up and slightly forward. The association with a fox/jackal was the number of jackals that were to found in the cemeteries. Sometimes he was shown seated on a pylon.

Anukis

This was the wife of Khnum and the mother of Sartis, the third member of the Elephantine Triad. She was the goddess of the first cataract area and was depicted wearing a high crown of feathers and carrying a sceptre of papyrus plant.

Apis Bulls
The sacred bulls of Memphis were all black bulls with a white triangle on the forehead and a crescent shape on the flank. A sacred bull was believed to contain the spirit of Ptah and lived in a palace and was present as guest of honour at state functions. When it died it was mummified and buried at the huge underground tomb of the Serapeum at Saqqara and a new younger bull, its reincarnation, took its place. On illustrations it was sometimes shown with a sun disc between its horns.

Apophis
This was a symbol of unrest and chaos in the form of a large serpent. It was kept under control by the stronger powers of good, in particular the cat-goddess Bastet and by Sekhmet the fierce lioness god.

Aten
He was the sun-god depicted as the solar disc emitting long bright rays which often terminated in human hands. For a brief time, under Akhenaton, worship of Aten was the state religion. He was considered the one true god. After the demise of Akhenaton he disappeared into obscurity.

Atum
This was one of the first forms of the sun-creator god. He was originally just a local deity of Heliopolis but joined with Re, as Atum-Re, he became more popular. Re took the part of the sun at the zenith and Atum was identified with the setting sun when it goes to the underworld. As this he was represented as a man, sometimes an old man, indicating the dying of the day.

Bastet
The famous cat goddess of the Delta region was the daughter of Re. She represented the power of the sun to ripen crops and was considered to be virile, strong and agile. Her home city was Bubastis (see page 170) but her fame spread widely. She was initially a goddess of the home but in the religion of the New Kingdom she became associated with the lioness war goddess. She was regarded as a friendly deity – the goddess of joy.

She was represented as a woman with a cat's head, carried an ancient percussion instrument, the sistrum, in her right hand, a breast plate in her left hand and had a small bag hung over her left arm. Numerous small cat figures were used in the home for worship or as amulets. Mummified cats (votive offerings) were buried in a vast cemetery at Bubastis. She was loosely connected with Mut and Sekhmet.

Bes
This was a strange creature, the god of dancing, merriment and music, being capable of playing many musical instruments. He was always portrayed as a jolly dwarf with a large head, a round face, round ears, goggle eyes, protruding tongue, sprouting lion's whiskers, which later became stylized as a fancy collar, under a tall headdress of feathers. He had short bow legs and a bushy tail. He was one of the few gods drawn front face rather than profile.

It is suggested his hideousness was to drive away evil spirits and hence pain and sorrow. As the guardian of women and children he kept the house free from snakes and evil spirits. He was portrayed on vases, mirrors, perfume jars and other toilet articles and even on the pillows of mummies. He was frequently represented in birth houses as the guardian of women in childbirth. It seems that at first he just protected the Royal family but later took on the care of all Egyptians.

Buto

This deity, also known as Wadjet, was a cobra goddess whose fame spread from the Delta to all of Lower Egypt. She was known as the green goddess (the colour of papyrus) and was said to be responsible for the burning heat of the sun.

Geb/Shu/Nut

These members of the Heliopolitan ennead, are frequently depicted together. Geb (god of the earth), son of Shu (god of the air or emptiness), was married to his sister Nut (goddess of the sky). The sun-god Re was displeased with this association although most gods seem to marry their sisters and ordered Shu to keep the two apart. Hence all three are represented together with Shu between Geb's green recumbent form and Nut arching in the sky.

Geb

As explained, this was the god of the earth, the physical support of the world. Along with his sister/wife Nut he was part of the second generation ennead of Heliopolis. He was usually drawn as a man without any distinguishing characteristics though sometimes had the head of a goose which was distinguishing enough. He could be also be depicted as a bull in contrast to Nut's cow. His recumbent form mentioned above represented the hills and valleys and the green colour the plants growing there.

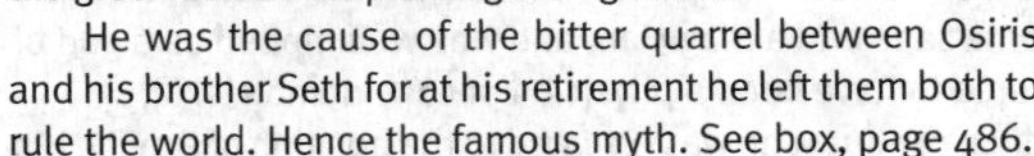

He was the cause of the bitter quarrel between Osiris and his brother Seth for at his retirement he left them both to rule the world. Hence the famous myth. See box, page 486.

Hapi/Hapy

He was the god who lived next to the river because he controlled the level of Nile and was responsible for the floods. He was even responsible for the dew that fell at night. He was represented as a bearded man with a female breast wearing a bunch of papyrus on his head and carrying offerings or leading a sacrifice. There was an association here with Apis.

There was another god Hapi who was one of the sons of Horus, the baboon headed guardian of the Canopic jar of the lungs.

Harpokrates

This was the name given to Horus as a child. In illustrations he was a naked child with a finger in his mouth. The side lock of hair he wore is an indication of youth.

Hathor

This was the goddess of the sky who was also known as the golden one. Her name means 'castle of the sky-god Horus'. She was a goddess of festivity, love and dance.

The original centre of her cult was Dendera and her importance spread to Thebes and Memphis. With the increase in her fame and contrary to her earlier nature she became known as a goddess of the dead and the region of the dead. She was believed to have been responsible for nearly destroying all mankind. See myths, page 203. On illustrations she was represented as a cow or a cow-headed woman or a woman with a headdress of a disc between two horns and large cow-like ears.

Heh

This lesser known god can be seen kneeling holding a palm branch notched with the number of the years in a king's life.

Heqet

This was a frog goddess who sometimes assisted at childbirth.

Horus

This was a very important god, the falcon headed sky god. Horus means 'he who is far above' and the hawk fits this image. Hence he was depicted as hawk-headed or even a full hawk often wearing the double crown of Egypt. The hawk's eyes are thought of as the sun and the moon. Horus' left eye was damaged in his conflict with Seth and this was thought to indicate the waxing and waning of the moon. He probably originated in the Delta region and the cult spread to all of Egypt. It was only later that he became associated with Isis and Osiris as their son.

Imhotep

He was a man, one of two mortals (the other was Amenhotep) who were totally deified. He was recorded as the designer of the first temple at Edfu and the official architect of Zoser's step pyramid. When he was later deified it was as a god of healing and made the honorary son of Ptah. He was known, not as a temple builder, but, as a patron of scribes, a healer, a sage and a magician, and was worshipped as a god of medicine. He was considered to have been a physician of considerable skill.

At the time of the Persian conquest he was elevated to the position of a deity. His cult reached its peak in Greaco-Roman times where his temples at Memphis and on the island of Philae in the River Nile were often crowded with unhealthy people who slept there hoping that a cure for their problems would be revealed to them in their dreams. He was depicted on wall illustrations as a seated man holding an open papyrus.

Isis

She was one of the most important ancient Egyptian goddesses, the most popular goddess in Egypt from around AD 650 right up to the introduction of Christianity. Originally the cult was in Lower Egypt but it spread to embrace eventually the whole of Egypt and parts of Nubia. Her name means 'throne' and because the word throne is feminine it was depicted by a woman's figure. This made her the mother of the king who sat on the throne. She receives a number of mentions as the grieving widow of Osiris. She was also the sister of Osiris, Seth and Nephthys.

She was held in high esteem as the perfect wife and mother

and became the goddess of protection. She was also an enchantress, using her power to bring Osiris back to life again. She was represented as a woman with the hieroglyph sign for a throne on her head, an orb or sun between two horns, and was generally sitting nursing her son Horus, or seen also kneeling at a coffin of Osiris. Her ability to give life to the dead meant she was the chief deity at all funerals.

There are temples to her at Dendera, on Philae and in the Nile Delta. Several temples were dedicated to her in Alexandria where she was the patroness of seafarers. She was guardian of the Canopic jar which held the viscera.

Khepri

He was the sun-god represented as a scarab beetle with a sun disc. As the scarab beetle rolls a ball of dung around so the Egyptians thought this was how the sun was moved. They thought the scarab possessed remarkable powers and used it as an amulet. See box, page 157.

Khnum

He was represented on wall drawings as a man with a ram's head with long twisted horns. The Egyptians believed he made the first man by moulding him in clay from the River Nile on a potter's wheel. Over time his area of responsibility changed. He lived at the first cataract on the Nile where he presided over all the cataracts of the Nile. He had the authority to decide whether or not the god Hapi 'rose' and the River Nile flooded. He was associated with temples at Elephantine and Esna.

Khonsu

He was regarded as the son of Amun and Mut. The three made up the Thebian Triad. He had the ability to cast a range of spells, dispel demons and act as an oracle. He travelled through the sky at night and sometimes assisted the scribe of the gods. As the moon god he was usually represented as a man wearing a disc of the full moon and horns on his head or the head of a falcon. He had a single lock of hair to show his youth.

Ma'at

This well loved deity was the goddess of order, truth and justice. She was the daughter of the sun-god Re and Thoth the goddess of wisdom. She can be seen at the ceremony of judgement, the balancing of the heart of the deceased against a feather. The scale was balanced by Ma'at or her ideogram, the single ostrich feather as a test of truthfulness. The priests with her were judges. She often appears, confusingly, as two identical goddesses, a case of double judgement. She was very popular with the other gods. She was also depicted on wall paintings in the solar barque.

Mertseger

This was the goddess of the west, a cobra goddess from Thebes. She was said to punish those who did not come up to scratch with illness or even death.

Min

This was the god of sexual prowess, of fertility and of good harvests. He was depicted bearded, wearing a crown of two feathers, phallus erect, a ceremonial flail in his raised right hand and a ribbon from his headdress reaching down to the ground at the back. He was worshipped at Luxor. His feast day was an important festival often associated with wild orgies. He was worshipped too as the guardian of travellers as he protected the routes to the Red Sea and in the Eastern Desert. The lettuce was his sacred plant.

Montu

The war god Montu who rose to importance in the 11th Dynasty protected the king in battle. He has a temple to the north of the main temple in Karnak. His image was hawk-headed with a sun disc between two plumes.

Mut

She was originally a very ancient vulture goddess of Thebes but during the 18th Dynasty was married to the god Amun and with their adopted son Khonsu made up the Thebian Triad. The marriage of Amun and Mut was a reason for great annual celebrations in Thebes. Her role as mistress of the heavens or as sky goddess often had her appearing as a cow, standing behind her husband as he rose from the primeval sea Nu to his place in the heavens. More often she was represented with a double crown of Egypt on her head, a vulture's head or lioness's head on her forehead. Another role was as a great divine mother. She has a temple south of the main temple at Karnak.

Nefertum

He was one of the Memphis deities most often associated with perfumes. He was represented as a man with a lotus flower on his head.

Neith

This was the goddess of weaving, war and hunting, among other things. She was also protector of the dead and the Canopic jars. She wore a red crown of Lower Egypt and a shield on her head (sometimes held in her hand), held two crossed arrows and an ankh in her hand. She was connected with Sobek and was worshipped at Memphis, Esna and Fayoum.

Nekhbet

In her more important guise she was the vulture or serpent goddess, protectress of Upper Egypt and especially of its rulers. She was generally depicted with spreading wings held over the pharaoh while grasping in her claw the royal ring or other emblems. She always appeared as a woman, sometimes with a vulture's head and always wearing a white crown. Her special colour was white, in contrast to her counterpart Buto (red) who was the goddess of Lower Egypt. In another aspect she was worshipped as goddess of the River Nile and consort of the river god. She was associated too with Mut.

Nephthys

Her name was translated as 'lady of the house'. She was the sister of Seth, Osiris and Isis. She was married to Seth. She had no children by her husband but a son, Anubis, by Osiris. She wears the hieroglyphs of her name on her head. She was one of the protector guardians of the Canopic jars and a goddess of the dead.

Nut

She was goddess of the sky, the vault of the heavens. She was wife/sister of Geb. The Egyptians believed that on five special days preceding the new year she gave birth on successive days to the deities Osiris, Horus, Seth, Isis and Nephthys. This was cause for great celebrations. She was usually depicted as a naked woman arched over Shu who supported her with upraised arms. She was also represented wearing a water pot or pear shaped vessel on her head, this being the hieroglyph of her name. Sometimes she was depicted as a cow, so that she could carry the sun-god Re on her back to the sky. The cow was usually spangled with stars to represent the night sky. It was supposed that the cow swallowed the sun which journeyed through her body during the night to emerge at sunrise. This was also considered a symbol of resurrection.

Osiris

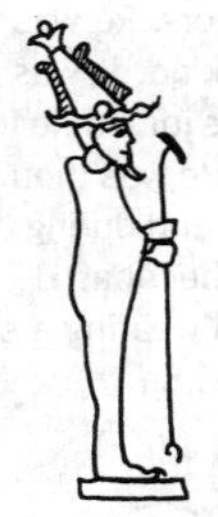

This was one of the most important gods in ancient Egypt, the god of the dead, the god of the underworld and the god of plenty. He had the power to control the vegetation (particular cereals because he began his career as a corn deity) which sprouted after the annual flooding of the River Nile. He originated in the Delta at Busiris and it is suggested that he was once a real ruler. His importance spread to the whole of Egypt.

Annual celebrations included the moulding of a clay body in the shape of Osiris, filled with soil and containing seeds. This was moistened with water from the River Nile and the sprouting grain symbolized the strength of Osiris. One of the main celebrations in the Temple at Abydos where he was very popular was associated with Osiris and it was fashionable to be buried or have a memorial on the processional road to Abydos and so absorb the blessing of Osiris. There are temples dedicated to Osiris at Edfu and on Bigah Island opposite Philae.

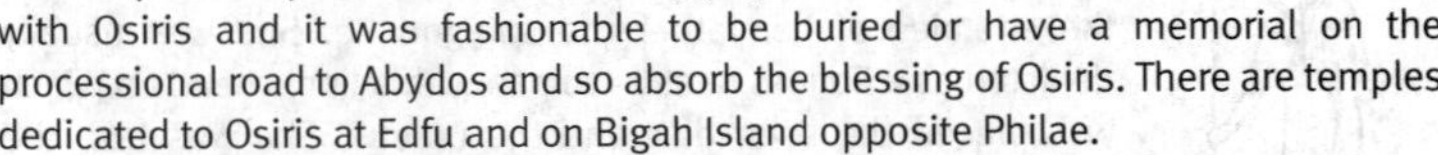

According to ancient Egyptian custom when a king and later any person died he became Osiris and thus through him mankind had a some hope of resurrection. The Apis bull at Memphis also represented Osiris. The names Osiris-apis and Sarapis are derived from this.

He was shown as a mummy with his arm crossed over his breast, one hand holding a royal crook the other a ceremonial flail. These crook and flail sceptres on his portraits and statues showed he was god of the underworld. He wore a narrow plaited beard and the white crown of Upper Egypt and two red feathers.

Ptah

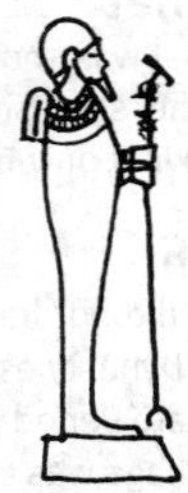

He was originally the local deity of the capital Memphis and his importance eventually spread over the whole of Egypt. He was very popular at Thebes and Abydos. He was worshipped as the creator of the gods of the Memphite theology. Ptah was the husband of Sekhmet and father of Nefertum. Only later was he associated with Osiris. He was the patron of craftsmen, especially sculptors. He was renowned for his skill as an engineer, stonemason, metal worker and artist.

He was always shown in human form, mummified or swathed in a winding sheet, with a clean shaven human head. He would be holding a staff and wearing an amulet. The Apis bull had its stall in the great temple of Ptah in Memphis.

Qebehsenuf

The falcon headed guardian of the Canopic jar of the intestines was the son of Horus.

Re

This was the sun-god of Heliopolis and the supreme judge. He was the main god at the time of the New Kingdom. His importance was great. His cult centre was Heliopolis and the cult reached the zenith in the fifth Dynasty when he had become the official god of the pharaohs and every king was both the son of Re and Re incarnate.

Re was the god who symbolized the sun. He appeared in many aspects and was portrayed in many different ways. He was found in conjunction with other gods Re-Horakhte, Amun-Re, Min-Re etc. As Amun-Re (Amun was the god from Thebes) he was king of the gods and responsible for the pharaoh on military campaigns where he handed the scimitar of conquest to the great warriors. Re was king and father of the gods and the creator of mankind. It was believed that after death, the pharaoh in his barge joined Re in the heavens.

He was thought to travel across the sky each day in his solar boat and during the night make his passage in the underworld in another boat. He was represented as man with a hawk or falcon's head wearing a sun disc or if dead with a ram's head. See also page 483.

Sekhmet

This was another aspect of the goddess Hathor. Sekhmet the consort of Ptah was a fierce goddess of war and the destroyer of the enemies of her father the sun-god Re. She was usually depicted as a lioness or as a woman with a lion's head on which was placed the solar disc and the uraeus. She was also the goddess who was associated with pestilence, and could bring disease and death to mankind but her task also was to do the healing and her priests were often doctors. She was said to have chained the serpent Apophis.

Selket

This was one of the four goddesses who protected the sources of the River Nile. As the guardian of the dead she was portrayed often with a scorpion on her head. She was put in charge of the bound serpent Apophis in the underworld.

Seshat

Seshat was shown as a woman with a seven point star on her head, and dressed in a panther skin. She was the goddess of writing and of recording the years. She carried a palm leaf on which she wrote her records.

Seth

Seth did not begin with such bad press. He was in favour in the 19th Dynasty especially in the Eastern Delta around Tanis but by the Late Period he was considered evil and on some monuments his image was effaced. By the Christian era he was firmly in place as the devil. The Egyptians thought Seth who was the brother of Osiris, Isis and Nephthys tried to prevent the sun from rising each dawn. As such an enemy of mankind they represented him as a huge serpent-dragon. He was sometimes depicted as a hippopotamus and sometimes took the form of a crocodile as he did to avoid the avenging Horus. More often he was depicted as an unidentified animal, a greyhound, dog, pig, ass, okapi, anteater or a man with the head of an animal. The head had an unusual long down curved snout and the ears were upstanding and square-tipped. The eyes were slanting and the tail long and forked. He was also seen in drawings standing at the prow of the sun-god's boat.

Shu

He and his twin sister and wife Tefnut were created by the sun-god Re by his own power without the aid of a woman. They were the first couple of the ennead of Heliopolis. He was father of Geb the earth god and Nut the sky goddess. He was the representation of air and emptiness, of light and space, the supporter of the sky.

He was portrayed in human form with the hieroglyph of his name, an ostrich feather on his head. Often he was drawn separating Geb and Nut for their union was not approved of by Re.

Sobek

He was known as the crocodile god, a protector of reptiles and of kings. Crocodile gods were very common in Fayoum, mainly at the time of the Middle Kingdom and also at Esna and Kom Ombo. The live crocodiles at the temples were believed to be this god incarnate and accordingly were treated very well. These sacred crocodiles were kept in a lake before the temples. They were pampered and bejewelled. After death they were mummified. Confusingly he was usually depicted with Amun's crown of rams' horns and feathers.

Taweret

This upright pregnant hippopotamus had pendant human breasts, lion's paws and a crocodile's tail. Sometimes she wore the horns of Hathor with a solar disc. She was also known as Apet/Opet. She was the goddess of childbirth and attended both royal births and the daily rebirth of the sun. She was a goddess at Esna.

Tefnut

She was the wife/sister of Shu, the lion-headed goddess of moisture and dew, one of the Heliopolitan ennead.

Thoth

His cult originated in the Nile Delta and was then mainly centred in Upper Egypt. He was held to be the inventor of writing, the founder of social order, the creator of languages, the patron of scribes, interpreter and adviser to the gods, and (in his spare time?) representative of the sun-god Re on earth. He gave the Egyptians knowledge of medicine and mathematics. He possessed a book in which all the wisdom of the world was recorded. In another aspect he was known as the moon god. He was also associated with the birth of the earth.

Thoth protected Isis during her pregnancy and healed the injury to Horus inflicted by Seth. He too was depicted in the feather/heart weighing judgement ceremonies of the diseased and as the scribe reported the results to Osiris. His sacred animals were the ibis and the baboon. Numerous mummified bodies of these two animals were found in cemeteries in Hermopolis and Thebes.

He was usually represented as a human with an ibis' head. The curved beak of the ibis was like the crescent moon so the two were connected and the ibis became the symbol of the moon god Thoth.

Wepwawet

He was the jackal-headed god of Middle Egypt, especially popular in the Assiut region. He was know as 'the opener of the ways'.

Glossary

A

Abbasids Muslim Dynasty ruled from Baghdad 750-1258
Agora Market/meeting place
Aïd/Eïd Festival
Aïn Spring
Almohads Islamic Empire in North Africa 1130-1269
Amir Mamluk military officer
Amulet Object with magical power of protection
Ankh Symbol of life
Apis bull A sacred bull worshipped as the living image of Ptah
Arabesque Geometric pattern with flowers and foliage used in Islamic designs

B

Bab City gate
Bahri North/northern
Baladiyah Municipality
Baksheesh Money as alms, tip or bribe
Baraka Blessing
Barbary Name of North Africa 16th-19th centuries
Basha See Pasha
Basilica Imposing Roman building, with aisles, later used for worship
Bazaar Market
Bedouin Nomadic desert Arab
Beni Sons of (tribe)
Berber Indigenous tribe of North Africa
Bey Governor (Ottoman)
Borj Fort
Burnous Man's cloak with hood – tradional wear

C

Caid Official
Calèche Horse drawn carriage
Canopic jars Four jars used to store the internal organs of the mummified deceased
Capital Top section of a column
Caravanserai Lodgings for travellers and animals around a courtyard
Cartouche Oval ring containing a king's name in hieroglyphics
Chechia Man's small red felt hat
Chotts Low-lying salt lakes
Colossus Gigantic statue

D

Dar House
Darj w ktaf Carved geometric motif of intersecting arcs with super-imposed rectangles
Deglet Nur High quality translucent date
Delu Water lifting device at head of well
Dey Commander (of janissaries)
Dikka Raised platform in mosque for Koramic readings
Djemma Main or Friday mosque
Djin Spirit
Dólmenes Prehistoric cave
Dour Village settlement

E

Eïd See Aïd
Eïn See Aïn
Erg Sand dune desert

F

Faqirs Muslim who has taken a vow of poverty
Fatimids Muslim dynasty 909-1171 AD claiming descent from Mohammed's daughter Fatimah
Fatwa Islamic district
Fellaheen Peasants
Felucca Sailing boat on Nile
Fondouk/Funduq Lodgings for goods and animals around a courtyard
Forum Central open space in Roman town
Fuul Fava beans

G

Gallabiyya Outer garment with sleeves and a hood - often striped
Garrigue Poor quality Mediterranean scrubland
Gymnasium Roman school for mind and body

H

Haikal Altar area
Hallal Meat from animals killed in accordance with Islamic law
Hamada Stone desert
Hammam Bath house
Harem Women's quarters
Harira Soup
Hypogeum The part of the building below ground, underground chamber

I

Iconostasis Wooden screen supporting icons
Imam Muslim religious leader

J

Jabal See Jebel
Jami' Mosque
Janissaries Elite Ottoman soldiery
Jarapas Rough cloth made with rags
Jebel Mountain
Jihad Holy war by Muslims against non-believers

K

Ka Spirit
Khedivate The realm of Mohammed Ali and his successors
Kilim Woven carpet

Kif Hashish
Kissaria Covered market
Koubba Dome on tomb of holy man
Kufic Earliest style of Arabic script
Kuttab Korami school for young boys or orphans

L

Lintel Piece of stone over a doorway
Liwan Vaulted arcade
Loculus Small compartment or cell, a recess

M

Mahboub Coins worn as jewellery
Malekite Section of Sunni Islam
Malqaf Wind vent
Maquis Mediterranean scrubland - often aromatic
Marabout Muslim holy man/his tomb
Maristan Hospital
Mashrabiyya Wooden screen
Mastaba Tomb
Mausoleum Large tomb building
Medresa School usually attached to a mosque
Médina Old walled town, residential quarter
Mellah Jewish quarter of old town
Menzel House
Mihrab Recess in wall of mosque indicating direction of Mecca
Minaret Slender tower of mosque which the muezzin calls the faithful to prayer
Minbar Pulpit in a mosque
Mosque Muslim place of worship
Moulid Religious festival – Prophet's birthday
Moussem Religious gathering
Muezzin Priest who calls the faithful to prayer
Mullah Muslim religious teacher
Murabtin Dependent tribe

N

Necropolis Cemetery
Noas Shrine or chapel
Nome District or province

O

Oasis Watered desert gardens
Obelisk Tapering monolithic shaft of stone with pyramidal apex
Ostraca Inscribed rock flakes and potsherds
Ottoman Muslim Empire based in Turkey 13th-20th centuries
Ouled Tribe
Outrepassé Horse-shoe shaped arch

P

Papyrus (papyri) Papers used by Ancient Egyptians
Pasha Governor
Phoenicians Important trading nation based in eastern Mediterranean from 1100 BC
Pilaster Square column partly built into, partly projecting from, the wall
Pisé Sun-baked clay used for building
Piste Unsurfaced road
Pylon Gateway of Egyptian temple
Pyramidion A small pyramid shaped cap stone for the apex of a pyramid

Q

Qarafah Graveyard
Qibla Mosque wall in direction of Mecca

R

Rabbi Head of Jewish community
Ramadan Muslim month of fasting
Reg Rock desert
Ribat Fortified monastery
Riwaq Arcaded aisle

S

Sabil Public water fountain
Sabkha Dry salt lake
Saggia Water canal
Sahel Coast/coastal plain
Sahn Courtyard
Salat Worship
Saqiya Water wheel
Sarcophagus Decorated stone coffin
Sebkha See Sabkha
Semi-columnar Flat on one side and rounded on the other
Serais Lodging for men and animals
Serir Sand desert
Shadoof Water lifting device
Shahada Profession of faith
Shawabti Statuette buried with deceased, designed to work in the hereafter for its owner
Shergui Hot, dry desert wind
Sidi Saint
Souk Traditional market
Stalactite An ornamental arrangement of multi-tiered niches, like a honeycomb, found in domes and portrals
Stele Inscribed pillar used as gravestone
Suani Small walled irrigated traditional garden
Sufi Muslim mystic
Sunni Orthodox Muslims

T

Tagine/tajine Meat stew
Taifa Sub-tribe
Tariqa Brotherhood/Order
Thòlos Round building, dome, cupola
Triclinium A room with benches on three sides
Troglodyte Underground/cave dweller

U

Uraeus Rearing cobra symbol, sign of kingship

V

Vandals Ruling empire in North Africa 429-534 AD
Vizier Governor

W

Wadi Water course, usually dry

Waqf Endowed land

Wikala Merchants' hostel

Wilaya/wilayat Governorate/district

Z

Zaouia/zawia/zawiya Shrine/Sennusi centre

Zellij Geometrical mosaic pattern made from pieces of glazed tiles

Zeriba House of straw/grass

Shorts index

Map index

T

V

W

Index

D

E

F

G

N

O

P

Footnotes Index

Q

R

S

T

U

V

W

Y

Z

Acknowledgements

Cherine would like to offer her heartfelt gratitude to all those who supported her in the research of this edition. Particular thanks go out to Pops, Chris, Sarah, Yasmine, Chad, Wendy, Con, Micky, Samir, Boxa, Dahlia, Victor, Shereef, Mahdi, Beheh, Ahmed, Mohammed, Shukri, Captain Ahmed, the Morcos family; the Bishay family, and especially her mom.

Thanks are also due to Anne and Keith McLachlan who researched and wrote previous editions of this guide.

The health section was written by **Dr Charlie Easmon** MBBS MRCP MSc Public Health DTM&H DOccMed, Director of Travel Screening Services.

Credits

Footprint credits

Editor: Sarah Thorowgood
Map editor: Sarah Sorensen

Publisher: Patrick Dawson
Editorial: Alan Murphy, Sophie Blacksell, Claire Boobbyer, Felicity Laughton, Davina Rungasamy, Laura Dixon
Proof reading: Stephanie Egerton
Cartography: Robert Lunn, Claire Benison, Kevin Feeney
Series development: Rachel Fielding
Design: Mytton Williams and Rosemary Dawson (brand)
Advertising: Debbie Wylde
Finance and administration: Sharon Hughes, Elizabeth Taylor

Photography credits

Front cover: *Felucca* on the Nile (Alamy)
Back cover: Tutankhamen mask (Powerstock)
Inside colour section: Imagestate, Images of Africa, Travel Ink, The Travel Library

Print

Manufactured in Italy by LegoPrint
Pulp from sustainable forests

Footprint feedback

We try as hard as we can to make each Footprint guide as up to date as possible but, of course, things always change. If you want to let us know about your experiences – good, bad or ugly – then don't delay, go to **www.footprintbooks.com** and send in your comments.

Publishing information

Footprint Egypt
4th edition

June 2004

ISBN 1 903471 77 X
CIP DATA: A catalogue record for this book is available from the British Library

Published by Footprint

6 Riverside Court
Lower Bristol Road
Bath BA2 3DZ, UK
T +44 (0)1225 469141
F +44 (0)1225 469461
discover@footprintbooks.com
www.footprintbooks.com

Distributed in the USA by

Publishers Group West

Map 1
Mediterranean Sea
Sollum
Sidi Barrani
Marsa Matruh
Sidi Abdel Rahman
El-Daba
El-Hammam
El-Alamein
Expressway
Main road
Connecting road
Other road, dirt track
Railway
International border
Seasonal river
Mountain
A
Qattara Depression
Siwa Oasis
Siwa
Bawati
Bahariyya Oasis
Great Sand Sea
Black Desert
White Desert
B
Farafra Oasis
Libyan Desert
Western Desert
LIBYA
Dakhla Oasis
Mut
C
Tropic of Cancer
Sahara Desert
N
0 km 30
0 miles 30
1
2
3

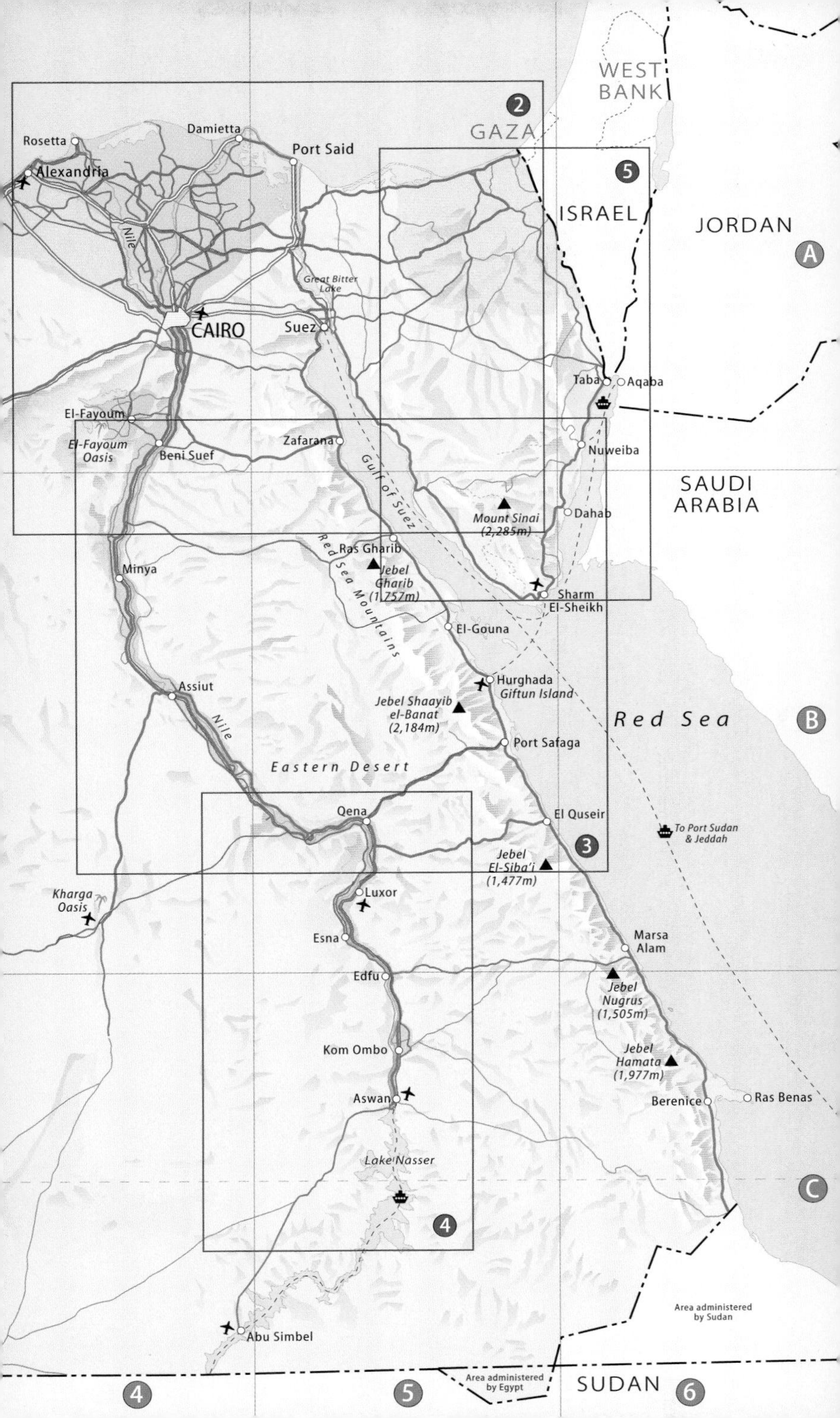

WEST BANK
GAZA
ISRAEL
JORDAN
SAUDI ARABIA
SUDAN
Rosetta
Damietta
Port Said
Alexandria
Nile
Great Bitter Lake
CAIRO
Suez
El-Fayoum
El-Fayoum Oasis
Beni Suef
Zafarana
Gulf of Suez
Taba
Aqaba
Nuweiba
Dahab
Mount Sinai (2,285m)
Sharm El-Sheikh
Ras Gharib
Jebel Gharib (1,757m)
Red Sea Mountains
Minya
El-Gouna
Hurghada
Giftun Island
Jebel Shaayib el-Banat (2,184m)
Assiut
Red Sea
Port Safaga
Eastern Desert
Qena
El Quseir
Jebel El-Siba'i (1,477m)
To Port Sudan & Jeddah
Luxor
Kharga Oasis
Esna
Marsa Alam
Edfu
Jebel Nugrus (1,505m)
Kom Ombo
Jebel Hamata (1,977m)
Aswan
Berenice
Ras Benas
Lake Nasser
Area administered by Sudan
Abu Simbel
Area administered by Egypt
2
3
4
5
A
B
C
4
5
6

Map 2

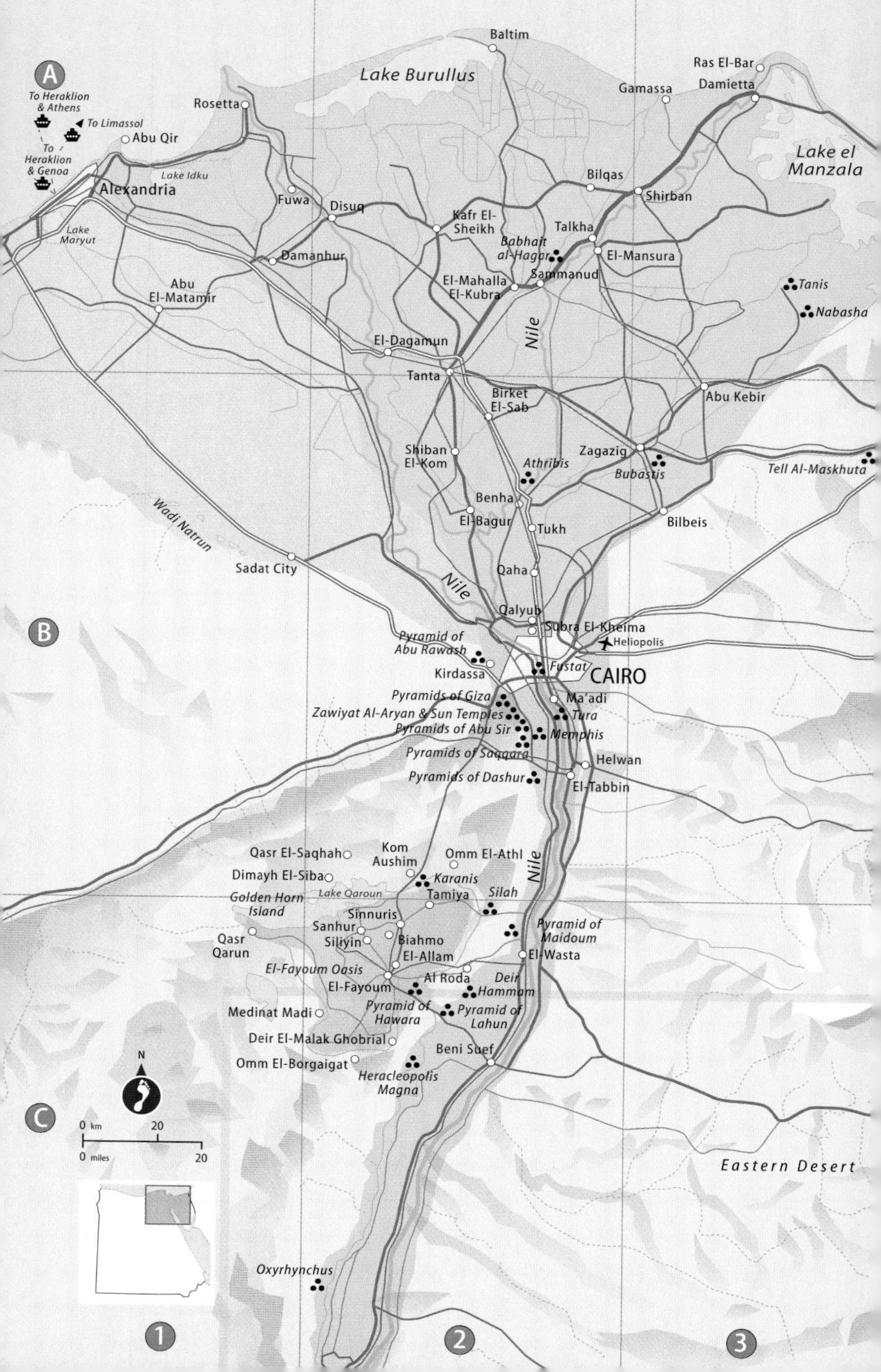

A
B
C
To Heraklion & Athens
To Limassol
To Heraklion & Genoa
Abu Qir
Rosetta
Alexandria
Lake Idku
Lake Maryut
Lake Burullus
Baltim
Gamassa
Ras El-Bar
Damietta
Lake el Manzala
Fuwa
Disuq
Damanhur
Abu El-Matamir
Kafr El-Sheikh
Bilqas
Shirban
Talkha
Babhait al-Hagar
El-Mansura
Sammanud
El-Mahalla El-Kubra
Tanis
Nabasha
Nile
El-Dagamun
Tanta
Birket El-Sab
Abu Kebir
Shiban El-Kom
Zagazig
Athribis
Bubastis
Tell Al-Maskhuta
Wadi Natrun
Benha
El-Bagur
Tukh
Bilbeis
Sadat City
Qaha
Qalyub
Subra El-Kheima
Heliopolis
Pyramid of Abu Rawash
Kirdassa
Fustat
CAIRO
Pyramids of Giza
Ma'adi
Zawiyat Al-Aryan & Sun Temples
Tura
Pyramids of Abu Sir
Memphis
Pyramids of Saqqara
Helwan
Pyramids of Dashur
El-Tabbin
Qasr El-Saqhah
Kom Aushim
Omm El-Athl
Dimayh El-Siba
Karanis
Golden Horn Island
Lake Qaroun
Tamiya
Silah
Sinnuris
Sanhur
Siliyin
Biahmo
Pyramid of Maidoum
Qasr Qarun
El-Allam
El-Wasta
El-Fayoum Oasis
Al Roda
Deir Hammam
El-Fayoum
Medinat Madi
Pyramid of Hawara
Pyramid of Lahun
Deir El-Malak Ghobrial
Beni Suef
Omm El-Borgaigat
Heracleopolis Magna
N
0 km 20
0 miles 20
Eastern Desert
Oxyrhynchus
1
2
3

Mediterranean Sea
To Limassol
To Rhodes & Athens
Port Said
Port Fouad
Ras El-'Ish
Suez Canal
El-Tina
El-Cap
Pelusium
Rumana
Katia
Bir Al-Abd
Lake Bardweel
Al-Mazar
El-Arish
Oruba
Rafah
GAZA
ISRAEL
Lahfan
El-Maqdaba
Abu Aweigila
Jebel El-Amrar (319m)
Risan Aneiza (368m)
Umm Girim (149m)
East Qantara
West Qantara
El-Ballah
El-Firdan Ferry
Ismailia
Lake Timsah
Khatmia Pass
Bir Gifgafa
El-Ousaima
Bir Hasana
Abu Sultan
Great Bitter Lake
Fayed
Kabrit
Little Bitter Lake
Bir El-Thamada
El-Shallufa
Ahmed Hamdi Tunnel
Suez
Mitla Pass
El-Shatt
Ayoun Moussa
Nakhl
Ain-Sudr
El-Thamad
Ras Sudr
Aïn Sukhana
Map 3
Sinai Peninsula
Zafarana
Monastery of St Paul
Monastery of St Anthony
To Port Sudan & Jeddah
Gulf of Suez
Feiran Oasis
Watiya Pass
Serabit
St Catherine's Monastery
Mount Sinai (2,285m)
Mount Catherine (2,637m)
Red Sea Mountains
Ras Gharib
A
B
C
4
5
6

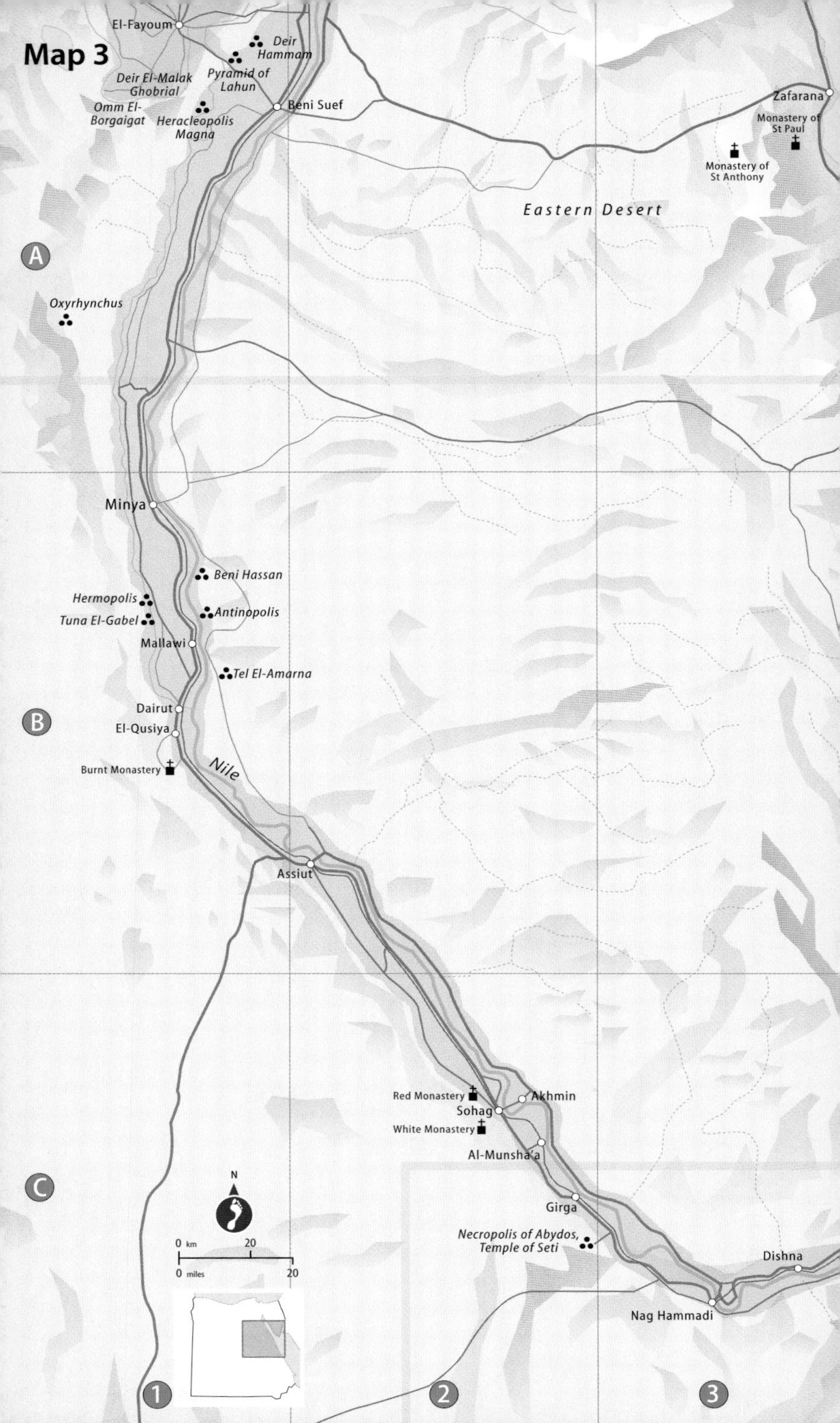

Map 3
El-Fayoum
Deir Hammam
Pyramid of Lahun
Deir El-Malak Ghobrial
Omm El-Borgaigat
Heracleopolis Magna
Beni Suef
Zafarana
Monastery of St Paul
Monastery of St Anthony
Eastern Desert
A
Oxyrhynchus
Minya
Beni Hassan
Hermopolis
Tuna El-Gabel
Antinopolis
Mallawi
Tel El-Amarna
Dairut
B
El-Qusiya
Burnt Monastery
Nile
Assiut
Red Monastery
Akhmin
Sohag
White Monastery
Al-Munsha'a
C
N
Girga
Necropolis of Abydos, Temple of Seti
0 km 20
0 miles 20
Dishna
Nag Hammadi
1
2
3

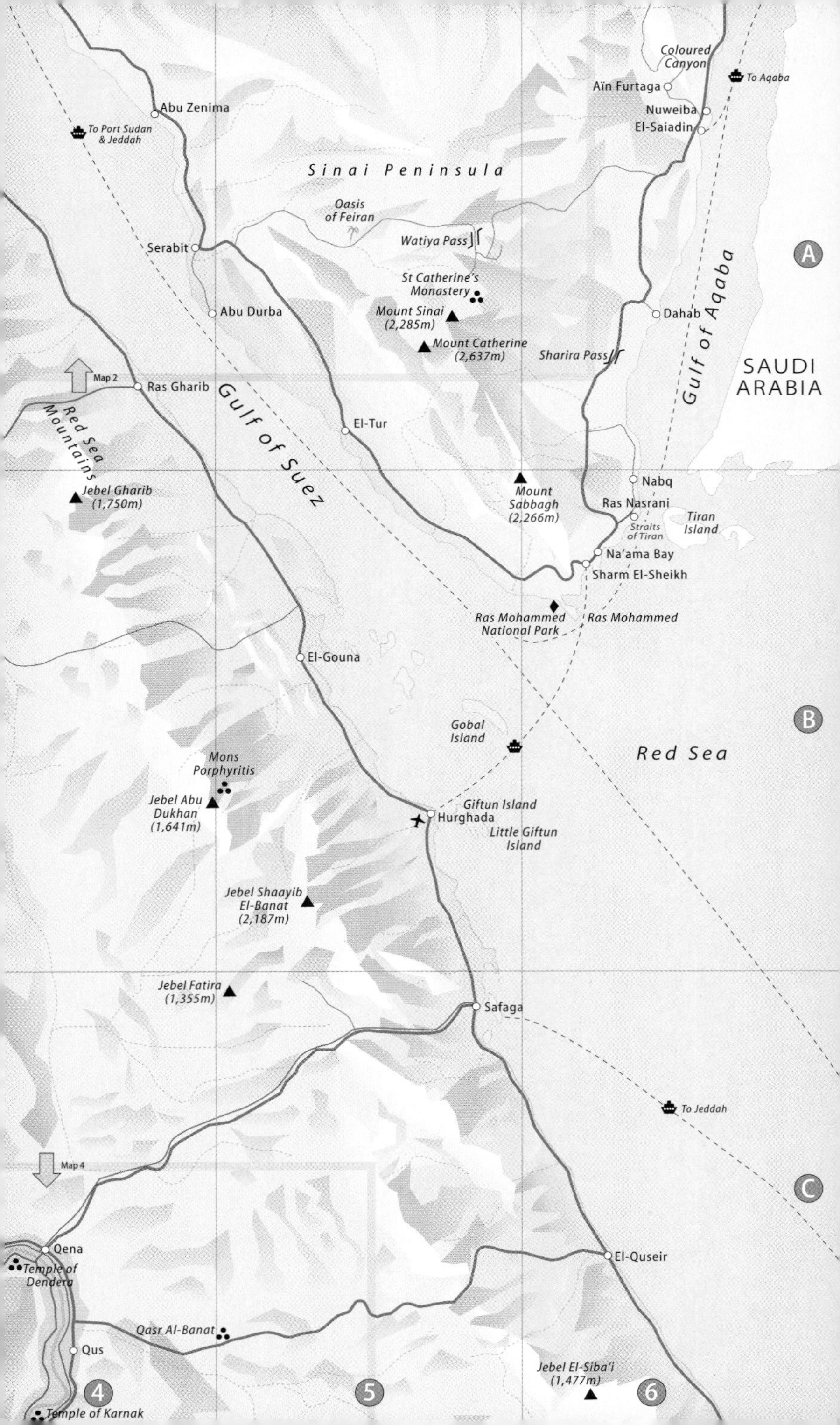

Coloured Canyon
To Aqaba
Aïn Furtaga
Abu Zenima
Nuweiba
To Port Sudan & Jeddah
El-Saiadin
Sinai Peninsula
Oasis of Feiran
Watiya Pass
Serabit
A
St Catherine's Monastery
Abu Durba
Mount Sinai (2,285m)
Dahab
Mount Catherine (2,637m)
Sharira Pass
Gulf of Aqaba
SAUDI ARABIA
Map 2
Ras Gharib
Red Sea Mountains
Gulf of Suez
El-Tur
Nabq
Jebel Gharib (1,750m)
Mount Sabbagh (2,266m)
Ras Nasrani
Straits of Tiran
Tiran Island
Na'ama Bay
Sharm El-Sheikh
Ras Mohammed National Park
Ras Mohammed
El-Gouna
B
Gobal Island
Red Sea
Mons Porphyritis
Jebel Abu Dukhan (1,641m)
Giftun Island
Hurghada
Little Giftun Island
Jebel Shaayib El-Banat (2,187m)
Jebel Fatira (1,355m)
Safaga
To Jeddah
Map 4
C
Qena
Temple of Dendera
El-Quseir
Qasr Al-Banat
Qus
Jebel El-Siba'i (1,477m)
4
5
6
Temple of Karnak

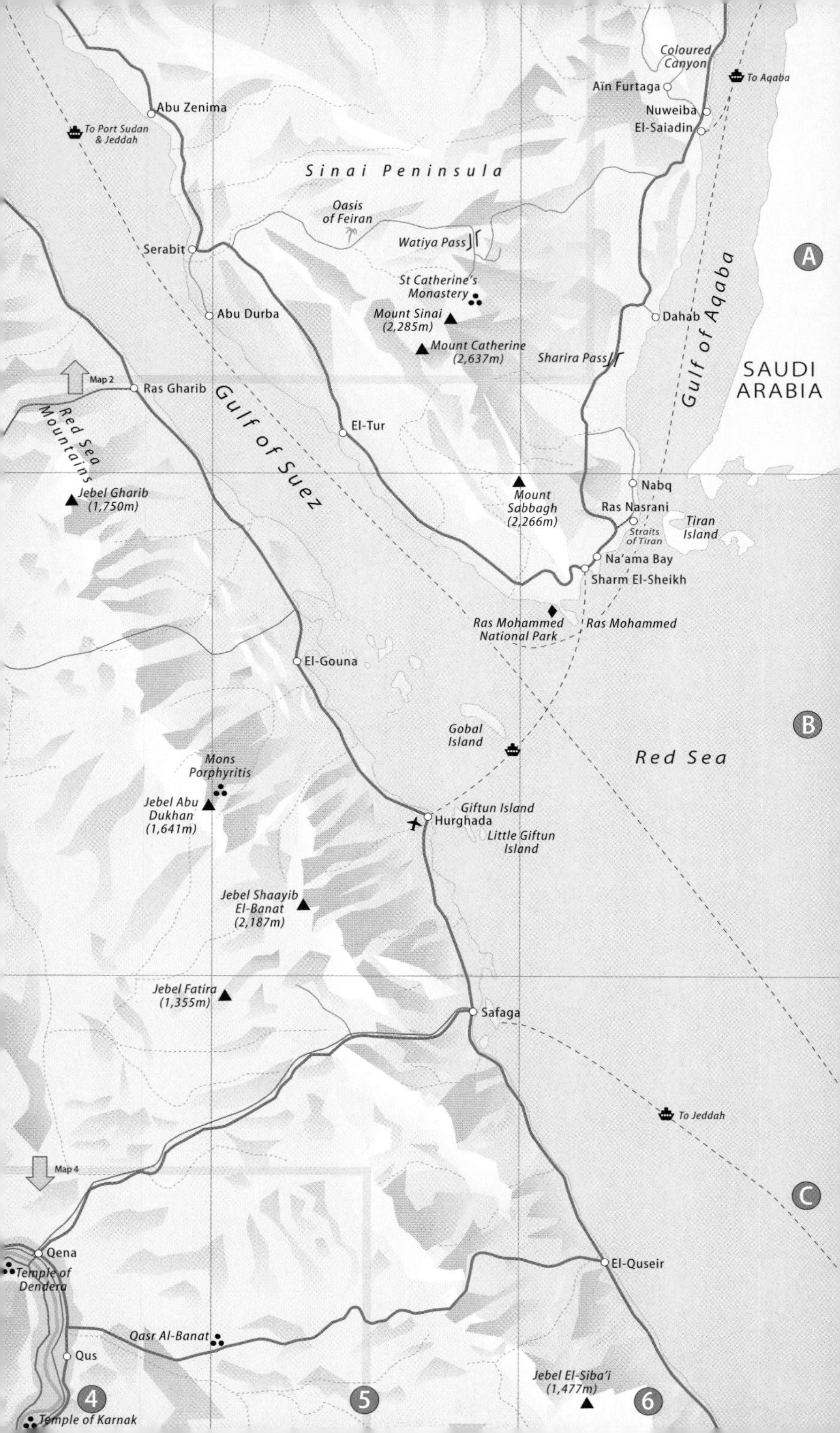

Coloured Canyon
Aïn Furtaga
To Aqaba
Nuweiba
El-Saiadin
Abu Zenima
To Port Sudan & Jeddah
Sinai Peninsula
Oasis of Feiran
Watiya Pass
Serabit
St Catherine's Monastery
Abu Durba
Mount Sinai (2,285m)
Dahab
Mount Catherine (2,637m)
Sharira Pass
Gulf of Aqaba
SAUDI ARABIA
Map 2
Ras Gharib
Red Sea Mountains
Gulf of Suez
El-Tur
Jebel Gharib (1,750m)
Mount Sabbagh (2,266m)
Nabq
Ras Nasrani
Straits of Tiran
Tiran Island
Na'ama Bay
Sharm El-Sheikh
Ras Mohammed National Park
Ras Mohammed
El-Gouna
Gobal Island
Red Sea
Mons Porphyritis
Jebel Abu Dukhan (1,641m)
Giftun Island
Hurghada
Little Giftun Island
Jebel Shaayib El-Banat (2,187m)
Jebel Fatira (1,355m)
Safaga
To Jeddah
Map 4
Qena
Temple of Dendera
El-Quseir
Qasr Al-Banat
Qus
Jebel El-Siba'i (1,477m)
Temple of Karnak
A
B
C
4
5
6

Map 5

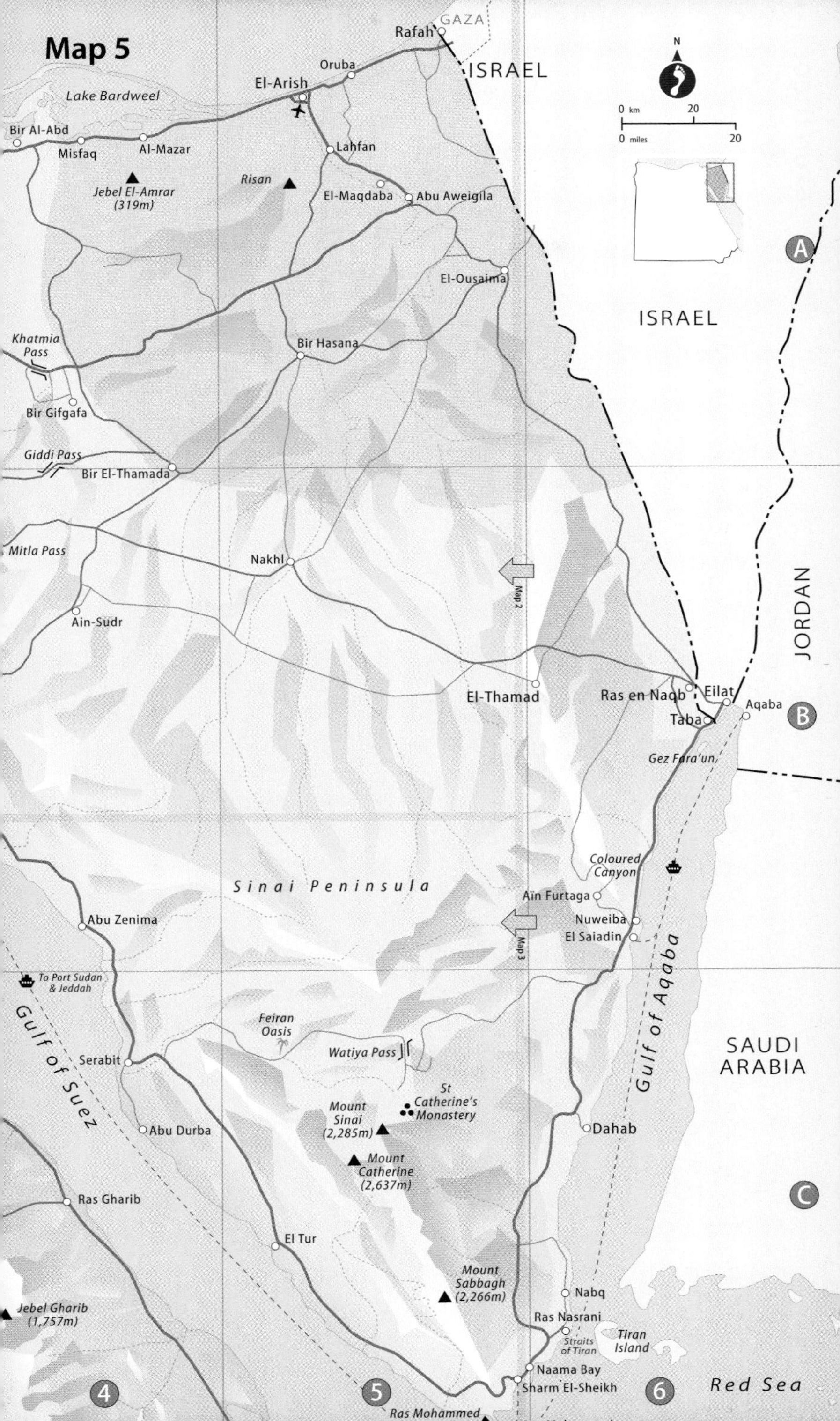

GAZA
Rafah
ISRAEL
Oruba
El-Arish
Lake Bardweel
Bir Al-Abd
Misfaq
Al-Mazar
Lahfan
Jebel El-Amrar
(319m)
Risan
El-Maqdaba
Abu Aweigila
El-Ousaima
ISRAEL
Khatmia
Pass
Bir Hasana
Bir Gifgafa
Giddi Pass
Bir El-Thamada
Mitla Pass
Nakhl
Map 2
Ain-Sudr
JORDAN
El-Thamad
Ras en Naqb
Eilat
Taba
Aqaba
Gez Fara'un
Coloured
Canyon
Sinai Peninsula
Aïn Furtaga
Nuweiba
El Saiadin
Map 3
Abu Zenima
To Port Sudan
& Jeddah
Gulf of Suez
Feiran
Oasis
Watiya Pass
SAUDI
ARABIA
Gulf of Aqaba
Serabit
St
Catherine's
Monastery
Mount
Sinai
(2,285m)
Abu Durba
Dahab
Mount
Catherine
(2,637m)
Ras Gharib
El Tur
Mount
Sabbagh
(2,266m)
Nabq
Jebel Gharib
(1,757m)
Ras Nasrani
Straits
of Tiran
Tiran
Island
Naama Bay
Sharm El-Sheikh
Red Sea
Ras Mohammed
A
B
C
4
5
6
N
0 km 20
0 miles 20

Map 6 Luxor/Thebes

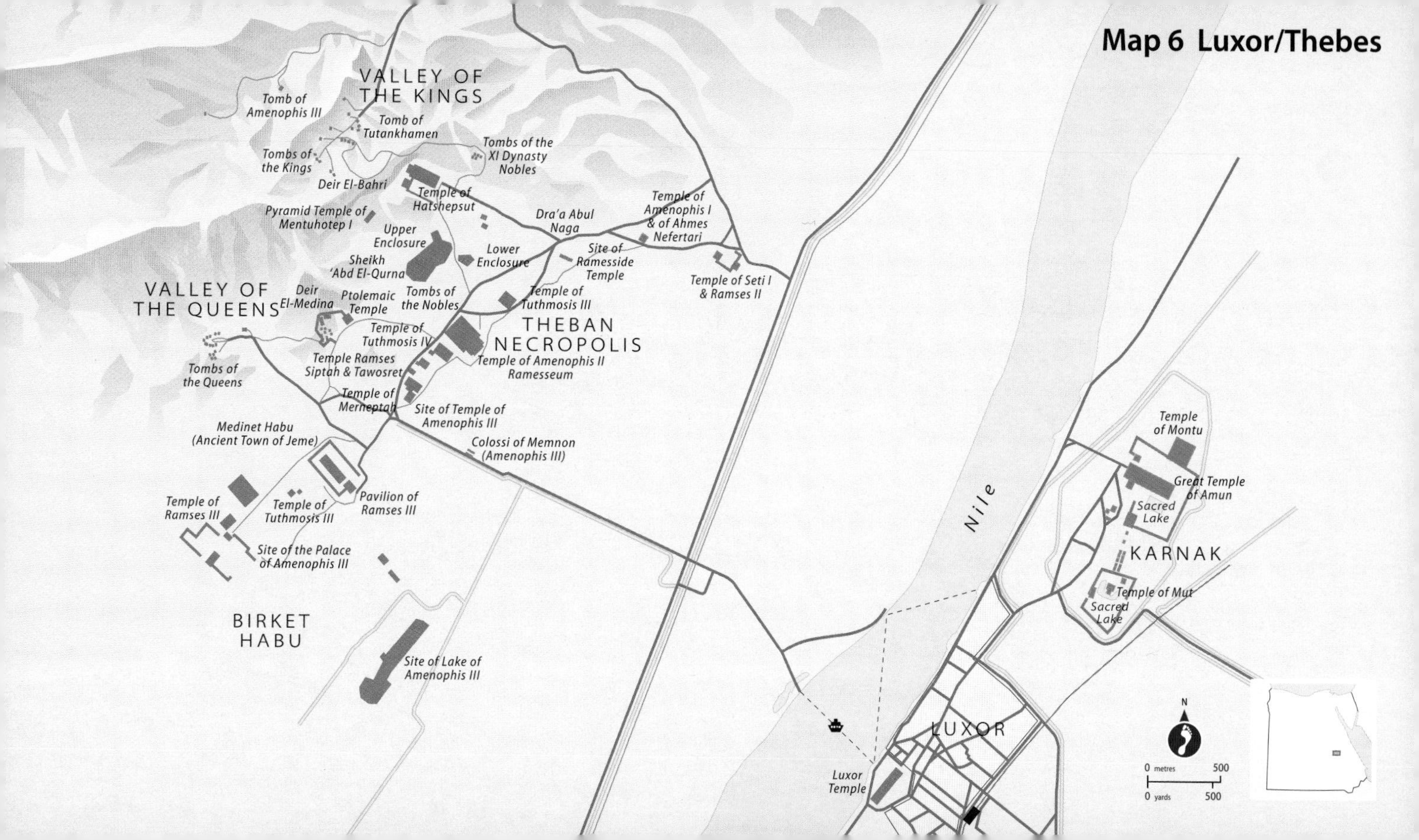

Map symbols

Administration

- Capital city
- Other city/town

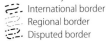

- International border
- Regional border
- Disputed border

Roads and travel

- Main road (National highway)
- Unpaved or *ripio* (gravel) road
- 4WD track
- Footpath
- Railway with station
- Airport
- Bus station
- Metro station
- Cable car
- Funicular
- Ferry

Water features

- River, canal
- Lake, ocean
- Seasonal marshland
- Beach, sand bank
- Waterfall

Topographical features

- Contours (approx)
- Mountain
- Volcano
- Mountain pass
- Escarpment
- Gorge
- Glacier
- Salt flat
- Rocks

Cities and towns

- Main through route
- Main street
- Minor street
- Pedestrianized street
- Tunnel
- One way street
- Steps
- Bridge
- Fortified wall
- Park, garden, stadium
- Sleeping
- Eating
- Bars & clubs
- Entertainment
- cp Casa particular
- Building
- Sight
- Cathedral, church
- Chinese temple
- Hindu temple
- Meru
- Mosque
- Stupa
- Synagogue
- Tourist office
- Museum
- Post office
- Police
- Bank
- Internet
- Telephone
- Market
- Hospital
- Parking
- Petrol
- Golf
- A Detail map
- A Related map

Other symbols

- Archaeological site
- National park, wildlife reserve
- Viewing point
- Campsite
- Refuge, lodge
- Castle
- Diving
- Deciduous/coniferous/palm trees
- Hide
- Vineyard
- Distillery
- Shipwreck
- Historic battlefield

Complete title listing

Footprint publishes travel guides to over 150 destinations worldwide. Each guide is packed with practical, concise and colourful information for everybody from first-time travellers to travel aficionados. The list is growing fast and current titles are noted below.

Available from all good bookshops and online

www.footprintbooks.com

(P) denotes pocket guide

Latin America and Caribbean
Argentina
Barbados (P)
Bolivia
Brazil
Caribbean Islands
Central America & Mexico
Chile
Colombia
Costa Rica
Cuba
Cusco & the Inca Trail
Dominican Republic
Ecuador & Galápagos
Guatemala
Havana (P)
Mexico
Nicaragua
Peru
Rio de Janeiro
South American Handbook
Venezuela

North America
Vancouver (P)
New York (P)
Western Canada

Africa
Cape Town (P)
East Africa
Libya
Marrakech & the High Atlas
Marrakech (P)
Morocco
Namibia
South Africa
Tunisia
Uganda

Middle East
Egypt
Israel
Jordan
Syria & Lebanon

Australasia

Australia
East Coast Australia
New Zealand
Sydney (P)
West Coast Australia

Asia

Bali
Bangkok & the Beaches
Cambodia
Goa
Hong Kong (P)
India
Indian Himalaya
Indonesia
Laos
Malaysia
Nepal
Pakistan
Rajasthan & Gujarat
Singapore
South India
Sri Lanka
Sumatra
Thailand
Tibet
Vietnam

Europe

Andalucía
Barcelona
Barcelona (P)
Berlin (P)
Bilbao (P)
Bologna (P)
Britain
Cardiff (P)
Copenhagen (P)
Croatia
Dublin
Dublin (P)
Edinburgh
Edinburgh (P)
England
Glasgow
Glasgow (P)
Ireland
Lisbon (P)
London
London (P)
Madrid (P)
Naples (P)
Northern Spain
Paris (P)
Reykjavík (P)
Scotland
Scotland Highlands & Islands
Seville (P)
Spain
Tallinn (P)
Turin (P)
Turkey
Valencia (P)
Verona (P)

Also available
Traveller's Handbook (WEXAS)
Traveller's Healthbook (WEXAS)
Traveller's Internet Guide (WEXAS)

What the papers say...

"I carried the South American Handbook from Cape Horn to Cartagena and consulted it every night for two and a half months. I wouldn't do that for anything else except my hip flask."
Michael Palin, BBC Full Circle

"My favourite series is the Handbook series published by Footprint and I especially recommend the Mexico, Central and South America Handbooks."
Boston Globe

"If 'the essence of real travel' is what you have been secretly yearning for all these years, then Footprint are the guides for you."
Under 26 magazine

"Who should pack Footprint-readers who want to escape the crowd."
The Observer

"Footprint can be depended on for accurate travel information and for imparting a deep sense of respect for the lands and people they cover."
World News

"The guides for intelligent, independently-minded souls of any age or budget."
Indie Traveller

Mail order
Available worldwide in bookshops and on-line. Footprint travel guides can also be ordered directly from us in Bath, via our website www.footprintbooks.com or from the address on the imprint page of this book.